LOCAL GOVERNMENT LAW

Second Edition

By

Gerald E. Frug

Samuel R. Rosenthal Professor of Law,
Harvard University

AMERICAN CASEBOOK SERIES®

WEST PUBLISHING CO.
ST. PAUL, MINN., 1994

COPYRIGHT © 1988 WEST PUBLISHING CO.

COPYRIGHT © 1994 By WEST PUBLISHING CO.
                        610 Opperman Drive
                        P.O. Box 64526
                        St. Paul, MN 55164–0526
                        1–800–328–9352

Library of Congress Cataloging-in-Publication Data
Frug, Gerald E., 1939–
    Local government law / by Gerald E. Frug. — 2nd ed.
      p.   cm. — (American casebook series)
    Includes index.
    ISBN 0–314–04219–9
    1. Municipal corporations—United States—Cases.
2. Decentralization in government—United States—Cases. I. Title.
II. Series.
KF5305.A4F78 1994
342.73 ' 09—dc20
[347.3029]   94–22599
                                                 CIP

ISBN 0–314–04219–9

Introduction

Studying local government law involves an investigation of two questions: What are the current legal rules governing decentralization of political power in the United States? And what are the possibilities for any further decentralization of power to American cities and towns?

Decentralization has always been a controversial topic in American political life. Many people, both on the right and the left of the American political spectrum, argue that decentralization of power is an essential — and increasingly threatened — ingredient of political freedom. Genuine democratic self-government, they claim, is possible only on a local level because only local government is close enough to its constituents to permit their participation in the decisionmaking that affects their lives. Moreover, only a local government can tailor its policies to the needs and desires of a particular community. Others, however, defend the long-standing effort in the United States to increase the power of state governments over cities and to increase the power of the federal government over both states and cities. Centralization, they contend, is necessary to regulate the effects of local decisionmaking on outsiders, to minimize conflicts between local policies, and to prevent the invasion of minority rights.

Local government law is one of the ways in which the legal system resolves this debate between proponents of decentralization and centralization. The Constitutional provisions, statutes and cases reproduced in this casebook not only raise but seek to answer critical questions about the proper organization of governmental power: Should local government law embody a view of society that favors centralization or decentralization? What justifications can be offered for either position? What, if anything, can (and should) be done to change the balance of power among federal, state and local governments?

To examine the answers offered by local government law to these questions, this casebook is organized into four parts. Chapter One introduces the basic arguments for and against decentralization that pervade the cases and materials found in the rest of the casebook. In addition, Chapter One provides an initial case-study of the way these arguments are resolved in local government law through an examination of the source of local government power. Chapter Two then addresses the relationships between cities and states and between cities and the federal government. Since local governments are subject to the exercise of both state and federal power, local authority depends in large part on limiting or controlling these higher levels of government. Chapter Two examines state-city and federal-city relationships not only in general terms but also through an inquiry into a number of specific problems, including state control over cities' freedom of speech and the application of federal antitrust and criminal law to local governments.

Chapter Three shifts the subject of inquiry to the problems of inter-local relationships. Because American metropolitan areas are divided into dozens of separate cities, decentralization of power requires an allocation of responsibilities not only between cities and higher levels of government but also among neighboring cities. Chapter Three focuses specifically on the city-suburb relationship, as well as on possible regional solutions to city-suburb conflict. Finally, Chapter Four investigates the legal relationship between city governments and their constituents. One of the traditional justifications for restraints on local power is the fear of the tyranny of the majority; the materials in Chapter Four examine how this fear has influenced American law. But Chapter Four also investigates the legal system's efforts to enable local citizens to initiate, and pay for, city policies that promote community empowerment.

This casebook thus concentrates on an examination of three relationships: the relationship between cities and higher levels of government, the relationship between neighboring cities, and the relationship between cities and the people who live within their boundaries. The problems engendered by these three relationships are the basic ingredients of local government law. In fact, similar problems are encountered in every attempt to decentralize power to groups in our society. For example, the power of private corporations can be understood through an examination of questions analogous to those this casebook asks of public (or "municipal") corporations: What are the limits on the power of state and federal governments to control corporate behavior? What are the rules of law (antitrust law, contract law, tort law, and property law) that govern intercorporate relationships? What is the legal relationship between a corporation and its shareholders and employees? The similarities between the issues confronted by different efforts to decentralize power allow one to gain insight into local government law by comparing the rules that apply to cities with those that apply to other mechanisms of decentralization. Consequently, this casebook includes references not only to the rules affecting private corporations but also to those that govern other groups that exercise decentralized power in America: unions, families, voluntary associations and religious organizations.

This casebook refers as well to another important source of comparison for local government law—the law that governs the power of states. Cities and states, after all, are the two principal devices in the United States for the decentralization of political power. But while this casebook includes references to the legal rules affecting states for comparative purposes, it treats the subject matter of local government law itself as dealing with cities rather than with states. There are several reasons for limiting the subject matter in this way. First of all, the general issue of federal-state relationships—of federalism—is traditionally covered in other law school courses, such as Constitutional Law and Federal Courts.

There would, I think, be too much of an overlap with other parts of the curriculum if this casebook sought to cover, as a primary focus of inquiry, materials that dealt with states as well as with cities. Moreover, the notion of decentralized political power may not be very meaningful in jurisdictions as large as states. If limits on size are essential for exercising democratic self-governance, only cities (perhaps, in large cities, only neighborhoods) are small enough to allow popular involvement in governmental decisionmaking. The issue of decentralization of power should be addressed specifically in the place where its promise and potential are greatest. Finally, as the materials in this casebook demonstrate, the law governing cities and the law governing states are not the same. Cities, for example, unlike states, are not even mentioned in the United States Constitution. Only by focusing on the power of cities directly, therefore, can the specific problems and prospects of local governmental power be examined in depth.

As with any casebook, the selection and organization of topics and materials in this casebook represent only one of the many possible ways to define the relevant subject matter. Some topics have been omitted that could well have been covered in a local government law course, and others have been included even though no one before me has thought them essential. Although this kind of partiality exists in all casebooks, I want to encourage readers of this casebook to be mindful of my prejudices. Question why the materials are presented in the way they are, and consider what kinds of issues and perspectives have been omitted. I have sought to emphasize the relevance of my partiality in this casebook by including a number of excerpts from my published work. I believe this form of presentation, rather than the more common method of writing unsigned notes on specific subjects, alerts readers to the fact that my discussion of an issue is not the only possible way to understand it. I expect these excerpts from my work to be read critically; they are included not only to persuade but also to provoke thinking about the subject.

This casebook also includes a number of excerpts from books and articles dealing with questions of political theory and urban history (as well as a few excerpts from a work of fiction). These excerpts are designed to introduce the reader to non-legal materials that illuminate—and are illuminated by—legal doctrine. I have included relatively substantial excerpts from these works in the belief that local government law can be understood only in the context of the historical development of cities in America and in terms of the political theories that the legal doctrines governing city power have relied on and incorporated. Not only are non-legal materials scattered throughout the casebook but a special section of each chapter of the casebook is devoted entirely to democratic theory. These sections are designed to suggest criticisms of the conceptions of democracy found in local government law and to offer ways of thinking about alternatives to these conceptions. To evaluate the possibility of decentralization of power in America, it is important to understand not only the versions of democracy that the law has embraced but also the versions that, although possible, the law has rejected.

There are many people to whom I am indebted for help in preparing this casebook. My book has been considerably influenced by a path-breaking earlier casebook published in the American Casebook Series, Frank Michelman and Terrance Sandalow's Materials on Government in Urban Areas (1970) and by teaching materials prepared by my colleague Kathleen Sullivan, now a Professor at Stanford Law School. I am also grateful to my students in local government law at Harvard Law School and the University of Pennsylvania Law School for contributing to my thinking about the issues covered in this casebook. Discussions with students and colleagues have caused me to do so much rethinking about the subject of local government law that only one case remains in this casebook from the materials I first prepared to teach the course (North City Area-Wide Council v. Romney, in Chapter Four). Finally, I want to thank Elizabeth Sponheim for her invaluable work in helping to prepare the manuscript for publication.

I need to make a technical point about the presentation of the materials. Citations and footnotes have been omitted from both the cases and the work of commentators—and concurring and dissenting opinions have been omitted from the cases—without specifically noting these omissions. When footnotes are include in the materials, they retain the original numbering.

GERALD E. FRUG

June, 1994

Acknowledgments

I am indebted to the following authors and publishers for their generosity in allowing me to include in this book excerpts from copyrighted materials, all of which are reprinted by permission:

Gregory Alexander, The Cornell Law Review, and Fred B. Rothman & Company for excerpts from Alexander, Dilemmas of Group Autonomy: Residential Associations and Community, 75 Cornell L.Rev. 1 (1989);

Keith Aoki and The Fordham Urban Law Journal for excerpts from Aoki, Race, Space, and Place: The Relation Between Architectural Modernism, Post-Modernism, Urban Planning, and Gentrification, 20 Fordham Urb.L.J. 699 (1993);

Yale University Press for excerpts from Philippe Aries, The Family and The City in the Old World and the New, contained in V. Tufte and B. Myerhoff, eds., CHANGING IMAGES OF THE FAMILY, copyright © 1979 by Yale University Press;

Princeton University Press for excerpts from Hadley Arkes, THE PHILOSOPHER IN THE CITY: THE MORAL DIMENSIONS OF URBAN POLITICS, copyright © 1981 by Princeton University Press;

The University of California Press and Benjamin Barber for excerpts from Barber, STRONG DEMOCRACY: PARTICIPATORY POLITICS FOR A NEW AGE, copyright © 1984 by The Regents of the University of California;

Derrick Bell, The Washington Law Review, and Fred B. Rothman & Company for excerpts from Bell, The Referendum: Democracy's Barrier to Racial Equality, 54 Wash.L.Rev. 1 (1978);

The Brookings Institution, Jeffrey Berry, Kent Portney, and Ken Thomson for excerpts from Berry, et al., THE REBIRTH OF URBAN DEMOCRACY, copyright © 1993 by The Brookings Institution;

Fred Bosselman, Nancy Stroud, and The Nova Law Journal for excerpts from Bosselman and Stroud, Mandatory Tithes: The Legality of Land Development Linkage, 9 Nova L.J. 383 (1985);

Richard Briffault and The Columbia Law Review for excerpts from Briffault, Our Localism: Part I—The Structure of Local Government Law, 90 Col.L.Rev. 1 (1990), and Briffault, Our Localism: Part II—Localism and Legal Theory, 90 Col.L.Rev. 346 (1990);

Harcourt Brace Jovanovich, Inc. for excerpts from Italo Calvino, INVISIBLE CITIES, translated from the Italian by William Weaver, copyright © 1972 by Giulio Einaudi s.p.a.; translation copyright © 1974 by Harcourt Brace Jovanovich, Inc.;

Alfred A. Knopf, Inc. and Robert A. Caro for excerpts from Caro, THE POWER BROKER, copyright © 1974 by Robert A. Caro;

Ronald Cass and The Marquette Law Review for excerpts from Cass, Privatization: Politics, Law and Theory, 71 Marquette L.Rev. 449 (1988);

The University of California Press and Manuel Castells for excerpts from Castells, THE CITY AND THE GRASS ROOTS: A CROSS-CULTURAL THEORY OF URBAN SOCIAL MOVEMENTS, copyright © 1984 by The Regents of the University of California;

Yale University Press for excerpts from Robert A. Dahl, DILEMMAS IN PLURALIST DEMOCRACY, copyright © 1982 by Yale University Press;

Columbia University Press for excerpts from Michael N. Danielson, THE POLITICS OF EXCLUSION, copyright © 1976 by Columbia University Press;

Basic Books, Inc. and John Donahue for excerpts from Donahue, THE PRIVATIZATION DECISION: PUBLIC ENDS, PRIVATE MEANS, copyright © 1989 by Basic Books, Inc., a division of HarperCollins Publishers, Inc.;

Robert Ellickson, The University of Pennsylvania Law Review, and Fred B. Rothman & Company for excerpts from Ellickson, Cities and Homeowners Associations, 130 U.Pa.L.Rev. 1519 (1982);

Basic Books, Inc. for excerpts from Robert Fishman, BOURGEOIS UTOPIAS, copyright © 1987 by Basic Books, Inc., a division of HarperCollins Publishers, Inc.;

Richard Ford and The Harvard Law Review Association for excerpts from Ford, The Boundaries of Race: The Assertion of Political Space in a Critical Jurisprudence, 107 Harv.L.Rev. 1841, copyright © 1994 by The Harvard Law Review Association;

Bantam, Doubleday, Dell Publishing Group, Inc. and Joel Garreau for excerpts from Garreau, EDGE CITY: LIFE ON THE NEW FRONTIER, copyright © 1991 by Doubleday, a division of Bantam, Doubleday, Dell Publishing Group, Inc.;

The University of Illinois Press and John Gaventa for excerpts from Gaventa, POWER AND POWERLESSNESS: QUIESCENCE AND REBELLION IN AN APPALACHIAN VALLEY, copyright © 1980 by John Gaventa;

Clayton Gillette and The Chicago-Kent Law Review for excerpts from Gillette, In Partial Praise of Dillon's Rule, or, Can Public Choice Theory Justify Local Government Law, 67 Chicago-Kent L.Rev. 959 (1991);

The Free Press, an imprint of Simon & Schuster for excerpts from Lani Guinier, THE TYRANNY OF THE MAJORITY: FUNDAMENTAL FAIRNESS IN REPRESENTATIVE DEMOCRACY, copyright © 1994 by Lani Guinier;

Basil Blackwell Ltd. and Peter Hall for excerpts from Hall, CITIES OF TOMORROW: AN INTELLECTUAL HISTORY OF URBAN PLANNING AND DESIGN IN THE TWENTIETH CENTURY, copyright © 1988 by Peter Hall.

Oxford University Press and Kenneth Jackson for excerpts from Jackson, CRABGRASS FRONTIER: THE SUBURBANIZATION OF THE UNITED STATES, copyright © 1985 by Oxford University Press, Inc.;

Harvard University Press and Rosabeth Moss Kanter for excerpts from Kanter, COMMITMENT AND COMMUNITY, copyright © 1972 by The President and Fellows of Harvard College;

Oxford University Press for excerpts from C.B. Macpherson, THE LIFE AND TIMES OF LIBERAL DEMOCRACY, copyright © 1977 by C.B. Macpherson;

Frank Michelman, The Indiana Law Journal and Fred B. Rothman & Company for excerpts from Michelman, Political Markets and Community Self Determination, 53 Ind.L.J. 145 (1977-78);

MacMillan Publishing Company and John Noonan for excerpts from Noonan, BRIBES, copyright © 1984 by MacMillan Publishing Company;

The Harvard Law Review Association for excerpts from Note, The Rule of Law in Residential Associations, 99 Harv.L.Rev. 472, copyright © 1985 by the Harvard Law Review Association;

Basic Books, Inc. and Robert Nozick for excerpts from Nozick, ANARCHY, STATE AND UTOPIA, copyright © 1974 by Basic Books, Inc., a division of HarperCollins Publishers, Inc.;

Addison-Wesley Publishing Company for excerpts from David Osborne and Ted Gaebler, REINVENTING GOVERNMENT, copyright © 1992 by David Osborne and Ted Gaebler;

Hanna Pitkin and Sara Shumer for excerpts from Pitkin and Shumer, On Participation, 2 democracy 43 (1992);

The Academy of Political Science, Steve Hanke, and James Ramsey for excerpts from Ramsey, Selling the New York Subway: Wild-eyed Radicalism or the Only Feasible Solution?, contained in Hanke, ed., PROSPECTS FOR PRIVATIZATION, PROCEEDINGS OF THE ACADEMY OF POLITICAL SCIENCE, vol. 36, copyright © 1987 by The Academy of Political Science;

Jamin Raskin, The University of Pennsylvania Law Review, and Fred B. Rothman & Company for excerpts from Raskin, Legal Aliens, Local Citizens: The Historical, Constitutional and Theoretical Meanings of Alien Suffrage, 141 U.Pa.L.Rev. 1391 (1993);

The Johns Hopkins University Press and The Woodrow Wilson Center Press for excerpts from David Rusk, CITIES WITHOUT SUB-URBS, copyright © 1993 by The Woodrow Wilson International Center for Scholars;

The University of Chicago Press, Susan Saegert, and Catharine Stimpson for excerpts from Saegert, Masculine Cities and Feminine Suburbs, contained in Stimpson, et al., eds., WOMEN AND THE AMERICAN CITY, copyright © 1981 by The University of Chicago Press;

Terrance Sandalow and the Minnesota Law Review for excerpts from Sandalow, The Limits of Municipal Power Under Home Rule: A Role for the Courts, 48 Minn.L.Rev. 632 (1964);

Gary Schwartz, the U.C.L.A. Law Review, and Fred B. Rothman & Company for excerpts from Schwartz, The Logic of Home Rule and the Private Law Exception, 20 U.C.L.A. L.Rev. 670 (1973);

The University of Chicago Press for excerpts from Tiebout, A Pure Theory of Local Expenditures, 64 J.Pol.Econ. 416 (1956);

The Free Press, A Division of MacMillan, Inc., and Roberto Unger for excerpts from Unger, THE DILEMMAS OF COMMUNITARIAN POLITICS, copyright © 1975 by Roberto Mangabeira Unger;

Joan Williams and The Wisconsin Law Review for excerpts from Williams, The Constitutional Vulnerability of American Local Government: The Politics of City Status in American Law, 1986 Wis.L.Rev. 83;

Princeton University Press and Iris Young for excerpts from Young, JUSTICE AND THE POLITICS OF DIFFERENCE, copyright © 1990 by Princeton University Press;

Alfred A. Knopf, Inc. and Michael Zuckerman for excerpts from Zuckerman, PEACEABLE KINGDOMS, copyright © 1970 by Michael Zuckerman.

Summary of Contents

*

Table of Contents

Chapter Four. The Relationship Between Cities and Their Citizens

Table of Cases

The principal cases are in bold type. Cases cited or discussed in the text are roman type. References are to pages. Cases cited in principal cases and within other quoted materials are not included.

*

Table of Authorities

The page numbers of works from which extracts have been taken appear in bold; all others appear in Roman

LOCAL GOVERNMENT LAW

Second Edition

[T]he strength of free nations resides in the local community. Local institutions are to liberty what primary schools are to science; they bring it within people's reach, they teach people to use and enjoy it. Without local institutions, a nation may establish a free government, but it cannot have the spirit of liberty. Transient passions, momentary interests, the chance of circumstances, may create the external forms of independence; but the despotic tendency which has been repressed into the interior of the social body will, sooner or later, appear on the surface.

> Alexis de Tocqueville,
> Democracy in America

[In a] pure democracy, by which I mean a society consisting of a small number of citizens, who assemble and administer the government in person, * * * [a] common passion or interest will, in almost every case, be felt by a majority of the whole; a communication and concert results from the form of government itself; and there is nothing to check the inducements to sacrifice the weaker party or an obnoxious individual. Hence it is that such democracies have ever been spectacles of turbulence and contention; have ever been found incompatible with personal security or the rights of property; and have in general been as short in their lives as they have been violent in their deaths.

> The Federalist No. 10
> (Madison)

*

Chapter One

INTRODUCTION TO THE PROBLEMS OF DECENTRALIZATION

SECTION A. DECENTRALIZATION OF POWER TO LOCAL GOVERNMENT: THE PROS AND CONS

Debates about the definition and desirability of decentralizing political power have taken place repeatedly throughout American history. The argument over the ratification of the Constitution of the United States was itself largely an argument over its impact on state and local power. Proponents of the Constitution argued that the Constitution properly strengthened the authority of the national government, while its opponents, the anti-federalists, argued that the Constitution threatened the primacy of the states and, as a consequence, endangered the preservation of individual liberty.[1] Since the adoption of the Constitution, debates about decentralization have recurred frequently, for example in the struggle between the Whigs and the Jacksonians in the 1830's, in the conflict over the extension of slavery in the territories in the 1850's, in the controversy over Progressivism at the beginning of the 20th century, and in the arguments over the enactment of Civil Rights legislation in the 1960's.[2]

1. For the federalists' argument, see The Federalist Papers (B. Wright ed. 1961); for the anti-federalists' argument, see The Anti Federalist: Writings by the Opponents of the Constitution (H. Storing and M. Dry eds. 1985); H. Storing, What The Anti Federalists Were For (1981). Selections from both sides of the debate have been conveniently collected in The American Constitution: For and Against (J.R. Pole ed. 1987). For more recent versions of the federalist/anti-federalist argument, see, e.g., McConnell, Federalism: Evaluating the Founders' Design, 54 U.Chi.L.Rev. 1484, 1491–1511 (1987); Rose, Planning and Dealing: Piecemeal Land Controls as a Problem of Local Legitimacy, 71 Calif.L.Rev. 837 (1983).

2. For a discussion of these debates, see, e.g., T. Brown, Politics and Statesmanship: Essays on the American Whig Party (1985), D. Howe, The Political Culture of the American Whigs (1979), and Social Theories of Jacksonian Democracy: Representative Writings of the Period (J. Blau ed. 1954); E. Foner, Free Soil, Free Labor, Free Men: The Ideology of the Republican Party Before the Civil War (1970) and E. Foner,

1

No participant in these recurrent debates about decentralization contended that governmental power in the United States should be fully centralized or fully decentralized. Everyone supported a role both for the national government and for state and local governments. The controversies instead concerned the relative importance of centralized or decentralized authority; it was in the process of articulating the comparative value of concentrating and dispersing power that a number of classic arguments for and against decentralization were developed. These arguments pervade local government law; indeed, local government law is one of the products of—as well as one of the contributors to—this debate. It is important here at the outset, therefore, to become familiar with the arguments about the values and dangers of decentralization.

Two important contributions to the debate over decentralization are excerpted below. The first is an excerpt from Alexis de Tocqueville's Democracy in America, an eloquent defense of decentralization of power to local government. The second is an excerpt from James Madison's Federalist 10, a highly influential (perhaps *the* most influential) argument against decentralization of power to American cities and towns. When reading these excerpts, try to identify both the appeal and the fear of decentralization of decisionmaking authority that the authors articulate. How does each side of the argument answer the points made by the other side?

My inclusion in this casebook of works such as Tocqueville's and Madison's assumes a significant relationship between political theory and legal doctrine. The chapter reproduced below from Invisible Cities, a novel by the great Italian writer Italo Calvino, does not directly address the question why studying theory is important to understanding local government law. But a consideration of the relationship that Calvino suggests between Eudoxia's carpet and the city in which it is housed might be helpful in thinking about the issue.

ITALO CALVINO, INVISIBLE CITIES
Pp. 96–97 (1974).

In Eudoxia, which spreads both upward and down, with winding alleys, steps, dead ends, hovels, a carpet is preserved in which you can observe the city's true form. At first sight nothing seems to resemble Eudoxia less than the design of that carpet, laid out in symmetrical motives whose patterns are repeated along straight and circular lines, interwoven with brilliantly colored spires, in a repetition that can be followed throughout the whole woof. But if you pause and examine it carefully, you become convinced that each place in the carpet corresponds to a place in the city and all the things contained in the city are

Politics and Ideology in the Age of the Civil War (1980); G. Mowry, The Era of Theodore Roosevelt 1900–1912 (1958), A. Link, Woodrow Wilson and the Progressive Era (1954), and G. Kolko, The Triumph of Conservatism (1963); B. Schwartz, Statutory History of the United States: Civil Rights, Part II, pp. 1089–1452 (1970).

included in the design, arranged according to their true relationship, which escapes your eye distracted by the bustle, the throngs, the shoving. All of Eudoxia's confusion, the mules' braying, the lampblack stains, the fish smell is what is evident in the incomplete perspective you grasp; but the carpet proves that there is a point from which the city shows its true proportions, the geometrical scheme implicit in its every, tiniest detail.

It is easy to get lost in Eudoxia: but when you concentrate and stare at the carpet, you recognize the street you were seeking in a crimson or indigo or magenta thread which, in a wide loop, brings you to the purple enclosure that is your real destination. Every inhabitant of Eudoxia compares the carpet's immobile order with his own image of the city, an anguish of his own, and each can find, concealed among the arabesques, an answer, the story of his life, the twists of fate.

An oracle was questioned about the mysterious bond between two objects so dissimilar as the carpet and the city. One of the two objects— the oracle replied—has the form the gods gave the starry sky and the orbits in which the worlds revolve; the other is an approximate reflection, like every human creation.

For some time the augurs had been sure that the carpet's harmonious pattern was of divine origin. The oracle was interpreted in this sense, arousing no controversy. But you could, similarly, come to the opposite conclusion: that the true map of the universe is the city of Eudoxia, just as it is, a stain that spreads out shapelessly, with crooked streets, houses that crumble one upon the other amid clouds of dust, fires, screams in the darkness.

ALEXIS DE TOCQUEVILLE, DEMOCRACY IN AMERICA

Volume 1, Pp. 74–76, 112–119, 302–304, 310, 313–332.
(F. Bowen ed., 1863, revised and edited).

It is not by accident that I examine the town first. The town is the only association which is so perfectly natural, that, wherever people come together, it seems to constitute itself.

Communal society, then, exists in all nations, whatever their laws and customs may be: it is man who makes monarchies and establishes republics, but the town seem to come directly from the hand of God. But although towns have existed as long as man, communal freedom is a rare and fragile thing. A nation can always establish great political assemblies, because it generally contains a certain number of individuals fitted by their talents, if not by their habits, for the direction of affairs. The town, on the contrary, is composed of coarser materials, which are less easily fashioned by the legislator. The difficulty of establishing its independence increases rather than diminishes with the increasing intelligence of the people. A highly civilized community can hardly tolerate a town's independence, is disgusted at its numerous blunders, and is apt to despair of success before the experiment is completed. Of all forms of liberty, that of the town, which is established with so much difficulty, is least of all protected against the encroachments of power. The institutions of a local community can hardly struggle against a strong and enterprising government on their own, and they cannot defend themselves with success unless they are identified with the customs of the nation and supported by public opinion. Thus, until local freedom has become part of the culture of a people, it is easily destroyed; and it can become part of the culture only after long existence in law. Communal freedom is not the fruit of human effort; it is rarely created; it somehow gives birth to itself. It develops almost in secret in the midst of a semi-barbarous state of society. The constant action of laws and national habits, peculiar circumstances, and, above all, time, may consolidate it; but there is certainly no nation on the continent of Europe which has experienced its advantages. Yet the strength of free nations resides in the local community. Local institutions are to liberty what primary schools are to science; they bring it within people's reach, they teach people how to use and enjoy it. Without local institutions, a nation may establish a free government, but it cannot have the spirit of liberty. Transient passions, momentary interests, or the chance of circumstances, may create the external forms of independence; but the despotic tendency which has been repressed into the interior of the social body, will, sooner or later, reappear on the surface. * * *

The partisans of centralization in Europe claim that the government can administer the affairs of each locality better than the citizens could for themselves: this may be true, when the central power is enlightened, and the local authorities are ignorant; when it is alert, and they are slow; when it is accustomed to act, and they to obey. Indeed, it is evident that this double tendency must grow with the growth of centralization, and that the readiness of the one and the incapacity of the others must become more and more prominent. But I deny that it is so, when the people are as enlightened, as awake to their interests, and as accustomed to reflect on them, as the Americans are. I am persuaded, on the contrary, that, in this case, the collective strength of the citizens will always more powerfully produce social welfare than the authority of the government. I know it is difficult to point out with certainty the means of arousing a sleeping population, and of giving it passions and knowledge which it does not possess; it is, I am well aware, an arduous task to persuade men to busy themselves about their own affairs. It would frequently be easier to interest them in the details of court etiquette, than in the repairs of their common dwelling. But whenever a central administration tries completely to supersede the persons most interested, I believe that it is either misled, or wants to mislead. However enlightened and skillful a central power may be, it cannot of itself embrace all the details of the life of a great nation. Such an achievement exceeds the powers of man. And when it attempts unaided to create and set in motion so many complicated springs, it must submit to a very imperfect result, or exhaust itself in futile efforts.

Centralization easily succeeds, indeed, in subjecting the external actions of men to a certain uniformity, which we come at last to love for its own sake, independently of the objects to which it is applied, like those devotees who worship the statue, and forget the deity it represents. Centralization imparts without difficulty an admirable regularity to the routine of business; provides skillfully for the details of social control; represses small disorders and petty misdemeanors; maintains society in a *statu quo* alike secure from improvement and decline; and perpetuates a drowsy regularity in the conduct of affairs, which the heads of the administration are apt to call good order and public tranquillity; in short, it excels in prevention, but not in action. Its force deserts it, when society is to be profoundly moved, or accelerated in its course; and if once the co-operation of private citizens is necessary to the furtherance of its measures, the secret of its impotence is disclosed. Sometimes the centralized power, in its despair, invokes the assistance of the citizens; it says to them: "You shall act just as I please, as much as I please, and in the direction which I please. You are to take charge of the details, without aspiring to guide the system; you are to work in darkness; and afterwards you may judge my work by its results." These are not the conditions on which the alliance of the human will is to be obtained; it must be free in its style, and responsible for its acts, or (such is the constitution of man) the citizen had rather remain a passive spectator, than a dependent actor, in schemes with which he is unacquainted. * * *

Granting, for an instant, that the villages and counties of the United States would be more usefully governed by a distant central authority than by functionaries taken from among them,—admitting, for the sake of argument, that there would be more security in America, and the resources of society would be better employed there, if the whole administration centered in a single arm,—still the *political* advantages which the Americans derive from their decentralized system would induce me to prefer it to the contrary plan. It profits me but little, after all, that a vigilant authority always protects the tranquillity of my pleasures, and constantly averts all dangers from my path, without my care or concern, if this same authority is the absolute master of my liberty and my life, and if it so monopolizes movement and life, that when it languishes everything languishes around it, that when it sleeps everything must sleep, and that when it dies the state itself must perish.

There are countries in Europe, where the natives consider themselves as a kind of settlers, indifferent to the fate of the spot which they inhabit. The greatest changes are effected there without their concurrence, and (unless chance may have apprised them of the event) without their knowledge; nay, more, the condition of his village, the policing of his street, the repairs of the church or the parsonage, do not concern him; for he looks upon all these things as unconnected with himself, and as the property of a powerful stranger whom he calls the government. He has only a life-interest in these possessions, without the spirit of ownership or any ideas of improvement. This want of interest in his own affairs goes so far, that if his own safety or that of his children is at last endangered, instead of trying to avert the peril, he will fold his arms, and wait till the whole nation comes to his aid. This man, who has so completely sacrificed his own free will, does not, more than any other person, love obedience; he cowers, it is true, before the pettiest officer; but he braves the law with the spirit of a conquered foe, as soon as its superior force is withdrawn: he perpetually oscillates between servitude and license.

When a nation has arrived at this state, it must either change its customs and its laws, or perish; for the source of public virtues is dried up; and though it may contain subjects, it has no citizens.   * * *

It is not the *administrative,* but the *political* effects of decentralization, that I most admire in America. In the United States, the interests of the country are everywhere kept in view; they are an object of solicitude from the village to the entire Union, and every citizen is as warmly attached to them as if they were his own. He takes pride in the glory of his nation; he boasts of its success, to which he conceives himself to have contributed; and he rejoices in the general prosperity by which he profits. The feeling he entertains toward the state is analogous to that which unites him to his family, and it is by a kind of selfishness that he interests himself in the welfare of his country.

To the European, a public official represents a superior force; to an American, he represents right. In America, then, it may be said that no one renders obedience to man, but to justice and to law. If the opinion which the citizen entertains of himself is exaggerated, it is at least salutary; he unhesitatingly confides in his own powers, which appear to him to be all-sufficient. When a private individual considers some enterprise, however directly connected it may be with the welfare of society, he never thinks of soliciting the co-operation of the government; but he publishes his plan, offers to execute it, courts the assistance of other individuals, and struggles mightily against all obstacles. Undoubtedly he is often less successful than the state might have been in his position; but in the end, the sum of these private undertakings far exceeds all that the government could have done.

As the administrative authority is within the reach of the citizens, whom in some degree it represents, it excites neither their jealousy nor hatred: as its resources are limited, every one feels that he must not rely solely on its aid. Thus, when the administration thinks fit to act within its own limits, it is not abandoned to itself, as in Europe; the duties of private citizens are not supposed to have lapsed because the state has come into action; but every one is ready, on the contrary, to guide and support it. This action of individuals, joined to that of the public authorities, frequently accomplishes what the most energetic centralized administration would be unable to do.   * * *

Aristocracies are infinitely more expert in the science of legislation than democracies ever can be. They are possessed of a self-control which protects them from the errors of temporary excitement; and they form far-reaching designs, which they know how to nurture until a favorable opportunity arrives. Aristocratic government proceeds with the dexterity of art; it understands how to make the collective force of all its laws converge at the same time to a given point. Such is not the case with democracies, whose laws are almost always ineffective or inopportune. The means of democracy are therefore more imperfect than those of aristocracy, and the measures which it unwittingly adopts are frequently opposed to its own cause; but the object it has in view is more useful.

Let us now imagine a community so organized by nature, or by its constitution, that it can support the transitory action of bad laws, and that it can await, without destruction, the *general tendency* of its legislation: we shall then conceive how a democratic government, notwithstanding its faults, may be best fitted to produce the prosperity of this community. This is precisely what has occurred in the United States; and I repeat, what I have before remarked, that the great advantage of the Americans consists in their being able to commit faults which they may afterwards repair. * * *

At the present time, civic spirit seems to me to be inseparable from the exercise of political rights; and I think that the number of citizens will be found to increase or decrease in Europe in proportion as those rights are extended.

How does it happen that in the United States, where the inhabitants arrived yesterday upon the soil which they now occupy, and brought neither customs nor traditions with them there; where they met each other for the first time with no previous acquaintance; where, in short, the instinctive love of country can scarcely exist;—how does it happen that every one takes as zealous an interest in the affairs of his township, his county, and the whole State, as if they were his own? It is because every one, in his sphere, takes an active part in the government of society.

The common man in the United States understand the influence exercised by the general prosperity upon his own welfare; simple as this observation is, it is too rarely made by the people. Besides, he usually considers this prosperity as his own achievement. The citizen looks upon the fortune of the public as his own, and he labors for the good of the State, not merely from a sense of pride or duty, but from what I dare to call greed. * * *

Democratic government brings the notion of political rights to the level of the humblest citizens, just as the dissemination of wealth brings the notion of property within the reach of all men; to my mind, this is one of its greatest advantages. I do not say it is easy to teach men how to exercise political rights; but I maintain that, when it is possible, the effects which result from it are highly important; and I add, that, if there ever was a time at which such an attempt ought to be made, that time is now. Do you not see that religious belief is shaken, and the divine notion of right is declining?—that morality is debased, and the notion of moral right is therefore fading away? Argument is substituted for faith, and calculation for the impulses of sentiment. If, in the midst of this general disruption, you do not succeed in connecting the notion of right with that of private interest, which is the only immutable point in the human heart, what means will you have of governing the world except by fear? When I am told that the laws are weak and the people are turbulent, that passions are excited and the authority of virtue is paralyzed, and therefore no measures must be taken to increase the rights of the democracy, I reply, that, for these very reasons, some measures of the kind ought to be taken; and I believe that governments are still more interested in taking them than society at large, for governments may perish, but society cannot die. * * *

It is not always feasible to consult the whole people, either directly or indirectly, in the formation of the law; but it cannot be denied that, when this is possible, the authority of the law is greatly increased. This popular origin, which impairs the excellence and the wisdom of legislation, contributes much to increase its power. There is an amazing strength in the expression of the will of a whole people; and when it declares itself, even the imagination of those who would wish to contest it is overawed. The truth of this fact is well known by parties; and they consequently strive to make out a majority whenever they can. If they have not the greater number of voters on their side, they assert that the true majority abstained from voting; and if they are foiled even there, they have recourse to those persons who had no right to vote.

In the United States, except slaves, servants, and paupers supported by the towns, there is no class of persons who do not exercise the elective franchise, and who do not indirectly contribute to make the laws. Those who wish to attack the laws must consequently either change the opinion of the nation, or trample upon its decision.

A second reason, which is still more direct and weighty, may be adduced: in the United States, every one is personally interested in enforcing the obedience of the whole community to the law; for as the minority may shortly rally the majority to its principles, it is interested in professing that respect for the decrees of the legislator which it may soon have occasion to claim for its own. However annoying an enactment may be, the citizen of the United States complies with it, not only because it is the work of the majority, but because it is his own, and he regards it as a contract to which he is himself a party.

In the United States, then, that numerous and turbulent multitude does not exist, who, regarding the law as their natural enemy, look upon it with fear and distrust. It is impossible, on the contrary, not to perceive that all classes display the utmost reliance upon the legislation of their country, and are attached to it by a kind of paternal love.

I am wrong, however, in saying all classes; for as, in America, the European scale of authority is inverted, the wealthy are there placed in a position analogous to that of the poor in the Old World, and it is the rich who frequently look upon the law with suspicion. I have already observed that the advantage of democracy is not, as has been sometimes asserted, that it protects the interests of all, but simply that it protects those of the majority. In the United States, where the poor rule, the rich have always something to fear from the abuse of their power. This natural anxiety of the rich may produce a secret dissatisfaction; but society is not disturbed by it, for the same reason which withholds the confidence of the rich from the legislative authority, makes them obey its mandates: their wealth, which prevents them from making the law, prevents them from withstanding it. In civilized nations, only those who have nothing to lose ever revolt; and if the laws of a democracy are not always worthy of respect, they are always respected; for those who usually infringe the laws cannot fail to obey those which they have themselves made, and by which they are benefited; and the citizens who might be interested in breaking them are induced, by their character and station, to submit to the decisions of the legislature, whatever they may be. Besides, the people in America obey the law, not only because it is their work, but because it may be changed if by any chance it is harmful; a law is observed because, first, it is a self-imposed evil, and, secondly, it is an evil of transient duration. * * *

On passing from a free country into one which is not free, the traveller is struck by the change; in the former, all is bustle and activity; in the latter, everything seems calm and motionless. In the one, amelioration and progress are the only topics; in the other, it seems as if the community wished only to repose in the enjoyment of advantages already acquired. Nevertheless, the country which exerts itself so strenuously to become happy, is generally more wealthy and prosperous than that which appears so contented with its lot; and when we compare them, we can scarcely conceive how so many new wants are daily felt in the former, while so few seem to exist in the latter.

If this remark is applicable to those free countries which have preserved monarchical forms and aristocratic institutions, it is still more so to democratic republics. In these States, it is not a portion only of the people who endeavor to improve the state of society, but the whole community is engaged in the task; and it is not the needs and convenience of a single class for which provision is to be made, but the needs and convenience of all classes at once.

It is not impossible to conceive the surprising liberty which the Americans enjoy; some idea may likewise be formed of their extreme equality; but the political activity which pervades the United States must be seen in order to be understood. No sooner do you set foot upon American ground, than you are stunned by a kind of tumult; a confused clamor is heard on every side; and a thousand simultaneous voices demand the satisfaction of their social wants. Everything is in motion around you; here, the people of one quarter of a town meet to decide upon the building of a church; there, the election of a representative is going on; a little further, the delegates of a district are rushing to the town in order to consult upon some local improvements; in another place, the laborers of a village quit their ploughs to deliberate upon the project of a road or a public school. Meetings are called for the sole purpose of declaring their disapproval of the conduct of the government; while in other assemblies, citizens salute the authorities of the day as the fathers of their country. Societies are formed which regard drunkenness as the principal cause of the evils of the state, and solemnly bind themselves to give an example of temperance.

The great political agitation of American legislative bodies, which is the only one that attracts the attention of foreigners, is a mere episode, or a sort of continuation, of that universal movement which originates in the lowest ranks of the people, and extends successively to all the classes of citizens. It is impossible to spend more effort in the pursuit of happiness.

It is hard to describe the place political concerns occupy in the life of a citizen of the United States; to involve himself in the government of society and to talk about it is his most important business and, so to speak, the only pleasure an American knows. This feeling pervades the most trifling habits of life; even the women frequently attend public meetings, and listen to political harangues as an escape from household troubles. Debating clubs are, to a certain extent, a substitute for theatrical entertainment: an American does not know how to converse, he argues; he does not speak, he holds forth. He speaks to you as if he were addressing a meeting; and if he happens to get excited, he will say "Gentlemen" to the person with whom he is conversing.

In some countries, the inhabitants only accept with a sort of repugnance the political rights which the law gives them; it would seem that they set too high a value upon their time to spent it on the interests of the community; and they shut themselves up in a narrow selfishness, marked out by four ditches topped by hedges. But if an American were condemned to confine his activity to his own affairs, he would be robbed of one half of his existence; he would feel an immense void in the life which he is accustomed to lead, and he would become incredibly unhappy. I am persuaded that, if ever a despotism should be established in America, it will be more difficult to overcome the habits which freedom has formed, than to conquer the love of freedom itself.

This ceaseless agitation which democratic government has introduced into the political world passes into civil society. I am not sure that, upon the whole, this is not the greatest advantage of democracy; and I am less inclined to applaud it for what it does, than for what it causes to be done.

It is incontestable that the people frequently conduct public business very poorly; but it is impossible that the people should take part in public business without extending the circle of their ideas and without their spirit emerging from the rut of ordinary routine. The common man who participates in the government of society acquires a certain degree of self-respect; and as he possess authority, he can command the services of minds more enlightened than his own. Constant efforts are made to enlist his support, and, in seeking to deceive him in a thousand ways, they really enlighten him. He takes a part in political undertakings which he did not originate, but which give him a taste for undertakings of the kind. New improvements are daily pointed out to him in the common property, and this gives him the desire of improving that property which is his own. He is perhaps neither happier nor better than those who came before him, but he is better informed and more active. I have no doubt that the democratic institutions of the United States, joined to the physical constitution of the country, are the cause (not the direct, as is so often asserted, but the indirect cause) of the prodigious commercial activity of the inhabitants. It is not created by the laws, but the people learn how to promote it by the experience derived from making the laws.

When the opponents of democracy assert that a single man performs what he undertakes better than the government of all, it appears to me that they are right. The government of an individual, supposing an equality of knowledge on either side, is more consistent, more persevering, more uniform, and more accurate in details, than that of a multitude, and it selects with more discrimination the men whom it employs. If any deny this, they have never seen a democratic government, or have judged upon partial evidence. It is true that, even when local circumstances and the dispositions of the people allow democratic institutions to exist, they do not display a regular and methodical system of government. Democratic liberty is far from accomplishing all its projects with the skill of an adroit despotism. It frequently abandons them before they have borne their fruits, or risks them when the consequences may be dangerous; but in the end, it produces more than any absolute government; if it does fewer things well, it does a greater number of things. Under its sway, the grandeur is not in what the public administration does, but in what is done without it or outside of it. Democracy does not give the people the most skillful government, but it produces what the ablest governments are frequently unable to create; namely, an all-pervading and restless activity, a superabundant force, and an energy which is inseparable from it, and which may, however unfavorable circumstances may be, produce wonders. These are the true advantages of democracy. * * *

We must first understand what is wanted of society and its government. Do you wish to give a certain elevation to the human mind, and teach it to regard the things of this world with generous feelings, to inspire men with a scorn of mere temporal advantages, to form and nourish strong convictions, and keep alive the spirit of honorable devotedness? Is it your object to refine the habits, embellish the manners, and cultivate the arts, to promote the love of poetry, beauty, and glory? Would you organize a nation so that it will act powerfully upon all other nations, and engage in those high enterprises which, whatever be their results, will leave a name forever famous in history? If you believe such to be the principal object of society, avoid democratic government, for it would not lead you with certainty to the goal.

But if it seems useful to you to divert the moral and intellectual activity of man to the production of comfort, and the promotion of general well-being; if a clear understanding be more profitable to man than genius; if your object is not to stimulate the virtues of heroism, but the habits of peace; if you had rather witness vices than crimes, and are content to meet with fewer noble deeds, provided offences are diminished in the same proportion; if, instead of living in the midst of a brilliant society, you are contented to have prosperity around you; if, in short, you are of the opinion that the principal object of government is not to confer the greatest possible power and glory upon the body of the nation, but to insure the greatest enjoyment, and to avoid the most misery, to each of the individuals who compose it,—if such be your desire, then equalize the conditions of men, and establish democratic institutions.

But if it is no longer the moment to make such a choice, and if some power superior to that of man already inclines you, without consulting your wishes, towards one or the other of these two governments, make the best of that which is allotted to you, and, by finding out both its good and its evil tendencies, foster the former and repress the latter to the utmost.   * * *

THE FEDERALIST

Number 10 (Madison).

Among the numerous advantages promised by a well-constructed Union, none deserves to be more accurately developed than its tendency to break and control the violence of faction. The friend of popular governments never finds himself so much alarmed for their character and fate as when he contemplates their propensity to this dangerous vice. He will not fail, therefore, to set a due value on any plan which, without violating the principles to which he is attached, provides a proper cure for it. The instability, injustice, and confusion introduced into the public councils, have, in truth, been the mortal diseases under which popular governments have everywhere perished; as they continue to be the favourite and fruitful topics from which the adversaries to liberty derive their most specious declamations. The valuable improvements made by the American constitutions on the popular models, both ancient and modern, cannot certainly be too much admired; but it would be an unwarrantable partiality, to contend that they have as effectually obviated the danger on this side, as was wished and expected. Complaints are everywhere heard from our most considerate and virtuous citizens, equally the friends of public and private faith, and of public and personal liberty, that our governments are too unstable, that the public good is disregarded in the conflicts of rival parties, and that measures are too often decided, not according to the rules of justice and the rights of the minor party, but by the superior force of an interested and overbearing majority. However anxiously we may wish that these complaints had no foundation, the evidence of known facts will not permit us to deny that they are in some degree true. * * *

By a faction, I understand a number of citizens, whether amounting to a majority or minority of the whole, who are united and actuated by some common impulse of passion, or of interest, adverse to the rights of other citizens, or to the permanent and aggregate interests of the community.

There are two methods of curing the mischiefs of faction: the one, by removing its causes; the other, by controlling its effects.

There are again two methods of removing the causes of faction: the one, by destroying the liberty which is essential to its existence; the other, by giving to every citizen the same opinions, the same passions, and the same interests.

It could never be more truly said than of the first remedy, that it was worse than the disease. Liberty is to faction what air is to fire, an aliment without which it instantly expires. But it could not be less folly to abolish liberty, which is essential to political life, because it nourishes faction, than it would be to wish the annihilation of air, which is essential to animal life, because it imparts to fire its destructive agency.

The second expedient is as impracticable as the first would be unwise. As long as the reason of man continues fallible, and he is at liberty to exercise it, different opinions will be formed. As long as the connection subsists between his reason and his self-love, his opinions and his passions will have a reciprocal influence on each other; and the former will be objects to which the latter will attach themselves. The diversity in the faculties of men, from which the rights of property originate, is not less an insuperable obstacle to a uniformity of interests. The protection of these faculties is the first object of government. From the protection of different and unequal faculties of acquiring property, the possession of different degrees and kinds of property immediately results; and from the influence of these on the sentiments and views of the respective proprietors, ensues a division of the society into different interests and parties.

* * * The regulation of these various and interfering interests forms the principal task of modern legislation, and involves the spirit of party and faction, in the necessary and ordinary operations of the government.

No man is allowed to be a judge in his own cause, because his interest would certainly bias his judgment, and, not improbably, corrupt his integrity. With equal, nay, with greater reason, a body of men are unfit to be both judges and parties at the same time; yet what are many of the most important acts of legislation but so many judicial determinations, not indeed concerning the rights of single persons, but concerning the rights of large bodies of citizens? And what are the different classes of legislators but advocates and parties to the causes which they determine? Is a law proposed concerning private debts? It is a question to which the creditors are parties on one side and the debtors on the other. Justice ought to hold the balance between them. Yet the parties are, and must be, themselves the judges; and the most numerous party, or, in other words, the most powerful faction must be expected to prevail.

Shall domestic manufactures be encouraged, and in what degree, by restrictions on foreign manufactures? are questions which would be differently decided by the landed and the manufacturing classes, and probably by neither with a sole regard to justice and the public good. The apportionment of taxes on the various descriptions of property is an act which seems to require the most exact impartiality; yet there is, perhaps, no legislative act in which greater opportunity and temptation are given to a predominant party to trample on the rules of justice. Every shilling with which they overburden the inferior number, is a shilling saved to their own pockets.

It is in vain to say that enlightened statesmen will be able to adjust these clashing interests, and render them all subservient to the public good. Enlightened statesmen will not always be at the helm. Nor, in many cases, can such an adjustment be made at all without taking into view indirect and remote considerations, which will rarely prevail over the immediate interest which one party may find in disregarding the rights of another or the good of the whole.

The inference to which we are brought is, that the *causes* of faction cannot be removed, and that relief is only to be sought in the means of controlling its *effects*.

If a faction consists of less than a majority, relief is supplied by the republican principle, which enables the majority to defeat its sinister views by regular vote. It may clog the administration, it may convulse the society; but it will be unable to execute and mask its violence under the forms of the Constitution. When a majority is included in a faction, the form of popular government, on the other hand, enables it to sacrifice to its ruling passion or interest both the public good and the rights of other citizens. To secure the public good and private rights against the danger of such a faction, and at the same time to preserve the spirit and the form of popular government, is then the great object to which our inquiries are directed. Let me add that it is the great desideratum by which this form of government can be rescued from the opprobrium under which it has so long laboured, and be recommended to the esteem and adoption of mankind.

By what means is this object obtainable? Evidently by one of two only. Either the existence of the same passion or interest in a majority at the same time must be prevented, or the majority, having such co-existent passion or interest, must be rendered, by their number and local situation, unable to concert and carry into effect schemes of oppression. If the impulse and the opportunity be suffered to coincide, we well know that neither moral nor religious motives can be relied on as an adequate control. They are not found to be such on the injustice and violence of individuals, and lose their efficacy in proportion to the number combined together, that is, in proportion as their efficacy becomes needful.

From this view of the subject it may be concluded that a pure democracy, by which I mean a society consisting of a small number of citizens, who assemble and administer the government in person, can admit of no cure for the mischiefs of faction. A common passion or interest will, in almost every case, be felt by a majority of the whole; a communication and concert results from the form of government itself; and there is nothing to check the inducements to sacrifice the weaker party or an obnoxious individual. Hence it is that such democracies have ever been spectacles of turbulence and contention; have ever been found incompatible with personal security or the rights of property; and have in general been as short in their lives as they have been violent in their deaths. Theoretic politicians, who have patronised this species of government, have erroneously supposed that by reducing mankind to a perfect equality in their political rights, they would, at the same time, be perfectly equalised and assimilated in their possessions, their opinions, and their passions.

A republic, by which I mean a government in which the scheme of representation takes place, opens a different prospect, and promises the cure for which we are seeking. Let us examine the points in which it varies from pure democracy, and we shall comprehend both the nature of the cure and the efficacy which it must derive from the Union.

The two great points of difference between a democracy and a republic are: first, the delegation of the government in the latter, to a small number of citizens elected by the rest; secondly, the greater number of citizens, and greater sphere of country, over which the latter may be extended.

The effect of the first difference is, on the one hand: to refine and enlarge the public views, by passing them through the medium of a chosen body of citizens, whose wisdom may best discern the true interest of their country, and whose patriotism and love of justice will be least likely to sacrifice it to temporary or partial considerations. Under such a regulation, it may well happen that the public voice, pronounced by the representatives of the people, will be more consonant to the public good than if pronounced by the people themselves, convened for the purpose. On the other hand, the effect may be inverted. Men of factious tempers, of local prejudices, or of sinister designs, may, by intrigue, by corruption, or by other means, first obtain the suffrages, and then betray the interests, of the people. The question resulting is, whether small or extensive republics are more favourable to the election of proper guardians of the public weal; and it is clearly decided in favour of the latter by two obvious considerations:

In the first place, it is to be remarked that, however small the republic may be, the representatives must be raised to a certain number, in order to guard against the cabals of a few; and that, however large it may be, they must be limited to a certain number, in order to guard against the confusion of a multitude. Hence the number of representatives in the two cases not being in proportion to that of the two constituents, and being proportionally greater in the small republic, it follows that, if the proportion of fit characters be not less in the large than in the small republic, the former will present a greater option, and consequently a greater probability of a fit choice.

In the next place, as each representative will be chosen by a greater number of citizens in the large than in the small republic, it will be more difficult for unworthy candidates to practise with success the vicious arts by which elections are too often carried; and the suffrages of the people being more free, will be more likely to centre in men who possess the most attractive merit and the most diffusive and established characters.

It must be confessed that in this, as in most other cases, there is a mean, on both sides of which inconveniences will be found to lie. By enlarging too much the number of electors, you render the representative too little acquainted with all their local circumstances and lesser interests; as by reducing it too much, you render him unduly attached to these, and too little fit to comprehend and pursue great and national objects. The federal Constitution forms a happy combination in this respect; the great and aggregate interests being referred to the national, the local and particular to the State legislatures.

The other point of difference is, the greater number of citizens and extent of territory which may be brought within the compass of republican than of democratic government; and it is this circumstance principally which renders factious combinations less to be dreaded in the former than in the latter. The smaller the society, the fewer probably will be the distinct parties and interests composing it; the fewer the distinct parties and interests, the more frequently will a majority be found of the same party; and the smaller the number of individuals composing a majority, and the smaller the compass within which they are placed, the more easily will they concert and execute their plans of oppression. Extend the sphere, and you take in a greater variety of parties and interests; you make it less probable that a majority of the whole will have a common motive to invade the rights of other citizens; or if such a common motive exists, it will be more difficult for all who feel it to discover their own strength, and to act in unison with each other. Besides other impediments, it may be remarked that, where there is a consciousness of unjust or dishonourable purposes, communication is always checked by distrust in proportion to the number whose concurrence is necessary.

Hence, it clearly appears that the same advantage which a republic has over a democracy, in controlling the effects of faction, is enjoyed by a large over a small republic—is enjoyed by the Union over the States composing it. Does the advantage consist in the substitution of representatives whose enlightened views and virtuous sentiments render them superior to local prejudices and to schemes of injustice? It will not be denied that the representation of the Union will be most likely to possess these requisite endowments. Does it consist in the greater security afforded by a greater variety of parties, against the event of any one party being able to outnumber and oppress the rest? In an equal degree does the increased variety of parties comprised within the Union increase this security. Does it, in fine, consist in the greater obstacles opposed to the concert and accomplishment of the secret wishes of an unjust and interested majority? Here, again, the extent of the Union gives it the most palpable advantage.

The influence of factious leaders may kindle a flame within their particular States, but will be unable to spread a general conflagration through the other States. A religious sect may degenerate into a political faction in a part of the Confederacy; but the variety of sects dispersed over the entire face of it must secure the national councils against any danger from that source. A rage for paper money, for an abolition of debts, for an equal division of property or for any other improper or wicked project, will be less apt to pervade the whole body of the Union than a particular member of it; in the same proportion as such a malady is more likely to taint a particular county or district, than an entire State.

In the extent and proper structure of the Union, therefore, we behold a republican remedy for the diseases most incident to republican government. And according to the degree of pleasure and pride we feel in being republicans, ought to be our zeal in cherishing the spirit and supporting the character of Federalists.

———

The kind of arguments for and against decentralization of power articulated by Tocqueville and Madison are not limited to the issue of political decentralization. Similar arguments are often made in the context of determining the proper roles of the private sector and the government in economic decisionmaking. Advocates of limiting governmental regulation of economic activity tend to stress the values of experimentation and creative energy that Tocqueville defends, while advocates of national planning tend to emphasize, as does Madison, the danger that self-interested groups (such as corporations) pose to the rights of other citizens and to the public interest.[1] Parallel arguments are also raised in the context of defining the proper role of voluntary associations. Consider, for example, the arguments made in the following case, Citizens Against Rent Control v. City of Berkeley. How do Chief Justice Burger's arguments in support of Citizens Against Rent Control and Justice White's counter-arguments defending the City of Berkeley's ordinance relate to the positions articulated by Tocqueville and Madison? Is there an argument, based on the excerpt from Tocqueville, that would justify the opposite result in the *Berkeley* case?

CITIZENS AGAINST RENT CONTROL
v. CITY OF BERKELEY
Supreme Court of the United States, 1981.
454 U.S. 290, 102 S.Ct. 434, 70 L.Ed.2d 492.

CHIEF JUSTICE BURGER delivered the opinion of the Court. * * *

---

1. Compare, for example, M. & R. Friedman, Free to Choose 54–64 (1979) with K. Mannheim, Freedom, Power and Democratic Planning 7–31 (1951).

The voters of Berkeley, California adopted the Election Reform Act of 1974, Ord.No. 4700–N.S., by initiative. The campaign ordinance so enacted placed limits on expenditures and contributions in campaigns involving both candidates and ballot measures. Section 602 of the ordinance provides:

> "No person shall make, and no campaign treasurer shall solicit or accept, any contribution which will cause the total amount contributed by such person with respect to a single election in support of or in opposition to a measure to exceed two hundred and fifty dollars ($250)."

Appellant Citizens Against Rent Control is an unincorporated association formed to oppose a ballot measure at issue in the April 19, 1977 election. The ballot measure would have imposed rent control on many of Berkeley's rental units. To make its views on the ballot measure known, Citizens Against Rent Control raised more than $108,000 from approximately 1,300 contributors. It accepted nine contributions over the $250 limit. Those nine contributions totaled $20,850, or $18,600 more than if none of the contributions exceeded $250. Pursuant to § 604 of the ordinance, appellee Berkeley Fair Campaign Practices Commission, 20 days before the election, ordered appellant Citizens Against Rent Control to pay $18,600 into the City treasury.

Two weeks before the election, Citizens Against Rent Control sought and obtained a temporary restraining order prohibiting enforcement of §§ 602 and 604. The ballot measure relating to rent control was defeated. The Superior Court subsequently granted Citizens Against Rent Control's motion for summary judgment, declaring that § 602 was invalid on its face because it violated the First Amendment of the United States Constitution and Art. I, § 2, of the California Constitution. * * *

We begin by recalling that the practice of persons sharing common views banding together to achieve a common end is deeply embedded in the American political process. The 18th Century Committees of Correspondence and the pamphleteers were early examples of this phenomena and the Federalist Papers were perhaps the most significant and lasting example. The tradition of volunteer committees for collective action has manifested itself in myriad community and public activities; in the political process it can focus on a candidate or on a ballot measure. Its value is that by collective effort individuals can make their views known, when, individually, their voices would be faint or lost.

The Court has long viewed the First Amendment as protecting a market place for the clash of different views and conflicting ideas. That concept has been stated and restated almost since the Constitution was drafted. The voters of the City of Berkeley adopted the challenged ordinance which places restrictions on that market place. It is irrelevant that the voters rather than a legislative body enacted § 602, because the voters may no more violate the Constitution by enacting a ballot measure than a legislative body may do so by enacting legislation.

The Court has acknowledged the importance of freedom of association in guaranteeing the right of people to make their voices heard on public issues:

> "Effective advocacy of both public and private points of view, particularly controversial ones, is undeniably enhanced by group association, as this Court has more than once recognized by remarking upon the close nexus between the freedoms of speech and assembly." *NAACP v. Alabama,* 357 U.S. 449, 460, 78 S.Ct. 1163, 1170, 2 L.Ed.2d 1488 (1958).

More recently the Court stated, "The First Amendment protects political association as well as political expression." *Buckley v. Valeo,* 424 U.S. 1, 15, 96 S.Ct. 612, 632, 46 L.Ed.2d 659 (1976).

Buckley also made clear that contributors cannot be protected from the possibility that others will make larger contributions:

> "[T]he concept that government may restrict the speech of some elements of our society in order to enhance the relative voice of others is wholly foreign to the First Amendment, which was designed 'to secure "the widest possible dissemination of information from diverse and antagonistic sources," and "to assure unfettered interchange of ideas for the bringing about of political and social changes desired by the people." ' The First Amendment's protection against governmental abridgment of free expression cannot properly be made to depend on a person's financial ability to engage in public discussion."

The Court went on to note that the freedom of association "is diluted if it does not include the right to pool money through contributions, for funds are often essential if 'advocacy' is to be truly or optimally 'effective.' " Under the Berkeley ordinance an affluent person can, acting alone, spend without limit to advocate individual views on a ballot measure. It is only when contributions are made in concert with one or more others in the exercise of the right of association that they are restricted by § 602.

There are, of course, some activities, legal if engaged in by one, yet illegal if performed in concert with others, but political expression is not one of them. To place a spartan limit—or indeed any limit—on individuals wishing to band together to advance their views on a ballot measure, while placing none on individuals acting alone, is clearly a restraint on the right of association. Section 602 does not seek to mute the voice of one individual and it cannot be allowed to hobble the collective expressions of a group.

Buckley identified a single narrow exception to the rule that limits on political activity were contrary to the First Amendment. The exception relates to the perception of undue influence of large contributors to a *candidate*:

"To the extent that large contributions are given to secure a political *quid pro quo* from current and potential office holders, the integrity of our system of representative democracy is undermined. * * * Congress could legitimately conclude that the avoidance of the appearance of improper influence 'is also critical * * * if confidence in the system of representative Government is not to be eroded to a disasterous extent.' "

Buckley thus sustained limits on contributions to candidates and their committees. * * *

In *First National Bank v. Bellotti,* 435 U.S. 765, 98 S.Ct. 1407, 55 L.Ed.2d 707 (1978), we held that a state could not prohibit corporations any more than it could preclude individuals from making contributions or expenditures advocating views on ballot measures. The *Bellotti* Court relied on *Buckley* to strike down state legislative limits on advocacy relating to ballot measures:

"Referenda are held on issues, not candidates for public office. The risk of corruption perceived in cases involving candidate elections simply is not present in a popular vote on a public issue. To be sure, corporate advertising may influence the outcome of the vote; this would be its purpose. But the fact that advocacy may persuade the electorate is hardly a reason to suppress it: The Constitution 'protects expression which is eloquent no less than that which is unconvincing.' "

Notwithstanding *Buckley* and *Bellotti,* the City of Berkeley argues that § 602 is necessary as a prophylactic measure to make known the identity of supporters and opponents of ballot measures. It is true that when individuals or corporations speak through committees, they often adopt seductive names that may tend to conceal the true identity of the source. Here there is no risk that the Berkeley voters will be in doubt as to the identity of those whose money supports or opposes a given ballot measure since contributors must make their identities known under § 112 of the ordinance, which requires publication of lists of contributors in advance of the voting.

Contributions by individuals to support concerted action by a committee advocating a position on a ballot measure is beyond question a very significant form of political expression. As we have noted, regulation of First Amendment rights is always subject to exacting judicial scrutiny. The public interest allegedly advanced by § 602—identifying the sources of support for and opposition to ballot measures—is insubstantial because voters may identify those sources under the provisions of § 112. In addition, the record in this case does not support the California Supreme Court's conclusion that § 602 is needed to preserve voters' confidence in the ballot measure process. Cf. *Bellotti,* supra, 435 U.S., at 789–790, 98 S.Ct., at 1422–1423. It is clear, therefore, that § 602 does not advance a legitimate governmental interest significant enough to justify its infringement on First Amendment rights.

Apart from the impermissible restraint on freedom of association, but virtually inseparable from it in this context, § 602 imposes a significant restraint on the freedom of expression of groups and those individuals who wish to express their views through committees. As we have noted, an individual may make expenditures without limit under § 602 on a ballot measure but may not contribute beyond the $250 limit when joining with others to advocate common views. The contribution limit thus automatically affects expenditures and limits on expenditures operate as a direct restraint on freedom of expression of a group or committee desiring to engage in political dialogue concerning a ballot measure.

Whatever may be the state interest or degree of that interest in regulating and limiting contributions to or expenditures of a candidate or a candidate's committees there is no significant state or public interest in curtailing debate and discussion of a ballot measure. Placing limits on contributions which in turn limit expenditures plainly impairs freedom of expression. The integrity of the political system will be adequately protected if contributors are identified in a public filing revealing the amounts contributed; if it is thought wise, legislation can outlaw anonymous contributions.

A limit on contributions in this setting need not be analyzed exclusively in terms of the right of association or the right of expression. The two rights overlap and blend; to limit the right of association places an impermissible restraint on the right of expression. The restraint imposed by the Berkeley Ordinance on rights of association and in turn on individual and collective rights of expression plainly contravenes both the right of association and the speech guarantees of the First Amendment. * * *

Justice White, dissenting. * * *

The Court * * * finds that the freedom of association is impermissibly compromised by not allowing persons to contribute unlimited funds to committees organized to support or oppose a ballot measure. However, in *Buckley,* the Court observed that contribution ceilings "leav[e] persons free to engage in independent political expression, to associate actively through volunteering their services, and to assist to a limited but nonetheless substantial extent in supporting candidates and committees with financial resources." Associational rights, it was thought, were seriously impinged only by expenditure ceilings—there by virtue of precluding associations from effectively amplifying the voice of their adherents, "the original basis for the recognition of First Amendment protection of the freedom of association." * * *

In *Bellotti,* the Court * * * suggested that some regulation of corporate spending might be justified if "corporate advocacy threatened imminently to undermine democratic processes, thereby denigrating rather than serving First Amendment interests." The Court suggested that such a situation would arise if it could be shown that "the relative voice of corporation ha[d] been overwhelming [and] * * * significant in influencing referenda." It is quite possible that such a test is fairly met in this case. Large contributions, mainly from corporate sources, have skyrocketed as the role of individuals has declined. Staggering disparities have developed between spending for and against various ballot measures. While it is not possible to prove that heavy spending "bought" a victory on any particular ballot proposition, there is increasing evidence that large contributors are at least able to block the adoption of measures through the initiative process. Recognition that enormous contributions from a few institutional sources can overshadow the efforts of individuals may have discouraged participation in ballot measure campaigns and undermined public confidence in the referendum process.

By restricting the size of contributions, the Berkeley ordinance requires major contributors to communicate directly with the voters. If the ordinance has an ultimate impact on speech, it will be to assure that a diversity of views will be presented to the voters. As such, it will "facilitate and enlarge public discussion and participation in the electoral process, goals vital to a self-governing people." *Buckley,* 424 U.S., at 92–93, 96 S.Ct., at 669–670. Of course, entities remain free to make major direct expenditures. But because political communications must state the source of funds, voters will be able to identify the source of such messages and recognize that the communication reflects, for example, the opinion of a single powerful corporate interest rather than the views of a large number of individuals. As the existence of disclosure laws in many states suggests, information concerning who supports or opposes a ballot measure significantly affects voter evaluation of the proposal. The Court asserts, without elaboration, that existing disclosure requirements suffice to inform voters of the identity of contributors. Yet, the inadequacy of disclosure laws was a major reason for the adoption of the Berkeley ordinance. Section 101 of the ordinance constitutes a finding by the people of Berkeley that "the influence of large campaign contributors is increased because existing laws for disclosure of campaign receipts and expenditures have proved to be inadequate." * * *

The interests which justify the Berkeley ordinance can properly be understood only in the context of the historic role of the initiative in California. "California's entire history demonstrates the repeated use of referendums to give citizens a voice on questions of public policy." *James v. Valtierra,* 402 U.S. 137, 141, 91 S.Ct. 1331, 1333, 28 L.Ed.2d 678 (1971). From its earliest days, it was designed to circumvent the undue influence of large corporate interests on government decisionmaking. It served, as President Wilson put it, as a "gun behind the door" to keep political bosses and legislators honest. In more recent years, concerned that the heavy financial participation by corporations in referendum contests has undermined this tool of direct democracy, the voters of California enacted by initiative in 1974 the Political Reform Act, which limited expenditures in statewide ballot measure campaigns, and Berkeley voters adopted the ordinance at issue in this case. The role of the initiative in California cannot be separated from its purpose of preventing the dominance of special interests. That is the very history and purpose of the initiative in California and similarly it is the purpose of ancillary regulations designed to protect it. Both serve to maximize the exchange of political discourse. As in *Bellotti*, "The Court's fundamental error is its failure to realize that the state regulatory interests * * * are themselves derived from the First Amendment." 435 U.S., at 803 804, 98 S.Ct., at 1429 1430 (White, J., dissenting). * * *

SECTION B. THE CITY AS A PUBLIC OR PRIVATE ENTITY

The preceding materials, by sketching the arguments for and against decentralization of power, introduced one of the basic themes of local government law. This section introduces another basic theme—the question whether cities, when they exercise decentralized power, should be treated as public or private entities. As an initial matter, the answer to this question may seem obvious. Of course, one might say, cities are public entities. Cities are governments, just like states; they are not at all like private entities, such as corporations.

As the doctrines of local government law covered in this book demonstrate, however, the answer to the question of the nature of city power is more complicated than it first appears. Cities can certainly be understood as exercising the coercive power of government. But cities have also traditionally been understood as corporations—as collective entities organized to pursue not the interests of the state but the interests of the people who live within them. Although cities are partly created by state law, they also are partly created by city residents seeking to exercise their own power independent of national or state control. Throughout our history, cities have been seen not only as governments but also as vehicles for the exercise of self-determination.

As an historical matter, this dual nature of cities can be traced to their ancestral roots in the medieval town. A medieval town was a corporation and, like other corporations (such as universities and the church), it was a device that enabled a group of people to exercise collective power. Moreover, the towns, like corporations generally, wielded both political and economic power; medieval theorists did not classify corporations as political or economic, as public or private. Instead, corporate (and, consequently, the towns') activity was understood in medieval society as raising the general question of the role of groups, as distinguished from the roles of individuals or the nation-state, in social life. Defending the autonomy of medieval towns against national control was a way to maintain individual liberty by securing the entitlements of a group. By ensuring the rights of a corporation, one could protect the group as a whole.[1]

---

1. For further discussion of the medieval town, see, e.g., O. Gierke, Political Theories of the Middle Ages (F.W. Maitland trans. 1958); F. Maitland, Township and

To be sure, since medieval towns and other corporations wielded considerable power, they often were under attack by those who wanted to curb their influence in social life. These critics generally sought to reallocate corporate (and thus the towns') power either to the central government or to individuals. In England, municipal corporations were able to resist this attack because of their economic strength and their status as entities with rights protected against the King. Ultimately, the nature of these rights themselves became the subject of a major controversy between the King and the cities. This controversy led, after the Glorious Revolution of 1688, to even further protection of municipal rights against the King.[2]

In colonial America, the rights of cities were also resolved as part of the question of the relationship between corporations in general and governmental power. Before the nineteenth century, it is important to emphasize, there was no legal distinction in England or in America between public and private corporations, between businesses and cities. All corporations had the same rights. But, although these corporate rights had been resolved in the corporations' favor against the King, the relationship between corporations and state legislatures remained unsettled. The problem of city power in early America lay in defining that relationship. The following excerpt, taken from an article of mine entitled The City as a Legal Concept, describes how the nature of the relationship between corporations and legislatures became established.

GERALD FRUG, THE CITY AS A LEGAL CONCEPT

93 Harv.L.Rev. 1057, 1098–1109 (1980).

The question of the appropriate extent of legislative power over the cities was decided as part of the larger issue of the desired extent of legislative power over all corporations, whether cities or other mercantile bodies. In late eighteenth century America, the larger issue was deeply troubling. On the one hand, corporate rights had been protected from the King by the Glorious Revolution; these rights, once recognized, seemed to deserve protection from legislative infringement as well. America had rejected the English notion of legislative supremacy in favor of the Lockean concept of a legislative power limited by natural rights. Legislative denial of these rights could be tolerated no more than could executive denial. On the other hand, corporations exercised power in society that seemed to limit the rights of individuals to earn their livelihood, and this power, wielded by an aristocratic elite to protect their monopolistic privileges, needed to be controlled by popular—that is,

Borough (1898); H. Pirenne, Medieval Cities (F. Halsey trans. 1925). See also G. Frug, The City as a Legal Concept, 93 Harv. L.Rev. 1057, 1083–90 (1980).

2. For materials on early modern towns, see, e.g., F. Braudel, Towns, in Capitalism and Material Life 1400–1800, at 373 (M.

Kochan trans. 1967); P. Clark & P. Slack, English Towns in Transition 1500–1700 (1974); J. Levin, The Charter Controversy in the City of London 1600–1688 and Its Consequences (1969). See also G. Frug, The City as a Legal Concept, 93 Harv. L.Rev. 1057, 1090–95 (1980).

legislative—action.   Thus, while the exercise of legislative power was perceived as a threat to corporate rights, the exercise of corporate rights risked the curtailment of legislative power thought necessary to protect the welfare of the people.

On a deeper level, the corporation represented an anomaly to liberal thinkers who envisioned the world as sharply divided between individual rightholders and state power, the ruled in conflict with the ruler.   The corporation exhibited traits of both poles: it was part ruled and part ruler, both an association of individuals and an entity with state-granted power.   * * *

Even more troublesome was that the corporation was in some aspects a protector of, while in other ways a threat to, both individual rights and state power.   In one capacity, the corporation not only protected individual property rights but also served as a useful vehicle for the exercise of state powers.   Yet, at the same time, the corporation, like the medieval town, restricted the freedom of individual enterprise and operated as a miniature republic, impervious to state power.   The dilemma created by the corporation, then, could be solved neither by retention of its present form nor by abolition in favor of individual rights, as urged by Adam Smith, or in favor of the state, as advocated by Hobbes.

To solve the problem created by the intermediate status of the corporation, early nineteenth century legal doctrine divided the corporation into two different entities, one assimilated to the role of an individual in society and the other assimilated to the role of the state.   The corporation as an entity that was simultaneously a rightholder and a power wielder thus disappeared. In its place emerged the private corporation, which was an individual rightholder,[165] and the public corporation, an entity that was identified with the state.   The very purpose of the distinction was to ensure that some corporations, called "private," would be protected against domination by the state and that others, called "public," would be subject to such domination.   In this way, the corporate anomaly was resolved so that corporations, like the rest of society, were divided into individuals and the state.

This public/private distinction for corporations was not purely a legal invention.   The distinction had been generally emerging since the American Revolution, and both the newly created public and private identities were the product of a pervasive liberal attack on the exclusive privileges and oligarchic power wielded by corporations.

The attack which established the "private" character of business corporations developed as their number expanded, rising from only eight in 1780 to several hundred by the time of the critical *Dartmouth College* opinion in 1819.   Even though these business corporations were public service enterprises, such as canals, bridges, water supply companies, and

---

165. This culminated in the recognition of the corporation as a person for purposes of the 14th amendment.   *See* Santa Clara   Co. v. Southern Pac. R.R., 118 U.S. 394 (1886).

banking enterprises, their creation raised troubling questions concerning the amount of protection afforded their investors and participants. As the courts gradually developed protections for the investors' property, pressure mounted on the legislature to expand the opportunities for incorporation from a favored few to the more general population.

Yet, as the legislature yielded to this drive for more incorporations, the demand for protection of property rights for those involved itself increased. As one commentary noted, "The process which multiplied the institution [of the corporation] and the unfoldment of its private character reacted upon each other in a reciprocal, accumulative fashion. Every new grant strengthened the grounds for considering it private; every new affirmation of privateness strengthened the hands of those who demanded new grants." This process gathered momentum, culminating in the middle of the nineteenth century in the Jacksonian effort to pass general incorporation laws, thus allowing the "privilege" of incorporation to be exercised by all.

The attack on the exclusiveness of city corporations worked in another direction. Although the number of city corporations could not be expanded, participation in their operation could be enlarged. With the sovereignty of the people as the emerging basis of republican politics, and with the need created by population growth to add new functions to city corporations, the pressure for state legislation to end aristocratic corporate governance mounted. The most important closed corporation in America, that of Philadelphia, was abolished by radical republican legislators in 1776, and it was replaced several years later with a modified, more broadly based, corporation.

This attack on the privileged control of city corporations and the concomitant expansion of participation in corporate governance made it increasingly difficult to separate the city corporation from the people as a whole, that is, to view city corporate rights as distinct from the rights of the public at large. The movement toward what was then considered universal suffrage, in the 1820's and 1830's, helped confirm the emerging public character of city corporations, thus setting them in contrast to the "private" business corporations.

Despite the developments, American courts in the early nineteenth century had great difficulty in establishing the public/private distinction for corporations. All corporations continued to have similar characteristics. Corporations, whether cities or mercantile entities, were chartered only to further public purposes, and many of their functions overlapped. All corporations were in one sense created by individuals and, in another sense, created by the state through the award of the franchise. Many mercantile corporations wielded the same powers as cities, such as eminent domain, while many cities received their income from the same sources as mercantile corporations, primarily commerce and trade. Both cities and mercantile corporations served to protect the private investments of individual founders and allowed those active in their governance a large degree of self-determination. Many cities and mercantile corporations were controlled by an elite, and consequently both were subject to popular attack. Finally, cities and mercantile corporations alike could be viewed as associations of individuals organized to achieve commercial ends. In short, all corporations wielded power and all corporations protected rights. The concepts of power and rights, so fully merged in the medieval town, had not yet been segregated into their public and private identities.

In determining where to draw the public/private distinction for corporations, the courts first decided what was important to protect against state power. In *Trustees of Dartmouth College v. Woodward*, decided in 1819, the United States Supreme Court gave its response to this question, an answer that came straight from Locke: what needed protection was property. The scope of property rights thus divided private from public corporations, private corporations being those founded by individual contributions of property, and public corporations being those founded by the government without such individual contributions.

Having decided the importance of property rights, the Court then sought to determine the status of cities under the public/private distinction. While three major opinions were delivered in the case, Justice Story, who had four years earlier first made the public/private distinction for corporations in a Supreme Court opinion, presented the most complete discussion of the issue:

> Another division of corporations is into public and private. Public corporations are generally esteemed such as exist for public political purposes only, such as towns, cities, parishes, and counties; and in many respects they are so, although they involve some private interests; but strictly speaking, public corporations are such only as are founded by the government for public purposes, where the whole interests belong also to the government.

This passage, however, is ambiguous. Justice Story may have been arguing that the critical distinction between private and public corporations was whether they were founded by individuals or "founded *by the government* for public purposes, where the *whole interests* belong to the government." This seems close to the positions taken by both Chief Justice Marshall and Justice Washington. Only if the corporation were completely a state creation, Justice Washington argued, would there be a diminished need to protect property rights from state domination; protection of contract rights would be unnecessary if there were but one party, the state, involved in the foundation of the corporation. Yet, if that were the definition of public corporations, most cities could not be public corporations: most were not founded by the government, nor did they belong wholly to the government. Alternatively, Justice Story may have accepted what was "generally esteemed" at the time if not "strictly speaking" true: that all cities were public corporations. In fact, he twice referred to "towns, cities, and counties" as examples of public corporations. Which of these positions Justice Story held with regard to the place of cities within the public/private distinction is unclear.

Moreover, the emphasis on property did not in itself provide a division between cities and other mercantile corporations. Many cities possessed property contributed by individual founders, and mercantile corporations could readily be created by governments for their own purposes. Indeed, Justice Story noted in *Dartmouth College* that even cities possessed certain property rights, although he did not indicate what, if any, additional legal protection from legislative interference cities should receive.

Seventeen years later in his *Commentaries on American Law*, Chancellor Kent offered his own view of the status of cities within the public/private distinction:

> Public corporations are such as are created by the government for political purposes, as counties, cities, towns and villages; they are invested with subordinate legislative powers to be exercised for local purposes connected with the public good, and such powers are subject to the control of the legislature of the state. They may also be empowered to take or hold private property for municipal uses, and such property is invested with the security of other private rights.

In this passage, Chancellor Kent apparently rejected the notion that, in order for an entity to constitute a public corporation, the "whole interest" must belong to the government. He simply asserted that cities were "created by the government," thus denying their actual history both in England and in America. Having taken that step, Kent then divided city authority into two parts: legislation for the public good, and the possession of property for municipal uses. Of these, only city property received protection from state control. Just as public and private corporations are distinguished by the need to protect private property, cities themselves became bifurcated by the same need—self-determination was retained only for the protection of their private property. It is this view that became, and remains, the law concerning the status of cities in the United States.

It is by no means self-explanatory why, once corporate property rights were protected, early nineteenth century writers like Chancellor Kent seemed to think it obvious that the other functions of cities would be subordinate to state power. Cities, like other corporations, had never based their resistance to state control simply on the protection of property. Freedom of association and the exercise of self-government had always been values sought to be protected by the defense of the corporation. It did not, therefore, follow from the need to protect property that property alone needed protection and that these other values could be sacrificed to state domination. Indeed, even at the time, these other values were seen as part of the definition of liberty, their defense being most clearly articulated in the defense of state power against federal control encapsulated in the doctrine of federalism.

In addition, such a notion of subordination would turn the political world as it then existed upside down. New England towns had controlled state legislatures since prior to the Revolution, and the move in other sections of the country to end aristocratic city governance in favor of democracy was not made with the intention of establishing state control over cities. Nor could subservience to the state be considered an inevitable product of liberal thought. The proper relationship of city to state was instead a hotly contested political issue. Some argued that the sovereignty of the people required control at the local level, but others feared the power of democratic cities over the allocation of property in America. Aristotle, Montesquieu, and Rousseau could be invoked in favor of power at the local level, while Madison and Hume could be cited to show the danger of local self-government. Thus, it is necessary to explain how legal theorists could classify cities as public corporations and thereby subject them to state control.

In seeking to understand why cities became subordinate to state power, I will not seek to isolate some factor as the "cause" of this change in city status. Instead, I will simply suggest how an early nineteenth century thinker could have conceived of state control of cities as a defense of freedom and other values rather than as a restriction of freedom.

Once the cities became synonymous with the people within them, one could acknowledge city rights only if one were willing to recognize the right of association and self-determination for any group of people, however large. Such a recognition would threaten many other important values. It would limit the nation's ability to establish a unified political system under the Federal Constitution, preventing the needed centralization of authority and perpetuating the idea that the nation was merely a loose federation of localities. Moreover, these groups, particularly small groups, could be seen as "factions" dangerous to the individuals within them, inhibiting the individual's free development and threatening his property rights. In other words, recognizing the rights of the city as an exercise of the freedom of association would frustrate both the interests of the state and the individual and would defy the liberal attempt to dissolve the power of groups in favor of the state and the individual. Recognizing the rights of the city as an association would thus bring to the surface what was sought to be denied: that corporations were the continuation of the group rights of the medieval town, protecting both the associational and property rights of its members.

Recognition of city rights would also bring to the surface the conflict between the values of association and of property rights themselves, a conflict that had been hidden by the fact that both values had traditionally been protected by the corporate form. Prior to the emergence of the public/private distinction, there was no difference between a corporation's property rights and its rights of group self-government. But now group self-government—or popular sovereignty—seemed a threat to property rights, and property rights seemed a necessary limit to popular sovereignty. Thus, any recognition of the rights of the city would require the courts to choose between associational rights and property rights in particular cases, rather than simply protecting property rights against the power of "governmental" collective action. All these problems seemed to disappear, however, if recognition of the rights of cities were avoided.

The amount of emphasis to put on the fear of democratic power in explaining the judicial decision to limit the power of cities is, of course, a matter of conjecture. Such fear plainly existed, however, even in the minds of such champions of local power as Jefferson and de Tocqueville. While Jefferson saw towns as the "elementary republics" of the nation that must be preserved so that "the voice of the whole people would be fairly, fully, and peaceably expressed * * * by the common reason" of all citizens, he also saw them as objects to be feared: "The mobs of great cities add just so much to the support of pure government, as sores do to the strength of the human body." For de Tocqueville, "the strength of free peoples resides in the local community," giving them both the "spirit of liberty" and the ability to withstand the "tyranny of the majority", but the size of American cities and the nature of their inhabitants were also so threatening to the future of the republic that they required "an armed force which, while remaining subject to the wishes of the national majority, is independent of the peoples of the towns and capable of suppressing their excesses." Indeed, the vision of cities as being the home of "mobs," the working class, immigrants, and, finally, racial minorities, is a theme that runs throughout much of nineteenth and twentieth century thought. Chancellor Kent's own fears of the democratic cities were surely no secret.

Yet one need not rely on the assertion that the subordination of cities was the product of the unwillingness to protect the cities' rights of association and the fear of democratic power. Since the issue of city power was decided as part of the issue of corporate power, the threatening ideas associated with the rights of association did not need to be brought to consciousness. It is for this reason that the classification of American cities as corporations mattered; it can be understood as helping to repress the notion that associational rights were being affected in defining the laws governing city rights. No rights of association needed to be articulated when discussing the rights of "private" corporations, since property rights were sufficient to protect them against state power, and there was nothing that required rights of association to be imagined in discussing the subordination of "public" corporations. Yet, if no rights of association were recognized, cities, increasingly deprived of their economic character—the basis of their power for hundreds of years—had little defense against the reallocation of their power to the individual and to the state. There was nothing left that seemed to demand protection; therefore, nothing could prevent the control of the cities by the state.

The developments in legal doctrine that led to the public/private distinction for corporations did not immediately alter the allocation of power between American states and cities. In fact, prior to the 1850's, local autonomy remained largely intact. The impetus for the assertion of state political power to curb local autonomy finally came when the desire to restrict city activity in favor of private activity increased. In light of the new conception of public and private activities, the investment by cities in business enterprises no longer seemed an appropriate "public" function, and local regulation of a city's business community seemed to invade the "private sphere." Hence, state control over these city activities was invoked. State control of cities during this period, however, was by no means limited to the assurance of a "laissez-faire" policy designed to prevent both cities and states, as governments, from intervening in the private sector. Much state legislation compelled the cities to raise and spend money for state-supported causes, including the promotion of economic enterprise. Other state legislation—so-called "ripper legislation"—simply sought to transfer control of the city government to state-appointed officials. For a wide variety of purposes, then, state power to control cities could now be exercised—and was being exercised—as a matter of law. * * *

The meaning of the public/private distinction was not definitively settled in the early nineteenth century. The first two cases that follow illustrate the difficulties in applying the distinction to the modern metropolis. In the first case, International Society for Krishna Consciousness v. Lee, the United States Supreme Court declined to treat a government-owned airport terminal as a "public forum" although the dissent analogized the terminal to a public street. In the second case, Lloyd Corporation v. Tanner, the Supreme Court rejected the contention that a shopping center performs a "public function" although the dissent argued that a shopping center is like a city downtown. In reading these cases, consider how the courts decide whether to treat an entity as "public" and, therefore, as subject to the application of Constitutional restraints. Does an entity become subject to the Constitution because it is awarded a state charter? Or does it become subject to the Constitution, whether or not it has a charter, if it acts like a public entity? What does "acting like a public entity" mean?

In the final case in the section, Board of Education of Kiryas Joel School District v. Grumet, the Supreme Court held unconstitutional New York State's creation of a school district comprised only of Hasidic Jews. The school district violated the Establishment Clause, the Court reasoned, because it unacceptably merged private religion and public power. What limits does the *Kiryas Joel* case impose on the ability of (private) individuals who profess the same religion to form a school district (or a city)? If a religious group lives together in a territorially defined community, would it be a city even if it didn't obtain a state charter? To provoke thought about this final question, I have reproduced below an excerpt from Joel Garreau's important book, Edge City. The excerpt describes a large private development called Sun City, Arizona. Is Sun City a "city"? Should Constitutional safeguards protect the residents of Sun City whether or not it is considered a "city"?

JOEL GARREAU, EDGE CITY

Pp. 184–185 (1991).

Sun City, Arizona, on the west side of metropolitan Phoenix, bills itself as the largest "adult" community in the world. It has ten shopping centers and forty-six thousand residents. It is a privately owned development that has fervently resisted incorporation into any municipality in order to avoid a new level of taxation. But, though private, it has taken on many trappings of a city. It runs everything from libraries to parks to swimming pools to an art museum to a crisis-counseling hotline to a fire department to a symphony orchestra. The squad cars of its legally franchised, armed, unpaid private posse routinely patrol the public streets. Its innocuously named Recreation Association, meanwhile, has the power to assess fees that are functionally indistinguishable from taxes. If a homeowner does not pay the fees, the association has the legal right—so far unexercised—to slap a lien on that person's house and sell it at auction.

Sun City is by no means an aberration. It represents several forms of private-enterprise governments—shadow governments, if you will—of which there are more than 150,000 in the United States. These shadow governments have become the most numerous, ubiquitous, and largest form of local government in America today, studies show. In their various guises shadow governments levy taxes, adjudicate disputes, provide police protection, run fire departments, provide health care, channel development, plan regionally, enforce esthetic standards, run buses, run railroads, run airports, build roads, fill potholes, publish newspapers, pump water, generate electricity, clean streets, landscape grounds, pick up garbage, cut grass, rake leaves, remove snow, offer recreation, and provide the hottest social service in the United States today: day care. They are central to the Edge City society we are building, in which office parks are in the childrearing business, parking-lot officials run police forces, private enterprise builds public freeways, and subdivisions have a say in who lives where.

These shadow governments have powers far beyond those ever granted rulers in this country before. Not only can they prohibit the organization of everything from a synagogue to a Boy Scout troop; they can regulate the color of a person's living room curtains. Nonetheless, the general public almost never gets the opportunity to vote its leaders out of office, and rarely is protected from them by the United States Constitution. * * *

INTERNATIONAL SOCIETY FOR KRISHNA CONSCIOUSNESS, INC. v. LEE

Supreme Court of the United States, 1992.
—— U.S. ——, 112 S.Ct. 2701, 120 L.Ed.2d 541.

JUSTICE REHNQUIST delivered the opinion of the Court. * * *

Petitioner International Society for Krishna Consciousness, Inc. (ISKCON) is a not-for-profit religious corporation whose members perform a ritual known as *sankirtan*. The ritual consists of " 'going into public places, disseminating religious literature and soliciting funds to support the religion.' " 925 F.2d 576, 577 (CA2 1991). The primary purpose of this ritual is raising funds for the movement.

Respondent Walter Lee, now deceased, was the police superintendent of the Port Authority of New York and New Jersey * * *. The Port Authority owns and operates three major airports in the greater New York City area: John F. Kennedy International Airport (Kennedy), La Guardia Airport (La Guardia), and Newark International Airport (Newark). The three airports collectively form one of the world's busiest metropolitan airport complexes. * * *

The airports are funded by user fees and operated to make a regulated profit. Most space at the three airports is leased to commercial airlines, which bear primary responsibility for the leasehold. The Port Authority retains control over unleased portions, including La Guardia's Central Terminal Building, portions of Kennedy's International Arrivals Building, and Newark's North Terminal Building (we refer to these areas collectively as the "terminals"). The terminals are generally accessible to the general public and contain various commercial establishments such as restaurants, snack stands, bars, newsstands, and stores of various types. Virtually all who visit the terminals do so for purposes related to air travel. * * *

The Port Authority has adopted a regulation forbidding within the terminals the repetitive solicitation of money or distribution of literature. * * * The regulation effectively prohibits petitioner from performing *sankirtan* in the terminals. As a result, petitioner brought suit seeking declaratory and injunctive relief under 42 U.S.C. § 1983, alleging that the regulation worked to deprive them of rights guaranteed under the First Amendment. * * *

It is uncontested that the solicitation at issue in this case is a form of speech protected under the First Amendment. But it is also well settled that the government need not permit all forms of speech on property that it owns and controls. Where the government is acting as a proprietor, managing its internal operations, rather than acting as lawmaker with the power to regulate or license, its action will not be subjected to the heightened review to which its actions as a lawmaker may be subject. Thus, we have upheld a ban on political advertisements in city-operated transit vehicles, *Lehman v. City of Shaker Heights*, 418 U.S. 298, 94 S.Ct. 2714, 41 L.Ed.2d 770 (1974), even though the city permitted other types of advertising on those vehicles. Similarly, we have permitted a school district to limit access to an internal mail system used to communicate with teachers employed by the district. *Perry*

Education Assn. v. Perry Local Educators' Ass'n, 460 U.S. 37, 103 S.Ct. 948, 74 L.Ed.2d 794 (1983).

These cases reflect, either implicitly or explicitly, a "forum-based" approach for assessing restrictions that the government seeks to place on the use of its property. Under this approach, regulation of speech on government property that has traditionally been available for public expression is subject to the highest scrutiny. Such regulations survive only if they are narrowly drawn to achieve a compelling state interest. The second category of public property is the designated public forum, whether of a limited or unlimited character—property that the state has opened for expressive activity by part or all of the public. Regulation of such property is subject to the same limitations as that governing a traditional public forum. Finally, there is all remaining public property. Limitations on expressive activity conducted on this last category of property must survive only a much more limited review. The challenged regulation need only be reasonable, as long as the regulation is not an effort to suppress the speaker's activity due to disagreement with the speaker's view. * * *

The suggestion that the government has a high burden in justifying speech restrictions relating to traditional public fora made its first appearance in *Hague v. Committee for Industrial Organization*, 307 U.S. 496, 515, 516, 59 S.Ct. 954, 963, 964, 83 L.Ed. 1423 (1939). Justice Roberts, concluding that individuals have a right to use "streets and parks for communication of views," reasoned that such a right flowed from the fact that "streets and parks * * * have immemorially been held in trust for the use of the public and, time out of mind, have been used for purposes of assembly, communicating thoughts between citizens, and discussing public questions." We confirmed this observation in *Frisby v. Schultz*, 487 U.S. 474, 481, 108 S.Ct. 2495, 2500, 101 L.Ed.2d 420 (1988), where we held that a residential street was a public forum.

Our recent cases provide additional guidance on the characteristics of a public forum. In *Cornelius* [*v. NAACP Legal Defense and Education Fund, Inc.*,] we noted that a traditional public forum is property that has as "a principal purpose * * * the free exchange of ideas." 473 U.S. [788], at 800, 105 S.Ct. [3439], at 3448. Moreover, consistent with the notion that the government—like other property owners—"has power to preserve the property under its control for the use to which it is lawfully dedicated," *Greer* [*v. Spock*], 424 U.S. [828], at 836, 96 S.Ct. [1211], at 1217, the government does not create a public forum by inaction. Nor is a public forum created "whenever members of the public are permitted freely to visit a place owned or operated by the Government." *Ibid.* The decision to create a public forum must instead be made "by intentionally opening a nontraditional forum for public discourse." *Cornelius, supra*, 473 U.S., at 802, 105 S.Ct., at 3449. Finally, we have recognized that the location of property also has bearing because separation from acknowledged public areas may serve to indicate that the separated property is a special enclave, subject to greater restriction.

These precedents foreclose the conclusion that airport terminals are public fora. Reflecting the general growth of the air travel industry, airport terminals have only recently achieved their contemporary size and character. But given the lateness with which the modern air terminal has made its appearance, it hardly qualifies for the description of having "immemorially * * * time out of mind" been held in the public trust and used for purposes of expressive activity. Moreover, even within the rather short history of air transport, it is only "[i]n recent years [that] it has become a common practice for various religious and non-profit organizations to use commercial airports as a forum for the distribution of literature, the solicitation of funds, the proselytizing of new members, and other similar activities." 45 Fed.Reg. 35314 (1980). Thus, the tradition of airport activity does not demonstrate that airports have historically been made available for speech activity. Nor can we say that these particular terminals, or airport terminals generally, have been intentionally opened by their operators to such activity; the frequent and continuing litigation evidencing the operators' objections belies any such claim. In short, there can be no argument that society's time-tested judgment, expressed through acquiescence in a continuing practice, has resolved the issue in petitioner's favor.

Petitioner attempts to circumvent the history and practice governing airport activity by pointing our attention to the variety of speech activity that it claims historically occurred at various "transportation nodes" such as rail stations, bus stations, wharves, and Ellis Island. Even if we were inclined to accept petitioner's historical account describing speech activity at these locations, an account respondent contests, we think that such evidence is of little import for two reasons. First, much of the evidence is irrelevant to *public* fora analysis, because sites such as bus and rail terminals traditionally have had private ownership. The development of privately owned parks that ban speech activity would not change the public fora status of publicly held parks. But the reverse is also true. The practices of privately held transportation centers do not bear on the government's regulatory authority over a publicly owned airport.

Second, the relevant unit for our inquiry is an airport, not "transportation nodes" generally. * * * To blithely equate airports with other transportation centers * * * would be a mistake. * * * As commercial enterprises, airports must provide services attractive to the marketplace. In light of this, it cannot fairly be said that an airport terminal has as a principal purpose "promoting the free exchange of ideas." *Cornelius v. NAACP Legal Defense and Educational Fund, Inc.*, 473 U.S. 788, 105 S.Ct. 3439, 87 L.Ed.2d 567 (1985). To the contrary, the record demonstrates that Port Authority management considers the purpose of the terminals to be the facilitation of passenger air travel, not the promotion of expression. * * * Thus, we think that neither by tradition nor purpose can the terminals be described as satisfying the standards we have previously set out for identifying a public forum.

The restrictions here challenged, therefore, need only satisfy a requirement of reasonableness. * * * We have no doubt that under this standard the prohibition on solicitation passes muster. * * *

JUSTICE O'CONNOR, concurring * * *.

I * * * agree that publicly owned airports are not public fora. * * * There is little doubt that airports are among those publicly owned facilities that could be closed to all except those who have legitimate business there. Public access to airports is thus not "inherent in the open nature of the locations," as it is for most streets and parks, but is rather a "matter of grace by government officials." *United States v. Kokinda,* 497 U.S. 720, 743, 110 S.Ct. 3115, 3128, 111 L.Ed.2d 571 (1990) (Brennan, J., dissenting). * * * The airports house restaurants, cafeterias, snack bars, coffee shops, cocktail lounges, post offices, banks, telegraph offices, clothing shops, drug stores, food stores, nurseries, barber shops, currency exchanges, art exhibits, commercial advertising displays, bookstores, newsstands, dental offices and private clubs. The International Arrivals Building at JFK Airport even has two branches of Bloomingdale's. * * * In my view, the Port Authority is operating a shopping mall as well as an airport. The reasonableness inquiry, therefore, is not whether the restrictions on speech are "consistent with * * * preserving the property" for air travel, *Perry,* 460 U.S. at 50–51, 103 S.Ct., at 958, but whether they are reasonably related to maintaining the multipurpose environment that the Port Authority has deliberately created. * * *

JUSTICE KENNEDY, with whom JUSTICE BLACKMUN, JUSTICE STEVENS, and JUSTICE SOUTER join as to Part I, concurring in the judgment. * * *

I

* * * [T]he Court's analysis * * * leaves the government with almost unlimited authority to restrict speech on its property by doing nothing more than articulating a non-speech-related purpose for the area, and it leaves almost no scope for the development of new public forums absent the rare approval of the government. The Court's error lies in its conclusion that the public-forum status of public property depends on the government's defined purpose for the property, or on an explicit decision by the government to dedicate the property to expressive activity. In my view, the inquiry must be an objective one, based on the actual, physical characteristics and uses of the property.

The First Amendment is a limitation on government, not a grant of power. Its design is to prevent the government from controlling speech. Yet under the Court's view the authority of the government to control speech on its property is paramount, for in almost all cases the critical step in the Court's analysis is a classification of the property that turns on the government's own definition or decision, unconstrained by an independent duty to respect the speech its citizens can voice there. The Court acknowledges as much, by reintroducing today into our First Amendment law a strict doctrinal line between the proprietary and regulatory functions of government which I thought had been abandoned long ago. * * *

The Court's analysis rests on an inaccurate view of history. The notion that traditional public forums are property which have public discourse as their principal purpose is a most doubtful fiction. The types of property that we have recognized as the quintessential public forums are streets, parks, and sidewalks. It would seem apparent that the principal purpose of streets and sidewalks, like airports, is to facilitate transportation, not public discourse, and we have recognized as much. Similarly, the purpose for the creation of public parks may be as much for beauty and open space as for discourse. Thus under the Court's analysis, even the quintessential public forums would appear to lack the necessary elements of what the Court defines as a public forum.

The effect of the Court's narrow view of the first category of public forums is compounded by its description of the second purported category, the so-called "designated" forum. The requirements for such a designation are so stringent that I cannot be certain whether the category has any content left at all. In any event, it seems evident that under the Court's analysis today few if any types of property other than those already recognized as public forums will be accorded that status.

The Court's answer to these objections appears to be a recourse to history as justifying its recognition of streets, parks, and sidewalks, but apparently no other types of government property, as traditional public forums. * * * In my view the policies underlying the doctrine cannot be given effect unless we recognize that open, public spaces and thoroughfares which are suitable for discourse may be public forums, whatever their historical pedigree and without concern for a precise classification of the property. * * * Without this recognition our forum doctrine retains no relevance in times of fast-changing technology and increasing insularity. In a country where most citizens travel by automobile, and parks all too often become locales for crime rather than social intercourse, our failure to recognize the possibility that new types of government property may be appropriate forums for speech will lead to a serious curtailment of our expressive activity.

One of the places left in our mobile society that is suitable for discourse is a metropolitan airport. It is of particular importance to recognize that such spaces are public forums because in these days an airport is one of the few government-owned spaces where many persons have extensive contact with other members of the public. Given that private spaces of similar character are not subject to the dictates of the First Amendment, see *Hudgens v. NLRB*, 424 U.S. 507, 96 S.Ct. 1029, 47 L.Ed.2d 196 (1976), it is critical that we preserve these areas for protected speech. In my view, our public forum doctrine must recognize this reality, and allow the creation of public forums which do not fit within the narrow tradition of streets, sidewalks, and parks. * * * Under the proper circumstances I would accord public forum status to other forms of property, regardless of its ancient or contemporary origins and whether or not it fits within a narrow historic tradition. If the objective, physical characteristics of the property at issue and the actual public access and uses which have been permitted by the government indicate that expressive activity would be appropriate and compatible with those uses, the property is a public forum. The most important considerations in this analysis are whether the property shares physical similarities with more traditional public forums, whether the government has permitted or acquiesced in broad public access to the property, and whether expressive activity would tend to interfere in a significant way with the uses to which the government has as a factual matter dedicated the property. In conducting the last inquiry, courts must consider the consistency of those uses with expressive activities in general, rather than the specific sort of speech at issue in the case before it; otherwise the analysis would be one not of classification but rather of case-by-case balancing, and would provide little guidance to the State regarding its discretion to regulate speech. Courts must also consider the availability of reasonable time, place, and manner restrictions in undertaking this compatibility analysis. The possibility of some theoretical inconsistency between expressive activities and the property's uses should not bar a finding of a public forum, if those inconsistencies can be avoided through simple and permitted regulations. * * *

Under this analysis, it is evident that the public spaces of the Port Authority's airports are public forums. First, the District Court made detailed findings regarding the physical similarities between the Port Authority's airports and public streets. These findings show that the public spaces in the airports are broad, public thoroughfares full of people and lined with stores and other commercial activities. An airport corridor is of course not a street, but that is not the proper inquiry. The question is one of physical similarities, sufficient to suggest that the airport corridor should be a public forum for the same reasons that streets and sidewalks have been treated as public forums by the people who use them.

Second, the airport areas involved here are open to the public without restriction. * * * [W]hile most people who come to the Port Authority's airports do so for a reason related to air travel, either because they are passengers or because they are picking up or dropping off passengers, this does not distinguish an airport from streets or sidewalks, which most people use for travel. * * *

Third, and perhaps most important, it is apparent from the record, and from the recent history of airports, that when adequate time, place, and manner regulations are in place, expressive activity is quite compatible with the uses of major airports. * * * In fact, the history of the Authority's own airports, as well as other major airports in this country, leaves little doubt that such a solution is quite feasible. The Port Authority has for many years permitted expressive activities by the plaintiffs and others, without any apparent interference with its ability to meet its transportation purposes. * * * [P]roblems have been dealt with in the past, and in other settings, through proper time, place, and manner restrictions; and the Port Authority does not make any showing that similar regulations would not be effective in its airports. * * *

LLOYD CORPORATION, LTD. v. TANNER

Supreme Court of the United States, 1972.
407 U.S. 551, 92 S.Ct. 2219, 33 L.Ed.2d 131.

MR. JUSTICE POWELL delivered the opinion of the Court. * * *

Lloyd Corp., Ltd. (Lloyd), owns a large, modern retail shopping center in Portland, Oregon. Lloyd Center embraces altogether about 50 acres, including some 20 acres of open and covered parking facilities which accommodate more than 1,000 automobiles. It has a perimeter of almost one and one-half miles, bounded by four public streets. * * * Lloyd owns all land and buildings within the Center, except * * * [the] public streets and sidewalks. There are some 60 commercial tenants, including small shops and several major department stores. * * * The stores are all located within a single large, multi-level building complex sometimes referred to as the "Mall." Within this complex, in addition to the stores, there are parking facilities, malls, private sidewalks, stairways, escalators, gardens, an auditorium, and a skating rink. Some of the stores open directly on the outside public sidewalks, but most open on the interior privately owned malls. * * *

Lloyd employs 12 security guards, who are commissioned as such by the city of Portland. The guards have police authority within the Center, wear uniforms similar to those worn by city police, and are licensed to carry handguns. They are employed by and subject to the control of Lloyd. Their duties are the customary ones, including shoplifting surveillance and general security. * * *

The Center is open generally to the public, with a considerable effort being made to attract shoppers and prospective shoppers, and to create "customer motivation" as well as customer goodwill in the community. * * * Groups and organizations are permitted, by invitation and advance arrangement, to use the auditorium and other facilities. * * * The Center also allows limited use of the malls by the American Legion to sell poppies for disabled veterans, and by the Salvation Army and Volunteers of America to solicit Christmas contributions. * * * The Center had been in operation for some eight years when this litigation commenced. Throughout this period it had a policy, strictly enforced, against the distribution of handbills within the building complex and its malls. * * *

On November 14, 1968, the respondents in this case distributed within the Center handbill invitations to a meeting of the "Resistance Community" to protest the draft and the Vietnam war. The distribution, made in several different places on the mall walkways by five young people, was quiet and orderly, and there was no littering. There was a complaint from one customer. Security guards informed the respondents that they were trespassing and would be arrested unless they stopped distributing the handbills within the Center. Respondents left the premises as requested "to avoid arrest" and continued the handbilling outside. Subsequently this suit was instituted in the District Court seeking declaratory and injunctive relief.

The District Court, emphasizing that the Center * * * is "the functional equivalent of a public business district" held that Lloyd's "rule prohibiting the distribution of handbills within the Mall violates * * * First Amendment rights." * * * [T]he Court of Appeals * * * concluded that the decisions of this Court in *Marsh v. Alabama*, 326 U.S. 501, 66 S.Ct. 276, 90 L.Ed. 265 (1946), and *Amalgamated Food Employees Union Local 590 v. Logan Valley Plaza, Inc.*, 391 U.S. 308, 88 S.Ct. 1601, 20 L.Ed.2d 603 (1968), compelled affirmance.

Marsh involved Chickasaw, Alabama, a company town wholly owned by the Gulf Shipbuilding Corp. The opinion of the Court, by Mr. Justice Black, described Chickasaw as follows:

"Except for [ownership by a private corporation] it has all the characteristics of any other American town. The property consists of residential buildings, streets, a system of sewers, a sewage disposal plant and a 'business block' on which business places are situated. A deputy of the Mobile County Sheriff, paid by the company, serves as the town's policeman. Merchants and service establishments have rented the stores and business places on the business block and the United States uses one of the places as a post office from which six carriers deliver mail to the people of Chickasaw and the adjacent area. The town and the surrounding neighborhood, which can not be distinguished from the Gulf property by anyone not familiar with the property lines, are thickly settled, and according to all indications the residents use the business block as their regular shopping center. To do so, they now, as they have for many years, make use of a company-owned paved street and sidewalk located alongside the store fronts in order to enter and leave the stores and the post office. Intersecting company-owned roads at each end of the business block lead into a four-lane public highway which runs parallel to the business block at a distance of thirty feet. There is nothing to stop highway traffic from coming onto the business block and upon arrival a traveler may make free use of the facilities available there. In short the town and its shopping district are accessible to and freely used by the public in general and there is nothing to distinguish them from any other town and shopping center except the fact that the title to the property belongs to a private corporation."

A Jehovah's Witness undertook to distribute religious literature on a sidewalk near the post office and was arrested on a trespassing charge. In holding that First and Fourteenth Amendment rights were infringed, the Court emphasized that the business district was within a company-owned town, an anachronism long prevalent in some southern States and now rarely found. * * *

The courts below considered the critical inquiry to be whether Lloyd Center was "the functional equivalent of a public business district." This phrase was first used in *Logan Valley*, but its genesis was in *Marsh*. It is well to consider what *Marsh* actually decided. As noted above, it involved an economic anomaly of the past, "the company town." One must have seen such towns to understand that "functionally" they were no different from municipalities of comparable size. They developed primarily in the Deep South to meet economic conditions, especially those which existed following the Civil War. Impoverished States, and especially backward areas thereof, needed an influx of industry and capital. Corporations attracted to the area by natural resources and abundant labor were willing to assume the role of local government. Quite literally, towns were built and operated by private capital with all of the customary services and utilities normally afforded by a municipal or state government: there were streets, sidewalks, sewers, public lighting, police and fire protection, business and residential areas, churches, postal facilities, and sometimes schools. In short, as Mr. Justice Black said, Chickasaw, Alabama, had "all the characteristics of any other American town." The Court simply held that where private interests were substituting for and performing the customary functions of government, First Amendment freedoms could not be denied where exercised in the customary manner on the town's sidewalks and streets. Indeed, as title to the entire town was held privately, there were no publicly owned streets, sidewalks, or parks where such rights could be exercised.

Logan Valley extended *Marsh* to a shopping center situation in a different context from the company town setting, but it did so only in a context where the First Amendment activity was related to the shopping center's operations. There is some language in *Logan Valley*, unnecessary to the decision, suggesting that the key focus of *Marsh* was upon the "business district," and that whenever a privately owned business district serves the public generally its sidewalks and streets become the functional equivalents of similar public facilities. * * * The holding in *Logan Valley* was not dependent upon the suggestion that the privately owned streets and sidewalks of a business district or a shopping center are the equivalent, for First Amendment purposes, of municipally owned streets and sidewalks. No such expansive reading of the opinion of the Court is necessary or appropriate. The opinion was carefully phrased to limit its holding to the picketing involved, where the picketing was "directly related in its purpose to the use to which the shopping center property was being put," and where the store was located in the center of a large private enclave with the consequence that no other reasonable opportunities for the pickets to convey their message to their intended audience were available. * * *

The basic issue in this case is whether respondents, in the exercise of asserted First Amendment rights, may distribute handbills on Lloyd's private property contrary to its wishes and contrary to a policy enforced against all handbilling. In addressing this issue, it must be remembered that the First and Fourteenth Amendments safeguard the rights of free speech and assembly by limitations on *state* action, not on action by the owner of private property used nondiscriminatorily for private purposes only. * * * [T]his Court has never held that a trespasser or an uninvited guest may exercise general rights of free speech on property privately owned and used nondiscriminatorily for private purposes only. * * *

Respondents contend, however, that the property of a large shopping center is "open to the public," serves the same purposes as a "business district" of a municipality, and therefore has been dedicated to certain types of public use. The argument is that such a center has sidewalks, streets, and parking areas which are functionally similar to facilities customarily provided by municipalities. It is then asserted that all members of the public, whether invited as customers or not, have the same right of free speech as they would have on the similar public facilities in the streets of a city or town.

The argument reaches too far. The Constitution by no means requires such an attenuated doctrine of dedication of private property to public use. The closest decision in theory, *Marsh v. Alabama, supra,* involved the assumption by a private enterprise of all of the attributes of a state-created municipality and the exercise by that enterprise of semiofficial municipal functions as a delegate of the State. In effect, the owner of the company town was performing the full spectrum of municipal powers and stood in the shoes of the State. In the instant case where is no comparable assumption or exercise of municipal functions or power.

Nor does property lose its private character merely because the public is generally invited to use it for designated purposes. Few would argue that a free-standing store, with abutting parking space for customers, assumes significant public attributes merely because the public is invited to shop there. Nor is size alone the controlling factor. The essentially private character of a store and its privately owned abutting property does not change by virtue of being large or clustered with other stores in a modern shopping center. This is not to say that no differences may exist with respect to government regulation or rights of citizens arising by virtue of the size and diversity of activities carried on within a privately owned facility serving the public. There will be, for example, problems with respect to public health and safety which vary in degree and in the appropriate government response, depending upon the size and character of a shopping center, an office building, a sports arena, or other large facility serving the public for commercial purposes. We do say that the Fifth and Fourteenth Amendment rights of private property owners, as well as the First Amendment rights of all citizens, must be respected and protected. The Framers of the Constitution certainly did not think these fundamental rights of a free society are incompatible with each other. There may be situations where accommodations between them, and the drawing of lines to assure due protection of both, are not easy. But on the facts presented in this case, the answer is clear. * * *

MR. JUSTICE MARSHALL, with whom MR. JUSTICE DOUGLAS, MR. JUSTICE BRENNAN, and MR. JUSTICE STEWART join, dissenting. * * *

This Court held in *Marsh v. Alabama* that even though property is privately owned, under some circumstances it may be treated as though it were publicly held, at least for purposes of the First Amendment. * * * The Court reasoned that "[t]he more an owner, for his advantage, opens up his property for use by the public in general, the more do his rights become circumscribed by the statutory and constitutional rights of those who use it." Noting that the stifling effect produced by any ban on free expression in a community's central business district was the same whether the ban was imposed by public or private owners, the Court concluded that:

> "When we balance the Constitutional rights of owners of property against those of the people to enjoy freedom of press and religion, as we must here, we remain mindful of the fact that the latter occupy a preferred position. As we have stated before, the right to exercise the liberties safeguarded by the First Amendment 'lies at the foundation of free government by free men' and we must in all cases 'weigh the circumstances and * * * appraise the * * * reasons * * * in support of the regulation * * * of the rights.' * * * In our view the circumstance that the property rights to the premises where the deprivation of liberty, here involved, took place, were held by others than the public, is not sufficient to justify the State's permitting a corporation to govern a community of citizens so as to restrict their fundamental liberties and the enforcement of such restraint by the application of a State statute." * * *

[T]he Lloyd Center is an integral part of the Portland community. From its inception, the city viewed it as a "business district" of the city and depended on it to supply much-needed employment opportunities. To insure the success of the Center, the city carefully integrated it into the pattern of streets already established and planned future development of streets around the Center. It is plain, therefore, that Lloyd Center is the equivalent of a public "business district" within the meaning of *Marsh* and *Logan Valley*. * * * Members of the Portland community are able to see doctors, dentists, lawyers, bankers, travel agents, and persons offering countless other services in Lloyd Center. They can buy almost anything that they want or need there. For many Portland citizens, Lloyd Center will so completely satisfy their wants that they will have no reason to go elsewhere for goods or services. If speech is to reach these people, it must reach them in Lloyd Center. * * *

For many persons who do not have easy access to television, radio, the major newspapers, and the other forms of mass media, the only way they can express themselves to a broad range of citizens on issues of general public concern is to picket, or to handbill, or to utilize other free or relatively inexpensive means of communication. The only hope that these people have to be able to communicate effectively is to be permitted to speak in those areas in which most of their fellow citizens can be found. One such area is the business district of a city or town or its functional equivalent. And this is why respondents have a tremendous need to express themselves within Lloyd Center. * * *

We noted in *Logan Valley* that the large-scale movement of this country's population from the cities to the suburbs has been accompanied by the growth of suburban shopping centers. In response to this phenomenon, cites like Portland are providing for large-scale shopping areas within the city. It is obvious that privately owned shopping areas could prove to be greatly advantageous to cities. They are totally self-sufficient, needing no financial support from local government; and if, as here, they truly are the functional equivalent of a public business area, the city reaps the advantages of having such an area without paying for them. Some of the advantages are an increased tax base, a drawing attraction for residents, and a stimulus to further growth.

It would not be surprising in the future to see cities rely more and more on private businesses to perform functions once performed by governmental agencies. The advantage of reduced expenses and an increased tax base cannot be overstated. As governments rely on private enterprise, public property decreases in favor of privately owned property. It becomes harder and harder for citizens to find means to communicate with other citizens. Only the wealthy may find effective communication possible unless we adhere to *Marsh v. Alabama* * * *.

BOARD OF EDUCATION OF KIRYAS JOEL VILLAGE SCHOOL DISTRICT v. GRUMET

Supreme Court of the United States, 1994.
___ U.S. ___, 114 S.Ct. 2481, ___ L.Ed.2d ___.

JUSTICE SOUTER delivered the opinion of the Court.

The Village of Kiryas Joel in Orange County, New York, is a religious enclave of Satmar Hasidim, practitioners of a strict form of Judaism. * * * The Satmar Hasidic sect takes its name from the town near the Hungarian and Romanian border where, in the early years of this century, Grand Rebbe Joel Teitelbaum molded the group into a distinct community. After World War II and the destruction of much of European Jewry, the Grand Rebbe and most of his surviving followers moved to the Williamsburg section of Brooklyn, New York. Then, 20 years ago, the Satmars purchased an approved but undeveloped subdivision in the town of Monroe and began assembling the community that has since become the Village of Kiryas Joel. When a zoning dispute arose in the course of settlement, the Satmars presented the Town Board of Monroe with a petition to form a new village within the town, a right that New York's Village Law gives almost any group of residents who satisfy certain procedural niceties. Neighbors who did not wish to secede with the Satmars objected strenuously, and after arduous negotiations the proposed boundaries of the Village of Kiryas Joel were drawn to include just the 320 acres owned and inhabited entirely by Satmars. The village, incorporated in 1977, has a population of about 8,500 today. * * *

The residents of Kiryas Joel are vigorously religious people who make few concessions to the modern world and go to great lengths to avoid assimilation into it. They interpret the Torah strictly; segregate the sexes outside the home; speak Yiddish as their primary language; eschew television, radio, and English-language publications; and dress in distinctive ways that include headcoverings and special garments for boys and modest dresses for girls. Children are educated in private religious schools * * *. These schools do not, however, offer any distinctive services to handicapped children, who are entitled under state and federal law to special education services even when enrolled in private schools. Starting in 1984 the Monroe-Woodbury Central School District provided such services for the children of Kiryas Joel * * * but a year later ended that arrangement in response to our decisions in *Aguilar v. Felton,* 473 U.S. 402, 87 L.Ed.2d 290, 105 S.Ct. 3232 (1985), and *School Dist. of Grand Rapids v. Ball,* 473 U.S. 373, 87 L.Ed.2d 267, 105 S.Ct. 3216 (1985). Children from Kiryas Joel who needed special education (including the deaf, the mentally retarded, and others suffering from a range of physical, mental, or emotional disorders) were then forced to attend public schools outside the village, which their families found highly unsatisfactory. Parents of most of these children withdrew them from the Monroe-Woodbury secular schools, citing "the panic, fear and trauma [the children] suffered in leaving their own community and being with people whose ways were so different," and some sought administrative review of the public-school placements. * * *

By 1989, only one child from Kiryas Joel was attending Monroe-Woodbury's public schools; the village's other handicapped children received privately funded special services or went without. It was then that the New York Legislature passed the statute at issue in this litigation, which provided that the Village of Kiryas Joel "is constituted a separate school district, * * * and shall have and enjoy all the powers and duties of a union free school district. * * *" 1989 N.Y. Laws, ch. 748. The statute thus empowered a locally elected board of education to take such action as opening schools and closing them, hiring teachers, prescribing textbooks, establishing disciplinary rules, and raising property taxes to fund operations. * * * Although it enjoys plenary legal authority over the elementary and secondary education of all school-aged children in the village, the Kiryas Joel Village School District currently runs only a special education program for handicapped children. The other village children have stayed in their parochial schools, relying on the new school district only for transportation, remedial education, and health and welfare services. If any child without handicap in Kiryas Joel were to seek a public-school education, the district would pay tuition to send the child into Monroe-Woodbury or another school district nearby. Under like arrangements, several of the neighboring districts send their handicapped Hasidic children into Kiryas Joel, so that two thirds of the full-time students in the village's public school come from outside. In all, the new district serves just over 40 full-time students, and two or three times that many parochial school students on a part-time basis.

Several months before the new district began operations, the New York State School Boards Association and respondents Grumet and Hawk brought this action against the State Education Department and various state officials, challenging Chapter 748 under the national and state constitutions as an unconstitutional establishment of religion. * * *

Larkin v. Grendel's Den, Inc., 459 U.S. 116, 74 L.Ed.2d 297, 103 S.Ct. 505 (1982), provides an instructive comparison with the litigation before us. There, the Court was requested to strike down a Massachusetts statute granting religious bodies veto power over applications for liquor licenses. * * * [T]he Court found that * * * the statute violated "the wholesome 'neutrality' of which this Court's cases speak" * * *. The Establishment Clause problem presented by Chapter 748 is more subtle, but it resembles the issue raised in *Larkin* to the extent that the earlier case teaches that a State may not delegate its civic authority to a group chosen according to a religious criterion. * * * What makes this litigation different from *Larkin* is the delegation here of civic power to the "qualified voters of the village of Kiryas Joel," 1989 N.Y. Laws, ch. 748, as distinct from a religious leader such as the village rov, or an institution of religious government like the formally constituted parish council in *Larkin*. In light of the circumstances of this case, however, this distinction turns out to lack constitutional significance.

It is, first, not dispositive that the recipients of state power in this case are a group of religious individuals united by common doctrine, not the group's leaders or officers. Although some school district franchise is common to all voters, the State's manipulation of the franchise for this district limited it to Satmars, giving the sect exclusively control of the political subdivision. In the circumstances of this case, the difference between thus vesting state power in the members of a religious group as such instead of the officers of its sectarian organization is one of form, not substance. It is true that religious people (or groups of religious people) cannot be denied the opportunity to exercise the rights of citizens simply because of their religious affiliations or commitments, for such a disability would violate the right to religious free exercise, which the First Amendment guarantees as certainly as it bars any establishment. * * * Where "fusion" is an issue, the difference lies in the distinction between a government's purposeful delegation on the basis of religion and a delegation on principles neutral to religion, to individuals whose religious identities are incidental to their receipt of civic authority.

Of course, Chapter 748 delegates power not by express reference to the religious belief of the Satmar community, but to residents of the "territory of the village of Kiryas Joel." 1989 N.Y. Laws, ch. 748. Thus the second (and arguably more important) distinction between this case and *Larkin* is the identification here of the group to exercise civil authority in terms not expressly religious. But our analysis does not end with the text of the statute at issue, and the context here persuades us that Chapter 748 effectively identifies these recipients of governmental authority by reference to doctrinal adherence, even though it does not do so expressly. We find this to be the better view of the facts because of the way the boundary lines of the school district divide residents according to religious affiliation, under the terms of an unusual and special legislative act.

It is undisputed that those who negotiated the village boundaries when applying the general village incorporation statute drew them so as to exclude all but Satmars, and that the New York Legislature was well aware that the village remained exclusively Satmar in 1989 when it adopted Chapter 748. The significance of this fact to the state legislature is indicated by the further fact that carving out the village school district ran counter to customary districting practices in the State. Indeed, the trend in New York is not toward dividing school districts but toward consolidating them. The thousands of small common school districts laid out in the early 19th century have been combined and recombined, first into union free school districts and then into larger central school districts, until only a tenth as many remain today. * * * Most of these cover several towns, many of them cross county boundaries, and only one remains precisely coterminous with an incorporated village. * * * The Kiryas Joel Village School District, in contrast, has only 13 local, full-time students in all (even including out-of-area and part-time students leaves the number under 200), and in offering only special education and remedial programs it makes no pretense to be a full-service district.

The origin of the district in a special act of the legislature, rather than the State's general laws governing school district reorganization, is likewise anomalous. Although the legislature has established some 20 existing school districts by special act, all but one of these are districts in name only, having been designed to be run by private organizations serving institutionalized children. * * * Because the district's creation ran uniquely counter to state practice, following the lines of a religious community where the customary and neutral principles would not have dictated the same result, we have good reasons to treat this district as the reflection of a religious criterion for identifying the recipients of civil authority. Not even the special needs of the children in this community can explain the legislature's unusual Act, for the State could have responded to the concerns of the Satmar parents without implicating the Establishment Clause * * *. We therefore find the legislature's Act to be substantially equivalent to defining a political subdivision and hence the qualification for its franchise by a religious test, resulting in a purposeful and forbidden "fusion of governmental and religious functions." *Larkin v. Grendel's Den,* 459 U.S., at 126.[6] * * *

The fact that this school district was created by a special and unusual Act of the legislature also gives reason for concern whether the benefit received by the Satmar community is one that the legislature will provide equally to other religious (and nonreligious) groups.   * * * Because the religious community of Kiryas Joel did not receive its new governmental authority simply as one of many communities eligible for equal treatment under a general law,[7] we have no assurance that the next similarly situated group seeking a school district of its own will receive one * * *.

We do not disable a religiously homogeneous group from exercising political power conferred on it without regard to religion.   Unlike the states of Utah and New Mexico (which were laid out according to traditional political methodologies taking account of lines of latitude and longitude and topographical features), the reference line chosen for the Kiryas Joel Village School District was one purposely drawn to separate Satmars from non-Satmars.   Nor do we impugn the motives of the New York Legislature, which no doubt intended to accommodate the Satmar community without violating the Establishment Clause; we simply refuse to ignore that the method it chose is one that aids a particular religious community, as such, rather than all groups similarly interested in separate schooling.   * * *

JUSTICE STEVENS, with whom JUSTICE BLACKMUN and JUSTICE GINSBURG join, concurring.

New York created a special school district for the members of the Satmar religious sect in response to parental concern that children suffered "panic, fear and trauma" when "leaving their own community and being with people whose ways were so different."   To meet those concerns, the State could have taken steps to alleviate the children's fear by teaching their schoolmates to be tolerant and respectful of Satmar customs.   Action of that kind would raise no constitutional concerns and would further the strong public interest in promoting diversity and understanding in the public schools.

Instead, the State responded with a solution that affirmatively supports a religious sect's interest in segregating itself and preventing its children from associating with their neighbors.   The isolation of these children, while it may protect them from "panic, fear and trauma," also unquestionably increased the likelihood that they would remain within the fold, faithful adherents of their parents' religious faith.   By creating

6. Because it is the unusual circumstances of this district's creation that persuade us the State has employed a religious criterion for delegating political power, this conclusion does not imply that any political subdivision that is coterminous with the boundaries of a religiously homogeneous community suffers the same constitutional infirmity.   The district in this case is distinguishable from one whose boundaries are derived according to neutral historical and geographic criteria, but whose population happens to comprise coreligionists.

7. This contrasts with the process by which the Village of Kiryas Joel itself was created, involving, as it did, the application of a neutral state law designed to give almost any group of residents the right to incorporate.

a school district that is specifically intended to shield children from contact with others who have "different ways," the State provided official support to cement the attachment of young adherents to a particular faith. It is telling, in this regard, that two thirds of the school's full-time students are Hasidic handicapped children from outside the village; the Kiryas Joel school thus serves a population far wider than the village—one defined less by geography than by religion.

Affirmative state action in aid of segregation of this character is unlike the evenhanded distribution of a public benefit or service, a "release time" program for public school students involving no public premises or funds, or a decision to grant an exemption from a burdensome general rule. It is, I believe, fairly characterized as establishing, rather than merely accommodating, religion. * * *

JUSTICE KENNEDY, concurring in the judgment. * * *

The real vice of the school district, in my estimation, is that New York created it by drawing political boundaries on the basis of religion. * * * [G]overnment may not use religion as a criterion to draw political or electoral lines. Whether or not the purpose is accommodation and whether or not the government provides similar gerrymanders to people of all religious faiths, the Establishment Clause forbids the government to use religion as a line-drawing criterion. In this respect, the Establishment Clause mirrors the Equal Protection Clause. Just as the government may not segregate people on account of their race, so too it may not segregate on the basis of religion. The danger of stigma and stirred animosities is no less acute for religious line-drawing than for racial. Justice Douglas put it well in a statement this Court quoted with approval just last Term:

> "When racial or religious lines are drawn by the State, the multiracial, multireligious communities that our Constitution seeks to weld together as one become separatist; antagonisms that relate to race or to religion rather than to political issues are generated; communities seek not the best representative but the best racial or religious partisan. Since that system is at war with the democratic ideal, it should find no footing here." *Wright v. Rockefeller*, 376 U.S. 52, 67, 11 L.Ed.2d 512, 84 S.Ct. 603 (1964) (Douglas, J., dissenting).

I agree with the Court insofar as it invalidates the school district for being drawn along religious lines. * * * There is no serious question that the legislature configured the school district, with purpose and precision, along a religious line. This explicit religious gerrymandering violates the First Amendment Establishment Clause.

It is important to recognize the limits of this principle. We do not confront the constitutionality of the Kiryas Joel Village itself, and the formation of the village appears to differ from the formation of the school district in one critical respect. As the Court notes, the village was formed pursuant to a religion-neutral self-incorporation scheme. Under New York law, a territory with at least 500 residents and not more than five square miles may be incorporated upon petition by at least 20 percent of the voting residents of that territory or by the owners of more than 50 percent of the territory's real property. Aside from insuring that the petition complies with certain procedural requirements, the supervisor of the town in which the territory is located has no discretion to reject the petition. The residents of the town then vote upon the incorporation petition in a special election. By contrast, the Kiryas Joel Village School District was created by state legislation. The State of New York had complete discretion not to enact it. The State thus had a direct hand in accomplishing the religious segregation.

As the plurality indicates, the Establishment Clause does not invalidate a town or a state "whose boundaries are derived according to neutral historical and geographic criteria, but whose population happens to comprise coreligionists." People who share a common religious belief or life style may live together without sacrificing the basic rights of self-governance that all American citizens enjoy, so long as they do not use those rights to establish their religious faith. Religion flourishes in community, and the Establishment Clause must not be construed as some sort of homogenizing solvent that forces unconventional religious groups to choose between assimilating to mainstream American culture or losing their political rights. There is more than a fine line, however, between the voluntary association that leads to a political community comprised of people who share a common religious faith, and the forced separation that occurs when the government draws explicit political boundaries on the basis of peoples' faith. In creating the Kiryas Joel Village School District, New York crossed that line, and so we must hold the district invalid. * * *

Justice Scalia, with whom The Chief Justice and Justice Thomas join, dissenting. * * *

Unlike most of our Establishment Clause cases involving education, these cases involve no public funding, however slight or indirect, to private religious schools. They do not involve private schools at all. The school under scrutiny is a public school specifically designed to provide a public secular education to handicapped students. The superintendent of the school, who is not Hasidic, is a 20–year veteran of the New York City public school system, with expertise in the area of bilingual, bicultural, special education. The teachers and therapists at the school all live outside the village of Kiryas Joel. While the village's private schools are profoundly religious and strictly segregated by sex, classes at the public school are co-ed and the curriculum secular. The school building has the bland appearance of a public school, unadorned by religious symbols or markings; and the school complies with the laws and regulations governing all other New York State public schools. * * * The only thing distinctive about the school is that all the students share the same religion. * * * None of our cases has ever suggested that there is anything wrong with that. * * * Justice Souter's opinion [therefore] does not focus upon the school, but rather upon the school district and the New York Legislature that created it. * * *

Justice Souter relies extensively, and virtually exclusively, upon *Larkin v. Grendel's Den, Inc.*, 459 U.S. 116, 74 L.Ed.2d 297, 103 S.Ct. 505 (1982). * * * The uniqueness of * * * [that] case stemmed from the grant of governmental power directly to a religious institution * * *. Justice Souter's steamrolling of the difference between civil authority held by a church, and civil authority held by members of a church, is breathtaking. To accept it, one must believe that large portions of the civil authority exercised during most of our history were unconstitutional, and that much more of it than merely the Kiryas Joel School District is unconstitutional today. The history of populating of North America is in no small measure the story of groups of people sharing a common religious and cultural heritage striking out to form their own communities. It is preposterous to suggest that the civil institutions of these communities, separate from their churches, were constitutionally suspect. And if they were, surely Justice Souter cannot mean that the inclusion of one or two nonbelievers in the community would have been enough to eliminate the constitutional vice. If the conferral of governmental power upon a religious institution as such (rather than upon American citizens who belong to the religious institution) is not the test of *Grendel's Den* invalidity, there is no reason why giving power to a body that is overwhelmingly dominated by the members of one sect would not suffice to invoke the Establishment Clause. That might have made the entire States of Utah and New Mexico unconstitutional at the time of their admission to the Union, and would undoubtedly make many units of local government unconstitutional today.[2] * * *

Perhaps appreciating the startling implications for our constitutional jurisprudence of collapsing the distinction between religious institutions and their members, Justice Souter tries to limit his "unconstitutional conferral of civil authority" holding by pointing out several features supposedly unique to the present case: that the "boundary lines of the school district divide residents according to religious affiliation"; that the school district was created by "a special act of the legislature"; and that the formation of the school district ran counter to the legislature's trend of consolidating districts in recent years. Assuming all these points to be true (and they are not), they would certainly bear upon whether the legislature had an impermissible religious motivation in creating the district * * *. But they have nothing to do with whether conferral of power upon a group of citizens can be the conferral of power upon a religious institution. It can not. * * *

[E]ven if the New York Legislature had never before created a school district by special statute (which is not true), and even if it had done nothing but consolidate school districts for over a century (which is not true), how could the departure from those past practices possibly demonstrate that the legislature had religious favoritism in mind? It

---

2. At the county level, the smallest unit for which comprehensive data is available, there are a number of counties in which the overwhelming majority of churchgoers are of a single religion: Rich County, Utah (100% Mormon); Kennedy County, Texas (100% Roman Catholic); * * * Graham County, North Carolina (93.7% Southern Baptist); Mora County, New Mexico (92.6% Roman Catholic). * * *

could not. * * * Justice Souter's case against the statute comes down to nothing more, therefore, than * * * the fact that all the residents of the Kiryas Joel Village School District are Satmars. But all its residents also wear unusual dress, have unusual civic customs, and have not much to do with people who are culturally different from them. * * * On what basis does Justice Souter conclude that it is the theological distinctiveness rather than the cultural distinctiveness that was the basis for New York State's decision? * * * The special district was created to meet the special educational needs of distinctive handicapped children, and the geographical boundaries selected for that district were (quite logically) those that already existed for the village. * * * What happened in the creation of the village is in fact precisely what happened in the creation of the school district, so that the former cannot possibly infect the latter, as Justice Souter tries to suggest. Entirely secular reasons (zoning for the village, cultural alienation of students for the school district) produced a political unit whose members happened to share the same religion. There is no evidence (indeed, no plausible suspicion) of the legislature's desire to favor the Satmar religion, as opposed to meeting distinctive secular needs or desires of citizens who happened to be Satmars. * * *

SECTION C. THE SOURCES OF LOCAL GOVERNMENT AUTHORITY

1. DILLON'S RULE

In this section, we begin examining an issue of fundamental importance in local government law—the source of city power. Given the materials on the public/private distinction just presented, cities might appear to have two possible sources of power: authorization for their actions could come from their own citizens or it could come from the state government. To appreciate the significance of the difference between these alternative sources of power, consider how other entities in our society, such as corporations, unions or churches, obtain authorization for their actions. Is their power limited to express or implied grants of authority by the states or do they have general authority, derived from their members, to do what they want to do unless prohibited by state law? What would be the impact on the power and freedom of these entities if they could only take actions authorized by state government? What would be the impact on your own power and freedom if you were able to engage in only those activities authorized by state law?

The reason for asking these questions about the source of the power of individuals and of groups other than cities will become apparent once you turn to the first reading in this section, an excerpt from an influential treatise on local government law written by John Dillon and published in 1872. The excerpt contains what is known in local government law as "Dillon's Rule", a rule that specifies the extent to which local government power is restricted to actions authorized by enabling legislation enacted by the state legislature. This section is devoted to an examination of the emphasis on enabling legislation found in Dillon's Rule; the next section will be devoted to an alternative understanding of the source of local government power, one based on the concept of home rule.

Dillon's Rule is a very important aspect of local government law;[1] it has been cited in hundreds and hundreds of cases. Because of its importance, some historical background about the rule, taken (again) from my article, The City as a Legal Concept, follows the excerpt from Dillon's treatise reproduced below.[2] Two cases then raise questions about the rule. The first case, County Board of Arlington County v. Brown, is a relatively strict application of Dillon's Rule and thus offers an opportunity to consider how (and whether) such an application might be justified. One possible way to think about these questions is suggested by Clayton Gillette in an article excerpted after the *Brown* decision. The second case, State v. Hutchinson, contains a full-scale debate about the desirability of Dillon's Rule.

In reading these materials, consider the relevance of the arguments about centralization and decentralization and about the public/private distinction discussed above in sections A and B. What is the impact of Dillon's Rule on the possibility of decentralization of power in America? How are the courts' (and your own) views of the wisdom of Dillon's Rule affected by different attitudes toward the exercise of decentralized power by public and private entities?

JOHN DILLON, MUNICIPAL CORPORATIONS

Vol. 1, pp. 448–455 (5th ed. 1911).

§ 237(89). **Extent of Power; Limitations; Canons of Construction.**—It is a general and undisputed proposition of law that *a municipal corporation possesses and can exercise the following powers, and no others:* First, those granted in *express words;* second, those *necessarily or fairly implied* in or *incident* to the powers expressly granted; third, those *essential* to the accomplishment of the declared objects and purposes of the corporation,—not simply convenient, but indispensable. Any fair, reasonable, substantial doubt concerning the

1. For a general discussion of the principles found in Dillon's Rule, see 3 Sands & Libonati, Local Government Law, Chapter 13 (1993); G. Clark, Judges and the Cities (1985). See also Gillette, In Partial Praise of Dillon's Rule, or, Can Public Choice Theory Justify Local Government Law, 67 Chi.-Kent L.Rev. 959 (1991); Briffault, Home Rule, Majority Rule, and Dillon's Rule, 67 Chi.-Kent L.Rev. 1011 (1991); Schwartz, Reviewing and Revising Dillon's Rule, 67 Chi.-Kent L.Rev. 1025 (1991); Comment: Redefining The Scope of Local Regulatory Power, State v. Hutchinson, 1981 Utah L.Rev. 617; Bruff, Judicial Review in Local Government Law: A Reappraisal, 60 Minn.

L.Rev. 669 (1976); Comment: The Dillon Rule A Limit on Local Government Powers, 41 Mo.L.Rev. 546 (1976).

2. For alternative interpretations of this history, see, e.g., Williams, The Constitutional Vulnerability of American Local Government: The Politics of City Status in American Law, 1986 Wis.L.Rev. 83, 90–100; Gere, Dillon's Rule and the Cooley Doctrine, 8 J.Urb.Hist. 271 (1982). See also H. Hartog, Public Property and Private Power: The Corporation of the City of New York in American Law 1730–1870, 220–24, 262–63 (1983).

existence of power is resolved by the courts against the corporation, and the power is denied. Of every municipal corporation the charter or statute by which it is created is its organic act. Neither the corporation nor its officers can do any act, or make any contract, or incur any liability, not authorized thereby, or by some legislative act applicable thereto. All acts beyond the scope of the powers granted are void. Much less can any power be exercised, or any act done, which is forbidden by charter or statute. *These principles are of transcendent importance, and lie at the foundation of the law of municipal corporations.* Their reasonableness, their necessity, and their salutary character have been often vindicated, but never more forcibly than by the learned Chief Justice Shaw, who, speaking of municipal and public corporations, says: *"They can exercise no powers* but those which are conferred upon them by the act by which they are constituted, or such as are necessary to the exercise of their corporate powers, the performance of their corporate duties, and the accomplishment of the purposes of their association. This principle is derived from the nature of corporations, the mode in which they are organized, and in which their affairs must be conducted."

§ 238(90). **Same Subject.**—"In aggregate corporations, as a general rule," continues Chief Justice Shaw, "the act and will of a majority is deemed in law the act and will of the whole,—as the act of the corporate body. The consequence is that a minority must be bound not only without, but against, their consent. Such an obligation may extend to every onerous duty,—to pay money to an unlimited amount, to perform services, to surrender lands, and the like. It is obvious, therefore, that if this liability were to extend to unlimited and indefinite objects, the citizen, by being a member of a corporation, might be deprived of his most valuable personal rights and liberties. The security against this danger is in a steady adherence to the principle stated, viz., *that corporations can only exercise their powers over their respective members, for the accomplishment of limited and defined objects.* And if this principle is important, as a general rule of social right and municipal law, it is of the highest importance in these States, where corporations have been extended and multiplied so as to embrace almost every object of human concern." The language of another learned judge on this subject is well chosen, and fittingly supplements that which we have quoted in the preceding section. "In this country," says Church, J., "all corporations, whether public or private, derive their powers from legislative grant, and can do no act for which authority is not expressly given, or may not be reasonably inferred. But if we were to say that they can do nothing for which a warrant could not be found in the language of their charters, we should deny them, in some cases, the power of self-preservation, as well as many of the means necessary to effect the essential objects of their incorporation. And therefore it has long been an established principle in the law of corporations, that they *may exercise all the powers within the fair intent and purpose of their creation which are reasonably proper to give effect to powers expressly granted.* In doing this, they must [unless restricted in this respect] have a choice of means adapted to ends, and are not to be confined to any one mode of operation."

§ 239(91). **Same Subject; Principles of Construction.**—The *extent of the powers of municipalities,* whether express, implied, or indispensable, is one of construction. And here the fundamental and universal rule, which is as reasonable as it is necessary, is, that while the construction is to be just, seeking first of all for the legislative intent in order to give it fair effect, yet any ambiguity or fair, reasonable, substantial doubt as to the extent of the power is to be determined in favor of the State or general public, and against the State's grantee. The rule of strict construction of corporate powers is not so directly applicable to the ordinary clauses in the charter or incorporating acts of municipalities as it is to the charters of private corporations; but it is equally applicable to grants of powers to municipal and public bodies which are out of the usual range, or which grant franchises, or rights of that nature, or which may result in public burdens, or which, in their exercise, touch the right to liberty or property, or, as it may be compendiously expressed, any common-law right of the citizen or inhabitant. * * * The rule of strict construction does not apply to the *mode adopted* by the municipality *to carry into effect powers expressly or plainly granted,* where the mode is not limited or prescribed by the legislature, and is left to the discretion of the municipal authorities. In such a case the usual test of the validity of the act of a municipal body is, Whether it is reasonable? and there is no presumption against the municipal action in such cases.

The general principles of law, stated in this and in the preceding sections, are indisputably settled, but difficulty is often experienced in their application, on account of the complex character of municipal duties, and the various, miscellaneous, and frequently indefinite purposes or objects which municipalities are authorized to execute or carry into operation.

GERALD FRUG, THE CITY AS A LEGAL CONCEPT

93 Harv.L.Rev. 1057, 1109–1115 (1980).

The legal doctrine that cities were subject to state authority was enthusiastically endorsed by John Dillon, who in 1872 wrote the first and most important American treatise on municipal corporations. Dillon did not seek to disguise the values he thought important in framing the law for municipal corporations. In speeches, law review articles, and books, Dillon eloquently defended the need to protect private property from attack and indicated his reservations about the kind of democracy then practiced in the cities.

It would be a mistake, however, to read Dillon's defense of strict state control of cities as simply a crude effort to advance the interests of the rich or of private corporations at the expense of the poor inhabitants of cities. Instead, it is more plausible to interpret Dillon as a forerunner of the Progressive tradition; he sought to protect private property not only against abuse by democracy but also against abuse by private economic power. To do so, he advocated an objective, rational government, staffed by the nation's elite—a government strong enough to curb the excesses of corporate power and at the same time help those who deserved help. It is important to understand how Dillon could consider state control of cities as a major ingredient in accomplishing these objectives.

According to Dillon, a critical impediment to the development of a government dedicated to the public good was the intermingling of the public and the private sectors. Strict enforcement of a public/private distinction was essential both to protect government from the threat of domination by private interests and to protect the activities of the private economy from being unfairly influenced by government intervention. Moreover, to ensure its fully "public" nature, government had to be organized so that it could attract to power those in the community best able to govern. Class legislation in favor of either the rich or the poor had to be avoided—neither a government of private greed nor one of mass ignorance could be tolerated. Instead, it was the role of the best people to assume responsibility by recognizing and fulfilling their communal obligations: "It is a duty of perpetual obligation on the part of the strong to take care of the weak, of the rich to take care of the poor."

This vision pervades Dillon's work on municipal corporations. From his perspective, cities presented problems that seemed almost "inherent" in their nature. By merging the public and private spheres, cities had extravagantly invested in private businesses, performing functions "better left to private enterprise." As both a state and federal judge, Dillon saw firsthand the problems engendered by municipal financing of railroads. He therefore advocated constitutional limitations and restriction of the franchise to taxpayers whenever any expenditure of money was at stake in order to prevent cities from engaging further in such transactions.

At the same time, Dillon believed that all of the functions properly undertaken by cities should be considered "public." He therefore criticized the courts for contributing to the division of city activities into public and private spheres. For half a century, courts had distinguished the city's governmental functions, which were subject to absolute state power, from its proprietary functions, which received the constitutional protection afforded to rights of private property. While conceding that such a distinction was "highly important" in municipal corporation law, Dillon found a city's retention of any private identity "difficult exactly to comprehend." Since a city was by definition created by the state, "which breathed into it the breath of life," there seemed nothing private about them at all.

Most troubling of all to Dillon, cities were not managed by those *"best fitted* by their intelligence, business experience, capacity and moral character." Their management was "too often both *unwise* and *extravagant.*" A major change in city government was therefore needed to achieve a fully public city government dedicated to the common good.

But how could this be achieved? To Dillon, the answer seemed to lie in state control of cities and in judicial supervision of that control. State control, though political, was purely public, and the "best fitted" could more likely be attracted to its government. Moreover, enforcement of the rule of law could play a role, since law was "the beneficence of civil society acting by rule, in its nature * * * opposed to all that [was] fitful, capricious, unjust, partial or destructive." The state and the law working together could thus curb municipal abuse by rigorously enforcing the public/private distinction.

In his treatise, Dillon could not have more broadly phrased the extent of state power over city functions. State power "is supreme and transcendent: it may erect, change, divide, and even abolish, at pleasure, as it deems the public good to require." In addition to legislative control, he argued for a major role for the courts:

> The courts, too, have duties, the most important of which is to require these corporations, in all cases, to show a plain and clear grant for the authority they assume to exercise; to *lean against constructive powers,* and, with firm hands, to hold them and their officers within chartered limits.

Once all these steps were taken, Dillon argued, the cities' governance could properly be left to democratic control.

It is hard for us to comprehend fully Dillon's confidence in noblesse oblige and in the expectation that state and judicial control would help ensure the attainment by cities of an unselfish public good. For us, the late nineteenth century legislature was as unwise and extravagant as the late nineteenth century city, and our definition of law would be somewhat more restrained than Dillon's. The important point, however, is that the legal doctrines emphasized by Dillon—state control of cities, restriction of cities to "public" functions and strict construction of city powers—are not necessarily tied to his vision of society. While for Dillon the law of cities and the goals of public policy formed a coherent whole, he stated the law so broadly and categorically that it could simply be extracted from its context and applied generally.

Indeed, although Dillon's vision of society may be gone forever, Dillon's statement of the law of municipal corporations, stripped of its ideological underpinnings, largely remains intact today. For example, in the current edition of his treatise, Professor Antieau's articulation of the subservience of cities to state power (absent specific state constitutional protection for cities) is no less emphatic than Dillon's in 1872. His emphasis upon the strict construction required of grants of power is simply a paraphrase of the so-called Dillon's Rule. He too criticizes the public/private distinction *within* municipal corporation law as "difficult to draw," although, like Dillon, he has no difficulty with the distinction between public and private corporations themselves. Only his statement of the law of what are now called public utilities seems more accepting than Dillon's version.

Dillon's thesis, however, did not go unchallenged at the time. The major challenge was launched by Judge Thomas M. Cooley, only three years after publishing his celebrated *Treatise on Constitutional Limitations*. In a concurring opinion in *People ex rel. Le Roy v. Hurlbut*,[235] Cooley denied the existence of absolute state supremacy over cities. Relying on American colonial history and on the importance of political liberty in the definition of freedom, he argued that local government was a matter of "absolute right," a right protected by an implied restriction on the powers of the legislature under the state constitution. Amasa Eaton advanced the same thesis in a series of articles entitled *The Right to Local Self–Government*. Eaton canvassed English and American history to demonstrate that this "right to local self-government" existed prior to state incorporations and could not be subjected to state restriction.

The most extensive rebuttal to Dillon was published in 1911 by Eugene McQuillin in his multivolume treatise, *The Law of Municipal Corporations*. In an exhaustive survey, McQuillin traced the historical development of municipal corporations and found the essential theme to be a right to local self-government. He rejected the suggestion that cities were created by the state, arguing that "[s]uch [a] position ignores well-established, historical facts easily ascertainable." McQuillin strongly criticized courts that failed to uphold the right of local self-government:

> The judicial decisions denying the right of local self-government without express constitutional guaranty, reject the rule of construction that all grants of power are to be interpreted in the light of the maxims of Magna Carta, or rather the development of English rights and governmental powers prior to that time; that is, the common law transmuted into our constitutions and laws. They ignore in toto the fact that local self-government does not owe its origin to constitutions and laws. * * * They disregard the fact that it is a part of the liberty of a community, an expression of community freedom, the heart of our political institutions. They refuse to concede, therefore, that it is a right in any just sense beyond unlimited state control, but rather it is nothing more than a privilege, to be refused or granted in such measure as the legislative agents of the people for the time being determine.

McQuillin also sought to buttress his argument by inventing a new rationale for the public/private distinction within municipal corporation law, the distinction that had so confused other writers. There was a general consensus, McQuillin noted, that absolute state power could only be exerted over a city's "public functions." Those functions, he argued, were those that in fact had been given the city by the state. Since the justification for state supremacy depends on the idea of state creation,

---

235. 24 Mich. 44, 93 (1871) (Cooley, J., concurring).

state control must be limited to those things so created. Powers not derived from legislative action must therefore be "private" and subject to the same constitutional protection as other private rights. The power of the locality that historically was exercised prior to a state charter—the right to local self-government—is, then, a "private" right and cannot be subject to state supremacy.

History has not been kind to the Cooley–Eaton–McQuillin thesis, although at first it was taken quite seriously. In a later edition of his treatise, Dillon himself specifically denied the theory's usefulness and noted its lack of judicial acceptance. Howard Lee McBain, a noted municipal law authority of the time, argued that most courts had properly rejected the right of self-government. In discounting the thesis, McBain seized upon the weak links in the way the proponents framed the right. He denounced the idea of an "implied limitation" on legislative power as dangerous and unworkable and argued that, even if the right to local self-government were a common law right, it would not therefore be beyond the legislative power to change the common law. He also denied that there was in fact an historical right to self-government, at least if interpreted as the right to democratic, popular control of local officials.

McBain's arguments were cleverly aimed at the phrasing, and not the substance, of the Cooley–Eaton–McQuillin thesis. The proponents of the thesis could have responded that the power of public corporations was a "liberty" interest expressly protected by the due process clause in the same way that the "property" interests of private corporations were protected. They could also have explained that this liberty interest was not the democratic control of corporations as understood in the nineteenth century, but instead the kind of local autonomy all corporations had exercised before the ideas of property and sovereignty were separated in the late eighteenth and the nineteenth centuries. But they did not do so. Nor would it have mattered. By the time of McBain's attack, courts were not willing to eliminate the distinction between public and private corporations—even Cooley, Eaton and McQuillin did not challenge *that* distinction. That state power over cities was different from state power over corporations had become an automatically accepted part of legal thought.

In 1923, William Munro, in his classic work, *The Government of American Cities,* stated that Dillon's position on state control of cities was "so well recognized that it is not nowadays open to question." McQuillin's thesis, on the other hand, has been substantially revised even in his own treatise by its current editor:

> [T]he municipal corporation is a creature of the legislature, from which, within constitutional limits, it derives all its rights and powers. Distinction should be made between the right of local self-government as inherent in the people, and the right as inherent in a municipal corporation; while as to the people, the right has quite commonly been assumed to exist, but as to the municipal corpora-

tion the right must be derived, either from the people through the constitution or from the legislature.

No other serious academic challenge to the Dillon thesis has ever been made. * * *

COUNTY BOARD OF ARLINGTON COUNTY v. BROWN

Supreme Court of Virginia, 1985.
229 Va. 341, 329 S.E.2d 468.

COMPTON, JUSTICE. * * *

Arlington County owns 6.4 acres of undeveloped land adjacent to its existing courthouse, jail, and County office complex. * * * The entire 6.4 acres presently is used for parking of County-owned vehicles and vehicles of County employees.

In 1979, the County inaugurated a study to determine the proper future use of this land. * * * The County determined that a mixture of high density office, hotel, retail, and residential uses would be appropriate, consistent with both the comprehensive plan and the zoning ordinance. * * * [A]fter full citizen participation, a selection panel recommended in October of 1982 that a proposal from Charles E. Smith Companies/Artery Organization, a private developer, be accepted. * * * Negotiations with the developer began in December 1982. The County staff was concerned with the future location of County office space, whether to sell or lease the subject parcel for the development, and the amount of remuneration the County should receive for the interest to be conveyed. A strong preference emerged for leasing much of the land, especially the land devoted to office use. One of the main reasons for the preference was the intention to keep the property under public control to assure its availability for long-term public use. * * *

This proposal was detailed in a letter of intent, which was accepted by the County Board in August of 1984. * * * According to the letter of intent, the land for the office buildings, and related retail space, will be let to Smith–Artery on a 75–year ground lease with a base rent and a percentage rent. At the end of the term, the improvements will revert to the County free of encumbrances. The County will receive as compensation for the land lease 50 percent of the net profit of the rental of the office space and retail space. * * * In addition, the County, as lessee, will lease no less than 140,000 square feet in the first office building to be constructed for an initial period of 15 years with multiple 10–year renewal periods. * * * The County will receive a favorable rate for rental of the office space and a period of rent-free occupancy.

Following approval of the proposal, the County Board directed the County Manager to sign the letter of intent on behalf of the Board and to commence preparations to complete the transaction. The Manager refused to follow the Board's orders, believing certain questions should be determined judicially before the County proceeded further. * * *

The Manager contends that the applicable statutes contain no express grant of power for the County to lease this property under these circumstances and that no such power can be fairly implied from the powers expressly conferred. We agree.

Virginia follows Dillon's Rule of strict construction and its corollary. The powers of county boards of supervisors are fixed by statute and are limited to those powers conferred expressly or by necessary implication.

The County Board relies on Code § 15.1–261.1 as one source of its power to lease the subject land. That statute provides, in pertinent part:

> "The governing body of any county, in its discretion, may lease to any responsible person, firm or corporation any unused lands owned or held by such county for any lawful purpose provided such governing body shall first hold a public hearing * * *."

The Board argues the parcel in question is "unused," as that term is employed in the statute. It claims the tract is "underdeveloped" and that its use for parking "is inefficient and an underutilization because the land is appropriate for high density private development." The Board also claims that, at the time the lease to Smith–Artery would become effective, the County will have ceased using the land for parking in order to prepare the tract for construction, thus making the land "unused," even if it be determined it is not presently "unused" because parking is allowed. We disagree.

We construe the term "unused lands" according to its plain meaning. Land that is "unused" is vacant, surplus, spare, and unemployed; it is not necessarily "underdeveloped" or "underutilized." "Unused land" may be raw land for which there is no current county need or it may be land improved with buildings, which are not currently, actively employed by the county. The parcel in question qualifies under none of the foregoing concepts. This land was acquired by the County for public purposes. It has been, and is, employed to provide parking facilities for those connected with the courthouse complex, according to the record. The parcel has a substantive, functional use and in no sense of the statutory term is it "unused." And we will not presume the General Assembly intended this Court to approve a subterfuge by holding, as the Board suggests, that land used for a legitimate public purpose suddenly becomes "unused," and susceptible to being leased, when the existing use must be stopped so construction can begin for a commercial development.

Alternatively, the Board relies on Code § 15.1–262 as a source of power to lease the subject parcel. As pertinent to this controversy, that statute provides:

> "The governing body of the county shall have power to sell, at public or private sale, or exchange and convey the real property, * * * of the county * * *."

The Board argues that the right to sell, exchange and convey under the statute includes the right to lease. We do not agree. * * * Nowhere in the statute is the power given to counties to grant less than fee simple title to county land. In contrast, under Code § 15.1–847 there is a specific grant of power to municipal corporations to lease. That statute provides:

"A municipal corporation may control and regulate the use and management of all of its property, real and personal, within and without the municipal corporation; and may sell, lease, mortgage, pledge or dispose of such property, * * * subject to such limitations as may be imposed by the Constitution of Virginia or general law."

Thus, as the County Manager contends, the grant to municipal corporations of a general power to lease government property to others, when compared to a restrictive grant to counties to deal with their property, demonstrates a clear legislative intent to withhold from counties any power to lease not otherwise specifically granted. * * *

CLAYTON GILLETTE, IN PARTIAL PRAISE OF DILLON'S RULE, OR, CAN PUBLIC CHOICE THEORY JUSTIFY LOCAL GOVERNMENT LAW

67 Chicago–Kent L. Rev. 959, 995–998 (1991).

* * * [T]he propriety of Dillon's Rule ultimately depends on whether the state legislature is more likely than the locality to make decisions that are attentive to local residents' preferences. That conclusion, in turn, depends on whether diverse views are likely to be made known to state legislators and whether those legislators are more or less likely than their local counterparts to engage in rent-seeking from privileged groups. * * *

One-sided lobbying might be thought to be more prevalent at the state level because, to be successful, interest groups are likely to require financial resources beyond the reach of many local or ad hoc organizations. At the local level, a relatively small sum of money is likely to have greater influence than a similar sum at the state level. This is true not only because more state legislators than city councillors will have to be contacted, but because the financial demands of the former are likely to be much greater. A city councillor will need relatively few funds to sustain an effective election campaign, given the number and geographic scope of constituents. Thus, the number of groups who can make a "meaningful" contribution (sufficient to sustain the incumbent's attention) at the local level will be far greater than the number that can make "meaningful" contributions at the state level. The group that seeks state legislation may also have incurred substantial costs at the local level to induce local officials to press the case at the state level. This "double dip" increases the need for resources to wage a successful bid for or against legislation, and hence limits the number of groups able to engage in the process.

Nevertheless, there are competing reasons to believe that the state legislature will be far less susceptible than its local counterpart to one-sided lobbying. Simply as a geographical matter, the state is more likely to contain a variety of perspectives that may be represented throughout the state but absent within any area within the state. Interests that are latent at the local level (for lack of numbers, organization, or funds) may be privileged at the state level or may attract an entrepreneurial leader who would not have been available at the local level. Additionally, the legislatures of most states are characterized by procedural safeguards against one-sided lobbying that are not available at the local level. At the state level, bills must survive a committee hearing, which may have no counterpart at the local level. Legislatures in all but one state are bicameral, so that investments made in lobbying must be directed at a larger and more geographically diffuse group of legislators. One effect of these safeguards is to increase the costs of capturing a large number of decision makers beyond the resources of groups that represent narrow interests. These safeguards increase the costs of obtaining legislation and hence serve to reduce the likelihood that any particular group will find pursuit of its interests worthwhile. Moreover, a bill that appears to favor a particular interest group may more readily find opposition from an alternative branch of government at the state level, i.e., a strong executive, that finds little analogue in any but the largest cities governed by mayors and city councillors.

Moreover, the groups likely to be successful at the state level are not necessarily the same as those likely to be successful at the local level. A local developer or zoning attorney may have superior access to local officials because she is a repeat player with respect to those officials. But this does not translate into an advantage at the state level, governed by a different set of officials with whom the local partisan has little prior contact. Nor, if the developer or attorney anticipates continued concentration in local projects, is it worthwhile to develop the relationship necessary to cultivate the statewide relationship. Certainly statewide organizations will exist, be they state bar associations or developer associations. But they are likely to concentrate on matters of statewide concern beyond the ken of Dillon's Rule in the first place (as their statewide effects would render them inappropriate for local initiative), rather than on parochial concerns of a particular locality.

It is difficult to determine which of these tendencies (towards one sided lobbying at the state or local level) dominates. The above considerations, however, lead at least to the following conclusion. The higher costs that attend lobbying at the state level likely mean that fewer groups concerned with parochial issues will have a sufficient advantage to dominate at that level. Initially, this suggests that local issues will receive a less biased hearing at that level, a vindication of Dillon's Rule. But this same logic suggests that those groups with sufficient resources to sift through to the state level are likely to be even more influential as they will face less opposition than they would at the local level. What is unclear is whether the balance between quantity and ultimate effectiveness nets out in favor of forcing localities to seek express authority from the legislature for issues most susceptible to lobbying efforts. * * *

STATE v. HUTCHINSON

Supreme Court of Utah, 1980.
624 P.2d 1116.

STEWART, JUSTICE.

Defendant, a candidate for the office of Salt Lake County Commissioner, was charged with having violated § 1–10–4, Revised Ordinances of Salt Lake County, which requires the filing of campaign statements and the disclosure of campaign contributions. * * * Defendant contends that because the Legislature has not specifically authorized counties to enact ordinances requiring disclosure of campaign contributions in county elections, Salt Lake County had no power to enact the ordinance in question. * * *

Concededly, * * * the Legislature has not expressly authorized enactment of an ordinance requiring disclosure of campaign contributions in county elections. However, the Legislature has conferred upon cities and counties the authority to enact all necessary measures to promote the general health, safety, morals, and welfare of their citizens. Section 17–5–77, U.C.A. (1953), as amended, provides:

> The board of county commissioners may pass all ordinances * * * not repugnant to law * * * *necessary and proper to provide for the safety, and preserve the health, promote the prosperity, improve the morals, peace and good order, comfort and convenience of the county and the inhabitants thereof,* * * * and may enforce obedience to such ordinances * * * by fine in any sum less than $300 or by imprisonment not to exceed six months, or by both such fine and imprisonment * * *. [Emphasis added.]

The Legislature has made a similar grant of power to the cities.

The specific issue in this case is whether § 17–5–77 by itself provides Salt Lake County legal authority to enact the ordinance for disclosure of campaign contributions, or whether there must be a specific grant of authority for counties to enact measures dealing with disclosures of campaign financing to sustain the ordinance in question. Defendant claims that the powers of municipalities must be strictly construed and that because Salt Lake County did not have specific, delegated authority to enact the ordinance in issue, the ordinance is invalid.

The rule requiring strict construction of the powers delegated by the Legislature to counties and municipalities is a rule which is archaic, unrealistic, and unresponsive to the current needs of both state and local governments and effectively nullifies the legislative grant of general police power to the counties. Furthermore, although the rule of strict construction is supported by some cases in this State, it is inconsistent with other cases decided by this Court—a situation that permits choosing between conflicting precedents to support a particular result.

Dillon's Rule, which requires strict construction of delegated powers to local governments, was first enunciated in 1868. The rule was widely adopted during a period of great mistrust of municipal governments and has been viewed as "the only possible alternative by which extensive governmental powers may be conferred upon our municipalities, with a measurable limit upon their abuse."

The courts, in applying the Dillon Rule to general welfare clauses, have not viewed the latter as an independent source of power, but rather as limited by specific, enumerated grants of authority. More recently, however, reasoned opinion regarding the validity of the rule has changed. One authority has noted the harmful effects that the rule of strict construction has had upon the effective exercise of appropriate municipal authority:

> Any vestige of inherent powers or liberality in construing delegated powers was soon swept away by the Dillon Rule. This rule was formulated in an era when farm-dominated legislatures were jealous of their power and when city scandals were notorious. It has been the authority, without critical analysis of it, for literally hundreds of subsequent cases.

> As it arose, the strict construction doctrine applied to municipal corporations but it has been extended to local government generally and it must be faced in any approach to liberalizing local powers. This rule sends local government to State legislatures seeking grants of additional powers; it causes local officials to doubt their power, and it stops local governmental programs from developing fully. The strict construction rule stimulated home rule efforts and is largely responsible for the erosion of home rule. Because of its importance the rule should be examined critically from time to time.[6]

As pointed out in Frug, *The City As A Legal Concept,* 93 Harvard L.Rev. 1059, 1111 (1980):

> Most troubling of all to Dillon, cities were not managed by those "*best fitted* by their intelligence, business experience, capacity and moral character." Their management was "too often both *unwise* and *extravagant*." A major change in city government was therefore needed to achieve a fully public city government dedicated to the common good. [Emphasis in original.]

If there were once valid policy reasons supporting the rule, we think they have largely lost their force and that effective local self-government, as an important constituent part of our system of government, must have sufficient power to deal effectively with the problems with which it must deal. In a time of almost universal education and of substantial, and sometimes intense, citizen interest in the proper functioning of local government, we do not share the belief that local officials are generally

---

6. Advisory Commission on Intergovernmental Relations, State Constitutional and Statutory Restrictions Upon the Structural, Functional, and Personnel Powers of Local Government, 24 (1962).

unworthy of the trust of those governed. Indeed, if democratic processes at the grassroots level do not function well, then it is not likely that our state government will operate much better. * * *

The fear of local governments abusing their delegated powers as a justification for strict construction of those powers is a slur on the right and the ability of people to govern themselves. Adequate protection against abuse of power or interference with legitimate statewide interests is provided by the electorate, state supervisory control, and judicial review. Strict construction, particularly in the face of a general welfare grant of power to local governments, simply eviscerates the plain language of the statute, nullifies the intent of the Legislature, and seriously cripples effective local government.

There are ample safeguards against any abuse of power at the local level. Local governments, as subdivisions of the State, exercise those powers granted to them by the State Legislature, and the exercise of a delegated power is subject to the limitations imposed by state statutes and state and federal constitutions. A state cannot empower local governments to do that which the state itself does not have authority to do. In addition, local governments are without authority to pass any ordinance prohibited by, or in conflict with, state statutory law. Also, an ordinance is invalid if it intrudes into an area which the Legislature has preempted by comprehensive legislation intended to blanket a particular field.

In view of all these restraints and corrective measures, it is not appropriate for this Court to enfeeble local governments on the unjustified assumption that strict construction of delegated powers is necessary to prevent abuse. The enactment of a broad general welfare clause conferring police powers directly on the counties was to enable them to act in every reasonable, necessary, and appropriate way to further the public welfare of their citizens.

The ultimate limitation upon potential abuses by local governments is the people themselves. It is their vigilance and sound judgment by which all democratic governments in the end, are restricted and directed. Officials who abuse the powers with which they have been entrusted ought not to be, and usually are not, long tolerated. * * *

This view is shared by the Advisory Commission on Intergovernmental Relations which has urged that local governments be given broad powers. The Commission's Report states:

> The Commission believes that legislatures should delegate local powers in broad terms. The abuse by local government of broad powers troubles the Commission minimally. It is not currently wide-spread in any serious way. The fact that abuse conceivably might occur is no more reason to deny broad delegations of power than it is to deny a Boy Scout a knife because he might cut himself. Additionally, we are of the opinion that if a broad functional delegation of power is a part of the total power residing in the local governing body it will be more responsive to popular control. * * *

The general welfare provision, § 17–5–77, grants county commissioners of each county two distinct types of authority. In the first instance, power is given *to implement specific grants of authority.* Second, the counties are granted *an independent source of power to act for the general welfare of its citizens.* * * * Nothing in § 17–5–77 * * * suggests that the general welfare clause should be narrowly or strictly construed. Its breadth of language demands the opposite conclusion. * * * When the State has granted general welfare power to local governments, those governments have independent authority apart from, and in addition to, specific grants of authority to pass ordinances which are reasonably and appropriately related to the objectives of that power, i.e., providing for the public safety, health, morals, and welfare. And the courts will not interfere with the legislative choice of the means selected unless it is arbitrary, or is directly prohibited by, or is inconsistent with the policy of, the state or federal laws or the constitution of this State or of the United States. Specific grants of authority may serve to limit the means available under the general welfare clause, for some limitation may be imposed on the exercise of power by directing the use of power in a particular manner. But specific grants should generally be construed with reasonable latitude in light of the broad language of the general welfare clause which may supplement the power found in a specific delegation.

Broad construction of the powers of counties and cities is consistent with the current needs of local governments. The Dillon Rule of strict construction is antithetical to effective and efficient local and state government. The complexities confronting local governments, and the degree to which the nature of those problems varies from county to county and city to city, has changed since the Dillon Rule was formulated. Several counties in this State, for example, currently confront large and serious problems caused by accelerated urban growth. The same problems however, are not so acute in many other counties. Some counties are experiencing, and others may soon be experiencing, explosive economic growth as the result of the development of natural resources. The problems that must be solved by these counties are to some extent unique to them. According a plain meaning to the legislative grant of general welfare power to local governmental units allows each local government to be responsive to the particular problems facing it.

Local power should not be paralyzed and critical problems should not remain unsolved while officials await a biennial session of the Legislature in the hope of obtaining passage of a special grant of authority. Furthermore, passage of legislation needed or appropriate for some counties may fail because of the press of other legislative business or the disinterest of legislators from other parts of the State whose constituencies experience other, and to them more pressing, problems. In granting cities and counties the power to enact ordinances to further the general welfare, the Legislature no doubt took such political realities into consideration.

We therefore hold that a county has the power to preserve the purity of its electoral process. The county was entitled to conclude that financial disclosure by candidates would directly serve the legitimate purpose of achieving the goal that special interests should not be able to exercise undue influence in local elections without their influence being brought to light. * * *

MAUGHAN, JUSTICE (dissenting): * * *

The analysis of the majority opinion utilizes the familiar technique of erecting a straw man, in this case, the abstract principle of law identified as Dillon's Rule, and throttling it with the evocative shibboleth of local control. The majority then interprets Section 17–5–77 as a carte blanche delegation of the state police power to local government, unless there be a specific and direct conflict between state and local law. This interpretation is inconsistent with the multiple statutes, wherein the legislature confers specific powers and duties on local government, and distorts the nature of the police power.

The State is the sole and exclusive repository of the police power, neither the federal nor local government has any such inherent power. The police power is awesome, for it confers the right to declare an act a crime and to deprive an individual of his liberty or property in order to protect or advance the public health, safety, morals, and welfare. The decision of whether a problem should be deemed one of local concern and should be regulated under the police power should initially be decided by the legislature representing all the citizens of this state. The legislature may then elect to delegate the power to local government to deal with the specific area of concern. It is equally a legislative judgment to deny delegating this power to local government.

The palliative suggested by the majority opinion that local citizens can change the law by electing new officials provides no relief for the individual previously convicted and avoids the basic issue of whether the police power has, in fact, been delegated under the specific circumstance. All exercise of the police power by local government is derivative, none is inherent, and it is the exclusive prerogative of the State to establish the conditions under which it will be exercised. If local government discerns a condition which merits control through the police power, this matter should be submitted to the legislature so that representatives of the entire state may resolve whether the problem should be addressed on a local level.

It is within the context of the foregoing principles that the specific delegation of the police power in Section 17–5–77 should be interpreted in this case. * * * The County advocates the view that the general welfare clause of Section 17–5–77 constitutes a broad, general grant of the state's police power to counties. This section is similar to Section 10–8–84, which grants the same powers to cities and has been interpreted by this court on a number of occasions. In *Lark v. Whitehead* the city urged, under the general welfare clause, a municipal legislative body had a broad grant of power in criminal matters. It was also alleged the city was better qualified to determine what would adversely affect the safety, peace and good order of its inhabitants than was the state legislature. This Court responded:

> In *Nasfell v. Ogden City* this court stated that it was committed to the principle that cities have none of the elements of sovereignty and that any fair, reasonable, substantial doubt concerning the existence of the power is resolved by the courts against the corporation (city) and the power denied; grants of power to cities are strictly construed to the exclusion of implied powers which are not reasonably necessary in carrying out the purposes of the express powers granted. * * *

The issue is thus reduced to the question of whether the challenged ordinances are *substantially and reasonably* related to the promotion of the prosperity and improvement of the morals, peace and good order, comfort and convenience of the county and its inhabitants. The circumstances of this case compel a negative answer; there is neither a substantial nor reasonable relationship between the aforecited purposes and the campaign disclosures of elected county officials. This matter is best illustrated by three cases: *Bohn v. Salt Lake City,*[14] *Salt Lake City v. Revene,*[15] and *Nance v. Mayflower Tavern, Inc.*[16]

In *Bohn* the issue concerned the authority of the city to include certain special provisions in a contract to construct storm sewers. These provisions were included solely for the purpose of alleviating the unemployment situation, which this Court described as a wholly collateral condition to the objects and purposes sought by the construction of storm sewers. This Court began its analysis by citing the principles that implied and incidental powers include those necessary to give effect to powers expressly granted, and the "General Welfare Clause" neither enlarges nor annuls the powers conferred upon the city by special grant.

This Court particularly concentrated on the provision in the contract concerning minimum wage. The power to fix a minimum wage and to prescribe the hours which constitute a day's labor are generally regarded as an exercise of the police power. The Court explained * * *

> There is in this state no express or implied power conferred upon a municipality which directly or by implication authorizes a city to dictate to a contractor the wages that he shall pay his employees * * *. In this jurisdiction, inasmuch as municipalities have none of the elements of sovereignty in exerting their given powers, we think the provision in the proposed contracts with respect to the minimum wage must be ruled out.

In the *Revene* case, the city urged, an ordinance, setting the closing hours of barbershops, was a valid exercise of the police power delegated by the Legislature to the city to regulate for the safety and preservation of health in the community. This Court characterized the issue as

---

14. 79 Utah 121, 8 P.2d 591 (1932). **16.** 106 Utah 517, 150 P.2d 773 (1944).

15. 101 Utah 504, 124 P.2d 537 (1942).

whether the fixing of the closing hours was a reasonable regulation within the scope of the *delegated* police power, i.e., did it have a reasonable relationship to the protection of the health of the public. * * * The opinion then recited and relied on the principle that any fair, reasonable, substantial doubt concerning the existence of the power is resolved by the courts against the corporation, and the power denied. * * *

In the *Nance* case the challenged ordinance provided for civil rights concerning restaurants. The Court said cities had no inherent or original legislative power. * * * The Court held:

> * * * The power to enact civil rights legislation is not granted in express words either by constitution or by statute, nor is it necessarily or fairly implied in or incident to the powers expressly granted. Likewise it cannot be held to be essential to the accomplishment of the declared objects and purposes of the corporation, or as Dillon states, "indispensable" to the accomplishment of the declared objects. We therefore hold that cities have no power to enact such civil rights legislation * * *.

In the matter at hand, there is no express grant conferring authority on Salt Lake County to enact a corrupt practices act concerning local elected officials. Such authority cannot be implied from the general welfare clause of Section 17–5–77 since it does not have a sufficiently direct, substantial, immediate effect on the specific general welfare interests set forth therein. * * *

2. HOME RULE INITIATIVE

Even at the time of the publication of Dillon's treatise, political efforts were already being undertaken to enable cities to engage in more extensive self-government than is permissible under Dillon's Rule. These political efforts, known as the home rule movement, had two different objectives. The first objective was to give cities a power of initiative in city affairs, allowing them to operate under a general grant of authority from the state instead of requiring them to rely on individualized delegations for particular purposes. The second objective was to give cities an area of autonomy immune from state control. These two objectives, it should be recognized, are not necessarily connected: cities could be given a broad power to initiate actions on their own ("Home Rule Initiative") without giving them immunity from the state's power to overrule these actions if the state chooses to do so ("Home Rule Immunity"). Only the first of these objectives is covered in this section of the book; the second is covered in Chapter Two, below.[1]

1. For general analyses of the concept of home rule, see, e.g., 3 Sands & Libonati, Local Government Law, § 13.03 (1993); 1 Antieau, Municipal Corporation Law, Chapter 3 (1980); Vaubel, Toward Principles of State Restraint Upon the Exercise of Municipal Power in Home Rule, 22 Stet.L.Rev. 643 (1993), 20 Stet.L.Rev.845 (1991), 20 Stet.L.Rev.5 (1990); Libonati, Home Rule: An Essay on Pluralism, 64 Wash.L.Rev. 51 (1989); Sebree, One Century of Home Rule: A Progress Report, 64 Wash. L. Rev. 155 (1989); Andersen, Resolving State/Local Governmental Conflict A Tale of Three Cit-

Missouri became the first state in the nation to include a home rule provision in its state constitution in 1875; since that time, most state constitutions have been amended to provide for municipal home rule. The first two cases reproduced below illustrate the contrasting attitudes that courts have taken toward these constitutional provisions: City of Ocala v. Nye offers a broad interpretation and McCrory Corporation v. Fowler offers a restrictive interpretation of home rule authority. Can the different results in the two cases be explained by differences in the language of the two state constitutions? Or are the different results a consequence of the same controversy about the desirability of city authority evident in the Dillon's Rule cases considered earlier? Following the two cases, an excerpt from Terrance Sandalow's influential article, The Limits of Municipal Power Under Home Rule: A Role for the Courts, presents an argument for judicial restrictions on home rule initiative. Are his arguments for a continuing restraint on cities' power of initiative persuasive? Under Professor Sandalow's analysis, what is the difference between Dillon's Rule and Home Rule?

CITY OF OCALA v. NYE

Supreme Court of Florida, 1992.
608 So.2d 15.

PER CURIAM.   * * *

This case involves the question of whether a municipality has the power of eminent domain to acquire an entire tract of land when only a portion of the tract is needed for a municipal purpose. * * * The City of Ocala (the City) sought to condemn property in order to widen a city street. * * * The City contends that under its home rule powers, article VIII, section 2(b), Florida Constitution,[2] * * * it may exercise any power for a municipal purpose except when expressly prohibited by law. The City argues that because the Department of Transportation (DOT) and counties, as political subdivisions of the state, are expressly permitted by statute to condemn more property than is necessary where they would save money by doing so, the City may likewise do so pursuant to its home rule powers. We agree.

ies, 18 Urban Law Annual 129 (1980); Vanlandingham, Constitutional Home Rule Since the AMA (NLC) Model, 17 Wm. & Mary L.Rev. 1 (1975); Vanlandingham, Municipal Home Rule in the United States, 10 Wm. & Mary L.Rev. 269 (1968); Fordham & Asher, Home Rule Powers in Theory and Practice, 9 Ohio St.L.J. 18 (1948); McGoldrick, Law and Practice of Municipal Home Rule, 1916–1930 (1933); McBain, The Law and Practice of Municipal Home Rule (1916). For analyses of home rule in specific states, see, e.g., Griffith, Connecticut's Home Rule: The Judicial Resolution of State and Local Conflicts, 4 U.Bridgeport L.Rev. 177 (1983); Michael & Norton, Home Rule in Illinois: A Functional Analy-

sis, 1978 U.Ill.L.F. 559 (1978); Vaubel, Municipal Home Rule in Ohio, 3 Ohio North. L.Rev. 1, 355 (1975).

2. Article VIII, section 2(b), Florida Constitution, states:

SECTION 2. Municipalities.—

(b) POWERS. Municipalities shall have governmental, corporate and proprietary powers to enable them to conduct municipal government, perform municipal functions and render municipal services, and may exercise any power for municipal purposes except as otherwise provided by law. * * *

The power of eminent domain is an attribute of the sovereign which is circumscribed by, rather than conferred by, constitution or statute. *Peavy-Wilson Lumber Co. v. Brevard County*, 159 Fla. 311, 31 So.2d 483 (1947). This power can only be exercised by counties and state agencies if the state delegates that power to those political subdivisions. Furthermore, "when the sovereign delegates the power [of eminent domain] to a political unit or agency a strict construction will be given against the agency asserting the power." 159 Fla. at 314, 31 So.2d at 485. Thus, it is only through another specific legislative grant that the DOT and the counties are authorized to acquire land in its entirety in order to reduce acquisition costs. * * *

Article VIII, section 2, Florida Constitution, expressly grants to every municipality the authority to conduct municipal government, perform municipal functions, and render municipal services. The only constitutional limitation placed on the municipalities' authority is that such powers be exercised for valid "municipal purposes." The "Municipal Home Rule Powers Act," enacted by the legislature in 1973, states that as provided by the Florida Constitution municipalities "may exercise any power for municipal purposes, except when expressly prohibited by law." Thus, municipalities are not dependent upon the legislature for further authorization, and legislative statutes are relevant only to determine limitations of authority. Although section 166.401, Florida Statutes (1989), purports to authorize municipalities to exercise eminent domain powers, municipalities could exercise those powers for a valid municipal purpose without any such "grant" of authority. If the state has the power to take particular land for public purposes, then a municipality may also exercise that power unless it is "expressly prohibited." Although section 166.401(2) does not expressly grant the taking of an entire parcel by a municipality to save money, it also does not expressly prohibit a municipality from doing so.

With regard to the taking of an entire parcel to avoid business damages, this Court has stated that "the purpose of cutting acquisition costs to expand the financial base for further public projects constitutes a valid public purpose." *Department of Transp. v. Fortune Fed. Sav. & Loan Ass'n*, 532 So.2d 1267, 1270 (Fla.1988). If it is a public purpose to save state and county money in road acquisition costs by taking an entire parcel rather than part of a parcel of land, then it is also a public purpose for municipalities to save taxpayers' money for the same type of acquisition. * * *

McCRORY CORPORATION v. FOWLER

Court of Appeals of Maryland, 1990.
319 Md. 12, 570 A.2d 834.

ELDRIDGE, JUDGE.

Pursuant to the Maryland Uniform Certification of Questions of Law Act, the United States District Court for the District of Maryland has certified to this Court the following * * * [question] concerning a Montgomery County ordinance:

"(1) Did enactment of Section 27–20(a) of the Montgomery County Code, which creates a private cause of action for employment discrimination entitling a claimant to sue for damages, injunctive or other civil relief, exceed the authority delegated to chartered home rule counties * * *?"

* * * Robert Fowler, a white male, managed a store for McCrory Corporation. Fowler alleged that one of McCrory's managers told him not to hire any more black persons or persons under thirty-five years of age, and that when Fowler requested McCrory executives to repudiate this directive, they refused to do so. Thereafter, Fowler claimed, he was harassed and eventually constructively discharged in retaliation for his protest. Fowler brought an action for money damages against McCrory in the Circuit Court for Montgomery County * * *. At McCrory's request, the case was removed to the United States District Court for the District of Maryland. Fowler filed an amended complaint in the United States District Court, * * * adding a count under § 27–20(a) of the Montgomery County Code * * *. Section 27–20(a) * * * [provides]:

"Any person who has been subjected to any act of discrimination prohibited under this division shall be deemed to have been denied a civil right and shall be entitled to sue for damages, injunction or other civil relief, including reasonable attorney's fees * * *."

Montgomery County has chartered home rule under Article XI–A of the Maryland Constitution. Article XI–A * * * known as the Home Rule Amendment, enabled counties, which chose to adopt a home rule charter, to achieve a significant degree of political self-determination. * * * Section 3 of Article XI–A provides (emphasis supplied):

"From and after the adoption of a charter by the City of Baltimore, or any County of this State, as hereinbefore provided, the Mayor of Baltimore and City Council of the City of Baltimore or the County Council of said County, subject to the Constitution and Public General Laws of this State, shall have full power to enact *local laws* of said city, or county * * * upon all matters covered by the express powers granted as above provided * * *."

Article XI–A "does not constitute a grant of absolute autonomy to local governments." *Ritchmount Partnership v. Board*, 283 Md. 48, 56, 388 A.2d 523, 529 (1978). This Court's decisions and the above-quoted passage make it clear that the Home Rule Amendment limits the Montgomery County Council to enacting "local laws" * * * .

Thus, it is first necessary to determine whether § 27–20(a) of the Montgomery County Code is a "local law." * * * In *Steimel v. Board*, 278 Md. 1, 5, 357 A.2d 386, 388 (1976), we stated that a local law "in subject matter and substance" is "confined in its operation to prescribed territorial limits* * *." A general law, on the other hand, " 'deals with the general public welfare, a subject which is of significant interest not just to any one county, but rather to more than one geographical subdivision, or even to the entire state.' " * * *

Section 27–20(a) of the Montgomery County Code authorizes a private citizen to seek redress for another private citizen's violation of a county anti-employment discrimination ordinance by instituting a judicial action in the courts of the State for, *inter alia*, unlimited money damages. Fowler, for example, is seeking over $1.8 million. * * * In creating a new judicial cause of action between private individuals, § 27–20(a) encroaches upon an area which heretofore had been the province of state agencies. In Maryland, the creation of new causes of action in the courts has traditionally been done either by the General Assembly or by this Court under its authority to modify the common law of this State. Furthermore, the creation of new judicial remedies has traditionally been done on a statewide basis.

Abusive employment practices constitute a statewide problem which has been addressed by the General Assembly in Article 49B of the Maryland Code * * *. It is true that the field has not been preempted by the State, and that home rule counties have concurrent authority to provide administrative remedies not in conflict with state law. Nevertheless, creating a remedy which has traditionally been the sole province of the General Assembly and the Court of Appeals, to combat a statewide problem such as employment discrimination, goes beyond a "matter[ ] of purely local concern." [T]he Montgomery County Code affects "matters of significant interest to the entire state" and cannot qualify as a "local law" under Article XI–A.

A contrary holding would open the door for counties to enact a variety of laws in areas which have heretofore been viewed as the exclusive province of the General Assembly and the Court of Appeals. For example, could a county ordinance authorize in the circuit court and the District Court negligence actions in which contributory negligence would not be a bar? Could a county ordinance provide for breach of contract suits upon "contracts" not supported by consideration, or where the parol evidence rule is inapplicable? We believe that the answer is "no." These, and many other legal doctrines, are matters of significant interest to the entire State, calling for uniform application in state courts. They are not proper subject matters for "local laws."

Chief Judge Cardozo recognized that certain areas of the law are matters of statewide concern when he wrote about a city home rule provision in New York's Constitution (*Adler v. Deegan*, 251 N.Y. 467, 167 N.E. 705, 713 (1929) (Cardozo, C.J., concurring)):

"In every case, 'it is necessary to inquire whether a proposed subject of legislation is a matter of State concern or of local concern.' * * *. There are * * * affairs exclusively those of the state, such as the law of domestic relations, of wills, of inheritance, of contracts, of crimes not essentially local * * *, the organization of courts, the procedure therein. None of these things can be said to touch the affairs that a city is organized to regulate, whether we have reference to history or to tradition or to existing forms of charters." * * *

Our holding today is in accord with the position taken in 6 McQuillin, *Municipal Corporations* (3rd Ed.Rev.), § 22.01:

> "The well-established general rule is that a municipal corporation cannot create by ordinance a right of action between third persons or enlarge the common law or statutory duty or liability of citizens among themselves. Under the rule, an ordinance cannot directly create a civil liability of one citizen to another or relieve one citizen from liability by imposing it on another." * * *

We hold, therefore, that an ordinance attempting to combat employment discrimination by creating a new private judicial cause of action is not a "local law" under Article XI–A of the Maryland Constitution, and thus is not within the power of Montgomery County to enact. * * *

TERRANCE SANDALOW, THE LIMITS OF MUNICIPAL POWER UNDER HOME RULE: A ROLE FOR THE COURTS

48 Minn.L.Rev. 643, 685–687, 691, 701–702, 705–710, 712–715, 717 (1964).

Judicially imposed limitations on municipal initiative under a grant of home rule power have not * * * been frequent or unduly restrictive of municipal power. Nevertheless, such limitations have occasionally been imposed. In recent years, commencing with Dean Fordham's draft of *Model Constitutional Provisions for Municipal Home Rule,* efforts have been made to formulate the grant of home rule powers in terms sufficiently comprehensive to extinguish, or at least considerably narrow, the opportunities for judicial limitation. Dean Fordham's proposal is that a home rule municipality be permitted to "exercise any power or perform any function which the legislature has power to devolve upon a non-home rule" municipality. The sixth edition of the National Municipal League's *Model State Constitution* goes even further; it would authorize a municipality to "exercise any legislative power or perform any function. * * *" Except for the recent Alaska constitution these proposals provide greater power than is granted in any state.

Two primary assumptions underlie the proposals. The first * * * involves the undesirability of fragmenting governmental power. Responsibility for the general welfare cannot, as appears to have been assumed in drafting the traditional home rule provisions, be neatly divided into areas of local and general concern. Fulfillment of municipal responsibility toward the local citizenry requires a broad range of powers. Specification is not only unwieldy, it ignores the obvious truth that constantly changing conditions require flexibility, a need which can best be met by permitting municipalities to assume new powers whenever, in the judgment of those most familiar with local problems, the necessity arises. The second assumption rests upon the indisputable premise that the allocation of governmental power is a political question. Judicial participation in the resolution of such political questions has, through the years, been the target of frequent criticism by commentators. Judges, it has been argued, lack both the training and experience requisite to wise judgment in such matters. Moreover, the critics continue, the adjudicative process is not adapted to the solution of such problems; it places too much reliance upon concept and precedent and not enough on administrative and practical implications. * * *

Closer analysis suggests, however, that the proposals may go too far in broadening the scope of municipal initiative and removing the courts from participation in the process of curbing possible abuses of municipal power. * * * The apparent theory of the proposals is that the legislature can be relied upon to protect the broader public interest against possible incursions by municipalities * * *. The question is whether legislation can carry so large a burden. To answer the question requires not only an analysis of the areas to which municipal power would extend under the proposals but a comparative assessment of the ability of the courts and the legislature to cope with the various problems. * * *

Virtually every substantive power exercised by municipalities—there is a temptation to say every power without qualification—may, under appropriate circumstances, have an impact upon surrounding areas. Legislative review of the possible uses of such power with a view toward imposition of limitations necessary to protect the general welfare is, of course, desirable. But in view of the broad range of powers exercised by municipalities, the various ways in which they are exercised, and the continuously changing circumstances which affect the extent of extra-territorial impact, the ability of the legislature to foresee all of the potential problems is extremely doubtful. A related consideration is that the relatively narrow impact of many local measures incompatible with the general welfare makes it difficult for the legislature to assume the primary responsibility for policing local action. Such measures do not arouse sufficient general interest to overcome legislative inertia. * * *

The inherent limitations of legislative oversight suggest that there may be a role for the courts in the protection of the larger community against municipal parochialism. Although the ad hoc and limited character of judicial intervention precludes any possibility that over-all "solutions" can be achieved through this device alone, partial reliance upon the courts does offer several advantages. The institution of lawsuits by individuals disadvantaged by municipal legislation provides an opportunity for continuous, if nonetheless episodic, review of such legislation to determine its consistency with the welfare of the larger community. In discharging this responsibility, the courts have the advantage of comparative freedom from local pressures. Equally important, issues almost invariably come before the courts in relatively concrete circumstances, permitting somewhat more particularized judgments than are likely to be made by the legislature. In the long run, this may permit greater flexibility and adaptability to changing circumstances * * * than would reliance upon the legislature for the formulation of statutory limitations upon municipal initiative. * * *

[A]s Professor Mishkin has pointed out * * *: "The rationale behind the presumption of validity generally is that political processes are adequate to assure representation of affected interests in the legislature and that, therefore, the court should not 'substitute its judgment' for that of the democratically chosen and responsible body." * * * [A]ffected interests often are not represented in the municipal council and, consequently, * * * courts may justifiably limit municipal initiative in situations where identical state legislation would be upheld * * *. Ultimately, a judgment must be made as to relative weights of the municipality's interest and other affected interests. Concededly, such judgments are difficult for courts. Frequently they lack the information necessary to a fully informed decision. There may be insufficient consensus as to the scale on which interests are to be weighed. Nevertheless, guides to decision are not entirely wanting. Some guidance may be obtained by reference to enabling legislation for non-home rule municipalities. The absence of legislation authorizing exercise of a power cannot, of course, be treated as conclusive without depriving home rule of all its meaning, but if the legislature has authorized exercise of the power in question or similar powers by non-home rule municipalities that would seem to settle the matter in favor of home rule municipalities. Similarly, some weight may be given to the permissibility *vel non* of a state exercising the power under the federal constitution. * * * In the absence of such guides there is no escape from the necessity of attempting to weigh the competing interests. * * *

The demand for local autonomy has been most insistent with respect to those matters as to which the impact of municipal action is thought to be confined to local residents. * * * The plea for unlimited municipal initiative (so long as there is no extraterritorial impact and general constitutional limitations are observed) conjures up visions of local democracy deeply rooted in American political ideology. * * * At least since Madison, however, there have been warnings that local democracy may also be destructive of important values. The municipal council is not necessarily the equivalent of the state legislature even though the impact of its actions is wholly intramural.

The argument of *Federalist* X is of particular relevance, for it suggests that a power which might be exercised by the legislature may reasonably be denied a municipal council because, for certain purposes, the municipality's political processes are less adequate than those at the state level. * * * The argument is occasionally made that the existence of constitutional guarantees, enforceable by the courts, is adequate to protect individuals or minorities against the oppressive use of local power. Some measure of protection is, of course, provided by constitutional restrictions upon the power of all government, but exclusive reliance upon these guarantees poses troublesome questions. Is it wise to increase the risk of constitutional decisions restrictive of individual freedom or contrary to minority interests solely at the instance of a local majority which well may not be representative of the larger community? Conversely, is there not a danger that if courts are limited to general constitutional guarantees in protecting individual or minorities from local majorities, precedent will be established which may impede governmental action if the time comes that the larger community, as represented in the state legislature, determines that the general welfare requires the interference with individual or minority interests? There is, of course, a possibility that courts might adopt a variable standard of constitutional interpretation under which the weight accorded a legislative judgment would be partially dependent upon the size (and presumptively, therefore, the diversity) of the population represented. Whatever the merits of such an approach in other contexts, it seems to offer no advantages over a formulation of home rule powers which permits courts to deny municipalities certain powers in the absence of enabling legislation. * * *

The area of possible municipal action is so broad, the range of potential experimentation so great, that the ability of the legislature to foresee all of the problems which may arise is highly improbable. Nor can reliance be placed upon legislative action after the exercise of municipal initiative. The relatively narrow impact of many local measures may not arouse sufficient general interest to overcome legislative inertia. * * * A more satisfactory accommodation of the competing values might be achieved by a broad but not unlimited grant of municipal initiative, in terms similar to those currently employed in most state constitutions. * * * [T]here appears to be no textual obstacle to reading the constitutional provisions as permitting the courts to limit municipal initiative so as to preclude a use of municipal power which threatens fundamental community values or established state policies. Either in terms or by construction constitutional home rule provisions authorize municipal action only with respect to "local" or "municipal" affairs. A use of governmental power which threatens fundamental values or established state policies might not be deemed a "local" or "municipal" affair for much the same reason that municipal regulations with too great an extraterritorial impact are not considered to be "local" or "municipal" affairs * * *.

A number of state constitutional home rule provisions expressly state that cities' home rule power does not include the power "to enact private or civil law governing civil relationships except as incident to an exercise of an independent municipal power." (This quotation is from the Massachusetts Constitution discussed in Marshal House, Inc. v. Rent Review Board of Brookline, reproduced below.) An excerpt from Gary Schwartz's article, The Logic of Home Rule and The Private Law Exception, offers a rationale for this limit on home rule cities' power of initiative. And the *Marshal House* case applies the private law exception to a city's effort to regulate the landlord-tenant relationship. Does Professor Schwartz or can you justify the limits on cities' home rule power imposed by the private law exception? Are city ordinances like the one considered above in McCrory Corporation v. Fowler "private law''? How much home rule power of initiative remains after the private law exception is applied?

GARY SCHWARTZ, THE LOGIC OF HOME RULE AND THE PRIVATE LAW EXCEPTION

20 U.C.L.A.L.Rev. 670, 687–690, 750–756 (1973).

While ''private law'' is a term employed by lawyers in several very different senses, the suggested home rule private law exception clearly is intended to refer to private law in the rough sense that contracts, property, and torts are private law. With these as examples of private law, we can formulate the following working definition: Private law consists of the substantive law which establishes legal rights and duties between and among private entities, law that takes effect in lawsuits brought by one private entity against another. The complement of private law is thus ''public law''—the substantive law defining the legal obligations of private individuals or entities to the government, and also establishing their liberties and opportunities in relation to the government. * * *

While the definition here advanced is understood as conforming to what lawyers generally mean by ''private law,'' it appears that at least some lawyers, somewhat contrary to the definition, may be inclined to block off entire subject matter areas—for example, corporations law, sales law—as innately ''private law.'' * * * [O]ne need only consult the first and still the foremost book-length treatment of home rule, Professor McBain's *The Law and Practice of Home Rule,* published in 1916. In this volume, after 672 pages influenced by a general sympathy for a generous interpretation of home rule, the following passage rather abruptly appears:

> By common understanding such general subjects as * * * domestic relations, wills and administration, mortgages, trusts, contracts, real and personal property, insurance, banking, corporations, and many others have never been regarded by any one, least of all by the cities themselves, as appropriate subjects of local control. No city has been so foolhardy as to venture generally into any one of these fields of law. It has simply been universally accepted that these matters are strictly of ''state concern.''

A leading contemporary law review assessment of home rule authority, published almost half a century after McBain, includes an affirmation of this ''common understanding.'' Since its ''many others'' element can presumably be supplied with meaning only if a content common to the specifically enumerated elements can be clarified, this Article will speak of the ''McBain nine,'' those nine legal subjects preceding the ''many others'' finale. * * *

The home rule literature has noted the useful if obvious point that cities are subject to * * * [the Commerce] clause in the sense that if a state statute is invalid as an ''undue burden'' on interstate commerce, a city ordinance containing the same requirements would be equally invalid. What has not so far received scholarly attention is the intriguing possibility that a burden on interstate commerce which is constitutionally "due" if imposed by a state can become "undue" if its source is a city, by virtue of the fact that the greater number and proximity of cities (as compared to states) signifies that the burden in the latter situation will be far more onerous. * * * To look back at the McBain nine * * *, it can now be said that certain city enactments covered by the nine might well be precluded in their application to intercity entities by federal commerce clause principles or their state counterparts. * * * Granted, home rule must generally be willing to live with substantial non-uniformity. Nevertheless * * * a home rule authority exception is appropriate and even necessary if there are serious disadvantages to home rule in application and if these disadvantages are convincingly shown to be in excess of the relevant home rule benefits; and there is ultimately no satisfying reason why extreme inefficiency should not be treated like any other functional disadvantage of city lawmaking for exception purposes. * * *

If the conclusion thus is that undue burden and extreme inefficiency do function as predicates for home rule exceptions, it is important to note that the private law component of a city ordinance will often significantly add to the overall magnitude of its burden or the extent of its inefficiency. The reason for this goes back to the fact noted earlier that because of the poor accessibility of city legal documents, the chances of inadvertent and excusable error in the ascertainment of city law are quite high. This fact standing alone applies, of course, to city public and private law alike; but the additional point is that with private law, far more than with public law, the consequences of accidental and minor violations can be enormous. Assume a major private arrangement on which many parties have heavily relied. It is bad enough if one party's innocent misperception of city law leads to a modest public fine; it is something else if this innocent misperception causes the entire arrangement to disastrously collapse. Under a system of city private law, a testator's intentions in disposing of his wealth could be negated by his lawyer's excusable city law mistake, a lender could find that all his mortgages are worthless because of an inadvertent and technical violation of a city ordinance, and so on. * * *

Courts are well suited, and legislatures rather poorly suited, to render low-level determinations that address themselves to the local interests involved in and the inefficiencies produced by particular local ordinances * * *. But if we desire generic determinations which concern themselves with entire legal subjects (for example, the law of contracts), the legislature would be the more appropriate institution to turn to. * * * As a way of testing out the generic approach, we can briefly look back upon the McBain nine. Inevitably, the extent of statutory suppression within the nine renders the home rule authority issues so hypothetical that meaningful comment, while not impossible, is difficult. Especially in these circumstances, it would be unduly ambitious to deal with each of the nine, but I will venture to comment on at least a few; even these comments will concededly be somewhat sketchy and summary. "Corporations" law seems generally lacking in characterization difficulties, and one can imagine relatively few city corporations ordinances that would advance legitimate city interests without entailing unacceptable inefficiencies; therefore, the legislature—or a court, if a proper case arises—should declare corporations law beyond home rule authority. Similar thinking suggests the appropriateness of "wills" and "trusts" exceptions; that these subjects almost always entail private law magnifies, for reasons indicated above, the potential inefficiency of city lawmaking. On the other hand, "contract" law and "real property" law exceptions would lead to significant characterization problems, and as home rule exceptions they would be significantly over-inclusive. One does not know, for example, whether landlord-tenant law sounds in "contract" or in "real property" or in both; whichever, it does not seem that the local interests furthered by city landlord-tenant lawmaking are plainly inferior to the resulting inefficiencies. Therefore a tentative judgment is that neither a categorical "contracts" exception nor a categorical "real property" exception would be a good idea; however, in light of the convincingly strong public interest against uncertainties ("clouds") in real property title, an exception limited to the law of title is warranted. For similar reasons, a full "domestic relations" exception would be inappropriate, but at least a "marital status" exception is probably justifiable. * * * As for the fair housing, cooling-off-period, landlord-tenant, rental-car liability, and comparative negligence ordinances, it is hardly clear that their inefficiencies exceed the benefits of local lawmaking, and therefore a particular approach would not place them within the extreme inefficiency exception. * * *

MARSHAL HOUSE, INC. v. RENT REVIEW AND GRIEVANCE BOARD OF BROOKLINE

Supreme Judicial Court of Massachusetts, 1970.
357 Mass. 709, 260 N.E.2d 200.

CUTTER, JUSTICE.

The plaintiff (Marshal House) owns more than ten units of housing accommodations in Brookline. It seeks declaratory relief against the board and the town concerning art. XXV (the by-law) of the Brookline by-laws, entitled "Unfair and Unreasonable Rental Practices in Housing Accommodations." * * *

The principal contentions of the town and the board are (a) that the town has been given by art. 89, § 6, of the Amendments to the Constitution of the Commonwealth very broad legislative power, subject only to the Legislature's power to supersede local legislation by general laws; (b) that these powers under § 6 include the power to adopt a rent control by-law without further authorization (by the Legislature or otherwise) than is found in § 6; and (c) that nothing in art. 89, § 7, so limits the power granted to the town by § 6 as to preclude the adoption of the by-law or to impair its validity. The Attorney General makes substantially similar contentions. Marshal House, on the other hand, takes the position that the by-law is invalid because of art. 89, § 7, which states that nothing in art. 89 grants to "any * * * town the power * * * (5) to enact private or civil law governing civil relationships except as an incident to an exercise of an independent municipal power." * * *

We quote (emphasis supplied) pertinent portions of art. 89. Section 1 provides, in part, "It is the intention of this article to reaffirm the * * * traditional liberties of the people with respect to the *conduct of their local government,* and to grant and confirm to the people of every * * * town the right of self-government *in local matters,* subject to the provisions of this article and to such standards and requirements as the general court may establish by law in accordance with the provisions of this article." Section 6 contains a broad grant of powers to cities and towns, "Any * * * town may, by the adoption * * * of local * * * by-laws, exercise any power * * * which the general court has power to confer upon it, *which is not inconsistent with the constitution* or laws enacted by the general court in conformity with powers reserved to the general court by section eight, and which is not denied * * * to the * * * town by its charter * * *." The powers, which at first glance seem to be granted by § 6, are limited substantially by § 7, which reads: "Nothing in this article [89] shall be deemed to grant to any * * * town the power to (1) regulate elections * * *; (2) to levy * * * taxes; (3) to borrow money or pledge the credit of the * * * town; (4) to dispose of park land; (5) *to enact private or civil law governing civil relationships except as an incident to an exercise of an independent municipal power;* or (6) to define and provide for the punishment of a felony or to impose imprisonment as a punishment for any violation of law; provided, however, that the *foregoing enumerated powers may be granted by the general court* in conformity with the constitution and with the powers reserved to the general court by section eight * * *." Section 8 defines certain legislative powers reserved to and possessed by the General Court. No contention appears to be made that there is any basis of authority other than art. 89, § 6, for the town's action in enacting the by-law.

Ambiguity exists concerning the meaning of the italicized language in § 7(5). This ambiguity is not substantially clarified by examination of the historical background of art. 89. See Fordham, Home Rule—AMA Model, 44 Natl. Municipal Rev. 137, 142; Sandalow, The Limits of Municipal Power under Home Rule, 48 Minn.L.Rev. 643, 674–679. * * * Professor Fordham, in his discussion of the particular language, * * * says, "This is a phase of home rule which has not generally been adequately considered. Obviously, we do not wish to give our cities the power to enact a distinctive law of contracts, for example. On the other hand, the exercise of municipal powers is very likely to have important bearings upon private interests and relationships. The approach of the * * * [language now in § 7(5)] is to strike a balance by enabling home rule units to enact private law only as an incident to the exercise of some independent municipal power." This court thus is faced with interpreting novel and very general language concerning which there exist only inconclusive indications concerning the intentions of the draftsmen.

It is within the power of the Legislature, where there is reasonable basis in fact for such a determination, to conclude that an emergency exists in certain areas with respect to residential housing and to take action "in the exercise of its police power," including provisions for rent control, to relieve the emergency. "Having adopted a policy of rent control by * * * emergency legislation it may also delegate to * * * towns as governmental agencies the administration of its details in respect to matters peculiarly affecting local interests." See Russell v. Treasurer & Recr. Gen., 331 Mass. 501, 506–507, 120 N.E.2d 388. We recognized in Answer of the Justices, 250 N.E.2d 450, 452–453, that the language of "§ 6 * * * standing by itself, is broad enough to authorize a * * * [town] to enact a rent control * * * by-law. The limitation in § 7(5) simultaneously withholds part of the authority prima facie conferred by § 6 * * *."

The town argues that art. 89, § 7(5), should be strictly construed. So far as § 7 removes specified subjects from the scope of municipal legislative action, the several exclusions must be interpreted broadly enough to accomplish their purposes. Certainly there is no basis for any limited interpretation of the exclusions found in § 7(1), concerning elections; in § 7(2), prohibiting local tax legislation; in § 7(3), with respect to borrowings; and in § 7(4), in the matter of disposing of park lands. The term "private or civil law governing civil relationships" is broad enough to include law controlling ordinary and usual relationships between landlords and tenants. The language is not so confined as clearly to apply only to general legislation like the Uniform Commercial Code, or the laws governing marriage or intestate succession to property.

The town contends that the "by-law is a public law governing the economic relationship between landlords and tenants, not a private [or civil] law governing civil relationships." It also is argued that it is "in substance a temporary substitute for market forces * * * distorted by unusual conditions," rendering unreliable the usual process of determining "the amount of rent for an apartment * * * by bargaining between the landlord and [the] tenant." The by-law gives power to the board to require a landlord to "desist from * * * [an] unfair * * * rental practice" (defined as receiving any "rent * * * excessive under the circumstances"), to prevent the receipt of such rent; and to regulate the "services * * * [to] be furnished" for such rent. In these aspects, although we assume the purpose of thus affecting the landlord-tenant relationship to be public, the method adopted is primarily civil in that it affords to the board power in effect to remake, in important respects, the parties' contract creating a tenancy. The by-law also imposes criminal penalties in the form of fines. * * *

The question for decision is a relatively narrow one of applying art. 89, § 7(5), in a particular situation. Does the by-law so directly affect the landlord-tenant relationship, otherwise than "as an incident to an

exercise of an independent municipal power," as to come within § 7(5)?
* * *

It is suggested that rent control is, in its nature, a purely local function and that, therefore, a town by-law, even though it directly affects a principal aspect of the landlord-tenant relationship, is incident to an exercise of an independent municipal power. Doubtless, under art. 89, § 6, a town possesses (subject to applicable constitutional provisions and legislation) broad powers to adopt by-laws for the protection of the public health, morals, safety, and general welfare, of a type often referred to as the "police" power. We assume that these broad powers would permit adopting a by-law requiring landlords (so far as legislation does not control the matter) to take particular precautions to protect tenants against injury from fire, badly lighted common passageways, and similar hazards. Such by-laws, although affecting the circumstances of a tenancy, would do so (more clearly than in the case of the present by-law) as an incident to the exercising of a particular aspect of the police power.

Rent control, in a general sense, is for the purpose of providing shelter at reasonable cost for members of the public, a matter comprised within the broad concept of the public welfare. Rent control, however, is also an objective in itself designed to keep rents at reasonable levels. Is the attempt to achieve this objective to be viewed as merely incident to the exercise of the whole range of the police power, or does art. 89, § 7(5), imply that the separate components of the police power are to be considered individually in determining whether the exercise of one of them enacts "civil law governing civil relationships except as an incident to an exercise of an independent municipal power"? The quoted vague language points, in our opinion, to viewing separately the various component powers making up the broad police power, with the consequence that a municipal civil law regulating a civil relationship is permissible (without prior legislative authorization) only as an incident to the exercise of some independent, individual component of the municipal police power. To construe § 7(5) otherwise might give it a very narrow range of application.

We conclude that it would be, in effect, a contradiction (or circuitous) to say that a by-law, the principal objective and consequence of which is to control rent payments, is also merely incidental to the exercise of an independent municipal power to control rents. We perceive no component of the general municipal police power, other than the regulation of rents itself, to which such regulation fairly could be said to be incidental. * * *

We apply the ambiguous exclusion in art. 89, § 7(5), in accordance with what appears to us to be the most probable meaning of the words of the exclusion, interpreted with reasonable breadth, as the nature of each other exclusion indicates should be done. In particular, we hold that § 7(5) prevents the adoption of local rent control by-laws in the absence of an explicit delegation to municipalities by the Legislature of power to engage in such regulation of the landlord-tenant relationship.   * * *

SECTION D.   THE CITY AND DEMOCRATIC THEORY: PART ONE

Three different approaches toward decentralization of power to cities are excerpted below.   The first is from an influential article on economic theory by Charles Tiebout, the second is from an eloquent statement of conservative political philosophy by Robert Nozick, and the third is from an important cross-cultural study of urban social movements by Manuel Castells.   These excerpts present contrasting justifications for decentralization of power and contrasting views of the public/private distinction.   What assumptions do the three authors make about the source of city power?   Would it be possible to foster any of their notions of decentralization under Dillon's Rule or Home Rule?   Should it be possible to do so?   What does the first excerpt below, another chapter from Italo Calvino's Invisible Cities, suggest about the value of imagining cities that are different from the kind that now exist?

ITALO CALVINO, INVISIBLE CITIES
Pp. 32–33 (1974).

In the center of Fedora, that gray stone metropolis, stands a metal building with a crystal globe in every room.   Looking into each globe, you see a blue city, the model of a different Fedora.   These are the forms the city could have taken if, for one reason or another, it had not become what we see today.   In every age someone, looking at Fedora as it was, imagined a way of making it the ideal city, but while he constructed his miniature model, Fedora was already no longer the same as before, and what had been until yesterday a possible future became only a toy in a glass globe.

The building with the globes is now Fedora's museum: every inhabitant visits it, chooses the city that corresponds to his desires, contemplates it, imagining his reflection in the medusa pond that would have collected the waters of the canal (if it had not been dried up), the view from the high canopied box along the avenue reserved for elephants (now banished from the city), the fun of sliding down the spiral, twisting minaret (which never found a pedestal from which to rise).

On the map of your empire, O Great Khan, there must be room both for the big, stone Fedora and the little Fedoras in glass globes.   Not because they are all equally real, but because all are only assumptions. The one contains what is accepted as necessary when it is not yet so; the others, what is imagined as possible and, a moment later, is possible no longer.

CHARLES TIEBOUT, A PURE THEORY OF LOCAL EXPENDITURES

64 J.Pol.Econ. 416, 418–420 (1956).

Consider for a moment the case of the city resident about to move to the suburbs. What variables will influence his choice of a municipality? If he has children, a high level of expenditures on schools may be important. Another person may prefer a community with a municipal golf course. The availability and quality of such facilities and services as beaches, parks, police protection, roads, and parking facilities will enter into the decision-making process. Of course, non-economic variables will also be considered, but this is of no concern at this point.

The consumer-voter may be viewed as picking that community which best satisfies his preference pattern for public goods. This is a major difference between central and local provision of public goods. At the central level the preferences of the consumer-voter are given, and the government tries to adjust to the pattern of these preferences, whereas at the local level various governments have their revenue and expenditure patterns more or less set. Given these revenue and expenditure patterns, the consumer-voter moves to that community whose local government best satisfies his set of preferences. The greater the number of communities and the greater the variance among them, the closer the consumer will come to fully realizing his preference position.

The implications of the preceding argument may be shown by postulating an extreme model. Here the following assumptions are made:

1. Consumer-voters are fully mobile and will move to that community where their preference patterns, which are set, are best satisfied.

2. Consumer-voters are assumed to have full knowledge of differences among revenue and expenditure patterns and to react to these differences.

3. There are a large number of communities in which the consumer-voters may choose to live.

4. Restrictions due to employment opportunities are not considered. It may be assumed that all persons are living on dividend income.

5. The public services supplied exhibit no external economies or diseconomies between communities.

Assumptions 6 and 7 to follow are less familiar and require brief explanations:

6. For every pattern of community services set by, say, a city manager who follows the preferences of the older residents of the community, there is an optimal community size. This optimum is defined in terms of the number of residents for which this bundle of services can be produced at the lowest average cost. This, of course, is closely analogous to the low point of a firm's average cost curve. Such a

cost function implies that some factor or resource is fixed. If this were not so, there would be no logical reason to limit community size, given the preference patterns. In the same sense that the average cost curve has a minimum for one firm but can be reproduced by another there is seemingly no reason why a duplicate community cannot exist. The assumption that some factor is fixed explains why it is not possible for the community in question to double its size by growth. The factor may be the limited land area of a suburban community, combined with a set of zoning laws against apartment buildings. It may be the local beach, whose capacity is limited. Anything of this nature will provide a restraint.

In order to see how this restraint works, let us consider the beach problem. Suppose the preference patterns of the community are such that the optimum size population is 13,000. Within this set of preferences there is a certain demand per family for beach space. This demand is such that at 13,000 population a 500–yard beach is required. If the actual length of the beach is, say, 600 yards, then it is not possible to realize this preference pattern with twice the optimum population, since there would be too little beach space by 400 yards.

The assumption of a fixed factor is necessary * * * in order to get a determinate number of communities. It also has the advantage of introducing a realistic restraint into the model.

7. The last assumption is that communities below the optimum size seek to attract new residents to lower average costs. Those above optimum size do just the opposite. Those at an optimum try to keep their populations constant.

This assumption needs to be amplified. Clearly, communities below the optimum size, through chambers of commerce or other agencies, seek to attract new residents. This is best exemplified by the housing developments in some suburban areas, such as Park Forest in the Chicago area and Levittown in the New York area, which need to reach an optimum size. The same is true of communities that try to attract manufacturing industries by setting up certain facilities and getting an optimum number of firms to move into the industrially zoned area.

The case of the city that is too large and tries to get rid of residents is more difficult to imagine. No alderman in his right political mind would ever admit that the city is too big. Nevertheless, economic forces are at work to push people out of it. Every resident who moves to the suburbs to find better schools, more parks, and so forth, is reacting, in part, against the pattern the city has to offer.

The case of the community which is at the optimum size and tries to remain so is not hard to visualize. Again proper zoning laws, implicit agreements among realtors, and the like are sufficient to keep the population stable.

Except when this system is in equilibrium, there will be a subset of consumer-voters who are discontented with the patterns of their community. Another set will be satisfied. Given the assumption about mobility and the other assumptions listed previously, movement will take place out of the communities of greater than optimal size into the communities of less than optimal size. The consumer-voter moves to the community that satisfies his preference pattern.

The act of moving or failing to move is crucial. Moving or failing to move replaces the usual market test of willingness to buy a good and reveals the consumer-voter's demand for public goods. Thus each locality has a revenue and expenditure pattern that reflects the desires of its residents. The next step is to see what this implies for the allocation of public goods at the local level.

Each city manager now has a certain demand for n local public goods. In supplying these goods, he and $m-1$ other city managers may be considered as going to a national market and bidding for the appropriate units of service of each kind: so many units of police for the ith community; twice that number for the jth community; and so on. The demand on the public goods market for each of the n commodities will be the sum of the demands of the m communities. In the limit, as shown in a less realistic model to be developed later, this total demand will approximate the demand that represents the true preferences of the consumer-voters—that is, the demand they would reveal, if they were forced, somehow, to state their true preferences. In this model there is no attempt on the part of local governments to "adapt to" the preferences of consumer-voters. Instead, those local governments that attract the optimum number of residents may be viewed as being "adopted by" the economic system. * * *

ROBERT NOZICK, ANARCHY, STATE AND UTOPIA

Pp. 297, 309–312, 316–317, 320–323, 329–331 (1974).

A FRAMEWORK FOR UTOPIA

* * * It would be disconcerting if there were only one argument or connected set of reasons for the adequacy of a particular description of utopia. Utopia is the focus of so many different strands of aspiration that there must be many theoretical paths leading to it. Let us sketch some of these alternate, mutually supporting, theoretical routes.

The first route begins with the fact that people are different. They differ in temperament, interests, intellectual ability, aspirations, natural bent, spiritual quests, and the kind of life they wish to lead. They diverge in the values they have and have different weightings for the values they share. (They wish to live in different climates—some in mountains, plains, deserts, seashores, cities, towns.) There is no reason to think that there is *one* community which will serve as ideal for all people and much reason to think that there is not. * * *

Wittgenstein, Elizabeth Taylor, Bertrand Russell, Thomas Merton, Yogi Berra, Allen Ginsburg, Harry Wolfson, Thoreau, Casey Stengel, The Lubavitcher Rebbe, Picasso, Moses, Einstein, Hugh Heffner, Socrates,

Henry Ford, Lenny Bruce, Baba Ram Dass, Gandhi, Sir Edmund Hillary, Raymond Lubitz, Buddha, Frank Sinatra, Columbus, Freud, Norman Mailer, Ayn Rand, Baron Rothschild, Ted Williams, Thomas Edison, H.L. Mencken, Thomas Jefferson, Ralph Ellison, Bobby Fischer, Emma Goldman, Peter Kropotkin, you, and your parents. Is there really *one* kind of life which is best for each of these people? Imagine all of them living in any utopia you've ever seen described in detail. * * *

No utopian author has everyone in his society leading exactly the same life, allocating exactly the same amount of time to exactly the same activities. *Why not?* Don't the reasons also count against just one kind of community?

The conclusion to draw is that there will not be *one* kind of community existing and one kind of life led in utopia. Utopia will consist of utopias, of many different and divergent communities in which people lead different kinds of lives under different institutions. Some kinds of communities will be more attractive to most than others; communities will wax and wane. People will leave some for others or spend their whole lives in one. Utopia is a framework for utopias, a place where people are at liberty to join together voluntarily to pursue and attempt to realize their own vision of the good life in the ideal community but where no one can *impose* his own utopian vision upon others. The utopian society is the society of utopianism. (Some of course may be content where they are. Not *everyone* will be joining special experimental communities, and many who abstain at first will join the communities later, after it is clear how they actually are working out.) * * *

If the ideas must actually be tried out, there must be many communities trying out different patterns. The filtering process, the process of eliminating communities, that our framework involves is very simple: people try out living in various communities, and they leave or slightly modify the ones they don't like (find defective). Some communities will be abandoned, others will struggle along, others will split, others will flourish, gain members, and be duplicated elsewhere. Each community must win and hold the voluntary adherence of its members. No pattern is *imposed* on everyone, and the result will be one pattern if and only if everyone voluntarily chooses to live in accordance with that pattern of community.

The design device comes in at the stage of generating specific communities to be lived in and tried out. Any group of people may devise a pattern and attempt to persuade others to participate in the adventure of a community in that pattern. Visionaries and crackpots, maniacs and saints, monks and libertines, capitalists and communists and participatory democrats, proponents of phalanxes (Fourier), palaces of labor (Flora Tristan), villages of unity and cooperation (Owen), mutualist communities (Proudhon), time stores (Josiah Warren), Bruderhof, kibbutzim, kundalini yoga ashrams, and so forth, may all have their try at building their vision and setting an alluring example. It should not be thought that every pattern tried will be explicitly designed *de novo*. Some will be planned modifications, however slight, of others already existing (when it is seen where they rub), and the details of many will be built up spontaneously in communities that leave some leeway. As communities become more attractive for their inhabitants, patterns previously adopted as the best available will be rejected. And as the communities which people live in improve (according to their lights), ideas for new communities often will improve as well. * * *

The operation of the framework has many of the virtues, and few of the defects, people find in the libertarian vision. For though there is great liberty to choose among communities, many particular communities internally may have many restrictions unjustifiable on libertarian grounds: that is, restrictions which libertarians would condemn if they were enforced by a central state apparatus. For example, paternalistic intervention into people's lives, restrictions on the range of books which may circulate in the community, limitations on the kinds of sexual behavior, and so on. But this is merely another way of pointing out that in a free society people may contract into various restrictions which the government may not legitimately impose upon them. Though the framework is libertarian and laissez-faire, *individual communities within it need not be,* and perhaps no community within it will choose to be so. Thus, the characteristics of the framework need not pervade the individual communities. In *this* laissez-faire system it could turn out that though they are permitted, there are no actually functioning "capitalist" institutions; or that some communities have them and others don't or some communities have some of them, or what you will.*

In previous chapters, we have spoken of a person's opting out of particular provisions of certain arrangements. Why now do we say that various restrictions may be imposed in a particular community? Mustn't the community allow its members to opt out of these restrictions? No; founders and members of a small communist community may, quite properly, refuse to allow anyone to opt out of equal sharing, even though it would be possible to arrange this. It is not a general principle that every community or group must allow internal opting out when that is feasible. For sometimes such internal opting out would itself change the character of the group from that desired. Herein lies an interesting theoretical problem. A nation or protective agency may not compel redistribution between one community and another, yet a community such as a kibbutz may redistribute within itself (or give to another community or to outside individuals). Such a community needn't offer its members an opportunity to opt out of these arrangements while remaining a member of the community. Yet, I have argued, a nation should offer this opportunity; people have a right to so opt out of a nation's requirements. Wherein lies the difference between a

---

* It is strange that many young people "in tune with" nature and hoping to "go with the flow" and not force things against their natural bent should be attracted to statist views and socialism, and are antagonistic to equilibrium and invisible-hand processes.

community and a nation that makes the difference in the legitimacy of imposing a certain pattern upon all of its members?

A person will swallow the imperfections of a package *P* (which may be a protective arrangement, a consumer good, a community) that is desirable on the whole rather than purchase a different package (a completely different package, or *P* with some changes), when no more desirable attainable different package is worth to him its greater costs over *P,* including the costs of inducing enough others to participate in making the alternative package. One assumes that the cost calculation for nations is such as to permit internal opting out. But this is not the whole story for two reasons. First, it may be feasible in individual communities also to arrange internal opting out at little administrative cost (which he may be willing to pay), yet this needn't always be done. Second, nations differ from other packages in that the individual himself isn't to bear the administrative costs of opting out of some otherwise compulsory provision. The other people must pay for finely designing their compulsory arrangements so that they don't apply to those who wish to opt out. Nor is the difference merely a matter of there being many alternative kinds of communities while there are many fewer nations. Even if almost everyone wished to live in a communist community, so that there weren't any viable noncommunist communities, no particular community need also (though it is to be hoped that one would) allow a resident individual to opt out of their sharing arrangement. The recalcitrant individual has no alternative but to conform. Still, the others do not force him to conform, and his rights are not violated. He has no right that the others cooperate in making his nonconformity feasible.

The difference seems to me to reside in the difference between a face-to-face community and a nation. In a nation, one knows that there are nonconforming individuals, but one need not be directly confronted by these individuals or by the fact of their nonconformity. Even if one finds it offensive that others do not conform, even if the knowledge that there exist nonconformists rankles and makes one very unhappy, this does not constitute being harmed by the others or having one's rights violated. Whereas in a face-to-face community one cannot avoid being directly confronted with what one finds to be offensive. How one lives in one's immediate environment is affected.

This distinction between a face-to-face community and one that is not generally runs parallel to another distinction. A face-to-face community can exist on land jointly owned by its members, whereas the land of a nation is not so held. The community will be entitled then, as a body, to determine what regulations are to be obeyed on its land; whereas the citizens of a nation do not jointly own its land and so cannot in this way regulate its use. If *all* the separate individuals who own land coordinate their actions in imposing a common regulation (for example, no one may reside on this land who does not contribute *n* percent of his income to the poor), the same *effect* will be achieved as if the nation had passed legislation requiring this. But since unanimity is only as strong as its weakest link, even with the use of secondary boycotts (which are perfectly legitimate), it would be impossible to maintain such a unanimous coalition in the face of the blandishments to some to defect.

But some face-to-face communities will not be situated on jointly held land. May the majority of the voters in a small village pass an ordinance against things that they find offensive being done on the *public* streets? May they legislate against nudity or fornication or sadism (on consenting masochists) or hand-holding by racially mixed couples on the streets? Any private owner can regulate his premises as he chooses. But what of the public thoroughfares, where people cannot easily avoid sights they find offensive? Must the vast majority cloister themselves against the offensive minority? If the majority may determine the limits on detectable behavior in public, may they, in addition to requiring that no one appear in public without wearing clothing, also require that no one appear in public without wearing a badge certifying that he has contributed n percent of his income to the needy during the year, on the grounds that they find it offensive to look at someone not wearing this badge (not having contributed)? And whence this emergent right of the majority to decide? Or are there to be no "public" place or ways? * * * Since I do not see my way clearly through these issues, I raise them here only to leave them. * * *

Nor do I assume that all problems about the framework are solved. Let us mention a few here. There will be problems about the role, if any, to be played by some central authority (or protective association); how will this authority be selected, and how will it be ensured that the authority does, and does only, what it is supposed to do? The major role, as I see it, would be to enforce the operation of the framework—for example, to prevent some communities from invading and seizing others, their persons or assets. Furthermore, it will adjudicate in some reasonable fashion conflicts between communities which cannot be settled by peaceful means. What the best form of such a central authority is I would not wish to investigate here. It seems desirable that one not be fixed permanently but that room be left for improvements of detail. I ignore here the difficult and important problems of the controls on a central authority powerful enough to perform its appropriate functions, because I have nothing special to add to the standard literature on federations, confederations, decentralization of power, checks and balances, and so on.

One persistent strand in utopian thinking, as we have mentioned, is the feeling that there is some set of principles obvious enough to be accepted by all men of good will, precise enough to give unambiguous guidance in particular situations, clear enough so that all will realize its dictates, and complete enough to cover all problems which actually will arise. Since I do not assume that there are such principles, I do not assume that the political realm will wither away. The messiness of the details of a political apparatus and the details of how *it* is to be controlled and limited do not fit easily into one's hopes for a sleek, simple utopian scheme.

Apart from the conflict between communities, there will be other tasks for a central apparatus or agency, for example, enforcing an individual's right to leave a community. But problems arise if an individual can plausibly be viewed as *owing* something to the other members of a community he wishes to leave: for example, he has been educated at their expense on the explicit agreement that he would use his acquired skills and knowledge in the home community. Or, he has acquired certain family obligations that he will abandon by shifting communities. Or, without such ties, he wishes to leave. What may he take out with him? Or, he wishes to leave after he's committed some punishable offense for which the community wishes to punish him. Clearly the principles will be complicated ones. Children present yet more difficult problems. In some way it must be ensured that they are *informed* of the range of alternatives in the world. But the home community might view it as important that their youngsters not be exposed to the knowledge that one hundred miles away is a community of great sexual freedom. And so on. I mention these problems to indicate a fraction of the thinking that needs to be done on the details of a framework and to make clear that I do not think its nature can be settled finally now either.

Even though the details of the framework aren't settled, won't there be some rigid limits about it, some things inalterably fixed? Will it be possible to shift to a nonvoluntary framework permitting the forced exclusion of various styles of life? If a framework could be devised that could not be transformed into a nonvoluntary one, would we wish to institute it? If we institute such a permanently voluntary general framework, are we not, to some extent, ruling out certain possible choices? Are we not saying in advance that people cannot choose to live in a certain way; are we setting a rigid range in which people can move and thus committing the usual fault of the static utopians? The comparable question about an individual is whether a free system will allow him to sell himself into slavery. I believe that it would. (Other writers disagree.) It also would allow him permanently to commit himself never to enter into such a transaction. But some things individuals may choose for themselves, no one may choose for another. So long as it is realized at what a *general* level the rigidity lies, and what diversity of particular lives and communities it allows, the answer is, "Yes, the framework should be fixed as voluntary." But remember that any individual may contract into any particular constraints over himself and so may use the voluntary framework to contract himself out of it. (If all individuals do so, the voluntary framework will not operate until the next generation, when others come of age.) * * *

MANUEL CASTELLS, THE CITY AND THE GRASS ROOTS
Pp. 318–331 (1983).

THE ALTERNATIVE CITY: THE STRUCTURE AND MEANING
OF CONTEMPORARY URBAN SOCIAL MOVEMENTS

Cities and space are the unfinished products of historical debates and conflicts involving meaning, function, and form. We have observed throughout the different situations presented in this book how grassroots mobilization has been a crucial factor in the shaping of the city, as well as the decisive element in urban innovation against prevailing social interests. While the situations which we researched were carefully selected to maximize the impact of urban change fostered by social mobilization, it is our theoretical perspective to consider all cities as being shaped by the outcome of social conflicts and contradictory projects. The structurally dominant interests prevail more often than not, and so shape the city. Yet, as the continuation of capitalist management does not diminish the crucial role of labour in affecting production and distribution, the trace of urban protest and alternative projects can also be recognized in the spatial forms and the meaning of cities. Any theory of the city must be, at its starting point, a theory of social conflict. Our cross-cultural evidence supports this fundamental hypothesis.

Yet urban situations can be so diverse, and the specificity of the processes we have observed has deliberately been so exceptional, that the theoretical usefulness of our findings must be considered in a broader context. Our main proposition is that there is an intimate connection between the themes, goals, and experiences of urban social movements and the overall process of historical conflict and change in our societies. Not that urban movements are the new historical actors creating social change, nor the pivotal source of alternative social forms. Rather, our statement is that urban movements are not random expressions of discontent, varying from city to city, but that they bear, in their structure and goals, the stigmas and projects of all the great historical conflicts of our time. If such a statement is true, historical change and urban change are intertwined, as assumed in our general theory. If this hypothesis is a social fact, we must find the trace of these debates and conflicts in the urban movements we have studied. Furthermore, the themes of these debates must be the crucial factors in explaining the behaviour and effects of urban movements as recorded in our research.

So let us turn to our case studies to determine what were the main elements present in these urban movements. To avoid repetition, we will analyse only the essential trends detected in each city and refer the reader to the relevant part for the details and verification of the social trends now presented.

We have found that, in accordance to the general hypothesis posed in the Introduction, urban movements making their interests and values materialize, are structured around three basic goals. By goals we mean purposive desires and demands present in the collective practice of the movement. They must be consciously expressed, but a declaration of intent or a list of demands is not sufficient to denote a goal, which must be collectively acted on, not just declared. Each goal opposes another project in the city, relying on a contradictory set of social interests and values.   Therefore each goal defines an adversary whose power and characteristics will profoundly influence the movement.   Not all the movements we observed had the three basic goals; nor did they pursue them with the same intensity.   In fact the articulation (or lack of articulation) of the three goals in any given movement is one of the major elements that explains our theory about the relationship between movements and cities.

The three goals, are as follows:

1.   To obtain for the residents a city organized around its use value, as against the notion of urban living and services as a commodity, the logic of exchange value.   The content of this use value changed considerably from place to place, city to city, or between classes within a given city.   It could be decent housing provided as a public service, the preservation of a historic building, or the demand for open space.   But wherever mobilization occurred, it was for improved collective consumption, in contradiction to the notion of the city for profit in which the desirability of space and urban services are distributed according to levels of income.   We name this type of mobilization *collective consumption trade unionism*.   (Please note that this is a theoretical type, and therefore a movement can be focused on collective consumption while pursuing other goals; it would then be a combination of two types of movements, and research would have to determine the consequences of such a combination).

2.   The second major goal we found present in the urban movements was the search for cultural identity, for the maintenance or creation of autonomous local cultures, ethnically-based or historically originated.   In other words, the defense of communication between people, autonomously defined social meaning, and face-to-face interaction, against the monopoly of messages by the media, the predominance of one-way information flows, and the standardization of culture on the basis of increasingly heteronomous sources for the neighbourhood residents.   We named the movement orientated towards this goal, *community*.

3.   The third goal we discovered was the search for increasing power for local government, neighbourhood decentralization, and urban self-management in contradiction to the centralized state and a subordinated and undifferentiated territorial administration.   We call the struggle for a free city, a *citizen movement*.

Our emphasis on goals stems from our general theoretical perspective that cities and societies are produced by the conflictive process of collective actors mobilized towards certain goals, that is, ways of structuring society and space.   Therefore a movement is first of all defined by its goals (as expressed in its conscious practice) or set of goals.   Each time a social actor defines or searches for a goal he finds an adverse one, as well as allies and enemies (that is allies of the adverse goal).   Then both movement and adversary are moving towards a historically defined confrontation over the object of their goals, which in our case is the city. Thus the structure of an urban movement, while generated by the definition of a goal, appears to become complex as soon as it begins the same social process by which a movement defines its goal.   * * *

But who are these urban actors? Are we not re-entering a structuralist paradigm, deprived of social actors and worked out by contradictions? Certainly not. The actors of the urban movements are the urban movements themselves, since we have defined movements by the goals they set up for themselves. The movements become social actors by being engaged in a mobilization towards an urban goal which is itself linked to the general struggle over the continuous restructuring of society. And the movements are different, according to the goals of each type of movement. Yet the question remains: who are they in terms of their social characteristics? At the empirical level, we have carefully answered the question in each observed situation. At the theoretical level, however, a major point needs to be made, based on our empirical observation: the movements are urban actors, defined by their goals and their urban condition. They are not, then, another form of class struggle, gender struggle, or ethnic struggle. The components of the urban movements come from a variety of social, gender, and ethnic situations, according to their urban and national contexts. And yet their urban themes are recurrent and the factors underlying their dynamics, successes, and failures are quite similar, as we were able to observe in our case studies. To be more specific, they are neither working class movements nor a middle class movement, as has been advanced, particularly by French researchers. First, this idea is empirically false, as witnessed by the American and British inner cities, the Spanish neighbourhood movements, and the Italian self-discount movement. Even in Paris our research on the Grands Ensembles showed the social diversity of the movement's participants, including, but not predominantly, the middle class. Second, and more significantly, when Dagnaud and Mehl among others, point out the role of the new middle class in the urban movements, they do not deny the participation of manual workers, or even unionized workers, in those movements, but emphasize the non-class basis of the urban movements, which is a fundamental and most useful observation. The fact that they can be associated with the petty-bourgeoisie, a non-class by definition in the classical sense of class, means that they are defined on another social dimension, cutting across the class structure. They are not middle class but multi-class movements for the very simple reason that they do not relate directly to the relationships of production, but to the relationships of consumption, communication, and power.

So the observed experience of urban movements points towards an alternative urban meaning, posing the alternative to the city emerging from the interests and values of the dominant class. The alternative city is therefore a network of cultural communities defined by time and space, and politically self-managed towards the maximization of use value for their residents; this use value is always decided and reexamined by the residents themselves. This new urban meaning is neither the ideal image nor the dream of a midsummer night: it is the set of goals that emerges from the practice of the urban movements we have observed, and its significance and existence is not contradicted by the amount of secondary data known about other urban movements in other cities and other societies. (We exclude the socialist countries because, as already stated, we do not have enough reliable information on them concerning our subject.) This urban profile is as real as the skyscrapers on the drawing boards of the corporate board rooms. The movements are projects of cities, social life, and urban functions and forms (predetermined by urban meaning) emerging from the capacity of the new urban dwellers to produce and control their own environment, space, and urban services. Another question, and a fundamental one, is the feasibility of such a city—the likelihood of its ever taking shape. In fact this outcome will depend on the conflict over the city and the conflict's links with social change and political struggle. This is the aim of our theoretical analysis: to unveil the mechanisms at work in the conflictive process that is shaping today's dramas, and tomorrow's heavens and hells.

The most important point, from this perspective, is to determine the conditions under which urban movements seem to achieve their maximum impact on the change of urban meaning. Or, in other words, under what conditions do they become urban social movements?

On the basis of a selected sample of major urban movements in four cultural areas in the last two decades, our research shows that the highest transformation of urban meaning occurred in Madrid, and we were able to establish the structural formula underlying the capacity of Madrid's Citizen Movement to become an urban social movement. To be sure, Madrid continues to be an extremely difficult city to live in, and therefore to say that urban movements accomplished a great deal might seem a subjective appreciation. Nevertheless, we provided enough empirical evidence in Part 5 to support a conclusion on the extent of the change in the urban meaning prevailing in Madrid, in spite of the setbacks experienced after 1980 (after our research had been concluded) because of the crisis in the Citizen Movement. So, for reasons that will become more evident, we propose the structural formula we discovered in our research in Madrid as the general structural formula able to foster the fulfillment of an urban social movement across different cultures of the capitalist-informational mode of production and in our epoch. * * * [L]et us remind ourselves of the four basic elements:

1. To accomplish the transformation of urban meaning in the full extent of its political and cultural implications, an urban movement must articulate in its praxis the three goals of collective consumption demands, community culture, and political self-management.

2. It must be conscious of its role as an urban social movement.

3.   It must be connected to society through a series of organizational operators, three in particular: the media, the professionals, and the political parties.

4.   A *sine qua non* condition: while urban social movements must be connected to the political system to at least partially achieve its goals, they must be organizationally and ideologically autonomous of any political party.   The reason is that social transformation and political struggle, negotiation, and management, although intimately connected and interdependent, do not operate at the same level of the social structure.   As Daniel Cohn–Bendit, the leader of the students' revolt in Nanterre in 1968, once said to his liberal professors, "For you to be successful reformists, we have to be failing revolutionaries."

On the basis of our observation of other experiences, we add a fifth rule for the development of an urban social movement: the first condition must command all the others.   If the three basic goals are not interconnected in the praxis of the movement, no other element will be able to accomplish a significant change in urban meaning.   * * *

Let us assume * * * that the structural formula underlying the formation and achievement of urban social movements is correct.   Why should it be so?   And where does it come from?   These two fundamental questions require careful answers.

First, what is the process of formation of urban social movements?   How, within the limits of our time and cultures, have urban movements come to integrate the goals and the means which have been discovered as necessary to produce a change in urban meaning?   It is here that the contribution of Ira Katznelson, John Rex and John Foster are invaluable.   They have all insisted on the necessity of considering the historical contexts in the formation of social classes in general, and social movements in particular. And that is in fact our answer: the production of the structural formula leading to urban social movements is specific to each national-cultural context, and any attempt to find a general formulation is to resort to metaphysics.   Let us point out, at the same time, that we maintain there is a general structural formula in our historical epoch of urban social movements as processes aimed at a given outcome the transformation of urban meaning.   This is because we live in a world-wide mode of production (capitalism) developing through two world-wide articulated modes of development (industrial and informational).   Therefore the raw materials of social change (and thus of urban change) are ubiquitous, while the social processes bringing together these raw materials are historically, and so nationally and culturally, specific.

How did the Citizen Movement in Madrid bring together the three basic goals aimed at multidimensional change?   The answer is paradoxical: Spain was a society oppressed in a totalitarian way that integrated the different social subsystems.   The state, blessed by the Church, was at the root of everything, destroying any remnant of political freedom or cultural autonomy. Multinational capital and local speculators took advantage of the freedom given to them to impose industrialization and urbanization at a cost that in Europe can only be rivalled by the early nineteenth century. The cultural backwardness of an illiterate army ensured that no popular cultural expression could flourish. Furthermore, the structure of Spanish society was not a historical accident linked to the Franquist dictatorship; it goes back to the Christian crusade, fighting for eight centuries to exterminate the superior Arab civilization; it goes back to the massive expulsion of over half-a-million Spanish Jews in the sixteenth century, throwing out forever the most enlightened Spaniards; it goes back to the Inquisition and the absolutist state; it goes back to the Catholic Church, the backbone of Spanish society, where bishops and priests ordered the kings to conquer more territories in order to determine whether their inhabitants' souls could be sent to paradise if they converted or to hell if they resisted. This context called for total, sudden, and violent revolution. The Spanish people tried several times in history until they learned that the institutions were so strong, so deeply embedded in the people themselves, any attempt to confront the system at its roots would cause civil war. This meant bloodshed and, in the European context, defeat. So they gave up the idea of total political revolution. But any movement knew, from the collective memory, that everything was linked. To have light in the city streets to which they were forced to migrate, they had both to fight the police and gather their neighbours to a street-dancing party where life could go on in spite of the harshness. This has been the Spanish way. And this was at the root of the Spanish urban movement.

In San Francisco things were very different. American society, and California in particular, is based upon ethnic fragmentation of the popular classes, a pluralist political system based on coalitions of interest groups, and a decentralized insulated state that works through integration and co-optation except when it feels threatened, in which case it uses the most extreme violence. The Mission Coalition collapsed because Latinos wanted to be ethnically defined in order to avoid sharing the benefits of social programmes with other communities, while the community activists, trying to unify all the poor people, became totally absorbed by the management of social programmes that would create their own power. Gays won their right to survival and their capacity to be themselves by concentrating spatially and mobilizing electorally. Yet, since they needed a space, they took it from the poor ethnic communities, triggering prejudice and hostility. They won their right to existence but at the expense of their capacity to transform the city and society in unison with the other oppressed minorities. Thus coalition politics led to a series of victories by different oppressed groups, but ended in a collective stalemate.   * * *

Thus each national-cultural context explains not only how but why different goals converged or became disjointed, as well as how the organizational operators of the movements connected, disconnected, or took over, the relationships between urban demands, state, and society.

Now the final and most important question. Are these goals constitutive of urban social movements and why do they generate a change of
urban meaning? And why these goals as opposed to others? Could
there be more or fewer goals? And why must they be clustered together
in the praxis of the movement to produce a significant effect?

Here we must recall the general analysis of social change in our
historical context. The three goals that are crucial factors in the
fulfillment of urban social movements are precisely the three alternative
projects to the modes of production and modes of development that
dominate our world. The city as a use value contradicts the capitalist
form of the city as exchange value. The city as a communication
network opposes the one-way information flow characteristic of the
informational mode of development. And the city as a political entity of
free self-management opposes the reliance on the centralized state as an
instrument of authoritarianism and a threat of totalitarianism.

Thus the fundamental themes and debates of our history are actually the raw material of the urban movements. Does this mean that
urban social movements are the core of the new processes of historical
change? Not at all; it is precisely because the alternative projects of
change in the dimensions of production, culture, and power have come to
a stalemate that urban social movements have been able to appear and
play a major social role. Let us develop this idea that is the keystone of
our analysis.

Cities in our societies are the expression of the different dimensions
of life, of the variety of social processes that form the intricate web of
our experience. Therefore people tend to consider cities, space, and
urban functions and forms as the mainspring for their feelings. This is
the basis for the urban ideology that assigns the causality of social
effects to the structure of spatial forms. Yet when people experience an
undefined force they react on one of several levels against the material
form that transfers to them the force they feel. Thus the less people
identify the source of their economic exploitation, cultural alienation,
and political oppression while still feeling their effects, the more they
will react against the material forms that introduce these experiences
into their lives. Furthermore, the spatial form is not simply a transmit-
ter of all these evils. It is an organizer of them and becomes an evil in
its own right. So popular reaction is two-fold, both against the unrecognized structural source of their exploitation-alienation-oppression, and
against the particular spatial form that expresses their condition as a
daily reminder: the wild city.

The source of urban movements in our societies is the absence of
effective channels for social change for each one of the basic dimensions
involved in the conflictive appropriation of production and history. The
labour movement has been, by and large, unable to address the issue of
the social wage and the negotiation of living conditions outside the work
place. So urban trade unionism has had to take its place outside
factories and offices. The overflow of one-way information has been met

only by marginal, alternative cultures, leaving to people to try and spontaneously defend their autonomous networks on the most primitive basis: territoriality. The centralization of the state and the obsession of political parties with the instrumental dimension of power has led to a growing distance between civil society and the state. The revival of local autonomy, the call for political self-management, decentralization, and participation is the last chance before the dramatic split between bureaucratic apparatuses and irreducible identities.

Because all these potential sources of conflict in our society do not have autonomous means of expression, organization, and mobilization they have come together in a negative and reactive way in the shape of urban movements. When they are primitive one-dimensional reactions, they take the form of urban protest. When they have developed an alternative global vision, they form a counter-culture, and feel more comfortable if they define their alternative in a territory: they propose an alternative social organization, an alternative space, an alternative city. They become an urban social movement. But such a movement cannot be "proactive", only "reactive", except in its Utopian dimension. It cannot, however, be a social alternative, only the symptom of a social limit, because the city it projects is not, and cannot be, connected to an alternative mode of production and development, nor to a democratic state adapted to the world-wide processes of power. Thus urban social movements are aimed at transforming the meaning of the city without being able to transform society. They are a reaction, not an alternative: they are calling for a depth of existence without being able to create that new breadth. They project the profile of the world they want, without knowing why, or how, or if. When institutions remain insulated or unresponsive, banks maintain their high interest rates, police take over the streets again, and meaningful space continues to disintegrate, and urban social movements no longer call for an alternative city. Instead their fragmented elements undertake the destruction of the city they reject. We observed and analysed their hope for society as projected by their desired space and cherished city. If such appeals are not heard, if the political avenues remain closed, if the new central social movements (feminism, new labour, self-management, alternative communication) do not develop fully, then the urban movements—reactive Utopias that tried to illuminate the path they could not walk—will return, but this time as urban shadows eager to destroy the closed walls of their captive city.

THE SOCIAL SIGNIFICANCE OF CONTEMPORARY URBAN MOVEMENTS

We have unveiled the structure and dynamics of the urban movements observed in a variety of cultural, economic, and institutional contexts. We have related these observations to a broader theoretical framework, whilst dealing simultaneously with the relationship between space and society, and with the formation and effects of social movements. A tentative theoretical framework has emerged, enabling us to understand the complex dialectics between the city and the grassroots.

We have therefore enough elements to address some more specific social and political concerns about the actual role that urban movements play in society. Are they marginal forms of protest, doomed to disappear as soon as parties, unions, and other institutionalized forms of social mobilization take care of the concerns voiced by urban movements? After all, several of the movements we studied disappeared or were seriously weakened after their defeat or victory. Furthermore, a number of very important movements, the Italian urban struggles of the early 1970s for example, have receded spectacularly in recent years. Nevertheless, on purely empirical grounds we could speak of the uneven development of urban movements, but of expansion to a broader geographical and cultural area. At the time the Italian movement was agonizing in the late 1970s, the Spanish neighbourhood associations strengthened and had greater impact. When, in 1980–81, the Citizen Movement in Madrid went through a devastating crisis, the squatter movements in Holland and Germany proposed many of the goals that had been forwarded by neighbourhood groups elsewhere. When the *pobladores* of Chile crumbled under the terror of Pinochet, new urban movements started to develop in Brazil, Venezuela, and Mexico, with a broader social basis and a higher consciousness of their autonomous role as agents of social change. And after the end of collective violent protest of the American inner cities in the 1960s, a steady flow of community organizations and neighbourhood groups demanding public services quietly irrigated the country's urban geography through the 1970s, from Cincinnati to Los Angeles, and from Crystal City, Texas, to New York. In spite of the absence of reliable, systematic information on the development of urban movements in different countries throughout history, our own knowledge as well as the amount of existing information suggest a clear, comparative upward trend.

Although the size and ubiquity of this development are important to the evaluation of its historical significance, the decisive point is the role that urban movements have played in the overall dynamics of a society. Are they another form of interest group? Have they become a new form of alternative society, that is a major contemporary social movement? Or do they tend to be, as we proposed in the last chapter, reactive Utopias? And why so?

First of all, let us make clear that we believe we are considering, in general, a somewhat homogenous phenomenon. To be sure, under the general term of urban movements (or urban struggles as we used to call them) we are considering very different forms of mobilization, from counter-cultural squatters to middle class neighbourhood associations and shanty town defense groups. Nevertheless they all seem to share some basic characteristics in spite of their diversity:

1. They consider themselves as urban, or citizen, or, in any case, related to the city (or to the community) in their self-denomination.

2. They are locally-based and territorially-defined, a feature that will be decisive in helping us to determine their significance.

3. They tend to mobilize around three major goals that we identified in our general overview and found to be crucial in our case studies: collective consumption, cultural identity, and political self-management. Furthermore, our tried and tested hypothesis is that only when the three themes combine in a movement's practice does it bring about social change, while the separation of any of the goals and a narrow self-definition turn it into an interest group that will be moulded into the established institutions of society, so losing most of its identity and impact. We also pointed out that these three goals were not arrived at by accident, but are the major points of opposition against the dominant logics of capitalism, informationalism, and statism.

Thus, we are convinced of some fundamental degree of homogeneity in urban movements in whatever societies they may occur. The diversity of their effects and development stems from the fact that their origin, social causation, and development are differential, according to the specificity of each historical context, and their singular pattern of behaviour. To some extent, this can all be said of the labour movement, a movement that is evident in all societies, but in different forms, behaving in divergent ways, and having diverse social effects.

Yet, while recognizing the generality of urban movements and their development, we have rejected the thesis that they might constitute a new central social movement able to transform our history. We have, furthermore, characterized urban movements as reactive Utopias. Why so?

The reason is not that they are incapable of being politically effective because of their distance to, or their subordination to, the political system. In fact, all social movements are unable to fully accomplish their project since they lose their identity as they become institutionalized, the inevitable outcome of bargaining for social reform within the political system. Such is the natural cycle of life and death in society so that the fate of urban movements is not unique. If they followed the experience of social movements, they would extinguish themselves in a struggle that would cause social change they would not survive to see. But this is not our thesis for today's urban movements. We argue that they are not agents of structural social change, but symptoms of resistance to the social domination even if, in their effort to resist, they do have major effects on cities and societies.

The reason for this defensive role is that they are unable to put forward any historically feasible project of economic production, communication, or government. Let us explain.

For any historical actor to handle satisfactorily the production and delivery of public goods and services, it has to be able to reorganize the relationship between production, consumption, and circulation. And this task is beyond any local community in a technologically sophisticated economy that is increasingly organized on a world scale and, at the same time, increasingly disguised within the labyrinths of the underground economy.

To maintain and develop cultural identity and autonomous forms of communication, communities and people must deal with the technology of mass media, as well as with the empires of image-producers that monopolise the codes, flows, and receivers, reinforcing the increasing impoverishment of inter-personal communication. The global village announced by Marshall McLuhan has become, instead, a collection of silent, individual receivers, and the lonely crowd has gone over to high technology. How could local communities match this satellite-related network, so well-supported by economic resources and so directly enforced by the state?

Furthermore, how to advance grassroots democracy when the state has become an overwhelming, centralized, and insulated bureaucracy, when the power game is being played all over the planet with nuclear stakes, and when political parties represent social interests and cultural values which bear an increasingly narrow spectrum? The more locally-based urban movements aim at local governments, but local communities are, in reality, powerless in the context of world empires and computerized bureaucracies.

So, why urban movements? Why the emphasis on local communities? Have people not understood that they need an international working class movement to oppose the multi-national corporations, a strong, democratic parliament, reinforced by participatory democracy, to control the centralized state, and a multiple, interactive communication system to use the new technologies of the media to express (not to suppress) the cultural diversity of society? Why, instead of choosing the right ones, do people insist on aiming at the local targets?

For the simple reason that, according to available information, people appear to have no other choice. The historical actors (social movements, political parties, institutions) that were supposed to provide the answers to the new challenges at the global level, were unable to stand up to them. The labour movement generated by the capitalist mode of production has largely lost its capacity to control the economy, given the internationalization of production, markets, labour, and management, the attack of the informal economy, and the entry of women to work that has shaken the male-dominated foundations of the labour unions. As a result, the relationships between production and consumption, the individual wage and social wage, and the labour process and the welfare state are increasingly out of the control of the labour movement that was the key social actor of the class struggle of the last hundred years. Private corporations and debt-ridden governments take advantage of their newly recovered freedom to cast off the burden of their social responsibility for collective consumption. But if the mechanisms of the welfare state disappear, people are still in need of its benefits in their homes, neighbourhoods, and cities.

At the level of communication patterns and cultural identity, the philosophical rationalism of the political left and the one-dimensional culture of the labour movement led the social movements of industrial capitalism to ignore subcultures, gender specificity, ethnic groups, religious beliefs, national identities, and personal experiences. All human diversity was generally considered a remnant of the past, and class struggle and human progress would help to supersede it until a universal fraternity was arrived at that would provide, paradoxically, the ideal stage both for bourgeois enlightenment and proletarian Marxism. Between times, people continued to speak their languages, pray to their saints, celebrate their traditions, enjoy their bodies, and refuse just to be labour or consumers. In fact, the real drift towards cultural uniformity did not originate with class consciousness or mass consumption, but with the new audio-visual technology, itself not a capitalist conspiracy, but the by-product of military communication that has been commercialized and used by some states for their propaganda. Once again, the existing social movements and forces of political change ignored the potential of these developments, and either switched-off the television or used it in a purely instrumental way to get their message on it. But there was no attempt to connect people's life, experience, and culture to the new world of images and sounds. As a result the sources of communication dried up, interpersonal channels became obsolete, and the mass media took over everybody's imaginary world. Although people did not necessarily like this development they did not find an alternative source of communication and information. So they became accustomed to it, while taking every opportunity to express themselves outside the mass media.

The increasing gap, in terms of political institutions, between people's concerns on the one hand, and parties and the state on the other, grew even greater. All over the world, the state developed a voracious, independent machinery, technologically sophisticated, and bureaucratically self-reproductive. In most nations, this state apparatus repressed the people, coercing them through the policing of their souls and torturing of their bodies. In the few remaining parliamentary democracies, the tragedy has been the increasing distance between citizens and political parties. On the one hand, parties have been historically produced by very different social movements or social interests from the new values and projects so that the established parties and new movements are consequently mismatched. On the other hand, the dominant parties tend to dilute their programmes to capture the middle ground of the political spectrum. As a result, the differences between parties and political coalitions, while still important, tend to diminish, so that the chances of encompassing the electorate's variety of interests are, in fact, reduced, and the distance between everyday life and electoral programmes increased.

As a result we can perceive a growing pattern of electoral abstention (almost 50 per cent in America), that is only counterbalanced when the law enforces the vote (Italy), or when there is a dramatic choice (France and Spain). While national politics are still crucial for the future of the country concerned, the citizens in all cases think the national state is too far removed from their problems. They therefore tend to oscillate in their vote, hoping that the alternance of apparently moderate formulae will yield results. But each time that the pendulum moves and little happens, belief in the political system is further undermined, and people dig a little bit deeper into their local trenches.

So, faced with an overpowered labour movement, an omnipresent one-way communication system indifferent to cultural identities, an all-powerful centralized state loosely governed by unreliable political parties, a structural economic crisis, cultural uncertainty, and the likelihood of nuclear war, people go home. Most withdraw individually, but the crucial, active minority, anxious to retaliate, organize themselves on their local turf. They react against the exploitation-alienation-oppression that the city has become to represent. They may be unable to control the international flows of capital, but they can impose conditions on any multinational wishing to set up in their community. Although not against the television networks they do insist that some broadcasts are made in their language at peak-viewing hours; and they do keep their local celebrations to which the media takes second place. They will support representative democracy, but they go to the city council meeting *en masse* both to remind their representatives that they are there to represent them, and so to exercise some control. So when people find themselves unable to control the world, they simply shrink the world to the size of their community.

Thus, urban movements do address the real issues of our time, although neither on the scale nor terms that are adequate to the task. And yet they do not have any choice since they are the last reaction to the domination and renewed exploitation that submerges our world. But they are more than a last, symbolic stand and desperate cry: they are symptoms of our contradictions, and therefore potentially capable of superseding these contradictions. They are the organizational forms, the live schools, where the new social movements of our emerging society are taking place, growing up, learning to breath, out of reach of the state apparatuses, and outside the closed doors of repressed family life. They are successful when they connect all the repressed aspects of the new, emerging life because this is their specificity: to speak the new language that nobody yet speaks in its multifaceted meaning. When the vocabulary becomes too restricted (a single focus on rent control, for instance) the movements lose their appeal and become yet another interest group in a pluralist society. When they try to impose their programme, they become a counter-society, and collapse under the combined pressure of multinational capital, a mass media system, and the bureaucratic state.

Urban movements do, however, produce new historical meaning in the twilight zone of pretending to build within the walls of a local community a new society they know to be unattainable. And they do so by nurturing the embryos of tomorrow's social movements within the local Utopias that urban movements have constructed in order never to surrender to barbarism.   * * *

Chapter Two

THE RELATIONSHIP BETWEEN CITIES AND STATES AND BETWEEN CITIES AND THE FEDERAL GOVERNMENT

SECTION A. THE RELATIONSHIP BETWEEN CITIES AND STATES

The heart of local government law has traditionally been an analysis of the relationship between cities and states. Much of this book has already been devoted to this topic. The materials dealing with the source of city power concentrated on the city-state relationship because city power is possible only if cities have at least some independence from state control. In the nineteenth century, as the essay in Chapter One concerning the historical background of Dillon's Rule suggests, the controversy over the nature of the city-state relationship involved a debate between Dillon's view that cities were creatures of the state and the view articulated by McQuillin and others that cities had a right to self-government. The materials that follow consider the choice between these two alternatives made by local government law.

1. THE CITY–STATE RELATIONSHIP AS A MATTER OF FEDERAL CONSTITUTIONAL LAW

According to the following case, states can exercise virtually limitless power over cities as a matter of federal Constitutional law. In reading the case, consider how the Supreme Court envisions the city-state relationship. What distinction does the Court suggest between cities and, for example, administrative departments of the state government (such as the state Department of Education)?

107

HUNTER v. CITY OF PITTSBURGH

Supreme Court of the United States, 1907.
207 U.S. 161, 28 S.Ct. 40, 52 L.Ed. 151.

Mr. Justice Moody * * * delivered the opinion of the court:

The plaintiffs in error seek a reversal of the judgment of the supreme court of Pennsylvania, which affirmed a decree of a lower court, directing the consolidation of the cities of Pittsburgh and Allegheny. This decree was entered by authority of an act of the general assembly of that state, after proceedings taken in conformity with its requirements. The act authorized the consolidation of two cities, situated with reference to each other as Pittsburgh and Allegheny are, if, upon an election, the majority of the votes cast in the territory comprised within the limits of both cities favor the consolidation, even though, as happened in this instance, a majority of the votes cast in one of the cities oppose it. The procedure prescribed by the act is that after a petition filed by one of the cities in the court of quarter sessions, and a hearing upon that petition, that court, if the petition and proceedings are found to be regular and in conformity with the act, shall order an election. If the election shows a majority of the votes cast to be in favor of the consolidation, the court "shall enter a decree annexing and consolidating the lesser city * * * with the greater city." The act provides, in considerable detail, for the effect of the consolidation upon the debts, obligations, claims, and property of the constituent cities; grants rights of citizenship to the citizens of those cities in the consolidated city; enacts that "except as herein otherwise provided, all the property * * * and rights and privileges * * * vested in or belonging to either of said cities * * * prior to and at the time of the annexation shall be vested in and owned by the consolidated or united city," and establishes the form of government of the new city. This procedure was followed by the filing of a petition by the city of Pittsburgh; by an election, in which the majority of all the votes cast were in the affirmative, although the majority of all the votes cast by the voters of Allegheny were in the negative; and by a decree of the court, uniting the two cities.

Prior to the hearing upon the petition the plaintiffs in error, who were citizens, voters, owners of property, and taxpayers in Allegheny, filed twenty-two exceptions to the petition. These exceptions were disposed of adversely to the exceptants by the court of quarter sessions, and the action of that court was successively affirmed by the superior and supreme courts of the state. The case is here upon writ of error.
* * *

Briefly stated, the assertion in the fourth assignment of error is that the act of assembly deprives the plaintiffs in error of their property without due process of law, by subjecting it to the burden of the additional taxation which would result from the consolidation. The manner in which the right of due process of law has been violated, as set forth in the first assignment of error and insisted upon in argument, is that the method of voting on the consolidation prescribed in the act has permitted the voters of the larger city to overpower the voters of the smaller city, and compel the union without their consent and against their protest. The precise question thus presented has not been determined by this court. It is important, and, as we have said, not so devoid of merit as to be denied consideration, although its solution by principles long settled and constantly acted upon is not difficult. This court has many times had occasion to consider and decide the nature of municipal corporations, their rights and duties, and the rights of their citizens and creditors. It would be unnecessary and unprofitable to analyze these decisions or quote from the opinions rendered. We think the following principles have been established by them and have become settled doctrines of this court, to be acted upon wherever they are applicable. Municipal corporations are political subdivisions of the state, created as convenient agencies for exercising such of the governmental powers of the state as may be intrusted to them. For the purpose of executing these powers properly and efficiently they usually are given the power to acquire, hold, and manage personal and real property. The number, nature, and duration of the powers conferred upon these corporations and the territory over which they shall be exercised rests in the absolute discretion of the state. Neither their charters, nor any law conferring governmental powers, or vesting in them property to be used for governmental purposes, or authorizing them to hold or manage such property, or exempting them from taxation upon it, constitutes a contract with the state within the meaning of the Federal Constitution. The state, therefore, at its pleasure, may modify or withdraw all such powers, may take without compensation such property, hold it itself, or vest it in other agencies, expand or contract the territorial area, unite the whole or a part of it with another municipality, repeal the charter and destroy the corporation. All this may be done, conditionally or unconditionally, with or without the consent of the citizens, or even against their protest. In all these respects the state is supreme, and its legislative body, conforming its action to the state Constitution, may do as it will, unrestrained by any provision of the Constitution of the United States. Although the inhabitants and property owners may, by such changes, suffer inconvenience, and their property may be lessened in value by the burden of increased taxation, or for any other reason, they have no right, by contract or otherwise, in the unaltered or continued existence of the corporation or its powers, and there is nothing in the Federal Constitution which protects them from these injurious consequences. The power is in the state, and those who legislate for the state are alone responsible for any unjust or oppressive exercise of it.

Applying these principles to the case at bar, it follows irresistibly that this assignment of error, so far as it relates to the citizens who are plaintiffs in error, must be overruled.

It will be observed that, in describing the absolute power of the state over the property of municipal corporations, we have not extended it beyond the property held and used for governmental purposes. Such corporations are sometimes authorized to hold and do hold property for the same purposes that property is held by private corporations or individuals. The distinction between property owned by municipal corporations in their public and governmental capacity and that owned by them in their private capacity, though difficult to define, has been approved by many of the state courts (Dill.Mun.Corp. 4th ed. §§ 66 to 66a inclusive), and it has been held that, as to the latter class of property, the legislature is not omnipotent. If the distinction is recognized it suggests the question whether property of a municipal corporation owned in its private and proprietary capacity may be taken from it against its will and without compensation. Mr. Dillon says truly that the question has never arisen directly for adjudication in this court. But it and the distinction upon which it is based have several times been noticed. Counsel for plaintiffs in error assert that the city of Allegheny was the owner of property held in its private and proprietary capacity, and insist that the effect of the proceedings under this act was to take its property without compensation and vest it in another corporation, and that thereby the city was deprived of its property without due process of law, in violation of the 14th Amendment. But no such question is presented by the record, and there is but a vague suggestion of facts upon which it might have been founded. In the sixth exception there is a recital of facts with a purpose of showing how the taxes of the citizens of Allegheny would be increased by annexation to Pittsburgh. In that connection it is alleged that while Pittsburgh intends to spend large sums of money in the purchase of the water plant of a private company and for the construction of an electric light plant, Allegheny "has improved its streets, established its own system of electric lighting, and established a satisfactory water supply." This is the only reference in the record to the property rights of Allegheny, and it falls far short of a statement that that city holds any property in its private and proprietary capacity. Nor was there any allegation that Allegheny had been deprived of its property without due process of law. The only allegation of this kind is that the taxpayers, plaintiffs in error, were deprived of their property without due process of law because of the increased taxation which would result from the annexation, an entirely different proposition. * * * [N]o question of the effect of the act upon private property rights of the city of Allegheny was considered in the opinions in the state courts or suggested by assignment of errors in this court. The question is entirely outside of the record and has no connection with any question which is raised in the record. For these reasons we are without jurisdiction to consider it, and neither express nor intimate any opinion upon it.

2. HOME RULE AS A PROTECTION AGAINST STATE POWER

Given the plenary nature of state power over cities as described in Hunter v. Pittsburgh, the autonomy of cities from states, to the extent it exists at all, depends on state constitutional law.[1] There are, in fact, a

---

1. It should be noted that some federal Constitutional restraints have been imposed on states' ability to control cities notwithstanding Hunter v. Pittsburgh. For example, the states' ability to draw city boundaries has been limited by the Fif-

teenth Amendment's prohibition on discrimination against voting on the basis of race. Gomillion v. Lightfoot, 364 U.S. 339, 81 S.Ct. 125, 5 L.Ed.2d 110 (1960). Other federal Constitutional restrictions on state power, based on the Fourteenth Amend-

wide variety of state constitutional provisions designed to create some degree of protection from state control for city decisionmaking. In this book we examine only two such provisions: home rule, covered in this section, and prohibitions against special legislation, covered in the next section.

The following materials take up the aspect of home rule mentioned, but not discussed, in Chapter One's section on Home Rule Initiative: the extent of immunity from state control provided by a grant of home rule. As the following materials demonstrate, before cities can be given any such immunity, a way has to be found to distinguish those city actions that are subject to state regulation from those that can be allocated to a sphere of local autonomy. States plainly have power to control *some* kinds of city activity. Many people have attempted to articulate how to divide decisionmaking power between centralized and decentralized governments. Four contrasting ways of doing so are presented below. The first is contained in an except from John Stuart Mill's influential book, On Representative Government; the other three are from court opinions—the majority and dissenting opinions in City of LaGrande v. Public Employes Retirement Board and the majority opinion in Johnson v. Bradley. What are the differences among the four approaches to the problem? What is the relationship between the effort to specify the scope of home rule for cities and the attempt to find an area of individual autonomy not subject to state control in the right of property (as in Lochner v. New York, 198 U.S. 45, 25 S.Ct. 539, 49 L.Ed. 937 (1905)) or the right of privacy (as in Roe v. Wade, 410 U.S. 113, 93 S.Ct. 705, 35 L.Ed.2d 147 (1973))? *Should* there be an area of city autonomy immune from state control? [2]

JOHN STUART MILL, ON REPRESENTATIVE GOVERNMENT

Chapter 15.

OF LOCAL REPRESENTATIVE BODIES.

* * * [A]fter subtracting from the functions performed by most European governments those which ought not to be undertaken by public authorities at all, there still remains so great and various an aggregate of duties that, if only on the principle of division of labour, it is indispensable to share them between central and local authorities. Not only are separate executive officers required for purely local duties (an amount of separation which exists under all governments), but the

ment, are covered below in Chapter 4. None of these federal Constitutional restrictions on state power, however, enable cities to engage in self-government in a manner immune from state control.

2. For an extended analysis of this issue, see Clark, Judges and the Cities (1985). See also 1 Sands & Libonati, Local Govern-

ment Law, Chapter 3 (1993); Libonati, Reconstructing Local Government, 19 The Urban Lawyer 645 (1987); Libonati, Do Local Governments Have Rights?, 10 Urban, State and Local Law Newsletter 1 (1987); and the references cited in Chapter One, Section C, above.

popular control over those officers can only be advantageously exerted through a separate organ. Their original appointment, the function of watching and checking them, the duty of providing, or the discretion of withholding, the supplies necessary for their operations, should rest, not with the national Parliament or the national executive, but with the people of the locality. * * * It is necessary, then, that in addition to the national representation there should be municipal and provincial representations: and the two questions which remain to be resolved are, how the local representative bodies should be constituted, and what should be the extent of their functions.

In considering these questions two points require an equal degree of our attention: how the local business itself can be best done; and how its transaction can be made most instrumental to the nourishment of public spirit and the development of intelligence. In an earlier part of this inquiry I have dwelt in strong language—hardly any language is strong enough to express the strength of my conviction—on the importance of that portion of the operation of free institutions which may be called the public education of the citizens. Now, of this operation the local administrative institutions are the chief instrument. Except by the part they may take as jurymen in the administration of justice, the mass of the population have very little opportunity of sharing personally in the conduct of the general affairs of the community. Reading newspapers, and perhaps writing to them, public meetings, and solicitations of different sorts addressed to the political authorities, are the extent of the participation of private citizens in general politics during the interval between one parliamentary election and another. Though it is impossible to exaggerate the importance of these various liberties, both as securities for freedom and as means of general cultivation, the practice which they give is more in thinking than in action, and in thinking without the responsibilities of action; which with most people amounts to little more than passively receiving the thoughts of someone else. But in the case of local bodies, besides the function of electing, many citizens in turn have the chance of being elected, and many, either by selection or by rotation, fill one or other of the numerous local executive offices. In these positions they have to act for public interests, as well as to think and to speak, and the thinking cannot all be done by proxy. It may be added, that these local functions, not being in general sought by the higher ranks, carry down the important political education which they are the means of conferring to a much lower grade in society. The mental discipline being thus a more important feature in local concerns than in the general affairs of the State, while there are not such vital interests dependent on the quality of the administration, a greater weight may be given to the former consideration, and the latter admits much more frequently of being postponed to it than in matters of general legislation and the conduct of imperial affairs. * * *

From the constitution of the local bodies I now pass to the equally important and more difficult subject of their proper attributions. This question divides itself into two parts: what should be their duties, and whether they should have full authority within the sphere of those duties, or should be liable to any, and what, interference on the part of the central government.

It is obvious, to begin with, that all business purely local—all which concerns only a single locality—should devolve upon the local authorities. The paving, lighting, and cleansing of the streets of a town, and in ordinary circumstances the draining of its houses, are of little consequence to any but its inhabitants. The nation at large is interested in them in no other way than that in which it is interested in the private well-being of all its individual citizens. But among the duties classed as local, or performed by local functionaries, there are many which might with equal propriety be termed national, being the share, belonging to the locality, of some branch of the public administration in the efficiency of which the whole nation is alike interested: the gaols, for instance, most of which in this country are under county management; the local police; the local administration of justice, much of which, especially in corporate towns, is performed by officers elected by the locality, and paid from local funds. None of these can be said to be matters of local, as distinguished from national, importance. It would not be a matter personally indifferent to the rest of the country if any part of it became a nest of robbers or a focus of demoralisations, owing to the maladministration of its police; or if, through the bad regulations of its gaol, the punishment which the courts of justice intended to inflict on the criminals confined therein (who might have come from, or committed their offences in, any other district) might be doubled in intensity, or lowered to practical impunity. The points, moreover, which constitute good management of these things are the same everywhere; there is no good reason why police, or gaols, or the administration of justice, should be differently managed in one part of the kingdom and in another, while there is great peril that in things so important, and to which the most instructed minds available to the State are not more than adequate, the lower average of capacities which alone can be counted on for the service of the localities might commit errors of such magnitude to be a serious blot upon the general administration of the country.

Security of person and property, and equal justice between individuals, are the first needs of society, and the primary ends of government: if these things can be left to any responsibility below the highest, there is nothing, except war and treaties, which requires a general government at all. Whatever are the best arrangements for securing these primary objects should be made universally obligatory, and, to secure their enforcement, should be placed under central superintendence. It is often useful, and with the institutions of our own country even necessary, from the scarcity in the localities of officers representing the general government, that the execution of duties imposed by the central authority should be entrusted to functionaries appointed for local purposes by the locality. But experience is daily forcing upon the public a conviction of the necessity of having at least inspectors appointed by the general government to see that the local officers do their duty. If prisons are under local management, the central government appoints inspectors of prisons to take care that the rules laid down by Parliament are observed, and to suggest others if the state of the gaols shows them to be requisite: as there are inspectors of factories, and inspectors of schools, to watch over the observance of the Acts of Parliament relating to the first, and the fulfilment of the conditions on which State assistance is granted to the latter.

But, if the administration of justice, police and gaols included, is both so universal a concern, and so much a matter of general science independent of local peculiarities, that it may be, and ought to be uniformly regulated throughout the country, and its regulation enforced by more trained and skillful hands than those of purely local authorities—there is also business, such as the administration of the poor laws, sanitary regulation, and others, which, while really interesting to the whole country, cannot consistently with the very purposes of local administration, be managed otherwise than by the localities. In regard to such duties the question arises, how far the local authorities ought to be trusted with discretionary power, free from any superintendence or control of the State.

To decide this question it is essential to consider what is the comparative position of the central and the local authorities to capacity for the work, and security against negligence or abuse. In the first place, the local representative bodies and their officers are almost certain to be of a much lower grade of intelligence and knowledge than Parliament and the national executive. Secondly, besides being themselves of inferior qualifications, they are watched by, and accountable to, an inferior public opinion. The public under whose eyes they act, and by whom they are criticised, is both more limited in extent, and generally far less enlightened, than that which surrounds and admonishes the highest authorities at the capital; while the comparative smallness of the interests involved causes even that inferior public to direct its thoughts to the subject less intently, and with less solicitude. Far less interference is exercised by the press and by public discussion, and that which is exercised may with much more impunity be disregarded in the proceedings of local than in those of national authorities.

Thus far the advantage seems wholly on the side of management by the central government. But, when we look more closely, these motives of preference are found to be balanced by others fully as substantial. If the local authorities and public are inferior to the central ones in knowledge of the principles of administration, they have the compensating advantage of a far more direct interest in the result. A man's neighbours or his landlord may be much cleverer than himself, and not without an indirect interest in his prosperity, but for all that his interests will be better attended to in his own keeping than in theirs. It is further to be remembered, that even supposing the central government to administer through its own officers, its officers do not act at the centre, but in the locality; and however inferior the local public may be to the central, it is the local public alone which has any opportunity of watching them, and it is the local opinion alone which either acts directly upon their own conduct, or calls the attention of the government to the points in which they may require correction. It is but in extreme cases that the general opinion of the country is brought to bear at all upon details of local administration, and still more rarely has it the means of deciding upon them with any just appreciation of the case. Now, the local opinion necessarily acts far more forcibly upon purely local administrators. They, in the natural course of things, are permanent residents, not expecting to be withdrawn from the place when they cease to exercise authority in it; and their authority itself depends, by supposition, on the will of the local public. I need not dwell on the deficiencies of the central authority in detailed knowledge of local persons and things, and the too great engrossment of its time and thoughts by other concerns, to admit of its acquiring the quantity and quality of local knowledge necessary even for deciding on complaints, and enforcing responsibility from so great a number of local agents. In the details of management, therefore, the local bodies will generally have the advantage; but in comprehension of the principles even of purely local management, the superiority of the central government, when rightly constituted, ought to be prodigious: not only by reason of the probably great personal superiority of the individuals composing it, and the multitude of thinkers and writers who are at all times engaged in pressing useful ideas upon their notice, but also because the knowledge and experience of any local authority is but local knowledge and experience, confined to their own part of the country and its modes of management, whereas the central government has the means of knowing all that is to be learnt from the united experience of the whole kingdom, with the addition of easy access to that of foreign countries.

The practical conclusion from these premises is not difficult to draw. The authority which is most conversant with principles should be supreme over principles, while that which is most competent in details should have the details left to it. The principal business of the central authority should be to give instruction, of the local authority to apply it. Power may be localised, but knowledge, to be most useful, must be centralised; there must be somewhere a focus at which all its scattered rays are collected, that the broken and coloured lights which exist elsewhere may find there what is necessary to complete and purify them. To every branch of local administration which affects the general interest there should be a corresponding central organ, either a minister, or some specially appointed functionary under him; even if that functionary does no more than collect information from all quarters, and bring the experience acquired in one locality to the knowledge of another where it is wanted. But there is also something more than this for the central authority to do. It ought to keep open a perpetual communication with the localities: informing itself by their experience, and them by its own; giving advice freely when asked, volunteering it when seen to be required; compelling publicity and recordation of proceedings, and enforcing obedience to every general law which the legislature has laid down on the subject of local management.

That some such laws ought to be laid down few are likely to deny. The localities may be allowed to mismanage their own interests, but not to prejudice those of others, nor violate those principles of justice between one person and another of which it is the duty of the State to maintain the rigid observance. If the local majority attempts to oppress the minority, or one class another, the State is bound to interpose. For example, all local rates ought to be voted exclusively by the local representative body; but that body, though elected solely by rate-payers, may raise its revenues by imposts of such a kind, or assess them in such a manner, as to throw an unjust share of the burden on the poor, the rich, or some particular class of the population: it is the duty, therefore, of the legislature, while leaving the mere amount of the local taxes to the discretion of the local body, to lay down authoritatively the modes of taxation, and rules of assessment, which alone the localities shall be permitted to use. Again, in the administration of public charity the industry and morality of the whole labouring population depend, to a most serious extent, upon adherence to certain fixed principles in awarding relief. Though it belongs essentially to the local functionaries to determine who, according to those principles, is entitled to be relieved, the national Parliament is the proper authority to prescribe the principles themselves; and it would neglect a most important part of its duty if it did not, in a matter of such grave national concern, lay down imperative rules, and make effectual provision that those rules should not be departed from. What power of actual interference with the local administrators it may be necessary to retain, for the due enforcement of the laws, is a question of detail into which it would be useless to enter. The laws themselves will naturally define the penalties, and fix the mode of their enforcement. It may be requisite, to meet extreme cases, that the power of the central authority should extend to dissolving the local representative council, or dismissing the local executive: but not to making new appointments, or suspending the local institutions. Where Parliament has not interfered, neither ought any branch of the executive to interfere with authority; but as an adviser and critic, an enforcer of the laws, and a denouncer to Parliament or the local constituencies of conduct which it deems condemnable, the functions of the executive are of the greatest possible value.

Some may think that however much the central authority surpasses the local in knowledge of the principles of administration, the great object which has been so much insisted on, the social and political education of the citizens, requires that they should be left to manage these matters by their own, however imperfect, lights. To this it might be answered, that the education of the citizens is not the only thing to be considered; government and administration do not exist for that alone, great as its importance is. But the objection shows a very imperfect understanding of the function of popular institutions as a means of political instruction. It is but a poor education that associates ignorance with ignorance, and leaves them, if they care for knowledge, to grope their way to it without help, and to do without it if they do not. What is wanted is, the means of making ignorance aware of itself, and able to profit by knowledge; accustoming minds which know only routine to act upon, and feel the value of, principles teaching them to compare different modes of action, and learn by the use of their reason, to distinguish the best. When we desire to have a good school, we do not eliminate the teacher. The old remark, "as the schoolmaster is, so will be the school," is as true of the indirect schooling of grown people by public business as of the schooling of youth in academies and colleges. A government which attempts to do everything is aptly compared by M. Charles de Remusat to a schoolmaster who does all the pupils' tasks for them; he may be very popular with the pupils, but he will teach them little. A government, on the other hand, which neither does anything itself that can possibly be done by any one else, nor shows any one else how to do anything, is like a school in which there is no schoolmaster, but only pupil teachers who have never themselves been taught.

CITY OF LA GRANDE v. PUBLIC EMPLOYES RETIREMENT BOARD

Supreme Court of Oregon, 1978.
281 Or. 137, 576 P.2d 1204.

LINDE, JUSTICE.

By a 1971 enactment, the legislative assembly required all police officers and firemen employed by any city, county, or district to be brought within the state's Public Employes Retirement System by July 1, 1973, unless the particular public employer provides them with equal or better retirement benefits. The same statute also required these public employers to pay the premiums on an insurance policy purchased by the state's Department of General Services, providing $10,000 to an officer's or fireman's beneficiaries in case of his or her job-related death, again unless the employer provides equal or better benefits.

The validity of the retirement provisions of the statute was attacked in separate declaratory judgment proceedings brought by the Cities of La Grande and Astoria against various state officials and against their respective police and firefighters as a class or as represented by their collective bargaining agents. Astoria also challenged the statutory requirement of insurance coverage. The cities claim that by requiring them to provide police officers and firemen with retirement and insurance benefits the legislature has invaded a domain reserved to local discretion by the Oregon Constitution. * * *

The issues in these cases arise from two provisions of the Oregon Constitution that together provide "home rule" for cities and towns. Enacted together by initiative amendment in 1906, they appear in two places in the constitution. The pertinent part of article XI, section 2, provides:

The Legislative Assembly shall not enact, amend or repeal any charter or act of incorporation for any municipality, city or town. The legal voters of every city and town are hereby granted power to enact and amend their municipal charter, subject to the Constitution and criminal laws of the State of Oregon * * *.

In article IV, section 1a (now 1(5)), the statewide initiative and referendum powers "reserved" to the people by amendment of article IV, section 1, in 1902 were "further reserved to the qualified voters of each municipality and district as to all local, special and municipal legislation of every character in or for their municipality or district." * * *

It is useful to recall the role of the amendments in the state's constitutional arrangements. With respect to local authority, their central object is to allow the people of the locality to decide upon the organization of their government and the scope of its powers under its charter without having to obtain statutory authorization from the legislature, as was the case before the amendments. Thus the validity of local action depends, first, on whether it is authorized by the local charter or by a statute, or if taken by initiative, whether it qualifies as "local, special [or] municipal legislation" under article IV, section 1(5); second, on whether it contravenes state or federal law. With respect to a state law, or action taken under it, on the other hand, it is elementary that the legislature has plenary authority except for such limits as may be found in the constitution or in federal law. Thus the validity of a state law vis-a-vis local entities does not depend upon a source of authority for the law, nor on whether a locality may have authority to act on the same subject; it depends on the limitations imposed by article XI, section 2.

Moreover, these constitutional provisions are concerned with the structural and organizational arrangements for the exercise of local self-government, with the power of local voters to enact and amend their own municipal charters and to employ the initiative and referendum for "local, special [or] municipal legislation." They address the manner in which governmental power is granted and exercised, not the concrete uses to which it is put. Except for the limits on the initiative and referendum implied in the quoted phrase of article IV, section 1(5), the amendments do not purport to divide areas of substantive policy between the levels of government. Accordingly, the accommodation of state and local authority most directly involves the amendments when a party invokes a state law as governing some process of local government, such as elections, the qualification and selection of local government personnel, taxation and finance or judicial procedures.

The important issue in the early disputes over the effects of the amendments was whether the prohibition of article XI, section 2, extended beyond laws changing a single municipal charter to laws amending such charters generally. * * * [T]he same issue was reexamined most recently in *State ex rel. Heinig v. City of Milwaukie*, 231 Or. 473, 479, 373 P.2d 680 (1962). There a state law requiring a city to establish a civil service system, administered by a prescribed city commission, was defended on the ground that it applied to all cities. The court rejected the argument that this fact of itself took the law outside article XI, section 2. Instead, Justice O'Connell wrote,

> we now expressly hold that the legislative assembly does not have the authority to enact a law relating to city government even though it is of general applicability to all cities in the state unless the subject matter of the enactment is of general concern to the state as a whole, that is to say that it is a matter of more than local concern to each of the municipalities purported to be regulated by the enactment. Borrowing the language from *Branch v. Albee,* 71 Or. 188, 193, 142 P. 598, 599 (1914), we hold that the people of a city are not "subject to the will of the legislature in the management of purely local municipal business in which the state at large is not interested, and which is not of any interest to any outside the local municipality."

But even with respect to a law prescribing municipal modes of government, the court concluded, a general law might be valid if it served a predominant social interest extending beyond the local municipality. This conclusion is consistent with many of the court's decisions in which state standards designed to safeguard the interest of private persons in the procedures of local government have generally been sustained.

The quoted holding of *Heinig* states the rule for testing general laws for the processes of city government. The opinion in *Heinig* went further, explaining this holding by a view of the state and its cities as competing sovereignties that seemed to extend to all conflicts of state and local policy. But we do not think that article XI, section 2, extends that far, nor that the *Heinig* formula should be extended beyond the context of laws for city government in which it was formulated. This is so for two reasons. First, constitutional provisions like those for home rule in the first instance are designed to formulate how government is to govern, not how judges are to exercise judicial review. Article XI, section 2, for instance, is addressed to the legislative assembly and to the cities, telling the legislature what it may not do and the voters of the several cities what they may do. Judicial interpretations of such a provision must strive to articulate these directives and avoid formulations that give no guidance to government and leave every policy dispute to judicial decision. Of course this does not mean that challenges to a state or local act under the home rule provisions are beyond judicial review. We are reviewing such a challenge in this very case. Rather, it bears on the proper interpretation of the provisions.

Secondly, however, when such a challenge does reach a court, the court's decision must be derived from a constitutional standard, not from the court's own view of competing public policies. The accommodation of state and local authority over the processes of city government at least involves comparable interests the citizens' interests in responsible government, in elections, in official accountability, in the procedures of policy planning and decision, taxing and borrowing, and the like. * * * These processes of government are the chief object of the municipal charters mentioned in article XI, section 2, as has been set forth more expressly in the more recently formulated constitutional provisions for county charters. They were the historical reason for the adoption of the constitutional amendments, as reviewed above. When a comparison of competing policies is pressed beyond this to all conflicts between state and local acts, however, it must often involve a choice among values that have no common denominator either in or outside the constitution. There is no agreed common measure to "weigh" or "balance," for instance, an esthetic environment against commercial profit or the prevention of caries against strongly felt objections to fluoridation of the water supply if state and local policy should differ on such matters. Such choices are the essence of political, not judicial, decision.

Outside the context of laws prescribing the modes of local government, both municipalities and the state legislature in many cases have enacted laws in pursuit of substantive objectives, each well within its respective authority, that were arguably inconsistent with one another. In such cases, the first inquiry must be whether the local rule in truth is incompatible with the legislative policy, either because both cannot operate concurrently or because the legislature meant its law to be exclusive. It is reasonable to interpret local enactments, if possible, to be intended to function consistently with state laws, and equally reasonable to assume that the legislature does not mean to displace local civil or administrative regulation of local conditions by a statewide law unless that intention is apparent. However, when a local enactment is found incompatible with a state law in an area of substantive policy, the state law will displace the local rule. * * *

It is therefore pertinent to the prohibition expressed in article XI, section 2, to determine whether the challenged law is addressed primarily to a concern of the state with the modes of local government or to substantive social, economic, or other regulatory objectives. * * * The provisions of ORS chapters 237 and 243 requiring retirement and insurance benefits for police officers and firemen * * * plainly embody a legislative concern with securing the postemployment living standards of persons in these occupations and their families, not with the cities' governmental organization. It is not essential to the legitimacy of this goal whether the legislature singled out police officers and firemen because it deemed these occupations particularly hazardous or the desired benefits difficult and costly to obtain piecemeal, nor whether its assumptions were well founded. In any event, the statutes are addressed to a statewide substantive, social objective rather than any asserted concern with the modes of local government.

The present legislation avoids the prescription of precise municipal organization involved in * * * *State ex rel. Heinig v. City of Milwaukie, supra.* * * * [W]hile the statute involved in *Heinig* did not single out one city, it * * * undertook by the act itself to create municipal civil service commissions, to be composed of three members selected in the manner prescribed by the act, which would be charged with supervising civil service systems, for firemen. Even apart from this direct prescription of an element in the city's administrative structure, the civil service law would have displaced the authority of the politically accountable local officials over the selection, assignment, discipline, and replacement of the employees for whose performance they were responsible, and done so not as a matter of the community's policy or negotiated agreement but by direction from the state. This is a substantially different interference with local self-government from an obligation to provide a measure of economic security to public employees. Thus the act was held to be an intervention into the powers of appointment, transfer, and discharge of personnel specified in the Milwaukie city charter, unjustified by any independent statewide concern, and therefore in violation of article XI, section 2.

In contrast, the present statutes do not create any agencies of local government, nor do they direct local communities to do so. They oblige local governments to bring their police officers and firemen under the benefits provided respectively by the state's retirement system and a statewide insurance policy, but even that obligation is made contingent upon an option to provide equal or better benefits by other means of the local government's choice. The administrative machinery of these statutes is state administration, not compelled local administration.

Though the legislature in these laws has not mandated city administration in the manner that proved fatal in * * * *Heinig,* its pursuit of its statewide social objective undeniably displaces the arrangements (or absence of arrangements) preferred by the local government. This is not uncommon, as many of our cited decisions show. Nor is it generally useful to define a "subject" of legislation and assign it to one or the other level of government. To treat "local personnel" as such a subject, for instance, would appear to sweep beyond the civil service law invalidated in *Heinig* and to raise doubt whether local employees also must be excluded from all state occupational qualifications or state protective laws, *e.g.,* workers' compensation, wage and hour standards, safety standards, nondiscrimination, or child labor laws. * * * But if these doubts can be made to disappear by defining the "subject" of the same laws to be safety, or nondiscrimination, or job security, the definition merely marks the desired conclusion of an argument rather than its premise. A search for a predominant state or local interest in the "subject matter" of legislation can only substitute for the political process to which we have referred the court's own political judgment whether the state or the local policy should prevail. Moreover, as the foregoing examples show, it misconceives the nature of a "state interest" to focus narrowly on the functions performed by particular groups of employees to the exclusion of a concern with the employees as citizens. The "state" as such has no interest apart from that of its inhabitants, present and future; and the legislature may, if it so chooses, consider the interests of those who perform the job as well as the interests of those dependent on that performance.

The geographic boundaries of local entities are not much more determinative in excluding state concerns. Arguments presented in these cases, as in *Heinig*, point out that city police officers and firemen are sometimes assigned duties beyond their cities, but this is hardly needed to demonstrate a state concern. Large complexes of state buildings and state personnel such as college campuses, and indeed the state Capitol, executive offices, and this court, depend on the quality of police and fire protection within city limits, and thousands of persons who frequent city streets and business districts every day are not city residents. The state relies on local governments for many functions deemed important to the state within local boundaries, most recently land use controls. The modern addition of home rule for counties would create additional complexities in employing a geographic criterion for allocating mutually exclusive constitutional authority.

Finally, as individuals we may differ with legislative policies that mandate substantive standards for programs and activities for which local taxpayers and local officials rather than state legislators will bear the fiscal responsibility. But if there are other constitutional limitations than the "home rule" amendments that preclude the particular financial effect of the statutes involved in these cases, the parties have not brought them to the court's attention. The simple provision of article XI, section 2, that "[t]he Legislative Assembly shall not enact, amend or repeal any charter or act of incorporation for any municipality, city or town" does not purport to sweep that broadly.

Thus neither the form in which the local policy is cast, nor the "subject" of the state law, nor the existence of local boundaries can by itself determine the validity of a statewide law. Instead, we conclude that the following principles for resolving a conflict between such a law and an inconsistent local provision for the conduct of city government are consistent with our past interpretations of the "home rule" amendments:

When a statute is addressed to a concern of the state with the structure and procedures of local agencies, the statute impinges on the powers reserved by the amendments to the citizens of local communities. Such a state concern must be justified by a need to safeguard the interests of persons or entities affected by the procedures of local government.

Conversely, a general law addressed primarily to substantive social, economic, or other regulatory objectives of the state prevails over contrary policies preferred by some local governments if it is clearly intended to do so, unless the law is shown to be irreconcilable with the local community's freedom to choose its own political form.[31] In that case, such a state law must yield in those particulars necessary to preserve that freedom of local organization.

31. Instances where general regulatory laws have this effect are probably rare, but hypothetical examples might be state laws that would impose policy responsibilities or recordkeeping, reporting, or negotiating requirements on persons or entities contrary to their allocation under the local charter.

As we have said, the statutes challenged by the cities in these cases are of the second, substantive kind. The provisions for financial security for police officers and firemen and their dependents in the event of retirement, disability, or death address a social concern with the living standards of these classes of workers, not with local governments as such. Various categories of employees are not placed beyond the reach of the state's social legislation merely because their occupational functions—here police and fire protection, elsewhere perhaps municipal transit or utility or library services—happen to be found in the public sector of local government. While the statewide retirement and insurance plans do displace other plans that local agencies have made, or might make, for these objectives, they are not irreconcilable with the freedom to charter their own governmental structures that are reserved to the citizens of Astoria and La Grande by article XI, section 2. Accordingly, the statutes are constitutional.

Tongue, Justice, dissenting.

I agree that, as a general rule, dissenting opinions should be restrained and respectful. It is difficult to do so, however, when, because of a purely fortuitous change in the membership of this court, there is now a majority which, by a margin of one vote, has prevailed by an opinion which:

(1) Drastically upsets the long-existing balance of power between Oregon cities and the state legislature in the critical area of "home rule" by abandonment of the long-established concept that the "home rule" amendments to the Oregon Constitution granted to Oregon cities exclusive power to legislate as to all matters of "local interest," i.e., a grant of "local autonomy," free from intervention by the state legislature, and with the courts as the arbiters of disputes between cities and the state as to what are matters of "local interest."

(2) Substitutes for that long-established concept of "local autonomy" a new rule of "legislative supremacy," to the effect that the state legislature may legislate as to all matters which *it* deems to involve some state-wide interest, with the single exception of some matters involving the "structure and procedures of local agencies." Despite the fact that the Oregon courts have long served as a protective "fence" between "the fox and the chickens," the majority has now removed most of the "fence," leaving the "chickens" at the mercy of the "fox." * * *

(5) Uses this case as a vehicle for a "judicial *tour de force*" by the adoption of that new and unprecedented rule despite the fact that the majority could have sustained the validity of state laws requiring cities to provide pensions for police officers and firemen by application of the rule previously recognized by this court for application in such cases. * * *

It has been recognized by authorities on this important subject that one of the basic purposes of "home rule" is to "stake out a limited area where local government could legislate for itself" and to "carve out an area in which the municipality enjoys a measure of *local autonomy* free from legislative interference or control * * *." It has also been recognized, however, that "[h]ome rule does not mean, and has never been intended to mean, complete local autonomy within the states, because home rule cities must always remain integral parts of state government and must assume, like non-home rule cities, responsibility for enforcement of state law," but that, "[o]rdinarily, a home rule grant transfers authority from the state legislature to the municipalities to enact measures of purely municipal concern." Thus, it has been more accurately stated that "home rule" is a method for "distribution of power by the people between two levels of government state and local." * * *

In *Heinig* this court held that "the real test" to be applied in determining whether a particular matter is one of "local" or "state" concern is "not whether the state or the city has an interest in the matter, for usually they both have, but whether the state's interest or that of the city is paramount." * * * In *Heinig* it was also held unanimously that it is for the courts of Oregon to determine what matters are of predominately state-wide interest, so as to be subject to the exclusive power of the legislature, and what matters are of predominately local interest, so as to be subject to the exclusive power of Oregon cities in holding that:

> " * * * [U]nder the theory of home rule which we have adopted there are involved two political agencies making conflicting claims to sovereignty, and the resolution of that conflict must be made by the courts." * * *

[T]he majority * * * announces a completely new concept namely, that the intended purpose of the Oregon "home rule" amendments was only to grant to the cities the limited power to legislate upon matters involving what the majority refers to variously as "processes" or "mode" of local government, or as "structure and organization" or "structure and procedures" of local government, as distinguished from "substantive social, economic, or other regulatory objectives."

It is obvious, of course, that this new concept by the majority * * * imposes a drastic limitation upon the area in which cities have exclusive power to legislate * * *. But aside from the drastic nature of this change, it is submitted, with all due respect, that this new concept, which is the foundation upon which the majority rests its opinion, is not only a curious hybrid of uncertain ancestry, but is unsound and should have been rejected by this court for the following reasons:

(1) Matters of "substance," as well as matters of "procedure," can be matters of "predominantly local interest." For example: the style of uniforms worn by firemen (an example referred to by this court in *Heinig*) or the number and location of benches or swings in a city park. On the other hand, matters of "procedure" of city government may be of "predominantly state-wide interest," such as the manner in which a ballot measure for a municipal tax measure is stated, for information of the voters.

(2) The fact that most previous cases presented to this court, including *Heinig*, may have involved "some process of local government" is, of itself, wholly insufficient to support the conclusion that the Oregon "home rule" amendments were *intended* to make a grant of home rule power to cities which was *limited* to matters of "organization," "structure" or "procedure," in the absence of a proper basis for such a conclusion in the terms of the Oregon "home rule" amendments.

(3) There is nothing in the terms of the Oregon "home rule" amendments which supports, or is claimed by the majority to support, its conclusion that the intended purpose of these constitutional amendments was to limit the grant of home rule powers to cities to matters of "organization," "structure" or "procedure" and to reserve to the state the exclusive power to legislate as to all other matters by general "civil" laws. On the contrary, Art. IV, § 1(a) (now § 1(5)), expressly reserves power to the voters of cities over *"all local, special and municipal legislation of every character"* and Art. XI, § 2, provided that the home rule process granted to cities was subject only to "the Constitution and *criminal* laws of the State of Oregon." * * *

The majority * * * holds * * * that the jurisdiction of the courts no longer extends to cases involving disputes over what it describes as "competing policies" for the reason that "such choices are the essence of political, not judicial, decision." * * * [But the] courts frequently apply a "balancing test" of weighing competing social interests under constitutional provisions which provide no more of a "standard." Examples, among others, are to be found in cases in which the courts must balance the interests of individuals as against the interest of the state in cases involving claims by individuals to freedom of speech, to equal protection of the laws, to an administrative hearing, and to an abortion, to mention but a few. Also, the problem confronted by the courts under the "balancing of interest" test as stated in *Heinig* * * * is no more difficult of application than the "fairness" test as adopted by this and other courts in cases involving the application of state "long arm" statutes, in the balancing of competing interests in child custody cases involving conflicts of competing state jurisdiction, or in negligence cases in which the "continuum" test is sometimes applied. * * *

[E]ven under the test as previously adopted by this court in *Heinig* (and now repudiated by the majority) it is arguable that state laws requiring the payment of pensions to police officers and firemen may be held valid upon the ground that the interest of the state in the protection of its citizens by proper police and fire protection requires the payment of wages, and including such "fringe benefits" sufficient to attract and retain qualified policemen and firemen. In *Heinig* it was stated:

> " * * * Each case requires a weighing of the state's interest against the interest of the municipality. In some instances the need for uniformity, or the benefit of a widespread application of the law, or the recognition that the matter dealt with is interrelated with other

functions of the state and similar considerations will require that the statute have preference over the charter * * *."

Indeed, although the cases are not without conflict, there are decisions by courts of other states holding that state laws requiring pension benefits for policemen and firemen involve such an interest of the state so as to prevail over that of the cities which employ them. * * *

Wholly aside from its finespun legal theory, and wholly as a practical matter, the majority opinion is simply "bad law," in my opinion. What the majority has done in adopting a rule of "legislative supremacy" as to all substantive matters, i.e., all matters which the legislature may deem to involve "societal policy," is to enable the legislature to require the cities of Oregon to adopt expensive social programs without being responsible for any part of the costs of such programs and without recourse to the courts in the event of "jurisdictional disputes." * * * The majority opinion, in my judgment, makes a mockery of the "home rule" amendments to the Oregon Constitution. * * *

JOHNSON v. BRADLEY

Supreme Court of California, 1992.
4 Cal.4th 389, 14 Cal.Rptr.2d 470, 841 P.2d 990.

LUCAS, CHIEF JUSTICE. * * *

In June 1988, State Assemblyman Ross Johnson and State Senator Quentin Kopp (two of the three petitioners in this action) successfully sponsored a statewide initiative, Proposition 73, which added chapter 5 to the Political Reform Act of 1974 (Gov. Code, §§ 81000–91015). Article 3 of chapter 5, entitled "Contribution Limitations," imposed various restrictions on contributions to and by candidates and political committees or parties (§§ 85301–85307), and also provided in section 85300: "No public officer shall expend and no candidate shall accept any public moneys for the purpose of seeking elective office."

Two years later, the voters of the City of Los Angeles amended the city charter by adopting Measure H, a comprehensive campaign, election and ethics reform plan. * * * [U]nlike Proposition 73, which imposed limits on *contributions* but not on *spending* by candidates, Measure H also imposed spending limitations. The drafters of Measure H apparently realized that under *Buckley v. Valeo* (1976) 424 U.S. 1, 46 L.Ed.2d 659, 96 S.Ct. 612, spending limitations are constitutionally invalid unless they are conditioned on a candidate's acceptance of public funds. Accordingly, Measure H provided for partial public funding of city political campaigns, and, correspondingly, spending limits on candidates who accept public funds. As codified, this provision is now found in section 313 of the Los Angeles City Charter (hereafter charter section 313). * * *

Petitioners invoked the original jurisdiction of the Court of Appeal to enjoin respondents from implementing and enforcing charter section 313. The Court of Appeal * * * agreed with respondents that a charter city's decision to provide its own public funds to finance city political campaigns is a "municipal affair" and not a matter of "statewide concern," and hence charter section 313 prevails over section 85300. * * * We granted review to address the municipal affairs issue. * * *

Article XI, section 5 of the state Constitution (hereafter article XI, section 5) addresses the "home rule" powers of charter cities * * *. Subdivision (a) sets out the general principle of local self-governance, and provides: "It shall be competent in any city charter to provide that the city governed thereunder may *make and enforce all ordinances and regulations in respect to municipal affairs*, subject only to the restrictions and limitations provided in their several charters and in respect to other matters they shall be subject to general laws. City charters adopted pursuant to this Constitution shall supersede any existing charter, and with respect to municipal affairs shall supersede all laws inconsistent therewith." (Italics added.) * * *

In *California Fed. Savings & Loan Assn. v. City of Los Angeles* (1991) 54 Cal.3d 1, 283 Cal.Rptr. 569, 812 P.2d 916 (*CalFed*), we * * * concluded [that] subdivision (a) does not permit a charter city to impose local income taxes on "savings banks" exempted from such taxes by general statewide law. * * * [I]n *CalFed* * * * [we] articulated a framework for resolving municipal affairs and statewide-concern questions under subdivision (a) of article XI, section 5. When the local matter under review "implicates a 'municipal affair' and poses a genuine conflict with state law, the question of statewide concern is the bedrock inquiry through which the conflict between state and local interests is adjusted. If the subject of the statute fails to qualify as one of statewide concern, then the conflicting charter city measure is a 'municipal affair' and 'beyond the reach of legislative enactment.' * * * If, however, the court is persuaded that the subject of the state statute is one of statewide concern and that the statute is reasonably related [and 'narrowly tailored'] to its resolution, then the conflicting charter city measure ceases to be a 'municipal affair' pro tanto and the Legislature is not prohibited by article XI, section 5 [, subdivision] (a), from addressing the statewide dimension by its own tailored enactments."

We further explained, "The phrase 'statewide concern' is thus nothing more than a conceptual formula employed in aid of the judicial mediation of jurisdictional disputes between charter cities and the Legislature, one that facially discloses a *focus on extramunicipal concerns* as the starting point for analysis. *By requiring, as a condition of state legislative supremacy, a dimension demonstrably transcending identifiable municipal interests, the phrase resists the invasion of areas which are of intramural concern only, preserving core values of charter city government.* As applied to state and charter city enactments in actual conflict, 'municipal affair' and 'statewide concern' represent, Janus-like, ultimate legal conclusions rather than factual descriptions. Their inherent ambiguity masks the difficult but inescapable duty of the court to, in the words of one authoritative commentator, 'allocate the governmental powers under consideration in the most sensible and appropriate fashion as between local and state legislative bodies.'"

We summarized the dispositive issue as follows: "In cases presenting a true conflict between a charter city measure * * * and a state statute, * * * the hinge of the decision is the identification of a convincing basis for legislative action originating in extramural concerns * * *." Turning to the question before us in *CalFed*, we stated, "We must decide whether * * * the showing before the superior court supports the Legislature's finding of a need for paramount state control over the aggregate income tax burden on financial corporations such as petitioner." After reviewing the legislative history of the statutory scheme, we concluded, "the Legislature's decision to modify the tax system by eliminating local taxes on savings banks finds substantial support in the regulatory and historical context summarized above, * * * and is *narrowly tailored* to resolve the problem at hand." * * *

[P]etitioners assert that because the drafters of Proposition 73 and those who voted for the measure *intended* to create a statewide rule barring public funding of all election campaigns, section 85300 addresses a matter of statewide concern. * * * This point need not detain us long. The assertion that a legislative body may define what is, and is not, a matter of statewide concern was rejected in *Bishop v. City of San Jose*, * * * [(1969) 1 Cal.3d 56, 81 Cal.Rptr. 465, 460 P.2d 137]: "[T]he fact, standing alone, that the Legislature has attempted to deal with a particular subject on a statewide basis is not determinative of the issue as between state and municipal affairs * * *; stated otherwise, the Legislature is empowered neither to determine what constitutes a municipal affair nor to change such an affair into a matter of statewide concern." As we explained in *CalFed*, our inquiry regarding statewide concern focuses not on the legislative body's intent, but on "the identification of a convincing basis for legislative action originating in extra-municipal concerns, one justifying legislative supersession based on sensible, pragmatic considerations." In other words, we must be satisfied that there are good reasons, grounded on statewide interests, to label a given matter a "statewide concern." * * *

In their effort to identify a statewide concern, petitioners advance various arguments relating to fiscal matters. First, they point to ballot arguments advising the voters that "too much money is being spent on political campaigns today." From these and other ballot statements, petitioners conclude the electorate was "clearly informed Proposition 73's aim was reducing the costs of political campaigns through a system of contribution limitations and prohibition on public funding." In other words, they identify as a statewide concern the protection of the public fisc.

We do not doubt that conservation of the state's limited funds is a statewide concern. But petitioners, understandably, do not attempt to justify the public funding ban on the ground that it is designed to protect state revenues, because a local public funding law that draws its revenues exclusively from local taxes would obviously not implicate a concern for protecting the state fisc. Instead, petitioners suggest there is a legitimate statewide concern in how local tax proceeds are expended.

On this point, we agree with the Court of Appeal below, which observed, "[W]e can think of nothing that is of greater municipal concern than how a city's tax dollars will be spent; nor anything which could be of less interest to taxpayers of other jurisdictions. [Charter section 313, subdivision (C)4] expressly limit[s] the monies to be utilized for campaign financing to city funds. Thus, payments received by the city from state or federal governmental agencies may not be used. These are the city taxpayers' own dollars and those taxpayers, together with their city council, have voted to utilize those dollars to help finance political campaigns for city elective offices as a central if not critical part of major political campaign and ethics reform. That Proposition 73 expressly dealt with this subject and intended that its prohibition extend to campaigns and candidates for local office does not convert the decision of the City of Los Angeles, to follow a different path with its own money, into a matter of statewide concern."

Petitioners also advance two variations on the fiscal concern described above in their attempt to establish a statewide concern. They focus on ballot arguments by the proponents of Proposition 73 to the effect that public funding might: (i) divert scarce tax funds from local needs such as "police protection, fire protection, or schools"; and (ii) be made available to "extremist candidates" such as "communists or members of the Ku Klux Klan" with whom many voters disagree.

We reject the first claim because it is merely a variation on the argument presented and rejected above, i.e., that the manner in which local tax proceeds are expended is a legitimate statewide concern. Moreover, it proves too much, by effectively negating the authority of charter cities to regulate any municipal affair that involves expenditure of funds. * * *

[P]etitioners appear to assert there is a legitimate statewide concern regarding the funding of political campaigns of candidates who are "extremists"—i.e., outside the mainstream of political thinking. They fail, however, to explain what legitimate interest the state might have in discriminating against "non-mainstream" candidates who otherwise qualify for matching funds under the objective eligibility criteria for receiving such funds. Accordingly, we reject this ground of alleged statewide concern.

Finally, petitioners assert: (i) the "integrity of the electoral process" is itself a statewide concern; (ii) section 85300's ban on public funding of election campaigns is reasonably calculated to resolve that statewide concern; and (iii) therefore section 85300 addresses a statewide concern.

We have no reason to doubt petitioners' major premise; the integrity of the electoral process, at both the state and local level, is undoubtedly a statewide concern. * * * Although we accept petitioners' major premise, we question their minor premise, that section 85300's ban on public financing of election campaigns is reasonably calculated to address the statewide concern regarding the integrity of the electoral process. * * * Petitioners cite nothing to support the proposition that section 85300's ban on public funding of political campaigns advances in any way the goal of enhancing the integrity of the electoral process. In fact, the opposite appears to be true. As the high court observed in *Buckley v. Valeo, supra*, 424 U.S. 1, 96 S.Ct. 612, 46 L.Ed.2d 659, concerning the federal "matching funds" program for Presidential candidates, "It cannot be gainsaid that public financing as a means of eliminating improper influence of large private contributions furthers a significant governmental interest. In addition, the limits on contributions necessarily increase the burden of fundraising, and Congress properly regarded public financing as an appropriate means of relieving major-party Presidential candidates from the rigors of soliciting private contributions."

The Court of Appeal below agreed: "[T]he use of public funds for campaign financing will not, almost by definition, have a corrupting influence. [Instead] * * * it seems obvious that public money reduces rather than increases the fund raising pressures on public office seekers and thereby reduces the undue influence of special interest groups. * * * [Moreover], the goals of campaign reform and reduction of election costs, including the reduction of the influence of special interest groups and large contributors, is in no way embarrassed by public financing. To the contrary, those goals can only be furthered. * * *"

For all of the above reasons, we conclude section 85300 is not reasonably related to the statewide concern of enhancing the integrity of the electoral process. Having reached this conclusion, we need not address whether the statute is also narrowly tailored to avoid unnecessary incursion into legitimate areas of local concern. * * * The judgment of the Court of Appeal is affirmed. * * *

3. STATE CONSTITUTIONAL PROHIBITIONS AGAINST LOCAL OR SPECIAL LEGISLATION

Most state constitutions include a specific provision prohibiting the enactment of "local" or "special" legislation. These provisions, like state constitutional protections for home rule, were first adopted in the nineteenth century as part of the political effort to restrict state power over cities. Despite the wide variety of forms these constitutional restrictions on local legislation have taken, all of them seem based on the belief that general legislation, rather than legislation aimed at specific cities, will curb state interference in city affairs. States, however, clearly have a legitimate interest in enacting legislation designed to solve problems found only in particular areas of the state; not every state law can appropriately be applied state-wide. The courts, therefore, have repeatedly had to determine when, in light of the constitutional prohibitions against special legislation, legislation limited to a specific category of cities is reasonable. The cases included in this section explore the difficulty of making this determination. The first two cases present contrasting understandings not only of the definition of special legislation but also of the relationship between the state constitutional prohibition against special legislation and the state (and federal) constitutional requirement of equal protection of the law. Is it helpful to think of the prohibition against special legislation as an aspect of anti-discrimination law?

The final case in this section—Powers v. Secretary of Administration—upheld the constitutionality of a state statute that substituted a state-appointed official for the elected Mayor of Chelsea, Massachusetts. According to the opinion, neither the prohibition against special legislation nor the grant of home rule protected Chelsea from this exercise of state power. Do you think that a state takeover of city hall should be permissible? What is the relationship between the difficulty in restricting state power to pass special legislation and the problem of defining an area of city home rule immune from state control?[1]

CHICAGO NATIONAL LEAGUE BALL CLUB, INC. v. THOMPSON

Supreme Court of Illinois, 1985.
108 Ill.2d 357, 91 Ill.Dec. 610, 483 N.E.2d 1245.

WARD, JUSTICE.

The Chicago National League Ball Club, Inc., is a corporation which owns and operates the Chicago Cubs, the major league baseball team, and the Cubs' home ball park, Wrigley Field. On December 19, 1984, the corporation (the Cubs) filed a complaint in the circuit court of Cook County seeking a declaratory judgment that a 1982 amendment to the Environmental Protection Act and a Chicago city ordinance violate the * * * equal protection and the special-legislation clause[s] of the Constitution of Illinois. * * * The statute, which amends title VI, section 25, of the Environmental Protection Act, provides:

> "The [Pollution Control] Board shall, by regulations under this Section, categorize the types and sources of noise emissions that unreasonably interfere with the enjoyment of life, or with any lawful business, or activity, and shall prescribe for each such category the maximum permissible limits on such noise emissions. * * *

> No Board standards for monitoring noise or regulations prescribing limitations on noise emissions shall apply to any organized amateur or professional sporting activity except as otherwise provided in this Section. Baseball, football or soccer sporting events played during nighttime hours, by professional athletes, in a city with more than

---

1. For an analysis of constitutional restrictions on special legislation, see, e.g., 1 Sands & Libonati, Local Government Law, Chapter 3 (1993); 2 McQuillin, Municipal Corporations, Chapter 4 (3d ed. 1979); Gillette, Expropriation and Institutional Design in State and Local Government Law, 80 Va.L.Rev. 625, 642–657 (1994); Clark, State Control of Local Government in Kansas; Special Legislation and Home Rule, 20 Kan.L.Rev. 631 (1972); Winters, Classification of Municipalities, 57 Nw.U.L.Rev. 279 (1962).

1,000,000 inhabitants, in a stadium at which such nighttime events were not played prior to July 1, 1982, shall be subject to nighttime noise emission regulations promulgated by the Illinois Pollution Control Board."

The provisions of the Chicago ordinance are:

"It shall be unlawful for any * * * person * * * to * * * present any athletic contest * * * if any part of such athletic contest * * * takes place between the hours of 8:00 p.m. and 8:00 a.m., and is presented in a stadium or playing field which is not totally enclosed and contains more than 15,000 seats where any such seats are located within 500 feet of 100 or more dwelling units."

The Cubs challenge the constitutionality of the statute, apparently considering that night baseball games at Wrigley Field would violate the nighttime-noise-emission regulations of the Pollution Control Board. * * * The parties * * * are agreed that the ordinance would have the effect of prohibiting night games at Wrigley Field. Wrigley Field is located on the north side of Chicago in the Lake View area. * * * It is an open-air ball park with a seating capacity of slightly over 37,000, and it is the only park in the major leagues that, because it does not have lights, does not have night games. * * * The area surrounding Wrigley Field is predominately residential, with some light industry to the south and west of the ball park. Most of the buildings in the area are multi-unit dwellings, which gives Lake View a highly concentrated population. There are no expressways in close proximity to Wrigley Field to accommodate the influx of spectators on days when games are played at the field, and there are few off-street parking facilities in the area. In general, only the neighborhood streets are available for parking. * * *

[T]he Cubs contend that Wrigley Field is the only stadium affected by the statute and ordinance, and therefore [that] the enactments violate the State and Federal equal protection clauses and the provision of the Constitution of Illinois prohibiting special legislation. * * * To be constitutional, the Cubs argue, the enactments would have to apply equally to all stadia in the State and not have exclusive application to Wrigley Field. But, of course, the equal protection clauses of our constitution and of the Constitution of the United States do not require uniform treatment in legislative classifications for all persons. That other stadia in the State might have been, but were not, affected by the legislation is not decisive on whether the legislation was intended to apply to Wrigley Field only, particularly when any stadia constructed in the future will have to comply with the legislation. The legislature need not choose between legislating against all evils of the same kind or not legislating at all. Instead it may choose to address itself to what it perceives to be the most acute need. * * *

The provision in the Constitution of Illinois prohibiting special legislation states: "The General Assembly shall pass no special or local law when a general law is or can be made applicable. Whether a general law is or can be made applicable shall be a matter of judicial determination."   Special legislation confers a special benefit or privilege on a person or group of persons to the exclusion of others similarly situated. It discriminates in favor of a select group without a sound, reasonable basis.   A denial of equal protection, on the other hand, is different.   It is an arbitrary and invidious discrimination that results when government withholds from a person or class of persons a right, benefit or privilege without a reasonable basis for the governmental action.   Legislation which confers a benefit on one class and denies the same to another may be attacked both as special legislation and as a denial of equal protection, but under either ground for challenge it is the duty of courts to decide whether classifications are unreasonable.   Though the constitutional protections involved are not identical, a claim that the special-legislation provision has been violated is generally judged by the same standard that is used in considering a claim that equal protection has been denied.

Unless legislation operates to the disadvantage of a suspect classification or infringes upon a fundamental right, the legislation, to be upheld as constitutional, must simply bear a rational relationship to a legitimate governmental interest.   * * * There is a presumption in favor of the validity of any legislation, including of course a legislative act enacted under the police power.   The burden of showing legislation to be an unreasonable exercise of the police power is on the party challenging it.   When a classification under a statute is called into question, if any state of facts can reasonably be conceived to sustain the classification, the existence of that state of facts at the time the statute was enacted must be assumed.

The declared purpose of title VI of the Environmental Protection Act is "to prevent noise which creates a public nuisance." * * * The purpose of * * * [the] amendment to the Act was to protect, within the comprehensive regulatory scheme, the property and other rights of residents who live near stadia by making the nighttime use of the stadia subject to the regulations of the Pollution Control Board.   * * * Only stadia in cities with more than one million inhabitants are subject to the regulations.   Chicago is the only city in our State that has a population of more than one million.   A legislative classification based upon population will be sustained "where founded on a rational difference of situation or condition existing in the persons or objects upon which [the classification] rests and there is a reasonable basis for the classification in view of the objects and purposes to be accomplished." (*People v. Palkes* (1972), 52 Ill. 2d 472, 477, 288 N.E.2d 469.)   Considering the terms of this amendment, there is a rationally founded difference between a less populous city and a city with a greater population.   It might be reasonably anticipated that in a typical urban setting more people would be affected in the larger city by the noise from spectators in a stadium for a nighttime event.   The problems attending a densely populated area would be exacerbated: limited areas for parking would become overburdened; neighborhood streets would become busier and thus potentially more dangerous to residents of the area and their children; and thoroughfares to and from the area would become more congested. Too, a rational basis may be found in the concern that there would be less open space in an area with a highly concentrated population that could serve as a buffer zone against the noise generated.

The same considerations serve as a proper basis for the distinction made by the legislature between nighttime and daytime sporting events. The General Assembly well might have concluded that the evening hours are traditionally spent in restful and quieter pursuits and should be protected by closer regulation. More residents would be at home during the evening hours, and there are variations in traffic patterns and in police patrol deployment between night and day hours which might have served as reasonable considerations by the legislature in enacting the statute.

The amendment distinguishes between professional and amateur sporting events. Amateur sports generally have shorter seasons than their professional counterparts and often attract fewer spectators. There also is a widely entertained opinion that amateur athletics benefit the public, and the legislature may therefore have decided to limit the applicability of the statute to professional sports, which are profit-oriented enterprises. Finally, a provision exempts stadia where night-time events were held prior to July 1, 1982. A legislature may, if it finds remedial measures necessary, address problems one step at a time. "The legislature may select one phase of one field and apply a remedy there, neglecting the others." (*Williamson v. Lee Optical of Oklahoma, Inc.* (1955), 348 U.S. 483, 489, 75 S.Ct. 461, 465, 99 L.Ed. 563, 573.) We are unwilling to strike down as constitutionally infirm a classification because the legislature may have chosen to regulate expectant interests and not established interests.

An ordinance adopted by the governing body of a city must satisfy the same requirement of reasonableness that is applicable to statutes enacted by the General Assembly. Here the ordinance distinguishes between the hours of use, whether the stadia are open-air or enclosed, the seating capacity of the stadia and the proximity to dwelling units. As we observed earlier in discussing the statute, a regulatory scheme intended to abate public nuisances may reasonably distinguish between the hours of permissible use of land when that use may operate to interfere with property and other rights of the community. The distinction between open-air stadia and enclosed stadia may be rationally based on the different volumes of decibels of noise coming from open and enclosed stadia. The noise from an enclosed stadium is muted and less intrusive on area residents.

The city council established 500 feet as the required distance between a stadium and the nearest dwelling unit. There is, of course, a reasonable relationship between the distance from the source of noise and the effect that the noise will have on the surrounding community. The city council also decided to restrict the ordinance's reach to stadia with seating capacities in excess of 15,000. The noise from smaller stadia with fewer spectators would not have the same intrusive effect on a neighborhood as the noise from larger stadia. The discretion of the council to create legislative classifications includes the authority to set permissible boundaries. The creation of classifications is for the judgment of the legislature, and its amending or modifying is not for courts to decide. * * *

REPUBLIC INVESTMENT FUND I v. TOWN OF SURPRISE

Supreme Court of Arizona, 1990.
166 Ariz. 143, 800 P.2d 1251.

GORDON, CHIEF JUSTICE.

These two cases, consolidated for our review, raise the issue of the constitutionality of the Arizona deannexation law, * * * A.R.S. § 9–471. The municipalities involved in both cases claim the statute is unconstitutional as a prohibited special or local law under Ariz. Const. art. 4, pt. 2, § 19(20), which provides:

> No local or special laws shall be enacted in any of the following cases, that is to say: * * *

20. When a general law can be made applicable. * * *

In 1978 the Town of Surprise annexed territory, pursuant to the then existing version of A.R.S. § 9–471, consisting of a ten-foot wide strip of land surrounding an area of approximately 21 square miles. The annexation effectively created an island of unincorporated land within the town's border. Part of the annexed property was acquired by Republic Investment Fund I in April 1987. Republic Investment subsequently petitioned the superior court to deannex its property from Surprise. Surprise challenged the deannexation statute's constitutionality and the sufficiency of Republic Investment's petition. * * * In the second case before us, Petitioners for Deannexation sought statutory deannexation from the City of Goodyear. Goodyear moved to dismiss the petition to deannex, claiming the law was unconstitutional because, among other reasons, it violated the local or special law prohibition * * *.

In the 1970s and 1980s, a large number of Arizona cities and towns engaged in "strip" annexation. Many municipalities artificially extended their boundaries by annexing long strips of property, sometimes only 10 feet wide. Such annexations had two general purposes: (1) to encompass, without actually incorporating, areas with potentially high tax values; and (2) to thwart neighboring municipalities from encroaching through similar actions. The legislature, in 1985, placed a statewide moratorium on all annexations and revised the annexation laws, making the statutory requirements for annexation more stringent. In recognition of past abuses, the legislature also enacted a provision permitting deannexation if certain conditions were met.

The original proposal for deannexation applied statewide. As subsequently passed, however, the deannexation provisions were significantly narrower in scope:

A. The superior court shall order the deannexation of territory from a city or town *having a population of less than ten thousand persons according to the 1980 United States decennial census within a county having a population in excess of one million two hundred thousand persons according to the 1980 United States decennial census and return the territory to the jurisdiction of the county if all of the following conditions are satisfied:* * * *

(Emphasis added). As enacted, the bill only affected thirteen cities within Maricopa County.

After the Governor signed the bill, it was further amended to provide that deannexation applied only to cities and towns having a population less than eleven thousand according to the last special United States census and required that petitions for deannexation pursuant to the act be filed before September 1, 1987. This resulted in the exclusion of Gilbert from the original list of cities affected and limited the application period to thirteen months. * * *

Goodyear Petitioners for Deannexation claim that the municipalities' complaint is properly characterized as an equal protection, not a special/local law, challenge. * * * This court distinguishes between the equal protection and special/local law provisions of the Arizona Constitution:

Although similar policies are involved, constitutional prohibitions against special legislation serve a purpose distinguishable from equal protection provisions. Equal protection is denied when the state unreasonably discriminates *against* a person or class. Prohibited special legislation, on the other hand, unreasonably and arbitrarily discriminates *in favor of* a person or class by granting them a special or exclusive immunity, privilege, or franchise.

Arizona Downs v. Arizona Horsemen's Foundation, 130 Ariz. 550, 557, 637 P.2d 1053, 1060 (1981) (emphasis in original). A statute may be challenged under each provision individually.

The deannexation statute clearly is intended to remedy problems arising from the abusive annexation practices. However, because the statute is limited in application to 12 small cities and towns in Maricopa County, it not only discriminates against those small municipalities, but also discriminates *in favor* of larger municipalities in Maricopa County, as well as all cities and towns in other counties. On its factual basis alone, therefore, the statute could be attacked as both violative of equal protection and as unconstitutional special legislation because it denies a benefit to one class while conferring a benefit on another. * * *

A statute may withstand equal protection review, yet still be found unconstitutional under the special/local law provision. A different and heightened standard of review is necessary because the two provisions were promulgated to address different evils. Our constitution's framers were well aware of the dangers inherent in special legislation. By including proscriptions against special laws, they sought to avoid the evils created by a patchwork type of legal system where some laws applied in a few locations while others applied elsewhere. The legislature may classify, but it cannot make a classification based on a decision that a law should apply to a particular individual or group. Rather, the legislature must enact laws that apply to all individuals who may benefit from its attempt to remedy a particular evil. Accordingly, we consistently review challenges under the equal protection and special/local law provisions separately. * * *

Although the constitutional analysis under both provisions begins in the same manner, the analysis under the special/local law provision encompasses more than an assessment of the statute's rational relationship to a legitimate legislative purpose. * * * To be general, a law need not operate on every person, place, or thing within the state; however, it must apply uniformly to all cases and to all members within the circumstances provided for by the law. In other words, it must * * * encompass a legitimate classification by population, geography, or time limitations. A law may be general and still apply to only one entity, if that entity is the only member of a legitimate class. *See generally* 2 E. McQuillin, [*The Law of Municipal Corporations*], § 4.44, at 109 [(3rd ed. 1988)] ("[A] general law may operate only in a particular county and only affect a small group of persons at the time of its enactment.... [T]he statute must apply equally to all in a similar situation coming within its scope."). * * *

A statute is special or local if it is worded such that its scope is limited to a particular case and it "looks to no broader application in the future." To be general, the classification must be elastic, or open, not only to admit entry of additional persons, places, or things attaining the requisite characteristics, but also to enable others to exit the statute's coverage when they no longer have those characteristics. * * * A statute worded so as to admit entry and exit from the class implies that the class formation was separate from consideration of particular persons, places, or things and, thus, not intended as special or local in operation. Although the number in the class is not determinative, as that number decreases in size, courts are more likely to find the classification invalid. A classification limited to a population as of a particular census or date is a typical form of defective closed class; such an act is a form of identification, not of classification, because it is impossible for entities to enter or exit the class with changes in population. To decide whether a statute legitimately classifies, we will consider the actual probability that others will come under the act's operation when the population changes. Where the prospect is only theoretical, and not probable, we will find the act special or local in nature.

Applying these standards to the deannexation statute, we * * * hold that the statute is a special or local law. Although the statute may be rationally related to a legitimate legislative objective, thus satisfying the equal protection test, the statute does not meet the remaining two special/local law standards.

As Division One noted, "the legislature might rationally perceive that areas annexed by small cities (population under 11,000) may have greater cause to deannex than those annexed to larger cities because of the smaller cities' inability to provide services." However, even if a rational basis exists, the deannexation statute is a special/local law. The statute was enacted in response to the abuse of the municipalities' power to strip annex. On that basis, the class affected by the statute should include all cities where annexation abuses may have occurred. Because the statute applies to only 12 cities within Maricopa County, it does not apply uniformly to all members of the class. Instead, the statute confers a benefit only on part of the class while immunizing larger cities in Maricopa County and all other similarly situated cities in other counties. Moreover, the statute's focus, limited to a particular census for only 13 months, prevents any municipality from either coming within or exiting from its operation in the future. Because a general law would have provided a remedy to individuals in all areas annexed by large or small cities within the state, as indicated by the original bill, the statute's limited application violates the special law prohibition.

The statute is not elastic, excludes similarly situated members of the class, and a general law could be made applicable. The deannexation statute, therefore, violates Ariz. Const. art. 4, pt. 2, § 19(20). * * *

POWERS v. SECRETARY OF ADMINISTRATION

Supreme Judicial Court of Massachusetts, 1992.
412 Mass. 119, 587 N.E.2d 744.

LIACOS, CHIEF JUSTICE.

On September 11, 1991, in response to a recommendation from the Governor, the Senate and the House of Representatives each passed * * * "An Act establishing a receivership for the city of Chelsea" (Receivership Act). The Receivership Act provided, inter alia, that: (1) a "fiscal crisis" existed in Chelsea; (2) a receivership must be established and a receiver appointed by the Governor to an initial one year term "[i]n order to institute a comprehensive long-term solution to [Chelsea's] financial problems"; (3) "[the] receiver shall be the chief executive officer of [Chelsea] and shall be responsible for the overall operation and administration of [Chelsea]"; (4) the office of the mayor of Chelsea shall be vacated and shall remain vacant during the term of the receivership; (5) the Chelsea "board of aldermen shall be vested only with the power to advise [the] receiver concerning matters previously within its jurisdiction under the [Chelsea] charter"; (6) the receiver shall be vested with all powers previously vested in the office of the mayor, as well as additional enumerated powers; and (7) the receiver shall report to the Secretary of Administration (Secretary), who "shall have authority to reappoint the receiver for additional one-year terms * * * [and] may also terminate the receiver for cause at any time." On September 12, 1991, the Governor signed the Receivership Act, the provisions of which became effective upon passage, and appointed a receiver for Chelsea.

On September 17, 1991, the plaintiffs, citizens of and homeowners in Chelsea, filed a complaint with the Supreme Judicial Court for the county of Suffolk alleging that * * * the Receivership Act was passed in violation of art. 89 of the Amendments to the Constitution of the Commonwealth, more commonly known as the Home Rule Amendment. Specifically, the plaintiffs argue that: (a) the Senate and the House failed to meet the procedural requirements of § 8 of the Home Rule Amendment in passing the Receivership Act; and (b) the provisions of the Receivership Act conflict with the intention of the Home Rule Amendment as expressed in § 1 of the amendment. * * *

As this court previously has noted, § 8 of the Home Rule Amendment, which limits the circumstances under which the Legislature can pass "special laws" which apply to only one particular city or town, "clearly evidenc[es] a concern that no city or town be singled out for special treatment." *Doris v. Police Comm'r of Boston*, 374 Mass. 443, 446, 373 N.E.2d 944 (1978). Accordingly, § 8 provides that, in the absence of explicitly defined special circumstances, the Legislature has the authority to "act in relation to cities and towns * * * only by general laws which apply alike to all cities or to all towns, or to all cities and towns, or to a class of not fewer than two." To the extent that the Legislature wants to pass a "special law," § 8 provides four separate procedures * * *. The parties do not dispute that the only § 8 procedure in issue before us is that procedure which provides the Legislature may pass a special law "by a two-thirds vote of each branch of the general court following a recommendation by the governor." * * * [T]he parties stipulate that "[e]ach branch of the Legislature passed the Act by a two-thirds vote." * * * The plaintiffs, however, point to the parties' additional stipulation that the Receivership Act was passed on a "voice vote" in both the Senate and the House. * * * [W]e reject the plaintiffs' contention that a voice vote does not meet the requirements of § 8. * * *

The plaintiffs also claim that the Receivership Act violates § 1 of the Home Rule Amendment, which is set forth in the margin.[8] * * * To the extent that the plaintiffs intend to argue that the Receivership Act violates the underlying purpose of the Home Rule Amendment because the act removed from the city's elected officials the authority to address Chelsea's fiscal crisis and vested it in an appointed receiver, this argument is without merit. This court has recognized in previous decisions that the Home Rule Amendment grants the Legislature extensive authority over municipal government. In *Arlington v. Board of Concilia-*

---

8. "It is the intention of this article to reaffirm the customary and traditional liberties of the people with respect to the conduct of their local government, and to grant and confirm to the people of every city and town the right of self-government in local matters, subject to the provisions of this article and to such standards and requirements as the general court may establish by law in accordance with the provisions of this article." Art. 89, § 1.

tion & Arbitration, 370 Mass. 769, 773, 352 N.E.2d 914 (1976) (1976), we stated that:

> "[Previous decisions of this court] and the text of art. 89 itself indicate that, while the scope of the authority granted to municipalities to act on municipal problems is very broad, the scope of the disability imposed on the Legislature by the amendment is quite narrow. Section 6 of the amendment, while providing the broad grant of governmental powers referred to above, *limits the municipal exercise of those powers to acts which are 'not inconsistent with the constitution or laws enacted by the general court in conformity with powers reserved to the general court by section eight' " (emphasis added).*

Section 1 prevents a municipality from exercising powers in a manner that is inconsistent with "such standards and requirements as the general court may establish by law in accordance with the provisions of [the Home Rule Amendment.]" We have held that the Receivership Act was passed in accordance with § 8. Therefore, to the extent that there was a conflict between exercise of the authority granted to the receiver and the authority held by Chelsea's elected government, § 1 required that the elected government give way. The Receivership Act does not conflict with § 1 of the Home Rule Amendment. * * *

The plaintiffs argue that the appointment of a receiver violates the "one person, one vote" rule of the equal protection clause of the Fourteenth Amendment to the United States Constitution because their "constitutional right" to elect their municipal officials has been ignored. This argument is without merit.

The plaintiffs have not referred us to any State or Federal constitutional provision to support their claim that they have a constitutional right to elective municipal officials, nor can we find one. As this court previously has held, the Home Rule Amendment recognizes the Legislature's broad authority over municipalities. This authority includes the power to choose to provide an appointive, rather than elective, form of municipal government. *Opinion of the Justices*, 368 Mass. 849, 854, 332 N.E.2d 896 (1975). Accordingly, "there is no [State] constitutional impediment to the creation of appointive rather than elective municipal offices." *Id.* With regard to Federal constitutional impediments to an appointive municipal government, the United States Supreme Court has stated that "[w]e see nothing in the [Federal] Constitution to prevent experimentation. At least as respects nonlegislative officers, a State can appoint local officials or elect them or combine the elective and appointive systems." *Sailors v. Board of Educ. of the County of Kent*, 387 U.S. 105, 111, 87 S.Ct. 1549, 1553, 18 L.Ed.2d 650 (1967). Because the plaintiffs do not have a constitutional right to an elective form of municipal government, and because the Legislature has chosen to provide Chelsea with an appointed receiver, the "one person, one vote" rule is inapplicable to the present case. * * *

4. STATE PREEMPTION OF LOCAL LAWS

In the absence of state constitutional provisions to the contrary (such as home rule or the prohibition against special legislation), states have the power to modify or reverse any city decision. In any particular case, however, it is necessary to decide whether a state has exercised this power. Even though the state and a city have adopted different policies to deal with the same problem, it doesn't necessarily follow that the state has forbidden local decisionmaking on the issue. Both state and local policies might be able to be pursued simultaneously. Determining whether they can be is the task of the doctrine of preemption. This section investigates *state* preemption of local laws; the related issue of federal preemption is covered below in Section B.

According to the doctrine of state preemption, state law prevails if there is a direct conflict between state and local law. Even if there is no direct conflict, a state law will still preempt a local law if state policy is interpreted to forbid local legislation of any kind (in the language of the preemption doctrine, the issue is whether the state intended "to occupy the field"). A state's silence on an issue can itself be interpreted to mean that no local legislation of any kind is permitted.[1]

In the first preemption case that follows, the state was found to have preempted the local law; in the second, it was found not to have preempted the local law. How did the courts decide whether a local law could be stricter than a state law? In explaining the result in these cases, how important are the different attitudes toward decentralization canvassed in Chapter One? How important are the facts of the cases?

ILC DATA DEVICE CORP. v. COUNTY OF SUFFOLK

New York Supreme Court, Appellate Division, 1992.
182 A.D.2d 293, 588 N.Y.S.2d 845, appeal denied, 81 N.Y.2d
952, 597 N.Y.S.2d 933, 613 N.E.2d 965 (1993).

SULLIVAN, JUSTICE PRESIDING. * * *

After conducting a series of public hearings and reviewing extensive testimonial and documentary submissions, the Suffolk County Legislature enacted Local Laws, 1988, No. 21 of the County of Suffolk (hereinafter Local Law No. 21), entitled "A local law providing employee protection against video display terminals". * * * Local Law No. 21 requires that those employers operating 20 or more VDTs in the County meet certain workplace standards, *inter alia*, for light, noise levels, and seating comfort for their employees who are VDT operators. Additionally, the law affords VDT operators the opportunity to have an annual eye examination and to receive corrective lenses necessitated by VDT usage,

---

1. For an analysis of preemption, see, e.g., Martin, Preemption in the Age of Local Regulatory Innovation: Fitting the Formula to a Different Kind of Conflict, 70 Tex. L.Rev. 1831 (1992); Hoke, Preemption Pathologies and Republican Values, 71 B.U.L.Rev. 685 (1992); Note, A Framework for Preemption Analysis, 88 Yale L.J. 363 (1978); Note, Conflict Between State Statutes and Municipal Ordinances, 72 Harv. L.Rev. 737 (1959).

with 80% of the cost therefor to be borne by the employer. Moreover, the legislation expressly authorizes the Commissioner of the Suffolk County Department of Health Services to promulgate regulations governing the inspection of employer premises and the enforcement of the Local Law.

By service of a summons and complaint dated July 20, 1988, the plaintiffs, corporations which claimed that they would be adversely affected by the provisions of Local Law No. 21, commenced the instant action against the defendant County of Suffolk * * *. The plaintiffs * * * maintain that Local Law No. 21 is inconsistent with and preempted by a host of Federal and State enactments, chief among these the New York State Labor Law. * * * In *Jancyn Mfg. Corp. v. County of Suffolk* (71 N.Y.2d 91, 96–97, 524 N.Y.S.2d 8, 518 N.E.2d 903), the Court of Appeals identified the parameters of the legislative authority conferred upon local governments and explained the related concepts of inconsistency and preemption as follows:

> "although the constitutional home rule provision confers broad police powers upon local governments relating to the welfare of [their] citizens, local governments may not exercise their police power by adopting a law inconsistent with the Constitution or any general law of the State. A local law may be ruled invalid as inconsistent with State law not only where an express conflict exists between the State and local laws, but also where the State has clearly evinced a desire to preempt an entire field thereby precluding any further local regulation. Where it is determined that the State has preempted an entire field, a local law regulating the same subject matter is deemed inconsistent with the State's overriding interests because it either (1) prohibits conduct which the State law, although perhaps not expressly speaking to, considers acceptable or at least does not proscribe or (2) imposes additional restrictions on rights granted by State law. Such laws, were they permitted to operate in a field preempted by State law, would tend to inhibit the operation of the State's general law and thereby thwart the operation of the State's overriding policy concerns."

Applying the foregoing principles to the matter before us, we find that Local Law No. 21 is "inconsistent" with a general law of the State because it constitutes an attempt to regulate in a field preempted by the Labor Law. Any express conflict between Local Law No. 21 and a specific provision of the Labor Law is largely obviated by the fact that there are no State-wide statutory or regulatory provisions governing the use of VDTs in the workplace. Nevertheless, it is well settled that inconsistency may be found, even in the absence of an express conflict, where the State Legislature has evinced a desire to preempt a given field and thereby to prohibit local regulation of the entire area. The intent to occupy an entire field of regulation need not be express. Rather, "that desire may be inferred from a declaration of State policy by the Legislature or from the legislative enactment of a comprehensive and detailed regulatory scheme in a particular area" (*New York State Club Assn. v.*

City of New York, 69 N.Y.2d 211, 217, 513 N.Y.S.2d 349, 505 N.E.2d 915 *aff'd*, 487 U.S. 1, 108 S.Ct. 2225, 101 L.Ed.2d 1). In the present case, the enacting of the comprehensive regulatory scheme embodied in the Labor Law and the vesting of broad rule-making and enforcement authority in the Commissioner of Labor of the State of New York (hereinafter the Commissioner) lead us to conclude that the State Legislature intended to preclude local regulation in the field of employee safety in the workplace.

The general powers and duties of the Commissioner, including the expansive authority to engage in inspections, investigations, and enforcement with regard to, *inter alia*, workplace safety and health, are set forth in Labor Law § 21. A desire on the part of the Legislature to foster a direct and cooperative relationship between the Commissioner, as a State officer, and individual employers and employees is discernible from the language of Labor Law § 21(5) and (6), which provide that the Commissioner * * * "[s]hall institute methods and procedures for the establishment of a program for voluntary compliance by employers and employees with the requirements of this act" * * * [and] "provide a method of encouraging employers and employees in their efforts to reduce the number of safety and health hazards * * *." Consistent with the foregoing duties, the Commissioner has the authority to establish and maintain local "branch offices" of the Department of Labor in such locations as he may determine, thereby facilitating the application of State-wide regulation by State officials at the local level. * * *

Furthermore, to the extent that it is not preempted by the United States Occupational Safety and Health Act of 1970, Labor Law § 27 regulates the adoption, implementation, and enforcement of safety and health standards for private employees in New York. That statute expressly authorizes the Commissioner to adopt "safety and health standards which provide reasonable and adequate protection to the lives, safety or health of employees", to require licenses and to establish a licensing fee schedule for any occupation "which the Commissioner finds contains special elements of danger to the lives, safety or health" of such employees, and to "promulgate such regulations as he shall consider necessary and proper to effectuate the purposes and provisions of this section". * * * Additionally, the State Legislature has provided the Commissioner with the authority to make, amend, and terminate "variations" from health and safety standards upon a showing of practical difficulties or unnecessary hardship, to inspect physical premises and books and records and to issue subpoenas and conduct hearings. The Labor Law and the regulations promulgated thereunder similarly set forth comprehensive procedures for administrative and judicial review, govern the employment of minors in the workplace, control work hours and wages and authorize the Commissioner to identify and ameliorate dangers in machinery and equipment.

The foregoing statutes, regulations, and legislative memorandum strongly suggest that the State Legislature intended the field of workplace safety to be exclusively occupied by the Labor Law to the extent that it is not already regulated by the Federal Occupational Safety and Health Act of 1970. In effect, the regulatory scheme set up by the Labor Law with regard to the subject of employee health and safety is so comprehensive and detailed as to render Local Law No. 21 "inconsistent" with State law under New York Constitution. * * *

The County * * * claims that it has the authority to regulate the operation of VDTs within its borders because the Labor Law is silent on this specific subject. It also contends that a finding of inconsistency cannot be premised on the mere fact that the State law and local law attempt to regulate the same general subject matter (i.e., employee safety in the workplace). These contentions are not without some support. Indeed, "silence on [an] issue should not be interpreted as an expression of intent by the Legislature. To interpret a statute in that manner would vitiate the concept of home rule; anytime a State is silent the likelihood exists that a local law will regulate the activity and will prohibit something permitted elsewhere in the State" (*Council For Owner Occupied Housing v. Koch*, 119 Misc.2d 241, 245, 462 N.Y.S.2d 762, *aff'd*. 61 N.Y.2d 942, 475 N.Y.S.2d 279, 463 N.W.2d 620). * * * However, where the State law preempts a particular field, such as the field of employee safety in this case, "a local law regulating the same subject matter is deemed inconsistent with the State's overriding interests because it * * * prohibits conduct which the State law, although perhaps not expressly speaking to, considers acceptable or at least does not proscribe" (*Jancyn Mfg. Corp. v. County of Suffolk*, 71 N.Y.2d 91, 97, 524 N.Y.S.2d 8, 518 N.E.2d 903, *supra*). Inasmuch as the Labor Law preempts the field of workplace safety, it permits, by reason of its silence on the subject, the operation of VDTs without any special regulations or safeguards. Hence, Local Law No. 21 impermissibly prohibits what the State law permits by providing that the use of VDTs must be accompanied by a panoply of safeguards which neither the State Legislature nor the Commissioner of Labor has seen fit to enact. * * *

Local Law No. 21 improperly attempts to add another layer of regulation in an area where comprehensive and detailed regulations already exist at the State level, and its enforcement "would tend to inhibit the operation of the State's general law and thereby thwart the operation of the State's overriding policy concerns" (*Jancyn Mfg. Corp. v. County of Suffolk*, 71 N.Y.2d 91, 97, 524 N.Y.S.2d 8, 518 N.E.2d 903, *supra*). Indeed, the insertion of local regulation into this field would certainly appear to inhibit the desirable goal, among others, of fostering a direct and cooperative relationship between New York State Department of Labor officials and employers (see, Labor Law § 21[5], [6]). Under these circumstances, the very nature of the field of employee safety in the workplace, and the comprehensive State regulatory scheme governing it, dictate that controls over workplace safety and health continue to be approached on a uniform, State-wide basis. Although Local Law No. 21 is undoubtedly well-intentioned and demonstrates laudable concern for employee safety, it cannot stand in view of our finding of State preemption. * * *

CITY OF PORTLAND v. JACKSON

Supreme Court of Oregon, 1993.
316 Or. 143, 850 P.2d 1093.

PETERSON, JUSTICE.

The issue in this case is this: When a state statute that forbids public exposure of genitalia has as an element "the *intent* of arousing the sexual desire of the person or another person," and a defendant is prosecuted under a city ordinance that forbids public exposure of genitalia, regardless of the defendant's culpable mental state, is the city ordinance in conflict with the statute and therefore invalid under the "home rule" provision of the Oregon Constitution, Article XI, section 2? We hold that the city ordinance is not invalid. * * *

In 1906, Article XI, section 2, and Article IV, section 1a (now section 1(5)), of the Oregon Constitution were added in order to provide "home rule" for cities and towns. For our purposes, we are concerned with Article XI, section 2, which in part provides:

> "The Legislative Assembly shall not enact, amend or repeal any charter or act of incorporation for any municipality, city or town. The legal voters of every city and town are hereby granted power to enact and amend their municipal charter, *subject to the Constitution and criminal laws of the State of Oregon * * *.*" (Emphasis added.)

Article XI, section 2, has long been interpreted to prohibit local governments from enacting legislation that conflicts with state criminal laws. * * * Local governments thus are barred from, *e.g.*, creating a "safe haven" for outlaws by legalizing, within the boundaries of the city, that which the legislature has made criminal statewide. This case, defendant claims, involves the converse of the foregoing scenario; here, a city ordinance is alleged to be "in conflict with" a state statute because the ordinance forbids conduct that, according to defendant, state law permits. We turn to that question.

The "not in conflict" interpretation of Article XI, section 2, was used by this court recently in *City of Portland v. Dollarhide*, 300 Or. 490, 714 P.2d 220 (1986). * * * The *Dollarhide* court stated a method for determining whether a criminal ordinance and statute are in conflict * * *. Under the *Dollarhide* test, if a statute *permits* conduct that an ordinance *prohibits*, the two laws are in conflict.

Statutes defining crimes normally are not written in terms of permitted conduct; they normally are written to prohibit conduct. If the criminal statutes of Oregon are interpreted to permit all conduct not prohibited, the interpretation would swallow Article XI, section 2, for it would bar all local governments from legislation in the area of criminal law unless the local legislation was identical to its state counterpart. The question, then, is one not asked or answered in *Dollarhide*: How does one determine whether a state law *permits* that which an ordinance prohibits? This question may be answered in several ways.

1.   The legislature expressly could occupy an entire field of legislation on a subject, and expressly preclude local legislation on the subject.   * * *

2.   The legislature could expressly permit specified *conduct*. *See, e.g.*, ORS 166.370(2)(d) (persons with a permit to carry a concealed handgun cannot be prosecuted for possessing a firearm in a public building).   By implication, local governments could not criminalize the specified conduct.

3.   The legislature could otherwise manifest its intent to permit specified *conduct*.   By implication, local governments could not prohibit the specified conduct.

City of Portland v. Lodi, 308 Or. 468, 474, 782 P.2d 415 (1989), is illustrative of legislative permission by implication.   In *Lodi*, a city ordinance prohibited the carrying of a pocketknife with a blade beyond a certain length.   The legislature had enacted a statute concerning concealed weapons.   The legislative history revealed that an earlier draft of the proposed law had listed as a dangerous weapon "any knife other than a pocketknife," along with a switchblade, dirk, or dagger.   A legislative subcommittee later amended the bill by removing all reference to knives other than switchblades, dirks, or daggers.   The *Lodi* court held that, because the legislative history showed that a decision had been made to permit the concealed carrying of any knife not a switchblade, dirk, or dagger, the city ordinance *prohibited* conduct that the legislature intended to *permit*, and the ordinance was displaced by the state statute. "The search is not for particular words but for a political decision, for what the state's lawmakers either did or considered and chose not to do."   *Id.* at 474, 782 P.2d 415.

Neither *Dollarhide* nor *Lodi* addressed the situation in which the statute and its legislative history are silent or unclear as to whether a decision to "permit" conduct has been made.   * * * [In] *Dollarhide* * * * [t]he court * * * stated that it is "reasonable to assume that the legislature does not mean to displace local civil or administrative regulation of local conditions by a statewide law unless that intention is apparent."   In a footnote, the court then stated the *dictum* that "[the] reservation in article XI, section 2, *supra*, regarding state criminal law reverses this assumption with respect to such laws."   That passage could be interpreted in the present case to mean that, if the legislature has not made a clear decision to permit *conduct* that an ordinance prohibits, we should nevertheless "assume" that the legislature intended to permit that conduct, and thus also "assume" that the ordinance is displaced by the statute.

We disavow such an interpretation.   * * * The people of Oregon, by amending Article XI, section 2, gave to the people of a municipality (acting through their local government) the right to pass laws, and restrict their own individual freedom and the freedom of others within their jurisdiction, subject only to the "Constitution and the criminal laws of the State of Oregon."   We cannot simply "assume" that, *by its silence,* the legislature intended to *permit* conduct made punishable under an ordinance. The state constitutional rights granted to the citizens of a municipality are not so easily discarded. When a local criminal ordinance prohibits conduct, unless the legislature has permitted that same conduct, either expressly or under circumstances in which the legislative intent to permit that conduct is otherwise apparent, the ordinance is not in conflict with state criminal law and is valid under Article XI, section 2, of the Oregon Constitution. * * *

We turn, then, to the ordinance and statutes at issue here. * * * Defendant was charged with "indecent exposure" under PCC § 14.24.-060, which provides:

> "It is unlawful for any person to expose his or her genitalia while in a public place or place visible from a public place, if the public place is open or available to persons of the opposite sex."

Defendant claims that the ordinance is in conflict with the state "public indecency" statute, ORS 163.465, which provides in part:

> "(1) A person commits the crime of public indecency if while in, or in view of, a public place the person performs: * * *

> "(c) An act of exposing the genitals of the person with the intent of arousing the sexual desire of the person or another person." * * *

[T]he Oregon legislature * * * has not, by legislation, expressly permitted public exposure of genitalia occurring without an intent to arouse. We examine the legislative history to see whether it has otherwise manifested its intent to allow such conduct.

In 1971, the legislature enacted ORS 163.465 and repealed *former* ORS 167.145, an "indecent exposure" statute, which had remained essentially unchanged since 1864. Arguably, *former* ORS 167.145 prohibited sexually motivated behavior *and* non-sexually motivated behavior. Thus, its repeal and replacement with a law that prohibits only sexually motivated public nudity is evidence that the legislature made a decision to permit non-sexually motivated public nudity. Repeal of a statute may be evidence of a political decision to permit conduct that was previously forbidden.

In the present case, however, *former* ORS 167.145 was *replaced*, and the commentary to its replacement, ORS 163.465, does not indicate that the legislature intended to permit non-sexually motivated public nudity. The commentary states that "[an] exposure that is not sexually motivated would not violate this section, but might be 'disorderly conduct.'" Whether or not public nudity would constitute "disorderly conduct," this commentary is insufficient to demonstrate a legislative political decision to permit non-sexually motivated public nudity. * * * We do not believe that the repeal of *former* ORS 167.145, without more, establishes a legislative political decision to permit non-sexually motivated public nudity. In the absence of stronger evidence of legislative intent, we are unconvinced that the legislature intended to permit the conduct prohibited in the city ordinance. Therefore, city's "indecent exposure" ordinance does not conflict with the state "public indecency" statute, and the ordinance is valid under Article XI, section 2, of the Oregon Constitution. * * *

FADELEY, JUSTICE, dissenting. * * *

This court has determined that under Article XI, section 2, local ordinances, whether civil or criminal, are displaced by "incompatible" state law. * * * This court's opinion in *City of Portland v. Dollarhide* discusses and applies the proper test for assessing the compatibility of a local criminal ordinance with state law (and thus, for assessing the validity of such ordinances). * * *

   " * * * In the area of civil or administrative ordinances regulating local conditions, it is reasonable to assume that the legislature did not mean to displace local ordinances, unless that intention is apparent. *The reservation in Article XI, section 2, however, reverses this assumption with respect to state criminal law.*

   "The analysis of compatibility begins then with the assumption that state criminal law displaces conflicting local ordinances which prohibit and punish the same conduct, absent an apparent legislative intent to the contrary." (emphasis added).

* * * As in *Dollarhide*, we must assume, in the face of a state statute dealing with "indecent exposure," that the state legislature intended to displace the conflicting local ordinance, absent some manifestation of contrary legislative intent. Proponents of the local ordinance have pointed to nothing that suggests any such contrary intent. * * *

That a conflict exists between the Portland indecent exposure ordinance and ORS 163.465 could not be more clear; while exposure of the genitals in a public place without any intent to sexually arouse either oneself or a viewer is lawful or "permissible" under the state criminal law, it is prohibited conduct under the local ordinance. * * *

The majority circumvents this obvious result by interpreting the term "permit" in the *Dollarhide* test as meaning "legislatively authorize," that is, expressly approved by the legislature. This is a test that the great majority of everyday activities taking place within the state could not meet under the civil statutes, let alone in the criminal code. Furthermore, the context and the very structure of the sentence in which the term appears make it clear that the *Dollarhide* court used "permit" in its simplest sense. It was meant to convey only an absence of prohibition—that the conduct under examination is "not prohibited."

By skewing the interpretation of the term to mean "legislatively authorized," the majority turns what was intended as a simple comparison of the elements of a crime into an examination of legislative intent. * * * [T]he majority's proposed test becomes downright disastrous in application because it empowers any home rule city to make any act criminal unless that very act is covered by and also expressly permitted by state criminal law.[2]

Furthermore, the Portland indecent exposure ordinance is invalid even under the majority's erroneous analysis. The majority opinion adverts to the fact that in 1971, the state legislature repealed a long-standing indecent exposure statute which criminalized both sexually motivated and nonsexually motivated exposure and replaced it with the statute that is now in effect, which criminalizes only exposure of genitalia that is sexually motivated. That fact, in itself, would seem to attest to a conscious decision by the legislature to permit uncovering the full body so long as that act of exposure was not intended to arouse sexual desire in another person or the actor. But given that the legislative history also indicates that the legislature affirmatively considered the element of sexual motivation before the present bill was passed, a conclusion that the legislature consciously intended to permit nonsexually motivated nudity seems obligatory. Therefore, even assuming for the sake of argument, that local criminal ordinances prohibiting some conduct are invalidated only when the state has manifested some intent to affirmatively permit the conduct in the sense of consciously repealing or changing its former criminal statutes, the record shows affirmative decriminalization by the state legislature of the conduct that Portland wishes to prohibit in this case. * * *

In the two cases reproduced above, the preemption issue arose because a city sought to regulate a subject more strictly than the state. Another question that might arise is whether a city can ever be more lenient than the state. For example, can a city impose a $5 fine for possession of marijuana even if state law provides a penalty of up to four years in prison, a $2000 fine, or both, for the same offense? For an argument that the answer to this question should be yes, see Note, The Concurrent State and Local Regulation of Marijuana: The Validity of the Ann Arbor Marijuana Ordinance, 71 Mich.L.Rev. 400 (1972).

5. STATE POWER TO ABRIDGE CITIES' FREEDOM OF SPEECH

This section raises a final topic in our examination of the state-city relationship: the extent of the state's ability to abridge cities' freedom of

---

2. Under the majority's analysis, nothing prevents Portland and other Oregon cities from passing criminal ordinances on other subjects to enforce majority attitudes within that given community, such as imposing abortion procedural delays and Saturday bank openings.

The majority assigns to state criminal laws the function of disclosing what human conduct is *permitted* conduct. But those passing such laws traditionally believe, instead, that they are deciding only what conduct is *prohibited*. Looking for what is "permitted" in criminal laws designed and intended to "prohibit" is at best like looking for a needle in a haystack. At worst, it suggests that the people of the state have no personal freedoms of conduct, *vis-a-vis*, city or town government, unless spelled out in the state criminal code.

speech. In recent years, a number of local governments have sought to influence the outcome of local or state-wide referenda on topics ranging from fluoridation of a city's water supply to the reallocation of the burden of local property taxation from homeowners to businesses. The question usually asked with respect to these city campaign efforts is whether local governments should ever be allowed to engage in speech designed to influence the outcome of an election.[1] The predominate answer given to this question has been "no", and state courts have employed a number of the doctrines analyzed in this chapter—such as Dillon's Rule and a finding of state preemption—to curb city speech.[2] Moreover, no federal Constitutional challenge to this form of state control over cities is usually made, presumably because it is assumed that cities, under Hunter v. Pittsburgh, have no federal Constitutional protection from state control. From this perspective, then, state control of city speech simply constitutes one more example of the exercise of state power over cities.

The materials that follow, however, are designed to question this traditional way of dealing with the issue of city speech. They are organized to investigate whether the prohibition of city speech is justifiable given the fact that corporate speech is allowed. The first case, Alabama Libertarian Party v. Birmingham, offers a vigorous (and rare) defense of city speech. The two subsequent cases then provide material on the distinction between city and corporate speech. In Anderson v. City of Boston, the Massachusetts Supreme Judicial Court upheld the state's power to deny Boston the ability to spend money to influence an election despite Boston's claim that this state prohibition of city speech was unconstitutional. In First National Bank of Boston v. Bellotti, on the other hand, the Supreme Court of the United States held that Massachusetts' attempt to limit corporate spending in an election was unconstitutional. To what extent do the arguments made by Justice Powell in *Bellotti* answer the *Anderson* decision's concerns about city speech? To what extent do the *Anderson* decision's concerns about city speech apply to the corporate speech at issue in *Bellotti*? Should both city and corporate speech be allowed? Should both be forbidden? Or does a public/private distinction justify allowing one but not the other? The final case in this section, Austin v. Michigan Chamber of Commerce, suggests that the critical distinction—for corporate speech—is between speech designed to influence voting on candidates and speech designed to influence voting on public issues. Should this distinction be applied to city speech as well? Or is the distinction unpersuasive even for corporations?

---

1. For insightful explorations of this question, see, e.g., Yudof, When Government Speaks: Politics, Law and Government Expression in America (1983); Schauer, Is Government Speech a Prob-lem?, 35 Stan.L.Rev. 373 (1983); Shiffrin, Government Speech, 27 U.C.L.A.L.Rev. 565 (1980).

2. See, e.g., Burt v. Blumenauer, 299 Or. 55, 699 P.2d 168 (1985).

ALABAMA LIBERTARIAN PARTY
v. BIRMINGHAM, ALABAMA

United States District Court, Northern District of Alabama, 1988.
694 F.Supp. 814.

PROPST, DISTRICT JUDGE.   * * *

A special election was held in the City of Birmingham, Alabama (City) on May 12, 1987. The purpose for this election was to submit a proposition to impose a one-half mill property tax for library enhancement and to levy a charge to all telephone subscribers for enhanced 911 emergency telephone service. Before this election, the City launched a promotional campaign to encourage passage of the propositions. This campaign included an advertisement in the Birmingham News on Sunday, May 10, 1987, which read "SAY YES to the Future. SAY YES to our Libraries, SAY YES to Enhanced 911 Service. VOTE YES on May 12! * * * Paid Political Advertisement[3] by the City of Birmingham." Plaintiffs allege that this same advertisement was also broadcast over radio station WERC.

Another special election was held on May 10, 1988 for the purpose of approving a $110,000,000 bond issue. Prior to this election, the City distributed leaflets headed "Build a Better Birmingham—Vote FOR Progress on May 10 * * * Vote FOR the bond issue and funding on May 10! * * * It's a small price to pay for so much progress!" * * * It is plaintiffs' contention that the funds utilized to promote the City's position at these elections came from the City's tax revenues, and that their use constituted a misuse of municipal funds and a violation of plaintiffs' First Amendment rights. By this action, plaintiffs seek to permanently enjoin the City from similar activities in the future, and an accounting and restitution of all expended funds. * * *

The gravamen of plaintiffs' complaint is that the City's expenditures in promoting the passage of the propositions violate their First Amendment rights. The U.S. Supreme Court considered the protection of an individual's right of association in *Abood v. Detroit Board of Education,* 431 U.S. 209, 97 S.Ct. 1782, 52 L.Ed.2d 261 (1977). Therein, the Court discussed whether organizations in which membership is mandatory, may utilize the mandatory dues paid to advance *political* causes opposed by some members. The Court held such a use violated * * * [union] members' First Amendment right of association: * * * "The fact that the appellants are compelled to make, rather than prohibited from making, contributions for political purposes works no less an infringement of their constitutional rights. For at the heart of the First Amendment is the notion that an individual should be free to believe as he will, and that in a free society one's beliefs should be shaped by his mind and his conscience rather than coerced by the State." * * * The Court ultimately held that these principles " * * * prohibit the appellees from requiring any of the appellants to contribute to the support of an

---

3. The fact that the advertisement was labeled as "political" does not necessarily make it so. The term is generally used by the media in connection with such advertisements.

ideological cause he may oppose * * * '' (Emphasis added) *Id.* at 235. The holding did not completely prohibit unions from expending funds for political purposes. "Rather, the Constitution requires only that such expenditures be financed from charges, dues, or assessments paid by employees who do not object to advancing those ideas and who are not coerced into doing so against their will by the threat of loss of governmental employment." *Id.* * * *

The critical distinction between *Abood* and the case *sub judice* is not whether the plaintiffs were compelled to contribute, but whether a portion of plaintiffs' tax funds were expended for "political" and "ideological" purposes. * * * In *Abood,* the Court emphasizes the political and ideological content of the matters at issue. * * * Here, the City leadership has determined to promote a cause consistent with the common needs of its citizens. It is not requiring plaintiffs to be the courier for an ideological or political message.

The Court does not believe that the City's advertising campaign was political or ideological in nature.[6] This was not a case where municipal funds were used to support a particular candidate, doctrine or ideology. Rather, the City merely solicited its citizens to provide funds to supply perceived needs common to all. The City and its officials not only have the right, but the duty, to determine the needs of its citizens and to provide funds to service those needs. The funds must come from some source. The City officials are charged with the responsibility of providing those funds by some means. If they cannot directly tax through ordinance, they have the incidental right to solicit the votes of citizens to provide those means. The City officials had already taken, through the passage of ordinances, public positions on the issues. The advertisements do no more than to publicize the positions they have previously taken.

As noted in *Buckley v. Valeo,* 424 U.S. 1, 90–93, 96 S.Ct. 612, 668–670, 46 L.Ed.2d 659, virtually every public expenditure will "to some extent involve a use of public money as to which some taxpayers may object. Nevertheless, this does not mean that those taxpayers have a constitutionally protected right to enjoin such expenditures." *FCC v. League of Women Voters of Calif.,* 468 U.S. 364, 385 n. 16, 104 S.Ct. 3106, 3120 n. 16, 82 L.Ed.2d 278 (1984). Here, the plaintiffs apparently disagreed with both the advertising expenditures and the expenditures which would have been allowed if the City had been successful at the elections. The question that might be posed is whether the City would have violated the plaintiffs' First Amendment rights if they had expended public funds to lobby the legislature for legislative authority to tax or had proposed constitutional amendments which would have allowed the City to levy taxes in order to provide the needed funds. The City in effect made a finding that the funds were needed and that it should seek

6. The court does not conclude that if the advertising were to be so deemed, that its conclusion would, of necessity, be different.

the support of its citizens in acquiring these funds. This is clearly a public function.

In *FCC, supra* the Court notes a distinction between a ban on political endorsements and a ban on editorial opinion. * * * While defendants might be forbidden to spend funds to support candidates, oppose initiative proposals, etc., they are not forbidden to publicize and seek public support for their own governmental proposals. Alleged First Amendment violations are subject to a content analysis. Defendants' actions pass muster.

Plaintiffs also rely on *District of Columbia Common Cause v. District of Columbia, et al.,* No. 85–3528 (D.C.1986) to support their First Amendment claim. *Common Cause* involved efforts by the District of Columbia to persuade voters to vote against an initiative measure which would require the local government to guarantee overnight shelter for homeless people. The pamphlets and flyers distributed "did not purport to present the pros and cons of the initiative but [were] devoted solely to a presentation of the reasons why D.C. voters should vote against Initiative 17 and an exhortation to Vote No on Initiative 17! * * * " These materials bore the statement "Distributed by the District of Columbia!" The court held that the promotion of only one side of a contested election issue amounted to "a content-based government subsidy" and was therefore violative of the First Amendment rights of D.C. voters. * * *

The *Common Cause* court repeatedly emphasizes that the election was called through an initiative process. The *Common Cause* opinion apparently proceeds on the basis that the District of Columbia had expended funds on behalf of only one of two opposing factions. * * * What is not significantly discussed is that the adoption of the measure "would require the District of Columbia government to guarantee overnight shelter for homeless people." The fact that some citizens would have one view of the subject and other citizens another view, would not appear to necessarily require that the governmental entity whose funds and services would be impacted remain neutral. * * * The *Common Cause* court emphasizes that "the challenged expenditures were made on the basis of *political ideas* not some content-neutral criteria. The government *aligned* itself in the *political fray* * * * thereby unfairly tipping the scales of the electoral balance in favor of *one side* of the *initiative* election." (emphasis added). The court concludes, "The government has an obligation to remain neutral and not spend public funds advocating or opposing an *initiative* on the ballot." (emphases added). The court also found a D.C. statutory basis for its decision.

What the *Common Cause* court appears to assume is that the District of Columbia was siding with opposing factions and ignored, discounted, rejected or did not hear an argument that it was entitled to its own position which, of necessity, coincided with that of one of the opposing factions. While this court may not agree that a governmental entity can never take sides in an initiative election, it certainly cannot agree that a governmental entity cannot expend funds to even publicly endorse its own measures.   * * *

The special elections at issue in the instant action originated from ordinance(s) of the Birmingham City Council. The elections were not "initiative elections," but rather were part of a process begun by the municipality which determined that the funds sought would be beneficial to the City. Defendants therefore argue that the City had the right, if not the duty, to advise its citizens of the benefits proposed. This court agrees. The library improvements and 911 enhancement were services which the City sought to provide to all of its citizens. Clearly, the City has the responsibility to determine when improvements are necessary or desirable and to express its determination of those needs to the public. In order to implement such proposed benefits, a municipality must attempt to secure the funds from its citizenry. The ads at issue in the instant action merely amount to a solicitation of the necessary funds. Those taxpayers who disapprove of the proposed benefits have two opportunities to dissent: (1) They may dissent at the polls on the issues involved and (2) they may dissent at the polls when City officials seek re-election.

One could reasonably suggest that to forbid defendants the right to support by advertising their position, initiated by their own resolution or ordinance, would be violative of their own First Amendment rights. * * * It would be a strange system indeed which would allow the City to determine its needs, allow it to adopt ordinances calling for elections to fulfill those needs, allow it to bear the expense of those elections, and then require it to stand silently by before the issues are voted on. Obviously, the City is not neutral under such circumstances and should not be required to appear so.

The court concludes that the City of Birmingham's use of tax revenues to promote passage of measures to enhance city services does not contravene the principles of the First Amendment.   * * *

ANDERSON v. CITY OF BOSTON

Supreme Judicial Court of Massachusetts, 1978.
376 Mass. 178, 380 N.E.2d 628, appeal dismissed, 439
U.S. 1060, 99 S.Ct. 822, 59 L.Ed.2d 26 (1979).

WILKINS, JUSTICE.

The plaintiffs, eleven taxable inhabitants of the city of Boston (city), seek a declaratory judgment and equitable relief concerning the legality of certain actions contemplated by the city in support of a referendum proposal which will be presented to the people at the November, 1978, general election. The referendum proposal concerns an amendment (the classification amendment) to Part II, c. 1, § 1, art. 4, of the Constitution of the Commonwealth which would authorize the Legislature to "classify real property according to its use in no more than four classes and to assess, rate and tax such property differently in the classes so established, but proportionately in the same class" and to grant reasonable exemptions. * * *

On May 30, 1978, the mayor submitted a proposed ordinance to the city council (council), which the council passed by a five-to-four vote on June 7, 1978. That ordinance authorized, subject to appropriation, the expenditure of city funds "for the purposes of providing educational materials and disseminating information urging the adoption by the people of a proposed amendment to the Massachusetts Constitution relating to the classification of property for purposes of taxation." [3] * * * The mayor has organized the Office of Public Information on Classification "for the purpose of collecting and disseminating information about the impact of 100% valuation on the residents of the City and on the potential of the classification amendment to mitigate that impact." That office would include in its information the fact that the city urges the voters to approve the classification question. * * *

Studies conducted by the City indicate that the implementation of 100% valuation in the City will effect a transfer of tax burden from commercial and industrial property to residential property in a gross amount of approximately $78,000,000. This transfer will practically double the tax burden on many single family homes in the City, increasing the tax on them by over $1,000. Other studies indicate that, "while many Boston voters understand the impact of 100% valuation on their taxes, few were acquainted with the Classification Amendment or had any idea of its possible impact in mitigating the effects of 100% valuation." There are persons and interests opposed to the passage of the classification amendment who will work to defeat it and who are raising funds from individuals and corporations for that purpose. * * *

We conclude that (1) the city does not have authority to appropriate funds to be expended in support of the classification amendment, and (2) the First Amendment to the Constitution of the United States, applicable to the States through the Fourteenth Amendment, does not require that the city be authorized to appropriate funds to influence the result of the vote on the classification amendment. * * *

The issue at the heart of the dispute concerning the city's authority to appropriate funds for the purpose of influencing the result on the referendum question is whether the city's purported home rule ordinance is inconsistent with any law enacted by the Legislature under the powers reserved to it under the Home Rule Amendment. On this point, we agree with the plaintiffs that the appropriation of funds by a municipality for the purpose of influencing the vote on a State-wide referendum question is "inconsistent with * * * laws enacted by the general court." We reach this result because comprehensive legislation, enacted after the adoption of the Home Rule Amendment, regulating election financing manifests an intention to bar municipalities from

---

3. The ordinance forbids the use of any such funds for the promotion of any individual. No public official may have his name or picture "individually displayed on any so-called educational material."

engaging in the expenditure of funds to influence election results. G.L. c. 55, as appearing in St.1975, c. 151, § 1. This comprehensive legislation requires the reasonable inference that the Legislature "intended to preclude the exercise of any local power or function on the same subject because otherwise the legislative purpose of that statute would be frustrated." *Bloom v. Worcester,* 293 N.E.2d at 280.

Chapter 55 is a detailed enactment entitled, "Disclosure and Regulation of Campaign Expenditures and Contributions." Its stated purposes are "to provide for public disclosure of political contributions and expenditures, and the regulation of said contributions and expenditures." * * * Chapter 55 also places restrictions on the expenditure of funds by corporations, making explicit reference to various kinds of corporations, although not to a municipal corporation.[9] * * * The absence of any reference to municipal corporations is significant, not as an indication that municipal action to influence election results was intended to be exempt from regulation, but rather as an indication that the Legislature did not even contemplate such municipal action could occur. We notice judicially that traditionally municipalities have not appropriated funds to influence election results. If the Legislature had expected that municipalities would engage in such activities or intended that they could, G.L. c. 55 would have regulated those activities as well. We thus construe G.L. c. 55 as preempting any right which a municipality might otherwise have to appropriate funds for the purpose of influencing the result on a referendum question to be submitted to the people at a State election. * * * [11]

We turn then to the defendants' assertion that, even in the presence of a legislative direction that no municipal funds be expended for the purpose of influencing the result of a referendum, the city has a First Amendment right to expend public funds in an attempt to obtain an affirmative vote on the classification amendment. * * * We abstain from expressing the issue before us in terms of whether a municipality "has" First Amendment rights and what the scope of those rights may be. "Instead, the question must be whether [the Commonwealth's denial of the right to the city to expend funds in support of the classification amendment] * * * abridges expression that the First Amendment was meant to protect." *First Nat'l Bank v. Bellotti,* ___ U.S. ___, ___, 98 S.Ct. 1407, 1415, 55 L.Ed.2d 707 (1978). In other

---

9. One restriction concerning the expenditure of corporate funds on a referendum question was held to be unconstitutional by a five-to-four vote in *First Nat'l Bank v. Bellotti,* 435 U.S. 765, 98 S.Ct. 1407, 55 L.Ed.2d 707 (1978) reversing *First Nat'l Bank v. Attorney Gen.,* ___ Mass. ___, 359 N.E.2d 1262 (1977).

11. We are not concerned here with the First Amendment or other right of a municipality to expend public funds to influence legislative action. Municipal action concerning legislation has statutory, traditional, and constitutional foundations which are not applicable to municipal action on questions submitted to the people. There is express authorization for the use of public funds for the purpose of influencing the legislative process. * * * Moreover, quite apart from legislative authorization, there is a tradition of localities acting through their officials and employees to obtain legislative action in their favor. Indeed, the Home Rule Amendment itself contains procedures by which an individual city or town may seek legislative authorization for particular action by it. * * *

words, is speech of the character involved here, expressed by a political subdivision of a State, speech which the First Amendment was intended to protect? The First Amendment, of course, restrains States from barring others from expressing ideas. By its terms and in its traditional applications, the First Amendment has nothing to do with a State's determination to refrain from speech on a given topic or topics and to bar its various subdivisions from expending funds in contravention of that determination. There are, no doubt, constitutional restrictions on governmental speech even where the subject under discussion is one at the heart of the First Amendment's protection.[14] On the other hand, there are a variety of instances in which government funds are used lawfully to express views and conclusions on matters of importance where various taxpayers may disagree with those views and conclusions. The Constitution of the United States, thus, does not forbid all government communications and publications which are not neutral and purely informative. We need not explore, however, how far constitutional considerations may limit the Federal and the State governments from expending otherwise lawfully appropriated funds to advance a partisan position by publication of documents and advertisements in support of that view. Here, we are presented with the issue whether constitutionally protected speech includes the right of a municipality to speak militantly about a referendum issue of admitted public importance where the Legislature of the State has said it may not. The Supreme Court has left open the possibility that restrictions on speech would be valid as to private corporations which would not be valid as to individuals. *First Nat'l Bank v. Bellotti,* 435 U.S. 765, 777 n. 13, 98 S.Ct. 1407, 1416 n. 13, 55 L.Ed.2d 707 (1978). Although we suspect that the First Amendment has nothing to do with this intra-state question of the rights of a political subdivision to disregard the mandate of the supreme legislative authority of the State, no matter how important the topic desired to be placed under discussion and even in the absence of a compelling State interest in suppressing discussion, we need not resolve this point. Even if we were to assume that the appropriation of funds by a municipal corporation to engage in robust, partisan speech is expression that the First Amendment was meant to protect, there are demonstrated, compelling interests of the Commonwealth which justify the "restraint" which the Commonwealth has placed on the city.

In this phase of our analysis we assume that the expenditure of municipal funds to promote adoption of the classification amendment involves expression protected by the First Amendment, and we conclude that a State-imposed restriction on such an expenditure survives the

---

14. Surely, the Constitution of the United States does not authorize the expenditure of public funds to promote the reelection of the President, Congressmen, and State and local officials (to the exclusion of their opponents), even though the open discussion of political candidates and elections is basic First Amendment material. Government domination of the expression of ideas is repugnant to our system of constitutional government. In this Commonwealth, we might find a constitutional bar to such an attempt at political self-perpetuation in art. 9 of the Declaration of Rights of our Constitution, concerning free elections, and in considerations of equal protection and due process of law.

exacting scrutiny to which such a restriction must be subjected. See *First Nat'l Bank v. Bellotti, supra* at 786, 98 S.Ct. at 1421. * * * The Commonwealth has a substantial, compelling interest in assuring the fairness of elections and the appearance of fairness in the electoral process. It may protect that interest by excluding its political subdivisions from partisan involvement in election questions, where the means employed are " 'closely drawn to avoid unnecessary abridgement * * * [of First Amendment freedoms].' " *First Nat'l Bank v. Bellotti, supra* at 786, 98 S.Ct. at 1421, quoting from *Buckley v. Valeo,* 424 U.S. 1, 25, 96 S.Ct. 612, 46 L.Ed.2d 659 (1976). * * *

Article 48 * * * [of the Constitution], concerning referenda, * * * assures disclosure to every voter of the nature of each referendum before the date of the election and places in the Legislature the determination of what "other information and arguments for and against" may be distributed. * * * The people have expressed a strong interest that the Legislature have the authority to determine what, if any, material will be disseminated on a referendum proposal. The Legislature may decide, as it has, that fairness in the election process is best achieved by a direction that political subdivisions of the State maintain a "hands off" policy. It may further decide that the State government and its various subdivisions should not use public funds to instruct the people, the ultimate authority, how they should vote. That determination avoids the possibility of a babel of municipal huckstering and reserves the financing of public debate for nongovernmental agencies and individuals. See *Buckley v. Valeo, supra* 424 U.S. at 57, 96 S.Ct. 612.

Fairness and the appearance of fairness are assured by a prohibition against using public tax revenues to advocate a position which certain taxpayers oppose. The Commonwealth's interest in fairness and in the appearance of fairness is particularly significant in the face of the defendants' argument that no limit may be imposed on the city's expenditure of tax revenue for vigorous advocacy on a referendum question. On this view, the Commonwealth is apparently powerless against political entities of its own creation.

Assuming that the Commonwealth has no right to restrict such advocacy where there is no opposition from any affected citizen, the Commonwealth has a compelling interest in restricting such advocacy where the affected citizenry are not in unanimity. The Commonwealth has an interest in assuring that a dissenting minority of taxpayers is not compelled to finance the expression on an election issue of views with which they disagree. Unlike the shareholders of a private corporation (see *First Nat'l Bank v. Bellotti,* 435 U.S. 765, 98 S.Ct. 1407, 55 L.Ed.2d 707 [1978]), real estate taxpayers such as the plaintiffs cannot avoid the financial consequences of the city's appropriation of funds. * * * The coercion which a majority of the Supreme Court found absent in *First Nat'l Bank v. Bellotti, supra* at 794 n. 34, 98 S.Ct. at 1425 n. 34, is thus present here. And the objectors are not hypothetical. They have identified themselves by bringing this action. This case is more analogous to *Abood v. Detroit Bd. of Educ.,* 431 U.S. 209, 235 236, 97 S.Ct.

1782, 52 L.Ed.2d 261 (1977), where the Supreme Court struck down involuntary contributions by government employees to a union's political expression.[20] * * *

FIRST NATIONAL BANK OF BOSTON v. BELLOTTI

Supreme Court of the United States, 1978.
435 U.S. 765, 98 S.Ct. 1407, 55 L.Ed.2d 707.

MR. JUSTICE POWELL delivered the opinion of the Court. * * *

The statute at issue, Mass.Gen.Laws Ann., ch. 55, § 8 (West Supp. 1977), prohibits appellants, two national banking associations and three business corporations, from making contributions or expenditures "for the purpose of * * * influencing or affecting the vote on any question submitted to the voters, other than one materially affecting any of the property, business or assets of the corporation." The statute further specifies that "[n]o question submitted to the voters solely concerning the taxation of the income, property or transactions of individuals shall be deemed materially to affect the property, business or assets of the corporation." * * * Appellants wanted to spend money to publicize their views on a proposed constitutional amendment that was to be submitted to the voters as a ballot question at a general election on November 2, 1976. The amendment would have permitted the legislature to impose a graduated tax on the income of individuals. After appellee, the Attorney General of Massachusetts, informed appellants that he intended to enforce § 8 against them, they brought this action seeking to have the statute declared unconstitutional. * * *

The court below framed the principal question in this case as whether and to what extent corporations have First Amendment rights. We believe that the court posed the wrong question. The Constitution often protects interests broader than those of the party seeking their vindication. The First Amendment, in particular, serves significant societal interests. The proper question therefore is not whether corporations "have" First Amendment rights and, if so, whether they are coextensive with those of natural persons. Instead, the question must be whether § 8 abridges expression that the First Amendment was meant to protect. We hold that it does.

The speech proposed by appellants is at the heart of the First Amendment's protection. * * * If the speakers here were not corporations, no one would suggest that the State could silence their proposed speech. It is the type of speech indispensable to decisionmaking in a democracy, and this is no less true because the speech comes from a

---

20. If the proper remedy in union cases is that the dissenting member should not be obligated to pay that portion of his dues attributable to political activities (see *First Nat'l Bank v. Bellotti, supra* at 794 n. 34, 98 S.Ct. at 1425 n. 34), the remedy here is that any dissenting taxpayer should not be obliged to pay that portion of his local real estate taxes attributable to the city's political activities on the referendum proposal. Such a result, however, can be achieved more effectively by striking the entire appropriation and letting those who wish to do so make their own contributions directly to the cause.

corporation rather than an individual. The inherent worth of the speech in terms of its capacity for informing the public does not depend upon the identity of its source, whether corporation, association, union, or individual. * * *

The question in this case, simply put, is whether the corporate identity of the speaker deprives this proposed speech of what otherwise would be its clear entitlement to protection. * * * The constitutionality of § 8's prohibition of the "exposition of ideas" by corporations turns on whether it can survive the exacting scrutiny necessitated by a state-imposed restriction of freedom of speech. * * *

Appellee * * * advances two principal justifications for the prohibition of corporate speech. The first is the State's interest in sustaining the active role of the individual citizen in the electoral process and thereby preventing diminution of the citizen's confidence in government. The second is the interest in protecting the rights of shareholders whose views differ from those expressed by management on behalf of the corporation. However weighty these interests may be in the context of partisan candidate elections, they either are not implicated in this case or are not served at all, or in other than a random manner, by the prohibition in § 8.

Preserving the integrity of the electoral process, preventing corruption, and "sustain[ing] the active, alert responsibility of the individual citizen in a democracy for the wise conduct of government" are interests of the highest importance.

Appellee advances a number of arguments in support of his view that these interests are endangered by corporate participation in discussion of a referendum issue. They hinge upon the assumption that such participation would exert an undue influence on the outcome of a referendum vote, and—in the end—destroy the confidence of the people in the democratic process and the integrity of government. According to appellee, corporations are wealthy and powerful and their views may drown out other points of view. If appellee's arguments were supported by record or legislative findings that corporate advocacy threatened imminently to undermine democratic processes, thereby denigrating rather than serving First Amendment interests, these arguments would merit our consideration. But there has been no showing that the relative voice of corporations has been overwhelming or even significant in influencing referenda in Massachusetts, or that there has been any threat to the confidence of the citizenry in government. * * *

Moreover, the people in our democracy are entrusted with the responsibility for judging and evaluating the relative merits of conflicting arguments. They may consider, in making their judgment, the source and credibility of the advocate. But if there be any danger that the people cannot evaluate the information and arguments advanced by appellants, it is a danger contemplated by the Framers of the First Amendment. In sum, "[a] restriction so destructive of the right of public discussion [as § 8], without greater or more imminent danger to the public interest than existed in this case, is incompatible with the freedoms secured by the First Amendment."

Finally, appellee argues that § 8 protects corporate shareholders, an interest that is both legitimate and traditionally within the province of state law. The statute is said to serve this interest by preventing the use of corporate resources in furtherance of views with which some shareholders may disagree. This purpose is belied, however, by the provisions of the statute, which are both underinclusive and overinclusive.

The underinclusiveness of the statute is self-evident. Corporate expenditures with respect to a referendum are prohibited, while corporate activity with respect to the passage or defeat of legislation is permitted, even though corporations may engage in lobbying more often than they take positions on ballot questions submitted to the voters. Nor does § 8 prohibit a corporation from expressing its views, by the expenditure of corporate funds, on any public issue until it becomes the subject of a referendum, though the displeasure of disapproving shareholders is unlikely to be any less.

The overinclusiveness of the statute is demonstrated by the fact that § 8 would prohibit a corporation from supporting or opposing a referendum proposal even if its shareholders unanimously authorized the contribution or expenditure. Ultimately shareholders may decide, through the procedures of corporate democracy, whether their corporation should engage in debate on public issues.[34] Acting through their power to elect the board of directors or to insist upon protective provisions in the corporation's charter, shareholders normally are presumed competent to protect their own interests. In addition to intracorporate remedies,

---

34. Appellee does not explain why the dissenting shareholder's wishes are entitled to such greater solicitude in this context than in many others where equally important and controversial corporate decisions are made by management or by a predetermined percentage of the shareholders. * * *

The dissent of Mr. Justice White relies heavily on *Abood v. Detroit Board of Education,* 431 U.S. 209, 97 S.Ct. 1782, 52 L.Ed.2d 261 (1977), and *International Assn. of Machinists v. Street,* 367 U.S. 740, 81 S.Ct. 1784, 6 L.Ed.2d 1141 (1961). These decisions involved the First Amendment rights of employees in closed or agency shops not to be compelled, as a condition of employment, to support with financial contributions the political activities of other union members with which the dissenters disagreed. * * *

The critical distinction here is that no shareholder has been "compelled" to contribute anything. Apart from the fact, noted by the dissent, that compulsion by the State is wholly absent, the [shareholder] invests in a corporation of his own volition and is [free to withdraw his investment at any time and for any reason.] A more relevant analogy, therefore, is to the situation where an employee voluntarily joins a union, or an individual voluntarily joins an association, and later finds himself in disagreement with its stance on a political issue. The *Street* and *Abood* Courts did not address the question whether, in such a situation, the union or association must refund a portion of the dissenter's dues or, more drastically, refrain from expressing the majority's views. In addition, even apart from the substantive differences between compelled membership in a union and voluntary investment in a corporation or voluntary participation in *any* collective organization, it is by no means an automatic step from the remedy in *Abood,* which honored the interests of the minority without infringing the majority's rights, to the position adopted by the dissent which would completely silence the majority because a hypothetical minority might object.

minority shareholders generally have access to the judicial remedy of a derivative suit to challenge corporate disbursements alleged to have been made for improper corporate purposes or merely to further the personal interests of management. * * *

MR. JUSTICE WHITE, with whom MR. JUSTICE BRENNAN and MR. JUSTICE MARSHALL join, dissenting. * * *

Although it is arguable that corporations make * * * expenditures because their managers believe that it is in the corporations' economic interest to do so, there is no basis whatsoever for concluding that these views are expressive of the heterogeneous beliefs of their shareholders whose convictions on many political issues are undoubtedly shaped by considerations other than a desire to endorse any electoral or ideological cause which would tend to increase the value of a particular corporate investment. This is particularly true where, as in this case, whatever the belief of the corporate managers may be, they have not been able to demonstrate that the issue involved has any material connection with the corporate business. Thus when a profitmaking corporation contributes to a political candidate this does not further the self-expression or self-fulfillment of its shareholders in the way that expenditures from them as individuals would. * * *

The governmental interest in regulating corporate political communications, especially those relating to electoral matters, also raises considerations which differ significantly from those governing the regulation of individual speech. Corporations are artificial entities created by law for the purpose of furthering certain economic goals. * * * It has long been recognized * * * that the special status of corporations has placed them in a position to control vast amounts of economic power which may, if not regulated, dominate not only the economy but also the very heart of our democracy, the electoral process. * * * The State need not permit its own creation to consume it. Massachusetts could permissibly conclude that not to impose limits upon the political activities of corporations would have placed it in a position of departing from neutrality and indirectly assisting the propagation of corporate views because of the advantages its laws give to the corporate acquisition of funds to finance such activities. Such expenditures may be viewed as seriously threatening the role of the First Amendment as a guarantor of a free marketplace of ideas. Ordinarily, the expenditure of funds to promote political causes may be assumed to bear some relation to the fervency with which they are held. Corporate political expression, however, is not only divorced from the convictions of individual corporate shareholders, but also, because of the ease with which corporations are permitted to accumulate capital, bears no relation to the conviction with which the ideas expressed are held by the communicator. * * *

There is an additional overriding interest related to the prevention of corporate domination which is substantially advanced by Massachusetts' restrictions upon corporate contributions: assuring that shareholders are not compelled to support and financially further beliefs with which they disagree where, as is the case here, the issue involved does not materially affect the business, property, or other affairs of the corporation. The State has not interfered with the prerogatives of corporate management to communicate about matters that have material impact on the business affairs entrusted to them, however much individual stockholders may disagree on economic or ideological grounds. Nor has the State forbidden management from formulating and circulating its views at its own expense or at the expense of others, even where the subject at issue is irrelevant to corporate business affairs. But Massachusetts *has* chosen to forbid corporate management from spending corporate funds in referenda elections absent some demonstrable effect of the issue on the economic life of the company. In short, corporate management may not use corporate monies to promote what does not further corporate affairs but what in the last analysis are the purely personal views of the management, individually or as a group. * * *

It is no answer to respond, as the Court does, that the dissenting "shareholder * * * is free to withdraw his investment at any time and for any reason." The employees in *Street* and *Abood* were also free to seek other jobs where they would not be compelled to finance causes with which they disagreed, but we held in *Abood* that First Amendment rights could not be so burdened. Clearly the State has a strong interest in assuring that its citizens are not forced to choose between supporting the propagation of views with which they disagree and passing up investment opportunities. * * *

Mr. Justice Rehnquist, dissenting. * * *

There can be little doubt that when a State creates a corporation with the power to acquire and utilize property, it necessarily and implicitly guarantees that the corporation will not be deprived of that property absent due process of law. * * * It cannot be so readily concluded that the right of political expression is equally necessary to carry out the functions of a corporation organized for commercial purposes. A State grants to a business corporation the blessings of potentially perpetual life and limited liability to enhance its efficiency as an economic entity. It might reasonably be concluded that those properties, so beneficial in the economic sphere, pose special dangers in the political sphere. Furthermore, it might be argued that liberties of political expression are not at all necessary to effectuate the purposes for which States permit commercial corporations to exist. So long as the Judicial Branches of the State and Federal Governments remain open to protect the corporation's interest in its property, it has no need, though it may have the desire, to petition the political branches for similar protection. Indeed, the States might reasonably fear that the corporation would use its economic power to obtain further benefits beyond those already bestowed. I would think that any particular form of organization upon which the State confers special privileges or immunities different from those of natural persons would be subject to like regulation, whether the organization is a labor union, a partnership, a trade association, or a corporation. * * *

AUSTIN v. MICHIGAN CHAMBER OF COMMERCE
Supreme Court of the United States, 1990.
494 U.S. 652, 110 S.Ct. 1391, 108 L.Ed.2d 652.

JUSTICE MARSHALL delivered the opinion of the Court. * * *

Section 54(1) of the Michigan Campaign Finance Act prohibits corporations from making contributions and independent expenditures in connection with state candidate elections. * * * The Act exempts from this general prohibition against corporate political spending any expenditure made from a segregated fund. A corporation may solicit contributions to its political fund only from an enumerated list of persons associated with the corporation.

The Michigan State Chamber of Commerce, a nonprofit Michigan corporation, challenges the constitutionality of this statutory scheme. The Chamber comprises more than 8,000 members, three-quarters of whom are for-profit corporations. The Chamber's general treasury is funded through annual dues required of all members. * * *

To determine whether Michigan's restrictions on corporate political expenditures may constitutionally be applied to the Chamber, we must ascertain whether they burden the exercise of political speech and, if they do, whether they are narrowly tailored to serve a compelling state interest. *Buckley v. Valeo,* 424 U.S. 1, 44–45, 96 S.Ct. 612, 646–647, 46 L.Ed.2d 659 (1976) (*per curiam*). Certainly, the use of funds to support a political candidate is "speech"; independent campaign expenditures constitute "political expression 'at the core of our electoral process and of the First Amendment freedom.' " *Id.,* at 39, 96 S.Ct., at 644. The mere fact that the Chamber is a corporation does not remove its speech from the ambit of the First Amendment. See, *e.g., First National Bank of Boston v. Bellotti,* 435 U.S. 765, 777, 98 S.Ct. 1407, 1416, 55 L.Ed.2d 707 (1978).

This Court concluded in *FEC v. Massachusetts Citizens for Life, Inc.,* 479 U.S. 238, 107 S.Ct. 616, 93 L.Ed.2d 539 (1986) (*MCFL*), that a federal statute requiring corporations to make independent political expenditures only through special segregated funds burdens corporate freedom of expression. The Court reasoned that the small nonprofit corporation in that case would face certain organizational and financial hurdles in establishing and administering a segregated political fund. * * * The Act imposes requirements similar to those in the federal statute involved in *MCFL*: a segregated fund must have a treasurer; and its administrators must keep detailed accounts of contributions, and file with state officials a statement of organization. * * * Although these requirements do not stifle corporate speech entirely, they do burden expressive activity. Thus, they must be justified by a compelling state interest.

The State contends that the unique legal and economic characteristics of corporations necessitate some regulation of their political expenditures to avoid corruption or the appearance of corruption. See *FEC v. National Conservative Political Action Comm.*, 470 U.S. 480, 496–497, 105 S.Ct. 1459, 1468, 84 L.Ed.2d 455 (1985) (*NCPAC*) ("[P]reventing corruption or the appearance of corruption are the only legitimate and compelling government interests thus far identified for restricting campaign finances"). State law grants corporations special advantages—such as limited liability, perpetual life, and favorable treatment of the accumulation and distribution of assets—that enhance their ability to attract capital and to deploy their resources in ways that maximize the return on their shareholders' investments. These state-created advantages not only allow corporations to play a dominant role in the nation's economy, but also permit them to use "resources amassed in the economic marketplace" to obtain "an unfair advantage in the political marketplace." *MCFL*, 479 U.S., at 257, 107 S.Ct., at 627. As the Court explained in *MCFL*, the political advantage of corporations is unfair because

> "[t]he resources in the treasury of a business corporation * * * are not an indication of popular support for the corporation's political ideas. They reflect instead the economically motivated decisions of investors and customers. The availability of these resources may make a corporation a formidable political presence, even though the power of the corporation may be no reflection of the power of its ideas." *Id.*, at 258, 107 S.Ct., at 628.

We therefore have recognized that "the compelling governmental interest in preventing corruption support[s] the restriction of the influence of political war chests funneled through the corporate form." *NCPAC, supra*, 470 U.S., at 500–501, 105 S.Ct., at 1470.

The Chamber argues that this concern about corporate domination of the political process is insufficient to justify restrictions on independent expenditures. Although this court has distinguished these expenditures from direct contributions in the context of federal laws regulating individual donors, *Buckley*, 424 U.S., at 47, 96 S.Ct., at 648, it has also recognized that a legislature might demonstrate a danger of real or apparent corruption posed by such expenditures when made by corporations to influence candidate elections, *Bellotti*, 435 U.S., at 788, n. 26, 98 S.Ct., at 1422, n. 26. Regardless of whether this danger of "financial *quid pro quo* " corruption, see *NCPAC, supra*, 479 U.S., at 497, 105 S.Ct., at 1468, may be sufficient to justify a restriction on independent expenditures, Michigan's regulation aims at a different type of corruption in the political arena: the corrosive and distorting effects of immense aggregations of wealth that are accumulated with the help of the corporate form and that have little or no correlation to the public's support for the corporation's political ideas. The Act does not attempt "to equalize the relative influence of speakers on elections," *post* (Kennedy, J., dissenting); rather, it ensures that expenditures reflect actual public support for the political ideas espoused by corporations. We emphasize that the mere fact that corporations may accumulate large amounts of wealth is not the justification for § 54; rather, the unique state-conferred corporate structure that facilitates the amassing of large treasuries warrants the limit on independent expenditures. Corporate wealth can unfairly influence elections when it is deployed in the form of independent expenditures, just as it can when it assumes the guise of political contributions. We therefore hold that the State has articulated a sufficiently compelling rationale to support its restriction on independent expenditures by corporations.

We next turn to the question whether the Act is sufficiently narrowly tailored to achieve its goal. We find that the Act is precisely targeted to eliminate the distortion caused by corporate spending while also allowing corporations to express their political views. Contrary to the dissents' critical assumptions, the Act does not impose an *absolute* ban on all forms of corporate political spending but permits corporations to make independent political expenditures through separate segregated funds. Because persons contributing to such funds understand that their money will be used solely for political purposes, the speech generated accurately reflects contributors' support for the corporation's political views. * * * [T]he Chamber differs * * * greatly from the Massachusetts organization [in *MCFL*]. MCFL was not established by, and had a policy of not accepting contributions from, business corporations. Thus it could not "serv[e] as [a] condui[t] for the type of direct spending that creates a threat to the political marketplace." *Ibid.* In striking contrast, more than three-quarters of the Chamber's members are business corporations, whose political contributions and expenditures can constitutionally be regulated by the State. * * * In sum, the Chamber does not possess the features that would compel the State to exempt it from restrictions on independent political expenditures. * * *

Justice Brennan, concurring. * * *

[T]he Michigan law protects dissenting shareholders of business corporations that are members of the Chamber to the extent that such shareholders oppose the use of their money, paid as dues to the Chamber out of general corporate treasury funds, for political campaigns.

Of course, a member could resign from the Chamber and a stockholder could divest from a business corporation that used the Chamber as a conduit, but these options would impose a financial sacrifice on those objecting to political expenditures. It is therefore irrelevant that "[t]o the extent that members disagree with their nonprofit corporation's policies, they can seek change from within, withhold financial support, cease to associate with the group, or form a rival group of their own." *Post* (Kennedy, J., dissenting). * * * While the State may have no constitutional *duty* to protect the objecting Chamber member and corporate shareholder in the absence of state action, cf. *Abood v. Detroit Board of Education,* 431 U.S. 209, 232–237, 97 S.Ct. 1782, 1798–1800, 52 L.Ed.2d 261 (1977), the State surely has a compelling interest in preventing a corporation it has chartered from exploiting those who do not wish to contribute to the Chamber's political message. * * *

JUSTICE SCALIA, dissenting. * * *

The Court's opinion says that political speech of corporations can be regulated because "[s]tate law grants [them] special advantages." This analysis seeks to create one good argument by combining two bad ones. Those individuals who form that type of voluntary association known as a corporation are, to be sure, given special advantages—notably, the immunization of their personal fortunes from liability for the actions of the association—that the State is under no obligation to confer. But so are other associations and private individuals given all sorts of special advantages that the State need not confer, ranging from tax breaks to contract awards to public employment to outright cash subsidiaries. It is rudimentary that the State cannot exact as the price of those special advantages the forfeiture of First Amendment rights. The categorical suspension of the right of any person, or of any association of persons, to speak out on political matters must be justified by a compelling state need. See *Buckley v. Valeo,* 424 U.S. 1, 44–45, 96 S.Ct. 612, 646–647, 46 L.Ed.2d 659 (1976) (*per curiam*). Which is why the Court puts forward its second bad argument, the fact that corporations "amas[s] large treasuries." But that alone is also not sufficient justification for the suppression of political speech, unless one thinks it would be lawful to prohibit men and women whose net worth is above a certain figure from endorsing political candidates. Neither of these two flawed arguments is improved by combining them and saying, as the Court in effect does, that "since the State gives special advantages to these voluntary associations, and since they thereby amass vast wealth, they may be required to abandon their right of political speech." * * *

Justice Brennan's concurrence would have us believe that the prohibition adopted by Michigan and approved by the Court is a paternalistic measure to protect the corporate shareholder of America. * * * But such solicitude is a most implausible explanation for the Michigan statute, inasmuch as it permits corporations to take as many ideological and political positions as they please, so long as they are not "in assistance of, or in opposition to, the nomination or election of a candidate." That is indeed the Court's sole basis for distinguishing *First National Bank of Boston v. Bellotti,* 435 U.S. 765, 98 S.Ct. 1407, 55 L.Ed.2d 707 (1978), which invalidated restriction of a corporation's general political speech. The Michigan law appears to be designed, in other words, neither to protect shareholders, not even (impermissibly) to "balance" general political debate, but to protect political candidates. Given the degree of political sophistication that ought to attend the exercise of our constitutional responsibilities, it is regrettable that this should come as a surprise.

But even if the object of the prohibition could plausibly be portrayed as the protection of shareholders (which the Court's opinion, at least, does not even assert), that would not suffice as a "compelling need" to support this blatant restriction upon core political speech. A person becomes a member of that form of association known as a for-profit corporation in order to pursue economic objectives, *i.e.,* to make money. Some corporate charters may specify the line of commerce to which the company is limited, but even that can be amended by shareholder vote. Thus, in joining such an association, the shareholder knows that management may take any action that is ultimately in accord with what the majority (or a specified supermajority) of the shareholders wishes, so long as that action is designed to make a profit. That is the deal. The corporate actions to which the shareholder exposes himself, therefore, include many things that he may find politically or ideologically uncongenial: investment in South Africa, operation of an abortion clinic, publication of a pornographic magazine, or even publication of a newspaper that adopts absurd political views and makes catastrophic political endorsements. His only protections against such assaults upon his ideological commitments are (1) his ability to persuade a majority (or the requisite minority) of his fellow shareholders that the action should not be taken, and ultimately (2) his ability to sell his stock. (The latter course, by the way, does not ordinarily involve the severe psychic trauma or economic disaster that Justice Brennan's opinion suggests.) It seems to me entirely fanciful, in other words, to suggest that the Michigan statute makes any significant contribution towards insulating the exclusively profit-motivated shareholder from the rude world of politics and ideology. * * *

JUSTICE KENNEDY, with whom JUSTICE O'CONNOR and JUSTICE SCALIA join, dissenting. * * *

The Act prohibits corporations from speaking on a particular subject, the subject of candidate elections. It is a basic precept that the State may not confine speech to certain subjects. Content-based restrictions are the essence of censorial power. * * *

[T]he Act [also] discriminates on the basis of the speaker's identity. Under the Michigan law, any person or group other than a corporation may engage in political debate over candidate elections; but corporations, even nonprofit corporations that have unique views of vital importance to the electorate, must remain mute. Our precedents condemn this censorship. * * * [I]n *Bellotti* * * * we rejected the assumption that "corporations are wealthy and powerful and their views may drown out other points of view" or "exert an undue influence" on the electorate in the absence of a showing that the relative voice of corporations was significant. 435 U.S., at 789, 98 S.Ct., at 1422. And even were we to assume that some record support for this assertion would make a constitutional difference, it has not been established here. The majority provides only conjecture. All censorship is suspect; but censorship based on vague surmise is not permissible in any case. * * *

SECTION B. THE RELATIONSHIP BETWEEN CITIES AND THE FEDERAL GOVERNMENT

The ability of cities to exercise any meaningful power requires independence not only from the states but also from the federal government. Of course, the task of establishing the proper relationship between the federal government and state and local governments is a major political issue in the United States. It is also, as this section reveals, a hotly debated issue of federal law.

Three different levels of government are potentially involved in a dispute over the allocation of governmental power—the federal government, the states, and the cities. A number of different federal relationships with cities are therefore possible. The federal government could, for example, align itself with cities against states by helping cities free themselves from state restraints. The first subsection below examines this federal role. Another, no doubt more frequent, option is for the federal government, like the states, to limit city power. The subsequent two subsections examine this use of federal power, first as matter of Constitutional law and then as a matter of preemption doctrine. These two subsections present issues similar to those raised above in determining, as a matter of state law, the relationship between states and cities. This is not surprising. Common problems confront all attempts to protect decentralized political power from the control of larger governmental units.

The final two subsections have no direct counterparts in the materials on state-city relationships. They deal with the application of federal anti-trust laws to cities and the enforcement of federal criminal law against city officials, two quite recent—and very important—examples of federal intervention in city affairs. The materials on federal anti-trust law and criminal law illustrate how the nature of the federal-city relationship depends not just on Constitutional issues but also on judicial interpretation of the numerous federal statutes applicable to local governments.

1. THE FEDERAL GOVERNMENT AS A SOURCE OF CITY POWER

In the two cases that follow, the Supreme Court interpreted, first, a federal statute and, subsequently, federal judicial remedies in ways that empowered cities against states. In reading these cases, consider whether the federal-state-city relationship that the Court envisions in these cases is consistent with the relationship articulated above in Hunter v. Pittsburgh. Is federal power likely to be a promising source for city protection against state power?

LAWRENCE COUNTY v. LEAD–DEADWOOD SCHOOL DISTRICT

Supreme Court of the United States, 1985.
469 U.S. 256, 105 S.Ct. 695, 83 L.Ed.2d 635.

JUSTICE WHITE delivered the opinion of the Court. * * *

The Payment in Lieu of Taxes Act compensates local governments for the loss of tax revenues resulting from the tax-immune status of federal lands located in their jurisdictions, and for the cost of providing services related to these lands. These "entitlement lands" include wilderness areas, national parks, and lands administered by the Bureau of Land Management. * * * [T]he Secretary of the Interior is required to make annual payments "to each unit of general local government in which entitlement land is located." The local unit "may use the payment for any governmental purpose." 31 U.S.C. § 6902(a). Appellant Lawrence County has received in excess of $400,000 under the Act.

In 1979, South Dakota enacted a statute requiring local governments to distribute federal payments in lieu of taxes in the same way they distribute general tax revenues. Since the county allocates approximately 60% of its general tax revenues to its school districts, the state statute would require the county to give the school districts 60% of the § 6902 payments it receives. The county, however, declined to distribute the funds in accordance with the state statute, claiming that the Payment in Lieu of Taxes Act gave it the discretion to spend the funds for any governmental purpose it chose. * * * Appellee, Lead–Deadwood School District No. 40–1, * * * filed a complaint in state court, seeking a writ of mandamus to compel the county to distribute the federal funds in accordance with the state statute. * * *

Even if Congress has not expressly pre-empted state law in a given area, a state statute may nevertheless be invalid under the Supremacy Clause if it conflicts with federal law or "stands as an obstacle to the accomplishment of the full purposes and objectives of Congress." *Silkwood v. Kerr McGee Corp.,* 464 U.S. ___, 104 S.Ct. 615, 78 L.Ed.2d 443 (1984). In determining whether the state statute at issue here impeded the operation of the federal Act, the South Dakota Supreme Court limited its inquiry to whether the funding of school districts was a "governmental purpose." Concluding that it was, the court found no inconsistency between the state and federal provisions. This plain language analysis, however, is seriously flawed.

The Act provides that "each unit of general local government"—in this case, the county—"may" use the moneys for "any" governmental purpose. This language appears to endow local governments with the discretion to spend in-lieu payments for any governmental purpose. It seems to say that if the local unit chooses to spend all of the money on roads, for example, it could do so. Under the state statute, however, that is forbidden: the funds must be allocated among the various services in the same manner as other revenues. The State insists that since money used as the law directs would be spent on proper governmental services, there is no inconsistency with § 6902. Under this interpretation, the word "may" confers no discretion on local governments that is immune from state control. The last sentence of § 6902(a) is drained of almost all meaning, since had it been omitted, the legal position of local governments would be precisely as described by the South Dakota Supreme Court. The sentence would become a mere admonition not to embezzle and to spend federal money on proper purposes. At the very least, § 6902 is ambiguous with respect to the degree of discretion it confers on local governments. Contrary to the views expressed in the court below, it does not of its own force dispose of the county's case. Resort to other indicia of the meaning of the statutory language is therefore appropriate. * * *

The Payment in Lieu of Taxes Act was passed in response to a comprehensive review of the policies applicable to the use, management, and disposition of federal lands. The Federal Government had for many years been providing payments to partially compensate state and local governments for revenues lost as a result of the presence of tax-exempt federal lands within their borders. But the Public Land Law Review Commission and Congress identified a number of flaws in the existing programs. Prominent among congressional concerns was that, under systems of direct payment to the States, local governments often received funds that were insufficient to cover the full cost of maintaining the federal lands within their jurisdictions. Where these lands consisted of wilderness or park areas, they attracted thousands of visitors each year. State governments might benefit from this federally inspired tourism through the collection of income or sales taxes, but these revenues would not accrue to local governments, who were often restricted to raising revenue from property taxes. Yet it was the local governments that bore the brunt of the expenses associated with federal lands, such as law enforcement, road maintenance, and the provision of public health services. * * *

The School District acknowledges that this legislative history evidences a clear intent to distribute funds directly to units of local government, bypassing the State. But it argues that the South Dakota statute poses no impediment to the accomplishment of this goal: federal money still flows directly to the county; none of it is thereafter "parcelled out" to other counties that have no federal lands within their borders; and the federal statute merely defines the "point of distribution" of funds, the State having authority to prescribe the "plan of distribution."

As we see it, however, Congress was not merely concerned that local governments receive adequate amounts of money, and that they receive these amounts directly. Equally as important was the objective of ensuring local governments the freedom and flexibility to spend the federal money as they saw fit. * * * The South Dakota statute, mandating that local governments spend these funds according to a specific formula, runs directly counter to this objective. If the State may dictate a "plan" of distribution, as the School District contends, it may impose exactly the kinds of restrictions on the use of funds that Congress intended to prohibit. * * *

Congress also recognized that the costs associated with maintaining and serving federal lands were varied and unpredictable, and that local governments needed the flexibility to allocate in-lieu payments to these needs as they arose. * * * The picture that emerges from the hearings on the Act is that there are many counties in which much of the land is owned by the Federal Government, and whose populations are markedly increased by tourists and hunters in the summer, in deer season, or on the weekends. These transients suffer accidents requiring emergency services or hospitalization for which they cannot always pay; commit crimes that call for police protection, prosecution, and incarceration; create waste that necessitates the construction of sewage treatment plants; use roads that must be paved and maintained; and generally impose a strain on a county's limited resources without providing much in the way of compensating revenues. One cost unlikely to increase with the presence of this largely uninhabited federal land, however, is that of education. * * *

Against this background, we have little trouble in concluding that Congress intended to prohibit the kind of state-imposed limitation on the use of in-lieu payments represented by the South Dakota statute challenged in this case. * * * [T]he allocation of federal payments in the same proportion as local revenue would most likely result in a windfall for school districts and other entities that are already fully funded by local revenues. The federal money would not serve its intended purpose of compensating local governments for extraordinary or additional expenditures associated with federal lands. A county conceivably could avoid this result, but the strong congressional concern that local governments have maximum flexibility in this area indicates that counties should not encounter substantial interference from the State in allocating funds to the area of greatest need.

The School District and the State also argue that because of concerns of federalism, the Federal Government may not intrude lightly into the State's efforts to provide fiscal guidance to its subdivisions. The Federal Government, however, has not presumed to dictate the manner in which the counties may spend *state* in-lieu-of-tax payments. Rather, it has merely imposed a condition on its disbursement of federal funds. The condition in this instance is that the counties should not be denied the discretion to spend § 6902 funds for any governmental purpose, including expenditures that are linked to federal lands within their borders. It is far from a novel proposition that pursuant to its powers under the Spending Clause, Congress may impose conditions on the receipt of federal funds, absent some independent constitutional bar. In our view, Congress was sufficiently clear in its intention to funnel § 6902 moneys directly to local governments, so that they might spend them for governmental purposes without substantial interference. * * *

The attempt of the South Dakota legislation to limit the manner in which counties or other qualified local governmental units may spend federal in-lieu-of-tax payments obstructs this congressional purpose and runs afoul of the Supremacy Clause. Congress intended the affected units of local government, such as Lawrence County, to be the managers of these funds, not merely the State's cashiers. * * *

JUSTICE REHNQUIST, with whom JUSTICE STEVENS joins, dissenting.

In *Hunter v. Pittsburgh,* 207 U.S. 161, 28 S.Ct. 40, 52 L.Ed. 151 (1907), this Court unanimously described the "settled doctrines of this Court" with respect to States, on the one hand, and counties and other municipal corporations within them, on the other:

> "Municipal corporations are political subdivisions of the State, created as convenient agencies for exercising such of the governmental powers of the State as may be entrusted to them. For the purpose of executing these powers properly and efficiently they usually are given the power to acquire, hold, and manage personal and real property. The number, nature and duration of the powers conferred upon these corporations and the territory over which they shall be exercised rests in the absolute discretion of the State."

Flying in the face of this settled doctrine, the Court today holds that Congress, by providing for payments of federal funds in lieu of taxes to counties in South Dakota, implicitly prohibited the State of South Dakota from regulating in any way the manner in which its counties might spend those funds. * * *

[The] two-sentence statutory provision enacted by Congress certainly does not proclaim by its language any single meaning, but one would be hard pressed to derive a more tortured meaning from it than that chosen by the Court. It may be that Congress, by providing that payments be made directly to the counties rather than to the States, implied a desire to have the money spent in the counties. But nothing in the South Dakota statute requires any contrary result; all the South Dakota statute requires is that the counties allocate a part of the money to school districts within the county, just as general tax revenues and state in-lieu payments are allocated. The Court's collection of reasons why Congress intended to prohibit this result is simply not convincing in the light of the long history of treatment of counties as being by law totally subordinate to the States which have created them. * * *

MISSOURI v. JENKINS

Supreme Court of the United States, 1990.
495 U.S. 33, 110 S.Ct. 1651, 109 L.Ed.2d 31.

JUSTICE WHITE delivered the opinion of the Court. * * *

In 1977, KCMSD [the Kansas City, Missouri, School District] and a group of KCMSD students filed a complaint alleging that the State of Missouri and surrounding school districts had operated a segregated public school system in the Kansas City metropolitan area. * * * After a lengthy trial, the District Court found that KCMSD and the State had operated a segregated school system within the KCMSD.

The District Court thereafter issued an order detailing the remedies necessary to eliminate the vestiges of segregation and the financing necessary to implement those remedies. The District Court originally estimated the total cost of the desegregation remedy to be almost $88,000,000 over three years, of which it expected the State to pay $67,592,072 and KCMSD to pay $20,140,472. The court concluded, however, that several provisions of Missouri law would prevent KCMSD from being able to pay its share of the obligation. The Missouri Constitution limits local property taxes to $1.25 per $100 of assessed valuation unless a majority of the voters in the district approve a higher levy, up to $3.25 per $100; the levy may be raised above $3.25 per $100 only if two-thirds of the voters agree.[5] The "Hancock Amendment" requires property tax rates to be rolled back when property is assessed at a higher valuation to ensure that taxes will not be increased solely as a result of reassessments. The Hancock Amendment thus prevents KCMSD from obtaining any revenue increase as a result of increases in the assessed valuation of real property. "Proposition C" allocates one cent of every dollar raised by the state sales tax to a schools trust fund and requires school districts to reduce property taxes by an amount equal to 50% of the previous year's sales tax receipts in the district. However, the trust fund is allocated according to a formula that does not compensate KCMSD for the amount lost in property tax revenues, and the effect of Proposition C is to divert nearly half of the sales taxes collected in KCMSD to other parts of the State.

The District Court believed that it had the power to order a tax increase to ensure adequate funding of the desegregation plan, but it hesitated to take this step. It chose instead to enjoin the effect of the Proposition C rollback to allow KCMSD to raise an additional $4,000,000 for the coming fiscal year. The court ordered KCMSD to submit to the voters a proposal for an increase in taxes sufficient to pay for its share of the desegregation remedy in following years.

The Court of Appeals for the Eighth Circuit affirmed the District Court's findings of liability and remedial order in most respects. The Court of Appeals agreed with the State, however, that the District Court had failed to explain adequately why it had imposed most of the cost of the desegregation plan on the State. The Eighth Circuit ordered the District Court to divide the cost equally between the State and KCMSD. We denied certiorari.

Proceedings before the District Court continued during the appeal. In its original remedial order, the District Court had directed KCMSD to prepare a study addressing the usefulness of "magnet schools" to promote desegregation. A year later, the District Court approved KCMSD's

---

5. KCMSD voters approved a levy of $3.75 per $100 in 1969, but efforts to raise the tax rate higher than that had consistently failed to obtain the approval of two-thirds of the voters, and the District Court found it unlikely that a proposal to raise taxes about $3.75 per $100 would receive the voters' approval.

proposal to operate six magnet schools during the 1986–1987 school year. The court again faced the problem of funding, for KCMSD's efforts to persuade the voters to approve a tax increase had failed, as had its efforts to seek funds from the Kansas City Council and the state legislature. Again hesitating to impose a tax increase itself, the court continued its injunction against the Proposition C rollback to enable KCMSD to raise an additional $6,500,000.

In November 1986, the District Court endorsed a marked expansion of the magnet school program. It adopted in substance a KCMSD proposal that every high school, every middle school, and half of the elementary schools in KCMSD become magnet schools by the 1991–1992 school year. It also approved the $142,736,025 budget proposed by KCMSD for implementation of the magnet school plan, as well as the expenditure of $52,858,301 for additional capital improvements.

The District Court next considered, as the Court of Appeals had directed, how to shift the cost of desegregation to KCMSD. The District Court concluded that it would be "clearly inequitable" to require the population of KCMSD to pay half of the desegregation cost, and that "even with Court help it would be very difficult for the KCMSD to fund more than 25% of the costs of the entire remedial plan." * * * Three months later, the District Court adopted a plan requiring $187,450,334 in further capital improvements. By then it was clear that KCMSD would lack the resources to pay for its 25% share of the desegregation cost. KCMSD requested that the District Court order the State to pay for any amount that KCMSD could not meet. The District Court declined to impose a greater share of the cost on the State, but it accepted that KCMSD had "exhausted all available means of raising additional revenue." Finding itself with "no choice but to exercise its broad equitable powers and enter a judgment that will enable the KCMSD to raise its share of the cost of the plan," and believing that the "United States Supreme Court has stated that a tax may be increased if 'necessary to raise funds adequate to * * * operate and maintain without racial discrimination a public school system,'" (quoting *Griffin v. Prince Edward County School Bd.*, 377 U.S. 218, 233, 84 S.Ct. 1226, 1234, 12 L.Ed.2d 256 (1964)), the court ordered the KCMSD property tax levy raised from $2.05 to $4.00 per $100 of assessed valuation through the 1991–1992 fiscal year. KCMSD was also directed to issue $150,000,-000 in capital improvement bonds. A subsequent order directed that the revenues generated by the property tax increase be used to retire the capital improvement bonds. * * *

The State appealed * * *. [W]e agree with the State that the tax increase contravened the principles of comity that must govern the exercise of the District Court's equitable discretion in this area.

It is accepted by all the parties, as it was by the courts below, that the imposition of a tax increase by a federal court was an extraordinary event. In assuming for itself the fundamental and delicate power of taxation the District Court not only intruded on local authority but circumvented it altogether. Before taking such a drastic step the District Court was obliged to assure itself that no permissible alternative would have accomplished the required task. * * * [O]ne of the most important considerations governing the exercise of equitable power is a proper respect for the integrity and function of local government institutions. Especially is this true where, as here, those institutions are ready, willing, and—but for the operation of state law curtailing their power—able to remedy the deprivation of constitutional rights themselves.

The District Court believed that it had no alternative to imposing a tax increase. But there was an alternative, the very one outlined by the Court of Appeals: it could have authorized or required KCMSD to levy property taxes at a rate adequate to fund the desegregation remedy and could have enjoined the operation of state laws that would have prevented KCMSD from exercising this power. The difference between the two approaches is far more than a matter of form. Authorizing and directing local government institutions to devise and implement remedies not only protects the function of those institutions but, to the extent possible, also places the responsibility for solutions to the problems of segregation upon those who have themselves created the problems. * * * The District Court therefore abused its discretion in imposing the tax itself. The Court of Appeals should not have allowed the tax increase to stand and should have reversed the District Court in this respect.

We stand on different ground when we review the modifications to the District Court's order made by the Court of Appeals. * * * [T]he Court of Appeals held that the District Court in the future should authorize KCMSD to submit a levy to the state tax collection authorities adequate to fund its budget and should enjoin the operation of state laws that would limit or reduce the levy below that amount.

The State argues that the funding ordered by the District court violates principles of equity and comity because the remedial order itself was excessive. As the State puts it, "[t]he only reason that the court below needed to consider an unprecedented tax increase was the equally unprecedented cost of its remedial programs." We think this argument aims at the scope of the remedy rather than the manner in which the remedy is to be funded and thus falls outside our limited grant of certiorari in this case. As we denied certiorari on the first question presented by the State's petition, which did challenge the scope of the remedial order, we must resist the State's efforts to argue that point now. We accept, without approving or disapproving, the Court of Appeals' conclusion that the District Court's remedy was proper. * * *

Finally, the State argues that an order to increase taxes cannot be sustained under the judicial power of Article III. Whatever the merits of this argument when applied to the District Court's own order increasing taxes, a point we have not reached, a court order directing a local government body to levy its own taxes is plainly a judicial act within the power of a federal court. We held as much in *Griffin v. Prince Edward County School Bd.,* 377 U.S., at 233, 84 S.Ct., at 1234, where we stated that a District Court, faced with a country's attempt to avoid desegregation of the public schools by refusing to operate those schools, could "require the [County] Supervisors to exercise the power that is theirs to levy taxes to raise funds adequate to reopen, operate, and maintain without racial discrimination a public school system * * *." *Griffin* followed a long and venerable line of cases in which this Court held that federal courts could issue the writ of mandamus to compel local governmental bodies to levy taxes adequate to satisfy their debt obligations. See, *e.g., Von Hoffman v. City of Quincy,* 4 Wall. 535, 18 L.Ed. 403 (1867).

The State maintains, however, that even under these cases, the federal judicial power can go no further than to require local governments to levy taxes *as authorized under state law.* In other words, the State argues that federal courts cannot set aside state-imposed limitations on local taxing authority because to do so is to do more than to require the local government "to exercise the power *that is theirs.*" We disagree. * * * [T]he KCMSD may be ordered to levy taxes despite the statutory limitations on its authority in order to compel the discharge of an obligation imposed on KCMSD by the Fourteenth Amendment. To hold otherwise would fail to take account of the obligations of local government, under the Supremacy Clause, to fulfill the requirements that the Constitution imposes on them. However wide the discretion of local authorities in fashioning desegregation remedies may be, "if a state-imposed limitation on a school authority's discretion operates to inhibit or obstruct the operation of a unitary school system or impede the disestablishing of a dual school system, it must fall; state policy must give way when it operates to hinder vindication of federal constitutional guarantees." *North Carolina State Bd. of Education v. Swann,* 402 U.S. 43, 45, 91 S.Ct. 1284, 1286, 28 L.Ed.2d 586 (1971). Even though a particular remedy may not be required in every case to vindicate constitutional guarantees, where (as here) it has been found that a particular remedy is required, the State cannot hinder the process by preventing a local government from implementing that remedy. * * *

JUSTICE KENNEDY with whom THE CHIEF JUSTICE, JUSTICE O'CONNOR, and JUSTICE SCALIA join, concurring in part and concurring in the judgment. * * *

The District Court's remedial plan was proposed for the most part by the Kansas City, Missouri, School District (KCMSD) itself, which is in name a defendant in the suit. Defendants, and above all defendants that are public entities, act in the highest and best tradition of our legal system when they acknowledge fault and cooperate to suggest remedies. But in the context of this dispute, it is of vital importance to note the KCMSD demonstrated little concern for the fiscal consequences of the remedy that it helped design.

As the District Court acknowledged, the plaintiffs and the KCMSD pursued a "friendly adversary" relationship. Throughout the remedial phase of the litigation, the KCMSD proposed ever more expensive capital improvements with the agreement of the plaintiffs, and the State objected. Some of these improvements involved basic repairs to deteriorating facilities within the school system. The KCMSD, however, devised a broader concept for district-wide improvement, and the District Court approved it. * * * It comes as no surprise that the cost of this approach to the remedy far exceeded KCMSD's budget, or for that matter, its authority to tax. * * *

I agree with the Court that the Eighth Circuit's judgment affirming the District Court's direct levy of a property tax must be reversed. I cannot agree, however, that we "stand on different ground when we review the modifications to the District Court's order made by the Court of Appeals." * * * The premise of the Court's analysis, I submit, is infirm. Any purported distinction between direct imposition of a tax by the federal court and an order commanding the school district to impose the tax is but a convenient formalism where the court's action is predicated on elimination of state law limitations on the school district's taxing authority. As the Court describes it, the local KCMSD possesses plenary taxing powers, which allow it to impose any tax it chooses if not "hinder[ed]" by the Missouri Constitution and state statutes. This puts the conclusion before the premise. Local government bodies in Missouri, as elsewhere, must derive their power from a sovereign, and that sovereign is the State of Missouri. Under Missouri law, the KCMSD has power to impose a limited property tax levy up to $1.25 per $100 of assessed value. The power to exact a higher rate of property tax remains with the people, a majority of whom must agree to empower the KCMSD to increase the levy up to $3.75 per $100, and two-thirds of whom must agree for the levy to go higher. The Missouri Constitution states that "[p]roperty taxes and other local taxes may not be increased above the limitations specified herein without direct voter approval as provided by this constitution." Mo. Const., Art. X, § 16.

For this reason, I reject the artificial suggestion that the District Court may by "prevent[ing] * * * officials from applying state law that would interfere with the willing levy of property taxes by KCMSD" cause the KCMSD to exercise power under *state* law. State laws, including taxation provisions legitimate and constitutional in themselves, define the power of the KCMSD. Absent a change in state law, no increase in property taxes could take place in the KCMSD without a federal court order. It makes no difference that the KCMSD stands "ready, willing, and * * * able" to impose a tax not authorized by state law. Whatever taxing power the KCMSD may exercise outside the boundaries of state law would derive from the federal court. The Court never confronts the judicial authority to issue an order for this purpose. Absent a change in state law, the tax is imposed by federal authority under a federal decree. The question is whether a district court possesses a power to tax under federal law, either directly or through delegation to the KCMSD. * * *

In my view, a taxation order should not even be considered, and this Court need never have addressed the question, unless there has been a finding that without the particular remedy at issue the constitutional violation will go unremedied. By this I do not mean that the remedy is, as we assume this one was, within the broad discretion of the district court. Rather, as a prerequisite to considering a taxation order, I would require a finding that any remedy less costly than the one at issue would so plainly leave the violation unremedied that its implementation would itself be an abuse of discretion. There is no showing in this record that, faced with the revenue shortfall, the District Court gave due consideration to the possibility that another remedy among the "wide range of possibilities" would have addressed the constitutional violations without giving rise to a funding crises. * * *

2. THE FEDERAL GOVERNMENT AS A THREAT TO CITY POWER

National League of Cities v. Usery and the case that overruled it nine years later, Garcia v. San Antonio Metropolitan Transit Authority, define the terms of the Constitutional debate about federal-city—and federal-state—relationships.[1] In reading the opinions in these cases, try to determine what the terms of this debate are. How do the arguments in these Supreme Court cases relate to the debate over home rule in City of LaGrande v. Public Employees Retirement Board? Indeed, how do the arguments in *National League of Cities* and *Garcia* relate to each other? Do Justice Rehnquist's opinion in *National League of Cities* and Justice Powell's opinion in *Garcia* state the proposed limit on federal power over states and cities in the same way? How does the most recent Tenth Amendment case, New York v. United States, change the nature of the Constitutional debate?[2] Does the *New York* case suggest that ultimately *National League of Cities*, and not *Garcia*, will prevail?

NATIONAL LEAGUE OF CITIES v. USERY

Supreme Court of the United States, 1976.
426 U.S. 833, 96 S.Ct. 2465, 49 L.Ed.2d 245.

MR. JUSTICE REHNQUIST delivered the opinion of the Court.

Nearly 40 years ago Congress enacted the Fair Labor Standards Act, and required employers covered by the Act to pay their employees a

---

1. There is an extensive literature on this debate. See, e.g., L. Tribe, American Constitutional Law 386–400 (2d ed. 1988); Stephenson & Levine, Vicarious Federalism: The Modern Supreme Court and the Tenth Amendment, 19 The Urban Lawyer 683 (1987); Lynch, Garcia v. San Antonio Metropolitan Transit Authority: An Alternate Opinion, 16 Seton Hall L.Rev. 74 (1986); Advisory Commission on Intergovernmental Relations, Reflections on Garcia and Its Implications for Federalism (1986); Field, Garcia v. San Antonio Metropolitan Transit Authority: The Demise of a Mis-

guided Doctrine, 99 Harv.L.Rev. 84 (1985); Howard, *Garcia* and the Values of Federalism: On the Need for a Recurrence to Fundamental Principles, 19 Ga.L.Rev. 789 (1985); Michelman, States' Rights and States' Roles: Permutations of "Sovereignty" in National League of Cities v. Usery, 86 Yale L.J. 1165 (1977).

2. See, e.g., Levy, New York v. United States: An Essay on the Uses and Misuses of Precedent, History, and Policy in Determining the Scope of Federal Power, 41 U.Kan.L.Rev. 493 (1993).

minimum hourly wage and to pay them at one and one-half times their regular rate of pay for hours worked in excess of 40 during a workweek. * * * The original Fair Labor Standards Act passed in 1938 specifically excluded the States and their political subdivisions from its coverage. In 1974, however, * * * Congress * * * extended the minimum wage and maximum hour provisions to almost all public employees employed by the States and by their various political subdivisions. Appellants in these cases include individual cities and States, the National League of Cities, and the National Governors' Conference; they brought an action in the District Court for the District of Columbia which challenged the validity of the 1974 amendments. They asserted in effect that when Congress sought to apply the Fair Labor Standards Act provisions virtually across the board to employees of state and municipal governments it "infringed a constitutional prohibition" running in favor of the States *as States*. * * *

It is established beyond peradventure that the Commerce Clause of Art. I of the Constitution is a grant of plenary authority to Congress. * * * Congressional power over areas of private endeavor, even when its exercise may preempt express state-law determinations contrary to the result which has commended itself to the collective wisdom of Congress, has been held to be limited only by the requirement that "the means chosen by [Congress] must be reasonably adapted to the end permitted by the Constitution." *Heart of Atlanta Motel v. United States,* 379 U.S. 241, 262, 85 S.Ct. 348, 360, 13 L.Ed.2d 258 (1964). * * * Appellants' essential contention is that the 1974 amendments to the Act, while undoubtedly within the scope of the Commerce Clause, encounter a similar constitutional barrier because they are to be applied directly to the States and subdivisions of States as employers. * * *

Appellee Secretary argues that the cases in which this Court has upheld sweeping exercises of authority by Congress, even though those exercises pre-empted state regulation of the private sector, have already curtailed the sovereignty of the States quite as much as the 1974 amendments to the Fair Labor Standards Act. We do not agree. It is one thing to recognize the authority of Congress to enact laws regulating individual businesses necessarily subject to the dual sovereignty of the government of the Nation and of the State in which they reside. It is quite another to uphold a similar exercise of congressional authority directed, not to private citizens, but to the States as States. We have repeatedly recognized that there are attributes of sovereignty attaching to every state government which may not be impaired by Congress, not because Congress may lack an affirmative grant of legislative authority to reach the matter, but because the Constitution prohibits it from exercising the authority in that manner. In *Coyle v. Oklahoma,* 221 U.S. 559, 31 S.Ct. 688, 55 L.Ed. 853 (1911), the Court gave this example of such an attribute:

"The power to locate its own seat of government, and to determine when and how it shall be changed from one place to another, and to appropriate its own public funds for that purpose, are essentially and peculiarly state powers. That one of the original thirteen states could now be shorn of such powers by an act of Congress would not be for a moment entertained."

One undoubted attribute of state sovereignty is the States' power to determine the wages which shall be paid to those whom they employ in order to carry out their governmental functions, what hours those persons will work, and what compensation will be provided where these employees may be called upon to work overtime. The question we must resolve here, then, is whether these determinations are " 'functions essential to separate and independent existence,' " *id.*, at 580, 31 S.Ct., at 695, so that Congress may not abrogate the States' otherwise plenary authority to make them.

In their complaint appellants advanced estimates of substantial costs which will be imposed upon them by the 1974 amendments. Since the District Court dismissed their complaint, we take its well-pleaded allegations as true, although it appears from appellee's submissions in the District Court and in this Court that resolution of the factual disputes as to the effect of the amendments is not critical to our disposition of the case.

Judged solely in terms of increased costs in dollars, these allegations show a significant impact on the functioning of the governmental bodies involved. * * * Quite apart from the[se] substantial costs * * *, the Act displaces state policies regarding the manner in which they will structure delivery of those governmental services which their citizens require. The Act, speaking directly to the States *qua* States, requires that they shall pay all but an extremely limited minority of their employees the minimum wage rates currently chosen by Congress. It may well be that as a matter of economic policy it would be desirable that States, just as private employers, comply with these minimum wage requirements. But it cannot be gainsaid that the federal requirement directly supplants the considered policy choices of the States' elected officials and administrators as to how they wish to structure pay scales in state employment. The State might wish to employ persons with little or no training, or those who wish to work on a casual basis, or those who for some other reason do not possess minimum employment requirements, and pay them less than the federally prescribed minimum wage. It may wish to offer part-time or summer employment to teenagers at a figure less than the minimum wage, and if unable to do so may decline to offer such employment at all. But the Act would forbid such choices by the States. The only "discretion" left to them under the Act is either to attempt to increase their revenue to meet the additional financial burden imposed upon them by paying congressionally prescribed wages to their existing complement of employees, or to reduce that complement to a number which can be paid the federal minimum wage without increasing revenue.

This dilemma presented by the minimum wage restrictions may seem not immediately different from that faced by private employers, who have long been covered by the Act and who must find ways to increase their gross income if they are to pay higher wages while maintaining current earnings. The difference, however, is that a State is not merely a factor in the "shifting economic arrangements" of the private sector of the economy, *Kovacs v. Cooper*, 336 U.S. 77, 95, 69 S.Ct. 448, 458, 93 L.Ed. 513 (1949) (Frankfurter, J., concurring), but is itself a coordinate element in the system established by the Framers for governing our Federal Union. * * *

This congressionally imposed displacement of state decisions may substantially restructure traditional ways in which the local governments have arranged their affairs. Although at this point many of the actual effects under the proposed amendments remain a matter of some dispute among the parties, enough can be satisfactorily anticipated for an outline discussion of their general import. The requirement imposing premium rates upon any employment in excess of what Congress has decided is appropriate for a governmental employee's workweek, for example, appears likely to have the effect of coercing the States to structure work periods in some employment areas, such as police and fire protection, in a manner substantially different from practices which have long been commonly accepted among local governments of this Nation. * * * Another example of congressional choices displacing those of the States in the area of what are without doubt essential governmental decisions may be found in the practice of using volunteer firemen, a source of manpower crucial to many of our smaller towns' existence. Under the regulations proposed by appellee, whether individuals are indeed "volunteers" rather than "employees" subject to the minimum wage provisions of the Act are questions to be decided in the courts. It goes without saying that provisions such as these contemplate a significant reduction of traditional volunteer assistance which has been in the past drawn on to complement the operation of many local governmental functions.

Our examination of the effect of the 1974 amendments, as sought to be extended to the States and their political subdivisions, satisfies us that both the minimum wage and the maximum hour provisions will impermissibly interfere with the integral governmental functions of these bodies. * * * [E]ven if we accept appellee's assessments concerning the impact of the amendments, their application will nonetheless significantly alter or displace the States' abilities to structure employer-employee relationships in such areas as fire prevention, police protection, sanitation, public health, and parks and recreation. These activities are typical of those performed by state and local governments in discharging their dual functions of administering the public law and furnishing public services. Indeed, it is functions such as these which governments are created to provide, services such as these which the States have traditionally afforded their citizens. If Congress may withdraw from the States the authority to make those fundamental employment decisions upon which their systems for performance of these functions must rest, we think there would be little left of the States' " 'separate and independent existence.' " *Coyle,* 221 U.S., at 580, 31 S.Ct., at 695. Thus, even if appellants may have overestimated the effect which the Act will have upon their current levels and patterns of governmental activity, the dispositive factor is that Congress has attempted to exercise its Commerce Clause authority to prescribe minimum wages and maximum hours to be paid by the States in their capacities as sovereign governments. In so doing, Congress has sought to wield its power in a fashion that would impair the States' "ability to function effectively in a federal system," *Fry [v. United States],* 421 U.S. [542], at 547, 95 S.Ct. [1792], at 1796 n. 7 [(1975)]. * * * This exercise of congressional authority does not comport with the federal system of government embodied in the Constitution. We hold that insofar as the challenged amendments operate to directly displace the States' freedom to structure integral operations in areas of traditional governmental functions, they are not within the authority granted Congress by Art. I, § 8, cl. 3. * * * The fire and police departments affected here * * * provide[ ] an integral portion of those governmental services which the States and their political subdivisions have traditionally afforded their citizens.[20] * * *

Mr. Justice Blackmun, concurring.

The Court's opinion and the dissents indicate the importance and significance of this litigation as it bears upon the relationship between the Federal Government and our States. Although I am not untroubled by certain possible implications of the Court's opinion—some of them suggested by the dissents—I do not read the opinion so despairingly as does my Brother Brennan. In my view, the result with respect to the statute under challenge here is necessarily correct. I may misinterpret the Court's opinion, but it seems to me that it adopts a balancing approach, and does not outlaw federal power in areas such as environmental protection, where the federal interest is demonstrably greater and where state facility compliance with imposed federal standards would be essential. With this understanding on my part of the Court's opinion, I join it.

Mr. Justice Brennan, with whom Mr. Justice White and Mr. Justice Marshall join, dissenting. * * *

The reliance of my Brethren upon the Tenth Amendment as "an express declaration of [a state sovereignty] limitation" not only suggests that they overrule governing decisions of this Court that address this question but must astound scholars of the Constitution. For not only early decisions, *Gibbons v. Ogden,* 9 Wheat., at 196; *McCulloch v. Maryland,* 4 Wheat., at 404–407; and *Martin v. Hunter's Lessee,* 1

---

20. As the denomination "political subdivision" implies, the local governmental units which Congress sought to bring within the Act derive their authority and power from their respective States. Interference with integral governmental services provided by such subordinate arms of a state government is therefore beyond the reach of congressional power under the Commerce Clause just as if such services were provided by the State itself.

Wheat. 304, 324–325, 4 L.Ed. 97 (1816), hold that nothing in the Tenth Amendment constitutes a limitation on congressional exercise of powers delegated by the Constitution to Congress. * * * Certainly the paradigm of sovereign action action *qua* State is in the enactment and enforcement of state laws. Is it possible that my Brethren are signaling abandonment of the heretofore unchallenged principle that Congress "can, if it chooses, entirely displace the States to the full extent of the far-reaching Commerce Clause"? *Bethlehem Steel Co. v. New York State Board,* 330 U.S. 767, 780, 67 S.Ct. 1026, 1033, 91 L.Ed. 1234 (1947) (opinion of Frankfurter, J.). * * * [T]he ouster of state laws obviously curtails or prohibits the States' prerogatives to make policy choices respecting subjects clearly of greater significance to the "State *qua* State" than the minimum wage paid to state employees. The Supremacy Clause dictates this result under "the federal system of government embodied in the Constitution."

My Brethren do more than turn aside longstanding constitutional jurisprudence that emphatically rejects today's conclusion. More alarming is the startling restructuring of our federal system, and the role they create therein for the federal judiciary. * * * It is unacceptable that the judicial process should be thought superior to the political process in this area. Under the Constitution the Judiciary has no role to play beyond finding that Congress has not made an unreasonable legislative judgment respecting what is "commerce." * * *

Judicial restraint in this area merely recognizes that the political branches of our Government are structured to protect the interests of the States, as well as the Nation as a whole, and that the States are fully able to protect their own interests in the premises. Congress is constituted of representatives in both the Senate and House *elected from the States.* Decisions upon the extent of federal intervention under the Commerce Clause into the affairs of the States are in that sense decisions of the States themselves. Judicial redistribution of powers granted the National Government by the terms of the Constitution violates the fundamental tenet of our federalism that the extent of federal intervention into the States' affairs in the exercise of delegated powers shall be determined by the States' exercise of political power through their representatives in Congress. * * *

Mr. Justice Stevens, dissenting.

The Court holds that the Federal Government may not interfere with a sovereign State's inherent right to pay a substandard wage to the janitor at the state capitol. The principle on which the holding rests is difficult to perceive.

The Federal Government may, I believe, require the State to act impartially when it hires or fires the janitor, to withhold taxes from his paycheck, to observe safety regulations when he is performing his job, to forbid him from burning too much soft coal in the capitol furnace, from dumping untreated refuse in an adjacent waterway, from overloading a state-owned garbage truck, or from driving either the truck or the

Governor's limousine over 55 miles an hour. Even though these and many other activities of the capitol janitor are activities of the State *qua* State, I have no doubt that they are subject to federal regulation. * * * Since I am unable to identify a limitation on that federal power that would not also invalidate federal regulation of state activities that I consider unquestionably permissible, I am persuaded that this statute is valid. Accordingly, with respect and a great deal of sympathy for the views expressed by the Court, I dissent from its constitutional holding.

GARCIA v. SAN ANTONIO METROPOLITAN TRANSIT AUTHORITY

Supreme Court of the United States, 1985.
469 U.S. 528, 105 S.Ct. 1005, 83 L.Ed.2d 1016.

Justice Blackmun delivered the opinion of the Court.

We revisit in these cases an issue raised in *National League of Cities v. Usery,* 426 U.S. 833, 96 S.Ct. 2465, 49 L.Ed.2d 245 (1976). In that litigation, this Court, by a sharply divided vote, ruled that the Commerce Clause does not empower Congress to enforce the minimum-wage and overtime provisions of the Fair Labor Standards Act (FLSA) against the States "in areas of traditional governmental functions." * * * In the present cases, a Federal District Court concluded that municipal ownership and operation of a mass-transit system is a traditional governmental function and thus, under *National League of Cities,* is exempt from the obligations imposed by the FLSA. * * * Our examination of this "function" standard [as] applied * * * over the last eight years now persuades us that the attempt to draw the boundaries of state regulatory immunity in terms of "traditional governmental function" is not only unworkable but is inconsistent with established principles of federalism and, indeed, with those very federalism principles on which *National League of Cities* purported to rest. That case, accordingly, is overruled. * * *

[A]ppellee San Antonio Metropolitan Transit Authority (SAMTA), a public mass-transit authority organized on a countywide basis, * * * currently is the major provider of transportation in the San Antonio metropolitan area * * *. On November 2[, 1979] * * *, SAMTA filed this action against the Secretary of Labor in the United States District Court for the Western District of Texas. It sought a declaratory judgment that * * * *National League of Cities* precluded the application of the FLSA's overtime requirements to SAMTA's operations. * * *

The prerequisites for governmental immunity under *National League of Cities* were summarized by this Court in *Hodel [v. Virginia Surface Mining & Recl. Assn.,* 452 U.S. 264, 276–277, 101 S.Ct. 2352, 2360–2361, 69 L.Ed.2d 1 (1981)]. Under that summary, four conditions must be satisfied before a state activity may be deemed immune from a particular federal regulation under the Commerce Clause. First, it is said that the federal statute at issue must regulate "the 'States as States.'" Second, the statute must "address matters that are indisputably 'attribute[s] of state sovereignty.' "   Third, state compliance with the federal obligation must "directly impair [the States'] ability 'to structure integral operations in areas of traditional governmental functions.' "   Finally, the relation of state and federal interests must not be such that "the nature of the federal interest * * * justifies state submission."

The controversy in the present cases has focused on the third *Hodel* requirement—that the challenged federal statute trench on "traditional governmental functions."   The District Court voiced a common concern: "Despite the abundance of adjectives, identifying which particular state functions are immune remains difficult."   Just how troublesome the task has been is revealed by the results reached in other federal cases. Thus, courts have held that regulating ambulance services, operating a municipal airport, performing solid waste disposal, and operating a highway authority, are functions *protected* under *National League of Cities*.   At the same time, courts have held that issuance of industrial development bonds, regulation of intrastate natural gas sales, regulation of traffic on public roads, regulation of air transportation, operation of a telephone system, leasing and sale of natural gas, operation of a mental health facility, and provision of in-house domestic services for the aged and handicapped are *not* entitled to immunity.   We find it difficult, if not impossible, to identify an organizing principle that places each of the cases in the first group on one side of a line and each of the cases in the second group on the other side.   The constitutional distinction between licensing drivers and regulating traffic, for example, or between operating a highway authority and operating a mental health facility, is elusive at best.   * * *

Many constitutional standards involve "undoubte[d] * * * gray areas," *Fry v. United States,* 421 U.S. 542, 558, 95 S.Ct. 1792, 1801, 44 L.Ed.2d 363 (1975) (dissenting opinion), and, despite the difficulties that this Court and other courts have encountered so far, it normally might be fair to venture the assumption that case-by-case development would lead to a workable standard for determining whether a particular governmental function should be immune from federal regulation under the Commerce Clause.   A further cautionary note is sounded, however, by the Court's experience in the related field of state immunity from federal taxation.   In *South Carolina v. United States,* 199 U.S. 437, 26 S.Ct. 110, 50 L.Ed. 261 (1905), the Court held for the first time that the state tax immunity recognized in *Collector v. Day,* 11 Wall. 113, 20 L.Ed. 122 (1870), extended only to the "ordinary" and "strictly governmental" instrumentalities of state governments and not to instrumentalities "used by the State in the carrying on of an ordinary private business." While the Court applied the distinction outlined in *South Carolina* for the following 40 years, at no time during that period did the Court develop a consistent formulation of the kinds of governmental functions that were entitled to immunity.   The Court identified the protected functions at various times as "essential," "usual," "traditional," or "strictly governmental."   While "these differences in phraseology * * * must not be too literally contradistinguished," *Brush v. Commissioner*, 300 U.S. 352, 362, 57 S.Ct. 495, 496, 81 L.Ed. 691 (1937), they reflect an inability to specify precisely what aspects of a governmental function made it necessary to the "unimpaired existence" of the States. *Collector v. Day*, 11 Wall., at 127. Indeed, the Court ultimately chose "not, by an attempt to formulate any general test, [to] risk embarrassing the decision of cases [concerning] activities of a different kind which may arise in the future." *Brush v. Commissioner,* 300 U.S., at 365, 57 S.Ct., at 498.

If these tax immunity cases had any common thread, it was in the attempt to distinguish between "governmental" and "proprietary" functions. To say that the distinction between "governmental" and "proprietary" proved to be stable, however, would be something of an overstatement. In 1911, for example, the Court declared that the provision of a municipal water supply "is no part of the essential governmental functions of a State." *Flint v. Stone Tracy Co.*, 220 U.S. 107, 172, 31 S.Ct. 342, 357, 55 L.Ed. 389. Twenty-six years later, without any intervening change in the applicable legal standards, the Court simply rejected its earlier position and decided that the provision of a municipal water supply *was* immune from federal taxation as an essential governmental function, even though municipal water works long had been operated for profit by private industry. At the same time that the Court was holding a municipal water supply to be immune from federal taxes, it had held that a state-run commuter rail system was *not* immune. Justice Black, in *Helvering v. Gerhardt,* 304 U.S. 405, 427, 58 S.Ct. 969, 978, 82 L.Ed. 1427 (1938), was moved to observe: "An implied constitutional distinction which taxes income of an officer of a state-operated transportation system and exempts income of the manager of a municipal water works system manifests the uncertainty created by the 'essential' and 'non-essential' test" (concurring opinion). It was this uncertainty and instability that led the Court shortly thereafter, in *New York v. United States,* 326 U.S. 572, 66 S.Ct. 310, 90 L.Ed. 326 (1946), unanimously to conclude that the distinction between "governmental" and "proprietary" functions was "untenable" and must be abandoned. * * *

The distinction the Court discarded as unworkable in the field of tax immunity has proved no more fruitful in the field of regulatory immunity under the Commerce Clause. Neither do any of the alternative standards that might be employed to distinguish between protected and unprotected governmental functions appear manageable. We rejected the possibility of making immunity turn on a purely historical standard of "tradition" in *[Transportation Union v.] Long Island [R.Co.,* 455 U.S. 678, 102 S.Ct. 1349, 71 L.E.2d 547 (1982)] and properly so. The most obvious defect of a historical approach to state immunity is that it prevents a court from accommodating changes in the historical functions of States, changes that have resulted in a number of once-private functions like education being assumed by the States and their subdivisions. At the same time, the only apparent virtue of a rigorous historical standard, namely, its promise of a reasonably objective measure for state immunity, is illusory. Reliance on history as an organizing principle results in linedrawing of the most arbitrary sort; the genesis of state governmental functions stretches over a historical continuum from before the Revolution to the present, and courts would have to decide by fiat precisely how longstanding a pattern of state involvement had to be for federal regulatory authority to be defeated.

A nonhistorical standard for selecting immune governmental functions is likely to be just as unworkable as is a historical standard. The goal of identifying "uniquely" governmental functions, for example, has been rejected by the Court in the field of governmental tort liability in part because the notion of a "uniquely" governmental function is unmanageable. Another possibility would be to confine immunity to "necessary" governmental services, that is, services that would be provided inadequately or not at all unless the government provided them. The set of services that fits into this category, however, may well be negligible. The fact that an unregulated market produces less of some service than a State deems desirable does not mean that the State itself must provide the service; in most if not all cases, the State can "contract out" by hiring private firms to provide the service or simply by providing subsidies to existing suppliers. It also is open to question how well equipped courts are to make this kind of determination about the workings of economic markets.

We believe, however, that there is a more fundamental problem at work here, a problem that explains why the Court was never able to provide a basis for the governmental/proprietary distinction in the intergovernmental tax immunity cases and why an attempt to draw similar distinctions with respect to federal regulatory authority under *National League of Cities* is unlikely to succeed regardless of how the distinctions are phrased. The problem is that neither the governmental/proprietary distinction nor any other that purports to separate out important governmental functions can be faithful to the role of federalism in a democratic society. The essence of our federal system is that within the realm of authority left open to them under the Constitution, the States must be equally free to engage in any activity that their citizens choose for the common weal, no matter how unorthodox or unnecessary anyone else—including the judiciary—deems state involvement to be. Any rule of state immunity that looks to the "traditional," "integral," or "necessary" nature of governmental functions inevitably invites an unelected federal judiciary to make decisions about which state policies it favors and which ones it dislikes. * * * We therefore now reject, as unsound in principle and unworkable in practice, a rule of state immunity from federal regulation that turns on a judicial appraisal of whether a particular governmental function is "integral" or "traditional." Any such rule leads to inconsistent results at the same time that it disserves principles of democratic self-governance, and it breeds inconsistency precisely because it is divorced from those principles. If there are to be limits on the Federal Government's power to interfere with state functions—as undoubtedly there are—we must look elsewhere to find them. We accordingly return to the underlying issue that confronted this Court in *National League of Cities*—the manner in which the Constitution insulates States from the reach of Congress' power under the Commerce Clause.

The central theme of *National League of Cities* was that the States occupy a special position in our constitutional system and that the scope of Congress' authority under the Commerce Clause must reflect that position. * * * What has proved problematic is not the perception that the Constitution's federal structure imposes limitations on the Commerce Clause, but rather the nature and content of those limitations. One approach to defining the limits on Congress' authority to regulate the States under the Commerce Clause is to identify certain underlying elements of political sovereignty that are deemed essential to the States' "separate and independent existence." *Lane County v. Oregon,* 7 Wall. 71, 76, 19 L.Ed. 101 (1869). * * * In *National League of Cities* itself, for example, the Court concluded that decisions by a State concerning the wages and hours of its employees are an "undoubted attribute of state sovereignty." The opinion did not explain what aspects of such decisions made them such an "undoubted attribute," and the Court since then has remarked on the uncertain scope of the concept. * * *

We doubt that courts ultimately can identify principled constitutional limitations on the scope of Congress' Commerce Clause powers over the States merely by relying on *a priori* definitions of state sovereignty. In part, this is because of the elusiveness of objective criteria for "fundamental" elements of state sovereignty, a problem we have witnessed in the search for "traditional governmental functions." There is, however, a more fundamental reason: the sovereignty of the States is limited by the Constitution itself. A variety of sovereign powers, for example, are withdrawn from the States by Article I, § 10. * * * By providing for final review of questions of federal law in this Court, Article III curtails the sovereign power of the States' judiciaries to make authoritative determinations of law. Finally, the developed application, through the Fourteenth Amendment, of the greater part of the Bill of Rights to the States limits the sovereign authority that States otherwise would possess to legislate with respect to their citizens and to conduct their own affairs. * * *

When we look for the States' "residuary and inviolable sovereignty," The Federalist No. 39, p. 285 (B. Wright ed. 1961) (J. Madison), in the shape of the constitutional scheme rather than in predetermined notions of sovereign power, a different measure of state sovereignty emerges. Apart from the limitation on federal authority inherent in the delegated nature of Congress' Article I powers, the principal means chosen by the Framers to ensure the role of the States in the federal system lies in the structure of the Federal Government itself. It is no novelty to observe that the composition of the Federal Government was designed in large part to protect the States from overreaching by Congress. The Framers thus gave the States a role in the selection both of the Executive and the

Legislative Branches of the Federal Government. The States were vested with indirect influence over the House of Representatives and the Presidency by their control of electoral qualifications and their role in presidential elections. U.S. Const., Art. I, § 2, and Art. II, § 1. They were given more direct influence in the Senate, where each State received equal representation and each Senator was to be selected by the legislature of his State. Art. I, § 3. The significance attached to the States' equal representation in the Senate is underscored by the prohibition of any constitutional amendment divesting a State of equal representation without the State's consent. Art. V. * * * State sovereign interests, then, are more properly protected by procedural safeguards inherent in the structure of the federal system than by judicially created limitations on federal power. * * *

We realize that changes in the structure of the Federal Government have taken place since 1789, not the least of which has been the substitution of popular election of Senators by the adoption of the Seventeenth Amendment in 1913, and that these changes may work to alter the influence of the States in the federal political process. Nonetheless, against this background, we are convinced that the fundamental limitation that the constitutional scheme imposes on the Commerce Clause to protect the "States as States" is one of process rather than one of result. Any substantive restraint on the exercise of Commerce Clause powers must find its justification in the procedural nature of this basic limitation, and it must be tailored to compensate for possible failings in the national political process rather than to dictate a "sacred province of state autonomy." *EEOC v. Wyoming,* 460 U.S., at 236, 103 S.Ct., at 1060.

Insofar as the present cases are concerned, then, we need go no further than to state that we perceive nothing in the overtime and minimum-wage requirements of the FLSA, as applied to SAMTA, that is destructive of state sovereignty or violative of any constitutional provision. SAMTA faces nothing more than the same minimum-wage and overtime obligations that hundreds of thousands of other employers, public as well as private, have to meet. * * * This analysis makes clear that Congress' action in affording SAMTA employees the protections of the wage and hour provisions of the FLSA contravened no affirmative limit on Congress' power under the Commerce Clause. * * *

Of course, we continue to recognize that the States occupy a special and specific position in our constitutional system and that the scope of Congress' authority under the Commerce Clause must reflect that position. But the principal and basic limit on the federal commerce power is that inherent in all congressional action—the built-in restraints that our system provides through state participation in federal governmental action. The political process ensures that laws that unduly burden the States will not be promulgated. * * *

JUSTICE POWELL, with whom THE CHIEF JUSTICE, JUSTICE REHNQUIST, and JUSTICE O'CONNOR join, dissenting. * * *

Much of the Court's opinion is devoted to arguing that it is difficult to define *a priori* "traditional governmental functions." *National League of Cities* neither engaged in, nor required, such a task. The Court discusses and condemns as standards "traditional governmental function[s]," "purely historical" functions, " 'uniquely' governmental functions," and " 'necessary' governmental services." But nowhere does it mention that *National League of Cities* adopted a familiar type of balancing test for determining whether Commerce Clause enactments transgress constitutional limitations imposed by the federal nature of our system of government. This omission is noteworthy, since the author of today's opinion joined *National League of Cities* and concurred separately to point out that the Court's opinion in that case "adopt[s] a balancing approach [that] does not outlaw federal power in areas * * * where the federal interest is demonstrably greater and where state * * * compliance with imposed federal standards would be essential." (Blackmun, J., concurring). * * * In overruling *National League of Cities,* the Court incorrectly characterizes the mode of analysis established therein and developed in subsequent cases.

Today's opinion does not explain how the States' role in the electoral process guarantees that particular exercises of the Commerce Clause power will not infringe on residual State sovereignty. Members of Congress are elected from the various States, but once in office they are members of the federal government.[8] Although the States participate in the Electoral College, this is hardly a reason to view the President as a representative of the States' interest against federal encroachment. We noted recently "the hydraulic pressure inherent within each of the separate Branches to exceed the outer limits of its power * * *." *Immigration and Naturalization Service v. Chadha,* 462 U.S. 919, ___, 103 S.Ct. 2764, 2784, 77 L.Ed.2d 317 (1983). The Court offers no reason to think that this pressure will not operate when Congress seeks to invoke its powers under the Commerce Clause, notwithstanding the electoral role of the States. * * *

The States' role in our system of government is a matter of constitutional law, not of legislative grace. "The powers not delegated to the United States by the Constitution, nor prohibited by it to the States, are reserved to the States, respectively, or to the people." U.S. Const., Amend. 10. * * * Far from being "unsound in principle," judicial enforcement of the Tenth Amendment is essential to maintaining the federal system so carefully designed by the Framers and adopted in the Constitution. * * * [T]he harm to the States that results from federal overreaching under the Commerce Clause is not simply a matter of dollars and cents. Nor is it a matter of the wisdom or folly of certain policy choices. Rather, by usurping functions traditionally performed by the States, federal overreaching under the Commerce Clause undermines

---

8. One can hardly imagine this Court saying that because Congress is composed of individuals, individual rights guaranteed by the Bill of Rights are amply protected by the political process. Yet, the position adopted today is indistinguishable in principle. The Tenth Amendment also is an essential part of the Bill of Rights.

the constitutionally mandated balance of power between the States and the federal government, a balance designed to protect our fundamental liberties. * * *

In *National League of Cities,* we spoke of fire prevention, police protection, sanitation, and public health as "typical of [the services] performed by state and local governments in discharging their dual functions of administering the public law and furnishing public services." Not only are these activities remote from any normal concept of interstate commerce, they are also activities that epitomize the concerns of local, democratic self-government. In emphasizing the need to protect traditional governmental functions, we identified the kinds of activities engaged in by state and local governments that affect the everyday lives of citizens. These are services that people are in a position to understand and evaluate, and in a democracy, have the right to oversee. * * * [M]embers of the immense federal bureaucracy are not elected, know less about the services traditionally rendered by States and localities, and are inevitably less responsive to recipients of such services, than are state legislatures, city councils, boards of supervisors, and state and local commissions, boards, and agencies. It is at these state and local levels— not in Washington as the Court so mistakenly thinks—that "democratic self-government" is best exemplified.

The question presented in this case is whether the extension of the FLSA to the wages and hours of employees of a city-owned transit system unconstitutionally impinges on fundamental state sovereignty. * * * The Court does not find in this case that the "federal interest is demonstrably greater." 426 U.S., at 856, 96 S.Ct., at 2476 (Blackmun, J., concurring). No such finding could have been made, for the state interest is compelling. The financial impact on States and localities of displacing their control over wages, hours, overtime regulations, pensions, and labor relations with their employees could have serious, as well as unanticipated, effects on state and local planning, budgeting, and the levying of taxes. As we said in *National League of Cities,* federal control of the terms and conditions of employment of State employees also inevitably "displaces state policies regarding the manner in which [States] will structure delivery of those governmental services that citizens require."

The Court emphasizes that municipal operation of an intracity mass transit system is relatively new in the life of our country. It nevertheless is a classic example of the type of service traditionally provided by local government. It is *local* by definition. It is indistinguishable in principle from the traditional services of providing and maintaining streets, public lighting, traffic control, water, and sewerage systems. Services of this kind are precisely those "with which citizens are more 'familiarly and minutely conversant.'" The Federalist, No. 46, p. 316. State and local officials of course must be intimately familiar with these services and sensitive to their quality as well as cost. Such officials also know that their constituents and the press respond to the adequacy, fair distribution, and cost of these services. It is this kind of state and local control and accountability that the Framers understood would insure the vitality and preservation of the federal system that the Constitution explicitly requires. * * *

JUSTICE REHNQUIST, dissenting.

I join both Justice Powell's and Justice O'Connor's thoughtful dissents. Justice Powell's reference to the "balancing test" approved in *National League of Cities* is not identical with the language in that case, which recognized that Congress could not act under its commerce power to infringe on certain fundamental aspects of state sovereignty that are essential to "the States' separate and independent existence." Nor is either test, or Justice O'Connor's suggested approach, precisely congruent with Justice Blackmun's views in 1976, when he spoke of a balancing approach which did not outlaw federal power in areas "where the federal interest is demonstrably greater." But under any one of these approaches the judgment in this case should be affirmed, and I do not think it incumbent on those of us in dissent to spell out further the fine points of a principle that will, I am confident, in time again command the support of a majority of this Court.

JUSTICE O'CONNOR, with whom JUSTICE POWELL and JUSTICE REHNQUIST join, dissenting. * * *

The problems of federalism in an integrated national economy are capable of more responsible resolution than holding that the States as States retain no status apart from that which Congress chooses to let them retain. The proper resolution, I suggest, lies in weighing state autonomy as a factor in the balance when interpreting the means by which Congress can exercise its authority on the States as States. It is insufficient, in assessing the validity of congressional regulation of a State pursuant to the commerce power, to ask only whether the same regulation would be valid if enforced against a private party. That reasoning, embodied in the majority opinion, is inconsistent with the spirit of our Constitution. It remains relevant that a *State* is being regulated, as *National League of Cities* and every recent case have recognized. As far as the Constitution is concerned, a State should not be equated with any private litigant. Instead, the autonomy of a State is an essential component of federalism. If state autonomy is ignored in assessing the means by which Congress regulates matters affecting commerce, then federalism becomes irrelevant simply because the set of activities remaining beyond the reach of such a commerce power "may well be negligible." * * * I would not shirk the duty acknowledged by *National League of Cities* and its progeny, and I share Justice Rehnquist's belief that this Court will in time again assume its constitutional responsibility.

NEW YORK v. UNITED STATES
Supreme Court of the United States, 1992.
___ U.S. ___, 112 S.Ct. 2408, 120 L.Ed.2d 120.

JUSTICE O'CONNOR delivered the opinion of the Court. * * *

We live in a world full of low level radioactive waste. Radioactive material is present in luminous watch dials, smoke alarms, measurement devices, medical fluids, research materials, and the protective gear and construction materials used by workers at nuclear power plants. * * * The waste must be isolated from humans for long periods of time, often for hundreds of years. Millions of cubic feet of low level radioactive waste must be disposed of each year. * * * [S]ince 1979 only three disposal sites—those in Nevada, Washington, and South Carolina—have been in operation. Waste generated in the rest of the country must be shipped to one of these three sites for disposal. * * *

[T]he Low–Level Radioactive Waste Policy Amendments Act of 1985 * * * directs: "Each State shall be responsible for providing, either by itself or in cooperation with other States, for the disposal of * * * low-level radioactive waste generated within the State" * * *. The Act authorizes States to "enter into such [interstate] compacts as may be necessary to provide for the establishment and operation of regional disposal facilities for low-level radioactive waste." For * * * seven years * * *, from the beginning of 1986 through the end of 1992, the three existing disposal sites "shall make disposal capacity available for low-level radioactive waste generated by any source" * * *. But the three States in which the disposal sites are located are permitted to exact a graduated surcharge for waste arriving from outside the regional com-pact * * *. After the seven-year transition period expires, approved regional compacts may exclude radioactive waste generated outside the region. The Act provides three types of incentives to encourage the States to comply with their statutory obligation to provide for the disposal of waste generated within their borders. * * * These three incentives are the focus of petitioners' constitutional challenge. * * * Petitioners—the State of New York and * * * two counties—filed this suit against the United States in 1990. * * * [A]s the case stands before us, petitioners claim only that the Act is inconsistent with the Tenth Amendment and the Guarantee Clause. * * *

[T]he task of ascertaining the constitutional line between federal and state power has given rise to many of the Court's most difficult and celebrated cases. * * * In some cases the Court has inquired whether an Act of Congress is authorized by one of the powers delegated to Congress in Article I of the Constitution. See, *e.g., McCulloch v. Maryland*, 4 Wheat. 316, 4 L.Ed. 579 (1819). In other cases the Court has sought to determine whether an Act of Congress invades the prov-ince of state sovereignty reserved by the Tenth Amendment. See, *e.g., Garcia v. San Antonio Metropolitan Transit Authority*, 469 U.S. 528, 105 S.Ct. 1005, 83 L.Ed.2d 1016 (1985). In a case like this one, involving the division of authority between federal and state governments, the two inquiries are mirror images of each other. If a power is delegated to Congress in the Constitution, the Tenth Amendment expressly disclaims any reservation of that power to the States; if a power is an attribute of state sovereignty reserved by the Tenth Amendment, it is necessarily a power the Constitution has not conferred on Congress. * * * The actual scope of the Federal Government's authority with respect to the States has changed over the years, * * * but the constitutional structure underlying and limiting that authority has not. In the end, * * * it makes no difference whether one views the question at issue in this case as one of ascertaining the limits of the power delegated to the Federal Government under the affirmative provisions of the Constitution or one of discerning the core of sovereignty retained by the States under the Tenth Amendment. Either way, we must determine whether any of the three challenged provisions of the Low–Level Radioactive Waste Policy Amendments Act of 1985 oversteps the boundary between federal and state authority.

Petitioners do not contend that Congress lacks the power to regulate the disposal of low level radioactive waste. * * * Petitioners likewise do not dispute that under the Supremacy Clause Congress could, if it wished, pre-empt state radioactive waste regulation. Petitioners contend only that the Tenth Amendment limits the power of Congress to regulate in the way it has chosen. Rather than addressing the problem of waste disposal by directly regulating the generators and disposers of waste, petitioners argue, Congress has impermissibly directed the States to regulate in this field.

Most of our recent cases interpreting the Tenth Amendment have concerned the authority of Congress to subject state governments to generally applicable laws. The Court's jurisprudence in this area has traveled an unsteady path. See *Maryland v. Wirtz*, 392 U.S. 183, 88 S.Ct. 2017, 20 L.Ed.2d 1020 (1968); *National League of Cities v. Usery*, 426 U.S. 833, 96 S.Ct. 2465, 49 L.Ed.2d 245 (1976) (overruling *Wirtz*); *Garcia v. San Antonio Metropolitan Transit Authority*, 469 U.S. 528, 105 S.Ct. 1005, 83 L.Ed.2d 1016 (1985) (overruling *National League of Cities*). This case presents no occasion to apply or revisit the holdings of any of these cases, as this is not a case in which Congress has subjected a State to the same legislation applicable to private parties.

This case instead concerns the circumstances under which Congress may use the States as implements of regulation; that is, whether Congress may direct or otherwise motivate the States to regulate in a particular field or a particular way. * * * While Congress has substantial powers to govern the Nation directly, including in areas of intimate concern to the States, the Constitution has never been understood to confer upon Congress the ability to require the States to govern according to Congress' instructions. * * * This is not to say that Congress lacks the ability to encourage a State to regulate in a particular way, or that Congress may not hold out incentives to the States as a method of influencing a State's policy choices. Our cases have identified a variety of methods, short of outright coercion, by which Congress may urge a State to adopt a legislative program consistent with federal interests. Two of these methods are of particular relevance here. First, under Congress' spending power, "Congress may attach conditions on the receipt of federal funds." *South Dakota v. Dole*, 483 U.S. [203], at 206, 107 S.Ct. [2793], at 2795. * * * Second, where Congress has the authority to regulate private activity under the Commerce Clause, we have recognized Congress' power to offer States the choice of regulating that activity according to federal standards or having state law pre-empted by federal regulation. * * * By either of these two methods, as by any other permissible method of encouraging a State to conform to federal policy choices, the residents of the State retain the ultimate decision as to whether or not the State will comply. If a State's citizens view federal policy as sufficiently contrary to local interests, they may elect to decline a federal grant. If state residents would prefer their government to devote its attention and resources to problems other than those deemed important by Congress, they may choose to have the Federal Government rather than the State bear the expense of a federal-ly mandated regulatory program, and they may continue to supplement that program to the extent state law is not preempted. Where Congress encourages state regulation rather than compelling it, state governments remain responsive to the local electorate's preferences; state officials remain accountable to the people.

By contrast, where the Federal Government compels States to regulate, the accountability of both state and federal officials is diminish-ed. If the citizens of New York, for example, do not consider that making provision for the disposal of radioactive waste is in their best interest, they may elect state officials who share their view. That view can always be preempted under the Supremacy Clause if is contrary to the national view, but in such a case it is the Federal Government that makes the decision in full view of the public, and it will be federal officials that suffer the consequences if the decision turns out to be detrimental or unpopular. But where the Federal Government directs the States to regulate, it may be state officials who will bear the brunt of public disapproval, while the federal officials who devised the regulatory program may remain insulated from the electoral ramifications of their decision. Accountability is thus diminished when, due to federal coer-cion, elected state officials cannot regulate in accordance with the views of the local electorate in matters not pre-empted by federal regulation.

With these principles in mind, we turn to the three challenged provisions of the Low–Level Radioactive Waste Policy Amendments Act of 1985. * * * The first set of incentives * * *, in which Congress has conditioned grants to the States upon the States' attainment of a series of milestones, is * * * well within the authority of Congress under the Commerce and Spending Clauses * * * [and thus] is not inconsistent with the Tenth Amendment.

In the second set of incentives, Congress has authorized States and regional compacts with disposal sites gradually to increase the cost of access to the sites, and then to deny access altogether, to radioactive waste generated in States that do not meet federal deadlines. As a simple regulation, this provision would be within the power of Congress to authorize the States to discriminate against interstate commerce.

* * * The affected States are not compelled by Congress to regulate, because any burden caused by a State's refusal to regulate will fall on those who generate waste and find no outlet for its disposal, rather than on the State as a sovereign. * * * The State need not expend any funds, or participate in any federal program, if local residents do not view such expenditures or participation as worthwhile. * * * The Act's second set of incentives thus represents a conditional exercise of Congress' commerce power, along the lines of those we have held to be within Congress' authority. As a result, the second set of incentives does not intrude on the sovereignty reserved to the States by the Tenth Amendment.

The take title provision is of a different character. This third so-called "incentive" * * * offers state governments a "choice" of either accepting ownership of waste or regulating according to the instructions of Congress. Respondents do not claim that the Constitution would authorize Congress to impose either option as a freestanding requirement. On one hand, the Constitution would not permit Congress simply to transfer radioactive waste from generators to state governments. Such a forced transfer, standing alone, would in principle be no different than a congressionally compelled subsidy from state governments to radioactive waste producers. The same is true of the provision requiring the States to become liable for the generators' damages. Standing alone, this provision would be indistinguishable from an Act of Congress directing the States to assume the liabilities of certain state residents. Either type of federal action would "commandeer" state governments into the service of federal regulatory purposes, and would for this reason be inconsistent with the Constitution's division of authority between federal and state governments. On the other hand, the second alternative held out to state governments—regulating pursuant to Congress' direction—would, standing alone, present a simple command to state governments to implement legislation enacted by Congress. As we have seen, the Constitution does not empower Congress to subject state governments to this type of instruction.

Because an instruction to state governments to take title to waste, standing alone, would be beyond the authority of Congress, and because a direct order to regulate, standing alone, would also be beyond the authority of Congress, it follows that Congress lacks the power to offer the States a choice between the two. * * * A choice between two unconstitutionally coercive regulatory techniques is no choice at all. * * * The take title provision appears to be unique. No other federal statute has been cited which offers a state government no option other than that of implementing legislation enacted by Congress. Whether one views the take title provision as lying outside Congress' enumerated powers, or as infringing upon the core of state sovereignty reserved by the Tenth Amendment, the provision is inconsistent with the federal structure of our Government established by the Constitution.

Respondents raise a number of objections to this understanding of the limits of Congress' power. * * * First, the United States argues that the Constitution's prohibition of congressional directives to state governments can be overcome where the federal interest is sufficiently important to justify state submission. This argument contains a kernel of truth: In determining whether the Tenth Amendment limits the ability of Congress to subject state governments to generally applicable laws, the Court has in some cases stated that it will evaluate the strength of federal interests in light of the degree to which such laws would prevent the State from functioning as a sovereign; that is, the extent to which such generally applicable laws would impede a state government's responsibility to represent and be accountable to the citizens of the State. See, *e.g., National League of Cities v. Usery*, 426 U.S., at 853, 96 S.Ct., at 2475. The Court has more recently departed from this approach. See, *e.g., Garcia v. San Antonio Metropolitan Transit Authority*, 469 U.S., at 556–557, 105 S.Ct., at 1020. But whether or not a particularly strong federal interest enables Congress to bring state governments within the orbit of generally applicable federal regulation, no Member of the Court has ever suggested that such a federal interest would enable Congress to command a state government to enact state regulation. No matter how powerful the federal interest involved, the Constitution simply does not give Congress the authority to require the States to regulate. * * *

[T]he United States, supported by the three sited regional compacts as amici, argues that the Constitution envisions a role for Congress as an arbiter of interstate disputes. * * * Respondents note that the Act embodies a bargain among the sited and unsited States, a compromise to which New York was a willing participant and from which New York has reaped much benefit. Respondents then pose what appears at first to be a troubling question: How can a federal statute be found an unconstitutional infringement of State sovereignty when state officials consented to the statute's enactment?

The answer follows from an understanding of the fundamental purpose served by our Government's federal structure. The Constitution does not protect the sovereignty of States for the benefit of the States or state governments as abstract political entities, or even for the benefit of the public officials governing the States. To the contrary, the Constitution divides authority between federal and state governments for the protection of individuals. * * * Where Congress exceeds its authority relative to the States, therefore, the departure from the constitutional plan cannot be ratified by the "consent" of state officials. * * * Indeed, the facts of this case raise the possibility that powerful incentives might lead both federal and state officials to view departures from the federal structure to be in their personal interests. Most citizens recognize the need for radioactive waste disposal sites, but few want sites near their homes. As a result, while it would be well within the authority of either federal or state officials to choose where the disposal sites will be, it is likely to be in the political interest of each individual official to avoid being held accountable to the voters for the choice of location. * * * The interests of public officials thus may not coincide with the Constitution's intergovernmental allocation of authority. Where state officials purport to submit to the direction of Congress in this manner, federalism is hardly being advanced. * * *

The Constitution * * * "leaves to the several States a residuary and inviolable sovereignty," The Federalist No. 39, p.245 (C. Rossiter ed. 1961), reserved explicitly to the States by the Tenth Amendment. * * * Whatever the outer limits of that sovereignty may be, one thing is clear: The Federal Government may not compel the States to enact or administer a federal regulatory program. * * *

JUSTICE WHITE, with whom JUSTICE BLACKMUN and JUSTICE STEVENS join, concurring in part and dissenting in part. * * *

The Court's distinction between a federal statute's regulation of States and private parties for general purposes, as opposed to a regulation solely on the activities of States, is unsupported by our recent Tenth Amendment cases. * * * Moreover, the Court makes no effort to explain why this purported distinction should affect the analysis of Congress' power under general principles of federalism and the Tenth Amendment. * * * Certainly one would be hard-pressed to read the spirited exchanges between the Court and dissenting Justices in *National League of Cities* and in *Garcia v. San Antonio Metropolitan Transit Authority* as having been based on the distinction now drawn by the Court. An incursion on state sovereignty hardly seems more constitutionally acceptable if the federal statute that "commands" specific action also applies to private parties. The alleged diminution in state authority over its own affairs is not any less because the federal mandate restricts the activities of private parties. * * *

I would also submit * * * that the Court's attempt to carve out a doctrinal distinction for statutes that purport solely to regulate State activities is especially unpersuasive after *Garcia*. * * * [T]he Court tacitly concedes that a failing of the political process cannot be shown in this case because it refuses to rebut the unassailable arguments that the States were well able to look after themselves in the legislative process that culminated in the 1985 Act's passage. Indeed, New York acknowledges that its "congressional delegation participated in the drafting and enactment of both the 1980 and the 1985 Acts." The Court rejects this process-based argument by resorting to generalities and platitudes about the purpose of federalism being to protect individual rights. * * * For me, the Court's civics lecture has a decidedly hollow ring at a time when action, rather than rhetoric, is needed to solve a national problem. * * *

JUSTICE STEVENS, concurring in part and dissenting in part. * * *

The notion that Congress does not have the power to issue "a simple command to state governments to implement legislation enacted by Congress," is incorrect and unsound. There is no such limitation in the Constitution. The Tenth Amendment surely does not impose any limit on Congress' exercise of the powers delegated to it by Article I. Nor does the structure of the constitutional order or the values of federalism mandate such a formal rule. To the contrary, the Federal Government directs state governments in many realms. The Government regulates state-operated railroads, state school systems, state prisons, state elections, and a host of other state functions. Similarly, there can be no doubt that, in time of war, Congress could either draft soldiers itself or command the States to supply their quotas of troops. I see no reason why Congress may not also command the States to enforce federal water and air quality standards or federal standards for the disposition of low-level radioactive wastes. * * *

With respect to the problem presented by the case at hand, if litigation should develop between States that have joined a compact, we would surely have the power to grant relief in the form of specific enforcement of the take title provision. Indeed, even if the statute had never been passed, if one State's radioactive waste created a nuisance that harmed its neighbors, it seems clear that we would have had the power to command the offending State to take remedial action. If this Court has such authority, surely Congress has similar authority. * * *

––––––––

The final two cases in this subsection are designed to raise questions about the *National League of Cities-Garcia-New York* line of cases. Both cases deal with racial discrimination. In the first case, City of Richmond v. Croson, the Supreme Court held a city's affirmative action policy unconstitutional. Why were the justices who joined the majority in *National League of Cities* and *New York* (and who dissented in *Garcia*) not supportive of local power in *Croson*? Did conservatives and liberals switch sides on the federalism issue because the case involved affirmative action rather than the minimum wage? Does the difference between the Fourteenth Amendment and the Commerce Clause adequately explain this shift of positions?

In the second case, Spallone v. United States, neither the majority nor the dissenting opinion seemed concerned about ordering a city to enact legislation to remedy acts of racial discrimination. The only dispute concerned the proper remedy against individual members of the city council. Given the majority opinion in the *New York* case, why was such an order found acceptable? Do the *Croson* and *Spallone* cases, taken together, suggest that Justice Scalia is right to claim (citing Madison's Federalist X) that race is not a proper subject for local decisionmaking?

CITY OF RICHMOND v. J. A. CROSON COMPANY

Supreme Court of the United States, 1989.
488 U.S. 469, 109 S.Ct. 706, 102 L.Ed.2d 854.

JUSTICE O'CONNOR announced the judgment of the Court and delivered the opinion of the Court with respect to Parts I, III–B, and IV, an opinion with respect to Part II, in which THE CHIEF JUSTICE and JUSTICE

WHITE join, and an opinion with respect to Parts III–A and V, in which THE CHIEF JUSTICE, JUSTICE WHITE and JUSTICE KENNEDY join.   * * *

I

On April 11, 1983, the Richmond City Council adopted the Minority Business Utilization Plan (the Plan). The Plan required prime contractors to whom the city awarded construction contracts to subcontract at least 30% of the dollar amount of the contract to one of more Minority Business Enterprises (MBEs).   * * * The Plan was adopted by the Richmond City Council after a public hearing.   * * * Proponents of the set-aside provision relied on a study which indicated that, while the general population of Richmond was 50% black, only .67% of the city's prime construction contracts had been awarded to minority businesses in the 5–year period from 1978 to 1983.   * * * The city's legal counsel indicated his view that the ordinance was constitutional under this Court's decision in *Fullilove v. Klutznick,* 448 U.S. 448, 100 S.Ct. 2758, 65 L.Ed.2d 902 (1980).   * * *

II

In *Fullilove,* we upheld the minority set-aside contained in § 103(f)(2) of the Public Works Employment Act of 1977 (the Act) against a challenge based on the equal protection component of the Due Process Clause. The Act authorized a four billion dollar appropriation for federal grants to state and local governments for use in public works projects.   * * * The Act also contained the following requirement: "Except to the extent the Secretary determines otherwise, no grant shall be made under this Act * * * unless the applicant gives satisfactory assurance to the Secretary that at least 10 per centum of the amount of each grant shall be expended for minority business enterprises." *Fullilove,* 448 U.S., at 454, 100 S.Ct., at 2762.   * * *

The principal opinion in *Fullilove,* written by Chief Justice Burger, * * * stressed two factors in upholding the MBE set-aside. First was the unique remedial powers of Congress under § 5 of the Fourteenth Amendment: * * * "Congress not only may induce voluntary action to assure compliance with existing federal statutory or constitutional anti-discrimination provisions, but also, where Congress has authority to *declare certain conduct unlawful,* it may, as here, authorize and induce state action to avoid such conduct." *Id.,* at 483–484, 100 S.Ct., at 2777 (emphasis added).   * * * The second factor emphasized by the principal opinion in *Fullilove* was the flexible nature of the 10% set-aside.   * * *

Appellant [City of Richmond] and its supporting *amici* rely heavily on *Fullilove* for the proposition that a city council, like Congress, need not make specific findings of discrimination to engage in race-conscious relief. Thus, appellant argues "[i]t would be a perversion of federalism to hold that the federal government has a compelling interest in remedying the effects of racial discrimination in its own public works program, but a city government does not." Brief for Appellant 32.

What appellant ignores is that Congress, unlike any State or political subdivision, has a specific constitutional mandate to enforce the dictates of the Fourteenth Amendment. The power to "enforce" may at times also include the power to define situations which *Congress* determines threaten principles of equality and to adopt prophylactic rules to deal with those situations. * * * That Congress may identify and redress the effects of society-wide discrimination does not mean that, *a fortiori,* the States and their political subdivisions are free to decide that such remedies are appropriate. Section 1 of the Fourteenth Amendment is an explicit *constraint* on state power, and the States must undertake any remedial efforts in accordance with that provision. To hold otherwise would be to cede control over the content of the Equal Protection Clause to the 50 state legislatures and their myriad political subdivisions. The mere recitation of a benign or compensatory purpose for the use of a racial classification would essentially entitle the States to exercise the full power of Congress under § 5 of the Fourteenth Amendment and insulate any racial classification from judicial scrutiny under § 1. We believe that such a result would be contrary to the intentions of the Framers of the Fourteenth Amendment, who desired to place clear limits on the States' use of race as a criterion for legislative action, and to have the federal courts enforce those limitations. * * *

It would seem equally clear, however, that a state or local subdivision (if delegated the authority from the State) has the authority to eradicate the effects of private discrimination within its own legislative jurisdiction. This authority must, of course, be exercised within the constraints of § 1 of the Fourteenth Amendment. * * * As a matter of state law, the city of Richmond has legislative authority over its procurement policies, and can use its spending powers to remedy private discrimination, if it identifies that discrimination with the particularity required by the Fourteenth Amendment. * * * Thus, if the city could show that it had essentially become a "passive participant" in a system of racial exclusion practiced by elements of the local construction industry, we think it clear that the city could take affirmative steps to dismantle such a system. It is beyond dispute that any public entity, state or federal, has a compelling interest in assuring that public dollars, drawn from the tax contributions of all citizens, do not serve to finance the evil of private prejudice. * * *

III–A

* * * [T]he standard of review under the Equal Protection Clause is not dependent on the race of those burdened or benefited by a particular classification. * * * Even were we to accept a reading of the guarantee of equal protection under which the level of scrutiny varies according to the ability of different groups to defend their interests in the representative process, heightened scrutiny would still be appropriate in the circumstances of this case. * * * [B]lacks comprise approximately 50% of the population of the city of Richmond. Five of the nine seats on the City Council are held by blacks. The concern that a political majority

will more easily act to the disadvantage of a minority based on unwarranted assumptions or incomplete facts would seem to militate for, not against, the application of heightened judicial scrutiny in this case. See Ely, The Constitutionality of Reverse Racial Discrimination, 41 U.Chi. L.Rev. 723, 379, n. 58 (1974) ("Of course it works both ways: a law that favors Blacks over Whites would be suspect if it were enacted by a predominately Black legislature"). * * *

III–B

* * * While there is no doubt that the sorry history of both private and public discrimination in this country has contributed to a lack of opportunities for black entrepreneurs, this observation, standing alone, cannot justify a rigid racial quota in the awarding of public contracts in Richmond, Virginia. * * * The District Court relied upon five predicate "facts" in reaching its conclusion that there was an adequate basis for the 30% quota: (1) the ordinance declares itself to be remedial; (2) several proponents of the measure stated their views that there had been past discrimination in the construction industry; (3) minority businesses received .67% of prime contracts from the city while minorities constituted 50% of the city's population; (4) there were very few minority contractors in local and state contractors' association; and (5) in 1977, Congress made a determination that the effects of past discrimination had stifled minority participation in the construction industry nationally.

None of these "findings," singly or together, provide the city of Richmond with a "strong basis in evidence for its conclusion that remedial action was necessary." *Wygant [v. Jackson Board of Education],* 476 U.S. [267,] 277, 106 S.Ct. [1842,] 1848 [(1986)] (plurality opinion). There is nothing approaching a prima facie case of a constitutional or statutory violation by *anyone* in the Richmond construction industry. * * * We, therefore, hold that the city has failed to demonstrate a compelling interest in apportioning public contracting opportunities on the basis of race. To accept Richmond's claim that past societal discrimination alone can serve as the basis for rigid racial preferences would be to open the door to competing claims for "remedial relief" for every disadvantaged group. The dream of a Nation of equal citizens in a society where race is irrelevant to personal opportunity and achievement would be lost in a mosaic of shifting preferences based on inherently unmeasurable claims of past wrongs. * * *

JUSTICE KENNEDY, concurring in part and concurring in the judgment. * * *

The process by which a law that is an equal protection violation when enacted by a State becomes transformed to an equal protection guarantee when enacted by Congress poses a difficult proposition for me; but as it is not before us, any reconsideration of that issue must await some further case. For purposes of the ordinance challenged here, it suffices to say that the State has the power to eradicate racial discrimination and its effects in both the public and private sectors, and the absolute duty to do so where those wrongs were caused intentionally by the State itself. The Fourteenth Amendment ought not to be interpreted to reduce a State's authority in this regard, unless, of course, there is a conflict with federal law or a state remedy is itself a violation of equal protection. The latter is the case presented here. * * *

Justice Scalia, concurring in the judgment. * * *

[I]t is one thing to permit racially based conduct by the Federal Government—whose legislative powers concerning matters of race were explicitly enhanced by the Fourteenth Amendment—and quite another to permit it by the precise entities against whose conduct in matters of race that Amendment was specifically directed. * * * A sound distinction between federal and state (or local) action based on race rests not only upon the substance of the Civil War Amendments, but upon social reality and governmental theory. It is a simple fact that what Justice Stewart described in *Fullilove* as "the dispassionate objectivity [and] the flexibility that are needed to mold a race-conscious remedy around the single objective of eliminating the effects of past or present discrimination"—political qualities already to be doubted in a national legislature—are substantially less likely to exist at the state or local level. The struggle for racial justice has historically been a struggle by the national society against oppression in the individual States. And the struggle retains that character in modern times. See *e.g., Brown v. Board of Education,* 349 U.S. 294, 75 S.Ct. 753, 99 L.Ed. 1083 (1955) (*Brown II*). Not all of that struggle has involved discrimination against blacks, and not all of it has been in the Old South. What the record shows, in other words, is that racial discrimination against any group finds a more ready expression at the state and local than at the federal level. To the children of the Founding Fathers, this should come as no surprise. An acute awareness of the heightened danger of oppression from political factions in small, rather than large, political units dates to the very beginning of our national history. As James Madison observed in support of the proposed Constitution's enhancement of national powers:

> "The smaller the society, the fewer probably will be the distinct parties and interests composing it; the fewer the distinct parties and interests, the more frequently will a majority be found of the same party; and the smaller the number of individuals composing a majority, and the smaller the compass within which they are placed, the more easily will they concert and execute their plan of oppression. Extend the sphere and you take in a greater variety of parties and interests; you make it less probable that a majority of the whole will have a common motive to invade the rights of other citizens; or if such a common motive exists, it will be more difficult for all who feel it to discover their own strength and to act in unison with each other." The Federalist No. 10, pp. 82–84 (C. Rossiter ed. 1961).

The prophesy of these words came to fruition in Richmond in the enactment of a set-aside clearly and directly beneficial to the dominant political group, which happens also to be the dominant racial group. The same thing has no doubt happened before in other cities (though the racial basis of the preference has rarely been made textually explicit)—and blacks have often been on the receiving end of the injustice. Where injustice is the game, however, turn-about is not fair play. * * *

JUSTICE MARSHALL, with whom JUSTICE BRENNAN and JUSTICE BLACKMUN join, dissenting.

It is a welcome symbol of racial progress when the former capital of the Confederacy acts forthrightly to confront the effects of racial discrimination in its midst. * * * A majority of this Court holds today, however, that the Equal Protection Clause of the Fourteenth Amendment blocks Richmond's initiative. The essence of the majority's position is that Richmond has failed to catalogue adequate findings to prove that past discrimination has impeded minorities from joining or participating fully in Richmond's construction contracting industry. I find deep irony in second-guessing Richmond's judgment on this point. As much as any municipality in the United States, Richmond knows what racial discrimination is; a century of decisions by this and other federal courts has richly documented the city's disgraceful history of public and private racial discrimination. In any event, the Richmond City Council *has* supported its determination that minorities have been wrongly excluded from local construction contracting. Its proof includes statistics showing that minority-owned businesses have received virtually no city contracting dollars and rarely if ever belonged to area trade associations; testimony by municipal officials that discrimination has been widespread in the local construction industry; and the same exhaustive and widely publicized federal studies relied on in *Fullilove,* studies which showed that pervasive discrimination in the Nation's tight-knit construction industry had operated to exclude minorities from public contracting. * * * [T]o suggest that the facts on which Richmond has relied do not provide a sound basis for its finding of past racial discrimination simply blinks credibility. * * *

The majority's perfunctory dismissal of the testimony of Richmond's appointed and elected leaders is also deeply disturbing. These officials—including councilmembers, a former mayor, and the present city manager—asserted that race discrimination in area contracting had been widespread, and that the set-aside ordinance was a sincere and necessary attempt to eradicate the effects of this discrimination. * * * By disregarding the testimony of local leaders and the judgment of local government, the majority does violence to the very principles of comity within our federal system which this Court has long championed. Local officials, by virtue of their proximity to, and their expertise with, local affairs, are exceptionally well-qualified to make determinations of public good "within their respective spheres of authority." *Hawaii Housing Authority v. Midkiff,* 467 U.S. 229, 244, 104 S.Ct. 2321, 2331, 81 L.Ed.2d 186 (1984). * * * When the legislatures and leaders of cities with histories of pervasive discrimination testify that past discrimination has infected one of their industries, armchair cynicism like that exercised by the majority has no place. It may well be that "the autonomy of state is an essential component of federalism," *Garcia v. San Antonio Metropoli-*

tan Transit Authority, 469 U.S. 528, 588, 105 S.Ct. 1005, 1037, 83 L.Ed.2d 1016 (1985) (O'Connor, J., dissenting), and that "each State is sovereign within its own domain, governing its citizens and providing for their general welfare," *FERC v. Mississippi,* 456 U.S., at 777, 102 S.Ct., at 2147 (O'Connor, J., dissenting), but apparently this is not the case when federal judges, with nothing but their impressions to go on, choose to disbelieve the explanations of these local governments and officials. * * *

I am also troubled by the majority's assertion that, even if it did not believe generally in strict scrutiny of race-based remedial measures, "the circumstances of this case" require this Court to look upon the Richmond City Council's measure with the strictest scrutiny. The sole such circumstance which the majority cites, however, is the fact that blacks in Richmond are a "dominant racial grou[p]" in the city. * * * It cannot seriously be suggested that nonminorities in Richmond have any "history of purposeful unequal treatment." Indeed, the numerical and political dominance of nonminorities within the State of Virginia and the Nation as a whole provide an enormous political check against the "simple racial politics" at the municipal level which the majority fears. * * *

In recent years, white and black councilmembers in Richmond have increasingly joined hands on controversial matters. When the Richmond City Council elected a black man Mayor in 1982, for example, his victory was won with the support of the City Council's four white members. The vote on the set-aside plan a year later also was not purely along racial lines. Of the four white councilmembers, one voted for the measure and another abstained. The majority's view that remedial measures undertaken by municipalities with black leadership must face a stiffer test of Equal Protection Clause scrutiny than remedial measures undertaken by municipalities with white leadership implies a lack of political maturity on the part of this Nation's elected minority officials that is totally unwarranted. Such insulting judgments have no place in constitutional jurisprudence. * * *

[T]here is simply no credible evidence that the Framers of the Fourteenth Amendment sought "to transfer the security and protection of all the civil rights * * * from the States to the Federal government." The *Slaughter-House Cases,* 16 Wall. 36, 77–78, 21 L.Ed. 394 (1873). The three Reconstruction Amendments undeniably "worked a dramatic change in the balance between congressional and state power": they forbade state-sanctioned slavery, forbade the state-sanctioned denial of the right to vote, and (until the content of the Equal Protection Clause was substantially applied to the Federal Government through the Due Process Clause of the Fifth Amendment) uniquely forbade States from denying equal protection. The Amendments also specifically empowered the Federal Government to combat discrimination at a time when the breadth of federal power under the Constitution was less apparent than it is today. But nothing in the Amendments themselves, or in our long history of interpreting or applying those momentous charters, suggests that States, exercising their police power, are in any way constitutionally inhibited from working alongside the Federal Government in the fight against discrimination and its effects. * * *

SPALLONE v. UNITED STATES

Supreme Court of the United States, 1990.
493 U.S. 265, 110 S.Ct. 625, 107 L.Ed.2d 644.

CHIEF JUSTICE REHNQUIST delivered the opinion of the Court. * * *

In 1980, the United States filed a complaint alleging * * * [that] the city of Yonkers and the Yonkers Community Development Agency * * * had intentionally engaged in a pattern and practice of housing discrimination, in violation of Title VIII of the Civil Rights Act of 1968 and the Equal Protection Clause of the Fourteenth Amendment. The Government and plaintiff-intervenor National Association for the Advancement of Colored People (NAACP) asserted that the city had, over a period of three decades, selected sites for subsidized housing in order to perpetuate residential racial segregation. * * * The District Court found the two named defendants liable, concluding that the segregative effect of the city's action had been "consistent and extreme" * * *. [It] enjoined "the City of Yonkers, its officers, agents, employees, successors and all persons in active concert or participation with any of them" from, *inter alia,* * * * blocking or limiting the availability of public or subsidized housing in east or northwest Yonkers on the basis of race or national origin. * * * Part IV of the order noted that the city previously had committed itself to provide acceptable sites for 200 units of public housing as a condition for receiving 1983 Community Development Block Grant funds from the Federal Government, but had failed to do so. Consequently, it required the city to designate sites for 200 units of public housing in East Yonkers, and to submit to the Department of Housing and Urban Development an acceptable Housing Assistance Plan for 1984–1985 and other documentation. Part VI directed the city to develop by November 1986 a long-term plan "for the creation of additional subsidized family housing units * * * in existing residential areas in east or northwest Yonkers." * * *

Under the Charter of the city of Yonkers all legislative powers are vested in the city council, which consists of an elected mayor and six councilmembers, including petitioners. * * * Pending appeal of the District Court's liability and remedial orders, * * * the city did not * * * propose sites for the public housing, and in November 1986, [it] informed the District Court that it would not present a long-term plan in compliance with Part VI. The United States and the NAACP then moved for an adjudication of civil contempt and the imposition of coercive sanctions, but the District Court * * * [instead] secured an agreement from the city to appoint an outside housing advisor to identify sites for the 200 units of public housing and to draft a long-term plan.

* * * [I]n January 1988, the parties agreed to a consent decree that set forth "certain actions which the City of Yonkers [would] take in

connection with a consensual implementation of Parts IV and VI'' of the housing remedy order. The decree was approved by the city council in a 5–to–2 vote (petitioners Spallone and Chema voting no), and entered by the District Court as a consent judgment on January 28, 1988. Sections 12 through 18 of the decree established the framework for the long-term plan and are the underlying bases for the contempt orders at issue in this case. Perhaps most significant was § 17, in which the city agreed to adopt, within 90 days, legislation conditioning the construction of all multifamily housing on the inclusion of at least 20 percent assisted units, granting tax abatements and density bonuses to developers, and providing for zoning changes to allow the placement of housing developments.

For several more months, however, the city continued to delay action toward implementing the long-term plan. * * * As a result of the city's intransigence, the United States and the NAACP moved the court for the entry of a Long Term Plan Order * * * [and, on] June 13, * * * the District Court entered the Long Term Plan Order, which provided greater detail for the legislation prescribed by § 17 of the decree. After several weeks of further delay the court, after a hearing held on July 26, 1988, entered an order requiring the city of Yonkers to enact on or before August 1, 1988, the "legislative package" described in a section of the earlier consent decree; the second paragraph provided:

> "It is further ORDERED that, in the event the City of Yonkers fails to enact the legislative package on or before August 1, 1988, the City of Yonkers shall be required to show cause at a hearing before this Court at 10:00 a.m. on August 2, 1988, why it should not be held in contempt, and each individual City Council member shall be required to show cause at a hearing before this court at 10:00 a.m. on August 2, 1988, why he should not be held in contempt."

Further provisions of the order specified escalating daily amounts of fines in the event of contempt, and provided that if the legislation were not enacted before August 10, 1988, any councilmember who remained in contempt should be committed to the custody of the United States Marshal for imprisonment. The specified daily fines for the city were $100 for the first day, to be doubled for each consecutive day of noncompliance; the specified daily fine for members of the city council was $500 per day.

Notwithstanding the threat of substantial sanctions, on August 1 the city council defeated a resolution of intent to adopt the legislative package, known as the Affordable Housing Ordinance, by a vote of 4 to 3 (petitioners constituting the majority). On August 2, the District Court held a hearing to afford the city and the councilmembers an opportunity to show cause why they should not be adjudicated in contempt. It rejected the city's arguments, held the city in contempt, and imposed the coercive sanctions set forth in the July 26 order. After questioning the individual council members as to the reasons for their negative votes, the court also held each of the petitioners in contempt and imposed sanctions. * * * On August 17, the Court of Appeals stayed the contempt sanctions pending appeal. Shortly thereafter, the court affirmed the adjudications of contempt against both the city and the councilmembers, but limited the fines against the city so that they would not exceed $1 million per day. * * * Both the city and the councilmembers requested this Court to stay imposition of sanctions pending filing and disposition of petitions for certiorari. We granted a stay as to petitioners, but denied the city's request. With the city's daily contempt sanction approaching $1 million per day, the city council finally enacted the Affordable Housing Ordinance on September 9, 1988, by a vote of 5 to 2, petitioners Spallone and Fagan voting no. * * *

The issue before us is relatively narrow. There can be no question about the liability of the city of Yonkers for racial discrimination * * *. Nor do we have before us any question as to the District Court's remedial order * * *. Our focus, then, is only on the District Court's order of July 26 imposing contempt sanctions on the individual petitioners if they failed to vote in favor of the ordinance in question. * * *

Given that the city had entered a consent judgment committing itself to enact legislation implementing the long-term plan, we certainly cannot say it was an abuse of discretion for the District Court to have chosen contempt sanctions against the city, as opposed to petitioners, as a means of ensuring compliance. The city, as we have noted, was a party to the action from the beginning, had been found liable for numerous statutory and constitutional violations, and had been subjected to various elaborate remedial decrees which had been upheld on appeal. Petitioners, the individual city councilmen, on the other hand, were not parties to the action, and they had not been found individually liable for any of the violations upon which the remedial decree was based. Although the injunctive portion of that decree was directed not only to the city but to "its officers, agents, employees, successors and all persons in active concert or participation with any of the them," the remaining parts of the decree ordering affirmative steps were directed only to the city.

It was the city, in fact, which capitulated. * * * While the District Court could not have been sure in late July that this would be the result, the city's arguments against imposing sanctions on it pointed out the sort of pressure that such sanctions would place on the city. After just two weeks of fines, the city's emergency financial plan required it to curtail sanitation services (resulting in uncollected garbage), eliminate part-time school crossing guards, close all public libraries and parks and lay off approximately 447 employees. In the ensuing four weeks, the city would have been forced to lay off another 1100 city employees. * * * The nub of the matter, then, is whether in the light of the reasonable probability that sanctions against the city would accomplish the desired result, it was within the court's discretion to impose sanctions on the petitioners as well under the circumstances of this case. * * *

Sanctions directed against the city for failure to take actions such as required by the consent decree coerce the city legislators and, or course, restrict the freedom of those legislators to act in accordance with their current view of the city's best interests. But we believe there are significant differences between the two types of fines. The imposition of sanctions on individual legislators is designed to cause them to vote, not with a view to the interest of their constituents or of the city, but with a view solely to their own personal interests. Even though an individual legislator took the extreme position—or felt that his constituents took the extreme position—that even a huge fine against the city was preferable to enacting the Affordable Housing Ordinance, monetary sanctions against him individually would motivate him to vote to enact the ordinance simply because he did not want to be out of pocket financially. Such fines thus encourage legislators, in effect, to declare that they favor an ordinance not in order to avoid bankrupting the city for which they legislate, but in order to avoid bankrupting themselves.

This sort of individual sanction effects a much greater perversion of the normal legislative process than does the imposition of sanctions on the city for the failure of these same legislators to enact an ordinance. In that case, the legislator is only encouraged to vote in favor of an ordinance that he would not otherwise favor by reason of the adverse sanctions imposed on the city. A councilman who felt that his constituents would rather have the city enact the Affordable Housing Ordinance than pay a "bankrupting fine" would be motivated to vote in favor of such an ordinance because the sanctions were a threat to the fiscal solvency of the city for whose welfare he was in part responsible. This is the sort of calculus in which legislators engage regularly.

We hold that the District Court, in view of the "extraordinary" nature of the imposition of sanctions against the individual councilmen, should have proceeded with such contempt sanctions first against the city alone in order to secure compliance with the remedial orders. Only if that approach failed to produce compliance within a reasonable time should the question of imposing contempt sanctions against petitioners even have been considered. "This limitation accords with the doctrine that a court must exercise '[t]he least possible power adequate to the end proposed.' " *Anderson v. Dunn,* 6 Wheat. 204, 231 5 L.Ed.242 (1821). * * *

JUSTICE BRENNAN, with whom JUSTICE MARSHALL, JUSTICE BLACKMUN, and JUSTICE STEVENS join, dissenting. * * *

While acknowledging that Judge Sand "could not have been sure in late July that this would be the result," the Court confidently concludes that Judge Sand should have been *sure enough* that fining the city would eventually coerce compliance that he should not have personally fined the councilmembers as well. In light of the information available to Judge Sand in July, the Court's confidence is chimerical. * * * [T]he recalcitrant councilmembers were extremely responsive to the strong segments of their constituencies that were vociferously opposed to racial residential integration. * * * Moreover, once Yonkers had gained national attention over its refusal to integrate, many residents made it clear to their representatives on the council that they preferred bankrupt martyrdom to integration. * * * It thus was not evident that petitioners opposed bankrupting the city; at the very least, capitulation by any individual councilmember was widely perceived as political suicide. As a result, even assuming that each recalcitrant member sought to avoid city bankruptcy, each still had a very strong incentive to play "chicken" with his colleagues by continuing to defy the Contempt Order while secretly hoping that at least one colleague would change his position and suffer the wrath of the electorate. * * * Moreover, acutely aware of these political conditions, the city attorney repeatedly warned Judge Sand *not* to assume that the threat of bankruptcy would compel compliance.

The Court, in addition to ignoring all of this evidence * * *, also inexplicably ignores the fact that imposing personal fines in addition to sanctions against the city would not only help ensure but actually *hasten* compliance. City sanctions, by design, impede the normal operation of local government. Judge Sand knew that each day the councilmembers remained in contempt, the city would suffer an ever-growing financial drain that threatened not only to disrupt many critical city services but also to frustrate the long-term success of the underlying remedial scheme. Fines assessed against the public fisc directly "diminish the limited resources which the city has to comply with the Decree," *United States v. Providence,* 492 F.Supp. 602, 610 (DRI 1980), and more generally curtail various public services with a likely disparate impact on poor and minority residents.

Given these ancillary effects of city sanctions, it seems to me entirely appropriate—indeed obligatory—for Judge Sand to have considered, not just whether city sanctions alone would *eventually* have coerced compliance, but also *how promptly* they would have done so. * * * The Court * * * [contends] that personal sanctions against city councilmembers effect a greater interference than city sanctions with the " 'interests of * * * local authorities in managing their own affairs, consistent with the Constitution.' " * * * But once a federal court has issued a valid order to remedy the effects of a prior, specific constitutional violation, the * * * Constitution itself imposes an overriding definition of the "public good," and a court's valid command to obey constitutional dictates is not subject to override by any countervailing preferences of the polity, no matter how widely and ardently shared. * * *

3. FEDERAL PREEMPTION OF LOCAL LAWS

Federal preemption doctrine is based on the Supremacy Clause of the United States Constitution, which provides that "this Constitution, and the Laws of the United States which shall be made in Pursuance thereof, * * * shall be the supreme Law of the Land." [1] As the *Associat-*

---

1. U.S. Constitution, Article VI, cl. 2. For a general analysis of federal preemption doctrine, see L. Tribe, American Constitutional Law 479–511 (2d ed. 1988).

ed Builders case, reprinted below, indicates, federal preemption operates to nullify a local law if "it conflicts with federal law or would frustrate the federal scheme, or * * * [if the Court] discern[s] from the totality of the circumstances that Congress sought to occupy the field to the exclusion of the States." This formulation is very similar to the one that governs state preemption of a local law. This subsection raises the question whether, notwithstanding this similarity, preemption should be interpreted differently in the federal and the state contexts. The first case, Gregory v. Ashcroft, requires Congress to make a "plain statement" of its intent to override a local law when Tenth Amendment issues are at stake. The second case, Building and Construction Trades Council v. Associated Builders and Contractors, relies on a public/private distinction to limit the extent of federal preemption. Do these restriction on the extent of federal preemption make sense? Should similar ideas be incorporated in the rules governing state preemption of local laws? Why shouldn't a "plain statement" always be required before federal *or* state preemption of a local law is found?[2] Given the final case in this subsection—which holds that a city will sometimes be liable in damages when they attempt to legislate in an area preempted by federal law—should a "plain statement" at least be required before damages can be awarded?

GREGORY v. ASHCROFT

Supreme Court of the United States, 1991.
501 U.S. 452, 111 S.Ct. 2395, 115 L.Ed.2d 410.

JUSTICE O'CONNOR delivered the opinion of the Court.

Article V, § 26 of the Missouri Constitution provides that "[a]ll judges other than municipal judges shall retire at the age of seventy years." We consider whether this mandatory retirement provision violates the federal Age Discrimination in Employment Act of 1967 (ADEA) * * *.

As every schoolchild learns, our Constitution establishes a system of dual sovereignty between the States and the Federal Government. * * * This federalist structure of joint sovereigns * * * assures a decentralized government that will be more sensitive to the diverse needs of a heterogenous society; it increases opportunity for citizen involvement in democratic processes; it allows for more innovation and experimentation in government; and it makes government more responsive by putting the States in competition for a mobile citizenry. * * * The Federal Government holds a decided advantage in this delicate balance: the Supremacy Clause. U.S. Const., Art. VI. As long as it is acting within the powers granted it under the Constitution, Congress may impose its will on the States. * * * This is an extraordinary power in a federalist

---

2. For a draft of a statute requiring a clear statement of the intent of Congress as a prerequisite to federal preemption, see Freilich, A Proposed Congressional "Statute of Federalism", 19 The Urban Lawyer 539, 545–46 (1987).

system. It is a power that we must assume Congress does not exercise lightly.

The present case concerns a state constitutional provision through which the people of Missouri establish a qualification for those who sit as their judges. This * * * is a decision of the most fundamental sort for a sovereign entity. Through the structure of its government, and the character of those who exercise government authority, a State defines itself as a sovereign. * * * Congressional interference with this decision of the people of Missouri, defining their constitutional officers, would upset the usual constitutional balance of federal and state powers. For this reason, "it is incumbent upon the federal courts to be certain of Congress' intent before finding that federal law overrides" this balance. *Atascadero [State Hospital v. Scanlon,* 473 U.S. 234,] 243, 105 S.Ct. [3142], 3147. We explained recently:

> * * * "Congress should make its intention clear and manifest 'if it intends to pre-empt the historic powers of the States.... In traditionally sensitive areas, such as legislation affecting the federal balance, the requirement of clear statement assures that the legislature has in fact faced, and intended to bring into issue, the critical matters involved in the judicial decision.'" *Will v. Michigan Dept. of State Police,* 491 U.S. 58, 65, 109 S.Ct. 2304, 2308, 105 L.Ed.2d 45 (1989). * * *

[T]he authority of the people of the States to determine the qualifications of their most important government officials * * * is an authority that lies at " 'the heart of representative government.' " [*Bernal v. Fainter,* 467 U.S. 216, 221, 104 S.Ct. 2312, 2316, 81 L.Ed.2d 175 (1984).] It is a power reserved to the States under the Tenth Amendment and guaranteed them by that provision of the Constitution under which the United States "guarantees to every State in this Union a Republican Form of Government." U.S. Const., Art. IV. * * * Here, we must decide what Congress did in extending the ADEA to the States, pursuant to its powers under the Commerce Clause. See *EEOC v. Wyoming,* 460 U.S. 226, 103 S.Ct. 1054, 75 L.Ed.2d 18 (1983) (the extension of the ADEA to employment by state and local governments was a valid exercise of Congress' powers under the Commerce Clause). As against Congress' powers "to regulate Commerce * * * among the several States," U.S. Const., Art. I, § 8, cl. 3, the authority of the people of the States to determine the qualifications of their government officials may be inviolate.

We are constrained in our ability to consider the limits that the state-federal balance places on Congress' powers under the Commerce Clause. See *Garcia v. San Antonio Metropolitan Transit Authority,* 469 U.S. 528, 105 S.Ct. 1005, 83 L.Ed.2d 1016 (1985) (declining to review limitations placed on Congress' Commerce Clause powers by our federal system). But there is no need to do so if we hold that the ADEA does not apply to state judges. Application of the plain statement rule thus may avoid a potential constitutional problem. Indeed, inasmuch as this

Court in *Garcia* has left primarily to the political process the protection of the States against intrusive exercises of Congress' Commerce Clause powers, we must be absolutely certain that Congress intended such an exercise. "To give the state-displacing weight of federal law to mere congressional ambiguity would evade the very procedure for lawmaking on which *Garcia* relied to protect states' interests." L. Tribe, American Constitutional Law § 6–25, p. 480 (2d ed. 1988).

In 1974, Congress extended the substantive provisions of the ADEA to include the States as employers. At the same time, Congress amended the definition of "employee" to exclude all elected and most high-ranking government officials. Under the Act, as amended:

> "The term 'employee' means an individual employed by any employer except that the term 'employee' shall not include any person elected to public office in any State or political subdivision of any State by the qualified voters thereof, or any person chosen by such officer to be on such officer's personal staff, or an appointee on the policymaking level or an immediate adviser with respect to the exercise of the constitutional or legal powers of the office." * * *

"[A]ppointee on the policymaking level," particularly in the context of the other exceptions that surround it, is an odd way for Congress to exclude judges; a plain statement that judges are not "employees" would seem the most efficient phrasing. But in this case we are not looking for a plain statement that judges are excluded. We will not read the ADEA to cover state judges unless Congress has made it clear that judges are included. This does not mean that the Act must mention judges explicitly, though it does not. Rather, it must be plain to anyone reading the Act that it covers judges. In the context of a statute that plainly excludes most important state public officials, "appointee on the policymaking level" is sufficiently broad that we cannot conclude that the statute plainly covers appointed state judges. Therefore, it does not. * * *

JUSTICE WHITE, with whom JUSTICE STEVENS joins, concurring in part, dissenting in part, and concurring in the judgment. * * *

If petitioners are "employees," Missouri's mandatory retirement provision clearly conflicts with the antidiscrimination provisions of the ADEA. * * * Pre-emption therefore is automatic, since "state law is pre-empted to the extent that it actually conflicts with federal law." *Pacific Gas & Electric Co. v. State Energy Resources Conservation and Development Comm'n,* 461 U.S. 190, 204, 103 S.Ct. 1713, 1722, 75 L.Ed.2d 752 (1983). The majority's federalism concerns are irrelevant to such "actual conflict" pre-emption. "The relative importance to the State of its own law is not material when there is a conflict with a valid federal law, for the Framers of our Constitution provided that the federal law must prevail." *Fidelity Federal Savings & Loan Assn. v. De la Cuesta,* 458 U.S. 141, 153, 102 S.Ct. 3014, 3022, 73 L.Ed.2d 664 (1982).

While acknowledging this principle of federal legislative supremacy, the majority nevertheless imposes upon Congress a "plain statement" requirement. * * * The majority's plain statement rule is not only unprecedented, it directly contravenes our decisions in *Garcia v. San Antonio Metropolitan Transit Authority,* 469 U.S. 528, 105 S.Ct. 1005, 83 L.Ed.2d 1016 (1985), and *South Carolina v. Baker,* 485 U.S. 505, 108 S.Ct. 1355, 99 L.Ed.2d 592 (1988). * * * The majority disregards those decisions in its attempt to carve out areas of state activity that will receive special protection from federal legislation.

The majority's approach is also unsound because it will serve only to confuse the law. * * * Is the rule limited to federal regulation of the qualifications of state officials? Or does it apply more broadly to the regulation of any "state governmental functions"? * * * [Does the] requirement that Congress' intent to regulate a particular state activity be "plain to anyone reading [the federal statute]" * * * mean that it is now improper to look to the purpose or history of a federal statute in determining the scope of the statute's limitations on state activities? * * * The vagueness of the majority's rule undoubtedly will lead States to assert that various federal statutes no longer apply to a wide variety of State activities if Congress has not expressly referred to those activities in the statute. Congress, in turn, will be forced to draft long and detailed lists of which particular state functions it meant to regulate. * * *

The majority asserts that its plain statement rule is helpful in avoiding a "potential constitutional problem." It is far from clear, however, why there would be a constitutional problem if the ADEA applied to state judges, in light of our decisions in *Garcia* and *Baker* * * *. In any event, * * * a straightforward analysis of the ADEA's definition of "employee" reveals that the ADEA does not apply here. * * * [B]ecause this case can be decided purely on the basis of statutory interpretation, the majority's announcement of its plain statement rule, which purportedly is derived from constitutional principles, violates our general practice of avoiding the unnecessary resolution of constitutional issues. * * *

BUILDING AND CONSTRUCTION TRADES COUNCIL v. ASSOCIATED BUILDERS AND CONTRACTORS

Supreme Court of the United States, 1993.
___ U.S. ___, 113 S.Ct. 1190, 122 L.Ed.2d 565.

JUSTICE BLACKMUN delivered the opinion of the Court. * * *

The Massachusetts Water Resources Authority (MWRA) is an independent government agency charged by the Massachusetts Legislature with providing water-supply services, sewage collection, and treatment and disposal services for the eastern half of Massachusetts. Following a lawsuit arising out of its failure to prevent the pollution of Boston

Harbor, in alleged violation of the Federal Water Pollution Control Act, MWRA was ordered to clean up the Harbor. * * *

In the spring of 1988, MWRA selected Kaiser Engineers, Inc., as its project manager. Kaiser * * * suggested to MWRA that Kaiser be permitted to negotiate an agreement with the Building and Construction Trades Council and affiliated organizations (BCTC) that would assure labor stability over the life of the project. MWRA accepted Kaiser's suggestion, and Kaiser accordingly proceeded to negotiate the Boston Harbor Wastewater Treatment Facilities Project Labor Agreement. The Agreement included: recognition of BCTC as the exclusive bargaining agent for all craft employees; use of specified methods for resolving all labor-related disputes; a requirement that all employees be subject to union-security provisions compelling them to become union members within seven days of their employment; the primary use of BCTC's hiring halls to supply the project's craft labor force; a 10–year no-strike commitment; and a requirement that all contractors and subcontractors agree to be bound by the Agreement. MWRA's Board of Directors approved and adopted the Agreement in May 1989 and directed that Bid Specification 13.1 be incorporated into its solicitation of bids for work on the project. Bid Specification 13.1 provides in pertinent part:

> "Each successful bidder and any and all levels of subcontractors, as a condition of being awarded a contract or subcontract, will agree to abide by the provisions of the Boston Harbor Wastewater Treatment Facilities Project Labor Agreement * * *."

In March 1990, * * * respondent Associated Builders and Contractors of Massachusetts/Rhode Island, Inc. (ABC), an organization representing nonunion construction industry employers, brought this suit against MWRA, Kaiser, and BCTC, seeking, among other things, to enjoin enforcement of Bid Specification 13.1. ABC alleged pre-emption under the NLRA [National Labor Relations Act] * * *.

The NLRA contains no express pre-emption provision. Therefore, in accordance with settled pre-emption principles, we should not find MWRA's bid specification pre-empted " ' " * * * unless it conflicts with federal law or would frustrate the federal scheme, or unless [we] discern from the totality of the circumstances that Congress sought to occupy the field to the exclusion of the States." ' " *Metropolitan Life Ins. Co. v. Massachusetts*, 471 U.S. 724, 747–748, 105 S.Ct. 2380, 2393, 85 L.Ed.2d 728 (1985). We are reluctant to infer pre-emption. "Consideration under the Supremacy Clause starts with the basic assumption that Congress did not intend to displace state law." *Maryland v. Louisiana*, 451 U.S. 725, 746, 101 S.Ct. 2114, 2129, 68 L.Ed.2d 576 (1981). With these general principles in mind, we turn to the particular pre-emption doctrines that have developed around the NLRA.

In *Metropolitan Life Ins. Co. v. Massachusetts*, 471 U.S., at 748, 105 S.Ct., at 2394, we noted: "The Court has articulated two distinct NLRA pre-emption principles." The first, "*Garmon* pre-emption," see *San Diego Building Trades Council v. Garmon*, [359 U.S. 236, 79 S.Ct. 773, 3

L.Ed.2d 775 (1959)], * * * is designed to prevent conflict between, on the one hand, state and local regulation and, on the other, Congress' "integrated scheme of regulation," embodied in §§ 7 and 8 of the NLRA, which includes the choice of the NLRB, rather than state or federal courts, as the appropriate body to implement the Act. * * * A second pre-emption principle, "*Machinists* pre-emption," see *Machinists v. Wisconsin Employment Relations Comm'n*, 427 U.S., at 147, 96 S.Ct., at 2556, prohibits state and municipal regulation of areas that have been left " 'to be controlled by the free play of economic forces.' " *Id.*, at 140, 96 S.Ct., at 2553 (citation omitted). See also *Golden State Transit Corp. v. Los Angeles*, 475 U.S. 608, 614, 106 S.Ct. 1395, 1398, 89 L.Ed.2d 616 (1986) (*Golden State I*); *Golden State Transit Corp. v. Los Angeles*, 493 U.S. 103, 111, 110 S.Ct. 444, 451, 107 L.Ed.2d 420 (1989) (*Golden State II*). * * *

When we say that the NLRA pre-empts state law, we mean that the NLRA prevents a State from regulating within a protected zone, whether it be a zone protected and reserved for market freedom, see *Machinists*, or for NLRB jurisdiction, see *Garmon*. A State does not regulate, however, simply by acting within one of these protected areas. When a State owns and manages property, for example, it must interact with private participants in the marketplace. In so doing, the State is not subject to pre-emption by the NLRA, because pre-emption doctrines apply only to state *regulation*.

Our decisions in this area support the distinction between government as regulator and government as proprietor. We have held consistently that the NLRA was intended to supplant state labor *regulation*, not all legitimate state activity that affects labor. * * * In *Golden State I*, we held that the reason Los Angeles could not condition renewal of a taxicab franchise upon settlement of a labor dispute was that "*Machinists* pre-emption * * * precludes state and municipal *regulation* 'concerning conduct that Congress intended to be *unregulated*.' " 475 U.S., at 614, 106 S.Ct., at 1398 (emphasis added) * * *. As petitioners point out, a very different case would have been presented had the city of Los Angeles purchased taxi services from Golden State in order to transport city employees. In that situation, if the strike had produced serious interruptions in the services the city had purchased, the city would not necessarily have been pre-empted from advising Golden State that it would hire another company if the labor dispute were not resolved and services resumed by a specific deadline. * * *

The conceptual distinction between regulator and purchaser exists to a limited extent in the private sphere as well. A private actor, for example, can participate in a boycott of a supplier on the basis of a labor policy concern rather than a profit motive. The private actor under such circumstances would be attempting to "regulate" the suppliers and would not be acting as a typical proprietor. The fact that a private actor may "regulate" does not mean, of course, that the private actor may be "pre-empted" by the NLRA; the Supremacy Clause does not require pre-emption of private conduct. Private actors therefore may "regulate"

as they please, as long as their conduct does not violate the law.   * * *
[But] States have a qualitatively different role to play from private
parties.   When the State acts as regulator, it performs a role that is
characteristically a governmental rather than a private role, boycotts
notwithstanding.   Moreover, as regulator of private conduct, the State is
more powerful than private parties.   These distinctions are far less
significant when the State acts as a market participant with no interest
in setting policy.   * * *

Permitting the States to participate freely in the marketplace is not
only consistent with NLRA pre-emption principles generally but also, in
this case, promotes the legislative goals that animated the passage of
* * * § 8(f) * * * [of the NLRA].   Section 8(f) explicitly permits employers in the construction industry—but no other employers—to enter into
prehire agreements.   Prehire agreements are collective-bargaining
agreements providing for union recognition, compulsory union dues or
equivalents, and mandatory use of union hiring halls, prior to the hiring
of any employees.   * * * It is undisputed that the Agreement between
Kaiser and BCTC is a valid labor contract under § * * * 8(f).   * * * It is
evident from the face of the statute that in enacting exemptions authorizing certain kinds of project labor agreements in the construction
industry, Congress intended to accommodate conditions specific to that
industry.   Such conditions include, among others, the short-term nature
of employment which makes post-hire collective bargaining difficult, the
contractor's need for predictable costs and a steady supply of skilled
labor, and a longstanding custom of prehire bargaining in the industry.

There is no reason to expect these defining features of the construction industry to depend upon the public or private nature of the entity
purchasing contracting services.   To the extent that a private purchaser
may choose a contractor based upon that contractor's willingness to
enter into a prehire agreement, a public entity *as purchaser* should be
permitted to do the same.   * * * In the absence of any express or
implied indication by Congress that a State may not manage its own
property when it pursues its purely proprietary interests, and where
analogous private conduct would be permitted, this Court will not infer
such a restriction.   Indeed, there is some force to petitioners' argument
that denying an option to public owner-developers that is available to
private owner-developers itself places a restriction on Congress' intended
free play of economic forces identified in *Machinists*.   * * *

GOLDEN STATE TRANSIT v.
CITY OF LOS ANGELES

Supreme Court of the United States, 1989.
493 U.S. 103, 110 S.Ct. 444, 107 L.Ed.2d 420.

JUSTICE STEVENS delivered the opinion of the Court.

In *Golden State Transit Corp. v. City of Los Angeles,* 475 U.S. 608,
106 S.Ct. 1395, 89 L.Ed.2d 616 (1986) *(Golden State I),* we held that the
respondent city had violated federal law by conditioning the renewal of

petitioner's taxi cab franchise on settlement of a pending labor dispute between petitioner and its union. On remand, the District Court enjoined the city to reinstate the franchise but concluded that 42 U.S.C. § 1983 did not authorize an award of compensatory damages. The court reasoned that "the supremacy clause does not create individual rights that may be vindicated in an action for damages under Section 1983," and that even though the city's conduct was preempted by the National Labor Relations Act (NLRA), a § 1983 cause of action did not lie because there had been no "direct violation" of the statute and because the Act's comprehensive enforcement scheme precluded resort to § 1983. * * *

Section 1983 provides a federal remedy for "the deprivation of any rights, privileges, or immunities secured by the Constitution and laws." As the language of the statute plainly indicates, the remedy encompasses violations of federal statutory as well as constitutional rights. * * * Respondent argues that the Supremacy Clause, of its own force, does not create rights enforceable under § 1983. We agree. * * * Given the variety of situations in which preemption claims may be asserted, in state court and in federal court, it would obviously be incorrect to assume that a federal right of action pursuant to § 1983 exists every time a federal rule of law preempts state regulatory authority. Conversely, the fact that a federal statute has preempted certain state action does not preclude the possibility that the same federal statute may create a federal right for which § 1983 provides a remedy.

In all cases, the availability of the § 1983 remedy turns on whether the statute, by its terms or as interpreted, creates obligations "sufficiently specific and definite" to be within "the competence of the judiciary to enforce," *Wright [v. Roanoke Redevelopment and Housing Authority]*, 479 U.S., at 432, 107 S.Ct., at 775, is intended to benefit the putative plaintiff, and is not foreclosed "by express provision or other specific evidence from the statute itself." *Id.,* at 423, 107 S.Ct., at 770.

The nub of the controversy between the parties is whether the NLRA creates "rights" in labor and management that are protected against governmental interference. * * * We agree with petitioner that * * * the NLRA gives it rights enforceable against governmental interference in an action under § 1983. * * * In the NLRA, Congress has not just "occupied the field" with legislation that is passed solely with the interests of the general public in mind. In such circumstances, when congressional pre-emption benefits particular parties only as an incident of the federal scheme of regulation, a private damages remedy under § 1983 may not be available. The NLRA, however, creates rights in labor and management both against one another and against the State. * * * The rights protected against state interference, moreover, are not limited to those explicitly set forth in § 7 as protected against private interference. * * *

Golden State I was based on the doctrine that is identified with our decision in *Machinists v. Wisconsin Employment Relations Comm'n,* 427 U.S. 132, 96 S.Ct. 2548, 49 L.Ed.2d 396 (1972). That doctrine is fundamentally different from the rule of *San Diego Building Trades Council v. Garmon,* 359 U.S. 236, 79 S.Ct. 773, 3 L.Ed.2d 775 (1959), that state jurisdiction over conduct arguably protected or prohibited by the NLRA is pre-empted in the interest of maintaining uniformity in the administration of the federal regulatory jurisdiction. In *Machinists,* we reiterated that Congress intended to give parties to a collective-bargaining agreement the right to make use of "economic weapons," not explicitly set forth in the Act, free of governmental interference. 427 U.S., at 150, 96 S.Ct., at 2558. * * * The *Machinists* rule creates a free zone from which all regulation, "whether federal or State," *id.,* at 153, 96 S.Ct., at 2559, is excluded.

The city's contrary argument, that the NLRA does not secure rights against the State because the duties of the State are not expressly set forth in the text of the statute, is not persuasive. * * * A rule of law that is the product of judicial interpretation of a vague, ambiguous or incomplete statutory provision is no less binding than a rule that is based on the plain meaning of a statute. The violation of a federal right that has been found to be implicit in a statute's language and structure is as much a "direct violation" of a right as is the violation of a right that is clearly set forth in the text of the statute.

The *Machinists* rule is not designed—as is the *Garmon* rule—to answer the question whether state or federal regulations should apply to certain conduct. Rather, it is more akin to a rule that denies either sovereign the authority to abridge a personal liberty. * * * [T]he interest in being free of governmental regulation of the "peaceful methods of putting economic pressure upon one another," *Machinists,* 427 U.S., at 154, 96 S.Ct., at 2560, is a right specifically conferred on employers and employees by the NLRA. Of course, Congress has the authority to retract the statutorily conferred liberty at will * * *. But while the rule remains in effect, it is a guarantee of freedom for private conduct that the State may not abridge. * * *

JUSTICE KENNEDY, with whom THE CHIEF JUSTICE and JUSTICE O'CONNOR join, dissenting. * * *

Section 1983 * * * distinguishes secured rights, privileges, and immunities from those interests merely resulting from the allocation of power between the State and Federal Governments. * * * Pre-emption concerns the federal structure of the Nation rather than the securing of individual rights, privileges, and immunities to individuals. Although the majority finds the *Machinists* pre-emption doctrine "akin to a rule that denies either sovereign the authority to abridge a personal liberty," and describes the interest of being free of governmental regulation as a right specifically conferred by the NLRA on employers and employees, I cannot agree that federal law secures this legal interest within the meaning of § 1983.

Golden State does not and cannot contend that a federal statute protects it from the city's primary conduct apart form its governmental character. *Machinists'* pre-emption * * * rests upon the allocation of power rather than upon individual rights, privileges, or immunities. The dispute between Golden State and the city exists because the Federal Government has exercised its power under the Commerce Clause to regulate Golden State's labor relations under the NLRA and thus has deprived the city of the power to effect its own regulations of these relations. * * * Golden State's immunity, as defined in *Machinists,* has nothing to do with the substance of the requirement imposed on its collective bargaining. The immunity for instance, would not prevent the United States from exercising its power under the Commerce Clause to authorize the actions taken by the city. The immunity, rather, permits the company to object only that the wrong sovereign has attempted to regulate its labor relations. Golden State's immunity does not benefit the company as an individual, but instead results from the Supremacy Clause's separate protection of the federal structure and from the division of power in the constitutional system. Federal law, as such, does not secure this immunity to Golden State within the meaning of § 1983. * * *

4. ANTITRUST LAW

In the important case of Parker v. Brown, 317 U.S. 341, 63 S.Ct. 307, 87 L.Ed. 315 (1943), the Supreme Court held that the Sherman Antitrust Act did not apply to anticompetitive action engaged in by states. Thirty-five years later, in City of Lafayette v. Louisiana Power & Light Co., 435 U.S. 389, 98 S.Ct. 1123, 55 L.Ed.2d 364 (1978), the Supreme Court held that the Sherman Act did apply to anticompetitive action engaged in by cities. None of the four opinions in the *Lafayette* case was joined by a majority of the court, however, so initially the rationale for applying the Sherman Act to cities but not to states remained in doubt. In Community Communications Co. v. Boulder, reproduced below, a majority of the Supreme Court articulated for the first time the reasons for distinguishing cities from states for purposes of applying the federal antitrust law.[1]

The reaction to cities' exposure to federal antitrust liability under the *Lafayette* and *Boulder* cases has been quite intense. Dozens of scholarly articles have analyzed and criticized the opinions in the cases.[2]

---

1. Both the plurality opinion in *Lafayette* and the majority opinion in *Boulder* were written by Justice Brennan. For an analysis of Justice Brennan's treatment of cities not only in these cases but also in other cases imposing limits on city power, see Williams, The Constitutional Vulnerability of American Local Government: The Politics of City Status in American Law, 1986 Wis.L.Rev. 83, 120–137. See also Balkin, Federalism and the Conservative Ideology, 19 The Urban Lawyer 458 (1987) (analyzing the relationship between notions of federalism and conservatism).

2. See, e.g., Elhauge, The Scope of Antitrust Process, 104 Harv.L.Rev. 667 (1991);

Garland, Antitrust and State Action: Economic Efficiency and the Political Process, 96 Yale L.J. 486 (1987); Wiley, Revision and Apology in Antitrust Federalism, 96 Yale L.J. 1277 (1987); Garland, Antitrust and Federalism: A Response to Professor Wiley, 96 Yale L.J. 1291 (1987); Wiley, A Capture Theory of Antitrust Federalism, 99 Harv.L.Rev. 713 (1986); Gifford, The Antitrust State Action Doctrine After Fisher v. Berkeley, 39 Vand.L.Rev. 1257 (1986); Hovenkamp and MacKerron, Municipal Regulation and Federal Antitrust Policy, 32 U.C.L.A.L.Rev. 719 (1985); Vanderstar, Liability of Municipalities under the Antitrust Laws: Litigation Strategies, 32 Cath.

In response to the *Boulder* case, Congress passed the Local Government Antitrust Act of 1984[3], exempting cities from treble damages actions under the Clayton Act (although not exempting them from injunctive relief).   Three later Supreme Court cases have sought to clarify the extent of municipal liability under the Sherman Act.   Two of these cases are described in a Note following the *Boulder* case; the third, Fisher v. City of Berkeley, is reproduced after the Note.

Most of the commentary on the municipal antitrust cases has been written from an antitrust law perspective.   But these cases also raise significant local government law issues.[4]   Consider, for example, how the cases use the public/private distinction and arguments about decentralization of power to determine the extent of municipal antitrust liability. In what ways do the opinions treat cities like states and in what ways do they treat them like corporations?   What impact do these cases have on the choice of basing local governmental power on Dillon's Rule or home rule?   Why did neither opinion in the *Boulder* case cite National League of Cities v. Usery?   In addition to these questions of local government law, also consider how the four cases relate to each other.   How, for example, does the analysis of municipal liability in Fisher v. City of Berkeley differ from that used in *Boulder*?   If the *Fisher* opinion had been decided first, would *Boulder* have come out the same way?

COMMUNITY COMMUNICATIONS CO. v. BOULDER

Supreme Court of the United States, 1982.
455 U.S. 40, 102 S.Ct. 835, 70 L.Ed.2d 810.

JUSTICE BRENNAN delivered the opinion of the Court.   * * *

Respondent City of Boulder is organized as a "home rule" municipality under the Constitution of the State of Colorado.   The City is thus entitled to exercise "the full right of self-government in both local and municipal matters," and with respect to such matters the City Charter and ordinances supersede the laws of the State.   Under that Charter, all municipal legislative powers are exercised by an elected City Council.   In 1964 the City Council enacted an ordinance granting to Colorado Televents, Inc., a 20–year, revocable, non-exclusive permit to conduct a cable television business within the City limits.   This permit was assigned to petitioner in 1966, and since that time petitioner has provided cable television service to the University Hill area of Boulder, an area where some 20% of the City's population lives, and where, for geographical reasons, broadcast television signals cannot be received.   * * * [M]arkedly improved technology became available in the late 1970s, enabling

U.L.Rev. 395 (1983); Areeda, Antitrust Immunity for "State Action" After *Lafayette,* 95 Harv.L.Rev. 435 (1981); Antitrust Symposium: Municipal Antitrust Liability, 1980 Ariz.St.L.J. 245.

3. 15 U.S.C. secs. 1, 34–36 (Supp. II 1984).

4. See, e.g., Sentell, The United States Supreme Court as Home Rule Wrecker, 34 Mercer L.Rev. 363 (1982); Freilich & Carlisle, The Community Communications Case: A Return to the Dark Ages Before Home Rule, 14 Urb.Law. v (1982).

petitioner to offer many more channels of entertainment than could be provided by local broadcast television. Thus presented with an opportunity to expand its business into other areas of the City, petitioner in May 1979 informed the City Council that it planned such an expansion. But the new technology offered opportunities to potential competitors, as well, and in July 1979 one of them, the newly formed Boulder Communications Company (BCC), also wrote to the City Council, expressing its interest in obtaining a permit to provide competing cable television service throughout the City.

The City Council's response, after reviewing its cable television policy, was the enactment of an "emergency" ordinance prohibiting petitioner from expanding its business into other areas of the City for a period of three months. The City Council announced that during this moratorium it planned to draft a model cable television ordinance and to invite new businesses to enter the Boulder market under its terms, but that the moratorium was necessary because petitioner's continued expansion during the drafting of the model ordinance would discourage potential competitors from entering the market.

Petitioner filed this suit in the United States District Court for the District of Colorado, and sought, *inter alia,* a preliminary injunction to prevent the City from restricting petitioner's proposed business expansion, alleging that such a restriction would violate § 1 of the Sherman Act. * * *

Parker v. Brown, [317 U.S. 341, 63 S.Ct. 307, 87 L.Ed.2d 315 (1943)], addressed the question whether the federal antitrust laws prohibited a State, in the exercise of its sovereign powers, from imposing certain anticompetitive restraints. * * * *Parker* * * * [held] that California's program * * * [was] exempt, by virtue of the Sherman Act's own limitations, from antitrust attack:

> "We find nothing in the language of the Sherman Act or in its history which suggests that its purpose was to restrain a state or its officers or agents from activities directed by its legislature. In a dual system of government in which, under the Constitution, the states are sovereign, save only as Congress may constitutionally subtract from their authority, an unexpressed purpose to nullify a state's control over its officers and agents is not lightly to be attributed to Congress."

The availability of this exemption to a State's municipalities was the question presented in *City of Lafayette.* In that case, petitioners were Louisiana cities empowered to own and operate electric utility systems both within and beyond their municipal limits. Respondent brought suit against petitioners under the Sherman Act, alleging that they had committed various antitrust offenses in the conduct of their utility systems, to the injury of respondent. * * * A plurality opinion for four Justices * * * addressed petitioners' argument that *Parker,* properly construed, extended to "all governmental entities, whether state agencies or subdivisions of a State, * * * simply by reason of their status as such." The plurality opinion rejected this argument, * * * [noting] that the *Parker* exemption reflects the federalism principle that we are a nation of *States,* a principle that makes no accommodation for sovereign subdivisions of States. The plurality opinion said that:

> "Cities are not themselves sovereign; they do not receive all the federal deference of the States that create them. *Parker*'s limitation of the exemption to 'official action directed by a state,' is consistent with the fact that the States' subdivisions generally have not been treated as equivalents of the States' themselves. In light of the serious economic dislocation which could result if cities were free to place their own parochial interests above the Nation's economic goals reflected in the antitrust laws, we are especially unwilling to presume that Congress intended to exclude anticompetitive municipal action from their reach."

The opinion emphasized, however, that the state as sovereign might sanction anticompetitive municipal activities and thereby immunize municipalities from antitrust liability. Under the plurality's standard, the *Parker* doctrine would shield from antitrust liability municipal conduct engaged in "pursuant to state policy to displace competition with regulation or monopoly public service." This was simply a recognition that a State may frequently choose to effect its policies through the instrumentality of its cities and towns. It was stressed, however, that the "state policy" relied upon would have to be "clearly articulated and affirmatively expressed." * * *

Our precedents thus reveal that Boulder's moratorium ordinance cannot be exempt from antitrust scrutiny unless it constitutes the action of the State of Colorado itself in its sovereign capacity or unless it constitutes municipal action in furtherance or implementation of clearly articulated and affirmatively expressed state policy. Boulder argues that these criteria are met by the direct delegation of powers to municipalities through the Home Rule Amendment to the Colorado Constitution. It contends that this delegation satisfies both the *Parker* and the *City of Lafayette* standards. We take up these arguments in turn.

Respondent's *Parker* argument emphasizes that through the Home Rule Amendment the people of the State of Colorado have vested in the City of Boulder "*every power* theretofore possessed by the legislature * * * in local and municipal affairs." The power thus possessed by Boulder's City Council assertedly embraces the regulation of cable television, which is claimed to pose essentially local problems. Thus, it is suggested, the City's cable television moratorium ordinance is an "act of government" performed by the City *acting as the state* in local matters, which meets the "state action" criterion of *Parker.*

We reject this argument: it both misstates the letter of the law and misunderstands its spirit. The *Parker* state action exemption reflects Congress' intention to embody in the Sherman Act the federalism principle that the States possess a significant measure of sovereignty under our Constitution. But this principle contains its own limitation:

Ours is a "*dual* system of government," *Parker, supra* (emphasis added), which has no place for sovereign cities. * * * The dissent in the Court of Appeals correctly discerned this limitation upon the federalism principle: "We are a nation not of 'city-states' but of States." *Parker* itself took this view. * * * *Parker* recognized Congress' intention to limit the state action exemption based upon the federalism principle of limited state sovereignty. * * * It was expressly recognized by the plurality opinion in *City of Lafayette* that municipalities "are not themselves sovereign" and that accordingly they could partake of the *Parker* exemption only to the extent that they acted pursuant to a clearly articulated and affirmatively expressed state policy. * * * We turn then to Boulder's contention that its actions were undertaken pursuant to a clearly articulated and affirmatively expressed state policy.

Boulder first argues that the requirement of "clear articulation and affirmative expression" is fulfilled by the Colorado Home Rule Amendment's "guarantee of local autonomy." * * * But plainly the requirement of "clear articulation and affirmative expression" is not satisfied when the State's position is one of mere *neutrality* respecting the municipal actions challenged as anticompetitive. A State that allows its municipalities to do as they please can hardly be said to have "contemplated" the specific anticompetitive actions for which municipal liability is sought. * * * Indeed, respondent argues that as to local matters regulated by a home rule city, the Colorado General Assembly is without power to act. Thus on respondent's view, Boulder can pursue its course of regulating cable television competition, while another home rule city can choose to prescribe monopoly service, while still another can elect free-market competition: and all of these policies are equally "contemplated," and "comprehended within the powers granted." Acceptance of such a proposition—that the general grant of power to enact ordinances necessarily implies state authorization to enact specific anticompetitive ordinances—would wholly eviscerate the concepts of "clear articulation and affirmative expression" that our precedents require.

Respondent argues that denial of the *Parker* exemption in the present case will have serious adverse consequences for cities, and will unduly burden the federal courts. But this argument is simply an attack upon the wisdom of the longstanding congressional commitment to the policy of free markets and open competition embodied in the antitrust laws. Those laws, like other federal laws imposing civil or criminal sanctions upon "persons," of course apply to municipalities as well as to other corporate entities. Moreover, judicial enforcement of Congress' will regarding the state action exemption renders a State "no less able to allocate governmental power between itself and its political subdivisions. It means only that when the State itself has not directed or authorized an anticompetitive practice, the State's subdivisions in exercising their delegated power must obey the antitrust laws." *City of Lafayette,* 435 U.S., at 416, 98 S.Ct., at 1138. * * *

JUSTICE REHNQUIST, with whom THE CHIEF JUSTICE and JUSTICE O'CONNOR join, dissenting.

The Court's decision in this case is flawed in two serious respects, and will thereby impede, if not paralyze, local governments' efforts to enact ordinances and regulations aimed at protecting public health, safety, and welfare, for fear of subjecting the local government to liability under the Sherman Act. First, the Court treats the issue in this case as whether a municipality is "exempt" from the Sherman Act under our decision in *Parker v. Brown,* 317 U.S. 341, 63 S.Ct. 307, 87 L.Ed. 315 (1943). The question addressed in *Parker* and in this case is not whether State and local governments are *exempt* from the Sherman Act, but whether statutes, ordinances, and regulations enacted as an act of government are *preempted* by the Sherman Act under the operation of the Supremacy Clause. Second, in holding that a municipality's ordinances can be "exempt" from antitrust scrutiny only if the enactment furthers or implements a "clearly articulated and affirmatively expressed state policy," the Court treats a political subdivision of a State as an entity indistinguishable from any privately owned business. As I read the Court's opinion, a municipality may be said to *violate* the antitrust laws by enacting legislation in conflict with the Sherman Act, unless the legislation is enacted pursuant to an affirmative state policy to supplant competitive market forces in the area of the economy to be regulated. * * *

Viewing the *Parker* doctrine in this manner will have troubling consequences for this Court and the lower courts who must now adapt antitrust principles to adjudicate Sherman Act challenges to local regulation of the economy. * * * In *National Society of Professional Engineers v. United States,* 435 U.S. 679, 695, 98 S.Ct. 1355, 1367, 55 L.Ed.2d 637 (1978), we held that an anticompetitive restraint could not be defended on the basis of a private party's conclusion that competition posed a potential threat to public safety and the ethics of a particular profession. * * * Instead, private entities may defend restraints only on the basis that the restraint is not unreasonable in its effect on competition or because its pro-competitive effects outweigh its anticompetitive effects.

Applying *Professional Engineers* to municipalities would mean that an ordinance could not be defended on the basis that its benefits to the community, in terms of traditional health, safety, and public welfare concerns, outweigh its anticompetitive effects. A local government would be disabled from displacing competition with regulation. Thus, a municipality would violate the Sherman Act by enacting restrictive zoning ordinances, by requiring business and occupational licenses, and by granting exclusive franchises to utility services, even if the city determined that it would be in the best interests of its inhabitants to displace competition with regulation. Competition simply does not and cannot further the interests that lie behind most social welfare legislation. * * * Surely, the Court does not seek to require a municipality to justify every ordinance it enacts in terms of its pro-competitive effects. If municipalities are permitted only to enact ordinances that are consistent with the pro-competitive policies of the Sherman Act, a municipality's power to regulate the economy would be all but destroyed. This country's municipalities will be unable to experiment with innovative social programs.

On the other hand, rejecting the rationale of *Professional Engineers* to accommodate the municipal defendant opens up a different sort of Pandora's Box. If the Rule of Reason were "modified" to permit a municipality to defend its regulation on the basis that its benefits to the community outweigh its anticompetitive effects, the courts will be called upon to review social legislation in a manner reminiscent of the *Lochner* era. Once again, the federal courts will be called upon to engage in the same wide-ranging, essentially standardless inquiry into the reasonableness of local regulation that this Court has properly rejected. * * * The Sherman Act should not be deemed to authorize federal courts to "substitute their social and economic beliefs for the judgment of legislative bodies, who are elected to pass laws." *Ferguson v. Skrupa,* 372 U.S. 726, 730, 83 S.Ct. 1028, 1031, 10 L.Ed.2d 93 (1963). * * *

[T]he majority comes to the startling conclusion that our Federalism is in no way implicated when a municipal ordinance is invalidated by the Sherman Act. I see no principled basis to conclude, as does the Court, that municipal ordinances are more susceptible to invalidation under the Sherman Act than are state statutes. The majority concludes that since municipalities are not States, and hence are not "sovereigns", our notions of federalism are not implicated when federal law is applied to invalidate otherwise constitutionally valid municipal legislation. I find this reasoning remarkable indeed. Our notions of federalism are implicated when it is contended that a municipal ordinance is preempted by a federal statute. This Court has made no such distinction between States and their subdivisions with regard to the preemptive effects of federal law. The standards applied by this Court are the same regardless of whether the challenged enactment is that of a State or one of its political subdivisions. See, *e.g., City of Burbank v. Lockheed Air Terminal, Inc.,* 411 U.S. 624, 93 S.Ct. 1854, 36 L.Ed.2d 547 (1973). I suspect that the Court has not intended to so dramatically alter established principles of Supremacy Clause analysis. Yet, this is precisely what it appears to have done by holding that a municipality may invoke the *Parker* doctrine only to the same extent as can a private litigant. Since the *Parker* doctrine is a matter of federal preemption under the Supremacy Clause, it should apply in challenges to municipal regulation in similar fashion as it applies in a challenge to a state regulatory enactment. The distinction between cities and States created by the majority has no principled basis to support it if the issue is properly framed in terms of preemption rather than exemption.

As with the States, the *Parker* doctrine should be employed to determine whether local legislation has been preempted by the Sherman Act. Like the State, a municipality should not be haled into federal court in order to justify its decision that competition should be replaced with regulation. The *Parker* doctrine correctly holds that the federal interest in protecting and fostering competition is not infringed so long as the state or local regulation is so structured to ensure that it is truly the government, and not the regulated private entities, which is replacing competition with regulation.

By treating the municipal defendant as no different from the private litigant attempting to invoke the *Parker* doctrine, the Court's decision today will radically alter the relationship between the States and their political subdivisions. Municipalities will no longer be able to regulate the local economy without the imprimatur of a clearly expressed state policy to displace competition. The decision today effectively destroys the "home rule" movement in this country, through which local governments have obtained, not without persistent state opposition, a limited autonomy over matters of local concern. The municipalities that stand most to lose by the decision today are those with the most autonomy. Where the State is totally disabled from enacting legislation dealing with matters of local concern, the municipality will be defenseless from challenges to its regulation of the local economy. In such a case, the State is disabled from articulating a policy to displace competition with regulation. Nothing short of altering the relationship between the municipality and the State will enable the local government to legislate on matters important to its inhabitants. In order to defend itself from Sherman Act attacks, the home rule municipality will have to cede its authority back to the State. It is unfortunate enough that the Court today holds that our Federalism is not implicated when municipal legislation is invalidated by a federal statute. It is nothing less than a novel and egregious error when this Court uses the Sherman Act to regulate the relationship between the States and their political subdivisions.

———

Note on Hallie and Omni

In Town of Hallie v. City of Eau Claire, 471 U.S. 34, 105 S.Ct. 1713, 85 L.Ed.2d 24 (1985), the Town of Hallie (Wisconsin) challenged the City of Eau Claire's condition for use of the City's sewage treatment facility: in order to use the facility, neighboring towns had to agree to be annexed by the City. The Supreme Court held the City's policy was state action and therefore exempt from the Sherman Act. Writing for a unanimous court, Justice Powell sought to clarify two issues raised by the *Boulder* case: (1) "how clearly a state policy must be articulated for a municipality to be able to establish that its anticompetitive activity constitutes state action," and (2) whether action by a municipality—like action by a private party—must satisfy the requirement that there be "active state supervision" of anticompetitive activity.

On the first issue, the Court noted that Wisconsin law had not only authorized the City's sewage treatment system but had allowed the city to "delineate the area within which service will be provided." This authorization, the Court said, empowered the city to refuse to serve unannexed areas and, therefore, "clearly contemplated that the city could engage in anticompetitive conduct." The Town, however, argued that *Boulder*'s "clear articulation" test required a state statute to say expressly that anticompetitive activity was authorized. The Court rejected this argument. Not only did this position take an "unrealistic view of how legislatures work[ed]", the Court said, but such a requirement would have "detrimental side effects upon municipalities' local autonomy and authority to govern themselves." To satisfy the clear articulation requirement of the state action test, all that was necessary, the Court held, was for the Wisconsin statute to "contemplate[ ] the kind of action complained of".

On the second issue, the Court rejected the notion that the anticompetitive activity of cities, like that of private parties, had to be actively supervised by the state. The active supervision requirement had been imposed on private parties in California Retail Liquor Dealers Assn. v. Midcal Aluminum, Inc., 445 U.S. 97, 100 S.Ct. 937, 63 L.Ed.2d 233 (1980). The Court reasoned:

> In *Midcal,* we stated that the active state supervision requirement was necessary to prevent a State from circumventing the Sherman Act's proscriptions "by casting * * * a gauzy cloak of state involvement over what is essentially a private price-fixing arrangement." Where a private party is engaging in the anticompetitive activity, there is a real danger that he is acting to further his own interests, rather than the governmental interests of the State. Where the actor is a municipality, there is little or no danger that it is involved in a *private* price-fixing arrangement. The only real danger is that it will seek to further purely parochial public interests at the expense of more overriding state goals. This danger is minimal, however, because of the requirement that the municipality act pursuant to a clearly articulated state policy. Once it is clear that state authorization exists, there is no need to require the State to supervise actively the municipality's execution of what is a properly delegated function.

In City of Columbia v. Omni Outdoor Advertising, 499 U.S. 365, 111 S.Ct. 1344, 113 L.Ed.2d 382 (1991), Omni Outdoor Advertising, Inc., challenged a city ordinance that restricted the size, location, and spacing of billboards on the grounds that it violated the Sherman Act. Omni charged that the mayor and members of the city council were personal friends of the majority owner of Columbia Outdoor Advertising (COA), a company that controlled more than 95% of Columbia's outdoor advertising market, and that COA officials were part of a "longstanding" "secret anticompetitive agreement" whereby "the City and COA would each use their [sic] respective power and resources to protect * * * COA's monopoly position," in return for which "City Council members received advantages made possible by COA's monopoly."

Justice Scalia, writing for the Court, found that Columbia was authorized by state law to pass the challenged ordinance. "In order to prevent *Parker* from undermining the very interests of federalism it is designed to protect," he said, "it is necessary to adopt a concept of authority broader than what is applied to determine the legality of the municipality's action under state law. * * * [N]o more is needed to establish, for *Parker* purposes, the city's authority to regulate than its unquestioned zoning power over the size, location, and spacing of billboards."

The Court also rejected the notion, advanced by the Court of Appeals in the case, that otherwise legitimate city action is invalid when it is taken pursuant to a conspiracy with private parties. The Court stated:

> The impracticality of such a principle is evident if, for purposes of the exception, "conspiracy" means nothing more than an agreement to impose the regulation in question. Since it is both inevitable and desirable that public officials often agree to do what one or another group of private citizens urges upon them, such an exception would virtually swallow up the *Parker* rule: All anticompetitive regulation would be vulnerable to a "conspiracy" charge.

Even an exception limited to instances of government corruption, the Court reasoned, would be impractical:

> Few governmental actions are immune from the charge that they are "not in the public interest" or in some sense "corrupt." * * * The fact is that virtually all regulation benefits some segments of the society and harms others; and that it is not universally considered contrary to the public good if the net economic loss to the losers exceeds the net economic gain to the winners. *Parker* was not written in ignorance of the reality that determination of "the public interest" in the manifold areas of government regulation entails not merely economic and mathematical analysis but value judgment, and it was not meant to shift that judgment from elected officials to judges and juries. If the city of Columbia's decision to regulate what one local newspaper called "billboard jungles" is made subject to *ex post facto* judicial assessment of "the public interest," with personal liability of city officials a possible consequence, we will have gone far to "compromise the States' ability to regulate their domestic commerce". * * * For these reasons, we reaffirm our rejection of any interpretation of the Sherman Act that would allow plaintiffs to look behind the actions of state sovereigns to base their claims on "perceived conspiracies to restrain trade," *Hoover [v. Ronwin],* 466 U.S., at 580, 104 S.Ct., at 2001. We reiterate that, with the possible market participant exception, *any* action that qualifies as state action is "*ipso facto* * * * exempt from the operation of the antitrust laws," *id.,* at 568, 104 S.Ct., at 1995.

Although *Omni* was decided after Fisher v. City of Berkeley, the case reproduced below, Justice Scalia did not cite the *Fisher* case. Justice Stevens, in a dissent in which Justices White and Marshall joined, said the following about *Fisher*:

> The Court's assumption that an agreement between private parties and public officials is an "inevitable" precondition for official action * * * is simply wrong.[8] Indeed, I am persuaded that such agreements are the exception rather than the rule, and that they are, and should be, disfavored. The mere fact that an official body adopts a position that is

---

8. No such agreement was involved in Hallie v. Eau Claire * * * In that case the plaintiffs challenged independent action— the determination of the service area of the city's sewage system—that had been expressly authorized by Wisconsin legislation. The absence of any such agreement provid- ed the basis for our decision in Fisher v. Berkeley ("[t]he distinction between unilateral and concerted action is critical here * * * [t]hus, if the Berkeley Ordinance stabilizes rents without this element of concerted action, the program it establishes cannot run afoul of § 1").

advocated by a private lobbyist is plainly not sufficient to establish an agreement to do so. See *Fisher v. Berkeley,* 475 U.S. 260, 266–267, 106 S.Ct. 1045, 1049, 89 L.Ed.2d 206 (1986). Nevertheless, in many circumstances, it would seem reasonable to infer—as the jury did in this case—that the official action is the product of an agreement intended to elevate particular private interests over the general good. * * *

FISHER v. CITY OF BERKELEY

Supreme Court of the United States, 1986.
475 U.S. 260, 106 S.Ct. 1045, 89 L.Ed.2d 206.

JUSTICE MARSHALL delivered the opinion of the Court. * * *

In June 1980, the electorate of the City of Berkeley, California, enacted an initiative entitled "Ordinance 5261–N.S., Rent Stabilization and Eviction for Good Cause Ordinance," (hereafter Ordinance). * * * [T]he Ordinance places strict rent controls on all real property that "is being rented or is available for rent for residential use in whole or in part". * * * [Under the Ordinance a] landlord may raise his rents * * * only pursuant to an annual general adjustment of rent ceilings by a Rent Stabilization Board of appointed commissioners or after he is successful in petitioning the Board for an individual adjustment. * * *

Shortly after the passage of the initiative, appellants, a group of landlords owning rental property in Berkeley, brought this suit in California Superior Court, claiming, *inter alia,* that the Ordinance violates their rights under the Due Process and Equal Protection Clauses of the Fourteenth Amendment, and seeking declaratory and injunctive relief. * * * [T]his Court's decision in *Community Communications Co. v. City of Boulder,* 455 U.S. 40, 102 S.Ct. 835, 70 L.Ed.2d 810 (1982), led certain *amici* to raise the question whether the Ordinance was unconstitutional because pre-empted by the federal antitrust laws. * * * We noted probable jurisdiction limited to the antitrust preemption question. * * *

Recognizing that the function of government may often be to tamper with free markets, correcting their failures and aiding their victims, this Court noted in *Rice v. Norman Williams Co.* [458 U.S. 654, 102 S.Ct. 3294, 73 L.E.2d 1042 (1982)] that a "state statute is not pre-empted by the federal antitrust laws simply because the state scheme may have an anticompetitive effect". We have therefore held that a state statute should be struck down on pre-emption grounds "only if it mandates or authorizes conduct that necessarily constitutes a violation of the antitrust laws in all cases, or if it places irresistible pressure on a private party to violate the antitrust laws in order to comply with the statute." 458 U.S., at 661, 102 S.Ct., at 3300.

While *Rice* involved a state statute rather than a municipal ordinance, the rule it established does not distinguish between the two. As in other pre-emption cases, the analysis is the same for the acts of both levels of government. Only where legislation is found to conflict "irreconcilably" with the antitrust laws, *Rice,* 458 U.S., at 659, 102 S.Ct., at

3298, does the level of government responsible for its enactment become important. Legislation that would otherwise be pre-empted under *Rice* may nonetheless survive if it is found to be state action immune from antitrust scrutiny under *Parker v. Brown,* 317 U.S. 341, 63 S.Ct. 307, 87 L.Ed. 315 (1943). The ultimate source of that immunity can be only the State, not its subdivisions. See *Community Communications Co. v. Boulder,* 455 U.S., at 50–51, 102 S.Ct., at 840; *Lafayette v. Louisiana Power & Light Co.,* 435 U.S. 389, 412–413, 98 S.Ct. 1123, 1136, 55 L.Ed.2d 364 (1978) (opinion of Brennan, J.).

Appellants argue that Berkeley's Rent Stabilization Ordinance is pre-empted under *Rice* because it imposes rent ceilings across the entire rental market for residential units. Such a regime, they contend, clearly falls within the *per se* rule against price fixing, a rule that has been one of the settled points of antitrust enforcement since the earliest days of the Sherman Act. * * * Certainly there is this much truth to appellants' argument: Had the owners of residential rental property in Berkeley voluntarily banded together to stabilize rents in the city, their activities would not be saved from antitrust attack by claims that they had set reasonable prices out of solicitude for the welfare of their tenants. Moreover, it cannot be denied that Berkeley's Ordinance will affect the residential housing rental market in much the same way as would the philanthropic activities of this hypothetical trade association. What distinguishes the operation of Berkeley's Ordinance from the activities of a benevolent landlords' cartel is not that the Ordinance will necessarily have a different economic effect, but that the rent ceilings imposed by the Ordinance and maintained by the Stabilization Board have been unilaterally imposed by government upon landlords to the exclusion of private control.

The distinction between unilateral and concerted action is critical here. Adhering to the language of § 1, this Court has always limited the reach of that provision to "unreasonable restraints of trade effected by a 'contract, combination * * *, or conspiracy' between *separate* entities." *Copperweld Corp. v. Independence Tube Corp.,* 467 U.S. 752, 768, 104 S.Ct. 2731, 2740, 81 L.Ed.2d 628 (1984) (emphasis in original). * * * Even where a single firm's restraints directly affect prices and have the same economic effect as concerted action might have, there can be no liability under § 1 in the absence of agreement. Thus, if the Berkeley Ordinance stabilizes rents without this element of concerted action, the program it establishes cannot run afoul of § 1.

Recognizing this concerted action requirement, appellants argue that the Ordinance "forms a combination between [the City of Berkeley and its officials], on the one hand, and the property owners on the other. It also creates a horizontal combination among the landlords." In so arguing, appellants misconstrue the concerted action requirement of § 1. A restraint imposed unilaterally by government does not become concerted action within the meaning of the statute simply because it has a coercive effect upon parties who must obey the law. The ordinary relationship between the government and those who must obey its regulatory commands whether they wish to or not is not enough to establish a conspiracy. Similarly, the mere fact that all competing property owners must comply with the same provisions of the Ordinance is not enough to establish a conspiracy among landlords. Under Berkeley's Ordinance, control over the maximum rent levels of every affected residential unit has been unilaterally removed from the owners of those properties and given to the Rent Stabilization Board. While the Board may choose to respond to an individual landlord's petition for a special adjustment of a particular rent ceiling, it may decide not to. There is no meeting of the minds here. The owners of residential property in Berkeley have no more freedom to resist the city's rent controls than they do to violate any other local ordinance enforced by substantial sanctions. * * * Adopted by popular initiative, the Ordinance can hardly be viewed as a cloak for any conspiracy among landlords or between the landlords and the municipality. Berkeley's landlords have simply been deprived of the power freely to raise their rents. That is why they are here. And that is why their role in the stabilization program does not alter the restraint's unilateral nature.

Because under settled principles of antitrust law, the rent controls established by Berkeley's Ordinance lack the element of concerted action needed before they can be characterized as a *per se* violation of § 1 of the Sherman Act, we cannot say that the Ordinance is facially inconsistent with the federal antitrust laws. See *Rice v. Norman Williams Co.*, 458 U.S., at 661, 102 S.Ct., at 3299. We therefore need not address whether, even if the controls were to mandate § 1 violations, they would be exempt under the state-action doctrine from antitrust scrutiny. See *Town of Hallie v. City of Eau Claire*, 471 U.S. ___, ___, 105 S.Ct. 1713, ___, 85 L.Ed.2d 24 (1985). * * *

JUSTICE BRENNAN, dissenting. * * *

In this case, by declaring maximum prices landlords may charge, Berkeley's Ordinance irresistably pressures landlords to fix prices for their rental units. Thus, the Ordinance "facially conflict[s] with the Sherman Act because it *mandate[s]* [price fixing], an activity that has long been regarded as a *per se* violation of the Sherman Act." *[Rice v. Norman Williams Co.*, 458 U.S. 654,] 659–60, 102 S.Ct. [3294,] at 3298–3299, [73 L.Ed.2d 1042 (1982)]. * * * Despite this, the Court holds that the Ordinance is not pre-empted by the Sherman Act because prices are fixed "unilaterally" by the city, rather than by "contract, combination, or conspiracy." I do not read our decisions necessarily to require proof of such concerted action as a prerequisite to a finding of pre-emption. * * *

Even if I accepted the Court's analysis of the antitrust preemption issue, I would find a functional "combination" in this case between the city of Berkeley and its officials, on the one hand, and the landlords on the other—a combination that operates to fix prices for rental units in Berkeley. To reach a contrary result, the Court simply states a conclusion—that "[a] restraint imposed unilaterally by government does not become concerted action within the meaning of the statute simply because it has a coercive effect upon parties who must obey the law." The Court doesn't explain why this is so * * *. The best I can make of this is that the Court apparently would interpret the Sherman Act to forbid only privately arranged price-fixing schemes. That interpretation would be plainly misguided. * * * [T]he city can compel landlords to do what the Sherman Act plainly forbids to fix prices for rental units in Berkeley. Regardless of whether the landlords "agree" to the prices charged, the circumstances here clearly "exclude the possibility that the [city and the landlords] were acting independently." *[Monsanto Co. v. Spray–Rite Service Corp.,]* 465 U.S. 752, 764, 104 S.Ct. 1464, 1471, [79 L.Ed.2d 775 (1984)]. The Ordinance eliminates price competition more effectively than any private "agreement" ever could, and is therefore preempted by the Sherman Act. The Court's contrary conclusion does not further, as it argues, but rather distorts "traditional antitrust principles." * * *

Appellees suggest that three considerations support their argument that the Ordinance implements a clearly articulated and affirmatively expressed state policy authorizing municipalities to enact rent control measures * * *. First, in 1972, Berkeley adopted a rent control charter amendment, which was approved by concurrent resolution of both houses of the state legislature. There are serious doubts that this purely *pro forma* approval would qualify the amendment for the *Parker* exemption. In any event, that amendment was subsequently invalidated by the California Supreme Court, [*Birkenfeld v. City of Berkeley,* 17 Cal.3d 129, 138, 130 Cal.Rptr. 465, 472, 550 P.2d 1001, 1008 (1976),] and the legislature's actions respecting its passage afford no support for the claimed exemption of the *current* Ordinance from antitrust scrutiny.

Second, the *Birkenfeld* decision, while invalidating Berkeley's rent control amendment, found state authority for such measures in constitutional provisions conferring upon cities the power to "make and enforce * * * all local, police, sanitary, and other ordinances and regulations not in conflict with general laws." But we have made clear that such general grants of authority do not constitute the required mandate to engage in conduct that necessarily constitutes a violation of the antitrust laws. See *Boulder,* 455 U.S., at 55, 102 S.Ct., at 842. * * *

Third, state law requires cities to "make adequate provision for the housing needs of all economic segments of the community." Cal.Govt. Code Ann. § 65580(d) (West 1983). But * * * [the] requirement of " 'clear articulation and affirmative expression' is not satisfied when the State's position is one of mere *neutrality* respecting the municipal actions challenged as anticompetitive." *Boulder,* 455 U.S., at 55, 102 S.Ct., at 843 (emphasis in original). * * *

Congress may ultimately agree with appellees' argument, and may choose to amend the antitrust laws to grant municipalities broad discretion to enact anticompetitive measures in the public interest. Pending such amendment, however, only a clearly articulated and affirmatively expressed state policy will exempt ordinances like this from the reach of the Sherman Act.

5. FEDERAL CRIMINAL LAW ENFORCEMENT AND CITY POLITICS

Municipal corruption is certainly not new; on the contrary, the (controversial) history of corruption in American cities—and of the efforts to control it—is well known.[1] What is new, however, as the following excerpt from John Noonan's study of bribes suggests, is the attempt by the federal government to use federal criminal law to combat this corruption. Justification for this use of federal power is not hard to find. The existence of corruption at all levels of government is widely recognized. Many people believe that municipal corruption is so pervasive that local law enforcement officials cannot control it; indeed, sometimes these officials themselves may be corrupt. Moreover, municipal corruption is costly and has a devastating impact on public confidence in government. Under these circumstances, federal officials could plausibly argue that the federal government has a responsibility to curb this abuse of public trust.

Yet federal criminal prosecution constitutes a massive federal intrusion into local decisionmaking. Through an expansive reading of federal criminal statutes, the federal government can impose its own code of behavior on local officials; indeed, partisan politics can influence who is selected to be subjected to this code of behavior. Consider the following remarks of Judge Winter of the United States Court of Appeals for the Second Circuit:

> Quite frankly, I shudder at the prospect of partisan political activists being indicted for failing to act "impartially" in influencing governmental acts. * * * Where Congress has not passed legislation specifying particular acts by the politically active as criminal, our reliance rather should be on public debate, a free press and an alert electorate. * * * The limitless expansion of the mail fraud statute subjects virtually every active participant in the political process to potential criminal investigation and prosecution. It may be a disagreeable fact but it is nevertheless a fact that political opponents not infrequently exchange charges of "corruption," "bias," "dishonesty," or deviation from "accepted standards of * * * fair play and right dealing." Every such accusation is now potentially translatable into a federal indictment. *U.S. v. Margiotta*, 688 F.2d 108, 143 (2d Cir.1982) (Winter, J. dissenting).

1. The classic contemporary critiques of late nineteenth century municipal corruption are Bryce, The American Commonwealth (1888) and Steffens, The Shame of the Cities (1904). For more general treatments of the subject, see, e.g., Brownell, Bosses and Reformers: Urban Politics in America, 1880–1920 (1973); Schiesl, The Politics of Efficiency, Municipal Administration and Reform in America, 1800–1920 (1977); Shefter, The Emergence of the Political Machine: An Alternative View, in Hawley et al., Theoretical Perspectives on Urban Politics (1976).

The cases reproduced below present contrasting views of the definition of extortion under the Hobbs Act and of the scope of the federal mail fraud statute. How expansively should federal criminal law be interpreted in the effort to weed out municipal corruption? Should concerns about local autonomy—or the partisan abuse of the criminal process—limit federal criminal prosecution of local officials? [2] What are the alternative ways to combat municipal corruption other than federal criminal prosecution?

JOHN NOONAN, BRIBES

584–587, 589–591, 598, 600–601 (1984).

THE LARGER THAN LOCAL CHAMPION

Federal entry on the local scene can be understood as a facet of the larger tendency to federalize provincial preserves, a trend that ever since the Civil War had brought more and more power to Washington. The federal income tax, the securities regulation enacted under the New Deal, the civil rights legislation of the 1960s, were other signs and embodiments of the same dynamism. The push toward the center was stronger than party principles. In the late 1960s one local area yet unaffected by federal expansion was criminal corruption. Ideologically, President Nixon presented himself as a believer in decentralization. Yet under his administration, a combination of old laws, prosecutorial ingenuity, judicial imperialism, and new legislation approved by Nixon began an effective federalization of the law of bribery. Much as in the eleventh century, to the admiring applause of reformers, the central administration of the Church assumed responsibility for suppressing simony everywhere in theory, and in fact did so selectively far from Rome, so the federal leviathan emerged as the general foe of all graft and the selective chastener of civic corruption. From the perspective of reform, it was the age of Ildebrando; that an age of Leo X and Luther would follow did not figure in the federal calculations.

The Equation of Bribery with Extortion. Harbinger of what was to come was the prosecution of the Kenny machine in Jersey City, the work of two Nixon-appointed district attorneys, Frederick Lacey and his successor, Herbert J. Stern. New Jersey, according to Lincoln Steffens, had always been corrupt; Jersey City seemed the corruptest part of all. A reform led by an undertaker in 1905 had been quickly snuffed out. From 1918 to 1949 the city had been ruled by Boss Frank Hague. John Kenny, a Hague henchman, beat the machine in 1949 in the guise of a reformer; and in a spectacular gesture of repudiation the city actually sued Hague for $15,000,000 taken as bribes from municipal employees in the thirty-one years of his incumbency. The theory of the suit was upheld by the New Jersey Supreme Court; the money was not collected before Hague died. Kenny soon showed himself a boss in the mold of his

---

2. For a debate on this topic, see Maass, Public Policy by Prosecution, 89 The Public Interest 107 (1987); Heymann, Reply: The Risks of Corruption, 89 The Public Interest 128 (1987).

mentor, and the law enforcement agencies of the state were unable to shake his hold. In 1970 the federal rescue was launched.

Put into play was the Anti–Racketeering Act of 1934. The law had been enacted after a Senate investigation of big city gangsterism. The statute did not mention bribery. By the Hobbs Act of 1946, aimed at racketeering labor unions, the statute was amended to outlaw extortion—defined as the obtaining of the property of another with the other's consent under circumstances where that consent was "induced by wrongful use of actual or threatened force, violence or fear, or under color of official right." The sanction for violation was serious—a maximum of twenty years' imprisonment. On its face the statute had no application to bribery, and before 1970 it had never been applied to bribery. The leaders of the Kenny machine in Jersey City were charged with violation of the Hobbs Act.

Kenny himself no longer held public office, but was, in the words of the court reviewing the evidence, "the absolute boss of the political party in power." He was seventy-seven, sure of his position, announcing that he would "spit in the eye" of the prosecutor who indicted him. Evidence developed at the trial showed that contractors with Jersey City or Hudson County were expected to pay 10 percent of the contract price to designated members of the machine. If they were known to be unwilling to pay, they were excluded from bidding. If they failed to pay after being hired, their final payments were delayed until the 10 percent was delivered. At the head of the recipients of the payments was Kenny. The liquid anonymity of large sums—$700,000 in bearer bonds in Kenny's possession; a secret bank account in Florida controlled by the mayor—were mute testimony to the success of the system and its criminal character. The defendants, with the exception of Kenny, were convicted. His trial was severed on the grounds of ill health. After his confederates were convicted, he pleaded guilty to tax evasion, was fined $30,000, and sentenced to prison for eighteen years. His sentence was then reduced to eighteen months; he spent most of his prison time in the prison hospital; and he was paroled within a year. His power was nonetheless broken. The main instrument of his machine's downfall had been the Hobbs Act.

Bribery had been established on a massive scale, but how had the Hobbs Act been violated? Kenny's associates appealed. Stern, the successful prosecutor, published in Newark in the *Seton Hall Law Review* an article with the pointed title, "Prosecutions of Local Political Corruption under the Hobbs Act: The Unnecessary Distinction between Bribery and Extortion." The act, Stern wrote, was a major statute under which the federal government could "combat local political corruption where the state is either unable or unwilling to do so." At the core of his article was the contention that "extortion" under color of official right was equivalent to bribery. Blackstone's definition of extortion, he asserted, supported this position. On this theory, it was apparent, he had prosecuted the Kenny crowd. On appeal, without discussion of the point, the Third Circuit Court of Appeals, speaking through Circuit Judge John Gibbons, upheld the convictions.

For almost two centuries it had been black letter law that there was no federal common law of crimes—that is, federal judges lacked the power to turn evils into crimes the way English judges had done; every act which counted as a federal crime had to be an act proscribed by Congress. To a substantial degree, broad federal statutes and judicial self-confidence had made the black letter rule a myth. The Sherman Act, for example, made criminal "every contract * * * in restraint of trade." As any contract in some degree restrains trade, the courts had been forced to construct "a standard of reason" based on the judges' reading of English common law and past American practice—in short, to write a kind of common law gloss on the criminal statute. The judges' freedom to interpret the criminal law gave them in fact the power, if they chose to exercise it, of making new law—of creating in effect a new federal common law of crime. With *Kenny* this judicial freedom was exercised in regard to bribery.

Stern's contention that Blackstone supported his interpretation was substantively inaccurate; and Congress had not treated extortion and bribery as the same. A statute banning extortion by federal officials had been on the books since 1909. It had never been interpreted to include bribery. In statutes enacted as recently as 1961 and 1970, Congress had continued to use "extortion" and "bribery" as distinct terms. As effectively as if there were federal common law crimes, the court in *Kenny* ignored Blackstone and congressional usage, for practical purposes amending the Hobbs Act and bringing into existence a new crime—local bribery affecting interstate commerce. Hereafter, for purposes of Hobbs Act prosecutions, such bribery was to be called extortion. The federal policing of state corruption had begun. * * *

In the context of labor racketeering, courts continued to maintain that Hobbs Act extortion was distinct from bribery. The distinction offered was that the payor of extortion feared economic *loss*. The distinction collapsed when applied to payments paid public officials. Bribers often paid officeholders to achieve economic *gain*. These acts were now regularly treated as Hobbs Act extortion. In *Hathaway*, for example, a consulting engineer from Philadelphia paid $25,000 or about 10 percent of his contract price, to the executive director of the New Bedford Redevelopment Authority to win the contract. At the trial of the director, the engineer testified that on other occasions he had bribed the majority leader of the Pennsylvania House, the treasurer of New Jersey, and the mayor of Lancaster, Pennsylvania. The engineer's *modus operandi*, in short, was bribery. If anyone was ready to pay, it was he. The First Circuit, per Levin Campbell, observed that he paid in New Bedford, Massachusetts, because he feared "preclusion from business with the Authority." The payee's conviction of Hobbs Act extortion was upheld. Similarly in *Salvitti*, the executive director of the Philadelphia Redevelopment Authority suggested that a certain lawyer be hired by a developer seeking a settlement of a disputed claim, and the developer hired the lawyer, agreeing to his fee with the understanding that he would not have to pay anyone else in City Hall. The developer observed, "When in Rome, do as the Romans do." The lawyer delivered $27,000 of his $75,000 fee in cash to the director, who was convicted of extortion: the "subtlety" of his communication to the payor was no defense when he clearly indicated that a payoff was expected.   * * *

Lacking any national directive to pursue bribery under the Hobbs Act (indeed national directives would seem to have indicated the contrary), the United States district attorneys, spread throughout the land, made individual decisions whether to bring local bribery within the Hobbs Act or not. Newark had led the way. New York, Baltimore, Chicago, Philadelphia, and Pittsburgh followed with particular vigor. In theory a crime anywhere in the nation, Hobbs Act bribery depended for its establishment on initiatives that varied with geography. By the mid–1970s, over 300 state officials were being prosecuted annually.   * * *

The case of Otto Kerner, Jr., governor of Illinois from 1961 to 1968, prosecuted under Nixon in 1973, illustrates how a basic crime of bribery could be made the subject of both tax evasion and mail fraud indictments. Governor Kerner and his bagman, Ted Isaacs, accepted stock in Chicago Thoroughbred Enterprises and in exchange favored the interests of the company's owner, Marjorie Lindheimer Everett, in setting racing dates, making appointments to the Harness Commission, and influencing legislation on horseracing. Kerner and Isaacs reported $159,000 apiece as long-term capital gain when they sold the stock in 1967. But they had received the stock in 1966. If it was a bribe, the stock was ordinary income to them in that year. To prove its tax case, the government proved the bribe. The failure to report in 1966 constituted evasion of the tax.

As for mail fraud, it was indisputable that they had used the mail to transmit checks and correspondence relating to their transactions with Mrs. Everett. But what fraud had they committed? Fraud, their lawyers argued, must involve depriving someone of something of "definable value." Mrs. Everett had paid willingly and knowingly. "To defraud" in the mail fraud statute meant what it meant at common law—to get an economic benefit from the victim. Whose money or property had they taken by dealing with her? The Seventh Circuit dismissed the argument. Their fraud consisted in depriving the citizens of Illinois of the governor's "honest and faithful service." As "defraud" in the conspiracy statute had been interpreted to include Manton taking money for the exercise of judicial power even when the power was exercised to reach a just result, so "defraud" in the mail fraud statute was read to include the exercise of executive power for money. No financial harm to anyone had to be shown. Corruption of a public official was itself a species of fraud. When the mail was used in the course of the transaction, the crime of federal mail fraud was committed. For the first time at an appellate level, bribery of a public official where no money or property was obtained from the state was treated as fraud in the sense of the statute. So holding, the Seventh Circuit innovatively enlarged the statute's scope and in effect created a new crime. * * *

The role of the federal judiciary—that mostly male, mostly white, mostly over forty, distinctly affluent elite—was critical in the expansion of federal supervision over local corruption. If the trial judges had not responded sympathetically to the new theories of the prosecutors and if the appellate courts had not sustained most convictions, the expansion would not have occurred. The federal judges felt little empathy for the bribetaking politician. No historical or technical distinction between bribery and extortion was to aid him to elude conviction in the way the ancient distinction between larceny and embezzlement had once aided white-collar thieves. The judges themselves were usually not innocent of political experience and connections; their first loyalty remained to the judicial system. Their corporate ethic spurned bribery. * * *

Common accord existed in the federal judiciary, it appeared, that local corruption was an evil now to be stamped out, almost as vigorously as racial discrimination. That bribery was a great evil had been the contention of American censors since the days of Henry Adams. The federal judges reflected the consensus of concerned citizens, novelists, journalists. Little dissent was heard as the Hobbs Act received a gloss creating a new federal crime of extortion, as mail fraud came to include breach of fiduciary duty to the state, and as the federal courts created a federal common law of bribery. * * *

At the level of political rather than anthropological explanation, the increase in prosecutions at a local level can be simply accounted for: federal supervision of local corruption removed the inhibitions on bribery prosecutions that often operated when bribery had to be prosecuted by local authorities. Not only outright corruption and not only the dictates of a political machine but also restraints imposed by friendship, political indebtedness, and political fear worked to discourage local prosecutors from pursuing local grafters. The agents of a superior system looking at those involved in an inferior system did not suffer the same inhibitions; and those in the inferior system were, often enough, insufficiently plugged into the higher system through congressmen or national party to influence it. Descending from above, supported by a judiciary sometimes called "imperial," the federal forces had an independence, an impartiality, and a sense of integrity that made the federal policing of bribery far more effective than the typical efforts of a state or city. The vigor of the supervision was testified to by the governors— Agnew of Maryland, Blanton of Tennessee, Hall of Oklahoma, Kerner of Illinois, Mandel of Maryland—who now fell within the federal net; and except in the exceptional circumstances of Vice President Agnew, the sanction actively applied was harsher than had been usual for high bribetakers. Imprisonment was prescribed for Blanton, Hall, Kerner, and Mandel. Although parole substantially reduced the time the governors served, their incarcerations were not nominal.

In the period 1970–1977, 43 mayors, 44 state judges, 60 state legislators, and 260 sheriffs or local police officers were federally indicted for corruption; most were convicted. In all, 369 state officials and 1,290 local officials were found guilty of corruption. There was no way of knowing whether more corruption existed in the 1970s than at earlier times in the United States. A fraction of the cases would have documented Baron Jacobi's gloomy assessment of America in *Democracy* or provided a book for Lincoln Steffens. Both Jacobi and Steffens believed that corruption was universal in the America they knew. They would not have been surprised at the statistics of the 1970s. What was clear was that corruption was being investigated and punished on a scale unknown before. That phenomenon was tied to the emergence of a champion bigger than the locality.   * * *

EVANS v. UNITED STATES

Supreme Court of the United States, 1992.
___ U.S. ___, 112 S.Ct. 1881, 119 L.Ed.2d 57.

JUSTICE STEVENS delivered the opinion of the Court.   * * *

Petitioner was an elected member of the Board of Commissioners of DeKalb County, Georgia. During the period between March 1985 and October 1986, as part of an effort by the Federal Bureau of Investigation (FBI) to investigate allegations of public corruption in the Atlanta area, particularly in the area of rezonings of property, an FBI agent posing as a real estate developer talked on the telephone and met with petitioner on a number of occasions. Virtually all, if not all, of those conversations were initiated by the agent and most were recorded on tape or video. In those conversations, the agent sought petitioner's assistance in an effort to rezone a 25–acre tract of land for high-density residential use. On July 25, 1986, the agent handed petitioner cash totaling $7,000 and a check, payable to petitioner's campaign, for $1,000. Petitioner reported the check, but not the cash, on his state campaign-financing disclosure form; he also did not report the $7,000 on his 1986 federal income tax return. Viewing the evidence in the light most favorable to the Government, as we must in light of the verdict, we assume that the jury found that petitioner accepted the cash knowing that it was intended to ensure that he would vote in favor of the rezoning application and that he would try to persuade his fellow commissioners to do likewise. Thus, although petitioner did not initiate the transaction, his acceptance of the bribe constituted an implicit promise to use his official position to serve the interests of the bribe-giver.   * * *

[P]etitioner was charged with extortion in violation of 18 U.S.C. § 1951 [the Hobbs Act] * * *. At common law, extortion was an offense committed by a public official who took "by colour of his office" money that was not due to him for the performance of his official duties. A demand, or request, by the public official was not an element of the offense. Extortion by the public official was the rough equivalent of what we would now describe as "taking a bribe." It is clear that petitioner committed that offense. The question is whether the federal statute, insofar as it applies to official extortion, has narrowed the common-law definition. * * *

The portion of the Hobbs Act that is relevant to our decision today provides:

"(a) Whoever in any way or degree obstructs, delays, or affects commerce or the movement of any article or commodity in commerce, by robbery or extortion or attempts or conspires so to do, or commits or threatens physical violence to any person or property in furtherance of a plan or purpose to do anything in violation of this section shall be fined not more than $10,000 or imprisoned not more than twenty years, or both.

"(b) As used in this section—

"(2) The term 'extortion' means the obtaining of property from another, with his consent, induced by wrongful use of actual or threatened force, violence, or fear, or under color of official right." 18 U.S.C. § 1951. * * *

Although the present statutory text is much broader than the common-law definition of extortion because it encompasses conduct by a private individual as well as conduct by a public official, the portion of the statute that refers to official misconduct continues to mirror the common-law definition. There is nothing in either the statutory text or the legislative history that could fairly be described as a "contrary direction" from Congress to narrow the scope of the offense. * * *

The two * * * [Circuit Courts] that have disagreed with the decision to apply the common-law definition have interpreted the word "induced" as requiring a wrongful use of official power that "begins with the public official, not with the gratuitous actions of another." *United States v. O'Grady*, 742 F.2d [682], at 691 ([(CA2 1984) (en banc)]; see *United States v. Aguon*, 851 F.2d [1158], at 1166 [(CA9 1988) (en banc)] ("'inducement' can be in the overt form of a 'demand,' or in a more subtle form such as 'custom' or 'expectation' "). If we had no common-law history to guide our interpretation of the statutory text, that reading would be plausible. For two reasons, however, we are convinced that it is incorrect.

First, we think the word "induced" is a part of the definition of the offense by the private individual, but not the offense by the public official. In the case of the private individual, the victim's consent must be "induced by wrongful use of actual or threatened force, violence or fear." In the case of the public official, however, there is no such requirement. The statute merely requires of the public official that he obtain "property from another, with his consent, * * * under color of official right." The use of the word "or" before "under color of official right" supports this reading.

Second, even if the statute were parsed so that the word "induced" applied to the public officeholder, we do not believe the word "induced" necessarily indicates that the transaction must be *initiated* by the recipient of the bribe. Many of the cases applying the majority rule have concluded that the wrongful acceptance of a bribe establishes all the inducement that the statute requires. They conclude that the coercive element is provided by the public office itself. And even the two courts that have adopted an inducement requirement for extortion under color of official right do not require proof that the inducement took the form of a threat or demand. See *United States v. O'Grady*, 742 F.2d, at 687; *United States v. Aguon*, 851 F.2d, at 1166.

Petitioner argues that the jury charge with respect to extortion allowed the jury to convict him on the basis of the "passive acceptance of a contribution." He contends that the instruction did not require the jury to find "an element of duress such as a demand," and it did not properly describe the *quid pro quo* requirement for conviction if the jury found that the payment was a campaign contribution.

We reject petitioner's criticism of the instruction, and conclude that it satisfies the *quid pro quo* requirement of *McCormick v. United States*, 500 U.S. ___, 111 S.Ct. 1807, 114 L.Ed.2d 307 (1991), because the offense is completed at the time when the public official receives a payment in return for his agreement to perform specific official acts; fulfillment of the *quid pro quo* is not an element of the offense. We also reject petitioner's contention that an affirmative step is an element of the offense of extortion "under color of official right" and need be included in the instruction. As we explained above, our construction of the statute is informed by the common-law tradition from which the term of art was drawn and understood. We hold today that the Government need only show that a public official has obtained a payment to which he was not entitled, knowing that the payment was made in return for official acts. * * *

An argument not raised by petitioner is now advanced by the dissent. It contends that common-law extortion was *limited* to wrongful takings under a false pretense of official right. It is perfectly clear, however, that although extortion accomplished by fraud was a well-recognized type of extortion, there were other types as well. * * * The dissent's theory notwithstanding, not one of the cases it cites holds that the public official is innocent unless he has deceived the payor by representing that the payment was proper. * * * The complete absence of support for the dissent's thesis presumably explains why it was not advanced by petitioner in the District Court or the Court of Appeals, is not recognized by any Court of Appeals, and is not advanced in any scholarly commentary. * * *

JUSTICE THOMAS, with whom THE CHIEF JUSTICE and JUSTICE SCALIA join, dissenting. * * *

The "under color of office" element of extortion * * * had a definite and well-established meaning at common law. "At common law it was essential that the money or property be obtained under color of office, *that is, under the pretense that the officer was entitled thereto by virtue of* *his office.* The money or thing received must have been claimed or accepted in right of office, and the person paying must have yielded to official authority." 3 R. Anderson, Wharton's Criminal Law and Procedure § 1393, pp. 790–791 (1957) (emphasis added). Thus, although the Court purports to define official extortion under the Hobbs Act by reference to the common law, its definition bears scant resemblance to the common-law crime Congress presumably codified * * *.

Because the Court misapprehends the "color of office" requirement, the crime it describes today is not the common-law crime that Congress presumably incorporated into the Hobbs Act. * * * The Court, therefore, errs in asserting that common-law extortion is the "rough equivalent of what we would now describe as 'taking a bribe.'" *Regardless* of whether extortion contains an "inducement" requirement, bribery and extortion are different crimes. An official who solicits or takes a bribe does *not* do so "under color of office"; *i.e.*, under any pretense of official entitlement. "The distinction between bribery and extortion seems to be that the former offense consists in offering a present or receiving one, the latter in *demanding* a fee or present *by color of office.*" *State v. Pritchard*, 107 N.C. 921, 929, 12 S.E. 50, 52 (1890) (emphasis added). Where extortion is at issue, the public official is the sole wrongdoer; because he acts "under color of office," the law regards the payor as an innocent victim and not an accomplice. With bribery, in contrast, the payor *knows* the recipient official is not entitled to the payment; he, as well as official, may be punished for the offense. Congress is well aware of the distinction between the crimes; it has always treated them separately. * * * By stretching the bounds of extortion to make it encompass bribery, the Court today blurs the traditional distinction between the crimes.

Perhaps because the common-law crime—as the Court defines it—is so expansive, the Court, at the very end of its opinion, appends a qualification: "We hold today that the Government need only show that a public official has obtained a payment to which he was not entitled, *knowing that the payment was made in return for official acts.*" This *quid pro quo* requirement is simply made up. The Court does not suggest that it has any basis in the common law or the language of the Hobbs Act, and I have found no treatise or dictionary that refers to any such requirement in defining "extortion."

Its only conceivable source, in fact, is our opinion last Term in *McCormick v. United States*, 500 U.S. ___, 111 S.Ct. 1807, 114 L.Ed.2d 307 (1991). Quite sensibly, we insisted in that case that, unless the Government established the existence of a *quid pro quo*, a public official could not be convicted of extortion under the Hobbs Act for accepting a campaign contribution. * * * "To hold otherwise would open to prosecution not only conduct that has long been thought to be well within the law but also conduct that in a very real sense is unavoidable so long as election campaigns are financed by private contributions or expenditures, as they have been from the beginning of the Nation. It would require statutory language more explicit than the Hobbs Act contains to

justify a contrary conclusion. *Id.*, at ___, 111 S.Ct., at 1816–1817."
* * * [I]t is [now] apparent that that limitation was in fact overly
modest: at common law, McCormick was innocent of extortion *not*
because he failed to offer a *quid pro quo* in return for campaign
contributions, but because he did not take the contributions under color
of official right. * * *

As serious as the Court's disregard for history is its disregard for
well-established principles of statutory construction. * * * Evans argues, in part, that he did not "induce" any payment. The Court rejects
that argument, concluding that the verb "induced" applies only to the
first portion of the definition. Thus, according to the Court, the statute
should read: "'The term "extortion" means the obtaining of property
from another, with his consent, *either* [1] induced by wrongful use of
actual or threatened force, violence, or fear, *or* [2] under color of official
right.'" That is, I concede, a conceivable construction of the words.
But it is—at the very least—forced, for it sets up an unnatural and
ungrammatical parallel between the *verb* "induced" and the *preposition*
"under."

The more natural construction is that the verb "induced" applies to
both types of extortion described in the statute. Thus, the unstated
"either" belongs *after* "induced": "The term 'extortion' means the
obtaining of property from another, with his consent, induced *either* [1]
by wrongful use of actual or threatened force, violence, or fear, *or* [2]
under color of official right." This construction comports with correct
grammar and standard usage by setting up a parallel between two
prepositional phrases, the first beginning with "by"; the second with
"under."

Our duty in construing this criminal statute, then, is clear: "The
Court has often stated that when there are two rational readings of a
criminal statute, one harsher than the other, we are to choose the
harsher only when Congress has spoken in clear and definite language."
McNally v. United States, 483 U.S. 350, 359–360, 107 S.Ct. 2875, 2881,
97 L.Ed.2d 292 (1987). Because the Court's expansive interpretation of
the statute is not the only plausible one, the rule of lenity compels
adoption of the narrower interpretation. * * *

Perhaps sensing the weakness of its position, the Court suggests an
alternative interpretation: even if the statute *does* set forth an "inducement" requirement for official extortion, that requirement is always
satisfied, because "the coercive element is provided by the public office
itself." I disagree. A particular public official, to be sure, may wield his
power in such a way as to coerce unlawful payments, even in the absence
of any explicit demand or threat. But it ignores reality to assert that
every public official, in *every* context, automatically exerts coercive influence on others by virtue of his office. If the Chairman of General
Motors meets with a local court clerk, for example, whatever implicit
coercive pressures exist will surely not emanate from the clerk. * * *

The Court's construction of the Hobbs Act is repugnant not only to the basic tenets of criminal justice reflected in the rule of lenity, but also to basic tenets of federalism. Over the past 20 years, the Hobbs Act has served as the engine for a stunning expansion of federal criminal jurisdiction into a field traditionally policed by state and local laws—acts of public corruption by state and local officials. * * * Our precedents, to be sure, suggest that Congress enjoys broad constitutional power to legislate in areas traditionally regulated by the States—power that apparently extends even to the direct regulation of the qualifications, tenure, and conduct of state governmental officials. See, *e.g., Garcia v. San Antonio Metropolitan Transit Authority*, 469 U.S. 528, 547–554, 105 S.Ct. 1005, 1015–1019, 83 L.Ed.2d 1016 (1985). As we emphasized only last Term, however, concerns of federalism require us to give a *narrow* construction to federal legislation in such sensitive areas unless Congress' contrary intent is "unmistakably clear in the language of the statute." *Gregory v. Ashcroft*, 501 U.S. __, __, 111 S.Ct. 2395, 2401, 115 L.Ed.2d 410 (1991). * * * *Gregory's* teaching is straightforward: because we "assume Congress does not exercise lightly" its extraordinary power to regulate state officials, we will construe ambiguous statutory provisions in the least intrusive manner that can reasonably be inferred from the statute. * * *

Similarly, in *McNally v. United States*, 483 U.S. 350, 107 S.Ct. 2875, 97 L.Ed.2d 292 (1987)—a case closely analogous to this one—we rejected the Government's contention that the federal mail fraud statute, 18 U.S.C. § 1341, protected the citizenry's "intangible right" to good government, and hence could be applied to all instances of state and local corruption. Such an expansive reading of the statute, we noted with disapproval, would "leav[e] its outer boundaries ambiguous and involv[e] the Federal Government in setting standards of disclosure and good government for local and state officials."

The reader of today's opinion, however, will search in vain for any consideration of the principles of federalism that animated *Gregory* * * * and *McNally*. * * * I have no doubt that today's opinion is motivated by noble aims. Political corruption at any level of government is a serious evil, and, from a policy perspective, perhaps one well suited for federal law enforcement. But federal judges are not free to devise new crimes to meet the occasion. * * * If the Court makes up this version of the crime today, who is to say what version it will make up tomorrow when confronted with the next perceived rascal? * * * Our criminal-justice system runs on the premise that prosecutors will respect and courts will enforce the boundaries on criminal conduct set by the legislature. Where, as here, those boundaries are breached, it becomes impossible to tell where prosecutorial discretion ends and prosecutorial abuse, or even discrimination, begins. The potential for abuse, of course, is particularly grave in the inherently political context of public-corruption prosecutions. * * *

McNALLY v. UNITED STATES

Supreme Court of the United States, 1987.
483 U.S. 350, 107 S.Ct. 2875, 97 L.Ed.2d 292.

Justice White delivered the opinion of the Court.

This action involves the prosecution of petitioner Gray, a former public official of the Commonwealth of Kentucky, and petitioner McNally, a private individual, for alleged violation of the federal mail fraud statute, 18 U.S.C. § 1341.[1] The prosecution's principal theory of the case, which was accepted by the courts below, was that petitioners' participation in a self-dealing patronage scheme defrauded the citizens and government of Kentucky of certain "intangible rights," such as the right to have the Commonwealth's affairs conducted honestly. We must consider whether the jury charge permitted a conviction for conduct not within the scope of the mail fraud statute.

We accept for the sake of argument the Government's view of the evidence, as follows. The petitioners and a third individual, Howard P. "Sonny" Hunt, were politically active in the Democratic Party in the Commonwealth of Kentucky during the 1970's. After Democrat Julian Carroll was elected Governor of Kentucky in 1974, Hunt was made chairman of the state Democratic Party and given *de facto* control over selecting the insurance agencies from which the State would purchase its policies. In 1975, the Wombwell Insurance Company of Lexington, Kentucky (Wombwell), which since 1971 had acted as the Commonwealth's agent for securing a workmen's compensation policy, agreed with Hunt that in exchange for a continued agency relationship it would share any resulting commissions in excess of $50,000 a year with other insurance agencies specified by him. The commissions in question were paid to Wombwell by the large insurance companies from which it secured coverage for the State.

From 1975 to 1979, Wombwell funneled $851,000 in commissions to 21 separate insurance agencies designated by Hunt. Among the recipients of these payments was Seton Investments, Inc. (Seton), a company controlled by Hunt and petitioner Gray and nominally owned and operated by petitioner McNally.

Gray served as Secretary of Public Protection and Regulation from 1976 to 1978 and also as Secretary of the Governor's Cabinet from 1977 to 1979. Prior to his 1976 appointment, he and Hunt established Seton for the sole purpose of sharing in the commissions distributed by Wombwell. Wombwell paid some $200,000 to Seton between 1975 and 1979, and the money was used to benefit Gray and Hunt. Pursuant to

---

1. Section 1341 provides in pertinent part:

"Whoever, having devised or intending to devise any scheme or artifice to defraud, or for obtaining money or property by means of false or fraudulent pretenses, representations, or promises, * * * for the purpose of executing such scheme or artifice or attempting so to do [uses the mails or causes them to be used,] shall be fined not more than $1,000 or imprisoned not more than five years, or both."

Hunt's direction, Wombwell also made excess commission payments to the Snodgrass Insurance Agency, which in turn gave the money to McNally.

On account of the foregoing activities, Hunt was charged with and pleaded guilty to mail and tax fraud and was sentenced to three years' imprisonment. The petitioners were charged with one count of conspiracy and seven counts of mail fraud, six of which were dismissed before trial. The remaining mail fraud count was based on the mailing of a commission check to Wombwell by the insurance company from which it had secured coverage for the State. This count alleged that petitioners had devised a scheme (1) to defraud the citizens and government of Kentucky of their right to have the Commonwealth's affairs conducted honestly, and (2) to obtain, directly and indirectly, money and other things of value by means of false pretenses and the concealment of material facts. * * * The jury convicted petitioners on both the mail fraud and conspiracy counts, and the Court of Appeals affirmed the convictions. * * *

The mail fraud statute clearly protects property rights, but does not refer to the intangible right of the citizenry to good government. As first enacted in 1872, as part of a recodification of the postal laws, the statute contained a general proscription against using the mails to initiate correspondence in furtherance of "any scheme or artifice to defraud." The sponsor of the recodification stated, in apparent reference to the anti-fraud provision, that measures were needed "to prevent the frauds which are mostly gotten up in the large cities * * * by thieves, forgers, and rapscallions generally, for the purpose of deceiving and fleecing the innocent people in the country." Insofar as the sparse legislative history reveals anything, it indicates that the original impetus behind the mail fraud statute was to protect the people from schemes to deprive them of their money or property. * * *

After 1909, * * * the mail fraud statute criminalized schemes or artifices "to defraud" or "for obtaining money or property by means of false or fraudulent pretenses, representation, or promises * * *." Because the two phrases identifying the proscribed schemes appear in the disjunctive, it is arguable that they are to be construed independently and that the money-or-property requirement of the latter phrase does not limit schemes to defraud to those aimed at causing deprivation of money or property. This is the approach that has been taken by each of the Courts of Appeals that has addressed the issue: schemes to defraud include those designed to deprive individuals, the people or the government of intangible rights, such as the right to have public officials perform their duties honestly. See, *e.g., United States v. Clapps,* 732 F.2d 1148, 1152 (CA3 1984); *United States v. States,* 488 F.2d 761, 764 (CA8 1973).

As the Court long ago stated, however, the words "to defraud" commonly refer "to wronging one in his property rights by dishonest methods or schemes," and "usually signify the deprivation of something of value by trick, deceit, chicane or overreaching." *Hammerschmidt v. United States,* 265 U.S. 182, 188, 44 S.Ct. 511, 512, 68 L.Ed. 968 (1924). * * * As we see it, adding the second phrase simply made it unmistakable that the statute reached false promises and misrepresentations as to the future as well as other frauds involving money or property.

We believe that Congress' intent in passing the mail fraud statute was to prevent the use of the mails in furtherance of such schemes. The Court has often stated that when there are two rational readings of a criminal statute, one harsher than the other, we are to choose the harsher only when Congress has spoken in clear and definite language. As the Court said in a mail fraud case years ago, "There are no constructive offenses; and before one can be punished, it must be shown that his case is plainly within the statute." *Fasulo v. United States,* 272 U.S. 620, 629, 47 S.Ct. 200, 202, 71 L.Ed. 443 (1926). Rather than construe the statute in a manner that leaves its outer boundaries ambiguous and involves the Federal Government in setting standards of disclosure and good government for local and state officials, we read § 1341 as limited in scope to the protection of property rights. If Congress desires to go further, it must speak more clearly than it has.

For purposes of this action, we assume that Hunt, as well as Gray, was a state officer. The issue is thus whether a state officer violates the mail fraud statute if he chooses an insurance agent to provide insurance for the State but specifies that the agent must share its commissions with other named insurance agencies, in one of which the officer has an ownership interest and hence profits when his agency receives part of the commissions. We note that as the action comes to us, there was no charge and the jury was not required to find that the Commonwealth itself was defrauded of any money or property. It was not charged that in the absence of the alleged scheme the Commonwealth would have paid a lower premium or secured better insurance. Hunt and Gray received part of the commissions but those commissions were not the Commonwealth's money. Nor was the jury charged that to convict it must find that the Commonwealth was deprived of control over how its money was spent. Indeed, the premium for insurance would have been paid to some agency, and what Hunt and Gray did was to assert control that the Commonwealth might not otherwise have made over the commissions paid by the insurance company to its agent. Although the Government now relies in part on the assertion that the petitioners obtained property by means of false representations to Wombwell, there was nothing in the jury charge that required such a finding. We hold, therefore, that the jury instruction on the substantive mail fraud count permitted a conviction for conduct not within the reach of § 1341. * * *

JUSTICE STEVENS, with whom JUSTICE O'CONNOR joins as to Parts I, II and III, dissenting. * * *

The mail fraud statute sets forth three separate prohibitions. It prohibits the use of the United States mails for the purpose of executing

"[1] *any* scheme or artifice to defraud, [2] *or* for obtaining money or property by means of false or fraudulent pretenses, representations, or promises, [3] *or* to sell, dispose of, loan, exchange, alter, give away, distribute, supply, or furnish or procure for unlawful use any counterfeit or spurious coin, obligation, security, or other article, or anything represented to be or intimated or held out to be such counterfeit or spurious article * * * " 18 U.S.C. § 1341 (emphasis and brackets added).

As the language makes clear, each of these restrictions is independent. One can violate the second clause—obtaining money or property by false pretenses even though one does not violate the third clause—counterfeiting. Similarly, one can violate the first clause—devising a scheme or artifice to defraud—without violating the counterfeiting provision. Until today it was also obvious that one could violate the first clause by devising a scheme or artifice to defraud, even though one did not violate the second clause by seeking to obtain money or property from his victim through false pretenses. Every court to consider the matter had so held. Yet, today, the Court, for all practical purposes, rejects this longstanding construction of the statute by imposing a requirement that a scheme or artifice to defraud does not violate the statute unless its purpose is to defraud someone of money or property. I am at a loss to understand the source or justification for this holding. * * * Can it be that Congress sought to purge the mails of schemes to defraud citizens of money but was willing to tolerate schemes to defraud citizens of their right to an honest government, or to unbiased public officials? Is it at all rational to assume that Congress wanted to ensure that the mails not be used for petty crimes, but did not prohibit election fraud accomplished through mailing fictitious ballots? * * *

———

Note: The Congressional Reaction to the McNally Opinion

On November 18, 1988, Congress enacted Title VII, 7603(a) of Pub.L. 100–960 (102 Stat. 4508), now codified as 18 U.S.C. § 1346, which provides as follows:

For the purposes of this chapter, the term "scheme or artifice to defraud" includes a scheme or artifice to deprive another of the intangible right of honest services.

The legislative history of this section is described and analyzed in Kurland, The Guarantee Clause as a Basis for Federal Prosecution of State and Local Officials, 62 S.C.L.Rev. 367, 489 n.452 (1989):

The brief legislative history of the actually enacted provision states that the legislation is intended to overrule *McNally* so that political corruption schemes at the federal, state, and local level that deprive the citizenry of honest government, as well as private fraud schemes, can be prosecuted under this intangible rights statute. See 134 Cong.Rec. H11251 (daily ed. Oct. 21, 1988) (Part II) (comments of Rep. Conyers); 134 Cong.Rec. S17308 (daily ed. Oct. 21, 1988) (comments of Senator

McConnell). Thus, the statute probably accomplishes what it obviously intended to accomplish. The potential problem with the statute is that the actual statutory language, as opposed to the legislative history, does not specifically refer to the intangible right of honest government and does not specifically set a federal standard for state and local officials. This is unlike most of the significant proposed intangible rights legislation of the last 18 years, virtually all of which included (in one form or another) statutory language referencing the citizenry's right to honest government and its application to state and local officials. Accordingly, whether the newly enacted statute satisfies the Supreme Court's federalism concern that if Congress wishes to regulate state and local corruption it must speak more clearly, see McNally v. United States, 107 S.Ct. 2875, 2881 (1987), as well as the court's admonition expressed in United States v. Bass, 404 U.S. 336, 349 (1972), that Congress must speak clearly when significantly altering the federal-state balance is problematical. See also 44 Crim.L.Rep. 2116 (Nov. 9, 1988) (summarizing *McNally* amendment and questioning whether "this measure simply restores pre-*McNally* law or has other effects will no doubt be a question for the courts to decide").

SECTION C.   THE CITY AND DEMOCRATIC THEORY: PART TWO

The materials in this chapter have raised in a variety of different ways one fundamental question: how can cities in America wield any power at all given their subjection to the state and federal government? What chance do cities have if (in the image of the Calvino story, printed below) they are "bound to the(se) two crests with ropes and chains and catwalks"? The principal hope for the possibility of city power offered by the cases in this chapter has been the creation of an area of city autonomy not subject to control by higher governments, an area defined, for example, in terms of home rule or (in National League of Cities v. Usery) in terms of "integral operations in areas of traditional governmental functions."

The books and articles excerpted in this section are designed to encourage reflection about this strategy of basing city power on judicial protection of a sphere of city autonomy invulnerable to encroachment by the state or federal government. The first two excerpts, one by Robert Dahl and one by me, relate the difficulty of identifying such an area of local autonomy to classic dilemmas of liberal democratic theory. The next two excerpts introduce an alternative notion of city-state or city-federal relations, one that seeks to protect decentralized power by reversing the flow of power between central governments and cities. This alternative version of city-state relations—empowering cities to control the state rather than the other way around—is presented in two dramatically different contexts, first in Michael Zuckerman's history of the early New England town and then in Karl Marx's celebration of the Paris Commune of 1870–71. This section concludes with an excerpt by the political theorist C.B. Macpherson that analyzes the possibility and problems of this alternative version of the relationship between decentralized and centralized governments.

In reading these materials, consider whether the dilemmas articulated in the readings accurately capture the problem of drawing a line between the appropriate spheres of centralized and decentralized governments and whether the alternative model of city-state relations could enhance the possibility of decentralized power. Could the alternative notion of decentralization be put into practice in today's society? What changes in local government law would be necessary to do so?

ITALO CALVINO, INVISIBLE CITIES

P. 75 (1974).

If you choose to believe me, good. Now I will tell how Octavia, the spider-web city, is made. There is a precipice between two steep mountains: the city is over the void, bound to the two crests with ropes and chains and catwalks. You walk on the little wooden ties, careful not to set your foot in the open spaces, or you cling to the hempen strands. Below there is nothing for hundreds and hundreds of feet: a few clouds glide past; farther down you can glimpse the chasm's bed.

This is the foundation of the city: a net which serves as passage and as support. All the rest, instead of rising up, is hung below: rope ladders, hammocks, houses made like sacks, clothes hangers, terraces like gondolas, skins of water, gas jets, spits, baskets on strings, dumbwaiters, showers, trapezes and rings for children's games, cable cars, chandeliers, pots with trailing plants.

Suspended over the abyss, the life of Octavia's inhabitants is less uncertain than in other cities. They know the net will last only so long.

ROBERT DAHL, DILEMMAS OF PLURALIST DEMOCRACY

Pp. 96–107 (1982).

Democratic Dilemmas

We seem to be trapped in a maze where, having reached the end, we discover ourselves at the beginning. Does this not hint at the possibility that large-scale democracy—indeed democracy on any scale—poses some fundamental dilemmas?

First dilemma: rights versus utility. This dilemma runs like a bright thread through all designs for dealing with the problem of democratic pluralism. Are solutions to be judged exclusively on utilitarian grounds, for their contributions to human well-being, welfare, happiness, satisfaction of wants, preferences, volitions, and so on? Are there not also questions of *rights* that are ultimately independent of utilitarian considerations, or at least cannot be finally settled on purely utilitarian grounds? Do not all human beings, for example, possess the fundamental moral *right* to have their interests taken equally into account? Even a utilitarian would acknowledge the validity of the claim to a certain basic moral equality, in insisting that utility to person A counts precisely the same as utility to person B. Thus Bentham's "Each person counts as one and no more than one".

But beyond this fundamental right there are others that might conflict with a utilitarian judgment. Does a people have a fundamental right to govern itself? If so, does not this fundamental right require all the subsidiary rights implied by the right of self-government? Are rights like these justified on other grounds? Must not utilitarian considerations therefore sometimes yield to considerations of rights?

Tested by mental experiments in the realm of hypothetical cases, it appears impossible to discover any right that can reasonably be justified in utter disregard for its consequences for the well-being of persons affected by the exercise of that right—including the possessor. Yet it is equally unreasonable to contend that rights must *always* give way to utilitarian considerations. Can we justify executing innocent prisoners in order to set an example to others? Is this not a violation of a human right so fundamental that it cannot be justified on utilitarian grounds?

Moral philosophers have struggled endlessly with this dilemma. Utilitarians remain convinced that they have successfully disposed of their critics' arguments. But they have failed to convince a substantial body of other philosophers. What is true of moral philosophy is a fortiori true of political life, as we are now about to see.

Second dilemma: a more exclusive versus a more inclusive demos. In practice, every demos is exclusive; no demos, no matter how large, has ever included all human beings. There simply is not and never has been an association of all human beings governed by the democratic process— or, for that matter, any single government.

The question arises: Why this demos rather than another? Might it not properly be more inclusive—or more exclusive? The question seems to admit of no definitive answer. That answers can be reached at all is the half-concealed mystery of democratic ideas and practices. The question is, in fact, an embarrassment to all normative theories of democracy, or would be were it not ignored. In practice, solutions call not upon theoretical reason, which is baffled by the question, but, as with Lincoln, on primordial attachments to tribe, town, city, subculture, nation, country. Though it is sometimes held that a more inclusive demos is always preferable to a less inclusive one, the argument is patently defective. For the argument logically implies that the only proper demos is all of humanity. But even those who defend an inclusive demos invariably accept, and without serious questioning, the limits on the demos imposed by primordial or historical boundaries— which nowadays are those of nation or country. But why draw the boundaries of the demos at the borders of a country? On the other hand, why not? Suppose we agree that maximum inclusion today really means the largest demos within the historically (and often arbitrarily) given boundaries of a country. There is still the second embarrassment:

No demos has ever included children, and those who contend that a more inclusive demos is better than a less inclusive one have no intention of demanding that children be included.

That no one seriously insists that the demos be *completely* inclusive suggests hidden premises at work. One kind of hidden premise often turns out to be utilitarian or expediential: demos X is better than Y because it leads to greater well-being, utility, satisfaction of preferences, welfare, happiness. An assumption of this kind is heir to all the usual defects of utilitarian moral reasoning. However elegant the efforts to quantify the relative utilities, or whatnot, the comparison never in practice leads to anything like an uncontestable conclusion. The quantities, even if precise, are fictitious; in fact, the greater their precision, the greater the fiction. There are also the usual problems of intensity and quality: *is* pushpin as good as poetry, *is* the satisfied fool better than Socrates dissatisfied? And there is the eternal challenge of nonutilitarian moral standards: rights, duties, personal integrity.

Both utilitarian and nonutilitarian arguments can be readily used either way: to justify a more inclusive demos or a more exclusive one. In the end, no solution to the problem can be better than the solution to the conflict between utilitarian and nonutilitarian moral standards.

Third dilemma: equality among individuals versus equality among organizations. The principle of equality in voting, which is central to the idea of democracy, refers to human beings, persons, individuals. Except under certain rare and all but irrelevant circumstances, the principle of voting equality is necessarily violated whenever units, associations, organizations, states, provinces, or countries, rather than individual persons, are granted equal votes. For, as we saw, unless the number of citizens is identical in all the units, then voting equality among units means inequality of votes among citizens. Except in rare cases, the number of citizens is not the same in all the units; if it were, there would be no reason to reject the principle of voting equality for the principle of organizational equality.

Should the principle of voting equality among citizens never be modified in order to allow for greater political equality among organizations (and so less among citizens)? Should a national legislature be designed to represent only citizens, or only provinces or states, or both? The American constitutional solution was, of course, to do both. Ought there to be functional representation? If so, should votes in a functional body be allocated according to the number of citizens in each functional group, in which case the body would not be all that different from one based on territorial constituencies; or should they be allocated equally among certain types of organizations, thereby violating the criterion of voting equality among citizens? Proponents of functional representations have never met this dilemma satisfactorily. Either their solution violates the principle of voting equality on grounds they are unable to justify; or else it does not, and if not, then functional representation offers few advantages over territorial representation.

The question remains: Is it ever justified to permit equality among organizations at the expense of equality among individual citizens? Arguments for doing so rest on considerations both of utility—indeed, often of expediency—and of rights. Systems of democratic corporatism, like the corporate pluralism of the Scandinavian countries, are thought to be justified because they are useful. Is there a better way to arrive at decisions involving the great nationwide interest organizations? Unless the government acts with the consent of the organizations, it is impotent. It cannot *impose* a solution. As is well known, cabinet officers and troops cannot mine coal. But if parliament *is* to act with the consent of the interest organizations, then some system of corporate pluralism seems necessary. But corporate pluralism means * * * that votes count but organizational resources decide. Likewise, consociational democracies may permit any one of several groups to veto policies its leaders think harmful. In effect, consociational democracy requires unanimity among certain major social aggregates and their organizations. These arrangements are held to be justified, not only because of their utility in gaining widespread consent in a segmented society, but also because they guarantee the *right* of each group to have its fundamental interests taken into account. Do Catholics and Calvinists, socialists and liberals, all have an equal right to their own subculture and community life? Do Francophone Walloons and Dutch-speaking Flemish have an equal right to their language and traditions? Should members of the small Italian-speaking minority in Switzerland have the same rights to cultural autonomy as members of the larger French-and German-speaking minorities? In the United Nations General Assembly, all countries are given equal votes. Is this justified only out of expediency, or is it also a matter of right? Would any foreseeable world government, even one much more nearly ideal than the U.N., operate exclusively under a system of majority rule where the demos consists simply of the human species? I do not say that satisfactory answers can never be found. But clearly there is a conflict of fundamental principles.

Fourth dilemma: uniformity versus diversity. As these examples suggest, diversity is precious, not only to groups that prize their own ways, religion, language, place, customs, traditions, history, and values, but also to everyone who holds that human diversity is good in itself or in its results. The protection of diversities can be justified on utilitarian grounds: It yields more satisfaction (or whatever) than uniformity— especially when one adds the costs of suppressing differences valued by their possessors. Protecting diversity can also be justified because one has a right to one's own identity, personhood, personality, culture. Am I to be punished because I insist on speaking my mother tongue? Do I not have a *right* to be different in that way from the majority of my fellow citizens?

In the modern world it is an easy and congenial task to defend diversity. If the idea of uniformity is superficially less attractive, uniformity is nonetheless desirable because not all differences among human beings are matters of right or have good consequences. Do we not advocate uniformity in the protection of fundamental rights? Oppose differences in the right of citizens to vote, to have a fair trial? When differences infringe on basic rights, one's appreciation of diversity crumbles. Should neighborhoods that want to preserve their special character be allowed to exclude anyone who does not fit in? There is also the question of the level at which differences ought to be permitted or protected: at the level of the individuals or the level of the group? If at the group level, what kind of group? With respect to what kinds of differences? To be sure, sometimes protection at the individual level necessarily requires protection at the group level. Religion is ordinarily not only a personal activity: It is social and organizational as well. Consequently, a government cannot protect the right of individuals to their religious beliefs without protecting their right to adhere to diverse religious organizations, to practice their rites in the presence of their coreligionists, and to exclude from membership those who reject the sect's beliefs. Applied to racial differences the same reasoning would require us to tolerate racial segregation in a neighborhood, school, university, workplace, trade union.

Equality means, precisely, identity. If A and B are to be treated as equal with respect to a thing of value, a right, opportunity, duty, or share in some social allocation, then the thing must be identical for A and B. If A and B have an equal right to vote, A's right to vote is identical with B's: the rights of A and B are theoretically interchangeable. Obviously, equality conflicts with diversity. In the steady march of the idea of equality throughout history that Tocqueville believed he discerned at work as a fundamental force in the world, many kinds of differences once widely thought acceptable are no longer. What might from an earlier perspective be justified as a proper difference, a desirable or ineradicable diversity, becomes an unjustified inequality, discrimination, unfairness, inequity. If equality is often desirable, then so is uniformity.

Fifth dilemma: centralization versus decentralization. Uniformity and diversity: centralization and decentralization. Although the two sets of terms are not symmetrical, uniformity often requires some centralization, and diversity often presupposes some decentralization. Let me now specify more precisely what I mean by centralization and decentralization. Suppose that subsystems exist within a more inclusive system of controls. Then the inclusive system—for the moment let me refer to it simply as the organization—is decentralized to the extent that the subsystems are autonomous in relation to other subsystems in the organization. If one subsystem controls all the others with respect to *x,* then with respect to *x* it is a center and the organization is centralized with respect to *x.* Sometimes one subsystem controls all the others over a large range of crucial actions. A subsystem of this kind might be designated *the* Center of the organization. Starting from any given situation, then, to decentralize means to increase the autonomy of subsystems in relation to *the* Center or *a* center. By definition, decentralization also means a decrease in control over the subsystems by a center, and in particular *the* Center. To centralize means exactly the reverse: when a center's control over subsystems increases, subsystem autonomy decreases. Since an organization may be centralized with respect to some matters and decentralized with respect to others, it is obvious that patterns of organization can be extraordinarily complex—a fact painfully familiar to all experienced students of organizations.

For example, every subsystem in the organization might be highly controlled by *a* center; in this sense the organization is highly centralized and might well appear so from the viewpoint of a member of any of the subsystems. But each of the centers might be relatively autonomous in relation to the others: in this sense, each center is also a somewhat independent subsystem. Thus the organization, though centralized, would be collegial rather than monocratic. To describe it in a different way: Control would be centralized in the joint leadership of the centers, but not among the leaders.

If organizations were the mechanisms of pure rationality they were often pictured to be in early theories of organization, and if centralization and decentralization had no other significant consequences than those immediately entailed in shifting control over certain matters toward or away from the Center, then a choice between centralization or decentralization would doubtless be simpler than it usually is. However, organizations are rarely if ever mechanisms of pure rationality; they are not constituted merely of rational actors striving only to maximize the efficient attainment of the organization's official goals. In practice, organizations depart from a model of pure rationality in several ways. For one thing, centralization and decentralization have consequences for communication, and thus for control. Centralized control requires a flow of accurate communications toward the Center. Centralized communication systems are not only in danger of jamming up from overload; they are highly susceptible to distortion. After the king executes the first messenger who brings bad tidings, the word quickly gets around. By decentralizing decisions to autonomous units, lengthy lines of communication can be shortened and the jam-up at the center can be reduced. But the big picture, the synoptic overview, may be destroyed; each unit makes its decisions without much awareness of what is happening elsewhere.

Centralization and decentralization also have consequences for power beyond those described in models of pure rationality. To centralize control is not merely to allocate resources for influencing others to a perfectly neutral incumbent of some central office. Centralization puts resources in the hands of specific human beings at the Center, persons with goals of their own. To decentralize is to allocate resources of influence away from the Center, and thus to convey them to other specific human beings. The problem is, of course, that these actors may very well not devote their resources simply to the ostensible purpose of the exercise, to see that the prescribed goals of the organization are attained more efficiently. They may also use their resources for their own particular purposes. They usually do. It is not going too far to say that leaders almost always use some of the resources available to them for self-aggrandizement. This is the essence of Acton's famous aphorism that power tends to corrupt, and absolute power corrupts absolutely. Is it reasonable to expect that any human beings, any team, group, sect, party, or stratum will long refrain from using the resources available to them in order to enhance their own distinct interests? Even where democratic forms remain, to allocate large resources to the Center may lead to a loss of control by citizens. Conversely, to shift resources away from the Center to more autonomous subsystems may prevent domination by the Center, but * * * decentralization may also allow domination *within* each subsystem.

In political life, at least, to centralize or decentralize is never simply a problem in engineering, where the strengths and tolerances can be nicely determined. It is a problem in political dynamics, where the consequences can only be guessed at. To increase the authority of the Presidency always increases the power of a person, or a group of people, in the White House. Decentralization to local communities increases the power of certain people more or less resident in certain localities. Although it is always uncertain how these various persons will use their power, human experience supports the hunch that they will use some of it to advance their own interests. And these interests may prove to be sharply adverse to the interests of others.

Sixth dilemma: concentration versus dispersion of power and political resources. Uniformity, centralization, concentration of power and resources; diversity, decentralization, dispersion of power and resources. If the last triad is the program of classical liberalism, what is the first? Liberalism, and in particular liberal ideas about democracy, were formulated in opposition to concentrated power. Liberal democracy represented a movement away from the uniformity of centralized regulation imposed by means of power concentrated in the crown, the royal ministers, and an unrepresentative parliament. By Tocqueville's time the liberal strategy had been so successful in the United States that it was necessary to sound a new liberal warning: By concentrating all power in the people, or rather in majorities, democracy also posed grave risks to liberty, most of all in a country where the citizens were more nearly equal in their conditions than had ever been true before among any numerous body of people.

The hostility of liberalism to concentration of power runs deep; as has often been observed, it may run deepest in that country where liberal ideas have always confronted the weakest challenge. Yet even in the United States, liberalism in the twentieth century yielded up a great deal of its earlier commitment to dispersion. Progressive liberalism, reform liberalism, the liberalism of Woodrow Wilson's New Freedom and Franklin Roosevelt's New Deal, all demanded that certain national policies be enforced uniformly throughout the United States. As a direct consequence, the new liberalism sought greater centralization of control over policies and decisions in federal agencies and a greater concentration of political resources at centers in Washington. Even more important, reform liberals quickly discovered that without strong presidential leadership no reform program could fight its way past the elaborate combination of checkpoints built into the American political process. These, of course, gave great advantages to defenders of the status quo. Liberal reform therefore required that political resources be concentrated in the hands of the president. Richard Nixon did not create the Imperial Presidency; he inherited it. In point of fact it was mainly liberals, not their conservative opponents, who designed, encouraged, supported, and brought about the shift of resources to the White House that finally facilitated the creation of an Imperial Presidency.

If this change took place in a country where hostility to concentrated power was stronger than elsewhere, the same process was bound to occur in other countries where the political traditions were far less monolithically liberal. It is a commonplace, but a valid one, to say that in all democratic countries concentration of power in the executive branch and the central bureaucracies has vastly increased in this century. Although the institutions of polyarchy have not collapsed under this new weight, it would be wrong to say that anxieties about the consequences of concentration have thereby been shown to be irrational. For one thing, the flourishing of dictatorships, sometimes in the extreme form of totalitarian rule, has once again demonstrated that democracy depends on a dispersion of power and resources.

Is this antinomy—concentration versus dispersion of power and resources—rather more lopsided than the others? Are we all really in favor of dispersion? Not necessarily. Once we accept the premise that there must be definite even if not perfectly clear limits to concentration in a polyarchy, then within these limits the dilemma becomes perfectly real.

For whenever (a) uniform enforcement of a policy is desirable, (b) uniformity cannot be attained without centralization, and (c) centralization requires a concentration of power and resources, then either one must forego a desirable uniformity or else accept concentration. Everyone who is not an anarchist is likely to agree that the risks of concentration are sometimes offset by the advantages of a uniform policy. The conflict between the advantages and risks of concentration is genuine, and citizens and leaders cannot escape the force of this dilemma in any democratic country. * * *

GERALD FRUG, THE CITY AS A LEGAL CONCEPT

93 Harv.L.Rev. 1057, 1120–1127 (1980).

THE PROBLEM OF DECENTRALIZING POWER

In Part III, I traced the development of the legal concept of the city, showing that the idea of the city as a powerless "creature of the state" derived from the liberal fracturing of all medieval corporate forms into spheres of the individual and of the state. The public/private distinction has perpetuated the liberal effort by assigning to private corporations the role of "persons" and to cities that of state subdivisions. In Part II, I emphasized the limited, although crucial, role I was claiming for the development of liberal thought: that these ideas have organized people's perception of the world and therefore their perception of which goals have been possible and desirable to achieve. In this way, they have influenced people's actions and, thereby, limited the institutional possibilities for the city.

Today, these ideas constrict our own actions, not only through our continued reliance on the legal status of the cities they helped create but through their influence on our ability to think about changing the city as an institution. Our ideas make the current status of the city seem such a natural and inevitable feature of modern society that any attempt to find, as a matter of law, a "local" function to be protected from state control, or to find, as a political matter, a way to decentralize real power to cities, seems defeated from the start. Changing our way of thinking about cities has become a necessary, although by no means sufficient, ingredient in increasing the power of cities.

1. Decentralization as a Dilemma Within Liberalism. —Our ability to change the status of cities is not, however, simply a matter of allocating more power to certain minor political subdivisions. The issue involves, instead, the fundamental question whether any decentralization of power is possible in a liberal society. The liberal attack against the city, traced in Part III, can be understood as illustrating the precariousness of establishing within liberalism any form of group power intermediate between a centralized state and the individual. Every example of group power—whether political or economic, public or private—permits the power wielder to invade the spheres of both the individual and the state, and is thus subject to the same liberal attack as has been waged against the cities. This attack may help explain the diminishing position in our society of forms of decentralized power as diverse as the family and the American states.

At the same time, the need to decentralize power is not widely questioned. Indeed, the history of the city repeatedly illustrates the idea that protection of entities intermediate between the state and the individual can be regarded as a defense of freedom, not simply as a danger to it. The creation of the medieval town as a protection for the merchants' way of life, the defense of the English corporation against the King in the name of rights of property, the vitality of the colonial town as an association, the defense of a "right of local self-government" against Dillon's support of state control of the cities, and the effort to gain "home rule" can all be seen as attempts to preserve intermediate entities in order to protect individuals from the power of a centralized state. Moreover, all these examples of the idea of group autonomy can contribute to the attempt to define the concept of "public freedom" discussed in Part I: the ability of a group of people, working together, to control actively the basic societal decisions that affect their lives.

Indeed, it is a paradox that while liberalism can be understood as an attempt to eradicate group power in favor of that of the individual and the state, most liberal thinkers seem convinced that the creation of a world without any intermediate bodies—a world in which the state is the only power wielder other than individuals themselves—would leave individuals powerless to prevent a centralized state from threatening their liberty. Liberal thinkers have sought to avoid this problem, principally by imagining that power can be allocated solely to individuals with the state all but withering away. An example is the pretense that a laissez-faire society could do away with a powerful state when, of course, such a state would be indispensable in creating, construing and enforcing "private rights." These days, however, the continued existence of a powerful state is too obvious for most liberal thinkers to ignore. They too, therefore, seek safety in the power of intermediate entities that can protect them from the power of the state.

Liberals, then, have been caught in a perilous contradiction: they have sought to destroy intermediate forms of power, but they also want to preserve them. Until recently, this contradiction had escaped the notice of many liberal thinkers. This was possible because private corporations, the principal remaining source of decentralized power in America, were portrayed as individuals—as persons—rather than as bodies exercising group power intermediate between the individual and the state.

But the image of major American corporations as individuals has become increasingly less convincing. The threats such corporations pose to real individuals are now being curbed, for example, by labor laws and civil rights legislation, as are the threats they pose to the state, by regulation and planning. Private corporations once again appear to be examples of the original meaning of "corporate" power—group power. As a result, they are now being subjected to the very attack already successfully waged against public corporations. Indeed, it is in the defense of private corporate power that the need for entities intermediate between the state and the individual is now most often expressed.

Those who now defend the need for some form of decentralized power do so, as did their predecessors, because of its connection with "freedom." As noted earlier, "public freedom" can only be achieved by preserving the authority of a group small enough to allow active participation by group members. Other definitions of freedom, such as "freedom of choice" and the maintenance of civil liberties, have also been tied to some form of independent corporate life. Yet immunizing, even to a limited extent, any definition of freedom is dangerous.

In supporting the need for decentralized power, one should not make the mistake of denying the force of the liberal attack against it. Independent corporate power of any kind does threaten individuals. We have seen examples of these threats in the history of the city outlined in Part III, and similar examples can be drawn from the more recent history of private corporations or even from the history of the family which in ancient times itself "was a Corporation."

Our choice, then, whether or not to have strong intermediate bodies is not a choice between vulnerability and protection. The exercise of state power infringes individual rights protected by independent corporations, yet the exercise of corporate power infringes individual rights protected by the state. Every time we seek state help to protect us from a corporate invasion of our rights, we strengthen one threat to liberty at the expense of another; yet every time we prevent the state from protecting us against corporate power, we accomplish the same result. Our only option is to choose which danger to liberty seems more tolerable, more controllable, or more worth defending.

2. *Decentralization as an Option Within Liberal Society.* —We can, of course, decentralize power if we decide to do so. We are not prisoners of our liberal ideology, forced by a mechanistic idealism to deny the preservation of group power. We can create any powerful entity we want to create. But if we wish to create powerful intermediate bodies, we must find a way to enable them to retain their power when challenged by individuals or by the state.

Any kind of absolute corporate immunity from state control, such as nineteenth century thinkers might have imagined in terms of home rule for cities or property rights for corporations, is, of course, a fantasy, as would be ceding to corporations absolute power over individuals. Yet corporations, once subjected to state power to some extent, cannot be defended against that power by seeking, in classic liberal terms, protection of corporate "rights." There will always be a good argument in favor of greater individual liberty from corporate power or greater state restriction of corporate power. And, if the state decides the conflict between these values and corporate rights (who else could?), the destruction of corporate power cannot be prevented. We know this not only because of the process of subordination that has already been completed in the case of cities but also from the history of the attempt to protect private corporate power through substantive due process. Independent group power is simply not an idea, whether clothed in the name of rights or sovereignty, that can be defended within a liberal legal system against liberal attack. The power of these intermediate entities must, therefore, be based on more than mere rights; it must rest on their actual ability to exercise power within society.

In fact, the power of intermediate groups, where it has occurred, has always been based on more than the protection of their legal rights. Two examples can illustrate this point. The current power of private corporations rests in part on their importance to the nation's economic system, so that any political or legal attempt to destroy their power would create what would seem to most people to be frightening instability. This degree of power can be self-protecting. When cities possessed real economic power in this sense, their ability to resist state control was much greater than today (notwithstanding the fact that their current "political" power to tax is "the power to destroy").

Second, as we have seen, cities, when they did not base their power merely on economic strength, rested it on their role in the daily lives of their citizens. Medieval towns were powerful because they represented an economic-political-communal unit that allowed their citizens to achieve a new status within feudal society. New England towns, at the height of their power, were religious and fraternal communities, and their ability to represent what seemed to be the fundamental interests of their citizens enabled the towns to control the state, rather than the other way around. The role of the polis in Greek life was so central that Aristotle could describe man as a political animal. Thus, the former power of cities depended, as the current power of corporations depends, on their actual place in social life. To protect any form of group power, therefore, such power must be based not simply on a legal status empty of an underlying rationale but on its importance—both as a matter of experience and as a matter of thought—to our lives.

3. *Cities as Possibilities for Decentralized Power.* —We seem, however, unable to conceive of a way in which cities could resume such importance. Our inability to imagine cities exercising real decentralized power stems in part from our tendency to reduce that possibility to the concept of political decentralization. There is, however, no meaningful possibility of purely political decentralization. To begin with, there has never been a concept of purely political local autonomy in Western thought. As we have just noted, all powerful local units, whether Greek cities, medieval towns or New England towns, combined their "political" identity with other forms of religious or fraternal cohesion or economic power.

Second, the liberal undermining of intermediate entities has nowhere been so effective as in presenting the danger involved in genuine decentralization of power to a purely political, purely governmental body. Decentralization of power to such an entity would make it, to the extent of its independence from state power, a sovereign political body. But to permit two sovereigns to function within the same state would create what is called *imperium in imperio,* "the greatest of all political solecisms." No area of political power can be left to the uncontrolled discretion of local authorities; every local action affects other localities; there must be a body to resolve local political conflict. Thus, the need for a single unified sovereign has become a fundamental premise of Western political thought.

Third, small units can be seen—as Madison saw them—as the greatest governmental danger to individual liberty. Indeed, it may not be enough merely to apply the Constitution to restrain the political power exercised by cities or to reform city power by making it more "rational." The mere delegation to cities of broad political power, even while leaving that power fully subject to state legislative control, can be considered an impermissible threat to individual liberties.

Finally, even if cities could exercise the amount of political power for their own jurisdiction that state legislatures exercise for the state as a whole, their ability to control effectively the future of their communities would be sharply limited by the independent exercise of economic power by private corporations. Not only would city power continue to be limited by the constitutional protections afforded private corporations (such as the commerce clause), but, as a practical matter, cities would still have to depend for their survival on the goodwill of the private corporations that did business within their boundaries. The influence on national political decisionmaking of the need to protect the economy is well recognized in modern political analysis, but that influence is vastly greater if the private sector decisionmaker can readily move his business across city boundaries to avoid political decisions he opposes. The very split between political and economic power, with political authorities dependent on their ability to tax economic entities in order to pay for government services, would thus determine much of the agenda of even a powerful local government.

Decentralization of power to cities need not, however, be limited to the transfer of purely political power. Cities could be given the kind of power that we are willing to decentralize in our society, the kind of power wielded by those entities that still exercise genuine decentralized power—private corporations. A start could be made, as some have suggested, by transferring a portion of the banking and insurance industries to city control. In having cities perform these functions, we need neither accept the current structure of American cities nor recreate a modern version of a hierarchical medieval town. We could create any form of city organization that seemed worth having. * * *

MICHAEL ZUCKERMAN, PEACEABLE KINGDOMS

Pp. 10–28, 35–38, 43–45 (1970).

THE CONTEXT OF COMMUNITY: THE TOWNS AND THE PROVINCE

The pre-eminence of the local community in provincial Massachusetts was, curiously, a new thing under the New England sun. The first Puritans who settled at the Bay had been congregationalists in ecclesiastical polity. They had set sail across the ocean only after decades of denunciation of bishops and synods as dead historical husks of Christianity to be peeled away before the churches could regain their primitive vitality, only after decades of disagreement with the Established Church, and the Presbyterian dissenters, over the scope of central surveillance of the churches of the realm. As the *Arbella* headed out from England, its passengers could hardly have conceived that they would flee the control of Canterbury and of London only to create a comparable one in Boston.

And yet, that was what they did. Under the necessity of governing and the temptation of power, availing themselves of the ambiguities of congregational theory and ignoring inconvenient aspects of its clarities, the magistrates and ministers established a degree of direction from the center that would have been unthinkable a hundred years later. It was only with the passage of decades that power passed to the communities; in the colonial era the assemblies and the synods exercised a close care over all that occurred in the communities and congregations.

Throughout the first generation, and in the very teeth of the principles of congregational autonomy which had guided the conception of the colony, the government at Boston practiced an ecclesiastical authority which spanned the settlement. Its control ranged from trifles, such as determination of closing times for services in a single church, to matters of real moment, such as the General Court's 1635 ruling that churches could not be organized at all unless they did "first acquainte the magistrates * * * & have their approbacon herein." Moreover, the ratification of the magistrates was required for all elected church officers, in new churches and in the established ones as well, which amounted to an overt invasion of congregational prerogatives since the minister was among the elected officers of the church. According to congregational theory, a minister was to be called by the communicants, his simple election establishing him in his station; but theory notwithstanding, the colonial magistrates successfully maintained for many years their claim "to approve the appointment of ministers and to suppress offending ones." * * *

In secular affairs the central government exercised an equally extensive authority. In the very first years of the colony, when the General Court "legislated on all local as well as general affairs," the magistrates actually continued to think of Massachusetts as a single community despite its geographic dispersion. In 1636 an act of the assembly did recognize the towns and empower them to manage their own business; yet even after this admission that the colony was no longer the single city on a hill which Winthrop had originally envisioned, the magistrates maintained their oversight of local affairs. Osgood referred as much to the period after 1636 as before when he insisted that "the legislation of Massachusetts affected the towns not only at the time of their organization, but continuously and in reference to their most important internal affairs."

Thus it was the Court, not the communities, which first made education a public obligation; and it did not do so until the 1640's. Thus, as late as 1647, more than a decade after their grant of local self-government, the legislators were still passing "minute provisions" for such minute matters as the ringing of swine and the fencing of common cornfields in particular communities, and before that their economic regulation had been even more extensive, touching trades, standards, and prices, and calling out the citizens to work on public projects such as roads and fortifications. In 1655 the Court chose one town's selectmen and installed them for double terms. In 1661 the magistrates went so far as to order an Ipswich man's land sold "because the distance of his home from the meetinghouse had caused him to absent himself from its service, 'in order that living nearer the meeting house he might more conveniently attend public worship.'" Such actions were apparently accepted in the seventeenth century. In the eighteenth, they were not even attempted.

Similarly in the matter of settlement policy, the Court often asserted an authority which unmistakably subordinated community to colony even in the years after the colony ceased to be thought of *as* a community. The affirmation of that authority began as early as 1630, when the Court ordered that "no person should plant in any place within the limits of the patent, without leave from the Governor and assistants, or the major part of them." In the midst of the antinomian excitement six years later the colony provided heavy fines for any town which even entertained a stranger longer than three weeks or allotted him any land without central consent, provisions which were made permanent the following year. And in 1639 the magistrates enunciated a still more sweeping form of interference with local settlement policy, declaring that they could "dispose of all onsettled p'sons into such towns as they shall judge to bee most fitt for the maintenance of such p'sons and families." * * *

In all these matters and in others less important, then, authority was not diffused at the outset. Its later localization was the essential institutional development of the era between settlement and the American Revolution. And it was supremely symptomatic of the shift that, as the importance of the central government declined, so too did the obligations that attached to its early rights disappear with decentralization. In the first generation the officers of the colony were commonly the leading participants in local projects, such as a 1636 subscription for the maintenance of a Boston schoolmaster which was "headed by the Governor, the Deputy Governor, the ex-deputy Governor, the colonial treasurer, and the selectmen"; later such cooperation became incomparably less common. Provincial governors came to consider themselves servants of the Crown, as indeed they were, and they were seldom able to work so easily with local selectmen. Nor did they ever truly desire to do so, or at least never so wholeheartedly. Winthrop, Dudley, and the others shared something of the same cause and something of the same dream with selectmen all around the Bay; men like Belcher and Bernard and the other eighteenth-century governors listened to different drummers.

The localization of authority was not an impulse altogether peculiar to the provincial era, of course. The process began with the very beginnings of settlement, as the American wilderness imposed its own imperatives, and a little later the dispersion of settlement added others. But deliberate effort and the traditional shape of thought held the tendency to decentralization in some degree of control so long as the colony continued under its original charter.

For almost sixty years from its establishment, the Massachusetts Bay Colony acknowledged no more than the merest shadow of colonial dependence on the mother country. Until the 1660's writs did not even run in the name of the King, and even after the restoration the men of

Massachusetts were not inclined to move much closer to the Crown. Royal agents did attempt, repeatedly, to secure some more substantial submission to English authority, but they were repulsed as repeatedly by Puritan ingenuity or intransigence. The result was an unprecedented era of independence for the infant colony, and where the synods and the central government were the inhabitants' own, men saw little reason to license change. In the Bay colony of the 1630's, or the 1650's or 1670's, the salutary application of coordinated guidance to a congregational polity often played an important part in the preservation of the New England Way.

But when the clouds of the Glorious Revolution cleared, William and Mary moved to reassert the authority of England. Massachusetts' original charter was repealed and a new one issued, reducing the almost autonomous colony to a royal province. Under the new instrument of government the settlers at the Bay were permitted to retain full control only over the lower house of their General Court. The Council was now merely nominated by the lower house, subject to the approval of the governor, and the governor himself was now to be appointed by the Crown rather than chosen by the colonists. By that considerable alteration the upper reaches of sovereignty in the province, the control of the executive, were removed from Massachusetts to the mother country. And lest the message of the new subordination be missed by any at the Bay, the new charter also afforded another unmistakable demonstration of change. Before 1691 the colonial franchise had been largely limited to church members; the limitation had been an integral part of the founders' designs for a Bible Commonwealth, and it had also and not incidentally prevented most Anglicans from voting in colonial elections. The charter of 1691 proscribed this religious test. Providing only for a moderate property qualification, it leveled what was left of Winthrop's city on a hill.

As long as the largest purposes of the central government had coincided with those of the communities and congregations around the colony, and as long as the colonial governors had been committed to the Puritan mission, the wide powers of the central government had posed no insoluble problems. But the case was not the same after the arrival of the provincial charter. No similar reliance could be placed in the new government which that charter had installed in Boston, crucially tied as it was to the mother country and her divergent interests and aspirations. For sixty years, against the forces of dispersion and ambition and the very continent itself, the dominance of the central government in Massachusetts had been maintained; with the issuance of the charter, the motives for its maintenance were removed. Central authority, growing gradually more distant in any case as settlement spread increasingly beyond the possibility of close surveillance from the center, grew very remote indeed when the separation between governors and governed became psychological as well as geographical. And as it did, an underlying tendency to the local communities as repositories of effective authority became manifest.

Thus, what was reluctantly admitted in the seventeenth century came to be openly acknowledged in the eighteenth: the public peace could not be entrusted to Boston, but would have to be separately secured in each town in the province. With the arrival of the new charter, a long-running drift toward devolution was licensed and legitimized. From that time forward to the era of the American Revolution, the locus of power and influence over the lives of the people lay primarily in the towns, not in the province. Provincial control contracted to an absorption in such matters as the management of imperial affairs and the very limited patronage that was dispensed from the center. The provincial government touched the daily life of the towns-people principally as a repository of favors and privileges, enacting into law what the townsmen wished to have enacted and granting what the townsmen wished granted. Local institutions, interposed between Boston and the people, became the prime political institutions of the new provincial society, and as the stakes of political play declined in the capital after 1691, they rose rapidly in the communities themselves.

One element of the new relationship between town and province was established at once and almost automatically. The removal of the executive from the election of the people eliminated the only elections which had ever called out the entire colony, those for the governor, deputy-governor, and assistants. With the governor appointed in England and the councillors chosen by the governor from the nominees of the lower legislative house, there remained not a single occasion which was shared by the whole political citizenry. No office could claim a provincial constituency, and no political pretext existed for mobilization, or even communication, that cut across all the communities of the colony. From the arrival of the new charter to the time of the Revolution, and with the exception only of a couple of insignificant county officials, no town chose any but its own officers or its own deputy to the General Court.

The confinement of the towns to the election of their own inhabitants, which was indeliberate with regard to the executive and his council, was quite conscious in the case of the legislative power, and the altered relationship of local to central authority that it presaged was even more profound. The early legislation which settled the structure of the new House of Representatives—the one branch of the legislature left unequivocally to the colonists—continued that body largely as it had been before, but it provided for one fundamental amendment which was a dramatic response to the imperatives of the new balance of power: a residence requirement was instituted for the representatives.

That requirement transformed the very character of the lower house. The meaning and the magnitude of the change were enunciated quite clearly in a protest signed by twenty-one representatives in 1693. The dissidents denounced the new requirements as

> contrary to the liberty granted in their Majesties' gracious and royal charter and to the usage and customs of their Majesties' kingdom of

> England and all his dominions and plantations and to the particular usage of this their province and that which will prove destructive to the same

and on almost every count their indictment was a true bill, even if the prophecy they drew from it was a false one. In the political theory and practice the colonists had carried across the Atlantic, a representative did not need to reside among the constituents of his own electoral district—and often had not done so—because his true constituency was considered to be the whole society. He was to speak for the general welfare.

The denial of that premise—a denial implicit in the residential qualification—appeared revolutionary to the twenty-one dissenters, and it was. Eighty years later it was still sufficiently revolutionary to constitute a prime point of contention between England and her rebellious colonies, which makes it all the more significant that the substitution of actual for virtual representation in Massachusetts was not an accident but a deliberate creation of policy, instituted over articulate opposition. The new residence requirement curtailed the tendency of the general assembly toward autonomy, reducing the House of Representatives to a virtual congress of communities, a body much more likely than its predecessor to be a creature of the towns to which its members thereby became bound. By the middle of the eighteenth century the principle of actual representation was so well established that a town could insist upon its "unalienable right" to a deputy chosen from among its own inhabitants. As a fundamental matter of political propriety, the petitioners insisted, no town ought to be represented by "a stranger to their interests and circumstances and whose interest is in no wise united with theirs."

The most striking institutional expression of the conviction that the representative must be bound in to his own local constituents was the town mandate. The mandate was an instruction or a set of instructions to the representative, drawn up by a committee of the town and then debated and voted upon in town meeting. There was little of the later *vox populi vox dei* about the mandate—New England Puritans did not conceive man's relation to God as the Jacksonians one day would—but within its sphere the mandate was authoritative. Under its injunction the deputy became a mere agent of the town, an embodiment of the conception of the attorneyship of representation.

Attorneyship of representation was thus an assertion of town sovereignty against invasion by the assembly. The Sunderland petitioners of 1754 said as much:

> Each town having naturally an equal right, so they might enjoy equal advantages to defend, secure, and promote their respective interests and privileges and not have it left to the pleasure of the general assembly to direct and appoint otherwise, for hereby an effectual door would be open for the great part of the province by degrees to be deprived of this privilege and consequently become

liable to be stripped of all other privileges and to be loaded with all manner of oppressions and burdens.

The assertion of *legislative* supremacy in the eighteenth century thus became, at least in Massachusetts, fundamentally an expression of *local* supremacy. As Samuel Eliot Morison has explained, "it was only natural to wish to entrust power to a body, every member of which was elected in town meeting and subject to its instructions."

Direct instruction was by no means the only manner in which towns sought to secure the subordination of their representatives to the wishes of the community. Mandates were merely a small part of a much larger pattern. Throughout the early eighteenth century, representatives were customarily required to render an account of the session's proceedings to the town meeting. Later in the provincial period some towns maintained an active correspondence with their agents while the assembly was in session. At least one town even sent a guardian to accompany its deputies to the General Court to be certain that they observed the town's wishes. And in the excise controversy of 1754 the theory of the attorneyship of representation was elaborated quite consciously in a number of pamphlets such as Daniel Fowle's *Appendix to the Late Total Eclipse of Liberty*, which he subtitled "Being some thoughts on the end and design of civil government; also the inherent power of the people maintained; that it is not given up to their representatives." Fowle called it "slavery" wherever "the representatives have an independent power," a note which was echoed elsewhere, while yet another pamphlet, *The Review,* simply professed amazement, as if unable to conceive of the deputies as independent. "No one suspected," its author declared, "that the representatives of a free people would dare to act contrary to the declared sense of their constituents."

Several other structural devices also curbed the autonomy of the delegates and helped assure their subjection to their own local communities. One of them was the printing and public distribution of the journals of the House of Representatives, a practice which began in Massachusetts in 1715, half a century before any other colony. Such publication was no mere quirk of Puritan intellectuality. A hardheaded determination to secure the fidelity of the deputies sustained it, just as the necessity of the deputies to prove their fidelity had initiated it. The first publication of the records of the assembly occurred in the aftermath of a controversy between the governor and the House, when the deputies decided to release their journals in order to vindicate themselves before their constituents. Thereafter, two copies of the journal were printed for each representative each year—one for himself, one for his town—a pattern which clearly emphasized the attachment of the representative to his community since distribution was wholly confined to those towns with representatives actually in attendance rather than to the full complement of towns in the province. No wider publication was provided because no wider audience was intended; the printed journal was simply an instrument of surveillance, by which the towns might see that their representatives were faithful.

Another instrument in the same strategy of subordination was the annual election of representatives. As *The Review* explained the principle during the excise controversy, "the month of May, which gladdens the face of nature, brings with it also the happy privilege of electing a new assembly." For in the uncommon case of a delegate's disregard of his community's wishes, a remedy was thereby rendered simple: reprisal at the polls. From the perspective of the prerogative that remedy, or at least the threat of its employment, was much more powerful and pervasive than the constraint of an occasional mandate: throughout his long tenure Governor Shirley attempted to prevent the representatives from currying the favor of their constituents by urging upon his English superiors the substitution of triennial elections for the annual ones to which the men of Massachusetts were accustomed. But Shirley never did convince Whitehall, and by 1776 the importance of annual elections was so well established that John Adams could claim that there was not "in the whole circle of the sciences a maxim more infallible than this, 'where annual elections end, there slavery begins.'"

Yet another instrument for the prevention of such "slavery" emerged late in the provincial period. In 1766, upon the urging of a deputy from Cambridge who was himself acting under instruction from his fellow townsmen, the House of Representatives erected a public gallery for visitors. In so doing, the House still further publicized that "special relationship that had always been understood to exist between the representative and his constituents." Displaying its proceedings thus to the public, the lower house gave tangible expression to its situation as an agent of public opinion; and where public opinion in the mother country was something discovered in Parliament, in Massachusetts that public opinion was something out in the country.

All the ties that bound representatives to their constituencies were significant, but it was equally significant that their constituencies were towns. In every colony outside New England the county was the unit of representation; east of the Hudson that unit was the town. Of course the Bay colonists had always conceived of representation in terms of towns, but through the three quarters of a century before independence, in legislation and in the assumptions implicit in their rhetoric, the preference for that aberrant pattern grew steadily firmer than it had ever been before.

The original legislation which established the House of Representatives under the new charter, in 1692, provided representation for every town with forty qualified inhabitants, but it also permitted any town with less than thirty qualified inhabitants to join another town in sending a representative. That permission obviously impaired the strict identity of the individual community and its deputy, however, and it was eliminated in the amendments of 1731, which declared towns with less than the requisite number of qualified voters "at liberty to send a representative, if they think fit," regardless of their size. Thereafter no demand was ever again made that one incorporated town join another in sending a delegate. * * *

Towns were more than merely the constituent elements in the structure of the House. They were also the foundation of financial support for its members, because the basic legislation of 1692 left responsibility for the payment of representatives almost totally to the towns. It reserved to the Court only the residual power to set the delegates' pay scale, and even that was often ignored in the towns, some of them paying as the province required but others giving more than the amount allotted, or less, or nothing at all. Even when subsequent legislative measures of 1726, 1730, and 1731 provided for payment of representatives out of the public treasury, they did not disturb accustomed modes. Towns could and did continue to add their own allowance or require the representative to refund his fees to the local coffer, and in any case the sums disbursed from the center were then added to the tax bills of the towns represented, so that the towns paid the money to the province, which passed it on to the deputies. The General Court and the province treasurer were simply intermediaries. Payment of representatives was never truly a public charge, because only the towns which sent delegates were ever assessed. When an effort was made, in the 1726–7 session of the legislature, to provide for payment of deputies by an assessment upon *all* the towns, "in proportion to their other Province tax," that effort was beaten back. Indeed, even a modest proposal of 1749—that at least the travel expenses of the delegates might be "at the public charge of the province and not laid on the several towns respectively who send a representative"—was defeated.

Thus the burden of financial support for members of the House rested steadily upon the towns throughout the provincial period. Whether the towns paid more or less than the province required, and whether they paid it directly, as they did before 1726, or indirectly, as they did thereafter, the essential element was the simple fact that they paid their own representatives. Such a situation meant that the assembly was not master even in its own lower house. It meant that representation depended on the situation of the towns, not of the province. Towns that considered themselves in sore circumstances might simply decline to send a delegate rather than bear the expense of his salary. Resources were scarce in the towns of eighteenth-century Massachusetts, and when there was more than one demand upon them, representation was unlikely to be accorded primacy. The issue was partly an issue of priority—the construction of a meetinghouse or the building of a road was, in actual fact, likely to take precedence over the dispatch of a deputy—but primarily it was an issue of protocol—the determination of precedence rested with the towns, whatever they decided. As the townsmen of Upton once testified, quite typically, "they are willing to do according to their abilities in supporting government, but their poverty renders them utterly unable to pay more than their common tax." That is, the town would send a delegate only according to its ability, and of that ability it set itself the judge.

In theory the General Court reserved to itself a superior judgment in the matter—the right to fine towns which failed to send a delegate—

but in fact such judgments tended to be mere ratifications of the prior determinations of the towns. As an official commentator on the *Journals of the House* noted, the Court was "more than lenient in accepting explanations from communities which did not care to go to the expense of sending a representative." In the session of which he spoke, only seven of the forty-six towns which had failed to send a representative were fined, and that proportion was not extraordinary in any way. * * *

In the face of such adamant insularity, the central government soon became, in practice, the creature of its constituents. The business that the deputies brought before the Court was basically the business of their fellow townsmen, and, in the absence of any initiative from the governor beyond his opening address and an occasional proposal, the legislative agenda was substantially set by petitions from the towns and their inhabitants. As J. R. Pole put it, the Court "dutifully attended to huge quantities of information and passed laws, after three readings each, on the pleas of innumerable townships, merchants, farmers, planters, clam-diggers, husbands, or wives."

Moreover, the Court's acquiescence in those local desires was quite regular, and in some of them it was unfailing. Administrative appointments were vested formally in higher authorities but actually left totally to the towns to settle for themselves. Appointments of commissioned officers in the militia, issued from Boston, were based in every case upon nominations made by a town committee of militia. Local judicial officers, placed in their seats of judgment by the higher tribunal agencies of the province, really owed their places to presentment to those authorities by their own towns. And even tavern proprietors were installed as the captains and commissioners were, being licensed by the General Court or the county courts but only upon the prior approbation and recommendation of the town of the town's selectmen.

Local wishes were likewise the province's commands in matters of policy, almost as consistently as in matters of personnel. Petitioners seeking to be sent off to another town nearly always had their pleas granted if they could show the approval of both their present and prospective communities. So too did applicants for a separate precinct, district, or town who were able to show a favorable vote of the town from which they sought separation.

Inhabitants of the towns were aware of the Court's disposition upon the appearance of local unanimity, and they acted accordingly. Men who spoke the sentiments of their communities steadily sought complete concurrence, in order "that we may carry our petition to the Great and General Court and the more easily get it granted." Men who found themselves in the opposition took pains to convey to the Court their circumstances, lest the legislators be "deceived" by a semblance of general agreement and mistake a majority vote for "the vote of the whole body of the town." * * *

Concord in the community was indeed the operative condition of effective authority in the province. Court and community alike subordinated provincial considerations to the particularistic demands of local unity. Towns quite commonly set the law aside, without ever a word that went beyond the town boundaries, when the law proved inconvenient for local purposes; and they did so without ever displaying any fundamental animus against the law as such. They simply set their own exigencies above it.

In the area of education the exercise of such local options was so advanced that the General Court itself admitted it. A legislative investigation of 1701 revealed that provincial school standards were "shamefully neglected" and that "the penalty thereof [was] not required." Another Court inquiry, seventeen years later, found "by sad experience" that non-compliance was still common; and, though those legislators thought the delinquent towns were at least paying the fines to which they were liable, more modern study of the subject has shown that evasion remained easy throughout the provincial era. As Bernard Bailyn put it, "the broad stream of enforcing legislation that flows through the statute books of the seventeenth century thinned out in the eighteenth as isolated rural communities * * * allowed the level to sink to local requirement."

In other affairs too, the province proposed and the community disposed; and not infrequently the local disposition was to ignore the edicts of Boston. Thus there were general laws which regulated the requirements for admission to the franchise, yet communities could decide, as Needham did decide in its election meeting of 1750, simply to let all freeholders vote. There was a law which forbade town meetings to consider any business not previously announced in the warning for the meeting, yet towns could with equal impunity set that prohibition aside as well. Indeed, though few towns intended to flaunt the central government and fewer still foresaw open confrontation with it when they did deviate, there was scarcely a law on the books which a town could not safely have neglected. Virtually all of them were, in practice, affairs of local option, on the model of the school requirements. Their enforcement was, as a student of public administration in Massachusetts has said, merely "a matter of local choice." * * *

According to Samuel Eliot Morison, the towns had become "in fact the several sovereigns of Massachusetts–Bay. Their relation to the General Court closely approximated that of the states to the Congress of the Confederation, with the important difference that there were not thirteen but almost three hundred of them." This sovereignty once established visibly to all, the towns went on about their business as they had come to see that business. They wrought a revolution.

The governor's authority now embraced little more than Boston; the royal treasurer soon failed to receive payments of recognition from the towns; by the towns had been brought about the end of the royal legislature; at their instance the royal courts had been abolished; and it is significant that in this general collapse the town system, and that alone, had maintained an existence and an activity that were practically continuous. By this element the government of the King had been destroyed; by it the reconstruction was to be effected. * * *

KARL MARX, THE CIVIL WAR IN FRANCE

* * * The centralised State power, with its ubiquitous organs of standing army, police, bureaucracy, clergy, and judicature—organs wrought after the plan of a systematic and hierarchic division of labour—originates from the days of absolute monarchy, serving nascent middle-class society as a mighty weapon in its struggles against feudalism. Still, its development remained clogged by all manner of medieval rubbish, seignorial rights, local privileges, municipal and guild monopolies and provincial constitutions. The gigantic broom of the French Revolution of the eighteenth century swept away all these relics of bygone times, thus clearing simultaneously the social soil of its last hindrances to the superstructure of the modern State edifice raised under the First Empire, itself the offspring of the coalition wars of old semi-feudal Europe against modern France. During the subsequent *régimes* the Government, placed under parliamentary control—that is, under the direct control of the propertied classes—became not only a hotbed of huge national debts and crushing taxes; with its irresistible allurements of place, pelf, and patronage, it became not only the bone of contention between the rival factions and adventurers of the ruling classes; but its political character changed simultaneously with the economic changes of society. At the same pace at which the progress of modern industry developed, widened, intensified the class antagonism between capital and labour, the State power assumed more and more the character of the national power of capital over labour, of a public force organised for social enslavement, of an engine of class despotism. After every revolution marking a progressive phase in the class struggle, the purely repressive character of the State power stands out in bolder and bolder relief. The Revolution of 1830, resulting in the transfer of Government from the landlords to the capitalists, transferred it from the more remote to the more direct antagonists of the working men. The bourgeois Republicans, who, in the name of the Revolution of February, took the State power, used it for the June massacres, in order to convince the working class that "social" republic meant the Republic ensuring their social subjection, and in order to convince the royalist bulk of the bourgeois and landlord class that they might safely leave the cares and emoluments of Government to the bourgeois "Republicans." However, after their one heroic exploit of June, the bourgeois Republicans had, from the front, to fall back to the rear of the "Party of Order"—a combination formed by all the rival fractions and factions of the appropriating class in their now openly declared antagonism to the producing classes. The proper form of their joint-stock Government was the *Parliamentary Republic,* with Louis Bonaparte for its President. Theirs was a *régime* of avowed class terrorism and deliberate insult

toward the "vile multitude." If the Parliamentary Republic, as M. Thiers said, "divided them (the different fractions of the ruling class) least," it opened an abyss between that class and the whole body of society outside their spare ranks. The restraints by which their own divisions had under former *regimes* still checked the State power, were removed by their union; and in view of the threatening upheaval of the proletariat, they now used that State power mercilessly and ostentatiously as the national war-engine of capital against labour. In their uninterrupted crusade against the producing masses they were, however, bound not only to invest the executive with continually increased powers of repression, but at the same time to divest their own parliamentary stronghold—the National Assembly—one by one, of all its own means of defence against the Executive. The Executive, in the person of Louis Bonaparte, turned them out. The natural offspring of the "Party-of-Order" Republic was the Second Empire.

The empire, with the *coup d'état* for its certificate of birth, universal suffrage for its sanction, and the sword for its sceptre, professed to rest upon the peasantry, the large mass of producers not directly involved in the struggle of capital and labour. It professed to save the working class by breaking down Parliamentarism, and, with it, the undisguised subserviency of Government to the propertied classes. It professed to save the propertied classes by upholding their economic supremacy over the working class; and, finally, it professed to unite all classes by reviving for all the chimera of national glory. In reality, it was the only form of government possible at a time when the bourgeoisie had already lost, and the working class had not yet acquired, the faculty of ruling the nation. It was acclaimed throughout the world as the saviour of society. Under its sway, bourgeois society, freed from political cares, attained a development unexpected even by itself. Its industry and commerce expanded to colossal dimensions; financial swindling celebrated cosmopolitan orgies; the misery of the masses was set off by a shameless display of gorgeous, meretricious and debased luxury. The State power, apparently soaring high above society, was at the same time itself the greatest scandal of that society and the very hotbed of all its corruptions. Its own rottenness, and the rottenness of the society it had saved, were laid bare by the bayonet of Prussia, herself eagerly bent upon transferring the supreme seat of that *régime* from Paris to Berlin. Imperialism is, at the same time, the most prostitute and the ultimate form of the State power which nascent middle-class society had commenced to elaborate as a means of its own emancipation from feudalism, and which full-grown bourgeois society had finally transformed into a means for the enslavement of labour by capital.

The direct antithesis to the empire was the Commune. The cry of "social republic," with which the revolution of February was ushered in by the Paris proletariat, did but express a vague aspiration after a Republic that was not only to supersede the monarchical form of class-rule, but class-rule itself. The Commune was the positive form of that Republic.

Paris, the central seat of the old governmental power, and, at the same time, the social stronghold of the French working class, had risen in arms against the attempt of Thiers and the Rurals to restore and perpetuate that old governmental power bequeathed to them by the empire. Paris could resist only because, in consequence of the siege, it had got rid of the army, and replaced it by a National Guard, the bulk of which consisted of working men. This fact was now to be transformed into an institution. The first decree of the Commune, therefore, was the suppression of the standing army, and the substitution for it of the armed people.

The Commune was formed of the municipal councillors, chosen by universal suffrage in the various wards of the town, responsible and revocable at short terms. The majority of its members were naturally working men, or acknowledged representatives of the working class. The Commune was to be a working, not a parliamentary, body, executive and legislative at the same time. Instead of continuing to be the agent of the Central Government, the police was at once stripped of its political attributes, and turned into the responsible and at all times revocable agent of the Commune. So were the officials of all other branches of the Administration. From the members of the Commune downwards, the public service had to be done at *workmen's wages*. The vested interests and the representation allowances of the high dignitaries of State disappeared along with the high dignitaries themselves. Public functions ceased to be the private property of the tools of the Central Government. Not only municipal administration, but the whole initiative hitherto exercised by the State was laid into the hands of the Commune.

Having once got rid of the standing army and the police, the physical force elements of the old Government, the Commune was anxious to break the spiritual force of repression, the "parson-power," by the disestablishment and disendowment of all churches as proprietary bodies. The priests were sent back to the recesses of private life, there to feed upon the alms of the faithful in imitation of their predecessors, the Apostles. The whole of the educational institutions were opened to the people gratuitously, and at the same time cleared of all interference of Church and State. Thus, not only was education made accessible to all, but science itself freed from the fetters which class prejudice and governmental force had imposed upon it.

The judicial functionaries were to be divested of that sham independence which had but served to mask their abject subserviency to all succeeding governments to which, in turn, they had taken, and broken, the oaths of allegiance. Like the rest of public servants, magistrates and judges were to be elective, responsible, and revocable.

The Paris Commune was, of course, to serve as a model to all the great industrial centres of France. The communal *régime* once established in Paris and the secondary centres, the old centralised Government would in the provinces, too, have to give way to the self-government of the producers. In a rough sketch of national organisation which the Commune had no time to develop, it states clearly that the Commune was to be the political form of even the smallest country hamlet, and that in the rural districts the standing army was to be replaced by a national militia, with an extremely short term of service. The rural communes of every district were to administer their common affairs by an assembly of delegates in the central town, and these district assemblies were again to send deputies to the National Delegation in Paris, each delegate to be at any time revocable and bound by the *mandat impératif* (formal instructions) of his constituents. The few but important functions which still would remain for a central government were not to be suppressed, as has been intentionally mis-stated, but were to be discharged by Communal, and therefore strictly responsible agents. The unity of the nation was not to be broken, but, on the contrary, to be organised by the Communal Constitution and to become a reality by the destruction of the State power which claimed to be the embodiment of that unity independent of, and superior to, the nation itself, from which it was but a parasitic excrescence. While the merely repressive organs of the old governmental power were to be amputated, its legitimate functions were to be wrested from an authority usurping pre-eminence over society itself, and restored to the responsible agents of society. Instead of deciding once in three or six years which member of the ruling class was to misrepresent the people in Parliament, universal suffrage was to serve the people, constituted in the Communes, as individual suffrage serves every other employer in the search for the workmen and managers in his business. And it is well known that companies, like individuals, in matters of real business generally know how to put the right man in the right place, and, if they for once make a mistake, to redress it promptly. On the other hand, nothing could be more foreign to the spirit of the Commune that to supersede universal suffrage by hierarchic investiture.

It is generally the fate of completely new historical creations to be mistaken for the counterpart of older and even defunct forms of social life, to which they may bear a certain likeness. Thus, this new Commune, which breaks the modern State power, has been mistaken for a reproduction of the medieval Communes, which first preceded, and afterwards became the substratum of, that very State power. The Communal Constitution has been mistaken for an attempt to break up into a federation of small States, as dreamt of by Montesquieu and the Girondins, that unity of great nations which, if originally brought about by political force, has now become a powerful coefficient of social production. The antagonism of the Commune against the State power has been mistaken for an exaggerated form of the ancient struggle against over-centralisation. Peculiar historical circumstances may have prevented the classical development, as in France, of the bourgeois form of government, and may have allowed, as in England, to complete the great central State organs by corrupt vestries, jobbing councillors, and ferocious poor-law guardians in the towns, and virtually hereditary magistrates in the counties. The Communal Constitution would have restored to the social body all the forces hitherto absorbed by the State parasite feeding upon, and clogging the free movement of, society. By this one act it would have initiated the regeneration of France. The provincial French middle class saw in the Commune an attempt to restore the sway their order had held over the country under Louis Philippe, and which, under Louis Napoleon, was supplanted by the pretended rule of the country over the towns. In reality, the Communal Constitution brought the rural producers under the intellectual lead of the central towns of their districts, and these secured to them, in the working men, the natural trustees of their interests. The very existence of the Commune involved, as a matter of course, local municipal liberty, but no longer as a check upon the, now superseded, State power. It could only enter into the head of a Bismarck, who, when not engaged on his intrigues of blood and iron, always likes to resume his old trade, so befitting his mental calibre, of contributor to *Kladderadatsch* (the Berlin *Punch*), it could only enter into such a head, to ascribe to the Paris Commune aspirations after that caricature of the old French municipal organisation of 1791, the Prussian municipal constitution which degrades the town governments to mere secondary wheels in the police-machinery of the Prussian State. The Commune made that catchword of bourgeois revolutions, cheap government, a reality, by destroying the two greatest sources of expenditure—the standing army and State functionarism. Its very existence presupposed the non-existence of monarchy, which, in Europe at least, is the normal incumbrance and indispensable cloak of class-rule. It supplied the Republic with the basis of really democratic institutions. But neither cheap Government nor the "true Republic" was its ultimate aim; they were its mere concomitants.

The multiplicity of interpretations to which the Commune has been subjected, and the multiplicity of interests which construed it in their favour, show that it was a thoroughly expansive political form, while all previous forms of government had been emphatically repressive. Its true secret was this. It was essentially a working-class government, the produce of the struggle of the producing against the appropriating class, the political form at last discovered under which to work out the economic emancipation of labour.

Except on this last condition, the Communal Constitution would have been an impossibility and a delusion. The political rule of the producer cannot coexist with the perpetuation of his social slavery. The Commune was therefore to serve as a lever for uprooting the economical foundations upon which rests the existence of classes, and therefore of class-rule. With labour emancipated, every man becomes a working man, and productive labour ceases to be a class attribute. * * *

C.B. MACPHERSON, THE LIFE AND TIMES OF LIBERAL DEMOCRACY
Pp. 108–114 (1977).

MODELS OF PARTICIPATORY DEMOCRACY

Let me turn finally to the question of how a participatory democracy might be run if we did achieve the prerequisites. How participatory could it be, given that at any level beyond the neighbourhood it would have to be an indirect or representative system rather than face-to-face direct democracy?

(i) Model 4A: an abstract first approximation

If one looks at the question first in general terms, setting aside for the present both the weight of tradition and the actual circumstances that might prevail in any country when the prerequisites had been sufficiently met, the simplest model that could properly be called a participatory democracy would be a pyramidal system with direct democracy at the base and delegate democracy at every level above that. Thus one would start with direct democracy at the neighbourhood or factory level—actual face-to-face discussion and decision by consensus or majority, and election of delegates who would make up a council at the next more inclusive level, say a city borough or ward or a township. The delegates would have to be sufficiently instructed by and accountable to those who elected them to make decisions at the council level reasonably democratic. So it would go on up to the top level, which would be a national council for matters of national concern, and local and regional councils for matters of less than national concern. At whatever level beyond the smallest primary one the final decisions on different matters were made, the issues would certainly have to be formulated by a committee of the council. Thus at whatever level the reference up stopped, it would stop in effect with a small committee of that level's council. This may seem a far cry from democratic control. But I think it is the best we can do. What is needed, at every stage, to make the system democratic, is that the decision-makers and issue-formulators elected from below be held responsible to those below by being subject to re-election or even recall.

Now such a system, no matter how clearly responsibilities are set out on paper, even if the paper is a formal national constitution, is no guarantee of effective democratic participation or control: the Soviet Union's "democratic centralism", which was just such a scheme, cannot be said to have provided the democratic control that had been intended. The question is whether such failure is inherent in the nature of a pyramidal councils system. I think it is not. I suggest that we can identify the sets of circumstances in which the system won't work as intended, that is, won't provide adequate responsibility to those below, won't be actively democratic. Three such sets of circumstances are evident.

(1) A pyramidal system will not provide real responsibility of the government to all the levels below in an immediately post-revolutionary situation; at least it will not do so if the threat of counter-revolution, with or without foreign intervention, is present. For in that case,

democratic control, with all its delays, has to give way to central authority. That was the lesson of the immediate aftermath of the 1917 Bolshevik revolution. A further lesson, to be drawn from the subsequent Soviet experience, is that, if a revolution bites off more than it can chew democratically, it will chew it undemocratically.

Now since we do not seem likely, in the Western liberal democracies, to try to move to full democracy by way of a Bolshevik revolution, this does not appear to be a difficulty for us. But we must notice that the threat of counter-revolution is present not only after a Bolshevik revolution but also after a parliamentary revolution, i.e. a constitutional, electoral, takeover of power by a party or popular front pledged to a radical reform leading to the replacement of capitalism. That this threat may be real, and be fatal to a constitutional revolutionary regime which tries to proceed democratically, is evident in the example of the counter-revolutionary overthrow of the Allende regime in Chile in 1973, after three years in office. We have to ask, therefore, whether the Chilean sequence could be repeated in any of the more advanced Western liberal-democracies. Could it happen in, say, Italy or France? If it could, the chances of participatory democracy in any such country would be slim.

There is no certainty that it could not happen there. We cannot rely on there being a longer habit of constitutionalism in Western Europe than in Latin America: indeed, in those European liberal democracies which are most likely to be in this situation in the forseeable future (e.g. Italy and France), the tradition of constitutionalism cannot be said to be much older or firmer than in Chile. We should, however, notice that Allende's popular front coalition was in control of only a part of the executive power (the presidency, but not the *contraloria,* which had power to rule on the legality of any executive action), and was in control of none of the legislative (including taxing) power. If a similar government elsewhere came into office with a stronger base it could proceed democratically without the same risk of being overthrown by counter-revolution.

(2) Another circumstance in which a responsible pyramidal councils system would not work would be a reappearance of an underlying class division and opposition. For, as we have seen, such division requires that the political system, in order to hold the society together, be able to perform the function of continual compromise between class interests, and that function makes it impossible to have clear and strong lines of responsibility from the upper elected levels downwards.

But this also is not as great a problem for us as it might seem. For if my earlier analysis is right, we shall not have reached the possibility of installing such a responsible system until we have greatly reduced the present social and economic inequalities. It is true that this will be possible only in the measure that the capital/labour relation that prevails in our society has been fundamentally changed, for capitalist relations produce and reproduce opposed classes. No amount of welfare-state redistribution of income will by itself change that relation. Nor will any amount of workers' participation or workers' control at the shop-floor level or the plant level: that is a promising breakthrough point, but it will not do the whole job. A fully democratic society requires democratic political control over the uses to which the amassed capital and the remaining natural resources of the society are put. It probably does not matter whether this takes the form of social ownership of all capital, or a social control of it so thorough as to be virtually the same as ownership. But more welfare-state redistribution of the national income is not enough: no matter how much it might reduce class inequalities of income it would not touch class inequalities of power.

(3) A third circumstance in which the pyramidal council system would not work is, of course, if the people at the base were apathetic. Such a system could not have been reached except by a people who had thrown off their political apathy. But might not apathy grow again? There can be no guarantee that it would not. But at least the main factor which I have argued creates and sustains apathy in our present system would by hypothesis be absent or at least greatly modified—I mean the class structure which discourages the participation of those in the lower strata by rendering it relatively ineffective, and which more generally discourages participation by requiring such a blurring of issues that governments cannot be held seriously responsible to the electorate.

To sum up the discussion so far of the prospects of a pyramidal councils system as a model of participatory democracy, we may say that in the measure that the prerequisite conditions for transition to a participatory system had been achieved in any Western country, the most obvious impediments to a pyramidal councils scheme being genuinely democratic would not be present. A pyramidal system might work. Or other impediments might emerge to prevent it being fully democratic. It is not worth pursuing these, for this simple model is too unrealistic. It can be nothing but a first approximation to a workable model, for it was reached by deliberately setting aside what must now be brought back into consideration—the weight of tradition and the actual circumstances that are likely to prevail in any Western nation at the time when the transition became possible.

The most important factor here is the existence of political parties. The simple model has no place for them. It envisages a no-party or one-party system. This was appropriate enough when such a model was put forward in the revolutionary circumstances of mid-seventeenth-century England and early twentieth-century Russia. But it is not appropriate for late twentieth-century Western nations, for it seems unlikely that any of them will move to the threshold of participatory democracy by way of a one-party revolutionary take-over. It is much more likely that any such move will be made under the leadership of a popular front or a coalition of social-democratic and socialist parties. Those parties will not wither away, at least not for some years. Unless all of them but one are put down by force, several will still be around. The real question then is, whether there is some way of combining a pyramidal council structure with a competitive party system.

(ii) Model 4B: a second approximation

The combination of a pyramidal direct/indirect democratic machinery with a continuing party system seems essential. Nothing but a pyramidal system will incorporate any direct democracy into a nation-wide structure of government, and some significant amount of direct democracy is required for anything that can be called participatory democracy. At the same time, competitive political parties must be assumed to be in existence, parties whose claims cannot, consistently with anything that could be called a liberal democracy, be overridden.

Not only is the combination of pyramid and parties probably unavoidable: it may be positively desirable. For even in a non-class-divided society there would still be issues around which parties might form, or even might be needed to allow issues to be effectively proposed and debated: issues such as the over-all allocation of resources, environmental and urban planning, population and immigration policies, foreign policy, military policy. Now supposing that a competitive party system were either unavoidable, or actually desirable, in a non-exploitive, non-class-divided society, could it be combined with any kind of pyramidal direct/indirect democracy?

I think it could. For the main functions which the competitive party system has had to perform, and has performed, in class-divided societies up to now, i.e. the blurring of class opposition and the continual arranging of compromises or apparent compromises between the demands of opposed classes, would no longer be required. And those are the features of the competitive party system which have made it up to now incompatible with any effective participatory democracy. With that function no longer required, the incompatibility disappears.

There are, in abstract theory, two possibilities of combining a pyramidal organization with competing parties. One, much the more difficult, and so unlikely as to deserve no attention here, would be to replace the existing Western parliamentary or congressional/presidential structure of government by a soviet-type structure (which is conceivable even with two or more parties). The other, much less difficult, would be to keep the existing structure of government, and rely on the parties themselves to operate by pyramidal participation. It is true, as I said earlier, that all the many attempts made by democratic reform movements and parties to make their leaders, when they became the government, responsible to the rank-and-file, have failed. But the reason for those failures would no longer exist in the circumstances we are considering, or at least would not exist to anything like the same degree. The reason for those failures was that strict responsibility of the party leadership to the membership does not allow the room for manoeuvre and compromise which a government in a class-divided society must have in order to carry out its necessary function of mediating between opposed class interests in the whole society. No doubt, even in a non-class-divided society, there would still have to be some room for compromise. But the amount of room needed for compromise on the sort of issues that might then divide parties would not be of the same order of magnitude as the amount now required, and the element of deception or concealment required to carry on the continual blurring of class lines would not be present.

It thus appears that there is a real possibility of genuinely participatory parties, and that they could operate through a parliamentary or congressional structure to provide a substantial measure of participatory democracy. This I think is as far as it is now feasible to go by way of a blueprint. * * *

Chapter Three

THE RELATIONSHIP AMONG NEIGHBORING CITIES

In Chapter Two, we explored the relationship between cities and the larger groups of which they are a part—the states and the nation. This chapter shifts our attention to the connections that cities have with each other. In examining these inter-city relationships, it would be a mistake simply to assume that every city is a separate, autonomous entity able to deal with other cities as it pleases. As the materials covered in Chapter Two suggest, states have considerable power to structure and control how cities deal with one another. Indeed, states even have the power to control the location and meaning of the geographic lines that separate cities from each other—the very lines that enable us to distinguish one city from another. To examine inter-city relationships, therefore, we need to recognize at the outset the complexities involved in any effort of a city's citizens to say to those outside its boundaries, "we want to choose our own way of life, to select our own leaders, and to use our resources for our own benefit." Who, for example, decides who is included in the term "we"? To respond that the citizens of each city can answer this question for themselves is circular. Who decides in the first instance who a city's citizens are?

This chapter's investigation of the complexities of inter-city relationships will concentrate on the most important contemporary location for inter-city conflict in America: metropolitan areas that include both a central city and its suburbs. The first subsection presents, from a number of contrasting perspectives, an introduction to the history and meaning of the city/suburb distinction in America. Two subsections then explore the ways in which residency within local boundaries now defines and maintains the crucial dividing line between cities and suburbs. To what extent can nonresidents be excluded from—or included in—the definition of those who can participate in local decisonmaking? To what extent does residency determine who can use publicly-owned facilities? To what extent can a locality favor its own residents over outsiders? After the importance of residency has been delineated, subsequent subsections examine possible changes in the composition of a city's (or a suburb's) residents. To what extent can a locality protect itself from such changes? Can it, for example, resist annexation by others or prevent sub-groups from seceding and forming new cities? Can it prevent outsiders who want to become residents from moving to town? Can it keep outsiders from benefiting from the resources that are located within its boundaries? Finally, the second half of the chapter changes the focus from questions, such as these, about current city-suburb relationships to contemporary attempts to find regional solutions to city-suburb conflicts. Are there ways of organizing our metropolitan areas better than we do now? If so, what are they?

SECTION A.   THE CITY–SUBURB RELATIONSHIP

1. AN INTRODUCTION TO THE RELATIONSHIP BETWEEN CITIES AND SUBURBS

What explains the vast expansion of suburbanization in the United States in the twentieth century? The readings that follow offer a number of contrasting explanations: government policy; class and ethnic conflict; crime and other "city problems"; racial segregation; conceptions of work, family and gender; desires for local control; the search for a sense of community. Which of these explanations seem persuasive?

PETER HALL, CITIES OF TOMORROW

Pp. 291–294 (1988).

There were four main foundations for the suburban boom. They were new roads to open up land outside the reach of the old trolley and commuter rail routes; land uses, to produce uniform essential tracts with stable property values; government-guaranteed mortgages, to make possible long-repayment low-interest mortgages that were affordable by families of modest incomes; and a baby boom, to produce a sudden surge in demand for family homes where young children could be raised. The first three of these were already in place, though sometimes only in embryonic form, a decade before the boom began. The fourth triggered it.

The first part, the roads, were embryonic. * * * [T]hey were there in one or two places: New York from the 1920s, Los Angeles from the 1940s. But, remarkably, developers do not seem to have appreciated their potential for a decade or more after they were in place. Still, in the 1930s, a majority of New Yorkers did not own cars. And many of those who did happen to work in Manhattan, to which car commuting was almost impossible; suburbanization must await the outward movement of jobs to places where the car was more convenient than the subway—which began to happen on any scale only in the 1950s. And in any event, generally the roads were not there. The Depression and the wartime years had brought a halt to the rise in car ownership; not until

1949 did registrations again exceed the level of 1929. And road-building, too, had stagnated.

It was the 1956 Federal–Aid Highway Act that marked the real beginning of freeway suburbanization. But at the beginning, it does not seem to have been meant that way at all. True, * * * an Inter–Regional Highways Committee * * * called for a 32,000–mile Interstate system, and Congress duly passed the Federal–Aid Highway Act of 1944. But that was to be a strictly inter-urban system, bypassing the cities; and, before it could be built, political splits emerged: between engineers who just wanted to pour concrete and city planners * * * who wanted to use new roads to cure urban blight, between those who wanted self-financing toll roads and those who wanted federal subsidy. Truman in 1949, Eisenhower in 1954, signed Urban Renewal Acts, but kept highways out of them.

Finally, Eisenhower—who believed that he had won the war on the German *Autobahnen*—accepted the argument that new roads were not only vital for national defense in an era of Cold War, but could also generate an economic boom. He called on a retired General, Lucius Clay, to head a committee of inquiry; most of the evidence came from the pro-roads side—including Robert Moses, who used the roads-fight-blight argument. But the fight over paying for them, which was essentially between fiscal conservatives and the highways lobby, almost killed the resulting bill. Finally, a compromise version, providing for the new roads to be built by a special fund through a tax on gasoline, oil, buses and trucks, was passed in June 1956; in the House of Representatives it went through without dissent, in the Senate one solitary vote was recorded against it. The greatest public-works programme in the history of the world—$41 billion for 41,000 miles of new roads—was under way.

The critical question, still, was what sort of road system it should be. Congress in 1944 had endorsed the principle that it should bypass the cities. Planners like Bartholomew and Moses argued on the contrary that it should penetrate into their hearts, thus removing blighted areas and improving accessibility from the suburbs to downtown offices and shops. In practice, given the strength of the urban renewal lobby in the 1950s and 1960s, there was little doubt about the outcome: the system would be used to create new corridors of accessibility from city centres to potential suburbs, as Moses had tried to do thirty years earlier. When the programme began in earnest, its chief Bertram D. Tallamy said that the new highways were built on principles that Moses had taught him as long ago as 1926; at that time and for long after, Moses was, after all, the only really experienced urban-highway builder in the United States.

The second requirement, zoning, had originated as early as 1880 in Modesto, California, where it had been used to remove Chinese laundries: a particularly apt beginning, since thereafter one of its principal functions was to safeguard property values by excluding undesirable land uses and undesirable neighbors. And * * * the city that took the lead in the zoning movement from 1913 on, New York City, was impelled to do so by the complaints of Manhattan retailers who, complaining that industrial incursions were threatening their profits, appealed loudly to 'every man who owns a home or rents an apartment'; the city's Commission on Building Heights accepted their argument that zoning secured 'greater safety and security in investment'. And the historic 1926 Supreme Court decision, *Euclid v. Ambler,* which confirmed the general validity of zoning seems to have accepted Alfred Bettman's argument that its point was to enhance property values. The point at issue, significantly, was whether land should be zoned industrial or residential.

Because it was meticulously designed as part of a general police power to safeguard 'public welfare' and 'public health, safety, morals and convenience', thus to avoid all suggestion of compulsory purchase with claims for compensation, New York's comprehensive zoning resolution of 1916 deliberately avoided long-term plans; Edward Bassett, the attorney in change, proudly declared 'We have gone at it block by block', invariably confirming the status quo. And most of America followed suit. Thus arose a paradox: land use control in the United States, in sharp contrast to much of Europe, came to be divorced from any kind of land-use planning; it could not be used to raise the level of design * * *.

The third precondition for the suburban boom was cheap long-term housing finance. In this regard, * * * America lagged strangely behind Britain. There, the permanent building societies had developed from the turn of the century, offering twenty- or twenty-five-year mortgages with low down payments, and powerfully fuelling the great suburban spread around London in the 1920s and 1930s. In contrast, until the 1930s, the typical American mortgage was only for five or ten years at 6 or 7 per cent interest: a ruinously high burden for the average family. It was an early New Deal experiment—the Home Owners Loan Corporation (HOLC), introduced as an emergency measure of April 1933 to stem farm foreclosures—that introduced into America the long-term, self-amortizing mortgage. The next year, the National Housing Act established the Federal Housing Authority (FHA) with powers to insure longer-term mortgage loans by private lenders for home construction and sale, with a down payment as low as 10 per cent and a period of twenty-five or thirty years at only 2 or 3 per cent. Between 1938 and 1941, it was insuring some 35 per cent of all home loans in the United States.

From 1934, then, the most powerful constraint to suburban home-building had been removed. For the FHA took over from the HOLC the notion of appraising whole neighborhoods, and thereby redlining those deemed to be undesirable; in practice, this meant the whole of America's inner cities. Further, the 'FHA exhorted racial segregation and endorsed it as a public policy'; as late as 1966, it had not insured a single mortgage in Paterson or Camden in New Jersey, two predominantly black cities. The central objective of the FHA was identical with that of zoning: it was to guarantee the security of residential real-estate values. And both worked through exclusion, to divert investment massively into new suburban house building at the expense of the central city.

Some of the consequences could already be glimpsed later in that decade. The National Resources Committee's report *Our Cities*, published in 1937 * * *, drew attention to the fact that even between 1920 and 1930, suburbs had grown twice as fast as central cities: 'the urbanite is rapidly becoming the suburbanite', as families fulfilled 'the urge to escape the obnoxious aspects of urban life without at the same time losing access to its economic and cultural advantages.' During that decade, some suburbs had grown at dizzy speed: Beverly Hills by 2,500 per cent; Shaker Heights outside Cleveland by 1,000 per cent. But then, the depression drastically cut new housing starts—by as much as 95 per cent between 1928 and 1933—and brought a huge crop of mortgage foreclosures. Not until after World War Two did the industry completely recover.

Given an almost complete moratorium on new construction—save for essential war-related building—between 1941 and 1945, the result at war's end was a huge accumulated shortage: an estimated 2.75–4.4 million families sharing, and another half-million in non-family quarters. On top of that came the baby boom, as the servicemen returned and the delayed crop of wartime babies coincided with the regular cohorts. The industry spectacularly responded: as against a mere 515,000 starts in 1939, there were 1,466,000 by 1949, 1,554,000 by 1959. And in the 1949 Housing Act—as well as initiating the urban renewal process * * *— Congress massively increased FHA's lending powers. As before, this money went into the suburbs. By 1950, the suburbs were found to be growing at ten times the rate of the central cities; by 1954, it was estimated that in the previous decade 9 million people had moved into the suburbs. The 1950s, as the 1960 Census showed, was the decade of the greatest suburban growth in American history: while the central cities grew by 6 million or 11.6 per cent, the suburbs grew by a dizzy 19 million, or by 45.9 per cent. And ominously, for the first time, some of the nation's greatest cities recorded actual population decline: Boston and St. Louis each lost 13 per cent of their population. * * *

MICHAEL DANIELSON, THE POLITICS OF EXCLUSION

Pp. 15–22 (1976).

POLITICAL FRAGMENTATION

The political separation of city and suburb is not the product of "natural" forces which caused the city to cease to expand and independent suburban jurisdictions to grow up around the urban core. Until the last decades of the nineteenth century, and much later in many cities, the steady exodus from the urban core typically was not accompanied by creation of politically independent suburbs. Quite the contrary, local political jurisdictions in the path of the decentralizing urban population commonly were swallowed up by the city. Milton Kotler has described the process in Philadelphia:

> Germantown originated as a chartered town of Quaker immigrants, founded concurrently with Philadelphia to its south. Germantown continued as a political unit until it was annexed by Philadelphia without the consent of its residents in the consolidation of 1854. After 171 years of independent growth, that neighborhood lost its political self-rule. * * * In 1854, twenty-eight cities, towns, and boroughs lost their local government and were incorporated into the city of Philadelphia. The present day neighborhoods of Philadelphia can be traced to these original political units.

Through annexation, cities extended their jurisdiction to encompass established communities, newly settled neighborhoods, and undeveloped land at the urban periphery. New areas usually welcomed annexation because the city was the only source of urban services. Cities, for their part, were eager to expand. The American credo assured city fathers that growth was good—to be bigger was to be better. Few cities could resist an expansion program that promised to bolster its image, expand the tax base, enhance the local economy, enlarge opportunities for political rewards, and enrich speculators, developers, and utility operators. Cincinnati's growth was typical of the era, as it expanded from six to twenty-one square miles between 1850 and 1880, and then annexed another twenty-eight square miles over the next thirty years.

As the spreading city sorted itself out along income, ethnic, and racial lines, however, political as well as spatial separation from the inner city became increasingly attractive in the middle-class neighborhoods. Independence promised neighborhood control over taxes and services, a homogeneous local political system responsive to community interests, an end to involvement with the city's complex politics and costly problems, and a more effective means of excluding the lower classes. Reinforcing the desire for autonomy was the rise of the political machine, whose strength was rooted in the lower-income and ethnic wards in the core of the differentiated metropolis. Opposition to the machine came primarily from the middle-class neighborhoods on the city's rim. "The boss," as Richard C. Wade notes, "fed on the problems and predicaments of the old congested center of the city while reform committees grew on the fears and anxieties of the new residential neighborhoods."

Resistance to annexation and demands for local autonomy in the outer neighborhoods became more insistent as immigrants poured into the city and machines consolidated their grip on the governmental machinery. At issue was the question of whether the urban community should maintain a single political system to encompass its diversity or permit its varied neighborhoods to go their own way, with different local governments for different social and economic groupings. Sam B. Warner, Jr., has described the debate in Boston during the late nineteenth century:

> Annexationists appealed to the idea of one great city where work and home, social and cultural activities, industry and commerce would be joined in a single political union. Boston, they said, would share the fate of Rome if the middle class, which heretofore had provided the governance of the city and the force of its reforms, abandoned the city for the suburbs.

> Opponents of annexation countered with the ideal of small town life: the simple informal community, the town meeting, the maintenance of the traditions of rural New England. They held out to their audience the idea of the suburban town as a refuge from the pressures of the new industrial metropolis. Nor were the opponents of annexation slow to point out that the high level of city services maintained by Boston meant higher taxes, and further, they frankly stated the independent suburban towns could maintain native American life free from Boston's waves of incoming poor immigrants.

> * * * It was already apparent in the 1880's that to join Boston was to assume all the burdens and conflicts of a modern industrial metropolis. To remain apart was to escape, at least for a time, some of these problems. In the face of this choice the metropolitan middle class abandoned their central city.

Almost everywhere, the advocates of suburban separation from the city prevailed. Boston was the first major city to stop growing, adding no new territory after 1873. Over the next half century, every major city in the Northeast, Midwest, and Far West was encircled by independent suburbs. Some cities stopped expanding because of natural barriers or the impediments imposed by state or county boundaries. A few city governments refused to annex new territory because of an unwillingness to underwrite costly capital improvements and service extensions in developing areas. In some instances, cities controlled by machines were willing to let middle-class areas go in order to dilute the electoral strength of the municipal reform movement. But the underlying cause of the end of annexation and the political containment of the city was the universal desire of the periphery for political autonomy from the core. This objective was rooted in class and ethnic conflict and the desire of middle-class areas for local control over their relatively homogeneous communities.

The division of the urban turf between city and suburb, of course, varied from metropolitan area to metropolitan area. A city's share of the newer residential, commercial, and industrial development—as well as of the middle- and upper-income families of the metropolis—depends primarily on its age and when it ceased annexing territory. Most of the older centers of the Northeast and Midwest stopped growing before the widespread introduction of the automobile. As a result, they encompass little low-density development and have relatively high proportions of lower-income and black residents, as well as stable or declining populations. The newer cities of the South and West, on the other hand, grew primarily during the automobile era. As a result, cities such as Albuquerque, El Paso, Orlando, Phoenix, Tampa, and Tucson are more "suburban" than "citylike" in terms of settlement patterns, residential densities, and commercial and industrial development. Neither foreign immigration nor the political machine was a significant factor in the development of most of these newer cities. As a result, differences between the center and the periphery tend to be less pronounced than in older metropolitan areas. Because differences are muted, there has been less reason to create independent suburbs, less need to use small-scale suburban political systems for exclusionary purposes, and a greater willingness on the part of the new areas to be annexed to the central city.

In separating themselves politically from the city, the residents of the newer neighborhoods superimposed a fragmented political system on the spatially differentiated population of the metropolis. The proliferation of suburban jurisdictions, each with independent control over access to residential, educational, and recreational opportunities within its borders, greatly reinforced the social, economic, ethnic, and racial differences among urban neighborhoods. Because of the local political boundaries which balkanize metropolitan areas into more than 20,000 units of government, no local jurisdiction encompasses the diversity of the typical metropolis. Given the spatial differentiation of residences and jobs in the metropolis, neither the need for services nor the ability to pay for them is evenly distributed among local governments whose activities are financed primarily by property and other locally based taxes. As a result, the metropolitan political economy is characterized by great variations in the costs and benefits of public services to residents of different communities. In the words of the Advisory Commission on Intergovernmental Relations, "political splintering along income and racial lines is akin to giving each rich, middle class, and poor neighborhood the power to tax, spend, and zone. Such decentralization of power can and does play hob with the goal of social justice."

Political separation of the city and suburbs has left central cities with twice as many poor residents as suburbia, four blacks for every one living in the suburbs, little room for growth, and a declining share of the metropolis's population and economic base. By cutting most cities off from the benefits of urban growth, and concentrating the most serious urban problems within city limits, the organization of autonomous suburbs has played a key role in the worsening plight of older cities. Independence from the city shields residents of suburbs from much of the public burden of providing for poor families who live in the city. Local autonomy also enhances the ability of suburbanites to exclude lower-income and minority groups, thus intensifying the concentration of the poor and blacks within the city limits. These developments, in turn, increase the attraction of independent suburbs which insulate their residents and businesses from the people and problems of older cities.

As a consequence of the political fragmentation of the metropolis, city taxpayers bear a substantially larger share of the public costs associated with lower income populations than residents of the suburbs, even though the ability of city dwellers to underwrite these expenditures usually is less than that of suburbanites. Higher taxes alone do not explain the flight of middle-income families and businesses to the suburbs, but they combine with poor schools, racial tensions, rising crime rates, and other problems in the older cities to accelerate the process. As the mayor of Camden, an aging industrial city across the Delaware River from Philadelphia, emphasized in explaining why his city lost one-fifth of its population during the 1950s and 1960s: "Business says it can't afford to locate here, and a homeowner with a $20,000 house is taxed over $1,500, about twice as much as if he owned a similar house in the suburbs."

Fiscal disparities between city and suburbs are only one result of the concentration of the poor and minority groups in the urban core. Mounting dependency has overwhelmed the public-welfare arrangements of most cities. Deteriorating city schools impel more and more middle-class families with school-age children to abandon the city for more attractive suburban school systems, while lower-income and minority families moving into neighborhoods abandoned by the middle class have found local schools ineffective and unresponsive to their needs. The concentration of blacks in the urban core means that most racial confrontation in the metropolis occurs in the central city. Competition for housing between blacks and whites takes place primarily within cities, with rapid racial neighborhood transition resulting far more often in cities than suburbs. As a result, "many central-city neighborhoods and housing markets have been in a state of frequent or continuous ferment for much of the past twenty-five years. This instability is an important qualitative difference between life in these central-city neighborhoods and in most suburban neighborhoods."

Racial concentration also makes central cities the scene of most struggles over school desegregation. Almost three-quarters of all black pupils in metropolitan areas live in the central city. Since areawide school districts are rare, almost all of these black youngsters are enrolled in central-city school systems, where they accounted for 31 per cent of all pupils in 1971. By contrast, less than seven per cent of the public-school population of the suburbs was black. Acceptance by federal courts of the boundaries of existing school districts in most metropolitan areas has made central cities the locus of almost all efforts to desegregate urban school districts. Confining integration to central cities has meant that the brunt of the busing issue—the most emotional and explosive political conflict of recent years—has been borne largely by city dwellers. School integration limited by the boundaries of the central city also is counter-productive, since whites with the means to move can escape integration by leaving the city for the sanctuary of the suburbs. In Boston, as a member of the school board points out, "no one wants to stay in the city * * * and risk busing their children to an integrated school, when they can move five miles outside of the city and send their kids to a nice, all-white neighborhood school.''

Whites who leave the city to avoid integrated schools illustrate how the combination of changing conditions in the city and the existence of the political boundary between city and suburbs push city dwellers in the direction of the suburbs. Once there, what the city has become in the bifurcated metropolis strongly reinforces the suburban desire to maintain the political separation of city and suburb. The independent suburb and local school district are widely perceived as the essential defense of the suburbanite's values which must be protected at all costs from the threat posed by the city and its dwellers. As a state legislator in the Atlanta area notes, "the suburbanite says to himself, 'The reason I worked for so many years was to get away from pollution, bad schools, and crime, and I'll be damned if I'll see it all follow me.'" In Cleveland, as in most metropolitan areas, the more recent arrivals in the suburbs often are the most hostile to those who remain in the city:

> Between 1950 and 1965 some 235,000 whites left Cleveland * * * for its suburbs. They left and continue to leave Cleveland, half with the feeling that they are being pushed out, half with the impression that they are refugees escaping to what they believe to be a liberated zone. They are not likely to be overly concerned about the plight of the city; rather they seem disposed to blame city people for their problems. * * * A large part of the hatred of the city stems from the characterization of its inhabitants as black, poor, and lawless—and thus, to most suburbanites, deserving of their plight.

Heightening suburban indifference and hostility to the city is the growing decentralization of the metropolis, which steadily reduces the number of suburbanites who come into direct contact with the city, its residents, and their problems. At the same time, the growth of crime, racial conflict, drug abuse, neighborhood decay, and other "city" problems in suburbia have not noticeably stimulated suburban concern with urban interdependence or the need for cooperative ventures with the central city. Quite the opposite has occurred in many instances. As social problems become more serious in the suburbs, suburban determination is reinforced to build the walls of political and social separation even higher in order to keep out a plague whose source is seen as the city and its lower-income and black residents.

As a result of these considerations, few in the suburbs believe that their local political jurisdiction has any obligation to contribute to the solution of the urban maladies which are concentrated in the inner city. "Responsibility?" asks a businessman in the St. Louis area, "I don't see why. What did the city ever do for us?" Similar thoughts are expressed by a suburban city manager in California: "Social problems in the city. People here would say, 'Sympathy, yes. But willingness to help? That's their tough luck. That's their problem.'" Even when the interdependence of city and suburb is perceived, it rarely leads to suburban recognition of the need for sharing of burdens. A member of the St.

Louis County Council articulates a common suburban perspective: "St. Louis has become just another neighborhood in the whole community. They're the poor cousin and we're the rich cousin and they have to accept that."

Suburbs are separated politically from each other as well as from the central city. In most metropolitan areas, suburbia is subdivided into a number of local jurisdictions, which vary in size, age, tax resources, major land uses, and, most important, the socio-economic composition of the population. Differentiation among suburbs results primarily from superimposing the small scale of the typical suburban jurisdiction on the spatial specialization of land uses and population in metropolitan areas. Differences among suburbs commonly are reinforced by the policies of local governments. Land-use controls which permit only the construction of single-family houses on large lots, or severely restrict the size and location of multiple-unit dwellings, or prohibit mobile homes affect the socio-economic composition and community character of suburban jurisdictions. So does local unwillingness to participate in subsidized housing programs, or zoning for major commercial or industrial developments.

Because neither affluent residents nor industry and commerce are equally distributed among suburban jurisdictions, wide variations exist in the tax resources available to individual units. These disparities in taxable wealth produce considerable differences in suburban tax rates and local governmental services. It is not uncommon for affluent residential suburbs, such as Weston and Dover in the Boston area, to have five times as much taxable property per capita as the poorest suburbs. Wealthy Great Neck in suburban Nassau County in the New York area can afford to spend almost three times as much per pupil as the school district which encompasses the modest homes of Levittown. In the suburbs of the Cleveland area, North Royalton can muster only half as much revenue for each of its students as Bratenahl. Inkster, a black working-class suburb in the Detroit area with almost no commercial or industrial development, has one of the highest school property-tax rates in Michigan, yet could raise only $171 per pupil in 1969. Nearby Dearborn, with a predominantly white, middle-class population and a large industrial base, had a tax rate two-thirds that of Inkster's, but raised five times as much per pupil. Even greater disparities exist between industrial enclaves and low-income bedroom suburbs. In Los Angeles County, Vernon had almost $13,000 in local revenue available for each of its 228 residents in 1965, compared with the less than $35 Baldwin Park could muster for each of its 45,000 inhabitants.

Differences in local resources, tax rates, and service levels increase the attractions of political independence and exclusionary policies in the suburbs. Jurisdictions which are well off seek to isolate themselves from the rest of the metropolis. A local official in a wealthy suburb in Southern California explains his constituents' parochialism in the following terms: "Newport Beach people don't want to identify with anything else. They came here because they don't like any other places. They like Newport Beach the way it is and they don't want it changed.'' Unwanted change can come from other suburbs as well as the central city, especially as the suburban population and economy diversify, so the walls of suburban exclusion in affluent jurisdictions are directed at outsiders from both city and suburbs. At the other end of the suburban spectrum, poor suburbs employ land-use controls to protect themselves from more lower-income residents.

As a result, lower-income and minority groups tend to be concentrated in the older and poorer suburban jurisdictions. These aging suburbs usually are adjacent to the central city, and, in the larger metropolitan areas, increasingly distant from the suburban periphery where more and more of the nation's economic growth occurs. By contrast, the expanding outer portions of the metropolis are populated primarily by middle- and upper-income families. Thus, within suburbia as in the metropolis as a whole, political fragmentation and suburban exclusion reinforce and institutionalize the spatial separation of groups along economic and social lines, and lengthen the distance between economic opportunities and the location of lower-income and black households. * * *

RICHARD FORD, THE PERPETUATION OF RACIALLY IDENTIFIED SPACES: AN ECONOMIC/STRUCTURAL ANALYSIS

From Richard Ford, The Boundaries of Race: Political Geography
in Legal Analysis, 107 Harv.L.Rev. 1841, 1849–1857 (1994).

Much traditional social and legal theory imagines that the elimination of public policies designed to promote segregation will eliminate segregation, or will at least eliminate any segregation that can be attributed to public policy and leave only the aggregate effects of individual biases (which are beyond the authority of government to remedy). This view fails, however, to acknowledge that racial segregation is embedded in and perpetuated by the social construction of racially identified political space.

TROUBLE IN PARADISE: AN ECONOMIC MODEL

Imagine a society with only two groups, blacks and whites, differentiated only by morphology (visible physical differences). Blacks, as a result of historical discrimination, tend, on average, to earn significantly less than whites. Imagine also that this society has recently (during the past twenty or thirty years) come to see the error of its discriminatory ways. It has enacted a program of reform that has totally eliminated any legal support for racial discrimination and, through a concentrated program of public education, has also succeeded in eliminating any vestige of racism from its citizenry. In short, the society has become color-blind. Such a society may feel itself well on its way to the ideal of racial justice and equality, if not already there.

Imagine also that, in our hypothetical society, small, decentralized and geographically defined governments exercise significant power to tax citizens, and use the tax revenues to provide certain public services (such as police and fire protection), public utilities (such as sewage, water and garbage collection), infrastructure development, and public education.

Finally, imagine that, before the period of racial reform, our society had in place a policy of fairly strict segregation of the races, such that every municipality consisted of two enclaves, one almost entirely white and one almost entirely black. In some cases, whites even re-incorporated their enclaves as separate municipalities to ensure the separation of the races. Thus, the now-color-blind society confronts a situation of almost complete segregation of the races—a segregation that also fairly neatly tracks a class segregation (because blacks earn, on average, far less than whites, in part because of their historical isolation from resources and job opportunities available in the wealthier and socially privileged white communities.)

We can assume that all members of this society are indifferent to the race of their neighbors, co-workers, social acquaintances, and so forth. However, we must also assume that most members of this society care a great deal about their economic well-being and are unlikely to make decisions that will adversely affect their financial situation.

Our (hypothetical) society may feel that, over time, racial segregation will dissipate in the absence of de jure discrimination and racial prejudice. But let us examine the likely outcome under these circumstances. Higher incomes in the white neighborhoods would result in larger homes and more privately financed amenities, although public expenditures would be equally distributed among white and black neighborhoods within a single municipality. However, in those municipalities that incorporated along racial lines, white cities would have substantially superior public services (or lower taxes and the same level of services) than the "mixed" cities, due to a higher average tax base. The all-black cities would, it follows, have substantially inferior public services or higher taxes as compared to the mixed cities. Consequently, the wealthier white citizens of mixed cities would have a real economic incentive to depart, or even secede, from the mixed cities, and whites in unincorporated areas would be spurred to form their own jurisdictions and resist consolidation with the larger mixed cities or all-black cities. Note that this pattern can be explained without reference to "racism": whites might be color-blind and yet prefer predominantly white or all-white neighborhoods on purely economic grounds, as long as the condition of substantial income differentiation obtains.

Of course, simply because municipalities begin as racially segregated enclaves does not mean that they will remain segregated. Presumably blacks would also prefer the higher public service amenities or lower tax burdens of white neighborhoods, and those with sufficient wealth would move in; remember, in this world there is no racism and there are no cultural differences between the races—people behave as purely rational economic actors. One might imagine that, over time, income levels will even out between the races, and blacks would move into the wealthier neighborhoods, while less fortunate whites would be outbid and would move to the formerly all-black neighborhoods. Hence racial segregation might eventually be transformed into a purely economic segregation.

This conclusion rests, however, on the assumption that residential segregation would not itself affect employment opportunities and economic status. But because the educational system is financed through local taxes, segregated localities would offer significantly different levels of educational opportunity: the poor, black cities would have poorer educational facilities than the wealthy, white cities. Thus, whites would, on average, be better equipped to obtain high-income employment than will blacks. Moreover, residential segregation would result in a pattern of segregated informal social networks; neighbors would work and play together in community organizations such as schools, PTAs, Little Leagues, Rotary Clubs, neighborhood-watch groups, cultural associations, and religious organizations. These social networks would form the basis of ties and communities of trust that open the doors of opportunity in the business world. All other things being equal, employers would hire people they know and like over people of whom they have no personal knowledge, good or bad. They would hire someone who comes with a personal recommendation from a close friend over someone without such a recommendation. Residential segregation substantially decreases the likelihood that such connections would be formed between members of different races. Finally, and more concretely, economic segregation would mean that the market value of black homes would be significantly lower than that of white homes; thus, blacks attempting to move into white neighborhoods would, on average, have less collateral with which to obtain new mortgages, or less equity to convert into cash.

Inequalities in both educational opportunity and the networking dynamic would result in fewer and less remunerative employment opportunities, and hence lower incomes, for blacks. Poorer blacks, unable to move into the more privileged neighborhoods and cities, would remain segregated; and few, if any, whites would forgo the benefits of their white neighborhoods to move into poorer black neighborhoods, which will be burdened by higher taxes or provided with inferior public services. This does not necessarily mean that income polarization and segregation would constantly increase (although at times they would), but only that they would not level out over time through a process of osmosis. Instead, every successive generation of blacks and whites would find itself in much the same situation as the previous generation, and in the absence of some intervening factor, the cycle would likely perpetuate itself. At some point an equilibrium might be achieved: generally better-connected and better-educated whites would secure the better, higher-income jobs and disadvantaged blacks would occupy the lower status and lower-wage jobs.

Thus, even in the absence of racism, race-neutral policy could be expected to entrench segregation and socio-economic stratification in a society with a history of racism. Political space plays a central role in this process. Spatially and racially defined communities perform the "work" of segregation silently. There is no racist actor or racist policy in this model, and yet a racially stratified society is the inevitable result. Although political space seems to be the inert context in which individuals make rational choices, it is in fact a controlling structure in which seemingly innocuous actions lead to racially detrimental consequences.

STRANGERS IN PARADISE: A COMPLICATED MODEL

* * * If we now introduce a few real-world complications into our model, we can see just how potent this race/space dynamic is. Suppose that (only) half of all whites in our society are in some measure racist or harbor some racial fear or concern, ranging from the open-minded liberal, who remains somewhat resistant, if only for pragmatic reasons, to mixed-race relations (Spencer Tracy's character in *Guess Who's Coming to Dinner*) to the avowed racial separatist and member of the Ku Klux Klan. Further suppose that the existence of racism produces a degree of racial fear and animosity in blacks, such that (only) half of blacks fear or distrust whites to some degree, ranging from a pragmatic belief that blacks need to "keep to their own kind," if only to avoid unnecessary confrontation and strife (Sidney Poitier's father in *Guess Who's Coming to Dinner*), to strident nationalist separatism. Let us also assume that significant cultural differences generally exist between whites and blacks.

In this model, cultural difference and socialization further entrench racial segregation. Even assuming that a few blacks would be able to attain the income necessary to move into white neighborhoods, it is less likely that they would wish to do so. Many blacks would fear and distrust whites and would be reluctant to live among them, especially in the absence of a significant number of other blacks. Likewise, many whites would resent the presence of black neighbors and would try to discourage them from entering white neighborhoods in ways both subtle and overt. The result is an effective "tax" on integration. The additional amenities and lower taxes of the white neighborhood would often be outweighed by the intangible but real costs of living as an isolated minority in an alien and sometimes hostile environment. Many blacks would undoubtedly choose to remain in black neighborhoods.

But importantly for our purposes, this dynamic would produce racially *identified* spaces. Because our hypothetical society is now somewhat racist, segregated neighborhoods would become identified by the race of their inhabitants; race would be seen as intimately related to the economic and social condition of political space. The creation of racially identified political spaces would make possible a number of regulatory activities and private practices that further entrench the segregation of the races. For example, because some whites would resent the introduction of blacks into their neighborhoods, real estate brokers would be unlikely to show property in white neighborhoods to blacks for fear that disgruntled white homeowners would boycott them.

Even within mixed cities, localities might decline to provide adequate services in black neighborhoods, and might divert funds to white neighborhoods to encourage whites with higher incomes to enter or remain in the jurisdiction. Thus, although our discussion has focused primarily on racially homogeneous jurisdictions with autonomous taxing power, the existence of such jurisdictions might affect the policy of racially heterogeneous jurisdictions, which would have to compete with the low-tax/superior-service homogeneous cities for wealthier residents. This outcome would be especially likely if the mixed jurisdictions were characterized by governmental structures resistant to participation by grassroots community groups or that are otherwise unresponsive to the citizenry as a whole. A dynamic similar to what I have posited for the homogeneous jurisdictions would occur *within* such racially mixed jurisdictions, with neighborhoods taking the place of separate jurisdictions.

Each of these phenomena would exacerbate the others, in a vicious circle of causation. The lack of public services would create a general negative image of poor, black neighborhoods; the inadequate police protection would lead to a perception of the neighborhoods as unsafe; uncollected trash would lead to a perception of the neighborhood as dirty, and so forth. Financial institutions would redline black neighborhoods—refuse to lend to property owners in these areas—because they would likely perceive them as financially risky. As a result, both real estate improvement and sale would often become unfeasible.

Strangers in a Strange Land

One might object that our model has ignored the existence of private developers who would find it profitable to build affordable housing in the white jurisdictions. These developers would be able to sell or to lease housing to blacks who would then reap the benefits of the higher tax base of their new jurisdiction. Developers would find such a venture profitable because blacks would be willing to pay a "premium" for such housing because of the lower taxes or superior public services that would come with it. Developers would have access to sufficient funds to purchase property in white neighborhoods although the individual blacks to whom they would eventually sell or lease may not. The developers would indirectly pool the resources of many blacks, thereby taking advantage of an economy of scale.

This mechanism might succeed in integrating localities and neighborhoods but for one additional real-world complication: the zoning power. Localities with the power to regulate land uses might limit the construction of multi-family housing and moderately priced detached units to certain areas of town, or might even exclude such development altogether. Localities would have a strong incentive to exclude such uses to keep lower-income individuals from diluting the municipal tax base. Again, a purely economic motivation would result in the exclusion of blacks from the municipality.

CONCLUSION: THE IMPLICATIONS FOR RACIAL HARMONY

Empirical study confirms the existence of racially identified space. The foregoing economic model demonstrates that race and class are inextricably linked in American society, and that both are linked to segregation and to the creation of racially identified political spaces. Even if racism could be magically eliminated, racial segregation would be likely to continue as long as we begin with significant income polarization and segregation of the races. Furthermore, even a relatively slight, residual racism severely complicates any effort to eliminate racial segregation that does not directly address political space and class-based segregation.

One might imagine that racism could be overcome by education and rational persuasion alone: because racism is irrational, it seems to follow that, over time, one can argue or educate it away. The model shows that even if such a project were entirely successful, in the absence of any further interventions, racial segregation would remain indefinitely.

Contemporary society imposes significant economic costs on non-segregated living arrangements. In the absence of a conscious effort to eliminate it, segregation will persist in this atmosphere (although it may appear to be the product of individual choices). The structure of racially identified space is more than the mere vestigial effect of historical racism; it is a structure that continues to exist today with nearly as much force as when policies of segregation were explicitly backed by the force of law. This structure will not gradually atrophy because it is constantly used and constantly reinforced. * * *

ROBERT FISHMAN, BOURGEOIS UTOPIAS: THE RISE AND FALL OF SUBURBIA

Pp. 3–4, 15–16 (1987).

Every civilization gets the monuments it deserves. The triumph of bourgeois capitalism seems most apparent in the massive constructions of iron and steel that celebrate the union of technology and profit: the railroad terminals, exposition halls, suspension bridges, and skyscrapers. * * * But if * * * we are seeking the architecture that best reveals "the spirit and character of modern civilization," then suburbia might tell us more about the culture that built the factories and skyscrapers than these edifices themselves can. For suburbia too was an archetypal middle-class invention, perhaps the most radical rethinking of the relation between residence and the city in the history of domestic architecture. It was founded on that primacy of the family and domestic life which was the equivalent in bourgeois society of the intense civic life celebrated by the public architecture of the ancient city. However modest each suburban house might be, suburbia represents a collective assertion of class wealth and privilege as impressive as any medieval castle. Most importantly, suburbia embodies a new ideal of family life, an ideal so emotionally charged that it made the home more sacred to the bourgeoisie than any place of worship.   * * * [T]he true center of any bourgeois society is the middle-class house.   If you seek the monuments of the bourgeoisie, go to the suburbs and look around.

Suburbia is more than a collection of residential buildings;   it expresses values so deeply embedded in bourgeois culture that it might also be called the bourgeois utopia.   Yet this "utopia" was always at most a partial paradise, a refuge not only from threatening elements in the city but also from discordant elements in bourgeois society itself. From its origins, the suburban world of leisure, family life, and union with nature was based on the principle of exclusion.   Work was excluded from the family residence;   middle-class villas were segregated from working-class housing;   the greenery of suburbia stood in contrast to a gray, polluted urban environment.   Middle-class women were especially affected by the new suburban dichotomy of work and family life.   The new environment supposedly exalted their role in the family, but it also segregated them from the world of power and productivity.   This self-segregation soon enveloped all aspects of bourgeois culture.   Suburbia, therefore, represents more than the bourgeois utopia, the triumphant assertion of middle-class values.   It also reflects the alienation of the middle classes from the urban-industrial world they themselves were creating.   * * *

If there is a single theme that differentiates the history of twentieth century suburbia from its nineteenth century antecedents, it is the attempt to secure for the whole middle class (and even for the working class as well) the benefits of suburbia, which in the classic nineteenth century suburb had been restricted to the bourgeois elite alone.   Inevitably, this attempt was to change the basic nature both of suburbia and of the larger city.   For how can a form based on the principle of exclusion include everyone?

This paradox is exemplified in the history of Los Angeles, the suburban metropolis of the twentieth century.   From its first building boom in the late nineteenth century, Los Angeles has been shaped by the promise of a suburban home for all.   The automobile and the highway when they came were no more than new tools to achieve a suburban vision that had its origins in the streetcar era.   But as population spread along the streetcar lines and the highways, the "suburbs" of Los Angeles began to lose contact with the central city, which so diminished in importance that even the new highways bypassed it.   In the 1920s, a new urban form evolved in which the industries, specialized shopping, and offices once concentrated in the urban core spread over the whole region.   By the 1930s Los Angeles had become a sprawling metropolitan region, the basic unit of which was the decentralized suburb.

This creation of a suburban metropolis signaled a fundamental shift in the relationship of the urban core and its periphery, with implications extending far beyond Los Angeles.   As we have seen, the suburb emerged during the era of urban concentration, when the limitations of communications and transportation combined to draw people and production into the crowded core. By the 1920s an interrelated technology of decentralization—of which the automobile was only one element—had begun to operate, which inexorably loosened the ties that once bound the urban functions of society to tightly defined cores. As the most important urban institutions spread out over the landscape, the suburb became part of a complex "outer city," which now included jobs as well as residences.

Increasingly independent of the urban core, the suburb since 1945 has lost its traditional meaning and function as a satellite of the central city. Where peripheral communities had once excluded industry and large scale commerce, the suburb now becomes the heartland of the most rapidly expanding elements of the late twentieth century economy. The basic concept of the suburb as a privileged zone between city and country no longer fits the realities of a posturban era in which high tech research centers sit in the midst of farmland and grass grows on abandoned factory sites in the core. As both core and periphery are swallowed up in seemingly endless multicentered regions, where can one find suburbia? * * *

SUSAN SAEGERT, MASCULINE CITIES AND FEMININE SUBURBS: POLARIZED IDEAS, CONTRADICTORY REALITIES

From C. Stimpson, E. Dixler, M. Nelson and K. Yatrakis,
Women and the American City 93–94, 108 (1981).

"Cities" and "suburbs," "men" and "women," are names of categories that encompass individual entities which are, in many ways, as different from each other as they are similar. Yet, because the commonalities that do exist are, for various reasons, important to us, we find the labels meaningful. In this paper, I will try to deal with three related uses of the words "women," "men," "suburbs," and "cities." First, they are symbols that our culture has construed as polar opposites: the city against the suburb, men against women. We have gone on to link the city with men, the suburbs with women. Next, they are both symbols and actual events in the lives of contemporary Americans who talk about themselves. Finally, they are the subjects of statistical descriptions of the distribution of people of various racial and socioeconomic groups in different residential locations, household types, and jobs. The pictures that emerge from each type of data—the cultural, the introspective self-report, and the demographic—have a certain apparent consistency. Yet, taken together, contradictions between symbols, lived experience, and demographic description become obvious. * * *

I would argue that a wide range of symbolic associations attach to women and suburbs versus men and cities, although it is not possible to document this fully in this essay. Urban life and men tend to be thought of as more aggressive, assertive, definers of important world events, intellectual, powerful, active, and sometimes dangerous. Women and suburbs share domesticity, repose, closeness to nature, lack of seriousness, mindlessness, and safety. Figuratively, women and suburbs tend to be more conservative about political and moral issues and norms. In his essay on the meaning of suburbs as a sociological concept, Barry Schwartz clearly recognizes our symbolic structuring of female/suburban and male/urban: "No wonder that male and female symbolism should distinguish city and suburb with such decisiveness. Not only to the gender of the daytime population does suburbia owe its essential femininity, but also to the domesticity which is its very *raison d'etre,* and to its corresponding alienation from the 'serious' work which has always taken place within the masculine province of the city * * *. The suburbs, in this sense, conform to the Freudian conception of femininity: passive, intellectually void, instinctually distractive * * *." When Paul Davidoff took Schwartz to task for "showing no signs of raised consciousness" in this statement, he was quite right. He was also, I think, responding from a phase of "raised consciousness" that is now giving way to a more complex analysis.

That analysis suggests that just as the female symbolism Schwartz evokes is too narrow to comprehend the real lives of women, so the suburban-urban dichotomy is too clean, too fictional, to describe their sociological, economic, and ecological actuality. Unfortunately, some of the pain and alienation women and men feel may well be engendered by the gap between the symbolic and the lived experience. Yet, these culturally bifurcated conceptions have power. They help to give rise to organizations of space and time that make real choices between domestic, private activities and public, productive ones difficult. Further, the symbolic dichotomy of female/male and suburban/urban may reinforce and reflect a variation of an actual segregation of much private life from public, socially organized productive life that perpetuates inequalities. * * *

The idealized opposition of female, domestic, private, often suburban worlds and male, productive, public, usually urban worlds does not really describe the lives of many people. Moreover, the convergence of changes in residential and occupational distribution and in female employment and family compositions suggests that a strong and intimate link, not a gap, exists between the domestic and the public spheres. Women's cheap labor, relative good manners, and educational distribution may presently make them desirable as workers from an employer's point of view, compared to the employer's image of unskilled, unruly minority workers in the city. Women, by accepting both low wages and major responsibility for domestic life, are a bargain. Here cultural and personal understandings of women and of domestic life become critical. Research shows that many women, even when they work, think of themselves first as homemakers. The vast majority of both men and women value the male world role more than the female domestic role for men. This continuing devaluation of domestic private life, and its assignment to women in the context of policies and environments, make the handling of both difficult indeed.

The segregation of public and private, male and female domains appears strongest as a guiding fiction, yet one that finds its way into public policy and planning and into women's and men's sense of who they are. This fiction places a burden of a kind of dual reality on many women: double duty at home and work, split loyalties, and too scanty a recognition of achievement in either sphere. Women's energy must go to holding together the necessary areas of life that are organized temporally and spatially to create separation. Existing separations are difficult for individuals to overcome on their own, even if they aim toward a new identity. Collective visions of an integrated life of domestic work, productive work, and leisure must inform public policy and physical planning in order to bring forth an organization of time and space in which that integration is fostered.

HADLEY ARKES, THE PHILOSOPHER IN THE CITY
Pp. 320–326 (1981).

The tendencies within American society—the interests of businesses, the preferences of householders—have moved people rather steadily out of the old central cities in the Northeast and the Midwest. Between 1960 and 1970, for example, the central cities in the fifteen largest metropolitan areas lost 836,000 civilian jobs while their suburbs gained 3,086,000. This movement to the suburbs has become so far advanced that some observers have finally urged us to acknowledge in our public policy that some cities, very plainly, may be "dying." In that event, a massive investment in these cities by the federal government might only skew the urban development of the country and waste the money of taxpayers. It may well be true, as it is often said, that the future of this nation is in our cities. But it does not follow from that aphorism that our future is bound up with the old central cities—with Newark, Philadelphia, Boston, Cleveland, and Detroit. In the movement of population in this country, in the new weights of numbers and influence in our politics, Houston has now surpassed Cleveland, Phoenix has overtaken Newark, and the 1980 census will show that Dallas has exceeded Boston in population.

But even apart from regional shifts, there has been a general move away from settlements of high density. Over 70 percent of the population does live in urban centers, and in that sense it could be said that America is an urban nation. Yet only one person in ten lives in a city with a population over one million, and it has become clear in recent years that the attraction to the city has become weaker rather than stronger. In one study carried out in the mid–60's, the Survey Research Center of the University of Michigan interviewed people in thirty-two metropolitan areas about the kinds of places in which they preferred to live. About 85 percent of the respondents said that they preferred to live in houses designed for single families (and the state of this arrangement as an ideal was underscored by the fact that two-thirds of the people in the sample did not live at the moment in single-family dwellings). Only 15 percent wished to live in the center of town; 25 percent preferred to live farther away from the city; and for four people out of ten even the suburbs were not far enough away (they preferred to live in the countryside).

At about the same time, a Gallup survey found that nearly half of the respondents living in cities of 50,000 or over said that they would like to live somewhere else (a suburb, small town, or farm area), and very few people in the suburbs expressed any wish to move back to the city. By the 1970's the metropolitan areas in the country were actually beginning to show a net loss of population to nonmetropolitan areas. As William Alonso noted, one-sixth of all metropolitan areas lost population in the period 1970–1974, and in 1974 the proportion increased to one-fourth. By 1978 half of the people who were living in metropolitan areas were living in places which were losing population. In this respect, the surveys seem to bear out the observation that the American notion of urban living has never been quite the same as that of Europeans. Even within the old central cities the tendency in America has been to recreate, in the outer sections of these areas, the aspect of a more spacious country life, dominated by the presence of small, independent households—the yeoman farmer, as it were, transferred to the urban setting. In 1960, over 60 percent of the dwelling units in the United States consisted of houses that were owned and occupied by single families, and as Daniel Elazar has pointed out, that was essentially comparable to the proportion of small, single-family farms that existed in the United States in 1900.

Some commentators have suggested that the American ethic may actually be "anti-urban" because of the persisting preference for smaller communities with less concentration. But then again, size was not always thought to be the most decisive condition for the things that were most important in the city—not, at least, in the period before cities were seen as little more than great mercantile centers. Nor is it clear that size is so critical any longer for the amenities that many people have found attractive in large cities. It has been estimated, for example, that a library meeting minimum professional standards may be supported with a population base of about 50,000 to 75,000. An art museum may be sustained with a base of 100,000, and the figure may be only somewhat higher for museums of science and history. We know that the support for institutions such as libraries, symphony orchestras, and the theater has usually come from a minority of the middle and upper classes, and there is no reason why some of these institutions cannot be recreated in suburbs of sufficient size, where like-minded people can concentrate their tastes and their purchasing power. In fact, there has been some suggestion in recent studies that the optimal size of an American community may be between 50,000 and 200,000. Apart from water and sewage, an increase in size does not seem to reduce unit costs for most services, and the slight gains in economy that occur in the supply of water and the tending of sewage may be offset very easily by larger expenses in other areas, such as welfare and police.

But in the classic view, and in the view that comes to us in more modern times from Rousseau, the availability of theater tickets is decidedly less important for the city than the possibilities for citizenship. And that view has not been so remote from the motives that have led many people to leave the cities for the suburbs and smaller communities. A good portion of that movement has been impelled, of course, by the search for better housing and for areas of lower density. But as Nathan Glazer has argued, that movement has also involved motives that reach back ultimately to the concern for community. There has been an evident desire for a simpler and more penetrable form of government, which is not as distant or as hard to deal with as the formidable bureaucracies in the central cities. There has been an aversion to the corruption and manipulation of machine politics, and there has been a concern, also, to create a community with a definition of its own, which can express its character in its public policies. In this perspective, the issue of size is important, and it raises the enduring question of appropriate inclusion or exclusion: who should be included in the community, and who should be excluded, if the community is to preserve its special character?

It would be a grave mistake, then, to interpret these population movements as little more than movements of convenience. Even if they had started out in that way for many people, it was in the nature of things that they would become something more. The decision as to whether to leave the central city (and where precisely to settle in the suburbs) implied a judgment about the kind of people one wished to live with, and the conditions under which one expected to live. It is not so surprising, therefore, that suburban areas have been very sensitive about guarding their control over matters that make a difference to the character of the local community. They have been willing to participate in metropolitan schemes for water, sewage, and transportation, but they have been reluctant to transfer powers over zoning, and they have been especially adamant in clinging to control over education. Even where so-called metropolitan governments have been created in the United States, the suburban areas have usually managed to secure considerable autonomy in the governance and funding of their own schools. In other words, the suburbs have been quite willing to make use of metropolitan schemes when they involve simply the provision of technical services, but they have been inclined to resist the creation of any institutions at the metropolitan level which could imply a serious amalgamation of purpose.

Of course, "metropolitan government" has had an enduring appeal to those people in the academy and government who identify "efficiency" with larger units, and who are prepared to find, in the abstract, that the proliferation of small governments is likely to create "irrational," "uncoordinated" policies. These people are also apt to show, in demonstrations that usually surprise no one, that the suburbs and the central city are "economically interdependent." But as Aristotle recognized, the fact that people trade with one another rather extensively does not mean that they care to be brought together in a more solemn association, as citizens in a common polity. Nor does it suggest that it would be good for them to be joined in that way. Local communities have shown on a number of occasions that, given a choice between efficiency and control, they would prefer governments closer to home even if they were a bit more expensive. And quite apart from the advantages that may flow in certain instances from economies of scale, the preference for keeping governments smaller may result quite often in expenditures that are far more disciplined and, by any reckoning, much more efficient.

Most people are likely to be immune, however, from the impulses that grip experts on public administration; and so, if a number of communities have talked themselves into forms of metropolitan government, it can usually be assumed that this change has little to do with any passion, lately conceived, for administrative "co-ordination." In many cases a more melancholy assessment would probably also be a more accurate one: viz., that schemes for metropolitan government have been more appealing when they have offered a device for neutralizing the political power of blacks, especially in those instances in which blacks have appeared to be on the verge of a political breakthrough in the central city. In that event, the black organizations in the city could be overcome by vesting decisions in a larger board or agency for the metropolitan region. And in that order of things the city could be outvoted by communities in the suburban ring, while the whole arrangement may be buttressed by federal grants for planning, along with federal regulations and procedures. The result may be to reduce even further the range of choice available to public officials, and to hem in political leaders in the inner cities as they try to extend their influence to the suburbs. The discussion of policy in this setting goes forward in a rather specialized, technical idiom, carried on by lawyers with experience in the most rarified callings. Altogether, the complex may simply be too formidable for a layman or a politician to penetrate, and it is not the kind of arena in which black politicians from the inner city are likely to do well.

The movement away from the cities cannot be understood, then, without recognizing that it is in part, at least, a flight from the political authority of the city; and those who have settled in the suburbs are not eager to be linked to the city again, either through devices for regional government or through the decisions, say, of courts to bus children to school across municipal lines. The current in recent years has been in the direction of smaller communities, where there may be a larger possibility for the sharing of public purposes. If public policy becomes unacceptable on any decisive point, there is the prospect of moving to another community; and so the problem of moral discordance may be softened by a combination of freedom of choice and the powers that are still preserved in local communities to define their own character. * * *

Who decides—who should decide—how many separate jurisdictions should be created in America? In most states, according to Professor Richard Briffault, "the principal criterion for deciding whether a municipality will be incorporated is whether the local people want it. There are few limits on local discretion." [1] The following case examines the constitutionality of a much more limited local voice in incorporation decisions. Given the analysis in the case, is what Professor Briffault describes as the general rule unconstitutional?

BOARD OF SUPERVISORS OF SACRAMENTO COUNTY v. LOCAL AGENCY FORMATION COMMISSION

Supreme Court of California, 1992.
3 Cal.4th 903, 13 Cal.Rptr.2d 245, 838 P.2d 1198, cert. denied,
___ U.S. ___, 113 S.Ct. 1588, 123 L.Ed.2d 154 (1993).

MOSK, JUSTICE.

Residents of an unincorporated area of Sacramento County seek to incorporate into a city. Government Code section 57103 provides that only the voters residing in the territory to be incorporated may vote to confirm the incorporation. The Court of Appeal found this law unconstitutional as applied, holding that it violates the guaranty of equal protection of the laws. We conclude that the law is constitutional, both on its face and as applied to the incorporation at issue.

The case before us illustrates the tension between California's financially beleaguered counties and the desire of residents of unincorporated areas to form cities and draw local government closer to home. With the fall in tax rates following the adoption of Proposition 13 in 1978, and a concomitant population-driven rise in demand for services, this tension has grown in recent years: at least one California county has considered bankruptcy and, like the state itself, all counties have had to make painful spending decisions. The counties fear that if tax-rich districts form cities, the counties will be deprived of revenue and their financial position further weakened. On the other hand, community residents and landowners often prefer to govern their local affairs insofar as possible, and cityhood provides them with greater opportunities for self-determination than does residence or ownership in a more amorphous unincorporated area. The evolution of cities is a natural

---

1. Briffault, Our Localism: Part I—The Structure of Local Government Law, 90 Colum.L.Rev. 1, 74 (1990).

In most states, general enabling legislation places municipal incorporation in the hands of local residents or landowners. State laws provide for the initiation of the process by petitions signed by some number or percentage of local residents or landowners. Thereafter, an election is held in which local residents or landowners participate, and if a requisite percent-

age of the local electorate approves the incorporation goes forward. Neighboring localities, regional entities and residents outside of the boundaries of the territory proposed to be incorporated generally have no role. Judicial or administrative review is usually ministerial and limited to a determination of whether the signature, voting and other formal requirements have been met.

Id.

process when population grows and communities begin to form their own identities.

Acknowledging the tension between fiscal concerns and the desire for self-government, the Legislature enacted the Cortese–Knox Local Government Reorganization Act of 1985. * * * The * * * Act requires that every unconsolidated county have a local agency formation commission, appointed by local lawmaking bodies, to "review and approve or disapprove with or without amendment, wholly, partially, or conditionally, proposals for changes of organization or reorganization* * *." * * * The commission cannot act on an incorporation petition unless signed by not less than 25 percent of the registered voters residing in the territory of the proposed city or by not less than 25 percent of the landowners, which latter group must also own not less than 25 percent of the assessed land value. * * * [T]he commission * * * [has] the power to approve or disapprove an incorporation in whole or in part. But the Cortese–Knox Act does not give the commission carte blanche to approve incorporations. Its discretion is limited by [the] requirement[ ], among others, * * * that the proposed city likely will be fiscally sound for three fiscal years following its incorporation. * * * In reviewing an incorporation proposal, the commission is required to consider a multitude of factors.[7] * * * The commission may make its approval conditional on a virtually limitless array of factors, which are set forth in detail in * * * [the Act].[8] * * * After the commission has completed its inquiry and issued a resolution approving or disapproving the proposal, a county, or others affected by the decision, may request reconsideration. * * * Once the commission has issued its final resolution, the matter is in the hands of the "conducting authority," which in this case is the Sacramento County Board of Supervisors. The board must conduct a public hearing on the proposal. If more than 50 percent of the voters in the territory to be incorporated protest the incorporation, the board must end the proceedings. Otherwise it must order the incorporation, subject to the voters' "confirmation."

As the foregoing recitation reveals, the voters' role under the Cortese–Knox Act in confirming an incorporation is rather like that of the masons who place a keystone at the apex of a high and intricate arch. The voters' approval is an essential piece, but as we have shown,

---

7. These include but are not limited to: "(a) Population, population density; land area and land use; per capita assessed valuation; topography [and] natural boundaries * * *; proximity to other populated areas; the likelihood of significant growth in the area, and in adjacent incorporated and unincorporated areas, during the next 10 years.

(b) * * * [T]he present cost and adequacy of governmental services * * *; probable future needs for those services. * * *

(c) The effect of the proposed action * * * on adjacent areas, on mutual social and economic interests, and on the local governmental structure of the county. * * *"

8. These include reimbursement for the acquisition or use of public property, apportionment of bond obligations between the county and the proposed city, the incurring of new debt, property transfers, employee discharges and modification or termination of employment contracts, and the transfer of authority and responsibility among any affected cities and counties for the administration of special tax and special assessment districts.

by the time the question reaches the electorate the incorporation proposal will already have undergone a labyrinthine process containing elaborate safeguards designed to protect the political and economic interests of affected local governments, residents, and landowners. * * *

In 1986 persons in the unincorporated Sacramento County community of Citrus Heights, containing a population of approximately 69,000, collected enough valid signatures to qualify an incorporation petition to the Sacramento County Local Agency Formation Commission (commission), which * * * [under the Cortese–Knox Act] supervises municipal incorporations in the county. Following an environmental review and other proceedings, the commission * * * approved a resolution * * * [which] contained a provision designed to mitigate the financial impact on the county: the proposed city limits were relocated to exclude a sales-tax-rich shopping center. Requests for reconsideration of that resolution followed, in part on the ground that the boundaries still unfairly impacted the county's tax base. The commission adopted a new resolution that moved another shopping center outside the proposed city limits, and then, to further mitigate the county's financial loss, amended that resolution to require that the new city's receipt of property taxes be phased in more slowly. In accordance with section 57103, the commission ordered a confirming election to be held only within the territory of the proposed city.

This lawsuit followed. Plaintiffs include the Sacramento County Board of Supervisors, the Sacramento County Deputy Sheriffs' Association, and Sacramentans to Save our Services. * * * Displeased, among other things, with the law's limitation of the confirming election to the voters in the territory to be incorporated, plaintiffs challenged the limitation's constitutionality on the ground that section 57103 denies them equal protection of the laws. (U.S. Const., Amend. XIV, § 1; Cal. Const., art. 1, § 7.) * * * The question we confront * * * is whether section 57103 impinges on the right to vote in a manner that requires the application of strict scrutiny. As will appear, the statute does not compel that standard of review.

We agree that section 57103 touches on the right to vote. As it happens, the right to vote does not include a right to compel the state to provide any electoral mechanism whatever for changes of municipal organization. Such line-drawing is a function that the Legislature may reserve to itself. But when the state has provided for the voters' direct input, the equal protection clause requires that those similarly situated not be treated differently unless the disparity is justified. * * * [F]ederal precedent requires that we view all Sacramento County residents as similarly situated, for all are affected to some degree by the proposed incorporation.

The mere fact, however, that a state law touches on the right to vote does not necessarily require the application of strict scrutiny. Rather, "the 'compelling interest' measure must be applied if a classification has a 'real and appreciable impact' upon the equality, fairness and integrity of the electoral process." (*Choudhry v. Free* (1976) 17 Cal.3d 660, 664, 131 Cal.Rptr. 654, 552 P.2d 438, quoting *Bullock v. Carter* (1972) 405 U.S. 134, 144, 92 S.Ct. 849, 856, 31 L.Ed.2d 92.) * * * [S]ection 57103's impact in the case before us falls well short of the "real and appreciable," for individual interests in voting are much attenuated by the state's plenary power to oversee and regulate the formation of its political subdivisions, and the same power entitles the state to identify as differing in degree the interests of those who may vote under section 57103 and those who may not.

In our federal system the states are sovereign but cities and counties are not; in California as elsewhere they are mere creatures of the state and exist only at the state's sufferance. Accordingly, the United States Supreme Court has long recognized the states' plenary power to create and dissolve their political subdivisions. In *Hunter v. Pittsburgh* (1907) 207 U.S. 161, 28 S.Ct. 40, 52 L.Ed. 151, * * * [t]he federal high court, noting that "[m]unicipal corporations are political subdivisions of the State," concluded, "The number, nature and duration of the powers conferred upon these corporations and the territory over which they shall be exercised rests in the absolute discretion of the State. * * *" The foregoing language is, of course, immediately noteworthy for the breadth of its scope, and to a certain extent it bespeaks the judicial confidence of a simpler era. But *Hunter's* fundamental holding survives. * * * Thus, though the right to vote is perforce implicated whenever the state specifies that certain people may vote and others may not, we conclude that the essence of this case is not the fundamental right to vote, but the state's plenary power to set the conditions under which its political subdivisions are created. For that reason, the impairment of the right to vote is insufficiently implicated to demand the application of strict scrutiny.

We reach the foregoing conclusion notwithstanding our prior decisions in this area. *Fullerton [Joint Union High School Dist. v. State Bd. of Education* (1982) 32 Cal.3d 779, 805, 187 Cal.Rptr. 398, 654 P.2d 168 (*Fullerton*)], considered the constitutionality of a State Board of Education * * * decision to carve a new school district in Yorba Linda from its Fullerton parent. The education board ordered an election to be held on the secession, and ordered the question submitted to the Yorba Linda electorate only. *Fullerton* overturned the education board's decision.

Fullerton's reasoning is embodied in a plurality opinion signed by three justices. The plurality concluded that the equal protection clause required strict scrutiny to be applied to the education board's decision to limit the vote to Yorba Linda residents. The plurality reasoned that because the decision impinged more than marginally or incidentally on the right to vote, it could be given effect only if the education board could show that it had a compelling interest in excluding the Fullerton residents and that the distinction was necessary to further its purpose. * * * *Fullerton's* plurality opinion evinces a great concern that failure to apply strict scrutiny to the election at issue could result in racial segregation. It acquiesces in but describes as "questionable" an administrative decision that the secession would not promote segregation. Hence, notwithstanding the agency finding, the plurality found an equal protection violation in part because "the racial and financial impact of that Plan are matters of great concern to the residents who will remain in the Fullerton [high school district]." In the case at bench the parties have not alluded to any similar racial impact: the impact is purely economic.

The issue in *Citizens [Against Forced Annexation v. Local Agency Formation Com.* (1982) 32 Cal.3d 816, 826, 187 Cal.Rptr. 423, 654 P.2d 193 (*Citizens*)] was whether the Municipal Organization Act of 1977 constitutionally entitled the state to limit an election to confirm an annexation to residents of the territory to be annexed. The city in question had about 40,000 voters, while the territory to be annexed had about a quarter as many. The Legislature had provided that although under certain circumstances, applicable in *Citizens*, the territory's voters must confirm the annexation, the annexing city's voters could also vote to confirm the joinder only if, as relevant to the analysis in *Citizens*, the number of registered voters in the territory was 50 percent or more of those in the city.

Unlike in *Fullerton*, a bare majority concurred in the reasoning of *Citizens*. We decided that "the establishment of the legal relationship contemplated in this case, like the dissolution of a legal relationship involved in *Fullerton*, has a substantial effect upon the residents of both territories involved. We therefore conclude that the relevant geographic confines, for the purpose of constitutional analysis, include[ ] both the affected territory and the affected city. We must therefore inquire whether the restrictions * * * serve a compelling state interest and are necessary to further that purpose."

Applying strict scrutiny, we noted that the government may have a compelling interest to limit the vote to those "specially interested in the matter at issue". * * * [W]e decided that the state has a compelling interest in permitting unincorporated areas to join cities "even if the city's residents oppose annexation", because the state's interest in "promoting orderly and logical community development, and of providing municipal services to newly urbanized regions" was "of compelling importance," and the state's interest would be thwarted if city residents could veto the annexation.

Because *Citizens* commanded a majority of this court, it requires our considered reexamination. As we now explain, we conclude in hindsight that the reasoning in that case was questionable.

For one, we now find faulty the holding of *Citizens* that a compelling interest in excluding less interested potential voters justified city voters' exclusion because the territory to be annexed contained less than half the number of voters residing in the city. If strict scrutiny is given to an exclusionary voting scheme, the interest of those excluded from the election must be substantially less than that of those included for the scheme to pass muster. (*Kramer v. Union School District* (1969) 395

U.S. 621, 632, 89 S.Ct. 1886, 1892, 23 L.Ed.2d 583.) It is impossible for us to now reconcile *Citizens* with the federal high court's prescription. We can no longer conclude that the city residents' interest in the election outcome was so insubstantial for equal protection purposes: the annexation would have increased the city's size by almost one-quarter. * * *

Given that conclusion, we also find constitutionally infirm the reliance of *Citizens* on the goals of orderly development and provision of municipal services to justify the city voters' exclusion from the election. As mentioned above, *Citizens* reasoned that the exclusion was justifiable because the city dwellers might veto the annexation, thereby interfering with those goals. But if the city residents have a fundamental right to vote, then the state's putative interest in excluding them from voting because they might veto the annexation is constitutionally impermissible. * * * As *Carrington* explained, " 'Fencing out' from the franchise a sector of the population because of the way they may vote is constitutionally impermissible." (*Carrington v. Rash* (1965) 380 U.S. 89, 94, 85 S.Ct. 775, 779, 13 L.Ed.2d 675.)

To the extent that *Citizens* is inconsistent with the constitutional principles set forth in this opinion, it is not to be followed. * * * If we were to follow *Citizens*, and apply strict scrutiny, we would now be compelled to declare section 57103 invalid on constitutional grounds. Such a holding would greatly unbalance the Legislature's careful accommodation of competing local governmental and private interests in the subsequently enacted Cortese–Knox Act and would undermine the lawmakers' power over the existence of cities and counties. In such circumstances stare decisis carries less weight. * * *

We conclude that under applicable precedent we should apply a deferential standard in evaluating the classification set forth on the face of section 57103. The Legislature's traditional power to regulate the formation of political subdivisions allows it to decide that the county residents living outside the territory to be incorporated have a lesser degree of interest in the proposed incorporation than those within, in which case the classification must be denied effect only if it lacks a rational basis. * * *

In section 56001 [of the Cortese–Knox Act] the Legislature announced a policy "to encourage orderly growth and development * * * essential to the social, fiscal, and economic well-being of the state," and stated that "the logical formation and determination of local agency boundaries is an important factor in promoting orderly development* * *. [T]he Legislature further finds and declares that this policy should be effected by the logical formation and modification of the boundaries of local agencies."

The foregoing sufficiently shows a legitimate purpose in enacting section 57103. And we conclude that section 57103 is fairly related to the Legislature's declared purpose, for, if large, relatively disinterested majorities could veto incorporations decided through the Cortese–Knox Act's elaborate process, the result might well hinder orderly growth and development. * * * Unlike in *Fullerton*, which involved a discretionary agency decision to hold an election, the Cortese–Knox Act was constructed with a mighty bulwark against the exercise of arbitrary discretion. The act accommodates competing local governmental and private interests, narrowly channeling the commission's ultimate determination before the territory's voters consider the decision. The election merely asks the affected residents to confirm that they desire self-government. To deny the Legislature the authority to let the potentially incorporating territory's voters have the final say in the matter would be to lessen political participation, not increase it. We do not believe that result is required by our federal and state Constitutions. * * *

2. THE DISTINCTION BETWEEN RESIDENTS AND NON–RESIDENTS

The following two cases begin our examination of the relationship between city residents and outsiders. The case of Holt Civic Club v. City of Tuscaloosa involves a city's exercise of regulatory power on people who live outside its borders and who have no voice in electing city officials or determining city policy. This kind of exercise of extraterritorial power over neighboring areas is very common in the United States.[1] Yet, as Justice Brennan argues in his dissenting opinion, such a practice of extraterritorial regulation raises fundamental questions about "our basic conception of a 'political community.'" Perhaps surprisingly, there is no Constitutional principle in the United States that prohibits regulation—or taxation—without representation. Should there be? How can an exercise of extraterritorial power be justified? What importance do the two opinions in the *Holt* case attribute to the boundary that divides those who live in a city from those who live outside it? What impact does the *Holt* case have on the ability of cities to regulate suburban residents?

HOLT CIVIC CLUB v. CITY OF TUSCALOOSA

Supreme Court of the United States, 1978.
439 U.S. 60, 99 S.Ct. 383, 58 L.Ed.2d 292.

Mr. Justice Rehnquist delivered the opinion of the Court.

Holt is a small, largely rural, unincorporated community located on the northeastern outskirts of Tuscaloosa, the fifth largest city in Alabama. Because the community is within the three-mile police jurisdiction circumscribing Tuscaloosa's corporate limits, its residents are subject to the city's "police and sanitary regulations." Ala.Code § 11–40–10 (1975). Holt residents are also subject to the criminal jurisdiction of the

---

1. See generally, Comment, The Constitutionality of the Exercise of Extraterritorial Powers by Municipalities, 45 Chi.L.Rev. 151 (1977); Becker, Municipal Boundaries and Zoning: Controlling Regional Land Development, 1966 Wash.U.L.Q. 1; Sengstock, Extraterritorial Powers in the Metropolitan Area (1962); Maddox, The Extraterritorial Powers of Municipalities in the United States (1955); Anderson, The Extraterritorial Power of Cities, 10 Minn.L.Rev. 475 (1926).

city's court, and to the city's power to license businesses, trades, and professions. Tuscaloosa, however, may collect from businesses in the police jurisdiction only one-half of the license fee chargeable to similar businesses conducted within the corporate limits.

In 1973 appellants, an unincorporated civic association and seven individual residents of Holt, brought this statewide class action in the United States District Court for the Northern District of Alabama, challenging the constitutionality of these Alabama statutes. They claimed that the city's extraterritorial exercise of police powers over Holt residents, without a concomitant extension of the franchise on an equal footing with those residing within the corporate limits, denies residents of the police jurisdiction rights secured by the Due Process and Equal Protection Clauses of the Fourteenth Amendment. * * *

The unconstitutional predicament in which appellants assertedly found themselves could be remedied in only two ways: (1) the city's extraterritorial power could be negated by invalidating the State's authorizing statutes or (2) the right to vote in municipal elections could be extended to residents of the police jurisdiction. * * *

Appellants focus their equal protection attack on § 11–40–10, the statute fixing the limits of municipal police jurisdiction and giving extraterritorial effect to municipal police and sanitary ordinances. Citing *Kramer v. Union Free School Dist.,* 395 U.S. 621, 89 S.Ct. 1886, 23 L.Ed.2d 583 (1969), and cases following in its wake, appellants argue that the section creates a classification infringing on their right to participate in municipal elections. The State's denial of the franchise to police jurisdiction residents, appellants urge, can stand only if justified by a compelling state interest.

At issue in *Kramer* was a New York voter qualification statute that limited the vote in school district elections to otherwise qualified district residents who (1) either owned or leased taxable real property located within the district, (2) were married to persons owning or leasing qualifying property, or (3) were parents or guardians of children enrolled in a local district school for a specified time during the preceding year. Without deciding whether or not a State may in some circumstances limit the franchise to residents primarily interested or primarily affected by the activities of a given governmental unit, the court held that the statute was not sufficiently tailored to meet that state interest since its classifications excluded many bona fide residents of the school district who had distinct and direct interests in school board decisions and included many residents whose interests in school affairs were, at best, remote and indirect.

On the same day, in *Cipriano v. City of Houma,* 395 U.S. 701, 89 S.Ct. 1897, 23 L.Ed.2d 647 (1969), the Court upheld an equal protection challenge to a Louisiana law providing that only "property taxpayers" could vote in elections called to approve the issuance of revenue bonds by a municipal utility system. Operation of the utility system affected virtually every resident of the city, not just property owners, and the bonds were in no way financed by property tax revenue. Thus, since the benefits and burdens of the bond issue fell indiscriminately on property owner and nonproperty owner alike, the challenged classification impermissibly excluded otherwise qualified residents who were substantially affected and directly interested in the matter put to a referendum. The rationale of *Cipriano* was subsequently called upon to invalidate an Arizona law restricting the franchise to property taxpayers in elections to approve the issuance of general obligation municipal bonds. *Phoenix v. Kolodziejski,* 399 U.S. 204, 90 S.Ct. 1990, 26 L.Ed.2d 523 (1970).

Appellants also place heavy reliance on *Evans v. Cornman,* 398 U.S. 419, 90 S.Ct. 1752, 26 L.Ed.2d 370 (1970). In *Evans* the Permanent Board of Registry of Montgomery County, Maryland, ruled that persons living on the grounds of the National Institute of Health (NIH), a federal enclave located within the geographical boundaries of the State, did not meet the residency requirement of the Maryland Constitution. Accordingly, NIH residents were denied the right to vote in Maryland elections. This Court rejected the notion that persons living on NIH grounds were not residents of Maryland:

> "Appellees clearly live within the geographical boundaries of the State of Maryland, and they are treated as State residents in the census and in determining congressional apportionment. They are not residents of Maryland only if the NIH grounds ceased to be a part of Maryland when the enclave was created. However, that 'fiction of a state within a state' was specifically rejected by this Court in *Howard v. Commissioners of Louisville,* 344 U.S. 624, 627, 73 S.Ct. 465, 467, 97 L.Ed. 617 (1953), and it cannot be resurrected here to deny appellees the right to vote."

Thus, because inhabitants of the NIH enclave were residents of Maryland and were "just as interested in and connected with electoral decisions as they were prior to 1953 when the area came under federal jurisdiction and as their neighbors who live off the enclave," the State could not deny them the equal right to vote in Maryland elections.

From these and our other voting qualifications cases a common characteristic emerges: the challenged statute in each case denied the franchise to individuals who were physically resident within the geographic boundaries of the governmental entity concerned. * * *

No decision of this Court has extended the "one man, one vote" principle to individuals residing beyond the geographic confines of the governmental entity concerned, be it the State or its political subdivisions. On the contrary, our cases have uniformly recognized that a government unit may legitimately restrict the right to participate in its political processes to those who reside within its borders.

Appellants' argument that extraterritorial extension of municipal powers requires concomitant extraterritorial extension of the franchise proves too much. The imaginary line defining a city's corporate limits cannot corral the influence of municipal actions. A city's decisions inescapably affect individuals living immediately outside its borders.

The granting of building permits for highrise apartments, industrial plants, and the like on the city's fringe unavoidably contributes to problems of traffic congestion, school districting, and law enforcement immediately outside the city. A rate change in the city's sales or ad valorem tax could well have a significant impact on retailers and property values in areas bordering the city. The condemnation of real property on the city's edge for construction of a municipal garbage dump or waste treatment plant would have obvious implications for neighboring nonresidents. Indeed, the indirect extraterritorial effects of many purely internal municipal actions could conceivably have a heavier impact on surrounding environs than the direct regulation contemplated by Alabama's police jurisdiction statutes. Yet no one would suggest that nonresidents likely to be affected by this sort of municipal action have a constitutional right to participate in the political processes bringing it about. And unless one adopts the idea that the Austinian notion of sovereignty, which is presumably embodied to some extent in the authority of a city over a police jurisdiction, distinguishes the direct effects of limited municipal powers over police jurisdiction residents from the indirect though equally dramatic extraterritorial effects of purely internal municipal actions, it makes little sense to say that one requires extension of the franchise while the other does not.

Given this country's tradition of popular sovereignty, appellants' claimed right to vote in Tuscaloosa elections is not without some logical appeal. We are mindful, however, of Justice Holmes' observation in *Hudson Water Co. v. McCarter,* 209 U.S. 349, 355, 28 S.Ct. 529, 531, 52 L.Ed. 828 (1906):

> "All rights tend to declare themselves absolute to their logical extreme. Yet all in fact are limited by the neighborhood of principles of policy which are other than those on which the particular right is founded, and which become strong enough to hold their own when a certain point is reached. * * * The boundary at which the conflicting interests balance cannot be determined by any general formula in advance, but points in the line, or helping to establish it, are fixed by decisions that this or that concrete case falls on the nearer or farther side."

The line heretofore marked by this Court's voting qualifications decisions coincides with the geographical boundary of the governmental unit at issue, and we hold that appellants' case, like their homes, falls on the farther side.

Thus stripped of its voting rights attire, the equal protection issue presented by appellants becomes whether the Alabama statutes giving extraterritorial force to certain municipal ordinances and powers bear some rational relationship to a legitimate state purpose. *San Antonio School Dist. v. Rodriguez,* 411 U.S. 1, 93 S.Ct. 1278, 36 L.Ed.2d 16 (1973). "The Fourteenth Amendment does not prohibit legislation merely because it is special, or limited in its application to a particular geographical or political subdivision of the state." *Fort Smith Light Co.*

v. Paving Dist., 274 U.S. 387, 391, 47 S.Ct. 595, 597, 71 L.Ed. 1112 (1927). Rather, the Equal Protection Clause is offended only if the statute's classification "rests on grounds wholly irrelevant to the achievement of the State's objective." *McGowan v. Maryland,* 366 U.S. 420, 425, 81 S.Ct. 1101, 1104, 6 L.Ed.2d 393 (1961).

Government, observed Mr. Justice Johnson, "is the science of experiment," *Anderson v. Dunn,* 6 Wheat. 204, 226, 5 L.Ed. 242, 247 (1821), and a State is afforded wide leeway when experimenting with the appropriate allocation of state legislative power. This Court has often recognized that political subdivisions such as cities and counties are created by the State "as convenient agencies for exercising such of the governmental powers of the state as may be entrusted to them." *E.g., Sailors v. Board of Education,* 387 U.S. at 108, 87 S.Ct. at 1552; *Reynolds v. Sims,* 377 U.S. 533, 575, 84 S.Ct. 1362, 12 L.Ed.2d 506 (1964); *Hunter v. City of Pittsburgh,* 207 U.S. 161, 178, 28 S.Ct. 40, 46, 52 L.Ed. 151 (1907). In *Hunter v. City of Pittsburgh,* the Court discussed at length the relationship between a State and its political subdivisions, remarking: "The number, nature and duration of the powers conferred upon [municipal] corporations and the territory over which they shall be exercised rests in the absolute discretion of the state." While the broad statements as to state control over municipal corporations contained in *Hunter v. City of Pittsburgh,* have undoubtedly been qualified by the holdings of later cases such as *Kramer v. Union Free School Dist.,* we think that the case continues to have substantial constitutional significance in emphasizing the extraordinarily wide latitude that states have in creating various types of political subdivisions and conferring authority upon them.[7]

The extraterritorial exercise of municipal powers is a governmental technique neither recent in origin nor unique to the State of Alabama. See R. Maddox, Extraterritorial Powers of Municipalities in the United States (1955). In this country 35 States authorize their municipal subdivisions to exercise governmental powers beyond their corporate limits. Comment, The Constitutionality of the Exercise of Extraterritorial Powers by Municipalities, 45 Chi.L.Rev. 151 (1977). Although the extraterritorial municipal powers granted by these States vary widely, several States grant their cities more extensive or intrusive powers over bordering areas than those granted under the Alabama statutes.[8]

---

7. In this case residents of the police jurisdiction are excluded only from participation in municipal elections since they reside outside of Tuscaloosa's corporate limits. This "denial of the franchise," as appellants put it, does not have anything like the far-reaching consequences of the denial of the franchise in *Evans v. Cornman,* 398 U.S. 419, 90 S.Ct. 1752, 26 L.Ed.2d 370 (1970). There the Court pointed out that "[i]n nearly every election, federal, state, and local, for offices from the Presidency to the school board, and on the entire variety

of other ballot propositions, appellees have a stake equal to that of other Maryland residents." Treatment of the plaintiffs in *Evans* as nonresidents of Maryland had repercussions not merely with respect to their right to vote in city elections, but with respect to their right to vote in national, state, school board, and referendum elections.

8. Municipalities in some States have most almost unrestricted governmental powers over surrounding unincorporated territories. * * * [W]e do not mean to

In support of their equal protection claim, appellants suggest a number of "constitutionally preferable" governmental alternatives to Alabama's system of municipal police jurisdictions. For example, exclusive management of the police jurisdiction by county officials, appellants maintain, would be more "practical." From a political science standpoint, appellants' suggestions may be sound, but this Court does not sit to determine whether Alabama has chosen the soundest or most practical form of internal government possible. Authority to make those judgments resides in the state legislature, and Alabama citizens are free to urge their proposals to that body. See, *e.g., Hunter v. City of Pittsburgh, supra.* Our inquiry is limited to the question whether "any state of facts reasonably may be conceived to justify" Alabama's system of police jurisdictions, *Salyer Land Co. v. Tulare Water Dist.,* 410 U.S., at 732, 93 S.Ct., at 1231 (1973), and in this case it takes but momentary reflection to arrive at an affirmative answer.

The Alabama Legislature could have decided that municipal corporations should have some measure of control over activities carried on just beyond their "city limit" signs, particularly since today's police jurisdiction may be tomorrow's annexation to the city proper. Nor need the city's interests have been the only concern of the legislature when it enacted the police jurisdiction statutes. Urbanization of any area brings with it a number of individuals who long both for the quiet of suburban or country living and for the career opportunities offered by the city's working environment. Unincorporated communities like Holt dot the rim of most major population centers in Alabama and elsewhere, and state legislatures have a legitimate interest in seeing that this substantial segment of the population does not go without basic municipal services such as police, fire, and health protection. Established cities are experienced in the delivery of such services, and the incremental cost of extending the city's responsibility in these areas to surrounding environs may be substantially less than the expense of establishing wholly new service organizations in each community.

imply that every * * * [state law] would pass constitutional muster. We do not have before us, of course, a situation in which a city has annexed outlying territory in all but name, and is exercising precisely the same governmental powers over residents of surrounding unincorporated territory as it does over those residing within its corporate limits. Nor do we have here a case like *Evans v. Cornman, supra,* where NIH residents were subject to such "important aspects of state powers" as Maryland's authority "to levy and collect [its] income, gasoline, sales, and use taxes" and were "just as interested in and connected with electoral decisions as * * * their neighbors who live[d] off the enclave."

Appellants have made neither an allegation nor a showing that the authority exercised by the city of Tuscaloosa within the police jurisdiction is no less than that exercised by the city within its corporate limits. The minute catalog of ordinances of the city of Tuscaloosa which have extraterritorial effect set forth by our dissenting Brethren is as notable for what it does not include as for what it does. While the burden was on appellants to establish a difference in treatment violative of the Equal Protection Clause, we are bound to observe that among the powers *not* included in the "addendum" to appellants' brief referred to by the dissent are the vital and traditional authorities of cities and towns to levy ad valorem taxes, invoke the power of eminent domain, and zone property for various types of uses.

Nor was it unreasonable for the Alabama Legislature to require police jurisdiction residents to contribute through license fees to the expense of services provided them by the city. The statutory limitation on license fees to half the amount exacted within the city assures that police jurisdiction residents will not be victimized by the city government.

"Viable local governments may need many innovations, numerous combinations of old and new devices, great flexibility in municipal arrangements to meet changing urban conditions." *Sailors v. Board of Education, supra.* This observation in *Sailors* was doubtless as true at the turn of this century, when urban areas throughout the country were temporally closer to the effects of the industrial revolution. Alabama's police jurisdiction statute, enacted in 1907, was a rational legislative response to the problems faced by the State's burgeoning cities. Alabama is apparently content with the results of its experiment, and nothing in the Equal Protection Clause of the Fourteenth Amendment requires that it try something new.

Appellants also argue that "government without franchise is a fundamental violation of the due process clause." * * * Appellants' argument proceeds from the assumption, earlier shown to be erroneous, that they have a right to vote in Tuscaloosa elections. Their conclusion falls with their premise.

In sum, we conclude that Alabama's police jurisdiction statutes violate neither the Equal Protection Clause nor the Due Process Clause of the Fourteenth Amendment. * * *

MR. JUSTICE BRENNAN, with whom MR. JUSTICE WHITE and MR. JUSTICE MARSHALL join, dissenting. * * *

Because "statutes distributing the franchise constitute the foundation of our representative society," *Kramer v. Union School Dist.,* 395 U.S. 621, 626, 89 S.Ct. 1886, 1889, 23 L.Ed.2d 583 (1969), we have subjected such statutes to "exacting judicial scrutiny." *Id.,* at 628, 89 S.Ct., at 1890. Indeed, "if a challenged statute grants the right to vote to some citizens and denies the franchise to others, 'the Court must determine whether the exclusions are *necessary* to promote a *compelling* state interest.' *Kramer v. Union Free School District,* 395 U.S., at 627, 89 S.Ct., at 1890 (emphasis added) * * *." *Dunn v. Blumstein,* 405 U.S. 330, 337, 92 S.Ct. 995, 1000, 31 L.Ed.2d 274 (1972). * * *

Our decisions before today have held that bona fide residency requirements are an acceptable means of distinguishing qualified from unqualified voters. *Dunn v. Blumstein,* 405 U.S. at 343, 92 S.Ct. at 1003. * * * [But] *Dunn v. Blumstein* was careful to exempt from strict judicial scrutiny only bona fide residency requirements that were "appropriately defined and uniformly applied." The touchstone for determining whether a residency requirement is "appropriately defined" derives from the purpose of such requirements, which, as stated in *Dunn,* is "to preserve the basic conception of a political community." At the heart of our basic conception of a "political community," however, is the notion of a reciprocal relationship between the process of government and those who subject themselves to that process by choosing to live within the area of its authoritative application. Statutes such as those challenged in this case, which fracture this relationship by severing the connection between the process of government and those who are governed in the places of their residency, thus undermine the very purposes which have led this Court in the past to approve the application of bona fide residency requirements.

There is no question but that the residents of Tuscaloosa's police jurisdiction are governed by the city.[10] Under Alabama law, a munici-

10. Appellants have included in their brief an unchallenged addendum listing the ordinances of the city of Tuscaloosa, Code of Tuscaloosa (1962, Supplemented, 1975), that have application in its police jurisdiction:

"*Licenses:*

4–1 ambulance

9–4, 9–18, 9–33 bottle dealers

19–1 junk dealers

20–5 general business license ordinance

20–67 florists

20–102 hotels, motels, etc.

20–163 industry

"*Buildings:*

10–1 inspection service enforces codes

10–10 regulation of dams

10–21 Southern Standard Building Code adopted

10–25 building permits

13–3 National Electrical Code adopted

14–23 Fire Prevention Code adopted

14–65 regulation of incinerators

14–81 discharge of cinders

Chapter 21A mobile home parks

25–1 Southern Standard Plumbing Code adopted

33–79 disposal of human waste

33–114, 118 regulation of wells

"*Public Health:*

5–4 certain birds protected

5–4C, 42, 55 dogs running at large and bitches in heat prohibited

14–4 no smoking on buses

14–15 no self-service gas stations

15–2 regulation of sale of produce from trucks

15–4 food establishments to use public water supply

15–16 food, meat, milk inspectors

15–37 thru 40 regulates boardinghouses

15–52 milk code adopted

17–5 mosquito control

"*Traffic Regulations:*

22–2 stop & yield signs may be erected by chief of police

22–3 mufflers required

22–4 brakes required

22–5 inspection of vehicle by police

22–6 operation of vehicle

22–9 hitchhiking in roadway prohibited

22–9.1 permit to solicit funds on roadway

22–11 impounding cars

22–14 load limit on bridges

22–15 police damage stickers required after accident

22–25 driving while intoxicated

22–26 reckless driving

22–27 driving without consent of owner

22–33 stop sign

22–34 yield sign

22–38 driving across median

22–40 yield to emergency vehicle

22–42 cutting across private property

22–54 general speed limit

22–72 thru 78 truck routes

"*Criminal Ordinances:*

23–1 adopts all state misdemeanors

23–7.1 no wrecked cars on premises

23–15 nuisances

23–17 obscene literature

23–20 destruction of plants

23–37 swimming in nude

23–38 trespass to boats

26–51 no shooting galleries in the police jurisdiction or outside fire limits (downtown area)

28–31 thru 39 obscene films

pality exercises "governing" and "law-making" power over its police jurisdiction. *City of Homewood v. Wofford Oil Co.*, 232 Ala. 634, 637, 169 So. 288, 290 (1936). Residents of Tuscaloosa's police jurisdiction are subject to license fees exacted by the city, as well as to the city's police and sanitary regulations, which can be enforced through penal sanctions effective in the city's municipal court. The Court seems to imply, however, that residents of the police jurisdiction are not governed enough to be included within the political community of Tuscaloosa, since they are not subject to Tuscaloosa's powers of eminent domain, zoning, or ad valorem taxation. *Ante* n. 8. But this position is sharply contrary to our previous holdings. In *Kramer v. Union Free School Dist.*, for example, we held that residents of a school district who neither owned nor leased taxable real property located within the district, or were not married to someone who did, or were not parents or guardians of children enrolled in a local district school, nevertheless were sufficiently affected by the decisions of the local school board to make the denial of their franchise and local school board elections a violation of the Equal Protection Clause. Similarly, we held in *Cipriano v. City of Houma* that a Louisiana statute limiting the franchise in municipal utility system revenue bond referenda to those who were "property taxpayers" was unconstitutional because all residents of the municipality were affected by the operation of the utility system.

The residents of Tuscaloosa's police jurisdiction are vastly more affected by Tuscaloosa's decisionmaking processes than were the plaintiffs in either *Kramer* or *Cipriano* affected by the decisionmaking processes from which they had been unconstitutionally excluded. * * * The Court today does not explain why being subjected to the authority to exercise such extensive power does not suffice to bring the residents of Tuscaloosa's police jurisdiction within the political community of the city. Nor does the Court in fact provide any standards for determining when those subjected to extraterritorial municipal legislation will have been "governed enough" to trigger the protections of the Equal Protection Clause.

The criterion of geographical residency relied upon by the Court is of no assistance in this analysis. Just as the State may not fracture the integrity of a political community by restricting the franchise to property taxpayers, so it may not use geographical restrictions on the franchise to accomplish the same end. This is the teaching of *Evans v. Cornman*. *Evans* held, contrary to the conclusion of the Maryland Court of Appeals, that those who lived on the grounds of the National Institutes of Health (NIH) enclave within Montgomery County were residents of Maryland for purposes of the franchise. Our decision rested on the grounds that inhabitants of the enclave were "treated as state residents in the census and in determining congressional apportionment," and that "residents

"*Miscellaneous:*

   20–120 thru 122 cigarette tax

   24–31 public parks and recreation

26–18 admission tax

Chapter 29 regulates public streets

30–23 taxis must have meters."

of the NIH grounds are just as interested in and connected with electoral decisions as they were prior to 1953 when the area came under federal jurisdiction and as are their neighbors who live off the enclave." Residents of Tuscaloosa's police jurisdiction are assuredly as "interested in and connected with" the electoral decisions of the city as were the inhabitants of the NIH enclave in the electoral decisions of Maryland. True, inhabitants of the enclave lived "within the geographical boundaries of the State of Maryland," but appellants in this case similarly reside within the geographical boundaries of Tuscaloosa's police jurisdiction. They live within the perimeters of the city's "legislative powers."

The criterion of geographical residency is thus entirely arbitrary when applied to this case. It fails to explain why, consistently with the Equal Protection Clause, the "government unit" which may exclude from the franchise those who reside outside of its geographical boundaries should be composed of the city of Tuscaloosa rather than of the city together with its police jurisdiction. It irrationally distinguishes between two classes of citizens, each with equal claim to residency (insofar as that can be determined by domicile or intention or other similar criteria), and each governed by the city of Tuscaloosa in the place of their residency.

The Court argues, however, that if the franchise were extended to residents of the city's police jurisdiction, the franchise must similarly be extended to all those indirectly affected by the city's actions. This is a simple non sequitur. There is a crystal-clear distinction between those who reside in Tuscaloosa's police jurisdiction, and who are therefore subject to that city's police and sanitary ordinances, licensing fees, and the jurisdiction of its municipal court, and those who reside in neither the city nor its police jurisdiction, and who are thus merely affected by the indirect impact of the city's decisions. This distinction is recognized in Alabama law and is consistent with, if not mandated by, the very conception of a political community underlying constitutional recognition of bona fide residency requirements.

Appellants' equal protection claim can be simply expressed: The State cannot extend the franchise to some citizens who are governed by municipal government in the places of their residency, and withhold the franchise from others similarly situated, unless this distinction is necessary to promote a compelling state interest. No such interest has been articulated in this case. Neither Tuscaloosa's interest in regulating "activities carried on just beyond [its] 'city limit' signs" nor Alabama's interest in providing municipal services to the unincorporated communities surrounding its cities are in any way inconsistent with the extension of the franchise to residents of Tuscaloosa's police jurisdiction. Although a great many States may presently authorize the exercise of extraterritorial lawmaking powers by a municipality, and although the Alabama statutes involved in this case may be of venerable age, neither of these factors, as *Reynolds v. Sims,* 377 U.S. 533, 84 S.Ct. 1362, 12 L.Ed.2d 506 (1964), made clear, can serve to justify practices otherwise impermissible under the Equal Protection Clause of the Fourteenth Amendment. * * *

The next case suggests the possibility of treating outsiders in the opposite way to that upheld in *Holt*. In Brown v. Board of Commissioners of the City of Chattanooga, the city permitted outsiders (or at least some of them) to vote in city elections. Is there a Constitutional way to include as voters some (but not all) outsiders affected by city policy? Would it be Constitutional to include only those who own real estate in the city? If a city includes outsiders as voters, would city residents have a Constitutional claim that their right to self-government was being diluted by the votes of people less affected by city policy than they are?

BROWN v. BOARD OF COMMISSIONERS OF THE CITY OF CHATTANOOGA

United States District Court, Eastern District of Tennessee, 1989.
722 F.Supp. 380.

EDGAR, DISTRICT JUDGE.

Plaintiffs, who are black citizens of Chattanooga, Tennessee, have brought this action challenging the system for selecting members of the Board of Commissioners, Chattanooga's governing body. * * * [P]laintiffs assert that Tennessee Code Annotated Section 2–2–107(a) and section 5.1 of the Chattanooga charter, which permit nonresident "property qualification" as a basis for voting in municipal elections, violate the First, Ninth, Thirteenth, Fourteenth and Fifteenth Amendments to the United States Constitution * * *. * * *

Tennessee Code Annotated § 2–2–107(a) (1985) provides that:

A person shall be registered as a voter of the precinct in which he is a resident, and, if provided for by municipal charter or general law, may be also registered in a municipality in which he owns real property in order to participate in that municipality's elections.

Section 5.1 of the Chattanooga city charter provides in part that:

Nonresident freeholders may vote in the wards in which their freehold is situated, and not elsewhere; provided, that if any nonresident freeholder may have a freehold in more than one ward he may vote in the ward of his choice in which his freehold is situated.

Thus, the City of Chattanooga, by virtue of the authority granted it by state statute, permits city property owners who are nonresidents of the city to vote in municipal elections. * * * In 1988, the assessed value of real property owned in Chattanooga by nonresident voters was $6,154,-315.00 or .05% of the total assessed value of all real property in Chattanooga. These nonresident voters pay a similar percentage of Chattanooga's property taxes.

Plaintiffs allege that the statute and ordinance are violative of the Fourteenth Amendment * * *. Plaintiffs, relying on the legislative and municipal reapportionment cases, chiefly *Reynolds v. Sims*, 377 U.S. 533, 84 S.Ct. 1362, 12 L.Ed.2d 506 (1964), contend that property qualified voting can never be permitted because it is only residency, and not any other interest (example—property ownership), which can be the basis for voting.

The plaintiffs' argument is not supported by the authority that they cite. *Reynolds v. Sims* and its progeny were concerned with equalizing deviations from the equal population principle in voting districts. These cases do not say that an economic interest, such as property ownership, is an impermissible criterion for apportioning voting power in municipal elections.

Plaintiffs also assert that the statute and the ordinance must fall because they fail to advance a "compelling" state interest. In fact, several cases hold that, absent a compelling state interest, laws which *deny* some residents the right to vote in general elections on grounds other than residence, age or citizenship, are violative of the Fourteenth Amendment's equal protection clause. *See Kramer v. Union Free School District*, 395 U.S. 621, 626–27, 89 S.Ct. 1886, 1889, 23 L.Ed.2d 583 (1969).

However, the Tennessee statute and Chattanooga charter *expand* rather than curtail the franchise. *Over* inclusiveness is a lesser constitutional evil than *under* inclusiveness. The Court concludes, therefore, that the equal protection analysis which should be applied here is the traditional "rational basis" test. The issue, then, is whether the plaintiffs have shown that there is no rational basis for allowing nonresident property owners to vote in Chattanooga's municipal elections.

The "rational basis" test was used by the Fifth Circuit in *Glisson v. Mayor and Councilmen of Savannah Beach*, 346 F.2d 135 (5th Cir.1965), and by the district court in *Spahos v. Mayor and Councilmen of Savannah Beach*, 207 F.Supp. 688 (S.D.Ga.), *aff'd* 371 U.S. 206, 83 S.Ct. 304, 9 L.Ed.2d 269 (1962), both of which arose from the same town and from the same factual situation. There, state law and a municipal charter permitted nonresident property owners to vote. Savannah Beach, a resort town, had a population of 1,385 in 1962, with a summer population of 2,500. Nonresident property owners owned real estate with an assessed valuation of $2,852,040. Permanent residents owned property assessed at $1,586,485. Nonresident voters were limited to those who owned property in Savannah Beach and who resided in Chatham County. There were 712 resident voters and 467 property qualified nonresident voters. The Georgia legislation under these facts was found to have a "rational" objective and to make a reasonable classification with respect to the right to vote in municipal elections.[23] * * *

23. While the Court concurs with the approach taken in Spahos and Glisson, the Court nevertheless concludes that the re- sult reached in those cases does not dictate the same result in this case. The nonresi- dent voters in Savannah Beach as a group

The Court views the issue in the instant case as being whether the plaintiffs have demonstrated that the Chattanooga charter is irrational in that it permits nonresident property owners to vote in city elections who do not have a *substantial interest* in the operation of the city.

There is no question that city property owners, including nonresident property owners, have an interest in the conduct of municipal affairs, including property taxes, zoning, public services such as sewage and garbage disposal, and other matters that may affect their property. The difficulty, however, with Chattanooga's charter provision is that it contains no limitation of the number of people who can "vote" on a piece of property or no limitation as to any minimum property value required for the exercise of the franchise. The record in this case shows that as many as 23 nonresidents have been registered to vote on a single piece of property in the city. By way of further example, 15 nonresidents are registered to vote as co-owners of one parcel of property which has an assessed value of $100.[24]

A nonresident who owns a one-fifteenth undivided interest in a lot assessed at $100 does not have a substantial interest in the operation of the city. Since the Chattanooga charter permits a nonresident who owns a trivial amount of property to vote in municipal elections, it does not further any rational governmental interest. The Court, therefore, concludes that section 5.1 of the Chattanooga city charter violates of the equal protection clause of the Fourteenth Amendment. If Chattanooga wishes to give nonresident property owners the right to vote in municipal elections, the city charter must use means "more finely tailored to achieve the desired goal." *Quinn v. Millsap*, ___ U.S. ___, ___, 109 S.Ct. 2324, 2333, 105 L.Ed.2d 74. * * *

The Court's ruling does not extend to T.C.A. § 2–2–107(a). * * * T.C.A. § 2–2–107(a) is merely permissive, in that it only authorizes municipalities to permit nonresidents to vote. Municipalities are not specifically advised by the statute about how this might be accomplished, and it would appear that municipalities have some discretion as to this. The action of the municipality ultimately determines whether and defines *which* nonresidents can vote. Therefore, T.C.A. § 2–2–107(a) will be construed only to authorize municipalities to permit nonresidents to vote consistent with the Fourteenth Amendment. * * *

3. THE ABILITY OF CITIES TO FAVOR THEIR RESIDENTS OVER OUTSIDERS

This section examines the extent to which cities can act in a way

had a much greater economic interest in the municipality than do the nonresident voters of Chattanooga. They were also required to be residents of Chatham County, although the Court does not deem the geographical limitation to be determinative of the constitutional issue in this case.

24. As plaintiffs have pointed out, the law currently would permit Muammar el-Qaddafi to buy a parcel of land in Chattanooga and deed it to thousands of Libyans who would then be able to control the outcome of Chattanooga's elections.

that favors their own residents over outsiders.[1] A similar issue could, of course, be posed for a group of any kind: to what extent can *any* group favor its members over non-members? If a group is not entitled to limit at least *some* of its benefits to members, what would be the difference between membership and non-membership? These questions reintroduce a subject raised in Chapter One—the application of the public/private distinction to cities. How does the legitimacy of cities' favoring insiders over outsiders relate to similar action by private entities (such as private property owners, religious communities, or group health plans)?[2] What is the relationship between a city's preference for its own citizens and comparable action by the United States government?

The cases below explore cities' attempts to favor their own residents in a variety of contexts: the exclusion of outsiders from city schools and a city beach; the protection of city residents from solid waste generated elsewhere; a requirement that a city's contractors hire a minimum percentage of city residents. In reading the cases, consider how the courts use the public/private distinction in interpreting the variety of Constitutional provisions (the Equal Protection Clause, the Commerce Clause, the Privileges and Immunities Clause) and common law doctrines (the "public trust doctrine") that potentially limit local parochialism. Consider as well whether the cases provide a consistent policy regarding a locality's ability to prefer its own residents to outsiders. Why should a city be allowed to exclude non-residents from its schools but not its beaches? Why should a city be allowed to exclude foreign students but not foreign waste? Exactly *when* should a city be permitted to advance their residents' interests over those of outsiders? Are cities entitled to exclude non-residents from parking on city streets?[3] From using (or selling goods in) public hospitals?

1. For a general analysis of this issue, see Neuman, Territorial Discrimination, Equal Protection and Self–Determination, 135 U.Pa.L.Rev. 261 (1987). See also Murchison, Local Government Law, 45 La. L.Rev. 357, 361 71 (1984); Varat, State "Citizenship" and Interstate Equality, 48 U.Chi.L.Rev. 487 (1981); Antieau, Paul's Perverted Privileges or the True Meaning of the Privileges and Immunities Clause of Article Four, 9 Wm. & Mary L.Rev. 1 (1967).

2. See generally, Rose, The Comedy of the Commons: Custom, Commerce and Inherently Public Property, 53 U.Chi.L.Rev. 711 (1986).

3. In County Board of Arlington County, Virginia v. Richards, 434 U.S. 5, 98 S.Ct. 24, 54 L.Ed.2d 4 (1977), the United States Supreme Court held that a local ordinance limiting parking in a residential area to local residents did not violate the Equal Protection Clause of the Fourteenth Amendment. The Court reasoned:

To reduce air pollution and other environmental effects of automobile commuting, a community reasonably may restrict on-street parking available to commuters, thus encouraging reliance on car pools and mass transit. The same goal is served by assuring convenient parking to residents who leave their cars home during the day. A community may also decide that restrictions on the flow of outside traffic into particular residential areas would enhance the quality of life there by reducing noise, traffic hazards, and litter. By definition, discrimination against nonresidents would inhere in such a restriction. * * * The Equal Protection Clause requires only that the distinction drawn by an ordinance like Arlington's rationally promotes the regulation's objectives. On its face, the Arlington ordinance meets this test.

In New York State Public Employees Federation v. City of Albany, 72 N.Y.2d 96, 531 N.Y.S.2d 770, 527 N.E.2d 253 (1988), on the other hand, the New York Court of Appeals held invalid the City's policy of limiting nonresident parking in designated areas to

MARTINEZ v. BYNUM

Supreme Court of the United States, 1983.
461 U.S. 321, 103 S.Ct. 1838, 75 L.Ed.2d 879.

JUSTICE POWELL delivered the opinion of the Court. * * *

Roberto Morales was born in 1969 in McAllen, Texas, and is thus a United States citizen by birth. His parents are Mexican citizens who reside in Reynosa, Mexico. He left Reynosa in 1977 and returned to McAllen to live with his sister, petitioner Oralia Martinez, for the primary purpose of attending school in the McAllen Independent School District. Although Martinez is now his custodian, she is not—and does not desire to become—his guardian. As a result, Morales is not entitled to tuition-free admission to the McAllen schools. Sections 21.031(b) and (c) of the Texas Education Code would require the local school authorities to admit him if he or "his parent, guardian, or the person having lawful control of him" resided in the school district, Tex. Educ. Code Ann. § 21.031(b) and (c) (Supp. 1982), but § 21.031(d) denies tuition-free admission for a minor who lives apart from a "parent, guardian, or other person having lawful control of him under an order of a court" if his presence in the school district is "for the primary purpose of attending the public free schools." Respondent McAllen Independent School District therefore denied Morales' application for admission in the fall of 1977.

In December 1977 Martinez, as next friend of Morales, and four other adult custodians of school-age children instituted the present action * * * [alleging] that § 21.031(d) violated * * * the Equal Protection Clause, the Due Process Clause, and the Privileges and Immunities Clause. * * *

This Court frequently has considered constitutional challenges to residence requirements. On several occasions the Court has invalidated requirements that condition receipt of a benefit on a minimum period of residence within a jurisdiction, but it always has been careful to distinguish such durational residence requirements from bona fide residence requirements. * * * Last Term, in *Plyler v. Doe*, 457 U.S. ___, 102 S.Ct.

---

90 minutes while allowing residents unlimited parking privileges. Sections 1600 and 1604 of the state's Vehicle and Traffic Law, the court said,

> prohibit localities from excluding persons from free use of the highways except to the extent such limitations are expressly authorized by statute. * * * [R]estrictions on highway use based upon residency—such as that found in the contested ordinance—are [thereby] prohibited. * * * [T]he City maintains that the * * * rule should only be construed as prohibiting distinctions between residents and nonresidents for matters involving travel;

that distinctions may be drawn for parking matters. * * * [But the] general rule is clear: residents of a community have no greater right to use the highways abutting their land—whether it be for travel or parking—than other members of the public * * *. The Legislature is free to create exceptions to the general rule or delegate the power to do so to localities, but we conclude that it did neither here. * * *

Accord: People v. Speakerkits, Inc., 83 N.Y.2d 814, 611 N.Y.S.2d 488, 633 N.E.2d 1092 (1994).

2382, 72 L.Ed.2d 786 (1982), we reviewed an aspect of Tex. Educ. Code Ann. § 21.031—the statute at issue in this case. Although we invalidated the portion of the statute that excluded undocumented alien children from the public free schools, we recognized the school districts' right "to apply * * * established criteria for determining residence." *Id.*, at 229, n. 22, 102 S.Ct., at 2400, n. 22. * * *

A bona fide residence requirement, appropriately defined and uniformly applied, furthers the substantial state interest in assuring that services provided for its residents are enjoyed only by residents. Such a requirement with respect to attendance in public free schools does not violate the Equal Protection Clause of the Fourteenth Amendment.[7] It does not burden or penalize the constitutional right of interstate travel, for any person is free to move to a State and to establish residence there. A bona fide residence requirement simply requires that the person *does* establish residence before demanding the services that are restricted to residents.

There is a further, independent justification for local residence requirements in the public-school context. As we explained in *Milliken v. Bradley*, 418 U.S. 717, 94 S.Ct. 3112, 41 L.Ed.2d 1069 (1974):

> "No single tradition in public education is more deeply rooted than local control over the operation of schools; local autonomy has long been thought essential both to the maintenance of community concern and support for public schools and to quality of the educational process. * * * [Local] control over the educational process affords citizens an opportunity to participate in decision-making, permits the structuring of school programs to fit local needs, and encourages 'experimentation, innovation, and a healthy competition for educational excellence.' " 418 U.S., at 741–742, 94 S.Ct., at 3126 (quoting *San Antonio Independent School District v. Rodriquez*, 411 U.S. 1, 50, 93 S.Ct. 1278, 1305, 36 L.Ed.2d 16 (1973)).

The provision of primary and secondary education, of course, is one of the most important functions of local government. Absent residence requirements, there can be little doubt that the proper planning and operation of the schools would suffer significantly.[9] The State thus has a

---

7. A bona fide residence requirement implicates no "suspect" classification, and therefore is not subject to strict scrutiny. Indeed, there is nothing invidiously discriminatory about a bona fide residence requirement if it is uniformly applied. Thus the question is simply whether there is a rational basis for it.

This view assumes, of course, that the "service" that the State would deny to nonresidents is not a fundamental right protected by the Constitution. A State, for example, may not refuse to provide counsel to an indigent nonresident defendant at a criminal trial where a deprivation of liberty occurs. As we previously have recognized,

however, "[public] education is not a 'right' granted to individuals by the Constitution." *Plyler v. Doe*, 457 U.S. ___, ___, 102 S.Ct. 2382, 2397, 72 L.Ed.2d 786 (1982) (citing *San Antonio Independent School District v. Rodriguez*, 411 U.S. 1, 35, 93 S.Ct. 1278, 1297, 36 L.Ed.2d 16 (1973)).

9. The Court of Appeals accepted the District Court's findings on the adverse impact that invalidating § 21.031(d) would have on the quality of education in Texas. The District Court explicitly found:

"28. Declaring the statute unconstitutional would cause substantial numbers of [inter-district] transfers, which would * * *

substantial interest in imposing bona fide residence requirements to maintain the quality of local public schools. * * *

Section 21.031 * * * compels a school district to permit a child such as Morales to attend school without paying tuition if he has a bona fide intention to remain in the school district indefinitely, for he then would have a reason for being there other than his desire to attend school: his intention to make his home in the district. Thus § 21.031 grants the benefits of residency to all who satisfy the traditional requirements. The statute goes further and extends these benefits to many children even if they (or their families) do not intend to remain in the district indefinitely. As long as the child is not living in the district for the sole purpose of attending school, he satisfies the statutory test. * * * In short, § 21.031 grants the benefits of residency to everyone who satisfies the traditional residence definition and to some who legitimately could be classified as nonresidents. Since there is no indication that this extension of the traditional definition has any impermissible basis, we certainly cannot say that § 21.031(d) violates the Constitution. * * *

———

To support its result, the *Martinez* Court cites Milliken v. Bradley, 418 U.S. 717, 94 S.Ct. 3112, 41 L.Ed.2d 1069 (1974). What do you think of the following argument, made by Chief Justice Burger writing for the Court in *Milliken*, defending a city's ability to limit admission to its schools to city residents (and thereby overturning a District Court's order encompassing 53 neighboring school districts in the effort to desegregate Detroit's school system)?

> * * * Here the District Court's approach to what constituted "actual desegregation" raises the fundamental question * * * as to the circumstances in which a federal court may order desegregation relief that embraces more than a single school district. The court's analytical starting point was its conclusion that school district lines are no more than arbitrary lines on a map drawn "for political convenience." Boundary lines may be bridged where there has been a constitutional violation calling for interdistrict relief, but the notion that school district lines may be casually ignored or treated as a mere administrative convenience is contrary to the history of public education in our country. No single tradition in public

cause school populations to fluctuate. * * *

"29. Fluctuating school populations would make it impossible to predict enrollment figures—even on a semester-by-semester basis, causing over-or-under-estimates on teachers, supplies, materials, etc.

"30. The increased enrollment of students would cause overcrowded classrooms and related facilities; over-large teacher-pupil ratios; expansion of bilingual pro-

grams; the purchase of books, equipment, supplies and other customary items of support; all of which would require a substantial increase in the budget of the school districts."

We do not suggest that findings of this degree of specificity are necessary in every case. But they do illustrate the problems that prompt States to adopt regulations such as § 21.031.

education is more deeply rooted than local control over the operation of schools; local autonomy has long been thought essential both to the maintenance of community concern and support for public schools and to quality of the educational process. Thus, in San Antonio Independent School District v. Rodriguez, 411 U.S. 1, 50, 93 S.Ct. 1278, 1305, 36 L.Ed.2d 16 (1973), we observed that local control over the educational process affords citizens an opportunity to participate in decision-making, permits the structuring of school programs to fit local needs, and encourages "experimentation, innovation, and a healthy competition for educational excellence."

The Michigan educational structure involved in this case, in common with most States, provides for a large measure of local control, and a review of the scope and character of these local powers indicates the extent to which the interdistrict remedy approved by the two courts could disrupt and alter the structure of public education in Michigan. The metropolitan remedy would require, in effect, consolidation of 54 independent school districts historically administered as separate units into a vast new super school district. Entirely apart from the logistical and other serious problems attending large-scale transportation of students, the consolidation would give rise to an array of other problems in financing and operating this new school system. Some of the more obvious questions would be: What would be the status and authority of the present popularly elected school boards? Would the children of Detroit be within the jurisdiction and operating control of a school board elected by the parents and residents of other districts? What board or boards would levy taxes for school operations in these 54 districts constituting the consolidated metropolitan area? What provisions could be made for assuring substantial equality in tax levies among the 54 districts, if this were deemed requisite? What provisions would be made for financing? Would the validity of long-term bonds be jeopardized unless approved by all of the component districts as well as the State? What body would determine that portion of the curricula now left to the discretion of local school boards? Who would establish attendance zones, purchase school equipment, locate and construct new schools, and indeed attend to all the myriad day-to-day decisions that are necessary to school operations affecting potentially more than three-quarters of a million pupils?

It may be suggested that all of these vital operational problems are yet to be resolved by the District Court, and that this is the purpose of the Court of Appeals' proposed remand. But it is obvious from the scope of the interdistrict remedy itself that absent a complete restructuring of the laws of Michigan relating to school districts the District Court will become first, a *de facto* "legislative authority" to resolve these complex questions, and then the "school superintendent" for the entire area. This is a task which few, if any, judges are qualified to perform and one which would deprive the people of control of schools through their elected representatives.   * * *

FORT GRATIOT SANITARY LANDFILL, INC. v. MICHIGAN DEPARTMENT OF NATURAL RESOURCES

Supreme Court of the United States, 1992.
___ U.S. ___, 112 S.Ct. 2019, 119 L.Ed.2d 139.

JUSTICE STEVENS delivered the opinion of the Court.

In *Philadelphia v. New Jersey*, 437 U.S. 617, 618, 98 S.Ct. 2531, 2532, 57 L.Ed.2d 475 (1978), we held that a New Jersey law prohibiting the importation of most " 'solid or liquid waste which originated or was collected outside the territorial limits of the State' " violated the Commerce Clause of the United States Constitution.   In this case petitioner challenges a Michigan law that prohibits private landfill operators from accepting solid waste that originates outside the county in which their facilities are located.   Adhering to our holding in the *New Jersey* case, we conclude that this Michigan statute is also unconstitutional.

In 1978 Michigan enacted its Solid Waste Management Act (SWMA). That Act required every Michigan county to estimate the amount of solid waste that would be generated in the county in the next 20 years and to adopt a plan providing for its disposal at facilities that comply with state health standards.   * * * On December 28, 1988, the Michigan Legislature amended the SWMA by adopting two provisions concerning the "acceptance of waste or ash generated outside the county of disposal area."   Those amendments (Waste Import Restrictions), which became effective immediately, provide:

> "A person shall not accept for disposal solid waste * * * that is not generated in the county in which the disposal area is located unless the acceptance of solid waste * * * that is not generated in the county is explicitly authorized in the approved county solid waste management plan." * * *

In February, 1989, petitioner submitted an application to the St. Clair County Solid Waste Planning Committee for authority to accept up to 1,750 tons per day of out-of-state waste at its landfill.   * * * In view of the fact that the county's management plan does not authorize the acceptance of any out-of-county waste, the Waste Import Restrictions in the 1988 statute effectively prevent petitioner from receiving any solid waste that does not originate in St. Clair County.   * * * Petitioner therefore commenced this action seeking a judgment declaring the Waste Import Restrictions unconstitutional and enjoining their enforcement. * * *

Philadelphia v. New Jersey provides the framework for our analysis of this case.   Solid waste, even if it has no value, is an article of commerce.   Whether the business arrangements between out-of-state generators of waste and the Michigan operator of a waste disposal site are viewed as "sales" of garbage or "purchases" of transportation and disposal services, the commercial transactions unquestionably have an interstate character. The Commerce Clause thus imposes some constraints on Michigan's ability to regulate these transactions.

As we have long recognized, the "negative" or "dormant" aspect of the Commerce Clause prohibits States from "advancing their own commercial interests by curtailing the movement of articles of commerce, either into or out of the state." *H.P. Hood & Sons, Inc. v. Du Mond*, 336 U.S. 525, 535, 69 S.Ct. 657, 663, 93 L.Ed. 865 (1949). A state statute that clearly discriminates against interstate commerce is therefore unconstitutional "unless the discrimination is demonstrably justified by a valid factor unrelated to economic protectionism." *New Energy Co. of Indiana v. Limbach*, 486 U.S. 269, 274, 108 S.Ct. 1803, 1808, 100 L.Ed.2d 302 (1988).

New Jersey's prohibition on the importation of solid waste failed this test:

> "The evil of protectionism can reside in legislative means as well as legislative ends. Thus, it does not matter whether the ultimate aim of ch. 363 is to reduce the waste disposal costs of New Jersey residents or to save remaining open lands from pollution, for we assume New Jersey has every right to protect its residents' pocketbooks as well as their environment. And it may be assumed as well that New Jersey may pursue those ends by slowing the flow of *all* waste into the State's remaining landfills, even though interstate commerce may incidentally be affected. But whatever New Jersey's ultimate purpose, it may not be accompanied by discriminating against articles of commerce coming from outside the State unless there is some reason, apart from their origin, to treat them differently. Both on its face and in its plain effect, ch. 363 violates this principle of nondiscrimination.

> "The Court has consistently found parochial legislation of this kind to be constitutionally invalid, whether the ultimate aim of the legislation was to assure a steady supply of milk by erecting barriers to allegedly ruinous outside competition; or to create jobs by keeping industry within the State; or to preserve the State's financial resources from depletion by fencing out indigent immigrants. In each of these cases, a presumably legitimate goal was sought to be achieved by the illegitimate means of isolating the State from the national economy." *Philadelphia v. New Jersey*, 437 U.S., at 626–627, 98 S.Ct., at 2536–2537.

The Waste Import Restrictions enacted by Michigan authorize each of its 83 counties to isolate itself from the national economy. Indeed, unless a county acts affirmatively to permit other waste to enter its jurisdiction, the statute affords local waste producers complete protection from competition from out-of-state waste producers who seek to use local waste disposal areas. In view of the fact that Michigan has not identified any reason, apart from its origin, why solid waste coming from outside the county should be treated differently from solid waste within the county, the foregoing reasoning would appear to control the disposition of this case.

Respondents Michigan and St. Clair County argue, however, that the Waste Import Restrictions—unlike the New Jersey prohibition on the importation of solid waste—do not discriminate against interstate commerce on their face or in effect because they treat waste from other Michigan counties no differently than waste from other States. Instead, respondents maintain, the statute regulates evenhandedly to effectuate local interests and should be upheld because the burden on interstate commerce is not clearly excessive in relation to the local benefits. We disagree, for our prior cases teach that a State (or one of its political subdivisions) may not avoid the strictures of the Commerce Clause by curtailing the movement of articles of commerce through subdivisions of the State, rather than through the State itself. * * *

In *Dean Milk Co. v. Madison*, 340 U.S. 349, 71 S.Ct. 295, 95 L.Ed. 329 (1951), * * * [an] Illinois litigant challenged a city ordinance that made it unlawful to sell any milk as pasteurized unless it had been processed at a plant "within a radius of five miles from the central square of Madison," *id.*, at 350, 71 S.Ct., at 296. * * * The fact that the ordinance also discriminated against all Wisconsin producers whose facilities were more than five miles from the center of the city did not mitigate its burden on interstate commerce. As we noted, it was "immaterial that Wisconsin milk from outside the Madison area is subjected to the same proscription as that moving in interstate commerce." * * *

Michigan and St. Clair County also argue that this case is different from *Philadelphia v. New Jersey* because the SWMA constitutes a comprehensive health and safety regulation rather than "economic protectionism" of the State's limited landfill capacity. * * * We may assume that all of the provisions of Michigan's SWMA prior to the 1988 amendments adding the Waste Import Restrictions could fairly be characterized as health and safety regulations with no protectionist purpose, but we cannot make that same assumption with respect to the Waste Import Restrictions themselves. Because those provisions unambiguously discriminate against interstate commerce, the State bears the burden of proving that they further health and safety concerns that cannot be adequately served by nondiscriminatory alternatives. Michigan and St. Clair County have not met this burden.

Michigan and St. Clair County assert that the Waste Import Restrictions are necessary because they enable individual counties to make adequate plans for the safe disposal of future waste. Although accurate forecasts about the volume and composition of future waste flows may be an indispensable part of a comprehensive waste disposal plan, Michigan could attain that objective without discriminating between in- and out-of-state waste. Michigan could, for example, limit the amount of waste that landfill operators may accept each year. There is, however, no valid health and safety reason for limiting the amount of waste that a landfill operator may accept from outside the State, but not the amount that the operator may accept from inside the State. * * *

CHIEF JUSTICE REHNQUIST, with whom JUSTICE BLACKMUN joins, dissenting.

When confronted with a dormant Commerce Clause challenge "the crucial inquiry * * * must be directed to determining whether [the challenged statute] is basically a protectionist measure, or whether it can fairly be viewed as a law directed to legitimate local concerns, with effects upon interstate commerce that are only incidental." *Philadelphia v. New Jersey*, 437 U.S. 617, 624, 98 S.Ct. 2531, 2536, 57 L.Ed.2d 475 (1978). Because I think the Michigan statute is at least arguably directed to legitimate local concerns, rather than improper economic protectionism, I would remand this case for further proceedings.

The substantial environmental, aesthetic, health, and safety problems flowing from this country's waste piles were already apparent at the time we decided *Philadelphia*. Those problems have only risen in the intervening years. * * * [W]hile many are willing to generate waste—indeed, it is a practical impossibility to solve the waste problem by banning waste production—few are willing to help dispose of it. Those locales that do provide disposal capacity to serve foreign waste effectively are affording reduced environmental and safety risks to the States that will not take charge of their own waste.

The State of Michigan has stepped into this quagmire in order to address waste problems generated by its own populace. It has done so by adopting a comprehensive approach to the disposal of solid wastes generated within its borders. * * * In adopting this legislation, the Michigan Legislature also appears to have concluded that, like the State, counties should reap as they have sown—hardly a novel proposition. It has required counties within the State to be responsible for the waste created within the county. It has accomplished this by prohibiting waste facilities from accepting waste generated from outside the county, unless special permits are obtained. In the process, of course, this facially neutral restriction (i.e. it applies equally to both interstate and intrastate waste) also works to ban disposal from out-of-state sources unless appropriate permits are procured. But I cannot agree that such a requirement, when imposed as one part of a comprehensive approach to regulating in this difficult field, is the stuff of which economic protectionism is made.

If anything, the challenged regulation seems likely to work to Michigan's economic disadvantage. This is because, by limiting potential disposal volumes for any particular site, various fixed costs will have to be recovered across smaller volumes, increasing disposal costs per unit for Michigan consumers. The regulation also will require some Michigan counties—those that until now have been exporting their waste to other locations in the State—to confront environmental and other risks that they previously have avoided. Commerce Clause concerns are at their nadir when a state act works in this fashion—raising prices for all the State's consumers, and working to the substantial disadvantage of other segments of the State's population—because in these circumstances " 'a State's own political processes will serve as a check against unduly burdensome regulations.' " *Kassel v. Consolidated Freightways Corp. of Delaware*, 450 U.S. 662, 675, 101 S.Ct. 1309, 1318–1319, 67 L.Ed.2d 580 (1981). In sum, the law simply incorporates the common-sense notion that those responsible for a problem should be responsible for its solution *to the degree they are responsible for the problem but not further*. At a minimum, I think the facts just outlined suggest the State must be allowed to present evidence on the economic, environmental and other effects of its legislation. * * * I see no reason in the Commerce Clause * * * that requires cheap-land States to become the waste repositories for their brethren, thereby suffering the many risks that such sites present. * * *

WHITE v. MASSACHUSETTS COUNCIL OF CONSTRUCTION EMPLOYERS, INC.

Supreme Court of the United States, 1983.
460 U.S. 204, 103 S.Ct. 1042, 75 L.Ed.2d 1.

JUSTICE REHNQUIST delivered the opinion of the Court.

In 1979 the mayor of Boston, Massachusetts, issued an executive order which required that all construction projects funded in whole or in part by city funds, or funds which the city had the authority to administer, should be performed by a work force consisting of at least half *bona fide* residents of Boston. The Supreme Judicial Court of Massachusetts decided that the order was unconstitutional, observing that the Commerce Clause "presents a clear obstacle to the city's order." We granted certiorari to decide whether the Commerce Clause of the United States Constitution, Art. I, § 8, cl. 3, prevents the city from giving effect to the mayor's order. * * *

We were first asked in *Hughes v. Alexandria Scrap Corp.*, 426 U.S. 794, 96 S.Ct. 2488, 49 L.Ed.2d 220 (1976), to decide whether state and local governments are restrained by the Commerce Clause when they seek to affect commercial transactions not as "regulators" but as "market participants." In that case, the Maryland legislature, in an attempt to encourage the recycling of abandoned automobiles, offered a bounty for every Maryland-titled automobile converted into scrap if the scrap processor supplied documentation of ownership. An amendment to the Maryland statute imposed more exacting documentation requirements on out-of-state than in-state processors, who in turn demanded more exacting documentation from those who sold the junked automobiles for scrap. As a result, it became easier for those in possession of the automobiles to sell to in-state processors. "The practical effect was substantially the same as if Maryland had withdrawn altogether the availability of bounties on hulks delivered by unlicensed suppliers to licensed non-Maryland processors." 426 U.S., at 803, n. 13, 96 S.Ct., at

2495, n. 13.   In upholding the Maryland statute in the face of a Commerce Clause challenge, we said that "[n]othing in the purpose animating the Commerce Clause prohibits a State, in the absence of congressional action, from participating in the market and exercising the right to favor its own citizens over others."   Because Maryland was participating in the market, rather than acting as a market regulator, we concluded that the Commerce Clause was not "intended to require independent justification" for the statutory bounty.

We faced the question again in *Reeves, Inc. v. Stake,* 447 U.S. 429, 100 S.Ct. 2271, 65 L.Ed.2d 244 (1980), when confronted with a South Dakota policy to confine the sale of cement by a state operated cement plant to residents of South Dakota.   We underscored the holding of *Hughes v. Alexandria Scrap Corp.,* saying:

> "The basic distinction drawn in *Alexandria Scrap* between States as market participants and States as market regulators makes good sense and sound law.   As that case explains, the Commerce Clause responds principally to state taxes and regulatory measures impeding free private trade in the national marketplace.   There is no indication of a constitutional plan to limit the ability of the States themselves to operate freely in the free market."   447 U.S., at 436– 437, 100 S.Ct., at 2277.[3]

We concluded that South Dakota, "as a seller of cement, unquestionably fits the 'market participant' label" and applied the "general rule of *Alexandria Scrap.*"

Alexandria Scrap and *Reeves,* therefore, stand for the proposition that when a state or local government enters the market as a participant it is not subject to the restraints of the Commerce Clause.   As we said in *Reeves,* in this kind of case there is "a single inquiry: whether the challenged 'program constituted direct state participation in the market.' "   We reaffirm that principle now.   * * *

The Supreme Judicial Court of Massachusetts expressed reservations as to the application of the "market participation" principle to the city here, reasoning that "the implementation of the mayor's order will have a significant impact on those firms which engage in specialized areas of construction and employ permanent works crews composed of out-of-State residents."   Even if this conclusion is factually correct, it is not relevant to the inquiry of whether the city is participating in the

---

3.   We also noted the policy in support of this limitation on the Commerce Clause:

"Restraint in this area is also counseled by considerations of state sovereignty, the role of each State 'as guardian and trustee for its people,' *Heim v. McCall,* 239 U.S. 175, 191, 36 S.Ct. 78, 83, 60 L.Ed. 206 (1915), and 'the long recognized right of trader or manufacturer, engaged in an entirely private business, freely to exercise his own independent discretion as to parties with whom he will deal.' *United*

States v. Colgate & Co., 250 U.S. 300, 307, 39 S.Ct. 465, 468, 63 L.Ed. 992 (1919).   Moreover, state proprietary activities may be, and often are, burdened with the same restrictions imposed on private market participants.   Evenhandedness suggests that, when acting as proprietors, States should similarly share existing freedoms from federal constraints, including the inherent limits of the Commerce Clause."

marketplace when it provides city funds for building construction. If the city is a market participant, then the Commerce Clause establishes no barrier to conditions such as these which the city demands for its participation. Impact on out-of-state residents figures in the equation only after it is decided that the city is regulating the market rather than participating in it, for only in the former case need it be determined whether any burden on interstate commerce is permitted by the Commerce Clause.

The same may be said of the Massachusetts court's finding that the executive order sweeps too broadly, creating more burden than is necessary to accomplish its stated objectives. While relevant if the Commerce Clause imposes restraints on the city's activity, this characterization is of no help in deciding whether those restraints apply. The Massachusetts court relied in part on our decision in *Hicklin v. Orbeck*, 437 U.S. 518, 98 S.Ct. 2482, 57 L.Ed.2d 397 (1978), saying that "as in *Hicklin*, there is a broadly drawn statute which sweeps far wider than merely favoring unemployed or underemployed local residents."

In *Hicklin* we considered an Alaska statute which required employment in all work connected with oil and gas leases to which the State was a party to be offered first to "qualified" Alaska residents in preference to nonresidents. The State sought to justify the "Alaska Hire" law on the ground that the underlying oil and gas were owned by the State itself. Analyzing the case under the Privileges and Immunities Clause of Art. IV, § 2, cl. 1, we held that mere ownership of a natural resource did not in all circumstances render a state regulation such as the "Alaska Hire" law immune from attack under that clause. We summarized our view of the Alaska statute in these words:

> "In sum, the Act is an attempt to force virtually all businesses that benefit in some way from the economic ripple effect of Alaska's decision to develop its oil and gas resources to bias their employment practices in favor of the State's residents."

Even though respondents no longer press the Privileges and Immunities Clause holding of *Hicklin* in support of their Commerce Clause argument, we note that on the record before us the application of the mayor's executive order to contracts involving only city funds does not represent the sort of "attempt to force virtually all businesses that benefit in some way from the economic ripple effect" of the city's decision to enter into contracts for construction projects "to bias their employment practices in favor of the [city's] residents." [7] * * *

---

7. Justice Blackmun's opinion dissenting in part argues that the mayor's order goes beyond market participation because it regulates employment contracts between public contractors and their employees. We agree with Justice Blackmun that there are some limits on a state or local government's ability to impose restrictions that reach beyond the immediate parties with which the government transacts business. We find it unnecessary in this case to define those limits with precision, except to say that we think the Commerce Clause does not require the city to stop at the boundary of formal privity of contract. In this case, the mayor's executive order covers a discrete, identifiable class of economic activity in which the city is a major participant. Everyone affected by the order is, in a substantial if informal sense, "working for the

We hold that on the record before us the application of the mayor's executive order to the contracts in question did not violate the Commerce Clause of the United States Constitution. Insofar as the city expended only its own funds in entering into construction contracts for public projects, it was a market participant and entitled to be treated as such under the rule of *Hughes v. Alexandria Scrap Corp.* * * *

JUSTICE BLACKMUN, with whom JUSTICE WHITE joins, concurring in part and dissenting in part. * * *

Neither *Reeves* nor *Alexandria Scrap* * * * went beyond ensuring that the States enjoy " 'the long recognized right of trader or manufacturer, engaged in an entirely private business, freely to exercise his own independent discretion as to parties with whom he will deal.' " *Reeves,* 447 U.S., at 438–439, 100 S.Ct., at 2278. * * * Boston's executive order goes much further. The city has not attempted merely to choose the "parties with whom [it] will deal." [2] Instead, it has imposed as a condition of obtaining a public construction contract the requirement that *private firms* hire only Boston residents for 50% of specified jobs. Thus, the order directly restricts the ability of private employers to hire nonresidents, and thereby curtails nonresidents' access to jobs with private employers. I had thought it well established that, under the Commerce Clause, States and localities cannot impose restrictions granting their own residents either the exclusive right, or a priority, to private sector economic opportunities.

Such restrictions are not immune from attack under the Commerce Clause solely because the city has imposed them as conditions to its contracts with private employers. * * * The line between regulation and market participation, for purposes of the Commerce Clause, should be drawn with reference to the constitutional values giving rise to the market participant exemption itself. As the Court recognized in *Reeves,* the most important of these is that historically the "Commerce Clause responds principally to state taxes and regulatory measures impeding private trade in the national marketplace"; it was not designed "to limit the ability of the States themselves to operate freely in the free market." The Court also observed that the distinction between participation and regulation rests on core notions of state sovereignty, coupled with the traditional right of private traders to determine the identities of their bargaining partners free from governmental interference. The legitimacy of a claim to the market participant exemption thus should turn primarily on whether a particular state action more closely resembles an attempt to impede trade among private parties, or an attempt, analogous to the accustomed right of merchants in the private sector, to govern the

city." Wherever the limits of the market participation exception may lie, we conclude that the executive order in this case falls well within the scope of *Alexandria Scrap* and *Reeves.*

2. Had the city decided to limit its *own* hiring to Boston residents, its decision

would almost certainly have been permissible under *McCarthy v. Philadelphia Civil Service Comm'n,* 424 U.S. 645, 96 S.Ct. 1154, 47 L.Ed.2d 366 (1976), as well as *Reeves* and *Alexandria Scrap.*

State's own economic conduct and to determine the parties with whom it will deal.

The simple unilateral refusals to deal the Court encountered in *Reeves* and *Alexandria Scrap* were relatively pure examples of a seller's or purchaser's simply choosing its bargaining partners, "long recognized" as the right of traders in our free enterprise system. The executive order in this case, in notable contrast, by its terms is a direct attempt to govern private economic relationships. The power to dictate to another those with whom *he* may deal is viewed with suspicion and closely limited in the context of purely private economic relations. When exercised by government, such a power is the essence of regulation.

Attempts directly to constrict private economic choices through contractual conditions are particularly akin to regulation because, unlike simple refusals to deal but like conventional market regulation, they threaten to extend their regulatory impact well beyond the transaction in which the State has an interest. A requirement that firms wishing to deal with the State hire a certain percentage of their workforce from among state residents in practice may constrict the opportunities of nonresidents to work on projects with no connection whatever with the governmental entity imposing the condition. A firm that relies to any significant degree on a permanent workforce will be compelled to favor local residents for these positions. An analogous requirement that such firms purchase only from in-state suppliers the goods used in state projects also might constrict interstate trade wholly unrelated to government business. If economic considerations counsel in favor of stable relationships with suppliers, a firm wishing to deal with the State will be compelled to favor local firms across the board. The effect of such "conditions" on the ability of nonresidents to deal with affected firms would be virtually identical to the effect of a conventional market regulation requiring such practices.

In *Reeves,* the Court cited "considerations of state sovereignty" as another factor counseling restraint in applying the Commerce Clause to "proprietary" activity. The States have a sovereign interest in some freedom from federal interference when hiring state employees. * * * In my view, the State's interest in managing its relations with its employees is fully safeguarded by its power to do the work itself if it so chooses, with such immunity from the Commerce Clause as attaches in that situation. * * * The Court indicates that it upholds the executive order on the understanding that, with the exception of the federal grant programs, it is applied solely to construction projects funded entirely by the city. Because many construction contractors hire a substantially different work crew for each project they undertake, applied to such projects the mayor's order is arguably limited, as the Court says, to a "discrete, identifiable class of economic activity in which the city is a major participant." This unique aspect of employment in the construction industry—and of public works construction projects—must also underlie the Court's related justification that "[e]veryone affected by the order is, in a substantial if informal sense, 'working for the city.'"

I am not persuaded, however, that even the comparatively limited terms of the executive order constitute "market participation" rather than "market regulation." The "sense" in which those affected by the mayor's order "work for the city" is so "informal," in my view, as to lack substance altogether. The city does not hire them, fire them, negotiate with them or their representative about the terms of their employment, or pay their wages. In the case of the employees of subcontractors regulated by the order, the city does not even pay, or contract directly with, their employers. In short, the economic choices the city restricts in favor of its residents are the choices of private entities engaged in interstate commerce. Thus, the executive order directly impedes "free private trade in the national marketplace," and for that reason I would not hold it immune from Commerce Clause scrutiny. * * *

UNITED BUILDING & CONSTRUCTION TRADES COUNCIL OF CAMDEN COUNTY v. CAMDEN

Supreme Court of the United States, 1984.
465 U.S. 208, 104 S.Ct. 1020, 79 L.Ed.2d 249.

JUSTICE REHNQUIST delivered the opinion of the Court.

A municipal ordinance of the city of Camden, New Jersey, requires that at least 40% of the employees of contractors and subcontractors working on city construction projects be Camden residents. Appellant, the United Building and Construction Trades Council of Camden County and Vicinity (Council), challenges that ordinance as a violation of the Privileges and Immunities Clause, Art. IV, § 2, cl. 1, of the United States Constitution.[1] * * *

We first address the argument, accepted by the Supreme Court of New Jersey, that the Clause does not even apply to a *municipal* ordinance such as this. Two separate contentions are advanced in support of this position: first, that the Clause only applies to laws passed by a *State* and, second, that the Clause only applies to laws that discriminate on the basis of *state* citizenship.

The first argument can be quickly rejected. The fact that the ordinance in question is a municipal, rather than a state, law does not somehow place it outside the scope of the Privileges and Immunities Clause. First of all, one cannot easily distinguish municipal from state action in this case: the municipal ordinance would not have gone into effect without express approval by the State Treasurer. * * * More fundamentally, a municipality is merely a political subdivision of the

---

1. "The Citizens of each State shall be entitled to all Privileges and Immunities of Citizens in the several States."

State from which its authority derives. It is as true of the Privileges and Immunities Clause as of the Equal Protection Clause that what would be unconstitutional if done directly by the State can no more readily be accomplished by a city deriving its authority from the State. Thus, even if the ordinance had been adopted solely by Camden, and not pursuant to a state program or with state approval, the hiring preference would still have to comport with the Privileges and Immunities Clause.

The second argument merits more consideration. The New Jersey Supreme Court concluded that the Privileges and Immunities Clause does not apply to an ordinance that discriminates solely on the basis of *municipal* residency. The Clause is phrased in terms of *state* citizenship and was designed "to place the citizens of each State upon the same footing with citizens of other States, so far as the advantages resulting from citizenship in those States are concerned." *Paul v. Virginia*, 8 Wall. 168, 180, 19 L.Ed. 357 (1869). * * * Municipal residency classifications, it is argued, simply do not give rise to the same concerns.

We cannot accept this argument. * * * Given the Camden ordinance, an out-of-state citizen who ventures into New Jersey will not enjoy the same privileges as the New Jersey citizen residing in Camden. It is true that New Jersey citizens not residing in Camden will be affected by the ordinance as well as out-of-state citizens. And it is true that the disadvantaged New Jersey residents have no claim under the Privileges and Immunities Clause. But New Jersey residents at least have a chance to remedy at the polls any discrimination against them. Out-of-state citizens have no similar opportunity, and they must not "be restricted to the uncertain remedies afforded by diplomatic processes and official retaliation." *Toomer v. Witsell*, 334 U.S. [385], at 395, 68 S.Ct. [1156], at 1162.[9] We conclude that Camden's ordinance is not immune from constitutional review at the behest of out-of-state residents merely because some in-state residents are similarly disadvantaged.

9. The dissent suggests that New Jersey citizens not residing in Camden will adequately protect the interests of out-of-state residents and that the scope of the Privileges and Immunities Clause should be measured in light of this political reality. What the dissent fails to appreciate is that the Camden ordinance at issue in this case was adopted pursuant to a comprehensive, state-wide program applicable in all New Jersey cities. The Camden resident-preference ordinance has already received state sanction and approval, and every New Jersey city is free to adopt a similar protectionist measure. Some have already done so. Thus, it is hard to see how New Jersey residents living outside Camden will protect the interests of out-of-state citizens.

More fundamentally, the dissent's proposed blanket exemption for all classifications that are less than state-wide would provide States with a simple means for evading the strictures of the Privileges and Immunities Clause. Suppose, for example, that California wanted to guarantee that all employees of contractors and subcontractors working on construction projects funded in whole or in part by state funds are state residents. Under the dissent's analysis, the California legislature need merely divide the State in half, providing one resident-hiring preference for Northern Californians on all such projects taking place in Northern California, and one for Southern Californians on all projects taking place in Southern California. State residents generally would benefit from the law at the expense of out-of-state residents; yet, the law would be immune from scrutiny under the Clause simply because it was not phrased in terms of *state* citizenship or residency. Such a formalistic construction would effectively write the Clause out of the Constitution.

Application of the Privileges and Immunities Clause to a particular instance of discrimination against out-of-state residents entails a two-step inquiry. As an initial matter, the Court must decide whether the ordinance burdens one of those privileges and immunities protected by the Clause. *Baldwin v. Montana Fish and Game Comm'n,* 436 U.S. 371, 383, 98 S.Ct. 1852, 1860, 56 L.Ed.2d 354 (1978). Not all forms of discrimination against citizens of other States are constitutionally suspect.

> "Some distinctions between residents and nonresidents merely reflect the fact that this is a Nation composed of individual States, and are permitted; other distinctions are prohibited because they hinder the formation, the purpose, or the development of a single Union of those States. Only with respect to those 'privileges' and 'immunities' bearing upon the vitality of the Nation as a single entity must the State treat all citizens, resident and nonresident, equally." *Ibid.*

As a threshold matter, then, we must determine whether an out-of-state resident's interest in employment on public works contracts in another State is sufficiently "fundamental" to the promotion of interstate harmony so as to "fall within the purview of the Privileges and Immunities Clause." *Id.,* at 388, 98 S.Ct., at 1862.

Certainly, the pursuit of a common calling is one of the most fundamental of those privileges protected by the Clause. *Baldwin v. Montana Fish and Game Comm'n,* 436 U.S. 371, 387, 98 S.Ct. 1852, 1862, 56 L.Ed.2d 351 (1978). Many, if not most, of our cases expounding the Privileges and Immunities Clause have dealt with this basic and essential activity. See, *e.g., Hicklin v. Orbeck,* 437 U.S. 518, 98 S.Ct. 2482, 57 L.Ed.2d 397 (1978). Public employment, however, is qualitatively different from employment in the private sector; it is a subspecies of the broader opportunity to pursue a common calling. We have held that there is no fundamental right to government employment for purposes of the Equal Protection Clause. *Massachusetts v. Murgia,* 427 U.S. 307, 313, 96 S.Ct. 2562, 2566, 49 L.Ed.2d 520 (1976) (*per curiam*). *Cf. McCarthy v. Philadelphia Civil Service Comm'n,* 424 U.S. 645, 96 S.Ct. 1154, 47 L.Ed.2d 366 (1976) (*per curiam*)(rejecting equal protection challenge to municipal residency requirement for municipal workers). And in *White* [*v. Massachusetts Council of Const. Employers,*] we held that for purposes of the Commerce Clause everyone employed on a city public works project is, "in a substantial if informal sense, 'working for the city.' "

It can certainly be argued that for purposes of the Privileges and Immunities Clause everyone affected by the Camden ordinance is also "working for the city" and, therefore, has no grounds for complaint when the city favors its own residents. But we decline to transfer mechanically into this context an analysis fashioned to fit the Commerce Clause. Our decision in *White* turned on a distinction between the city acting as a market participant and the city acting as a market regulator. The question whether employees of contractors and subcontractors on public works projects were or were not, in some sense, working for the city was crucial to that analysis. The question had to be answered in order to chart the boundaries of the distinction. But the distinction between market participant and market regulator relied upon in *White* to dispose of the Commerce Clause challenge is not dispositive in this context. The two Clauses have different aims and set different standards for state conduct.

The Commerce Clause acts as an implied restraint upon state regulatory powers. Such powers must give way before the superior authority of Congress to legislate on (or leave unregulated) matters involving interstate commerce. When the State acts solely as a market participant, no conflict between state *regulation* and federal regulatory authority can arise. *White,* 103 S.Ct., at 1044; *Reeves, Inc. v. Stake,* 447 U.S. 429, 436–437, 100 S.Ct. 2271, 2277–2278, 65 L.Ed.2d 244 (1980); *Hughes v. Alexandria Scrap Corp.,* 426 U.S. 794, 810, 96 S.Ct. 2488, 2498, 49 L.Ed.2d 220 (1976). The Privileges and Immunities Clause, on the other hand, imposes a direct restraint on state action in the interests of interstate harmony. *Hicklin v. Orbeck,* 437 U.S. 518, 523–524, 98 S.Ct. 2482, 2486–2487, 57 L.Ed.2d 397 (1978). This concern with comity cuts across the market regulator-market participant distinction that is crucial under the Commerce Clause. It is discrimination against out-of-state residents on matters of fundamental concern which triggers the Clause, not regulation affecting interstate commerce. Thus, the fact that Camden is merely setting conditions on its expenditures for goods and services in the marketplace does not preclude the possibility that those conditions violate the Privileges and Immunities Clause.

In *Hicklin v. Orbeck,* 437 U.S. 518, 98 S.Ct. 2482, 57 L.Ed.2d 397 (1978), we struck down as a violation of the Privileges and Immunities Clause an "Alaska Hire" statute containing a resident hiring preference for all employment related to the development of the State's oil and gas resources. Alaska argued in that case "that because the oil and gas that are the subject of Alaska Hire are *owned* by the State, this ownership, of itself, is sufficient justification for the Act's discrimination against nonresidents, and takes the Act totally without the scope of the Privileges and Immunities Clause." We concluded, however, that the State's interest in controlling those things it claims to own is not absolute. "Rather than placing a statute completely beyond the Clause, a State's ownership of the property with which the statute is concerned is a factor—although often the crucial factor—to be considered in evaluating whether the statute's discrimination against noncitizens violates the Clause." Much the same analysis, we think, is appropriate to a city's efforts to bias private employment decisions in favor of its residents on construction projects funded with public monies. The fact that Camden is expending its own funds or funds it administers in accordance with the terms of a grant is certainly a factor—perhaps the crucial factor—to be considered in evaluating whether the statute's discrimination violates the Privileges and Immunities Clause. But it does not remove the Camden ordinance completely from the purview of the Clause.

In sum, Camden may, without fear of violating the Commerce Clause, pressure private employers engaged in public works projects funded in whole or in part by the city to hire city residents. But that same exercise of power to bias the employment decisions of private contractors and subcontractors against out-of-state residents may be called to account under the Privileges and Immunities Clause. A determination of whether a privilege is "fundamental" for purposes of that Clause does not depend on whether the employees of private contractors and subcontractors engaged in public works projects can or cannot be said to be "working for the city." The opportunity to seek employment with such private employers is "sufficiently basic to the livelihood of the Nation," *Baldwin v. Montana Fish and Game Comm'n,* 436 U.S. 371, 388, 98 S.Ct. 1852, 1863, 56 L.Ed.2d 354 (1978), as to fall within the purview of the Privileges and Immunities Clause even though the contractors and subcontractors are themselves engaged in projects funded in whole or part by the city.

The conclusion that Camden's ordinance discriminates against a protected privilege does not, of course, end the inquiry. We have stressed in prior cases that "[l]ike many other constitutional provisions, the privileges and immunities clause is not an absolute." *Toomer v. Witsell,* 334 U.S. 385, 396, 68 S.Ct. 1156, 1162, 92 L.Ed. 1460 (1948). It does not preclude discrimination against citizens of other States where there is a "substantial reason" for the difference in treatment. "[T]he inquiry in each case must be concerned with whether such reasons do exist and whether the degree of discrimination bears a close relation to them." *Ibid.* As part of any justification offered for the discriminatory law, nonresidents must somehow be shown to "constitute a peculiar source of the evil at which the statute is aimed." *Id.,* at 398, 68 S.Ct., at 1163.

The city of Camden contends that its ordinance is necessary to counteract grave economic and social ills. Spiralling unemployment, a sharp decline in population, and a dramatic reduction in the number of businesses located in the city have eroded property values and depleted the city's tax base. The resident hiring preference is designed, the city contends, to increase the number of employed persons living in Camden and to arrest the "middle class flight" currently plaguing the city. The city also argues that all nonCamden residents employed on city public works projects, whether they reside in New Jersey or Pennsylvania, constitute a "source of the evil at which the statute is aimed." That is, they "live off" Camden without "living in" Camden. Camden contends that the scope of the discrimination practiced in the ordinance, with its municipal residency requirement, is carefully tailored to alleviate this evil without unreasonably harming nonresidents, who still have access to 60% of the available positions.

Every inquiry under the Privileges and Immunities Clause "must * * * be conducted with due regard for the principle that the states should have considerable leeway in analyzing local evils and in prescribing appropriate cures." *Toomer v. Witsell,* 334 U.S. 385, 396, 68 S.Ct.

1156, 1162, 92 L.Ed. 1460 (1948). This caution is particularly appropriate when a government body is merely setting conditions on the expenditure of funds it controls. The Alaska Hire statute at issue in *Hicklin v. Orbeck,* 437 U.S. 518, 98 S.Ct. 2482, 57 L.Ed.2d 397 (1978), swept within its strictures not only contractors and subcontractors dealing directly with the State's oil and gas; it also covered suppliers who provided goods and services to those contractors and subcontractors. We invalidated the Act as "an attempt to force virtually all businesses that benefit in some way from the economic ripple effect of Alaska's decision to develop its oil and gas resources to bias their employment practices in favor of the State's residents." No similar "ripple effect" appears to infect the Camden ordinance. It is limited in scope to employees working directly on city public works projects.

Nonetheless, we find it impossible to evaluate Camden's justification on the record as it now stands. No trial has ever been held in the case. No findings of fact have been made. The Supreme Court of New Jersey certified the case for direct appeal after the brief administrative proceedings that led to approval of the ordinance by the State Treasurer. It would not be appropriate for this Court either to make factual determinations as an initial matter or to take judicial notice of Camden's decay. We, therefore, deem it wise to remand the case to the New Jersey Supreme Court. That court may decide, consistent with state procedures, on the best method for making the necessary findings. * * *

JUSTICE BLACKMUN, dissenting.

For over a century the underlying meaning of the Privileges and Immunities Clause of the Constitution's Article IV has been regarded as settled: at least absent some substantial, noninvidious justification, a State may not discriminate between its own residents and residents of other States on the basis of state citizenship. * * * Today, however, the Court casually extends the scope of the Clause by holding that it applies to laws that discriminate *among* state residents on the basis of *municipal* residence, simply because discrimination on the basis of municipal residence disadvantages citizens of other States "*ipso facto.*" This novel interpretation arrives accompanied by little practical justification and no historical or textual support whatsoever. * * *

Contrary to the Court's tacit assumption, discrimination on the basis of municipal residence is substantially different in this regard from discrimination on the basis of state citizenship. The distinction is simple but fundamental: discrimination on the basis of municipal residence penalizes persons within the State's political community as well as those without. The Court itself points out that while New Jersey citizens who reside outside Camden are not protected by the Privileges and Immunities Clause, they may resort to the State's political processes to protect themselves. What the Court fails to appreciate is that this avenue of relief for New Jersey residents works to protect residents of other States as well; disadvantaged state residents who turn to the state legislature to displace ordinances like Camden's further the interests of nonresidents as well as their own. Nor is this mechanism for relief merely a theoretical one; in the past decade several States, including California and Georgia, have repealed or forbidden protectionist ordinances like the one at issue here. In short, discrimination on the basis of municipal residence simply does not consign residents of other States, in the words of *Toomer,* to "the uncertain remedies afforded by diplomatic processes and official retaliation." The Court thus has applied the Privileges and Immunities Clause without regard for the political ills that it was designed to cure. * * *

MATTHEWS v. BAY HEAD IMPROVEMENT ASSOCIATION

Supreme Court of New Jersey, 1984.
95 N.J. 306, 471 A.2d 355, cert. denied, 469 U.S. 821, 105 S.Ct. 93, 83 L.Ed.2d 39.

SCHREIBER, J.

The public trust doctrine acknowledges that the ownership, dominion and sovereignty over land flowed by tidal waters, which extend to the mean high water mark, is vested in the State in trust for the people. The public's right to use the tidal lands and water encompasses navigation, fishing and recreational uses, including bathing, swimming and other shore activities. *Borough of Neptune City v. Borough of Avon-by-the-Sea,* 61 *N.J.* 296, 309, 294 *A.*2d 47 (1972). In *Avon* we held that the public trust applied to the municipally-owned dry sand beach immediately landward of the high water mark. The major issue in this case is whether, ancillary to the public's right to enjoy the tidal lands, the public has a right to gain access through and to use the dry sand area not owned by a municipality but by a quasi-public body.

The Borough of Point Pleasant instituted this suit against the Borough of Bay Head and the Bay Head Improvement Association (Association), generally asserting that the defendants prevented Point Pleasant inhabitants from gaining access to the Atlantic Ocean and the beachfront in Bay Head. The proceeding was dismissed as to the Borough of Bay Head because it did not own or control the beach. Subsequently, Virginia Matthews, a resident of Point Pleasant who desired to swim and bathe at the Bay Head beach, joined as a party plaintiff, and Stanley Van Ness, as Public Advocate, joined as plaintiff-intervenor. * * *

The Borough of Bay Head (Bay Head) borders the Atlantic Ocean. Adjacent to it on the north is the Borough of Point Pleasant Beach, on the south the Borough of Mantoloking, and on the west Barnegat Bay. Bay Head consists of a fairly narrow strip of land, 6,667 feet long (about 1¼ miles). A beach runs along its entire length adjacent to the Atlantic Ocean. There are 76 separate parcels of land that border the beach. All except six are owned by private individuals. Title to those six is vested in the Association.

The Association was founded in 1910 and incorporated as a nonprofit corporation in 1932. Its certificate of incorporation states that its purposes are

> the improving and beautifying of the Borough of Bay Head, New Jersey, cleaning, policing and otherwise making attractive and safe the bathing beaches in said Borough, and the doing of any act which may be found necessary or desirable for the greater convenience, comfort and enjoyment of the residents.

Its constitution delineates the Association's object to promote the best interests of the Borough and "in so doing to own property, operate bathing beaches, hire life guards, beach cleaners and policemen * * *."

Nine streets in the Borough, which are perpendicular to the beach, end at the dry sand. The Association owns the land commencing at the end of seven of these streets for the width of each street and extending through the upper dry sand to the mean high water line, the beginning of the wet sand area or foreshore. In addition, the Association owns the fee in six shore front properties, three of which are contiguous and have a frontage aggregating 310 feet. Many owners of beachfront property executed and delivered to the Association leases of the upper dry sand area. These leases are revocable by either party to the lease on thirty days' notice. Some owners have not executed such leases and have not permitted the Association to use their beaches. Some also have acquired riparian grants from the State extending approximately 1,000 feet east of the high water line.

The Association controls and supervises its beach property between the third week in June and Labor Day. It engages about 40 employees, who serve as lifeguards, beach police and beach cleaners. * * * Beach police are stationed at the entrances to the beaches where the public streets lead into the beach to ensure that only Association members or their guests enter. Some beach police patrol the beaches to enforce its membership rules.

Membership is generally limited to residents of Bay Head. Class A members are property owners. Class B are non-owners. Large families (six or more) pay $90 per year and small families pay $60 per year. Upon application residents are routinely accepted. Membership is evidenced by badges that signify permission to use the beaches. Members, which include local hotels, motels and inns, can also acquire badges for guests. The charge for each guest badge is $12. Members of the Bay Head Fire Company, Bay Head Borough employees, and teachers in the municipality's school system have been issued beach badges irrespective of residency.

Except for fishermen, who are permitted to walk through the upper dry sand area to the foreshore, only the membership may use the beach between 10:00 a.m. and 5:30 p.m. during the summer season. The public is permitted to use the Association's beach from 5:30 p.m. to 10:00 a.m. during the summer and, with no hourly restrictions, between Labor Day and mid-June. * * *

Association membership totals between 4,800 to 5,000. The Association President testified during depositions that its restrictive policy, in existence since 1932, was due to limited parking facilities and to the overcrowding of the beaches. The Association's avowed purpose was to provide the beach for the residents of Bay Head. * * *

In *Borough of Neptune City v. Borough of Avon-by-the-Sea,* 61 *N.J.* 296, 303, 294 A.2d 47 (1972), Justice Hall alluded to the ancient principle "that land covered by tidal waters belonged to the sovereign, but for the common use of all the people." * * * He observed that the public has a right to use the land below the mean average high water mark where the tide ebbs and flows. These uses have historically included navigation and fishing. In *Avon* the public's rights were extended "to recreational uses, including bathing, swimming and other shore activities." * * * In order to exercise these rights guaranteed by the public trust doctrine, the public must have access to municipally-owned dry sand areas as well as the foreshore. The extension of the public trust doctrine to include municipally-owned dry sand areas was necessitated by our conclusion that enjoyment of rights in the foreshore is inseparable from use of dry sand beaches. In *Avon* we struck down a municipal ordinance that required nonresidents to pay a higher fee than residents for the use of the beach. We held that where a municipal beach is dedicated to public use, the public trust doctrine "dictates that the beach and the ocean waters must be open to all on equal terms and without preference and that any contrary state or municipal action is impermissible." * * *

In *Van Ness v. Borough of Deal,* 78 *N.J.* 174, 393 A.2d 571 (1978), we stated that the public's right to use municipally-owned beaches was not dependent upon the municipality's dedication of its beaches to use by the general public. The Borough of Deal had dedicated a portion of such beach for use by its residents only. We found such limited dedication "immaterial" given the public trust doctrine's requirement that the public be afforded the right to enjoy all dry sand beaches owned by a municipality.

In *Avon* and *Deal* our finding of public rights in dry sand areas was specifically and appropriately limited to those beaches owned by a municipality. We now address the extent of the public's interest in privately-owned dry sand beaches. This interest may take one of two forms. First, the public may have a right to cross privately owned dry sand beaches in order to gain access to the foreshore. Second, this interest may be of the sort enjoyed by the public in municipal beaches under *Avon* and *Deal,* namely, the right to sunbathe and generally enjoy recreational activities. * * *

Exercise of the public's right to swim and bathe below the mean high water mark may depend upon a right to pass across the upland beach. Without some means of access the public right to use the foreshore would be meaningless. To say that the public trust doctrine entitles the public to swim in the ocean and to use the foreshore in connection therewith without assuring the public of a feasible access route would seriously impinge on, if not effectively eliminate, the rights of the public trust doctrine. This does not mean the public has an unrestricted right to cross at will over any and all property bordering on the common property. The public interest is satisfied so long as there is reasonable access to the sea. * * *

[T]he particular circumstances must be considered and examined before arriving at a solution that will accommodate the public's right and the private interests involved. Thus an undeveloped segment of the shore may have been available and used for access so as to establish a public right of way to the wet sand. Or there may be publicly-owned property, such as in *Avon,* which is suitable. Or, as in this case, the public streets and adjacent upland sand area might serve as a proper means of entry. The test is whether those means are reasonably satisfactory so that the public's right to use the beachfront can be satisfied.

The bather's right in the upland sands is not limited to passage. Reasonable enjoyment of the foreshore and the sea cannot be realized unless some enjoyment of the dry sand area is also allowed. The complete pleasure of swimming must be accompanied by intermittent periods of rest and relaxation beyond the water's edge. The unavailability of the physical situs for such rest and relaxation would seriously curtail and in many situations eliminate the right to the recreational use of the ocean. This was a principal reason why in *Avon* and *Deal* we held that municipally-owned dry sand beaches "must be open to all on equal terms * * *." We see no reason why rights under the public trust doctrine to use of the upland dry sand area should be limited to municipally-owned property. It is true that the private owner's interest in the upland dry sand area is not identical to that of a municipality. Nonetheless, where use of dry sand is essential or reasonably necessary for enjoyment of the ocean, the doctrine warrants the public's use of the upland dry sand area subject to an accommodation of the interests of the owner. * * *

Today, recognizing the increasing demand for our State's beaches and the dynamic nature of the public trust doctrine, we find that the public must be given both access to and use of privately-owned dry sand areas as reasonably necessary. While the public's rights in private beaches are not co-extensive with the rights enjoyed in municipal beaches, private landowners may not in all instances prevent the public from exercising its rights under the public trust doctrine. The public must be afforded reasonable access to the foreshore as well as a suitable area for recreation on the dry sand. * * * The question that we must address is whether the dry sand area that the Association owns or leases should be open to the public to satisfy the public's rights under the public trust doctrine. Our analysis turns upon whether the Association may restrict its membership to Bay Head residents and thereby preclude public use of the dry sand area. * * *

The general rule is that courts will not compel admission to a voluntary association. Ordinarily, a society or association may set its own membership qualifications and restrictions. However, that is not an inexorable rule. Where an organization is quasi-public, its power to exclude must be reasonably and lawfully exercised in furtherance of the public welfare related to its public characteristics. * * * [A] nonprofit association that is authorized and endeavors to carry out a purpose serving the general welfare of the community and is a quasi-public institution holds in trust its powers of exclusive control in the areas of vital public concern. When a nonprofit association rejects a membership application for reasons unrelated to its purposes and contrary to the general welfare, courts have "broad judicial authority to insure that exclusionary policies are lawful and are not applied arbitrarily or discriminately." *Greisman,* 40 *N.J.* at 395, 192 A.2d 817. That is the situation here. * * *

Shortly after the Association was incorporated and had established a plan to operate beaches that would be open to all residents of Bay Head, the Bay Head Borough Council, after discussion with the Association's members, adopted resolutions approving the plan and agreeing to cooperate with the Association in carrying out this plan "insofar as it lies within the power of the Council so to do." The municipality evidenced its cooperation thereafter in a number of ways. It provided office space without charge in the Borough Hall between 1934 and 1973. Until 1975 seven parcels that ran from public streets to the mean high tide, all owned by the Association, were not assessed and the Association paid no realty taxes for those properties. The Borough's blanket liability insurance policies in effect between 1962 and 1968 covered the Association's activities on the beach area. The Borough appropriated public funds for the Association's benefit, $600 annually between 1936 and 1941, and $1,000 in 1969. Six groins (stone jetties) have been installed on the beach. The Borough paid one quarter of their cost; Ocean County, one quarter; and the State, one half.

The Association's activities paralleled those of a municipality in its operation of the beachfront. The size of the beach was so great that it stationed lifeguards at five separate locations. The beach serviced about 5,000 members. The lifeguards performed the functions characteristic of those on a public beach. * * * The beach was maintained and kept clean by crews who worked each day. These crews cleaned the beach from end to end, including properties not leased to the Association. Membership badges were sold and guards were stationed at entrances to the beach to make certain that only those licensed could gain admittance. Further, some guards patrolled the beach to make certain that members and guests complied with the Association's rules and regulations. When viewed in its totality—its purposes, relationship with the municipality, communal characteristic, activities, and virtual monopoly over the Bay Head beachfront—the quasi-public nature of the Association is apparent. The Association makes available to the Bay Head public access to the common tidal property for swimming and bathing and to the upland dry sand area for use incidental thereto, preserving the residents' interests in a fashion similar to *Avon*.

There is no public beach in the Borough of Bay Head. If the residents of every municipality bordering the Jersey shore were to adopt the Bay Head policy, the public would be prevented from exercising its right to enjoy the foreshore. The Bay Head residents may not frustrate the public's right in this manner. By limiting membership only to residents and foreclosing the public, the Association is acting in conflict with the public good and contrary to the strong public policy "in favor of encouraging and expanding public access to and use of shoreline areas." *Gion v. City of Santa Cruz,* 2 *Cal.*3d 29, 43, 465 *P.*2d 50, 59, 84 *Cal.Rptr.* 162, 171 (1970). Indeed, the Association is frustrating the public's right under the public trust doctrine. It should not be permitted to do so.

Accordingly, membership in the Association must be open to the public at large. In this manner the public will be assured access to the common beach property during the hours of 10:00 a.m. to 5:30 p.m. between mid-June and September, where they may exercise their right to swim and bathe and to use the Association's dry sand area incidental to those activities. Although such membership rights to the use of the beach may be broader than the rights necessary for enjoyment of the public trust, opening the Association's membership to all, nonresidents and residents, should lead to a substantial satisfaction of the public trust doctrine. However, the Association shall also make available a reasonable quantity of daily as well as seasonal badges to the nonresident public. Its decision with respect to the number of daily and seasonal badges to be afforded to nonresidents should take into account all relevant matters, such as the public demand and the number of bathers and swimmers that may be safely and reasonably accommodated on the Association's property, whether owned or leased. The Association may continue to charge reasonable fees to cover its costs of lifeguards, beach cleaners, patrols, equipment, insurance, and administrative expenses. The fees fixed may not discriminate in any respect between residents and nonresidents. The Association may continue to enforce its regulations regarding cleanliness, safety, and other reasonable measures concerning the public use of the beach. In this connection, it would be entirely appropriate, in the formulation and adoption of such reasonable regulations concerning the public's use of the beaches, to encourage the participation and cooperation of all private beachfront property owners, regardless of their membership in or affiliation with the Association.

The Public Advocate has urged that all the privately-owned beachfront property likewise must be opened to the public. Nothing has been developed on this record to justify that conclusion. We have decided that the Association's membership and thereby its beach must be open to the public. That area might reasonably satisfy the public need at this time. We are aware that the Association possessed, as of the initiation of this litigation, about 42 upland sand lots under leases revocable on 30 days' notice. If any of these leases have been or are to be terminated, or if the Association were to sell all or part of its property, it may necessitate further adjudication of the public's claims in favor of the public trust on part or all of these or other privately-owned upland dry sand lands depending upon the circumstances. However, we see no necessity to have those issues resolved judicially at this time since the beach under the Association's control will be open to the public and may be adequate to satisfy the public trust interests. We believe that the Association and property owners will act in good faith and to the satisfaction of the Public Advocate. * * *

It is not necessary for us to determine under what circumstances and to what extent there will be a need to use the dry sand of private owners who either now or in the future may have no leases with the Association. Resolution of the competing interests, private ownership and the public trust, may in some cases be simple, but in many it may be most complex. * * * All we decide here is that private land is not immune from a possible right of access to the foreshore for swimming or bathing purposes, nor is it immune from the possibility that some of the dry sand may be used by the public incidental to the right of bathing and swimming. * * *

4. THE ABILITY OF CITIES TO ANNEX OUTSIDERS

This section raises a critical issue about inter-city relationships both as a matter of history and a matter of theory: who needs to agree before one city can annex another?[1] Four answers to this question seem possible:

1. Citizens of both the annexing and annexed city could vote, with all ballots counted together according to the principle of one person, one vote.

2. Only citizens of the annexing city could vote; no one in the annexed city would be entitled to vote.

3. Only citizens of the annexed city could vote; no one in the annexing city would be entitled to vote.

4. Citizens of both the annexing and annexed city could vote, but the ballots would be counted separately. Annexation would require both a majority of the vote of the annexing city and a majority of the vote of the annexed city.

Each of the following cases examines one of these four positions about the appropriate vote in an annexation. (Admittedly, not all of the

---

1. For a history of annexation, see, e.g., Teaford, City and Suburb: The Political Fragmentation of Metropolitan America, 1850–1970, pp. 32–63 (1979); see also Warner, Streetcar Suburbs: The Process of Growth in Boston, 1870–1900 (1962). For a consideration of the legal issues raised by annexation, see, e.g., Reynolds, Rethinking Municipal Annexation Powers, 24 The Urban Lawyer 247 (1992); Waite, Annexation and the Voting Rights Act, 28 How.L.J. 565 (1985); Lipsig, Annexation Elections and the Right to Vote, 20 U.C.L.A.L.Rev. 1093 (1973); Woodrooff, Systems and Standards of Municipal Annexation Review: A Comparative Analysis, 58 Geo.L.Rev. 743 (1970); National League of Cities, Adjusting Municipal Boundaries (1962). See also Fleischmann, The Politics of Annexation: A Preliminary Assessment of Competing Paradigms, 67 Soc.Sci.Q. 1 (1986).

cases are strictly-speaking annexation cases). In reading the cases, consider the possible grounds on which one might choose among the four possible ways of deciding annexation issues. What would justify giving a small city a veto on being annexed by a larger city (as in positions 3 and 4, above)? What would justify letting a large city annex a smaller city when a majority of the smaller city opposes the annexation (as in positions 1 and 2 above)? What do the results in these four cases suggest about the significance of the boundary line between cities?

HUNTER v. PITTSBURGH

Page 108, supra.

MURPHY v. KANSAS CITY, MISSOURI

United States District Court, Western District of Missouri, 1972.
347 F.Supp. 837.

ELMO B. HUNTER, DISTRICT JUDGE. * * *

On May 15, 1970, Ordinance No. 38354 was introduced in the City Council of the City of Kansas City, Missouri. This ordinance proposes the submission to the electorate of Kansas City of an amendment to the City Charter extending Kansas City's corporate boundaries to include an area in Platte County, Missouri, a third class county presently adjacent to Kansas City, Missouri. * * * Since the proposed area to be annexed is not an incorporated area, pursuant to Article VI, Section 20, of the Constitution of 1945 and Section 5 of the Kansas City Charter, its inclusion in the city limits of Kansas City, Missouri must be accomplished by an amendment to the Kansas City Charter. Thus, the annexation need be approved only by the voters of the City of Kansas City, and persons residing in the area to be annexed have no vote. * * * Plaintiffs [residents of the area to be annexed] claim that the method by which the proposed annexation of the area in which they reside is to be accomplished is violative of the equal protection clause of the Fourteenth Amendment to the United States Constitution. * * *

Defendants contend that plaintiffs' complaint presents a nonjusticiable political question. Defendants rely primarily on *Hunter v. City of Pittsburgh*, 207 U.S. 161, 28 S.Ct. 40, 52 L.Ed. 151 (1907). * * * In accordance with *Hunter* plaintiffs' challenge under the Fourteenth Amendment to the procedure for annexation established for the City of Kansas City, Missouri by that city's charter and by the Constitution and Laws of the State of Missouri, is not justiciable. * * * However, in view of the important questions presented by the complaint, they will be discussed on the merits. * * *

[P]laintiffs point to the fact that the proposed annexation will, under Article VI, Section 20, of the Missouri Constitution and under Section 5 of the Kansas City Charter, be accomplished without plaintiffs having the right to vote on the matter while the voters of Kansas City are entitled to vote on and must approve the annexation proposal. This, they contend, denies them equal protection of the laws in that they are denied the right to participate in this governmental decision even though they are directly affected and have a substantial interest. They further contend such practice is discrimination in favor of the voters of Kansas City, and that such discrimination is invidious, without rational basis, and is not necessary to promote any compelling state interest.

In support of this initial contention, plaintiffs attempt to equate their position with that of the plaintiffs in the voting rights cases of *Cipriano v. City of Houma*, 395 U.S. 701, 89 S.Ct. 1897, 23 L.Ed.2d 647 (1969), and *Kramer v. Union Free School Dist.*, 395 U.S. 621, 89 S.Ct. 1886, 23 L.Ed.2d 583 (1969), and assert that even though a question need not be submitted to the voters, once the legislature provides for a popular vote the equal protection clause applies and the vote must be granted to all persons substantially affected, and any exclusion of these persons from the election process must be shown to be necessary to promote a compelling state interest.

Plaintiffs' reliance on the above mentioned voting rights cases is misplaced. The defect that the Supreme Court found in those cases lay in the denial or dilution of voting because of group characteristics that bore no valid relationship to the interest in the subject matter of the election. * * * In the instant case plaintiffs are *not residents* of the City of Kansas City being denied the right to vote in that city's elections on the grounds of race, wealth, ownership of property, tax status, military status, or period of residency. Rather, plaintiffs are residents of an unincorporated area in Platte County, Missouri. They have no statutory or constitutional right to participate in the governmental processes of the City of Kansas City, for they do not reside within the boundaries of that governmental subdivision. In annexing adjacent territory, the City of Kansas City, Missouri is exercising power entrusted to it by the State of Missouri. The case of *Hunter v. City of Pittsburgh* establishes that the State of Missouri is empowered to alter municipal boundaries "with or without the consent of the citizens, or even against their protests." The City of Kansas City, as an agency of the state exercising this power, has, as a part of its internal governmental process, a method by which its electorate exercises a vote on the matter of whether or not to extend its city limits and numerous city services to an adjacent area. This in no way violates the principles of the voting rights cases relied on by plaintiffs. Plaintiffs make no claim that the proposed annexation is designed purposefully to dilute or exclude some qualified voters from an area. Thus neither the *Cipriano* nor the *Kramer* case is applicable to limit the power of the State of Missouri or the City of Kansas City regarding annexation proceedings as declared in *Hunter*. The State of Missouri has not provided that persons situated as the plaintiffs herein shall have a voice in the matter of the annexation of the territory in which they reside. The establishment of the present procedure is within the discretion of the State under the doctrine of *Hunter* and is not in violation of the equal protection clause of the fourteenth amendment. * * *

MOORMAN v. WOOD

United States District Court, Eastern District of Kentucky, 1980.
504 F.Supp. 467.

BERTELSMAN, DISTRICT JUDGE.   * * *

The 1980 session of the Kentucky General Assembly enacted K.R.S. 81A.430, which authorizes any city to designate for annexation a contiguous part of another city.   If there is an objection, the matter can be placed on the ballot and the citizens of the annexation area then vote on the matter and a majority of those voting decide the issue.

Plaintiffs here are citizens of the City of Covington, portions of which are sought to be annexed by the defendants, the smaller cities of Ft. Wright and Crescent Springs.   Plaintiffs seek to block the annexation on the ground that K.R.S. 81A.430 is unconstitutional in that it contravenes their right to equal protection under the Fourteenth Amendment to the Constitution of the United States.   They contend that the law must fall because it does not permit all of the voters of Covington to vote on what amounts to the deannexation of part of their city, a matter in which they claim a substantial interest.

The rationale of the 1980 annexation statutes cannot be understood in a vacuum.   Some background is essential.

Annexation wars have been rife in Kentucky for generations.   They have been the subject of particularly bitter controversies in the northern area of the state in which this court sits.   This northern area is composed of some 50 cities, contained in three counties.[4]   The largest of the cities, Covington, has a population of about 50,000 and the smallest contains only a few hundred residents.

It is important to an understanding of the statutes here involved and of this decision to grasp that these disputes have no racial overtones.[5]   Nor do they usually involve conflicting class interests of wealth and poverty.

Although the plaintiffs here claim that the annexations are the result of the efforts of two "affluent subdivisions" to attempt to avoid their fair share of urban problems, this is not always, nor even usually the case in local annexation controversies.   The court has known citizens of an unincorporated area with no municipal services whatever and a blue collar population to resist annexation to an affluent city of 15,000 and, in another case, a ferocious court battle to be waged to resist annexation to a city with a population of 3,000 or less, where neither the annexors nor the annexees could be described as affluent.

4. The total population of the three counties is approximately 260,000.   The area is principally urban or suburban and is a part of a larger metropolitan area consisting of the City of Cincinnati, Ohio, and its environs.

5. The black population of Northern Kentucky is between 1 and 3%.   The Oriental and Hispanic populations are minute.

Although, of course, there may be some desire to escape higher taxes and urban problems, in many instances, the motivation for resisting annexation in this vicinity is that many of the people like to live in their small towns where they can know the mayor, city council members and other officials personally, and where they can live their lives, as they see it, relatively free from regulation and have a direct voice in such municipal matters as zoning or the granting of a liquor license.

Where financial considerations are a primary motive in opposing annexations, frequently they involve a conscious desire to accept fewer municipal services as a trade off for lower taxes. For example, many of the smaller communities, both incorporated and unincorporated, keep taxes rather low by utilizing volunteer fire departments, part-time police forces, septic tanks instead of sewers, no city manager or engineer, etc. From this point of view, the prevention of annexation enables those with limited financial resources better to own their own homes. To such people terms like "metro government" and "annexation" are calls to a holy war of resistance.

The annexing cities, on the other hand, are often motivated by a desire to expand their tax base and a perceived need to end the confusion and inefficiency which they contend results from the profusion of small government entities. The court expresses no opinion as to the wisdom of either of these positions. They are described here solely to explain the emotionally charged dilemma with which the legislature was presented.

It is out of this history that the present controversy arises. In 1962 the City of Covington, certain citizens of which are individual plaintiffs here, commenced efforts to annex extensive unincorporated areas of Kenton County. At that time annexations were resisted in Kentucky by remonstrance suits, under which the state court in the context of an equitable action determined, under prescribed statutory tests, whether an annexation was appropriate.

The 1962 annexation litigation worked its tortuous way through the courts until it finally concluded in 1979, with a decision in favor of the annexing City of Covington. The proceedings are too complicated even to attempt to describe here. In 1979 Covington was ultimately successful in finalizing the annexation of these large unincorporated areas. Some of this territory which went to Covington at the conclusion of this 18 years of forensic hostilities is now sought to be detached from Covington and joined to Crescent Springs and Ft. Wright by what amounts to a preemptive strike.

This was made possible because such bitter animosities had been engendered by the prolonged conflict that the vanquished citizens of these areas, refusing to accept their defeat, set up a type of underground resistance movement, sought aid from the General Assembly of the Commonwealth and induced it to repeal the old annexation statutes and enact the one at issue here.

These citizens, who regard themselves as freedom fighters of a sort, then formed an alliance with the smaller cities of Ft. Wright and Crescent Springs to annex them away from Covington under the new law. The annexation was challenged by the filing of appropriate petitions, and the issue scheduled to be placed on the ballot at the general election of November 4, 1980, pursuant to the new statute. The plaintiffs here as citizens of Covington attacked the new law and sought to enjoin the holding of the election, claiming the statute violated their equal protection rights in that it did not permit all the citizens of Covington to vote in the annexation election, although all had a substantial interest in the result.

A preliminary injunction was sought from, but denied by this court, and the election held. There were other annexation issues on the ballot, through which Covington was attempting to annex certain unincorporated areas of Kenton County. The results are in the margin. In interpreting them, it must be recalled that a vote *for* the Ft. Wright and Crescent Springs annexation is actually an *anti*-annexation vote with respect to the City of Covington.[6] As these results show, popular local enthusiasm for annexation to Covington is somewhat restrained.

Thus the issue is presented:

Does a violation of the Equal Protection Clause of the Fourteenth Amendment result from the efforts of the legislature of the Commonwealth of Kentucky to resolve the difficult political problems of annexation by providing that the residents of an annexation area, to the exclusion of other affected citizens, decide by popular referendum the city in which they shall live? * * *

Defendants suggest that this case involves a non-justiciable controversy under the doctrine of *Hunter v. City of Pittsburgh*. * * * This court's reading of *Hunter* is not that it concerned political questions in the sense of the justiciability doctrine, but rather that it has to do with the principles of division of powers between the state and federal government, and is a "political question" decision only in that sense. *Hunter's* holding was not that an annexation question is non-justiciable under the Federal Constitution, but in more modern constitutional parlance that there is no property right or liberty interest in living within a particular political subdivision. Thus, a state statute directly placing a citizen in a particular city or county, or changing by the redrawing of boundary lines the political subdivision in which he resides, or providing some procedure where that may be done, may not be

---

6. **Are You in Favor of Being Annexed to the City of Ft. Wright?**

Fort Wright Ordinance
204–1980
YES: 504 votes
NO: 18 votes

Fort Wright Ordinance
217–1980
YES: 494 votes
NO: 15 votes

Are You in Favor of Being Annexed to the City of Crescent Springs?

Crescent Springs Ordinance 1980–38
YES: 108 votes
NO: 2 votes

Crescent Springs Ordinance 1980–39
YES: 16 votes
NO: 2 votes

* * *

attacked under the due process or equal protection clauses of the Fourteenth Amendment, except in certain very restricted circumstances. * * *

As applied to annexation elections, an analysis of the facts of all the cases cited by the parties or found by the court indicates that, so long as the residents of the affected areas are treated alike within those areas, statutory provisions for a wide variety of voting schemes will be upheld against an equal protection attack, and the vote of one *area* may be given more weight than that of the other, or the franchise may even be granted to one area and denied to another if a rational basis exists for so providing. These cases dovetail with the view of the voting rights cases that *residence* is a legitimate criterion for limiting the right to vote, as discussed in the next section of this opinion.

In the last analysis, what these cases are saying is that annexation has its pros and cons, and is a political question in the sense that under our Constitution's principles of federalism, it is the prerogative of the individual states to resolve the conflicting interests involved in annexation disputes as they see fit. It is true that the prerogative is subject to limitations of equal protection and due process, but *Hunter* requires that these limitations be interpreted in the light of that federalism. * * *

Defendants argue that it is not a denial of equal protection to limit the right to vote to residents of an affected area and that an annexation election is a special interest election in which it is permissible to permit only those specially affected to vote. * * * Plaintiffs, although they recognize that the right to vote may be limited to residents of "the geographic confines of the governmental entity concerned," argue that governmental entity is the entire City of Covington, rather than just the areas sought to be detached therefrom. They contend further that the cases permitting classification of voters in special interest elections are not applicable, because they concerned special purpose districts, rather than a municipal entity of general governmental powers, such as a city.

Construing the equal protection clause in the light of the principles of federalism discussed in the preceding part of this opinion, this court holds that defendants have the better of the argument, that these annexation elections are special interest elections, and that there is not only a rational basis, but a compelling state interest for limiting the right to vote in them to the residents of the annexation area.

The overall purpose of the equal protection clause is to preserve the dignity of the individual by protecting him from invidious prejudicial treatment at the hands of his government. This is the reason why classifications which burden fundamental rights or suggest prejudice against minorities are subjected to strict scrutiny. In the present case, since there is no suggestion of a suspect classification such as race, the strict scrutiny of the court is directed to whether the fundamental right of the citizen to reasonably equal participation in his government has been unduly burdened by the statute at issue. The court holds that it has not. * * *

Not only a rational basis, but a compelling state interest for the new statute is found in the following considerations. First, annexation battles, in this part of the state at least, were tearing the community apart and generating hostility to such a degree that some solution had to be found. The point had been reached where, even after it had been determined that an area was to be annexed to a particular city, harmony was destroyed, and the annexed citizens were devoting substantial civic energies to reversing the annexation. The procedure of committing annexation problems to the judiciary had not worked. The judiciary, the legislature apparently concluded, was not suited for the task of regulating annexations. There was no reason to believe an administrative procedure would work any better, and it would only result in returning the matter to the judiciary once again, because the Constitution of Kentucky guarantees judicial review of administrative action.

Therefore, the state had a compelling interest in finding some way to provide a fast, certain answer to annexation controversies. Experience demonstrated that such an immediate, certain solution, which would avoid years of litigation and uncertainty as to the status of a given area, was more desirable than one which nicely balanced all the relevant theoretical considerations of political science, but at the cost of decade-long, bitterly divisive court battles.

The legislature determined that voting is a workable answer. Having chosen voting as the best available, though certainly not a perfect solution to the problem of resolving annexation controversies, the state also had a compelling interest in limiting the right to vote in annexation elections to residents of the geographic area of the proposed annexation. The answer to plaintiffs' argument that all of the residents of the City of Covington must be given the right to vote, because they are substantially affected, is the same as that given by the Court in *Holt Civic Club v. Tuscaloosa* to a similar argument, that is, that such an argument proves too much.

Many persons other than residents of the annexation areas have a substantial interest at least equal to that of the citizens of Covington in the outcome of these annexations. A non-resident who works in an area may be subjected to or relieved from a substantial payroll tax. A non-resident who owns a valuable piece of real property in an area may find the tax rate imposed on it substantially altered by the annexation. In the present case, the citizens of the cities to which the annexed areas are sought to be attached have a substantial interest. In the annexation of an unincorporated area, the citizens of the county would have a very real interest. In fact, since the three counties of Northern Kentucky are in essence one integral metropolitan area, all of its citizens may be more than minimally affected by the results of these annexations. Once you go beyond the residents of the annexation area, where are you going to stop?

Such considerations as these explain why residence has always been recognized as a proper criterion for defining voting rights. It is impossible to permit everyone who is affected by an election of any kind to vote. Therefore, in the context of most elections the limitation of the franchise to residents satisfies a compelling state interest per se. * * *

It can be argued that liberal annexation is the most practical solution to our pressing urban problems and that to permit people to fence themselves off in suburban enclaves is to guarantee lack of interest in these problems, to facilitate the erosion of the core areas, and to promote urban blight and racial and class strife.

Those who oppose such arguments contend that size in municipal government is no guarantor of efficiency, that smaller towns or unincorporated communities are more in accord with democracy, and indeed that almost pure democracy, as exemplified by the New England town meeting, can be approached there. They cite stories of illegal public employee strikes and the inefficiencies inherent in bureaucratic government in support of their opposition to metropolitan government.

In short, there is much to be said both for and against liberal annexation procedures. Plaintiffs here claim that the statute under attack authorizes a war of attrition by the smaller surrounding cities against the core city, but this assumes that the outlying areas of Covington are eager to be detached from it. Perhaps the legislature believed that submitting annexation questions to a vote would require the core cities to do a better selling job, and indeed be more efficient. The legislature might also have meant to encourage cities to work out plans for consolidation of services.

It should be noted that in the annexation of unincorporated territory, the legislature weighted the scales heavily in favor of annexation, requiring a vote of 75 percent of all the registered voters in an area to defeat it. This again exemplifies a nice balancing of conflicting political interests with which a federal court has no authority to interfere.

Advocates of each side of this controversy are unlikely to be convinced by the arguments of those of the opposing persuasion. What *Hunter* and the similar cases cited herein are saying is that these difficult policy problems of local government are matters for the individual states to resolve, and the federal courts should stay out of them if principles of due process and equal protection are observed, as construed in light of federalism.

The Constitution of the United States enacts neither principles of consolidated metropolitan government nor those of decentralized government in villages and small towns. It is silent on these subjects. It grants the federal courts no power to construct solutions to urban blight or suburban sprawl, or to invalidate solutions reached by a state, if racial discrimination or some other unconstitutional factor is not involved. * * *

TOWN OF LOCKPORT v. CITIZENS
FOR COMMUNITY ACTION

Supreme Court of the United States, 1977.
430 U.S. 259, 97 S.Ct. 1047, 51 L.Ed.2d 313.

MR. JUSTICE STEWART delivered the opinion of the Court. * * *

County government in New York has traditionally taken the form of a single-branch legislature, exercising general governmental powers. General governmental powers are also exercised by the county's constituent cities, villages, and towns. The allocation of powers among these subdivisions can be changed, and a new form of county government adopted, pursuant to referendum procedures specified in Art. IX of the New York Constitution and implemented by § 33 of the Municipal Home Rule Law. Under those procedures a county board of supervisors may submit a proposed charter to the voters for approval. If a majority of the voting city dwellers and a majority of the voting noncity dwellers both approve, the charter is adopted.

In November 1972, a proposed charter for the county of Niagara was put to referendum. The charter created the new offices of County Executive and County Comptroller, and continued the county's existing power to establish tax rates, equalize assessments, issue bonds, maintain roads, and administer health and public welfare services. No explicit provision for redistribution of governmental powers from the cities or towns to the county government was made. The city voters approved the charter by a vote of 18,220 to 14,914. The noncity voters disapproved the charter by a vote of 11,594 to 10,665. A majority of those voting in the entire county thus favored the charter. * * *

[E]ver since the seminal case of *Reynolds v. Sims,* 377 U.S. 533, 84 S.Ct. 1362, 12 L.Ed.2d 506, it has been established that the Equal Protection Clause cannot tolerate the disparity in individual voting strength that results when elected officials represent districts of unequal population, since "the fundamental principle of representative government in this country is one of equal representation for equal numbers of people, without regard to race, sex, economic status, or place of residence within a State." * * * Beginning with *Reynolds v. Sims,* cases in which the principle emerged involved challenges to state legislative apportionment systems that gave "the same number of representatives to unequal numbers of constituents". 377 U.S., at 563, 84 S.Ct., at 1382. The Court concluded that in voting for their legislators, all citizens have an equal interest in representative democracy, and that the concept of equal protection therefore requires that their votes be given equal weight.

The equal protection principles applicable in gauging the fairness of an election involving the choice of legislative representatives are of limited relevance, however, in analyzing the propriety of recognizing distinctive voter interests in a "single-shot" referendum. In a referendum, the expression of voter will is direct, and there is no need to assure that the voters' views will be adequately represented through their representatives in the legislature. The policy impact of a referendum is also different in kind from the impact of choosing representatives— instead of sending legislators off to the state capitol to vote on a multitude of issues, the referendum puts one discrete issue to the voters. That issue is capable, at least, of being analyzed to determine whether its adoption or rejection will have a disproportionate impact on an identifiable group of voters. If it is found to have such a disproportionate impact, the question then is whether a State can recognize that impact either by limiting the franchise to those voters specially affected or by giving their votes a special weight. This question has been confronted by the Court in two types of cases: those dealing with elections involving "special-interest" governmental bodies of limited jurisdiction, and those dealing with bond referenda.

The Court has held that the electorate of a special purpose unit of government, such as a water storage district, may be apportioned to give greater influence to the constituent groups found to be most affected by the governmental unit's functions. *Salyer Land Co. v. Tulare Lake Basin Water Storage District,* 410 U.S. 719, 93 S.Ct. 1224, 35 L.Ed.2d 659. But the classification of voters into "interested" and "non-interested" groups must still be reasonably precise, as *Kramer v. Union Free School District No. 15,* 395 U.S. 621, 89 S.Ct. 1886, 23 L.Ed.2d 583, demonstrates. The Court assumed in that case that the voting constituency in school district elections could be limited to those "primarily interested in school affairs," but concluded that the State's classification of voters on the asserted basis of that interest was so imprecise that the exclusion of otherwise qualified voters was impermissible.

In the bond referenda cases, the local government had either limited the electoral franchise to property owners, or weighted property owners' votes more heavily than those of nonproperty owners by using a "dual box" separate majority approval system quite similar to the one at issue in the present case. *Cipriano v. City of Houma,* 395 U.S. 701, 89 S.Ct. 1897, 23 L.Ed.2d 647; *Phoenix v. Kolodziejski,* 399 U.S. 204, 90 S.Ct. 1990, 26 L.Ed.2d 523; *Hill v. Stone,* 421 U.S. 289, 95 S.Ct. 1637, 44 L.Ed.2d 172.

In the *Cipriano* case, involving revenue bonds, it was apparent that all voters had an identity of interest in passage of the bond issue, and limitation of the electoral franchise to "property taxpayers" was, plainly, invidiously discriminatory. The other two cases, however, involved general obligation bonds. There, as in *Salyer* and *Kramer,* the validity of the classification depended upon whether the group interests were sufficiently different to justify total or partial withholding of the electoral franchise from one of them. In support of the classifications, it was argued that property owners have a more substantial stake in the adoption of obligation bonds than do nonproperty owners, because the taxes of the former directly and substantially fund the bond obligation. The Court rejected that argument for limiting the electoral franchise, however, noting that nonproperty owners also share in the tax burden when the tax on rental property or commercial businesses is passed on in the form of higher prices. Although the interests of the two groups are concededly not identical, the Court held that they are sufficiently similar to prevent a state government from distinguishing between them by artificially narrowing or weighting the electoral franchise in favor of the property taxpayers.

These decisions do not resolve the issues in the present case. Taken together, however, they can be said to focus attention on two inquiries: whether there is a genuine difference in the relevant interests of the groups that the state electoral classification has created; and if so, whether any resulting enhancement of minority voting strength nonetheless amounts to invidious discrimination in violation of the Equal Protection Clause.

The argument that the provisions of New York law in question here are unconstitutional rests primarily on the premise that all voters in a New York county have identical interests in the adoption or rejection of a new charter, and that any distinction, therefore, between voters drawn on the basis of residence and working to the detriment of an identifiable class is an invidious discrimination. If the major premise were demonstrably correct—if it were clear that all voters in Niagara County have substantially identical interests in the adoption of a new county charter, regardless of where they reside within the county—the District Court's judgment would have to be affirmed under our prior cases. That major premise, however, simply cannot be accepted. To the contrary, it appears that the challenged provisions of New York law rest on the State's identification of the distinctive interests of the residents of the cities and towns within a county rather than their interests as residents of the county as a homogeneous unit. This identification is based in the realities of the distribution of governmental powers in New York, and is consistent with our cases that recognize both the wide discretion the States have in forming and allocating governmental tasks to local subdivisions, and the discrete interests that such local governmental units may have *qua* units.

General purpose local government in New York is entrusted to four different units: counties, cities, towns and villages. The State is divided into 62 counties; each of the 57 counties outside of New York City is divided into towns, or towns and one or more cities. Villages, once formed, are still part of the towns in which they are located. The New York Legislature has conferred home rule, and general governmental powers on all of these subdivisions, and their governmental activities may on occasion substantially overlap. The cities often perform functions within their jurisdiction that the county may perform for noncity residents; similarly villages perform some functions for their residents that the town provides for the rest of the town's inhabitants. Historically towns provided their areas with major social services that more recently have been transferred to counties; towns exercise more regulatory power than counties; and both towns and counties can create special taxing and improvement districts to administer services.

Acting within a fairly loose state apportionment of political power, the relative energy and organization of these various subdivisions will often determine which one of them in a given area carries out the major tasks of local government. Since the cities have the greatest autonomy within this scheme, changes serving to strengthen the county structure may have the most immediate impact on the functions of the towns as deliverers of government services.

The provisions of New York law here in question clearly contemplate that a new or amended county charter will frequently operate to transfer "functions or duties" from the towns or cities to the county, or even "[to] abolish one or more offices, departments, agencies or units of government." Although the 1974 Charter does not explicitly transfer governmental functions or duties from the towns to Niagara County, the executive-legislative form of government it provides would significantly enhance the county's organizational and service delivery capacity, for the purpose of "greater efficiency and responsibility in county government." Niagara County Charter, 1972. The creation of the offices of County Executive and County Comptroller clearly reflect this purpose. Such anticipated organizational changes, no less than explicit transfers of functions, could effectively shift any pre-existing balance of power between town and county governments towards county predominance. In terms of efficient delivery of government services such a shift might be all to the good, but it may still be viewed as carrying a cost quite different for town voters and their existing town governments from that incurred by city voters and their existing city governments.

The ultimate question then is whether, given the differing interests of city and noncity voters in the adoption of a new county charter in New York, those differences are sufficient under the Equal Protection Clause to justify the classifications made by New York law. If that question were posed in the context of annexation proceedings, the fact that the residents of the annexing city and the residents of the area to be annexed formed sufficiently different constituencies with sufficiently different interests could be readily perceived. The fact of impending union alone would not so merge them into one community of interest as constitutionally to require that their votes be aggregated in any referendum to approve annexation. Cf. *Hunter v. City of Pittsburgh,* 207 U.S. 161, 28 S.Ct. 40, 52 L.Ed. 151. Similarly a proposal that several school districts join to form a consolidated unit could surely be subject to voter approval in each constituent school district.

Yet in terms of recognizing constituencies with separate and potentially opposing interests, the structural decision to annex or consolidate is similar in impact to the decision to restructure county government in New York. In each case, separate voter approval requirements are based on the perception that the real and long-term impact of a restructuring of local government is felt quite differently by the different county constituent units that in a sense compete to provide similar governmental services. Voters in these constituent units are directly and differentially affected by the restructuring of county government, which may make the provider of public services more remote and less subject to the voters' individual influence.

The provisions of New York law here in question no more than recognize the realities of these substantially differing electoral interests.[18] Granting to these provisions the presumption of constitutionality to which every duly enacted state and federal law is entitled, we are unable to conclude that they violate the Equal Protection Clause of the Fourteenth Amendment. * * *

––––––––

Controversy over annexation procedures involves not just the question of who is entitled to approve an annexation but also who is entitled to propose one. In many states, property owners—rather than citizens generally—are given this right of initiation. The following case presents a debate about the constitutionality of such a process. Which opinion has the better argument? Is giving such a power to property owners, rather than voters, a bad idea even if it is constitutional?

GOODYEAR FARMS v. THE CITY OF AVONDALE

Supreme Court of Arizona, 1986.
148 Ariz. 216, 714 P.2d 386, appeal dismissed, 477
U.S. 901, 106 S.Ct. 3268, 91 L.Ed.2d 559.

CAMERON, JUSTICE. * * *

In 1981, petitions were circulated among owners of property adjacent to the City of Avondale and owned in part by the petitioners. The petitions were signed by property owners representing more than one-half of the real and personal property subject to taxation in the area and then presented to the City of Avondale (Avondale) requesting annexation. Consequently, Avondale noticed and held a public hearing on the proposed annexation.

Goodyear Farms, Litchfield Park Properties, and Litchfield Park Service Company (Goodyear Farms), corporations owning property in the area to be annexed, were specifically invited to the public hearing. Following the hearing, on 26 May 1981, Avondale passed Annexation Ordinance No. 301 which annexed certain portions of the Litchfield Park community contiguous to its boundaries. Goodyear Farms filed suit challenging the validity of the annexation ordinance. * * * In Arizona, a city or town may annex property according to the procedure provided in A.R.S. § 9–471. Annexation can only be initiated:

–––––

18. There is no indication that the classifications created by New York law work to favor city to town voter, or town to city voter. In some New York counties, city voters outnumber town voters; in other counties, the reverse is true. * * * The constitutional and statutory provisions in this case also do not appear to be the sustained product of either an entrenched minority or a willful majority. Instead they have been subject historically to fairly frequent revision. * * *

On presentation of a petition in writing signed by the owners of not less than one half in value of the real and personal property as would be subject to taxation by the city or town in the event of annexation, in any territory contiguous to the city or town, as shown by the last assessment of the property, and not embraced within the city or town limits, the governing body of the city or town may, by ordinance, annex the territory to such city or town * * *. * * *

Goodyear Farms argues that this method of annexation is unconstitutional, as a violation of equal protection, because it denies non-property owners residing in the area to be annexed the right to participate in the annexation decision.

The legislature has broad power over municipal annexations. This power was clearly recognized by the United States Supreme Court in *Hunter v. City of Pittsburgh*, 207 U.S. 161, 28 S.Ct. 40, 52 L.Ed. 151 (1907) * * *. In the instant case, Goodyear Farms does not maintain that there is an inherently suspect classification involved. Goodyear Farms does maintain that the annexation petitioning process is analogous to the fundamental right to vote, *e.g. Curtis v. Board of Supervisors,* 7 Cal.3d 942, 104 Cal.Rptr. 297, 501 P.2d 537 (1972) (statutes that touch upon or burden the right to vote); *Town of Fond du Lac v. City of Fond du Lac*, 22 Wis.2d 533, 126 N.W.2d 201 (1964) (the right of an elector to participate in an annexation proceeding is analogous to voting upon the question) and that it, therefore, infringes on a fundamental right. We do not agree.

Admittedly, the expansive power given to the legislature over municipal corporations in *Hunter* is not unrestrained where voting is concerned. In several voting rights cases, the United States Supreme Court has used the equal protection clause to strike down as unfair voter classifications where important municipal decisions were to be made by voters in an election. *See Kramer v. Union Free School District*, 395 U.S. 621, 89 S.Ct. 1886, 23 L.Ed.2d 583 (1969); *Cipriano v. City of Houma*, 395 U.S. 701, 89 S.Ct. 1897, 23 L.Ed.2d 647 (1969); *City of Phoenix v. Kolodziejski*, 399 U.S. 204, 90 S.Ct. 1990, 26 L.Ed.2d 523 (1970).

A.R.S. § 9–471 does not, however, provide for an election on the issue of annexation. The United States Court of Appeals in *Berry v. Bourne*, 588 F.2d 422, 424 (4th Cir.1978), noted that since the electors in the area to be annexed are not given the right to vote under the challenged statute, its application poses no equal protection issue. The statute in that case was very similar to ours, in that it required a petition of three-fourths of the freeholders requesting annexation before the governing body of the annexing city could annex the area. Without an election, the voting rights cases are not directly applicable. Also, there is "no federal constitutional right to vote on annexation matters."

Goodyear Farms argues, however, that an actual election is not required to trigger strict scrutiny. They contend that it is enough if the annexation procedure is analogous to voting, *Town of Fond du Lac, supra*, or touches upon or burdens the right to vote. *Curtis v. Board of Supervisors, supra.* We believe that both of these cases are distinguishable.

The finding in *Town of Fond du Lac* that the signing of an annexation petition is analogous to voting arose where the annexation petition required the signatures of resident electors. Therefore, it was held that the signature of an elector on an annexation petition was the exercise of a political right to participate in a governmental process like voting. In a later case, the Wisconsin Court of Appeals enunciated the distinction between a property owner as opposed to an elector signing an annexation petition. *Town of Medary v. City of La Crosse*, 88 Wis.2d 101, 277 N.W.2d 310 (App.1979).

> Ownership itself, detached from the personal benefits or detriments that accompany residency in a municipality, is more of a private right than the political right a resident may have in annexation. * * * The two types of interests are treated differently because they are different. Thus the political nature of annexation petitions recognized as applicable to electors in *De Bauche [v. Green Bay*, 227 Wis. 148, 153–154, 277 N.W. 147 (1938)] and *Fond du Lac* is not applicable to property owners.

Id. at 105, 277 N.W.2d at 314. We do not believe that the Arizona annexation petition process, which is signed by property owners, would be a political right analogous to voting.

In *Curtis v. Board of Supervisors, supra*, the California Supreme Court invalidated a statute which allowed landowners to bar an incorporation election. Under the California statute, after incorporation proceedings have begun but before the statutorily required incorporation election, a petition could be submitted, signed by fifty-one percent of the owners of the total assessed value of land in the area, which would deprive the county board of supervisors of jurisdiction to call for an incorporation election and no further incorporation could be initiated for one year. The court found that barring an election touched upon and burdened the right to vote and applied the compelling state interest test. * * * The Arizona annexation statute provides for neither an annexation election nor a veto by property owners over such an election. Such a procedure, therefore, should not be invalid under *Curtis*. * * * The Arizona annexation statute provides for the actual annexation to be by the governing body of the annexing city or town. The petitioners are mere supplicants and have no power or right to require annexation. The decision to annex is entirely discretionary with the city or town's governing body. It has been said that the voting rights cases " 'create no constitutional rights in affected citizens concerning the procedure for creating or altering' any type of state district." *Township of Jefferson v. City of West Carrollton*, 517 F.Supp. at 420, (emphasis added). * * *

We conclude that the petitioning process utilized in A.R.S. § 9–471 is not analogous to voting, and therefore does not infringe on a fundamental right. Therefore, the proper test to apply in the case before us is the rational basis test. In reaching this decision, we agree with the *Berry* court that " 'the Supreme Court's decision in *Hunter v. City of Pittsburgh* * * * continues to be the law, and we are not at liberty to limit the effect of this decision by grafting the voting rights decisions on to this annexation body of law.' " *Berry v. Bourne*, 588 F.2d at 424. * * *

We agree that there are rational bases for the property owner, non-property owner classification; namely, the effects of annexation such as susceptibility to property taxes and bond liens apply only to landowners; property owners face more of an increased financial burden; and municipalities will be severely handicapped if annexation required the approval of all voters in the area and it would hinder the orderly growth of Arizona cities and towns. The legislature intended that the permanency associated with a property owner be present in a signer of an annexation petition. * * * Also in *Adams v. City of Colorado Springs,* [308 F.Supp. 1397 (D.Colo.1970), *affirmed per mem.* 399 U.S. 901, 90 S.Ct. 2197, 26 L.Ed.2d 555 (1970)], it was recognized that a municipality is severely handicapped by annexation procedures requiring approval of all property owners and electors in the area. It would be unable to deal with the people living just outside the city, enjoying its advantages without having to pay for them. Such persons would seldom consent to annexation and their nonconsent could threaten the core city.

We point out that by finding a rational basis for this classification and upholding the annexation procedure provided in A.R.S. § 9–471, we are not depriving non-property owners from any voice in the annexation process. First, non-property owners may express their opinions, pro or con, to the governing body of the annexing city or town. It is who has the real power of approval or rejection over the annexation. Second, the legislature has provided that any interested party may contest the validity of an annexation for failure to comply properly with the procedure set forth in A.R.S. § 9–471. By this provision, a non-property owner can protect himself against an illegal annexation. Therefore, even though we recognize that non-property owners have an interest in whether or not the area in which they reside is annexed, we find that the classification drawn by the legislature in A.R.S. § 9–471 is rational and furthers a legitimate state interest in the orderly and prosperous growth of Arizona cities and towns. The Arizona annexation statute, A.R.S. § 9–471, is constitutional. * * *

FELDMAN, JUSTICE, dissenting. * * *

The majority quotes extensively from *Hunter v. City of Pittsburgh.* I believe that in the context of this present case *Hunter* does not stand for the proposition of absolute power for which it is cited. * * * Not only have concepts of due process and equal protection evolved in the past 80 years, but in *Hunter* all voters in both cities were allowed to vote on the proposition. The premise of *Hunter* is that cities are creatures of the state, which I do not dispute. However, the issue in the present case is whether the legislature can deprive the class of resident non-landowners of a voice in the initial decision to become part of a city while granting it to non-resident landowners. *Hunter* is inapposite to this issue.

The ability to participate in the determination of the nature of the governmental entity that is to exercise power over one's person and one's family is a right of a fundamental nature. It is a right that is shared by residents and property owners in the area. *Curtis v. Board of Supervisors of Los Angeles County*, 7 Cal.3d 942, 960, 104 Cal.Rptr. 297, 309, 501 P.2d 537, 549 (1972). In my view, therefore, although the right denied non-property owners in the present case is not an electoral right, it is one of fundamental importance in its impact upon residents and property owners alike. * * * The California statute in *Curtis* allowed landowners to control the culmination of the annexation process—an election—while the Arizona statute allows landowners to control the initiation of an annexation which culminates in a vote by the city council. Both statutes interfere with the citizen's right of participation in the political process. The Arizona statute, like that held unconstitutional by the California court, touches upon fundamental political interests. It can be found valid only by applying strict scrutiny—the compelling state interest test. The majority errs in adopting and applying the rational basis test.

The majority also errs in holding that the statute passes even the rational basis test. The annexation statute makes two unconstitutional classifications. First it distinguishes between those who own taxable property and those who do not, excluding those who do not. The majority has identified no state interest to justify this exclusion. While the initial burdens of increased property taxation are placed on landowners, they are immediately passed on to consumers through increased rents and via increased prices. Further, landowners share equally with non-landowners the need for and benefits from all public services.

The second major defective classification is that § 9–471 distinguishes by wealth even among the eligible landowners themselves by providing that owners of at least "one-half *in value*" of the property sign the petition. The greater the assessed value of a parcel land, the greater the weight of that owner's signature. This classification cannot withstand any scrutiny. One landowner with substantial holdings could effectively block all action by a much greater number of people. This is fundamentally at odds with all notions of fairness and participation in the political process. It is patently exclusionary. This statute discriminates against all residents and small property owners who have the same interests in government services as wealthier owners. The state has no interest which can justify this exclusion. * * *

The majority argues that there is a rational basis for the property—non-property classification because property owners pay taxes, must bear the financial burdens of annexation, and, therefore, have a real interest in whether their property is annexed or not. I concur in these sentiments, but find in them only a rational basis for *inclusion* of property owners in the process of determining whether a property should be annexed.

The question before us, however, is whether there is a rational basis for *exclusion* of residents in the areas who happen not to own property. While the majority argues that non-property owners have some voice in the annexation process because they can argue to the city council or mount a court contest to the validity or legality of the annexation, I find the reasoning unpersuasive. It fails to explain why a non-resident owner who has never set foot in Arizona, and who may never intend to do so, may have the sole voice in determining whether the property is to be annexed; it fails to explain why those who reside on the property and whose vital interests will be affected by the question of annexation have no voice whatsoever and no method by which to even attempt to determine who will provide them with necessary governmental services. * * *

5. SECESSION: THE ABILITY TO BECOME OUTSIDERS

In 1986, the citizens of an area of Boston that includes the city's principal Black neighborhoods voted in a nonbinding referendum on a proposal that they incorporate themselves as a new city, to be called Mandela. The referendum failed by a 3–1 margin.[1] What is the relationship between the effort of members of Boston's Black community to secede from Boston and the decision in 1873 by the residents of Brookline, a wealthy neighborhood surrounded by the city of Boston, to remain separate from the city?[2] Who should be entitled to vote on these questions of separation—only the residents of "Mandela" (or Brookline) or all the residents of Boston as a whole? Are the problems of identifying the proper decisionmakers for the "Mandela" secession and the Brookline resistance to annexation different from each other because of the difference in the timing between separating from a city and remaining separate from it? Should the difference in the relative wealth and power of the two communities affect the decision about the proper franchise?

The two cases that follow do not directly confront the questions just raised about the proper electorate for secession issues. In their decisions dealing with Staten Islanders' attempt to secede from the City of New York and with a similar attempt by residents of Weirs Beach (New Hampshire) to secede from the City of Laconia, the courts instead addressed a issue considered above in Chapter Two: does state legislation concerning secession invade the home rule immunities of cities? What is the relationship between the home rule issue and the voting rights issue? Is it a sufficient protection of the interests of those who live in the areas of the city not targeted for secession that the state

1. See Boston Globe, November 5, 1986, pp. 1, 23.

2. See Warner, Streetcar Suburbs: The Process of Growth in Boston, 1870–1900, p. 163 (1962).

legislature, as well as those in the potential secession area, must approve the secession before it is allowed? [3]

CITY OF NEW YORK v. STATE OF NEW YORK

Court of Appeals of New York, 1990.
76 N.Y.2d 479, 561 N.Y.S.2d 154, 562 N.E.2d 118.

PER CURIAM:

At issue on this appeal is the constitutionality of chapter 773 of the Laws of 1989 * * *. Chapter 773 requires that, in the next general election, voters of the borough of Staten Island, one of New York City's five boroughs, be asked the following question: "Shall a charter commission to provide for the separation of the borough of Staten Island from the city of New York and for the establishment of the city of Staten Island be created?" If a majority answers yes, a commission composed only of Staten Island residents and legislators will be organized to draft a proposed charter and consider any subject it deems relevant to the organization of a new city of Staten Island. The law further specifies that, within roughly two years, this commission must submit a proposed charter to the governor, the temporary president of the senate, the speaker of the assembly and the president of the borough of Staten Island, and must hold public hearings throughout Staten Island for at least six months thereafter.

The charter commission may, in its discretion, then submit to Staten Island voters the question whether to adopt the proposed charter and, if not, whether the commission should continue, in order to redraft a charter proposal. If Staten Island voters answer yes, the charter is "adopted," and the commission must submit proposed legislation enabling Staten Island to separate from New York City. If they answer no, the commission continues briefly in order to consider an alternative proposed charter for the City of Staten Island; in the event of a second negative vote, the commission is to dissolve.

Chapter 773 further contemplates the appointment of three "advisory committees" with five members each, to study and report on the creation of school districts, civil service rights and retirement benefits, and tax and finance matters. These committees are also charged with responsibility for submitting proposed legislation to implement their recommendations. An additional commission of state legislators from

---

3. In November, 1993, Staten Islanders voted in favor of secession by more than a 2–1 margin. New York Times, November 8, 1993, Page 1, col. 5. Legislative officials, however, have stated that, because of home rule, the state legislature can authorize the secession only with the consent of the City of New York. New York Times, March 5, 1994, Section 1, page 27, col. 4. For an analysis of the issues involved in the Staten Island secession, see, e.g., Briffault, Voting Rights, Home Rule, and Metropolitan Government: The Secession of Staten Island as a Case Study in the Dilemmas of Local Self-Determination, 92 Colum.L.Rev. 775 (1992); Cavanna, Home Rule and the Secession of Staten Island: City of New York v. State of New York, 6 Touro L.Rev. 795 (1992). See generally, Sunstein, Constitutionalism and Secession, 58 U.Chi.L.Rev. 633 (1991).

Staten Island is to be organized by the charter commission to apportion any local legislative body established by the proposed charter.

All committees and commissions are to be named without input from the other boroughs of New York City, with a single exception. Appointment of one member of the civil service rights and retirements benefits committee is to be made on the recommendation of the Mayor of the City of New York. Thus, as chapter 773 has been designed and formulated, upon completion of the referenda, hearing and drafting processes, what the Legislature will have is the view of Staten Islanders as to whether they desire separation from New York City, and the basis on which they would see it accomplished.

Significantly, as was made explicit by later amendment to chapter 773, no act or proposal of the various Staten Island committees or commissions can have the force of law. The charter, or alternative charter, for the city of Staten Island can become law only if the Legislature enacts legislation enabling Staten Island to disengage and separate from the City of New York. The law specifically directs that until such time, "the borough of Staten Island shall remain a part of the city of New York."

Upon New York City's challenge to the constitutionality of chapter 773, Supreme Court granted the State's cross-motion for summary judgment and declared the special law constitutional, holding that the State has plenary power to change municipal boundaries without home rule constraints. * * * We now affirm, but on different grounds. In particular, we expressly decline to decide as unnecessary and premature whether genuine secession legislation, if ever it were to come before the Legislature, would require a home rule message. * * *

The City makes a plausible argument that chapter 773 is not "advisory only." A State-sponsored referendum merely soliciting the interest of Staten Islanders in secession might, for example, be deemed advisory only, because by definition it has no effect on the property, affairs or government of New York City, and therefore outside the home rule requirement. Chapter 773, however, does more than that. It authorizes the commitment of public funds and other public resources, potentially extending over a period of several years, to conduct studies, hold hearings and submit legislation that would effectuate Staten Island's separation from the city of New York if the Legislature ever passed such a law and the Governor ever signed it. Chapter 773 is in this respect more than "advisory only," and is surely ripe for review.

That conclusion does not, however, answer the dispositive question whether the special law is an "act in relation to the property, affairs or government" of New York City requiring a home rule message under article IX, § 2(b)(2) of the State Constitution. By their very nature, special laws ordinarily will have an effect on the subject locality. However, not every special law in and of itself requires a home rule message, as the effect may be at most incidental, not a direct impact on the property, affairs or government of that entity. "The intent of these provisions of the Constitution was to provide some measure of protection to a city from possible danger of ill-considered interference by the legislature in its local affairs." (*City of New York v. Village of Lawrence.* 250 N.Y. 429, 439.)

Here we discern no State interference in New York City property, affairs or government, and we therefore need not reach the next step of determining whether there is any substantial State interest in the matter. Chapter 773 does not authorize secession; it does not authorize the voters of Staten Island to decide the secession issue; it does not initiate secession, or commit the State to support it; it does not represent any relinquishment by the Legislature of any power it may have with respect to secession; and it in no way circumscribes whatever protections exist in the State constitution home rule provision with respect to an act formally triggering secession.

Indeed, rather than any direct effect of chapter 773 on the property, affairs or government of New York City, the impact of the law as the City portrays it is either wholly speculative, or simply the anticipated response to Staten Island's already publicized interest in secession. In the category of speculative, for example, are the City's references to the loss of population, acreage and investment in Staten Island's infrastructure, none of which could result from the present legislation. Likewise, any anticipated uncertainties in City planning or financing are not the direct consequence of chapter 773, which commits to no binding law of any sort; Staten Island's expressed interest in secession after *Morris v. Board of Estimate* (707 F.2d 686, *affd.* 489 U.S. 688) itself suggested planning for that contingency even without chapter 773.

Nor does the dissent add any material consideration to the factors relied on by the City. That New York City may choose to incur expense in a desire to track the various Staten Island processes can hardly be deemed the State's intrusion into New York City's property, affairs or government; similarly, commission authorization to "request and receive" assistance is not tantamount to license to requisition resources or commandeer City agencies, and plainly does not constitute "open-ended" or "unbridled" intrusion into City affairs.

The City's equal protection argument is also unavailing. Even in voter classification, a State is not prohibited from recognizing the distinctive interests of the residents of its political subdivisions (*see, e.g., Town of Lockport v. Citizens for Community Action*, 430 U.S. 259, 268–269). The legislative choice to allow Staten Island voters to express their views as to whether, and how, they might wish to separate from New York City—while affording them no unilateral right to do so—is a reasonable classification based on the distinct interest of that subdivision of the State. * * * The virtual exclusivity of Staten Islanders in the process marks chapter 773 for what it is—not as a procedure aimed at dividing New York City without the voice of its other boroughs but as a procedure that allows Staten Island to explore its publicized interest in

secession, stripped of any force without further act of the Legislature.
* * *

HANCOCK, J. (dissenting):

The court today holds that a measure which establishes a detailed process aimed at splitting New York City into two separate cities—while depriving four of its five boroughs from any voice in the process—does not affect its property, affairs or government. I cannot agree. * * * Realistically, no subject more directly concerns the affairs and government of a city than whether the integrity of its boundaries and of its existing governmental structure should be altered. There can be no question that chapter 773 sets in motion a process that has one purpose: to disengage Staten Island from New York City and establish it as a separate and independent City of Staten Island. * * *

The charter commission—the statute's guiding component—is not a study group charged with investigating and reporting on the advisability of secession; it is the official body created by the Legislature for the purpose of directing the continuing process toward secession. It must support secession, hold hearings, do research, gather information and draft the complex bill that will be necessary to effectuate it. (See Chapter 773, § 4[e] [mandating that within "three months of adoption of the charter by the voters of Staten Island, the *commission shall submit* * * * proposed legislation enabling the borough of Staten Island to disengage and separate from the City of New York" (emphasis added)]).

All thirteen-members of the charter commission must come from Staten Island. Each of the five Staten Island legislators, all of whom are on record as favoring the legislation, is automatically a member of the commission. Each legislator is empowered to appoint one member to the commission. The three other commission members—also Staten Island residents—are to be appointed by the Governor, the temporary President of the Senate and the Speaker of the Assembly. The commission members are to be reimbursed by the state for their actual and necessary expenses.

The commission is vested with broad powers and prerogatives for carrying out its function. It may employ and set the compensation for such employees and consultants as it shall require. It is empowered to conduct private hearings, take testimony, subpoena witnesses and require the production of books, papers and records. Significantly, the commission may demand from any state or city department or bureau, commission, office, agency or other instrumentality such facilities, assistance, data and personnel as may be necessary or desirable for the proper execution of its powers and duties. It must establish advisory committees on the creation of school districts for Staten Island, on civil service rights and retirement benefits for city employees who will become employees of the Staten Island municipal government, and on the various tax and financial problems that will arise.

There can be no doubt that—irrespective of the ultimate possibility of secession—the very pendency of the process and the activities of the commission will have, at least, the following immediate effects:

Uncertainty and Confusion—by creating this secession-aimed legislation, the future makeup of the city's legislative body, and the configurations of its civil service system, its school system, its public works, its pension and retirement funds, its entire public debt structure, and its solid waste disposal scheme are put in question. This widespread uncertainty necessarily impairs effective present-day city planning for the future in several governmental areas.

Conscription of Resources and Personnel—from the very beginning of this multi-year process, the city's resources and personnel are affected. The referendum to poll Staten Island's interest in secession is to be supervised by the city board of election. The board must prepare the ballots, canvass the results and certify the results to the Senate and Assembly. Although the city's expenditures are to be reimbursed by the state, the city must initially lay out its money, assign its personnel, detail its expenses, and submit them to the state, subject to audit by the comptroller. Finally and most significantly, the unbridled authorization vested in the commission to "request and receive from *any* * * * city * * * *agency* or other instrumentality such *facilities, assistance, data and personnel as may be* necessary or *desirable* (to the commission) * * *" (*id.* § 4[e] [emphasis added]) amounts to an open-ended license for commandeering virtually every agency of city government.

Resultant Costs to the City—that there are direct and indirect costs to the city incident to its compliance with section 4(e)'s command to assist the charter commission is self-evident. Notably, no provision is made for state reimbursement of these costs. Beyond that, to protect its vital interests, the city—because it is excluded from any participation in the commission's proceedings—must now create and fund a parallel process in preparation for evaluating and reacting to any Staten Island secession bill emanating from the chapter 773 process.

Once the effect on city affairs, property or government is demonstrated, as it is here, a special act can be passed without a Home Rule message only where a concern exists "of sufficient importance to the State, transcendent of local or parochial interests" (*Wambat Realty Corp. v. State of New York,* 41 N.Y.2d 490, 494).

With no showing of a perceptible state interest, chapter 773 is before us as a measure that is quintessentially local in its effect. Under these circumstances, there can be no question that under governing case law, a home rule message was mandated. * * *

OPINION OF THE JUSTICES (WEIRS BEACH)

Supreme Court of New Hampshire, 1991.
134 N.H. 711, 598 A.2d 864.

The following Resolution No. 19, requesting an opinion of the justices, was adopted by the House of Representatives on March 21, 1991, and filed with the Supreme Court on March 27, 1991:

"Whereas, there is pending in the House, House Bill 762–FN, 'An Act to incorporate the inhabitants of the northeasterly part of Laconia into a separate town to be known as Weirs Beach, with all the privileges and immunities of other cities and towns in this state'; and * * *

"Whereas, enactment of HB 762–FN would, by establishing a new town of Weirs Beach within the current boundaries of the city of Laconia, effect a change of the boundaries of the city of Laconia; and * * *

"Whereas, HB 762–FN contains a provision requiring a referendum of the inhabitants of that portion of the city of Laconia which would become the new town of Weirs Beach, as a precondition to the bill's taking effect if enacted; and * * *

"Whereas, it is important that the question of the constitutionality of said provisions should be settled in advance of its enactment; now, therefore, be it

"Resolved by the house:

"That the Justices of the Supreme Court be respectfully requested to give their opinion on the following questions of law:

1. Would the change of the current boundaries of the city of Laconia, effected by enactment of HB 762–FN, constitute a change to 'the charter or form of government' of the city of Laconia, as that phrase is contemplated by Part I, Article 39 of the New Hampshire Constitution * * *?

2. Would enactment of HB 762–FN, by establishing a new town of Weirs Beach and causing those inhabitants of the new town of Weirs Beach who were formerly inhabitants of the city of Laconia to become inhabitants of a town as opposed to a city, change 'the charter or form of government' of the city of Laconia, as that phrase is contemplated by Part I, Article 39 of the New Hampshire Constitution? * * *

4. If the answer to question 1, 2, or 3 is in the affirmative, does the provision contained in HB 762–FN, requiring a referendum of the inhabitants of that portion of the city of Laconia which would become the new town of Weirs Beach as a precondition to the bill's taking effect, satisfy the requirements of Part I, Article 39 of the New Hampshire Constitution? * * *"

The following response is respectfully returned.

To the Honorable House of Representatives: * * *

House Bill ("HB") 762–FN proposes to incorporate a new town of Weirs Beach and partition portions of two existing wards of the city of Laconia for the new town's territorial jurisdiction. The memoranda filed with this court demonstrate that this partition is earnestly sought by at least some Weirs Beach area residents, who perceive themselves geographically and politically isolated from Laconia. It is earnestly opposed by the city of Laconia. The existing Laconia city charter includes a detailed description of the boundaries of each ward of the city, as well as a more generalized statement of what areas constitute the city. * * * HB 762–FN * * * would define new boundaries for Laconia and, although not expressly amending the Laconia charter, would cause those sections of the Laconia charter which purport to delineate the city boundaries to be obsolete. The issue which arises is whether this redrawing of boundaries changes the "charter" of Laconia in the integral manner which would trigger the referendum requirement of part I, article 39 of the New Hampshire Constitution, or whether such redrawing is a legitimate exercise of legislative power outside the scope of the charter change requirements.

Municipalities in the State of New Hampshire are divisions of the State, and they derive their authority from the legislature. As recently as 1962, in addressing similar partition legislation, this court held that the traditional "plenary control by the Legislature over municipalities" included the power to create, modify, or divide them for the advancement of the public interest. *Lisbon v. Lisbon Village District*, 104 N.H. 255, 258, 183 A.2d 250, 253 (1962). * * * In 1966, however, partly in response to a perception that the legislature was becoming a forum for concerns better handled at the level of local government, the legislature's plenary control over municipalities was constitutionally limited. In that year, our constitution was amended to provide * * *:

> "No law changing the charter or form of government of a particular city or town shall be enacted by the legislature except to become effective upon the approval of the voters of such city or town upon a referendum to be provided for in said law.

> The legislature may by general law authorize cities and towns to adopt or amend their charters or forms of government in any way which is not in conflict with general law, provided that such charters or amendments shall become effective only upon the approval of the voters of each such city or town on a referendum."

N.H. Const. pt. I, art. 39.

This amendment to our constitution has never been interpreted as a grant to municipalities of the supreme legislative authority over all municipal affairs, even when such affairs are memorialized by charter. This broader authority is exclusively vested in the legislature by part II, article 2 of our constitution. Nor does the amendment have the effect of completely insulating municipalities from legislative control. It does not render inviolate, or subject to the constitutionally prescribed referendum procedure, any matter or issue that the municipality chooses to include in its charter. Rather, what part I, article 39 does is grant municipal citizens the right to approve a proposed change to "the form of their local government *as enacted in their charters*." *Seabrook Citizens v. Yankee Greyhound Racing, Inc.*, 123 N.H. 103, 108, 456 A.2d 973, 975

(1983) (emphasis added).   The amendment to our constitution did not remove from the legislature its traditionally unrestricted authority over other aspects of municipal functions.   This traditional legislative authority, unaffected by the constitutional provision, includes the power to create new municipalities or to modify the boundaries of existing ones in furtherance of the public interest.   Although HB 762–FN includes what are in effect textual changes to the Laconia city charter, the only elements of a particular municipality's charter which are constitutionally insulated from legislative change, absent referendum, are those provisions concerned with the form of local government.   The alteration of city boundaries proposed by the bill does not fall within the constitutional prohibition.   Therefore, we return a negative answer to question one.

Question two inquires whether the enactment of HB 762–FN would "change the charter or form of government" of the city of Laconia because the inhabitants of the new town of Weirs Beach would become inhabitants of a town as opposed to a city.   We return a negative answer. Under the proposal, Laconia will continue with its present form of government intact, and there will be no change in the form of local government as enacted in its charter.   Article 39 prohibits a change to the form of government of a *particular* city or town.   A comparison of the city charter with the proposed legislation demonstrates that the city government of the territory remaining under the jurisdiction of Laconia would remain unchanged.   The constitutional prohibition only bars a legislative change of Laconia's form of government.   The proposed formation of the town of Weirs Beach, separate and apart from the newly legislatively defined Laconia, does not violate article 39.   Legislation does not offend article 39 when it establishes the form of government of persons living outside the territorial jurisdiction of the charter city. * * *

As our answers to questions one and two are in the negative, we do not address question four.   The matter of whether to hold referenda remains strictly a legislative consideration.   * * *

6. EXCLUSIONARY ZONING

In previous sections, we have examined the relationship between city residents and outsiders.   In this section, we examine a city's power to prevent outsiders from *becoming* city residents.   In local government law, this issue is rarely confronted directly.   Citizens of a city (unlike, say, residents of many condominiums) do not have a formal veto power over who can live in the city.   Nevertheless, a wide variety of zoning restrictions—mandating a minimum lot size, prohibiting multi-family housing, or excluding mobile homes, for example—can have the effect of controlling the kind of people able to move into a city (creating what is often called an "exclusive" community).   This practice of exclusionary zoning has spawned an enormous literature.[1]

1. See, e.g., Hartnett, Affordable Housing, Exclusionary Zoning, and American   Apartheid: Using Title VIII to Foster Statewide Racial Integration, 68 N.Y.U.L.Rev. 89

The cases included below offer two different legal responses to exclusionary zoning, one articulated by the United States Supreme Court interpreting the United States Constitution and the other articulated by the Supreme Court of New Jersey interpreting the New Jersey Constitution. These two responses suggest alternative visions of inter-city relations. Moreover, they suggest that the legitimacy of exclusionary zoning practices is predicated on a particular conception of cities. Remember that one of the traditional ingredients of the (private) property right is the right to exclude others[2] and that the United States has immigration laws. Do (and should) the cases treat cities like private property associations, like the nation as a whole, or like some other entity? Should all forms of city exclusion be considered identical? For example, should cities' ability to control the *character* of their population be treated in the same way as the ability to control the *size* of their population? In reading the following cases, consider as well the role of the courts in dealing with subjects like exclusionary zoning. Can the New Jersey decisions be defended on the ground that judicial intervention to force legislative action is necessary because suburban representatives can effectively block any legislative proposal to curb exclusionary practices? Is there an alternative solution to the problems generated by exclusionary zoning other than state or federal control of zoning decisions?

The legitimacy of exclusionary zoning practices might also usefully be compared with the legitimacy of local policies to prevent gentrification—that is, to prevent affluent people from taking over neighborhoods and thereby displacing those not able to keep up with the higher prices.[3] One way to prevent gentrification, for example, is to regulate condominium conversions (as in the Massachusetts case reproduced above in Chapter One, Section C.) Should the legal rules dealing with exclusion-

(1993); Schill, Deconcentrating the Inner City Poor, 67 Chi.-Kent L.Rev. 795 (1992); Stockman, Anti–Snob Zoning in Massachusetts: Assessing One Attempt at Opening the Suburbs to Affordable Housing, 78 Va. L.Rev. 535 (1992); Briffault, Our Localism: Part I—The Structure of Local Government Law, 90 Colum.L.Rev. 1, 39–58 (1990); Kmiec, Exclusionary Zoning and Purposeful Racial Segregation in Housing: Two Wrongs Deserving Separate Remedies, 18 The Urban Lawyer 393 (1986); M.A. Huls, Exclusionary and Inclusionary Zoning: A Bibliography (1985); M.D. Gelfand, Federal Constitutional Law and American Local Government 281–312 (1984); Salsich, Displacement and Urban Reinvestment: A Mt. Laurel Perspective, 53 U.Cinn.L.Rev. 333 (1984); Symposium—Mount Laurel II and Development in New Jersey, 15 Rutgers L.J. 513 (1984); Mount Laurel II Symposium, 14 Seton Hall L.Rev. 829 (1984); McDougal, Contemporary Authoritative Conceptions of Federalism and Exclusion-

ary Land Use Planning: A Critique, 21 B.C.L.Rev. 301 (1980); Mandelker, Racial Discrimination and Exclusionary Zoning: A Perspective on Arlington Heights, 55 Tex. L.Rev. 1217 (1977); Ellickson, Suburban Growth Controls: An Economic and Legal Analysis, 86 Yale L.J. 385 (1977); Payne, Delegation Doctrine in the Reform of Local Government Law: The Case of Exclusionary Zoning, 29 Rutgers L.Rev. 803 (1976).

2. See, e.g., Cohen, Dialogue on Private Property, 9 Rutgers L.Rev. 357, 374 (1954).

3. See generally, K. Nelson, Gentrification and Distressed Cities: An Assessment of Trends in Intrametropolitan Migration (1988); N. Smith & P. Williams, Gentrification of the City (1986); J. Palen & B. London, Gentrification, Displacement and Neighborhood Revitalization (1984); Bryant & McGee, Gentrification and the Law: Combatting Urban Displacement, 25 Wash.Univ.J.Urb. & Contemp.L. 43 (1983).

ary zoning and the prevention of gentrification be the same? If not, how can these two forms of exclusion be distinguished?

VILLAGE OF ARLINGTON HEIGHTS v. METROPOLITAN HOUSING DEVELOPMENT CORPORATION

Supreme Court of the United States, 1977.
429 U.S. 252, 97 S.Ct. 555, 50 L.Ed.2d 450.

MR. JUSTICE POWELL delivered the opinion of the Court. * * *

Arlington Heights is a suburb of Chicago, located about 26 miles northwest of the downtown Loop area. Most of the land in Arlington Heights is zoned for detached single-family homes, and this is in fact the prevailing land use. The Village experienced substantial growth during the 1960's, but, like other communities in northwest Cook County, its population of racial minority groups remained quite low. According to the 1970 census, only 27 of the Village's 64,000 residents were black.

The Clerics of St. Viator, a religious order (Order), own an 80-acre parcel just east of the center of Arlington Heights. Part of the site is occupied by the Viatorian high school, and part by the Order's three-story novitiate building, which houses dormitories and a Montessori school. Much of the site, however, remains vacant. Since 1959, when the Village first adopted a zoning ordinance, all the land surrounding the Viatorian property has been zoned R-3, a single-family specification with relatively small minimum lot-size requirements. On three sides of the Viatorian land there are single-family homes just across a street; to the east the Viatorian property directly adjoins the backyards of other single-family homes.

The Order decided in 1970 to devote some of its land to low- and moderate-income housing. Investigation revealed that the most expeditious way to build such housing was to work through a nonprofit developer experienced in the use of federal housing subsidies under § 236 of the National Housing Act.

MHDC is such a developer. It was organized in 1968 by several prominent Chicago citizens for the purpose of building low- and moderate-income housing throughout the Chicago area. * * * After some negotiation, MHDC and the Order entered into a 99-year lease and an accompanying agreement of sale covering a 15-acre site in the southeast corner of the Viatorian property. * * * MHDC engaged an architect and proceeded with the project, to be known as Lincoln Green. The plans called for 20 two-story buildings with a total of 190 units, each unit having its own private entrance from outside. One hundred of the units would have a single bedroom, thought likely to attract elderly citizens. The remainder would have two, three, or four bedrooms. A large portion of the site would remain open, with shrubs and trees to screen the homes abutting the property to the east.

The planned development did not conform to the Village's zoning ordinance and could not be built unless Arlington Heights rezoned the parcel to R–5, its multiple-family housing classification. Accordingly, MHDC filed with the Village Plan Commission a petition for rezoning, accompanied by supporting materials describing the development and specifying that it would be subsidized under § 236. The materials made clear that one requirement under § 236 is an affirmative marketing plan designed to assure that a subsidized development is racially integrated. MHDC also submitted studies demonstrating the need for housing of this type and analyzing the probable impact of the development. * * *

During the spring of 1971, the Plan Commission considered the proposal at a series of three public meetings, which drew large crowds. Although many of those attending were quite vocal and demonstrative in opposition to Lincoln Green, a number of individuals and representatives of community groups spoke in support of rezoning. Some of the comments, both from opponents and supporters, addressed what was referred to as the "social issue"—the desirability or undesirability of introducing at this location in Arlington Heights low- and moderate-income housing, housing that would probably be racially integrated.

Many of the opponents, however, focused on the zoning aspects of the petition, stressing two arguments. First, the area always had been zoned single-family, and the neighboring citizens had built or purchased there in reliance on that classification. Rezoning threatened to cause a measurable drop in property value for neighboring sites. Second, the Village's apartment policy, adopted by the Village Board in 1962 and amended in 1970, called for R–5 zoning primarily to serve as a buffer between single-family development and land uses thought incompatible, such as commercial or manufacturing districts. Lincoln Green did not meet this requirement, as it adjoined no commercial or manufacturing district.

At the close of the third meeting, the Plan Commission adopted a motion to recommend to the Village's Board of Trustees that it deny the request. * * * Two members voted against the motion and submitted a minority report, stressing that in their view the change to accommodate Lincoln Green represented "good zoning." The Village Board met on September 28, 1971, to consider MHDC's request and the recommendation of the Plan Commission. After a public hearing, the Board denied the rezoning by a 6–1 vote.

The following June MHDC and three Negro individuals filed this lawsuit against the Village, seeking declaratory and injunctive relief. * * *

At the outset, petitioners challenge the respondents standing to bring the suit. * * * In *Warth v. Seldin,* 422 U.S. 490, 95 S.Ct. 2197, 45 L.Ed.2d 343 (1975), a case similar in some respects to this one, we reviewed the constitutional limitations and prudential considerations that guide a court in determining a party's standing, and we need not repeat that discussion here. The essence of the standing question, in its constitutional dimension, is "whether the plaintiff has 'alleged such a personal stake in the outcome of the controversy' [as] to warrant *his* invocation of federal-court jurisdiction and to justify exercise of the court's remedial powers on his behalf." *Id.,* at 498–499, 95 S.Ct. at 2205. * * * Here there can be little doubt that MHDC meets the constitutional standing requirements. The challenged action of the petitioners stands as an absolute barrier to constructing the housing MHDC had contracted to place on the Viatorian site. If MHDC secures the injunctive relief it seeks, that barrier will be removed. An injunction would not, of course, guarantee that Lincoln Green will be built. MHDC would still have to secure financing, qualify for federal subsidies, and carry through with construction. But all housing developments are subject to some extent to similar uncertainties. When a project is as detailed and specific as Lincoln Green, a court is not required to engage in undue speculation as a predicate for finding that the plaintiff has the requisite personal stake in the controversy.

Respondent Ransom, a Negro, works at the Honeywell factory in Arlington Heights and lives approximately 20 miles away in Evanston in a 5–room house with his mother and his son. The complaint alleged that he seeks and would qualify for the housing MHDC wants to build in Arlington Heights. Ransom testified at trial that if Lincoln Green were built he would probably move there, since it is closer to his job.

The injury Ransom asserts is that his quest for housing nearer his employment has been thwarted by official action that is racially discriminatory. If a court grants the relief he seeks, there is at least a "substantial probability," *Warth v. Seldin,* 422 U.S., at 504, 95 S.Ct., at 2208, that the Lincoln Green project will materialize, affording Ransom the housing opportunity he desires in Arlington Heights. His is not a generalized grievance. Instead, as we suggested in *Warth,* it focuses on a particular project and is not dependent on speculation about the possible actions of third parties not before the court. Unlike the individual plaintiffs in *Warth,* Ransom has adequately averred an "actionable causal relationship" between Arlington Heights' zoning practices and his asserted injury. We therefore proceed to the merits.

Our decision last Term in *Washington v. Davis,* 426 U.S. 229, 96 S.Ct. 2040, 48 L.Ed.2d 597 (1976), made it clear that official action will not be held unconstitutional solely because it results in a racially disproportionate impact. "Disproportionate impact is not irrelevant, but it is not the sole touchstone of an invidious racial discrimination." *Id.,* at 242, 96 S.Ct., at 2049. Proof of racially discriminatory intent or purpose is required to show a violation of the Equal Protection Clause. Although some contrary indications may be drawn from some of our cases, the holding in *Davis* reaffirmed a principle well established in a variety of contexts.

Davis does not require a plaintiff to prove that the challenged action rested solely on racially discriminatory purposes. Rarely can it be said that a legislature or administrative body operating under a broad mandate made a decision motivated solely by a single concern, or even that a particular purpose was the "dominant" or "primary" one. In fact, it is because legislators and administrators are properly concerned with balancing numerous competing considerations that courts refrain from reviewing the merits of their decisions, absent a showing of arbitrariness or irrationality. But racial discrimination is not just another competing consideration. When there is a proof that a discriminatory purpose has been a motivating factor in the decision, this judicial deference is no longer justified.

Determining whether invidious discriminatory purpose was a motivating factor demands a sensitive inquiry into such circumstantial and direct evidence of intent as may be available. The impact of the official action—whether it "bears more heavily on one race than another," *Washington v. Davis,* 426 U.S., at 242, 96 S.Ct., at 2049—may provide an important starting point. Sometimes a clear pattern, unexplainable on grounds other than race, emerges from the effect of the state action even when the governing legislation appears neutral on its face. *Yick Wo v. Hopkins,* 118 U.S. 356, 6 S.Ct. 1064, 30 L.Ed. 220 (1886); *Gomillion v. Lightfoot,* 364 U.S. 339, 81 S.Ct. 125, 5 L.Ed.2d 110 (1960). The evidentiary inquiry is then relatively easy. But such cases are rare. Absent a pattern as stark as that in *Gomillion* or *Yick Wo,* impact alone is not determinative, and the Court must look to other evidence. * * *

We have reviewed the evidence. The impact of the Village's decision does arguably bear more heavily on racial minorities. Minorities constitute 18% of the Chicago area population, and 40% of the income groups said to be eligible for Lincoln Green. But there is little about the sequence of events leading up to the decision that would spark suspicion. The area around the Viatorian property has been zoned R–3 since 1959, the year when Arlington Heights first adopted a zoning map. Single-family homes surround the 80–acre site, and the Village is undeniably committed to single-family homes as its dominant residential land use. The rezoning request progressed according to the usual procedures. The Plan Commission even scheduled two additional hearings, at least in part to accommodate MHDC and permit it to supplement its presentation with answers to questions generated at the first hearing.

The statements by the Plan Commission and Village Board members, as reflected in the official minutes, focused almost exclusively on the zoning aspects of the MHDC petition, and the zoning factors on which they relied are not novel criteria in the Village's rezoning decisions. There is no reason to doubt that there has been reliance by some neighboring property owners on the maintenance of single-family zoning in the vicinity. The Village originally adopted its buffer policy long before MHDC entered the picture and has applied the policy too consistently for us to infer discriminatory purpose from its application in this case. Finally, MHDC called one member of the Village Board to the stand at trial. Nothing in her testimony supports an inference of invidious purpose.

In sum, the evidence does not warrant overturning the concurrent findings of both courts below. Respondents simply failed to carry their burden of proving that discriminatory purpose was a motivating factor in the Village's decision.[21] This conclusion ends the constitutional inquiry. * * *

SOUTHERN BURLINGTON COUNTY N.A.A.C.P. v. TOWNSHIP OF MT. LAUREL

Supreme Court of New Jersey, 1975.
67 N.J. 151, 336 A.2d 713.

HALL, J.

This case attacks the system of land use regulation by defendant Township of Mount Laurel on the ground that low and moderate income families are thereby unlawfully excluded from the municipality. * * * The implications of the issue presented are indeed broad and far-reaching, extending much beyond these particular plaintiffs and the boundaries of this particular municipality.

There is not the slightest doubt that New Jersey has been, and continues to be, faced with a desperate need for housing, especially of decent living accommodations economically suitable for low and moderate income families. The situation was characterized as a "crisis" and fully explored and documented by Governor Cahill in two special messages to the Legislature * * *.

Plaintiffs represent the minority group poor (black and Hispanic) seeking such quarters. But they are not the only category of persons barred from so many municipalities by reason of restrictive land use regulations. We have reference to young and elderly couples, single persons and large, growing families not in the poverty class, but who still cannot afford the only kinds of housing realistically permitted in most places—relatively high-priced, single-family detached dwellings on sizeable lots and, in some municipalities, expensive apartments. We will, therefore, consider the case from the wider viewpoint that the effect of Mount Laurel's land use regulation has been to prevent various categories of persons from living in the township because of the limited extent of their income and resources. In this connection, we accept the representation of the municipality's counsel at oral argument that the regulatory scheme was not adopted with any desire or intent to exclude prospective residents on the obviously illegal bases of race, origin or believed social incompatibility.

21. Proof that the decision by the Village was motivated in part by a racially discriminatory purpose would not necessarily have required invalidation of the challenged decision. Such proof would, however, have shifted to the Village the burden of establishing that the same decision would have resulted even had the impermissible purpose not been considered. If this were established, the complaining party in a case of this kind no longer fairly could attribute the injury complained of to improper consideration of a discriminatory purpose. In such circumstances, there would be no justification for judicial interference with the challenged decision. But in this case respondents failed to make the required threshold showing.

As already intimated, the issue here is not confined to Mount Laurel. The same question arises with respect to any number of other municipalities of sizeable land area outside the central cities and older built-up suburbs of our North and South Jersey metropolitan areas (and surrounding some of the smaller cities outside those areas as well) which, like Mount Laurel, have substantially shed rural characteristics and have undergone great population increase since World War II, or are now in the process of doing so, but still are not completely developed and remain in the path of inevitable future residential, commercial and industrial demand and growth. Most such municipalities, with but relatively insignificant variation in details, present generally comparable physical situations, courses of municipal policies, practices, enactments and results and human, governmental and legal problems arising therefrom. It is in the context of communities now of this type or which become so in the future, rather than with central cities or older built-up suburbs or areas still rural and likely to continue to be for some time yet, that we deal with the question raised.

Extensive oral and documentary evidence was introduced at the trial, largely informational, dealing with the development of Mount Laurel. * * * This evidence was not contradicted by the township, except in a few unimportant details. Its candid position is that, conceding its land use regulation was intended to result and has resulted in economic discrimination and exclusion of substantial segments of the area population, its policies and practices are in the best present and future fiscal interest of the municipality and its inhabitants and are legally permissible and justified. * * *

Mount Laurel is a flat, sprawling township, 22 square miles, or about 14,000 acres, in area, on the west central edge of Burlington County. * * * [I]ts southerly side * * * is about seven miles from the boundary line of the city of Camden and not more than 10 miles from the Benjamin Franklin Bridge crossing the river to Philadelphia. * * * In 1950, the township had a population of 2817, only about 600 more people than it had in 1940. It was then, as it had been for decades, primarily a rural agricultural area with no sizeable settlements or commercial or industrial enterprises. * * * After 1950, as in so many other municipalities similarly situated, residential development and some commerce and industry began to come in. By 1960 the population had almost doubled to 5249 and by 1970 had more than doubled again to 11,221. * * * The township is now definitely a part of the outer ring of the South Jersey metropolitan area * * *. The growth of the township has been spurred by the construction or improvement of main highways through or near it. * * * This highway network gives the township a most strategic location from the standpoint of transport of goods and people by truck and private car. There is no other means of transportation.

The location and nature of development has been, as usual, controlled by the local zoning enactments. * * * Under the present ordinance, 29.2% of all the land in the township, or 4,121 acres, is zoned for industry. * * * Only industry meeting specified performance standards is permitted. The effect is to limit the use substantially to light manufacturing, research, distribution of goods, offices and the like. * * * At the time of trial no more than 100 acres * * * were actually occupied by industrial uses. * * * The rest of the land so zoned has remained undeveloped. If it were fully utilized, the testimony was that about 43,500 industrial jobs would be created, but it appeared clear that, as happens in the case of so many municipalities, much more land has been so zoned than the reasonable potential for industrial movement or expansion warrants. At the same time, however, the land cannot be used for residential development under the general ordinance.

The amount of land zoned for retail business use under the general ordinance is relatively small—169 acres, or 1.2% of the total. * * * [T]here is no major shopping center or concentrated retail commercial area—"downtown"—in the township. * * * The balance of the land area, almost 10,000 acres, has been developed until recently in the conventional form of major subdivisions. * * * All permit only single-family, detached dwellings, one house per lot—the usual form of grid development. Attached townhouses, apartments (except on farms for agricultural workers) and mobile homes are not allowed anywhere in the township under the general ordinance. * * * The result has been quite intensive development of * * * [some] sections, but at a low density. The dwellings are substantial; the average value in 1971 was $32,500 and is undoubtedly much higher today.

The general ordinance requirements, while not as restrictive as those in many similar municipalities, nonetheless realistically allow only homes within the financial reach of persons of at least middle income. The R–1 zone requires a minimum lot area of 9,375 square feet, a minimum lot width of 75 feet at the building line, and a minimum dwelling floor area of 1,100 square feet if a one-story building and 1,300 square feet if one and one-half stories or higher. * * * [I]n the R–3 zone * * *—slightly more than half of the total municipal area—requirements are substantially higher * * * in that the minimum lot size is increased to about one-half acre (20,000 square feet). * * * Lot width at the building line must be 100 feet. Minimum dwelling floor area is as in the R–1 zone. Presently this section is primarily in agricultural use; it contains as well most of the municipality's substandard housing. * * *

A variation from conventional development has recently occurred in some parts of Mount Laurel, as in a number of other similar municipalities, by use of the land use regulation device known as "planned unit development" (PUD). This scheme differs from the traditional in that the type, density and placement of land uses and buildings, instead of being detailed and confined to specified districts by local legislation in advance, is determined by contract, or "deal," as to each development between the developer and the municipal administrative authority, under broad guidelines laid down by state enabling legislation and an implementing local ordinance. The stress is on regulation of density and permitted mixture of uses within the same area, including various kinds of living accommodations with or without commercial and industrial enterprises. * * * While multi-family housing in the form of rental garden, medium rise and high rise apartments and attached townhouses is for the first time provided for, as well as single-family detached dwellings for sale, it is not designed to accommodate and is beyond the financial reach of low and moderate income families, especially those with young children. The aim is quite the contrary; as with the single-family homes in the older conventional subdivisions, only persons of medium and upper income are sought as residents. * * * The approvals * * * sharply limit the number of apartments having more than one bedroom. Further, they require that the developer must provide in its leases that no school-age children shall be permitted to occupy any one-bedroom apartment and that no more than two such children shall reside in any two-bedroom unit. * * * In addition, low density, required amenities, such as central air conditioning, and specified developer contributions help to push rents and sales prices to high levels. These contributions include fire apparatus, ambulances, fire houses, and very large sums of money for educational facilities, a cultural center and the township library. * * *

There cannot be the slightest doubt that the reason for this course of conduct has been to keep down local taxes on *property* (Mount Laurel is not a high tax municipality) and that the policy was carried out without regard for non-fiscal considerations with respect to *people,* either within or without its boundaries. * * * This policy of land use regulation for a fiscal end derives from New Jersey's tax structure, which has imposed on local real estate most of the cost of municipal and county government and of the primary and secondary education of the municipality's children. The latter expense is much the largest, so, basically, the fewer the school children, the lower the tax rate. Sizeable industrial and commercial ratables are eagerly sought and homes and the lots on which they are situate are required to be large enough, through minimum lot sizes and minimum floor areas, to have substantial value in order to produce greater tax revenues to meet school costs. Large families who cannot afford to buy large houses and must live in cheaper rental accommodations are definitely not wanted, so we find drastic bedroom restrictions for, or complete prohibition of, multi-family or other feasible housing for those of lesser income.

This pattern of land use regulation has been adopted for the same purpose in developing municipality after developing municipality. Almost every one acts solely in its own selfish and parochial interest and in effect builds a wall around itself to keep out those people or entities not adding favorably to the tax base, despite the location of the municipality or the demand for varied kinds of housing. There has been no effective intermunicipal or area planning or land use regulation. * * * One incongruous result is the picture of developing municipalities rendering it impossible for lower paid employees of industries they have eagerly sought and welcomed with open arms (and, in Mount Laurel's case, even some of its own lower paid municipal employees) to live in the community where they work.

The other end of the spectrum should also be mentioned because it shows the source of some of the demand for cheaper housing than the developing municipalities have permitted. Core cities were originally the location of most commerce and industry. Many of those facilities furnished employment for the unskilled and semi-skilled. These employees lived relatively near their work, so sections of cities always have housed the majority of people of low and moderate income, generally in old and deteriorating housing. Despite the municipally confined tax structure, commercial and industrial ratables generally used to supply enough revenue to provide and maintain municipal services equal or superior to those furnished in most suburban and rural areas.

The situation has become exactly the opposite since the end of World War II. Much industry and retail business, and even the professions, have left the cities. Camden is a typical example. The testimonial and documentary evidence in this case as to what has happened to that city is depressing indeed. For various reasons, it lost thousands of jobs between 1950 and 1970, including more than half of its manufacturing jobs (a reduction from 43,267 to 20,671, while all jobs in the entire area labor market increased from 94,507 to 197,037). A large segment of retail business faded away with the erection of large suburban shopping centers. The economically better situated city residents helped fill up the miles of sprawling new housing developments, not fully served by public transit. In a society which came to depend more and more on expensive individual motor vehicle transportation for all purposes, low income employees very frequently could not afford to reach outlying places of suitable employment and they certainly could not afford the permissible housing near such locations. These people have great difficulty in obtaining work and have been forced to remain in housing which is overcrowded, and has become more and more substandard and less and less tax productive. There has been a consequent critical erosion of the city tax base and inability to provide the amount and quality of those governmental services—education, health, police, fire, housing and the like—so necessary to the very existence of safe and decent city life. This category of city dwellers desperately needs much better housing and living conditions than is available to them now, both in a rehabilitated city and in outlying municipalities. They make up, along with the other classes of persons earlier mentioned who also cannot afford the only generally permitted housing in the developing municipalities, the acknowledged great demand for low and moderate income housing.

The legal question before us * * * is whether a developing municipality like Mount Laurel may validly, by a system of land use regulation, make it physically and economically impossible to provide low and moderate income housing in the municipality for the various categories of persons who need and want it and thereby, as Mount Laurel has, exclude such people from living within its confines because of the limited extent of their income and resources. Necessarily implicated are the broader questions of the right of such municipalities to limit the kinds of available housing and of any obligation to make possible a variety and choice of types of living accommodations.

We conclude that every such municipality must, by its land use regulations, presumptively make realistically possible an appropriate variety and choice of housing. More specifically, presumptively it cannot foreclose the opportunity of the classes of people mentioned for low and moderate income housing and in its regulations must affirmatively afford that opportunity, at least to the extent of the municipality's fair share of the present and prospective regional need therefor. These obligations must be met unless the particular municipality can sustain the heavy burden of demonstrating peculiar circumstances which dictate that it should not be required so to do.[10]

We reach this conclusion under state law and so do not find it necessary to consider federal constitutional grounds urged by plaintiffs. * * * It is elementary theory that all police power enactments, no matter at what level of government, must conform to the basic state constitutional requirements of substantive due process and equal protection of the laws. These are inherent in Art. I, par. 1 of our Constitution, the requirements of which may be more demanding than those of the federal Constitution. It is required that, affirmatively, a zoning regulation, like any police power enactment, must promote public health, safety, morals or the general welfare. * * *

The demarcation between the valid and the invalid in the field of land use regulation is difficult to determine, not always clear and subject to change. * * * This court has * * * plainly warned, even in cases decided some years ago sanctioning a broad measure of restrictive municipal decisions, of the inevitability of change in judicial approach and view as mandated by change in the world around us. * * * The warning implicates the matter of *whose* general welfare must be served or not violated in the field of land use regulation. Frequently the decisions in this state * * * have spoken only in terms of the interest of the enacting municipality, so that it has been thought, at least in some quarters, that such was the only welfare requiring consideration. It is, of course, true that many cases have dealt only with regulations having little, if any, outside impact where the local decision is ordinarily entitled to prevail. However, it is fundamental and not to be forgotten that the zoning power is a police power of the state and the local authority is acting only as a delegate of that power and is restricted in the same manner as is the state. So, when regulation does have a substantial external impact, the welfare of the state's citizens beyond the borders of the particular municipality cannot be disregarded and must be recognized and served. * * *

---

10. While, as the trial court found, Mount Laurel's actions were deliberate, we are of the view that the identical conclusion follows even when municipal conduct is not shown to be intentional, but the effect is substantially the same as if it were.

It is plain beyond dispute that proper provision for adequate housing of all categories of people is certainly an absolute essential in promotion of the general welfare required in all local land use regulation. Further the universal and constant need for such housing is so important and of such broad public interest that the general welfare which developing municipalities like Mount Laurel must consider extends beyond their boundaries and cannot be parochially confined to the claimed good of the particular municipality. It has to follow that, broadly speaking, the presumptive obligation arises for each such municipality affirmatively to plan and provide, by its land use regulations, the reasonable opportunity for an appropriate variety and choice of housing, including, of course, low and moderate cost housing, to meet the needs, desires and resources of all categories of people who may desire to live within its boundaries. Negatively, it may not adopt regulations or policies which thwart or preclude that opportunity. * * *

We have spoken of this obligation of such municipalities as "presumptive." The term has two aspects, procedural and substantive. Procedurally, we think the basic importance of appropriate housing for all dictates that, when it is shown that a developing municipality in its land use regulations has not made realistically possible a variety and choice of housing, including adequate provision to afford the opportunity for low and moderate income housing, or has expressly prescribed requirements or restrictions which preclude or substantially hinder it, a facial showing of violation of substantive due process or equal protection under the state constitution has been made out and the burden, and it is a heavy one, shifts to the municipality to establish a valid basis for its action or non-action. The substantive aspect of "presumptive" relates to the specifics, on the one hand, of what municipal land use regulation provisions, or the absence thereof, will evidence invalidity and shift the burden of proof and, on the other hand, of what bases and considerations will carry the municipality's burden and sustain what it has done or failed to do. Both kinds of specifics may well vary between municipalities according to peculiar circumstances. * * *

Without further elaboration at this point, our opinion is that Mount Laurel's zoning ordinance is presumptively contrary to the general welfare and outside the intended scope of the zoning power in the particulars mentioned. A facial showing of invalidity is thus established, shifting to the municipality the burden of establishing valid superseding reasons for its action and non-action. We now examine the reasons it advances.

The township's principal reason in support of its zoning plan and ordinance housing provisions, advanced especially strongly at oral argument, is the fiscal one previously adverted to, *i.e.*, that by reason of New Jersey's tax structure which substantially finances municipal governmental and educational costs from taxes on local real property, every municipality may, by the exercise of the zoning power, allow only such uses and to such extent as will be beneficial to the local tax rate. In other words, the position is that any municipality may zone extensively to seek and encourage the "good" tax ratables of industry and commerce and limit the permissible types of housing to those having the fewest school children or to those providing sufficient value to attain or approach paying their own way taxwise. * * * We have no hesitancy in now saying, and do so emphatically, that, considering the basic importance of the opportunity for appropriate housing for all classes of our citizenry, no municipality may exclude or limit categories of housing for that reason or purpose. While we fully recognize the increasingly heavy burden of local taxes for municipal governmental and school costs on homeowners, relief from the consequences of this tax system will have to be furnished by other branches of government. It cannot legitimately be accomplished by restricting types of housing through the zoning process in developing municipalities.

The propriety of zoning ordinance limitations on housing for ecological or environmental reasons seems also to be suggested by Mount Laurel in support of the one-half acre minimum lot size in that very considerable portion of the township still available for residential development. It is said that the area is without sewer or water utilities and that the soil is such that this plot size is required for safe individual lot sewage disposal and water supply. The short answer is that, this being flat land and readily amenable to such utility installations, the township could require them as improvements by developers or install them under the special assessment or other appropriate statutory procedure. The present environmental situation of the area is, therefore, no sufficient excuse in itself for limiting housing therein to single-family dwelling on large lots. * * *

By way of summary, what we have said comes down to this. As a developing municipality, Mount Laurel must, by its land use regulations, make realistically possible the opportunity for an appropriate variety and choice of housing for all categories of people who may desire to live there, of course including those of low and moderate income. It must permit multi-family housing, without bedroom or similar restrictions, as well as small dwellings on very small lots, low cost housing of other types and, in general, high density zoning, without artificial and unjustifiable minimum requirements as to lot size, building size and the like, to meet the full panoply of these needs. Certainly when a municipality zones for industry and commerce for local tax benefit purposes, it without question must zone to permit adequate housing within the means of the employees involved in such uses. (If planned unit developments are authorized, one would assume that each must include a reasonable amount of low and moderate income housing in its residential "mix," unless opportunity for such housing has already been realistically provided for elsewhere in the municipality.) The amount of land removed from residential use by allocation to industrial and commercial purposes must be reasonably related to the present and future potential for such purposes. In other words, such municipalities must zone primarily for the living welfare of people and not for the benefit of the local tax rate.

We have earlier stated that a developing municipality's obligation to afford the opportunity for decent and adequate low and moderate income housing extends at least to "* * * the municipality's fair share of the present and prospective regional need therefor." Some comment on that conclusion is in order at this point. Frequently it might be sounder to have more of such housing, like some specialized land uses, in one municipality in a region than in another, because of greater availability of suitable land, location of employment, accessibility of public transportation or some other significant reason. But, under present New Jersey legislation, zoning must be on an individual municipal basis, rather than regionally. So long as that situation persists under the present tax structure, or in the absence of some kind of binding agreement among all the municipalities of a region, we feel that every municipality therein must bear its fair share of the regional burden. (In this respect our holding is broader than that of the trial court, which was limited to Mount Laurel-related low and moderate income housing needs.)

The composition of the applicable "region" will necessarily vary from situation to situation and probably no hard and fast rule will serve to furnish the answer in every case. Confinement to or within a certain county appears not to be realistic, but restriction within the boundaries of the state seem practical and advisable. (This is not to say that a developing municipality can ignore a demand for housing within its boundaries on the part of people who commute to work in another state.) Here we have already defined the region at present as "those portions of Camden, Burlington and Gloucester Counties within a semicircle having a radius of 20 miles or so from the heart of Camden City." The concept of "fair share" is coming into more general use and, through the expertise of the municipal planning adviser, the county planning boards and the state planning agency, a reasonable figure for Mount Laurel can be determined, which can then be translated to the allocation of sufficient land therefor on the zoning map. We may add that we think that, in arriving at such a determination, the type of information and estimates, which the trial judge directed the township to compile and furnish to him, concerning the housing needs of persons of low and moderate income now or formerly residing in the township in substandard dwellings and those presently employed or reasonably expected to be employed therein, will be pertinent.

There is no reason why developing municipalities like Mount Laurel, required by this opinion to afford the opportunity for all types of housing to meet the needs of various categories of people, may not become and remain attractive, viable communities providing good living and adequate services for all their residents in the kind of atmosphere which a democracy and free institutions demand. They can have industrial sections, commercial sections and sections for every kind of housing from low cost and multi-family to lots of more than an acre with very expensive homes. Proper planning and governmental cooperation can prevent over-intensive and too sudden development, insure against future suburban sprawl and slums and assure the preservation of open space and local beauty. We do not intend that developing municipalities shall be overwhelmed by voracious land speculators and developers if they use the powers which they have intelligently and in the broad public interest. Under our holdings today, they can be better communities for all than they previously have been. * * *

It is the local function and responsibility, in the first instance at least, rather than the court's, to decide on the details of * * * [corrective legislation] within the guidelines we have laid down. * * * Courts do not build housing nor do municipalities. That function is performed by private builders, various kinds of associations, or, for public housing, by special agencies created for that purpose at various levels of government. The municipal function is initially to provide the opportunity through appropriate land use regulations and we have spelled out what Mount Laurel must do in that regard. It is not appropriate at this time, particularly in view of the advanced view of zoning law as applied to housing laid down by this opinion, to deal with the matter of the further extent of judicial power in the field or to exercise any such power. The municipality should first have full opportunity to itself act without judicial supervision. We trust it will do so in the spirit we have suggested, both by appropriate zoning ordinance amendments and whatever additional action encouraging the fulfillment of its fair share of the regional need for low and moderate income housing may be indicated as necessary and advisable. (We have in mind that there is at least a moral obligation in a municipality to establish a local housing agency pursuant to state law to provide housing for its resident poor now living in dilapidated, unhealthy quarters.) * * * Should Mount Laurel not perform as we expect, further judicial action may be sought by supplemental pleading in this cause. * * *

SOUTHERN BURLINGTON COUNTY N.A.A.C.P. v. TOWNSHIP OF MT. LAUREL

Supreme Court of New Jersey, 1983.
92 N.J. 158, 456 A.2d 390.

WILENTZ, C.J.

This is the return, eight years later, of *Southern Burlington County N.A.A.C.P. v. Township of Mount Laurel,* 67 N.J. 151, 336 A.2d 713 (1975) (*Mount Laurel I*). We set forth in that case, for the first time, the doctrine requiring that municipalities' land use regulations provide a realistic opportunity for low and moderate income housing. The doctrine has become famous. The *Mount Laurel* case itself threatens to become infamous. After all this time, ten years after the trial court's initial order invalidating its zoning ordinance, Mount Laurel remains afflicted with a blatantly exclusionary ordinance. Papered over with studies, rationalized by hired experts, the ordinance at its core is true to nothing but Mount Laurel's determination to exclude the poor. Mount Laurel is not alone; we believe that there is widespread non-compliance with the constitutional mandate of our original opinion in this case.

To the best of our ability, we shall not allow it to continue. This Court is more firmly committed to the original *Mount Laurel* doctrine than ever, and we are determined, within appropriate judicial bounds, to make it work. The obligation is to provide a realistic opportunity for housing, not litigation. We have learned from experience, however, that unless a strong judicial hand is used, *Mount Laurel* will not result in housing, but in paper, process, witnesses, trials and appeals. We intend by this decision to strengthen it, clarify it, and make it easier for public officials, including judges, to apply it.

This case is accompanied by five others, heard together and decided in this opinion. All involve questions arising from the *Mount Laurel* doctrine. They demonstrate the need to put some steel into that doctrine. The deficiencies in its application range from uncertainty and inconsistency at the trial level to inflexible review criteria at the appellate level. The waste of judicial energy involved at every level is substantial and is matched only by the often needless expenditure of talent on the part of lawyers and experts. The length and complexity of trials is often outrageous, and the expense of litigation is so high that a real question develops whether the municipality can afford to defend or the plaintiffs can afford to sue.

There is another side to the story. We believe, both through the representations of counsel and from our own research and experience, that the doctrine has done some good, indeed, perhaps substantial good. We have tried to make the doctrine clearer for we believe that most municipal officials will in good faith strive to fulfill their constitutional duty. There are a number of municipalities around the State that have responded to our decisions by amending their zoning ordinances to provide realistic opportunities for the construction of low and moderate income housing. Further, many other municipalities have at least recognized their obligation to provide such opportunities in their ordinances and master plans. Finally, state and county government agencies have responded by preparing regional housing plans that help both the courts and municipalities themselves carry out the *Mount Laurel* mandate. Still, we are far from where we had hoped to be and nowhere near where we should be with regard to the administration of the doctrine in our courts. * * *

The constitutional basis for the *Mount Laurel* doctrine remains the same. The constitutional power to zone, delegated to the municipalities subject to legislation, is but one portion of the police power and, as such, must be exercised for the general welfare. When the exercise of that power by a municipality affects something as fundamental as housing, the general welfare includes more than the welfare of that municipality and its citizens: it also includes the general welfare—in this case the housing needs—of those residing outside of the municipality but within the region that contributes to the housing demand within the municipality. * * * It would be useful to remind ourselves that * * * [this] doctrine does not arise from some theoretical analysis of our Constitution, but rather from underlying concepts of fundamental fairness in the exercise of governmental power. The basis for the constitutional obligation is simple: the State controls the use of land, *all* of the land. In exercising that control it cannot favor rich over poor. It cannot legislatively set aside dilapidated housing in urban ghettos for the poor and decent housing elsewhere for everyone else. The government that controls this land represents everyone. While the State may not have the ability to eliminate poverty, it cannot use that condition as the basis for imposing further disadvantages. And the same applies to the municipality, to which this control over land has been constitutionally delegated.

The clarity of the constitutional obligation is seen most simply by imagining what this state could be like were this claim never to be recognized and enforced: poor people forever zoned out of substantial areas of the state, not because housing could not be built for them but because they are not wanted; poor people forced to live in urban slums forever not because suburbia, developing rural areas, fully developed residential sections, seashore resorts, and other attractive locations could not accommodate them, but simply because they are not wanted. It is a vision not only at variance with the requirement that the zoning power be used for the general welfare but with all concepts of fundamental fairness and decency that underpin many constitutional obligations.

Subject to the clear obligation to preserve open space and prime agricultural land, a builder in New Jersey who finds it economically feasible to provide decent housing for lower income groups will no longer find it governmentally impossible. Builders may not be able to build just where they want—our parks, farms, and conservation areas are not a land bank for housing speculators. But if sound planning of an area allows the rich and middle class to live there, it must also realistically and practically allow the poor. And if the area will accommodate factories, it must also find space for workers. The specific location of such housing will of course continue to depend on sound municipal land use planning.

While *Mount Laurel I* discussed the need for "an appropriate variety and choice of housing," the specific constitutional obligation addressed there, as well as in our opinion here, is that relating to low and moderate income housing. All that we say here concerns that category alone; the doctrine as we interpret it has no present applicability to other kinds of housing. It is obvious that eight years after *Mount Laurel I* the need for satisfaction of this doctrine is greater than ever. Upper and middle income groups may search with increasing difficulty for housing within their means; for low and moderate income people, there is nothing to search for.

No one has challenged the *Mount Laurel* doctrine on these appeals. Nevertheless, a brief reminder of the judicial role in this sensitive area is appropriate, since powerful reasons suggest, and we agree, that the matter is better left to the Legislature. We act first and foremost because the Constitution of our State requires protection of the interests involved and because the Legislature has not protected them. We recognize the social and economic controversy (and its political consequences) that has resulted in relatively little legislative action in this field. We understand the enormous difficulty of achieving a political consensus that might lead to significant legislation enforcing the constitutional mandate better than we can, legislation that might completely remove this Court from those controversies. But enforcement of constitutional rights cannot await a supporting political consensus. So while we have always preferred legislative to judicial action in this field, we shall continue—until the Legislature acts—to do our best to uphold the constitutional obligation that underlies the *Mount Laurel* doctrine. That is our duty. We may not build houses, but we do enforce the Constitution.

We note that there has been some legislative initiative in this field. We look forward to more. The new Municipal Land Use Law explicitly recognizes the obligation of municipalities to zone with regional consequences in mind; it also recognizes the work of the Division of State and Regional Planning in the Department of Community Affairs (DCA), in creating the State Development Guide Plan (1980) (SDGP), which plays an important part in our decisions today. Our deference to these legislative and executive initiatives can be regarded as a clear signal of our readiness to defer further to more substantial actions.

The judicial role, however, which could decrease as a result of legislative and executive action, necessarily will expand to the extent that we remain virtually alone in this field. In the absence of adequate legislative and executive help, we must give meaning to the constitutional doctrine in the cases before us through our own devices, even if they are relatively less suitable. That is the basic explanation of our decisions today.

Our rulings today have several purposes. First, we intend to encourage voluntary compliance with the constitutional obligation by defining it more clearly. We believe that the use of the State Development Guide Plan and the confinement of all *Mount Laurel* litigation to a small group of judges, selected by the Chief Justice with the approval of the Court, will tend to serve that purpose. Second, we hope to simplify litigation in this area. While we are not overly optimistic, we think that the remedial use of the SDGP may achieve that purpose, given the significance accorded it in this opinion. Third, the decisions are intended to increase substantially the effectiveness of the judicial remedy. In most cases, upon determination that the municipality has not fulfilled its constitutional obligation, the trial court will retain jurisdiction, order an immediate revision of the ordinance (including, if necessary, supervision of the revision through a court appointed master), and require the use of effective affirmative planning and zoning devices. The long delays of interminable appellate review will be discouraged, if not completely ended, and the opportunity for low and moderate income housing found in the new ordinance will be as realistic as judicial remedies can make it. We hope to achieve all of these purposes while preserving the fundamental legitimate control of municipalities over their own zoning and, indeed, their destiny.

The following is a summary of the more significant rulings of these cases:

(1) *Every* municipality's land use regulations should provide a realistic opportunity for decent housing for at least some part of its resident poor who now occupy dilapidated housing. The zoning power is no more abused by keeping out the region's poor than by forcing out the resident poor. In other words, each municipality must provide a realistic opportunity for decent housing for its indigenous poor except where they represent a disproportionately large segment of the population as compared with the rest of the region. This is the case in many of our urban areas.

(2) The existence of a municipal obligation to provide a realistic opportunity for a fair share of the region's present and prospective low and moderate income housing need will no longer be determined by whether or not a municipality is "developing." The obligation extends, instead, to every municipality, any portion of which is designated by the State, through the SDGP as a "growth area." This obligation, imposed as a remedial measure, does not extend to those areas where the SDGP discourages growth—namely, open spaces, rural areas, prime farmland, conservation areas, limited growth areas, parts of the Pinelands and certain Coastal Zone areas. The SDGP represents the conscious determination of the State, through the executive and legislative branches, on how best to plan its future. It appropriately serves as a judicial remedial tool. The obligation to encourage lower income housing, therefore, will hereafter depend on rational long-range land use planning (incorporated into the SDGP) rather than upon the sheer economic forces that have dictated whether a municipality is "developing." Moreover, the fact that a municipality is fully developed does not eliminate this obligation although, obviously, it may affect the extent of the obligation and the timing of its satisfaction. The remedial obligation of municipalities that consist of both "growth areas" and other areas may be reduced, based on many factors, as compared to a municipality completely within a "growth area."

There shall be a heavy burden on any party seeking to vary the foregoing remedial consequences of the SDGP designations.

(3) *Mount Laurel* litigation will ordinarily include proof of the municipality's fair share of low and moderate income housing in terms of the number of units needed immediately, as well as the number needed for a reasonable period of time in the future. "Numberless" resolution of the issue based upon a conclusion that the ordinance provides a realistic opportunity for *some* low and moderate income housing will be insufficient. Plaintiffs, however, will still be able to prove a *prima facie* case, without proving the precise fair share of the municipality, by proving that the zoning ordinance is substantially affected by restrictive devices, that proof creating a presumption that the ordinance is invalid.

The municipal obligation to provide a realistic opportunity for low and moderate income housing is not satisfied by a good faith attempt. The housing opportunity provided must, in fact, be the substantial equivalent of the fair share.

(4) Any future *Mount Laurel* litigation shall be assigned only to those judges selected by the Chief Justice with the approval of the Supreme Court. * * * Since the same judge will hear and decide all *Mount Laurel* cases within a particular area and only three judges will do so in the entire state, we believe that over a period of time a consistent pattern of regions will emerge. * * *

(5) The municipal obligation to provide a realistic opportunity for the construction of its fair share of low and moderate income housing may require more than the elimination of unnecessary cost-producing requirements and restrictions. Affirmative governmental devices should be used to make that opportunity realistic, including lower-income density bonuses and mandatory set-asides. Furthermore the municipality should cooperate with the developer's attempts to obtain federal subsidies. For instance, where federal subsidies depend on the municipality providing certain municipal tax treatment allowed by state statutes for lower income housing, the municipality should make a good faith effort to provide it. Mobile homes may not be prohibited, unless there is solid proof that sound planning in a particular municipality requires such prohibition.

(6) The lower income regional housing need is comprised of both low and moderate income housing. A municipality's fair share should include both in such proportion as reflects consideration of all relevant factors, including the proportion of low and moderate income housing that make up the regional need.

(7) Providing a realistic opportunity for the construction of least-cost housing will satisfy a municipality's *Mount Laurel* obligation if, and only if, it cannot otherwise be satisfied. In other words, it is only after *all* alternatives have been explored, *all* affirmative devices considered, including, where appropriate, a reasonable period of time to determine whether low and moderate income housing is produced, only when everything has been considered and tried in order to produce a realistic opportunity for low and moderate income housing that least-cost housing will provide an adequate substitute. Least-cost housing means what it says, namely, housing that can be produced at the lowest possible price consistent with minimal standards of health and safety.

(8) Builder's remedies will be afforded to plaintiffs in *Mount Laurel* litigation where appropriate, on a case-by-case basis. Where the plaintiff has acted in good faith, attempted to obtain relief without litigation, and thereafter vindicates the constitutional obligation in *Mount Laurel*-type litigation, ordinarily a builder's remedy will be granted, provided that the proposed project includes an appropriate portion of low and moderate income housing, and provided further that it is located and designed

in accordance with sound zoning and planning concepts, including its environmental impact.

(9) The judiciary should manage *Mount Laurel* litigation to dispose of a case in all of its aspects with one trial and one appeal, unless substantial considerations indicate some other course. This means that in most cases after a determination of invalidity, and prior to final judgment and possible appeal, the municipality will be required to rezone, preserving its contention that the trial court's adjudication was incorrect. If an appeal is taken, all facets of the litigation will be considered by the appellate court including both the correctness of the lower court's determination of invalidity, the scope of remedies imposed on the municipality, and the validity of the ordinance adopted after the judgment of invalidity. The grant or denial of a stay will depend upon the circumstances of each case. The trial court will appoint a master to assist in formulating and implementing a proper remedy whenever that course seems desirable.

(10) The *Mount Laurel* obligation to meet the prospective lower income housing need of the region is, by definition, one that is met year after year in the future, throughout the years of the particular projection used in calculating prospective need. In this sense the affirmative obligation to provide a realistic opportunity to construct a fair share of lower income housing is met by a "phase-in" over those years; it need not be provided immediately. Nevertheless, there may be circumstances in which the obligation requires zoning that will provide an immediate opportunity—for instance, zoning to meet the region's present lower income housing need. In some cases, the provision of such a realistic opportunity might result in the immediate construction of lower income housing in such quantity as would radically transform the municipality overnight. Trial courts shall have the discretion, under those circumstances, to moderate the impact of such housing by allowing even the present need to be phased in over a period of years. Such power, however, should be exercised sparingly. The same power may be exercised in the satisfaction of prospective need, equally sparingly, and with special care to assure that such further postponement will not significantly dilute the *Mount Laurel* obligation.

We reassure all concerned that *Mount Laurel* is not designed to sweep away all land use restrictions or leave our open spaces and natural resources prey to speculators. Municipalities consisting largely of conservation, agricultural, or environmentally sensitive areas will not be required to grow because of *Mount Laurel*. No forests or small towns need be paved over and covered with high-rise apartments as a result of today's decision.

As for those municipalities that may have to make adjustments in their lifestyles to provide for their fair share of low and moderate income housing, they should remember that they are not being required to provide more than their *fair* share. No one community need be concerned that it will be radically transformed by a deluge of low and moderate income developments. Nor should any community conclude that its residents will move to other suburbs as a result of this decision, for those "other suburbs" may very well be required to do their part to provide the same housing. Finally, once a community has satisfied its fair share obligation, the *Mount Laurel* doctrine will not restrict other measures, including large-lot and open area zoning, that would maintain its beauty and communal character.

Many of these points will be discussed later in this opinion. We mention them now only to reassure all concerned that any changes brought about by this opinion need not be drastic or destructive. Our scenic and rural areas will remain essentially scenic and rural, and our suburban communities will retain their basic suburban character. But there will be *some* change, as there must be if the constitutional rights of our lower income citizens are ever to be protected. That change will be much less painful for us than the status quo has been for them. * * *

HILLS DEVELOPMENT COMPANY v. BERNARDS TOWNSHIP IN SOMERSET COUNTY

Supreme Court of New Jersey, 1986.
103 N.J. 1, 510 A.2d 621.

WILENTZ, C.J.

In this appeal we are called upon to determine the constitutionality and effect of the "Fair Housing Act," the Legislature's response to the *Mount Laurel* cases. The Act creates an administrative agency (the Council on Affordable Housing) with power to define housing regions within the state and the regional need for low and moderate income housing, along with the power to promulgate criteria and guidelines to enable municipalities within each region to determine their fair share of that regional need. The Council is further empowered, on application, to decide whether proposed ordinances and related measures of a particular municipality will, if enacted, satisfy its *Mount Laurel* obligation, *i.e.,* will they create a realistic opportunity for the construction of that municipality's fair share of the regional need for low and moderate income housing. *Southern Burlington County N.A.A.C.P. v. Mount Laurel,* 92 N.J. 158, 208–09, 456 A.2d 390 (1983). The agency's determination that the municipality's *Mount Laurel* obligation has been satisfied will ordinarily amount to a final resolution of that issue; it can be set aside in court only by "clear and convincing evidence" to the contrary. The Act includes appropriations and other financial means designed to help achieve the construction of low and moderate income housing.

In order to assure that the extent and satisfaction of a municipality's *Mount Laurel* obligation are decided and managed by the Council through this administrative procedure, rather than by the courts, the Act provides for the transfer of pending and future *Mount Laurel* litigation to the agency. Transfer is required in all cases except, as to cases commenced more than 60 days before the effective date of the Act

(July 2, 1985), when it would result in "manifest injustice to any party to the litigation."

The statutory scheme set forth in the Act is intended to satisfy the constitutional obligation enunciated by this Court in the *Mount Laurel* cases. The Act includes an explicit declaration to that effect in section 3.

I.

OVERVIEW OF ACT; SUMMARY OF THE COURT'S DECISION

The Act that we review and sustain today represents a substantial effort by the other branches of government to vindicate the *Mount Laurel* constitutional obligation. This is not ordinary legislation. It deals with one of the most difficult constitutional, legal and social issues of our day—that of providing suitable and affordable housing for citizens of low and moderate income. In *Mount Laurel II,* we did not minimize the difficulty of this effort—we stressed only its paramount importance—and we do not minimize its difficulty today. But we believe that if the Act before us works in accordance with its expressed intent, it will assure a realistic opportunity for lower income housing in all those parts of the state where sensible planning calls for such housing.

Most objections raised against the Act assume that it will not work, or construe its provisions so that it cannot work, and attribute both to the legislation and to the Council a mission, nowhere expressed in the Act, of sabotaging the *Mount Laurel* doctrine. On the contrary, we must assume that the Council will pursue the vindication of the *Mount Laurel* obligation with determination and skill. If it does, that vindication should be far preferable to vindication by the courts, and may be far more effective.

Instead of depending on chance—the chance that a builder will sue—the location and extent of lower income housing will depend on sound, comprehensive statewide planning, developed by the Council and aided by the State Development and Redevelopment Plan (SDRP) to be prepared by the newly formed State Planning Commission pursuant to L.1985, c. 398. Conceptually, the Fair Housing Act is similar to CAFRA (Coastal Area Facility Review Act), the Pinelands Act (Pinelands Protection Act), and the Meadowlands Act (Hackensack Meadowlands Reclamation & Development Act), in its regional approach to questions of appropriate land use. Its statewide scope is an extensive departure from the unplanned and uncoordinated municipal growth of the past.

The Council will determine the total need for lower income housing, the regional portion of that need, and the standards for allocating to each municipality its fair share. The Council is charged by law with that responsibility, imparting to it the legitimacy and presumed expertise that derives from selection by the Governor and confirmation by the Senate, in accordance with the will of the Legislature. Instead of varying and potentially inconsistent definitions of total need, regions, regional need, and fair share that can result from the case-by-case determinations of courts involved in isolated litigation, an overall plan for the entire state is envisioned, with definitions and standards that will have the kind of consistency that can result only when full responsibility and power are given to a single entity. Municipalities will have both the means and motives to determine, using the same standards, what is required of them, what their fair share is, and what combination of ordinances and other measures will achieve that fair share. The means consist of the rules, criteria, and guidelines of the Council, along with the Council's determination that the municipal fair share plan complies, or, if it does not, what steps must be taken. The motives are the municipalities' strong preference to exercise their zoning powers independently and voluntarily as compared to their open hostility to court-ordered rezoning; the motives also include the municipalities' desire to avoid such litigation, a goal best achieved by voluntary compliance through conformance with the standards adopted by the Council.

The Council's work is intended to produce ordinances and other measures that will fit together as part of a statewide plan, among other things, a plan that provides a real chance, a realistic "likelihood," *Mount Laurel II,* 92 N.J. at 222, 456 A.2d 390, for the construction or rehabilitation of lower income housing. And where necessary, financing may be available to help, for the Act includes appropriations and other financial measures that will provide needed subsidies.

The Act recognizes that zoning and planning for lower income housing is a long-range task, that goals must be changed periodically, revisions made accordingly, and results regularly evaluated. This continuing nature of the planning process is given explicit recognition in the Act.

When supplemented by the SDRP, the Act amounts to an overall plan for the state, rationally conceived, to be implemented through governmental devices that hold the promise that the outcome—the provision of lower income housing—will substantially conform to the plan. It is a plan administered by an administrative agency with a broad grant of general power, providing the flexibility necessary for such an undertaking; it is a plan that will necessarily reflect competing needs and interests resolved through value judgments whose public acceptability is based on their legislative source. Most important of all to the success of the plan is this public acceptance and, hence, the municipal acceptance that it should command.

That is the general outline of how this Act and the Council created by it are intended to operate, and the results they are intended to achieve. It is a description at variance with the prediction of some who oppose the Act. Our opinion and our rulings today, significantly reducing the courts' function in this field, are based on this outline, based, that is, on the Council's ability, through the Act, to approach the results described above. If, however, as predicted by its opponents, the Act, despite the intention behind it, achieves nothing but delay, the judiciary will be forced to resume its appropriate role.

This Act represents an unprecedented willingness by the Governor and the Legislature to face the *Mount Laurel* issue after unprecedented decisions by this Court. Even with ordinary legislation, the rule is firmly settled that a law is presumed constitutional. * * *

We hold that the Act is constitutional and order that all of the cases pending before us be transferred to the Council. Those transfers, however, shall be subject to such conditions as the trial courts may find necessary to preserve the municipalities' ability to satisfy their *Mount Laurel* obligation. * * *

————

Note on Hills

Later in the *Hills* opinion, the Supreme Court of New Jersey described one important feature of the New Jersey Fair Housing Act in the following terms:

The Act * * * allows municipalities to share *Mount Laurel* obligations by entering into regional contribution agreements. This device requires either Council or court approval to be effective. Under this provision, one municipality can transfer to another, if that other agrees, a portion, under 50%, of its fair share obligation, the receiving municipality adding that to its own. The Act contemplates that the first municipality will contribute funds to the other, presumably to make the housing construction possible and to eliminate any financial burden resulting from the added fair share. The provisions seem intended to allow suburban municipalities to transfer a portion of their obligation to urban areas (see § 2g, evincing a legislative intent to encourage construction, conversion, or rehabilitation of housing in urban areas), thereby aiding in the construction of decent lower income housing in the area where most lower income households are found, provided, however, that such areas are "within convenient access to employment opportunities," and conform to "sound comprehensive regional planning." * * *

Do you think that these agreements accomplish or undermine the goal of the *Mt. Laurel* cases?

————

In evaluating the appropriateness of government action—whether legislative or judicial—to eliminate exclusionary zoning, one factor to consider is the historic role that the government played in promoting housing segregation along race and class lines in the first place. An important historical account of the federal government's policy of fostering housing segregation is excerpted below. Does this excerpt influence your view about the comparative wisdom of the *Arlington Heights* and *Mt. Laurel* approaches to exclusionary zoning?

KENNETH JACKSON, THE FEDERAL HOUSING ADMINISTRATION

From K. Jackson, Crabgrass Frontier: The Suburbanization
of the United States 203–209, 213–218 (1985).

No agency of the United States government has had a more pervasive and powerful impact on the American people over the past half-century than the Federal Housing Administration (FHA). It dates from the adoption of the National Housing Act on June 27, 1934. * * * [I]t was intended "to encourage improvement in housing standards and conditions, to facilitate sound home financing on reasonable terms, and to exert a stabilizing influence on the mortgage market." The primary purpose of the legislation, however, was the alleviation of unemployment, which stood at about a quarter of the total work force in 1934 and which was particularly high in the construction industry. * * * The FHA effort was later supplemented by the Servicemen's Readjustment Act of 1944 (more familiarly known as the GI Bill), which created a Veterans Administration (VA) program to help the sixteen million soldiers and sailors of World War II purchase a home after the defeat of Germany and Japan. * * *

Between 1934 and 1968, and to a lesser extent until the present day, both the FHA and the VA (since 1944) have had a remarkable record of accomplishment. Essentially, they insure long-term mortgage loans made by private lenders for home construction and sale. To this end, they collect premiums, set up reserves for losses, and in the event of a default on a mortgage, indemnify the lender. They do not build houses or lend money. Instead, they induce lenders who have money to invest it in residential mortgages by insuring them against loss on such instruments, with the full weight of the United States Treasury behind the contract. And they have revolutionized the home finance industry in the following ways:

Before the FHA began operation, first mortgages were limited to one-half or two-thirds of the appraised value of the property. * * * By contrast, the fraction of the collateral that the lender was able to lend for an FHA-secured loan was about 93 percent. Thus, down payments of more than 10 percent were unnecessary.

Continuing a trend begun by the Home Owners Loan Corporation, FHA extended the repayment period for its guaranteed mortgages to twenty-five or thirty years and insisted that all loans be fully amortized. * * *

FHA established minimum standards for home construction that became almost standard in the industry. * * *

In the 1920s, the interest rate for first mortgages averaged between 6 and 8 percent. * * * Under the FHA (and later Veterans Administration) program, by contrast, there was very little risk to the banker if a loan turned sour. Reflecting this government guarantee, interest rates fell by two or three percentage points.

These four changes substantially increased the number of American families who could reasonably expect to purchase homes. Builders went back to work, and housing starts and sales began to accelerate rapidly in 1936. * * * Quite simply, it often became cheaper to buy than to rent. * * * Long Island builder Martin Winter recalled that in the early 1950s families living in the Kew Gardens section of Queens were paying about ninety dollars per month for small two-bedroom apartments. For less money, they could and often did, move to the new Levittown-type developments springing up along the highways from Manhattan. * * * Not surprisingly, the middle-class suburban family with the new house and the long-term, fixed-rate, FHA-insured mortgage became a symbol, and perhaps a stereotype, of the American way of life.

Unfortunately, the corollary to this achievement was the fact that FHA programs hastened the decay of inner-city neighborhoods by stripping them of much of their middle-class constituency. In practice, FHA insurance went to new residential developments on the edges of metropolitan areas, to the neglect of core cities. This occurred for three reasons. First, although the legislation nowhere mentioned an antiurban bias, it favored the construction of single-family projects and discouraged construction of multi-family projects through unpopular terms. Historically, single-family housing programs have been the heart of FHA's insured loan activities. * * *

Second, loans for the repair of existing structures were small and for short duration, which meant that a family could more easily purchase a new home than modernize an old one. * * *

The third and most important variety of suburban, middle-class favoritism had to do with the "unbiased professional estimate" that was a prerequisite to any loan guarantee. Required because maximum mortgage amounts were related to "appraised value," this mandatory judgment included a rating of the property itself, a rating of the mortgagor or borrower, and a rating of the neighborhood. The aim was to guarantee that at any time during the term of the mortgage the market value of the dwelling would exceed the outstanding debt. The lower the valuation placed on properties, the less government risk and the less generous the aid to the potential buyers (and sellers). The purpose of the neighborhood evaluation was "to determine the degree of mortgage risk introduced in a mortgage insurance transaction because of the location of the property at a specific site." And unlike the Home Owners Loan Corporation, which used a similar procedure, the Federal Housing Administration allowed personal and agency bias in favor of all-white subdivisions in the suburbs to affect the kinds of loans it guaranteed—or, equally important, refused to guarantee. In this way, the bureaucracy influenced the character of housing at least as much as the 1934 enabling legislation did.

The Federal Housing Administration was quite precise in teaching its underwriters how to measure quality in residential areas. Eight criteria were established (the numbers in parentheses reflect the percentage weight given to each):

Relative economic stability (40 percent)

Protection from adverse influences (20 percent)

Freedom from special hazards (5 percent)

Adequacy of civic, social, and commercial centers (5 percent)

Adequacy of transportation (10 percent)

Sufficiency of utilities and conveniences (5 percent)

Level of taxes and special assessments (5 percent)

Appeal (10 percent)

Although FHA directives insisted that no project should be insured that involved a high degree of risk with regard to any of the eight categories, "economic stability" and "protection from adverse influences" together counted for more than the other six combined. Both were interpreted in ways that were prejudicial against heterogeneous environments. The 1939 *Underwriting Manual* taught that "crowded neighborhoods lessen desirability," and "older properties in a neighborhood have a tendency to accelerate the transition to lower class occupancy." Smoke and odor were considered "adverse influences," and appraisers were told to look carefully for any "inferior and non-productive characteristics of the areas surrounding the site." The agency endorsed restrictive zoning and insisted that any single-family residence it insured could not have facilities that allowed the dwelling to be used as a store, an office, or a rental unit.

Obviously, prospective buyers could avoid many of these so-called undesirable features by locating in suburban sections. In 1939 FHA asked each of its fifty regional offices to send in plans for six "typical American houses." The photographs and dimensions were then used for a National Archives exhibit. Virtually all of the entries were bungalows or colonials on ample lots with driveways and garages.

In an attempt to standardize such ideal homes, the Federal Housing Administration set up minimum requirements for lot size, setback from the street, separation from adjacent structures, and even for the width of the house itself. While such requirements did provide light and air for new structures, they effectively eliminated whole categories of dwellings, such as the traditional 16–foot-wide row houses of Baltimore, from eligibility for loan guarantees. Even apartment-house owners were encouraged to look to suburbia: "Under the best of conditions a rental development under the FHA program is a project set in what amounts to a privately owned and privately controlled park area."

Reflecting the racist tradition of the United States, the Federal Housing Administration was extraordinarily concerned with "inharmonious racial or nationality groups." It feared that an entire area could lose its investment value if rigid white-black separation was not maintained. Bluntly warning, "If a neighborhood is to retain stability, it is necessary that properties shall continue to be occupied by the same social and racial classes," the *Underwriting Manual* openly recommended "subdivision regulations and suitable restrictive covenants" that would be "superior to any mortgage." Such covenants, which were legal provisions written into property deeds, were a common method of prohibiting black occupancy until the United States Supreme Court ruling in 1948 *(Shelley v. Kraemer)* that they were "unenforceable as law and contrary to public policy." Even then, it was not until 1949 that FHA announced that as of February 15, 1950, it would not insure mortgages on real estate subject to covenants. Although the press treated the FHA announcement as a major advancement in the field of racial justice, former housing administrator Nathan Straus noted that "the new policy in fact served only to warn speculative builders who had not filed covenants of their right to do so, and it gave them a convenient respite in which to file."

In addition to recommending covenants, FHA compiled detailed reports and maps charting the present and most likely future residential locations of black families. In a March 1939 map of Brooklyn, for example, the presence of a single, non-white family on any block was sufficient to mark that entire block black. Similarly, very extensive maps of the District of Columbia depicted the spread of the black population and the percentage of dwelling units occupied by persons other than white. As late as November 19, 1948, Assistant FHA Commissioner W. J. Lockwood could write that FHA "has never insured a housing project of mixed occupancy" because of the expectation that "such projects would probably in a short period of time become all-Negro or all-white." * * *

The precise extent to which the agency discriminated against blacks and other minority groups is difficult to determine. Although FHA has always collected reams of data regarding the price, floor area, lot size, number of bathrooms, type of roof, and structural characteristics of the single-family homes it has insured, it has been quite secretive about the location of these loans. * * * Such data as are available indicate that the neighborhood appraisals were very influential in determining "where it would be reasonably safe to insure mortgages." * * * The result was a degree of suburban favoritism even greater than the documentary analysis would have suggested. * * *

For its part, the Federal Housing Administration usually responded that it was not created to help cities, but to revive home building, to stimulate homeownership, and to reduce unemployment. And it concentrated on convincing both the Congress and the public that it was, as its first Administrator, James Moffett, remarked, "a conservative business operation." The agency emphasized its concern over sound loans no higher than the value of the assets and the repayment ability of the borrower would support. And FHA was unusual in the vast array of

Washington programs because of its record of earning a small profit for the federal government.

But FHA also helped to turn the building industry against the minority and inner-city housing market, and its policies supported the income and racial segregation of suburbia. For perhaps the first time, the federal government embraced the discriminatory attitudes of the marketplace. Previously, prejudices were personalized and individualized; FHA exhorted segregation and enshrined it as public policy. Whole areas of cities were declared ineligible for loan guarantees; as late as 1966, for example, FHA did not have a mortgage on a single home in Camden or Paterson, New Jersey, both declining industrial cities. This withdrawal of financing often resulted in an inability to sell houses in a neighborhood, so that vacant units often stood empty for months, producing a steep decline in value.

Despite the fact that the government's leading housing agency openly exhorted segregation throughout the first thirty years of its operation, very few voices were raised against FHA red-lining practices. * * * Not until the civil-rights movement of the 1960s did community groups realize that red lining and disinvestment were a major cause of community decline and that home-improvement loans were the "life-blood of housing." In * * * [1968] Senator Paul Douglas of Illinois reported for the National Commission on Urban Problems on the role of the federal government in home finance:

> The poor and those on the fringes of poverty have been almost completely excluded. These and the lower middle class, together constituting the 40 percent of the population whose housing needs are greatest, received only 11 percent of the FHA mortgages* * *. Even middle-class residential districts in the central cities were suspect, since there was always the prospect that they, too, might turn as Negroes and poor whites continued to pour into the cities, and as middle and upper-middle-income whites continued to move out.

Moreover, as urban analyst Jane Jacobs has said, "Credit blacklisting maps are accurate prophecies because they are self-fulfilling prophecies."

In 1966, FHA drastically shifted its policies with a view toward making much more mortgage insurance available for inner-city neighborhoods. Ironically, the primary effect of the change was to make it easier for white families to finance their escape from areas experiencing racial change. At the same time, the relaxed credit standards for black applicants meant that home improvement companies could buy properties at low cost, make cosmetic improvements, and sell the renovated home at inflated prices approved by FHA. Many of the minority purchasers could not afford the cost of maintenance, and FHA had to repossess thousands of homes. The final result was to increase the speed with which areas went through racial transformation and to victimize those it was designed to help. The only people to benefit were contractors and white, middle-class homeowners who were assisted in escaping from a distress position. * * *

Any serious indictment of federal lawmakers and federal officials for the miserable state of many American cities must take cognizance of two important points. First, and most obviously, it is hazardous to condemn a government for adopting policies in accord with the preference of a majority of its citizens. As novelist Anthony Trollope put it in 1867: "It is a very comfortable thing to stand on your own ground. Land is about the only thing that can't fly away." FHA helped to build houses, and where they were put was less important than that they were built. For more than a century, Americans have had a strong affinity for a detached home on a private lot. Obviously, some popular measures, such as gun control, are not adopted because of special-interest lobbies. But suburbanization was not willed on an innocent peasantry. Without a substantial amount of encouragement from the mainstream of public opinion, the bureaucrats would never have been able to push their projects as far as they did. The single-family house responded to the psychic value of privacy or castlehood. In fact, suburbanization was an ideal government policy because it met the needs of both citizens and business interests and because it earned the politicians' votes. It is a simple fact that homeownership introduced equity into the estates of over 35 million families between 1933 and 1978. The tract houses they often bought may have been dismissed as hopeless by highbrow architectural purists, but they were a lot less dreary to the people who raised families there and then sold to new families at a profit.

Federal housing policies were also not the *sine qua non* in the mushrooming of the suburbs. Mortgage insurance obviously made it easier for families to secure their dream houses, but the dominant residential drift in American cities had been toward the periphery for at least a century before the New Deal, and there is no reason to assume that the suburban trend would not have continued in the absence of direct federal assistance.

The lasting damage done by the national government was that it put its seal of approval on ethnic and racial discrimination and developed policies which had the result of the practical abandonment of large sections of older, industrial cities. More seriously, Washington actions were later picked up by private interests, so that banks and savings-and-loan institutions institutionalized the practice of denying mortgages "solely because of the geographical location of the property." The financial community saw blighted neighborhoods as physical evidence of the melting-pot mistake. To them, cities were risky because of their heterogeneity, because of their attempt to bring various people together harmoniously. Such mixing, they believed, had but two consequences— the decline of both the human race and of property values. As Mark Gelfand has observed, "Given the chance, bankers would do for their business what they had already done for themselves—leave the city." * * *

[T]he * * * broad patterns of downtown decline, inner-city deterioration, and exurban development * * * are * * * typical of the large population centers of the United States. This same result might have been achieved in the absence of all federal intervention, but the simple fact is that the various government policies toward housing have had substantially the same result from Los Angeles to Boston. The poor in America have not shared in the postwar real-estate boom, in most of the major highway improvements, in property and income-tax write-offs, and in mortgage insurance programs. Public housing projects were intended to redress the imbalance. Unfortunately, * * * it did not work out that way. * * *

7. THE DISTRIBUTION AND REDISTRIBUTION OF LOCAL WEALTH

Exclusionary zoning is one method a city can use to promote the prosperity of its current residents over that of outsiders. An alternative way of accomplishing the same result is to ensure that the income generated by city taxation is used solely for the benefit of city residents. This section explores the limits on a city's ability to spend its tax-generated income exclusively on its own citizens. It explores, in other words, the extent to which cities are required to redistribute locally-generated wealth to outsiders. Of course, the idea that those who are better off should be required to share (at least some of) their advantages with others is highly controversial. In local government law, the extent of the obligation to share financial resources has principally arisen in the context of financing local school systems.[1] A number of state courts (and some state legislatures) have sought to reduce the gap between the richest and poorest school districts.[2] It should be noted that, at least in the view of some experts, these efforts have so far made very little progress in accomplishing their objective.[3]

1. For an analysis of the analogous problem of *intra-group* obligations to share resources, see Haar & Fessler, The Wrong Side of the Tracks (1986).

2. Cases that have declared school financing systems unconstitutional include: Dupree v. Alma School Dist., 279 Ark. 340, 651 S.W.2d 90 (1983); Serrano v. Priest, 5 Cal.3d 584, 96 Cal.Rptr. 601, 487 P.2d 1241 (1971); Horton v. Meskill, 172 Conn. 615, 376 A.2d 359 (1977); Rose v. Council for Better Educ., 790 S.W.2d 186 (Ky. 1989); Helena Elementary School v. State, 236 Mont. 44, 769 P.2d 684 (1989); Abbott v. Burke, 119 N.J. 287, 575 A.2d 359 (1990); Carrollton–Farmers Branch Independent School Dist. v. Edgewood Independent School District, 826 S.W.2d 489 (Tex. 1992); Seattle School Dist. v. State, 90 Wash.2d 476, 585 P.2d 71 (1978); Pauley v. Kelly, 162 W.Va. 672, 255 S.E.2d 859 (1979); Washakie County School Dist. v. Herschler, 606 P.2d 310 (Wyo.1980), cert. denied, 449 U.S. 824, 101 S.Ct. 86, 66 L.Ed.2d 28. Those that have rejected constitutional challenges include: Shofstall v. Hollins, 110 Ariz. 88, 515 P.2d 590 (1973); Lujan v. Colorado State Bd. of Educ., 649 P.2d 1005 (Colo.1982); Thompson v. Engelking, 96 Idaho 793, 537 P.2d 635 (1975); Hornbeck v. Somerset County Bd. of Educ., 295 Md. 597, 458 A.2d 758 (1983); Board of Educ., Levittown Union Free School Dist. v. Nyquist, 57 N.Y.2d 27, 453 N.Y.S.2d 643, 439 N.E.2d 359 (1982); Board of Educ. v. Walter, 58 Ohio St. 368, 390 N.E.2d 813 (1979); Fair School Finance Council v. State, 746 P.2d 1135 (Okl.1987); Olsen v. State, 276 Or. 9, 554 P.2d 139 (1976); Danson v. Casey, 484 Pa. 415, 399 A.2d 360 (1979); Kukor v. Grover, 148 Wis.2d 469, 436 N.W.2d 568 (1989).

3. See Note, Unfulfilled Promises: School Finance Remedies and State Courts, 104 Harv. L.Rev. 1072 (1991); "Efforts Are Failing to Close Gaps Separating Rich and

Two judicial views of inter-city obligations concerning school financing are presented in the first two cases reproduced below. As with the cases on exclusionary zoning, alternative conceptions of inter-city relations and of the value of local sovereignty underlie the different opinions. The United States Supreme Court articulates one of these conceptions in San Antonio Independent School District v. Rodriguez; following the case, an excerpt from Joan Williams' article, The Constitutional Vulnerability of American Local Government, offers an interpretation of the *Rodriguez* opinion's concept of "local control." [4] Then, in Edgewood Independent School District v. Kirby, the Texas Supreme Court—reviewing a later challenge by the same school district involved in *Rodriguez*—suggests an alternative vision of local autonomy and inter-city obligations. What definition of "local control" does the *Kirby* opinion advance? Does either case suggest that rich school districts are entitled to spend money derived from their larger tax base only on themselves? Does either case suggest that poorer school districts are entitled to share in the resources of the richer districts? What relevance do the arguments about reallocation of wealth in these cases have to other services—such as health care or police protection?

The ideas debated in these cases reflect the influence of important scholarly writings [5] and the cases themselves have generated a large literature. [6] One of the most influential ideas advanced in the school financing litigation was the concept of district power equalizing proposed by John Coons, William Clune and Stephen Sugarman; this concept was

Poor Schools", New York Times, February 19, 1985, page C1, col. 1; "Illinois School District Votes to Disband: Poor Chicago Suburb Wants to Send Its Pupils to Its More Affluent Neighbors", The Boston Globe, April 15, 1993, p.9, col. 1.

4. For another analysis of the Supreme Court's recent invocation of the notion of local control, see Gelfand, The Constitutional Position of American Local Government: Retrospect for the Burger Court and Prospects for the Rehnquist Court, 19 Hastings Const. L.Q. 635 (1987); Gelfand, Local Government in the American Federal System: The Bicentennial as a Time of Crisis and Opportunity, 19 The Urban Lawyer 568 (1987); Gelfand, The Burger Court and the New Federalism: Preliminary Reflections on the Roles of Local Government Actors in the Political Drama of the 1980s, 21 B.C.L.Rev. 763 (1980).

5. See, e.g., A. Wise, Rich Schools, Poor Schools: The Promise of Equal Educational Opportunity (1968); Horowitz & Neitring, Equal Protection Aspects of Inequalities in Public Education and Public Assistance Programs from Place to Place Within a State, 15 U.C.L.A.L.Rev. 787 (1968); J. Coons, W. Clune & S. Sugarman, Private Wealth and Public Education (1970).

6. See, e.g., Mahtesian, School Finance: Is Equity the Answer, 6 Governing 43 (1993); Clune, New Answers to Hard Questions Posed by Rodriguez, 24 Conn.L.Rev. 721 (1992); Briffault, The Role of Local Control in School Finance Reform, 24 Conn. L.Rev. 773 (1992); Symposium: Investing in Our Children's Future: School Finance Reform in the '90's, 28 Harv.J.Legis. 293 (1991); Note, Unfulfilled Promises: School Finance Remedies and State Courts, 104 Harv. L.Rev. 1072 (1991); Neuman, Territorial Discrimination, Equal Protection, and Self–Determination, 135 U.Pa.L.Rev. 261, 372–82 (1987); Kaden, Courts and Legislatures in a Federal System: The Case of School Finance, 11 Hofstra L.Rev. 1205 (1983); Elmore, Reform and Retrenchment: The Politics of California's School Finance Reform (1982); Inman & Rubinfeld, The Judicial Pursuit of Local Fiscal Equity, 92 Harv.L.Rev. 1662 (1979); Andersen, School Finance Litigation—The Styles of Judicial Intervention, 55 Wash.L.Rev. 137 (1979); Future Directions for School Finance Reform, 38 Law & Contemp.Probs. 293 (1974); Glickstein & Want, Inequality in School Financing: The Role of Law, 25 Stan.L.Rev. 335 (1973); Goldstein, Interdistrict Inequalities in School Financing: A Critical Analysis of Serrano v. Priest and Its Progeny, 120 U.Pa.L.Rev. 504 (1972).

designed to assure "true local fiscal control" of school financing by cutting the tie between the amount of money that can be raised by a locality and the amount of district wealth. Under district power equalizing, school financing would depend on the tax rate of each district but it would not depend on the size of its tax base. The following excerpt [7] offers a brief articulation of the idea:

> The essence of district power equalizing is the simple elimination of wealth from the formula determining a school district's offering. Instead of offering being a function of both wealth and effort, it becomes a function of effort alone. The easiest way to perceive this is to suppose that the legislature has developed a table which specifies how much per pupil each district will be permitted to spend for each level of (locally chosen) tax effort against local wealth (preferably income, but, more realistically, property). Such a table might look like this:

Local Tax Rate	Permissible Per Pupil Expenditure
10 mills (minimum rate permitted)	$ 500
11 mills	550
12 mills	600
13 mills	650
14 mills	700
29 mills	1450
30 mills (maximum rate permitted)	1500

> Irrespective of the amount of the local collections the district would be permitted to spend that amount and only that amount per pupil fixed by law for the tax rate chosen. Rich districts and poor districts taxing at 12 mills would provide a $600 education. Poor districts and rich districts taxing at 30 mills would provide a $1500 education. Obviously this might require the redistribution of excess local collections from rich districts and the subvention of insufficient collections in poor districts. The magnitude of such effects would depend on the degree to which the state wishes to pay for the total cost of education; this in turn is related to the extent to which the state wishes to stimulate district effort. The formulas for controlling total cost and the respective state and local shares are infinitely variable and can incorporate many refinements. One that deserves mention would be an adjustment for municipal overburden in the case of large cities. Such fine tuning is easily handled under a power equalized system and could be employed to eliminate vestiges of wealth discrimination associated with certain economic and social differences among the districts other than differences in assessed wealth. Other examples of such differences are transportation costs and variations from area to area in cost of services such as salaries.

> The effect, then, is to make all districts equal in their *power* to raise dollars for education. The variations from district to district in

7. From Coons, Clune & Sugarman, Educational Opportunity: A Workable Constitutional Test for State Financial Structures, 57 Calif.L.Rev. 303, 319–21 (1969).

dollars per pupil spent upon education would thus be a function simply of local interest in public education. Power equalizing would not guarantee equal dollars per pupil—a goal we consider fatuous and counter-productive; it would merely make the money raising game a fair one and maximize the incentive for political effort at the local level. Its potential relevance to the movement for "community control" is obvious. * * *

The final case in this section, Buse v. Smith, considers the question of the constitutionality of a district power equalizing system. What view of inter-city relationships does the court adopt in declaring the system unconstitutional? If district power equalizing is impermissible, does that leave federal or state control of local financing decisions as the only remaining alternative to permitting local school districts to base their financing on district wealth?

SAN ANTONIO INDEPENDENT SCHOOL DISTRICT v. RODRIGUEZ

Supreme Court of the United States, 1973.
411 U.S. 1, 93 S.Ct. 1278, 36 L.Ed.2d 16.

Mr. Justice Powell delivered the opinion of the Court.

This suit attacking the Texas system of financing public education was initiated by Mexican–American parents whose children attend the elementary and secondary schools in the Edgewood Independent School District, an urban school district in San Antonio, Texas. They brought a class action on behalf of schoolchildren throughout the State who are members of minority groups or who are poor and reside in school districts having a low property tax base. Named as defendants were the State Board of Education, the Commissioner of Education, the State Attorney General, and the Bexar County (San Antonio) Board of Trustees. * * *

Until recent times, Texas was a predominantly rural State and its population and property wealth were spread relatively evenly across the State. Sizable differences in the value of assessable property between local school districts became increasingly evident as the State became more industrialized and as rural-to-urban population shifts became more pronounced. The location of commercial and industrial property began to play a significant role in determining the amount of tax resources available to each school district. These growing disparities in population and taxable property between districts were responsible in part for increasingly notable differences in levels of local expenditure for education. * * * Recognizing the need for increased state funding to help offset disparities in local spending and to meet Texas' changing educational requirements, the state legislature in the late 1940's undertook a thorough evaluation of public education with an eye toward major reform. * * * [These] efforts led to the passage of the * * * Texas Minimum Foundation School Program. Today, this Program accounts for approximately half of the total educational expenditures in Texas.

The Program calls for state and local contributions to a fund earmarked specifically for teacher salaries, operating expenses, and transportation costs. The State, supplying funds from its general revenues, finances approximately 80% of the Program, and the school districts are responsible—as a unit—for providing the remaining 20%. The districts' share, known as the Local Fund Assignment, is apportioned among the school districts under a formula designed to reflect each district's relative taxpaying ability. * * * Today every school district * * * [imposes] a property tax from which it derives locally expendable funds in excess of the amount necessary to satisfy its Local Fund Assignment under the Foundation Program. * * *

The school district in which appellees reside, the Edgewood Independent School District, has been compared throughout this litigation with the Alamo Heights Independent School District. This comparison between the least and most affluent districts in the San Antonio area serves to illustrate the manner in which the dual system of finance operates and to indicate the extent to which substantial disparities exist despite the State's impressive progress in recent years. Edgewood is one of seven public school districts in the metropolitan area. Approximately 22,000 students are enrolled in its 25 elementary and secondary schools. The district is situated in the core-city sector of San Antonio in a residential neighborhood that has little commercial or industrial property. The residents are predominantly of Mexican–American descent: approximately 90% of the student population is Mexican–American and over 6% is Negro. The average assessed property value per pupil is $5,960—the lowest in the metropolitan area—and the median family income ($4,686) is also the lowest. At an equalized tax rate of $1.05 per $100 of assessed property—the highest in the metropolitan area—the district contributed $26 to the education of each child for the 1967–1968 school year above its Local Fund Assignment for the Minimum Foundation Program. The Foundation Program contributed $222 per pupil for a state-local total of $248. Federal funds added another $108 for a total of $356 per pupil. * * *

Alamo Heights is the most affluent school district in San Antonio. Its six schools, housing approximately 5,000 students, are situated in a residential community quite unlike the Edgewood District. The school population is predominantly "Anglo," having only 18% Mexican–Americans and less than 1% Negroes. The assessed property value per pupil exceeds $49,000, and the median family income is $8,001. In 1967–1968 the local tax rate of $.85 per $100 of valuation yielded $333 per pupil over and above its contribution to the Foundation Program. Coupled with the $225 provided from that Program, the district was able to supply $558 per student. Supplemented by a $36 per-pupil grant from federal sources, Alamo Heights spent $594 per pupil. * * *

The case comes to us with no definitive description of the classifying facts or delineation of the disfavored class. Examination of the District Court's opinion and of appellees' complaint, briefs, and contentions at oral argument suggests, however, at least three ways in which the discrimination claimed here might be described. The Texas system of school financing might be regarded as discriminating (1) against "poor" persons whose incomes fall below some identifiable level of poverty or who might be characterized as functionally "indigent," or (2) against those who are relatively poorer than others, or (3) against all those who, irrespective of their personal incomes, happen to reside in relatively poorer school districts. Our task must be to ascertain whether, in fact, the Texas system has been shown to discriminate on any of these possible bases and, if so, whether the resulting classification may be regarded as suspect. * * *

Even a cursory examination * * * demonstrates that neither of the two distinguishing characteristics of wealth classifications can be found here. First, in support of their charge that the system discriminates against the "poor," appellees have made no effort to demonstrate that it operates to the peculiar disadvantage of any class fairly definable as indigent, or as composed of persons whose incomes are beneath any designated poverty level. Indeed, there is reason to believe that the poorest families are not necessarily clustered in the poorest property districts. A recent and exhaustive study of school districts in Connecticut * * * found, not surprisingly, that the poor were clustered around commercial and industrial areas—those same areas that provide the most attractive sources of property tax income for school districts. Whether a similar pattern would be discovered in Texas is not known, but there is no basis on the record in this case for assuming that the poorest people—defined by reference to any level of absolute impecunity—are concentrated in the poorest districts.

Second, neither appellees nor the District Court addressed the fact that * * * lack of personal resources has not occasioned an absolute deprivation of the desired benefit. The argument here is not that the children in districts having relatively low assessable property values are receiving no public education; rather, it is that they are receiving a poorer quality education than that available to children in districts having more assessable wealth. Apart from the unsettled and disputed question whether the quality of education may be determined by the amount of money expended for it, a sufficient answer to appellees' argument is that, at least where wealth is involved, the Equal Protection Clause does not require absolute equality or precisely equal advantages. Nor indeed, in view of the infinite variables affecting the educational process, can any system assure equal quality of education except in the most relative sense. Texas asserts that the Minimum Foundation Program * * * assures "every child in every school district an adequate education." No proof was offered at trial persuasively discrediting or refuting the State's assertion.

For these two reasons—the absence of any evidence that the financing system discriminates against any definable category of "poor" people or that it results in the absolute deprivation of education—the disadvantaged class is not susceptible of identification in traditional terms. * * * However described, it is clear that appellees' suit asks this Court to extend its most exacting scrutiny to review a system that allegedly discriminates against a large, diverse, and amorphous class, unified only by the common factor of residence in districts that happen to have less taxable wealth than other districts. * * * We thus conclude that the Texas system does not operate to the peculiar disadvantage of any suspect class. * * *

Education, of course, is not among the rights afforded explicit protection under our Federal Constitution. Nor do we find any basis for saying it is implicitly so protected. As we have said, the undisputed importance of education will not alone cause this Court to depart from the usual standard for reviewing a State's social and economic legislation. It is appellees' contention, however, that education * * * is itself a fundamental personal right because it is essential to the effective exercise of First Amendment freedoms and to intelligent utilization of the right to vote. * * * Even if it were conceded that some identifiable quantum of education is a constitutionally protected prerequisite to the meaningful exercise of either right, we have no indication that the present levels of educational expenditures in Texas provide an education that falls short. Whatever merit appellees' argument might have if a State's financing system occasioned an absolute denial of educational opportunities to any of its children, that argument provides no basis for finding an interference with fundamental rights where only relative differences in spending levels are involved and where—as is true in the present case—no charge fairly could be made that the system fails to provide each child with an opportunity to acquire the basic minimal skills necessary for the enjoyment of the rights of speech and of full participation in the political process. * * * Furthermore, the logical limitations on appellees' nexus theory are difficult to perceive. How, for instance, is education to be distinguished from the significant personal interests in the basics of decent food and shelter? Empirical examination might well buttress an assumption that the ill-fed, ill-clothed, and ill-housed are among the most ineffective participants in the political process, and that they derive the least enjoyment from the benefits of the First Amendment. * * *

It should be clear, for the reasons stated above and in accord with the prior decisions of this Court, that this is not a case in which the challenged state action must be subjected to the searching judicial scrutiny reserved for laws that create suspect classifications or impinge upon constitutionally protected rights.

We need not rest our decision, however, solely on the inappropriateness of the strict-scrutiny test. A century of Supreme Court adjudication under the Equal Protection Clause affirmatively supports the application of the traditional standard of review, which requires only that the State's system be shown to bear some rational relationship to legitimate state purposes. This case represents far more than a challenge to the manner in which Texas provides for the education of its children. We have here nothing less than a direct attack on the way in which Texas has chosen to raise and disburse state and local tax revenues. We are asked to condemn the State's judgment in conferring on political subdivisions the power to tax local property to supply revenues for local interests. In so doing, appellees would have the Court intrude in an area in which it has traditionally deferred to state legislatures. * * * In addition to matters of fiscal policy, this case also involves the most persistent and difficult questions of educational policy, another area in which this Court's lack of specialized knowledge and experience counsels against premature interference with the informed judgments made at the state and local levels. * * *

It must be remembered, also, that every claim arising under the Equal Protection Clause has implications for the relationship between national and state power under our federal system. Questions of federalism are always inherent in the process of determining whether a State's laws are to be accorded the traditional presumption of constitutionality, or are to be subjected instead to rigorous judicial scrutiny. While "[t]he maintenance of the principles of federalism is a foremost consideration in interpreting any of the pertinent constitutional provisions under which this Court examines state action," it would be difficult to imagine a case having a greater potential impact on our federal system than the one now before us, in which we are urged to abrogate systems of financing public education presently in existence in virtually every State. * * *

In its reliance on state as well as local resources, the Texas system is comparable to the systems employed in virtually every other State. * * * The "foundation grant" theory * * * [was] devoted to establishing a means of guaranteeing a minimum statewide educational program without sacrificing the vital element of local participation. * * * As articulated by Professor Coleman:

> "The history of education since the industrial revolution shows a continual struggle between two forces: the desire by members of society to have educational opportunity for all children, and the desire of each family to provide the best education it can afford for its own children."

The Texas system of school finance is responsive to these two forces. While assuring a basic education for every child in the State, it permits and encourages a large measure of participation in and control of each district's schools at the local level. In an era that has witnessed a consistent trend toward centralization of the functions of government, local sharing of responsibility for public education has survived. * * * The persistence of attachment to government at the lowest level where education is concerned reflects the depth of commitment of its supporters. In part, local control means, as Professor Coleman suggests, the freedom to devote more money to the education of one's children. Equally important, however, is the opportunity it offers for participation in the decisionmaking process that determines how those local tax dollars will be spent. Each locality is free to tailor local programs to local needs. Pluralism also affords some opportunity for experimentation, innovation, and a healthy competition for educational excellence. An analogy to the Nation–State relationship in our federal system seems uniquely appropriate. Mr. Justice Brandeis identified as one of the peculiar strengths of our form of government each State's freedom to "serve as a laboratory; and try novel social and economic experiments." No area of social concern stands to profit more from a multiplicity of viewpoints and from a diversity of approaches than does public education.

Appellees do not question the propriety of Texas' dedication to local control of education. To the contrary, they attack the school-financing system precisely because, in their view, it does not provide the same level of local control and fiscal flexibility in all districts. Appellees suggest that local control could be preserved and promoted under other financing systems that resulted in more equality in educational expenditures. While it is no doubt true that reliance on local property taxation for school revenues provides less freedom of choice with respect to expenditures for some districts than for others, the existence of "some inequality" in the manner in which the State's rationale is achieved is not alone a sufficient basis for striking down the entire system. * * * It is also well to remember that even those districts that have reduced ability to make free decisions with respect to how much they spend on education still retain under the present system a large measure of authority as to how available funds will be allocated. They further enjoy the power to make numerous other decisions with respect to the operation of the schools. The people of Texas may be justified in believing that other systems of school financing, which place more of the financial responsibility in the hands of the State, will result in a comparable lessening of desired local autonomy. * * *

Appellees further urge that the Texas system is unconstitutionally arbitrary because it allows the availability of local taxable resources to turn on "happenstance." They see no justification for a system that allows, as they contend, the quality of education to fluctuate on the basis of the fortuitous positioning of the boundary lines of political subdivisions and the location of valuable commercial and industrial property. But any scheme of local taxation—indeed the very existence of identifiable local governmental units—requires the establishment of jurisdictional boundaries that are inevitably arbitrary. It is equally inevitable that some localities are going to be blessed with more taxable assets than others. Nor is local wealth a static quantity. Changes in the level of taxable wealth within any district may result from any number of events, some of which local residents can and do influence. For instance, commercial and industrial enterprises may be encouraged to locate within a district by various actions—public and private.

Moreover, if local taxation for local expenditures were an unconstitutional method of providing for education then it might be an equally impermissible means of providing other necessary services customarily financed largely from local property taxes, including local police and fire protection, public health and hospitals, and public utility facilities of various kinds. We perceive no justification for such a severe denigration of local property taxation and control as would follow from appellees' contentions. It has simply never been within the constitutional prerogative of this Court to nullify statewide measures for financing public services merely because the burdens or benefits thereof fall unevenly depending upon the relative wealth of the political subdivisions in which citizens live.

In sum, to the extent that the Texas system of school financing results in unequal expenditures between children who happen to reside in different districts, we cannot say that such disparities are the product of a system that is so irrational as to be invidiously discriminatory. * * *

Mr. Justice Marshall, with whom Mr. Justice Douglas concurs, dissenting.

The Court today decides, in effect, that a State may constitutionally vary the quality of education which it offers its children in accordance with the amount of taxable wealth located in the school districts within which they reside. * * * The only justification offered by appellants to sustain the discrimination in educational opportunity caused by the Texas financing scheme is local educational control. * * * I do not question that local control of public education, as an abstract matter, constitutes a very substantial state interest. * * * The State's interest in local educational control—which certainly includes questions of educational funding—has deep roots in the inherent benefits of community support for public education. Consequently, true state dedication to local control would present, I think, a substantial justification to weigh against simply interdistrict variations in the treatment of a State's schoolchildren. But I need not now decide how I might ultimately strike the balance were we confronted with a situation where the State's sincere concern for local control inevitably produced educational inequality. For, on this record, it is apparent that the State's purported concern with local control is offered primarily as an excuse rather than as a justification for interdistrict inequality.

In Texas, statewide laws regulate in fact the most minute details of local public education. For example the State prescribes required courses. All textbooks must be submitted for state approval, and only approved textbooks may be used. The State has established the qualifications necessary for teaching in Texas public schools and the procedures for obtaining certification. The State has even legislated on the length of the school day. * * *

Moreover, even if we accept Texas' general dedication to local control in educational matters, it is difficult to find any evidence of such dedication with respect to fiscal matters. It ignores reality to suggest— as the Court does—that the local property tax element of the Texas financing scheme reflects a conscious legislative effort to provide school districts with local fiscal control. If Texas had a system truly dedicated to local fiscal control, one would expect the quality of the educational opportunity provided in each district to vary with the decision of the voters in that district as to the level of sacrifice they wish to make for public education. In fact, the Texas scheme produces precisely the opposite result. Local school districts cannot choose to have the best education in the State by imposing the highest tax rate. Instead, the quality of the educational opportunity offered by any particular district is largely determined by the amount of taxable property located in the district—a factor over which local voters can exercise no control. * * *

[I]t is essential to recognize that an end to the wide variations in taxable district property wealth inherent in the Texas financing scheme would entail none of the untoward consequences suggested by the Court or by the appellants.

First, affirmance of the District Court's decisions would hardly sound the death knell for local control of education. It would mean neither centralized decisionmaking nor federal court intervention in the operation of public schools. Clearly, this suit has nothing to do with local decisionmaking with respect to educational policy or even educational spending. It involves only a narrow aspect of local control— namely, local control over the raising of educational funds. * * * [T]he District Court's decision [does not] even necessarily eliminate local control of educational funding. The District Court struck down nothing more than the continued interdistrict wealth discrimination inherent in the present property tax. Both centralized and decentralized plans for educational funding not involving such interdistrict discrimination have been put forward.[98] The choice among these or other alternatives would remain with the State, not with the federal courts. * * *

98. Centralized educational financing is, to be sure, one alternative. On analysis, though, it is clear that even centralized financing would not deprive local school districts of what has been considered to be the essence of local educational control. Central financing would leave in local hands the entire gamut of local educational policymaking—teachers, curriculum, school sites, the whole process of allocating resources among alternative educational objectives.

A second possibility is the much-discussed theory of district power equalization put forth by Professors Coons, Clune, and Sugarman in their seminal work, Private Wealth and Public Education 201–242 (1970). Such a scheme would truly reflect a dedication to local fiscal control. Under their system, each school district would receive a fixed amount of revenue per pupil for any particular level of tax effort regardless of the level of local property tax base. Appellants criticize this scheme on the rather extraordinary ground that it would encourage poorer districts to overtax themselves in order to obtain substantial revenues for education. But under the present discriminatory scheme, it is the poor districts that are already taxing themselves at the highest rates, yet are receiving the lowest returns.

District wealth reapportionment is yet another alternative which would accomplish directly essentially what district power equalization would seek to do artificially. Appellants claim that the calculations concerning state property required by such a scheme would be impossible as a practical matter. Yet Texas is already making far more complex annual calculations involving not only local property values but also local income and other economic factors in conjunction with the Local Fund Assignment portion of the Minimum Foundation School Program.

A fourth possibility would be to remove commercial, industrial, and mineral property from local tax rolls, to tax this property on a statewide basis, and to return the resulting revenues to the local districts in a fashion that would compensate for remaining variations in the local tax bases.

None of these particular alternatives are necessarily constitutionally compelled;

JOAN WILLIAMS, THE CONSTITUTIONAL VULNERABILITY OF AMERICAN LOCAL GOVERNMENT: THE POLITICS OF CITY STATUS IN AMERICAN LAW

1986 Wis.L.Rev. 83, 104–113, 118–119.

THE TENSION BETWEEN NINETEENTH AND TWENTIETH CENTURY CONSERVATIVES' FORMULATIONS OF CITY STATUS

Recent decisions of the Burger Court provide an intriguing contrast to Dillon's basic framework of city powerlessness. In these recent cases, the Court has used local sovereignty language to support an internal limit on the reach of the fourteenth amendment and, for a time, to limit Congress' ability to regulate under the Commerce Clause. In sharp contrast to the traditional local government law doctrines crystallized by Dillon, Burger Court decisions setting out the principle of local government sovereignty reveal a pattern of solicitude for localities' structural integrity and a broad judicial deference to their programmatic choices. * * *

The principle of local government sovereignty offers contemporary conservatives a powerful rhetorical strategy because it allows them to mobilize resonant Jeffersonian imagery. Thomas Jefferson, "the first, and also the foremost, advocate of local self government," originated the theory of local self-government. Like many of his contemporaries, Jefferson viewed all government as a potential threat to freedom. Yet, most of his fears were focused upon the federal government, whereas most of his hopes for democracy were focused on government at a local level. * * *

Jefferson * * * advocated division of counties into "wards" of five or six square miles each. Each ward would function as a "little republic," exercising self-government in a broad range of duties. In 1816, Jefferson said:

> In government, as well as in every other business of life, it is by division and subdivision of duties alone, that all matters, great and small, can be managed to perfection * * *. And the whole is cemented by giving to every citizen, personally, a part in the administration of public affairs.

Jefferson's linkage of local self-government and republican virtue has proved an enormously influential source of political imagery since its inception. As initially formulated, Jefferson's exaltation of local government did not apply to cities, which he abhorred. Jefferson envisioned his localities as semi-rural farming communities where yeomen met to agree on those matters that would be burdensome for each to handle alone.

rather, they indicate the breadth of choice which would remain to the State if the present interdistrict disparities were eliminated.

The Burger Court's principle of local sovereignty is heavily dependent on imagery derived from the Jeffersonian tradition. Two distinct themes emerge in the Court's Jeffersonian rhetoric. In one set of cases, involving schools and zoning, the Burger Court has stressed the positive side of the Jeffersonian vision. These opinions, many of them written by Justices Burger and Powell, will be called the "local autonomy decisions." They consistently stress the virtues of "local autonomy," "community" and "local control" in terms that recall the Jeffersonian romance with self-government at the local level. Although Justice Rehnquist joined these opinions, and has at times himself expressed concern for local control, his own opinions stress a second aspect of the Jeffersonian vision. While the local autonomy opinions stress the positive value of local control, Rehnquist stresses the negative consequences of excessive federal power. These two themes act in concert in Burger Court jurisprudence to provide a rationale for the existence of a core area of local government sovereignty.

In the local autonomy opinions, the Court's Jeffersonian rhetoric is used to support decisions that limit the scope of the fourteenth amendment. Two important early examples were *San Antonio v. Rodriguez* (per Justice Powell) and *Milliken v. Bradley* (per Justice Burger).

San Antonio v. Rodriguez illustrates the central role played by the Court's Jeffersonian rhetoric in its abandonment of Warren Court activism. * * * For our purposes, the crucial part of Powell's opinion in *Rodriguez* is not the decision's technical holding, but rather its use of the Jeffersonian rhetoric of local sovereignty as a rationale for limiting the reach of the fourteenth amendment. Powell asserted that a major reason for refusing to extend the equal protection clause to school financing was his concern to preserve the autonomy of local schools, and of localities in general * * *. A notable irony is that the fiscal scheme involved in *Rodriguez* was not imposed on the local level: the plaintiffs were challenging a mechanism of school financing imposed by the state of Texas. Why did Powell shy away from formulating the issue in *Rodriguez* as a clash between state autonomy and federal requirements, and characterize the case instead as involving issues of local autonomy?

The short answer is that established constitutional theory made it difficult for the Court to argue that the scope of the fourteenth amendment was constrained by considerations of autonomy. During the battle in the 1960's over whether the Bill of Rights had been incorporated into the fourteenth amendment, Justices Frankfurter and Harlan argued that the Bill of Rights should not be applied to the states in the interests of preserving the states as "laboratories" for innovation. Their position was ultimately rejected by the majority of the Court.

The outcome of the incorporation battle made it awkward for Powell to argue that the fourteenth amendment's scope should be constricted in the interest of preserving state autonomy. Powell's focus on the need for the Court to defer to local autonomy is an attempt to avoid this pitfall. The attempt fails because the Supreme Court has long since accepted Dillon's principle that cities are mere subdivisions of the states. If the need to preserve state autonomy is not a valid reason to constrict the scope of the fourteenth amendment, the need to preserve the autonomy of the state's (subservient) subdivisions surely is not a valid consideration in limiting the amendment's reach.

Powell's incantation of the sanctity of local as opposed to state autonomy submerges these difficult problems. They nonetheless persist, for if states have absolute power over their subdivisions, and federal courts have full authority to invade state sovereignty (including, presumably, the sovereignty of states' subdivisions) in order to enforce constitutional mandates, it seems illogical for the Court to cite considerations of local autonomy in constricting the scope of the fourteenth amendment.

In *Milliken v. Bradley,* a second case that highlights the doctrinal difficulties of the local autonomy opinions, Justice Burger used a rhetorical structure similar to that used by Powell in *Rodriguez.* *Milliken* involved a federal court order to desegregate Detroit schools. Because Detroit's school-age population was overwhelmingly black, the district court ordered a metropolitan-wide remedy that involved busing city children into the suburbs, where most students were white. The Court, in an opinion written by Justice Burger, reversed the district court order, noting:

> No single tradition in public education is more deeply rooted than local control over the operation of schools; local autonomy has long been thought essential both to the maintenance of community concern and support for public schools and to the quality of the educational process.

This language is reminiscent of Powell's Jeffersonian rhetoric in *Rodriguez.* Moreover, it functions in a similar way. The local sovereignty language in *Rodriguez* was used to support creation of an internal limit on the coverage of the fourteenth amendment. In *Milliken,* similar language was used to limit a court's ability to remedy a constitutional violation.

The analysis in *Milliken* highlights the acute doctrinal tension between Dillon's formulation of city status and the Court's local sovereignty principle. *Milliken* holds that although courts are free to enforce the fourteenth amendment against the states, they cannot enforce it against local government units in a way that treats those units as entities of "mere administrative convenience." Yet according to Dillon's formulation of municipal law, that is exactly what local units are: not only school districts, but also general-purpose governments such as cities, are units of "mere administrative convenience." Under municipal law, the boundaries of school districts, and of cities as well, may be rewritten by states at will.

Milliken v. Bradley and *San Antonio v. Rodriguez* appear to reinvigorate Cooley's argument (expressly rejected by state courts in the period 1870–1900) that a core of local government sovereignty should be accorded constitutional status. These cases conflict sharply with Dillon's premise that the people delegated all their sovereignty to the states. Yet, these cases explicitly embrace Dillon's basic tenet that cities are subdivisions of the states. Consequently, a central contradiction recurs: if local units such as municipalities and school districts are mere subdivisions of the states, how can their inviolable core of local sovereignty function to limit federal courts' ability to enforce fourteenth amendment mandates on the states? Perhaps the Court senses the severe doctrinal difficulties in *Milliken* and *Rodriguez,* for in neither case is its deference to local autonomy elevated to the level of a formal holding. Instead, * * * the quasi-constitutional principle of local sovereignty serves to divert attention from the fact that established federalism principles are not available to justify constrictions on the ability of plaintiffs to recover under the fourteenth amendment.

Rodriguez and *Milliken* are part of a larger trend in which the Burger Court extols local autonomy to constrict the scope of the fourteenth amendment. Many of these cases involve zoning. In six cases, the right of a municipality to zone out low- and moderate-income people, student households, and pornographic theaters has been upheld in the face of fourteenth amendment challenges. In two additional cases, the conservative members of the Court joined dissenting opinions upholding towns' right to zone out extended families and nude dancing. * * * In the zoning opinions * * *, the Court set up a rhetorical universe in which the exclusionary choices of municipalities are canonized as self-rule, while fourteenth amendment mandates are characterized as intrusive central government controls. The Court's use of Jeffersonian rhetoric serves to blur the underlying issue of how to define the "community" entitled to self-determination. Of the myriad possible "communities" available—from the neighborhood to the nation—the Court chose to focus its solicitude upon predominantly white, relatively affluent suburbs that were opposing the introduction of low- and moderate-income housing or other "undesirable" uses. The Court's imagery is powerful because, whereas an argument defending the self-determination of an individual bigot is no longer a strong rhetorical position, the need to preserve a town's right to control its community life, without conformity enforced by Big Brother, resonates with pervasive contemporary concerns. * * *

The Court has used the principle of local autonomy to refuse relief for discrimination in housing or schools whenever such relief requires changes in a city's basic metropolitan structure. The Court's local sovereignty principle enabled it to eviscerate fourteenth amendment equal protection requirements in the large number of cases in which discrimination in housing or schools cannot be remedied without alteration of local boundaries or local duties.

The Court's use of the local sovereignty principle to protect suburban spheres in some sense parallels Dillon's use of his formulation of city status. Both served to protect private property (the taxpayer's wallet or the suburban enclave) against redistributive intrusions—taxation to finance bonds (in the case of Dillon) or federal courts' efforts to enforce constitutional requirements (in the Burger Court opinions). * * *

EDGEWOOD INDEPENDENT SCHOOL DISTRICT v. KIRBY

Supreme Court of Texas, 1989.
777 S.W.2d 391.

MAUZY, JUSTICE. * * *

There are approximately three million public school children in Texas. The legislature finances the education of these children through a combination of revenues supplied by the state itself and revenues supplied by local school districts which are governmental subdivisions of the state. Of total education costs, the state provides about forty-two percent, school districts provide about fifty percent, and the remainder comes from various other sources including federal funds. School districts derive revenues from local ad valorem property taxes, and the state raises funds from a variety of sources including the sales tax and various severance and excise taxes.

There are glaring disparities in the abilities of the various school districts to raise revenues from property taxes because taxable property wealth varies greatly from district to district. * * * The 300,000 students in the lowest-wealth schools have less than 3% of the state's property wealth to support their education while the 300,000 students in the highest-wealth schools have over 25% of the state's property wealth; thus the 300,000 students in the wealthiest districts have more than eight times the property value to support their education as the 300,000 students in the poorest districts. * * * Edgewood I.S.D. has $38,854 in property wealth per student; Alamo Heights I.S.D. in the same county, has $570,109 in property wealth per student.

The state has tried for many years to lessen the disparities through various efforts to supplement the poorer districts. Through the Foundation School Program, the state currently attempts to ensure that each district has sufficient funds to provide its students with at least a basic education. Under this program, state aid is distributed to the various districts according to a complex formula such that property-poor districts receive more state aid than do property-rich districts. However, the Foundation School Program does not cover even the cost of meeting the state-mandated minimum requirements. Most importantly, there are no Foundation School Program allotments for school facilities or for debt service. * * * Low-wealth districts use a significantly greater proportion of their local funds to pay the debt service on construction bonds while high-wealth districts are able to use their funds to pay for a wide array of enrichment programs.

Because of the disparities in district property wealth, spending per student varies widely, ranging from $2,112 to $19,333. Under the existing system, an average of $2,000 more per year is spent on each of the 150,000 students in the wealthiest districts than is spent on the 150,000 students in the poorest districts.

The lower expenditures in the property-poor districts are not the result of lack of tax effort. Generally, the property-rich districts can tax low and spend high while the property-poor districts must tax high merely to spend low. In 1985–86, local tax rates ranged from \$.09 to \$1.55 per \$100 valuation. The 100 poorest districts had an average tax rate of 74.5 cents and spent an average of \$2,978 per student. The 100 wealthiest districts had an average tax rate of 47 cents and spent an average of \$7,233 per student. * * * Many districts have become tax havens. The existing funding system permits "budget balanced districts" which, at minimal tax rates, can still spend above the statewide average; if forced to tax at just average tax rates, these districts would generate additional revenues of more than \$200,000,000 annually for public education.

Property-poor districts are trapped in a cycle of poverty from which there is no opportunity to free themselves. Because of their inadequate tax base, they must tax at significantly higher rates in order to meet minimum requirements for accreditation; yet their educational programs are typically inferior. The location of new industry and development is strongly influenced by tax rates and the quality of local schools. Thus, the property-poor districts with their high tax rates and inferior schools are unable to attract new industry or development and so have little opportunity to improve their tax base.

The amount of money spent on a student's education has a real and meaningful impact on the educational opportunity offered that student. High-wealth districts are able to provide for their students broader educational experiences including more extensive curricula, more up-to-date technological equipment, better libraries and library personnel, teacher aides, counseling services, lower student-teacher ratios, better facilities, parental involvement programs, and drop-out prevention programs. They are also better able to attract and retain experienced teachers and administrators.

The differences in the quality of educational programs offered are dramatic. For example, San Elizario I.S.D. offers no foreign language, no pre-kindergarten program, no chemistry, no physics, no calculus, and no college preparatory or honors program. It also offers virtually no extra-curricular activities such as band, debate, or football. At the time of trial, one-third of Texas school districts did not even meet the state-mandated standards for maximum class size. The great majority of these are low-wealth districts. In many instances, wealthy and poor districts are found contiguous to one another within the same county. * * *

Article VII, section 1 of the Texas Constitution provides:

A general diffusion of knowledge being essential to the preservation of the liberties and rights of the people, it shall be the duty of the Legislature of the State to establish and make suitable provision for the support and maintenance of an efficient system of public free schools. * * *

The State argues that, as used in article VII, section 1, the word "efficient" was intended to suggest a simple and inexpensive system. * * * While there is some evidence that many delegates wanted an economical school system, there is no persuasive evidence that the delegates used the term "efficient" to achieve that end. It must be recognized that the constitution requires an "efficient," not an "economical," "inexpensive," or "cheap" system. The language of the Constitution must be presumed to have been carefully selected. The framers used the term "economical" elsewhere and could have done so here had they so intended.

There is no reason to think that "efficient" meant anything different in 1875 from what is now means. "Efficient" conveys the meaning of effective or productive of results and connotes the use of resources so as to produce results with little waste; this meaning does not appear to have changed over time. One dictionary used by the framers defined efficient as follows:

> Causing effects; producing results; actively operative; not inactive, slack or incapable; characterized by energetic and useful activity * * *.

N. Webster, *An American Dictionary of the English Language* 430 (1864). * * * Considering "the general spirit of the times and the prevailing sentiments of the people," it is apparent from the historical record that those who drafted and ratified article VII, section 1 never contemplated the possibility that such gross inequalities could exist within an "efficient" system. At the Constitutional Convention of 1875, delegates spoke at length on the importance of education for *all* the people of this state, rich and poor alike. * * *

The 1876 Constitution provided a structure whereby the burdens of school taxation fell equally and uniformly across the state, and each student in the state was entitled to exactly the same distribution of funds. The state's school fund was initially apportioned strictly on a per capita basis. Also, a poll tax of one dollar per voter was levied across the state for school purposes. These per capita methods of taxation and of revenue distribution seem simplistic compared to today's system; however they do indicate that the people were contemplating that the tax burden would be shared uniformly and that the state's resources would be distributed on an even, equitable basis.

If our state's population had grown at the same rate in each district and if the taxable wealth in each district had also grown at the same rate, efficiency could probably have been maintained within the structure of the present system. That did not happen. Wealth, in its many forms, has not appeared with geographic symmetry. The economic development of the state has not been uniform. Some cities have grown dramatically, while their sister communities have remained static or have shrunk. Formulas that once fit have been knocked askew. Although local conditions vary, the constitutionally imposed state responsibility for an efficient education system is the same for all citizens regardless of where they live.

We conclude that, in mandating "efficiency," the constitutional framers and ratifiers did not intend a system with such vast disparities as now exist. Instead, they stated clearly that the purpose of an efficient system was to provide for a "*general* diffusion of knowledge." (Emphasis added.) The present system, by contrast, provides not for a diffusion that is general, but for one that is limited and unbalanced. The resultant inequalities are thus directly contrary to the constitutional vision of efficiency. * * *

By statutory directives, the legislature has attempted through the years to reduce disparities and improve the system. There have been good faith efforts on the part of many public officials, and some progress has been made. However, as the undisputed facts of this case make painfully clear, the reality is that the constitutional mandate has not been met.

The legislature's recent efforts have focused primarily on increasing the state's contributions. More money allocated under the present system would reduce some of the existing disparities between districts but would at best only postpone the reform that is necessary to make the system efficient. A band-aid will not suffice; the system itself must be changed.

We hold that the state's school financing system is neither financially efficient nor efficient in the sense of providing for a "general diffusion of knowledge" statewide, and therefore that it violates article VII, section 1 of the Texas Constitution. Efficiency does not require a per capita distribution, but it also does not allow concentrations of resources in property-rich school districts that are taxing low when property-poor districts that are taxing high cannot generate sufficient revenues to meet even minimum standards. There must be a direct and close correlation between a district's tax effort and the educational resources available to it; in other words, districts must have substantially equal access to similar revenues per pupil at similar levels of tax effort. Children who live in poor districts and children who live in rich districts must be afforded a substantially equal opportunity to have access to educational funds. Certainly, this much is required if the state is to educate its populace efficiently and provide for a general diffusion of knowledge statewide.

Under article VII, section 1, the obligation is the legislature's to provide for an efficient system. In setting appropriations, the legislature must establish priorities according to constitutional mandate; equalizing educational opportunity cannot be relegated to an "if funds are left over" basis. We recognize that there are and always will be strong public interests competing for available state funds. However, the legislature's responsibility to support public education is different because it is constitutionally imposed. Whether the legislature acts directly or enlists local government to help meet its obligation, the end product must still be what the constitution commands—i.e. an efficient system of public free schools throughout the state. This does not mean that the state may not recognize differences in area costs or in costs associated with providing an equalized educational opportunity to atypical students or disadvantaged students. Nor does it mean that local communities would be precluded from supplementing an efficient system established by the legislature; however any local enrichment must derive solely from local tax effort.

Some have argued that reform in school finance will eliminate local control, but this argument has no merit. An efficient system does not preclude the ability of communities to exercise local control over the education of their children. It requires only that the funds available for education be distributed equitably and evenly. An efficient system will actually allow for more local control, not less. It will provide property-poor districts with economic alternatives that are not now available to them. Only if alternatives are indeed available can a community exercise the control of making choices. * * *

BUSE v. SMITH

Supreme Court of Wisconsin, 1976.
74 Wis.2d 550, 247 N.W.2d 141.

CONNOR T. HANSEN, Justice. * * *

As a result of the introduction of the district power equalization factor into the procedure for financing school districts, certain of the school districts in the state will not receive any state aid. Instead, they will be required to pay a portion of their property tax revenues into the general state fund to ultimately be redistributed to other school districts in the state. The districts so required to make payments into the state fund have become known as "negative-aid districts." The school districts receiving state aid have become known as "positive-aid districts." * * *

Sec. 121.08, Stats., is intended to achieve equalization of taxing power among the school districts of Wisconsin. Power equalization legislation is based on the premise that student equality of opportunity results when: (a) Regardless of a school district's actual property valuation, its tax levy rate for school purposes produces the same net amount of available school revenue as the same tax levy rate in every other like school district; and (b) there are no per-pupil spending disparities between districts. * * *

At the time the briefs were filed in this case, there were 19 negative-aid districts in the state. Pursuant to secs. 121.07 and 121.08, Stats., they were required to pay into the state fund a portion of the revenues raised by their local tax levies. The funds received from the districts are commingled with state revenues and ultimately disbursed by the state as state school aids to the positive-aid districts throughout the state. * * *

The levying of taxes constitutes the enforcement of proportional contributions from persons and property, levied by the state or municipality for the support of its government and its public needs.

The genesis of the rules of taxation are found in art. VIII, sec. 1, of the Wisconsin Constitution, which provides in pertinent part: "The rule of taxation shall be uniform * * *." * * *

Cooley states the general rule concerning the requirement of equality and uniformity:

"The requirement of equality and uniformity of taxation relates to the rate of taxation, the valuation for taxation, territorial equality, and, according to one view, the inclusion of all property as the subject of taxation. The rate of taxation must be the same, at least as to the same class * * * The valuation must be based upon the same percentage, at least as to the same class of property * * * There must be territorial equality throughout the taxing district." * * *

It is well established that there are certain inherent limitations and restrictions on the power to tax, particularly as they relate to territorial equality or uniformity. Cooley states two of them to be: " * * * [the] inherent limitation on the power of the legislature to tax a local subdivision for a purely local purpose, or to compel such subdivision to tax itself for such a purpose. * * *" A state purpose must be accomplished by state taxation, a county purpose by county taxation, and a public purpose for an inferior district by taxation on such district.

Wisconsin has long recognized this rule of constitutional interpretation, *i.e.,* the purpose of the tax must be one which pertains to the public purpose of the district within which the tax is to be levied and raised. * * * [T]he theory of equality of taxation is that the taxpayer is compensated for the taxes he pays in some public purpose by the unit of government which imposes the tax. * * *

In *Lund v. Chippewa County* (1896), 93 Wis. 640, 648, 649, 67 N.W. 927, 930, the legislature authorized the state to receive funds for buying land and constructing a state institution in Chippewa county. Chippewa county responded to this legislation and raised money by issuing bonds to be amortized out of future tax levies. The action of the county was challenged. This court found the legislation not to be violative of art. VIII, sec. 1, and in so doing held that the state legislature could authorize the county to give money for this purpose [state institution] but " " * * * the legislature has no power, against the will of the municipal corporation, to compel it to contract debts for local purposes in which the state has no concern, or to assume obligations not within the ordinary functions of municipal government * * *.' "

In *State ex rel. Owen v. Donald,* 160 Wis. 126, 127, 151 N.W. 331, 366, it was stated:

"There may lurk in the field of present protection to person or property or both, or, in what seems quite idealistic, a high moral duty to mankind, in general, without regard to place or time, the essential element of consideration, yet it must be remembered that even the demands of charity, springing from dire distress in some foreign jurisdiction, or any outside of the particular taxing unit, are not a legitimate basis for taxation of property in the particular jurisdiction, because of the absence of reciprocal obligations and benefits, in a governmental sense. 'There can be no legitimate taxation unless for the uses of the government' levying it. 2 Dillon, Mun.Corp. (4th ed.) § 736.''

More recently, in *State ex rel. Wisconsin Development Authority v. Dammann* (1938), 228 Wis. 147, 183, 277 N.W. 278, 280 N.W. 698, 709, the rule was simply stated as ''It is the general rule applicable to appropriations that a tax must be spent at the level at which it is raised.'' * * *

Regardless of the merits of the legislative enactments or the worthiness of the cause, we conclude that the state cannot compel one school district to levy and collect a tax for the direct benefit of other school districts, or for the sole benefit of the state. The statutes here under consideration are violative of art. VIII, sec. 1, of the Wisconsin Constitution. * * *

ABRAHAMSON, DAY and HEFFERNAN, JUSTICES (dissenting). * * *

The heart of the majority opinion is that the negative aids law * * * compels ''one school district to levy and collect a tax for the direct benefit of other school districts, or for the sole benefit of the state'' in violation of art. VIII, sec. 1, Wis. Const. As one can see from the holding of the majority and from the cases following, the rule that ''taxes must be spent at the level at which they are raised'' means only that there must be some correspondence between the taxing district or districts upon whom the burden of a given tax rests and the district or districts thought to be benefited by the expenditure of the proceeds. One taxing district cannot be taxed for the sole benefit of another taxing district. This court has said '' 'there can be no legitimate taxation unless for the uses of the government' levying it.'' * * *

Lund v. Chippewa County, 93 Wis. 640, 67 N.W. 927 (1896), and *State ex rel. Board of Education of City of Oshkosh v. Haben,* 22 Wis. 629 (1868), are cited by the majority for the rule the state could not require one or more counties of the state, less than the whole, to support a state institution. * * * The rule established was that all local units—all taxpayers—should make a contribution to support the state purpose.

The negative aid law in question here applies across the state to all school districts. No one school district is singled out to support another school district or state education. Thus the negative aids legislation is substantially different from the statutes in the cases cited by the majority, and the application of those cases to our question is therefore questionable. However, it is important to note that the negative aids law does not contravene the quoted black-letter doctrines set forth in these cases. No taxpayer is relieved of his proportional contribution to the support of education. The goal of the legislation is that all Wisconsin taxpayers shall contribute their fair share to the support of public education, and all will be, relative to any given spending level, equally burdened. The fact that the result of the negative aid provision will be that some but not all districts will pay negative aid is not grounds for its invalidation. The rules governing aid payments apply to all school districts alike which meet the terms and conditions of the statute. * * *

The next issue is whether the legislature is requiring the local school districts to raise and expend funds for a purpose which is not germane to the local school district in violation of the public purpose doctrine. * * * The majority opinion assumes—without any discussion—that a payment by a school district to the state for redistribution for education is not germane to any purpose of the school district making the payment. However, the *Lund* and *Haben* cases recognize the power of the local unit to raise funds for a state purpose. A local government raising funds for a state purpose does not violate the uniformity clause or public purpose doctrine—if it can be shown that the unit also has an interest in the state purpose.

That expenditures are made outside the district do not render the appropriation invalid because such expenditures may still be a valid school district purpose. * * * If the majority (and petitioner) are saying that the payments to the state are invalid because property receiving no direct benefit from a tax for a particular purpose should not be taxed for that purpose, this position is not defensible. A citizen must pay a proportion of a school tax although he or she has no children. * * *

We are unwilling to say that school districts, as a matter of constitutional law, have an absolute, unqualified right to the full revenues raised by the property tax within their districts. * * * We believe the legislature has reasonable grounds to conclude that contribution by a school district to the Department of Public Instruction of part of its locally raised property tax revenue which shall then be distributed as state educational aids to school districts, is in the interest of and is germane to the purposes of the contributing school district. The taxpayers should not be heard to complain because a fraction of the taxes they pay for school purposes benefit the state's school system, of which the school districts in which they reside are a part.

School districts are merely quasi-municipal bodies and agents of the state for the purpose of administering the state's system of public education and have only such powers as are conferred upon them expressly or by necessary implication. Public education is a state, not a local function, by virtue of the explicit command of the state constitution, the express enactment of the legislature, and the repeated pronouncements of this court over the years.

It is true that school boards have a very large measure of local control, but it is the legislature, and not the constitution, which creates the specific dimensions of this local control. Over the years the legislature has encouraged local control of the educational system. Nevertheless each local school unit is not an isolated entity unto itself. Each unit must meet state requirements and is subject to the supervision of the Department of Public Instruction. Each unit is part of the whole state educational system.

We believe it an inevitable conclusion that the purpose of each school district is not only to educate its own children but also to participate in a state-wide educational system. Local school district purposes, for which local tax revenues may properly be spent, are not circumscribed by school district boundaries. * * * Activities within a given school district are of interest and concern to and serve a purpose common to other districts. There is mobility of population and transfer of students; there is movement of children within the state and students attend school outside the school district of residence. Moreover one school district may provide education of its pupils in another school district on a tuition basis. * * *

Some might argue that the reasoning set forth above, pushed to its logical conclusion, means that every state benefit is of local concern and that any state direction for a local unit to turn over funds raised at the local level will therefore be valid. Such a conclusion does not necessarily follow from this opinion. In large part, it is the uniqueness of education among all public activities which supports this negative-aid system. * * *

SECTION B.   REGIONAL SOLUTIONS TO INTERLOCAL CONFLICT

1.   JOINT UNDERTAKINGS

INTERLOCAL AGREEMENTS

Advisory Commission on Intergovernmental Relations, Metropolitan America: Challenge to Federalism, pp. 87–88 (1966).

Intergovernmental agreements are arrangements under which a local community conducts an activity jointly or cooperatively with one or more other governmental units, or contracts for its performance by another governmental unit. The agreements may be permanent or temporary; pursuant to special act or general law; effective with or without voter approval; and may be formal or informal in character. Intergovernmental agreements may be for the provision of direct services to citizens of two or more jurisdictions, such as water supply or police protection; or they may be for governmental housekeeping activities, such as joint purchasing or personnel administration activities.

Local governments in California make extensive use of this approach, with counties contracting to provide services to cities. This procedure has become known as the Lakewood plan, since Lakewood on becoming a city contracted to have practically all its governmental services provided by Los Angeles County. In March 1959, there were

887 contracts between cities and Los Angeles County, covering functions from assessing to dog control and street maintenance. Other types of intergovernmental agreements are also popular in California. Under the Joint Powers Act, two or more public agencies exercising common powers may agree that one of them should exercise power for all of them.

Elsewhere, a survey of intermunicipal contracts indicated that between 1950 and 1957, Cleveland had 30 contracts with 12 of its suburbs, and the 12 suburbs had 43 contracts with one another to provide services. And between 1950 and 1959, 81 of St. Louis County's 98 municipalities signed a total of 241 contracts for provision of municipal services by the county, including law enforcement, health and sanitation, and building regulation.

Intergovernmental agreements are useful in broadening the geographic base for planning and administering governmental services and controls. By enlarging the scale of administration, they make it possible to lower unit costs. Further, the boundaries are flexible and can be enlarged without difficulty when additional governments want to join an agreement. Where agreements are used to extend city services to developing fringe areas, they may be helpful in guiding orderly metropolitan growth.

A basic weakness of joint agreements is that they are practical only when the immediate local interest of each community receiving service is not in conflict with the interest responsible for providing it. Yet in providing areawide services such as public transportation or water supply, conflicts are likely to arise over the location of facilities or priorities for investment. Since agreements are voluntary, each community in effect has veto power within its own borders and can withdraw when its interests are affected adversely by decisions concerning areawide services. Intergovernmental agreements are thus not suited to effective decisionmaking on issues which transcend local interests; under a system of agreements such issues would require unanimity among the governments involved rather than decision by majority vote.

On issues that are more local in character, intergovernmental agreements may interfere with the citizens' ability to take part in making policy. Even though individual governments retain their freedom to pull out of an agreement, and thus retain ultimate control over their own policies, the weaving of a network of intergovernmental agreements tends to confuse the lines of actual responsibility to the point where effective local control may be seriously eroded. Further, the tendency is for each agreement to be made on an ad hoc basis for a particular need, so that the complete view is never brought into focus, making it more difficult to coordinate services and achieve a balance of needs and resources.

Intergovernmental contracts may be objectionable on other grounds where the seller municipality has a virtual monopoly on the service. If one community controls the water supply in an area, for example, only its own self-restraint protects the purchasing communities from being exploited on price and service. Where monopoly conditions exist, some outside authority is needed to protect the purchasers—a role performed in some States by utility regulatory bodies that review water contracts. * * *

———

As the concluding paragraphs of the preceding excerpt suggest, cities may sometimes consider joint action not to be in their own interest. But if cities *want* to engage in some cooperative activity, how could anyone object? In reading Oakland v. Williams, consider what the possible objections to interlocal cooperation might be. Do interlocal agreements square with the conception of cities embodied in Dillon's Rule? Do long-term interlocal agreements threaten to undermine democratic accountability of city governments to city voters? Do interlocal agreements— such as the Lakewood plan mentioned in the excerpt—promote or reduce the fragmentation of America's metropolitan areas? [1]

In evaluating the desirability and likelihood of interlocal agreements, the preceding except takes for granted that the agreements are voluntary—that is, that they are entered into only if each contracting party considers the contract to be in its own interest. How is this concept of city self-interest to be understood? To what extent are cities entitled to act as if they owe no obligation to neighboring cities? This, of course, is the question underlying the materials in the last two sections on exclusionary zoning and school financing. The relevance of the cases in those sections to the likelihood of interlocal agreements is explored in an article of mine excerpted below. Should more interlocal agreements be encouraged? If so, what is the right strategy for doing so? What would be the impact on our current understanding of city-state and city-federal relations if interlocal agreements became more common and more ambitious?

CITY OF OAKLAND v. WILLIAMS

Supreme Court of California, 1940.
15 Cal.2d 542, 103 P.2d 168.

SHENK, JUSTICE.

This is an application for a peremptory writ of mandate directing Harry G. Williams, as Auditor of the City of Oakland, to countersign and endorse his certificate upon a certain contract for and on behalf of said city, as required by sections 125 and 131 of its charter. * * * Briefly, the parties hereto seek an adjudication of the validity of said contract

1. For a general analysis of interlocal agreements, see, e.g., 1 Sands & Libonati, Local Government Law, Chapter 6 (1994); 1 McQuillin, Municipal Corporations, Chapter 3A (3d ed. 1987); Hall & Wallack, Intergovernmental Cooperation and the Transfer of Powers, 1981 U.Ill.L.Rev. 775; Advisory Commission on Intergovernmental Relations, A Handbook for Interlocal Agreements and Contracts (1967). On the Lakewood Plan, see, e.g., Davis, City of Quartz 165–169 (1990).

and of the contemplated expenditure thereunder of some $60,000 for an extended survey of the sewage disposal problem of the signatories thereto, some seven municipalities situated on the east side of San Francisco Bay.

It appears that the seven interested municipalities * * * are contiguous and presently discharge their sewage by many outlets into San Francisco Bay, several of such outlets being jointly used by two or more cities. By reason of the proximity of these outlets, dispersion has proved highly unsatisfactory, and admittedly a grave condition exists threatening both health and property. * * * In an effort to overcome and terminate such unhealthy and unsatisfactory condition, each of the named municipalities in 1937 appointed an official to a body known as the East Bay Executives' Association, whose province it was to investigate and find the facts. * * * These investigations and studies disclosed that the problem could not be satisfactorily solved by independent action of each of the municipalities, but, instead, required a joint survey and investigation of conditions in all the area and of the suitability of different methods of disposal to the peculiar circumstances there existing. It was also reported that such a survey would require approximately seven months and would involve an expenditure of $60,000. Thereupon the seven named municipalities, by appropriate action of their governing bodies, approved such recommendation and respectively authorized the execution of a proposed agreement among them looking to such joint survey and study and directed the appropriate officers to execute the same on their behalf, each agreeing to pay its share of the expenses incident thereto. * * * Admittedly, ample funds remain in the Oakland treasury for the performance and discharge of its obligation under the contract here involved, but Williams, as auditor, nevertheless has refused to countersign the contract on the ground generally that the City of Oakland is without authority under its charter to enter into such a contract with its neighboring cities for a joint survey of the sewage disposal problem. * * *

Preliminarily, it is well to state that * * * any independent action of one or more of said cities looking to the solution of the problem would, because of the action of the tides and currents of San Francisco Bay, still leave unabated the obnoxious nuisance and health menace resulting from sewage deposited on the common shores by the neighboring cities continuing to discharge their sewage into the bay. This and the further fact that there is a present interlocking or common use of certain sewers and outfalls by the named cities makes it readily apparent that the proposed joint solution of the problem is the only feasible and practical one. Therefore, the Executive Association above mentioned proposed a form of contract, later agreed upon and approved by the governing bodies of the several cities, by which said cities would contract with one of their number to do the work under certain restrictive conditions and subject to the approval and supervision of an executive committee whose membership would consist of one representative from each of the contracting cities. * * * By its terms the City of Berkeley will become the sponsor of the proposed survey and the depository of the funds agreed by the several signatories to be paid toward the cost and completion of such survey. All contentions of Williams to the contrary notwithstanding, it may generally be stated that by the terms of the agreement the City of Berkeley is to be the employer of all persons engaged upon the survey. * * * But, in order to give each of the cities contributing to the fund the right to approve the expenditures and to determine that the agreement is being carried out as intended, the City of Berkeley agrees that none of the money will be disbursed except upon approval of the executive committee. * * * However, the executive committee itself is without authority to incur any expense, execute any contract or employ any person. The committee's approval is merely a condition precedent to the exercise of the powers conferred by the agreement on the City of Berkeley. * * *

The statute under which the above contract was drafted was enacted in 1921 and is entitled "An act providing for the joint exercise of powers by counties, by municipalities or by municipalities and counties." Section 1 thereof, among other things, provides that two or more municipalities "by agreement entered into respectively by them and authorized by their legislative bodies, may jointly exercise any power or powers common to the several contracting parties." * * *

In substance, Williams, as auditor of the City of Oakland, urges that the statute above referred to authorizing the joint exercise by municipalities of powers "common" to them does not contemplate or permit the joint exercise of powers that may be separately or independently exercised by them, but only permits of the joint exercise of powers already possessed in common. Such a construction of the statute is strained and would render it meaningless. In other words, if municipalities possessed a power in common there would be no need for a statute authorizing their joint exercise. The statute means nothing if it does not mean that cities may contract in effect to delegate to one of their number the exercise of a power or the performance of an act in behalf of all of them, and which each independently could have exercised or performed. A statute thus authorizing the joint exercise of powers separately possessed by municipalities cannot be said to enlarge upon the charter provisions of said municipalities. It grants no new powers but merely sets up a new procedure for the exercise of existing powers. * * *

An assault is made upon the contract based on the declaration that it would permit the expenditure of Oakland tax funds for non-municipal purposes in that a portion of said funds may assertedly be expended outside the territorial limits of Oakland and for the purpose of surveying the tidelands of one or more of the other contracting cities. It is hinted that such result would likewise run counter to the constitutional inhibition against the gift of public funds. We cannot approve the contention. * * * Among other things, the city in reply [argues] * * * that sewage disposal technically presents more than a municipal problem and is of statewide interest. It is urged that cities daily expend their funds in a legal manner in the enforcement of various state laws which in the strict sense of the word do not involve municipal purposes but, on the contrary, involve public purposes or state affairs. Be that as it may, we are satisfied that if in the solution of their respective municipal sewage problems it becomes necessary, as here, for several contiguous cities to contribute to the conduct of a joint survey of the entire affected area, the expenditure of the funds of each such city in this manner is a proper municipal expenditure.

We are likewise constrained to reject the argument that the joint survey agreement does violence to the civil service provisions of the charter of the City of Oakland. This contention is in effect premised upon the theory that the City of Berkeley is not, under the agreement, to carry out the survey and that the persons to be engaged in the project must therefore necessarily be employees of the City of Oakland and subject to its civil service requirements. Earlier in this opinion we rejected this theory, pointing out that the City of Berkeley under the agreement was to be the sponsor of the survey and was to enter into all necessary contracts and obligations, pay all appropriate expenses out of the sewage disposal fund and employ all persons essential to the project, subject only to the approval of the executive committee. This being so, the civil service provisions of the City of Oakland are without relevancy. * * *

The contention is made that the joint survey agreement does violence to section 125 and other sections of the Oakland charter calling for competitive bids on public work contracts. We cannot accede to the application of said charter provisions under an agreement such as we have here, in which one of the several contracting cities undertakes to carry on the survey. If the conceivably conflicting charter provisions of all the contracting cities were held to be applicable and relevant, the effect would be to vitiate the statute authorizing joint and cooperative action. In other words, there could only be joint action under such a theory when the charter provisions of all contracting cities are identical. To state the matter is to reveal its absurdity. * * *

Let a peremptory writ of mandate issue directing Harry G. Williams, as auditor of the City of Oakland, to countersign the agreement and to endorse thereon his certificate, as required by sections 125 and 131 of the city charter.

GERALD FRUG, EMPOWERING CITIES IN A FEDERAL SYSTEM

19 The Urban Lawyer 553, 557–564, 565–566 (1987).

One way to see the importance of intercity cooperation is to look at the constitutional status of interstate cooperation. Some early federalists might have thought that there was no distinction between creating the federal government and ensuring cooperation among states—that action by the federal government was the same thing as action by the united states. But clearly others recognized, as we do, that these two concepts can be very different from each other; our current federal government represents only one possible form of interstate cooperation. Indeed, the only reference to interstate relationships in the Constitution treats cooperation among states as suspect: article I, section 10 provides: "No state shall, without the Consent of Congress, * * * enter into any Agreement or Compact with another State. * * *"

Why did the federalists who framed the Constitution want centralized control of interstate cooperation? Did they fear that interstate compacts could create a powerful counterforce to the national government? If Congress could not control the relationship among the states, would a very different form of federalism emerge?

I think it would, just as I think that the most effective way to strengthen cities' power is for cities to engage in joint activity and to learn to deal with intercity conflict on their own. The power that can be generated by collective action is widely recognized, as is the effort of centralized authorities to limit it. The ability of employees to increase their power by moving from individual employment contracts to unions—and the efforts of employers to prevent unionization—is one well-known example. The power that private corporations can create through agreements with each other—and the attempt by antitrust laws to limit these agreements—is another. Article I, section 10 of the Constitution, then, is not unusual in its attempt to empower centralized authorities to control collective activity. Efforts to create power through collective organization are generally threatened by countervailing efforts to restrain it. But these attempts to impose centralized control on collective action simply increase its importance; organizing strengthens the ability of individuals and groups to resist centralized power. The defense of local democracy can thus be enhanced if cities work together to advance their common interests.

In order to consider the chances of increasing intercity cooperation, we need to look more closely at the entitlements of individual cities considered separately. The prospects for any agreement depend on the powers that each potential party to the agreement can exercise on its own. This is a matter of basic contract and property law: there is no reason to negotiate over anything to which one is already entitled as a matter of law before the negotiation begins. How, then, should we understand the entitlements of one locality vis-à-vis those of another in the absence of agreement between them? Two different answers have been given to this question, answers that are based on very different ideas about the reason for and value of local democracy. I shall call these conceptions the "free choice" and "participation" theories of democracy.

The free choice theory of democracy is an individualist theory: it envisions the relationship among localities in the way people often imagine the relationship among self-interested individuals. Each locality is free to choose its own destiny, according to its own views of its own self-interest, unless and until it is regulated by law. Indeed, from this point of view, the very reason for establishing a local democracy is to allow the people within it to choose for themselves the kind of life they want to live. Thus advocates of free choice theory might defend exclusionary zoning—a city's decision to permit only certain kinds of housing within its border—as an example of local democratic decision making. They might argue as well that property-rich school districts—those who can support themselves with a low tax rate imposed on highly valued property—owe no obligations to property-poor school districts, even though the poor school districts could never achieve the same amount of income because they do not have adequate property to tax. If a locality cannot decide for itself the kind of community it is to have and cannot control the way it spends its own money on local education, a free choice advocate might argue, local democracy would have no meaning at all. From the free choice view, inter-local agreements are just another example of voluntary agreements between parties who meet each other at arm's length. When cities (like individuals) meet to contract, they can refuse to go along with any proposal they don't like; what each city agrees to will depend on what the people within it want.

The participation theory of democracy, by contrast, envisions local democracy not in terms of individual choice but in terms of a citizen's ability to participate as an equal in the decisions that affect her or his life. Participation theory rejects the relationship among individuals or groups—the sharp separation between self and others—that free choice theory espouses. Defenders of participation theory see such an "arm's-length" version of human relationships as incompatible with democratic existence. Every individual decision, they argue, produces external effects that need to be taken into account in decision making. Participation theory thus describes democracy in terms of a conversation designed to find a satisfactory resolution of differences; indeed, participation theory presents democracy not merely as a decision-making process but as a form of education, a way of creating a sense of self and an understanding of human relationships constructed through political conflict, negotiation, compromise, and disagreement.

Much of the attention of participation theory has focused on internal city organization. Participation theorists have argued that if democracy is to mean more in American life than simply choosing from time to time the individuals who will govern us—if democracy is to mean involvement by the members of a community themselves in the decision making that affects their lives—institutions need to be created that can foster citizen participation. In areas as large as American states and the nation as a whole, elections may be the only form democracy can take; if so, only in cities (and in large cities, only in neighborhoods) can people have the experience of engaging in democratic activity themselves. For participation theorists, the reason for having powerful local governments is to promote this kind of activity. * * *

This process of building democratic city institutions is critically important, but it should be clear that democracies cannot exist merely by perfecting their internal organization. Democratic institutions, like other entities, need to establish ways of living together. Indeed, any theory of democracy must confront the problem of establishing a relationship among individual democracies that is consistent with its democratic ideals. Advocates of participation theory, therefore, are likely to see the relationship among communities as similar to the relationship among people within any single community: both must be built on the recognition of connection and interdependence. Thus a participation theorist might treat the issue of exclusionary zoning as a problem of establishing a mechanism that will allow dialogue among the communities affected by the zoning action; both those excluded and those seeking to exclude must be allowed to participate in the process of resolving their interconnected housing problems. In such a dialogue there can be no automatic assumption that one community has a right to exclude the other's residents. Similarly, a defender of participation theory might deny that the question of school financing can be resolved by assuming that a property-rich school district has an entitlement to use "its own" resources on education without regard to the needs of others; instead, she or he might argue that both property-rich and property-poor school districts are entitled to no more than participation as an equal in working out how school funds are to be allocated. According to participation theory, when individuals or groups meet for the purposes of potential cooperation, they have to learn to understand themselves not as maximizers of their own self-interest but as people who are engaged as equals in the task of resolving their differences.

To be sure, it would be a mistake to overstate the contrast between the free choice and participation theories of democracy. If a local community did not have some degree of freedom of choice, it would not have many decisions to make; thus no one would want to participate in its affairs. Conversely, for a local community to make an informed and representative choice, some degree of popular participation in the decision-making process is indispensable. Thus there is no reason to believe that defenders of free choice necessarily oppose participation or that believers in participation reject the notion of choice. Nonetheless, as the exclusionary zoning and school financing examples are designed to illustrate, the two theories have very different points of emphasis. Indeed, the two theories suggest quite different strategies for promoting the kind of intercity cooperation that, I contend, is so essential to city empowerment.

To date, modern local government law has largely adopted a strategy based on free choice theory.[9] At first glance, this appears to be the right decision: free choice theory seems to provide a far more promising way to increase city power than does participation theory. In fact, participation theory hardly seems to permit any local power at all. According

---

9. *See, e.g.,* Village of Arlington Heights v. Metropolitan Dev. Corp., 429 U.S. 252 (1977); Milliken v. Bradley, 418 U.S. 717 (1974); San Antonio Indep. School Dist. v. Rodriguez, 411 U.S. 1 (1973). *But see, e.g.,* Serrano v. Priest, 557 P.2d 929 (Cal.Sup.Ct. 1977); Southern Burlington County NAACP v. Township of Mount Laurel, 336 A.2d 713 (N.J.Sup.Ct.1975).

to the way I have presented the theory, a community can make virtually no decision about its own future by itself. Local decisions appear to be made only by some sort of romantic transcending of differences between cities—even the very stark differences between inner cities with black majorities and suburbs with white majorities. This process of transcending differences appears pretty vague and farfetched. By contrast, free choice theory seems understandable and in touch with what people are really like. If the object is to increase city power, then the idea of providing each city with some sort of autonomy to make choices—autonomy not only against the state and federal government but against other cities as well—seems the most sensible way to achieve the desired goal. Intercity cooperation would occur in the same way that cooperation occurs in other contexts—whenever the benefits of agreement to each contracting party outweighs the benefits of acting alone. The way to increase cooperation would be to encourage individual cities to see that their own self-interest will be advanced by it. If the benefits of cooperation actually exist, intercity agreements will be able to increase city power against state and federal governments.

The difficulty with the free choice strategy, however, lies in the power that it cedes to the state. If cities are understood, like self-interested individuals, to have entitlements against each other as well as against the state, some entity other than the cities will have to have the authority both to decide what these entitlements are and to resolve the conflicts that they will generate. Traditionally, this authority has been exercised by the state legislature and state courts. But ceding authority to these state agencies in an effort to establish city power simultaneously gives them authority to limit it. The cities' effort to gain autonomy threatens that very autonomy by empowering a central government to decide what it is. The only solution free choice theory offers to this dilemma is the concept of federalism: federalist theory is supposed to specify the limits on centralized control of cities. As we have seen, however, no defensible limits have been found. On the contrary, as article I, section 10, of the Constitution suggests, federalist theory can be interpreted to permit a central government to restrict even cities' ability to cooperate with each other—and many states do.

Self-interested cooperation between cities is likely to be jeopardized by more than assertions of power by the states. Mutual suspicion can also undermine the possibility of inner city cooperative ventures. Because cities seek power from the state that can be used against one another, those that see themselves as well off may be unwilling to help others gain any power that might threaten what they see as "theirs." Cities might also think that they will gain more by trying to win power from the state than by trying to deal with their neighbors. This mutual suspicion can reduce cities' experience of dealing with intercity conflict—particularly the kind of conflict that requires one entity to sacrifice itself in the interest of others. When such a conflict arises, cities will routinely feel that their only real choice is to ask the state to resolve it rather than try to deal with it themselves. Thus a strategy based on free choice theory can lead to increasing state control not simply because of state aggrandizement but because of city abandonment of decision-making responsibility. To be sure, such a process is not inevitable. Cities might understand, and act to reverse, a trend toward city subservience to the state. To do so, however, will require a spirit of cooperation that a self-interested city might find rubs against the grain.

Perhaps, then, a better strategy to encourage more city cooperation and a strong city position against the state is suggested by participation theory. Rather than defining freedom in terms of the entitlements that separate one city from another, cities should recognize that protecting their freedom requires them to resolve their differences themselves. If they do not resolve their own differences, they have to ask some higher authority to do it for them, and every abandonment of their own role in the decision-making process is a gamble that the entity empowered to decide their fate will itself not threaten their interests. Every time a decision is made to defer decision-making responsibility to someone else, there is a loss of freedom—a loss of the ability to have a voice in determining one's own future. Since it is a fantasy to think that, in a world filled with others, a city can determine its future by itself, all it can reasonably expect is the ability to participate with others in the decision-making process. Indeed, whenever such joint decision making works, it strengthens the power of both parties, enabling them to live together in ways that they themselves create.

Of course, a joint decision will often require a city to sacrifice advantages it has over others. But reliance on these advantages is risky because they contain the seeds of their own destruction: they will continue to exist only as long as the state, from which they derive, permits them to. Cities, after *Hunter v. Pittsburgh,* have no constitutional protection from a state's reallocation of their entitlements to others. Advantages secured by using state power to perpetuate a city's privileged position are thus less secure than advantages won through mutual agreement: mutual agreement is likely to produce joint action designed to protect the agreed-upon result from invasion by the state, while advantages won by one city at the expense of another will remain in jeopardy as long as the loser has a chance to influence the state to reverse its decision. Paradoxically, then, compromise with others might lead to more city empowerment than assertions of autonomy and independence even for cities comparatively well off. If so, cities need to create mechanisms that enable them to engage in conflict resolution on their own. Few institutional forums now exist that permit cities to resolve mutual problems without resort to outside intervention. Creating institutions of this kind is a first priority for those who adopt a participation strategy.

A major problem people usually find with a strategy based on participation theory is that they do not believe it is realistic to expect individuals or groups to deal with each other in the way the theory proposes. Is not this a kind of compromise and mutual vulnerability against human nature? Defenders of participation theory respond to this kind of objection by emphasizing that the kind of intercity relationship envisioned by a participation strategy *is* unrealistic—and it will remain unrealistic unless cities are organized internally as participatory democracies. Only if people learn to relate to others within their own community in a democratic fashion—only if they learn how to deal with conflict in their daily lives—will they be able to treat relationships between cities in a similar fashion. Thus the nature of the internal organization of cities is an indispensable ingredient in creating a participatory intercity relationship. The participatory strategy for inter-governmental relations is a strategy for relations among *democracies,* not a strategy that can be adopted by anyone. According to participation theory, one should recall, democracy is not just a decision-making process but a form of education, a form of learning how to deal with others. Of course nonparticipatory institutions are unable to deal with each other democratically, advocates of participation theory might say; people who have never participated in joint decision-making cannot know what it means to engage in democratic self-governance.

Another problem people often find with a strategy based on participation theory stems from the homogenous nature of so many American cities. How can the citizens of modern suburbia find people sufficiently different from themselves to engage in the kind of intracity debate and compromise participation theory envisions? What intracity debate could possibly prepare them to confront the kind of dramatic differences that exist between cities—those, for example, between wealthy suburbs and impoverished inner cities? Defenders of participation theory respond to these questions by agreeing that adequate intracity experience is often unavailable. After all, many cities have been formed and continue to be operated in accordance with free choice theory; citizens of these cities cannot have an adequate democratic experience because they have defined their intercity boundaries antagonistically, excluding different kinds of people. For these cities, the possibility of any genuine democratic participation depends on establishing participatory intercity relationships. Opening oneself to people across city boundaries can thus be as indispensable to enabling a city to function democratically as building a democratic internal organization is to the creation of participatory intercity relationships. Indeed, since participatory intercity and participatory intracity relationships can both be seen as a prerequisite to each other, a major puzzle for theorists has been trying to figure out how a participatory democratic experience can possibly begin. The answer, it seems, is that there is no logical place: barriers to democratic self-governance must be confronted everywhere at once, whenever and however they can. * * *

Let us consider, as a concrete example, the issues of exclusionary zoning and school financing mentioned earlier. The present national strategy of dealing with these issues treats cities as self-interested entities, able to engage in whatever zoning or education decisions they want unless modified by legislative or judicial intervention. Since the federal courts have ruled against federal judicial intervention into these areas of decision-making (in order to honor state policies fostering local democracy), the entitlements of cities engaged in exclusionary zoning practices and property-rich school districts have been protected at the national level. In a number of states, however, judicial or legislative intervention has invalidated exclusionary zoning practices and ordered redistribution of revenues for education. In the case of school financing, this reallocation has been done in the name of local democracy, but this time the localities sought to be empowered are the property-poor school districts that are unable, given their property values, to raise the money for education that their citizens want. (Even restrictions on exclusionary zoning could be defended in the name of local democracy, although normally they are not discussed in these terms. Cities in which the people who are excluded by exclusionary zoning live have no voice in matters that powerfully affect their future.)

Although both federal and state decisions appeal to the virtues of local control, in neither case is the appeal very convincing. Under either the federal or state decisions, some cities have been stripped of their ability to participate in the decision making that vitally affects their interests, let alone of the ability to decide their future by themselves. Those protected by the federal courts might feel satisfied that their "autonomy" has been protected until state legislative or judicial decisions overturn their victory. When that happens, the losers in federal court can feel protected by the help they have won from the state, but only as long as the state continues to act in their interest. In fact, it should be clear that neither side actually has much to say about its own future; it is simply up to one court or another, one legislature or another, to decide what that future is. Given the absence of participatory democratic structures within most of these jurisdictions, little progress is likely to be made immediately by having cities work together to solve the problems of exclusionary zoning or school financing. Too much self-interest and mutual suspicion will distort the bargaining process. Yet there will never be a system of local power until localities attempt to work out these problems themselves. Even now, some form of intercity discussions can be helpful, if only to alleviate the effects of state intervention or federal nonintervention. * * *

———

Neither theory of democracy explored above makes clear whether, in creating inter-city joint ventures, cities should relate to each other in terms of the number of individuals in each city or simply as city entities. This is the question raised in the next case in terms of the Constitutional requirement of one person/one vote. Which of the opinions in the case has the better argument about how councils of government have to be organized? Will large communities deal with small communities as equals only if each of them has equal representation? Alternatively, will communities deal with each other as equals only if representation is weighted according to population?

EDUCATION/INSTRUCCION v. MOORE

United States Court of Appeals, Second Circuit, 1974.
503 F.2d 1187, cert. denied, 419 U.S. 1109, 95 S.Ct. 783, 42 L.Ed.2d 806 (1975).

Before LUMBARD, OAKES and TIMBERS, CIRCUIT JUDGES.

PER CURIAM: * * *

Plaintiffs are a non-profit Connecticut corporation organized for educational, charitable and cultural purposes, together with three individual citizens of Connecticut, two of whom reside in the City of Hartford and one in the Town of Windsor. Defendants are the Chairman of the Capitol Regional Planning Agency (CRPA), the Chairman of the Capitol Region Council of Governments (CRCOG), the Secretary of the United States Department of Housing and Urban Development (HUD), the Regional Director of that Department and twenty-nine individuals who are the chief elected officials of the twenty-nine towns which comprise the Capitol Region (i.e. the Hartford area). * * *

Plaintiffs challenge on equal protection grounds Public Act 821 which provides for the restructuring of the existing CRPA and CRCOG to create a new regional council of government if approved by at least 60% of the towns within the planning region—here, the Hartford area. Each member town of the new council is entitled to one representative on the council, such representative to be the chief elected official of that town.

The gravamen of plaintiffs' claim is that the Act's restructuring of the present regional bodies to create a new regional council in the Hartford area will result in under-representation of the City of Hartford on the new council. In the past Hartford has had five representatives on CRPA, or 8% of that body's membership. On the new council Hartford will have four representatives. A 1973 amendment gave Hartford four representatives on the council instead of the one initially provided, the three additional council members to be appointed by Hartford's city council. Hartford has a population of approximately 160,000, or about 24% of the regional population. Thus, plaintiffs argue, Hartford's vote will be greatly diluted, as compared for example with the Town of Andover, whose population is approximately 2,000, which will have one vote. Plaintiffs' claim in essence is that the legislature's failure to apportion the new regional council on a one man, one vote basis denies them the equal protection of the laws in violation of the Fourteenth Amendment. * * *

The critical question raised by defendants' motion to dismiss the complaint for failure to state a claim upon which relief can be granted is whether the proposed regional council of government for the Hartford area is subject to the one man, one vote requirement. The district court held that it is not. We agree.

The statute in question does not provide for elective bodies.[3] The councils do not exercise general governmental powers, nor do they perform governmental functions, within the meaning of *Hadley v. Junior College District*, 397 U.S. 50 (1970), and *Avery v. Midland County*, 390 U.S. 474 (1968). Indeed, the councils do not have even the minimal governmental powers found insufficient to invoke the one man, one vote principle in the Supreme Court's most recent decisions in *Salyer Land Co. v. Tulare Water District*, 410 U.S. 719, 728 n. 7, 729 (1973), and *Associated Enterprises, Inc. v. Toltec District*, 410 U.S. 743 (1973).

The powers and functions of the councils are essentially to acquire information, to advise, to comment and to propose. As Judge Clarie aptly put it:

> "To the extent that the [council] is able to provide a forum for an interchange of ideas and an atmosphere conducive to the development of solutions to regional problems which know no geographic boundaries, its importance should not be minimized. But this does not bar recognition of the fact that it would be essentially advisory and non-governmental in both purpose and function, and the type of body which need not be apportioned on a strict numerical basis. As such, the [council] represents the kind of flexible experimentation which the Supreme Court has consistently recognized as being both desirable and constitutionally permissible."

We agree.   * * *

OAKES, CIRCUIT JUDGE (dissenting):   * * *

On the crucial question whether the new Council of Governments established in the Hartford area (COG) pursuant to the above state provisions exercises general governmental powers within the ambit of *Avery v. Midland County* and *Hadley v. Junior College District*, it seems to me that neither the COG nor its predecessor bodies, the Capitol Region Planning Agency (CRPA) and Capitol Region Council of Governments (CRCOG), can be considered solely in the light of the statutory authority delegated by the State of Connecticut, as the majority considers them. Rather, we must look to the overall role of the agency in question in the federal system as a whole. A regional planning body such as COG, though a creature of state law, is established with a view to its functions under federal law and the federal system. A regional planning agency cannot be looked at while wearing state-oriented blinders when one of its principal purposes is to play a substantial role in the

---

3. The district court did not find it necessary to determine whether members of the council are elected or appointed, since the council clearly does not exercise general governmental powers nor does it perform governmental functions.

We do note, however, that at least some members of the council do not automatically become council members by virtue of their election to office in their respective towns. The three additional members from Hartford, referred to above, are appointed by the city council under Special Act 73–79. And at least the members from West Hartford, Wethersfield and Glastonbury are selected by the respective town councils after the voters elect the councils themselves.

decision-making process involved in the dispensation of federal funds affecting all the citizens of the affected area.

The test of performing governmental powers must be one based on economic reality, not the mechanical application of nineteenth century municipal law. For example, 42 U.S.C. § 3334 requires that any application for a federal loan or grant for the planning or construction of hospitals, libraries, sewers, water and sewage treatment facilities, highways, mass transit, airports or other transportation facilities, recreation, or open-space development must be submitted for review to an areawide agency, which in this case would be COG. COG may then comment and make its recommendations whether the application should be granted or not. Primary emphasis is given to whether the project would be consistent with comprehensive planning and whether the project contributes to the fulfillment of such planning. Supplementary grants, amounting to as much as any original grant, can be made, but only when there is a showing that the project will be "carried out in accord with areawide [comprehensive] planning and programming." In making the determination whether a project is in accord with an areawide plan, "the Secretary shall obtain, and give full consideration to, the comments of [the areawide planning bodies]." In other words, federal law provides a carrot and stick approach to insure that local governments comply with the area plan. Thus, while COG may have no statutory power under state law to affect local governments, being limited to planning functions, in light of the federal statutes COG's plans themselves can affect local government's abilities to receive federal funds and COG's comments on localities' applications may be altogether determinative.

Not only does the Connecticut COG have an ability to affect the approval of individual municipalities' applications for grants by the exercise of its planning function, but also the local municipalities are dependent upon the COG for establishment of a proper plan in the first instance. Thus, if COG does not do its job—failing to create an areawide plan or creating an areawide plan which does not meet federal requirements—even a non-member municipality's application for a grant for water and sewer facilities or an open space land program may be disapproved for failure to be part of a proper areawide plan.

This control of the purse strings for the building of such a large assortment of facilities is essentially "governmental" in nature in a day and age when municipalities are frequently financially incapable of total self-reliance. In *Hadley,* the power to tax and spend was an important governmental power had by the district; in the year 1974 having a principal hand on the faucet of federal grants must be treated as at least as important as the local power to tax, especially where federal grants may pay up to 80 per cent of facilities' costs, especially since in so many cases the municipalities' powers to tax are often being exercised to their outer limits.

Beyond this, the COG has important powers under, *e.g.,* the Intergovernmental Cooperation Act, 42 U.S.C. § 4201 et seq., and NEPA, 42

U.S.C. § 4321 et seq. In this instance it also happens to operate a regional crime squad (with the help of LEAA money), engages in joint purchasing efforts and otherwise performs important functions that may properly be characterized as governmental in nature. * * *

None of this, of course, is to say that there must be the same precision in formulating a proper system of apportionment of representation on a regional planning agency as in a state legislature, just as state legislative reapportionment is not subject to the same strict standards as congressional reapportionment. Nor is it to fail to recognize the point underlying Mr. Justice Harlan's dissent in *Avery* that in a given case a regional planning agency may be of more concern to the rural members thereof than to the urban residents involved. These are considerations which could be taken into account, however, in establishing a formula which more equally protects or represents the people of Hartford than the one ultimately adopted, under the threat of this law suit, by the Connecticut Assembly by special act. Under the majority decision today, regional planning agencies for metropolitan areas may be weighted in representational makeup one-sidedly against the urban area in favor of the outlying suburbs and towns, and thus the central cities of states with a state legislature dominated by rural or suburban towns left behind the door when facilities or services requiring federal funding are established.

While the district court did not reach the question and the majority mentions it only in passing, a subsidiary question is whether, since there is no direct election of the members of the new COG as such, this case falls within the rule of *Sailors v. Board of Education*, 387 U.S. 105, 87 S.Ct. 1549, 18 L.Ed.2d 650 (1967), that makes the one-man one-vote doctrine of *Reynolds v. Sims* inapplicable to non-elected officials. The Connecticut statutes, however, make it very clear the COG will be basically composed of the "chief elected official" from each member town or city. Conn.Gen.Stat.Ann. § 4–124k. The "chief elected official" means "the highest ranking elected governmental official of any town, city or borough," and the term "elected official" means "any selectman, mayor, alderman or member of a common council or other similar legislative body * * *." While the case is one not precisely controlled by precedent in this respect, it seems closest to *Bianchi v. Griffing*, 393 F.2d 457 (2d Cir.1968), where persons elected as town supervisors automatically became members of the county board of supervisors. Here as there the fact is that these officials are *elected*, they are not appointed, and the one office (that of "chief elected official") carries with it automatic membership on the regional council.

From all this it seems clear to me that there is a sufficiently substantial question of constitutionality as to require the convening of a three-judge court.

2. PUBLIC AUTHORITIES AND SPECIAL DISTRICTS

One of the most common forms of local governmental organization is the "public authority" or "special district". These are entities created by the state to provide a service (or a combination of services) to a local community independent of city control. Indeed, housing authorities, highway authorities, port authorities, independent school boards, hospital corporations, redevelopment authorities, park districts and similar governmental organizations often provide a substantial percentage (sometimes most) of local services.[1] The independence of these public authorities and special districts from city government is often thought to take important public services out of politics, allowing them to be run in a more business-like manner. Moreover, as the case of Municipal Building Authority v. Lowder (reproduced below) illustrates, cities can evade a number of state-imposed restrictions on their operations by transferring city functions to a special district or public authority. Is the *Lowder* opinion persuasive in its argument that state-imposed restrictions on city borrowing should not apply to borrowing by a public authority? Should cities be able to exempt themselves from other state-imposed requirements, such as civil service rules for hiring personnel or competitive bidding rules for purchasing goods and services, by transferring functions to public authorities or special districts?

The jurisdictions of many public authorities and special districts extend across individual city boundaries. These entities therefore provide an alternative to inter-local agreements as vehicles for regional cooperation. The following is a (relatively typical) defense of the creation of regional or multicounty authorities as a means of providing regional services:

> (T)he strengths of multicounty authorities lie in increased efficiency and flexibility of jurisdiction. Among the services that are best suited for administration by this kind of body are those that require accumulated expertise and technological sophistication in their management. Continuity of management, attraction of superior personnel, and corporate powers and decisionmaking will be most beneficial in such areas as transportation, water supply and sewerage, port direction, and pollution control. Services in which area-wide administration and planning would result in significant economies of scale and integration of separate facilities are also likely to benefit from administration by multicounty authorities. An area-wide policy is mandatory, for instance, if a transportation plan is effectively to coordinate bus, train, and subway services with auto travel on the roads, ferries, and bridges, and through tunnels.[2]

The final two cases in this section are designed to raise questions about the use of public authorities and special districts as forms of regional organization, questions similar to those explored in other contexts earlier in this casebook. Are the cities' home rule objections to the

---

1. See generally, 3A Antieau, Municipal Corporation Law, Chapters 30C–Q (1979); Comment, An Analysis of Authorities: Traditional and Multicounty, 71 Mich.L.Rev. 1376 (1973); Quirk & Wein, A Short Constitutional History of Entities Commonly Known as Authorities, 56 Cornell L.Rev. 521 (1971).

2. Comment, An Analysis of Authorities: Traditional and Multicounty, 71 Mich. L.Rev. 1376, 1429 (1973).

power of regional authorities convincingly answered in the *Younger* case? Is the concern about democratic accountability of regional authorities persuasively dealt with by Ball v. James? What difference does it make whether inter-local agreements or regional authorities are chosen as a means of providing regional services?

RICHARD BRIFFAULT, OUR LOCALISM: PART II—LOCALISM AND LEGAL THEORY

90 Col.L.Rev. 346, 375–378 (1990).

Since the turn of the century, state legislatures have invented a "baffling array" of "pseudo governments" to provide infrastructure services to the suburbs without disturbing suburban political autonomy. These entities—variously christened boards, districts, authorities and commissions—are authorized to construct, operate or finance physical infrastructure services, usually water supply services, sewers, parks or transportation, over an area including many general-purpose governments. These limited-purpose entities can pool the resources of a number of localities in an area, but solely to provide one or a handful of specified services.

Where the board's jurisdiction includes both the city and the suburbs and the city has already installed its own water supply or sewers out of its own funds, the board effectively redistributes city revenues to the installation and support of suburban services. Where the board or district includes only developing areas in need of the initial installation of new services, the creation of a single area-wide water or sewer system and the combination of revenues from numerous localities lead to substantial economies of scale, reducing the per capita cost of providing new infrastructure systems but undermining the competitive advantage of the central city and permitting suburbs to enjoy municipal services without submitting to annexation or consolidation.

The structure and design of these special-purpose units minimize the intrusion on suburban autonomy. First, they are limited-purpose governments. The metropolitan unit overlaps cities and suburbs but has no general governmental authority over the territory or residents within its jurisdiction. Cities and suburbs are not merged, and the city gains no lawmaking authority over the suburbs. Rather, different municipalities are linked only for a particular purpose, such as supplying water or removing wastes.

Second, these units provide services that facilitate separate suburban political existence without disrupting suburban class or ethnic homogeneity. In Oliver Williams's terminology, the metropolitan special districts perform "system-maintenance functions" without impinging on suburban "lifestyles." The physical infrastructure that metropolitan districts provide usually lacks broader implications for the economic or social demography of suburban communities. Special districts supply engineering solutions to technical problems; they do not directly engage in area-wide social or economic policymaking. Metropolitan districts do not zone or provide police, housing or schools on an area-wide city-suburb basis. Suburbs that have accepted regional provision of certain transportation facilities, like airports, have been able to reject other area-wide services, like metropolitan mass transit systems, because of the concern that the latter would increase the ability of central city residents to travel to the suburbs.

Third, special districts' financial and governance arrangements minimize their regional redistributive and political potential. The operation of these agencies is usually funded through service fees or user charges, with local service recipients paying a specified amount for each unit of service they receive. Local tax bases are generally not exposed to the public service needs of the region or of people residing outside local political boundaries.

The metropolitan boards generally lack regional popular political constituencies. Often their members are unelected, and are, instead, appointees or officials of the affected municipalities serving ex officio. The board members do not serve as representatives of a regional electorate, but either represent their home locality to the regional unit—where they vote on a "one government, one vote" and not a "one person, one vote" basis—or they are not locally representative at all. There are few political ties linking metropolitan districts directly to the residents of the metropolitan area, so that these districts do not significantly disturb the existing political alignment of cities and suburbs.

As metropolitan areas have grown, special districts have proliferated. There are now more than 28,000, and the special district is the most common form of local government. In most areas there are more special districts than municipalities. At one time, political scientists saw these metropolitan boards and districts as a bridge from local independence to regional government. They predicted that as local governments developed institutions for interlocal cooperation and saw the need for regional solutions to area-wide problems, metropolitan consolidation would follow. Instead, the opposite has occurred. State-authorized limited-purpose governments have provided suburbs with an alternative to annexation, consolidation to the central city or acceptance of full-fledged metropolitan governments. A suburb can maintain political independence, including control of its tax base, schools and lands, while still sharing in the economies of scale provided by infrastructure services organized and funded on a regional basis.   * * *

MUNICIPAL BUILDING AUTHORITY v. LOWDER

Supreme Court of Utah, 1985.
711 P.2d 273.

ZIMMERMAN, JUSTICE:

Defendants, the auditor, treasurer and clerk of Iron County, appeal from a district court decision upholding the Utah Municipal Building Authority Act ("the Act") against a variety of constitutional challenges and finding that the actions proposed by the Iron County Board of Commissioners and the Iron County Municipal Building Authority ("the Authority") to finance construction of a new jail facility under that Act are lawful. * * *

Testimony before the district court indicated that the fifty-year-old Iron County jail has not met even minimum state and federal standards of habitability for some time. * * * Lengthy studies have underscored the need to build an entirely new jail. To finance its construction, the Iron County Commissioners proposed issuing general obligation bonds. Article XIV, section 3 of the Utah Constitution requires that such bonds be approved by the voters because they would be a long-term debt of the county. In December of 1981, a bond election was held and the proposal was defeated, leaving the county in a difficult dilemma. As a practical matter, the new facility had to be built; yet the Iron County taxpayers were unwilling to pay for the facility through the traditional means of financing major capital improvements—general obligation bonds.

The Board of Commissioners devised a plan which would permit a jail to be built without prior voter approval. Article XIV, section 3 requires voter approval of long-term indebtedness only when the indebted entity is a county or a subdivision of a county. The commissioners, acting under the Utah Municipal Building Authority Act, created the Iron County Building Authority, a quasi-municipal governmental entity designed *not* to be a "subdivision" of the county and, therefore, to be free from the voter-approval requirement of article XIV, section 3. As required by the Act, the Authority's board of trustees consists of all of the Iron County commissioners. The Authority is empowered to finance and construct a new jail facility and lease it to the county. Because the Authority, not the county, will borrow money for the construction, voter approval of its bond issue will not be necessary, yet a new jail will be made available to the county.

To implement the plan, the county and the Authority propose to enter into several related agreements. For a nominal consideration, the existing jail facility will be transferred to the Authority in fee; in effect, the present jail will be donated to the Authority. That property, now appraised at $124,000, will be traded by the Authority to a private developer for another site upon which the new jail facility will be constructed. Should there be some legal obstacle to this transfer in fee, the county proposes to lease a project site to the Authority. In either event, once the Authority has secured a site, it will issue revenue bonds with a term of twenty years to finance construction, pledging as security its interest in the project site and the facility to be constructed. As part of the same transaction, the county will lease the new jail facility from the Authority for twenty years, on a year-to-year basis. After the twenty years have passed and the bonds are paid in full, the Authority will transfer title to the new facility to the county. The agreements between the county and the Authority provide that in the event the Authority defaults on the bonds before they are paid off, the bond holders may foreclose upon the new jail facility and whatever interest the Authority has in the site, but they will have no recourse against the county or its taxpayers.   * * *

We first address defendants' contention that the Act allows counties to evade the constitution's debt limitations. Some background is necessary. Article XIV, section 3 of the Utah Constitution prohibits, *inter alia,* any county from incurring debt in excess of the current year's tax revenues without prior approval of a majority of the property taxpayers. A companion provision, article XIV, section 4, limits the debt a county can incur even with taxpayer approval to two percent of the assessed valuation. These two provisions demonstrate the drafters' concern in 1895 that absent limits on total debt and a requirement that any debt to be paid from future revenues be approved by taxpayers, local governmental units might be fiscally irresponsible. Members of the constitutional convention expressed strong concern about the tendency of local governments to provide present benefits to voters and to pay for them from future revenues. Sections 3 and 4 of article XIV were a direct response to that concern.

Historically, local governments, often aided and abetted by the state legislature, have tried to find ways to provide facilities needed by an increasingly urbanized society without being hobbled by the strict limitations in sections 3 and 4 of article XIV. This Court has often been receptive to such efforts. For example, the court-created "special fund doctrine" excludes certain bonds from section 3's election requirement if those bonds are repaid from revenues generated by the facilities constructed with the bond proceeds, rather than from general tax revenues. The underlying theory is that the bond holders have no recourse to the general tax revenues and, therefore, the bonds are not "debt" of the governmental entity in question.

Another means of avoiding the debt limitations is the creation of a special district. This Court has held that such a district is exempt from the limitations of sections 3 and 4 of article XIV because it is a quasi-municipal entity rather than a "city, county, town or subdivision thereof." Despite some attempts by this Court to limit the use of such districts on varying grounds, they have continued to proliferate. In fact, article XIV was amended in 1975 to clarify the status of such districts and to provide for legislative control over them.

There is no question that the Utah Municipal Building Authority Act is yet another attempt to develop a means for financing needed capital improvements without being restricted by the rigid debt ceiling of article XIV, section 4 or by the taxpayer approval requirement of section 3. Defendants contend that the Act must be struck down as inconsistent with article XIV, sections 3 and 4. We find these arguments without merit.

Defendants contend that the Authority's debt is debt of the county, within the meaning of article XIV, section 3. This Court has rejected similar arguments in the past, and we see no reason to depart from those precedents. The express terms of sections 3 and 4 of article XIV apply only to specified entities, including counties and their subdivisions; they do not apply to quasi-municipal entities such as building authorities. Therefore, a debt of the Authority for which the county is not responsible is not subject to the restrictions of article XIV, sections 3 and 4. * * *

Defendants assert that the proposed plan of action works a fraud upon the taxpayers because they expressly disapproved construction of a new jail. This mischaracterizes the election. The voters only expressed an unwillingness to incur a general obligation debt to finance the jail's construction; they were not asked whether the facility should be built if general obligation bonding could be avoided. The difference is significant. Under the constitution, it is only the former proposal that must be put before the voters.

Defendants next argue that there is no real difference between the proposed method of financing and general obligation bonding. This is not true. General obligation bonds would irretrievably obligate future taxpayers to pay off the debt incurred to build the jail; financing construction through the Authority will not. Under the proposed arrangement, the county will lease the jail facility on a year-to-year basis. The county retains the option of terminating the lease at the end of each year. Should this occur, neither the Authority nor the bond holders will have any recourse against the county or the taxpayers for the amount remaining unpaid on the bonded indebtedness.

In addition to the practical differences between a long-term bond indebtedness and a year-to-year obligation, there is a constitutionally significant legal difference: under article XIV, section 3, a contractual obligation that can be discharged within one year is not considered a debt that must be submitted to the voters. Our cases have held that the aggregate amount that may ultimately be paid under a multi-year contract or lease need not be taken into account in determining whether the debt represented by the contract or lease exceeds the current year's revenues so long as the actual amount due under the contract accrues only as the services are provided and the municipality cannot be coerced into paying for services not yet rendered.

In the present case, the county has the right to terminate the contract at the end of any year. The amount due in any one year is only for services provided during that year. Therefore, the proposed lease qualifies for treatment on a year-to-year basis. Of course, as a practical matter the county will renew the lease for the next twenty years. But that does not affect the analysis so long as the county cannot be held legally responsible for other than the services it receives during the current tax year.

We conclude that the proposed arrangement between the county and the Authority does not work a fraud, injustice or inequity upon the bond holders or the taxpayers. * * *

The next contention advanced by defendants in an attempt to bring the transaction before us within the prohibitions of article XIV, sections

3 and 4 is that the Act has an impermissible purpose—it allows municipalities to evade constitutional debt limits and create debt indirectly where it cannot be created directly. Defendants' argument belabors the obvious. Of course the Act is intended to permit avoidance of the constitutional debt limitations. It is the very rigidity of those limitations that has led the courts to narrowly construe them and the legislature to actively assist local government in avoiding them. We reject defendants' argument. If the express terms of an enactment do not offend the constitution, its purpose alone will not render it unconstitutional. And nothing prohibits local governments from lawfully avoiding these constitutional limitations.

Defendants' final argument under article XIV, sections 3 and 4 is that the use of general tax revenues to make the yearly rental payments under the jail lease will have the same economic result as if general obligation bonds had been issued; therefore, the jail lease payments should be considered debt subject to the constitution's restrictions. They reason that the use of general tax revenues to make the annual rental payments will result in a reduction of funds otherwise available to the county and will require the county to raise taxes to compensate for the expenditure on the jail. The net result is that the taxpayers will pay higher taxes just as if they had approved the original bond proposal. Defendants' assumptions may be correct, but their conclusion—that transactions resulting in the same economic burdens must be treated similarly for purposes of article XIV, sections 3 and 4—is not.

It is true that if the county continues with the lease for its full term, the taxpayers will pay as much for the jail facility as if general obligation bonds had been issued. In fact, they almost certainly will pay more, since general obligation bonds probably would have carried a lower interest rate than the somewhat riskier bonds being issued by the Authority. But that fact is not relevant to the legal inquiry—will the technical requirements of the constitution be violated by the proposed transaction?

As noted above, so long as the county's liability is limited to the annual rental installment for the current year, only that payment is considered in determining whether article XIV, section 3's debt limitation is exceeded. The full amount due over the term of the lease is not considered. The question here raised is whether the fact that taxes may have to be raised to cover the annual lease payment invalidates the transaction. Article XIV, sections 3 and 4 limit the indebtedness that can be incurred without a vote to "debt [not] in excess of the taxes for the current year." Under our decisions, compliance with this provision requires that the debt contracted for, taken together with all other debts of the county at the time of contracting, cannot exceed the amount of revenue the county anticipates it will receive during the tax year. So long as the anticipated revenues are sufficient to cover the annual payment, the debt incurred is valid under article XIV, section 3. Thus, the fact that the county will have to raise taxes in order to pay the jail rental does not invalidate the annual rental debt, so long as at the time the county becomes obligated to pay the debt it has sufficient anticipated revenues for that year to pay all of its debts. * * *

PEOPLE EX REL. YOUNGER v. COUNTY OF EL DORADO

Supreme Court of California, 1971.
5 Cal.3d 480, 96 Cal.Rptr. 553, 487 P.2d 1193.

SULLIVAN, JUSTICE.

The Attorney General, on behalf of the People of the State of California, seeks a writ of mandate commanding the Counties of El Dorado and Placer to pay to the Tahoe Regional Planning Agency (Agency) the amounts of money respectively allotted to them by the Agency as being necessary to support its activities. * * * The issues thus presented to us are of great concern to California, to its neighbors and, indeed, to the entire country.

The controversy which we are required to review focuses upon the Lake Tahoe Basin—an area of unique and unsurpassed beauty situated high in the Sierras along the California–Nevada border. Mark Twain, an early visitor to the region, viewed the lake as "a noble sheet of blue water lifted six thousand three hundred feet above the level of the sea * * * with the shadows of the mountains brilliantly photographed upon its still surface * * * the fairest picture the whole earth affords." Year after year the lake and its surrounding mountains have attracted and captivated countless visitors from all over the world.

However, there is good reason to fear that the region's natural wealth contains the virus of its ultimate impoverishment. A staggering increase in population, a greater mobility of people, an affluent society and an incessant urge to invest, to develop, to acquire and merely to spend—all have combined to pose a severe threat to the Tahoe region. Only recently has the public become aware of the delicate balance of the ecology, and of the complex interrelated natural processes which keep the lake's waters clear and fresh, preserve the mountains from unsightly erosion, and maintain all forms of wildlife at appropriate levels. Today, and for the foreseeable future, the ecology of Lake Tahoe stands in grave danger before a mounting wave of population and development.

In an imaginative and commendable effort to avert this imminent threat, California and Nevada, with the approval of Congress, entered into the Tahoe Regional Planning Compact (Compact) the provisions of which are found in Government Code section 66801. The basic concept of the Compact is a simple one—to provide for the region as a whole the planning, conservation and resource development essential to accommodate a growing population within the region's relatively small area without destroying the environment.

To achieve this purpose, the Compact establishes the Tahoe Regional Planning Agency with jurisdiction over the entire region. The Agency has been given broad powers to make and enforce a regional plan of an unusually comprehensive scope. This plan, to be adopted on or before September 1, 1971, must include, as correlated elements, plans for land-use, transportation, conservation, recreation, and public services and facilities. The Compact emphasizes that in formulating and maintaining this regional plan, the Agency "shall take account of and shall seek to harmonize the needs of the region as a whole * * *."

The Agency is given the power to "adopt all necessary ordinances, rules, regulations and policies to effectuate the adopted regional * * *" plan. While ordinances so enacted establish minimum standards applicable throughout the region, local political subdivisions may enact and enforce equal or higher standards. "The regulations shall contain general, regional standards including but not limited to the following: water purity and clarity; subdivision; zoning; tree removal; solid waste disposal; sewage disposal; land fills, excavations, cuts and grading; piers, harbors, breakwaters, or channels and other shoreline developments; waste disposal in shoreline areas; waste disposal from boats; mobilehome parks; house relocation; outdoor advertising; flood plain protection; soil and sedimentation control; air pollution; and watershed protection. Whenever possible without diminishing the effectiveness of the * * * general plan, the ordinances, rules, regulations and policies shall be confined to matters which are general and regional in application, leaving to the jurisdiction of the respective states, counties and cities the enactment of specific and local ordinances, rules, regulations and policies which conform to the * * * general plan." The Compact also provides that "[v]iolation of any ordinance of the [A]gency is a misdemeanor." Finally, it states that "all public works projects shall be reviewed prior to construction and [except for certain state public works projects] approved by the [A]gency as to the project's compliance with the adopted regional general plan."

The governing body of the Agency is composed of ten members, five from California and five from Nevada. The Boards of Supervisors of El Dorado and Placer Counties and the City Council of the City of South Lake Tahoe each appoint one member; "[e]ach [such] member shall be a member of the city council or county board of supervisors which he represents and, in the case of a supervisor, shall be a resident of a county supervisorial district lying wholly or partly within the region." The Boards of County Commissioners of the Counties of Douglas, Ormsby and Washoe in the State of Nevada each select one member; each member must be a resident of the county from which he is appointed and may be, in the discretion of the board of county commissioners, but is not required to be, a member of the board which appoints him and a resident or owner of real property in the region. The Administrator of the California Resources Agency, or his designee, and the Director of the Nevada Department of Conservation and Natural Resources, or his designee, are *ex officio* members of the board. Finally, the Governors of California and Nevada each appoint one member, who "shall not be a resident of the region and shall represent the public at large."

The Compact permits the Agency to receive fees for its services, gifts, grants and other financial aids. It also provides for Agency financing as follows: " * * * [O]n or before December 30 of each calendar year the agency shall establish the amount of money necessary to support its activities for the next succeeding fiscal year commencing July 1 of the following year. The agency shall apportion not more than $150,000 of this amount among the counties within the region on the same ratio to the total sum required as the full cash valuation of taxable property within the region in each county bears to the total full cash valuation of taxable property within the region. Each county in California shall pay the sum allotted to it by the agency from any funds available therefor and may levy a tax on any taxable property within its boundaries sufficient to pay the amount so allocated to it. Each county in Nevada shall pay such sum from its general fund or from any other moneys available therefor." * * *

The positions of the parties before us may be summarized as follows: the Attorney General contends that the respondent counties have a clear duty, imposed by the Compact, to pay their share of the funds necessary to support the activities of the Agency and that we should compel the performance of this duty by a writ of mandate. The counties contend * * * that they are not required to make any payments to the Agency because the Compact is unconstitutional and void. * * *

The counties first contend that the Compact violates former sections 11, 12 and 13 of article XI of the California Constitution. * * * Generally speaking, these sections confer upon specified local governmental bodies broad powers over purely local affairs. But, as we shall point out, the Compact is unaffected by any of the above provisions since its subject matter is of regional, rather than local, concern. * * * [T]he purpose of the Compact is to conserve the natural resources and control the environment of the Tahoe Basin as a whole through area-wide planning. * * * Only an agency transcending local boundaries can devise, adopt and put into operation solutions for the problems besetting the region as a whole. Indeed, the fact that the Compact is the product of the cooperative efforts and mutual agreement of two states is impressive proof that its subject matter and objectives are of regional rather than local concern.

Respondent counties * * * contend that the Compact violates former section 11 of article XI of the California Constitution. That section provided: "Any county, city, town or township may make and enforce within its limits all such local, police, sanitary and other regulations as are not in conflict with general laws." The counties argue that the Compact gives the Agency power to adopt local, police and sanitary ordinances, rules and regulations, violations of which are declared misdemeanors by section 66801, article VI, subdivision (f). According to their argument, "[t]hese powers have been granted to respondent counties by the California Constitution and there is, therefore, a violation of Article XI, section 11, of the California Constitution in any attempt to grant these same powers to the Agency." In support of this contention, the counties cite *In re Werner* (1900) 129 Cal. 567, 574, 62 P. 97.

In *Werner,* this court struck down a state statute which purported inter alia to grant a sanitary district the power "[t]o make and enforce all necessary and proper regulations for suppressing disorderly and disreputable resorts and houses of ill fame within the district, and to determine the qualifications of persons authorized to sell liquors at retail * * *." This court * * * held that section 11 prohibited the Legislature from granting a sanitary district a power "which clearly falls within the police powers possessed by cities and other like corporations formed and organized for governmental purposes. * * *." Certain broad language in *Werner* * * * appears to support the proposition that no power to make regulations having a local effect may be conferred upon public corporate bodies not enumerated in section 11. However, *Werner* * * * involved only the power to enact penal ordinances, and they have consistently been interpreted as forbidding only the delegation of power to prescribe penalties for violations of ordinances. * * * The instant case is clearly distinguishable from *Werner* * * * since the Legislature has not delegated to the Agency the power of enacting penal legislation. It is the Legislature itself which has properly declared that: "Violation of any ordinance of the agency is a misdemeanor."

Nor has the Legislature, as it is claimed, granted to the Agency the same powers which have been granted to respondent counties by section 11. * * * It is sufficient to point out that the powers exercised by respondents are for local purposes, within the limits of the county. But, as we have explained, the broad powers conferred upon the Agency are not for *local* purposes, but solely to achieve the *regional* goal of preserving the Lake Tahoe Basin—a goal which local bodies have been unable to attain. Indeed, the Compact specifically reserves to local entities matters within their proper sphere of action: "Whenever possible without diminishing the effectiveness of the * * * general plan, the ordinances, rules, regulations and policies [of the Agency] shall be confined to matters which are general and regional in application, leaving to the jurisdiction of the respective states, counties and cities the enactment of specific and local ordinances, rules, regulations and policies which conform to the * * * general plan." * * *

The counties next contend that the Compact legislation unconstitutionally imposes a tax on them in violation of former section 12 of article XI (now § 37 of art. XIII). Former section 12 provided: "Except as otherwise provided in this Constitution, the Legislature shall have no power to impose taxes upon counties, cities, towns or other public or municipal corporations, or upon the inhabitants or property thereof, for county, city, town, or other municipal purposes, but may, by general laws, vest in the corporate authorities thereof the power to assess and collect taxes for such purposes." Pursuant to section 66801, article VII, subdivision (a), the counties must pay to the Agency the amounts of money allotted to them by the Agency to support its activities, which amounts the counties may raise by levying taxes on property within their jurisdiction. It is argued that contrary to the mandate of section 12, such taxes are imposed for "county * * * purposes," since the functions for which the Agency will spend the money "are those traditionally assumed by appropriate units of local government." The point of the argument is that the Legislature, although indirectly, is attempting "to impose taxes upon counties * * * for county * * * purposes." * * * Contrary to the above claim, we have held that "[t]he limitations of section 12 do not prevent the Legislature from authorizing a district to impose taxes for a state purpose, nor for a purpose that transcends the boundaries of the various municipalities that may be included within the limits of a larger district." * * *

Finally, we consider the claim that the Compact violates former section 13 of article XI. That section provided: "The Legislature shall not delegate to any special commission, private corporation, company, association or individual any power to make, control, appropriate, supervise or in any way interfere with any county, city, town or municipal improvement, money, property, or effects, whether held in trust or otherwise, or to levy taxes or assessments or perform any municipal function whatever * * *." The counties assert that the Agency is a "special commission" within the purview of the section and that the Legislature has unconstitutionally delegated to it the power to "interfere with" county improvements and to "perform" municipal functions. We find no merit in the contention. * * *

Although section 13 was intended primarily to prevent legislative interference with the financial affairs of municipalities, its prohibition extends to other forms of interference. However, our cases have recognized "that the section was intended to prohibit only legislation interfering with purely local matters. Special commissions have been upheld if they either fulfill a more than local purpose, under the 'larger municipality' doctrine, or promote a 'statewide purpose.' " * * * In the case at bench, the Compact was enacted to serve regional, not merely local, purposes. Indeed, here, one of the reasons for the establishment of the Agency was the inability of the myriad of local entities to cope with the problem of preserving the Tahoe Basin. The Compact does not give the Agency power to build or maintain local parks or other improvements; it merely grants the Agency authority to assure that public works which are planned, built and maintained by appropriate local bodies do not interfere with the fulfillment of the regional plan. Any restriction upon local improvements is merely incidental to the execution of the Agency's regional duties. Consequently, the Compact does not violate former section 13 of article XI of the California Constitution. * * *

BALL v. JAMES

Supreme Court of the United States, 1981.
451 U.S. 355, 101 S.Ct. 1811, 68 L.Ed.2d 150.

JUSTICE STEWART delivered the opinion of the Court.

This appeal concerns the constitutionality of the system for electing the directors of a large water reclamation district in Arizona, a system which, in essence, limits voting eligibility to landowners and apportions voting power according to the amount of land a voter owns. The case requires us to consider whether the peculiarly narrow function of this local governmental body and the special relationship of one class of citizens to that body releases it from the strict demands of the one-person-one-vote principle of the Equal Protection Clause of the Fourteenth Amendment.

The public entity at issue here is the Salt River Project Agricultural Improvement and Power District (District), which stores and delivers untreated water to the owners of land comprising 236,000 acres in Central Arizona. The District, formed as a governmental entity in 1937, subsidizes its water operations by selling electricity, and has become the supplier of electric power for hundreds of thousands of people in an area including a large part of metropolitan Phoenix. Nevertheless, the history of the District began in the efforts of Arizona farmers in the 19th century to irrigate the arid lands of the Salt River Valley, and, as the parties have stipulated, the primary purposes of the District have always been the storage, delivery, and conservation of water.

As early as 1867, farmers in the Salt River Valley attempted to irrigate their lands with water from the Salt River. In 1895, concerned with the erratic and unreliable flow of the river, they formed a "Farmers Protective Association," which helped persuade Congress to pass the Reclamation Act of 1902, 43 U.S.C. § 371 *et seq*. Under that Act, the United States gave interest-free loans to help landowners build reclamation projects. The Salt River Project, from which the District developed, was created in 1903 as a result of this legislation. In 1906, Congress authorized projects created under the Act to generate and sell hydroelectric power, and the Salt River Project has supported its water operations by this means almost since its creation. The 1902 act provided that the water users who benefited from the reclamation project had to agree to repay to the United States the costs of constructing the project, and the Salt River Valley Water Users Association was organized as an Arizona corporation in 1903 to serve as the contracting agent for the landowners. The Association's Articles, drafted in cooperation with the Federal Reclamation Service, gave subscribing landowners the right to reclamation water and the power to vote in Association decisions in proportion to the number of acres the subscribers owned. The Articles also authorize acreage-proportionate stock assessments to raise income for the Association, the assessments becoming a lien on the subscribing owners' land until paid. * * *

The Association faced serious financial difficulties during the Depression as it built new dams and other works for the project, and it sought a means of borrowing money that would not overly encumber the subscribers' lands. The means seemed to be available in Arizona's Agricultural Improvement District Act of 1922, which authorized the creation of special public water districts within federal reclamation projects. Such districts, as political subdivisions of the State, could issue bonds exempt from federal income tax. Nevertheless, many Association members opposed creating a special district for the project, in part because the state statute would have required that voting power in elections for directors of the District be distributed per capita among landowners, and not according to the acreage formula for stock assessments and water rights. In 1936, in response to a request from the Association, the state legislature amended the 1922 statute. Under the new statutory scheme, which is essentially the one at issue in this case, the legislature allowed the District to limit voting for its directors to voters, otherwise regularly qualified under state law, who own land within the District, and to apportion voting power among those landowners according to the number of acres owned. The Salt River Project Agricultural Improvement and Power District was then formed in 1937, its boundaries essentially the same as the Association's. Under the 1937 agreement, the Association made the District its contracting agent, and transferred to the District all its property, and the Association in turn agreed to continue to operate and maintain the Salt River Project. Under the current agreement, the District itself manages the power and water storage work of the project, and the Association, as agent for the District, manages water delivery. As for financing, the statute now permits the special districts to raise money through an acreage-proportionate taxing power that mirrors the Association's stock assessment scheme or through bonds secured by liens on the real property within the District, though the bonds can simultaneously be secured by District revenues.

This lawsuit was brought by a class of registered voters who live within the geographic boundaries of the District, and who own either no land or less than an acre of land within the District. The complaint alleged that the District enjoys such governmental powers as the power to condemn land, to sell tax-exempt bonds, and to levy taxes on real property. It also alleged that because the District sells electricity to virtually half the population of Arizona, and because, through its water operations, it can exercise significant influence on flood control and environmental management within its boundaries, the District's policies and actions have a substantial effect on all people who live within the District, regardless of property ownership. Seeking declaratory and injunctive relief, the respondents claimed that the acreage-based scheme for electing directors of the District violates the Equal Protection Clause of the Fourteenth Amendment. * * *

Reynolds v. Sims held that the Equal Protection Clause requires adherence to the principle of one-person-one-vote in elections of state legislators. *Avery v. Midland County,* 390 U.S. 474, 88 S.Ct. 1114, 20 L.Ed.2d 45, extended the *Reynolds* rule to the election of officials of a county government, holding that the elected officials exercised "general governmental powers over the entire geographic area served by the body." The Court, however, reserved any decision on the application of *Reynolds* to "a special purpose unit of government assigned the performance of functions affecting definable groups of constituents more than other constituents." In *Hadley v. Junior College District,* 397 U.S. 50,

90 S.Ct. 791, 25 L.Ed.2d 45, the Court extended *Reynolds* to the election of trustees of a community college district because those trustees "exercised general governmental powers" and "performed important governmental functions" that had significant effect on all citizens residing within the district. But in that case the Court stated: "It is of course possible that there might be some case in which a State elects certain functionaries whose duties are so far removed from normal governmental activities and so disproportionately affect different groups that a popular election in compliance with *Reynolds* * * * might not be required * * *." *Id.,* at 56, 90 S.Ct., at 795.

The Court found such a case in *Salyer*. The Tulare Lake Basin water district involved there encompassed 193,000 acres, 85% of which were farmed by one or another of four corporations. *Salyer Land Co. v. Tulare Lake Basin Water Storage District,* 410 U.S. [719], at 723, 93 S.Ct. [1224], at 1227. Under California law, public water districts could acquire, store, conserve, and distribute water, and though the Tulare Lake Basin district had never chosen to do so, could generate and sell any form of power it saw fit to support its water operations. The costs of the project were assessed against each landowner according to the water benefits the landowner received. At issue in the case was the constitutionality of the scheme for electing the directors of the district, under which only landowners could vote, and voting power was apportioned according to the assessed valuation of the voting landowner's property. The Court recognized that the Tulare Lake Basin district did exercise "some typical governmental powers," including the power to hire and fire workers, contract for construction of projects, condemn private property, and issue general obligation bonds. Nevertheless, the Court concluded that the district had "relatively limited authority," because "its primary purpose, indeed the reason for its existence, is to provide for the acquisition, storage, and distribution of water for farming in the Tulare Lake Basin." The Court also noted that the financial burdens of the district could not but fall on the landowners, in proportion to the benefits they received from the district, and that the district's actions therefore disproportionately affected the voting landowners. The *Salyer* Court thus held that the strictures of *Reynolds* did not apply to the Tulare district, and proceeded to inquire simply whether the statutory voting scheme based on land valuation at least bore some relevancy to the statute's objectives. The Court concluded that the California legislature could have reasonably assumed that without voting power apportioned according to the value of their land, the landowners might not have been willing to subject their lands to the lien of the very assessments which made the creation of the district possible.

As noted by the Court of Appeals, the services currently provided by the Salt River District are more diverse and affect far more people than those of the Tulare Lake Basin District. Whereas the Tulare district included an area entirely devoted to agriculture and populated by only 77 persons, the Salt River District includes almost half the population of the State, including large parts of Phoenix and other cities. Moreover, the Salt River District, unlike the Tulare District, has exercised its statutory power to generate and sell electric power, and has become one of the largest suppliers of such power in the State. Further, whereas all the water delivered by the Tulare Lake Basin District went for agriculture, roughly 40% of the water delivered by the Salt River district goes to urban areas or is used for nonagricultural purposes in farming areas. Finally whereas all operating costs of the Tulare District were borne by the voting landowners through assessments apportioned according to land value, most of the capital and operating costs of the Salt River District have been met through the revenues generated by the selling of electric power. Nevertheless, a careful examination of the Salt River District reveals that, under the principles of the *Avery, Hadley,* and *Salyer* cases, these distinctions do not amount to a constitutional difference.

First, the District simply does not exercise the sort of governmental powers that invoke the strict demands of *Reynolds*. The District cannot impose ad valorem property taxes or sales taxes. It cannot enact any laws governing the conduct of citizens, nor does it administer such normal functions of government as the maintenance of streets, the operation of schools, or sanitation, health, or welfare services.

Second, though they were characterized broadly by the Court of Appeals, even the District's water functions, which comprise the primary and originating purpose of the District, are relatively narrow. The District and Association do not own, sell, or buy water, nor do they control the use of any water they have delivered. The District simply stores water behind its dams, conserves it from loss, and delivers it through project canals. It is true, as the Court of Appeals noted, that as much as 40% of the water delivered by the District goes for nonagricultural purposes. But the distinction between agricultural and urban land is of no special constitutional significance in this context. The constitutionally relevant fact is that all water delivered by the Salt River District, like the water delivered by the Tulare Lake Basin district, is distributed according to land ownership, and the District does not and cannot control the use to which the landowners who are entitled to the water choose to put it. As repeatedly recognized by the Arizona courts, though the state legislature has allowed water districts to become nominal public entities in order to obtain inexpensive bond financing, the districts remain essentially business enterprises, created by and chiefly benefiting a specific group of landowners. As in *Salyer,* the nominal public character of such an entity cannot transform it into the type of governmental body for which the Fourteenth Amendment demands a one-person-one-vote system of election.

Finally, neither the existence nor size of the District's power business affects the legality of its property-based voting scheme. As this Court has noted in a different context, the provision of electricity is not a traditional element of governmental sovereignty, *Jackson v. Metropolitan Edison Co.,* 419 U.S. 345, 353, 95 S.Ct. 449, 454, 42 L.Ed.2d 477, and so is not in itself the sort of general or important governmental function that would make the government provider subject to the doctrine of the *Reynolds* case. In any event, since the electric power functions were stipulated to be incidental to the water functions which are the District's primary purpose, they cannot change the character of that enterprise. The Arizona Legislature permitted the District to generate and sell electricity to subsidize the water operations which were the beneficiaries intended by the statute. A key part of the *Salyer* decision was that the voting scheme for a public entity like a water district may constitutionally reflect the narrow primary purpose for which the District is created. In this case, the parties have stipulated that the primary legislative purpose of the District is to store, conserve, and deliver water for use by District landowners, that the sole legislative reason for making water projects public entities was to enable them to raise revenue through interest-free bonds, and that the development and sale of electric power was undertaken not for the primary purpose of providing electricity to the public, but "to support the primary irrigation functions by supplying power for reclamation uses and by providing revenues which could be applied to increase the amount and reduce the cost of water to Association subscribed lands."

The appellees claim, and the Court of Appeals agreed, that the sheer size of the power operations and the great number of people they affect serve to transform the District into an entity of general governmental power. But no matter how great the number of nonvoting residents buying electricity from the District, the relationship between them and the District's power operations is essentially that between consumers and a business enterprise from which they buy. Nothing in the *Avery, Hadley,* or *Salyer* cases suggests that the volume of business or the breadth of economic effect of a venture undertaken by a government entity as an incident of its narrow and primary governmental public function can, of its own weight, subject the entity to the one-person-one-vote requirements of the *Reynolds* case.

The functions of the Salt River District are therefore of the narrow, special sort which justifies a departure from the popular election requirement of the *Reynolds* case. And as in *Salyer,* an aspect of that limited purpose is the disproportionate relationship the District's functions bear to the specific class of people whom the system makes eligible to vote. The voting landowners are the only residents of the District whose lands are subject to liens to secure District bonds. Only these landowners are subject to the acreage-based taxing power of the District, and voting landowners are the only residents who have ever committed capital to the District through stock assessments charged by the Association. The *Salyer* opinion did not say that the selected class of voters for a special public entity must be the only parties at all affected by the operations of the entity, or that their entire economic well-being must depend on that entity. Rather, the question was whether the effect of the entity's operations on them was disproportionately greater than the effect on those seeking the vote.

As in the *Salyer* case, we conclude that the voting scheme for the District is constitutional because it bears a reasonable relationship to its statutory objectives. Here, according to the stipulation of the parties, the subscriptions of land which made the Association and then the District possible might well have never occurred had not the subscribing landowners been assured a special voice in the conduct of the District's business. Therefore, as in *Salyer,* the State could rationally limit the vote to landowners. Moreover, Arizona could rationally make the weight of their vote dependent upon the number of acres they own, since that number reasonably reflects the relative risks they incurred as landowners and the distribution of the benefits and the burdens of the District's water operations. * * *

JUSTICE WHITE, with whom JUSTICE BRENNAN, JUSTICE MARSHALL, and JUSTICE BLACKMUN join, dissenting. * * *

The District involved here clearly exercises substantial governmental powers. The District is a municipal corporation organized under the laws of Arizona and is not, in any sense of the word, a private corporation. Pursuant to the Arizona Constitution, such districts are "political subdivisions of the State, and vested with all the rights, privileges and benefits, and entitled to the immunities and exemptions granted municipalities and political subdivisions under this Constitution or any law of the State or of the United States." Under the relevant statute controlling agricultural improvement districts, the District is "a public, political, taxing subdivision of the state, and a municipal corporation to the extent of the powers and privileges conferred by this chapter or granted generally to municipal corporations by the constitution and statutes of the state, including immunity of its property and bonds from taxation." The District's bonds are tax exempt, and its property is not subject to state or local property taxation. This attribute clearly indicates the governmental nature of the District's function. The District also has the power of eminent domain, a matter of some import. The District has also been given the power to enter into a wide range of contractual arrangements to secure energy sources. Inherent in this authorization is the power to control the use and source of energy generated by the District, including the possible use of nuclear power. Obviously, this broad authorization over the field of energy transcends the limited functions of the agricultural water storage district involved in *Salyer.*

The District here also has authority to allocate water within its service area. It has veto power over all transfers of surface water from one place or type of use to another, and this power extends to any "watershed or drainage area which supplies or contributes water for the irrigation of lands within [the] district. * * *" 45 Ariz.Rev.Stat.Ann. § 172.5 (Supp.1980).

Like most "private" utilities, which are often "natural monopolies," private utilities in Arizona are subject to regulation by public authority. The Arizona Corporation Commission is empowered to prescribe "just and reasonable rates" as well as to regulate other aspects of the business operations of private utilities. The rate structure of the District now before us, however, is not subject to control by another state agency because the District is a municipal corporation and itself purports to perform the public function of protecting the public interest that the Corporation Commission would otherwise perform. Its power to set its own rates and other conditions of service constitutes important attributes of sovereignty. When combined with a consideration of the District's wide-ranging operations which encompass water for agricultural and personal uses, and electrical generation for the needs of hundreds of thousands of customers, it is clear that the District exercises broad governmental power. With respect to energy management and the provision of water and electricity, the District's power is immense and authority complete.

It is not relevant that the District does not do more—what is detailed above is substantially more than that involved in the water storage district in *Salyer,* and certainly enough to trigger application of the strict standard of the Fourteenth Amendment under our prior cases. Previous cases have expressly upheld application of the strict requirements of the Fourteenth Amendment in situations where somewhat limited functions were involved. *Salyer* itself suggested that it would be a different case if a water district like the one involved in that case generated and sold electricity. In concluding that the Tulare District did not exercise normal governmental authority, the court specifically noted that the District provided "no other general public services such as schools, housing, transportation, *utilities,* roads, or anything else of the type ordinarily financed by a municipal body." 410 U.S., at 728–729, 93 S.Ct., at 1230 (emphasis supplied). In *Cipriano,* we held that a bond election which concerned only a city's provision of utilities involved a sufficiently broad governmental function. In *Kramer,* the Court noted that the "need for close judicial examination" did not change "because the district meetings and the school board do not have 'general' legislative powers. Our exacting examination is not necessitated by the subject of the election; rather, it is required because some resident citizens are permitted to participate and some are not." In *Hadley v. Junior College District,* 397 U.S. 50, 90 S.Ct. 791, 25 L.Ed.2d 45 (1970), the Court applied *Kramer* despite the fact that the powers exercised by the trustees of a junior college district were substantially less significant than those exercised in *Avery v. Midland County,* 390 U.S. 474, 88 S.Ct. 1114, 20 L.Ed.2d 45 (1969). It was sufficient that the trustees performed important governmental functions with sufficient impact throughout the District.

I therefore cannot agree that this line of cases is not applicable here. The authority and power of the District are sufficient to require application of the strict scrutiny required by our cases. This is not a single purpose water irrigation district, but a large and vital municipal corporation exercising a broad range of initiatives across a spectrum of operations. Moreover, by the nature of the state law, it is presently exercising that authority without direct regulation by state authorities charged with supervising privately owned corporations involved in the same business. The functions and purposes of the Salt River District represent important governmental responsibilities that distinguish this case from *Salyer.*

In terms of the relative impact of the Salt River District's operations on the favored landowner voters and those who may not vote for the officers of this municipal corporation, the contrast with the water district in *Salyer* is even more pronounced. * * *

With these facts in mind, it is indeed curious that the Court would attempt to characterize the District's electrical operations as "incidental" to its water operations, or would consider the power operations to be irrelevant to the legality of the voting scheme. The facts are that in *Salyer* the burdens of the water district fell entirely on the landowners who were served by the District. Here the landowners could not themselves afford to finance their own project and turned to a public agency to help them. That agency now subsidizes the storage and delivery of irrigation water for agricultural purposes by selling electricity to the public at prices that neither the voters nor any representative public agency has any right to control. Unlike the situation in *Salyer,* the financial burden of supplying irrigation water has been shifted from the landowners to the consumers of electricity. At the very least, the structure of the District's indebtedness together with the history of the District's operations compels a finding that the burdens placed upon the lands within the District are so minimal that they cannot possibly serve as a basis for limiting the franchise to property owners.

It is apparent in this case that landowning irrigators are getting a free ride at the expense of the users of electricity. It would also seem apparent that except for the subsidy, utility rates would be lower. Of course, subsidizing agricultural operations may well be in the public interest in Arizona, but it does not follow that the amount of the subsidy and the manner in which it is provided should be totally in the hands of a selected few.

To conclude that the effect of the District's operations in this case is substantially akin to that in *Salyer* ignores reality. As recognized in *Salyer,* there were "no towns, shops, hospitals, or other facilities designed to improve the quality of life within the district boundaries, and it does not have a fire department, police, buses, or trains." In short, there was nothing in the water storage district for its operations to effect except the land itself. The relationship between the burdens of the District and the land within the District's boundaries was strong. Here, the District encompasses one of the major metropolitan areas in the country. The effects of the provision of water and electricity on the citizens of the city are as major as they are obvious. There is no strong relationship between the District's operation and the land *qua* land. The District's revenues and bonds are tied directly to the electrical operation. Any encumbrance on the land is at best speculative. Certainly, any direct impact on the land is no greater than in *Phoenix* where we rejected the same argument presented today. Simply put, the District is an integral governmental actor providing important governmental services to residents of the District. To conclude otherwise is to ignore the urban reality of the District's operations.

Underlying the Court's conclusion in this case is the view that the provision of electricity and water is essentially a private enterprise and not sufficiently governmental—that the District "simply does not exercise the sort of governmental powers that invoke the strict demands" of the Fourteenth Amendment because it does not administer "such normal functions of government as the maintenance of streets, the operation of schools, or sanitation, health, or welfare services." This is a distinctly odd view of the reach of municipal services in this day and age. Supplying water for domestic and industrial uses is almost everywhere the responsibility of local government, and this function is intimately connected with sanitation and health. Nor is it any more accurate to consider the supplying of electricity as essentially a private function. The United States Government and its agencies generate and sell substantial amounts of power; and in view of the widespread existence of municipal utility systems, it is facetious to suggest that the operation of such utility systems should be considered as an incidental aspect of municipal government. Nor will it do, it seems to me, to return to the proprietary-governmental dichotomy in order to deliver into wholly private hands the control of a major municipal activity which acts to subsidize a limited number of landowners.

In *Indian Towing Co. v. United States,* 350 U.S. 61, 67–68, 76 S.Ct. 122, 125–126, 100 L.Ed. 48 (1955), the Court remarked:

> " 'Government is not partly public or partly private, depending upon the governmental pedigree of the type of a particular activity or the manner in which the Government conducts it.' *Federal Crop Insurance Corp. v. Merrill,* 332 U.S. 380, 383–384, 68 S.Ct. 1, 2–3, 92 L.Ed. 10. On the other hand, it is hard to think of any governmental activity on the 'operational level,' our present concern, which is 'uniquely governmental,' in the sense that its kind has not at one time or another been, or could not conceivably be, privately performed."

In *Lafayette v. Louisiana Power & Light Co.,* 435 U.S. 389, 98 S.Ct. 1123, 55 L.Ed.2d 364 (1978), Justice Stewart, after quoting the above passage from *Indian Towing Co.,* described the distinction between "proprietary" and "governmental" activities as a "quagmire" involving a distinction " 'so finespun and capricious as to be almost incapable of being held in the mind for adequate formulation.' " 435 U.S., at 433, 98 S.Ct., at 1147 (Stewart, J., dissenting) (quoting *Indian Towing Co.,* 350 U.S., at 65–68, 76 S.Ct., at 124–126). Justice Stewart went on to conclude that whether proprietary or not, the action of providing electrical utility services "is surely an act of government."

In *Salyer,* the Court nowhere suggested that the provision of water for agricultural purposes was anything but governmental action for a public purpose. The Court expressly recognized that the water district was a public entity. The question presented, in part, was whether its operations and authority were so narrow as not to require application of the *Kramer* rule. In *Cipriano,* the Court necessarily held that the provision of electrical, water, and gas utility services was a sufficiently important governmental service to require application of the Fourteenth Amendment's strict scrutiny safeguards. If the provision of electrical and other utility services by a municipal corporation was so "proprietary" or "private" as not to require application of the stricter standards of the Fourteenth Amendment, *Cipriano* could not have been decided as it was. The Court's facile characterization of the electrical service provided by the municipal corporation in this case as essentially a private function is a misreading of our prior holdings. * * *

3. REGIONAL GOVERNMENT

The excerpts by David Rusk and Kenneth Brunetti, reproduced below, introduce a third institutional structure—beyond interlocal agreements and public authorities—that might deal with problems in our metropolitan areas that cross local boundaries, namely, regional government.[1] Regional governments are less common in the United States than interlocal agreements or public authorities. Nevertheless, versions of regional government do exist, and the excerpts describe a number of them: Los Angeles County (California), Indianapolis–Marion County (Indiana), Dade County (Florida), the Twin Cities' Metropolitan Council (Minnesota), and the Metropolitan Government of Toronto (Canada). Moreover, both excerpts are advocacy pieces—they are written by people who want to expand the current (relatively modest) forms of regional government into a major new type of local government organization. The excerpts therefore provide an opportunity to consider the arguments for creating strong regional governments in America. Do the authors persuade you that regional governments are a good idea? If we created strong regional governments in our metropolitan areas, would it be accurate to describe them as exercising "decentralized" or "local" power?

DAVID RUSK, CITIES WITHOUT SUBURBS

Pp. 85, 91–95, 122–124 (1993).

Reversing the fragmentation of urban areas is an essential step in ending severe racial and economic segregation. The "city" must be redefined to reunify city and suburb. Ideally, such reunification is achieved through metropolitan government. * * * Having a metropoli-

---

1. For additional reading on regional governments, see, e.g., Gustely, The Allocational and Distributional Impacts of Governmental Consolidation: The Dade County Experience, 14 Urb.Aff.Q. 349 (1977); J. Horan & G. Taylor, Experiments in Metropolitan Government (1977); Freilich, Robards & Wilson, Home Rule for the Urban County: Observations on the New Jackson County Constitutional Charter, 39 UMKC L.Rev. 297 (1971); Note, The Urban County: A Study of New Approaches to Local Government in Metropolitan Areas, 73 Harv.L.Rev. 526 (1960).

tan government is much better than trying to get multiple local governments to act like a metropolitan government. The former is a more lasting and stable framework for sustained, long-term action. * * *

There are three different ways metropolitan governments can be created. In single-county metro areas, urban county governments can be fully empowered and municipal governments abolished; or county and municipal governments can be consolidated into new, unified governments. In multicounty metro areas, cities and existing counties can be combined into a single, regional government. Each of these three options will be discussed in turn.

Empowering urban counties. Except in New England, counties have been the basic framework of local government within which municipalities (a more intensive form of local government) come into being. Counties typically predate urban development. They are the creation of a state or territorial legislature, which initially partitioned the state or territory's land into large governing units. County jurisdictions are remarkably stable. There are today 3,042 counties in the United States; forty years ago there were 3,052 counties. (Such stability has given rise to the adage that "the legislature may create municipalities, but only God can create a county.")

County government has been the government of rural and small-town America. As urbanization occurs, municipalities are formed to control development through planning and zoning and to provide a more intensive level of local services. Generally, county government continues to be responsible countywide (including within municipalities) for certain services—the county courts (state criminal trials), county assessor (property tax assessment), county treasurer (property tax collection), county clerk (records and elections), and often a county hospital (indigent health care). In addition, counties provide public services (roads, parks, fire and police protection) to unincorporated areas of the county.

Over the decades, however, as areas have urbanized around older cities, counties have been empowered by legislatures to provide full municipal-type services to unincorporated areas. Urban county governments often rival or exceed major city governments in size and scope. Moreover, although county government is often more limited in the array of taxes it can levy, its tax base is much broader than that of municipal governments within its boundaries. (County government bond ratings are typically one full level above bond ratings of inelastic central cities located within them.)

County government, when developed to the greatest extent, becomes a major deliverer of urban services, such as the government of Los Angeles County. County government may become the dominant local unit of government, both providing services and controlling area development. Montgomery County, Maryland, is an outstanding example * * *.

The most direct—and probably most efficient—path to creating metropolitan government in the majority of metro areas is to empower urban county government, have it absorb the functions and responsibilities of all municipal governments within its boundaries, and abolish all municipalities. This is an action that is fully within the legal powers of most state legislatures even if at present such sweeping urban reorganization is beyond legislators' desires and political powers.

Consolidating cities and counties. Typically, movements to create area wide governmental units have focused on consolidating municipal governments with their surrounding county governments. In recent decades the most notable consolidations have merged the central city with single counties. Indianapolis–Marion County, Nashville–Davidson County, Jacksonville–Duval County are examples. * * *

Each city-county consolidation has been custom-made for its area. The ultimate structure represents a compromise with tradition and political realities. Traditional functions of county government may be absorbed into the new, unified government (Nashville–Davidson) or continued as independent functions while the new government assumes service-providing functions for all unincorporated areas (Indianapolis–Marion County). Bowing to political reality, certain municipal enclaves may remain (for example, the town of Speedway within Indianapolis), and rural residents may have to be reassured through creation of lower service, lower tax zones (Nashville).

Despite such compromises, city-county consolidations do initially achieve the key goals: unification of the tax base and centralization of planning and zoning authority. With the continued spread of suburbia and long-distance commuting, the long-term dilemma is that metro areas often grow beyond the consolidated boundaries of the consolidated governments. Indianapolis–Marion County, Nashville–Davidson County, and Jacksonville–Duval County were all highly successful consolidations of the 1960s. Today Indianapolis–Marion County is 59 percent of its ten-county metro area; Nashville–Davidson, 50 percent of its six-county area; and Jacksonville–Duval County, 70 percent of its five-county area. With the populations of outlying counties growing rapidly, their metropolitanization must be updated.

Combining counties into regional governments. The most significant multicounty combination is also the least remembered: the creation of New York City in 1898 * * *. Several independent local communities in what are now New York City's five boroughs were combined. For its first fifty years the consolidated result—New York City—functioned very well. Since the 1950s, however, the consequences of the White middle-class movement to the suburbs and the burgeoning low-income Black and Hispanic populations within the city have largely obscured New York City's earlier success as a consolidated, multicounty regional government. * * *

CONCLUSION AND RECOMMENDATIONS

* * * Throughout history cities have been the arena of opportunity and upward mobility. In America the "city" has been redefined since World War II. The real city is now the whole urban area—city and

suburb—the metropolitan area. Redeeming inner cities and the urban underclass requires reintegration of city and suburb.

This is the toughest political issue in American society. It goes right to the heart of Americans' fears about race and class. There will be no short-term, politically comfortable solutions.

The organization of metro areas into local governments has greatly affected the degree of racial and economic segregation. Within their expanding municipal boundaries, elastic cities have captured much of the growth of the suburbs. Elastic cities minimize city-suburb disparities, thereby lessening the separations between racial and economic groups.

Inelastic cities, in the battle over middle-class America, have lost to their suburbs. Some never even fought the good fight. Whatever the success of their downtown as regional employment centers, inelastic city neighborhoods have increasingly housed most of the metro area's poor Blacks and Hispanics.

How can responsibility for poor minorities be made a metropolitan-wide responsibility? How can all jurisdictions—city and suburb—assume a "fair share"?

Traditionally, the primary purpose of regional cooperation among local governments has been the delivery of public services. Regional arrangements usually avoid policies and programs that share the social burdens of inner-city residents. Yet this is the heart of the challenge. Areawide compacts on transportation planning, solid waste management, sewage treatment, and air quality management may be "good government," but they address the urban problem only if they attack racial and economic segregation.

For many small and medium-sized metro areas, the surest way to avoid or reverse patterns of racial and economic segregation is to create metro governments. This can be achieved by expanding the central city through aggressive annexation policies, by consolidating the city and county, or by fully empowering county government and abolishing or reducing the role of municipalities.

For larger, more complex metro areas, metro government may be neither politically feasible nor administratively desirable. Larger government is not necessarily more efficient government. At any scale, efficiency is largely a function of good management. Given the bureaucratic impulse of many large systems, metro government may be less efficient and less responsive as a deliverer of services than smaller governments.

It is not important that local residents have their garbage picked up by a metrowide garbage service or their parks managed by a metrowide parks and recreation department. It is important that all local governments pursue common policies that will diminish racial and economic segregation. The following four policies are essential:

1. "fair share" housing policies (supported by planning and zoning policies) that will encourage low- and moderate income housing in all jurisdictions;

2. fair employment and fair housing policies to ensure full access by minorities to the job and housing markets;

3. housing assistance policies to disperse low-income families to small-unit, scattered-site housing projects and to rent-subsidized private rental housing throughout a diversified metro housing market; and

4. tax-sharing arrangements that will offset tax-base disparities between the central city and its suburbs.

In baldest terms, sustained success requires moving poor people from bad city neighborhoods to good suburban neighborhoods and moving dollars from relatively wealthy suburban governments to poorer city governments. The long-term payoff will be an overall reduction in poverty, dependency, and crime areawide, and "prosperous cities [which] are the key to vital regional economies and to safe and healthy suburbs."

State government must play the leading role. Local government is the creature of state government, which sets the ground rules for local initiative and can create new local governments and merge old ones. Furthermore, governors and state legislators can and do act as metro-wide policymakers. State government also plays an increasingly important role in revenue sharing for local government. With the purse comes additional power (and responsibility) to make the organization of metro areas more rational and equitable.

State government must act. It must

1. improve annexation laws to facilitate continuous central city expansion into urbanizing areas;

2. enact laws to encourage city-county consolidation through local initiative or to reorganize local government by direct state statute;

3. empower county governments with all municipal powers so that they can act as de facto metro governments, where appropriate;

4. require all local governments in metro areas to have "fair share" affordable housing laws; and

5. establish metro wide tax-sharing arrangements for local governments or utilize state aid as a revenue-equalizing mechanism.

As I stated earlier, reorganizing local government is primarily a task for initiative and hard work at the state and local levels. There are key roles, however, for the federal government. Since World War II the federal government's "urban policy" has been "suburban policy." It is past time for the federal government to deal with the consequences of its handiwork in terms of helping bridge the city-suburb gap. * * *

KENNETH BRUNETTI, IT'S TIME TO CREATE A BAY AREA REGIONAL GOVERNMENT

42 Hastings L.J. 1103, 1124–1133 (1991).

TYPES OF METROPOLITAN GOVERNMENT

Although regional government rarely has been implemented in the United States, it has been studied thoroughly and scholars have developed several basic models for regional government. The one-government approach involves consolidating all the smaller government entities in an area into one large supergovernment. The "two-tier" approach retains local governments to handle local matters but creates a secondary government to handle matters of regional concern. Two examples of a two-tier approach are the "urban county," in which some powers are transferred to the county level, and the "federation," in which a new metropolitan government is created with powers to address regional matters and municipal governments retain control over local matters. A third type of metropolitan government is the regional umbrella agency which creates a regional plan of development and then coordinates the different single-power special districts in the area to ensure compliance with the plan. This type of agency usually will have indirect powers, such as the power to veto any major development projects or the power to block state or federal funds to the special purpose agencies. * * *

There are basically three ways to establish a single government for a metropolitan area: annexation of unincorporated land to form a larger city, consolidation of two or more cities to create a larger city, or consolidation of all the cities in a county into a city-county government. None of these alternatives is a realistic possibility for the [San Francisco] Bay Area, which encompasses ninety-eight municipalities and nine counties. To form a single government for the Bay Area, all nine counties and all ninety-eight municipalities would have to consolidate into one Bay Area city-county supergovernment. The California Constitution would require a popular vote at both the county and city levels, meaning that the measure would have to be passed in 107 separate elections. It is unlikely that the measure would pass in a single one of these elections; the chance of it passing in all 107 is virtually nonexistent. Furthermore, such a supergovernment would be too large to be effective. * * *

In an urban county the county government takes on matters of regional concern and the municipal governments retain their autonomy, exercising control over local issues. In essence, the urban county is the same as a federation, explained below, except that the urban county does not require the creation of a new government. This type of regional government is politically much easier to establish; the county simply authorizes amendment of its charter to allow the transfer of certain powers from the municipal governments to the county government. The urban county would be completely ineffective, however, in a metropolitan region that extends beyond the boundaries of a single county, as is the case in the Bay Area.

One example of an urban county government in the United States can be found in metropolitan Miami, Florida. In 1957 the voters of Dade County, in which the entire Metropolitan Statistical Area of Miami was located, passed a new county charter transferring many of the powers of the twenty-six existing municipalities to a new county government. The county government took charge of expressways, public transportation (including airports), traffic control, air pollution control, construction of an integrated water and sewer system, and regulation of building codes in unincorporated areas; the municipalities retained control of local services not specifically transferred over to the County government. The Dade County Metropolitan Government has had its share of hurdles, but it generally has been considered successful in addressing many of the regional problems of that area. Although such a government is not a possibility in the Bay Area, it demonstrates how a regional government successfully can address regional problems. * * *

A federation essentially is no different than an urban county except that a new layer of government is created to assume control of matters of regional concern. Numerous attempts to create federation-type regional governments in United States cities have failed to pass in referendum votes. A good example of a metropolitan federation is found in Toronto, Ontario. In 1953 the Ontario Legislature passed a bill creating a metropolitan federation government for the Toronto metropolitan area. The federation then consisted of thirteen municipalities: Toronto and twelve suburban municipalities. In 1967 the federation act was amended to consolidate the thirteen municipalities into Toronto and five boroughs.

Because "home rule traditions are not nearly as strong in Canada as they are in United States," and also because there was no requirement of a popular vote, the Ontario Provincial Government did not give the people of metropolitan Toronto an opportunity to vote on the creation of a regional government. In fact, in 1967 the Provincial Government even rearranged city lines and eliminated certain smaller cities without a popular vote. Thus, one of the main reasons for the successful implementation of Toronto's federation government is that it was created without the referendum process, something that has foiled many attempts at government reorganization in the United States.

When it was first created, the Metropolitan Government of Toronto (Metro) consisted of an executive council composed of twelve members from Toronto, one member from each of the twelve suburbs, and an independent chairperson to be elected by the council. Membership on the executive council since has increased to forty, with a much higher number representing the boroughs.

Initially, Metro's power was limited. Its major responsibility was borrowing money to finance the construction of a sewer system for the suburbs, new expressways, sidewalks, and schools. Eventually, Metro began taking over more and more regional responsibilities, including development and operation of a unified transportation system, provision of water for the entire region, disposal of solid waste, operation of a metropolitan police force, operation of emergency services, housing for the elderly, developmental control, and operation of regional parks.

Metro has been widely regarded as a great success. By the mid-seventies Metro had developed an integrated system of highways and public transportation, including subways, streetcars, and buses. Its handling of sewage and water supply problems has been even more impressive. Before Metro existed, Toronto's water supply was very limited and demand was increasing rapidly as the region continued to grow. Raw sewage was being dumped into rivers because the few treatment plants in the region could not handle the increased amount of sewage. With its financial clout Metro was able to undertake the massive project of building reservoirs, water purification plants, and sewage treatment plants. Within a few years metropolitan Toronto had more than enough available water and a complete sewage treatment system able to handle the area's rapid growth over the past three decades.

Metro also consolidated solid waste disposal operations in the region beginning in 1966. Before 1966 each municipality disposed of its own solid waste. This was not a significant problem because there was ample open space on which to deposit the waste. As the population grew, however, available dump sites began filling up and land for disposal sites no longer was available. When Metro took control of operations, it located large disposal sites far beyond its geographical limits. As people began moving near these sites, Metro located disposal sites further and further away from the Metro limits. Solid waste disposal always will be a problem because people do not like living near garbage dumping sites. With its greater financial resources, however, Metro was able to purchase bigger disposal sites, located beyond its boundaries, and to operate several incinerators.

Metro also has authority to plan residential subdivisions and large developments. Metro is required to submit plans for the region to the Ontario Provincial Government. As soon as these plans are accepted by the Provincial Government, they become binding and Metro may enforce them. This authority enables Metro to control urban sprawl. Rather than allowing municipalities to build huge subdivisions or office parks at their own discretion, Metro has planned for certain large suburban office developments and has provided the transportation necessary to serve these developments. Metro also has been able to plan for dense housing and office development in the city of Toronto, allowing more people to walk to work or take public transportation. Although Metro has had problems, overall it provides and excellent example of how a regional federation government can succeed in a large metropolitan area. * * *

The regional umbrella agency is not so much a government as it is a planning agency and coordinating body with limited powers to enforce its regional plan. The best example of this type of regional body is found in the Minneapolis–St. Paul metropolitan area (Twin Cities), which encompasses seven counties and close to 200 municipalities. The Minnesota Legislature created a Metropolitan Council (Metro Council) in 1967. Like Toronto's Metro government, Metro Council was not put to a referendum vote.

Metro Council has three basic functions: to review all metropolitan plans and projects of municipalities and special districts, and to suspend any project that it finds not in compliance with its development guidelines; to review and comment on any long-term municipal comprehensive plans that will have a substantial effect on metropolitan area development; and to review applications of local governments for federal grants, and to reject an application if Metro Council does not approve of the project.

The main purpose of Metro Council is to plan for the region and to oversee other agencies, cities, and counties, which implement actual operations. Examples of agencies that operate under Metro Council are a waste control commission, a unified transit commission, and an airport commission. Metro Council does not have the authority to create any operating agencies; all operating agencies are created by the Minnesota Legislature.

Perhaps the most important element of Metro Council's success is a fiscal disparities law, which reduces competition between municipalities for new development. The law requires every municipality to contribute forty percent of its commercial-industrial tax base growth since 1971 into a common pool that then is redistributed to every municipality in the region according to its population and overall tax base. This law enables Metro Council to implement its plan for the region by avoiding the political fighting of municipalities eager to overdevelop their communities to increase their tax bases.

Despite its progress, Metro Council has faced some difficulties. For example, Metro Council did not participate in the battle between Bloomington, the largest suburb of the Twin Cities, and Minneapolis over which city would build a new stadium. The Minnesota Legislature bypassed Metro Council and appointed a sports commission to decide where the new stadium should be located. Thus, Metro Council had no control or input on an important regional issue. More recently, Metro Council failed to exert any control over Bloomington's plans to construct the world's largest shopping center. Minneapolis Planning Director Oliver Byrum criticized Metro Council for failing "to look at the socioeconomic impacts or the long-range impacts on transportation. It's treating one of the largest development proposals in the area's history as a question of whether we do or don't need another freeway interchange."

Byrum believes that a massive shopping center in the suburbs will undermine the vitality of the two downtowns in the Twin Cities and is inconsistent with the long-term plans of Metro Council for the region. Exactly why Metro Council was not more involved in the decision to build the Bloomington shopping center is unclear. Although Metro

Council technically has the power to veto large development projects, it often appears reluctant to do so.

Overall, however, Metro Council is considered successful. With the help of the waste control commission, Metro Council established an efficient sewage network throughout the entire metropolitan area. Also, despite some disagreement between Metro Council and its subsidiary transit commission, they have implemented an effective regional bus system and now are planning construction of a light rail line. The Council also has taken control of selecting sites for dumping the region's solid waste and sewage. Like the Miami urban county government and the federation government of Toronto, the regional umbrella agency of the Twin Cities demonstrates how regional government can succeed.

WHAT TYPE OF REGIONAL GOVERNMENT SHOULD THE BAY AREA ADOPT?

After eliminating the supergovernment—which is neither desirable nor feasible—and the urban county—which though desirable, is not a realistic possibility for the nine-county Bay Area—two alternatives remain: the federation government and the umbrella agency models. The umbrella agency is easier to establish because it leaves intact many existing agencies and simply requires the formation of a new agency with limited powers over the other agencies. An umbrella agency will not be successful, however, if the number of competing subsidiary agencies is too large.

The Twin Cities Metro Council is successful because it deals with one agency for each problem area; there is only one waste control commission, one transportation commission, and one airport commission. These agencies do not compete against each other since they serve different functions; competition between municipalities is limited due to the shared tax pool. Yet Metro Council still faces some political fighting with these agencies as well as with municipalities. In the Bay Area an umbrella agency could not be successful if it had to deal with twenty-three transportation districts, three major airports, and a multitude of water districts, sewer districts, park districts, and other special purpose agencies.

The California Legislature would have to consolidate the many different agencies of the Bay Area into a few large agencies for an umbrella agency to succeed. In addition, legislation would be needed to form some type of tax-sharing pool, like that of the Twin Cities. The umbrella agency thus could carry out its plan without municipalities competing for tax revenues. The necessity of this legislation complicates its normally relatively simple creation, eliminating the main advantage of an umbrella agency. The federation government then becomes a more attractive alternative because it is more powerful and more efficient.

The California Legislature should adopt a limited federation regional government for the Bay Area. The new government could be modeled after Toronto's Metro government, which has been successful for the most part. Each large special district of the Bay Area, including trans-portation districts, water districts, sewage districts, and waste disposal districts, would be consolidated into departments of the new metropoli-tan government. All cities and counties in the Bay Area would retain their autonomy and continue governing matters of local concern. Since neither the city nor the county status would change, a popular election would not be required.

The new metropolitan government would be responsible for all matters of regional concern, including water supply, transportation, sewage and waste disposal, airport and seaport development, Bay conser-vation, and large-scale land use development. The experience in Toron-to has shown that a regional, federation government on this scale can work.

The Bay Area is certainly far more complex now than metropolitan Toronto was when Metro was formed in 1953. Toronto then was in the beginning stages of metropolization, whereas the Bay Area already has experienced years of urban growth. Toronto was the central city and only twelve other municipalities were in the region, whereas the Bay Area has three central cities and a total of ninety-eight municipalities. The Bay Area also has an established, though piecemeal, infrastructure, whereas Toronto had the luxury of planning its development when there was little established infrastructure.

Still, there is a strong need to take regional control of these problems before they become considerably worse. The Bay Area already has more than six million people and can be expected to absorb more than one million more by the year 2000. This will require more water, disposal of more sewage and waste, and an extensive overhaul of the region's public transportation system. A regional entity would tackle most efficiently these concerns. * * *

4. BEYOND REGIONAL GOVERNMENT

Are there ways of organizing our metropolitan areas other than through interlocal agreements, public authorities or regional govern-ment? In the excerpt reproduced below, I suggest that there are. But in order to consider such alternatives, we need to discard two basic ideas on which much of this chapter has been built: the meaningfulness of the city/suburb distinction in contemporary America and the policy of mak-ing residence the critical test for locating people in our metropolitan areas. The excerpt begins with a critique of these two basic ideas; the alternative forms of metropolitan organization I describe are based on this critique. In my view, we need to create a form of metropolitan organization that allows us to introduce regional thinking into local decisionmaking without abandoning the locality (that is, the city or the neighborhood) as the locus of decisionmaking. Do my proposals accom-plish this goal? Are there other ways of doing so?

GERALD FRUG, DECENTERING DECENTRALIZATION

60 U.Chi. L. Rev. 253, 295–297, 313–334 (1993).

The city/suburb distinction is often used to contrast two images: a congested, dangerous, deteriorating inner city and a quiet, prosperous residential suburb. Such a picture misrepresents life in contemporary American metropolitan areas. Parts of America's cities are certainly characterized by congestion, poverty and urban decay, but so are many suburbs. Indeed, these suburbs are often worse off than inner cities because their property values are so low that they cannot afford even the limited social services that cities offer their poorest residents. Similarly, if we think of a suburb as a homogeneous residential area dominated by well-kept single family houses set in yards, "almost all large cities," as Robert Fishman has noted, "have suburbs * * * within their borders." These residential areas within cities (Riverdale in New York, West Roxbury in Boston, Chestnut Hill in Philadelphia, Chevy Chase D.C. in Washington, Sauganash in Chicago, Palmer Woods in Detroit, River Oaks in Houston, Sea Cliff in San Francisco) are indistinguishable from neighborhoods on the other side of the city line. Moreover, people of color live in both kinds of neighborhoods. One-third of African Americans live in middle class suburbs; in some suburbs a majority of residents are African Americans, Chinese, or Latino. To be sure, lines of race divide American metropolitan areas as sharply as the Berlin Wall formerly divided Berlin and the green line divided Beirut. But these racial lines are more often found within cities and between suburbs than along the city/suburb boundary (96th Street and Howard Beach in New York, South Side and Bridgeport in Chicago, Roxbury and South Boston in Boston, Compton/Watts and the Westside in Los Angeles). Finally, it's not just the middle-class and the underclass who live on both sides of the border: there are working class suburbs just as there are working class neighborhoods within cities.

The other characteristic that has traditionally been associated with cities—a central business district with offices and stores—similarly describes suburbs as well as cities. "Most large metropolitan areas have ten to thirty urban cores, the downtown being just one of them." Two thirds of American offices are currently located outside of city downtowns. Tyson's Corner, Virginia has more office space than downtown Miami; Southfield, Michigan has more office space than Detroit. "By 1980, 38 percent of the nation's workers commuted to their jobs from suburb-to-suburb, while only half as many made the stereotypical suburb to city trek." Moreover, shopping malls have not only brought the density and feel of city commercial life to the suburbs but suburban stores now outsell their city competitors. Some of these suburban malls are as big as city downtowns. (On Route 202 in King of Prussia (Pennsylvania), the sign reads: MALL NEXT FOUR LEFTS.) The aggregation of restaurants, entertainment, shopping, and pedestrian walkways in suburban shopping malls has, in fact, so captured the image of America's commercial life that cities have begun to restructure their own commercial areas by copying them (Quincy Market in Boston; the Inner Harbor in Baltimore; Watertown Place in Chicago; the Skyways in Minneapolis; Ghiradelli Square in San Francisco; pedestrian zones everywhere).

In sum, in the words of the urban historian James Vance, "today it is hard to draw a significant concrete distinction between a Clayton and a St. Louis." Except, of course, most of us have never heard of Clayton. The only difference between St. Louis and Clayton is a legal distinction—local government law treats these two parts of the same region as separate and independent sovereignties. Indeed, during the course of my argument that the city/suburb distinction no longer describes American metropolitan areas, I have repeatedly invoked this legal distinction myself. I have used the words "city" and "suburb" to refer to one side or the other of the invisible line that marks the legally-recognized boundary between them. My use of these terms has masked the plurality and heterogeneity on both sides of the line. * * * To promote an alternative to this * * * [imagery], we must start by recognizing the arbitrariness of the city/suburb lines that now fracture America's metropolitan areas. We must look at our metropolitan areas anew, without focusing on the legally recognized borders between localities.

Most Americans who live in America's metropolitan areas already disregard these jurisdictional boundaries. Instead of sharply dividing city and suburb, residents create their own idea of the region in which they live by organizing it in terms of the places they know. They think nothing of crossing city lines for child care, work, shopping, recreation, entertainment, visiting friends, and the like. Their relevant space "is defined by the locations they can conveniently reach in their cars." They often don't even know the names of the towns where the mall they shop in is located; all they need to know is the name of the mall. Areas that do have names are commonly identified in a way that ignores local government boundaries: Route 128 in Massachusetts, Silicon Valley in Northern California, King of Prussia in Eastern Pennsylvania, the Galleria in Houston, Tyson's Corner in Virginia. Other areas both in the city and the suburbs—even some close by—are so unfamiliar that people get lost if they try to go there. The metropolitan area as a whole is a hodgepodge of elements—shopping/office/hotel complexes, strip shopping malls, industrial parks, office buildings, department stores, neighborhoods, subdivisions, condominium communities—that is "impossible to comprehend", "vertigo-inducing". For many Americans the symbol of this contemporary form of metropolis is Los Angeles. And, as Joel Garreau reports, "every single American city that is growing, is growing in the fashion of Los Angeles, with multiple urban cores."

This reference to Los Angeles suggests more than simply the absence of a metropolitan center. Los Angeles symbolizes another feature of contemporary urban life as well: issues of ethnicity, race and class cross-cut America's metropolitan areas without stopping at jurisdictional borders. Los Angeles has aptly been labeled the capital of the third world: immigrants from El Salvador, Guatemala, Mexico, the Philippines, Korea, Thailand, Vietnam, Iran, India, Pakistan, Armenia, Russia, and Israel (among other places) have formed communities in the area in both the city and the suburbs. Similar communities are being created across America. This influx of immigrants has not merely changed the character of the neighborhoods where the immigrants reside. As in Los Angeles, many immigrants do business in the region's poorest neighborhoods (Korean and Latino stores in African American neighborhoods); others work in minimum-wage jobs in the area's shopping/office/hotel complexes; others still spend most of their time in the region's fanciest neighborhoods because they have come to serve as the indispensable maids and babysitters for the upper-middle class. Los Angeles is also famous these days as the site of recent riots and of gang warfare in its South Central neighborhood. Fears of this kind of urban unrest and gang violence have increased throughout the country, and the proximity between the neighborhoods where the civil unrest and violence have occurred (or threaten to occur) and other neighborhoods has increased with the extent of this fear. Neighborhoods close by were once virtually forgotten ("no one lives in Detroit," someone who lived in a nearby suburb once informed me); now, they seem all too close.

As early as 1923, Frank Lloyd Wright declared that "the big city is no longer modern." He was right: as Garreau points out, "we have not built a single old-style downtown from raw dirt in seventy-five years." It's harder to realize—but it is also true—that the suburban era, the era of lawns and cul-de-sacs, has reached its end as well. Now, as Michael Sorkin argues, people live in "a wholly new kind of city, a city without a place attached to it," one that Sorkin calls the "ageographical city." Sorkin uses the term to describe the pastiche of highways, skyscrapers, malls, housing developments, and chain stores—the endless urban landscape of copies without an original—that constitute the place-bites (the spatial equivalent of sound-bites) of modern America. These place-bites can be combined in an infinite variety of ways, each of which makes equal sense, to represent the metropolitan area. The ageographical city, Sorkin suggests, is the urban form of the 800–number: the area code for no-place-in-particular. * * *

Local government law, however, now gives priority to a single place-bite within the metropolitan area: the place where people live. Indeed, residency has always been at the center of local government law's conception of people's relationship to the space around them. Perhaps this emphasis on residency was justifiable when, once upon a time, home, work, family, friends, market, past, present, and future, were (so we imagine) linked together in one community. But these days some people don't even live at their place of residence: students who spend full-time out-of-state, people who are serving in the military, and business-people who are assigned abroad are all residents of the town they're never in. And those who do live in the area are not found solely at home. Most people spend most of their day in other parts of the region.

If the neighborhood where people work deteriorates or their mall closes down, their lives will be just as affected as it would be by an event three blocks away from their residence. In an era when people often don't even know the name of neighbors who live a block away, a person's territorial identity should not be reduced to his or her address.

By locating people in their houses or apartments, local government law romanticizes the home as a haven in a heartless world. But in contemporary America one's place of residence provides "no defense, no retreat * * * The overexposure and transparence of the world which traverses * * * [people] without obstacle" leaves only a weak sense of "home". The ageographical city is, in other words, the urban form not just of the 800–number but also of the 700–number—the telephone number that is yours regardless of where you live. The average American moves twelve times in a lifetime. I was born and went to school in Berkeley, California; I met and married my wife (who was from St. Joseph, Missouri) in Washington, D.C.; our son was born in New York City; our daughter was born in Philadelphia; most recent family vacations have been taken in the same house in Westport, Massachusetts; I now live in Cambridge, Massachusetts. Where am I from? Where are you from? Most people recognize that the millions of new immigrants in our metropolitan areas are fractured by attachments to their country of origin, their current neighborhood, the place where they work, and the place where they hope to move—feeling "at home" in none of these locations. But in the age of the jet plane, the modem, the fax machine, satellite disks, and USA Today, it's not just recent immigrants who feel more linked to areas far away than close to home. Someone in the upper-middle-class in Boston is likely to be more connected to, and know more about, mid-town Manhattan than Medford.

Of course, many people still feel an attachment to their neighborhood. Sometimes this attachment is linked with commonalities of race, ethnicity or class; sometimes it is attributed to the fact that a family has lived in the same community for generations; sometimes it is expressed in terms of maintaining property values; sometimes it is expressed as a negative—residents feel trapped, by poverty and exclusion, in an area from which they cannot escape. But local government law has never given legal protection to neighborhoods. On the contrary, recent developments in local government law have presided over the destruction of many neighborhoods to which people have felt connected. In the 1960's and 1970's, some reformers sought to re-center local government law's sense of place from the city or suburb to the neighborhood. They wanted neighborhood to play the role for territorial identity that biology has played for racial and gender identity—to be the common core that unites the group. But * * * like the reliance on biology (and like the mirror image of the self), the concept of neighborhood provides no stable basis for either personal or group identity.

The image of neighborhood conjures up the ideal of community, but it is a fantasy community—a (comm)unity that is never achievable. One can succeed in maintaining an inside/outside distinction that delimits a neighborhood only by failing to see people who are there but do not fit in. Property owners who own property in the area but rent it to others, workers who spend more hours in the area than residents, residents whose violence or addiction threaten neighborhood stability, the homeless who live on the street, part-time residents who spend much of the year elsewhere, maids who "live in", undocumented aliens living with family—which of these are included in the sense of "neighborhood"? Some local people have always been treated as outside the definition of the community, while outsiders have often been included as community members. Even the definition a neighborhood is contestable: people who have lived in a neighborhood for years often disagree about its borders. * * *

To replace our current legal conception of localities with one that embraces the ageographical city, we have to stop building local government law on residency and on the importance of local jurisdictional boundaries. We must treat people not as located solely in one jurisdiction but as "switching center(s) for all the networks of influence" within the region that affect their lives. Under current law, residency within city limits determines people's legal rights on issues ranging from voting to their entitlement to participate in government programs. And the location of property within city limits determines who pays for these government programs through the property tax, still the predominant source of local government revenue. To illustrate how local government law would be transformed by embracing the * * * [ageographical city], I turn to a discussion of two specific local government doctrines: one dealing with residency (eligibility for government services) and one with the property tax (school financing).

Many local services are now available only to the people inside specified jurisdictional borders. Schools attendance requires living within the school district; police and fire protection stop at the city line; city hospitals exclude non-residents. One justification offered for these policies analogizes local government services to property rights: only those who pay for services are entitled to receive them. * * * But those who pay for local services are not the same people as those eligible to receive them. Non-residents who are property-owners pay the property tax, but they cannot send their children to city schools or use city hospitals. On the other hand, residents who own no property and therefore do not pay property taxes (at least directly) can use city services. Moreover, many city services are supported by state and federal as well as locally-generated revenue. Yet residency remains a qualification for services no matter where the funding comes from. The reason that services are allocated only to residents is not the source of financing but the equation of residency and decentralization: local control means control by residents.

A local government law organized in terms of the * * * [ageographical city] would recognize that the maids who clean the residents' houses, the grocery store family that provide their milk, and the consumers who drive to the area to shop are also connected to a neighborhood. * * * In the ageographical city, residency within invisible boundary lines should not determine who can use schools, hospitals, addiction treatment centers or the like. Local services should be open to all local people. The problem is to decide who they are and how to do so. * * *

Building local government law on * * * [the ageographical city] would * * * [also] transform local government financing. At present, only property located within jurisdictional boundaries is subject to tax, and only people who live within the same boundaries benefit from the tax. School financing provides the best known example of the impact of this inside/outside distinction. * * * [But] even those state courts that have held school financing systems unconstitutional have continued to recognize the importance of boundary lines. The Texas Supreme Court, for example, has made clear that its decision to invalidate the state's school financing system does not require localities to educate people who live outside their borders. And, the court indicated, once the state adds enough to money to the system to ensure that there is an efficient system of public schools throughout the state, school districts will be able to supplement the education of their residents through locally raised property taxes. Other state courts have similarly permitted this kind of local supplementation, thereby perpetuating the idea that the property located inside jurisdictional borders exists for the benefit of residents.

By defining the tax base in terms of the property found within a jurisdiction and by defining the beneficiaries of the tax base in terms of residency, local government law creates and intensifies inequality within the metropolitan area. It's no accident that the locations of major sources of tax revenue, such as large suburban malls and office complexes, are often at some distance from the locations where the revenue is most needed. Localities within the region compete for these sources of revenue, just as they compete for the ability to exclude those who need government services. But it is not necessary to organize the imposition and the dispersion of the property tax in terms of jurisdictional lines. Nor is it necessary to treat taxes on sales or income—taxes often paid by people who are not residents—as benefiting only residents. The current mismatch between the ability to raise revenue and the need for the money would be undermined by a local government law that embraced the * * * [ageographical city]. Again, the critical issue (discussed below) is determining how best to do so.

It should be clear by now, I hope, that the transformation of local government law envisioned in this section would be dramatic. Almost no local government law issue would remain unaffected. To date only a few local government services—such as beaches—have been required to be open to residents and non-residents alike, and property-based tax schemes have been invalidated only in the area of school financing. But it is no more justifiable, in my view, for the quality of police protection, hospitals, or welfare programs to vary with district wealth that it is for the quality of the schools. And the ability to support social programs in innovative ways should, like the power to raise taxes, not depend on where developers choose to put their office complexes. Some localities, for example, now condition zoning approvals for office buildings on the developers' agreement to subsidize low and moderate income housing—a practice known as "exactions". But they can do so only if they can attract the developer, and developers have an incentive to shop around for a jurisdiction not interested in imposing such an exaction. If, however, an exaction could be imposed for the benefit of the region's poor wherever the development is located, more such exactions would be possible and, as a result, more low and moderate income housing could be generated.

In the interest of preserving a national economy, the Commerce Clause has long been invoked to prevent cities from favoring their own residents over outsiders. But court decisions relying on the Commerce Clause have simply invalidated local ordinances; they have not created a basis for a regional system of revenue-sharing and service-entitlement. A local government law [that embraces the ageographical city] * * * has a chance of doing so. To be sure, as Justice Brennan suggested in *Holt*, a decision not to center local government law on local boundary lines and residency challenges our basic conception of what is means to be a political community. "At the heart of our basic conception of a 'political community,' " Justice Brennan asserted, "is the notion of a reciprocal relationship between the process of government and those who subject themselves to that process by choosing to live within the area of its authoritative application." Indeed, building local government law in terms of the ageographical city raises the question of what decentralization means. To whom would power be decentralized if not to people defined within local boundaries? And where would people participate in the democratic process if not at their place of residence? * * *

[One way to build local government law on the notion of the ageographical city would be to create] a regional legislature authorized to allocate entitlements to the area's cities and suburbs. The purpose of such a regional legislature would not be to act as a regional government or ape the powers of the state. Instead, it would be a democratic version of the idea of regional planning embodied in federal legislation of the 1960's and 1970's. These federal statutes sought to inject a regional voice into local decisionmaking by requiring local decisions to be consistent with a regional plan; Congress hoped that such a requirement would overcome the selfish pursuit of local self-interest by forcing each locality to consider the impact of their actions on the region as a whole. The effect of these federal statutes was limited by making regional considerations relevant only in the context of allocating federal grants, by creating as many different regional planning agencies as there were subject matters to plan for, by concentrating on the preparation of a written plan rather than on an ongoing process of regional negotiations, and by organizing the regional planning process in terms of existing political boundaries. Nevertheless the germ of the idea was sound. The object was not to have regional bodies replace local decisionmaking but to require localities, when making their decisions, to take the interests of other localities within the region into account.

As just mentioned, the task of the regional legislature would be to perform a specific function of the state legislature (and the state courts): the allocation of entitlements to local governments. An example of such an allocation is the articulation of standards—such as the *Mt. Laurel* standard—that describe the extent to which localities must accommodate the interest of others in the region when they decide their land-use policies. But there are also countless other entitlement issues facing local governments: what portion of the funds derived from the property tax can a locality use solely for its own schools? can a locality exclude a facility the region needs (a waste dump)? what incentives can a locality offer a business in a neighboring jurisdiction to move across the border? are stricter gun control laws more appropriate in one area of the region than elsewhere? Current local government law has clearly established that the kinds of entitlement questions I have just proposed cannot be distinguished "in principle" from substantive local decisionmaking. One could frame every issue as an entitlement question and thereby eliminate city decisionmaking altogether (and frame every issue as suitable for local resolution and thereby eliminate regional decisionmaking altogether). When, then, is the distinction that I am making between the entitlement allocation function of a regional legislature and a regional government?

The answer to this question must be found not in an analytical distinction between entitlement allocation and governance but in the way the regional legislature is organized. The regional legislature itself (and not the courts or the cities) should have the power to determine which questions it (rather than the localities) can decide, but the legislature should be structured to encourage its members not to exercise power themselves but to turn the legislature into a forum for * * * negotiations about how to decentralize power. * * * Institutional innovations might well be necessary to prevent legislators from becoming so enamored with their own power that they attempt to transform the regional legislature into a regional government. Requiring legislators to appear regularly before neighborhood meetings to report on legislative activity, allowing those at the meeting to vote on the kinds of compromises that the legislators are authorized to make, enabling neighborhood residents to control legislative salaries and perks, establishing term limits for those serving in the legislature—ideas such as these, from sources as varied as the history of New England towns and Marx's analysis of the Paris Commune, suggest that regional legislatures can be organized to frustrate the dynamic of centralization. Localities will not be able to get everything they want from such a structure, but they are likely to be able to gain more power than they now have or than they would have if they ceded authority to a regional (or state) government. * * *

[[I]t might also help if we change the rules that determine who is entitled to vote in local elections.] Consider a plan, for example, in which everyone gets five votes that they can cast in whatever local elections they feel affect their interest ("local" still being defined by the traditional territorial boundaries of city, suburb, or neighborhood). They can define their interests differently in different elections, and any form of connection that they think expresses an aspect of themselves at the moment will be treated as adequate. Under such an electoral system, representatives in the regional legislature, mayors and city council members would have a constituency made up not only of residents but of workers, shoppers, property owners, residents of neighboring jurisdictions, the homeless, and so forth. People are unlikely to vote in a jurisdiction they don't care about, but there are a host of possible motives for voting (racial integration, racial solidarity, redistribution of wealth, desire for gentrification, etc.) Indeed, there is no reason to think that the constituency would be limited solely to those who live in the region. These days, as I have already argued, people feel connected to areas far away as well as close to home. Puerto Ricans in New York, therefore, may want to vote not only in New York but in San Juan; of course, if they do, that would leave them one less vote for local elections in the New York region. On the other hand, the voting system might also mimic the idea of proportional representation by allowing someone to cast all five votes in a one locality if that's where her/his attachments are felt to be.

What exactly would happen under such a electoral allocation is hard to say: indeed its unpredictability might be felt to reproduce the sense of "vertigo" that life in metropolitan areas is now said to induce. * * * It seems likely to me, however, that the property tax generated by giant shopping malls and office complexes will be allocated to more than simply those who live within the borders where they are located. Indeed, the rules for the allocation of all property taxes by the regional legislature could easily have a better chance of meeting the needs of people throughout the metropolitan area than negotiations between the city and the suburbs (defined in terms of residency). The attempt to limit services to those "inside" an area are also likely to be rethought and, perhaps, replaced with another form of allocation. Most importantly, such a electoral scheme would radically change the idea of what a neighborhood or suburb or city is—of who is included in a reference to such a locality. The "self" in the phrase local self-interest would become a gesture toward an unknown and unspecifiable multiplicity.

Still, the change would not be quite as radical as it might first appear. The idea that Puerto Ricans who live outside of San Juan have an interest in being represented in its governance is not mine. Attempts have already been made to recognize their interests in the organization of San Juan's municipal government. Even the Supreme Court recognized, in *Kramer v. Union Free School District*, that those who vote in school board elections could not be limited to people who own or lease property in the area, their spouses, and the parents or guardians of the children who attend the schools. Many others, the court reasoned, have a direct and distinct interest in school decisions: "senior citizens and others living with children or relatives; clergy, military personnel, and others who live on tax-exempt property; boarders and lodgers; parents who neither own nor lease qualifying property and whose children are too young to attend school; parents who neither own nor lease property and whose children attend private schools." But why stop there? Many more—including many non-residents the Court did not consider—are just as interested: teachers and staff who work at the school; parents who would like to send their children to the school system if they weren't excluded by residency requirements; parents who are sending their children to schools with fewer resources; citizens who believe in school integration. Of course, adding this group to the list of residents that the Court did include would make the school's constituency very uncertain and unstable. But school constituencies are already uncertain and unstable: residents are constantly moving in and out. In our mobile society, the notion of residency has provided an ever-shifting referent for the population of school districts, neighborhoods, and cities; in fact, reliance on residency has demonstrated that a fixed population is unnecessary to define a political constituency. Constituencies are defined tautologically: a locality includes whoever is defined by its rules of inclusion. And there is no reason to interpret the Constitution as requiring the rule of inclusion to be residency.

A local government law based on * * * [the ageographical city] also need not respect the current territorial boundaries of cities and towns, as has so far been assumed. Even now the residents of America's metropolitan areas live in a multitude of jurisdictions with different borders: the areas defined by school districts, transportation districts, redevelopment authorities, park districts and the like often differ not only from city borders but from each other. Currently, however, each of these * * * special districts and public authorities serve those defined by *their* borders. Thus the experience of the loss of boundaries that might have been produced by the multiple definitions of each citizen's location within the metropolitan area has been eclipsed by the reassuring sense that one's location is defined by the purpose of each territorial definition (the fact that you're in the same Congressional district as someone else doesn't mean her kids can go to your school). * * * [We need to] replace this comforting feeling with an intensified experience of geographic dissonance. Bringing even just the current multiplicity of boundaries to consciousness can help undermine the boundary-fixation that characterizes so much of present-day local government law.

One form this consciousness-raising could take would be to increase the level of popular participation in the multitude of territorially-defined governmental bodies that now exist within a metropolitan area. At present their bureaucratic structure renders the differences among their boundary definitions virtually invisible; only insiders pay much attention to how the area is divided up. If, however, members of the public worked together on education, parks, transportation and similar issues, they would begin to recognize the uncertainties of defining who counts as part of their community. Moreover, this experience need not be confined to currently existing agencies. Often it would be better to set up a series of temporary task forces—ad-hoc organizations—created to solve specific problems and disbanded after the task is completed. The temporary character of these task forces would make it easier for people to participate than in permanent organizations. And the task forces could divide up the region in new ways to examine aspects of metropolitan life now largely left untouched: the need for better working conditions in offices (a region of buildings), the need for health and retirement benefits for people who work in others' houses (a region of domestic workers), the need for child-care facilities (a region of kids), the need for consumer protection (a region of shoppers). * * *

Another * * * [approach] would question not whom the locality includes but the kinds of functions it performs. So far, the discussion of localities has referred only to the traditional tasks of municipal governments, such as zoning, condominium conversion, school financing, and allocation of public services. But this limited view of the role of local government is by no means necessary. David Osborne and Ted Gaebler, for example, have sought to "reinvent government" on a model of entrepreneurial activity. Localities, they argue, should see themselves as profit-oriented market-innovators and entrepreneurs, not as regulators and law-makers. They should serve as catalysts for economic development, foster community-run organizations, and organize their own activates to increase worker participation. I have made similar proposals for this kind of change myself. But my ideas, like theirs, treated local territorial boundaries as given. I now think it would be better to combine these ideas with the other proposals advanced in this section, spreading their risk and benefits across the region rather having each locality undertake entrepreneurial activities as a separate entity (defined in terms of residency). But whether organized locally or inter-locally, these proposal illustrate one more way to destabilize the identity of localities: Osborne and Gaebler (and I) make the application of the public/private distinction to local governments impossible. * * *

SECTION C.   THE CITY AND DEMOCRATIC THEORY: PART THREE

The materials in this chapter have focused attention on the significance of inter-group boundaries. Are the lines that separate cities from each other barriers to inter-city cooperation or necessary forms of protection from threatening outsiders? City boundaries can easily be understood in both ways. Indeed, many of the cases in each section (such as the exclusionary zoning and school financing cases) illustrate both perspectives simultaneously. One explanation for the ambivalent nature of city boundaries is that they reproduce in the context of groups the familiar problem often raised about individuals: how do we establish a relationship with others if we need and desire their friendship yet fear that their power and influence can overwhelm our sense of self? The barriers that separate one person from another help define them as individuals, but they also isolate people from each other. A provocative reworking of the relationship between the self and others is the subject of the Calvino story reproduced below. Is his picture frightening or inspiring?

The five excerpts that follow the Calvino story conclude our exploration of the nature and value of inter-group boundaries. First, Richard Briffault offers a full-scale attack on the importance we attach to locally-defined boundaries, arguing instead for an increased role for the states in governmental decisionmaking. Rosabeth Moss Kanter's analysis of nineteenth-century utopian communities and Philippe Aries' analysis of the relationship between the family and the city then present alternative conceptions of the history and significance of the boundaries between groups. Consider whether, according to these readings, group boundaries have been progressively strengthened or progressively weakened over the last two centuries. Which of these options do the authors seem to favor? An excerpt from a review by Hanna Pitkin and Sara Shumer of an important recent book on local democracy [1] then raises a related question: to what extent should the defense of local boundaries be based on the value of fostering consensus? Finally, the excerpt from Roberto Unger's Knowledge and Politics offers a schematic view of the dilemmas of inter-group relations explored not only by the other readings in this section but by all the materials covered in this chapter.

ITALO CALVINO, INVISIBLE CITIES
Pp. 64–65 (1974).

When he enters the territory of which Eutropia is the capital, the traveler sees not one city but many, of equal size and not unlike one another, scattered over a vast, rolling plateau. Eutropia is not one, but all these cities together; only one is inhabited at a time, the others are empty; and this process is carried out in rotation. Now I shall tell you how. On the day when Eutropia's inhabitants feel the grip of weariness and no one can bear any longer his job, his relatives, his house and his life, debts, the people he must greet or who greet him, then the whole citizenry decides to move to the next city, which is there waiting for them, empty and good as new; there each will take up a new job, a different wife, will see another landscape on opening his window, and will spend his time with different pastimes, friends, gossip. So their life is renewed from move to move, among cities whose exposure or declivity or streams or winds make each site somehow different from the others. Since their society is ordered without great distinctions of wealth or authority, the passage from one function to another takes place almost without jolts; variety is guaranteed by the multiple assignments, so that in the span of a lifetime a man rarely returns to a job that has already been his.

Thus the city repeats its life, identical, shifting up and down on its empty chessboard. The inhabitants repeat the same scenes, with the

---

1. J. Mansbridge, Beyond Adversary De-   mocracy (Basic Books, 1980).

actors changed; they repeat the same speeches with variously combined accents; they open alternate mouths in identical yawns. Alone, among all the cities of the empire, Eutropia remains always the same. Mercury, god of the fickle, to whom the city is sacred, worked this ambiguous miracle.

RICHARD BRIFFAULT, OUR LOCALISM: PART II—LOCALISM AND LEGAL THEORY

90 Col.L.Rev. 346, 382–386, 388–389, 441–454 (1990).

Contemporary courts and legislators frequently appear to model their notions of local governments on the small size, homogeneous populations and residential nature of suburbs. Questions of local power are often resolved by an implicit reliance on the idealized residential suburb as the paradigm locality. In a sense, "the city as a legal concept," has become a suburb. * * *

The essence of the suburban model is the association of local government with the values of home and family. The suburb, the most common form of local government today, is conceived of as a small, primarily middle-class residential community, a place for domestic consumption rather than industrial production and a haven from the heartless political and economic world beyond local borders. The central function of local government is to protect the home and family—enabling residents to raise their children in "decent" surroundings, servicing home and family needs and insulating home and family from undesirable changes in the surrounding area.

This association of the municipal corporation with home and family provides a stronger foundation for legal localism than did the older notion of the locality as a complex urban ministate. At the same time, it obscures the perception of local government as a state institution and thus erodes the longstanding legal rule that local government actions are attributable to the state. In cases of head-to-head conflict with the state or of clear local violations of constitutional norms, the legal status of localities as state subdivisions will operate to limit local power. But when local governments conflict with individuals, particularly outsiders, or even when local governments prove fiscally unable to fulfill their responsibilities, then, so long as constitutional norms limiting government power are not clearly at issue, the locality may be seen as an agent not of the state but of local families, acting to defend the private sphere surrounding home and family.

The frequent linkage of local government to home and family leads to a deferential or protective attitude toward local power and a reluctance to mandate state intervention in local arrangements. As extensions of home and family, local governments appear to be less of a threat to personal liberty and less subject to central state control. Rather, local governments merit legal protection because of their close association with the home and family interests of their residents.

This is clear from the United States Supreme Court's opinion in *Village of Belle Terre v. Boraas*,[161] not simply in the holding sustaining local zoning authority to exclude nontraditional households, but in the Court's broader evocation of local government as a kind of moat protecting home and family from the crime, congestion and alien influences of the outside world. The local government in *Belle Terre* was an extension of the home, not an arm of the state, a defender of the family rather than an oppressor of individual liberty. The locality's exclusion of people who practiced an alternative lifestyle was unobjectionable because it was seen as an action similar to that of a family choosing not to welcome an unwanted guest into its home. Nor was Belle Terre's authority undermined by its position as a component of an economically and socially heterogeneous and interdependent metropolitan region. Rather, the village was, in Justice Douglas's words, "a sanctuary for people," a sort of national park for homes and families threatened by state power and urban ills.

The idea of local government as a "sanctuary for people" helps explain judicial and legislative support for local autonomy in zoning and school finance. Of all government activities, land use regulation and education have perhaps the greatest implications for home and family; these are the areas in which the local government as suburb may be presumed to be most effective in vindicating home and family values.

In the exclusionary zoning setting, * * * the new suburban paradigm was critical in redefining the concept of a residential area and of the role of local government in protecting "the well-being of our most important institution, the home." Courts justified local laws restricting land use to large, private, owner-occupied, single-family houses situated on large lots as home-protection policies, with the courts implicitly accepting the suburban definition of "home." Even courts troubled by exclusionary zoning did not doubt the legitimacy of local efforts to support the socioeconomic interests of suburban homeowners.

The courts' underlying assumption that protecting the home requires policies that mandate an affluent homogeneity in the surrounding community drew on the suburban model of local government, which differs profoundly from the traditional concept of a city as a place of diverse incomes, lifestyles and land uses. American cities are not exclusive communities but rather heterogeneous microcosms of the larger society that surrounds them. Judicial legitimation of local zoning that seeks residential homogeneity as a home-protection policy suggests the influence of suburban settlement patterns. Even today, *Mount Laurel* and a handful of cases like it notwithstanding, the association of home protection with local control and homogeneous residential communities remains powerful.

Similarly, the school finance cases reflect the influence of the suburban model and the transformation of local government from subordinate arm of the state to protector of family interests. For many courts

---

161. 416 U.S. 1 (1974). [See Chapter   Four, Part A, infra.]

the central issue in these cases was not interlocal inequality but local control. The courts that defended local control, accepted wealth-based spending differences and rejected demands that the states assume a greater fiscal responsibility, did so not because of any assumption that local governments possessed technical superiority in funding or operating schools but because they equated local control with parental involvement in the education of children. Not only would local control permit a larger parental role than under a system providing for greater state responsibility, but local control was also treated, at least metaphorically, as identical to parental control.

The association of local control over school financing with family or parental control of education may be more likely to occur when suburbs, not cities, are the focus of attention. The association may, in fact, be more accurate when applied to the suburbs. Residents of suburban communities focus on family and school issues; schools and taxes, along with land use, are the chief subjects of suburban political discourse. Suburban school districts tend to be smaller and have smaller bureaucracies than urban ones, so the structure of suburban school governance makes it easier for suburban parents and families to get involved in educational decision-making than it is for their counterparts in the cities. Suburban districts also commonly have more money to spend on local needs. Local tax revenues are devoted primarily to schools, and the smaller percentage of suburban children who are poor, who do not speak English, come from broken homes or need special educational assistance in the suburbs minimizes the local need for outside financial support. For cities, local fiscal autonomy—in education as in other areas—is often an illusion, and parents' interests would be better served by greater state fiscal responsibility for local schools.

Local control of education is more likely to be seen as a means of protecting the family interest in public schools if suburbs, rather than cities, are the norm in thinking about local governments. The tendency to conceptualize local government after the model of suburbs as centers of families and homes facilitates the equation of local control with family control, encourages deference to state decisions devolving educational, administrative and financial responsibilities to the local level and makes it more difficult for concerns about interlocal inequality and the external effects of local actions to overcome the decentralization endemic to the system. * * *

Of course, not all courts have adopted the suburban model of local government. The state courts that invalidated local property-tax-based school finance systems did so, in part, by hearkening back to the traditional notion of local governments as arms of the state. Treating education as the responsibility of the state and emphasizing that local school districts were created to carry out the state's educational duty, these courts held the state accountable for interlocal spending differences and mandated state action to improve the quality of education in the poorest districts. Similarly, the handful of courts that challenged exclusionary zoning returned to the concept of local power as delegated state power, and held that exclusionary measures could be invalidated since there was no state interest in local exclusion. The *Mount Laurel* doctrine, mandating that developing suburbs plan and provide for their "fair share" of regional low- and moderate-income housing needs, invoked the older notion of the locality as a microcosm of the larger society. *Mount Laurel* sought to require suburbs—as political arms of the state—to wield their state-delegated zoning power to allow people of different backgrounds to live among them and become socially and economically integrated communities.

Belle Terre and *Mount Laurel* exemplify the different approaches to local government and to the relationship between locality and state. Both have a place in thinking about local government law. Local governments are state-created and state-empowered, yet particularly responsive local residents' social concerns. Local governments can be heterogeneous microcosms of the larger society or class-segregated residential enclaves. But as the review of the law in the areas of school finance, land use and local government formation indicates, the approach taken in *Belle Terre* appears to be dominant. And the power of the *Belle Terre* approach is consonant with the role of the suburb as a paradigm for thinking about local governments. * * *

The protection of home and family is not simply about assuring domestic privacy and individual autonomy, it also tends to become associated with efforts to preserve interlocal class differences and the economic and social benefits of residence in high-income, high-status localities.

Internally, this results in a local politics aimed at the maintenance of class and ethnic homogeneity. Local homogeneity is attained by separate incorporation, often followed by the adoption of exclusionary land-use policies. Although most common in affluent areas, exclusion is not the prerogative of the wealthy; less well-to-do communities are just as concerned about maintaining community status against the deterioration usually attributed to the influx of racial and ethnic minorities and poorer people. The protection of turf through the prevention of internal racial or income differentiation is an important feature of suburban politics. Observers of suburban life have noted, "[O]ne need only attend a few public hearings on controversial zoning changes in suburban areas to realize that the people consider their right to pass judgment upon their future neighbors as sacred." Similarly, the insistence on separate suburban school districts reflects a determination to shield local children from exposure to economic, social and cultural differences that are perceived as a threat to family values.

Externally, suburban policies frequently seek to deny the suburb's membership in the metropolitan community or its responsibility for the economic and social ills of the region, especially those of the central city. Suburbs often refuse to permit facilities necessary for the economic development or social order of the region to be located within their borders. Solid-waste disposal sites, power plants, transportation facili-

ties, low-cost housing for area workers, shelters for the homeless, half-
way houses for the mentally ill and convalescent homes for AIDS
patients; all lead to cries of "NIMBY"—"not in my back yard." NIMBY
is certainly not a uniquely suburban phenomenon. City-dwellers are no
more altruistic than suburbanites, and the residents of city neighborhoods also frequently resist locally unwanted facilities, but they usually
lack the legal authority to enforce NIMBY attitudes: they may be
overruled by city governments. But suburbs, as independent municipal
corporations, usually have presumptive authority to exclude regionally
necessary but locally undesirable facilities. States have the formal
power to displace such local decision making, but such state action is
unusual, and is focused more on controlling development or permitting
the siting of industrial infrastructure rather than superseding local
decisions that exclude facilities intended to serve the disadvantaged.

Suburban autonomy and the focus of suburban politics on internal
concerns may contribute to a declining interest in cooperative interlocal
approaches to regional economic development or the solution of the
social problems of metropolitan areas. Suburbs compete with each other
and with the cities to attract desirable residents and nonpolluting
industries and to exclude undesirable production facilities, subsidized
housing and all programs to assist the poor. In most metropolitan areas
there is little interest in cooperation among municipalities concerning
local taxes, schools, housing or economic development. Integrated regional policies on these matters are uncommon, as the suburbs prefer to
rely on their own resources, protect their own values and shun fiscally
draining and socially threatening ties to the cities.

Most striking is the emergence of what historian Kenneth Jackson
calls "a new suburban consciousness," which denies the historic association of suburbs with their cities and treats cities and their residents with
a mixture of fear and disdain. At one time, the central cities set the
tone for their metropolitan areas. The city was the primary center of
jobs and commercial and cultural institutions for the region. The
prosperity of the suburbs was linked to that of the cities, suburbanites
knew it, and suburbs cooperated with policies aimed at promoting
regional interests. The movement of industry out of the city and the
creation of centers of commerce and employment in the suburbs has
reduced suburban dependence on the city and has made it possible for
residents to deny the economic links that integrate a region. Whereas
formerly "suburban" implied a relationship to the city, it now suggests a
distinction from the city and from the problems the city has come to
symbolize. So, too, the widening gap between suburban and urban
incomes and the polarization of the races between city and suburb
sharpen the suburban sense of city-suburb differences and heighten the
suburban tendency to treat the city as an alien place, one which merits
little assistance, support or cooperation. Local politics in the suburbs is
aimed at keeping the city and its concerns out, and the law of local
autonomy—the rules governing local government formation, land use,

school finance and local taxation—enables many suburbs to attain these goals.

The privatization of suburban public life, the class and race homogeneity of many suburbs, the parochialization of the local relationship to outsiders and the legal rules that permit and sustain the insulation of suburbs from regional problems, all breed an ideology of localism—a belief that land-use regulation, schools and tax policy ought to be controlled locally, with the interests of local residents as the exclusive desideratum of local decision makers. Localism reifies local borders, using invisible municipal boundary lines to delimit the range of local concern and the proper subjects of local compassion and treating the creation and maintenance of local borders as a basic right.

Localism translates questions about the proper structure of government and the proper relationship between different levels of government (and between different governments at the same level) into a language of rights. The focus of local public policy on home and family and the use of local public powers to advance these private interests lead to an association of the locality with individual autonomy. Local self-government within existing borders and effective local powers over land use and schools are treated as a right much like the personal right to privacy in one's home and to make family decisions immune from state interference.

Localism as a set of beliefs adds to the existing legal restrictions that inhibit the realignment of local boundaries to better match local wealth to local needs or the adoption of area-wide approaches to regional problems. Local borders, once created, reinforce local identification, become a focus of sentiment and symbolism and create a powerful legal bulwark for the preservation of local interests. Localism provides a normative basis for excluding regionally necessary but locally undesirable facilities and for treating problems that originate outside local borders as unworthy of local concern or the expenditure of local resources.

The suburbanization of local government thus presents a paradox for the participationist case for local autonomy. By their size, homogeneity and power over issues of basic importance to local residents, suburbs are optimal places for participatory government. Suburbanites have greater opportunities to participate in local decision making and suburban governments are particularly responsive to the values and interests of their residents. Local autonomy empowers residents of suburban communities—but does so at great cost to other localities and to the public values participation theory holds dear.

The appeal of participation theory is the promise it offers for the transformation of public life: the vision of people actively engaged in an ongoing discussion over issues fundamental to their collective lives, reconciling their differences through dialogue and mutual accommodation and creating a community of public-spirited citizens. It assumes that local participation will provide the experience in community-regarding decision making that can provide a basis for a more participatory national political life. But participatory activity on the suburban model is unlikely to fulfill that promise or advance the realization of that goal. Many critical public issues relating to the operation and regulation of the economy and the nature and structure of work are off the suburban agenda. Greater local autonomy would make it even more difficult to raise these issues; further, the intensity of the interlocal competition for development assures that when most local governments address economic issues, they do so to satisfy the demands of business or wealthy residents.

Moreover, the combination of jurisdictional boundaries with residential segregation along ethnic and economic lines contributes to the polarization of races and classes. Local approaches to interlocal or regional problems are too often shaped by an apparent tendency to adopt an "us against them" mentality. Participation in suburban local governments thus may result in the opposite of what the participationist argument for local autonomy anticipates. Instead of promoting the reconciliation of ethnic and economic differences, political participation may lead to policies and attitudes that seek to insulate the smaller, relatively more homogeneous locality and to deny its connection to a more heterogeneous nation.

Localism in this setting enables residents to believe that their range of concerns is, and ought to be, limited by local boundary lines. Poverty, crime, deteriorating school systems and the lack of affordable housing outside the home community are defined as the private, local problems of other communities and not as subjects of public concern. Local participation may drive communities apart, intensify the sense of interlocal difference and reduce the possibilities of fashioning regional solutions to regional problems.

This objection to local autonomy derives not from the potential internal oppressiveness of local majorities that troubled Madison, but rather from the function-, race- and income-segregated nature of the contemporary polis. The suburb can be a very private polis, both in terms of the issues that are the focus of local politics and the desire to avoid extralocal problems. The fragmentary nature of localities and the interlocal differences in personal wealth and municipal fiscal capacity mean that local autonomy will be worth a great deal more to some localities than others. Interlocal ethnic and class differences shape local decision making, leading to the adoption of land-use, tax and spending policies that perpetuate inequities and maintain residential separation. The private nature of local public values leads to the narrowing of local politics, the disclaiming of responsibility for problems beyond local borders and the rejection of interlocal cooperation on matters of social significance. They tend to lead as well to the pursuit of localist objectives at higher levels of government.

Local autonomy, thus, should be seen as normatively ambiguous. Although it may provide opportunities for political participation and responsive government, local autonomy also contributes to the preservation of the political, economic and social status quo and to the privatization of American politics. In empowering some, local autonomy disempowers others. Given the political economy of contemporary metropolitan areas and the resulting implications for local politics, the contention that greater local power and a categorically localist resolution of questions of local government law would enhance the quality of American political life and create new opportunities for the advancement of a progressive political agenda simply cannot be justified. * * *

Localism generally deprecates the states. The states are seen as too big and too remote from the ordinary citizen to permit either voice or exit, and state power is equated with excessive centralization and the loss of participation and efficiency. State governments are frequently treated as backward, rural-dominated institutions, hostile to cities and prone to intervene in local matters for partisan, political purposes. Even Robert Dahl, whose support for local autonomy is tempered by a recognition of local limitations, assumes that the states are "destined for a kind of limbo of quasi-democracy * * * [W]henever we are compelled to choose between city and state, we should always keep in mind, I think, that the city, not the state, is the better instrument of popular government."

But much as the fragmentation of the contemporary metropolis into multiple local governments changes the significance of local autonomy, it also provides a different perspective on the place of the states in local government law. The states are larger and far more politically, economically and socially complex than are individual localities. States are usually demographically diverse, and include both businesses and homes. They consist of many localities, cities as well as suburbs, so that an aggregation of internally homogeneous localities will constitute a heterogeneous state.

Moreover, the states have greater resources than most local governments. States contain and therefore can tax the corporations and affluent residents beyond the reach of most localities. Their larger and more diversified tax bases and superior administrative capabilities enable them to tax personal and corporate income and sales—sources of revenue beyond the reach of most localities' fiscal powers.

The states' greater geographic scope, superior fiscal resources and social and economic heterogeneity give them a greater capacity to control local externalities and address interlocal and interpersonal wealth differences. Because they include many localities, the states can internalize a wider range of decisions and can take a regional perspective on regional problems. The states are potentially subject to the political influence of low income and poor as well as affluent residents, to the demands of cities as well as suburbs. The larger size and smaller numbers of the states make it harder for taxpayers to exit their states and may reduce state vulnerability to the flight of capital. Interstate wealth and tax differences are smaller than such interlocal differences, making it more difficult for businesses to play the states off against each other and to find state tax havens.

The states in recent decades have, in fact, become somewhat more progressive, certainly when compared to local governments and the federal government. Reapportioned state legislatures and modernized state governments have experimented with innovative economic development, social services, environmental, educational and housing programs. Following the Reagan budget cuts, the states assumed some financial responsibility for many health, social service and training programs that had previously been funded by the federal government.

In terms of interlocal relations, some states have taken modest steps toward addressing interlocal externalities and fiscal disparities. * * * Only a minority of states have been active in any of these areas. * * * State legislatures remain attentive to the suburban interest in local autonomy, particularly in land use, and state programs of intergovernmental assistance are only modestly redistributive, often providing general support for all local governments rather than directing aid to communities most in need.

Moreover, the states, like localities, are constrained by the mobility of capital and the decreasing significance of particular places in the location of economic activity. The fact that there are fewer states may entail longer, costlier moves than interlocal relocation, but state redistributive activity, too, is restricted by the ability of investors, industries and affluent residents to decamp to states with lower taxes and less of a commitment to redistribution. Although less pressed than many localities, the states are also in competition for economic development, investment and tax base. * * *

A more compelling objection to a greater state role would be that the states have always had the nominal authority to control the local government system and typically have exercised that authority by delegating power to local governments—just the phenomenon this Article has criticized. How, in other words, can states be the solution when they are the source of the problem? The answer is that what is needed is not greater state power—states already have ample underlying authority—but a greater willingness on the part of state governments to exercise that power and take a state-centered approach in policy making. States must take more active responsibility for government decisions, state and local, within their borders, either by making more decisions at a state level or by making greater efforts to ameliorate or control the consequences of interlocal inequality and the external effects of local actions. State power is not, by itself, sufficient to remedy the harmful effects of localism since state power has often been exercised to promote localism; a state-oriented perspective in state decision making is also necessary. But greater use of state power provides the essential prerequisite for controlling local autonomy. Without greater recourse to the states and greater state activism in pursuit of statewide goals, the problems of interlocal inequities and local externalities cannot be satisfactorily addressed.

The real barrier to addressing the problems of the local government system, and the most significant constraint on state action, is not local autonomy per se but the ideology of localism. In theory, local autonomy is purely a matter of state legal and political decisions to vest certain state powers in local governments. Local authority, according to blackletter law, is merely a delegation from the state, to be exercised by the locality as agent on behalf of the state as principal. But, sustained by legal doctrines, embraced by powerful economic and political interests and legitimated by academic theorists, local autonomy has been transformed from a principle of administration to a faith in the decentralization of responsibility for the provision of public services and the exercise of public power. Local electorates have become the principals and local self-interest the principle governing the actions of local government agents. Localist ideology masks local power and hides the privatization of local public life behind the rhetoric of efficiency, participation, community and local self-determination. The contingency of local authority, the linkage of location to wealth, class, race and status and the parochial nature of local political activity are obscured by the nostalgia for the polis and the New England town and by abstract assumptions about the marketplace for municipal services.

Localist ideology has a hegemonic effect, imbuing localities with a belief in the justice of their freedom from extralocal concerns while crippling the willingness of states to take a statewide perspective and displace local authority when considerations of equity or efficiency make it appropriate to do so. The localist faith imposes a conceptual obstacle to the framing of public policies for the manifold economic and social ills pressing on cities, states and metropolitan areas.

Local autonomy is not always wrong; state displacement of local authority is no panacea for public policy. Although this Article has been critical of local government decision making, that is due in part to a desire to rectify the prolocal bias reflected in both state law and the existing academic literature. Many matters are, in fact, inappropriate for uniform state-wide treatment and are better suited to local decisions that reflect particular local beliefs and local needs. Many areas of public action benefit from the opportunities for experimentation that the decentralization of law-making and regulatory authority provides. It is understandable that land use and schools form the heart of local autonomy since they are closely connected to core areas of personal autonomy and many people want the locus of decision making over these matters vested in the governments they feel are closest to the community.

Local autonomy as community-based governance would be an attractive, indeed a compelling vision in a more equal society or even in a society composed of more racially and economically integrated communities. In such a society, interlocal wealth differences would play a lesser role in determining the quality of public services, and local participation would entail efforts to find common ground out of ethnic and economic diversity. Participation could mean empowerment for all.

But in contemporary America, where local boundaries mark racial and class inequalities as well as the divisions between jurisdictions, the value of local autonomy is fundamentally uncertain. By championing autonomy even in settings where local action without state monitoring or support is inappropriate, localism is too often a recipe for the perpetuation of injustice. The proliferation of municipalities in metropolitan areas translates race and wealth differences into territorial segregation and fiscal separation. The interplay of local incorporation law and state decentralization of fiscal and regulatory responsibilities turns poor places into poor municipalities. By forcing residents of these poorer municipalities to rely primarily on local resources and discrediting their claim to a share of the resources of the region, state or nation, localism further disempowers the weak. By enabling affluent localities and their residents to separate themselves from their poorer neighbors and by providing them with an ideology that justifies their resistance to the claims of the larger society outside their borders, localism further empowers the already powerful. Given the extent of place-related inequality in American society, an absolute commitment to local autonomy is not a basis for a progressive social transformation but rather can be an obstacle to efforts to reduce inequality and ameliorate class and race antagonisms.

Rather than seeking a state-local relationship characterized by either complete state dominance or one of complete local autonomy, elements of both perspectives should be combined. We must strive to develop legal doctrines and governmental structures that combine local initiative, participation and voice with state financial support, state oversight and statewide perspectives for evaluating local action. Such an integration of state and local concerns would be more appropriate than either a general expansion of local power or a centralization of authority in the states.

But to achieve such a pragmatic stance, the ideology of localism must be jettisoned and state and local problems examined without a preexisting commitment to the normative superiority of local power.
* * *

ROSABETH MOSS KANTER, COMMITMENT AND COMMUNITY

Pp. 148–161, 169–175 (1972).

Two Pulls in Social Life

Utopian communities in the nineteenth century sought both to enhance meaningful interpersonal relationships and to provide political, economic, and other services for their members. They attempted both to express values and to implement practical concerns in a single social unit. If the term utopian has come to connote impractical and impossible, it may be owing to what many have felt to be an inherent contradiction between these two sets of aims of utopian communities. Criticisms have been leveled at utopian communities to the effect that social life cannot be both "human" and "efficient," that brotherhood and economics do not mix, that it is impossible both to satisfy individual needs and to work toward the collective good, and that value expression is incompatible with pragmatism. This theme of the incompatibility of two strains in social life is also central to sociological thought in the distinction between *Gemeinschaft* and *Gesellschaft*.

Gemeinschaft relations include the nonrational, affective, emotional, traditional, and expressive components of social action, as in a family; Gesellschaft relations comprise the rational, contractual, instrumental, and task-oriented actions, as in a business corporation. In Gemeinschaft relations, actors are said to interact as whole persons; in Gesellschaft relations, as specific parts of their personalities, interacting for specific and limited purposes. Three early social theorists, Ferdinand Toennies, Max Weber, and Emile Durkheim, were responsible for first formulating elements of this dichotomy.

Though Gemeinschaft and Gesellschaft refer to ideal types rather than actual social groups and are old-fashioned sociological terms, they are useful in describing the two pulls experienced by utopian communities. The Gemeinschaft aspects of a utopian community consist of those mutually expressive, supportive, value-oriented, emotion-laden, personally-directed, loving social relations often called "community." They include mutual recognition of the values, temperament, character, and human needs of group members. Their highest priority is maintenance of values and close relations, and they are based on commitment, the personal involvement of participating members. In contrast, the Gesellschaft elements in a utopian community consist of those relations that are functional for dealing with environments, whether physical, social, or supernatural; for "getting the job done"; for acquiring things the group needs from its environment; for maximizing feedback and exchange with other systems in the form of information, resources, or acceptance. They include any activity that is relevant to conducting environmental exchanges regardless of the specific people involved. Gesellschaft systems organize group relations around the demands of tasks. Since any group that forms a "community" must also produce something or manage exchanges with an environment, and since these aims may require different and possibly incompatible forms of organization, a tension is set up that can force the group to make a choice of emphasis. The predominant movement of many of the successful nineteenth-century groups was away from a heavy initial emphasis on community toward the predominance of Gesellschaft. This change meant the end of the community and its transformation into a specialized organization. Amana, for example, evolved from a highly value-oriented Gemeinschaft community, in which production was secondary and designed only to meet subsistence requirements of the group, to a business-oriented system, hoping nevertheless to maintain its now secondary spiritual and human concerns: "The new Amana [after its dissolution and reorganization] is something more than a modern business structure with emphasis on methods and efficiency and the earning power of the dollar * * * There is a manifest desire to keep intact, as far as possible, the Community consciousness born of a precious heritage—a wealth of common aspirations and memories, and of spiritual assets that cannot be weighed, nor measured, nor tabulated, nor charted." The evolution of Oneida in a similar direction, ending in a joint-stock company carrying on a silverware-manufacturing business, is strikingly demonstrated by changes in the community's newspaper, *The Circular,* noted by Maren Lockwood. In 1851, three years after the founding of Oneida, almost all of *The Circular* was devoted to religion. By 1861, about half dealt with religion, and by 1870, less than a third. In 1876 *The Circular* was renamed *The American Socialist.*

This tension between the two pulls in social life was a factor in practically all of the nineteenth century communes studied, for the great majority of them were more than simple agricultural societies; they were to some extent concerned not only about production of enough goods and services for the community but also about their commercial and political relations with the larger society. Most of them had businesses of one kind or another, sometimes servicing the community primarily but also exchanging goods with the outside society. Zoar had both agriculture and industry, including woolen, linen, and flour mills, a timber planing business, and a wagon shop. Oneida in its early years engaged in farming and silk-jobbing besides running a flour mill, saw mill, and machine shop. It then began successful fruit-canning, bag-manufacturing, and animal trap businesses, and still later a successful silverware factory. Saint Nazianz sold cheese, beer, straw hats, shoes, and wheat. Among Harmony's items of commerce were hides, grains, furs, waxes, linen, tobacco, and cheese. The Shakers are still known for the furniture they manufactured.

The kinds of organization that are functional for production and business operations may often conflict with the commitment mechanisms that serve to maintain community feeling. This issue is being faced by communal groups today. As the Israeli kibbutzim, for example, industrialize and build modern factories on their grounds, they are coping with the issue of maintaining a value-oriented, communal society that at the same time permits efficient industrial production and remains fully a part of the modern world. So far they have avoided the several dilemmas arising from the two pulls in social life that contributed to the weakening of commitment and the dissolution of the successful nineteenth-century groups. These dilemmas involved pulls toward permeability, isomorphism, value indeterminism, and perpetuation strategies that undermined community.

Permeability refers to the degree to which community boundaries are open and permit penetration of movement across them, that is, the ease with which people can pass over the group's boundaries. Such easy passage is functional for economic and political tasks for several reasons.

The necessity of dealing with external systems requires an organizational structure that is not totally encapsulated. For one thing, commercial enterprises need information about the state of the environmental systems with which they must deal—about market conditions, for example. Permeability facilitates the garnering of information and the attainment of feedback, for it is relatively easy for information and feedback-bearers to pass in and out of the organization. Similarly, organizations can exchange personnel if easy passage into the system is possible and can thereby learn about external systems. Furthermore, when boundaries between the organization and its environments are not well defined or rigid, the line between what constitutes the organization's and the environment's interests may appear to be erased, so that helping the organization meet its goals may at the same time fulfill more general public interests.

Permeability can further aid dealings with the environment through the creation of boundary roles for the organization—roles such as salesman, customer relations specialist, or ambassador—which must often operate both within and outside the organization simultaneously. Many nineteenth-century groups, for example, had salesmen. In order for these roles to be effective and to facilitate exchange with the external systems with which they deal, organization boundaries must be relatively permeable. In addition, organizations must perform jobs for their members, and to this end they require resources and personnel. If necessary, these must be quickly attainable and deployable without requiring a difficult passage through a rigid boundary. If labor is required to meet immediate needs, for example, it is not altogether functional to insist that manpower wait through a six-month probationary period or that it make financial contributions. If boundaries are relatively permeable, appropriate experts, resources, and staff can be more easily imported. The most production-oriented of the successful nineteenth-century groups (Amana, Oneida, Harmony, the Shakers, and Zoar) all opened their boundaries and waived their usual requirements in the hiring of outside labor at periods of peak demand. In Oneida in 1880 there were 200 hired workers at peak times in a community otherwise totaling only 288. Finally, permeable boundaries make it possible for the organization to co-opt threatening elements from the outside, since they may be more easily incorporated into the system.

Permeability, while it may aid exchange goals, nevertheless conflicts with many commitment mechanisms that help to maintain communal relations. For example, insulation from the outside is a major renunciation mechanism, but permeable boundaries are almost diametrically opposed to insulated boundaries. The community's distinctiveness and social isolation may be lost when boundaries are relatively permeable. Permeability means almost by definition that stringent entrance requirements, such as investment and ideological conversion, which serve as commitment mechanisms, can no longer exist. Furthermore, permeable boundaries interfere with the cross-boundary control that is functional for communal relations, since the social limits of an organization and its demarcation from the environment are somewhat vague. An organization with permeable boundaries tends to become more heterogeneous, because it more readily admits diverse elements to its ranks, whereas homogeneity is the attribute that facilitates communion in utopian communities. The provision of boundary roles further tends to create people who have at least two allegiances—inside and outside the system—but what is required by utopian communities to maintain their communality are strong exclusive loyalties. Since occupants of boundary roles are not encapsulated within the organization, they need not be totally committed to it. Finally, if it is easy to import relevant experts and personnel, if people can pass in and out of the system with relatively little difficulty, the organization will tend to become staffed by a corps of "professionals," personnel who are relatively disinterested in the purposes of the organization and have little personal stake in its success or failure. Nineteenth century groups had such personnel late in their lives in the form of hired labor. Yet the required characteristics for maintaining communal relations are just the opposite: a strong interest and involvement with the community qua community, as well as a sizable stake in its future.

Isomorphism refers to the structural similarity between the community and its environment. Such parallelism facilitates cross-boundary dealings and exchanges for several reasons. In the first place, social systems that attempt to conduct relations with one another should generally share language, symbols, and media of exchange, which isomorphism implies. Second, labor and experts imported from the outside are more easily deployable in organizations that are isomorphic with respect to the environment, since these personnel need not be resocialized in order to participate in the system; roles in such a system are familiar and can be adopted by new members with less elaborate preparation than in nonisomorphic systems. Similarly, resources and information can be imported without having to transmute them. To offer a simple example, if outsiders speak the same language, communication with them does not require translation. Structural isomorphism may also aid the attainment of exchange goals, since organizations find it easier to deal with each other if they are set up in a similar fashion. If there is point to point correspondence, through similar structures and roles, it will be easier to form a relationship: for example, there will be a purchasing agent to deal with salesmen. An organization may also find itself in a more competitive position if it imitates other organizations of similar type. Finally, a certain amount of similarity to external systems is necessary for an organization to have dealings with other social systems, for being different in a cultural sense poses a threat to other systems at the most, and at the least hampers outstanding and public relations.

Isomorphism for purposes of exchanging with environments interferes to an extent with organization for the attainment of communal goals, however. For utopian communities, the sharing of symbols and media of exchange often means accepting the terms of the larger society and thereby subverting their own ideals and values. Sometimes it forces them to give up a distinctive language and dress, or to end job rotation. It creates practical problems as well. One such problem arises when utopian communities that do not use money in their internal dealings and do not reimburse their own members for labor must pay outside labor in money, becoming in this respect isomorphic with other employing organizations. Internal conflicts and value conflicts may ensue when outsiders are paid in cash and members are not, as happened in Zoar. Isomorphism owing to the pressure for favorable public relations may be similarly detrimental to communal goals and commitment mechanisms. One of several pressures for the transformation of Oneida from a group-marriage commune into a joint-stock company resembling other production organizations was unfavorable publicity and the threat of legal action concerning its practice of free love. Isomorphism also obviates the need for resocialization, since the community already parallels the outside, but in so doing it eliminates the resocialization practices that have value as mortification and surrender mechanisms. While isomorphism may aid environmental and exchange goals, therefore, it may also interfere with the maintenance of communal systems, whose purpose in existing may be their expression of unique and different values.

Value indeterminism is a third functional characteristic of production and exchange systems, one which aids organizational flexibility, especially in light of the need to deal with environments that may be continually changing. In order to ensure the ability to meet the challenge of such change, production organizations may either divorce values from actions and decisions, or adopt values of such wide scope that they encompass a large number of alternative courses of action. In either event, the organization is left free, at least in terms of its values, to make decisions and take actions with respect to external systems. This value indeterminism of organizations is similar in concept to the indeterminism of the collective conscience in modern society described by Emile Durkheim. Communal systems, however, are supported by the opposite phenomenon, value determinism, characterized by elaborate ideologies, detailed specification of rules and procedures, and the basing of decisions on values and ideals. For utopian communities, then, the requirements of community versus those of outside relations provide a possible source of conflict. I am making no judgments about rationality or irrationality here, merely about the guiding and determining role of values.

Communes can take several paths to resolve this dilemma. One strategy is to make values highly determinate of the personal conduct of members but relatively indeterminate of organizational policies, that is, to make them specific with respect to the appropriate behavior of individual members but relatively vague with respect to appropriate organizational behavior. This solution tended to characterize the accommodation of the Shakers. Another solution is to have dual leadership: one set of leaders can interpret and protect the community's values, serving as ideological spokesmen and watchmen; the other set can take care of the day-to-day dealings of the community, free from any otherwise desirable ideological coercion. This arrangement was generally characteristic of Harmony, Zoar, Oneida, and Amana, all of which had business managers as well as spiritual leaders. Saint Nazianz also developed a dual leadership after its founder's death. In addition, however, all of the successful utopias toward the end of their lives (with the exception of Jerusalem, which dissolved much earlier) faced environments quite different in nature from those that existed when the utopias were founded. In order to deal with these changes, value indeterminism became increasingly prevalent in all of the communities. The fact that in Oneida the amount of space devoted to spiritual matters and ideology in community newspapers decreased over the years of the community's existence indicated that increasing attention was paid to practical matters. Even when rules proliferated, as with the Shakers, values tended to become obsolete. In fact, Joseph Eaton pointed out with respect to the Hutterites that a rule proliferation in itself represents an accommodation to a changing environment.

The use of perpetuation strategies represents another way in which social systems can be organized to facilitate cross-boundary exchanges. Provision for leadership succession and for recruitment are two such strategies. Not only do these mechanisms ensure adequate personnel and leadership for the Gesellschaft-type system to accomplish its ends in the external relationship, but they also make the organization appear to have a life extending into the indefinite future, which facilitates its entering into stable and relatively permanent contracts, obligations, and networks of ties with outside environments. Such organizations must make provision for the continual availability of leadership and personnel, as well as acceptance of them by current members. In contrast, communal relations in the abstract require no such provisions, for they need no personnel, accomplish no tasks, and need not outlive the community of the committed, since it was founded to satisfy the needs of a specific group of people. If a communal system expresses the symbolic outputs and emotional feelings of particular people, then as a group it need not continue when those people are no longer present. In fact, in one sense a communal relation is by definition a relationship among particular people who are committed not only to the system as such but also to each other as the system's participants. Commercial and political orders, however, are often required by their systemic nature to continue even when particular leaders and particular personnel are no longer available, for they have in a sense contracted with their members and with the outside world to continue to serve their needs with respect to the environment, and to continue to bring in the appropriate resources or feedback, regardless of which particular personnel cooperate to perform these tasks. In addition, such systems may have entered into contractual relations with the environmental sources of feedback and must continue to exist in order to carry out their contracts.

For nineteenth-century utopian communities, the problem of leadership succession was an acute one. Many, both successful and unsuccessful in terms of number of years of existence, fell apart when their founder and charismatic leader died. Those that provided for continuity of leadership, however, managed to outlive their founders. Charismatic leaders thus may facilitate commitment and sustain communal relations, but they are somewhat dysfunctional for the perpetuation of other kinds of organization, such as Gesellschaft systems.

Recruitment is another general means of ensuring perpetuation, but it too may interfere with communal relations. Member homogeneity and communion may be disturbed by the addition of new elements into the community. New recruits may not be moved by the same values as the original members, and elaborate selection and processing procedures may be required. Recruitment itself represents a relationship between an organization and an environmental system, in this case the utopia's "public," and by virtue of the decision to recruit, such communities may find themselves changing in order to be competitive in the personnel market. This phenomenon characterized many nineteenth-century utopias.

These are a few of the dilemmas faced by utopian communities of the past owing to the dual pulls in their social life between Gemeinschaft and Gesellschaft processes. Early in their histories the successful communes had concentrated on building community, on developing strong commitment, and gave only secondary importance to production and other goals with respect to their environment. As they grew, however, these secondary goals also grew in importance, and "conducting business" began to conflict with maintaining community feeling. By the end of their histories, many commitment mechanisms had disappeared, and commitment itself was eroding.

Prosperity and Decline

One indication of the increasing attention shown to practical matters in the successful nineteenth century groups is the fact that they tended, on the whole, to become financially prosperous. Whereas in their early years they had suffered through periods of struggle and hardship, by the time they dissolved they were often wealthy, or if they had many outstanding debts, these had followed a period of prosperity. For nineteenth century communities at least, financial prosperity may be associated with the decline of community—partly because it indicated the growth of efficient Gesellschaft organization and partly because of the social consequences of prosperity, such as emphasis on individual consumption. Prosperity may lead to bureaucracy and privatism. Richard Ely wrote in 1885 that whereas poverty can knit members into a compact whole, "prosperity can be fatal." Charles Gide stated: "Perhaps the gravest [peril] of all lies in the fact that these colonies are threatened as much by success as by failure * * * If they attain prosperity they attract a crowd of members who lack the enthusiasm and faith of the earlier ones and are attracted only by self-interest. Then there is a conflict between the older element and the new."

There is evidence that if financial prosperity is not associated with a utopian community's failure, then at least it is unrelated to its ability to continue in existence. A number of both successful and unsuccessful utopias weathered periods of hardship and suffered financial losses without dissolving, but then broke up at a time when they had accumulated great wealth and showed a profit. Bethel, for example, began in 1844 with $30,000 in assets and, when it dissolved in 1880, had over $3,000,000 to distribute. Hopedale started in 1841 with under $5,000 in property and suffered a loss the following year, but in 1856, the year it broke up, it earned a net profit of $7,000 for the year and had a quarter of a million dollars in assets. The North American Phalanx increased its assets from $8,000 to $67,000 in addition to paying dividends of about five percent a year to stockholders, yet it dissolved after thirteen years. The Wisconsin Phalanx not only showed profits but also increased its assets from $1,000 to $33,000 over a six-year lifetime. Skaneateles doubled its assets in its two-and-one-half year history, and Communia increased its assets by more than a third. Oneida, after many years of losses, dissolved in 1881 at a time when profits were at an all-time high. Amana distributed well over two million dollars when it broke up in 1933, even though it also faced mounting debts. This evidence suggests that at the very least one can agree with Ralph Albertson's conclusion that American utopias with few exceptions were successful in earning their living: "Few colonies, if any, failed because they could not make their living * * * They failed to like communal housekeeping. They failed to hold their young people. They failed to compete with growing industry and commerce in a new, unexploited country. But they did not fail to make an independent subsistence living—and pay off a lot of debts and help a lot of stranded people."

With prosperity came not only reinforcement of forms of organization that were often in tension with community but also other kinds of conflict that contributed to the death of successful nineteenth-century groups. In particular, competition between individuals and families increased, as did the desire for private rather than shared ownership. In 1895 in Zoar, a few years before its final dissolution, the newspaper, *Nugitna,* began agitating for the right to withdraw from the communal society and to acquire property. As forms of organization oriented toward production, commerce, and exchange superceded commitment mechanisms, the old zeal and devotion to communal ideals declined, the will to continue the community in its utopian, communal form decreased, and the end was in sight.

Prosperity is enough of an issue for communal groups even today that not only do many communes self-consciously choose austerity and poverty rather than affluence, but also some refuse to work at making any more money than will meet their immediate needs. The Bruderhof, for example, have a successful toy-manufacturing business and could sell as much as they produce; but they often stop production when they feel they have earned enough to meet their daily needs.

All of the factors described—environmental change, population aging, and a growing tendency away from community toward organizational efficiency—intertwined to erode the commitment that had held successful communes together in the nineteenth century. Jerusalem had grown and become wealthy, but after the death of Jemimah Wilkinson, celibacy declined and hence the community. Bethel and Aurora suffered a similar fate after thirty-six years of existence. In Harmony by the 1870s only a few dozen old people were left, so that the group had to stop running its factories and start buying. By 1892 it faced large debts and lawsuits by ex-members and would-be heirs. It dissolved formally in 1904 after one hundred years. Saint Nazianz faced confusion after Father Ambrose Ochswald's death, for he had such complete authority that there was no one to replace him. The community property had been held in his name and willed to the community, but it could not be inherited because the community was not incorporated. At the same time, the population was aging and there were few recruits, while the remaining members desired changes in the commune's financial arrangements. What resulted was a dual management structure, with temporal and spiritual leaders. Litigation over division of the property and inheritance led to the formation of a joint-stock company to be administered by a board of directors. Saint Nazianz ended in 1896 after forty-two years.

Zoar, too, faced internal dissension and a decline in the desire for communal property. There were strains over the fact that title to the land was in Joseph Bimeler's name. Hiring of outside workers led to a money economy in which outsiders were paid but Zoarites were not. Although visitors were discouraged in the early years, they were encouraged after 1850, the period of the community's decline. A general store and hotel were built in the village to cater to neighboring settlements and visitors; the tourist trade was encouraged to increase income. Families began to sell surpluses to visitors, and competition was introduced. The management of the hotel was a cause of dissension, in that there were complaints that the members associated with it had special privileges. In general, the second generation was less committed to communal ownership; the third even less so. When business prosperity declined and expenses exceeded income, the membership began agitating for a division of property. Finally in 1898, after eighty-one years of existence, about $2,500 per person was distributed, and the utopian community of Zoar became the village of Zoar.

Oneida began to face difficulties in the 1870s. Attention was increasingly directed toward practical social and economic concerns, away from spiritual matters. The businesses were flourishing. There was a growing "generation gap" over the issue of science versus religion. Oneida's concern with education conflicted with commitment to the community. Youth who had been educated on the outside returned to the commune but with an undercurrent of discontent. In 1874 a newcomer named James William Towner, a lawyer, led a faction opposing John Humphrey Noyes's leadership, and Towner gained authority over business matters. In 1879 Noyes left for Canada because of the threat of legal action by local ministers with regard to the community's practice of complex marriage. In 1880 the adult members of the community signed an Agreement to Divide and Reorganize, giving up communal property and complex marriage, and in 1881, after thirty-three years as a commune, the Oneida Community became a joint-stock company, Oneida, Ltd.

The commitment that had enabled the successful nineteenth-century utopian communities to withstand threats to their existence early in their history, which had provided members with the determination to continue, which had developed relationships that could weather disagreement, dissatisfaction, or defections, and which had reinforced firm belief in the community's ideals and values, had declined by the time they dissolved. They faced a set of forces that grew in magnitude as the communities progressed, and which eventually proved too much for even the strongest. Some groups died slowly (like the Shakers), others dissolved formally, and still others reorganized to perform a specialized job. But whatever the issues, problems, and concerns that first brought these utopian communities together, the world they faced at their conclusion was very different from that existing at their beginning. In today's world, a new set of communes has arisen, growing out of the issues and concerns of today, but with much still to be learned about their problems and prospects by examining the lessons of the past.
* * *

The major difference between establishing a new community in the nineteenth and twentieth centuries is the degree of difficulty a group encounters in constructing strong boundaries and creating a coherent group. Whereas it was relatively easy for groups to develop clearcut boundaries in the nineteenth century, it is relatively difficult today. Although the strength of a commune today is still contingent on the presence of commitment mechanisms, the problems of employing these mechanisms have been exaggerated by the difficulties of developing and maintaining boundaries in an urban era of mass communication, easy mobility, and rapid social change. Strong communities today can generate and maintain commitment because of their adaptive solutions to boundary problems, while weak communes succumb to the boundary-denying forces in the society and become limited communities of narrow scope.

Boundary Problems

Boundaries define a group, set it off from its environment, and give it a sharp focus, which facilitates commitment. Strong communities tend to have strong boundaries—physical, social, and behavioral. What goes on within the community is sharply differentiated from what goes on outside. As with the secret societies described by Georg Simmel, events inside the community may even be kept hidden from outsiders and reserved for members alone to know, witness, and perform. One kind of boundary may help to define another. Physical boundaries, as of location and territory, might define those people with whom a person may legitimately engage in a relationship. Social boundaries may define behavioral ones, as in a monogamous marriage, where the two people who have defined themselves through the relationship behave toward each other in ways that they do not exhibit toward others.

With strong boundaries, it is clear who belongs to the group and who does not. The outside may treat members as a unit for many purposes. Passing in and out of the community, both for new recruits and for old members, may be relatively difficult. The definition of a communal group as an expressive unit concerned with interchanges between its members, as a group of people interested in mutual support and a shared way of life, indicates in part the importance of boundaries, because of their value in preserving the uniqueness of interaction between the specific set of people comprising the community.

Many of the commitment mechanisms that differentiated successful from unsuccessful nineteenth-century communes revolved around erecting and maintaining strong affirmative boundaries, which distinguished the group from its environment, so that members created for themselves psychic boundaries that encompassed the community—no more and no less—as the object of commitment and fulfillment. The commitment-generating problems of some unsuccessful groups can even be pinpointed as boundary issues, such as the fact that New Harmony let anyone in, exercising no selectivity and no socialization, or the fact that members of Brook Farm practically commuted to Boston. Many of the difficulties that successful groups later encountered stemmed in part from a weakening of the boundaries: hiring outside workers, educating children on the outside, increasing numbers of visitors, adopting the fruits of outside social change, and most important, engaging in expanded commerce and trade or decreased internal production and consumption, which destroyed the kind of self-sufficiency that itself constitutes a boundary.

Communes are conscious and purposeful in their attempt to separate from the larger society and create a special group. In the nineteenth century, conditions were such that distinct boundaries could be erected with relative ease. Physical isolation was possible, as well as a relatively self-sufficient farm and light industry economy. Technological needs were low, and contact with the outside minimized, so that a group could become institutionally complete, a comprehensive community comprised of all social institutions. Communication was slow, so that it was possible for a group to remain hidden, developing and maintaining a distinctive culture. Travel was generally confined to small geographic areas. There were fewer options for life in the society—from choice of career to choice of life style—so that it was possible to find a homogeneous group of people who were willing to share beliefs, without the confusion and pressure of constant subjection to opposing views. Some commitment mechanisms even arose unintentionally: the distinctive language and dress style of such groups as Harmony and Amana were a function of the fact that they were immigrant groups with a transplanted culture, but could, in the nineteenth century, experience few pressures for assimilation.

Twentieth-century American society provides a very different kind of environment, one that is constantly intruding and penetrating the borders of groups, which contributes to the fact that the boundaries of most contemporary communes are weak and constantly shifting. Four characteristics of contemporary society are primarily responsible: urbanization, advanced technology, instant communication, and a white middle-class culture that is increasingly both national (fairly uniform across the country) and pluralistic and eclectic within the range of options provided nationally. More people live in cities and want to stay in cities, which has given rise to urban communes, a new phenomenon of this century, for evidence is lacking of any urban utopias in the last century. Advanced technology makes it less possible for any group to supply all or most of its needs by itself or for a small group easily to develop an economic base as a complete production unit. Thus, many communes today do not even attempt to constitute an economic unit, concentrating rather on being a family, which typifies the diminishment of scope characterizing a large proportion of the new communes. Institutional comprehensiveness is no longer as possible as it was in the nineteenth century. Instant communication means that new ideas and new stimuli can intrude constantly, increasing the difficulty of generating and maintaining a distinctive set of beliefs. Most communes today do not develop their own ideologies, and even when they do, they often borrow and incorporate bits and pieces from other people and other groups. The problems of ideological completeness, therefore—of any one group developing a unique, comprehensive ideology—are intensified.

These three factors—urbanization, technology, and mass communication—have supported the development of a national middle class culture that is increasingly both uniform across regions and pluralistic in terms of styles available. People are more mobile—particularly the young, who are the ripest recruits for the new communes. As they move, they carry with them across the nation the counterculture of which communes are one part. In addition, people and places are increasingly interchangeable. If strong utopian communities in fact resemble secret societies, then in the twentieth century most communes participate in a culture that has become too pervasive and widespread to develop such a secret, shared truth. Developing a distinctive culture, set off from that of the surrounding environment, is much more difficult today than in the nineteenth century; many contemporary communes choose not even to try, again retreating from their former scope. Rather than separating themselves from society, as did the communes of the last century, many become a link in a chain of the national counterculture, exchanging members with other communes. The fact that modern American culture is at the same time pluralistic and eclectic, surrounding the person with a much greater number of options than in the last century—with respect to careers, consumption, relationships—makes it harder for the individual both to make definitive choices (as of one group or one culture and life style within that group) and to find one set of people with whom he can share every aspect of his life, since everyone else has the same large number of options from which to extract a life style. The individual constructs his own social world out of the myriad choices confronting him, and the chance that many others will construct theirs in exactly the same way is much more limited than in the less diverse environment of the last century. Without a strong set of beliefs to indicate to the person why he should suspend his options, he generally continues to exercise them in the new communes. And most new communes, given the increased difficulty of placing limits on options, choose not to do so.

The boundary problems of today's communes are exacerbated by the fact that communes as a unique social arrangement lack definition and legitimacy in American society. For legal and official purposes, they must define themselves in terms of some other form such as a nonprofit corporation, a business, a church, an educational institution, or a family. Sunrise Hill set itself up as a trust fund; Synanon defined itself as a charitable foundation; the Fort Hill commune is organized into a holding corporation, "United Illuminating." Moreover, whereas the norms of the larger society indicate the ways in which legitimate social institutions are to be approached, there are not yet such established guidelines for communes. There are socially delimited ways of entering a family, for example—through marriage, birth, or legal adoption—but no similar guidelines for joining a commune. In America as a whole, strangers do not knock at the doors of residences asking for a place to sleep or inquiring whether they can become a member of that particular family, but they do approach communes with these requests. To some extent, communes are considered fair game for anyone, and their borders are easily penetrable.

Thus, it is more difficult today to develop strong boundaries than it was in the nineteenth century, and territorial or spatial limits no longer suffice to give a group coherence. Today's communes have had to develop other kinds of group-environment relations and other means of handling their boundary problems, for as Eric Berne pointed out, the existence of a group is in part dependent on being able to predict who will or will not be present and behaving in particular ways at specific events. That is, the very definition of a group is to some extent dependent on the existence of boundaries: "constitutional, psychological or spatial distinctions between members and non-members."

Boundaries transcend people, however; they also distinguish between events that occur within a group and those that do not. Boundary distinctions can be established on two principles, affirmative and negative. Affirmative principles define the group by what it accepts; negative, by what it rejects. Affirmative boundaries encompass only that which is accepted by the group; all events or people are excluded except those specifically included. A person is not "in" unless the group defines him as "in." Norms are positive, specifically defining appropriate behavior and events. Negative boundaries, in contrast, encompass everything but what the group specifically rejects; all events or people are included except those explicitly excluded. A person is not "out" unless the group defines him as "out." All behavior is permitted except that defined as inappropriate. Affirmative boundaries, then, are characteristic of secret societies in being exclusive and strict. Negative boundaries are characteristic of open societies in that they are inclusive and permissive. Affirmative boundaries are more conducive to building commitment than are negative boundaries.

Today's communes can be placed in two general categories, depending on the predominance of negative or affirmative boundaries. One set of communes, in line with today's diminishing scope and retreat themes, has primarily negative boundaries. I call these "retreat" communes. They tend to be small, anarchistic, and easily dissolved, predominantly rural and youth-oriented. Some urban communes also fall into this category, since they choose to specialize in domestic life rather than to develop a complete set of social institutions. They limit their goals to relationships, and like the rural retreat groups, they tend to be permissive, inclusive, and temporary. But the rural communes tend to be more purposeful and organized than the urban ones, and also to have some minimal shared economy, which urban houses generally lack. Thus, urban communes must be considered a different phenomenon, representing alternative forms of the family rather than new communities.

The other set of communes has affirmative boundaries. Rather than shrinking into a small family or avoiding the issue of boundaries altogether, these communes choose interaction with the wider society through service. Their mission gives them the focus around which to erect affirmative boundaries. They are either urban or rural, tend to have a strong core group holding the community together, and incorporate in their structure ways of coping with the mobility and turnover characteristic of today. They may also be larger and more enduring than retreat communes. More traditional utopias, such as the Bruderhof and Twin Oaks, and religious missionary communes are similar to the service communes in that they, too, have affirmative boundaries. In the twentieth century, however, affirmation alone may not be enough to give a group strength, and to the extent that a commune can define a special way in which it helps or transforms the larger social environment, it may gain added strength and ability to endure.

The distinction between retreat and service communes corresponds roughly to those made by other observers of the contemporary commune movement. Retreat groups tend to be what Bennett Berger called "noncreedal," in that they generally lack a shared ideology or creed; service communes more often are "creedal." Retreat communes tend to be solidarity-based and unintentional; service communes are generally ideology-based and intentional. Service communes are more similar to the utopias of the past, and many of the lessons of the past apply to them. Retreat communes, in contrast, are part of the new contemporary movement to regain Eden. * * *

PHILIPPE ARIES, THE FAMILY AND THE CITY IN THE OLD WORLD AND THE NEW

From V. Tufte & B. Myerhoff, Changing Images of the Family.
Pp. 29–41 (1979).

I should like to make some observations in this essay about the relationship between family history and urban history. My central theme will be that when the city (and earlier, the rural community) deteriorated and lost its vitality, the role of the family overexpanded like a hypertrophied cell. In an attempt to fill the gap created by the decline of the city and the urban forms of social intercourse it had once provided, the omnipotent, omnipresent family took upon itself the task of trying to satisfy all the emotional and social needs of its members. Today, it is clear that the family has failed in its attempts to accomplish that feat, either because the increased emphasis on privacy has stifled the need for social intercourse or because the family has been too completely alienated by public powers. People are demanding that the family do everything that the outside world in its indifference or hostility refuses to do. But we should now ask ourselves why people have come to expect the family to satisfy all their needs, as if it had some kind of all-encompassing power.

First, let us take a brief look at Western traditional societies from the Middle Ages to the eighteenth century, that is, before they had been affected by the Enlightenment and the Industrial Revolution. Each individual grew up in a community of relatives, neighbors, friends, enemies, and others with whom he or she had interdependent relationships. The community was more important in determining the individual's fate than was the family. When a young boy left his mother's apron strings, it was his responsibility to make a place for himself. Like an animal or a bird, he had to establish a domain, and he had to get the community to recognize it. It was up to him to determine the limits of his authority, to decide what he could do and how far he could go before encountering resistance from others his parents, his wife, his neighbors. Securing his domain in this way depended more on the skillful use of natural talents than on knowledge or savoir-faire. It was a game in which the venturesome boy gifted in eloquence and with a dramatic flair had the advantage. All life was a stage: if a player went too far, he was put in his place; if he hesitated, he was relegated to an inferior role.

Since a man knew that his wife would be his most important and faithful collaborator in maintaining and expanding his role, he chose his bride with care. On her part, the woman accepted the domain she would have to protect, along with the man with whom she would live. Marriage strengthened the husband's position, as a result not only of his wife's work, but also of her personality, her presence of mind, her talents as player, actress, storyteller, her ability to seize opportunities and to assert herself.

The important concept, then, is that of *domain*. But this domain was neither private nor public, as these terms are understood today; rather, it was both simultaneously: private because it had to do with individual behavior, with one's personality, one's manner of being alone or in society, one's self-awareness and inner being; public because it fixed the individual's place within the community and established one's rights and obligations. Individual maneuvering was possible because the social space was not completely filled. The fabric was loose, and it behooved each person to adjust the seams to suit himself or herself within the limits set by the community. The community recognized the existence of the empty space surrounding people and things. It is worth remarking that the word *play* can mean both the act of playing and freedom of movement within a space. Perhaps, by the act of playing, the free space to play in was created and maintained. The state and society intervened in a person's life only infrequently and intermittently, bringing with them either terror and ruin or miraculous good fortune. But for the most part, individuals had to win their domains by coming to terms only with the men and women in their own small community.

The role of the family was to strengthen the authority of the head of the household, without threatening the stability of his relationship with the community. Married women would gather at the wash house, men at the cabaret. Each sex had its special place in church, in processions, in the public square, at celebrations, and even at the dance. But the family as such had no domain of its own; the only real domain was that each male won by his maneuvering, with the help of his wife, friends, and dependents.

In the course of the eighteenth century the situation began to change, influenced by three important trends. The first is the loss of "frontiers," to use American parlance; we might say that in earlier centuries the community had a frontier—or rather several frontiers—that could be pushed back by the audacious. Free areas were allowed to exist, and adventurous individuals were permitted to explore them. But in the eighteenth century, society—or more properly, the state—was loath to accept the fact that there were certain areas beyond its sphere of control and influence. Following upon the Enlightenment and industrialization, the state, with its sophisticated technology and organization, wiped out those frontiers: there was no longer an open area for the venturesome. Today the state's scrutiny and control extend, or are supposed to extend, into every sphere of activity. Today there is no free space for individuals to occupy and claim for themselves. To be sure, liberal societies allow individuals some initiative, but for the most part only in specific areas, such as school and work, where there is a preestablished order of promotion. This is a situation totally different from that in traditional society. In the new society, the concepts of play and free space are no longer accepted; society must be too well regulated.

The second phenomenon that produced this change is directly related to the first: this is the division of space into areas assigned to work and areas assigned to living. The worker is now required to leave what had been the domain in traditional society, the space where *all* activities had taken place, to go to work far away, sometimes very far away, in a very different environment. There the worker becomes subject to a system of rules and to a hierarchy of power. In this new world, the worker may, for all we know, be happier and more secure, involved in association with others, for example, through trade unions.

This specialized place devoted to work was invented by the new society in its abhorrence of uncontrolled space. To run industrial, commercial, and business enterprises successfully requires systems of tight control. Free-enterprise capitalism has demonstrated its ability to adapt, but this flexibility has nothing in common with the old concept of free space; rather it depends on the precise functioning of the unit as a whole. Although enterprises in a free-market economy may not be controlled by the state, they are no less controlled by society at large. One could reasonably argue that this displacement of workers was a form of "surveillance and punishment," as Foucault phrased it, similar to locking up children in school, the insane in asylums, and delinquents in prison. It was certainly, at the very least, a means of maintaining order and control.

The third and last important phenomenon that affected the transformations of the eighteenth and nineteenth centuries is different from the first two; it is psychological. But the chronological correlation with the other two is significant. The era witnessed not only an industrial revolution but an emotional revolution as well. Previously, feelings were diffuse, spread out over numerous natural and supernatural objects, including God, saints, parents, children, friends, horses, dogs, orchards, and gardens. Henceforth, they would be focused within the immediate family. The couple and their children became the objects of a passionate and exclusive love that transcended even death.

From that time on, a working man's life was polarized between job and family. But the people who did not go out to work (women, children, old men) were concerned exclusively with family life. Nor was the division between job and family either equal or symmetrical. Although there was no doubt some room for emotional involvement at work, the family was a more conducive setting; whereas the working world was subject to constant, strict surveillance, the family was a place of refuge, free from outside control. The family thus acquired some similarities to the individual domain in traditional society, but with an important distinction: the family is not a place for individualism. The individual must recede into the background for the sake of the family unit, and especially for the sake of the children. Furthermore, the family had become more removed from the community than in earlier times, and it tended to be rather hostile to the external world, to withdraw into itself. Thus, it became *the* private domain, the only place where a person could legitimately escape the inquisitive stare of industrial society. Even now, industrial society has not given up trying to fill the gaps created by the decline of traditional society; it does, nevertheless, show some respect for the new entity—the family—which has grown up in its midst as a place of refuge. Thus, the separation of space into work areas and living areas corresponds to the division of life into public sector and private sector. The family falls within the private sector.

These, then, were the main features of the new way of life. They evolved slowly in the industrialized West, and were not equally accepted in all places. Two important periods must be distinguished: the nineteenth century before the automobile conquered space, and the first half of the twentieth. The difference between the two lies in the degree of privacy that people enjoyed and in the nature of the public sector.

During the first period, roughly the whole of the nineteenth century, family life among the bourgeoisie and the peasantry was already much as it is today, that is, it was a private domain. But—and this distinction is very important—only women (including those who worked) were affected by the increased privacy; men were able to escape at times, and they no doubt considered it a male prerogative to do so. Women and children had virtually no life outside the family and the school; these comprised their entire universe. Men, on the other hand, had a lively meeting place outside their families and jobs—to wit, the city.

In peasant societies, age-old tradition and the innovations of the industrial era are so intertwined that it is difficult for the analyst to distinguish among them. Still, it should be noted that historians today agree that, thanks to the agricultural prosperity in Western Europe during the nineteenth century, a flourishing rural civilization developed there. This was no doubt true of the United States as well. Is it not said that in certain regions of the Midwest immigrants have maintained traditions that have long since disappeared in their original homelands? These flourishing subcultures testify to the enormous vitality of the rural communities at a time when privacy, the family, and the school were making great inroads upon them. The rural exodus had not yet destroyed peasant life; rather, it had made it easier. This was the era of the beautiful costumes and regional furniture we find displayed today in folk museums. It was a time when folk tales were easily collected. It was also, however, a time when, thanks to the schools, many peasants were trying desperately to force open the doors to government careers for their children (who by then had grown fewer in number). The elementary school teacher was an important person in nineteenth-century rural communities; this is not true today. But it is the urban, not the rural, development that I should now like to discuss.

The long nineteenth century marked a high point in the development of the city and its urban civilization. No doubt urban populations had already increased to frightening levels; the poor immigrants who descended en masse upon them from the villages appeared as a threat to the bourgeois property owners, who watched them encamp in their towns and viewed them as an army of criminals and rebels. But this image borne of fear need not deceive us today. To be sure, the large city was no longer what it had been in the seventeenth century, that is, a group of separate neighborhoods or streets, each constituting a community with a character of its own. In eighteenth-century Paris, the arrival of a transient population without a fixed place of residence upset this way of life. Traditional patterns of social intercourse based on neighborhoods and streets began to disappear. But new ones that maintained and developed the city's basic functions replaced them.

Central to these new patterns were the café and the restaurant, public meeting places where conversation flowed as abundantly as food and drink. The café was a place for discussion, an invention of the late eighteenth century. Previously there had been eating places, inns, and hostels, places to serve meals in the home or to provide food and lodging for transient guests. There were also taverns and cabarets where people went to drink, and often for the low life to be found there. But they were places of ill-repute, sometimes brothels. Cafés, on the other hand, were something completely new and different. They were strictly an urban phenomenon, unknown in rural areas. The cafés were meeting places in cities, which were growing very rapidly and where people did not know one another as they had before. In England the cafés were enclosed like cabarets, but the name *pub* describes their function well. In continental Europe, cafés opened onto the street and came to dominate them, thanks to their terraces. Cafés with their large terraces were in fact one of the most striking features of nineteenth-century cities. They were all but nonexistent in the medieval and Renaissance sections of the old cities, such as Rome, but they were very much in evidence in those same Italian cities around the large public squares that owe their existence to Cavour's vast urbanization and Italian unity. In Vienna, too, cafés were, and still are, the heart of the city. In Paris the opening of the cafés was probably the reason behind the shift to public life from closed places, like the famous gallery at the Palais Royal, to the linear, open space of the boulevard, the center of the city's night life.

Cafés no doubt originally served the aristocracy rather than the bourgeoisie. But they were quickly popularized and extended to all classes of society and to all neighborhoods. In nineteenth-century cities, there was not a neighborhood without at least one café, and more often several. In working-class neighborhoods, the small café played a vital role; it enabled communication that would otherwise have been impossible among the poorly housed residents who were often away at their jobs: the café served as message center. That is why the telephone became so immediately accessible after its advent. The café became the place where steady customers could make and receive telephone calls, leave and receive messages. It is easy to understand Maurice Aguilhon's surprise at the extraordinary number of small cafés in a city like Marseilles, each with its little network of neighbors and friends gathered around the counter and the telephone. The number and popularity of these cafés suggest that a new public sector had spontaneously developed in the nineteenth-century city.

Needless to say, the state's desire for control extended even to this new public sector. The state immediately understood the danger represented by the cafés and sought to limit it by establishing and enforcing codes and regulations. But it never completely succeeded. In addition self-righteous people, concerned with order and morality, were suspicious of the cafés, which they considered to be hotbeds of alcoholism, anarchy, laziness, vice, and political wrangling. In France even today urban planners relegate cafés to shopping districts in residential areas and at a good distance from any elementary or secondary schools. But the mistrust of the authorities and of the self-righteous has still failed to diminish the popularity of the cafés. In the nineteenth century, civilization was based on them.

Now let us compare the role played by the café in that era to that played by the family. The family was a private place, the café a public one. But they had one thing in common: they both managed to escape society's control. The family did so by right, the café in actual fact. These were the only two exceptions to the modern system of surveillance and order which came to include all social behavior. Thus, alongside the growing privacy of the family during the nineteenth and early twentieth centuries, a new and lively form of social intercourse developed in even the largest cities. This explains why the cities of the era were so full of life, and why the increased amount of privacy did not weaken the forms of social intercourse, at least among males.

Toward the middle of the twentieth century, these forms of social intercourse began to break down in Western industrialized societies. The social and socializing function of the city disappeared. The more the urban population grew, the more the city declined. I am reminded of the words of the comedian who suggested moving the cities to the countryside. That, in fact, was exactly what happened. Immense continuous urban areas developed in all countries, but especially in the United States, where they have replaced the city. There cities in the old sense have ceased to exist. This phenomenon, one of the most important in the history of our society, must be seen in the light of what we know about the family and the ways it has changed. I should like to show how the decay of the city and the loss of its socializing function have affected contemporary family life.

From the late nineteenth century, even before the advent of the automobile, rich city-dwellers began to regard the crowded cities as unwholesome and dangerous and to flee in search of purer air and more decent surroundings. En masse they began to settle in those neighborhoods on the outskirts of cities that were still sparsely populated, such as the sixteenth and seventeenth *arrondissements* in Paris, near the greenery of the Parc Monceau and the Bois de Boulogne. Later, thanks to the railroad, the streetcar, and, in time, the automobile, they pushed farther and farther out. This trend occurred in all Western industrialized societies, but it was in North America that it developed most fully and reached its most extreme proportions; so we shall examine it there.

Neighborhoods are segregated not only by social class but also by function. Thus, just as there are rich, bourgeois neighborhoods and poor, working-class ones, so, too, there are business districts and residential ones. Offices, businesses, factories, and shops are found in one location, houses and gardens in the other. The means of transportation most often used to get from one place to the other is the private car. In this scheme of things there is no longer room for the forum, the agora, the piazza, the corso. There is no room, either, for the café as meeting place. The only thing there is room for is the drive-in and the fast-food outlet. Eating establishments are to be found in both business and residential districts; depending on their location, they are busy at different times of the day. In business and industrial districts they are humming with activity at lunchtime; in residential neighborhoods they do most of their business at night. During the off-hours, in both places, they are empty and silent.

What is truly remarkable is that the social intercourse which used to be the city's main function has now entirely vanished. The city is either crowded with the traffic of people and cars in a hurry or it is empty. Around noontime, office workers in business districts sometimes take an old-fashioned stroll when the weather is nice, and enjoy a piece of cake or an ice cream cone in the sun. But after five o'clock the streets are deserted. Nor do the streets in residential neighborhoods become correspondingly crowded, except around shopping centers and their parking lots. People return to their homes, as turtles withdraw into their shells. At home they enjoy the warmth of family life and, on occasion, the company of carefully chosen friends. The urban conglomerate has become a mass of small islands—houses, offices, and shopping centers— all separated from one another by a great void. The interstitial space has vanished.

This evolution was precipitated by the automobile and by television, but it was well underway before they had even appeared, thanks to the growth of the cult of privacy in the bourgeois and middle classes during the nineteenth century. To people born between 1890 and 1920 (now between sixty and ninety years old), the green suburb represented the ideal way of life, an escape from the bustle of the city to more rural, more natural surroundings. This shift to the suburbs, far from the noise and crowds of the city streets, was caused by the growing attraction of a warm private family life. In those areas where private family living was less developed, as in the working-class areas along the Mediterranean, societies dominated by obstinate males, community life fared better.

During the nineteenth and early twentieth centuries, the results of the increased privacy and the new family style of living were kept in check by the vitality of community life in both urban and rural areas. A balance was achieved between family life in the home and community life in the café, on the terrace, in the street. But this balance was destroyed and the family carried the day, thanks to the spread of suburbia that came with the new technology: the automobile and television. When that happened, the whole of social life was absorbed by private, family living.

Henceforth, the only function of the streets and cafés was to enable the physical movement between home and work or restaurant. For the most part, these ceased to be places of meeting, conversation, or recreation as the home, the couple, the family came to fulfill most of those functions. Today when a couple or a family leave the house to do something that cannot be done at home, they go in a mobile extension of the house, namely, the car. As the ark permitted Noah to survive the Flood, so the car permits its owners to pass through the hostile and dangerous world outside the front door.

Some of my American friends have suggested that in America the churches for a long time filled a public social function, somewhat as the café had done in Europe. Even today, many churches not only bring the faithful together to worship, but also organize suppers, banquets, and other get-togethers for various age groups, separate from religious services. This function, in my opinion, implies an identity between church and community: certainly it used to be that one went to the church of one's community or parents and did not change. The individual's church was not chosen but given by birth. We might, however, ask whether the socializing function of the church has diminished with the growth of religious mobility. Freedom of choice, the ability to change churches as one changes houses, jobs, or towns, may thus have transformed the church from a public space, or gathering place for the community, into a private club.

I believe I recognize in American society today a tendency to substitute, for public and anonymous socializing, a socializing in private clubs and special groups. The problem then is whether to regard this private socializing as an extension of the family or a substitute for it, and whether it is still providing, in the private sector, a festive function such as was formerly provided by the distractions of the street, the town square, the café, and places of accidental and unexpected meetings. One significant difference in the two sectors is that in the private sector everything is more or less predictable; in the public sector, as I have defined it, all events—even the most banal—have an unexpected and unplanned aspect.

Not long ago I found myself in Rome at midnight in the working-class neighborhood of Trastevere. There were still crowds of people in the streets, but there were no adults, only *ragazzi* of eighteen or twenty. They were mostly boys, because people there have not yet got into the habit, at least in working-class neighborhoods, of letting girls run around at night. Although children and adults are content to sit in front of the television set, adolescents are more interested in the life around them, in personal, spontaneous experiences. The young people of Trastevere were greeted by the marvelous Roman street, still the warm, picturesque setting of their daily life. But what about places where the setting no longer exists? Where do adolescents gather then? In the basements of houses, in underground garages, in the rooms of friends, usually enclosed. They may very well reject their families, but they still retain their tendency to seek seclusion. Today's frontier is this internal wall: it continues to exist even though it no longer has much to protect.

In the so-called postindustrial age of the mid-twentieth century, the public sector of the nineteenth century collapsed and people thought they could fill the void by extending the private, family sector. They thus demanded that the family see to all their needs. They demanded that it provide the passionate love of Tristan and Yseult and the tenderness of Philemon and Baucis; they saw the family as a place for raising children, but, at the same time, as a means of keeping them in a prolonged network of exclusive love. They considered the family a self-sufficient unit, though at times they were willing to enlarge the circle to include a few close friends. In the family, they hoped to recover the nostalgic world of the Jalna novels and to experience the pleasures of family warmth; from the private fortress of the family car they sought to discover the world outside. And they cherished the family as a place for all the childish things that continue even beyond childhood. These trends were intensified by the baby boom. Since then, the family has had a monopoly on emotions, on raising children, and on filling leisure time. This tendency to monopolize its members is the family's way of coping with the decline of the public sector. One can well imagine the uneasiness and intolerance that the situation has created.

Although people today often claim that the family is undergoing a crisis, this is not, properly speaking, an accurate description of what is happening. Rather, we are witnessing the inability of the family to fulfill all the many functions with which it has been invested, no doubt temporarily, during the past half-century. Moreover, if my analysis is correct, this overexpansion of the family role is a result of the decline of the city and of the urban forms of social intercourse that it provided. The twentieth-century postindustrial world has been unable, so far, either to sustain the forms of social intercourse of the nineteenth century or to offer something in its place. The family has had to take over in an impossible situation; the real roots of the present domestic crisis lie not in our families, but in our cities.

HANNA PITKIN & SARA SHUMER, ON PARTICIPATION

2 democracy 43, 46–48, 50 (1982).

Politics always concerns both the competitive distribution of scarce resources and the community's shared way of life—competing needs and shared principles. Neglect either aspect, and you lose the dynamic potential of democracy. * * *

That becomes clearer when one examines Jane Mansbridge's *Beyond Adversary Democracy*.[2] Mansbridge also sets out to challenge the dominant contemporary understanding, which she calls "adversary democracy," in the name of the participatory "unitary democracy" she observed in two small self-governing groups: a New England town meeting and an urban "crisis center" collective.

Unitary democracy, she says, is based on friendship and a "rough equality of mutual respect" among the members, who make decisions by consensus after face-to-face discussion. The crucial feature that "determines" which model of democracy is appropriate is the degree to which members share common interests. While the adversary model can accommodate conflicting interests, since each member is most concerned to protect himself, in unitary democracy the predominant concern must be promoting the common interest. So unitary democracy can only work where significant conflicts are few; ideally it "would, over time, require" unanimity on "every conceivable" policy question, while the adversary model ideally assumes agreement only on "the peaceful settlement of disputes." Neither model, of course, ever actually exists in its pure form; and Mansbridge urges small groups to mix or alternate between them. But for national, or even state and urban politics, she takes it as obvious that only adversary democracy makes sense. Since conflicting interests are unavoidable there, the unitary model could only be a sham, cloaking the oppression of minorities behind a show of consensus.

As a result, Mansbridge defines participation as pernicious just where democracy might really matter politically. In her understanding, there is no way for either model of democracy to resolve serious conflicts into anything like justice or the common good, since unitary democracy cannot have serious conflicts to resolve, and adversary democracy knows no common good. Having dissected the concept in this way, Mansbridge cannot restore it to life by her suggestion to mix or combine the two models.

She has accepted too many liberal assumptions, notably a definition of interest as "enlightened policy preference": the policy one would prefer if perfect information were available about all possible consequences. By stressing "policy preference," she blocks from view the very real stake people have in the manner and principles by which policy decisions are reached. Mutuality, openness, dignity, persuasive deliberation, justice, are not mere procedures for the "peaceful settlement of disputes," yet they are not policy preferences either. They are intrinsically valuable because they define how we live together: who we, as a community, are.

Democratic politics is an encounter among people with differing interests, perspectives, and opinions—an encounter in which they reconsider and mutually revise opinions and interests, both individual and

2. Jane J. Mansbridge, *Beyond Adversary Democracy* (New York: Basic Books, 1980).

common. It happens always in a context of conflict, imperfect knowledge, and uncertainty, but where community action is necessary. The resolutions achieved are always more or less temporary, subject to reconsideration, and rarely unanimous. What matters is not unanimity but discourse. The substantive common interest is only discovered or created in democratic political struggle, and it remains contested as much as shared. Far from being inimical to democracy, conflict— handled in democratic ways, with openness and persuasion—is what makes democracy work, what makes for the mutual revision of opinions and interest.

Rightly stressing that interests need not be selfish, can be "altruistic," "public-regarding," "ideal-regarding," Mansbridge employs the model of personal friendship. But that provides no escape from the liberal dilemma between self-interest and self-sacrifice. Sometimes, to counter selfishness, Mansbridge makes membership even in a unitary democracy sound like a dutiful burden; at other times she construes its unity as so intense that—as she says of friendship—"the separate individuals fuse, in a sense, into one." No wonder, then, if its extension to large and diverse groups seems to imply the crushing of minorities, and anything short of unanimity seems to indicate a failure in "fusion."

Small groups of the like-minded are useful to democrats, for instance as a context where oppressed people might first dare to articulate their real thoughts. But as a model of democracy such groups will not do, and they suggest the wrong strategy for democrats. Rather than seeking doctrinal purity and regarding internal dissent as pathological, democratic groups must welcome diversity and dispute. For the real revolutionizing power of democracy lies not in deploying a massive army of unanimous, disciplined followers for this or that radical policy preference, but in transforming people from consumers, victims, and exploiters into responsible citizens, extending their horizons and deepening their understanding, engaging their capacities, their suppressed anger and need in the cause of justice. As Mansbridge acknowledges, democracy is a matter of "what happens to the citizens themselves" rather than of "policy outcomes."

Democratic movements become stronger and potentially more radical as they diversify and reach out to other groups: when workers join with peasants, antinuclear ecologists join with nuclear plant workers and the unemployed, civil rights activists join with blue-collar workers and feminists. Not only do they acquire new members and allies, but they grow more political, and more just. As the group becomes more inclusive, members move beyond scapegoating toward increasing sophistication about the true social causes of their pain, and toward a more principled justification of who should pay what price to relieve it. So members discover their connectedness—and forge new connections— with others, with principle, and with their own capacities. Democrats must be as committed to fostering participatory politics within their movements as they are to the intrinsic value of participation in democratic government. * * *

ROBERTO UNGER, KNOWLEDGE AND POLITICS

Pp. 284–289 (1975).

THE DILEMMAS OF COMMUNITARIAN POLITICS

In developing a conception of the social ideal and of its relationship to the actual condition of society there is always the danger of glossing over the risks and difficulties that accompany the birth of a form of life. One passes all too easily from remorseless savagery in the criticism of the past to child-like innocence in the anticipation of the future. Thus, one encourages the mistaken belief that the ideal can be fully realized in history.

The opposite error would be to suppose that the hard choices faced by a society of organic groups are really the same as those of the society it seeks to displace. The dilemmas of communitarian politics may indeed resist solution. Yet they shift the focus of political struggle so as to draw out the ultimate conflicts among different aspects of the social ideal. These conflicts reveal and establish the outer limits of our ability to attain the end philosophy prescribes for us.

The first dilemma goes to the relations among groups. The second deals with the relationships between communal bodies and the higher-level organizations that coordinate them, or, more concretely, with the tie between community and state. The third dilemma has to do with disputes between established and emergent communities. The fourth is concerned with the reciprocal position of group values and universal culture and therefore with the place of philosophy in politics.

Two polar images might describe relations among organic groups. Each of those images has important attractions and fatal weaknesses. The first of them is the model of vertical integration. It sees each group as a relatively self-sufficient and closely-knit community, a commune very different from present occupational bodies. This means that there may be little division of labor among groups, but a great deal of it within them. The alternative pole is the model of horizontal integration according to which each association performs a narrowly limited range of activities, but interacts constantly with other communities. Consequently, there may be scant division of labor within groups, but much of it among them. The horizontal-integration model might focus on existing occupational groups as starting points of political action.

The policy of vertical integration seems hardly consistent with the commitment to an industrial civilization, for it imposes a strong barrier to the dimensions of collaborative work. Moreover, vertical integration represents a threat to individual autonomy: it seems that a system of vertically integrated communities could work only if there were significant restrictions on the freedom to join and leave them. At the same time, vertical integration keeps us from resolving the problem of self and others in our relationships to all but the persons who belong to the same group as we do. As a corollary, there will be no context for a universal moral experience upon which universally shared values might be based. And the extreme diversity of experience may encourage a destructive antagonism among the groups and deny them the criteria by which to choose among their competing ideals.

The dangers of horizontal integration seem just as serious. If there is a marked division of labor among groups, membership in each group will require the mastery of specialized skills or talents and the performance of particular tasks. Will not the group become an association of role players rather than a community of common purpose? And must not their specialization, like their isolation, produce moral conflicts favorable to war?

Another dilemma arises when we try to think of a hierarchy as well as of a plurality of associations. There are two extreme ways of conceiving the relationship between the groups and the state or, more generally, between the groups and higher-level institutions. On one view, the higher organizations are simply coordinating devices, with little reality of their own as communities; the state is just the constitutional order of the organic groups. On the opposite view, the superior institutions are real groups in their own right; the state is a community of communities.

An objection to the idea of the state as the constitutional order of the organic groups is that the weakness of the higher-order institutions would make it difficult to avoid the eruption of conflict among the baseline collectivities. This difficulty is merely the symptom of a deeper problem: unless the ideal of community is embodied in associations ever more extensive than the small group, the spiral may not only stop advancing but start to unwind. One of the conditions for the authority of communal beliefs and allocations of power is their progressive corroboration or revision in the light of the emerging consensus of a more universal community. Without such an appeal, the organic group turns into a solipsistic moral universe, caught in the trap of subjective value.

These difficulties may tempt us to grasp at the opposite idea of the state as a community in itself. But insofar as the higher-level agencies become more than instruments of coordination, they threaten to sap the vitality of the organic groups. A community makes demands upon the time of its members; it cannot survive unless they are constantly involved in its politics and thereby irresistably drawn away from the concerns of their original groups. The scarcity of time and the primacy of politics in communal life conspire against the division of loyalties that a hierarchy of communities implies. Still more disturbing is the possibility that the state may be incapable of becoming a true community even if one would want it to. Because it is by hypothesis an association of strangers, it cannot rely on the face-to-face coexistence and the common experience that might encourage shared purpose and the recognition of concrete individuality.

The third dilemma grows out of the competing demands made by old and new communities. Every community sets its seal upon the social world; it orders the activities of its members and their relations to the members of other groups. If all groups are free to move into the territory of an established association or to exert influence upon it in other ways, the disruption of communal experience may be so frequent and far-reaching as to be destructive of community existence. Each organic group may have the power to pass a death sentence upon the others by simply intruding upon their internal forms of life.

Nevertheless, the spiral of domination and community progresses through constant experiments in association. Unless emergent groups are free to develop and are not disadvantaged in relation to existing ones, there is the danger that a partial vision of the good will be petrified and the spiral arrested. Fundamental changes in moral vision may be more difficult to consummate within established communities than within new ones. Indeed, it seems likely that the threat to turn one's back on the community and join or create another one is a factor in making the group sensitive to criticism and capable of transformation.

The fourth major tension opposes the demands of group cohesion to the ideal of a critical education that instructs in the past and present beliefs and creations of mankind in their richest and fullest variety. Community requires cohesion; it can survive only in an atmosphere of strongly felt, though relative and shifting, moral agreement. At the same time, however, individuals must have access to a culture that transcends what any one group can perceive or accomplish on its own. The different traditions of thought or work constitute the deposits of the species nature in history. For that reason, they represent, despite their distortion by the vices of dominance, parts of the good and indispensable aids to its further realization. Moreover, without a basis for the criticism of shared values, there will be the tendency to sacrifice autonomy to moral union, and transcendence to imminence.

Notwithstanding its indispensability, a critical education may have a permanently subversive effect on all group cohesion. With the diversity and the excellence of the ideals of culture forever before their eyes, the members of the group may find themselves repeatedly torn apart from each other and torn away from the politics of their community. Thus, despairing of a public good, each may seek the illusions of private enlightenment and salvation.

The four dilemmas I have described present similar problems for a politics of community. In each case, either of the polar views, carried to the extreme, would destroy the communitarian ideal. In none of the cases, however, does there seem to be a theoretical criterion for determining where and how to strike the balance. Nor indeed can we be sure that a balance can be struck; it may turn out that no possible mix of the two pairs is consistent with the characteristic features of the social ideal, because the ideal demands more than half of what each of the countervailing models provides. In that event, we would have to reject the idea of a society of organic groups as utopian, and revise our theoretical ideas in the light of our new experience. More probably, political practice would yield a changing blend, in which the temporary predominance of one side of the spectrum would give way periodically to the hegemony of the other side. We might even hope that this cycle would itself become a spiral, and that each oscillation would combine more perfectly the virtues of the contrasting trends.

Theory can define the tensions and suggest the factors that should be taken into account in dealing with them. But only prudence can teach us what to do about them at each moment. And only practice can yield the insights needed to correct the decisions we make.

The reason why the dilemmas create similar difficulties is that they arise from the same underlying conflict. The first two problems present the antagonism between the apparent ideal situation within a community and the desirable form of relations among communities. Vertical integration and the confinement of the state to a coordinative role may seem best for the organic group as an isolated entity. But they make satisfactory group relations impossible and thereby ultimately corrupt the internal life of the group, endangering its survival and robbing it of an indispensable source of moral guidance. On the other hand, horizontal integration and communal hierarchy may appear best suited to the foreign affairs of organic groups, but they tend to efface the communitarian character of the associations they are meant to join.

The second pair of dilemmas represents a conflict between what seems most important to the perpetuation of a society of organic groups and what appears indispensable to its progress. The protection of established communities and of group cohesion may seem requirements of the structure of a communitarian society. But they can constitute obstacles to the process by which communities are formed and improved. The emphasis on associational renewal and critical education may be basic to the development of communitarian politics, but it threatens to destroy with one hand what it has created with another.

The tensions between what is best for the group and what is best for the society of groups, and between the structure of that society and the process of its growth, express a still deeper and more general struggle between a politics of particularism and one of universalism. Vertical integration, decentralization, the emphasis on established groups, and the defense of consensus all point toward the maintenance of the particularity of each association. Horizontal integration, communal hierarchy, institutional inventiveness, and critical understanding all turn toward the ideal of the transcendence of existing collectivities by increasingly universal associations.

The study of the institutional principles of the organic group has already shown us that there is irreplaceable truth in both tendencies. The community needs to remain a particular group, yet it must also become a universal one. Thus, we rediscover on the larger screen of politics the same predicament of a universality at once desired and forbidden so characteristic of human love, the same irreconcilability of the universal and the particular that holds all human thought and life in its grip. It is this disharmony, diminished but never undone, that makes politics incapable of ever fully redressing the imperfections of existence and of reaching the ideal in history.

Theories of community have traditionally suffered from a blend of utopian flavor and totalitarian insinuation because of their failure to acknowledge the force of these dilemmas. By focusing on the static, isolated group, they have cast aside issues about the relations among groups and the political construction of community over time. But these issues stand in fact at the core of communitarian politics, and lend it depth and force by connecting it with the major concerns of human existence. (See Figure 2.)

Figure 2

The Dilemmas of Communitarian Politics

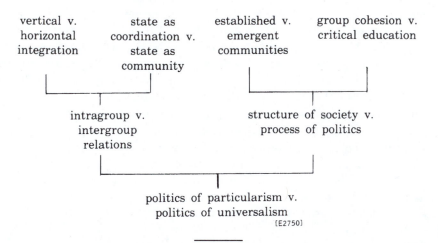

[E2750]

The excerpt from Professor Unger's Knowledge and Politics suggests that it is important to connect the subject of this Chapter—the relationship among neighboring cities—with the materials on federal-city and state-city relationship covered in Chapter Two. My own attempt to do so—the conclusion of the article excerpted above in Section B—is reproduced below.

GERALD FRUG, EMPOWERING CITIES IN A FEDERAL SYSTEM

19 The Urban Lawyer 553, 567–568 (1987).

We are now at the end of the essay, and I have not yet described the relationship between cities and the federal government (or between cities and states) at all. My discussion of cities' external relations has focused entirely on intercity relationships. The reason for this glaring omission is that the relationship among cities determines the relationship between cities and centralized governments. As long as we rely on free choice theory, we will continue to have to separate out the entitlements of cities, states, and the federal government. Some way must be found to protect the localities' entitlements not only from centralized control but also from each other. Under free choice theory, in short, all the puzzles of federalism will continue to recur. We have to be able to provide localities sufficient immunities from the national and state governments and from neighboring communities to protect their freedom of choice while not giving them so many immunities that the nation (and the state) will be threatened with unresolvable conflict.

On the other hand, consider the relationship between localities and the central government if a participation strategy has begun to work. The federal legislature can then be understood as one more mechanism for inter-local relationships, one more level of government on which issues of an inter-local conflict have to be worked out. The distinction between the federal government and the united localities will diminish, not because the Constitution says it should or because of the mere existence of local representation in the legislature, but because cooperation on the federal level will profit from the experience of cooperation gained through the multitude of intercity links (and intracity links) on the local level. Federalism will be created, not by the division of powers among geographic levels of government, but by building a structure of government from the bottom up, with the federal government simply being the final stage of inter-local resolution of conflict. Of course, some conflict between localities will seem unresolvable, and the temptation to seek a solution to the conflict from a higher authority will not go away. But the localities will learn that to the extent they cede power to a federal agency because of their failure to agree among themselves, they will be subject to centralized control. The way to avoid this centralized control is to come to an agreement themselves. Resolving federal-local relationships, in other words, will not be a matter of principle—not a question of allocation of authority by the courts—but a question of day-to-day decisionmaking by the localities. Thus, under a participation strategy, we might finally be able to put aside the classic federalism issue of drawing a "line" between local interests and federal interests; we will not have solved the problem of line drawing, but the question will no longer seem so important. Governmental relationships, like individual relationships, will remain difficult, helpful, threatening, and necessary for survival. But the important question will no longer be how to divide a group from a larger group of which it is a part. It will become instead how to find ways for individuals and groups to establish democratic relationships among themselves.

Chapter Four

THE RELATIONSHIP BETWEEN CITIES AND THEIR CITIZENS

The existence of federal and state power over cities, analyzed in Chapter Two, provides the background for the exploration in this chapter of the law governing the internal operations of cities. Much of the law examined in this chapter is federal Constitutional and statutory law designed to prevent city governments from invading citizens' rights. Indeed, fear of city restrictions on the freedom of its citizens—Madison's fear of the tyranny of the majority—pervades the cases reproduced below. This fear arises whenever cities try to control the character of city life, alter the nature of particular neighborhoods, or raise revenue from their citizens. It also influences the rules that govern voting, popular participation in city decisionmaking, citizens' rights to become informed about government activities, and the interpretation of Section 1983, the federal statute protecting citizens from violation of their Constitutional rights. A central question examined in this chapter, therefore, is the extent to which federal and state control of city government effectively protects citizens against the abusive exercise of city governmental power.

But this chapter raises another basic issue as well. The value of decentralizing political power—if it has any value at all—must be found in the internal operation of city government. Local power is desirable to the extent that it provides individuals with the ability to work together to control their own lives. Indeed, fostering the democratic operation of city governments can be seen as the central task of local government law. This point of view can be found in this chapter in the efforts of communities (and neighborhoods) to control their own character, in their attempts to increase citizen influence and participation in forming city policy, and in their search for new ways to ensure their economic viability. This chapter's cases, therefore, can be read not only to determine whether federal and state law effectively protects minority rights against city power but also to investigate whether local government law encourages or inhibits the emergence of a vital form of local democracy.

The two perspectives I have suggested for approaching this chapter restate Madison's and Tocqueville's contrasting views of decentralization of power presented in Chapter One. These two perspectives constitute the theoretical background for understanding the materials that follow.

SECTION A. CITY CONTROL OF COMMUNITY CHARACTER

Many people treat a city's ability to control its own character as the fundamental ingredient of local self-government. For them, local self-governance means the ability of citizens to create for themselves the kind of city they want to live in.[1] As we have already seen, however, this version of local self-governance is by no means unproblematic. In our examination of exclusionary zoning and school financing, for example, we saw that a city's attempt to control its own character had a negative impact on outsiders. Here, we examine how such an exercise of a city's power might be seen as a threat to its own citizens' Constitutional rights. The following cases and materials examine the extent to which the Constitution restricts a city's ability either to regulate who can live in the city (Village of Belle Terre v. Boraas, Moore v. East Cleveland, Kirsch v. Prince George's County, City of Cleburne, Texas v. Cleburne Living Center, and Bannum, Inc. v. City of St. Charles) or to impose zoning restrictions on pornographic movie theaters (City of Renton v. Playtime Theatres) and fast food restaurants (Taco Bell v. City of Mission). Why does the notion of community self-governance receive more attention in these cases than it did in the cases dealing with federal-city and state-city relations covered in Chapter Two? What does community self-governance mean in these cases? Is an ability to exclude "undesirables", pornographic movie theaters or fast food shops a necessary, justifiable—or Constitutional—part of the notion of community self-governance?

VILLAGE OF BELLE TERRE v. BORAAS

Supreme Court of the United States, 1974.
416 U.S. 1, 94 S.Ct. 1536, 39 L.Ed.2d 797.

MR. JUSTICE DOUGLAS delivered the opinion of the Court.

1. For a general analysis of this version of the concept of local self-governance, see, e.g., Neuman, Territorial Discrimination, Equal Protection and Self–Determination, 135 U.Pa.L.Rev. 261 (1987); Marshall, Discrimination and the Right of Association, 81 Nw.U.L.Rev. 68 (1986). For an analysis of this idea in particular contexts, see, e.g., Brest & Vandenberg, Politics, Feminism and the Constitution: The Anti–Pornography Movement in Minneapolis, 39 Stan. L.Rev. 607 (1987) (community efforts to eliminate pornography); Stein, Regulation of Adult Businesses Through Zoning After *Renton*, 18 Pac.L.J. 351 (1987) (same); Rose, Preservation and Community: New Directions in the Law of Historic Preservation, 33 Stan.L.Rev. 473 (1981) (an interpretation of the historical preservation movement as an effort to foster community cohesion).

Belle Terre is a village on Long Island's north shore of about 220 homes inhabited by 700 people. Its total land area is less than one square mile. It has restricted land use to one-family dwellings excluding lodging houses, boarding houses, fraternity houses, or multiple-dwelling houses. The word "family" as used in the ordinance means, "[o]ne or more persons related by blood, adoption, or marriage, living and cooking together as a single housekeeping unit, exclusive of household servants. A number of persons but not exceeding two (2) living and cooking together as a single housekeeping unit though not related by blood, adoption, or marriage shall be deemed to constitute a family."

Appellees, the Dickmans, are owners of a house in the village and leased it in December 1971 for a term of 18 months to Michael Truman. Later Bruce Boraas became a colessee. Then Anne Parish moved into the house along with three others. These six are students at nearby State University at Stony Brook and none is related to the other by blood, adoption, or marriage. When the village served the Dickmans with an "Order to Remedy Violations" of the ordinance, the owners plus three tenants thereupon brought this action under 42 U.S.C. § 1983 for an injunction and a judgment declaring the ordinance unconstitutional. * * *

This case brings to this Court a different phase of local zoning regulations from those we have previously reviewed. *Village of Euclid v. Ambler Realty Co.*, 272 U.S. 365, 47 S.Ct. 114, 71 L.Ed. 303, involved a zoning ordinance classifying land use in a given area into six categories. * * * The Court sustained the zoning ordinance under the police power of the State, saying that the line "which in this field separates the legitimate from the illegitimate assumption of power is not capable of precise delimitation. It varies with circumstances and conditions." And the Court added: "A nuisance may be merely a right thing in the wrong place, like a pig in the parlor instead of the barnyard. If the validity of the legislative classification for zoning purposes be fairly debatable, the legislative judgment must be allowed to control." * * * The main thrust of the case in the mind of the Court was in the exclusion of industries and apartments, and as respects that it commented on the desire to keep residential areas free of "disturbing noises"; "increased traffic"; the hazard of "moving and parked automobiles"; the "depriving children of the privilege of quiet and open spaces for play, enjoyed by those in more favored localities." The ordinance was sanctioned because the validity of the legislative classification was "fairly debatable" and therefore could not be said to be wholly arbitrary.

Our decision in *Berman v. Parker*, 348 U.S. 26, 75 S.Ct. 98, 99 L.Ed. 27, sustained a land use project in the District of Columbia against a landowner's claim that the taking violated the Due Process Clause and the Just Compensation Clause of the Fifth Amendment. The essence of the argument against the law was, while taking property for ridding an area of slums was permissible, taking it "merely to develop a better balanced, more attractive community" was not. We refused to limit the concept of public welfare that may be enhanced by zoning regulations. We said:

> "Miserable and disreputable housing conditions may do more than spread disease and crime and immorality. They may also suffocate the spirit by reducing the people who live there to the status of cattle. They may indeed make living an almost insufferable burden. They may also be an ugly sore, a blight on the community which robs it of charm, which makes it a place from which men turn. The misery of housing may despoil a community as an open sewer may ruin a river.

> "We do not sit to determine whether a particular housing project is or is not desirable. The concept of the public welfare is broad and inclusive. * * * The values it represents are spiritual as well as physical, aesthetic as well as monetary. It is within the power of the legislature to determine that the community should be beautiful as well as healthy, spacious as well as clean, well-balanced as well as carefully patrolled."

If the ordinance segregated one area only for one race, it would immediately be suspect under the reasoning of *Buchanan v. Warley*, 245 U.S. 60, 38 S.Ct. 16, 62 L.Ed. 149 where the Court invalidated a city ordinance barring a black from acquiring real property in a white residential area by reason of an 1866 Act of Congress, 14 Stat. 27, now 42 U.S.C. § 1982, and an 1870 Act, § 17, 16 Stat. 144, now 42 U.S.C. § 1981, both enforcing the Fourteenth Amendment. * * *

The present ordinance is challenged on several grounds: that it interferes with a person's right to travel; that it interferes with the right to migrate to and settle within a State; that it bars people who are uncongenial to the present residents; that it expresses the social preferences of the residents for groups that will be congenial to them; that social homogeneity is not a legitimate interest of government; that the restriction of those whom the neighbors do not like trenches on the newcomers' rights of privacy; that it is of no rightful concern to villagers whether the residents are married or unmarried; that the ordinance is antithetical to the Nation's experience, ideology, and self-perception as an open, egalitarian, and integrated society.

We find none of these reasons in the record before us. It is not aimed at transients. Cf. *Shapiro v. Thompson*, 394 U.S. 618, 89 S.Ct. 1322, 22 L.Ed.2d 600. It involves no procedural disparity inflicted on some but not on others such as was presented by *Griffin v. Illinois*, 351 U.S. 12, 76 S.Ct. 585, 100 L.Ed. 891. It involves no "fundamental" right guaranteed by the Constitution, such as voting, *Harper v. Virginia State Board*, 383 U.S. 663, 86 S.Ct. 1079, 16 L.Ed.2d 169; the right of association, *NAACP v. Alabama ex rel. Patterson*, 357 U.S. 449, 78 S.Ct. 1163, 2 L.Ed.2d 1488; the right of access to the courts, *NAACP v. Button*, 371 U.S. 415, 83 S.Ct. 328, 9 L.Ed.2d 405; or any rights of privacy, cf. *Griswold v. Connecticut*, 381 U.S. 479, 85 S.Ct. 1678, 14 L.Ed.2d 510; *Eisenstadt v. Baird*, 405 U.S. 438, 453 454, 92 S.Ct. 1029,

1038–1039, 31 L.Ed.2d 349. We deal with economic and social legislation where legislatures have historically drawn lines which we respect against the charge of violation of the Equal Protection Clause if the law be " 'reasonable, not arbitrary' " and bears "a rational relationship to a [permissible] state objective." *Reed v. Reed*, 404 U.S. 71, 76, 92 S.Ct. 251, 254, 30 L.Ed.2d 225.

It is said, however, that if two unmarried people can constitute a "family," there is no reason why three or four may not. But every line drawn by a legislature leaves some out that might well have been included. That exercise of discretion, however, is a legislative, not a judicial, function.

It is said that the Belle Terre ordinance reeks with an animosity to unmarried couples who live together. There is no evidence to support it; and the provision of the ordinance bringing within the definition of a "family" two unmarried people belies the charge.

The ordinance places no ban on other forms of association, for a "family" may, so far as the ordinance is concerned, entertain whomever it likes.

The regimes of boarding houses, fraternity houses, and the like present urban problems. More people occupy a given space; more cars rather continuously pass by; more cars are parked; noise travels with crowds.

A quiet place where yards are wide, people few, and motor vehicles restricted are legitimate guidelines in a land-use project addressed to family needs. This goal is a permissible one within *Berman v. Parker*, *supra*. The police power is not confined to elimination of filth, stench, and unhealthy places. It is ample to lay out zones where family values, youth values, and the blessings of quiet seclusion and clean air make the area a sanctuary for people. * * *

Mr. Justice Marshall, dissenting. * * *

In my view, the disputed classification burdens the students' fundamental rights of association and privacy guaranteed by the First and Fourteenth Amendments. Because the application of strict equal protection scrutiny is therefore required, I am at odds with my Brethren's conclusion that the ordinance may be sustained on a showing that it bears a rational relationship to the accomplishment of legitimate governmental objectives.

I am in full agreement with the majority that zoning is a complex and important function of the State. It may indeed be the most essential function performed by local government, for it is one of the primary means by which we protect that sometimes difficult to define concept of quality of life. I therefore continue to adhere to the principle of *Village of Euclid v. Ambler Realty Co.*, 272 U.S. 365, 47 S.Ct. 114, 71 L.Ed. 303 (1926), that deference should be given to governmental judgments concerning proper land-use allocation. That deference is a principle which has served this Court well and which is necessary for the continued development of effective zoning and land-use control mechanisms. Had the owners alone brought this suit alleging that the restrictive ordinance deprived them of their property or was an irrational legislative classification, I would agree that the ordinance would have to be sustained. Our role is not and should not be to sit as a zoning board of appeals.

I would also agree with the majority that local zoning authorities may properly act in furtherance of the objectives asserted to be served by the ordinance at issue here: restricting uncontrolled growth, solving traffic problems, keeping rental costs at a reasonable level, and making the community attractive to families. The police power which provides the justification for zoning is not narrowly confined. See *Berman v. Parker*, 348 U.S. 26, 75 S.Ct. 98, 99 L.Ed. 27 (1954). And, it is appropriate that we afford zoning authorities considerable latitude in choosing the means by which to implement such purposes. But deference does not mean abdication. This Court has an obligation to ensure that zoning ordinances, even when adopted in furtherance of such legitimate aims, do not infringe upon fundamental constitutional rights.
* * *

My disagreement with the Court today is based upon my view that the ordinance in this case unnecessarily burdens appellees' First Amendment freedom of association and their constitutionally guaranteed right to privacy. Our decisions establish that the First and Fourteenth Amendments protect the freedom to choose one's associates. Constitutional protection is extended, not only to modes of association that are political in the usual sense, but also to those that pertain to the social and economic benefit of the members. The selection of one's living companions involves similar choices as to the emotional, social, or economic benefits to be derived from alternative living arrangements.

The freedom of association is often inextricably entwined with the constitutionally guaranteed right of privacy. The right to "establish a home" is an essential part of the liberty guaranteed by the Fourteenth Amendment. *Meyer v. Nebraska*, 262 U.S. 390, 399, 43 S.Ct. 625, 626, 67 L.Ed. 1042 (1923); *Griswold v. Connecticut*, 381 U.S. 479, 495, 85 S.Ct. 1678, 1687, 14 L.Ed.2d 510 (1965) (Goldberg, J., concurring). And the Constitution secures to an individual a freedom "to satisfy his intellectual and emotional needs in the privacy of his own home." *Stanley v. Georgia*, 394 U.S. 557, 565, 89 S.Ct. 1243, 1248, 22 L.Ed.2d 542 (1969). Constitutionally protected privacy is, in Mr. Justice Brandeis' words, "as against the Government, the right to be let alone * * * the right most valued by civilized man." *Olmstead v. United States*, 277 U.S. 438, 478, 48 S.Ct. 564, 572, 72 L.Ed. 944 (1928) (dissenting opinion). The choice of household companions—of whether a person's "intellectual and emotional needs" are best met by living with family, friends, professional associates, or others—involves deeply personal considerations as to the kind and quality of intimate relationships within the home. That decision surely falls within the ambit of the right to privacy protected by the Constitution. * * *

The instant ordinance discriminates on the basis of just such a personal lifestyle choice as to household companions. It permits any number of persons related by blood or marriage, be it two or twenty, to live in a single household, but it limits to two the number of unrelated persons bound by profession, love, friendship, religious or political affiliation, or mere economics who can occupy a single home. Belle Terre imposes upon those who deviate from the community norm in their choice of living companions significantly greater restrictions than are applied to residential groups who are related by blood or marriage, and compose the established order within the community. The village has, in effect, acted to fence out those individuals whose choice of lifestyle differs from that of its current residents.

This is not a case where the Court is being asked to nullify a township's sincere efforts to maintain its residential character by preventing the operation of rooming houses, fraternity houses, or other commercial or high-density residential uses. Unquestionably, a town is free to restrict such uses. Moreover, as a general proposition, I see no constitutional infirmity in a town's limiting the density of use in residential areas by zoning regulations which do not discriminate on the basis of constitutionally suspect criteria. This ordinance, however, limits the density of occupancy of only those homes occupied by unrelated persons. It thus reaches beyond control of the use of land or the density of population, and undertakes to regulate the way people choose to associate with each other within the privacy of their own homes. * * *

Because I believe that this zoning ordinance creates a classification which impinges upon fundamental personal rights, it can withstand constitutional scrutiny only upon a clear showing that the burden imposed is necessary to protect a compelling and substantial governmental interest, *Shapiro v. Thompson*, 394 U.S. 618, 634, 89 S.Ct. 1322, 1331, 22 L.Ed.2d 600 (1969). * * * A variety of justifications have been proffered in support of the village's ordinance. It is claimed that the ordinance controls population density, prevents noise, traffic and parking problems, and preserves the rent structure of the community and its attractiveness to families. As I noted earlier, these are all legitimate and substantial interests of government. But I think it clear that the means chosen to accomplish these purposes are both overinclusive and underinclusive, and that the asserted goals could be as effectively achieved by means of an ordinance that did not discriminate on the basis of constitutionally protected choices of lifestyle. The ordinance imposes no restriction whatsoever on the number of persons who may live in a house, as long as they are related by marital or sanguinary bonds—presumably no matter how distant their relationship. Nor does the ordinance restrict the number of income earners who may contribute to rent in such a household, or the number of automobiles that may be maintained by its occupants. In that sense the ordinance is underinclusive. On the other hand, the statute restricts the number of unrelated persons who may live in a home to no more than two. It would therefore prevent three unrelated people from occupying a dwelling even if among them they had but one income and no vehicles. While an extended family of a dozen or more might live in a small bungalow, three elderly and retired persons could not occupy the large manor house next door. Thus the statute is also grossly overinclusive to accomplish its intended purposes.

There are some 220 residences in Belle Terre occupied by about 700 persons. The density is therefore just above three per household. The village is justifiably concerned with density of population and the related problems of noise, traffic, and the like. It could deal with those problems by limiting each household to a specified number of adults, two or three perhaps, without limitation on the number of dependent children. The burden of such an ordinance would fall equally upon all segments of the community. It would surely be better tailored to the goals asserted by the village than the ordinance before us today, for it would more realistically restrict population density and growth and their attendant environmental costs. Various other statutory mechanisms also suggest themselves as solutions to Belle Terre's problems—rent control, limits on the number of vehicles per household, and so forth, but, of course, such schemes are matters of legislative judgment and not for this Court. Appellants also refer to the necessity of maintaining the family character of the village. There is not a shred of evidence in the record indicating that, if Belle Terre permitted a limited number of unrelated persons to live together, the residential, familial character of the community would be fundamentally affected.

By limiting unrelated households to two persons while placing no limitation on households of related individuals, the village has embarked upon its commendable course in a constitutionally faulty vessel. I would find the challenged ordinance unconstitutional. But I would not ask the village to abandon its goal of providing quiet streets, little traffic, and a pleasant and reasonably priced environment in which families might raise their children. Rather, I would commend the village to continue to pursue those purposes but by means of more carefully drawn and even-handed legislation.

FRANK MICHELMAN, POLITICAL MARKETS AND COMMUNITY SELF–DETERMINATION

53 Ind.L.J. 145, 189–194 (1977–78).

Three years after upholding the Belle Terre ordinance, the Court again confronted a suburban single-family zoning restriction. This time, in *Moore v. East Cleveland*,[154] civil liberties prevailed and the ordinance was ruled invalid. East Cleveland's somewhat unusual and complicated regulation could be roughly described as excluding not only nonfamilial household groupings, but also "extended" as distinguished from "nuclear" families. One of its particular features was to distinguish among households containing a grandparent and more than one grandchild, admitting such households if all the grandchildren were one another's

---

154.   431 U.S. 494 (1977).

siblings but excluding them if any pair were first cousins. The appellant was an East Cleveland homeowner appealing from a criminal conviction and fine for having harbored two grandchildren, first cousins, in her home.

Writing for a plurality of four Justices,[156] Justice Powell relied on a civil-libertarian position similar to that which had been unavailing with the *Belle Terre* majority of which he had been a member—the position that, "[as] this Court has long recognized * * * freedom of personal choice in matters of marriage and family life is one of the liberties [particularly] protected by the Due Process Clause of the Fourteenth Amendment." Because the East Cleveland ordinance "intrudes on choices concerning family living arrangements, [the] Court must examine carefully the importance of the governmental interests advanced and the extent to which they are served by the challenged regulation." Examined from that standpoint, various anticongestion goals cited by East Cleveland could not justify its ordinance, because "the ordinance * * * serves them marginally at best." Of course, the same was true of the Belle Terre ordinance, but it was distinguished as not encroaching on a "private realm of family life,"—evidently meaning by "family" not simply a domestic household group, but a group mutually linked by "blood, adoption, or marriage." The only reason offered in defense of this distinction was that "the Constitution protects the sanctity of the family because the institution of the family is deeply rooted in this Nation's history and tradition. It is through the family that we inculcate and pass down many of our most cherished values, moral and cultural."

Two Belle Terre dissenters who joined Justice Powell's *East Cleveland* opinion also, through Justice Brennan, contributed some additional views of their own. Although they might consistently have dealt with the Belle Terre case by simply sticking to their earlier position that it was wrongly decided,[161] they instead said that it was distinguishable because the Belle Terre ordinance did not, as the East Cleveland ordinance did, "inhibit [in any manner] the choice of *related* individuals to constitute a family, whether in the 'nuclear' or 'extended' form." But they offered no account at all of the constitutional relevance of this distinction.

One more vote—that of Justice Stevens—was needed to swing the Court's five-to-four decision against the validity of the East Cleveland ordinance. In Justice Stevens' view, the constitutionally protected right infringed by that regulation was not a special right of self-determination in matters relating to family life, but a general property owners' "fundamental right"—"to decide who may reside on [one's] property," or, still more generally,—"to use [one's] own property as [one] sees fit," short of creating a "nuisance" that "impair[s] the enjoyment of other property in

156. Including Justices Brennan, Marshall, and Blackmun.

161. Justice Marshall had dissented on the merits, 416 U.S. 1, 12, while Justice Brennan had declined to reach the merits, *id.* at 10.

the vicinity" or violating a community land-use scheme having a "substantial relation to the public health, safety, morals or general welfare." The challenged feature of the East Cleveland ordinance could not satisfy this "substantial relation to general welfare" test because the city could not possibly "explain the need for a rule which would allow a homeowner to have two grandchildren live with her if they are brothers, but not if they are cousins." Apparently perceiving that families-only type ordinances—including Belle Terre's—would be generally vulnerable to like objection, Justice Stevens expressed sympathy for a series of "well reasoned" state court decisions protecting the rights of "unrelated persons to occupy single-family residences notwithstanding an ordinance prohibiting, either expressly or implicitly, such occupancy." Even so, he defended the Belle Terre decision (in a footnote) as "upholding a single-family ordinance as one primarily concerned with the prevention of transiency in a small, quiet suburban community."

All of the reasons advanced by the majority Justices for distinguishing between the East Cleveland and Belle Terre ordinances are deeply unsatisfying. The difficulty with Justice Stevens' "transiency" point is its stark nakedness. No explanation is offered either of why or how transiency might be regarded as an evil, or of why unaffiliated households might be thought more prone than "families" to be transient in whatever sense is supposed to be relevant. The Belle Terre decision itself sheds no light on these questions, because it made no reference to any interest on the villagers' part in avoiding transiency, relying rather on their interests in avoiding congestion and in maintaining "family values"—interests on which Justice Stevens, evidently, thought it inappropriate to rely.

Justice Brennan's concurring opinion simply makes no attempt to defend the plurality's distinction between "families" and household groupings of unrelated persons, accepting the former but rejecting the latter as bearers of constitutionally protected interests in domestic self-determination. So Justice Powell's opinion for the plurality must bear the entire burden of that defense. Now doubtless there are policy arguments for trying to preserve the strength of traditional family forms in society, and doubtless these are strong enough that a finding of constitutional impediment to certain governmental efforts in that direction is not "lightly" to be made. Doubtless, too, "the institution of the family is deeply rooted in this Nation's history and tradition." But from none of these premises does the conclusion follow that "the Constitution protects the sanctity of the family" in the sense required by the joint results of the *Belle Terre* and *East Cleveland* cases—that is, validating governmental direct censorship of nontraditional ("unrelated") in favor of traditional ("related") household groupings in favor of traditional ("related") household groupings. In fact Justice Powell's proposition that "the Constitution protects the sanctity of the family"—in that or any other sense—is certainly false if taken as a literal report of anything the Constitution says. Such constitutional protection, if detectable at all, can only be an inference from the document viewed as a whole—as a presumably coherent plan having underlying moral premises, themselves implicit but intelligible through a parsing of the constitutional plan's overall "structure and relationships." And when we consider that a main pillar—if not a keystone—in that structure is the first amendment, an inference that governments are not only constitutionally bound to respect traditional household forms, but are also constitutionally authorized to censor nontraditional ones, becomes problematic to say the least.[177] The difficulty is only aggravated, not alleviated, when—in the light cast by the first amendment—one heeds Justice Powell's injunction to open "our eyes to the basic reasons why certain rights associated with the family have been accorded shelter under the Fourteenth Amendment's Due Process Clause," and reflects on his suggestion that a crucial reason is that "it is through the family that we inculcate and pass down many of our most cherished values, moral and cultural." While none of this quite proves that the *Belle Terre* decision is wrong, it does, I believe, amply show that Justice Powell's defense of that decision in *East Cleveland* is inadequate and unconvincing as it stands.   * * *

KIRSCH v. PRINCE GEORGE'S COUNTY, MARYLAND

Court of Appeals of Maryland, 1993.
331 Md. 89, 626 A.2d 372, cert. denied, ___ U.S.
___, 114 S.Ct. 600, 126 L.Ed.2d 565.

KARWACKI, JUDGE.

In this case, we are asked whether the Prince George's County "mini-dorm" zoning ordinance codified within Subtitle 27 of the Prince George's County Code (1991), regulating the rental of residential property to three or more students pursuing higher education, deprives such students of equal protection of the law by discriminating against a class of persons in violation of the Fourteenth Amendment of the United States Constitution and Article 24 of the Maryland Declaration of Rights.   * * *

The Prince George's County "mini-dorm" ordinance * * * took effect on July 1, 1990. The ordinance's preamble states:

---

177. "[A]s with the first amendment, lifestyle protection may require defense of the most idiosyncratic among us in order to discourage, at the outer perimeter, the state's natural inclination to compel its citizens to think and behave in orthodox patterns." Wilkinson & White, [Constitutional Protection for Personal Life Styles, 62 Cornell L.Rev. 563,] at 613 (1977).

"*Pierce* struck down an Oregon law requiring all children to attend the State's public schools, holding that the Constitution 'excludes any general power of the State to standardize its children by forcing them to accept instruction from public teachers only.' * * * By the same

token the Constitution prevents East Cleveland from standardizing its children—and its adults—by forcing all to live in certain narrowly defined family patterns."

But why doesn't the same apply if we substitute "Belle Terre" for "East Cleveland" in that last sentence? "There will," after all, "always be some Americans who resist traditional conceptions of family life and regard the favored legal status of the nuclear family as economically oppressive and a source of indignity and affront." Wilkinson & White, *supra*. Why is it that governments are free to "standardize" them?

"AN ORDINANCE concerning Mini–Dormitories

FOR the purpose of defining a mini-dormitory; establishing criteria for regulating this use; allowing it as a permitted use or by Special Exception in certain zones, subject to certain criteria; prohibiting the Board of Appeals from granting certain variances for mini-dormitories; prohibiting the Planning Board from approving departures from the required number of parking spaces for mini-dormitories; and requiring all existing uses to be in conformance with these regulations by July 1, 1991." * * *

The ordinance defines a "mini-dormitory" as:

"An off-campus residence, located in a building that is, or was originally constructed as a one-family, two-family, or three-family dwelling which houses at least three (3), but not more than five (5), individuals, *all or part of whom are unrelated to one another by blood, adoption or marriage and who are registered full-time or part-time students at an institution of higher learning.*"

§ 27–107.1 (a) (150.1) (emphasis added). * * *

On July 3, 1990, Donald P. Kirsch and Martha Kaye Dunn, individual owners of residential property they wish to rent to persons including students, and Stephanie Stockman and Daniel Cones, both students at the University of Maryland residing off campus in housing subject to the ordinance, ("the petitioners"), filed suit in the Circuit Court for Prince George's County, seeking declaratory relief from the ordinance. * * *

No fundamental right or suspect class has been infringed upon by the "mini-dorm" ordinance's classification of housing on the basis of the occupation of the tenants. The petitioners do not argue otherwise. Therefore, we must apply the rational basis standard. To withstand such equal protection scrutiny, the zoning ordinance in question, classifying rental property on the basis of the occupations pursued by the lessees away from their residence, must be rationally related to a legitimate governmental purpose. * * *

The stated purpose of the Prince George's County "mini-dorm" ordinance is to "prevent or control detrimental effects upon neighboring properties, such as illegal parking and saturation of available parking by residents of mini-dormitories, litter, and noise." § 27–249.1(b). In order to qualify as a resident of a mini-dormitory one must be a student enrolled full or part time in an institution of higher learning. At argument, the County Attorney conceded that the ordinance was passed to address complaints regarding noise, litter, and parking problems from residents of the College Park area, the site of the principal campus of the University of Maryland, an internationally recognized university community that is expanding in the number of students and scope of degree offerings on an annual basis. Notwithstanding the county-wide effect of the ordinance, the County failed to identify any other neighborhoods in the County where similar off-campus student housing created noise, litter or parking problems.

The crucial question for this Court is whether the County by adopting the ordinance's classification advances its objective of clearing residential neighborhoods of noise, litter, and parking congestion within the command of the Equal Protection Clause of the Fourteenth Amendment and Article 24 of the Declaration of Rights. We hold that it does not. To differentiate between permissible residential tenant classes by creating more strenuous zoning requirements for some and less for others based solely on the occupation which the tenant pursues away from that residence is that sort of arbitrary classification forbidden under our constitutions.

The County has placed strong reliance on the Supreme Court's holding in *Village of Belle Terre v. Boraas*, 416 U.S. 1, 94 S.Ct. 1536, 39 L.Ed.2d 797 (1974) arguing that as in *Boraas*, "the ordinance affects only unrelated individuals and does not impermissibly infringe upon the associational rights of the students." * * * Unlike the zoning ordinance analyzed in *Boraas*, the Prince George's County "mini-dorm" ordinance does not differentiate based on the nature of the use of the property, such as a fraternity house or a lodging house, but rather on the occupation of the persons who would dwell therein. Therefore, under the ordinance a landlord of a building originally constructed as a one, two or three family dwelling is permitted to rent the same for occupancy by three to five unrelated persons so long as they are not pursuing a higher education without incurring the burdens of complying with the arduous requirements of the ordinance. Such occupancy would equally add motor vehicles to a congested parking situation and pose the threat of increased noise and litter. Such a zoning classification of residential property is wholly unrelated to the stated purpose of the ordinance, and its impact upon persons who are registered as full-time or part-time students at an institution of higher learning denies those students equal protection of the laws under the Fourteenth Amendment to the United States Constitution and Article 24 of the Declaration of Rights. * * *

CHASANOW, dissenting. * * *

It is not arbitrary or irrational for the Prince George's County Council to assume that, generally, residential college students will wish to live as close to their college campus as possible. It is not arbitrary or irrational for that legislative body to further assume college dormitories housing college students will, unless regulated, tend to be most highly concentrated in residential neighborhoods surrounding a college campus, whereas other non-student similar group residences will probably be more uniformly disbursed throughout the county. Because non-student group residences probably will not be as concentrated in any single geographic area as will student group residences near a college campus, there is a basis for zoning regulations addressing these student mini-dorms. It is not irrational to regulate student mini-dorms by requiring a special exception so as to avoid too high a concentration of unregulated, possibly substandard, student mini-dormitories in residential neighborhoods adjacent to institutions of higher learning. * * *

Several states of facts reasonably can be conceived that would justify the student/non-student classification. We can conceive that some students of the University of Maryland and Bowie State University might not like to live in the campus dormitories and would prefer to live off campus but close to their universities. We can conceive that as full or part-time students, they may only have limited funds and are therefore more willing to tolerate crowded, inferior living quarters. Real estate speculators, seizing upon this market, may buy small, inexpensive single-family residences close to these institutions of higher learning and rent formerly single-family homes to several students per house. Many of these students have cars which they might park on the street. As only nine-month tenants, the students may not be concerned about maintaining the property. Intolerant neighbors inconvenienced by the shortage of parking spaces and concerned about declining aesthetics of their neighborhoods may put their homes up for sale. Prospective buyers may not be eager to move into a neighborhood with neglected, crowded student group residences, so the speculators may be able to purchase more houses at deflated prices. The speculators, without doing anything more than is minimally necessary to rent the properties, can create more mini-dorms in close proximity to these two Universities. Soon there may be a real danger that many quiet college residential neighborhoods will be saturated with student mini-dorms. These assumed justifications are not irrational or arbitrary.

It is also easy to conceive that there is no such problem with non-students or people with other occupations. These non-students are more likely to be employed full-time than are students, and with more money to spend on housing, they presumably may be less willing to tolerate crowded, inferior living conditions. Also, since they will live in the same residence all year long, rather than only for nine months of the year, the premises are less likely to be neglected. Non-student group residences are more likely to be disbursed throughout the county and not clustered around the two Universities.

These hypotheses are conceivable and should not be dismissed as irrational. This Court may believe that the hypothetical justifications for the zoning ordinance are not probable or not likely to occur, but that is not the issue. The issue is whether these hypothetical justifications for the legislation are irrational—they are not. There has been no showing that the County Council was wrong in believing there was a particular problem with student mini-dorms or assuming that, because of their concentration around college campuses, student group residences could be a significant problem unless regulated. * * *

CITY OF CLEBURNE, TEXAS v. CLEBURNE LIVING CENTER

Supreme Court of the United States, 1985.
473 U.S. 432, 105 S.Ct. 3249, 87 L.Ed.2d 313.

JUSTICE WHITE delivered the opinion of the Court. * * *

In July, 1980, respondent Jan Hannah purchased a building at 201 Featherston Street in the city of Cleburne, Texas, with the intention of leasing it to Cleburne Living Centers, Inc. (CLC), for the operation of a group home for the mentally retarded. It was anticipated that the home would house 13 retarded men and women, who would be under the constant supervision of CLC staff members. The house had four bedrooms and two baths, with a half bath to be added. * * * The city informed CLC that a special use permit would be required for the operation of a group home at the site, and CLC accordingly submitted a permit application. * * * After holding a public hearing on CLC's application, the city council voted three to one to deny a special use permit.

CLC then filed suit in Federal District Court against the city and a number of its officials, alleging, *inter alia*, that the zoning ordinance was invalid on its face and as applied because it discriminated against the mentally retarded in violation of the equal protection rights of CLC and its potential residents. * * *

[W]e conclude for several reasons that the Court of Appeals erred in holding mental retardation a quasi-suspect classification calling for a more exacting standard of judicial review than is normally accorded economic and social legislation. First, it is undeniable, and it is not argued otherwise here, that those who are mentally retarded have a reduced ability to cope with and function in the everyday world. * * * They are thus different, immutably so, in relevant respects, and the states' interest in dealing with and providing for them is plainly a legitimate one. How this large and diversified group is to be treated under the law is a difficult and often a technical matter, very much a task for legislators guided by qualified professionals and not by the perhaps ill-informed opinions of the judiciary. * * *

Second, the distinctive legislative response, both national and state, to the plight of those who are mentally retarded demonstrates not only that they have unique problems, but also that the lawmakers have been addressing their difficulties in a manner that belies a continuing antipathy or prejudice and a corresponding need for more intrusive oversight by the judiciary. Thus, the federal government has not only outlawed discrimination against the mentally retarded in federally funded programs, see § 504 of the Rehabilitation Act of 1973, 29 U.S.C. § 794, but it has also provided the retarded with the right to receive "appropriate treatment, services, and habilitation" in a setting that is "least restrictive of [their] personal liberty." Developmental Disabilities Assistance and Bill of Rights Act, 42 U.S.C. §§ 6010(1), (2). * * * The State of Texas has similarly enacted legislation that acknowledges the special status of the mentally retarded by conferring certain rights upon them, such as "the right to live in the least restrictive setting appropriate to [their] individual needs and abilities," including "the right to live * * * in a group home." Mentally Retarded Persons Act of 1977, Tex.Rev.Civ.

Stat.Ann., Art. 5547 300, § 7 (Vernon Supp.1985). * * * It may be, as CLC contends, that legislation designed to benefit, rather than disadvantage, the retarded would generally withstand examination under a test of heightened scrutiny. * * * Even assuming that many of these laws could be shown to be substantially related to an important governmental purpose, merely requiring the legislature to justify its efforts in these terms may lead it to refrain from acting at all. Much recent legislation intended to benefit the retarded also assumes the need for measures that might be perceived to disadvantage them. The Education of the Handicapped Act, for example, requires an "appropriate" education, not one that is equal in all respects to the education of non-retarded children; clearly, admission to a class that exceeded the abilities of a retarded child would not be appropriate. Similarly, the Developmental Disabilities Assistance Act and the Texas act give the retarded the right to live only in the "least restrictive setting" appropriate to their abilities, implicitly assuming the need for at least some restrictions that would not be imposed on others. Especially given the wide variation in the abilities and needs of the retarded themselves, governmental bodies must have a certain amount of flexibility and freedom from judicial oversight in shaping and limiting their remedial efforts.

Third, the legislative response, which could hardly have occurred and survived without public support, negates any claim that the mentally retarded are politically powerless in the sense that they have no ability to attract the attention of the lawmakers. Any minority can be said to be powerless to assert direct control over the legislature, but if that were a criterion for higher level scrutiny by the courts, much economic and social legislation would now be suspect.

Fourth, if the large and amorphous class of the mentally retarded were deemed quasi-suspect for the reasons given by the Court of Appeals, it would be difficult to find a principled way to distinguish a variety of other groups who have perhaps immutable disabilities setting them off from others, who cannot themselves mandate the desired legislative responses, and who can claim some degree of prejudice from at least part of the public at large. One need mention in this respect only the aging, the disabled, the mentally ill, and the infirm. We are reluctant to set out on that course, and we decline to do so.

Doubtless, there have been and there will continue to be instances of discrimination against the retarded that are in fact invidious, and that are properly subject to judicial correction under constitutional norms. But the appropriate method of reaching such instances is not to create a new quasi-suspect classification and subject all governmental action based on that classification to more searching evaluation. Rather, we should look to the likelihood that governmental action premised on a particular classification is valid as a general matter, not merely to the specifics of the case before us. Because mental retardation is a characteristic that the government may legitimately take into account in a wide range of decisions, and because both state and federal governments have recently committed themselves to assisting the retarded, we will not presume that any given legislative action, even one that disadvantages retarded individuals, is rooted in considerations that the Constitution will not tolerate.

Our refusal to recognize the retarded as a quasi-suspect class does not leave them entirely unprotected from invidious discrimination. To withstand equal protection review, legislation that distinguishes between the mentally retarded and others must be rationally related to a legitimate governmental purpose. This standard, we believe, affords government the latitude necessary both to pursue policies designed to assist the retarded in realizing their full potential, and to freely and efficiently engage in activities that burden the retarded in what is essentially an incidental manner. The State may not rely on a classification whose relationship to an asserted goal is so attenuated as to render the distinction arbitrary or irrational. See *United States Department of Agriculture v. Moreno*, 413 U.S. 528, 535, 93 S.Ct. 2821, 2826, 37 L.Ed.2d 782 (1973). Furthermore, some objectives—such as "a bare * * * desire to harm a politically unpopular group," *Moreno*, 413 U.S., at 534, 93 S.Ct., at 2826—are not legitimate state interests. Beyond that, the mentally retarded, like others, have and retain their substantive constitutional rights in addition to the right to be treated equally by the law.

We turn to the issue of the validity of the zoning ordinance insofar as it requires a special use permit for homes for the mentally retarded. We inquire first whether requiring a special use permit for the Featherston home in the circumstances here deprives respondents of the equal protection of the laws. If it does, there will be no occasion to decide whether the special use permit provision is facially invalid where the mentally retarded are involved, or to put it another way, whether the city may never insist on a special use permit for a home for the mentally retarded in an R–3 zone. This is the preferred course of adjudication since it enables courts to avoid making unnecessarily broad constitutional judgments.

The constitutional issue is clearly posed. The City does not require a special use permit in an R–3 zone for apartment houses, multiple dwellings, boarding and lodging houses, fraternity or sorority houses, dormitories, apartment hotels, hospitals, sanitariums, nursing homes for convalescents or the aged (other than for the insane or feeble-minded or alcoholics or drug addicts), private clubs or fraternal orders, and other specified uses. It does, however, insist on a special permit for the Featherston home, and it does so, as the District Court found, because it would be a facility for the mentally retarded. May the city require the permit for this facility when other care and multiple dwelling facilities are freely permitted?

It is true, as already pointed out, that the mentally retarded as a group are indeed different from others not sharing their misfortune, and in this respect they may be different from those who would occupy other facilities that would be permitted in an R–3 zone without a special permit. But this difference is largely irrelevant unless the Featherston home and those who would occupy it would threaten legitimate interests of the city in a way that other permitted uses such as boarding houses and hospitals would not. Because in our view the record does not reveal any rational basis for believing that the Featherston home would pose any special threat to the city's legitimate interests, we affirm the judgment below insofar as it holds the ordinance invalid as applied in this case.

The District Court found that the City Council's insistence on the permit rested on several factors. First, the Council was concerned with the negative attitude of the majority of property owners located within 200 feet of the Featherston facility, as well as with the fears of elderly residents of the neighborhood. But mere negative attitudes, or fear, unsubstantiated by factors which are properly cognizable in a zoning proceeding, are not permissible bases for treating a home for the mentally retarded differently from apartment houses, multiple dwellings, and the like. * * *

Second, the Council had two objections to the location of the facility. It was concerned that the facility was across the street from a junior high school, and it feared that the students might harass the occupants of the Featherston home. But the school itself is attended by about 30 mentally retarded students, and denying a permit based on such vague, undifferentiated fears is again permitting some portion of the community to validate what would otherwise be an equal protection violation. The other objection to the home's location was that it was located on "a five hundred year flood plain." This concern with the possibility of a flood, however, can hardly be based on a distinction between the Featherston home and, for example, nursing homes, homes for convalescents or the aged, or sanitariums or hospitals, any of which could be located on the Featherston site without obtaining a special use permit. The same may be said of another concern of the Council—doubts about the legal responsibility for actions which the mentally retarded might take. If there is no concern about legal responsibility with respect to other uses that would be permitted in the area, such as boarding and fraternity houses, it is difficult to believe that the groups of mildly or moderately mentally retarded individuals who would live at 201 Featherston would present any different or special hazard.

Fourth, the Council was concerned with the size of the home and the number of people that would occupy it. The District Court found, and the Court of Appeals repeated, that "[i]f the potential residents of the Featherston Street home were not mentally retarded, but the home was the same in all other respects, its use would be permitted under the city's zoning ordinance." Given this finding, there would be no restrictions on the number of people who could occupy this home as a boarding house, nursing home, family dwelling, fraternity house, or dormitory. The question is whether it is rational to treat the mentally retarded differently. It is true that they suffer disability not shared by others; but why this difference warrants a density regulation that others need not observe is not at all apparent. At least this record does not clarify how, in this connection, the characteristics of the intended occupants of the Featherston home rationally justify denying to those occupants what would be permitted to groups occupying the same site for different purposes. Those who would live in the Featherston home are the type of individuals who, with supporting staff, satisfy federal and state standards for group housing in the community; and there is no dispute that the home would meet the federal square-footage-per-resident requirement for facilities of this type. In the words of the Court of Appeals, "The City never justifies its apparent view that other people can live under such 'crowded' conditions when mentally retarded persons cannot."

In the courts below the city also urged that the ordinance is aimed at avoiding concentration of population and at lessening congestion of the streets. These concerns obviously fail to explain why apartment houses, fraternity and sorority houses, hospitals and the like, may freely locate in the area without a permit. So, too, the expressed worry about fire hazards, the serenity of the neighborhood, and the avoidance of danger to other residents fail rationally to justify singling out a home such as 201 Featherston for the special use permit, yet imposing no such restrictions on the many other uses freely permitted in the neighborhood.

The short of it is that requiring the permit in this case appears to us to rest on an irrational prejudice against the mentally retarded, including those who would occupy the Featherston facility and who would live under the closely supervised and highly regulated conditions expressly provided for by state and federal law.

The judgment of the Court of Appeals is affirmed insofar as it invalidates the zoning ordinance as applied to the Featherston home. The judgment is otherwise vacated. * * *

Justice Marshall, with whom Justice Brennan and Justice Blackmun join, concurring in the judgment in part and dissenting in part. * * *

In my view, it is important to articulate, as the Court does not, the facts and principles that justify subjecting this zoning ordinance to the searching review—the heightened scrutiny—that actually leads to its invalidation. * * * [T]he interest of the retarded in establishing group homes is substantial. The right to "establish a home" has long been cherished as one of the fundamental liberties embraced by the Due Process Clause. See *Meyer v. Nebraska*, 262 U.S. 390, 399, 43 S.Ct. 625, 626, 67 L.Ed. 1042 (1923). For retarded adults, this right means living together in group homes, for as deinstitutionalization has progressed, group homes have become the primary means by which retarded adults can enter life in the community. * * * Excluding group homes deprives the retarded of much of what makes for human freedom and fulfillment—the ability to form bonds and take part in the life of a community.

Second, the mentally retarded have been subject to a "lengthy and tragic history" of segregation and discrimination that can only be called grotesque. During much of the nineteenth century, mental retardation was viewed as neither curable nor dangerous and the retarded were largely left to their own devices. By the latter part of the century and during the first decades of the new one, however, social views of the retarded underwent a radical transformation. Fueled by the rising tide of Social Darwinism, the "science" of eugenics, and the extreme xenophobia of those years, leading medical authorities and others began to portray the "feeble minded" as a "menace to society and civilization * * * responsible in a large degree for many, if not all, of our social problems." A regime of state-mandated segregation and degradation soon emerged that in its virulence and bigotry rivaled, and indeed paralleled, the worst excesses of Jim Crow. Massive custodial institutions were built to warehouse the retarded for life; the aim was to halt reproduction of the retarded and "nearly extinguish their race." Retarded children were categorically excluded from public schools, based on the false stereotype that all were ineducable and on the purported need to protect nonretarded children from them. State laws deemed the retarded "unfit for citizenship."

Segregation was accompanied by eugenic marriage and sterilization laws that extinguished for the retarded one of the "basic civil rights of man"—the right to marry and procreate. Marriages of the retarded were made, and in some states continue to be, not only voidable but also often a criminal offense. The purpose of such limitations, which frequently applied only to women of child bearing age, was unabashedly eugenic: to prevent the retarded from propagating. To assure this end, 29 states enacted compulsory eugenic sterilization laws between 1907 and 1931.

Prejudice, once let loose, is not easily cabined. As of 1979, most states still categorically disqualified "idiots" from voting, without regard to individual capacity and with discretion to exclude left in the hands of low-level election officials. Not until Congress enacted the Education of the Handicapped Act were "the door[s] of public education" opened wide to handicapped children. *Hendrick Hudson District Board of Education v. Rowley,* 458 U.S. 176, 192, 102 S.Ct. 3034, 3043, 73 L.Ed.2d 690 (1982). But most important, lengthy and continuing isolation of the retarded has perpetuated the ignorance, irrational fears, and stereotyping that long have plagued them.

In light of the importance of the interest at stake and the history of discrimination the retarded have suffered, the Equal Protection Clause requires us to do more than review the distinctions drawn by Cleburne's zoning ordinance as if they appeared in a taxing statute or in economic or commercial legislation. The searching scrutiny I would give to restrictions on the ability of the retarded to establish community group homes leads me to conclude that Cleburne's vague generalizations for classifying the "feebleminded" with drug addicts, alcoholics, and the insane, and excluding them where the elderly, the ill, the boarder, and the transient are allowed, are not substantial or important enough to overcome the suspicion that the ordinance rests on impermissible assumptions or out-moded and perhaps invidious stereotypes. * * *

BANNUM, INC. v. CITY OF ST. CHARLES

United States Court of Appeals, Eighth Circuit, 1993.
2 F.3d 267.

MAGILL, CIRCUIT JUDGE. * * *

Bannum is a company in the business of operating * * * [community treatment centers (CTCs)] throughout the United States pursuant to contracts with the Federal Bureau of Prisons (BOP). CTCs are half-way houses for convicted criminals in the last stage of their sentences before release. CTC participants work in the community during the day and reside in a supervised residential facility at night. In the past, Bannum has located some CTCs in motels, using the motel rooms both to house CTC participants and for offices to provide the participants with counseling and other support services.

In 1987, Bannum received a request from the BOP to submit a proposal for a CTC in the St. Louis area. After contacting hotels and motels in the area, Bannum chose the Town House Inn in the City as a potential CTC site. Bannum contacted the City police department to inform them it intended to open a CTC in the area, and contacted the City development department regarding zoning. One of the City's employees sent Bannum a letter stating that as she understood the proposed use, it would be permitted as a matter of right in the City's C2 district. * * * The City has a permissive zoning scheme; any use not expressly permitted by the zoning ordinances is prohibited. Among the uses permitted as a matter of right in the C2 General Business District was the use as "hotels, motels or motor lodges." The ordinance also listed conditional uses for the C2 district. Conditional uses are permitted if approved by the board of adjustment. CTCs or half-way houses were not expressly permitted in the City's zoning ordinances for any district as either a permitted use or a conditional use.

Bannum's proposed use of the Town House Inn was made public in late November 1988, and some opposition to it was raised. * * * On February 23, 1989, the City amended the zoning ordinances by adding half-way houses to the list of conditional uses in the C2 district. The City also enacted another ordinance which added to the ordinances definitions of "half-way house" and "transient," and substituted a new definition of "motel (motor court, tourist court or motor lodge)." Bannum's proposed CTC falls within the new definition of half-way house, and thus is allowed under the amended ordinances as a conditional use in the C2 district. Bannum did not apply for a conditional permit to operate its CTC.

The BOP's contract with Bannum was conditioned on the proposed CTC being in compliance with local zoning law. Because the City would not provide the BOP with documentation that the CTC was a permitted use under the zoning ordinances, the BOP notified Bannum that its contract to operate the CTC was terminated for convenience of the government.

Bannum brought a claim against the City under 42 U.S.C. § 1983, claiming, inter alia, the City violated its rights under the Equal Protection Clause. * * *

Bannum * * * contends the amended zoning ordinances violate the Equal Protection Clause both facially and as applied because Bannum is required to apply for a conditional use permit to operate a CTC. Bannum contends that other "similar and identical uses of property" are permitted as a matter of right and may operate without a conditional use permit. These uses which Bannum claims are similar and identical include hotels, convalescent homes, hospitals, apartment buildings, and multiple family housing. Because these uses do not need to apply for a conditional use permit, Bannum claims, imposing this requirement on half-way houses, which house prisoners, ex-prisoners, and juvenile offenders,[8] is arbitrary and irrational, violating Bannum's equal protection rights.

* * * [B]ecause no suspect class or fundamental right is involved, we review Bannum's claim under the rational basis test, and uphold the ordinance if it "bears a rational relation to a legitimate government objective," *Kadrmas v. Dickinson Pub. Sch.*, 487 U.S. 450, 461–62, 108 S.Ct. 2481, 101 L.Ed.2d 399 (1988). * * * We first address whether the amended ordinances which list half-way houses as conditional uses facially violate the Equal Protection Clause. The record does not contain articulated reasons from the city council for amending the zoning ordinances to include half-way houses as a conditional use. However, we need inquire only whether "any state of facts reasonably may be conceived to justify" the classification of half-way houses as conditional uses. *Holt Civic Club v. Tuscaloosa*, 439 U.S. 60, 74, 58 L.Ed.2d 292, 99 S.Ct. 383 (1978). * * *

Half-way houses, as defined by the amended ordinance, would include facilities for any prisoner, former prisoner, or juvenile offender. Persons who had been convicted of any state or federal crime could be placed in a half-way house. This population could include persons who had been convicted of violent crimes such as second degree murder or rape. If half-way houses were allowed as permitted uses, the City would have no control over where within a given district a half-way house was located. It is easy to envision many situations which the City would want to prevent, such as locating near a school a half-way house

---

8. Bannum apparently rests its claim that a CTC is similar and identical to hotels, convalescent homes, apartment buildings, and multiple family housing on the common factor that they are all used for multiple or temporary housing. However, Bannum regards as unimportant a key difference: CTCs are intended to house a certain population—convicted prisoners who are serving the final portion of their sentence. Additionally, we note that not all multiple housing uses are permitted uses, as the City also allows boarding and rooming houses only as conditional uses.

containing persons who had been convicted of dealing in drugs or of child molestation. Because of legitimate concerns for public welfare, the City could rationally want to control where within a district a half-way house could be located. It can accomplish this legitimate purpose by requiring a conditional permit for operation of a half-way house.

Bannum argues that under *City of Cleburne v. Cleburne Living Ctr., Inc.*, 473 U.S. 432, 87 L.Ed.2d 313, 105 S.Ct. 3249 (1985), negative attitudes and fear of offenders in the last stage before release are not permissible bases for treating a CTC or half-way house differently from apartment houses and other multiple person uses of property. The Cleburne Court held that "requiring [a] permit [for a home for the mentally retarded] appears to us to rest on an irrational prejudice against the mentally retarded...." *Id.* at 450. Among the concerns which the Court considered to be irrational bases for requiring a permit were the citizens' negative attitudes and fears of the mentally retarded, the number of persons which the home would contain, and population congestion.

However, *Cleburne* is inapposite. The concerns the City of Cleburne relied on to require a permit would be irrational bases as applied to any home for the mentally retarded, and the Court concluded that the permit requirement was really based on irrational prejudice. Here, the classification in the amended ordinance is addressed to half-way houses which serve any prisoner, ex-prisoner, or juvenile offender. The City could rationally believe that some groups in this classification could pose a threat to the public welfare. Such concerns are not based on irrational prejudice, but rather on a realistic view that some members of these groups could pose a threat in some locations. It is not irrational for the City to believe that recidivism could be a problem with some persons served by half-way houses. This is a legitimate concern which can be addressed on a case-by-case basis through application for conditional permits. * * *

Bannum claims its proposed CTC would house only nonviolent, white-collar offenders, and claims these criminals pose no threat to the public welfare. Thus, Bannum argues, it is irrational for the City to require that it apply for a conditional permit for this CTC. However, the City does not violate the Equal Protection Clause just because the classifications contained in its ordinances are not perfect. See *Gregory v. Ashcroft*, 115 L.Ed.2d 410, 111 S.Ct. 2395, 2407 (1991). The zoning ordinance was not written to apply only to Bannum's CTC; it was written to have broad application to any half-way houses which house prisoners, former prisoners, or juvenile offenders. It is not arbitrary or irrational for the City to create this broad category, and then draw fine lines between different types of half-way houses when an application for a permit is submitted. After a person wishing to operate a half-way house applies for a permit, the City will have the opportunity to examine at length what type of offenders will be housed at that half-way house and consider whether any threat to the public welfare exists at that particular location. * * * For the reasons discussed above, the former and the amended zoning ordinances do not violate the Equal Protection Clause.

CITY OF RENTON v. PLAYTIME THEATRES, INC.

Supreme Court of the United States, 1986.
475 U.S. 41, 106 S.Ct. 925, 89 L.Ed.2d 29.

JUSTICE REHNQUIST delivered the opinion of the Court.   * * *

In May 1980, the Mayor of Renton, a city of approximately 32,000 people located just south of Seattle, suggested to the Renton City Council that it consider the advisability of enacting zoning legislation dealing with adult entertainment uses. No such uses existed in the city at that time. Upon the Mayor's suggestion, the City Council referred the matter to the city's Planning and Development Committee.   * * * In April 1981, acting on the basis of the Planning and Development Committee's recommendation, the City Council enacted Ordinance No. 3526. The ordinance prohibited any "adult motion picture theater" from locating within 1,000 feet of any residential zone, single- or multiple-family dwelling, church, or park, and within one mile of any school. The term "adult motion picture theater" was defined as "[a]n enclosed building used for presenting motion picture films, video cassettes, cable television, or any other such visual media, distinguished or characteri[zed] by an emphasis on matter depicting, describing or relating to 'specified sexual activities' or 'specified anatomical areas' * * * for observation by patrons therein."

In early 1982, respondents acquired two existing theaters in downtown Renton, with the intention of using them to exhibit feature-length adult films. The theaters were located within the area proscribed by Ordinance No. 3526. At about the same time, respondents filed * * * [a] lawsuit challenging the ordinance on First and Fourteenth Amendment grounds, and seeking declaratory and injunctive relief. While the federal action was pending, the City Council amended the ordinance in several respects, adding a statement of reasons for its enactment and reducing the minimum distance from any school to 1,000 feet.   * * *

In our view, the resolution of this case is largely dictated by our decision in *[Young v.] American Mini Theatres* [427 U.S. 50, 96 S.Ct. 2440, 49 L.Ed.2d 310 (1976)]. There, although five Members of the Court did not agree on a single rationale for the decision, we held that the city of Detroit's zoning ordinance, which prohibited locating an adult theater within 1,000 feet of any two other "regulated uses" or within 500 feet of any residential zone, did not violate the First and Fourteenth Amendments. 427 U.S., at 72–73, 96 S.Ct., at 2453 (plurality opinion of Stevens, J., joined by Burger, C.J., and White and Rehnquist, JJ.); *id.,* at 84, 96 S.Ct., at 2459 (Powell, J., concurring). The Renton ordinance, like the one in *American Mini Theatres*, does not ban adult theaters altogether, but merely provides that such theaters may not be located within 1,000 feet of any residential zone, single- or multiple-family dwelling, church, park, or school. The ordinance is therefore properly analyzed as a form of time, place, and manner regulation.

Describing the ordinance as a time, place, and manner regulation is, of course, only the first step in our inquiry. This Court has long held that regulations enacted for the purpose of restraining speech on the basis of its content presumptively violate the First Amendment. On the other hand, so-called "content-neutral" time, place, and manner regulations are acceptable so long as they are designed to serve a substantial governmental interest and do not unreasonably limit alternative avenues of communication.

At first glance, the Renton ordinance, like the ordinance in *American Mini Theatres,* does not appear to fit neatly into either the "content-based" or the "content-neutral" category. To be sure, the ordinance treats theaters that specialize in adult films differently from other kinds of theaters. Nevertheless, as the District Court concluded, the Renton ordinance is aimed not at the *content* of the films shown at "adult motion picture theatres," but rather at the *secondary effects* of such theaters on the surrounding community. The District Court found that the City Council's *"predominate* concerns" were with the secondary effects of adult theaters, and not with the content of adult films themselves. But the Court of Appeals, relying on its decision in *Tovar v. Billmeyer,* 721 F.2d 1260, 1266 (CA9 1983), held that this was not enough to sustain the ordinance. According to the Court of Appeals, if *"a motivating factor"* in enacting the ordinance was to restrict respondents' exercise of First Amendment rights the ordinance would be invalid, apparently no matter how small a part this motivating factor may have played in the City Council's decision. This view of the law was rejected in *United States v. O'Brien,* 391 U.S. 367, 382–386, 88 S.Ct. 1673, 1681–1684, 20 L.Ed.2d 672 (1968) * * *. The District Court's finding as to "predominate" intent, left undisturbed by the Court of Appeals, is more than adequate to establish that the city's pursuit of its zoning interests here was unrelated to the suppression of free expression. The ordinance by its terms is designed to prevent crime, protect the city's retail trade, maintain property values, and generally "protec[t] and preserv[e] the quality of [the city's] neighborhoods, commercial districts, and the quality of urban life," not to suppress the expression of unpopular views. As Justice Powell observed in *American Mini Theatres,* "[i]f [the city] had been concerned with restricting the message purveyed by adult theaters, it would have tried to close them or restrict their number rather than circumscribe their choice as to location."

In short, the Renton ordinance is completely consistent with our definition of "content-neutral" speech regulations as those that "are *justified* without reference to the content of the regulated speech." *Virginia Pharmacy Board v. Virginia Citizens Consumer Council, Inc.,* 425 U.S. 748, 771, 96 S.Ct. 1817, 1830, 48 L.Ed.2d 346 (1976) (emphasis added). The ordinance does not contravene the fundamental principle that underlies our concern about "content-based" speech regulations: that "government may not grant the use of a forum to people whose views it finds acceptable, but deny use to those wishing to express less favored or more controversial views.'' [*Police Dept. of Chicago v.*] *Mosley,* 408 U.S., at 95–96, 92 S.Ct., at 2289–2290.

It was with this understanding in mind that, in *American Mini Theatres,* a majority of this Court decided that, at least with respect to businesses that purvey sexually explicit materials, zoning ordinances designed to combat the undesirable secondary effects of such businesses are to be reviewed under the standards applicable to ''content-neutral'' time, place, and manner regulations. Justice Stevens, writing for the plurality, concluded that the city of Detroit was entitled to draw a distinction between adult theaters and other kinds of theaters ''without violating the government's paramount obligation of neutrality in its regulation of protected communication,'' noting that ''[i]t is th[e] secondary effect which these zoning ordinances attempt to avoid, not the dissemination of 'offensive' speech''. Justice Powell, in concurrence, elaborated:

> ''[The] dissent misconceives the issue in this case by insisting that it involves an impermissible time, place, and manner restriction based on the content of expression. It involves nothing of the kind. We have here merely a decision by the city to treat certain movie theaters differently because they have markedly different effects upon their surroundings * * *. Moreover, even if this were a case involving a special governmental response to the content of one type of movie, it is possible that the result would be supported by a line of cases recognizing that the government can tailor its reaction to different types of speech according to the degree to which its special and overriding interests are implicated.''

The appropriate inquiry in this case, then, is whether the Renton ordinance is designed to serve a substantial governmental interest and allows for reasonable alternative avenues of communication. It is clear that the ordinance meets such a standard. As a majority of this Court recognized in *American Mini Theatres,* a city's ''interest in attempting to preserve the quality of urban life is one that must be accorded high respect.'' 427 U.S., at 71, 96 S.Ct., at 2453 (plurality opinion); see *id.,* at 80, 96 S.Ct., at 2457 (Powell, J., concurring) (''Nor is there doubt that the interests furthered by this ordinance are both important and substantial''). Exactly the same vital governmental interests are at stake here.

The Court of Appeals ruled, however, that because the Renton ordinance was enacted without the benefit of studies specifically relating to ''the particular problems or needs of Renton,'' the city's justifications for the ordinance were ''conclusory and speculative.'' We think the Court of Appeals imposed on the city an unnecessarily rigid burden of proof. The record in this case reveals that Renton relied heavily on the experience of, and studies produced by, the city of Seattle. In Seattle, as in Renton, the adult theater zoning ordinance was aimed at preventing the secondary effects caused by the presence of even one such theater in a given neighborhood. See *Northend Cinema, Inc. v. Seattle,* 90 Wash.2d 709, 585 P.2d 153 (1978). * * * We hold that Renton was entitled to rely on the experiences of Seattle and other cities, and in particular on the "detailed findings" summarized in the Washington Supreme Court's *Northend Cinema* opinion, in enacting its adult theater zoning ordinance. The First Amendment does not require a city, before enacting such an ordinance, to conduct new studies or produce evidence independent of that already generated by other cities, so long as whatever evidence the city relies upon is reasonably believed to be relevant to the problem that the city addresses. That was the case here. Nor is our holding affected by the fact that Seattle ultimately chose a different method of adult theater zoning than that chosen by Renton, since Seattle's choice of a different remedy to combat the secondary effects of adult theaters does not call into question either Seattle's identification of those secondary effects or the relevance of Seattle's experience to Renton.

We also find no constitutional defect in the method chosen by Renton to further its substantial interests. Cities may regulate adult theaters by dispersing them, as in Detroit, or by effectively concentrating them, as in Renton. "It is not our function to appraise the wisdom of [the city's] decision to require adult theaters to be separated rather than concentrated in the same areas * * *. [T]he city must be allowed a reasonable opportunity to experiment with solutions to admittedly serious problems." *American Mini Theatres, supra,* 427 U.S., at 71, 96 S.Ct., at 2453 (plurality opinion). Moreover, the Renton ordinance is "narrowly tailored" to affect only that category of theaters shown to produce the unwanted secondary effects, thus avoiding the flaw that proved fatal to the regulations in *Schad v. Mount Ephraim,* 452 U.S. 61, 101 S.Ct. 2176, 68 L.Ed.2d 671 (1981), and *Erznoznik v. City of Jacksonville,* 422 U.S. 205, 95 S.Ct. 2268, 45 L.Ed.2d 125 (1975).

Respondents contend that the Renton ordinance is "under-inclusive," in that it fails to regulate other kinds of adult businesses that are likely to produce secondary effects similar to those produced by adult theaters. On this record the contention must fail. There is no evidence that, at the time the Renton ordinance was enacted, any other adult business was located in, or was contemplating moving into, Renton. In fact, Resolution No. 2368, enacted in October 1980, states that "the City of Renton does not, at the present time, have any business whose primary purpose is the sale, rental, or showing of sexually explicit materials." That Renton chose first to address the potential problems created by one particular kind of adult business in no way suggests that the city has "singled out" adult theaters for discriminatory treatment. We simply have no basis on this record for assuming that Renton will not, in the future, amend its ordinance to include other kinds of adult businesses that have been shown to produce the same kinds of secondary effects as adult theaters. See *Williamson v. Lee Optical Co.,* 348 U.S. 483, 488–489, 75 S.Ct. 461, 464–465, 99 L.Ed. 563 (1955).

Finally, turning to the question whether the Renton ordinance allows for reasonable alternative avenues of communication, we note that the ordinance leaves some 520 acres, or more than five percent of the entire land area of Renton, open to use as adult theater sites. The District Court found, and the Court of Appeals did not dispute the finding, that the 520 acres of land consists of "[a]mple, accessible real estate," including "acreage in all stages of development from raw land to developed, industrial, warehouse, office, and shopping space that is crisscrossed by freeways, highways, and roads."

Respondents argue, however, that some of the land in question is already occupied by existing businesses, that "practically none" of the undeveloped land is currently for sale or lease, and that in general there are no "commercially viable" adult theater sites within the 520 acres left open by the Renton ordinance. The Court of Appeals accepted these arguments, concluded that the 520 acres was not truly "available" land, and therefore held that the Renton ordinance "would result in a substantial restriction" on speech.

We disagree with both the reasoning and the conclusion of the Court of Appeals. That respondents must fend for themselves in the real estate market, on an equal footing with other prospective purchasers and lessees, does not give rise to a First Amendment violation. And although we have cautioned against the enactment of zoning regulations that have "the effect of suppressing, or greatly restricting access to, lawful speech," *American Mini Theatres,* 427 U.S., at 71, n. 35, 96 S.Ct., at 2453, n. 35 (plurality opinion), we have never suggested that the First Amendment compels the Government to ensure that adult theaters, or any other kinds of speech-related businesses for that matter, will be able to obtain sites at bargain prices. See *id.,* at 78, 96 S.Ct., at 2456 (Powell, J., concurring) ("The inquiry for First Amendment purposes is not concerned with economic impact"). In our view, the First Amendment requires only that Renton refrain from effectively denying respondents a reasonable opportunity to open and operate an adult theater within the city, and the ordinance before us easily meets this requirement.

In sum, we find that the Renton ordinance represents a valid governmental response to the "admittedly serious problems" created by adult theaters. See *id.,* at 71, 96 S.Ct., at 2453 (plurality opinion). Renton has not used "the power to zone as a pretext for suppressing expression," *id.,* at 84, 96 S.Ct., at 2459 (Powell, J., concurring), but rather has sought to make some areas available for adult theaters and their patrons, while at the same time preserving the quality of life in the community at large by preventing those theaters from locating in other areas. This, after all, is the essence of zoning. Here, as in *American Mini Theatres,* the city has enacted a zoning ordinance that meets these goals while also satisfying the dictates of the First Amendment.   * * *

JUSTICE BRENNAN joined by JUSTICE MARSHALL, dissenting.   * * *

The ordinance discriminates on its face against certain forms of speech based on content. Movie theaters specializing in "adult motion pictures" may not be located within 1,000 feet of any residential zone, single- or multiple-family dwelling, church, park, or school. Other motion picture theaters, and other forms of "adult entertainment," such as bars, massage parlors, and adult bookstores, are not subject to the same restrictions. This selective treatment strongly suggests that Renton was interested not in controlling the "secondary effects" associated with adult businesses, but in discriminating against adult theaters based on the content of the films they exhibit. * * * The ordinance's underinclusiveness is cogent evidence that it was aimed at the *content* of the films shown in adult movie theaters.

Shortly *after* this lawsuit commenced, the Renton City Council amended the ordinance, adding a provision explaining that its intention in adopting the ordinance had been "to promote the City of Renton's great interest in protecting and preserving the quality of its neighborhoods, commercial districts, and the quality of urban life through effective land use planning." The amended ordinance also lists certain conclusory "findings" concerning adult entertainment land uses that the Council purportedly relied upon in adopting the ordinance. The city points to these provisions as evidence that the ordinance was designed to control the secondary effects associated with adult movie theaters, rather than to suppress the content of the films they exhibit. However, the "legislative history" of the ordinance strongly suggests otherwise.

Prior to the amendment, there was no indication that the ordinance was designed to address any "secondary effects" a single adult theater might create. In addition to the suspiciously coincidental timing of the amendment, many of the City Council's "findings" do not relate to legitimate land use concerns. As the Court of Appeals observed, "[b]oth the magistrate and the district court recognized that many of the stated reasons for the ordinance were no more than expressions of dislike for the subject matter." That some residents may be offended by the *content* of the films shown at adult movie theaters cannot form the basis for state regulation of speech. * * * In sum, the circumstances here strongly suggest that the ordinance was designed to suppress expression, even that constitutionally protected, and thus was not to be analyzed as a content-neutral time, place, and manner restriction. The Court allows Renton to conceal its illicit motives, however, by reliance on the fact that other communities adopted similar restrictions. The Court's approach largely immunizes such measures from judicial scrutiny, since a municipality can readily find other municipal ordinances to rely upon, thus always retrospectively justifying special zoning regulations for adult theaters. Rather than speculate about Renton's motives for adopting such measures, our cases require that the ordinance, like any other content-based restriction on speech, is constitutional "only if the [city] can show that [it] is a precisely drawn means of serving a compelling [governmental] interest." *Consolidated Edison Co. v. Public Service Comm'n of N.Y.,* 447 U.S., at 540, 100 S.Ct., at 2334. Only this strict approach can insure that cities will not use their zoning powers as a pretext for suppressing constitutionally protected expression.

Applying this standard to the facts of this case, the ordinance is patently unconstitutional. Renton has not shown that locating adult movie theaters in proximity to its churches, schools, parks, and residences will necessarily result in undesirable "secondary effects," or that these problems could not be effectively addressed by less intrusive restrictions. * * * The Court finds that the ordinance was designed to further Renton's substantial interest in "preserv[ing] the quality of urban life." As explained above, the record here is simply insufficient to support this assertion. The city made no showing as to how uses "protected" by the ordinance would be affected by the presence of an adult movie theater. Thus, the Renton ordinance is clearly distinguishable from the Detroit zoning ordinance upheld in *Young v. American Mini Theatres, Inc.,* 427 U.S. 50, 96 S.Ct. 2440, 49 L.Ed.2d 310 (1976). The Detroit ordinance, which was designed to disperse adult theaters throughout the city, was supported by the testimony of urban planners and real estate experts regarding the adverse effects of locating several such businesses in the same neighborhood. *Id.,* at 55, 96 S.Ct., at 2445; see also *Northend Cinema Inc. v. Seattle,* 90 Wash.2d 709, 711, 585 P.2d 1153, 1154–1155 (1978), cert. denied, *sub nom. Apple Theatre, Inc. v. Seattle,* 441 U.S. 946, 99 S.Ct. 2166, 60 L.Ed.2d 1048 (1979) (Seattle zoning ordinance was the "culmination of a long period of study and discussion"). Here, the Renton Council was aware only that some residents had complained about adult movie theaters, and that other localities had adopted special zoning restrictions for such establishments. These are not "facts" sufficient to justify the burdens the ordinance imposed upon constitutionally protected expression.

Finally, the ordinance is invalid because it does not provide for reasonable alternative avenues of communication. The District Court found that the ordinance left 520 acres in Renton available for adult theater sites, an area comprising about five percent of the city. However, the Court of Appeals found that because much of this land was already occupied, "[l]imiting adult theater uses to these areas is a substantial restriction on speech." Many "available" sites are also largely unsuited for use by movie theaters. Again, these facts serve to distinguish this case from *American Mini Theatres,* where there was no indication that the Detroit zoning ordinance seriously limited the locations available for adult businesses. * * *

TACO BELL v. CITY OF MISSION

Supreme Court of Kansas, 1984.
234 Kan. 879, 678 P.2d 133.

Herd, Justice: * * *

In September, 1981, Taco Bell entered into a contract to purchase a vacant lot on the northeast corner of Johnson Drive and Walmer in Mission, Kansas, from Arthur Treacher's Fish & Chips, Inc., for $150,-000, subject to rezoning for a drive-thru fast-food restaurant.

The Taco Bell site has been vacant for many years. Prior to Taco Bell's application the site was zoned special class for retail development as an automobile service station. Taco Bell requested special class zoning to construct its drive-thru window restaurant pursuant to Chapter 18.34 of the Mission Zoning Regulations.

The Mission planning commission and city council have consistently rejected applications for retail use of the vacant site, including a request for a Kentucky Fried Chicken restaurant, a Wylie's Fast–Food restaurant and an automatic car wash.

Johnson Drive, upon which the site fronts, is a four-lane highway through the City of Mission. It is capable of handling up to 23,000 vehicles a day. The City's most recent traffic count is approximately only 20,800 vehicles a day. Johnson Drive cannot be expanded to increase its capacity for additional traffic without great financial cost. Toward the west end of Mission, three residential streets intersect Johnson Drive from the north. * * * These streets provide access to a stable residential area to the north of Johnson Drive. * * *

The Taco Bell site plan satisfied all of the City's requirements pertaining to parking, signage and elevations. Taco Bell's proposed facility would have a seating capacity of forty persons. Its hours of operation were until midnight during the week and later on weekends. The environmental or aesthetic impact of the proposed Taco Bell operation is not of any different kind or degree than the developments already present along the north side of Johnson Drive except Taco Bell would contain a drive-through facility. The adjoining businesses of Winchell's Donuts and Arthur Treacher's are separated from the residential area by only a chainlink and wooden fence respectively.

The Taco Bell application was heard by the City Planning Commission on January 18, 1982. The Planning Commission unanimously recommended to the City Council that the application for the rezoning be denied. On March 10, 1982, after further review by the planning commission, the City Council also unanimously denied Taco Bell's application for rezoning. * * * On April 6, 1982, after the City denied its application, Taco Bell filed suit alleging the City was arbitrary, capricious and unreasonable in denying its application. * * *

In judging the actions of the City to be arbitrary and unreasonable in denying Taco Bell's application, the trial court utilized the appropriate scope of review and applied the test of reasonableness established by this court in *Golden v. City of Overland Park,* 224 Kan. 591, 584 P.2d 130 (1978). Prior to *Golden* the standard for determining "unreasonable" was so general and nondescript a court was helpless in applying any comprehensible standards to test the validity of zoning determinations. The results of applying such ambiguities as "beyond the realm of fair debate" and "reasonableness" often resulted in the City prevailing merely by presenting *some* evidence to support its action. Such is no longer the case. This court in *Golden* defined the factors which it suggested "would be well for a zoning body to bear in mind when hearing requests for change." These factors are:

"1. The character of the neighborhood;

"2. the zoning and uses of properties nearby;

"3. the suitability of the subject property for the uses to which it has been restricted;

"4. the extent to which removal of the restrictions will detrimentally affect nearby property;

"5. the length of time the subject property has remained vacant as zoned; and

"6. the relative gain to the public health, safety, and welfare by the destruction of the value of plaintiff's property as compared to the hardship imposed upon the individual landowner."

To these the court added: "the recommendations of permanent or professional staff, and the conformance of the requested change to the adopted or recognized master plan being utilized by the city."

Further, this court in *Golden* instructed that a City's rezoning determination on a particular tract rose or fell not on the use of generalized complaints against commercial development such as "noise", "litter", and "traffic", but rather on the defensibility of the City's stated reasons for its actions. The traditional tests of reasonableness were not abandoned but are enhanced by the eight factors which provide a reviewing court with a basis for testing the action of a governing body in a meaningful way.

Let us now review the denial of Taco Bell's application on the basis of the *Golden* criteria.

"The character of the neighborhood." The City argues the area north of Johnson Drive is mainly residential with some light commercial activity. The entire area, however, both north and south of Johnson Drive, is composed of retail business. Fast-food restaurants are quite predominant. On each side of the Taco Bell lot is a fast-food retailer, Winchell's Donuts to the west with Arthur Treacher's to the east. While there are no drive-thru restaurants on the north side of Johnson Drive, there are many to the south which are quite close to the Taco Bell lot.
* * *

The City speculates, without support, that one lone drive-thru fast-food restaurant will disrupt the peace and quiet of this entire area, as if there were not other commercial activity nearby. In actuality, the entire neighborhood is commercial/retail with the exception of the private homes to the north of the businesses which are situated on the north of Johnson Drive. The Taco Bell lot is surrounded on all sides, except to the north, by busy retail establishments. The trial court did not err in finding the character of the neighborhood was strong retail-commercial.

"The zoning and uses of property nearby." Prior to this action the Taco Bell lot was zoned for a gasoline service station. In considering the effect of the restaurant proposed by Taco Bell on the nearby property, the trial court found "the planned fast-food store with a drive-thru capacity appears to be a less intensive use than a gasoline service station." Substantial evidence was introduced at trial in support of this finding. Further, the trial court held: "Whatever impact the commerce of Johnson Drive may have on the adjacent residential area, the addition of one further restaurant should not significantly alter that impact."

The testimony at trial established the residential property adjacent to the businesses on the north side of Johnson Drive, while affected by the retail activity there, would not be harmed by the addition of the Taco Bell as compared to all the other retail businesses.

"The suitability of the subject property for the uses for which it has been restricted." The property, although zoned for use as a service station, was never developed as such. Testimony was offered at trial showing gas stations are not being built or purchased these days due to market conditions. The property, however, is now zoned C–O (office building). The City states this action was taken in order to provide better transitional zoning between the retail businesses and the residential area. While it is true office buildings provide transitional zoning, there was overwhelming evidence at trial that a demand for office buildings in Mission does not exist. The City admits this is currently true but speculates the future may have a need for such development. * * *

Experts from the fields of real estate sales, construction and real estate appraising all testified office buildings in Mission were vacant; tremendous rent concessions were being made by landlords in order to keep tenants; there had been no activity on some office building listings for over a year; no office buildings were being constructed on Johnson Drive; and finally, it would be extremely difficult to lease office space in a building located between two fast-food restaurants. The witnesses agreed any office building on the Taco Bell site would be a losing proposition.

The trial court's finding it is not feasible to develop the Taco Bell site as an office building is supported by substantial competent evidence.

"The extent to which removal of the restrictions will detrimentally affect nearby property." The City contends the economic value of the residential area will be decreased by the placement of a fast-food restaurant on the vacant lot. The evidence at trial, however, was that selling time could possibly be delayed but selling price would not be hurt. Other expert testimony was offered showing any decrease in value occurred years ago when Johnson Drive was developed commercially and one more restaurant could not realistically be linked to a decrease in property values.

The City also argued Taco Bell could not provide proper screening for lights or automobile odors or provide for other aesthetic considerations. Expert testimony was admitted which demonstrated substantial planning for green areas to include trees, shrubbery, fences and landscaping, all of which would result in effective screening. It was pointed out that Arthur Treacher's and Winchell's have only fences, one wooden and one chain link, to separate their property from the residential properties adjacent to them. Taco Bell's plan provided substantially more than a fence. * * *

The major detriment the City urges would result from the Taco Bell restaurant is increased traffic. * * * The lone Taco Bell restaurant in this case should not be disallowed merely because it might have an impact on traffic. We warned in *Golden* of the danger of a governing body relying on such general considerations as "traffic problems" and "traffic congestion" to control zoning decisions.

The City traffic engineer testified no new traffic signals would be needed after the Taco Bell was built because the traffic increase would be insignificant. The City's evidence that nearby property would be detrimentally affected by the Taco Bell restaurant is not persuasive.

"The length of time the subject property has remained vacant as zoned." For thirteen years, from 1969 to 1982, the property was zoned to allow a gasoline service station and remained undeveloped. The office district zoning has only been in effect since June 23, 1982. The evidence nevertheless demonstrated the City has an oversupply of office space, as previously discussed, and the area is thus not adaptable to that use.

"The relative gain to the public health, safety, and welfare by the destruction of the value of the plaintiff's property as compared to the hardship imposed to the individual landowner." When analyzing the gain to the public it must be remembered who constitutes the "public". This court has previously held: "Zoning is not to be based upon a plebiscite of the neighbors, and although their wishes are to be considered, the final ruling is to be governed by consideration of the benefit or harm involved to the community at large." *Waterstradt v. Board of Commissioners,* 203 Kan. 317, 454 P.2d 445 (1969). Thus, while residents neighboring the proposed Taco Bell site have protested its development, the benefit to the community as a whole must be considered. The neighbors argue there would be traffic, noise, light and odor problems. These have already been addressed and the evidence shows they can be alleviated by screening. The benefit to the public in not developing seems to be minimal. The benefit to the public in developing is great in the way of jobs, taxes, and use of previously unproductive property. * * *

In this case, the evidence supporting the granting of the zoning change was overwhelming. The evidence in opposition was minimal. The trial court properly applied the correct rules of law. After examining the entire record, we hold the trial judge did not err in finding the city council's action in denying rezoning unreasonable as a matter of law. * * *

LOCKETT, JUSTICE, concurring and dissenting. * * *

The zoning authority's action was not unreasonable and/or arbitrary. * * * The neighborhood north of Johnson Drive adjacent to the area was single family residences. The neighborhood had maintained high quality residential characteristics. Expert witnesses and neighboring property owners voiced serious concerns about the effect the proposed Taco Bell would have on property values. Expert witnesses testified that traffic along Johnson Drive is approaching the saturation point.

The city, through the years, has consistently denied requests for zoning changes on the north side of Johnson Drive to fast-food restaurants which included drive-thru window facilities. Reasons for the denials are contained in the record.

Other than being fast-food restaurants, the two adjoining restaurants are not really comparable in operation according to the evidence before the administrative board. Taco Bell's proposed facility would have a seating capacity twice the size of Arthur Treacher's or Winchell's Donuts. The peak hours of business were shown to be different between the three facilities. Taco Bell would have a greater volume than the other two restaurants during the late night hours. Taco Bell's night hours of operation would exceed those of the other two restaurants. Taco Bell's hours of operation would last until 12:00 midnight during the week and until 2:00 a.m. on the weekends. The parking lot and drive-thru area, situated adjacent to the residential area, would be properly lighted for the safety of customers during the night hours of operation, and the lighting in the parking area may be on all night to protect the property.

Other expert witnesses testified to the additional cost to the city to maintain the area, the availability of other sites on the south side of Johnson Drive, and the economic impact on the value of surrounding land. * * * I cannot say that the zoning authority's action was so arbitrary that it was unreasonable under the guidelines outlined in *Golden*.

SECTION B. PRIVATE CONTROL OF COMMUNITY CHARACTER

This section, like the previous section, is devoted to an analysis of a community's power to control its own character. Here, however, we investigate the exercise of this power when it is lodged in the hands of a private homeowners association rather than a city. We thus return to an issue first addressed in Chapter One: the impact of the public/private distinction on local government law. The materials begin with excerpts from four law review articles debating whether there are important differences between cities and homeowners associations and, if so, what these differences might be.[1] Three cases then raise issues parallel to

---

1. For further analyses of the legal issues raised by homeowners associations, see, e.g., Natelson, Consent, Coercion, and "Reasonableness" in Private Law: The

those raised in the preceding section. Maryland Commission on Human Relations v. Greenbelt Homes and 1733 Estates Association v. Randolph, like Village of Belle Terre v. Boraas, concern the community's ability to exclude unrelated adults; Omega Corporation of Chesterfield v. Malloy, like City of Cleburne, Texas v. Cleburne Living Center, deals with the community's power to exclude group homes for the mentally retarded. In reading the decisions in these three cases, consider whether a community's ability to exclude those whom its members consider "undesirable" should be different if the community is "private" rather than "public"— as well as whether the public/private distinction should determine whether a community is allowed to exclude pornographic movie theaters or fast food restaurants. Note too that the three cases present contrasting views concerning the meaning of terms like "family", "single-family dwelling" and "discrimination on the basis of marital status". A final case in the series, McMinn v. Town of Oyster Bay, addresses the definition of one of these terms—"family"—in a city ordinance. Should the definition of "family" be different for homeowners associations and cities? For example, should a community's ability to exclude gay or lesbian couples be different depending on whether the restriction to "family occupancy" is expressed in a homeowners association contract or a city ordinance? [2]

ROBERT ELLICKSON, CITIES AND HOMEOWNERS ASSOCIATIONS

130 U.Pa.L.Rev. 1519, 1519–1520, 1521–1523, 1526–1527 (1982).

In his recent article, *The City as a Legal Concept,* Professor Gerald Frug compared the city and the business corporation as possible vehicles for the exercise of decentralized power. In the course of his analysis, Frug asserted that American law is deeply biased against the emergence of powerful cities and, by implication, is less restrictive on corporate power. * * * Frug never directed his attention at a third candidate for the exercise of decentralized power: the private homeowners association. The association, not the business corporation, is the obvious private alternative to the city. Like a city, an association enables households that have clustered their activities in a territorially defined area to enforce rules of conduct, to provide "public goods" (such as open space), and to pursue other common goals they could not achieve without some form of potentially coercive central authority. Although they were relatively exotic as recently as twenty years ago, homeowners associa-

Special Case of the Property Owners Association, 51 Ohio St.L.J. 41 (1990); Guernsey, The Mentally Retarded and Private Restrictive Covenants, 25 Wm. & Mary L.Rev. 421 (1984); Rosenberry, The Application of the Federal and State Constitutions to Condominiums, Cooperatives and Planned Developments, 19 Real Prop.Prob. & Tr.J. 1 (1984); Geiss, Residential Private Governments and the Law, 67 A.B.A.J. 1418 (1981); Reichman, Residential Private Governments: An Introductory Survey, 43 U.Chi.L.Rev. 253 (1976).

2. For an inquiry into the relationship between gay and lesbian relationships and the term "family", see, e.g, Braschi v. Stahl Assoc., 74 N.Y.2d 201, 543 N.E.2d 49 (1989); Rubenstein, Lesbians, Gay Men, and the Law 377–474 (1993).

tions now outnumber cities. Developers create thousands of new associations each year to govern their subdivisions, condominiums, and planned communities.

American law currently treats the city and the homeowners association dramatically differently. One is "public"; the other, "private." In law, as Frug correctly points out, much now turns on this distinction. Frug emphasizes the relative "powerlessness" of cities, a legal phenomenon he discovers not so much by observation as by logical deduction from the "dualities" of "liberal thought."

This Article compares the legal status of cities and homeowners associations. In contrast to Professor Frug, I generally rely on empirical methods to identify legal phenomena. Part I of the Article examines the fundamental characteristics of cities and homeowners associations. Although cities are considered "public" and homeowners associations "private," I discern only one important difference between the two forms of organization—the sometimes involuntary nature of membership in a city versus the perfectly voluntary nature of membership in a homeowners association. I assert that this difference explains why cities are more active than associations are in undertaking coercive redistributive programs. * * *

Professor Frank Michelman, unquestionably the preeminent legal mind on community governance, has offered a characteristically useful one-sentence guide for identifying the existence of a "governmental" organization:

> We know perfectly well, granting that there are intermediate hard cases, how to distinguish governmental from non-governmental *powers* and *forms of organization:* governments are distinguished by their acknowledged, lawful authority—not dependent on property ownership—to coerce a territorially defined and imperfectly voluntary membership by acts of regulation, taxation, and condemnation, the exercise of which authority is determined by majoritarian and representative procedures.

Although this particular quotation was an aside in an article mainly addressed to other issues, a scholar as careful as Michelman no doubt crafted the sentence to encapsulate insights gained through years of puzzling over the essence of governmental organizations.

The homeowners association, although certainly one of Michelman's "intermediate hard cases," is currently viewed by both ordinary and legal observers as a "private" organization, not a "government." In fact, it is sufficiently "private" that it has rarely been granted any intermediate legal status that a hard case might be thought to deserve, but instead has been treated much like any other private organization. This is so even though the modern homeowners association has virtually all of the indicia that Michelman would have us associate with a government. First, a homeowners association rules a "territorially defined" area, and, in the usual case, obtains its power to do so through no form of property ownership. For example, when the members of a condominium association own the common areas as tenants in common, the association itself owns no real property at all.

Nor does Michelman's list of the tell-tale governmental powers do much to distinguish a homeowners association from a city. An association is typically entitled to undertake acts of both regulation and taxation, as those terms are ordinarily used. Associations, for example, may restrict to whom a member may sell his unit, prohibit certain kinds of conduct (not only in common areas but also within the confines of individual homes), and tightly control the physical alteration of a member's unit. An association's "taxation" takes the form of monthly assessments on members. Assessments can be raised without the unanimous consent of the membership. Payment of an assessment is secured by a lien on a member's unit, making the assessment is almost as hard to evade as a municipal property tax is. To be sure, association powers are not as extensive as those possessed by "public" bodies. The regulations of a homeowners association in sum are likely to be less intrusive and comprehensive than what one finds in a typical municipal code. Cities have far more ways to raise revenue than associations do. Lastly, it would be highly unusual for an association to have the power to condemn a member's unit—the third governmental power Michelman lists. Some homeowners associations do have the power to expel members for misbehavior—a power that comes close to the power of condemnation. But even if they did not, exercise of eminent domain power by a local government is rare; it would be remarkable if the presence of this power were a necessary condition for the use of the adjective "public" in ordinary or legal language.

Nor does one stretch ordinary language out of shape to describe an association as having "majoritarian and representative procedures." Much as citydwellers choose a city council, association members elect a board of directors to manage association affairs.

Only one part of Michelman's description of a government remains: its "imperfectly voluntary membership." Public entities have involuntary members when they are first formed. For example, the statutory procedures for incorporating a new city invariably authorize a majority (perhaps only concurrent or extraordinary majorities) to coerce involuntary minorities to join their organization. By contrast, membership in a private organization is wholly voluntary. A central thesis of this Article is that the presence of *involuntary members* is both a necessary condition for the use of the adjective "public" in ordinary language, and also a powerful explanation for the different legal treatment currently accorded public and private organizations. * * *

The initial members of a homeowners association, by their voluntary acts of joining, unanimously consent to the provisions in the association's original governing documents. In the language of Buchanan and Tullock, this unanimous ratification elevates those documents to the legal status of a private "constitution." The original documents—which today typically include a declaration of covenants, articles of association (or incorporation), and by-laws—are a true social contract. The feature of unanimous ratification distinguishes these documents from and gives them greater legal robustness than non-unanimously adopted public constitutions, not to mention the hypothetical social contracts of Rousseau or Rawls. * * *

GERALD FRUG, CITIES AND HOMEOWNERS ASSOCIATIONS: A REPLY

130 U.Pa.L.Rev. 1589, 1589–1591 (1982).

Professor Ellickson wants to convince us that homeowners associations are a better vehicle for decentralized power than are cities. To do so, he must make a convincing distinction between the two forms of associations, a convincing public/private distinction. This he bases on the voluntary/involuntary distinction—homeowners associations are formed voluntarily, while cities are formed at least in part involuntarily. But to persuade us that homeowners associations are formed voluntarily, he needs to have us think of them as a miniature version of the liberal society envisioned by John Locke. Thus, Professor Ellickson describes the homeowners association as an example of a Lockean social contract: a unanimous agreement of property owners that creates a constitution for (at least part of) the social order. It is this unanimous agreement that makes the association voluntary. Like Locke before him, however, Professor Ellickson simply invents this "wholly voluntary" contract as a postulate on which to base his argument. Although he asserts that the original membership in homeowners associations is wholly voluntary and that cities have involuntary members when first formed, this assertion has no empirical support. Cities can be, and have been, formed by the voluntary association of their citizens, while the original constitution of a homeowners association might well be the work of a developer without the participation of a single person who becomes a resident of the community. To support his voluntary/involuntary distinction, Professor Ellickson treats homeowners associations as if they come into existence by the voluntary agreement of the original settlers and treats cities as if they are created only after the residents are already in place. Yet, this public/private distinction is hypothesis and nothing more.

Perhaps Professor Ellickson is suggesting not that we simply accept this hypothesis, but that we make an inquiry in each case to determine whether the association was in fact originally formed by its residents, a developer, or some other group of people. But that kind of inquiry would not distinguish cities from homeowners associations: instead it would distinguish some of each from others of each. It thus would not reproduce the current public/private distinction at all. It also would be hard to do, because exactly when cities were formed is a matter open to considerable debate. We certainly need not accept the positivist definition of the formation of a city in terms of its being granted a corporate charter. Moreover, the circumstances of the original formation rapidly lose relevance as new residents move in, children take over their parents' homes, and the like. It therefore seems unlikely that Professor Ellickson would allow an historical proof that Plymouth, Mass., was formed by a social contract to determine the city's legal status today. But without history, we are left simply with his liberal postulate, one that we are free to reject. I do reject it. I can see no difference at all—no legitimate public/private distinction at all—between cities and home-owners associations.   * * *

GREGORY ALEXANDER, DILEMMAS OF GROUP AUTONOMY: RESIDENTIAL ASSOCIATIONS AND COMMUNITY

75 Cornell L. Rev. 1, 40–46, 56–60 (1989).

On the surface, residential associations appear to be straightforward examples of voluntary associations rather than communities. Residential associations are created explicitly by contract. Membership is overtly based on consent, which members express by purchasing their property interest in the development. In this context, the social contract is not a metaphor; the legal documents, which typically include a declaration of covenants, articles of incorporation, and by-laws, all evidence agreement to the rules of the group.

At the same time, however, the contractarian model of residential associations is incomplete. Its focus on the formal mode of creation leads it to ignore the character of social relations within residential groups. As a result, it fails to distinguish between residential groups that are held together only by mutual collaboration and convenience, and those in which individuals choose to live together because of more deeply shared values. That is, it ignores the distinction between *gemeinschaft* and *gesellschaft*. More specifically, its contractarian analysis overlooks the *combination* of these aspects in the creation of a residential group. Some empirical work done on the character of social relations within residential associations suggests that this combination exists in modern American residential groups.

Frances Fitzgerald's recent account of Sun City Center details the social experience of members of one residential association, an age-segregated retirement development in Florida. Her study reveals that although some social differentiation does exist in within the group, the population of Sun City Center is strikingly homogeneous in virtually all respects. "They came to Sun City," Fitzgerald observes, "for all of the amenities spelled out in the advertising brochures and for a homogeneity that had little to do with age. In a country where class is rarely discussed, they had found their own niche like homing pigeons." Because of that homogeneity, relationships form easily in Sun City, and the inhabitants feel quite comfortable with each other. They regularly socialize with each other, making isolation from other residents virtually non-existent. They are attracted to each other by their shared values and preferences, and they have created a mode of existence consciously based on that sharing of values and preferences. The effect is that residents of Sun City exhibit a deep sense of belonging there and belonging with each other.

Residential groups like Sun City Center are best understood as a type of constitutive group, that is, a community. The concept of a constitutive group implies an element of involuntariness. What binds the group together is a shared characteristic that is unchosen, or chosen only in a weak sense, such as cultural identity. But it is erroneous to suppose that community contradicts voluntariness. Two crucial insights lay behind the notion of constitutive groups. First, individuals define themselves according to some shared good; second, that good gives to each member of the group a sense of belonging. The experience of belonging can be based on a shared good that individuals have chosen. Consider * * * [the] example of a monastery. Monasteries are residential communities based on shared characteristics that some people suppose individuals have the power to choose, *i.e.*, religious commitment. Members of the monastery interpret their personal identities on the basis of that characteristic, which each defines as a good. The self-identity created by that interpretation virtually impels monks to live in close proximity with each other. In a similar, albeit, weaker, sense, Fitzgerald's account suggests the possibility that the residents of Sun City Center experience the need to live together with other older adults who have made the same life-style choices. Voluntariness and involuntariness are combined in the constitution of such groups.

To be sure, residential associations vary widely in the mixture of communal and contractarian ties that they exhibit. On the surface, many appear to be predominately contractarian aggregations of individuals who exhibit few affective ties with each other. One may react skeptically toward the typical promotional literature that advertises residential associations as "communities" on the basis of shared swimming pools and security patrols. Reliance on these factors alone as evidence of community is, as Thomas Bender states, a "cynical manipulation of symbols of community" that trivializes the very ideal of community. But shared resources, like swimming pools, do affect the social relationships among users, shaping the character of those relationships into one that can be called communitarian. Residents of common unit developments have commented that their arrangements are "more friendly than in a single family home development * * * because we see each other more often at the pool, and we see each other a lot at board meetings, and we've had some problems that we've all had to work out together. I think there's a feeling of togetherness." At the same time, as Constance Perin remarks in her study of the culture of condominium ownership, "Feelings of goodwill notwithstanding, condo owners act on the market-driven reciprocity expressly built into their relationship from the start."

Perhaps more than in any other group in modern American society, residential associations overtly blend contractarian and communitarian dimensions of group relationships. Common ownership requires that residents sacrifice individual autonomy for sharing. They choose to be

tied together, and, although that choice may initially have been motivated by instrumental reasons, the experience of being tied together creates new, qualitatively different layers in their personal relationships. While at one level sharing in common unit developments is explicitly collaborative, required by the residents' contracts, it generates other levels of sharing that transcend mere collaboration. Describing life within residential associations requires that we identify the multiple layers of the residents' relationships and understand how they can affect each other.
* * *

Since de Tocqueville, it has been common to praise voluntary associations for the "public values of the private association." The claim is that voluntary associations represent pockets of participation and self-governance in a society otherwise characterized by powerlessness and indifference. This argument for ceding strong autonomy to voluntary associations deserves serious attention, especially in the context of residential associations. If there are good reasons to believe that residential associations represent laboratories of undominated participation and self-governance, then we ought to be vary reluctant to interfere with them, not in the interest of freedom of contract, but out of a commitment to communitarian values. The crucial question is whether residential associations on the whole provide appropriate conditions for nurturing participatory governance.

Recent empirical studies on residential associations suggest that the vision of self-governance and participatory democracy within these groups often is illusory. It indicates that in some common unit developments residents are at best uninvolved in their homeowners association, and at worst frustrated and disillusioned with their private governance structures. Apparently, association boards often make little effort to involve residents, in part because they want to avoid the increased likelihood of disagreement, but more fundamentally because board members do not view themselves as occupying authoritative roles. Rather, they perceive their function as a combination of property managers and neighbors. Neither the citizens nor the managers of these "private residential governments" display an awareness of their experience in overtly political terms.

The failure of residential associations to realize the image of participatory democracy is not due simply to a rational choice by owners to forego opportunities to participate in the association's civic affairs. The gap that exists between the Panglossian image of many residential associations and reality stems, at least in part, from the unequal allocation of power within these developments. Private residential governments too often represent a dominated mode of residential life in modern America.

Several factors undermine the participatory and self-governing character of some residential associations. One obvious source of domination is developer control. Association by-laws enable developers to control crucial aspects of governance, not only at the inception of the project, but also after most of the units in the development have been sold. A development's "constitution," initially provided by the developer, typically may be amended only with the concurrence of both mortgage lenders and owners or by super-majorities (*i.e.*, 75%) of owners. Developers also frequently remain on the association board for many years after it formally has passed to the control of homeowners. Their longevity gives them substantial clout within the nominally independent board.

I do not suggest that all, or perhaps even most, residential associations are tainted by fraud or other distorting influences. The caricature of developers as villains dressed in black and twirling their mustaches while purchasers sign residential association agreements is, of course, only that—a caricature. But just as we ought to resist depicting common-unit developments as thoroughly tainted by duress or ill-considered choices, so we must reject portraits of residential associations as unqualified realms of enlightened individual preference-maximizing behavior. People buying into common-unit developments not infrequently have stated that they experienced coercion in agreeing to association rules and in joining the association itself. A finding of no legal coercion cannot eliminate this experienced reality. That these individuals experienced coercion is itself a truth. We will move much closer to a full understanding of social experiences within common-unit developments if we say, at the risk of stating the obvious, that people's experiences in this context are extremely complex. The desire for communal ties accompanies financial motives; regret, ambivalence, and misunderstanding accompany rational choice; domination accompanies autonomy.

A second factor belying the participatory character of residential associations is the virtually standard restriction of voting rights to owners—a practice that simultaneously disenfranchises renting residents and enhances the power of non-resident owners who own more than one unit in the development. Theories of participatory democracy stress the importance of widely-held voting rights, not because of the economic value that individuals attach to that right, but to enable individuals to gain control over their lives by "distributing 'voice' through which individuals may have their say in the social determinations of the structure of coercion and restraint." On this view, it is quite beside the point that renters do not value the franchise as much as owners, assuming for the moment that this assertion is justified. The rules of a residential association, a "structure of coercion and restraint," clearly affect renters, and the participatory objective of avoiding conditions of personal domination apply to these persons as fully as they do to owners. * * * The vision of common-unit developments as laboratories of small-scale democracy and civic participation, then, distorts social reality. * * *

[T]he role of the legal system is to connect * * * [these] groups with the rest of society even while recognizing their separateness. Disputes over the enforcement of group restrictions present opportunities for a dialogue about the group's shared values and the extent to which they advance the ideal of community or impede it by creating relations of domination.

This conception of the judicial role requires a form of legal involvement that is itself open-ended. * * * [It] suggests that the recent decisional trend replacing *per se* rules with the norm of reasonableness is appropriate to the group-character of common interest developments. *Per se* rules, either sustaining or invalidating association restrictions, would preclude courts from the dialogic inquiry that the ideal of community demands. A rule of *per se* invalidity would deny group autonomy altogether; its polar opposite risks community becoming self-defeating. The reasonableness standard harmonizes with the communitarian conception by requiring that decisions concerning the enforceability of association restrictions be made deliberately and socially.

That the reasonableness norm is open-ended and conversation-inducing does not imply that it provides no direction. Reasonableness is to be judged within a particular normative context or culture. The relevant normative culture is not that of any specific group, but the culture of a society committed to the ideal of community. * * * Legal intervention in the form of an open-ended standard is not a matter of groups ceding autonomy to courts, but a matter of groups remaining open to a continuing public conversation that, by connecting and reconnecting groups and others, progressively reiterates and reinforces the ideal of community. * * *

NOTE, THE RULE OF LAW IN RESIDENTIAL ASSOCIATIONS

99 Harv.L.Rev. 472, 485–490 (1985).

When a resident fails to conform to an association's rules, or challenges an association's actions, either the resident or the association is likely to invoke the power of the outside government to void or enforce the covenants and bylaws that define the association's power. The dissenter may claim that "unconstitutional" rules should be unenforceable, while the association may claim that it is just to enforce the rules because they reflect the consent of all members. When the constitutionalist and consent theories conflict in this way, legislatures and courts must determine the relative merits of the competing theories as applied to different sorts of association rules.

Legislatures and courts must consider this issue from the points of view both of association members and of the broader political community within which a residential association resides. The balance of harms and benefits that illiberal association government could bring, both within the association itself and to the outside community, suggest that state legislatures and courts should embrace the constitutionalist vision; they should require residential associations to respect the basic civil liberties embodied in the Bill of Rights and the fourteenth amendment. * * *

Residential associations offer valuable opportunities for those who choose to opt out of certain restrictions on their ways of life. The consent theorist would insist that only those who seek the benefits of an illiberal community need join and that, therefore, the balance of harms and benefits in a private residential association favors the enforcement of illiberal rules. Even though some individuals or families may lose their enthusiasm for the special goals or procedures of the association, the rest of the association will remain faithful to the polity; because the association is a self-selected community, government can be sure here— as it cannot in the case of a city—that dissenters are the exception, and believers the rule.

It is impossible, however, to evaluate the extent of harm illiberal associations do to their members. First, even though a disempowered dissident may be drastically outnumbered by contented conformists at the time she calls on the government for protection, other members of her association may at a later date find themselves in her position. Second, conformity in the face of potential sanctions does not necessarily reflect endorsement of the illiberal regime. The very existence of state-enforced association rules discourages the exercise of civil rights by association members; indeed, such regulations are designed to discourage residents from attempting to exercise certain rights. Finally, the existence of illiberal rules may, over time, have a more profound influence in stifling heterogeneity: by promoting conformity of conduct in the short term, state-enforced rules may prevent residents from recognizing that certain rights have value. The state, by placing its power behind illiberal association rules, would help create the very habits of obedience and conformity that consent theorists would use to justify holding residents to these rules.

Given this uncertainty about the actual consequences of enforcing illiberal association rules, government should lend its power to residential associations only in accordance with the same norms of individual rights that guide the direct use of state power. The residential association poses much the same danger to individuals and families as would local government unrestrained by constitutional norms. The jurisdiction of residential associations, like that of traditional governments, extends over a particularly sensitive and important location in most people's lives: their homes. If a person is subject to surveillance or intimidation in her home, she usually has no escape, no refuge. Unlike the workplace, the home is a place of privacy from the outside world for most individuals and families. Moreover, the risk of losing one's home represents a powerful disincentive to dissent on political and social issues within an association. Furthermore, residential associations may hold power over significant public spaces, such as common areas, streets, and parks, that could allow them to regulate the access of outsiders to members of a community, and communication among association residents.

By enforcing the rules and decisions of a private association, government grants the association something it would not otherwise have: the legitimate coercive power of the state. This power transforms private force into the maintenance of public order, private trespass or theft into the just vindication of the law. The constitutional tradition in the United States has demanded that public power be restrained in certain ways. This tradition embodies a belief that the harms suffered by nonconformists who cannot claim certain minimal protections, and ultimately by the community as a whole where democratic government is undermined by illiberal laws, are of greater weight than the accompanying loss to those who believe that constitutional liberties stand in the way of the form of community they find most valuable. Because an illiberal residential association would present the same kinds of dangers to dissidents and to democratic politics within the association that local governments present to a broader community, this premise of American constitutionalism has equal application to residential associations. * * *

The arguments from consent are further undermined by consideration of the wider public consequences likely to flow from permitting residential associations to ignore fourteenth amendment norms. Residential covenants effectively waiving liberties of constitutional magnitude should not be enforceable because the creation of illiberal enclaves in which the exercise of civil rights is burdened with onerous sanctions threatens the broader political communities of the city, the state, and the nation.

An illiberal enclave harms the process of government in the larger polity because it diminishes or distorts the role in this process of those within the enclave. For example, the existence of illiberal regulations may discourage a member's recognition of her power to participate outside the association; the association may limit its members' access to information and discussion about political issues in the broader society; and the association may attempt to use quasi-governmental powers to influence individual members of the association to support particular political programs outside the association.

The Supreme Court's incorporation of the most significant provisions of the Bill of Rights into the due process clause of the fourteenth amendment reflects the need for national uniformity in the enforcement of basic constitutional standards. Incorporation may be justified on the ground that local obstruction of civil rights may pose as great a threat to the political process in the state and the nation as does obstruction of civil rights by the federal government. The power of a municipal police force could prove a greater threat to free congressional elections than the power of the F.B.I.; local regulation of speech in public places may over time hinder national political debate as severely as might a president's attempt to restrain the publication of news. A residential association may exercise jurisdiction over its members' homes and may control significant public forums, such as parks and roads. There is no reason to assume that the powers of larger residential associations are less of a threat to the political life of the region, state, or nation than is the power of a typical municipality. Nor should government assume that residential associations of any size present less of a threat to the politics of the city than an illiberal state presents to the nation.

Residential associations may provide an escape for those who seek a community free of the liberal norms that dominate American society. But the private association can form a basis for alternative communities only to the extent that government enforces the community's rules and covenants—that is, only to the extent that government lends these associations its power to exclude and suppress nonconformists within the new communities. If residential associations were *simply* voluntary associations, there would be no need of rules and covenants; in fact, however, they are also coercive associations. And if residential associations can draw upon the support of government, they can exercise a coercive power very much like the power of the city they are meant to supplant, or at least to supplement. To conclude that government should not enforce rules that violate the norms embodied in constitutional civil rights, one need not believe that those who enter an illiberal association, and choose to burden activities protected in the outside world, necessarily make themselves less free in every case. Rather, government should not participate in illiberal associations because residential associations are so like a city, both within their own borders and in relation to the larger polities of which they are parts, that government should limit its own power to enforce the rules of private associations according to the same presumptions and values that favor constitutional civil liberties within our traditional polities.

MARYLAND COMMISSION ON HUMAN RELATIONS v. GREENBELT HOMES

Court of Appeals of Maryland, 1984.
300 Md. 75, 475 A.2d 1192.

COLE, JUDGE.

In this case we must determine whether enforcing a housing cooperative regulation that operates to prohibit a female resident from having an unrelated adult male reside with her constitutes discrimination on the basis of "marital status" proscribed by Maryland Code Art. 49B, § 20. The relevant facts are not disputed.

Greenbelt Homes, Inc. (Greenbelt) is a Maryland corporation operating a housing cooperative in Greenbelt, Maryland. In 1976, Raymond and Marguerite Burgess (Burgess) applied for a Greenbelt membership. Their daughter, C. Lynn Kuhr (Kuhr), and her son were to be the residents of the unit; therefore, Kuhr also was required to file an application with Greenbelt. On this application, Kuhr indicated that only she and her son would be living in the unit. The Greenbelt board of directors granted Burgess permission to have their daughter and her son dwell in their unit and on November 15, 1976, Burgess entered into a mutual ownership contract with Greenbelt purchasing the equity and perpetual use of a housing unit in the Greenbelt Housing Project. This contract provided that the corporation could impose reasonable rules and regulations in managing the project and specifically noted that occupancy of the unit was only for the cooperative member and "his immediate family." If the member violated any provisions of the agreement, the corporation could terminate the contract. Furthermore, a Greenbelt occupancy regulation specifically defined "family members."

Kuhr and her son moved into the unit shortly after her parents executed the contract. Sometime thereafter Richard Searight, an unrelated adult male, also moved into the unit. Neither Kuhr nor her parents ever sought a waiver of the contractual provision limiting occupancy to immediate family members. In May of 1978, Greenbelt became aware of Mr. Searight's presence in the unit after receiving complaints from other cooperative members about parking and other problems relating to the occupancy of the Kuhr unit. Greenbelt advised Kuhr and her parents that having this unrelated adult occupy the unit violated the mutual ownership contract and urged them to "straighten out" the situation. When the matter had not been resolved by September of 1978, Greenbelt notified Burgess of a board of directors meeting at which they could explain why their contract should not be terminated. Before this meeting, Kuhr notified Greenbelt that Mr. Searight would be vacating the unit (which he in fact did "against his will and against the will of [Kuhr]").

Prior to Searight's exodus, Kuhr filed a housing discrimination complaint with the Maryland Commission on Human Relations (Commission) pursuant to Maryland Code Art. 49B, § 9(a), alleging that Greenbelt's conduct constituted discrimination on the basis of her "marital status, single." * * * Greenbelt argues that Kuhr breached the mutual ownership contract and, thus, it has the right to terminate her occupancy. The mutual ownership contract provides, in pertinent part, as follows:

> 7(a). *Occupancy:* The Member shall occupy the dwelling unit covered by this contract as a private dwelling from the date of occupancy * * * for himself and his immediate family * * *.

> 7(b). *Rules and Regulations Relating to Occupancy and Care of the Dwelling:* This Corporation reserves the right to impose any reasonable rules and regulations not inconsistent with the provisions of this contract * * * as in its judgment may be necessary or desirable for the management and control of Greenbelt and the Member's dwelling unit and surrounding premises, and for the preservation of good order and comfort therein, and the Member agrees faithfully to observe and comply with such rules and regulations and further agrees that all persons living in the dwelling unit also will observe and comply with such rules and regulations * * *.

> 13. *Termination of Contract by Corporation for Default or for Cause:* In the event of default by the Member * * * or violation of any of the provisions hereof, the Corporation may terminate this contract. * * * The Corporation may terminate this Contract * * * if its board of directors * * * shall determine that the Member for

sufficient cause is undesirable as a resident in Greenbelt because of objectionable conduct on the part of the Member or of a person living in his dwelling unit. To violate or disregard the rules and regulations provided for in paragraph 7(b) hereof, after due warning, shall be deemed to be objectionable conduct. * * *

We had occasion to review these contractual provisions in *Green v. Greenbelt Homes,* 232 Md. 496, 194 A.2d 273 (1963). In that case Greenbelt sought to terminate its contract with a woman who, among other violations, was living with an unrelated adult man. The Court addressed the question "whether the provisions of the contract relating to termination were valid." The Court held that the member had breached her contract with Greenbelt sufficiently to "warrant the corporation exercising its right to terminate the interests of the member in the dwelling unit." In examining the issue presented in that case, the Court focused on the nature of the cooperative and its relationship to members:

> An important factor in the maintenance of a cooperative housing project is the control of the activities of the cooperative members living within the project. In a recent article, *Restrictions on the Use of Cooperative Apartment Property,* by Arthur E. Wallace, 13 Hastings Law Journal, 357, 363, it is said:

> "The economic and social interdependence of the tenant-owners demands cooperation on all levels of cooperative life if a tolerable living situation is to be maintained. Each tenant-owner is required to give up some of the freedoms he would otherwise enjoy if he were living in a private dwelling and likewise is privileged to demand the same sacrifices of his cotenant-owners with respect to his rights.

> "By analogy, the cooperative agreement is really a community within a community governed, like our municipalities, by rules and regulations for the benefit of the whole. Whereas the use of lands within a city is controlled by zoning ordinances, the use of apartments within the cooperative project is controlled by restrictive covenants. The use of the common facilities in the project is controlled on the same theory that the use of city streets and parks is regulated. In both situations compliance with the regulations is the price to be paid to live in and enjoy the benefits of the particular organization."

For these reasons, the Court recognized that the activities of cooperative members may be contractually regulated and that these regulations should be enforced.

The case *sub judice* is strikingly similar. Here, the undisputed facts demonstrate that Kuhr violated a provision of the mutual ownership contract executed by her parents, yet also governing the conduct of all those living in the project. She knew from the date the contract was signed that only her immediate family members were authorized to occupy the dwelling unit. Despite such knowledge, she allowed Mr. Searight, unrelated by blood or marriage, to live with her and at no time sought a waiver from the board of directors so as to justify his presence in the dwelling unit. Greenbelt maintains this breach should be dispositive of the issue before us.

However, as we see it, even this conduct cannot determine the issue if, indeed, the contractual covenant prohibiting persons from residing with unrelated adults violates the State anti-discrimination law. The real issue is whether Greenbelt was precluded from seeking to enforce its membership regulation because such conduct constituted an unlawful discriminatory practice under Maryland Code Art. 49B, § 20. Section 20 * * * means precisely what it says: no person shall be discriminated against in regard to housing because of that person's marital status. As we see it, "marital status" connotes whether one is married or not married.

Here, the fact that Kuhr was not married to Mr. Searight was irrelevant. It would have made no difference under the circumstances of this case if Searight had been Kuhr's best girlfriend, her favorite aunt, her destitute cousin, or her infant nephew. The point is that no one of these people, including Mr. Searight, falls within the defined class of family members in the regulation. * * * Our conclusion that Kuhr was not discriminated against because of her marital status is buttressed by an analysis of similar cases from other jurisdictions. For instance, the New York courts have addressed a similar issue in *Hudson View Properties v. Weiss,* 106 Misc.2d 251, 431 N.Y.S.2d 632 (1980), *rev'd,* 109 Misc.2d 589, 442 N.Y.S.2d 367 (1981), *rev'd,* 86 A.D.2d 803, 448 N.Y.S.2d 649 (1982), *rev'd,* 59 N.Y.2d 733, 463 N.Y.S.2d 428, 450 N.E.2d 234 (1983). In that case, * * * the New York Court of Appeals * * * stated:

> In this case, the issue arises not because the tenant is unmarried, but because the lease restricts occupancy of her apartment, as are all apartments in the building, to the tenant and the tenant's immediate family. Tenant admits that an individual not part of her immediate family currently occupies the apartment as his primary residence. Whether or not he could by marriage or otherwise become a part of her immediate family is not an issue. The landlord reserved the right by virtue of the covenant in the lease to restrict the occupants and the tenant agreed to this restriction. Were the additional tenant a female unrelated to the tenant, the lease would be violated without reference to marriage. The fact that the additional tenant here involved is a man with whom the tenant has a loving relationship is simply irrelevant. The applicability of that restriction does not depend on her marital status. * * *

Accordingly, we hold that § 20's prohibition against marital status discrimination does not preclude a housing cooperative from enforcing a contractual obligation restricting occupancy to persons in the member's immediate family. Thus, Greenbelt did not discriminate against Kuhr based on her "marital status." * * *

1733 ESTATES ASSOCIATION v. RANDOLPH

Court of Appeals of Nebraska, 1992.
485 N.W.2d 339.

SIEVERS, CHIEF JUDGE.

The appellant, 1733 Estates Association, Inc., brought suit in the district court for Buffalo County, Nebraska, seeking to enjoin Loretta Jean Randolph from renting the basement portion of her home to tenants. The appellant was seeking to enforce a restrictive covenant of record which provided: "I. USE OF LOTS: All of said lots in said subdivision shall be used for residential purposes only and shall be restricted to single family dwellings." * * *

Randolph is the owner of a residence located on a lot in Buffalo County, Nebraska. The residence and the lot are outside the city limits of Kearney. When Randolph and her former husband moved into the residence, the basement of the home was not finished in any way. Before the Randolphs separated and divorced, Randolph's former husband began finishing the basement, and he constructed a bedroom and a family room. After the first tenant, Joan Tarrell, began her occupancy in October 1987, additional construction was undertaken and completed. The result was that the basement had a kitchen, three bedrooms, a family room, a bathroom, and a private stairway entrance from the garage down to the basement. Tarrell shared this basement space with a college student and paid $425 per month rent for the two of them. Tarrell testified that she "resided primarily in the basement area of the house." She also testified that she was not prohibited from using the entire residence, but the record is silent on the extent to which she used the upstairs portion, although Tarrell's cat slept "most of the time in Jean's red velvet chair upstairs."

There were other tenants after Tarrell, usually women that were not related to Randolph. Some of the tenants paid rent, while others lived there in exchange for work they performed for a cleaning service which Randolph operated. * * *

We begin our analysis by noting that covenants restricting the use of property are not favored in law. If restrictive covenants are ambiguous, they will be construed in a manner permitting the maximum unrestricted use of the property. *Knudtson v. Trainor*, 216 Neb. 653, 345 N.W.2d 4 (1984).

Knudtson was the first Nebraska case to define the meaning and implication of the phrase "single-family dwelling," and in so doing, the court placed heavy reliance on *Sissel v. Smith*, 242 Ga. 595, 250 S.E.2d 463 (1978). The Georgia court held that the words "single-family dwelling" operate as a restriction on the type of building that can be constructed on a lot, but not as a limitation on the type of activity that can take place in the building so constructed.

The Nebraska Supreme Court, in *Knudtson*, was faced with a suit to enjoin the operation of a group home for five mentally retarded persons in a residential subdivision having a restrictive covenant which provided: " '1. No lot shall be used except for residential purposes. No building shall be erected, altered, placed or permitted to remain on any lot other than one detached single family dwelling. * * *' " *Knudtson*, 216 Neb. at 654, 345 N.W.2d at 5. The court approved the trial court's conclusions that the house at issue would " 'appear no different than any of the other houses in the neighborhood to any persons passing by' " and, further, that " 'the five women and their houseparents will live together as a family unit.' " *Id.* at 659–60, 345 N.W.2d at 8. As a result, the denial of the injunction was upheld.

Accordingly, we view *Knudtson* as requiring a two-part test when construing a restrictive covenant such as is involved here: (1) whether the *use* of the home was for a residential purpose and (2) whether the *physical structure* on the lot was a single-family dwelling. *Knudtson* defines the following key terms: "residential purpose" refers to the way the property is used and "residential" means a place where people reside, dwell, or make their homes. "Single-family dwelling" refers to the type of building which may be constructed and not to the use of such building. See *Knudtson, supra.* * * *

In applying *Knudtson* to the instant case in our de novo review, we find that at all times the house was used for residential purposes, both by Randolph and her tenants. This is where they lived and made their homes. There was no evidence that any commercial or business transactions were conducted on the premises. The restrictive covenants do not expressly prohibit the leasing for residential purposes of a portion or a share of the structure to unrelated persons, and we must construe the covenant in the least restrictive manner. If appellant association wished to prevent the leasing of space within a residence to unrelated parties, specific covenants could have been adopted. Therefore, in applying the first prong of the test from *Knudtson*, we find no violation of the covenant concerning Randolph's use of the structure, since it was used for residential purposes.

The second prong of the *Knudtson* test deals with the physical character of the building erected on the lot. We find that the physical structure of the home remained at all times a single-family dwelling, even though there may have been tenants living in the basement. There were no alterations made to the exterior of the home that changed its appearance or character. There was no evidence introduced by appellant association to show that Randolph's house would appear different " 'than any of the other houses in the neighborhood to any persons passing by.' " *Knudtson*, 216 Neb. at 659, 345 N.W.2d at 8. Therefore, we find that Randolph's home remained a single-family dwelling, even though she remodeled the basement so that others could live there and added an entrance from the garage. Clearly, outward appearance is the hallmark of the second prong of the test in *Knudtson*. Here, the alterations and finishing of the basement do not affect the outward appearance of the structure. With respect to the separate entrance constructed in the garage, there is no evidence which this court can use in its de novo review to conclude that adding the entrance was such a substantial change that it would make this home's appearance other than that of a single-family dwelling or outwardly different than the others in the neighborhood. Accordingly, we find no violation of the restrictive covenants. * * *

OMEGA CORPORATION OF CHESTERFIELD v. MALLOY

Supreme Court of Virginia, 1984.
228 Va. 12, 319 S.E.2d 728, cert. denied, 469 U.S.
1192, 105 S.Ct. 967, 83 L.Ed.2d 971 (1985).

CARRICO, CHIEF JUSTICE.

This appeal involves a proposal to construct and operate group homes for the mentally retarded in subdivisions subject to restrictive covenants which limit uses to "residential purposes" and prohibit buildings other than "single-family" dwellings. The subdivisions in question are Providence Pines and Scottingham, both located in Chesterfield County.

The Omega Corporation of Chesterfield, a nonstock, nonprofit Virginia corporation (Omega), owns one lot in each subdivision. Omega proposed to build a dwelling on each lot "to provide mentally retarded adults with normal residential housing in a community setting including the activities and life-style incident to such a setting."

On June 12, 1981, D. Duane Malloy and his wife and other owners of lots in Providence Pines filed a bill of complaint seeking to restrain Omega from using its lot in the subdivision for a group home for the mentally retarded. On July 13, 1981, Robert Lee Cobb and his wife and other homeowners in Scottingham filed a bill of complaint seeking similar relief against Omega with respect to the lot it owned in that subdivision. (The plaintiffs in the two suits will be referred to collectively as Homeowners.) Both suits were based upon alleged violations of the subdivisions' restrictive covenants, which run with the land. The pertinent portions read as follows:

> No lot shall be used except for residential purposes. No building shall be erected, altered, placed, or permitted to remain on any lot other than one detached single-family dwelling not to exceed two stories in height. * * *

The record shows that the Virginia Housing Development Authority has loaned Omega the funds to purchase the lots and has committed to lend the money to construct the group homes. The United States Department of Housing and Urban Development has approved the homes and has agreed to provide rent subsidies to those mentally retarded residents whose incomes qualify them for assistance. The residents would contribute one-fourth of their adjusted incomes toward rent.

The homes would be licensed by the Commonwealth, and the occupants would be supervised by counselors employed by the Chesterfield Mental Retardation Services. Three counselors would be assigned to each home on "rotation," with one counselor "there at all times."

Omega proposed to assign four mentally retarded adults to each home. Eligibility standards require each applicant for admission to be "a resident of Chesterfield County, eighteen years of age or older, and moderately mentally retarded."

Some of the prospective occupants are presently inmates of state institutions, but the majority live with their families or in "some other kind of situation." It is contemplated that, after staying in the group homes, some of the occupants would be "able to move out and go on * * * their own, and a few [would] go back into institutions, and the majority [would] stop at the group home level"; all are expected to remain two or three years, and "some may live in the homes for the rest of their lives."

On weekdays, the residents would leave the homes in early morning for work, vocational training, or "some [other] day activity," returning in late afternoon. Assisted by counselors, the occupants would spend their time at home cleaning house, cooking, and performing similar chores. Time at home would also be spent watching television, listening to music, and playing games. On weekends, the residents would go to the movies or on shopping or field trips, in addition to their usual leisure-time activities.

Aside from the assistance furnished by the counselors, no training of any kind would be provided the residents in the homes, and they would not receive any medical attention there. The residents and counselors would "function together as a single housekeeping unit." Except for the mental capacity of the occupants, the homes would operate like typical suburban households in "virtually all respects." * * *

The covenants must be read as a whole. When so read, the covenants specify that only dwellings designed structurally for single-family occupancy may be erected and that the buildings may be used only for single-family residential purposes.

Homeowners appear to concede that Omega's use of the buildings in question will be for residential purposes. This leaves for consideration, therefore, the question whether Omega's proposal to house mentally retarded persons in the buildings constitutes single family use. * * * In this case, Omega argues, there is nothing in the language of the restrictive covenants which makes clear that "persons unrelated by blood or marriage are to be excluded from the subdivisions"; further, the chancellor "found as fact that the intention of the developers was *not* to limit residency * * * to persons related by blood or marriage" (emphasis in original). Under these circumstances, Omega concludes, the chancellor's ruling that "the restrictive covenants prohibit persons unrelated by blood or marriage from living in the subdivision[s] is clearly wrong."

The difficulty with this argument is that the chancellor did not rule, as Omega claims, that the restrictive covenants in question prohibit persons unrelated by blood or marriage from living in the subdivisions. What the chancellor did rule is that "[a] single family use does not include occupancy by unrelated persons *who live in the home with a counselor*"(emphasis added).

There is a world of difference between Omega's interpretation of the chancellor's ruling and his actual holding. All the chancellor's holding means is that the single-family nature of a use is destroyed when the element of supervision by counselors is added to the occupancy of unrelated persons. The holding does not mean, as Omega suggests, that "three unrelated school-teachers" cannot live together in the subdivisions or that the restrictive covenants prohibit "housekeepers, governesses, tutors, butlers, valets, and the like" from living with families in the subdivisions.

Even so, Omega declares, the chancellor's definition of the word "family" is unduly restrictive. The "commonly accepted" meaning of the word, Omega submits, is "[t]he collective body of persons who live in one house." Furthermore, Omega asserts, respectable judicial authority supports both a broader meaning of the word "family" and a recognition that homes for the mentally retarded do not violate single-family provisions of restrictive covenants.

We agree with Omega that the word "family" should be interpreted broadly in favor of permitting the proposed use; this is the natural corollary of the rule that restrictive covenants must be construed strictly against those seeking to enforce them. The result sought by Omega, however, would require that we give an unrealistic meaning to the word "family."

The record shows that counselors who are public employees qualified by training and experience to handle handicapped persons would be present in the homes on a rotating basis "providing needed supervision" at all times, even while the residents of the homes are asleep. We can conceive of nothing more antithetical to the concept of family homelife than the constant surveillance of purported family members by government employees assigned to supervise them.

The presence of the counselors in the homes and their supervision of the occupants would convert what might otherwise have been a single-family use into what the chancellor termed "a facility." While the effort to provide "a facility" for the care of the mentally retarded is praiseworthy indeed, the fact remains that the use to which Omega wishes to put its property is institutional in nature and not familial.

Omega insists, however, that we cannot ignore the "many cases" from other jurisdictions in which homes for the mentally retarded have been held to satisfy the requirement of single-family provisions of zoning ordinances. Omega also points to Virginia's public policy that mentally retarded persons "should not be excluded by county or municipal zoning ordinances from the benefits of normal residential surroundings." Code § 15.1–486.2. Omega then argues that this statement of public policy cannot be frustrated by the undefined term "single-family dwelling" in restrictive covenants.

We deal in this case, however, with private contractual rights arising from restrictive covenants, and not with provisions of zoning ordinances. The parties apparently interpret Chesterfield County's zoning ordinance to permit the group homes proposed by Omega; if this interpretation is correct, the ordinance would promote the public policy declared in Code § 15.1–486.2. But Chesterfield's zoning ordinance cannot relieve the lots in question from the restrictive covenants to which they are subject. The zoning decisions cited by Omega, therefore, are inapposite. * * *

THOMAS, JUSTICE, dissenting.

The restrictive covenant relied on by the Homeowners cannot be fairly read to prohibit the activity complained of. The majority opinion marks a sharp departure from the way in which the Court has traditionally looked at restrictive covenants * * *. Traditionally, in Virginia, we have strictly construed restrictive covenants. Moreover, we have placed upon those who would enforce a restrictive covenant the burden of proving that the activity complained of falls within the terms of the restriction relied upon. * * * In addition to the foregoing, historically, we have focused upon the precise language used in the restriction without adding to or subtracting therefrom. Further, we have been careful not to imply that which was clearly stated. The majority opinion ignores these well-developed principles.

It would be difficult to image or to draft a restrictive covenant which more clearly sets forth a use restriction on the one hand and a structural restriction on the other. Both of the restrictive covenants considered in this appeal contained the following language:

> No lot shall be used except for residential purposes. No building shall be erected, altered, placed, or permitted to remain on any lot other than one detached single-family dwelling not to exceed two stories in height.

The first sentence contains the word "used." This means that where the drafter intended to limit use he knew exactly what to write in order to accomplish that result. The majority concedes that Omega's use of the property would comply with the residential use restriction contained in the first sentence. * * *

When the restrictive covenant is read as a whole, it is obviously a two-part restriction with the first part relating to use and the second part relating to structure. Nevertheless, the majority claims that by reading the covenant as a whole it finds a use restriction in the second sentence. What the majority has actually done is read language into the second sentence which cannot be found there. According to the majority, when read as a whole, "the covenants specify that only dwellings designed structurally for single-family occupancy may be erected and that the buildings may be used only for *single-family residential purposes*." The italicized language pinpoints the critical flaw in the majority opinion; that language cannot be found in the restrictive covenants here under review. That language was created and supplied by the majority. The majority's "reading" of the covenant can be more properly characterized as a re-write of that covenant. The majority's treatment of the restrictive covenant directly contravenes the rules this Court has evolved over the centuries concerning construction of restrictive covenants. * * *

The majority opinion is also disturbing because of the classification it develops. The majority states that it is willing to accept a broad definition of the word family. As a result, the majority accepts as a single-family three unrelated school teachers who live together in a house, households containing maids, governesses, tutors, butlers and others. Indeed, the majority does not attempt to say what groups will be included in its broad definition of family. All it concludes is that four unrelated mentally retarded persons and a counselor do not fall within that broad definition. The explanation for the exclusion of the family group proposed by Omega is that the counselors will surveil and supervise the mentally retarded family members. The suggestion is that watching over and supervising individuals is somehow antithetical to the concept of family. In my view, watching over and supervising members of a family who need such attention is central to families. The majority's explanation for excluding from the definition of family a group made up of a counselor and four individuals is unsatisfactory. The majority has drawn a line which will exclude appellants while including virtually everybody else. The facts and circumstances of this case do not support this result. * * *

McMINN v. TOWN OF OYSTER BAY

Court of Appeals of New York, 1985.
66 N.Y.2d 544, 498 N.Y.S.2d 128, 488 N.E.2d 1240.

SIMONS, JUDGE. * * *

The Town of Oyster Bay zoning ordinance establishes a number of use districts, including a "D Residence" district, in which single-family houses are permitted as of right but rooming and boarding houses are allowed only if approved by the Town Board after a public hearing. The ordinance also contains the following definition of "family":

"(a) Any number of persons, related by blood, marriage, or legal adoption, living and cooking on the premises together as a single, nonprofit housekeeping unit; or

"(b) Any two (2) persons not related by blood, marriage, or legal adoption, living and cooking on the premises together as a single, nonprofit housekeeping unit, both of whom are sixty-two (62) years of age or over, and residing on the premises."

Plaintiffs Robert and Joan McMinn purchased their house in 1973. It is in a D Residence district. On June 1, 1976, they leased the house to four unrelated young men between the ages of 22 and 25 who had grown up in the area and wanted to remain near their families but not reside with them. Shortly after the tenants moved in, a criminal information was filed against the McMinns in District Court, Nassau County, charging them with violating the zoning ordinance because the house was occupied by more than one family. The McMinns and the tenants then commenced this action seeking declaratory and injunctive relief * * *.

In order for a zoning ordinance to be a valid exercise of the police power it must survive a two-part test: (1) it must have been enacted in furtherance of a legitimate governmental purpose, and (2) there must be a "reasonable relation between the end sought to be achieved by the regulation and the means used to achieve that end". If the ordinance fails either part of this test, it is unreasonable and constitutes a deprivation of property without due process of law under our State Constitution.

Indisputably, this ordinance was enacted to further several legitimate governmental purposes, including preservation of the character of traditional single-family neighborhoods, reduction of parking and traffic problems, control of population density and prevention of noise and disturbance. The dispute centers on whether the means the local legislature has chosen, the challenged ordinance and more specifically the definition of "family" contained in it, are reasonably related to the achievement of these legitimate purposes.

Manifestly, restricting occupancy of single-family housing based generally on the biological or legal relationships between its inhabitants bears no reasonable relationship to the goals of reducing parking and traffic problems, controlling population density and preventing noise and disturbance. Their achievement depends not upon the biological or legal relations between the occupants of a house but generally upon the size of the dwelling and the lot and the number of its occupants. Thus, the definition of family employed here is both fatally overinclusive in prohibiting, for example, a young unmarried couple from occupying a four-bedroom house who do not threaten the purposes of the ordinance and underinclusive in failing to prohibit occupancy of a two-bedroom home by 10 or 12 persons who are related in only the most distant manner and who might well be expected to present serious overcrowding and traffic problems.

Nor is the ordinance's restrictive definition of family saved by the desire to preserve the character of the traditional single-family neighborhood in Oyster Bay. That is a legitimate governmental objective (see, *Group House v. Board of Zoning & Appeals*, 45 N.Y.2d 266, 271, 408 N.Y.S.2d 377, 380 N.E.2d 207; *City of White Plains v. Ferraioli*, 34 N.Y.2d 300, 305, 357 N.Y.S.2d 449, 313 N.E.2d 756; *see also, Village of Belle Terre v. Boraas*, 416 U.S. 1, 9, 4 S.Ct. 1536, 1541, 39 L.Ed.2d 797;

and *see generally, Validity of Ordinance Restricting Number of Unrelated Persons Who Can Live Together in Residential Zone*, Ann., 12 A.L.R.4th 238), but a municipality may not seek to achieve it by enacting a zoning ordinance that "[limits] the definition of family to exclude a household which in every but a biological sense is a single family" (*City of White Plains v. Ferraioli, supra*, 34 N.Y.2d at p. 306, 357 N.Y.S.2d 449, 313 N.E.2d 753). Zoning is "intended to control types of housing and living and not the genetic or intimate internal family relations of human beings" (*City of White Plains v. Ferraioli, supra*, at p. 305, 357 N.Y.S.2d 449, 313 N.E.2d 753) and if a household is "the functional and factual equivalent of a natural family" (*Group House v. Board of Zoning & Appeals, supra,* 45 N.Y.2d at p. 272, 357 N.Y.S.2d 449, 313 N.E.2d 756), the ordinance may not exclude it from a single-family neighborhood and still serve a valid purpose. This ordinance, by limiting occupancy of single-family homes to persons related by blood, marriage or adoption or to only two unrelated persons of a certain age, excludes many households who pose no threat to the goal of preserving the character of the traditional single-family neighborhood, such as the households involved in *White Plains* and *Group House*, and thus fails the rational relationship test.

Plaintiffs rely principally on the claimed invalidity of paragraph (a) of the definition of family. Zoning ordinances may define the term family alternatively to include various circumstances and relationships, as the present ordinance does, but only so long as the ordinance, when read in its entirety, does not exclude any households that due process requires be included. Thus, paragraph (a) of the provision, which defines family as "[any] number of persons, related by blood, marriage, or legal adoption", is not per se unconstitutional provided the ordinance contains an alternative definition of family as any number of unrelated persons living together who meet the indicia we set forth for the functional equivalent of a traditional family in *Group House v. Board of Zoning & Appeals, supra*, at pp. 272–273, 357 N.Y.S.2d 449, 313 N.E.2d 756 and *City of White Plains v. Ferraioli, supra*, 34 N.Y.2d at pp. 305–306, 357 N.Y.S.2d 449, 313 N.E.2d 753. Because the only alternative definition contained in this ordinance—"[any] two (2) persons not related by blood, marriage, or legal adoption * * * both of whom are sixty-two (62) years of age or over"—is more restrictive, both as to the number of unrelated persons and their ages, than is constitutionally permissible, however, the entire definition of family contained in the ordinance violates our State constitutional guarantee that no person shall be deprived of property without due process of law. * * *

For many people (Professor Ellickson, for example), the exercise of "private" power seems more benign than the exercise of "public" power. Homeowners associations, they argue, should be given rights to control the nature of their communities more readily than cities. The following excerpt from Frank Michelman's important article, Political Markets and Community Self–Determination, suggests the opposite way of under-standing the public/private distinction.   The excerpt describes three classic cases of neighborhood land-use control in which the exercise of "public" power appears more benign than the exercise of "private" power.   What difference do the cases suggest between public legislation and (to adopt the title of Professor Louis Jaffe's classic article) law making by private groups? [1]   When (under the cases) would a neighbor-hood veto over private land-use be acceptable?   How do the answers to these questions affect the analysis of the homeowners association cases considered above?

FRANK MICHELMAN, POLITICAL MARKETS AND COMMUNITY SELF–DETERMINATION

53 Ind.L.J. 145, 164–167 (1977–78).

Case I: *Eubank v. Richmond* (1912). The Virginia legislature had by statute authorized city councils "to make regulations concerning the building of houses * * *, and in their discretion, * * * in particular districts * * * to prescribe and establish building lines * * *." The Richmond City Council thereupon adopted an ordinance providing, in effect, a procedure whereby two-thirds of the owners along any block could adopt their own building setback line for their block. That procedure was used to establish a line that would have required the plaintiff to alter his plans for a house not yet built. The Supreme Court held that allowing the ordinance thus to be enforced against the plaintiff would unconstitutionally deprive him of his property.

Although the Court's opinion hints at a straight substantive due process objection to legislative regulation of building lines (the year, remember, was 1912), the opinion as a whole (and subsequent decisions) makes clear that the decision does not rest on that. The crucial objection was, rather, to the delegation feature of the Richmond ordi-nance which "enable[d] the convenience or purposes of one set of property owners to control the property rights of others." Because the ordinance "create[d] no standard by which [this] power [was] to be exercised," those exercising it might "do so solely for their own interest or even capriciously."

Case II: *Cusack v. Chicago* (1916). The Supreme Court upheld a city ordinance which excluded billboards from predominantly residential blocks except when a majority of the owners in the block would give written consent. The unsuccessful plaintiff was a would-be sign builder who, apparently unable to garner majority consent, attacked the ordi-nance on delegation grounds, complaining that it left his fate to "the whims and caprices" of his "neighbors." Not surprisingly, he leaned heavily on *Eubank*. The Court pulled this prop from under him by reasoning that the delegation feature of the Chicago ordinance could

1. Jaffe, Law Making by Private Groups, 51 Harv.L.Rev. 201 (1937).

only help him, not hurt him. *Eubank* was distinguished on the ground that there it was the unofficial body of self-interested neighbors who did the dirty work of imposing the prohibition, while in *Cusack* it was the city councillors who did that, while the neighbors were simply empowered to confer the favor of an exception: "The one ordinance permits two-thirds of the lot owners to impose restrictions upon the other property in the block, while the other permits one-half of the lot owners to remove a restriction from the other property owners. This is not a delegation of legislative power * * *." Justice McKenna, author of the *Eubank* opinion, dissented.

Case III: *Washington ex rel. Seattle Title & Trust Co. v. Roberge* (1928). A landowner wishing to construct a charitable home for aged poor persons in a residentially zoned area, but apparently unable to gain the consent of neighboring landowners, successfully challenged the constitutionality of Seattle's zoning provision permitting "a philanthropic home for children or for old people * * * in first residence district when the written consent shall have been obtained of the owners of two thirds of the property within four hundred (400) feet of the proposed building." This provision was a 1925 amendment to a pre-existing ordinance which had simply omitted such homes from the list of uses allowed in the first residence district. Given the less-than-satisfying earlier decisions with which the Court had to cope, perhaps it is not surprising that its *Roberge* opinion is a welter of confusion and inconsistency from which it is impossible to extract any precise, uncontradicted statement of the constitutional defect found in the Seattle ordinance:

> The right of the [owner] to devote its land to any legitimate use is property within the protection of the Constitution. The facts disclosed by the record make it clear that the exclusion of the new home from the first district is not indispensable to the general zoning plan. And there is no legislative determination that the proposed building and use would be inconsistent with * * * general welfare. The enactment itself plainly implies the contrary. * * * The section purports to give the owners of less than one-half the land within 400 feet of the proposed building authority—uncontrolled by any standard or rule prescribed by legislative action—to prevent the [owner] from using its land for the proposed home * * *. They are not bound by any official duty, but are free to withhold consent for selfish reasons or arbitrarily, and may subject the [plaintiff] to their will or caprice * * *. The delegation so attempted is repugnant to the due process clause of the 14th Amendment. *Eubank v. Richmond* * * *.
>
> *Thomas Cusack v. Chicago* * * * was held unlike *Eubank v. Richmond*, supra, and the ordinance [there] was fully sustained. The facts found were sufficient to warrant the conclusion that such billboards would or were liable to endanger the safety and decency of [residential] districts * * *. It is not suggested that the proposed new home for aged poor would be a nuisance * * *. The facts shown clearly distinguish the proposed building and use from such bill-

boards or other uses which by reason of their nature are liable to be offensive.

As the attempted delegation cannot be sustained, and the restriction thereby sought to be put upon the permission is arbitrary and repugnant to the due process clause * * * the [owner] is entitled to have the permit applied for.

We need not decide whether, consistently with the 14th Amendment, it is within the power of the state or municipality by a general zoning law to exclude the proposed new home from a district defined as is the first district in the ordinance under consideration.

Highlighted and reduced to its essentials, the logic of the Court's discussion comes to this: (1) The facts do not themselves suggest that the plaintiff's proposed rest home would be so disturbing to neighboring land uses as to call for restrictions on the plaintiff's free use of its property. (2) Nor has the city legislature exercised the responsibility of determining that the potential disturbance to others is such as to justify restricting the plaintiff's freedom. (3) So the Seattle scheme is simply one for sacrificing the plaintiff's freedom to the caprice of his neighbors. It is thus just like the scheme condemned in *Eubank* and it is, just as that one was, an improper attempt to delegate legislative power which violates the due process guaranty. (4) Of course the form of the Seattle scheme is of the kind which the Court held in *Cusack* is not a delegation of legislative power at all (that is, it empowers neighbors to lift a legislatively imposed restriction, not to impose a restriction themselves)—which was admittedly the reason given in *Cusack* for distinguishing that case from *Eubank*. (5) But this case differs from *Cusack* in that there the facts showed billboards to be noxious intruders in residential neighborhoods, while here the facts fail to indicate that the plaintiff's rest home would be a noxious intruder in its neighborhood. So the plaintiff's property rights prevail and it does not matter whether the scheme is labeled a delegation or not. (6) Given the delegation feature in the Seattle scheme, it is unnecessary to decide in this case whether this Seattle ordinance would have violated this plaintiff's constitutional property rights if the ordinance had flatly excluded all rest homes from the first residence district. (7) On this inconclusive and mystifying note the Court ends.

Now one wants to think that there must be better, truer reasoning than that to support the Court's conclusion not only that the Seattle ordinance should be struck down but also that both the *Eubank* and *Cusack* decisions should be reaffirmed. As presented, after all, the three cases form a puzzling triangle. The *Cusack* Court's professed reason for upholding the Chicago scheme, while reaffirming disapproval of the Richmond one, seems an unconvincing triumph of form over substance. But if that formal distinction is taken seriously, the Seattle scheme is like Chicago's not Richmond's; and yet Seattle's scheme is treated like Richmond's, not Chicago's—that is, it is invalidated. * * *

SECTION C.   COMMUNITY SELF–DEFENSE AGAINST CHANGES IN CHARACTER

The preceding sections have examined the relationship between a city and its citizens; this section investigates the relationship between a city and its neighborhoods. If a neighborhood were a legal entity, its relationship to the city could be understood in the way that federal-city and state-city relationships were treated in Chapter Two. But neighborhoods have no legal status, and the defense of neighborhood integrity against city power has relied not on notions of home rule but on the existence of individual Constitutional rights.

The first three readings below—an excerpt from an article by Keith Aoki, the important case of Poletown Neighborhood Council v. City of Detroit, and an excerpt from Robert Caro's book, The Power Broker— examine the ability of cities to change the character of neighborhoods through condemnation. The Aoki excerpt offers a history of the "urban renewal" movement in the 1950's; the *Poletown* case upholds Detroit's condemnation of a large section of one of its neighborhoods to make room for a General Motors plant; [1] the Caro excerpt presents a vivid account of the impact of the construction of a one mile segment of the Cross–Bronx Expressway on the East Tremont neighborhood. In reading these materials, consider whether neighborhoods have the power—or should have the power—to defend themselves against these kinds of city action. Does the current law governing eminent domain adequately immunize neighborhoods from changes in character? [2] If not, is there a way to protect neighborhoods other than by imposing legal restraints on the power of eminent domain? To what extent does the obviousness of what is permanent and what is transitory in city life, the subject of the Italo Calvino story that begins the section, affect the possibility of neighborhood self-defense against city control?

Some portions of the first three readings in this section—above all the Caro excerpt—portray the ethnic neighborhoods being subjected to city condemnation in very supportive, sometimes even romantic, terms. Do these neighborhoods in fact represent a form of life worth defending? Or are they too insular, too exclusionary? An excerpt from an important book by Iris Young, following the Caro reading, provides a critique of the idea of community relied on by Caro (and others) and offers an alterna-

---

1. See generally, Wylie, Poletown: Community Betrayed (1989).

2. See generally, Lunney, A Critical Reexamination of Takings Jurisprudence, 90 Mich.L.Rev. 1892 (1992); Paul, The Hidden Structure of Takings Law, 64 S.Cal.L.Rev. 1393 (1991); Symposium, 88 Colum.L.Rev. 1581 (1988); Epstein, Takings: Private Property and the Power of Eminent Domain (1985); Ackerman, Private Property and the Constitution (1977); Michelman, Property, Utility and Fairness: Comments on the Ethical Foundations of the "Just Compensation" Law, 80 Harv.L.Rev. 1165 (1967); Sax, Takings, Private Property and Public Rights, 81 Yale L.J. 149 (1971); Sax, Takings and the Police Power, 74 Yale L.J. 36 (1964). See also Freilich & Chinn, Transportation Corridors: Shaping and Financing Urbanization Through Integration of Eminent Domain, Zoning and Growth Management Techniques, 55 UMKC L.Rev. 153 (1987).

tive normative ideal of city life. The section then concludes with two cases that explore the relationship between Young's ideal of city life and neighborhood feelings of community. Asian Americans for Equality v. Koch concerns the efforts of residents of New York City's Chinatown to protect low income residents from displacement by developers; United States v. Starrett City Associates deals with the effort of a large private housing project to maintain an integrated neighborhood by using racial quotas. Should a neighborhood be more entitled to defend its existing character if it is seeking to remain economically or racially integrated rather than to preserve its isolation from outsiders (whether the isolation is sought for reasons of race, ethnicity or social class)? What is the appropriate geographic location for resolving the tension between community and diversity—the neighborhood or the city?

ITALO CALVINO, INVISIBLE CITIES

P. 63 (1974).

The city of Sophronia is made up of two half-cities. In one there is the great roller coaster with its steep humps, the carousel with its chain spokes, the Ferris wheel of spinning cages, the death-ride with crouching motorcyclists, the big top with the clump of trapezes hanging in the middle. The other half-city is of stone and marble and cement, with the bank, the factories, the palaces, the slaughterhouse, the school, and all the rest. One of the half-cities is permanent, the other is temporary, and when the period of its sojourn is over, they uproot it, dismantle it, and take it off, transplanting it to the vacant lots of another half-city.

And so every year the day comes when the workmen remove the marble pediments, lower the stone walls, the cement pylons, take down the Ministry, the monument, the docks, the petroleum refinery, the hospital, load them on trailers, to follow from stand to stand their annual itinerary. Here remains the half-Sophronia of the shooting-galleries and the carousels, the shout suspended from the cart of the headlong roller coaster, and it begins to count the months, the days it must wait before the caravan returns and a complete life can begin again.

KEITH AOKI, RACE, SPACE, AND PLACE: THE RELATION BETWEEN ARCHITECTURAL MODERNISM, POST–MODERNISM, URBAN PLANNING, AND GENTRIFICATION

20 Fordham Urb. L.J. 699, 766–772 (1993).

URBAN RENEWAL

During the 1950s, the real or imaginary horrors of urban existence * * * captured the attention of the public. Medical analogies proliferated, lingering as a vestige of an earlier generation's dread of urban disease and crime. Slums were seen as pathological malignancies that had to be removed by the scalpel of urban planning. Eventually, a relatively unified response to urban problems arose out of several factors: concerns about poor housing in the inner cities; fears about the economic costs of urban blight, such as loss of rich residents to the suburbs, loss of businesses and industries, and increasing social costs; pressures for office expansion; and major financial incentives from the federal government. The interaction of these factors were responsible for the genesis of the movement toward large-scale urban renewal projects. Coined in the late 1940s to replace the more accurate expression Slum Clearance, urban renewal was considered by its advocates as describing a type of radical surgery that would purge the city of unsafe, unsanitary, overcrowded buildings and replace them with a mixture of high-rise and walk-up apartments arranged geometrically in open blocks. Such projects would then generally operate under the administration of a municipal housing authority.

Urban renewal was widely supported in the nominally optimistic postwar era. Planners were considered to be working in the name of social and scientific progress, and even entrenched social problems might be solved through the intervention of enlightened modern design. * * * [U]rban renewal razed entire neighborhoods of nineteenth century tenements and row houses, which had been occupied by poor ethnic and minority communities. These structures were deemed unfit for habitation and were eliminated in the name of promoting public health, safety, and convenience. They were replaced by large geometric apartment blocks surrounded by asphalt and concrete—bleak embodiments of Le Corbusier's "tower in the park." These blocks were often bordered by major expressways that physically barred the new residents from entering the areas adjoining their new neighborhoods.

This inner city refurbishment was a manifestation of the planners' objective to once again make the central city attractive to those who could reconstruct its eroded tax base and infrastructure. The rapidly developing highway network, the expanding ring of suburban bedroom communities, and the flight of industry to the suburbs and other regions had brought about a decentralization of the metropolis and an erosion of its tax base. Revenue was needed to pay for expensive city services as well as to halt the city's imminent decline.

Accordingly, while officials and planners may have had certain altruistic motives in advancing urban renewal schemes, economic considerations were foremost in their minds. In their efforts to placate powerful interest groups, redevelopment planners allowed the predatory motives of developers and contractors to manipulate urban renewal plans to serve their own ends.

Sometimes, for example, powerful developers would persuade the government to demolish an area of the city and would then buy the land from the government at a low price. Another common strategy was for a developer to influence a municipality to preserve as "historic" the city land adjoining the developer's properties, greatly increasing the value of the developer's properties. Any low- or moderate-income housing located thereon would be promptly converted to luxury housing and expensive commercial leases. All such schemes resulted in both the displacement of poorer residents and a further decline in the city's affordable housing stock, all in the name of urban renewal.

Accordingly, the poor, who tended to be disproportionately racial and ethnic minorities, suffered in the brave new urban world built over their former homes. From 1949 to 1961, urban renewal displaced 85,000 families in 200 American cities, while federally funded renewal and highway programs displaced about 100,000 families and 15,000 businesses per year.

People who were displaced in this way quickly lost their ability to secure satisfactory replacement housing. Despite developers' promises to relocate them, many did not receive relocation services and were forced to bear the substantial costs of moving and living in more expensive apartment units. Such expenses could exhaust the savings of older residents. Resident purchasing power was also harmed by their forced withdrawal from neighborhood credit networks and business arrangements that had evolved over the years and which were often related to practices in the resident's country of origin. Such arrangements were often informal and thus not easily transferrable to new locations. In addition, re-establishing credit and a course of dealing in new surroundings could be an expensive hardship.

In disregard of such potential consequences, urban planners of this period placed much of their faith in the supposed deterministic power of the geometric modern environment. They appeared to assume, as had Le Corbusier in the 1920s, that the numerous problems of the slums stemmed from poor design and that a clean, new, modern environment would inevitably lead to a healthy new social order. Reminiscent of William Morris and other nineteenth century reformers who equated good morals with good design, the urban planners adopted the pleasing syllogism that poor housing quality demoralized its inhabitants and, therefore, better structures would introduce former slum dwellers to a better moral quality of life. Threaded through these rationales was a paternalistic hubris and confidence in the planners' own abilities to assist slum dwellers up from their dark, squalid nineteenth century lifestyles into the bright, modern planned world of the mid-twentieth century.

Criticism of urban renewal projects escalated in the 1960s, when urban historian Jane Jacobs accused these schemes of destroying virtually all that was vital in urban life. Jacobs articulated an alternate vision of slum life in which the old neighborhoods supported a spontaneous, interactive, street-oriented communal lifestyle among the residents of these areas. Jacobs described how doors of row houses and brownstones opened directly onto the street, allowing interactions with passers-by and with the mixed use street and its stores and businesses. In this way, social relations developed in semipublic open spaces, and the entry of strangers was readily noticed. Jacobs claimed urban renewal uprooted and shattered such organic communities, scattering former neighbors into whatever substandard housing was available elsewhere, and helping to create a culture of disaffection and an environment of violence and vandalism.

The catastrophic failure of several large scale public housing projects gave critics such as Jacobs credibility and caused many observers to begin developing dim views of the validity of government intervention in housing markets. The Pruitt–Igoe housing project in St. Louis was one such failure, and it became a lightning rod for commentary on the fate of modern architecture and urban planning.

In the early 1950s, the inner city of St. Louis had contained extremely dilapidated slum housing, which in 1954, was demolished and replaced by the Pruitt–Igoe projects. Twelve thousand people were relocated into forty-three eleven-story high-rise structures covering fifty-seven acres. Initially racially integrated, the project's inhabitants rapidly became exclusively black. Eventually, the residents' fear of crime and the rapid deterioration of the physical plant brought about by poor maintenance resulted in almost complete resident abandonment of large areas of the Pruitt–Igoe projects, despite the availability of subsidized low rents. President Nixon's HUD Secretary, George Romney, presided at the project's demolition in 1972.

Pruitt–Igoe's failure was perhaps not so much a failure of the modernist architectural paradigm, but rather a situation of unstable equilibrium in which project managers virtually ignored early warning signs of problems. The misery of massive forced relocation combined with poor design and inadequate maintenance set off a downward vicious circle. Cheap materials, inadequate maintenance, and poor design contributed to building deterioration, provoking resident dissatisfaction. Elevators, for example, were frequently out of service and became easy targets for vandalism. Residents of upper floors, who had to use the elevators to reach their apartments, quickly abandoned them. When units became deserted, remaining residents scavenged them for working fixtures to replace those that had broken in their own apartments.

The project administrators, who were perhaps feeling overconfident about their new "machine for living," had not addressed such problems early enough. By the time they noticed that something was wrong, it was too late in the downward vicious circle to correct the damage.

Such disasters were products of a combination of hubris and inadvertence. The planners of projects like Pruitt–Igoe failed to understand and accommodate the drastically different culture and context of the 1950s slum neighborhood and its residents. An apartment super-block that minimized the amount of semi-private interior spaces in which social interactions between residents could occur, may have worked for white middle-class individuals without children, but was inadequate for extended families of relocatees from the slums. Slum dwellers, many of whom were connected with large families, were accustomed to a social and spatial environment that encouraged constant use of the streets, sidewalks, and corners as semiprivate meeting grounds or territories for interacting with one another. While architects initially praised Pruitt–Igoe for its absence of wasted space between dwelling units, it was precisely in such spaces that neighboring relations had developed in "normal" slums. This aspect of the culture of the development's inhabitants had been invisible to and went completely unaddressed by the planners.

The sudden loss of the community to which they were accustomed posed other problems for Pruitt–Igoe's residents. While parents liked the in-home conveniences, the inability to watch their children when the latter were outside the apartment was unsettling. Furthermore, the new setting lacked what Oscar Newman has called "defensible spaces": stairwells, elevators, and corridors that could be controlled or informally surveyed from within private spaces. Overall, the rapid transition from the strong, informal neighboring system of the slum to a quasi-institutional setting that spatially discouraged informal interactions between neighbors was traumatic. While dissatisfied with the slum's overcrowded conditions, physical danger from cold weather, poor wiring, bad plumbing, and fire, residents had become accustomed to and depended on its dense network of social relations.

In sum, the residents of Pruitt–Igoe felt justifiably alienated and dislocated by the poorly considered design decisions that had been imposed on them. Indeed, the planners had built structures that had nothing to do with the actual social context of the people who lived within them. Instead of allowing functions that occurred within the building to determine the nature of its structure, as prescribed by early modernist architectural theory, they simply crammed a predetermined geometric package full of fungible apartment units, pouring the largely involuntary residents in to complete the mix.

Somewhere in translation from early twentieth century Europe to mid-twentieth century United States, geometric form had been reified into a stock building prototype, which looked the same regardless of whether it housed a prison, hospital, apartments, corporate offices, or a school. To the growing number of critics of the modernist style its geometric forms and reductionist approach were seen as villains, responsible for dehumanizing and abstracting away human problems. However, it was the deviation from modernist functionalism, not modernist functionalism itself, that resulted in some of the worst embarrassments for which modern architecture has been held responsible. Housing projects built during the 1950s were riddled with problems: they were often energy gluttons, their flat roofs leaked, elevators broke down frequently, and interior isolated spaces were open invitations to muggings and violence. However, these horrors were due more to hack misapplications and distortions of the tenets of modernist architecture than to any a priori flaw at its theoretical core. After embarrassments like Pruitt–Igoe, the term urban renewal gradually slipped from the urban planner's vocabulary to be replaced by phrases like "urban revitalization" and "urban design."

In the rush to disclaim responsibility for widely-publicized fiascoes like Pruitt–Igoe as well as the growing tendency to villify modern architecture in general, many important social issues raised by the critics of urban renewal were left unaddressed. Given the relative powerlessness of inner city populations and their lack of a meaningful political input in urban planning decisions, the cultural and psychological problems of forced relocation were largely ignored and sidestepped by planners and other public officials. The public soon lost faith in the ability of urban planners to control the social consequences of publicly funded housing projects. Unfortunately, many valid insights about the important and vital interaction between structures and inhabitants that lie at the core of the modernist architectural paradigm disappeared as well. * * *

POLETOWN NEIGHBORHOOD COUNCIL v. CITY OF DETROIT

Supreme Court of Michigan, 1981.
410 Mich. 616, 304 N.W.2d 455.

PER CURIAM.

This case arises out of a plan by the Detroit Economic Development Corporation to acquire, by condemnation if necessary, a large tract of land to be conveyed to General Motors Corporation as a site for construction of an assembly plant. * * * This case raises a question of paramount importance to the future welfare of this state and its residents: Can a municipality use the power of eminent domain granted to it by the Economic Development Corporations Act to condemn property for transfer to a private corporation to build a plant to promote industry and commerce, thereby adding jobs and taxes to the economic base of the municipality and state? * * *

[T]he legislature has authorized municipalities to acquire property by condemnation in order to provide industrial and commercial sites and the means of transfer from the municipality to private users.

Plaintiffs-appellants do not challenge the declaration of the legislature that programs to alleviate and prevent conditions of unemployment and to preserve and develop industry and commerce are essential public purposes. Nor do they challenge the proposition that legislation to accomplish this purpose falls within the Constitutional grant of general legislative power to the legislature in Const.1963, Art. 4, § 51. * * * What plaintiffs-appellants do challenge is the constitutionality of using the power of eminent domain to condemn one person's property to convey it to another private person in order to bolster the economy. They argue that whatever incidental benefit may accrue to the public, assembling land to General Motors' specifications for conveyance to General Motors for its uncontrolled use in profit making is really a taking for private use and not a public use because General Motors is the primary beneficiary of the condemnation.

The defendants-appellees contend, on the other hand, that the controlling public purpose in taking this land is to create an industrial site which will be used to alleviate and prevent conditions of unemployment and fiscal distress. The fact that it will be conveyed to and ultimately used by a private manufacturer does not defeat this predominant public purpose.

There is no dispute about the law. All agree that condemnation for a public use or purpose is permitted. All agree that condemnation for a private use or purpose is forbidden. Similarly, condemnation for a private use cannot be authorized whatever its incidental public benefit and condemnation for a public purpose cannot be forbidden whatever the incidental private gain. The heart of this dispute is whether the proposed condemnation is for the primary benefit of the public or the private user. * * *

In the court below, the plaintiffs-appellants challenged the necessity for the taking of the land for the proposed project. In this regard the city presented substantial evidence of the severe economic conditions facing the residents of the city and state, the need for new industrial development to revitalize local industries, the economic boost the proposed project would provide, and the lack of other adequate available sites to implement the project.

As Justice Cooley stated over a hundred years ago "the most important consideration in the case of eminent domain is the necessity of accomplishing some public good which is otherwise impracticable, and * * * the law does not so much regard the means as the need." *People ex rel. Detroit & Howell R. Co. v. Salem Twp. Board*, 20 Mich. 452, 480–481 (1870). * * *

In the instant case the benefit to be received by the municipality invoking the power of eminent domain is a clear and significant one and is sufficient to satisfy this Court that such a project was an intended and a legitimate object of the Legislature when it allowed municipalities to exercise condemnation powers even though a private party will also, ultimately, receive a benefit as an incident thereto.

The power of eminent domain is to be used in this instance primarily to accomplish the essential public purposes of alleviating unemployment and revitalizing the economic base of the community. The benefit to a private interest is merely incidental.

Our determination that this project falls within the public purpose, as stated by the Legislature, does not mean that every condemnation proposed by an economic development corporation will meet with similar acceptance simply because it may provide some jobs or add to the industrial or commercial base. If the public benefit was not so clear and significant, we would hesitate to sanction approval of such a project. The power of eminent domain is restricted to furthering public uses and purposes and is not to be exercised without substantial proof that the public is primarily to be benefited. Where, as here, the condemnation power is exercised in a way that benefits specific and identifiable private interests, a court inspects with heightened scrutiny the claim that the public interest is the predominant interest being advanced. Such public benefit cannot be speculative or marginal but must be clear and significant if it is to be within the legitimate purpose as stated by the Legislature. We hold this project is warranted on the basis that its significance for the people of Detroit and the state has been demonstrated. * * *

RYAN, JUSTICE (dissenting). * * *

The real controversy which underlies this litigation concerns the propriety of condemning private property for conveyance to another private party because the use of it by the new owner promises greater public "benefit" than the old use. The controversy arises in the context of economic crisis. While unemployment is high throughout the nation, it is of calamitous proportions throughout the state of Michigan, and particularly in the City of Detroit, whose economic lifeblood is the now foundering automobile industry. * * *

Thus it was to a city with its economic back to the wall that General Motors presented its highly detailed "proposal" for construction of a new plant in a "green field" location in the City of Detroit. In addition to the fact that Detroit had virtually no "green fields", the requirements of the "proposal" were such that it was clear that no existing location would be suitable unless the city acquired the requisite land one way or another and did so within the General Motors declared time schedule. The corporation told the city that it must find or assemble a parcel 450 to 500 acres in size with access to long-haul railroad lines and a freeway system with railroad marshalling yards within the plant site. As both General Motors and the city knew at the outset, no such "green field" existed. Unquestionably cognizant of its immense political and economic power, General Motors also insisted that it must receive title to the assembled parcel by May 1, 1981.

In a most impressive demonstration of governmental efficiency, the City of Detroit set about its task of meeting General Motors' specifications. Nine possible sites were identified and suggested to General Motors. Only one was found adequate—a parcel consisting of 465 acres straddling the Detroit–Hamtramck border that has come to be known as Central Industrial Park (CIP). * * *

Behind the frenzy of official activity was the unmistakable guiding and sustaining, indeed controlling, hand of the General Motors Corporation. The city administration and General Motors worked in close contact during the summer and autumn of 1980 negotiating the specifics for the new plant site. * * * The evidence then is that what General Motors wanted, General Motors got. The corporation conceived the project, determined the cost, allocated the financial burdens, selected the site, established the mode of financing, imposed specific deadlines for clearance of the property and taking title, and even demanded 12 years of tax concessions.

From the beginning, construction of the new assembly plant in Detroit was characterized by the city administration as a do or die proposition. * * * Faced with the unacceptable prospect of losing two automotive plants and the jobs that go with them, the city chose to march in fast lock-step with General Motors to carve a "green field" out of an urban setting which ultimately required sweeping away a tightly-knit residential enclave of first- and second-generation Americans, for many of whom their home was their single most valuable and cherished asset and their stable ethnic neighborhood the unchanging symbol of the security and quality of their lives. * * *

Stripped of the justifying adornments which have universally attended public description of this controversy, the central jurisprudential issue is the right of government to expropriate property from those who do not wish to sell for the use and benefit of a strictly private corporation. It is not disputed that this action was authorized by statute. The question is whether such authorization is constitutional. * * *

Section 2 of Art. 10 of the state constitution, the taking clause, provides in pertinent part, "[p]rivate property shall not be taken for public *use* without just compensation". (Emphasis added.) * * * Not to be confused is a separate provision of our constitution respecting an altogether different governmental power, one not in question in this case—the power of taxation. That provision limits the use of the power, including the expenditure of tax revenues, to "public purposes": "Each city and village is granted power to levy * * * taxes for public purposes". Const.1963, Art. 7, § 21.

Well over a century ago, a clear line of demarcation was drawn between the powers of eminent domain and taxation, setting the jurisprudences of the taking clause and, if you will, the "taxing clause" on separate, independent courses. What is "public" for one is not necessarily "public" for the other: * * * As a general proposition * * * in the realm of aid to private corporations, "public purpose" (taxation) has been construed less restrictively than "public use" (eminent domain). The distinction is fully justified. The character of governmental interference with the individual in the case of taxation is wholly different from the case of eminent domain. The degree of compelled deprivation of property is manifestly less intrusive in the former case: it is one thing to disagree with the purposes for which one's tax money is spent; it is quite another to be compelled to give up one's land and be required, as in this case, to leave what may well be a lifelong home and community. * * *

It is plain, of course, that condemnation of property for transfer to private corporations is not wholly proscribed. For many years, and probably since the date of Michigan's statehood, an exception to the general rule has been recognized. The exception, which for ease of reference might be denominated the instrumentality of commerce exception, has permitted condemnation for the establishment or improvement of the avenues of commerce—highways, railroads, and canals, for example—and can be traced to the common law where it was considered an exception to a general rule:

> "This right, it has been held, may be exercised on behalf of railways in the hands of private parties. But there can be no doubt, I think, that this holding was a considerable modification of common law principles." *People ex rel. Detroit & Howell R. Co. v. Salem Twp. Board,* 20 Mich. 452, 479 (1870). * * *

It cannot for an instant be maintained, however, nor has anyone suggested, that the case before us falls within the instrumentality of commerce exception.

In fact, the only authorities that even arguably support or justify the use of eminent domain in this case are the "slum clearance" cases. These cases hold that slum clearance is a public use for which eminent domain may be employed. The distinction, however, between those cases and the one at hand is evident. The fact that the private developers in the cited cases, to whom the city sold the cleared land, eventually benefitted from the projects does not lend validity to the condemnation under consideration here. * * * Simply put, the object of eminent domain when used in connection with slum clearance is not to convey land to a private corporation as it is in this case, but to erase blight, danger and disease.

The inapplicability of the slum clearance cases is evident. In the case before us the reputed public "benefit" to be gained is inextricably bound to ownership, development and use of the property in question by one, and only one, private corporation, General Motors, and then only in *the* manner prescribed by the corporation. The public "benefit" claimed by defendant to result can be achieved only if condemnation is executed upon an area, within a timetable, essentially for a price, and entirely for a purpose determined not by any public entity, but by the board of directors of General Motors. There may never be a clearer case than this of condemning land for a private corporation. * * *

There are at least two compelling considerations that weigh decisively against the similar expansion of "public use" accomplished so precipitously by the majority.

First, as discussed earlier, the deprivations of property that result from the exercise of the powers of taxation and eminent domain are different in kind. Eminent domain is a far more intrusive power. Like taxation, it can entail financial loss, although "just compensation" is required. But more important, it can entail, as it did in this case, intangible losses, such as severance or personal attachments to one's domicile and neighborhood and the destruction of an organic community of a most unique and irreplaceable character.

Second, when the private corporation to be aided by eminent domain is as large and influential as General Motors, the power of eminent domain, for all practical purposes, is in the hands of the private corporation. The municipality is merely the conduit. In contrast, the broader view of the notion of "public purpose" has not effected a comparable transfer of the power of taxation to the private sector. Government still determines how tax liability is computed and how and under what conditions tax revenues are spent.

Eminent domain is an attribute of sovereignty. When individual citizens are forced to suffer great social dislocation to permit private corporations to construct plants where they deem it most profitable, one is left to wonder who the sovereign is.

The sudden and fundamental change in established law effected by the Court in this case, entailing such a significant diminution of constitutional rights, cannot be justified as a function of judicial construction; the only proper vehicle for change of this dimension is a constitutional amendment. What has been done in this case can be explained by the overwhelming sense of inevitability that has attended this litigation from the beginning; a sense attributable to the combination and coincidence of the interests of a desperate city administration and a giant corporation willing and able to take advantage of the opportunity that presented itself. The justification for it, like the inevitability of it, has been made to seem more acceptable by the "team spirit" chorus of approval of the project which has been supplied by the voices of labor, business, industry, government, finance, and even the news media. Virtually the only discordant sounds of dissent have come from the miniscule minority of citizens most profoundly affected by this case, the Poletown residents whose neighborhood has been destroyed.

With this case the Court has subordinated a constitutional right to private corporate interests. As demolition of existing structures on the future plant site goes forward, the best that can be hoped for, jurisprudentially, is that the precedential value of this case will be lost in the accumulating rubble. * * *

ROBERT CARO, THE POWER BROKER

Pp. 850–854, 859, 863–864, 868–869, 872–873, 875, 877–878 (1974).

One Mile

Robert Moses built 627 miles of roads in and around New York City. This is the story of one of those miles.

There is something strange about that mile. It is one of seven that make up the great highway known as the Cross–Bronx Expressway, but the other six, like most of the other miles of Moses' expressways, are—roughly—straight, on a road map a heavy red line slashing inexorably across the delicate crosshatch of streets in the borough's central expanse. There is logic—the ruthless, single-minded logic of the engineer, perhaps, but logic—in that line. When it curves, the curves are shallow, the road hastening to resume its former course. But during that one mile, the road swerves, bulging abruptly and substantially toward the north.

A closer look does not explain that bulge. It makes it not less puzzling but more. Detailed maps show the entire area blanketed with rectangles that represent city blocks—except for one open space, running east-west, parallel to the expressway, that represents an unusually wide avenue, and, directly adjacent to and below that open space, another, colored green, that represents a 148–acre park. And these empty spaces lie directly in the path that the expressway would have followed had it just continued on its former straight course. All it had to do to take advantage of that corridor—to utilize for right-of-way the avenue roadbed, together with a very narrow strip at the very top edge of the park—was to keep on the way it had been going.

If the location of that one mile of expressway was puzzling on maps when Moses first proposed it in 1946, it was more puzzling in reality. For while the maps showed rectangles, reality was what was on those rectangles: apartment houses lined up rank upon rank, a solid mile of apartment houses, fifty-four of them, fifty-four structures of brick and steel and mortar piled fifty, sixty and seventy feet high and each housing thirty or forty or fifty families. Walk through the area, the proposed route of the expressway and the blocks around it, and it was impossible not to see that keeping the road straight would hurt little. Only six small buildings—dilapidated brownstone tenements—would have to be torn down. Most of the right-of-way—the park and the avenue—was already in the city's possession. While turning the road to the north would destroy hundreds upon hundreds of homes, homes in which lived thousands of men, women and children. And it would cost millions upon millions of dollars—in condemnation costs for fifty-four apartment houses, in demolition costs for the tearing down of those buildings, in tax revenue that would otherwise be paid, year after year for generations, into city coffers by the buildings' owners.

If the bulge in the expressway was puzzling to anyone studying it, it was tragic to those who didn't have to study it, to the people who lived in or near that right-of-way. For to these people, the fifty-four apartment buildings that would have to be destroyed were not just buildings but homes. That mile of buildings was the very heart of the neighborhood in which they lived, a section of the Bronx known as "East Tremont."

The people of East Tremont did not have much. Refugees or the children of refugees from the little *shtetls* in the Pale of Settlement and from the ghettos of Eastern Europe, the Jews who at the turn of the century had fled the pogroms and the wrath of the Tsars, they had first settled in America on the Lower East Side. The Lower East Side had become a place to which they were tied by family and friends and language and religion and a sense of belonging—but from whose damp and squalid tenements they had ached to escape, if not for their own sake then for the sake of their children, whose every cough brought dread to parents who knew all too well why the streets in which they lived were called "lung blocks." Jews from the Lower East Side who made enough money to escape in style escaped to "the Jewish half-mile" of Central Park West, "the Golden Ghetto." Jews who made enough money to escape—but not that much—escaped to the Grand Concourse. The Jews of East Tremont were luckier than those who had to stay behind on the Lower East Side, but not so lucky as the Grand Concourse Jews. They were not the milliners or the cloak-and-suiters but the pressers, finishers and cutters who worked in the bare workrooms behind the ornate showrooms of the garment district. They were a long way from being rich, and their neighborhood proved it. There were no elevators in most of the five- and six-story buildings into which they began to flood (stopping at 182nd Street, southern border of an Italian neighborhood, as abruptly as if a fence had stood there) after the extension of the IRT elevated line just before World War I linked East Tremont to the downtown garment district. By the end of World War II, the buildings' galvanized iron pipes were corroding, causing leaks and drops in water pressure; a few still had bathtubs that sat up on legs. With some 60,000 persons living along its narrow streets, its "population density"—441 persons "per residential acre"—was considered "undesirable" by social scientists. "In moving through East Tremont one senses a feeling of crowdedness brought on by the lack of open space and close location of buildings," one wrote.

But the neighborhood provided its residents with things that were important to them.

Transportation was important to the fathers who worked downtown, and the neighborhood had good transportation. With the Third Avenue El and the IRT White Plains Road line running right through it, it was only a few easy blocks from anywhere in East Tremont to a subway that took you right down to the garment district.

Jobs were important to the fathers who didn't work downtown, and the neighborhood had jobs available—good jobs by East Tremont standards—in a miniature garment and upholstery manufacturing district that had sprung up around Park Avenue, just ten minutes away.

Shopping was important to the mothers who stayed home and took care of the kids, and the neighborhood had good shopping. East Tremont Avenue, which ran conveniently right across its center, was a bright, bustling mile of bakeries which didn't bother advertising that they baked only with butter because all of them did, of groceries where your order was sliced and measured out and weighed ("You didn't get everything in packages like you do now"), of kosher butcher shops ("We weren't, but I bought kosher for my mother's sake. And it's the kind of meat you know in the pot"), of mama-and-papa candy stores, of delicatessens, filled always with the pungent aroma from the pickle barrels, whose owners got up before dawn to mix olives and pimentos and chives—or dates or caviar—into manufactured cream cheese to create individualized loaves they named "Paradise" or "Dark Jewel." You might go to Alexander's on the Concourse for clothes, but you didn't have to; Janowitz's on Tremont was just as good. You didn't even have to leave the neighborhood for a dress for a real "fancy" affair; "they had *high-priced* stores on Tremont, too; Held's [at the intersection of Southern Boulevard] was very expensive—as good as any store on the Concourse." If you didn't feel like going out, the "better" stores on Marmion delivered, and the stuff they delivered was just as good as if you had been there to feel it yourself, and for many items you didn't even have to pick up the telephone: a few pushcart peddlers still roamed the streets of East Tremont as if to remind the residents of where they had come from.

Parks were important to the mothers, too. There were no playgrounds in the neighborhood—mothers' delegations had attempted in the past to talk to the Park Department about the situation but Moses' aides had never even deigned to grant them an appointment—but running down its length was Southern Boulevard, whose broad center mall had grass plots plenty big enough for little children to play on, and surrounded by benches so mothers could keep their eyes on them to make sure they didn't run into the street. And the southwestern border of the neighborhood was Crotona Park. "Beautiful. Lovely. Playgrounds. There was a lake—Indian Lake. Nice. We used to sit there—under the trees. We raised our children in Crotona Park." Social scientists, who had never lived on the Lower East Side, might consider East Tremont "crowded." The people of East Tremont, who had, considered it open and airy, wonderfully open and airy.

Thanks to Crotona Park, young adults as well as children didn't have to leave the neighborhood for recreation. "It was a *great* park. Twenty tennis courts right *there*. Where you could walk to them. Baseball diamonds, magnificent playgrounds with baskets—three-man games would be going on all weekend, you know. A big swimming pool that Moses had built during the Depression. Indian Lake. And kept really clean then, you know. And safe. *Sure* people walked there at night. You never worried then. A *great* park!" And thanks to Tremont Avenue, you didn't have to leave the neighborhood for entertainment. On the avenue's one mile in the neighborhood were seven movie houses. The Bronx Zoo—with its animals roaming behind moats instead of bars—was one stop away on the White Plains El, the New York Botanical Garden was three; you could *walk* with your children to those two perfect places to spend a Sunday with the kids.

The neighborhood provided the things that were important to its old people. "The benches over on Southern Boulevard were beautiful, gorgeous. On sunny days, you could always find the girls over there, just chatting, you know, and having a good time. On weekends, they'd be so crowded, you couldn't sit down." Old men would sit there in the sun playing chess with men with whom they had been playing chess for thirty years. (Kibitzers had to stand.) There was a place to play chess—or cards—or just sit and talk over a cup of coffee in cold weather, too. The "Y"—the East Tremont Young Men's Hebrew Association—listed more than four hundred "senior citizens" on its active membership roles. "There was no reason for an older person to be lonely in that neighborhood," says one who lived there.

"You knew where your kids were at night, too," says one mother. They were at the Y, which had 1,700 families as members. "There were so many programs out of the Y for kids. At night—before—you never used to know where they were, what they were doing. You always used to hear about gangs—you had to worry, was he with a gang? Now you always knew where your kids were at night." Children who lived on Central Park West might be sent to expensive day camps and, when they got older, to sleep-away camps in the Adirondacks; the Y provided inexpensive day-camp and sleep-away programs—the largest run by any single institution in New York City—for children who lived on Crotona Park North.

Schools were terribly important to the people of East Tremont (a quarter of a century after their kids had graduated, some parents could still remember the precise student-teacher ratio in their classes), and East Tremont had good schools. They were old—PS 44, at 176th and Prospect, the neighborhood's junior high school, had been built in 1901, and the city said there was simply no money to replace it but there were no double sessions and standards were high. PS 67, off Southern Boulevard, was the first elementary school in New York to offer lessons—and supply instruments—for any child who wanted to learn to play the violin. And all the schools were close, close enough for kids to walk to.

To the people of East Tremont, East Tremont was family. In its bricks were generations. Raised in the neighborhood, Lillian Roberts married a boy from the neighborhood. They made their first apartment in a supposedly "nicer" section over on Fordham Road. When their first child was born, they moved back. "Why? Because my husband had— oh, we both had, I guess—nostalgic feelings. The reason we moved back to that area was that we loved it so much." Lillian and her husband moved into an apartment on the third floor of a walkup at 845 West 176th Street. On the first floor of that building, Lillian's mother, Ida Rozofsky, born in Russia, was living—with Lillian's grandmother. East Tremont was friends—real friends, not just acquaintances you happened to meet because they took their children to the same playground to which you took your children, or because they belonged to the same PTA as you, but friends whom you had grown up with and were going to grow old with, boys and girls—turned men and women—who knew and understood you and whom you knew and understood. Says Mrs. Helen Lazarcheck: "Everyone seemed to help one another. If there was trouble, everyone would do something for you if they could. They were always coming in and sharing what they had. If they were going away, they would give you food that you could use and they couldn't." East Tremont was a feeling of being known—in the streets and in the stores, where shopkeepers like big gruff Saul Janowitz, "the Mayor of East Tremont," had been selling to neighborhood families for decades. (The owner of one Crotona Avenue vegetable stand had been selling vegetables in Tremont when it still largely consisted of the three large "mount" farming estates—Mount Hope, Mount Eden and Fairmount—

that had given "Tremont" its name; he had gone from house to house with a horse and wagon then.) East Tremont was a sense of continuity, of warmth, of the security that comes—and only comes—with a sense of belonging. Even families that could afford to have their "simchas"— weddings and bar mitzvahs—in the Concourse Plaza, generally had them instead in the neighborhood's little, somewhat shabby, social halls. No one would have called East Tremont a *united* community. It possessed, one study observed, a "myriad of social systems covering religious *Landsmannschaft* groups, fraternal, educational, political and fund-raising groups" engaged in "a constant and shrill competition for loyalty," a competition which was not even resolved in the two areas where East Tremont might have been expected to be solid: politics and religion. FDR's hold was absolute—but only so far as FDR was concerned; in nonpresidential elections, men who once, long ago, had preached from soapboxes were loyal to an older faith: Socialist, Communist, American Labor and Progressive parties could all count on substantial votes in East Tremont. "In East Tremont," the study noted, "the Yiddishist and Hebraist each had his following with a supporting system of cultural clubs, bookstores, debating societies, etc." The neighborhood's seven synagogues were constantly competing for members and prestige. East Tremont may have been a loud community, a shrill community, a materialistic, money-conscious community. But it was a community. * * *

The letters came on December 4, 1952.

For years, East Tremont had been vaguely aware that one of Robert Moses' highways was going to run through the neighborhood, that part of it was already under construction over in the East Bronx somewhere. But there had been no hard facts available, and, as Mrs. Lillian Edelstein says, "it had gone on so long, and you keep hearing and hearing and nothing happens, and after a while it doesn't mean anything to you." When they thought about it—if they thought about it—they were sure it would run along the edge of Crotona Park; "I mean, it was so obvious you just figured it was going to go there," Mrs. Edelstein says. "It was in the wind for a long time that he was going to come through the apartment houses. But we just didn't believe it."

But on December 4, a Tuesday, the letters were there in hundreds of mailboxes, letters signed by "Robert Moses, City Construction Coordinator," informing each recipient that the building in which he or she lived was in the right-of-way of the Cross–Bronx Expressway, that it would be condemned by the city and torn down—and that they had ninety days to move. * * *

But East Tremont's panic was soon replaced by hope.

The hope was based on faith in Robert Moses, or, more accurately, in the Moses mystique. East Tremont's pious Jews still held the campaign of 1934 against him—"I hated him since the time he said he wasn't Jewish," one says—but they still believed in his image as a man above politics and bureaucrats. Believing in that image, the people of

East Tremont were sure that if they could only present Moses with an alternate route through their neighborhood that was truly better than the route he had chosen, he would accept it. And it did not take them very long to find out that such a route was indeed available.

Bronx Borough President James J. Lyons; Lyons' chief engineer, Moses' old Planning Commission ally Arthur V. Sheridan; and Sheridan's veteran aides had all been in on the laying out of the route Moses had chosen. But when the East Tremont committee asked for an appointment with Lyons, Lyons aide Charles F. Rodriguez recalls, "Lyons fobbed them off to Sheridan, and Sheridan fobbed them off to someone else"—and the someone else happened to be a recent addition to the staff named Edward J. Flanagan, who was, Rodriguez admits, "a capable engineer" but who had never, during a long engineering career, been associated with Moses and who was "very cocksure of himself" (by which Rodriguez apparently means he was not afraid to say what he thought). And when the housewives mentioned the possibility of an alternate route, Flanagan, without letting them finish, said of course there was, took out a pen, said, "There's no reason the route couldn't go this way," and sketched on a map before him the route through Crotona Park that was precisely what they had had in mind.

Flanagan was silenced—no one from East Tremont ever got an appointment with him again—but he had given the housewives conviction that the alternate route was feasible. The Bronx County Chapter of the New York State Society of Professional Engineers agreed to make a formal study of it.

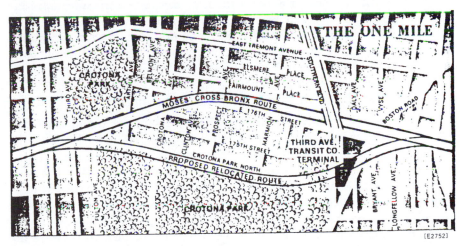

[E2752]

And one member of the society had enough experience with large-scale highway construction to do so—experience garnered working, indirectly, for Robert Moses. Bernard Weiner, a refugee with a heavy accent, was the brilliant engineer who, after working during the 1920's on the Westchester parkway system, had gone to work for Madigan Hyland and designed, among other Moses projects, all the concrete bridges on the

Circumferential Parkway—although he could not pronounce "Circumferential"—and the revolutionary three-span skew frame interchange that carries the Whitestone Expressway and Grand Central Parkway across each other in Queens. Then his independent outlook—he kept insisting that if Moses did not increase the grades on the Circumferential, it was going to flood in heavy rains—got him dropped from the team. Weiner, who had found it impossible, despite his experience and acknowledged brilliance, to get a good job since, had learned the price of opposing Moses, and he was not willing to pay it in full any more, but he was willing to pay part of it. When the Bronx Chapter asked him to do studies of the alternate route, he agreed only "on condition that I would be anonymous" (another engineer's name was signed to them), but he did do them—with his usual thoroughness, drawing up not just a sketch but a complete engineering study that demonstrated that the route through the park was not only feasible but met every federal and state standard for expressway design.

The arguments in favor of the park route were clear. By making only a gentle alteration in the road's route—swinging it just two blocks (one block in some places) to the south, 1,530 apartments would be saved at no cost to anyone: the road would not be made longer, its curves would not be made sharper—its efficiency as a traffic-moving device would not be harmed in the least. "We were happy then," recalls Lillian Edelstein. "We had been worried, but when we found there was a feasible alternate route, we figured we were in business."

The arguments in favor of the alternate route were so clear. Believing in the myth of Moses, the housewives of East Tremont were sure he would accept them. And it wasn't until they tried to present them to him that panic set in again. For neither he nor any of his aides would even listen to those arguments. There would be no point in any meeting, Moses' office told Mrs. Edelstein when she telephoned after letters and telegrams had gone unanswered. The Coordinator had already decided on the route. It would not be changed. * * *

Mrs. Edelstein had been informed at the very beginning of her fight that there were ample grounds for a full-scale legal, court battle, a battle which would, even if not successful in changing the expressway route, force the city to give tenants comparable new apartments. But, she was also informed, the legal fees could run to ten thousand dollars. Had a single one of the threatened tenants been a lawyer, with a personal interest in the case, legal help might have been available free, but not one was. In the Bronx of Ed Flynn and Charlie Buckley, there were no political dividends—and quite a few political disadvantages—to be reaped from opposing a project that Ed Flynn and Charlie Buckley favored. Several young attorneys did come forward with offers of legal assistance, but invariably their interest waned quickly.

Ten thousand dollars? Lillian Edelstein had difficulty raising amounts far smaller than that. "The feeling among people was, what's the use," explains Arthur Katz. "You can't lick City Hall. And even if you could, you certainly can't lick Robert Moses. We were told by the politicians we saw that when Robert Moses wanted his way, that was it. For a while at the start—with Lyons, when he promised—they had hope. But now * * *'' "You'd think people would fight for their homes," says Saul Janowitz. But Mrs. Edelstein had to beg and plead to persuade families to chip in a dollar bill at a time, and each time the dollar bills were harder to come by.

Nonetheless, a small band fought. Most of its members were businessmen who knew the mass evictions of their customers would destroy their businesses, but it was more than businessmen. Among the men and women of East Tremont were the sons and daughters of the revolutionaries who had preached socialism and Zionism in the Pale of Settlement, and on the Lower East Side, and some of them hadn't lost their faith in justice. "At that time there were a lot of lefts around here," recalls Saul Janowitz.

But mostly, it was Lillian Edelstein who fought.

Finding engineers willing to defy Moses, the housewife put them to work drawing maps detailed enough to prove from every engineering standpoint that their route was technically feasible. Then she put them to work obtaining hard figures: exactly how much more Moses' mile would cost than theirs. When they came up with those figures—Moses' route would require the demolition of fifty-four apartment houses, ninety one- or two-family homes and fifteen one-story "taxpayers" housing sixty stores, for a total of 159 separate buildings; condemning and demolishing them would cost more than $10,000,000 more than would be required if the road ran where they wanted it to, even without the cost of relocating 1,530 families and the loss of the real estate taxes (close to $200,000 per year at current rates) from the demolished buildings, income the city would be losing year after year forever she undertook the harder fight of bringing those maps and figures to the attention of the public and of public officials. * * *

The City Planning Commission gave the tenants the type of public hearing that might have been expected from a body controlled by a man who, if given his way, would have abolished public hearings. A large delegation had taken the day to ask the commission not to approve the Moses route—a long day. Commission chairman John J. Bennett, at that moment secretly negotiating a Title I transaction for which he needed that man's approval, refused to let even one tenant speak, saying that no public hearing was required. But there was a whole series of hearings before the Board of Estimate. Sometimes Moses was present himself. "He always looked surprisingly young and vigorous," Katz recalls. "He was very cool and detached. He didn't say anything. He had his assistants to do the talking for him. He sat and listened. He made some notes. My greatest anger at him was that he didn't seem to be affected by all this—people were getting up and telling these stories of hardship." But, despite Moses' presence, the Board kept postponing a final vote on his request to have the city authorize condemnation proceedings. After an emotional meeting with the ETNA group and several Bronx councilmen in Wagner's office at which the Mayor was visibly moved (and at which he said, "Every member of the Board will want to know the difficulties facing each family in the path of the expressway"), the Mayor interrupted one Board session—at which Moses had confidently expected the issue to be resolved—to order McCullough, who had done a "study" of the tenants' alternate route for Impellitteri in a matter of minutes, to give it a little more consideration. The engineer returned a month later with a report stating that while the alternate route would spare the protesters' homes, it would require the condemnation of almost as many homes belonging to other people. You see, Moses told the Board, it was just as he was always trying to explain to them: changing a route would just "trade in" one group of protesters for another; no matter where you tried to build a highway in the city, there would be protests, so the only way to handle them was to ignore them. ETNA's leaders, who had been certain that not a single home would have to be touched for the alternate route they had proposed, were shocked by McCullough's findings until they realized the trick that the engineer had played. He had studied an alternate route, all right, but not *their* alternate route. Instead, he had selected a route that would require large-scale condemnation and studied that instead. Epstein explained this to Wagner. Over Hodgkiss' violent objections, the Mayor ordered McCullough to study the right alternate route this time, to let Epstein oversee the study to make sure it was fair, and to complete the study before the Board's next meeting when a final decision would be made.

"A defeat for Moses," the *Post* reported. The tenants felt it was. "We felt we had won," Lillian Edelstein recalls. Epstein, trying to reassure her, had told her, in her words, "It's like a jury trial. If they stay out long enough, they won't convict you. Because it was dragging so—month after month, I figured something is happening to hold him and his crew."

On the day of the final hearing before McCullough, assembled in his office in the Municipal Building was a full panoply of Moses Men: Arthur S. Hodgkiss, assistant general manager of the Triborough Bridge and Tunnel Authority; Stuart Constable, acting executive officer of the New York City Department of Parks; W. Earle Andrews and Ernest J. Clark of Andrews, Clark and Buckley, consulting engineers; Milton Goul, district engineer, State Department of Public Works District Number 10, designated to represent the State Department of Public Works by Bertram Tallamy, Superintendent; Arthur B. Williams, liaison engineer, New York State Department of Public Works—and, representing Lyons, Edward J. Flanagan, who, during the entire proceedings, would utter not one word. These engineers and a dozen assistants had been assembled for the occasion on the orders of Robert Moses. * * * Lyons moved the question, saying, "This is an engineer's problem, not a layman's problem, and all the engineers unanimously support this route." One by one the Board members voted—in the affirmative. The last man to vote was Robert F. Wagner, Jr. He voted in the affirmative, too.

"It was so fast," Lillian Edelstein would recall years later. "I was positive at that last hearing that we would win. Because of Wagner. He had said so straight out that he would never let them do it. He had *promised.*" Lillian Edelstein wanted to ask the Mayor what care had been taken for the families, what the relocation plans were. But she couldn't. She was crying. Katz asked instead. Lyons tried to stop him from speaking, but he went ahead anyway. Quoting Wagner's words that he would not vote for acquisition until he had been satisfied as to the relocation plans, he asked the Mayor what those plans were. The Mayor said he did not know. * * *

Why *wouldn't* Moses shift the route of the Cross–Bronx Expressway slightly, thereby saving 1,530 apartments, millions in state and city money, months of aggravation and delay—and making his expressway straighter as well?

"I asked George Spargo that," says Joseph Ingraham, the *Times* reporter who was occasionally on Moses' payroll and who spent so much time socializing with the Moses team that he sometimes seemed to be one of its members. "On the day of the ribbon cutting they were opening a whole bunch of sections of different expressways, and it was raining, really pouring. George said, 'Let's sit this out, and we'll catch up to them at the next stop.' We went into a small bar in the Bronx and I asked him there. He said, 'Oh, one of Jimmy Lyons' relatives owns a piece of property up there and we would have had to take it if we used that other route, and Jimmy didn't want it taken, and RM had promised him we wouldn't.' At the time, George even told me the piece of property involved, but I've forgotten."

The people of East Tremont also wondered why Moses wouldn't shift the route. "I mean, we heard lots of rumors about the bus terminal," Lillian Edelstein recalls. "The politicians were always trying to tell us that was the reason. But we could never find out anything about it. And, I mean, I never believed that. I could never believe that even Robert Moses would take fifteen hundred homes just to save a bus terminal."

Spargo's statement may have been untrue. So may the rumors. If any relative of Bronx Borough President James J. Lyons owned property along either the alternate or actual expressway route, the author was unable to find evidence of that fact—although, since, in the Bronx, politicians' ownership of property was habitually concealed through a many-layered network of intermediaries and bag men, a network baffling even to contemporary investigators and all but impenetrable twenty years later, his failure is not conclusive. Moses' refusal to alter the route—unexplainable on the basis of his given reasons, all of which are demonstrably false—may have had nothing to do with the fact that the "bus terminal" of which Lillian Edelstein speaks—actually the "Tremont Depot" of the Third Avenue Transit Company, at the northeast corner of Crotona Park—lies in the path of the alternate route and would have had to be condemned if that route was adopted. It is possible that Moses' selection of the original route—it was he, not any engineer, who selected it—was based on no more than whim, and that his subsequent refusal to alter it was due to nothing more than stubbornness, although if so it was a whim quite inconsistent with Moses' customary whims: almost invariably over a period of forty years, whenever he had a choice of routes, he selected the one that would keep his road straight, not the one that would make the road curve.

However, in attempting to find an explanation for Moses' refusal to change the route, the Third Avenue Transit depot stands out. With the exception of six old, small, dilapidated brownstone tenements, housing a total of nineteen families, it was the only structure of any type that would have had to be condemned if the alternate route was used. In effect, for whatever reason, Robert Moses elected to tear down 159 buildings housing 1,530 families instead of tearing down six buildings housing nineteen families—and the terminal. It is a fact that the Third Avenue Transit Company secretly told Moses it was very anxious not to have the terminal condemned, for its location was strategic for its buses. And it is also a fact that for twenty years it was considered an open secret in Bronx political circles that key borough politicians held large but carefully hidden interests in Third Avenue Transit. And it is also a fact that, in Bronx politics of the period, what Third Avenue Transit wanted, Third Avenue Transit got.

But the unfortunate element in searching for the explanation of Moses' refusal is that in the perspective of the history of New York City it is unimportant. Whether Moses refused to change the route for a personal or political reason, the point is that his reason was the only one that counted. Neighborhood feelings, urban planning considerations, cost, aesthetics, common humanity, common sense—none of these mattered in laying out the routes of New York's great roads. The only consideration that mattered was Robert Moses' will. He had the power to impose it on New York. * * *

IRIS YOUNG, CITY LIFE AND DIFFERENCE

From I. Young, Justice and the Politics of Difference.
Pp. 234–241 (1990).

UNDESIRABLE POLITICAL CONSEQUENCES OF THE IDEAL OF COMMUNITY

* * * In ordinary speech in the United States, the term community refers to the people with whom one identifies in a specific locale. It refers to neighborhood, church, schools. It also carries connotations of ethnicity, race, and other group identifications. For most people, insofar as they consider themselves members of communities at all, a community is a group that shares a specific heritage, a common self-identification, a common culture and set of norms. * * * [S]elf-identification as a member of such a community also often occurs as an oppositional

differentiation from other groups, who are feared, despised, or at best devalued. Persons feel a sense of mutual identification only with some persons, feel in community only with those, and fear the difference others confront them with because they identify with a different culture, history, and point of view on the world. The ideal of community, I suggest, validates and reinforces the fear and aversion some social groups exhibit toward others. If community is a positive norm, that is, if existing together with others in relations of mutual understanding and reciprocity is the goal, then it is understandable that we exclude and avoid those with whom we do not or cannot identify.

Richard Sennett discusses how a "myth of community" operates perpetually in American society to produce and implicitly legitimate racist and classist behavior and policy. In many towns, suburbs, and neighborhoods people do have an image of their locale as one in which people all know one another, have the same values and life style, and relate with feelings of mutuality and love. In modern American society such an image is almost always false; while there may be a dominant group with a distinct set of values and life style, within any locale one can usually find deviant individuals and groups. Yet the myth of community operates strongly to produce defensive exclusionary behavior: pressuring the Black family that buys a house on the block to leave, beating up the Black youths who come into "our" neighborhood, zoning against the construction of multiunit dwellings.

The exclusionary consequences of valuing community, moreover, are not restricted to bigots and conservatives. Many radical political organizations founder on the desire for community. Too often people in groups working for social change take mutual friendship to be a goal of the group, and thus judge themselves wanting as a group when they do not achieve such commonality. Such a desire for community often channels energy away from the political goals of the group, and also produces a clique atmosphere which keeps groups small and turns potential members away. Mutual identification as an implicit group ideal can reproduce a homogeneity that usually conflicts with the organization's stated commitment to diversity. In recent years most socialist and feminist organizations, for example, have taken racial, class, age, and sexual diversity as an important criterion according to which the success of political organizations should be evaluated. To the degree that they take mutual understanding and identification as a goal, they may be deflected from this goal of diversity.

The exclusionary implications of a desire for face-to-face relations of mutual identification and sharing present a problem for movements asserting positive group difference * * *. [T]he effort of oppressed groups to reclaim their group identity, and to form with one another bonds of positive cultural affirmation around their group specificity, constitutes an important resistance to the oppression of cultural imperialism. It shifts the meaning of difference from otherness and exclusion to variation and specificity, and forces dominant groups to acknowledge their own group specificity. But does not such affirmation of group identity itself express an ideal of community, and is it not subject to exclusionary impulses?

Some social movements asserting positive group difference have found through painful confrontation that an urge to unity and mutual identification does indeed have exclusionary implications. Feminist efforts to create women's spaces and women's culture, for example, have often assumed the perspective of only a particular subgroup of women—white, or middle class, or lesbian, or straight—thus implicitly excluding or rendering invisible those women among them with differing identifications and experiences. Similar problems arise for any movement of group identification, because in our society most people have multiple group identifications, and thus group differences cut across every social group.

These arguments against community are not arguments against the political project of constructing and affirming a positive group identity and relations of group solidarity, as a means of confronting cultural imperialism and discovering things about oneself and others with whom one feels affinity. Critique of the ideal of community, however, reveals that even in such group-specific contexts affinity cannot mean the transparency of selves to one another. If in their zeal to affirm a positive meaning of group specificity people seek or try to enforce a strong sense of mutual identification, they are likely to reproduce exclusions similar to those they confront. Those affirming the specificity of a group affinity should at the same time recognize and affirm the group and individual differences within the group.

City Life as a Normative Ideal

Appeals to community are usually antiurban. Much sociological literature diagnoses modern history as a movement to the dangerous bureaucratized *Gesellschaft* from the manageable and safe *Gemeinschaft*, nostalgically reconstructed as a world of lost origins. Many others follow Rousseau in romanticizing the ancient *polis* and the medieval Swiss *Bürger* deploring the commerce, disorder, and unmanageable mass character of the modern city. Throughout the modern period, the city has often been decried as embodying immorality, artificiality, disorder, and danger—as the site of treasonous conspiracies, illicit sex, crime, deviance, and disease. The typical image of the modern city finds it expressing all the disvalues that a reinstantiation of community would eliminate.

Yet urbanity is the horizon of the modern, not to mention the postmodern, condition. Contemporary political theory must accept urbanity as a material given for those who live in advanced industrial societies. Urban relations define the lives not only of those who live in the huge metropolises, but also of those who live in suburbs and large towns. Our social life is structured by vast networks of temporal and spatial mediation among persons, so that nearly everyone depends on the activities of seen and unseen strangers who mediate between oneself and one's associates, between oneself and one's objects of desire. Urbanites find themselves relating geographically to increasingly large regions, thinking little of traveling seventy miles to work or an hour's drive for an evening's entertainment. Most people frequently and casually encounter strangers in their daily activities. The material surroundings and structures available to us define and presuppose urban relationships. The very size of populations in our society and most other nations of the world, coupled with a continuing sense of national or ethnic identity with millions of other people, supports the conclusion that a vision of dismantling the city is hopelessly utopian.

Starting from the given of modern urban life is not simply necessary, moreover; it is desirable. Even for many of those who decry the alienation, bureaucratization, and mass character of capitalist patriarchal society, city life exerts a powerful attraction. Modern literature, art, and film have celebrated city life, its energy, cultural diversity, technological complexity, and the multiplicity of its activities. Even many of the most staunch proponents of decentralized community love to show visiting friends around the Boston or San Francisco or New York in or near which they live, climbing up towers to see the glitter of lights and sampling the fare at the best ethnic restaurants.

I propose to construct a normative ideal of city life as an alternative to both the ideal of community and the liberal individualism it criticizes as asocial. By "city life" I mean a form of social relations which I define as the being together of strangers. In the city persons and groups interact within spaces and institutions they all experience themselves as belonging to, but without those interactions dissolving into unity or commonness. City life is composed of clusters of people with affinities— families, social group networks, voluntary associations, neighborhood networks, a vast array of small "communities." City dwellers frequently venture beyond such familiar enclaves, however, to the more open public of politics, commerce, and festival, where strangers meet and interact. City dwelling situates one's own identity and activity in relation to a horizon of a vast variety of other activity, and the awareness that this unknown, unfamiliar activity affects the conditions of one's own.

City life is a vast, even infinite, economic network of production, distribution, transportation, exchange, communication, service provision, and amusement. City dwellers depend on the mediation of thousands of other people and vast organizational resources in order to accomplish their individual ends. City dwellers are thus together, bound to one another, in what should be and sometimes is a single polity. Their being together entails some common problems and common interests, but they do not create a community of shared final ends, of mutual identification and reciprocity.

A normative ideal of city life must begin with our given experience of cities, and look there for the virtues of this form of social relations. Defining an ideal as unrealized possibilities of the actual, I extrapolate from that experience four such virtues.

(1) *Social differentiation without exclusion.* City life in urban mass society is not inconsistent with supportive social networks and subcultural communities. Indeed, for many it is their necessary condition. In the city social group differences flourish. Modernization theory predicted a decline in local, ethnic, and other group affiliations as universalist state institutions touch people's lives more directly and as people encounter many others with identifications and life styles different from their own. There is considerable evidence, however, that group differences are often reinforced by city life, and that the city even encourages the formation of new social group affinities. Deviant or minority groups find in the city both a cover of anonymity and a critical mass unavailable in the smaller town. It is hard to imagine the formation of gay or lesbian group affinities, for example, without the conditions of the modern city. While city dwelling as opposed to rural life has changed the lives and self-concepts of Chicanos, to take another example, city life encourages group identification and a desire for cultural nationalism at the same time that it may dissolve some traditional practices or promote assimilation to Anglo language and values. In actual cities many people express violent aversions to members of groups with which they do not identify. More than those who live in small towns, however, they tend to recognize social group difference as a given, something they must live with.

In the ideal of city life freedom leads to group differentiation, to the formation of affinity groups, but this social and spatial differentiation of groups is without exclusion. The urban ideal expresses difference * * *, a side-by-side particularity neither reducible to identity nor completely other. In this ideal groups do not stand in relations of inclusion and exclusion, but overlap and intermingle without becoming homogeneous. Though city life as we now experience it has many borders and exclusions, even our actual experience of the city also gives hints of what differentiation without exclusion can be. Many city neighborhoods have a distinct ethnic identity, but members of other groups also dwell in them. In the good city one crosses from one distinct neighborhood to another without knowing precisely where one ended and the other began. In the normative ideal of city life, borders are open and undecidable.

(2) *Variety.* The interfusion of groups in the city occurs partly because of the multiuse differentiation of social space. What makes urban spaces interesting, draws people out in public to them, gives people pleasure and excitement, is the diversity of activities they support. When stores, restaurants, bars, clubs, parks, and offices are sprinkled among residences, people have a neighborly feeling about their neighborhood, they go out and encounter one another on the streets and chat. They have a sense of their neighborhood as a "spot" or "place," because of that bar's distinctive clientele, or the citywide reputation of the pizza at that restaurant. Both business people and residents tend to have more commitment to and care for such neighborhoods than they do for single-use neighborhoods. Multifunctional streets, parks, and neigh-

borhoods are also much safer than single-use functional spaces because people are out on the streets during most hours, and have commitment to the place.

(3) *Eroticism*. City life also instantiates difference as the erotic, in the wide sense of an attraction to the other, the pleasure and excitement of being drawn out of one's secure routine to encounter the novel, strange, and surprising. The erotic dimension of the city has always been an aspect of its fearfulness, for it holds out the possibility that one will lose one's identity, will fall. But we also take pleasure in being open to and interested in people we experience as different. We spend a Sunday afternoon walking through Chinatown, or checking out this week's eccentric players in the park. We look for restaurants, stores, and clubs with something new for us, a new ethnic food, a different atmosphere, a different crowd of people. We walk through sections of the city that we experience as having unique characters which are not ours, where people from diverse places mingle and then go home.

The erotic attraction here is precisely the obverse of community. In the ideal of community people feel affirmed because those with whom they share experiences, perceptions, and goals recognize and are recognized by them; one sees oneself reflected in the others. There is another kind of pleasure, however, in coming to encounter a subjectivity, a set of meanings, that is different, unfamiliar. One takes pleasure in being drawn out of oneself to understand that there are other meanings, practices, perspectives on the city, and that one could learn or experience something more and different by interacting with them.

The city's eroticism also derives from the aesthetics of its material being: the bright and colored lights, the grandeur of its buildings, the juxtaposition of architecture of different times, styles, and purposes. City space offers delights and surprises. Walk around the corner, or over a few blocks, and you encounter a different spatial mood, a new play of sight and sound, and new interactive movement. The erotic meaning of the city arises from its social and spatial inexhaustibility. A place of many places, the city folds over on itself in so many layers and relationships that it is incomprehensible. One cannot "take it in," one never feels as though there is nothing new and interesting to explore, no new and interesting people to meet.

(4) *Publicity*. Political theorists who extol the value of community often construe the public as a realm of unity and mutual understanding, but this does not cohere with our actual experience of public spaces. Because by definition a public space is a place accessible to anyone, where anyone can participate and witness, in entering the public one always risks encounter with those who are different, those who identify with different groups and have different opinions or different forms of life. The group diversity of the city is most often apparent in public spaces. This helps account for their vitality and excitement. Cities provide important public spaces—streets, parks, and plazas—where people stand and sit together, interact and mingle, or simply witness one

another, without becoming unified in a community of "shared final ends."

Politics, the critical activity of raising issues and deciding how institutional and social relations should be organized, crucially depends on the existence of spaces and forums to which everyone has access. In such public spaces people encounter other people, meanings, expressions, issues, which they may not understand or with which they do not identify. The force of public demonstrations, for example, often consists in bringing to people who pass through public spaces those issues, demands, and people they might otherwise avoid. As a normative ideal city life provides public places and forums where anyone can speak and anyone can listen.

Because city life is a being together of strangers, diverse and overlapping neighbors, social justice cannot issue from the institution of an Enlightenment universal public. On the contrary, social justice in the city requires the realization of a politics of difference. This politics lays down institutional and ideological means for recognizing and affirming diverse social groups by giving political representation to these groups, and celebrating their distinctive characteristics and cultures. In the unoppressive city people open to unassimilated otherness. We all have our familiar relations and affinities, the people to whom we feel close and with whom we share daily life. These familial and social groups open onto a public in which all participate, and that public must be open and accessible to all. Contrary to the communitarian tradition, however, that public cannot be conceived as a unity transcending group differences, nor as entailing complete mutual understanding. In public life the differences remain unassimilated, but each participating group acknowledges and is open to listening to the others. The public is heterogeneous, plural, and playful, a place where people witness and appreciate diverse cultural expressions that they do not share and do not fully understand. * * *

ASIAN AMERICANS FOR EQUALITY v. KOCH

Court of Appeals of New York, 1988.
72 N.Y.2d 121, 531 N.Y.S.2d 782, 527 N.E.2d 265.

SIMONS, JUDGE. * * *

Plaintiff Asian Americans for Equality is a not-for-profit corporation engaged in supporting the rights of men and women of all races for improved housing, job opportunities and working conditions. The individual plaintiffs are now or formerly were residents of the area known as Chinatown, a center of Chinese culture and services in New York City where persons of Chinese and Asian ancestry reside. The individual plaintiffs allege either that they live in substandard housing there or that they were compelled to leave because of their inability to find suitable housing. They are persons of low income and none own property in Chinatown. Defendants are the City of New York, various officers and agencies of the City and a private developer.

The Special Manhattan Bridge District was created in 1981 by amendment to the City's Zoning Resolution. The District encompasses 14 blocks in the area of the Manhattan Bridge and includes a part, but by no means all, of Chinatown. One area south of Monroe and Madison Streets and west of St. James Place, was excluded from the District because it had been redeveloped with public or publicly assisted housing. Others were excluded because they were commercial.

The amendment was preceded by a study of the Manhattan Bridge area which confirmed that Chinatown contains a substantial proportion of high density, substandard housing occupied by low-income groups who work there in the garment, tourist and related industries. The amendment sought to correct these housing conditions by encouraging construction of new residential facilities, the rehabilitation of existing structures and the expansion of community facilities. To achieve those aims, it authorized development of mixed-income housing on land vacant or substantially vacant at the time the amendment was enacted. The amendment provides that new construction must be authorized by special permit and regulated by a system of bonus points permitting increased density in new housing units for those developers who agree to do one or a combination of the following: (1) donate space for community facilities such as senior citizen or day care centers, educational facilities, or a combination of these; (2) construct low-income dwelling units; or (3) rehabilitate existing substandard housing. * * *

Recognizing that the stated goals of the City's study of the Manhattan Bridge area and the amendment creating the District are "very similar" to their own, plaintiffs nevertheless contend that the amendment is invalid because the means adopted to achieve them are inadequate. They charge that the bonuses awarded to permit high density housing favor moderate and high-income development and do not provide sufficient incentive to encourage construction of low-cost housing. They ask the court to require defendants to (1) improve existing housing in the Special Manhattan Bridge District, (2) provide more affordable low-income housing, (3) minimize the adverse affects of rehabilitation and (4) assure that the present residents who wish to stay in Chinatown are able to do so. * * *

Zoning, as first devised, was a means of dividing the whole territory of a municipality into districts and imposing restrictions on the uses permitted in them. Restrictions on size and density of construction to control fire and traffic hazards, for example, or to eliminate offensive uses from residential districts were deemed a reasonable exercise of the police power (*see, Euclid v. Ambler Co.*, 272 U.S. 365, 47 S.Ct. 114, 71 L.Ed. 303). Such traditional zoning is both restrictive and passive, providing minimum encouragement for development of the municipality as a whole.

Special district zoning—exemplified by the Manhattan Bridge District questioned here—represents a significant departure from this traditional *Euclidian* zoning concept. It is based on the idea that zoning can be used as an incentive to further growth and development of the community rather than as a restraint. It is one of several imaginative legislative schemes intended to encourage, or even coerce, private developers into making the City a more pleasant and efficient place to live and work. Incentive zoning is based on the premise that certain uneconomic uses and amenities will not be provided by private development without economic incentive. The economic incentive frequently used, and the one used in the Manhattan Bridge District amendment, is the allowance of greater density within a proposed building, more floor area than permitted under general zoning rules, if developers provided certain amenities for the community. The amendment awards bonus points which entitle developers to expand their construction in return for increased construction of other, uneconomic projects such as low-cost housing, slum rehabilitation or public facilities. The bonus awarded for each amenity must be carefully structured, however, to make the cost-benefit equation favorable enough to induce the developer to provide the desired uneconomic benefit to the city but sufficiently limited to avoid a windfall to it. * * *

Because zoning is a legislative act, zoning ordinances and amendments enjoy a strong presumption of constitutionality and the burden rests on the party attacking them to overcome that presumption beyond a reasonable doubt. * * * [I]f the zoning ordinance is adopted for a legitimate governmental purpose and there is a " 'reasonable relation between the end sought to be achieved by the regulation and the means used to achieve that end' ", it will be upheld. An amendment which has been carefully studied, prepared and considered meets the general requirement for a well-considered plan and satisfies the statutory requirement. * * * Manifestly, this legislation was reasonably related to its goals: the development of needed housing and the rehabilitation of existing housing in one area of Chinatown. There is no allegation that it was not consistent with the City's general planning or that the City had failed to make provision for low-cost housing. That being so, and inasmuch as the amendment was enacted after study and consideration, it met the requirements for a well-considered plan * * *.

Plaintiffs * * * seek[ ] a mandatory injunction compelling the City to amend the Special Manhattan District Zoning to create greater opportunity for the construction of low-income housing. Plaintiffs do not attack the purpose of the amendment but rather the adequacy of the legislative scheme. They claim that the incentives offered will not provide sufficient low-cost housing because the rewards for doing so are too low compared to the rewards the amendment authorizes for other amenities. As pleaded, the cause of action seeks relief from exclusionary zoning similar to that granted in *Southern Burlington County N.A.A.C.P v. Township of Mount Laurel* (67 N.J. 151, 336 A.2d 713, *appeal dismissed* 423 U.S. 808, 96 S.Ct. 18, 46 L.Ed.2d 28 [*Mount Laurel I*]; 92 N.J. 158, 456 A.2d 390 [*Mount Laurel II*]: a mandatory injunction compelling the City to correct the problem. On appeal plaintiffs rely primarily on the rule in *Berenson v. Town of New Castle*, 38 N.Y.2d 102,

378 N.Y.S.2d 672, 341 N.E.2d 236, a decision of this court which held that a zoning ordinance would be annulled if it did not include districts for multiple housing when community and regional needs required such housing. * * *

Exclusionary zoning may occur either because the municipality has limited the permissible uses within a community to exclude certain groups, or has imposed restrictions so stringent that their practical effect is to prevent all but the wealthy from living there. It is a form of racial or socioeconomic discrimination which we have repeatedly condemned. If the party attacking the ordinance establishes that it was enacted for an exclusionary purpose or has an exclusionary effect, then the ordinance will be annulled.

In *Berenson* we reviewed an ordinance which made no provision for low- or moderate-income housing in undeveloped areas of the municipality. We held that there must be a legitimate basis for such exclusions; limitations on development will be permitted only if the ordinance satisfies the needs of the community and also reflects a consideration of regional needs and requirements. We stated, however, that our concern was not "whether the zones, in themselves, are balanced communities, but whether the town itself, as provided by its zoning ordinances, will be a balanced and integrated community" (*Berenson v. Town of New Castle, supra*, 38 N.Y.2d at 109, 378 N.Y.S.2d 672, 341 N.E.2d 236). Constitutional principles are not necessarily offended if one or several uses are not included in a particular area or district of the community as long as adequate provision is made to accommodate the needs of the community and the region generally.

Applying these decisions plaintiffs' second cause of action does not state a claim of exclusionary zoning. New York City does not now nor has it ever excluded low-cost housing in Chinatown or in the City generally. Low-income families now live in the District and will continue to live there, hopefully in rehabilitated or newly constructed low-cost housing, if the purposes of the amendment are fulfilled.

Plaintiffs nevertheless contend that the amendment must be annulled because its effect will be exclusionary. They assert that not only will presently available sites be limited to luxury housing but they predict that new development will force them from their homes and, because the change in zoning favors construction of mixed-income apartments, present structures will be replaced by living accommodations they cannot afford. They note that the constitutional validity of zoning rests on the exercise of the police power for the general welfare and that the general welfare is no more abused by zoning which excludes the poor from a community than by zoning which forces them out of the community. Thus, their complaint seeks an order of the court compelling the City to provide low-cost housing, relief similar to that afforded in the *Mount Laurel* cases. Having failed to sustain that argument in the Appellate Division, they have adopted in this court the position of the Appellate Division dissenters that the *Berenson* rule prohibiting exclusionary zoning must be modified to define the "community" for zoning purposes as the 14–block area of the Special Manhattan Bridge District.

Berenson cannot reasonably be extended to the facts presented here. The City is the governing authority, not the District and this action challenges its laws. When enacting them, City officials must address the needs of the broader community and must act not only for benefit of the District and its residents, but for the benefit of the City as a whole. Requiring City planners to include particular uses in every district may be truly obnoxious to the City's over-all development, however, and applying the *Berenson* rule to a district as small as this 14–block area could defeat the intended purpose of special district zoning. The interpretation plaintiffs seek also runs counter to the rationale underlying the *Berenson* decision. That holding was deemed necessary to avoid the parochialism of elected local officials in communities which excluded minorities and socioeconomic groups from undeveloped areas of their municipalities to cater to a favored constituency. But here the question of exclusion relates to a Special District in the most highly developed municipality in the Nation, one which already has made extensive allowance for a variety of housing opportunities within its boundaries. * * *

Both *Mount Laurel* and *Berenson* examined the limits expanding suburban communities could impose on the type of growth within their boundaries. This action, however, concerns a densely developed area in New York City with substantial low-cost housing, deteriorating to be sure, but bordering on an area of Chinatown containing modern public housing and in a City containing much more. Plaintiffs seek not to overcome exclusionary practices or to correct some past inequity by implementing an existing lawful State-wide legislative policy, as in *Mount Laurel*, but to overturn the considered decision of the executive and legislative branches of New York City's government because they believe the City's chosen remedy for this established area will prove inadequate. * * *

In our prior decisions we have not compelled the City to facilitate the development of housing specifically affordable to lower-income households; a zoning plan is valid if the municipality provides an array of opportunities for housing facilities. We conclude that we should not extend that rule in this case. Those charged with the duty of addressing the problems of Chinatown chose to rezone the Manhattan Bridge area and provide housing incentives they deemed most suitable. They have attempted to use incentive zoning to provide realistic housing opportunities which include new apartments for the poor. Nothing in the legislative plan suggests that it will fail its purpose and plaintiffs do not allege that the solution is arbitrary or capricious or undertaken for an improper purpose, only that they would have zoned the area differently, or better, to avoid a potential future problem. Their allegations fail to state a cause of action entitling them to judicial relief. * * *

UNITED STATES v. STARRETT CITY ASSOCIATES

United States Court of Appeals, Second Circuit, 1988.
840 F.2d 1096, cert. denied, 488 U.S. 946, 109 S.Ct. 376, 102 L.E.2d. 365.

MINER, CIRCUIT JUDGE:

The United States Attorney General, on behalf of the United States ("the government"), commenced this action under Title VIII of the Civil Rights Act of 1968 ("Fair Housing Act" or "the Act") against defendants-appellants Starrett City Associates, Starrett City, Inc. and Delmar Management Company (collectively, "Starrett") in the United States District Court for the Eastern District of New York. The government maintained that Starrett's practices of renting apartments in its Brooklyn housing complex solely on the basis of applicants' race or national origin, and of making apartments unavailable to black and hispanic applicants that are then made available to white applicants, violate section 804(a), (b), (c) and (d) of the Act.

The parties made cross-motions for summary judgment based on extensive documentary submissions. The district court granted summary judgment in favor of the government and permanently enjoined appellants from discriminating on the basis of race in the rental of apartments. Starrett appeals from this judgment. * * *

Appellants constructed, own and operate "Starrett City," the largest housing development in the nation, consisting of 46 high-rise buildings containing 5,881 apartments in Brooklyn, New York. The complex's rental office opened in December 1973. Starrett has made capital contributions of $19,091,000 to the project, the New York State Housing Finance Agency has made $362,720,000 in mortgage loans, and the U.S. Department of Housing and Urban Development subsidizes Starrett's monthly mortgage interest payments. The United Housing Foundation abandoned a project to build a development of cooperative apartments at the Starrett City site in 1971. Starrett proposed to construct rental units on the site on the condition that the New York City Board of Estimate approve a transfer to Starrett of the city real estate tax abatement granted to the original project. The transfer created "substantial community opposition" because "the neighborhood surrounding the project and past experience with subsidized housing" created fear that "the conversion to rental apartments would result in Starrett City's becoming an overwhelmingly minority development." *United States v. Starrett City Assocs.*, 660 F.Supp. 668, 670 (E.D.N.Y.1987). The transfer was approved, however, "upon the assurance of Starrett City's developer that it was intended to create a racially integrated community." *Id.*

Starrett has sought to maintain a racial distribution by apartment of 64% white, 22% black and 8% hispanic at Starrett City. Starrett claims that these racial quotas are necessary to prevent the loss of white tenants, which would transform Starrett City into a predominantly minority complex. Starrett points to the difficulty it has had in attracting an integrated applicant pool from the time Starrett City opened, despite extensive advertising and promotional efforts. Because of these purported difficulties, Starrett adopted a tenanting procedure to promote and maintain the desired racial balance. This procedure has resulted in relatively stable percentages of whites and minorities living at Starrett City between 1975 and the present.

The tenanting procedure requires completion of a preliminary information card stating, *inter alia,* the applicant's race or national origin, family composition, income and employment. The rental office at Starrett City receives and reviews these applications. Those that are found preliminarily eligible, based on family composition, income, employment and size of apartment sought, are placed in "the active file," in which separate records by race are maintained for apartment sizes and income levels. Applicants are told in an acknowledgement letter that no apartments are presently available, but that their applications have been placed in the active file and that they will be notified when a unit becomes available for them. When an apartment becomes available, applicants are selected from the active file for final processing, creating a processed applicant pool. As vacancies arise, applicants of a race or national origin similar to that of the departing tenants are selected from the pool and offered apartments.

In December 1979, a group of black applicants brought an action against Starrett in the United States District Court for the Eastern District of New York. * * * Plaintiffs alleged that Starrett's tenanting procedures violated federal and state law by discriminating against them on the basis of race. The parties stipulated to a settlement in May 1984, and a consent decree was entered subsequently, *see Arthur v. Starrett City Assocs.,* No. 79–CV–3096 (E.D.N.Y. April 2, 1985). The decree provided that Starrett would, depending on apartment availability, make an additional 35 units available each year for a five-year period to black and minority applicants.

The government commenced the present action against Starrett in June 1984, "to place before the [c]ourt the issue joined but left expressly unresolved" in the *Arthur* consent decree: the "legality of defendants' policy and practice of limiting the number of apartments available to minorities in order to maintain a prescribed degree of racial balance." *United States v. Starrett City Assocs.,* 605 F.Supp. 262, 263 (E.D.N.Y. 1985). The complaint alleged that Starrett, through its tenanting policies, discriminated in violation of the Fair Housing Act. * * *

Title VIII of the Civil Rights Act of 1968 ("Fair Housing Act" or "the Act") was enacted pursuant to Congress' thirteenth amendment powers "to provide, within constitutional limitations, for fair housing throughout the United States." 42 U.S.C. § 3601. Section 3604 of the statute prohibits discrimination because of race, color or national origin in the sale or rental of housing by, *inter alia:* (1) refusing to rent or make available any dwelling; (2) offering discriminatory "terms, conditions or privileges" of rental; (3) making, printing or publishing "any notice, statement, or advertisement * * * that indicates any preference, limitation, or discrimination based on race, color * * * or national origin"; and (4) representing to any person "that any dwelling is not available for * * * rental when such dwelling is in fact so available."

Housing practices unlawful under Title VIII include not only those motivated by a racially discriminatory purpose, but also those that disproportionately affect minorities. Section 3604 "is designed to ensure that no one is denied the right to live where they choose for discriminatory reasons." *See Southend Neighborhood Improv. Ass'n v. County of St. Clair,* 743 F.2d 1207, 1210 (7th Cir.1984). Although "not every denial, especially a temporary denial, of low-income public housing has a discriminatory impact on racial minorities" in violation of Title VIII, an action leading to discriminatory effects on the availability of housing violates the Act, *see Southend Neighborhood Improv. Ass'n,* 743 F.2d at 1209–10.

Starrett's allocation of public housing facilities on the basis of racial quotas, by denying an applicant access to a unit otherwise available solely because of race, produces a "discriminatory effect * * * [that] could hardly be clearer." *Burney v. Housing Auth.,* 551 F.Supp. 746, 770 (W.D.Pa.1982). Appellants do not contend that the plain language of section 3604 does not proscribe their practices. Rather, they claim to be "clothed with governmental authority" and thus obligated, under *Otero v. New York City Housing Auth.,* 484 F.2d 1122 (2d Cir.1973), to effectuate the purpose of the Fair Housing Act by affirmatively promoting integration and preventing "the reghettoization of a model integrated community." We need not decide whether Starrett is a state actor, however. Even if Starrett were a state actor with such a duty, the racial quotas and related practices employed at Starrett City to maintain integration violate the antidiscrimination provisions of the Act.

Both Starrett and the government cite to the legislative history of the Fair Housing Act in support of their positions. This history consists solely of statements from the floor of Congress. These statements reveal "that at the time that Title VIII was enacted, Congress believed that strict adherence to the antidiscrimination provisions of the [A]ct" would eliminate "racially discriminatory housing practices [and] ultimately would result in residential integration." *Burney,* 551 F.Supp. at 769. Thus, Congress saw the antidiscrimination policy as the means to effect the antisegregation-integration policy. While quotas promote Title VIII's integration policy, they contravene its antidiscrimination policy, bringing the dual goals of the Act into conflict. The legislative history provides no further guidance for resolving this conflict.

We therefore look to analogous provisions of federal law enacted to prohibit segregation and discrimination as guides in determining to what extent racial criteria may be used to maintain integration. Both the thirteenth amendment, pursuant to which Title VIII was enacted, and the fourteenth amendment empower Congress to act in eradicating racial discrimination, and both the fourteenth amendment and Title VIII are informed by the congressional goal of eradicating racial discrimination through the principle of antidiscrimination. Further, the parallel between the antidiscrimination objectives of Title VIII and Title VII of the Civil Rights Act of 1964 has been recognized. Thus, the Supreme Court's analysis of what constitutes permissible race-conscious affirmative action under provisions of federal law with goals similar to those of Title VIII provides a framework for examining the affirmative use of racial quotas under the Fair Housing Act.

Although any racial classification is presumptively discriminatory, a race-conscious affirmative action plan does not necessarily violate federal constitutional or statutory provisions. However, a race-conscious plan cannot be "ageless in [its] reach into the past, and timeless in [its] ability to affect the future." *Wygant v. Jackson Bd. of Educ.,* 106 S.Ct. 1842, 1848 (1986) (plurality opinion). A plan employing racial distinctions must be temporary in nature with a defined goal as its termination point. Moreover, we observe that societal discrimination alone seems "insufficient and over expansive" as the basis for adopting so-called "benign" practices with discriminatory effects "that work against innocent people," *Wygant,* 106 S.Ct. at 1848, in the drastic and burdensome way that rigid racial quotas do. Furthermore, the use of quotas generally should be based on some history of racial discrimination or imbalance within the entity seeking to employ them. Finally, measures designed to increase or ensure minority participation, such as "access" quotas, have generally been upheld. However, programs designed to maintain integration by limiting minority participation, such as ceiling quotas, are of doubtful validity.

Starrett's use of ceiling quotas to maintain integration at Starrett City lacks each of these characteristics. First, Starrett City's practices have only the goal of integration maintenance. The quotas already have been in effect for ten years. Appellants predict that their race-conscious tenanting practices must continue for at least fifteen more years, but fail to explain adequately how that approximation was reached. In any event, these practices are far from temporary. Since the goal of integration maintenance is purportedly threatened by the potential for "white flight" on a continuing basis, no definite termination date for Starrett's quotas is perceivable. Second, appellants do not assert, and there is no evidence to show, the existence of prior racial discrimination or discriminatory imbalance adversely affecting whites within Starrett City or appellants' other complexes. On the contrary, Starrett City was initiated as an integrated complex, and Starrett's avowed purpose for employing race-based tenanting practices is to maintain that initial integration. Finally, Starrett's quotas do not provide minorities with access to Starrett City, but rather act as a ceiling to their access. Thus, the impact of appellants' practices falls squarely on minorities, for whom Title VIII was intended to open up housing opportunities. Starrett claims that its use of quotas serves to keep the numbers of minorities entering Starrett City low enough to avoid setting off a wave of "white flight." Although the "white flight" phenomenon may be a factor "take[n] into account in the integration equation," *Parent Ass'n of Andrew Jackson High School v. Ambach,* 598 F.2d 705, 720 (2d Cir. 1979), it cannot serve to justify attempts to maintain integration at Starrett City through inflexible racial quotas that are neither temporary in nature nor used to remedy past racial discrimination or imbalance within the complex.

Appellants' reliance on *Otero* is misplaced. In *Otero* the New York City Housing Authority ("NYCHA") relocated over 1800 families in the Lower East Side of Manhattan to make way for the construction of new apartment buildings. Pursuant to its regulations, NYCHA offered the former site occupants first priority of returning to any housing built within the urban renewal area. However, because the response by the largely minority former site residents seeking to return was nearly seven times greater than expected, NYCHA declined to follow its regulation in order to avoid creating a "pocket ghetto" that would "tip" an integrated community towards a predominantly minority community. It instead rented up half of these apartments to non-former site occupants, 88% of whom were white.

In a suit brought by former site occupants who were denied the promised priority, the district court held as a matter of law that "affirmative action to achieve racially balanced communities was not permitted where it would result in depriving minority groups" of public housing, and thus granted summary judgment in favor of plaintiffs. This court reversed the grant of summary judgment, stating that public housing authorities had a federal constitutional and statutory duty "to fulfill, as much as possible, the goal of open, integrated residential housing patterns and to prevent the increase of segregation, in ghettos," but we recognized that "the effect in some instances might be to prevent some members of a racial minority from residing in publicly assisted housing in a particular location." *Id.* at 1133–34.

Otero does not, however, control in this case. The challenge in *Otero* did not involve procedures for the long-term maintenance of specified levels of integration, but rather, the rental of 171 of 360 new apartments to non-former site occupants, predominantly white, although former site residents, largely minority, sought those apartments and were entitled to priority under NYCHA's own regulation. The *Otero* court did not delineate the statutory or constitutional limits on permissible means of integration, but held only that NYCHA's rent-up practice could not be declared invalid as a matter of law under those limits. In fact, the court in *Otero* observed that the use of race-conscious tenanting practices might allow landlords "to engage in social engineering, subject only to general undefined control through judicial supervision" and could "constitute a form of unlawful racial discrimination." *Id.* at 1136.

It is particularly important to note that the NYCHA action challenged in *Otero* only applied to a single event—the initial rent up of the new complexes—and determined tenancy in the first instance alone. NYCHA sought only to prevent the immediate creation of a "pocket ghetto" in the Lower East Side, which had experienced a steady loss of white population, that would tip the precarious racial balance there, resulting in increased white flight and inevitable "non-white ghettoization of the community." *Id.* at 1124. Further, the suspension of NYCHA's regulation did not operate as a strict racial quota, because the former site residents entitled to a rental priority were approximately 40% white. As a one-time measure in response to the special circumstances of the Lower East Side in the early 1970's, the action challenged in *Otero* had an impact on non-whites as a group far less burdensome or discriminatory than Starrett City's continuing practices.

We do not intend to imply that race is always an inappropriate consideration under Title VIII in efforts to promote integrated housing. We hold only that Title VIII does not allow appellants to use rigid racial quotas of indefinite duration to maintain a fixed level of integration at Starrett City by restricting minority access to scarce and desirable rental accommodations otherwise available to them. * * *

JON O. NEWMAN, CIRCUIT JUDGE, dissenting:

Congress enacted the Fair Housing Act to prohibit racial segregation in housing. Starrett City is one of the most successful examples in the Nation of racial integration in housing. I respectfully dissent because I do not believe that Congress intended the Fair Housing Act to prohibit the maintenance of racial integration in private housing. * * *

The development of Starrett City as an apartment complex committed to a deliberate policy of maintained racial integration has at all times occurred with the knowledge, encouragement, and financial support of the agency of the United States directly concerned with housing, the Department of Housing and Urban Development (HUD). Under a contract between HUD and Starrett City, the federal government pays all but one percent of the debt service of the mortgage loan extended to Starrett City by the New York State Housing Finance Agency (HFA). By March 1986 HUD had paid HFA more than $211 million on Starrett City's behalf. In exchange for this interest subsidy, Starrett City agreed to limit the rent for eligible tenants to a monthly figure specified by HUD or to a stated percentage of the tenant's monthly income (initially 25%, now 30%), whichever is greater. In addition, HUD has provided rental subsidies for tenants with low incomes. Since 1981 these rental subsidies have been nearly $22 million a year.

Despite its close cooperation in the development of Starrett City as an integrated housing complex, the United States now sues Starrett City to force it to abandon the rental policies that have enabled it to maintain racial integration. The bringing of the suit raises a substantial question as to the Government's commitment to integrated housing. The timing of the suit puts that commitment further in doubt. In 1979 a class of Black applicants for housing at Starrett City brought suit to challenge on federal statutory and constitutional grounds the same tenant selection policies at issue in this case. *Arthur v. Starrett City Associates,* 79 Civ. 3096 (ERN) (E.D.N.Y.1979). With the federal government observing from the sidelines, the parties to the *Arthur* litigation engaged in protracted settlement negotiations. More than four years later, a mutually advantageous settlement was reached. Starrett City was permitted to continue its policy of maintaining integration through its tenant selection policies. In return, Starrett City agreed to increase by three percent over five years the proportion of rental units occupied by minority tenants. At the same time, DHCR, the state housing agency, which was also a defendant in the *Arthur* litigation, agreed to take affirmative steps to promote housing opportunities for minorities in DHCR-supervised housing projects in New York City. Specifically, the State agency agreed to give a priority in other projects to minority applicants on the Starrett City waiting list. No member of the class of minority applicants for housing at Starrett City objected to the settlement. Thus, the needs of the minority class for whose benefit the suit had been brought were met to their satisfaction by providing for more rental opportunities both at Starrett City and elsewhere. Just one month after that settlement was reached, the United States filed this suit, ostensibly concerned with vindication of the rights of the same minority applicants for housing who had just settled their dispute on favorable terms.

The only issue in this case is whether Starrett City's rental policies violate Title VIII of the Civil Rights Act of 1968, generally known as the "Fair Housing Act." * * * In my view, the defendants are entitled to prevail simply on the statutory issue to which the Government has limited its lawsuit. Though the terms of the statute literally encompass the defendants' actions, the statute was never intended to apply to such actions. This statute was intended to bar perpetuation of segregation. To apply it to bar maintenance of integration is precisely contrary to the congressional policy "to provide, within constitutional limitations, for fair housing throughout the United States." 42 U.S.C. § 3601. * * *

Title VIII bars discriminatory housing practices in order to end segregated housing. Starrett City is not promoting segregated housing. On the contrary, it is maintaining integrated housing. It is surely not within the spirit of the Fair Housing Act to enlist the Act to bar integrated housing. Nor is there any indication that application of the statute toward such a perverse end was within the intent of those who enacted the statute. * * * Starrett City is committed to the proposition that Blacks and Whites shall live next to each other. A law enacted to enhance the opportunity for people of all races to live next to each other should not be interpreted to prevent a landlord from maintaining one of the most successful integrated housing projects in America.

None of the legislators who enacted Title VIII ever expressed a view on whether they wished to prevent the maintenance of racially balanced housing. Most of those who passed this statute in 1968 probably could not even contemplate a private real estate owner who would deliberately set out to achieve a racially balanced tenant population. Had they thought of such an eventuality, there is not the slightest reason to believe that they would have raised their legislative hands against it.

This Circuit has previously ruled that Title VIII does not apply literally to prohibit racially based rental policies adopted to promote integration. *Otero v. New York City Housing Authority,* 484 F.2d 1122 (2d Cir.1973). * * * Our case is much easier than *Otero.* Starrett City is not seeking to be released from a commitment it has previously made to any of the applicants for housing. To prevail it need not find in Title VIII some affirmative obligation compelling it to promote integration. It has freely chosen to promote integration and is entitled to prevail unless something in Title VIII forbids its voluntary policy. If anything in Title VIII prohibited race-conscious rental policies adopted to promote integration, *Otero* would have been summarily decided against the defendant.

Acknowledging the significance of the ruling in *Otero,* the Court distinguishes it essentially on the ground that *Otero* involved a policy of limited duration, applicable only to the period in which those displaced from the site were applying for housing in the new project, whereas Starrett City seeks to pursue a long-term policy of maintaining integration. I see nothing in the text or legislative history of Title VIII that supports such a distinction. If, as the Court holds, Title VIII bars Starrett City's race-conscious rental policy, even though adopted to promote and maintain integration, then it would bar such policies whether adopted on a short-term or a long-term basis. Since the Act makes no distinction among the durations of rental policies alleged to violate its terms, *Otero's* upholding of a race-conscious rental policy adopted to promote integration cannot be ignored simply because the policy was of limited duration.[4] * * *

Whether integration of private housing complexes should be maintained through the use of race-conscious rental policies that deny minorities an equal opportunity to rent is a highly controversial issue of social policy. There is a substantial argument against imposing any artificial burdens on minorities in their quest for housing. On the other hand, there is a substantial argument against forcing an integrated housing complex to become segregated, even if current conditions make integration feasible only by means of imposing some extra delay on minority applicants for housing. Officials of the Department of Justice are

---

4. The Court, drawing a parallel between Title VIII and Title VII, which bars discrimination in employment, supports its view of Title VIII with Supreme Court decisions approving only limited use of race-conscious remedies under statutory and constitutional standards in the employment context. Though Titles VIII and VII share a common objective of combatting discrimination, their differing contexts preclude the assumption that the law of affirmative action developed for employment is readily applicable to housing. The Title VII cases have not been concerned with a "tipping point" beyond which a work force might become segregated. Yet that is a demonstrated fact of life in the context of housing. *Cf. Parent Ass'n of Andrew Jackson High School v. Ambach,* 598 F.2d 705, 718–20 (2d Cir.1979) (recognizing validity of a "tipping point" concern in the public school context in the course of framing a remedial desegregation decree). The statutory issue arising under Title VIII should be decided on the basis of what practices Congress was proscribing when it enacted this provision. Whether the constitutional standards for affirmative action differ between the employment and housing contexts need not be considered since the Government has explicitly declined in this litigation to advance any claim of unconstitutional action.

entitled to urge the former policy. Respected civil rights advocates like the noted psychologist, Dr. Kenneth Clark, are entitled to urge the latter policy, as he has done in an affidavit filed in this suit. That policy choice should be left to the individual decisions of private property owners unless and until Congress or the New York legislature decides for the Nation or for New York that it prefers to outlaw maintenance of integration. I do not believe Congress made that decision in 1968, and it is a substantial question whether it would make such a decision today. Until Congress acts, we should not lend our authority to the result this lawsuit will surely bring about. In the words of Dr. Clark:

> [I]t would be a tragedy of the highest magnitude if this litigation were to lead to the destruction of one of the model integrated communities in the United States.

Because the Fair Housing Act does not require this tragedy to occur, I respectfully dissent.

SECTION D.　PAYING THE CITY'S EXPENSES

1.　RAISING REVENUE BY IMPOSING COSTS ON OR OFFERING INDUCEMENTS TO BUSINESS ACTIVITY

The manner in which a city exercises its power to raise and spend revenue affects the internal life of cities just as crucially as its regulation of city activity or its condemnation of city property. The topic of city taxation and finance, however, is so vast and complex that it can easily fill an entire casebook.[1] In order to avoid a truncated (and therefore inadequate) treatment of the problems raised by local taxation, borrowing and expenditures, this section will focus solely on a number of innovative methods cities are now employing in the effort to solve their fiscal problems.

Chapter Two of this casebook explored the most important current limitation on a city's ability to generate revenue: the state power's to control city decisionmaking. States not only control the nature and extent of city taxation[2] but also commonly restrict cities' authority to borrow money.[3] The exercise of this state power to decide how much revenue cities can raise contributes to many cities' chronic lack of funds.

---

1. See, e.g., J. Hellerstein and W. Hellerstein, Cases on State and Local Taxation (5th ed. 1988); O. Oldman and F. Schoettle, State and Local Taxes and Finance: Text, Problems and Cases (1974).

2. See generally, Advisory Commission on Intergovernmental Relations, Significant Features of Fiscal Federalism 1992 Edition, Volume 1, p. 18; 4 Sands & Libonati, Local Government Law, Chapter 23 (1993); Cohn, Municipal Revenue Powers in the Context of Constitutional Home Rule, 51 Nw.U.L.Rev. 27 (1956).

3. See, e.g., Municipal Building Authority v. Lowder, in Chapter Three. See generally, 3 Sands & Libonati, Local Government Law, Chapter 25 (1993); Gelfand (ed.), State and Local Government Debt Financing (1985); Bowman, The Anachronism Called Debt Limitation, 52 Iowa L.Rev. 863 (1967); Advisory Commission on Intergovernmental Relations, State Constitutional Restrictions on Local Government Debt (1961).

Moreover, as we have seen, state mandates of city expenditures[4] and state-imposed reallocation of city-generated funds to neighboring jurisdictions[5] add to this pervasive strain on city budgets.

State-imposed controls on city income and expenditures, however, constitute only one of the reasons that many cities have begun to seek innovative ways to raise revenue. Another impetus derives from the problem of relying on taxation as a principal source of funds. The defects in the property tax—the traditional (and still most important) source of local income—have become the subject of an enormous literature. The National Commission on Urban Problems, for example, has criticized the property tax for imposing a disproportionately heavy burden on housing (residential property makes up roughly half of the tax base), for deterring housing maintenance (taxes increase as the value of the property increases), for imposing an unfair burden on the poor (the poor spend a larger percentage of their income on housing than do the rich), and for being unfairly administered (the task of assessing property values is fraught with complexity and the risk of unequal treatment.)[6] In many states, however, shifting the burden of the property tax from homeowners to businesses involves a constitutional amendment because the state constitutions require uniform property taxes on all property within any single jurisdiction.[7] (One city's effort to promote a constitutional amendment that would permit the classification of property for tax purposes was examined above in Anderson v. Boston.)[8] To be sure, the validity of the complaints against the property tax are hotly debated in the economics literature.[9] Nevertheless it seems clear that the widespread popular resentment against local property taxes has fueled a considerable reaction against them, as exemplified by California's Proposition 13, which added a state constitutional limitation on property tax increases.[10] Reliance on the property tax has thus declined over the last forty years and is likely to continue to do so in the future.[11]

The normal alternatives to the property tax—the sales and income taxes—have, however, generated considerable problems of their own. Local sales taxes have risen sharply in recent years and now constitute 6% of local revenue.[12] But many experts argue that local sales taxes

---

4. See, e.g., City of La Grande v. Public Employees Retirement Board in Chapter Two. See generally, Advisory Commission on Intergovernmental Relations, Mandates: Cases in State–Local Relations (1990).

5. See, e.g., Edgewood Independent School District v. Kirby in Chapter Three.

6. National Commission on Urban Problems, Building the American City 358–59 (1969).

7. See, e.g., Idaho Telephone Co. v. Baird, 91 Idaho 425, 423 P.2d 337 (1967).

8. See Chapter Two.

9. See, e.g., Aronson & Hilley, Financing State and Local Governments 120–41 (4th ed. 1986); R. & P. Musgrave, Public Finance in Theory and Practice 469–94 (4th ed. 1984); Oldman & Schoettle, State and Local Taxation and Finance 348–386 (1974).

10. See generally, Stocker, Proposition 13: A Ten Year Retrospective (1991); Heckart, Proposition 13 Ten Years Later: A Selected Bibliography (1988).

11. Advisory Commission on Intergovernmental Relations, Significant Features of Fiscal Federalism 1992 Edition, Volume 2, Table 61.

12. Advisory Commission on Intergovernmental Relations, Significant Features of Fiscal Federalism 1992 Edition, Volume 2, Table 61.

cause a decline in the amount of retail business activity in the city levying the tax [13] and that the sales tax (like the property tax) imposes a disproportionate burden on the poor.[14]   Similar criticisms have been expressed about the efforts of an increasing number of cities to impose local income taxes (particularly if only city residents are taxed).[15]   Given the many alternative places to shop or to live in regional areas, these critics argue, imposition of local sales or income taxes can easily be counterproductive: they can lead not to city prosperity but to city decline.

Although reliance on city taxes obviously cannot be eliminated in the foreseeable future, many cities have begun to explore alternatives. In the 1960's and 1970's, the most popular alternative consisted of obtaining grants-in-aid from the federal government; over the last twenty-five years, however, the percentage of local budgets supported by these federal grants has substantially declined.[16]   Another alternative— borrowing money to pay for essential city services—is clearly not a viable option, although New York City had to learn this lesson the hard way.[17] Counting on transfer payments from other governments or on borrowing money just to keep even leaves cities in a vulnerable position.   Cities have to find ways of obtaining their own funds without raising taxes.

The first two cases reproduced below explore two devices designed to avoid imposing general taxes on a city's citizens (or property owners or wage earners).   In both cases, the cities sought to levy charges solely on selected individuals or businesses.   In Simmons v. City of Moscow, the city sought to fund the reconstruction of its downtown area through a

---

13. For a discussion of this and other economic policy aspects of the tax, see, e.g., Oldman & Schoettle, State and Local Taxation and Finance 483–522 (1974); see also Fox, The Personal Income Tax as a Component of State Tax Structure, 39 Vand. L.Rev. 1081, 1089 (1986).

14. See, e.g., J. Aronson & J. Hilley, Financing State and Local Governments 86–102 (4th ed. 1986).   For a general review of legal issues involved in the imposition of local sales taxes, see Hellerstein, Significant Sales and Use Tax Developments During the Past Half Century, 39 Vand.L.Rev. 961 (1986).

15. Id.   See generally, Oakland, Central Cities: Fiscal Plight and Prospects for Reform, in Mieszkowski & Straszheim, Current Issues in Urban Economics 322–58 (1979); Legislative Developments, The Limits of Municipal Income Taxation: The Response in Ohio, 7 Harv.J.Legis. 271 (1970). For statistical data concerning local income taxes, see Advisory Commission on Intergovernmental Relations, Significant Features of Fiscal Federalism 1992 Edition, Volume 1, Tables 23–24 and Volume 2, Table 61.

16. Advisory Commission on Intergovernmental Relations, Significant Features of Fiscal Federalism 1992 Edition, Volume 2, Table 61.   For an analysis of the legal issues raised by federal grants-in-aid, see Michelman & Sandalow, Materials on Government in Urban Areas: Cases, Comments, Questions 970–1212 (1970); Cappalli, Restoring Federalism Values in the Federal Grant System, 19 The Urban Lawyer 493 (1987); Cappalli, The Emerging Law of Federal Assistance, 59 Wash.U.L.Q. 1153 (1982); Cappalli, Mandates Attached to Federal Grants: Sweet and Sour Federalism, 13 The Urban Lawyer 143 (1981); Cappalli, Federal Grants and the New Statutory Tort: State and Local Officials Beware!, 12 The Urban Lawyer 445 (1980). See also, Lawrence County v. Lead–Deadwood School District in Chapter Two.

17. See generally, Gelfand, Seeking Local Government Financial Integrity Through Debt Ceilings, Tax Limitations, and Expenditures Limits: The New York City Fiscal Crisis, the Taxpayers' Revolt, and Beyond, 63 Minn.L.Rev. 545 (1979). See also Griffith, The Federal Guaranty of Municipal Debt: Will Federalism Survive? 19 The Urban Lawyer 583 (1987).

special assessment on neighboring property owners. In Emerson College v. City of Boston, the city sought to pay for its fire services by charging owners of large buildings (but not the average property owner) for fire protection. Although the devices employed by these cities—special assessment and user charges—are by no means new ideas,[18] both cases represent innovative attempts to expand these sources of income. In reading the cases, consider the meaning of (and the justification for) the different standards that the courts articulate in deciding whether a city is allowed to obtain additional revenue from some of its citizens or property owners but not others. When are such selectively imposed revenue exactions appropriate?

The same question is raised by the law review excerpt that follows the two cases. The excerpt is from an article by Fred Bosselman and Nancy Stroud analyzing the attempts of San Francisco and Boston to require office building developers to build (or pay for) additional city housing as a condition to proceeding with their commercial ventures.[19] Is the "rational nexus" test that the authors discuss the same as the "rough proportionality test" announced in Dolan v. City of Tigard, the case that follows the excerpt? Are the kinds of exactions that Bosselman and Stroud describe unconstitutional under *Dolan*? Could *Dolan* also invalidate New York City's proposed contract, considered in Municipal Art Society v. City of New York, conditioning city zoning approval of a high density office building on the builder's agreement both to improve a subway station and to pay the city more for its land? What impact does *Dolan* have on the ability of cities to impose special assessments and user fees?

Of course, a more fundamental question is whether it is a good idea for cities to seek to improve their financial condition by imposing taxes or charges on selected business activity. Are these kinds of impositions on the private sector counter-productive? In fact, would cities better improve their own (and their citizens') financial status if they adopted the opposite policy—giving businesses inducements to move to town rather than exacting money from them if they do? The final case in this section, Common Cause v. State, considers the legality of this alternative strategy. Instead of raising money from the private sector to pay for city programs, the city of Portland (with the state's help) raised money to support a business venture. Is it (and should it be) easier for cities to raise money *for* specific companies in the private sector than to raise

18. For a general survey of the law governing special assessments, see 4 Sands & Libonati, Local Government Law, Chapter 24 (1993); 14 McQuillin, Municipal Corporations, Chapter 38 (3d ed. 1985).

19. For an analysis of exactions of this kind, see e.g., Sterk, Competition Among Municipalities as a Constraint on Land Use Exactions, 45 Vand. L. Rev. 831 (1992); Been, "Exit" as a Constraint on Land Use Exactions: Rethinking the Unconstitutional Conditions Doctrine, 91 Colum. L. Rev. 473 (1991); Note, Municipal Exactions, the Rational Nexus Text, and the Federal Constitution, 102 Harv. L. Rev. 992 (1989); Frank & Rhodes, (eds.) Development Exactions (1987); Exactions: A Controversial New Source for Municipal Funds, 50 Law & Contemporary Problems (1987).

money *from* specific companies in the private sector? Is this type of city strategy likely to pay off in the long run? [20]

SIMMONS v. CITY OF MOSCOW

Supreme Court of Idaho, 1986.
111 Idaho 14, 720 P.2d 197.

HUNTLEY, JUSTICE.

This case arises from challenges by property owners to assessments levied by the City of Moscow ("the City") pursuant to I.C. §§ 50–1701 through 50–1770. In June, 1980, the City formed Local Improvement District No. 94 to pay approximately one-half of the $1,600,000 cost of a downtown revitalization project, the other one-half being supplied by federal matching funds. The project consisted of construction of new downtown improvements, reconstruction of deteriorated facilities, and addition of other downtown amenities, such as landscaping, street furniture, signage, and lighting. The project also included increased parking and expansion of an area known as "Friendship Square" to facilitate downtown activities and draw customers to the area.

The project was a response by business owners and civic leaders to their perception that downtown Moscow was losing business to two retail shopping malls on the outskirts of town, with the result that the downtown area was deteriorating. The major goal of the project was to maintain the downtown business district as a significant retail shopping area by (1) encouraging pedestrian traffic in the area; (2) improving access to and parking in the downtown area; (3) preventing further relocation of existing downtown businesses to the retail malls; (4) preventing a slide in property and rental values and in fact facilitating the enhancement of property values; (5) increasing safety by replacing an inadequate lighting system; (6) creating a fundamental unity downtown by providing consistent landscaping, lighting and street furnishings; (7) providing a downtown focus with the Friendship Square area; and (8) encouraging preservation and restoration of downtown buildings.

In the late 1970's a number of workshops and studies focused on goals and strategies for downtown revitalization. * * * The city council passed a resolution of intention to create the Local Improvement District, pursuant to I.C. § 50–1707, on May 22, 1980. That resolution provided notice that property assessments would be made "in proportion to the benefits derived to such property by said improvements." After notice and hearing (the "formation hearing"), the LID was duly formed by ordinance on June 7, 1980.

The city council * * * determined that benefits derived from the improvements were to be related to proximity to the central part of the district. The assessment plan consisted of three zones within the

20. For an argument rejecting such a strategy, see J. Jacobs, Cities and the Wealth of Nations (1984); for a limited endorsement, see Malloy, The Political Economy of Co–Financing America's Urban Renaissance, 40 Vand.L.Rev. 67 (1987).

district: primary, secondary and tertiary. Within each zone, costs would be assessed based on square footage of each parcel of property. The primary zone, consisting of the "core" area of downtown, was assessed at 100 percent of the cost per square foot of the improvements. The secondary zone, the area surrounding the primary zone, was assessed at 40 percent of per square foot cost, and the tertiary zone was assessed at 20 percent of per square foot cost. As a result, a parcel of property in the primary zone would be assessed at five times the amount assessed to a similar parcel in the tertiary zone and two-and-one-half times the amount assessed to a similar parcel in the secondary zone.   * * *

It is fundamental to assessment law that in order to validly assess costs of an improvement to affected property, the property must receive a special benefit, one that is more intense than that received by the rest of the municipality. 14 McQuillin, [Municipal Corporations] at §§ 38.31 and 38.32; 2 Antieau, *Municipal Corporation Law,* § 14.02. An assessment must be reasonably proportional to the special benefit derived, but the law does not require that an assessment correspond exactly to the benefits received. 14 McQuillin at § 38.05; *Bitter v. City of Lincoln,* 165 Neb. 201, 85 N.W.2d 302 (1957). "Benefits capable of easy demonstration and mathematical exactness are not necessary to support an assessment. The most any officer or tribunal can do in this regard is to estimate the benefits as to each tract of land upon as uniform a plan as may be in the light afforded by available information." *Bitter, supra,* at 308.

The term "benefit" is not defined by Idaho's local assessment statutes. While many other jurisdictions primarily measure special benefits by the difference between the fair market value of the property before and after assessment, "courts are increasingly acknowledging that the special benefit to property assessed if [sic] not to be measured solely by the changes in market value, if any, before and after the improvement." 2 Antieau, *supra,* at 14.34. It has been noted, too, that the broad question concerning an assessment is whether the general value of the property has been enhanced rather than whether the present owner receives advantage.   * * *

The fact that benefits conferred on property might not immediately be reflected in increased market value does not overcome the presumption of benefit. *Soo Line RR Co. v. City of Wilton,* 172 N.W.2d 74, 83 (N.D.1969). In *Soo Line,* the railroad urged that because its property was devoted to the business of operating the railroad, it did not derive any benefits from paving and other improvements to the street parallel to its property. In response to this argument the court responded:

> It certainly does not mean that before such an assessment can be levied and enforced the city must be able to show that by reason of the paving the abutting property has been advanced in market value to the extent of the assessment, or point out in detail the specific way and manner in which the requisite benefits are to be realized in the future. Were such to be the rule, few, if any, schemes of local

improvement at the expense of the property immediately affected could ever be accomplished. It is natural for the average property owner to resent the burden thus laid upon him, and he easily persuades himself that the thing for which he is asked to pay is a detriment, rather than a benefit, to his land, and ordinarily it is not difficult for him to find plenty of sympathizing neighbors who will unite in supporting his contention. Indeed, the benefits to be derived in such cases are ordinarily not instant upon the inception or completion of the improvement, but materialize with the developments of the future. They are none the less [sic] benefits because their full fruition is postponed, or because the present use to which the property is devoted is not of a character to be materially affected by the improvement.

In the instant case, the city has recognized that the goal and benefit envisioned by the business community, the downtown steering committee and the Moscow City Council was not simply an immediate increase in property values. The city identified a number of special benefits to the assessed property, including stabilization of property values and rents; improved access to downtown businesses; enhanced ability to use the downtown area for public activities; increased safety for downtown pedestrians and business customers; improved appearance of the downtown area; and increased likelihood of preservation and restoration of historic downtown buildings. There is extensive testimony which indicates that the city council considered these benefits in determining the method of assessment and the apportionment of costs. The city did not appraise the affected property before and after the improvements. Given the intangible and long-term nature of most of the benefits the city projected, such action would have been a purposeless effort and a useless expenditure of resources. Appraisal immediately after these improvements were completed would not be expected to show an immediate increase in market value—it may be years before the revitalization effort will yield the particular benefit, only one of many, of increased property values. We hold that the trial court's requirement of a "before and after" appraisal as the measure of benefits derived does not comport with a *practical* operation of the LID statutory scheme when a city selects the benefits derived method of assessment. * * *

A basic qualification of an assessment method is that there must be a factual correlation between the result of an assessment formula and the actual benefit conferred. The mere fact that area or frontage has been considered will not invalidate an assessment if it has been guided by the principle of apportioning expenses according to benefits. The "benefits derived" method of assessment provides a more flexible method of apportioning costs than the front or square footage methods. The front and square foot methods may be satisfactory where an improvement is limited in scope and of proportionally equal benefit to all affected properties. A sewer, a roadway or a water line are examples of such improvements. Where, as in the instant case, benefits are contemplated to be less immediate and measurable, a method of assessment based *solely* on front or square footage will be inadequate. Area (square footage) may, however, be considered as a factor in determining benefits. As such, square footage is simply one of many factors a tool which a municipality may use to reach an equitable distribution of costs in relation to benefits.

The use of zones based on proximity is also a common tool in assessing benefits of many types of improvements. The more distant a property is from major improvements, the less benefit that property realizes. * * * In *Wing v. City of Eugene,* the Eugene City Council established four zones based on proximity to a downtown parking garage, the closest property paying the largest assessment, the more distant properties paying lesser assessments. In confirming this method of assessment, the Oregon Supreme Court stated:

> Inevitably, some land uses will be more benefited than others, and some presently not at all. But if the city council's plan for assessing the cost reasonably takes into consideration these differences, a court will not strike it down because it is not exactly fitted to the prospective benefit of each. The special assessments are not bound by "a system of delusive exactness." * * * It is not necessary to refine the concept of benefits so as to make it serve equally each of the lots in the area. * * *

A number of cases also approve the use of square footage as a measure of benefits *within* zones.

We also disagree with the trial court's finding that the City was unable to supply any basis for applying the ratio of 100–40–20 to allocate improvement costs. Mr. Benson Neilson, an architect employed by TSG Architects, testified that the architectural firm had described to the steering committee and the city council a number of assessment methods, including use of a ratio. The city council deliberated over the methods available, considering a 100–50–20 ratio as well as the one ultimately selected. A ratio was chosen as a fair and equitable way to distribute improvement costs among the zones of proximity. * * *

The city presented ample evidence that the city council, in good faith and with adequate information before it, considered and selected a reasonable method of assessment. The method of assessment was in fact a "benefits derived" method, and the assessments levied appear to be reasonable approximations of value of the benefits derived by each property owner.

The property owners have not shown that the city council action in apportioning costs was fraudulent, oppressive, arbitrary, unjust, unreasonable or an abuse of discretion. In the absence of such a showing, the council's determination of assessment methodology must be affirmed. * * *

BISTLINE, JUSTICE, dissenting. * * *

The Court as a whole now recognizes that in circumstances such as those here present there are benefits which are general and there are benefits which are special.   * * * The majority speaks of a general enhancement to the "locality."   The "locality" here, in the majority view, is that encompassed by the three zones which have been assessed. I do not agree, but see instead that the entire environs encompassed in the Moscow city limits are the generally benefited "locality."   Anyone living in Moscow can point with pride to a revamped downtown district. Special benefits undoubtedly do accrue to those properties which are within the spruced-up area, and those properties should be assessed for those special benefits but only after all the property within the city has made a proper contribution for the general benefit.   This philosophy of fairness is in line with the majority's * * *: "It is fundamental to assessment law that in order to validly assess costs of improvement to affected property, the property must receive a special benefit, *one that is more intense than that received by the rest of the municipality.*" * * *

EMERSON COLLEGE v. CITY OF BOSTON

Supreme Judicial Court of Massachusetts, 1984.
391 Mass. 415, 462 N.E.2d 1098.

ABRAMS, JUSTICE.

In 1982, the Legislature conferred authority on the city of Boston to impose a charge for fire protection against the owners of certain buildings that "by reason of their size, type of construction, use and other relevant factors * * * require the city to employ additional firefighters, deploy additional equipment and purchase equipment different in kind from that required to provide fire protection for the majority of structures."   St.1982, c. 190, § 30.   Under the statute, the city "is authorized to impose a fee for augmented fire services availability pursuant to [St.1982, c. 190, § 30] or pursuant to an ordinance enacted by the city of Boston not inconsistent with [St.1982, c. 190, § 30]."

On February 16, 1983, after the plaintiff's suit was initiated, the Boston city council, acting pursuant to the statute, promulgated an ordinance establishing augmented fire services availability (AFSA).   The plaintiff's motion for a preliminary injunction against imposition of the AFSA charge was denied on February 24, 1983.   On the same date, the mayor of Boston approved the AFSA ordinance.   City of Boston Code, Ordinances, Title 14, § 459, as amended February 24, 1983.

The plaintiff, a tax exempt educational institution, owns fourteen buildings in the city, containing classrooms, administrative offices and dormitories.   These buildings were inspected by the fire department in December, 1982, to determine whether they were subject to the charge. On January 27, 1983, the plaintiff brought an action requesting a declaratory judgment and injunctive relief.   The plaintiff's complaint alleged that the AFSA charge is in effect a tax on real property from which Emerson is exempt.   The plaintiff also alleged that the AFSA charge violates the constitutional requirement that property taxes be "proportional and reasonable," Part II, C. 1, § 1, art. 4, of the Massachusetts Constitution.   * * * On April 1, 1983, the judge issued a memorandum and order declaring the statute and the ordinance invalid as applied to the plaintiff and facially unconstitutional, and enjoined their enforcement. * * *

The judge declared "that the money sought to be collected by the city under sec. 30 of Chapter 190 of the Acts of 1982 and/or Title 14, sec. 459 of the Ordinances of the City of Boston, approved by the Mayor on February 24, 1983 is a tax and not a fee." He noted that the plaintiff is a tax exempt institution. He then declared that the money "sought to be raised [was] a real estate tax and not an excise tax," and, further, that the tax was not "proportional and reasonable." See Part II, C. 1, § 1, art. 4, of the Massachusetts Constitution.[5] * * * We conclude that the AFSA charge is a chimera, bearing features of both a fee and a tax, but not valid in either form. Therefore, we affirm the judgment invalidating the statute and the ordinance.

We summarize the relevant provisions of the AFSA statute and ordinance, as well as pertinent testimony presented at the Superior Court hearing. The proclaimed purpose of the statute "is to assure the city's continued ability to provide the availability of fire fighting services in excess of the degree of such services provided to the general public by imposing the cost of making available such extra services on those to whom such extra services are made available." The statute thus distinguishes two classes of building owners. In one class are owners of buildings who are deemed members of the "general public," to whom fire protection services are made available without any charge beyond the annual property tax. In a distinct class are building owners who, by implication, are not considered members of the "general" public, and who, in addition to the property tax, if any, assessed against them, must pay an AFSA charge for the availability of fire protection. A building-owner is subject to the AFSA charge if the "total fire fighting capacity * * * necessary to extinguish a fully involved fire" in the building exceeds 3,500 "gallons per minute."

The statutory scheme is based on a legislative determination that a disproportionate percentage of the city of Boston's firefighting budget is

---

5. The city does not challenge the judge's determination that the AFSA charge, if classified as a real property tax rather than as a fee or excise, violates the requirements for real estate taxation set forth in Part II, C. 1, § 1, art. 4, of the Massachusetts Constitution. Because it is imposed on a minority of property owners, the charge fails to comport with the requirement that real estate taxation be proportional. Additionally, the charge is not imposed on an ad valorem basis. Cf. *Fairmont v. Pitrolo Pontiac–Cadillac Co.,* 308 S.E.2d 527 (W.Va.1983) (fire protection "fee" imposed on all buildings within city at rate of fifty-five cents per $100 of building's value constitutes ad valorem property tax, but invalid because in excess of constitutional limitations).

The city correctly refrains from arguing that the AFSA charge is a special assessment or amount due for a betterment. Cf. G.L. c. 80, § 1. Special assessments may be imposed for local improvements which enhance the value of real property, provided the assessments are not in substantial excess of the benefits received. The maintenance of eight and one-half fire companies necessary to extinguish fires at various buildings distributed throughout Boston is not a local improvement. Nor is any increase in the value of property containing AFSA structures apparent—instead, fire protection once included within the general property tax has been reclassified as a special service and an incremental cost imposed.

consumed by expenses related to the maintenance of equipment and personnel capable of protecting buildings with physical characteristics requiring, in the event of a fire, the presence of more than fourteen fire companies. The fire commissioner said that 3,500 gallons per minute is the functional equivalent of fourteen fire companies, the personnel and equipment necessary to combat a three-alarm fire. * * *

The statute requires that, prior to March 1 of each year, the fire commissioner determine not only which buildings in Boston are subject to the AFSA charge, but also the amount of the charge to be assessed each such building. A formula set forth in the statute establishes three principal factors to be considered by the fire commissioner in establishing whether, in the event of fire, a building would require more than 3,500 gallons per minute of firefighting capacity.

One factor, the "needed fire flow" (NFF), measures the personnel and equipment necessary to extinguish a fire in the building. The NFF is determined by reference to various subfactors: the building's construction type, including the fire resistance of its constituent materials; the effective area of the building in square footage; the use of the building, including the combustibility of its contents; and "exposure" and "connecting passageways" subfactors, which measure the risk that a fire would spread to adjacent buildings.

The second factor, the "life risk factor" (LRF), measures the personnel and equipment necessary to ensure the safety of the occupants of the burning building. The LRF takes into account the building's density of occupancy, hours of occupancy, number of stories, and whether the building contains smoke removal equipment.

The third factor is a "suppression credit" (SC), which operates to reduce the gallons per minute computation by an amount that reflects a building's existing fire suppression and detection equipment. The department's consultant indicated that a suppression credit is granted for smoke and heat detectors connected to an alarm at the fire department. A larger suppression credit may be obtained if a building has standpipes with outlets to which fire hoses can be connected. A building's sprinkler systems also reduce the total gallons per minute computation.

The three factors, as incorporated in the statutory formula, yield a "total fire flow" (TFF) computation expressed in gallons per minute. * * *

Our initial inquiry pertains to the nature of the monetary exaction imposed by the AFSA statute. The city argues that the judge erred in rejecting the statutory characterization of the charge as a fee, and in holding that the charge is a property tax. Consequently, the city alleges, the judge's conclusion that the plaintiff is insulated from paying the charge by the G.L. c. 59, § 5, property tax exemption was erroneous, as was the judge's determination that the statute is facially inconsistent with constitutional limitations on the taxing power.

In reviewing the statute, we are bound, as was the judge, to treat with deference the classification of the charge as a fee. "In any doubtful case, the intention of the Legislature, as it may be expressed in part through its characterization [of the charge] * * * deserves judicial respect, and especially so where the constitutionality of the exaction depends on its proper characterization", *Associated Indus. of Mass., Inc. v. Commissioner of Revenue,* 378 Mass. 657, 667 668, 393 N.E.2d 812 (1979). Ultimately, however, the nature of a monetary exaction "must be determined by its operation rather than its specially descriptive phrase." *Thomson Elec. Welding Co. v. Commonwealth,* 275 Mass. 426, 429, 176 N.E. 203 (1931).

With these considerations in mind, we turn to the question whether the AFSA charge is a fee. Fees imposed by a governmental entity tend to fall into one of two principal categories: user fees, based on the rights of the entity as proprietor of the instrumentalities used, or regulatory fees (including licensing and inspection fees), founded on the police power to regulate particular businesses or activities. Such fees share common traits that distinguish them from taxes: they are charged in exchange for a particular governmental service which benefits the party paying the fee in a manner "not shared by other members of society," *National Cable Television Ass'n v. United States,* 415 U.S. 336, 341, 94 S.Ct. 1146, 1149, 39 L.Ed.2d 370 (1974); they are paid by choice, in that the party paying the fee has the option of not utilizing the governmental service and thereby avoiding the charge, *Vanceburg v. Federal Energy Regulatory Comm'n,* 571 F.2d 630, 644 n. 48 (D.C.Cir.1977), cert. denied, 439 U.S. 818, 99 S.Ct. 79, 58 L.Ed.2d 108 (1978), and the charges are collected not to raise revenues but to compensate the governmental entity providing the services for its expenses.

The city emphasizes that the factors used to determine the amount of each AFSA assessment are related to the city's costs in providing AFSA protection and urges that, on this basis alone, the charge be characterized a fee. We agree that, in its correlation to the costs of funding the personnel and equipment constituting eight and one-half of Boston's fire companies, the AFSA charges bears some similarity to a user fee.

The AFSA charge fails, however, to comply with another essential characteristic of a fee. Fees are legitimate to the extent that the services for which they are imposed are sufficiently particularized as to justify distribution of the costs among a limited group (the "users," or beneficiaries, of the services), rather than the general public. The benefits of "augmented" fire protection are not limited to the owners of AFSA buildings. The capacity to extinguish a fire in any particular building safeguards not only the private property interests of the owner, but also the safety of the building's occupants as well as that of surrounding buildings and their occupants. In more sparsely populated areas, it may be possible to isolate private property interests in fire suppression from the property and safety interests of the public at large. In a large, densely populated city like Boston, "the prevention of damage to buildings by fire is an object which affects the interest of all the inhabitants and relieves them from a common burden and danger." *Fisher v. Boston,* 104 Mass. 87, 93 (1870).

That a particular building requires "augmented" rather than regular fire protection does not change the nature of the benefit conferred by the suppression of a fire in that building from one that is public to one that is limited to the owner of the building. The statutory formula controlling the assessment and computation of AFSA charges illustrates this by factoring in not only the firefighting capacity necessary to preserve a particular structure in the event of fire, but also the personnel and equipment necessary to safeguard the building's occupants and to prevent the spread of fire to adjacent buildings.

Further confirmation of the public nature of the benefit conferred by AFSA services may be derived from the fact that "use" of AFSA protection is compelled. Fees generally are charged for services voluntarily requested. If the benefits for which AFSA charges are imposed were limited to the owners of AFSA structures, rather than being essential to the public welfare, there would be no reason to depart from the optional character of a traditional fee.

Although we need go no further to sustain the judge's conclusion that the AFSA charge is not a fee, we note additionally that, by statutory command, the amounts collected through AFSA assessments are targeted not for the maintenance of the eight and one-half fire companies attributed to AFSA protection but to general "police and fire services." That revenue obtained from a particular charge is not used exclusively to meet expenses incurred in providing the service but is destined instead for a broader range of services or for a general fund, "while not decisive, is of weight in indicating that the charge is a tax." *Opinion of the Justices,* 250 Mass. at 597, 148 N.E. 889. The statutory earmarking of proceeds for non-AFSA services is more consistent with a revenue raising purpose than with an intent to recover AFSA-related expenditures. The AFSA charge thus resembles not a fee, but a tax, which has been defined as "an enforced contribution to provide for the support of government." *United States v. Tax Com'n of Miss.,* 421 U.S. 599, 606, 95 S.Ct. 1872, 1877, 44 L.Ed.2d 404 (1975). * * *

The AFSA charge does not conform to any constitutionally permissible form of monetary exaction. The judgment of the Superior Court, declaring St.1982, c. 190, § 30, and City of Boston Code, Ordinances, Title 14, § 459, as amended February 24, 1983, invalid, is affirmed.

FRED BOSSELMAN & NANCY STROUD, MANDATORY TITHES: THE LEGALITY OF LAND DEVELOPMENT LINKAGE

9 Nova L.J. 383, 390–392, 396–398, 404, 407–411 (1985).

In 1980 the City of San Francisco began implementing a linkage program to encourage office developers to build housing. Specifically, under the Office Housing Production Program developers of office buildings containing more than 50,000 square feet are required to build or finance the amount of new housing in the City that will be needed to house the office workers generated by the development. The requirement is based on the following assumptions: office use generates one employee per two hundred and fifty square feet; forty percent of all office employees in San Francisco reside in San Francisco; and 1.8 working adults occupy each residential unit. This generates a requirement of approximately nine new dwelling units per 10,000 square feet of office space.

The new housing can be for people of any income level, but the developers are given incentives to produce modestly priced housing by allowing them to provide fewer units if the units are for moderate income people. There are no restrictions on the location in San Francisco in which the housing must be built. As alternative to building housing, the developer may contribute to a municipal housing trust—known as the Shared Appreciation Mortgage Pool. The amount of contribution is 6,000 dollars for each housing unit required. The trust funds are used to reduce mortgage payments of low and middle income house buyers. As of April 1984, the City of San Francisco states that its program has generated almost 3000 units of housing, a majority of which were for low and moderate income families. In addition, the trust fund has accrued approximately five million dollars. Despite its success, critics have continued to argue that San Francisco's program ought to be oriented exclusively toward moderately priced housing, and studies are currently underway that may lead to revision of the program.

Boston has now adopted a linkage program based on a somewhat similar analysis. The Boston program applies to developers of office, retail, hotel and institutional facilities and to developers of any use which will reduce the amount of existing low and moderate income housing. The threshold for application of the program is 100,000 square feet of floor area. Each such developer must pay a fee of forty-two dollars per square foot of floor area at the time the certificate of occupancy is issued, and must contract to pay a similar fee in each of the subsequent eleven years. The fee is to be turned over to a neighborhood housing trust to be used for the development of low and moderate income housing. The fee amounts to five dollars per square foot spread out over a twelve-year period in equal payments. The first major project to which the fee is being applied is a 326 million dollar International Place office complex built by the Chiofaro Company in downtown Boston. * * *

In a field such as land use law, where the courts of different states take widely varying positions, it is risky to generalize on the prospects of a new regulatory technique. Nevertheless, there do seem to be some common trends in the analysis of development exactions by the courts of a number of prominent states. An examination of these trends may yield some useful speculation on the way that state courts will determine the validity of linkage programs. * * *

Over the past twenty years the courts of virtually all of the states have come to use the term "rational nexus" to describe the test used to measure the validity of development exactions. The early court decisions adopting the rational nexus formulation were viewed by most commentators as a liberation of local governments from the strictures of earlier rules. The scholars who first proposed the test saw it as a "cost-accounting approach" that would make it "possible to determine the costs generated by new residents and thus to avoid charging the new-comers more than a proportionate share." The succeeding years witnessed a number of opinions, particularly in California, that applied the rational nexus test to uphold exactions using the loosest possible type of nexus. This led some commentators to treat the rational nexus test much like the rational basis test for equal protection—as a test the government always passes. At other times the court decisions incorporating the rational nexus test seemed to use it in such a widely varying manner that the term seems to represent nothing more than a loosening of the more restrictive standards used to evaluate the financing of local improvements through special assessments. More recently, however, courts have begun to put more meat on the rational nexus bones so that it becomes the basis for fairly rigorous analysis, in the manner that its original proponents intended, rather than a slogan used to justify any currently popular municipal policy.

The more rigorous version of the rational nexus test, as currently applied, requires a two-part analysis. First, it requires some real showing that the particular development will create a "need" and that the amount of the exaction bears some roughly proportional relationship to the share of the overall need that is contributed by this particular development. The second part of the test requires that the funds or property exacted from the developer be earmarked to be used in a way that provides some degree of "benefit" to the development from which the exaction was received. When the exaction relates to traditional public services and facilities usually provided to new residential development, the courts have generally accepted the proposition that the new development causes some need for new facilities such as streets, sewers, water, parks, and schools. * * *

How will linkage programs fare under the more rigorous analysis required by the evolving test of rational nexus? * * * The extent to which exactions may be imposed for housing-related linkage programs should depend on the local government's ability to show (1) that there is a need for housing, (2) that the need is caused by new development, (3) that the exaction is proportional to the need caused, (4) that the exaction will be used to remedy the need, and (5) that the remedy will benefit the occupants of the new development.

Both Boston and San Francisco experience a high demand for housing, and few would argue that these cities meet any objective test for housing need. Other cities, however, may have a difficult time meeting such a test, particularly if they are experiencing a net outflow of population.

Assuming that a need for housing exists, what is its cause? Proof of causation in the development process is no simple matter and can be the source of endless debate. The key issue is the determination of what causes a need for new housing. San Francisco and Boston both believe that the need for housing is stimulated by the new employment that results from the construction of new office buildings. This argument has been challenged at both tiers of its logic. Does the construction of office buildings create jobs? Do jobs create a need for housing?

San Francisco economist Claude Gruen argues that "additions to the supply of office space don't make office employment any more than cribs made babies." Any private developer of speculative facilities, whether office or retail or housing, can argue that the facilities themselves do not create the demand—they are only responding to a demand caused by overall economic conditions. The argument is reminiscent of the slogan "guns don't kill people, people kill people," which suggests that an instrumentality is being forced unfairly to bear the blame that should be attached to the operator. The equivalent of the trigger-puller is the in-migrant. Is it the in-migrant who causes the impact? If so, should he or she bear the burden directly?

In a chain of causation it is always possible to argue that the preceding link should bear responsibility. An argument that development does not cause economic impact, however, would also undermine the public purpose behind such programs for subsidizing development as industrial revenue bonds and tax increment financing. Whatever philosophical merits this argument may or may not have, it has garnered little judicial support. The Supreme Court has exhibited increasing concern about discrimination against out-of-state residents, but has thus far restricted its concern to regulations having a direct rather than an indirect impact on outsiders. Should the court begin to examine the indirect effect of development financing methods on interstate migration it will be necessary to re-examine not only linkage programs but other well accepted types of user charges and development exactions.

If the argument that development creates new jobs is accepted, one reaches the issue of whether the new jobs create a need for new housing. The answer is not as simple as it appears. Jobs come and go in a never-ending stream as businesses open and close, expand and contract. The peculiar value of cities may stem from the very flexibility with which their job market can respond to constant change. In such an environment, the addition of any new job does not necessarily mean that the net number of jobs is increased because the job may have been transferred from another location in the community. If the business is moving to promote efficiency in operation, on balance more jobs may have been lost than gained, which would suggest that future out-migration might cause a decline in housing demand.

Even if the total number of jobs does increase, the demand for housing does not necessarily increase along with it. A city's population is constantly changing through in-migration and out-migration, birth and death. Recent years have seen dramatic decreases in average household size, which has to some extent been accompanied by the splitting up of larger dwelling units. The existing housing stock is constantly changing as people build additions or convert housing to non-residential use or vice versa. New housing units are built while others are demolished. Few large cities have trustworthy statistical measures that keep tract of such small-scale changes in the housing supply as conversions and abandonments.

The complexity of the housing market does not mean that a relationship between jobs and housing cannot be shown, but it does mean that a fairly sophisticated analysis will be needed to meet the emerging tests in states like Utah, Texas and Florida. Whether the office-housing linkage in cities like San Francisco or Boston would be able to pass the causation element of a modern rational nexus test will depend on whether the documentation by the planning department of the relationship between office development and the need for housing can survive the scrutiny of litigation.

The causal connection needed to justify inclusionary zoning programs—that new housing creates a need for new low-income housing—is even less clear. Its proponents argue that if developers can be required to provide streets, sewers and other facilities needed to service their development they should also be required to provide housing for the workers who would be needed to operate these facilities and services. If a state accepts even the loosest causal connection as a basis for development exactions this argument may be satisfactory, so it is not surprising to find that California is the site of many inclusionary zoning programs. Other states might find it harder to accept the argument that new housing causes a need for jobs for lower income people.

If a causal relation between the development and the need for housing is established, the next step is to measure the proportional share of the need attributed to the particular development. Would the linkage programs in Boston and San Francisco meet a test of proportionality? Neither program explicitly credits the new development with any of the property tax or other revenue it will generate toward potential housing programs. On the other hand, the city may be able to argue that the exaction is so small in relation to the need that even with such credits the fee is not disproportionately high.

Finally, the earmarking test must be met. Whether the housing to be built by the San Francisco and Boston programs will mitigate the need for low-income housing, and do so in a way that benefits the developments that make the contributions, remains to be seen. In those states that demand strict assurance in advance on these issues, the programs of both cities may be excessively loose. A more cautiously designed linkage program would earmark the funds collected in a manner that guarantees that the funds are used to meet the identified need, and are used in accordance with an overall plan that ensures that the funds will be spent in a manner that benefits the developments from which they are collected. * * *

DOLAN v. CITY OF TIGARD

Supreme Court of the United States, 1994.
___ U.S. ___, 114 S.Ct. 2309, ___ L.Ed.2d ___.

CHIEF JUSTICE REHNQUIST delivered the opinion of the Court. * * *

The State of Oregon enacted a comprehensive land use management program in 1973. The program required all Oregon cities and counties to adopt new comprehensive land use plans that were consistent with the statewide planning goals. * * * Pursuant to the State's requirements, the city of Tigard, a community of some 30,000 residents on the southwest edge of Portland, developed a comprehensive plan and codified it in its Community Development Code (CDC). The CDC requires property owners in the area zoned Central Business District to comply with a 15% open space and landscaping requirement, which limits total site coverage, including all structures and paved parking, to 85% of the parcel. After the completion of a transportation study that identified congestion in the Central Business District as a particular problem, the city adopted a plan for a pedestrian/bicycle pathway intended to encourage alternatives to automobile transportation for short trips. The CDC requires that new development facilitate this plan by dedicating land for pedestrian pathways where provided for in the pedestrian/bicycle pathway plan.

The city also adopted a Master Drainage Plan (Drainage Plan). The Drainage Plan noted that flooding occurred in several areas along Fanno Creek, including areas near petitioner's property. The Drainage Plan also established that the increase in impervious surfaces associated with continued urbanization would exacerbate these flooding problems. To combat these risks, the Drainage Plan suggested a series of improvements to the Fanno Creek Basin, including channel excavation in the area next to petitioner's property. Other recommendations included ensuring that the floodplain remains free of structures and that it be preserved as greenways to minimize flood damage to structures. The Drainage Plan concluded that the cost of these improvements should be shared based on both direct and indirect benefits, with property owners along the waterways paying more due to the direct benefit that they would receive. * * *

Petitioner Florence Dolan owns a plumbing and electric supply store located on Main Street in the Central Business District of the city. The store covers approximately 9,700 square feet on the eastern side of a 1.67–acre parcel, which includes a gravel parking lot. Fanno Creek flows through the southwestern corner of the lot and along its western boundary. The year-round flow of the creek renders the area within the creek's 100–year floodplain virtually unusable for commercial development. The city's comprehensive plan includes the Fanno Creek floodplain as part of the city's greenway system.

Petitioner applied to the city for a permit to redevelop the site. Her proposed plans called for nearly doubling the size of the store to 17,600 square feet, and paving a 39–space parking lot. The existing store, located on the opposite side of the parcel, would be razed in sections as construction progressed on the new building. In the second phase of the project, petitioner proposed to build an additional structure on the northeast side of the site for complementary businesses, and to provide more parking. The proposed expansion and intensified use are consistent with the city's zoning scheme in the Central Business District.

The City Planning Commission granted petitioner's permit application subject to conditions imposed by the city's CDC. * * * [T]he Commission required that petitioner dedicate the portion of her property lying within the 100–year floodplain for improvement of a storm drainage system along Fanno Creek and that she dedicate an additional 15–foot strip of land adjacent to the floodplain as a pedestrian/bicycle pathway. The dedication required by that condition encompasses approximately 7,000 square feet, or roughly 10% of the property. In accordance with city practice, petitioner could rely on the dedicated property to meet the 15% open space and landscaping requirement mandated by the city's zoning scheme. The city would bear the cost of maintaining a landscaped buffer between the dedicated area and the new store. * * *

The Commission made a series of findings concerning the relationship between the dedicated conditions and the projected impacts of petitioner's project. First, the Commission noted that "it is reasonable to assume that customers and employees of the future uses of this site could utilize a pedestrian/bicycle pathway adjacent to this development for their transportation and recreational needs." The Commission noted that the site plan has provided for bicycle parking in a rack in front of the proposed building and "it is reasonable to expect that some of the users of the bicycle parking provided for by the site plan will use the pathway adjacent to Fanno Creek if it is constructed." In addition, the Commission found that creation of a convenient, safe pedestrian/bicycle pathway system as an alternative means of transportation "could offset some of the traffic demand on [nearby] streets and lessen the increase in traffic congestion."

The Commission went on to note that the required floodplain dedication would be reasonably related to petitioner's request to intensify the use of the site given the increase in the impervious surface. The Commission stated that the "anticipated increased storm water flow from the subject property to an already strained creek and drainage basin can only add to the public need to manage the stream channel and floodplain for drainage purposes." Based on this anticipated increased storm water flow, the Commission concluded that "the requirement of dedication of the floodplain area on the site is related to the applicant's plan to intensify development on the site." * * *

Petitioner appealed to the Land Use Board of Appeals (LUBA) on the ground that the city's dedication requirements were not related to the proposed development, and, therefore, those requirements constituted an uncompensated taking of their property under the Fifth Amendment. * * * LUBA concluded that "there is a 'reasonable relationship' between the proposed development and the requirement to dedicate land along Fanno Creek for a greenway." With respect to the pedestrian/bicycle pathway, LUBA * * * found a "reasonable relationship" between alleviating the impacts of increased traffic from the development and facilitating the provision of a pedestrian/bicycle pathway as an alternative means of transportation. The Oregon Court of Appeals * * * [and] Oregon Supreme Court affirmed. * * *

The Takings Clause of the Fifth Amendment of the United States Constitution, made applicable to the States through the Fourteenth Amendment, provides: "Nor shall private property be taken for public use, without just compensation." One of the principal purposes of the Takings Clause is "to bar Government from forcing some people alone to bear public burdens which, in all fairness and justice, should be borne by the public as a whole." *Armstrong v. United States,* 364 U.S. 40, 49, 80 S.Ct. 1563, 4 L.Ed.2d 1554 (1960). Without question, had the city simply required petitioner to dedicate a strip of land along Fanno Creek for public use, rather than conditioning the grant of her permit to redevelop her property on such a dedication, a taking would have occurred. Such public access would deprive petitioner of the right to exclude others, "one of the most essential sticks in the bundle of rights that are commonly characterized as property." *Kaiser Aetna v. United States,* 444 U.S. 164, 176, 100 S.Ct. 383, 62 L.Ed.2d 332 (1979).

On the other side of the ledger, the authority of state and local governments to engage in land use planning has been sustained against constitutional challenge as long ago as our decision in *Euclid v. Ambler Realty Co.,* 272 U.S. 365, 47 S.Ct. 114, 71 L.Ed. 303 (1926). "Government hardly could go on if to some extent values incident to property could not be diminished without paying for every such change in the general law." *Pennsylvania Coal Co. v. Mahon,* 260 U.S. 393, 413, 43 S.Ct. 158, 67 L.Ed. 322 (1922). A land use regulation does not effect a taking if it "substantially advances legitimate state interests" and does not "deny an owner economically viable use of his land." *Agins v. Tiburon,* 447 U.S. 255, 260, 100 S.Ct. 2138, 65 L.Ed.2d 106 (1980).

The sort of land use regulations discussed in the cases just cited, however, differ in two relevant particulars from the present case. First, they involved essentially legislative determinations classifying entire areas of the city, whereas here the city made an adjudicative decision to condition petitioner's application for a building permit on an individual parcel. Second, the conditions imposed were not simply a limitation on the use petitioner might make of her own parcel, but a requirement that she deed portions of the property to the city. In *Nollan [v. California Coastal Comm'n,* 483 U.S. 825, 107 S.Ct. 3141, 97 L.Ed.2d 677 (1987)], we held that governmental authority to exact such a condition was circumscribed by the Fifth and Fourteenth Amendments. Under the well-settled doctrine of "unconstitutional conditions," the government may not require a person to give up a constitutional right—here the right to receive just compensation when property is taken for a public use—in exchange for a discretionary benefit conferred by the government where the property sought has little or no relationship to the benefit.

Petitioner contends that the city has forced her to choose between the building permit and her right under the Fifth Amendment to just compensation for the public easements. Petitioner does not quarrel with the city's authority to exact some forms of dedication as a condition for the grant of a building permit, but challenges the showing made by the city to justify these exactions. She argues that the city has identified "no special benefits" conferred on her, and has not identified any "special quantifiable burdens" created by her new store that would justify the particular dedications required from her which are not required from the public at large.

In evaluating petitioner's claim, we must first determine whether the "essential nexus" exists between the "legitimate state interest" and the permit condition exacted by the city. *Nollan*, 483 U.S., at 837. * * * [In *Nollan*], [t]he California Coastal Commission demanded a lateral public easement across the Nollan's beachfront lot in exchange for a permit to demolish an existing bungalow and replace it with a three-bedroom house. The public easement was designed to connect two public beaches that were separated by the Nollan's property. The Coastal Commission had asserted that the public easement condition was imposed to promote the legitimate state interest of diminishing the "blockage of the view of the ocean" caused by construction of the larger house. * * * We resolved, however, that the Coastal Commission's regulatory authority was set completely adrift from its constitutional moorings when it claimed that a nexus existed between visual access to the ocean and a permit condition requiring lateral public access along the Nollan's beachfront lot. * * * The absence of a nexus left the Coastal Commission in the position of simply trying to obtain an easement through gimmickry, which converted a valid regulation of land use into "an out-and-out plan of extortion."

No such gimmicks are associated with the permit conditions imposed by the city in this case. Undoubtedly, the prevention of flooding along Fanno Creek and the reduction of traffic congestion in the Central Business District qualify as the type of legitimate public purposes we have upheld. It seems equally obvious that a nexus exists between preventing flooding along Fanno Creek and limiting development within the creek's 100–year floodplain. Petitioner proposes to double the size of her retail store and to pave her now-gravel parking lot, thereby expanding the impervious surface on the property and increasing the amount of stormwater run-off into Fanno Creek. * * * The same may be said for the city's attempt to reduce traffic congestion by providing for alternative means of transportation. In theory, a pedestrian/bicycle pathway provides a useful alternative means of transportation for workers and shoppers * * *.

The second part of our analysis requires us to determine whether the degree of the exactions demanded by the city's permit conditions bear the required relationship to the projected impact of petitioner's proposed development. * * * The city relies on the Commission's rather tentative findings that increased stormwater flow from petitioner's property "can only add to the public need to manage the [floodplain] for drainage purposes" to support its conclusion that the "requirement of dedication of the floodplain area on the site is related to the applicant's plan to intensify development on the site."

The city made the following specific findings relevant to the pedestrian/bicycle pathway:

"In addition, the proposed expanded use of this site is anticipated to generate additional vehicular traffic thereby increasing congestion on nearby collector and arterial streets. Creation of a convenient, safe pedestrian/bicycle pathway system as an alternative means of transportation could offset some of the traffic demand on these nearby streets and lessen the increase in traffic congestion."

The question for us is whether these findings are constitutionally sufficient to justify the conditions imposed by the city on petitioner's building permit. Since state courts have been dealing with this question a good deal longer than we have, we turn to representative decisions made by them.

In some States, very generalized statements as to the necessary connection between the required dedication and the proposed development seem to suffice. * * * Other state courts require a very exacting correspondence, described as the "specific and uniquely attributable" test. The Supreme Court of Illinois first developed this test in *Pioneer Trust & Savings Bank v. Mount Prospect,* 22 Ill.2d 375, 380, 176 N.E.2d 799, 802 (1961). Under this standard, if the local government cannot demonstrate that its exaction is directly proportional to the specifically created need, the exaction becomes "a veiled exercise of the power of eminent domain and a confiscation of private property behind the defense of police regulations." *Id.,* at 381, 176 N.E.2d, at 802. * * *

A number of state courts have taken an intermediate position, requiring the municipality to show a "reasonable relationship" between the required dedication and the impact of the proposed development. Typical is the Supreme Court of Nebraska's opinion in *Simpson v. North Platte,* 206 Neb. 240, 245, 292 N.W.2d 297, 301 (1980), where that court stated:

"The distinction, therefore, which must be made between an appropriate exercise of the police power and an improper exercise of eminent domain is whether the requirement has some reasonable relationship or nexus to the use to which the property is being made or is merely being used as an excuse for taking property simply because at that particular moment the landowner is asking the city for some license or permit."

Thus, the court held that a city may not require a property owner to dedicate private property for some future public use as a condition of obtaining a building permit when such future use is not "occasioned by the construction sought to be permitted." *Id.*, at 248, 292 N.W.2d, at 302. * * * Some form of the reasonable relationship test has been adopted in many other jurisdictions. * * *

We think the "reasonable relationship" test adopted by a majority of the state courts is closer to the federal constitutional norm than either of those previously discussed. But we do not adopt it as such, partly because the term "reasonable relationship" seems confusingly similar to the term "rational basis" which describes the minimal level of scrutiny under the Equal Protection Clause of the Fourteenth Amendment. We think a term such as "rough proportionality" best encapsulates what we hold to be the requirement of the Fifth Amendment. No precise mathematical calculation is required, but the city must make some sort of individualized determination that the required dedication is related both in nature and extent to the impact of the proposed development. * * *

We turn now to analysis of whether the findings relied upon by the city here, first with respect to the floodplain easement, and second with respect to the pedestrian/bicycle path, satisfied these requirements. * * * It is axiomatic that increasing the amount of impervious surface will increase the quantity and rate of stormwater flow from petitioner's property. Therefore, keeping the floodplain open and free from development would likely confine the pressures on Fanno Creek created by petitioner's development. In fact, because petitioner's property lies within the Central Business District, the Community Development Code already required that petitioner leave 15% of it as open space and the undeveloped floodplain would have nearly satisfied that requirement. But the city demanded more—it not only wanted petitioner not to build in the floodplain, but it also wanted petitioner's property along Fanno Creek for its Greenway system. The city has never said why a public greenway, as opposed to a private one, was required in the interest of flood control.

The difference to petitioner, of course, is the loss of her ability to exclude others. As we have noted, this right to exclude others is "one of the most essential sticks in the bundle of rights that are commonly characterized as property." *Kaiser Aetna*, 444 U.S., at 176. It is difficult to see why recreational visitors trampling along petitioner's floodplain easement are sufficiently related to the city's legitimate interest in reducing flooding problems along Fanno Creek, and the city has not attempted to make any individualized determination to support this part of its request.

The city contends that recreational easement along the Greenway is only ancillary to the city's chief purpose in controlling flood hazards. It further asserts that unlike the residential property at issue in *Nollan,* petitioner's property is commercial in character and therefore, her right to exclude others is compromised. * * * Admittedly, petitioner wants to build a bigger store to attract members of the public to her property. She also wants, however, to be able to control the time and manner in which they enter. * * * Petitioner would lose all rights to regulate the time in which the public entered onto the Greenway, regardless of any interference it might pose with her retail store. Her right to exclude would not be regulated, it would be eviscerated.

If petitioner's proposed development had somehow encroached on existing greenway space in the city, it would have been reasonable to require petitioner to provide some alternative greenway space for the public either on her property or elsewhere. * * * But that is not the case here. We conclude that the findings upon which the city relies do not show the required reasonable relationship between the floodplain easement and the petitioner's proposed new building.

With respect to the pedestrian/bicycle pathway, we have no doubt that the city was correct in finding that the larger retail sales facility proposed by petitioner will increase traffic on the streets of the Central Business District. The city estimates that the proposed development would generate roughly 435 additional trips per day. Dedications for streets, sidewalks, and other public ways are generally reasonable exactions to avoid excessive congestion from a proposed property use. But on the record before us, the city has not met its burden of demonstrating that the additional number of vehicle and bicycle trips generated by the petitioner's development reasonably relate to the city's requirement for a dedication of the pedestrian/bicycle pathway easement. The city simply found that the creation of the pathway "could offset some of the traffic demand . . . and lessen the increase in traffic congestion."

As Justice Peterson of the Supreme Court of Oregon explained in his dissenting opinion, however, "the findings of fact that the bicycle pathway system 'could offset some of the traffic demand' is a far cry from a finding that the bicycle pathway system will, or is likely to, offset some of the traffic demand." No precise mathematical calculation is required, but the city must make some effort to quantify its findings in support of the dedication for the pedestrian/bicycle pathway beyond the conclusory statement that it could offset some of the traffic demand generated.

Cities have long engaged in the commendable task of land use planning, made necessary by increasing urbanization particularly in metropolitan areas such as Portland. The city's goals of reducing flooding hazards and traffic congestion, and providing for public greenways, are laudable, but there are outer limits to how this may be done. "A strong public desire to improve the public condition [will not] warrant achieving the desire by a shorter cut than the constitutional way of paying for the change." *Pennsylvania Coal,* 260 U.S., at 416. * * *

JUSTICE STEVENS, with whom JUSTICE BLACKMUN and JUSTICE GINSBURG join, dissenting. * * *

The enlargement of the Tigard unit in Dolan's chain of hardware stores will have an adverse impact on the city's legitimate and substantial interests in controlling drainage in Fanno Creek and minimizing traffic congestion in Tigard's business district. That impact is sufficient to justify an outright denial of her application for approval of the expansion. The city has nevertheless agreed to grant Dolan's application if she will comply with two conditions, each of which admittedly will mitigate the adverse effects of her proposed development. * * *

[A]lthough * * * [the] state cases do lend support to the Court's reaffirmance of *Nollan's* reasonable nexus requirement, the role the Court accords them in the announcement of its newly minted second phase of the constitutional inquiry is remarkably inventive. * * * [T]he Court ignores the state courts' willingness to consider what the property owner gains from the exchange in question. The Supreme Court of Wisconsin, for example, found it significant that the village's approval of a proposed subdivision plat "enables the subdivider to profit financially by selling the subdivision lots as home-building sites and thus realizing a greater price than could have been obtained if he had sold his property as unplatted lands." *Jordan v. Village of Menomonee Falls,* 28 Wis.2d 608, 619–620, 137 N.W.2d 442, 448 (1965). The required dedication as a condition of that approval was permissible "in return for this benefit." In this case, moreover, Dolan's acceptance of the permit, with its attached conditions, would provide her with benefits that may well go beyond any advantage she gets from expanding her business. As the United States pointed out at oral argument, the improvement that the city's drainage plan contemplates would widen the channel and reinforce the slopes to increase the carrying capacity during serious floods, "conferring considerable benefits on the property owners immediately adjacent to the creek."

The state court decisions also are enlightening in the extent to which they required that the entire parcel be given controlling importance. * * * It is not merely state cases, but our own cases as well, that require the analysis to focus on the impact of the city's action on the entire parcel of private property. * * * The Court's narrow focus on one strand in the property owner's bundle of rights is particularly misguided in a case involving the development of commercial property. As Professor Johnston has noted:

> "The subdivider is a manufacturer, processer, and marketer of a product; land is but one of his raw materials. In subdivision control disputes, the developer is not defending hearth and home against the king's intrusion, but simply attempting to maximize his profits from the sale of a finished product. As applied to him, subdivision control exactions are actually business regulations." Johnston, Constitutionality of Subdivision Control Exactions: The Quest for A Rationale, 52 Cornell L.Q. 871, 923 (1967).

The exactions associated with the development of a retail business are likewise a species of business regulation that heretofore warranted a strong presumption of constitutional validity.

In Johnston's view, "if the municipality can demonstrate that its assessment of financial burdens against subdividers is rational, impartial, and conducive to fulfillment of authorized planning objectives, its action need be invalidated only in those extreme and presumably rare cases where the burden of compliance is sufficiently great to deter the owner from proceeding with his planned development." The city of Tigard has demonstrated that its plan is rational and impartial and that the conditions at issue are "conducive to fulfillment of authorized planning objectives." Dolan, on the other hand, has offered no evidence that her burden of compliance has any impact at all on the value or profitability of her planned development. Following the teaching of the cases on which it purports to rely, the Court should not isolate the burden associated with the loss of the power to exclude from an evaluation of the benefit to be derived from the permit to enlarge the store and the parking lot. * * * The correct inquiry should instead concentrate on whether the required nexus is present and venture beyond considerations of a condition's nature or germaneness only if the developer establishes that a concededly germane condition is so grossly disproportionate to the proposed development's adverse effects that it manifests motives other than land use regulation on the part of the city. * * *

The Court has made a serious error by abandoning the traditional presumption of constitutionality and imposing a novel burden of proof on a city implementing an admittedly valid comprehensive land use plan. * * * If the government can demonstrate that the conditions it has imposed in a land-use permit are rational, impartial and conducive to fulfilling the aims of a valid land-use plan, a strong presumption of validity should attach to those conditions. The burden of demonstrating that those conditions have unreasonably impaired the economic value of the proposed improvement belongs squarely on the shoulders of the party challenging the state action's constitutionality. That allocation of burdens has served us well in the past. The Court has stumbled badly today by reversing it. * * *

MUNICIPAL ART SOCIETY OF NEW YORK v. CITY OF NEW YORK

Supreme Court, New York County, 1987.
137 Misc.2d 832, 522 N.Y.S.2d 800.

EDWARD H. LEHNER, JUDGE. * * *

These proceedings involve the site of the New York Coliseum and an adjoining office building located on the west side of Columbus Circle in Manhattan extending from 58th to 60th Street.

In 1953 the City of New York (the "City") acquired the property by eminent domain, and sold it to the Triborough Bridge and Tunnel

Authority ("TBTA"), an affiliate of the Metropolitan Transportation Authority ("MTA"), both of which are public authorities created by the State. On that site, the TBTA constructed and operated the office building and Coliseum, which was employed as a convention center prior to the opening of the Javits Convention Center in 1986. The City has a contingent reversionary interest in the property, which ripens only in the event the corporate existence of the TBTA terminates.

In 1982 a report was issued by the New York City Planning Commission ("CPC") recommending changes in zoning affecting the west side of Manhattan (including the Coliseum site), intended to shift development away from the crowded east side. In May 1982 the Board of Estimate approved the recommended changes, which included incentive zoning.

The Coliseum is located in a zone which permits construction as of right of floor space up to a maximum of 15 times the square footage of the lot. This floor area ratio ("FAR") is subject to being increased by up to 20% in exchange for the developer agreeing to "provide major improvements for adjacent subway stations," provided that "the zoning lot for the development * * * on which a floor area bonus is requested shall be adjacent to the mezzanine or concourse of the subway station for which the improvement is proposed or an existing connecting passageway to the station." (Zoning Resolution of The City of New York, § 81–53).

In December 1984 the City and the TBTA agreed to sell the site for private development. In February 1985, TBTA, which was to be the "lead agency" for review under the State Environmental Quality Review Act (SEQRA), offered the property for sale pursuant to a Request for Proposals ("RFP").

The RFP provided that: i) the amount of the purchase price offered "will be the primary consideration", and the criteria for acceptance would also include "the economic viability of the proposal, the developer's experience and financial capacity" as well as "the overall benefit to the City"; ii) the designated developer "must apply for and use its best efforts to obtain the maximum twenty percent Subway Bonus" (448,500 additional square feet); iii) if any FAR bonus is granted, the developer must agree to construct the subway station improvements as set forth "in concept" in the RFP, with such obligation to exist even if the maximum bonus is not granted, so long as any FAR bonus is approved; iv) the amount of the bid "must assume the maximum twenty percent FAR Subway Bonus will be granted"; v) the purchase price will be reduced by a specified formula if the full 20% FAR bonus is not granted, with such amount to be $57 million if no bonus is granted; vi) the City and the TBTA will, pursuant to their memorandum of agreement dated December 19, 1984, each receive one half of the net proceeds, with the TBTA to "spend its proceeds solely for MTA capital projects in the City of New York", while the City "will spend its proceeds over a five year period solely for TA capital projects", with 28% to be spent in the first year and 18% in each of the subsequent four years; and vii) if no FAR bonus is granted, the City and TBTA will have no obligation to convey the site.

By May 1, 1985 fifteen proposals were received in response to the RFP, and although one bid was received for $477 million, a committee of City and MTA officials selected the bid of $455,100,000 from Boston Properties. A contract of sale dated September 30, 1985 was thereafter entered into which provides for a mixed use project, including the headquarters for the brokerage firm of Salomon Brothers, Inc., (which subsequently became an equity participant in the project and was expected to occupy over half the building), additional office space, residences, motion picture theatres, retail stores, and a parking garage. The building would have two towers, one 925 feet (68 stories) and the other 802 feet (58 stories), with a total of 9,300 people expected to be employed at the site.

The contract provides that if no FAR bonus is granted, the purchase price will be reduced by $57 million. The estimated cost of improvements to be made by the purchaser to the adjoining Columbus Circle (59th Street) subway station is between $35 and $40 million, although the estimated cost at the time of the execution of the contract is claimed to have been between $20 and $25 million. * * *

By amendment dated February 6, 1987 among the City, MTA and TBTA, the prior agreement with respect to the application of the proceeds of the sale was altered. Rather than one half being payable to the TBTA for MTA capital projects, said half is to be paid to the TBTA, as escrow agent, to be dispersed at the direction of the City to the New York City Transit Authority ("TA") for operating purposes. Such payments are to be deemed payments by the City under its obligation under Section 18–b of the Transportation Law to make operating subsidies to the TA, matching monies appropriated by the State.

In the Article 78 proceeding instituted by the Municipal Art Society of New York ("MAS") and others, the following arguments are raised:

1) The City illegally sold a zoning bonus because the price is reduced by $57 million in the event a subway bonus is not granted * * *

Section 81–53 of the Zoning Resolution provides that, when granting a FAR bonus, the zoning lot for which the bonus is requested must be adjacent to the subway station to be improved. In the March 1982 report of the CPC entitled "Midtown Zoning", which proposed the zoning changes which were adopted in May of that year, the following is said rejecting a suggestion for a bonus for a non-adjacent improvement:

> "Subway Improvements. A floor area bonus is provided for a substantial subway entrance improvement adjacent to a development site. * * * An off-site subway-station improvement does not provide any compensating reduction in density. The proposed bonus is justified because it improves direct access to the larger

development. For off-site subway improvements direct financial incentives appear to be more appropriate than zoning measures."

In its "Plain English" summary of § 81–535 of the Zoning Resolution, the CPC sets forth the basis for determining the amount of the bonus as follows:

"The amount of the floor area bonus subject to a 20 percent maximum over basic FAR will be in the City Planning Commission's discretion and will depend on findings made by the Commission that relate to the benefits the public will derive from the improvement."

In its June 1981 report entitled "Midtown Development", the CPC states:

"A major subway entrance improvement can benefit the building as well as the public. To encourage this, we will sanction a floor area bonus up to 20 percent of base FAR, depending upon the nature and cost of the station improvement."

Petitioners state that they "do not question whether the amount to be spent on these improvements * * * is sufficient to justify a bonus in some amount." Rather, the claim of illegality relates solely to the $57 million. This sum, which the City and the TBTA will receive as a result of the grant of the bonus, is not earmarked for the improvement of any local facility. Moreover, pursuant to the February 6, 1987 amendment to the agreement between the City, MTA and TBTA, one half of the money is no longer to be used for mass transit capital improvements, but is to be applied to the City's statutory obligation to provide operating subsidies to the MTA.

Although the transaction may well have been structured to paint a different picture, the clear fact of the matter is that in return for the grant by the CPC of the twenty percent floor area ratio bonus, the City is obtaining not only $35 to $40 million of local subway improvements, but an additional $57 million in cash to be employed for other purposes. This is not contemplated by the Zoning Resolution.

Zoning is a " 'vital tool for maintaining a civilized form of existence' for the benefit and welfare of an entire community" (*Little Joseph Realty, Inc. v. Town of Babylon*, 41 N.Y.2d 738, 745, 395 N.Y.S.2d 428, 363 N.E.2d 1163), and is "designed to preserve the character of zoned areas from encroachments of uses which devaluate living conditions" (*Lavere v. Board of Zoning Appeals of the City of Syracuse*, 39 A.D.2d 639, 331 N.Y.S.2d 141, aff'd 33 N.Y.2d 873, 352 N.Y.S.2d 442, 307 N.E.2d 559), with its goal being "to provide for the development of a balanced, cohesive community which will make efficient use of a town's available land." (*Berenson v. Town of New Castle*, 38 N.Y.2d 102, 109, 378 N.Y.S.2d 672, 341 N.E.2d 236).

When disposing of its property, government, of course, has an obligation to maximize the revenue it receives, consistent with its governmental responsibilities. Increasing the bulk of a project imposes a certain burden on the local community. The Zoning Resolution provides a means by which, in return for the imposition of that burden, a benefit is granted to the community.

Here, the major portion of the benefit which the purchaser is willing to pay for the right to construct a building of greater density than is permitted "as of right" is to be paid to the City to be employed for purposes other than local improvements. A proper *quid pro quo* for the grant of the right to increase the bulk of a building may not be the payment of additional cash into the City's coffers for citywide use.

Although the members of the CPC may well in good faith have approved the full 20% FAR bonus as a fair incentive for the developer agreeing to make $35 to $40 million of subway station improvements, the developer and the City officials who approved the contract obviously recognized that this bonus was worth a great deal more. However, government may not place itself in the position of reaping a cash premium because one of its agencies bestows a zoning benefit upon a developer. Zoning benefits are not cash items.

Although the court today is ruling that the City is prohibited from making what, in effect, is a "cash sale" of a zoning bonus, it should be noted that even without a higher sales price, construction of a larger building will, over the years, result in increased revenues to the City. Undoubtedly, such a building will receive a higher assessed valuation, with consequently greater annual payments of real estate taxes, and will presumably also generate additional income tax payments from the owner.

In conclusion, the court finds that the contract with the developer provides for an illegal payment. Consequently, the approvals thereof by the City and TBTA are null and void. * * *

COMMON CAUSE v. STATE

Supreme Court of Maine, 1983.
455 A.2d 1.

GODFREY, JUSTICE.

Early in 1981, Bath Iron Works Corporation (BIW), a subsidiary of Congoleum Corporation, was negotiating with officials of the city of Boston to lease parts of the Boston Navy Yard. BIW wanted to expand its business by undertaking the repair and overhaul of large ocean-going vessels, work that could not be carried out in the confines of BIW's location on the river in Bath, Maine. The facilities at Boston, which were complete and immediately available, included a permanent dry dock capable of handling the largest ships, extensive pier, warehouse and manufacturing facilities, and living quarters for seamen from ships under repair.

Officials of the city of Portland learned of the negotiations and sought out BIW to inquire whether it would entertain a competing proposal from Portland. On obtaining a favorable response, the city solicited and obtained the state's participation in making a proposal.

There followed a series of meetings of state, city and BIW officials, out of which evolved a joint proposal from the state and city to BIW under which the state and city would create in Portland harbor a comprehensive facility for ship repairs to be operated by BIW. Portland and the state had been engaged for several years in efforts to restore the vitality of the port, and the officials concerned regarded the creation of a major ship repair and overhaul facility as consistent with the already identified goals of improving the harbor, attracting more marine commerce, and, in general, redeveloping the economic potential of the Portland waterfront.

In July, 1981, officers of BIW, the state and the city executed a "Memorandum of Intent" outlining their tentative tripartite agreement for development of a dry dock facility at the Maine State Pier in Portland. On August 1, 1981, they entered into a further set of related agreements: namely, a "Comprehensive Commitment," a dry dock lease, and a pier lease—all contingent on approval by the Legislature and Maine electorate of the state's commitment to the project, by the city council and electorate of Portland for the participation of the city, and by the boards of directors of BIW and Congoleum Corporation.

In broad outline, the Memorandum of Intent called for the following acts to be done: (1) the state was to obtain title to a large floating dry dock meeting certain specifications. It was expected that the acquisition would be effected by a gratuitous transfer from the federal government to the state of Maine of such a dry dock, an "AFDB–3", having an adjusted capacity of 81,000 tons. (2) The state was to transfer its title in the Maine State Pier to the city of Portland for $4.6 million dollars. (3) The state and BIW were to share the cost of acquiring and rehabilitating the floating dry dock, the first $9 million dollars of that cost to be borne equally by BIW and the state, the next $15.1 million to be borne by the state alone, using for this purpose the $4.6 million paid by the city for the pier. All costs of rehabilitating the dry dock in excess of $24.1 million dollars were to be borne by BIW. (4) The state was to provide an additional $.5 million dollars to defray miscellaneous costs in initial planning, acquisition of land and issuance of bonds. (5) The state of Maine was to retain title to the dry dock, which was to be leased to BIW for 20 years, with an option in BIW to purchase it under certain conditions. No dollar amount of rent for the dock was provided for. (6) BIW was to install equipment and operate the dry dock at its own expense in accordance with the agreement, subject to United States Navy regulations. (7) The city was to acquire certain land adjacent to the pier property and lease it, with the pier itself, to BIW for stated amounts of annual rent, funding the improvement of the pier and adjacent submerged lands and shoreland with the $10.4 million remaining after purchase of the pier. (8) The city was to improve and lease to BIW the city hospital to provide suitable dormitory quarters for the berthing of seamen, the rental to be determined according to actual use by crew members. (9) The state's costs under the project, aside from $.5 million for start-up costs and the $4.6 million received from the city for transfer of the pier, were to be met by the issuance of general obligation bonds of the state; the city's costs were to be met by issuance of general obligation bonds of the city of Portland.

The Governor called a special session of the Legislature for August 3, 1981, to consider legislation authorizing the issuance of bonds to implement the state's participation. * * *

After the Legislature enacted authorization for the bond issue, the project and the desirability of issuing general obligation bonds to aid in carrying it out were the subject of debate in the newspapers and on television and radio, including a televised debate by the counsel for Common Cause and the president of BIW. On November 3, 1981, the bond issues were approved by the voters of the state and city.

On January 18, 1982, the parties entered into agreements in final form. * * * The financing provisions of the January, 1982, agreements resemble closely those described in the July, 1981, Memorandum of Intent and the August, 1981, Comprehensive Commitment.[2] In addition, BIW agrees to invest working capital, to buy all necessary capital equipment to operate the dock, to waive any state-jobs credit it might become entitled to on its state income tax arising from its investment in completing the dry dock, and to pay the operating costs of the dry dock until the agreement terminates, including utilities, taxes, maintenance, repair, and insurance.

BIW has the exclusive right to use the dry dock for up to forty years, without rent and without obligation to repay any of the money spent by the state for renovation of the dock. Although it has no general option to purchase, BIW has a right of first refusal for a three-year period after the forty-year term, whereby it may acquire the dry dock for $1,667,000 if the state decides to sell the dry dock during that period. BIW has the right to terminate the agreement at the end of certain years, beginning as early as 1986, upon at least thirty days' notice to the state. If BIW so terminates, it must pay maintenance costs for the six months following the termination. The state may terminate the agreement without cause at stated times beginning as early as 2006, upon six months' notice to BIW. If the state so terminates, BIW has a 90 day option to purchase the dry dock for $1,667,000. The agreement provides for sharing of proceeds of transfer of the dock by the state in the event of expiration or termination of the agreement under certain conditions. The agreement provides for audit of BIW's expenditures in renovating the dock and contains remedies for the state and city in the event of default by BIW in its performance under the dock agreement or the pier lease.

The dry dock has an estimated current salvage value of about $875,000. Yearly maintenance costs are projected roughly at $720,000. It has a useful life of between forty and fifty years, and perhaps longer if

---

2. The principal change is that instead of a twenty-year lease with option in BIW to purchase, as proposed in the July, 1981 Memorandum of Intent, the dry dock operating agreement of January, 1982 provides for a 40–year term without option to pur-chase but with certain rights of first refusal in BIW. Also, the January agreement is not denominated a "lease." It contains no provision for rent, and the rights of the state on default by BIW are different from the customary rights of a landlord.

well-maintained. At the end of forty years, the dry dock, if well-maintained and modernized, will be worth between five percent and thirty percent of its value after renovation in accordance with the terms of the agreements.

On April 19, 1982, the plaintiffs began this action in Superior Court, Kennebec County, for declaratory and injunctive relief. * * * Plaintiffs asked the Superior Court to issue a declaratory judgment holding the terms of the agreements to be in violation of the state and federal constitutions and hence without effect; to enjoin the state and the defendant officials from transferring funds to BIW under the terms of the agreements, and from borrowing funds on the credit of the state for that purpose; and to order such further relief as would "do substantial justice and protect and preserve the rights and interests of both plaintiffs and defendants and of the people of the State of Maine." * * *

To be constitutionally valid, taxation at either the state or local level must be for a public purpose. A corollary of that proposition is that the expenditure of public funds must be for a public purpose. The requirement of public purpose operates as a limitation on the power granted to the Legislature by article IV, part third, section 1 of the Maine Constitution, the legislative powers clause. * * *

The preamble and statement of purpose in chapter 75 of the Private and Special Laws of 1981, authorizing the state bond referendum, reveal the following declarations, among others, by the Maine Legislature:

There is a statewide need to provide for a greater utilization of the public ports and harbors * * * and to increase the flow of commerce, to thereby provide enlarged opportunities for gainful employment by the people of Maine and to thus ensure the preservation and betterment of the economy of the State for the benefit of its people.

It is determined to be a public purpose of the State to * * * cause to be operated either by lease, sale, transfer or other conveyance to public or private users, in cooperation with the State Government, port facilities * * * owned or leased by the State and to encourage and assist in the acquisition, financing, construction, renovation and operation of other port facilities * * * within the State, to the end that the public ports and harbors, the port facilities located therein * * * shall be utilized in a manner which will further the economic development of the State. * * *

Plaintiffs contend that judicial precedents in Maine clearly mark such an arrangement as one for a nonpublic purpose because neither will the shipyard be available for use by members of the public nor will its development and operation directly benefit the public, as, for instance, by eliminating conditions hazardous to public health or safety. The heart of plaintiffs' position is that the tripartite agreement calls for the state and city to subsidize a private profit-making project where the resulting industrial activity will benefit members of the public only indirectly and where there is no provision for direct recovery of the investment from the industry subsidized.

Plaintiffs go further. They assert not merely that the arrangements create a state subsidy to BIW but that the tripartite agreement itself is a fictitious contract under which the state and city obtain no real benefits in return for the benefits they confer on BIW. In plaintiffs' view, BIW has merely to carry on its business, doing essentially what it would have done anyhow but aided by the subsidy, while the state and city gain only the incidental benefits that may come from having the shipyard located in Portland. The plaintiffs argue that BIW's financial commitments to renovation of the dry dock, installation of capital equipment and operation of the shipyard obligate BIW to do nothing more than what good management of its own interests would have called for without any agreement. With respect to BIW's obligation to pay substantial annual rent on the pier lease, plaintiffs say that the amount of rent reserved will be inadequate to pay the debt and carrying charges created by the city bond issue covering the pier facilities.

We first consider plaintiffs' latter argument—that the tripartite agreement is a mere fiction to benefit BIW. We do not agree with plaintiffs that the agreement is fictitious or that BIW's legal obligation to carry out its financial and other commitments under the agreement may be ignored in deciding this case. The realities of the situation include the facts that BIW *is* legally obligated, that the state and city have bargained to have it so, and that BIW's obligations under the agreement go well beyond a mere commitment to locate a shipyard in Portland. The arrangements give the state and city a certain measure of assurance about the time, place, and manner of installation and operation of the shipyard facilities. The state and city promised to pay money and provide facilities in return for BIW's legal obligations to bring its new operation to Portland, renovate the dry dock, develop the pier, and operate the shipyard in certain ways and for certain times. This bargained-for exchange of obligations is not a gift, or even "in essence" a gift, nor can it be regarded as "fictitious" in any useful sense of the term. However, the question remains, whether the expenditures the state and city are obligated to make under the agreement will be for a public purpose. * * *

If there were no Maine precedents relating to legislation authorizing public financial aid to private business, it would be difficult for this Court, applying a deferential standard of review, to overturn the Legislature's characterization of the stated purposes of the Portland project as "public" in nature or its finding that the project is "for the benefit of the people." Revival of Portland's seaborne commerce and enhancement of Maine's employment opportunities are beyond question desirable ends. Reviewing the legislative and executive actions with the normal judicial deference on the question of their constitutional validity, we would find that the Legislature's statement of purpose was rationally supported by a state economic study and expert testimony tending to show that the projected arrangements would promote the announced legislative objectives. * * *

Although a public subsidy is involved, certain features of the Portland project set this case apart from any prior Maine case or advisory opinion involving public subsidy of a private enterprise. The project is unique in its potential for extensive, long-term, favorable economic impact; in the detailed arrangements under which a large private industry has been committed to long-term obligations in support of a major industrial development; and in the expert testimony at trial, tending to show that the project will improve commerce and create jobs, generating sufficient tax revenues to repay the state's investment. In short, the present case is without comparable Maine precedent. * * *

The question remains, however, whether the Legislature has exceeded its power to tax and spend by subsidizing an activity that does not confer some form of direct benefit on the public. In other words, may an indirect benefit to the economy of the state ever constitute a public purpose to validate a subsidy to private enterprise?

The chief indirect benefit predicted for the Portland project will consist of the jobs provided by the project itself and the economic "ripple effect" of introducing new business into the state. No Maine case has held as yet that public spending to stimulate the economy or create jobs has a public purpose. * * *

To be sure, there is some merit in a blanket rule that ignores indirect economic benefits. Such a rule, by focusing on more easily measurable direct benefits such as rental payments or public use, would help ensure that the public gets its money's worth for its investment. Moreover, the rule helps avoid the risk of approving transactions sponsored by legislators who may have been unduly dominated by the private enterprise. *See* Michelman, *Political Markets and Community Self-Determination: Competing Judicial Models of Local Government Legitimacy,* 53 Ind.L.J. 145, 163 (1977–1978).

But these concerns can be met without the drastic remedy of ignoring all indirect economic benefits. Ultimately, in examining the constitutionality of a tax or spending measure, the Court should focus on whether the plan threatens a detriment to the public which outweighs the benefit that could have been anticipated. In such a weighing, both direct and indirect benefits are relevant. Accordingly, we now hold that indirect economic benefits may be taken into consideration in deciding whether public spending by the state is justified.

Although the public-purpose inquiry turns on whether the likely costs of the Portland project outweigh the likely benefits, the scope of judicial review is narrow. The courts must treat such legislation as constitutional unless it is clearly demonstrated to be otherwise. The weighing of costs and benefits is for the Legislature in the first instance, and this Court should invalidate expenditures only when the Legislature's decision has no rational basis.

Though plaintiffs have pointed out aspects of the project that raise specific doubts about its ultimate effectiveness, they have not convinced us that the arrangements for this unique project at Portland are clearly unreasonable as a means for achieving the stated purposes. The rationality of the Legislature's and voters' decision is supported by the following facts: that Bath Iron Works is a large concern with strong ties to Maine and with long experience in the type of operation that it will be conducting in Portland; that operations of the type projected require many employees; and that the project is supported by expert testimony to the effect that the availability of facilities for ship repair will make Portland more attractive to seaborne commerce. Moreover, Bath Iron Works itself is contractually bound to invest several million dollars in the Portland project. That substantial private investment serves as an added measure of assurance of the soundness of the project, distinguishing this case from an outright donation, which would permit a private enterprise to take a risk-free, speculative gamble at public expense.

The Legislature's adoption of the arrangements is not rendered irrational simply because BIW has not agreed to create any certain number of jobs, or to service all ships in need of repair, or to subject its operations in Portland to more state control than the agreement provides. The Legislature could reasonably decide that, in the circumstances, the agreement sufficiently serves the public interest without additional restrictions on BIW.

Whether this Court would have made the same choice as the Legislature is irrelevant. After carefully considering all the facts of record in this case, we cannot say that the legislative choice was irrational. * * *

2. CITY PROPERTY OWNERSHIP

In this section, we examine the possibility of advancing city welfare by increasing the economic power of cities rather than (as in the previous section) having cities depend on income derived from taxing (or imposing charges on) the economic power of others.[1] One way to increase city influence and income is through a greater use of the entitlements that cities have as property owners. Another option, also examined in this section, is the use of the power of eminent domain to prevent local businesses from leaving town and thereby contributing to a city's economic decline.

The first excerpt below is a summary of Hendrik Hartog's important book, Public Property and Private Power: The Corporation of the City of New York in American Law, 1730–1870 (1983). Professor Hartog emphasizes the historic importance of city property ownership as a vehicle for the exercise of power by the City of New York.[2] An excerpt from a

---

1. For a classic argument for such an approach, see F. Howe, The City: The Hope of Democracy (1905).

2. For an analysis of Professor Hartog's argument, see, e.g., Williams, Review–The Development of the Public/Private Distinction in American Law, 64 Tex.L.Rev. 225

recent book by David Osborne and Ted Gaebler then suggests that the idea that cities can derive income from property ownership rather than from taxes is not simply a matter of history. Osborne and Gaebler list a multitude of current profit-making ventures by American cities. One question one might ask about the kinds of city activity that these two excerpts describe is whether "public" competition with "private" business is desirable. Should cities be allowed to engage in business—in *any* kind of business? A second line of inquiry addresses the legal rules that currently govern city business activity. The four cases that follow the Osborne and Gaebler excerpt explore a variety of legal reactions to a range of city actions: charging AT & T for laying a cable on city streets;[3] selling asphalt made in a city asphalt plant to other cities; running a city-owned cable television station; and taxing private parking lots while offering, at a lower price, public parking facilities. Do the cases adequately deal with the complexities involved in city business activity? What rules *should* govern city competition with, or attempts to earn money from, private business?

A city might also attempt to promote its prosperity by maintaining its current level of private business activity rather than by engaging in business itself. The final two cases deal with Oakland's attempt use the power of eminent domain to keep the Oakland Raiders from moving to Los Angeles. Other cities have contemplated similar action. Boston, for example, considered using its eminent domain power to prevent the closing of a private meat-packing plant, Colonial Provisions Co.; Boston planned to condemn the plant and transfer it to another owner, thereby preventing the loss of city residents' jobs. Because the city's corporation counsel advised the city council that such a use of eminent domain was unlawful, however, the city's proposed condemnation never took place and the plant closed.[4] Is it desirable (or lawful) to use the eminent domain power to prevent a city business from leaving town? Do the Oakland cases persuasively analyze the legal issues in this kind of situation? Would it put a city in a stronger or a weaker position if it were to take over and run the football team or the meat-packing plant

(1985); Rose, Public Property, Old and New, 79 Nw.U.L.Rev. 216 (1984).

3. The *AT & T* case presents a rare opportunity to read two alternative majority opinions—one written before and one after a petition for rehearing was granted.

4. New York Times, February 9, 1986, page 53, col. 1. For a criticism of the corporation counsel's position, see, e.g., Gillette & Singer, Colonial's Plant and Eminent Domain, The Boston Globe, February 23, 1986, page A25, col. 2:

[T]he corporation counsel's opinion * * * concludes that taking property from one owner and transferring it to another is both without precedent and outside the scope of the eminent domain power. On both points, the opinion is open to serious question. * * * The Supreme Judicial Court has upheld arrangements in which government borrows money from some private parties and lends it to others (home buyers or commercial enterprises) because the ultimate use of such funds is expected to redound to the public benefit by providing habitable living space, or jobs, or economic growth. The eminent domain power is simply another—albeit more invasive—mechanism to achieve similar public purposes.

See also Lazarus, The Commerce Clause Limitation on the Power to Condemn a Relocating Business, 96 Yale L.J. 1343 (1987); Note, Keeping the Home Team At Home, 74 Calif.L.Rev. 1329 (1986).

itself rather than transfer these businesses from one private owner to another?

My own suggestions for increasing the cities' use of their power as property owners are included as the last item in this section. Do these suggestions transgress the line that separates the proper functioning of the public and the private sectors?

GERALD FRUG, PROPERTY AND POWER: HARTOG ON THE LEGAL HISTORY OF NEW YORK CITY

1984 Am.Bar Foundation Research J. 673, 673–678.

PUBLIC PROPERTY AND PRIVATE POWER

Hendrik Hartog's *Public Property and Private Power* describes the "conceptual transformation" that radically altered the legal status and powers of the city of New York in the eighteenth and nineteenth centuries. According to this interesting and well-written account, the legal doctrines that affected New York City changed over a 140–year period in two significant ways. First, the legal system fractured the originally close connection between the city's property ownership and its power. Although in the eighteenth century the city was a corporation whose "property and governmental rights were blurred and mixed", in the nineteenth century it was stripped of its ability to use its ownership of property as a tool of governance. Second, the eighteenth-century conception of the city as neither a public nor a private entity was replaced with an understanding of it as a "public" corporation whose powers were significantly different from those of "private" business corporations. Thus Professor Hartog describes the transformation of the city's legal status in terms of two pairs of legal concepts: property and power, and public and private.

Professor Hartog organizes his account of the changing legal status of the city into three periods: the eighteenth century, the early nineteenth century, and the mid-nineteenth century. In the eighteenth century, he tells us, the City of New York was not characterized as a "public" as distinguished from a "private" corporation because no such general conceptual categories of corporations existed. Instead, every corporation, including the city, was viewed as a unique institution whose powers were understandable only in terms of the specific charter granted it by the state. The most important of New York City's charters, the one granted by Governor John Montgomerie in 1730, allowed the city to pass regulations for the public good, run jails and courthouses, maintain an exclusive franchise to operate ferries between Manhattan and Long Island, and own and manage a vast amount of real estate—including most of Manhattan Island north of Canal Street, the underwater land that surrounded Manhattan, and the waterfront of Brooklyn. All of these powers were understood together as the city's property. Accordingly, the city had the autonomy allowed any other property owner to shape its own identity independent of state control; its status as a property owner gave the city its power. This was true even though the city's authority to act as a property owner was based on a delegation of governmental power; such a delegation was the source of the authority exercised by every corporate property owner.

Of all the city's grants of power from the state, the most important was its ability to own real property. In the eighteenth century, city officials, like the officials of other corporations, did not concentrate their attention on providing services to the public; instead, "[t]he proper business of the [city] corporation was the management, care, and disposal of the real estate it owned". In part, this emphasis stemmed from the fact that real estate was the source of the city's revenue; until the 1760s, the city rarely resorted to direct taxation to provide city income. But the more important reason for the city's concentration on the management of its real property, according to Professor Hartog, was that the city used its property rights as a major vehicle for performing its functions of planning and governance. In the eighteenth century, there was no distinction between a corporation's property ownership and its governmental power, between property and sovereignty. Far from being divided into separate components—a private sphere of property management and a public sphere of government—the city used its property as a way of making governmental policy.

Professor Hartog's most original contribution to the study of the eighteenth-century city is his discussion of how New York City used its disposal of waterlots in lower Manhattan as a vehicle for effectuating public policy. In the deeds conveying waterlots to wealthy and favored citizens, the city imposed conditions requiring the purchasers to engage in construction—of streets and docks, for example—timed to coincide with the city's development plans. In this way, the city shifted the burden of expensive capital projects on to private individuals and relieved the government both of the cost of the projects and the need to build a bureaucracy to implement them. Moreover, it redistributed wealth from the rich to the larger community without transgressing the political ideology demanding limits on the role of government in society.

> Waterlot grants offered the possibility of achieving positive governmental goals—paving the streets, developing the harbor—at a time when there was no theory of direct government action. How do you get something done if you do not know how, or rather, if you cannot conceive of doing it yourself? You get someone else to do it for you * * * a chartered city with a substantial estate could use its wealth to achieve goals, to induce change * * *. The promised reward of the waterlot (and its profits) gave the city the power to coerce grantees to do things that they were not obliged as citizens to do.

By the early nineteenth century, this vision of the city as a legitimate property owner capable of wielding power through the exercise of its property rights had virtually disappeared. Instead of its property being the source of city power, the city became divided into separate spheres: its "public" nature allowed it to exercise "power," while its separate "private" sphere allowed it to exercise "property rights."

Indeed, property ownership, rather than enhancing the city's governmental powers, became an anomaly: property ownership seemed to make the corporation both a public and a private institution simultaneously. Accordingly, the corporation's exercise of property rights became more narrowly construed, and arguments were advanced to take the city out of the landowning business altogether. The use of city property was limited to its generation of revenue, and waterlot grants were awarded without conditions. "The corporation of the city of New York had become a public institution, financed largely by public taxation and devoting its energy to distinctively public concerns".

Even the source of the city's ability to exercise power had changed. The city began to seek the enactment of specific state legislation to authorize its actions even when authority for its actions might have been found in the Montgomerie charter.

> By the early nineteenth century, some city leaders had already concluded that "it would be altogether unsafe and erroneous to resort to the charter solely, upon any question of power, or its mode of exercise." As a government, its only "charter" was the accumulated relevant statutes of the New York legislature. The Montgomerie Charter still protected the city from legislative intervention into its property; but it was only the starting point for an evolving city government.

For the first third of the nineteenth century, these state legislative acts were "invariably drafted by city employees" and were passed only with the consent of the city. Thus no state infringement of city autonomy seemed to result from the practice of petitioning the state to authorize city activity. Indeed, reliance on state authorization seemed a more secure basis for city power than its corporate status, given the widespread antagonism of the time to the monopolistic power of corporate enterprise. Moreover, reliance on state legislative authorization allowed the city to avoid its previously excessive dependence on wealthy private citizens for effectuation of city policy. By creating a "public" sphere separate from that of the private interests of its citizens, the city could avoid being corrupted by private interests and ensure that it did not favor some of its citizens over others. It could instead become "an autonomous planner creating a stable context for private decision making".

For Professor Hartog, this early nineteenth-century vision of the city's "public" role is symbolized by its decision to obtain legislative authorization to lay out the streets of Manhattan according to a uniform rectangular grid. The city's imposition of a uniform plan for Manhattan, regardless of private boundaries, topographical differences, or potential uses of the land, was a bold assertion of public power. Such an exercise of "public" authority was sharply distinguishable from the kind of "private" authority property owners had to make decisions about their own property. Only the city could create the proper structure for land development; only property owners could make choices about the nature of that development. "The formal design of the city was public; but that design remained only a context for private decision making". Indeed the rhetoric used to defend the city's plan was

> a model for the justification of republican public authority: deferential toward private initiative, concerned to remain within the limits of proper public authority, yet insistent on the legitimacy of public control of a public sphere. The commissioners left largely unstated their own preferences as to the most proper, appropriate, or attractive development of city streets, for those were all areas of private choice. But they made it absolutely clear that private landowners had no right to expect the map to incorporate their particular plans or streets, for that was an area of public choice.

Not only was the city corporation divided into its public (governmental) and private (property owning) spheres, but all social decision making was organized around the same public/private distinction: some kinds of decisions were appropriate for government while others were appropriate for property owners, and the two kinds of decisions constantly had to be distinguished from each other.

Yet in the early nineteenth century one important aspect of the public/private distinction had still not been developed: there were still no separate bodies of law regulating "municipal corporations" and business corporations. Both kinds of corporations remained part of an "undifferentiated 'law' of corporations". As a result, the Corporation of the City of New York retained a number of the advantages and disadvantages generally attributed to corporations. All corporations retained areas of autonomy immune from state control, and all corporations were limited to those powers specifically delegated to them by the state, whether through legislation or the award of a charter. Indeed, legal theorists contrasted the Corporation of the City of New York not with other kinds of corporations but with unincorporated cities and towns. These entities, unlike corporations, were subject to unrestricted legislative power; moreover, unlike corporations, their authority was not limited to carrying out specific delegations from the state. It was not until the 1820s that the distinction between incorporated cities and unincorporated towns disappeared. Even then, important legal questions remained unresolved: Would the new general category of local governments be subject to unlimited state power (like unincorporated towns) or have rights against the state (like corporations)? Would local governments be able to exercise the full range of governmental power (like the state) or be limited to narrowly construed delegations (like corporations)?

The answers to these questions were not settled until the mid-nineteenth century when the courts began to develop a uniform system of local government law. In the final part of his book, Professor Hartog describes this development, one that made yet another dramatic change in the legal conception of city power. The courts held that the state had an unlimited amount of control over cities (making cities, unlike private corporations, merely creatures of the state) and that cities could not exercise the full range of governmental powers (making cities more like private corporations than the state).

> In place of local autonomy and political decentralization, the new law of municipal corporations posed the absolute centrality of state power and the insignificance of local publics in the political order. In place of the distinctive chartered rights of cities and the particular customs of local communities—both of which earlier served to frustrate the designs of central authorities—the new "law" held localities to explicit delegations of legislative power.

Moreover, rather than following the tradition of judicial deference to legislative decision making, the courts began to scrutinize delegations of power to local governments, construing narrowly the powers of municipal corporations (just as they did the powers of business corporations). The courts interposed themselves between the legislature and the cities, interpreting local power in terms of uniform judicial standards rather than particular legislative intent.

One method the courts used to regulate the cities was to redefine the ways cities were simultaneously public and private. Rather than seeing the private sphere as based on a local government's ownership of private property, the courts divided city governance functions into "proprietary" and "governmental" functions. If a function was defined as proprietary, the courts could treat a city like a private corporation; conversely, if a function was defined as governmental, the courts could treat a city as being just like the state. Courts even treated certain functions—such as the building of an aqueduct for New York City's water supply—as proprietary for some purposes and as governmental for others. By asserting that the city was acting as a proprietor in building the aqueduct, the courts denied the city the defense of sovereign immunity when it was sued in tort; by labeling the operation of the aqueduct a governmental function, the courts could ensure control over how the city operated the aqueduct.

This new form of applying the public/private distinction to the city put a double constraint on city power. In refusing to allow the city to protect its power under sovereign immunity by labeling activities "proprietary," the courts assumed that only in its public capacity was the city exercising independent power: "[They] identified a municipal corporation as a public entity for purposes of liability when it exercised judgment and discretion and characterized it as a 'private' entity whenever it was bound strictly by the dictates of legislation. As an autonomous decision maker, it was public; as a dependent agency it was private".

But when dealing with the question of state authority over city activities, it became clear that the "public" nature of the city's power also required control. For example, Professor Hartog describes how New York City's franchise to operate ferries to Brooklyn, considered by Chancellor Kent in 1836 to be " 'an absolute grant of vested property, or an estate in fee, which could not lawfully be questioned or disturbed, except by due process of law' ", became understood later in the century to be part of the public sphere of the corporation, subject to legislative repeal and intervention.   "By 1865," he writes, "the corporation of the city of New York had become legally indistinguishable from propertyless institutions of derivative public administration * * *. [E]ven its corporate capacity to own property existed only as a function of its representation of the interests of the state".   During the same time that the courts were tightening their restrictions on local authority, the state legislature stopped seeking the city's consent before enacting legislation affecting local interests and, in 1857, declared that it was free to intervene at will in the city's affairs.   "From then on, 'domination over the affairs of New York City went merrily and perniciously on from session to session of the legislature' ".

In summary, then, Professor Hartog describes a dramatic transformation of the legal status of the City of New York during the years 1730 to 1870:

> The eighteenth-century corporation had regarded property as essential to an autonomous government.   The corporation of the early nineteenth century had worked to separate corporate property from dependent republican government, leaving that property in a residual sphere of private, corporate autonomy.   But (by the mid-nineteenth century) * * * the private sphere of the corporation (as distinguished from the "proprietary" sphere of the municipal corporation) no longer existed.

New York City changed from being considered a corporation exercising the rights of a property owner to being considered a governmental entity threatening to the rights of property owners, one that required strict legislative and judicial supervision.   In its status as a "creature of the state," the city could still sometimes act in a proprietary capacity and thus be seen as more a private corporation than a government.   But even this private aspect of its nature no longer gave the city substantial protection from state control.   * * *

DAVID OSBORNE & TED GAEBLER, ENTERPRISING GOVERNMENT: EARNING RATHER THAN SPENDING

From D. Osborne & T. Gaebler: Reinventing Government.
Pp. 196–197, 200–202, 214–216 (1992).

Pressed hard by the tax revolts of the 1970s and 1980s and the fiscal crisis of the early 1990s, entrepreneurial governments are increasingly * * * searching for nontax revenues.   They are measuring their return on investment.   They are recycling their money, finding the 15 or 20 percent that can be redirected.   Some are even running for-profit enterprises.

> The Milwaukee Metropolitan Sewerage District transforms 60,000 tons of sewage sludge into fertilizer every year and sells it—generating $7.5 million in revenue.

Phoenix earns $750,000 a year by siphoning off the methane gas generated by a large wastewater treatment plant and selling it to the city of Mesa, for home heating and cooking.

Chicago turned a $2 million annual cost into a $2 million source of revenue by contracting with a private company to tow away abandoned cars. The city once spent $24 per car to tow cars; now a private company pays $25 a car for the privilege.

The St. Louis County Police developed a system that allows officers to call in their reports, rather than write them up. The department then licensed the software to a private company—earning $25,000 every time it sells to another police department.

The Washington State ferry system generated $1 million a year in new revenues during the early 1980s by rebidding its food service contract; more than $150,000 a year by bidding out a contract to sell advertising in the terminal building; and another $150,000 a year by letting a contract to operate duty-free shops on its two international boats.

Paulding County, Georgia, built a 244–bed prison, when it needed only 60 extra beds, so it could charge other jurisdictions $35 a night to handle their overflow. In the jail's first year of business, it brought in $1.4 million, $200,000 more than its operating costs.

Enterprising police departments in California are earning money by renting out motel rooms as weekend jails. The courts often let those convicted of drunk driving serve their time on weekends. So some police departments reserve blocks of cheap motel rooms, pay someone to sit outside and make sure everyone stays in their room, and rent the rooms to convicted drivers as jail cells at $75 a night.
* * *

Fairfield [California] * * * [was] the city that invented the mission-driven budget * * *. In 1976, a developer approached then city manager Gale Wilson for permission to develop a small shopping center. Wilson and his staff believed that Fairfield—which sits astride Highway 80, halfway between San Francisco and Sacramento—would grow into a perfect location for a large regional mall. (Fairfield had 51,700 people in 1976; today it has 80,000.) So they created a Redevelopment Authority, which bought 90 acres of land for $3.6 million, sold 48 to the developer for a $2 million profit, and built a new highway interchange. The developer put in a "super regional mall" with more than a million square feet and five large department stores. As part of the agreement, Fairfield negotiated a piece of the action: 10 to 17 percent of net cash flow for 65 years. When Proposition 13 limited the city's take from property taxes, Wilson negotiated a 55–cent-per-acre assessment for off-site improvements—roads, sewers, and the like—for 25 years. It now brings in between $400,000 and $500,000 a year and covers the cost of the bonds floated to pay for the improvements.

After the mall opened, in 1985, the city began leasing and selling off its other parcels. Overall, according to Fairfield's calculations, its investment of $8 million in land purchases and relocation costs had generated, by mid-1991, $6.4 million in sales, $9.4 million in increased property taxes, and $15.4 million in sales taxes. The profit-sharing agreement is generating $120,000 a year, and ground leases from the second major parcel developed, the Gateway Plaza, will kick in soon. The city still owns about 35 acres, which it intends to sell or lease as the market can absorb them.

Fairfield has since taken a similar approach to its other development projects. When a developer tried to build a large residential development just outside city limits, for instance, the city backed a county proposition that made it difficult to develop land outside a city, then proposed a deal that convinced the developer to build in Fairfield. The city built a public golf course around which the developer could build, then allowed him to increase the number of homes in the project from 800 to 1,200. The only catch: the developer had to donate land for the golf course and a public school, build a public road into the project, and put in the storm drainage system.

The city used revenue from the course and clubhouse to pay off the $7 million it borrowed to build the course. The result: The developer got higher value building lots, because they surrounded a golf course, and the city built its first public golf course with no subsidy from the taxpayers.

The project worked so well, in fact, that the city then negotiated a similar deal with another developer—in which the developer not only donated land but built a reservoir. As we write, Fairfield is studying the option of selling the first course and investing the profit of $20 to $25 million in some other amenity, such as a sports complex. "We intervened in the market by creating more value," explains City Manager Charlie Long. "The golf course created higher home prices because it created more value, and we then take that increment of profit and put it in the public sector to pay for more amenities."

Lest you think this kind of entrepreneurship can happen only in California, Cincinnati earns 17 percent of the profits from a hotel and office complex in the city center, for which the city assembled the land and arranged the financing; San Antonio is a partner in several real estate projects, including a Sheraton hotel; and the Metropolitan Area Transit Authority in Washington, D.C., has developed lucrative real estate above and around some of its subway stations. Orlando, Florida, even struck a deal in which a developer built a new city hall.

Orlando Mayor Bill Frederick, first elected in 1980 in the wake of a nationwide tax revolt, understood that his citizens wanted lower taxes. (He pushed property taxes down by 29 percent over the next decade.) He knew that if he wanted to accomplish anything, he would have "to look to new solutions—especially when it comes to finances."

"If Orlando had taken 5 percent of its General Fund revenue in 1980 and used it to finance a 30–year series of bonds," he explains, "we could have built only $30 million worth of capital projects." Instead Orlando used a series of profit-making authorities and funds to build nearly $2.5 billion worth of facilities—an expanded airport, a new basketball arena, wastewater treatment plants, a performing arts center—with virtually no subsidy from local taxpayers.

The crowning achievement was city hall. To avoid dipping into general revenues, the city used seven acres around the old city hall as a lure—asking developers to compete for the right to develop the land. The winner, Lincoln Property Company, agreed to build a $32.5 million, 246,000–square-foot, state-of-the-art city hall, complete with its own closed-circuit television system. In exchange, it got the right to build two office towers adjacent to city hall. Ground rents from the towers will pay off the city's construction bonds.

In addition, the city will receive 20 percent of the net proceeds from office and retail rents over a set income level, plus 20 percent of the proceeds from any sale or refinancing. (If Lincoln fails to build city hall to the city's satisfaction, or fails to begin paying ground rents on the first office tower in 1992 and the second in 1996, it will forfeit a $750,000 deposit.) The city expects the project's revenues to pay off its 30–year bonds in 10 to 12 years. * * *

The San Francisco suburb of San Bruno owns its cable television system * * *. David Thomas, who runs it, is a typical entrepreneur. He has pride of ownership. He is mission-driven. He plans ahead. He strives to please his customers. He is aware of his competitors—and he beats the pants off them. In 1991, San Bruno charged its 11,200 subscribers $12.55 for a 31–channel package.

Private cable companies in the county charged an average of $19.57 for the comparable package. Yet even at San Bruno's low price, the system generated enough money to upgrade all its hardware—cables, boxes, everything—every 10 years, without borrowing a dime. (This is after it returns 5 percent of gross revenues to the city.) "We don't use the word *profit*," Thomas smiles, "but we do use the term retained earnings."

We saw the same mind-set in Santa Clara. Like San Bruno's cable company, Santa Clara's publicly owned electric utility returns 5 percent of gross revenues to the city, but still charges 30 to 40 percent less than its private competitor does in surrounding communities. Thirty years ago, it spearheaded a group of other municipal utilities to form the Northern California Power Agency, which then built a large, 200–megawatt geothermal energy project, as well as the last major dam in California. When tax credits favored wind energy, the utility bought 2,600 acres and leased them out to private companies to build windmills.

Santa Clara's Water and Sewer Utility created a solar division—in effect, the nation's first solar utility. It provides hot water units for apartment buildings and swimming pools. The utility buys, installs, and maintains the equipment, charging the customer a monthly fee for six months of the year to cover the costs.

When the city's housing market became extremely tight, Santa Clara's Redevelopment Agency leased the existing city golf course to developers, who are putting in 2,000 apartment units; used the lease revenues to pay for a new golf and tennis club built over the city's old landfill; and put in wells to tap the natural gas generated by the buried garbage. The new course anchors the Santa Clara Trade and Convention Center (built next to Great America), which includes a 240,000–square-foot convention center, a 502–room hotel, and an office building. "One of our major goals was to create a long-term revenue stream for the city," says City Manager Jennifer Sparacino, "and it is definitely accomplishing that." Despite problems filling up the office building, the entire deal is already generating a positive return.

The private sector often complains about public enterprise, arguing that government should not compete with business. And many public leaders buy the argument. Lewis V. Pond, city manager of San Bruno, wants to sell the cable system. "We can't make money," he told us, "because we're a government." But where is it written that government should handle only lemons, while business gets all the profit centers? As Don Von Raesfeld said during the Great America debate, "It's been awfully interesting to me in my career as a city manager here that the people are always willing to push on to government losers in this country. The winners are always to be preserved to the private enterprise system."

In reality, there are several good reasons why government *should* sometimes compete with the private sector. Some services are natural monopolies. It is inefficient to string two or three sets of electrical lines and or bury two or three sets of gas lines in a city, for example. In such cases, governments can grant a private monopoly and regulate its prices, or they can create a public monopoly. The latter option often delivers a better deal to the public. For 100 years, publicly owned utilities have sold electricity at lower prices than their private counterparts. Today, publicly owned cable television systems do the same.

In other areas, where there is insufficient private competition, public enterprise can act as a competitive yardstick, forcing private firms to lower their prices and pursue greater efficiency. The Phoenix Department of Public Works does this by competing in garbage collection.

Finally, there are some occasions on which the private sector chooses to abandon a profitable business. Marriott sold Great America even though it was profitable, because industrial development would have been *more* profitable. (Being private, Marriott could ignore the public costs, which would have been enormous.) The Mets dropped a minor league franchise they owned in Visalia not because it was unprofitable, but because they decided to limit their farm system to the eastern United States. When no private buyers turned up, Visalia did just what

Santa Clara did. It took over the franchise, proved it could make money for six years, and sold it to local owners for a profit. * * *

AMERICAN TELEPHONE AND TELEGRAPH COMPANY v. THE VILLAGE OF ARLINGTON HEIGHTS

Supreme Court of Illinois, 1993.
156 Ill.2d 399, 189 Ill.Dec. 723, 620 N.E.2d 1040.

JUSTICE HEIPLE delivered the opinion of the court:

The question presented by this case is whether municipal governments can extort toll charges or franchise fees for the crossing of public ways. They cannot. The factual context of this case is that AT & T is laying an underground fiber optic cable along an 85–mile line in northern Illinois between Glenview and Rockford. The line is being laid along railroad right-of-way of the Chicago and North Western Transportation Company (CNW) pursuant to an easement granted by CNW. The cable is designed to carry only long distance telephone communications. Additionally, telecommunications traffic can enter or leave the cable only at AT & T's terminal points in Glenview, Rockford, and Rolling Meadows.

In transversing the 85–mile cable route following the railroad right-of-way, the cable must pass under more than 140 travelled public ways subject to the jurisdiction of five counties, six townships, 13 cities and villages, plus the Illinois Department of Transportation, the Corps of Engineers and the Illinois Toll Authority. Five cities and villages in the path of this cable will not permit street crossings unless AT & T agrees to so-called franchise agreements or tolls which AT & T refused to pay. Various demands were made upon AT & T including a percentage of gross revenues and $2.50 per foot of cable within the municipalities regardless of whether the cable was crossing the street or located entirely on CNW's property. It is to be noted that none of the municipalities object to the installation of the cable *per se*. They simply want to collect a toll for it.

In an action by the telephone company, the trial court initially entered a preliminary injunction in favor of the telephone company allowing the installation of the fiber optic cable without a franchise agreement. The appellate court, on an interlocutory appeal taken by the municipalities, affirmed the granting of the preliminary injunction, and the cause was subsequently returned to the trial court for a ruling on the permanent injunction. A permanent injunction barring the municipalities' interference with the installation of the fiber optic cable was entered by the trial court and the municipalities again appealed. The appellate court concluded that municipalities do not have an absolute right to require a franchise agreement as a prerequisite to a telephone company's utilization of the public streets. We allowed the municipalities' petition for leave to appeal and, in a split decision, reversed the appellate court. A majority of this court held that the municipalities have the right to prohibit AT & T from crossing public streets without a franchise agreement, and that the franchise agreement could require AT & T to pay rent for the crossing of the streets. Thereafter, AT & T's petition for rehearing was allowed, and the case was reargued. Today we rule that municipalities do not have a proprietary interest in the public streets and may not raise revenue by coercing telephone companies into franchise agreements. * * *

Defendants claim that they have the right to require revenue-raising franchise agreements or tolls as a pre-condition to the use of public streets by telephone companies. While municipalities have the authority to enact regulations relating to the use of the public streets and to charge reasonable regulatory fees for such use, they do not have the authority to hold the public streets hostage as a means of raising revenue. Defendants, by classifying their current attempt to raise revenue as franchise agreements, are attempting to circumvent both this court's previous holdings prohibiting municipalities from charging rent for the use of city streets and the statutory requirement that the taxing of a telecommunications company must be based upon the business originating within the corporate limits of the municipality.

It needs to be borne in mind that AT & T is not seeking permission to use city streets for the operation of a business within city limits such as a garbage collection service, a street railway, a cable TV franchise, etc. That is to say, they do not seek to garner revenue from the use of city streets. What is sought here is different in character from what would normally be considered a franchise-type business seeking protection, licensing and special privileges for the use of city streets. No person or entity within any of the municipalities in this case is to be connected to or have the use of the fiber optic cable which is sought to be laid. All that plaintiffs seek here is to get from one side of town to the other.

Regardless of the name given to this particular method of revenue enhancement, whether it is called a franchise, a rental fee or a tax, it is, in its essence, a toll. Parenthetically, it is to be noted that there are 1,281 cities and villages in Illinois, 102 counties and 1,434 townships, each of which maintain travelled ways. If each of these governmental units had the right to charge tolls for conduits going under and over their streets, the effect would amount to legalized extortion and a crippling of communication and commerce as we know it.

Municipalities do not possess proprietary powers over the public streets. They only possess regulatory powers. The public streets are held in trust for the use of the public. While numerous powers and rights regarding public streets have been granted to municipalities by the General Assembly, they are all regulatory in character, and do not grant any authority to rent or to lease parts, or all, of a public street. * * *

The villages of Arlington Heights and Palatine are both home rule municipalities. As such, their powers are to be liberally construed. However, the power of a home rule municipality to levy a tax is limited to issues of local rather than statewide concern. A telephone company which is running a fiber optic cable across the State and through various municipalities is not a matter of purely local concern and is an issue of statewide concern. Thus, the fact that the villages of Arlington Heights and Palatine are home rule municipalities does not permit this type of franchise agreement to be imposed upon AT & T. * * *

The fact that AT & T seeks to undercross certain streets in this case with a fiber optic cable results in no intrusion on, or diminution of, the use or safety of the streets. * * * Municipal governments, whether home rule or non-home-rule, are creatures of the Illinois Constitution. They have no other powers. Nothing in the Illinois Constitution or Illinois statutory law authorizes cities and villages to charge tolls for the crossing of the streets. If the plaintiffs were carrying phone messages in trucks commuting between Glenview and Rockford (if such can be imagined), instead of carrying the messages on a fiber optic cable, the municipalities would not be authorized to stop the plaintiffs' trucks and charge them tolls as they crossed municipal boundaries. The streets exist for the benefit of the entire public and are subject only to reasonable regulations regarding usage. Streets do not exist and were not created as either obstructions or revenue-producing property for municipalities. * * *

JUSTICE BILANDIC, dissenting:

As the sole survivor of the *old majority* (*AT & T v. Village of Arlington Heights* (December 4, 1992)), it is incumbent upon me to respond. (Justices Clark, Moran and Cunningham retired in December 1992.) The three-member *old minority* did not suffer any attrition. With the addition of two new members to their ranks, the *old minority* has been transformed into the *new majority*. I hasten to add my congratulations and respectful dissent.

The *new majority* opinion is substantially the same as the *old dissent*. The few changes did not, in my judgment, rehabilitate a fatally flawed argument.

There is no need to unduly burden this dissent with a restatement of the arguments made in the prior majority opinion, which is attached as an appendix to this dissent, since they can be incorporated by reference to the December 4, 1992, opinion. This dissent will be confined to additional argument. * * *

The new majority, by its opinion, is, in effect, levying a tax upon the citizens of the defendant municipalities. Pursuant to the majority's mandate, these municipalities must grant AT & T a valuable easement, an estate in land, *for free*. Generally, the grantor of an easement is entitled to receive consideration in return for such a grant. This is true even in the instant case where AT & T has paid a substantial sum of money to the railroad for its grant of an easement to AT & T. The new majority's opinion, however, requires the municipalities to grant AT & T an easement and receive nothing in return. The new majority's opinion, in effect, deprives the municipalities of revenue they otherwise would have received. The new majority is forcing these municipalities to subsidize AT & T.

Since the municipalities hold their streets in trust for the benefit of their citizens, the forced subsidy, in effect, amounts to an exactment of a tax upon the local, individual inhabitants of the defendant municipalities who receive no benefit. The new majority's imposition of this tax is in the nature of a taking, without just compensation, for a private purpose and runs afoul of the fourteenth amendment rights of these citizens in numerous respects. * * *

The result of the new majority's opinion is solely a private benefit to AT & T. The legislature has already granted telephone companies like AT & T the power of eminent domain to acquire easements from private property owners necessary to the construction of its cable. Along with this power, however, comes the corresponding duty to provide just compensation. The utility's statutory power of eminent domain, however, does not extend to municipal property. The municipalities neither solicited nor invited AT & T to use their streets. They were content to be left alone. However, it was AT & T which chose to go through the municipalities because it was more profitable for it and would give it an advantage over its competition.

Although it admits to paying a "substantial" fee to a railroad for an easement, AT & T refuses to pay any compensation to the municipalities for the extraordinary use of their streets. AT & T could have avoided going through the municipalities by exercising its power of eminent domain to obtain easements from private property owners beyond the municipal boundaries. However, AT & T would be required to pay "just compensation" for those easements. It would also be delayed because of the constitutional requirement of compliance with "due process" in any eminent domain proceedings against private property owners. The end result of the new majority's opinion is to save AT & T both money and time. Clearly, saving a private, profit-motivated company money and time does not serve any public purpose. Therefore, the new majority's opinion exacts a tax from the municipal inhabitants in violation of their fourteenth amendment due process rights. * * *

APPENDIX TO DISSENT

JUSTICE BILANDIC delivered the opinion of the court: * * *

The question presented in this appeal is whether the defendant municipalities may require a franchise agreement as a precondition to AT & T's use of public streets for private gain. * * *

Municipal corporations possess a double character—one governmental, regulatory or public, and the other proprietary or private. The defendant municipalities here argue that they have both regulatory and proprietary powers over the streets. They argue that they may, pursuant to their proprietary power over streets within their control, impose franchise fees, in the nature of rent, upon those who seek to use such streets for purposes other than ordinary travel. AT & T, on the other hand, argues that municipalities have only regulatory authority (or police powers) over public streets and have no right to prohibit AT & T from using public streets to install its fiber optic cable system. AT & T claims that a municipality's authority is limited to enacting regulations relating to the use of public streets and to charging reasonable *regulatory* fees for such use. This court's previous decisions and applicable State statutes, however, directly repudiate AT & T's argument.

In Illinois, fee simple title to the streets is vested in municipal corporations. It is well established that municipalities hold title to streets in trust for the benefit of use by the public, and on principle, such trust property can be disposed of by the municipality only in accordance with the public interest. Because municipalities hold title to the streets for the benefit of the public, this court has recognized that all citizens are vested with the right to use public streets for travel from one place to another in the ordinary court of business or pleasure. No person or company, however, has an unfettered right to make a greater use of public streets for his or its own private gain. Here, AT & T seeks the privilege of using public streets in an extraordinary manner. AT & T does not want to use the streets as a means of travel. Rather, AT & T wants to tear up the streets and permanently install its cable underneath them, with the obvious goal of increasing its market share of long distance telephone service.

A special right or privilege conferred upon a private corporation to use public streets in an extraordinary manner is commonly referred to as a "franchise." * * * This court has consistently recognized that municipalities have statutory authority to prohibit a public utility from using public streets without a franchise agreement. * * * More specific to this case, our decisions have recognized that, where the enjoyment of a franchise depends upon the consent of a municipality, its right to impose conditions authorizes it to exact payment of a fee, as compensation for the privilege of using public streets in an extraordinary manner. * * *

AT & T argues, however, that municipalities are limited to charging regulatory fees for the privilege of using public streets. As support for this claim, AT & T argues that municipalities have only regulatory, and not proprietary, powers over public streets. However, decisions of this court have specifically stated that the right to demand a franchise fee is an exercise of the municipality's *proprietary* power over public property. * * * [I]n *Broeckl v. Chicago Park District* (1989), 131 Ill.2d 79, 86, 136 Ill.Dec. 106, 544 N.E.2d 792 * * * plaintiffs * * *, boat owners, challenged the park district's practice of charging mooring fees in excess of costs actually incurred. The plaintiffs in *Broeckl*, like the plaintiffs in this case, argued that the park districts held the harbors in trust for the benefit of the public and that the mooring fees charged must be based upon the actual cost of regulating the services provided. The court rejected this claim, finding that the park district was not exercising a police power function when it imposed the mooring fee. Rather, the park district, *pursuant to its proprietary powers over public property,* was renting the mooring facilities and could charge reasonable fees for the use of the facilities. This court concluded that the amount of the fees charged was a matter within the park commissioners' discretion.

Thus, our decisions have conclusively established the two propositions necessary to decide this case. First, municipalities have statutory authority to prohibit a company, such as AT & T, from using public streets for extraordinary purposes without a franchise agreement. * * * Second, this court, in a long line of decisions, has recognized that municipalities, pursuant to their *proprietary* powers over public property, may require payment of compensation in the nature of rental fees, for the privilege of using public streets. * * *

We next consider whether the municipalities involved in this dispute that are *home rule units* (Arlington Heights, Palatine and the City of Chicago, as intervenor) have the power to prohibit AT & T from using public streets within their control pending negotiation of a franchise agreement, and to require AT & T to pay compensation for the privilege of installing its fiber optic cable under their streets. * * * We conclude that home rule municipalities have inherent constitutional authority to require AT & T to enter a negotiated franchise agreement, which exacts fees, in the nature of rent, as a precondition to AT & T's extraordinary use of streets wholly within the control of those municipalities. * * *

ASSOCIATED PENNSYLVANIA CONSTRUCTORS v. CITY OF PITTSBURGH

Commonwealth Court of Pennsylvania, 1990.
134 Pa.Cmwth. 536, 579 A.2d 461, appeal denied,
527 Pa. 618, 590 A.2d 759 (1991).

PALLADINO, JUDGE.

Associated Pennsylvania Constructors, Constructors Association of Western Pennsylvania, Allegheny Asphalt & Paving, Inc., Burrell Construction & Supply Company, Carnegie Tar & Asphalt Company, Northern Industries, Russell Industries, Inc., and Trumbull Corporation, (Appellants) appeal an order of the Court of Common Pleas of Allegheny County (trial court) which denied Appellants' application for an injunction and declaratory relief.

The parties stipulated the following pertinent facts. The City of Pittsburgh (City) * * * has owned and operated a plant which produces asphalt since 1982. The City Council enacted the Resolution No. 78 of 1988 (Resolution) which authorizes the City to enter into agreements to sell asphalt to other municipalities and governmental agencies outside of the City. The Resolution has not been specifically authorized by the Pennsylvania General Assembly (Assembly).

Appellants filed a complaint in equity seeking a declaration that the Resolution is illegal and seeking a permanent injunction against any agreements entered into pursuant to the Resolution. The Trial Court denied the request for an injunction and declared that the Resolution is valid. The Trial Court held that the construction of public roads is a clear governmental function, that the production of asphalt is necessary and incidental to carry out this governmental function and that Act of July 12, 1972, P.L. 762, *as amended*, 53 P.S. §§ 481–490 [4] (Act) permits the City to engage in governmental functions with other municipalities.

On appeal, Appellants renew the argument rejected by the trial court that the Resolution authorizes the City to engage in a proprietary function not approved by the Assembly in violation of Section 1–302(b) of the Law which provides in pertinent part as follows:

> (b) No municipality shall (i) engage in any proprietary or private business except as authorized by the General Assembly * * *.

Appellants do not challenge the City's right to produce asphalt for its own use under the Law. Appellants contend only that the sale of asphalt by the City to other municipalities is a proprietary function and therefore is a violation of the Law. Appellants argue that selling asphalt to other municipalities to raise revenue is not part of the governmental function of roadbuilding.

The only issue before this court is whether the sale of asphalt by the City to other municipalities is a proprietary or private business and therefore prohibited by the Law.

The term "proprietary or private business" is not defined in the Law. However, the proprietary-governmental function distinction has been frequently utilized but seldom clearly defined. * * * In *Morris v. School District of Township of Mount Lebanon*, 393 Pa. 633, 637–8, 144 A.2d 737, 739 (1958), *rev'd on other grounds*, 453 Pa. 584, 305 A.2d 877 (1973), the supreme court, examining the proprietary-governmental function distinction in the context of governmental immunity, stated as follows:

> Perhaps there is no issue known to the law which is surrounded by more confusion than the question whether a given municipal operation is governmental or proprietary in nature. * * * In general, (and perhaps unhelpfully), it has been said that if a given activity is one which a local governmental unit is not statutorily required to perform, or if it may also be carried on by private enterprise, or if it is used as a means of raising revenue, the function is proprietary.

Applying the *Morris* factors to the instant case, we conclude that the sale of asphalt by the City to other municipalities is a proprietary act or private business act. No statute exists that requires municipalities to produce and sell asphalt to each other. Clearly, the enterprise of supplying asphalt for the construction of roads can be and is performed

---

4. Section 3 of the Act, 53 P.S. § 483 states as follows:

Two or more municipalities in this Commonwealth may jointly cooperate, or any municipality or municipalities may jointly cooperate with any municipality or municipalities located in any other state, in the exercise or in the performance of their respective governmental functions, powers or responsibilities. For the purpose of carrying the provisions of this act into effect the municipalities cooperating shall enter into such joint agreements as may be deemed appropriate for such purposes.

by private parties such as Appellants. Furthermore, there is no dispute that the purpose of the Resolution is to increase revenue for the City. Therefore, we conclude that the City seeks to engage in a proprietary or private business in selling asphalt to other municipalities.

The Resolution has the effect of placing the City in direct competition with Appellants in the business of supplying asphalt for road construction. Such a result is prohibited under the Law without authorization from the General Assembly. The General Assembly has not approved the Resolution. Consequently, we hold that the Resolution violates section 1–302(b) of the Home Rule Charter and Optional Plans Law and is invalid. * * *

WARNER CABLE COMMUNICATIONS, INC. v. CITY OF NICEVILLE

United States Court of Appeals, Eleventh Circuit, 1990.
911 F.2d 634.

TJOFLAT, CHIEF JUDGE: * * *

The City of Niceville is a municipal corporation chartered, organized, and existing under the constitution and laws of the State of Florida. Warner is a corporation organized under the laws of the State of Illinois. Warner, through its predecessor corporation, began supplying cable television services to the City in 1971, pursuant to a franchise agreement with the City. The current franchise agreement between the parties was enacted by the Niceville City Council in 1980 as Ordinance 438. It is a nonexclusive franchise, expiring in 1995.

Subsequent to the City's enactment of Ordinance 438, Congress passed the Cable Communications Policy Act of 1984, which authorizes local governments to own and operate their own cable television systems. In 1985, after receiving numerous consumer complaints about Warner's service, the City began to explore the possibility of constructing and operating its own system. Following a favorable preliminary report form the outside firm commissioned by the city council to investigate the feasibility of such a system, a resolution concerning a City-owned cable system was submitted to the voters on July 15, 1985. The resolution passed by an overwhelming majority. * * *

In October 1985, the city council * * * enacted Ordinance 583, which authorized the City to issue revenue bonds for the purpose of constructing and operating a cable television system. * * * On November 5, 1985, Warner filed suit against the City, alleging that the City's conduct violated Warner's constitutional rights to freedom of speech and due process. * * *

Warner challenges the constitutionality of Ordinance 581 on first amendment grounds. Warner's attack anticipates the eventual success of the City's entry into the cable business as Warner's competitor. According to Warner, the city will be able to offer lower prices to cable subscribers, which "will create a press owned and controlled by the government, and will silence the only private cable operator, thereby 'muzzl[ing] one of the very agencies the Framers of our Constitution thoughtfully and deliberately selected to improve our society and keep it free.' " * * *

Warner's argument is essentially as follows. If the state or a state agent, here the City of Niceville, prevents a cable speaker from communicating its message to the public, the state or state agent "silences" the speaker. Where the prevention is only partial and stems from the state's regulation of the time, place, or manner in which the speech is conducted, the first amendment is violated unless the state demonstrates that the regulation is necessary to serve an important government interest. Ordinance 581, enacted by the City, will have the direct and foreseeable effect of diminishing—perhaps eliminating—Warner's share of the Niceville cable audience and is not necessary to serve an important government interest. Therefore, the ordinance will violate Warner's first amendment rights by preventing Warner from freely communicating its message to the citizens of Niceville. * * *

Warner claims that, because the City's plan "abridges Warner's right to speak" without furthering an important governmental interest, it does not meet the standard set forth in *United States v. O'Brien,* 391 U.S. 367, 88 S.Ct. 1673, 20 L.Ed.2d 672 (1968) (four-part test for justifying governmental regulation that incidentally impacts upon first amendment interests). Invocation of this standard, however, only reveals the unusual nature of Warner's prevention argument. Not only does Ordinance 581 not interfere in any way with Warner's programming decisions and editorial policies, it neither regulates the conduct through which Warner communicates its message nor restricts Warner's access to its audience. Whether or not the City's cable system becomes operative, Warner will continue to have access to the Niceville cable television market unimpeded by any newly imposed restrictions as to time, place, or manner. The assertion that the City's plan "abridges Warner's *right* to speak" (emphasis added) is simply inaccurate.

What the City's ordinance does abridge is the continuation of Warner's profitable position as the only speaker in a captive cable market. A City-owned cable system, if successful, will no doubt reduce the audience for Warner's speech and diminish the profitability of that speech. Such economic loss, however, does not constitute a *first amendment injury.* "The inquiry for First Amendment purposes is not concerned with economic impact; rather, it looks only to the effect of this ordinance upon freedom of expression." *Young v. American Mini Theatres, Inc.,* 427 U.S. 50, 78, 96 S.Ct. 2440, 2456, 49 L.Ed.2d 310 (1976) (Powell, J., concurring). Warner's freedom of expression remains unimpaired by the City's plan. As the district court put it, "while the first amendment protects Warner's right to make its programming decisions, its right to disseminate its speech, and its viewers' concomitant right to receive the speech, the first amendment does not guarantee that someone will listen to Warner's speech, nor pay to listen."

When the competing speaker is the government, that speaker is not itself protected by the first amendment, but "[t]o find that the government is without First Amendment protection is not to find that the government is prohibited from speaking." *Muir v. Alabama Educ. Television Comm'n,* 688 F.2d 1033, 1038 (5th Cir.1982) (en banc), *cert. denied,* 460 U.S. 1023, 103 S.Ct. 1274, 75 L.Ed.2d 495 (1983). "Even without First Amendment protection government may 'participate in the marketplace of ideas' and 'contribute its own views to those of other speakers.'" *Id.* Warner, however, raises the specter of government speech becoming so dominant as to "drown out" the voice of private speakers. This concern is misplaced in the context of the current case. We agree that the government may not speak so loudly as to make it impossible for other speakers to be heard by their audience. The government would then be preventing the speakers' access to that audience, and first amendment concerns would arise. For instance, if a city government builds a better soapbox, equipped with spotlights and powerful loudspeakers, next to the longstanding antique soapbox in the city square, and if government speakers dominate the new soapbox, then speakers on the first soapbox do not truly have the opportunity to communicate their views even to those who might with to hear them. The city would indeed be "drowning out" the voice of the private speakers. But if the soapboxes are equal and the city speakers simply attract more listeners because the listeners prefer the city's message, there is no "drowning out," no denial of access, and no first amendment violation. Although the government does not have a constitutionally-protected right to speak, its actions may promote the first amendment interest of making more speech available to the citizenry: the speaker on the first soapbox cannot demand to monopolize the information-seeking audience in the name of the first amendment. Like that speaker, under the City's plan, Warner retains unimpeded access to the Niceville cable television viewers. It can decide for itself whether and what it wishes to continue to communicate to them. * * * [W]e need apply no balancing test to the City's action. Because Warner retains the uninfringed right to send its messages to the Niceville audience, we hold that Warner's feared loss of profits, due to competition by the City-owned system, does not constitute a first amendment injury. * * *

Although we recognize Warner's legitimate concerns over the City's potential misuse of its position, we do not consider its due process claim ripe for adjudication at this time. * * * [W]e do not foreclose the possibility that the City's dual role as Warner's regulator and competitor might, in particular circumstances, give rise to a valid due process claim. If a dispute arises in which the City is called upon to the " 'complainant, jury, judge and executioner,' " *Cruz v. Ferre,* 755 F.2d 1415, 1422 (11th Cir.1985), there may exist an intolerably high risk of self-interested, unfair governmental action, particularly since the city's competitor in this case is a first amendment speaker. We recognized in *Cruz* that, because of the "potentially great impact upon first amendment rights[,] * * * regulation of a communicative activity must adhere to more narrowly drawn procedures than regulation of ordinary commercial activity." Currently, however, Warner has brought no matter before the City for decision, and the City is threatening no regulatory action that will result in redressable injury to Warner. In the absence of any such controversy involving actual or threatened injury to Warner, our consideration of its procedural due process claim would be premature. * * *

CITY OF PITTSBURGH v. ALCO PARKING CORPORATION

Supreme Court of the United States, 1974.
417 U.S. 369, 94 S.Ct. 2291, 41 L.Ed.2d 132.

MR. JUSTICE WHITE delivered the opinion of the Court.

The issue in this case is the validity under the Federal Constitution of Ordinance No. 704, which was enacted by the Pittsburgh, Pennsylvania, City Council in December 1969, and which placed a 20% tax on the gross receipts obtained from all transactions involving the parking or storing of a motor vehicle at a nonresidential parking place in return for a consideration. The ordinance superseded a 1968 ordinance imposing an identical tax, but at the rate of 15%, which in turn followed a tax at the rate of 10% imposed by the city in 1962. Soon after its enactment, 12 operators of offstreet parking facilities located in the city sued to enjoin enforcement of the ordinance, alleging that it was invalid under the Equal Protection and Due Process Clauses of the Fourteenth Amendment, as well as Art. VIII, § 1, of the Pennsylvania Constitution, which requires that taxes shall be uniform upon the same class of subjects. It appears from the findings and the opinions in the state courts that, at the time of suit, there were approximately 24,300 parking spaces in the downtown area of the city, approximately 17,000 of which the respondents operated. Another 1,000 were in the hands of private operators not party to the suit. The balance of approximately 6,100 was owned by the Parking Authority of the city of Pittsburgh. * * * The trial court also found that there was then a deficiency of 4,100 spaces in the downtown area.

The Court of Common Pleas sustained the ordinance. Its judgment was affirmed by the Commonwealth Court by a four-to-three vote, but the Pennsylvania Supreme Court reversed, also four to three. That court rejected challenges to the ordinance under the Pennsylvania Constitution and the Equal Protection Clause, but invalidated the ordinance as an uncompensated taking of property contrary to the Due Process Clause of the Fourteenth Amendment. Because the decision appeared to be in conflict with the applicable decisions of this Court, we granted certiorari, and we now reverse the judgment.

In the opinion of the Supreme Court of Pennsylvania, two aspects of the Pittsburgh ordinance combined to deprive the respondents of due process of law. First, the court thought the tax was "unreasonably high" and was responsible for the inability of nine of 14 different private parking lot operators to conduct their business at a profit and of the

remainder to show more than marginal earnings. Second, private operators of parking lots faced competition from the Parking Authority, a
public agency enjoying tax exemption (although not necessarily from this
tax) and other advantages which enabled it to offer offstreet parking at
lower rates than those charged by private operators. The average all-
day rate for the public lots was $2 as compared with a $3 all-day rate for
the private lots. The court's conclusion was that "[w]here such an
unfair competitive advantage accrues, generated by the use of public
funds, to a local government at the expense of private property owners,
without just compensation, a clear constitutional violation has occurred.
* * * [T]he unreasonably burdensome 20 percent gross receipts tax,
causing the majority of private parking lot operators to operate their
businesses at a loss, in the special competitive circumstances of this case,
constitutes an unconstitutional taking of private property without due
process of law in violation of the Fourteenth Amendment of the United
States Constitution."

We cannot agree that these two considerations, either alone or
together, are sufficient to invalidate the parking tax ordinance involved
in this case. The claim that a particular tax is so unreasonably high and
unduly burdensome as to deny due process is both familiar and recurring, but the Court has consistently refused either to undertake the task
of passing on the "reasonableness" of a tax that otherwise is within the
power of Congress or of state legislative authorities, or to hold that a tax
is unconstitutional because it renders a business unprofitable.   * * *
The premise that a tax is invalid if so excessive as to bring about the
destruction of a particular business, the Court said, had been "uniformly
rejected as furnishing on juridical ground for striking down a taxing
act." *Veazie Bank v. Fenno*, 8 Wall. 533, 548, 19 L.Ed. 482 (1869).
* * *

Nor are we convinced that the ordinance loses its character as a tax
and may be stricken down as too burdensome under the Due Process
Clause if the taxing authority, directly or through an instrumentality
enjoying various forms of tax exemption, competes with the taxpayer in a
manner thought to be unfair by the judiciary. This approach would
demand not only that the judiciary undertake to separate those taxes
that are too burdensome from those that are not, but also would require
judicial oversight of the terms and circumstances under which the
government or its tax-exempt instrumentalities may undertake to compete with the private sector. The clear teaching of prior cases is that
this is not a task that the Due Process Clause demands of or permits to
the judiciary. We are not now inclined to chart a different course.
* * *

[D]irectly in point is *Puget Sound Power & Light Co. v. Seattle*, 291
U.S. 619, 54 S.Ct. 542, 78 L.Ed. 1025 (1934), where the city imposed a
gross receipts tax on a power and light company and at the same time
actively competed with that company in the business of furnishing power
to consumers. The company's contention was that "constitutional limitations are transgressed * * * because the tax affects a business with

which the taxing sovereign is actively competing." Calling on prior cases in support, the Court rejected the contention, holding that "the Fourteenth Amendment does not prevent a city from conducting a public waterworks in competition with private business or preclude taxation of the private business to help its rival to succeed." The holding in *Puget Sound* remains good law and, together with the other authorities to which we have already referred, it is sufficient to require reversal of the decision of the Pennsylvania Supreme Court.

Even assuming that an uncompensated and hence forbidden "taking" could be inferred from an unreasonably high tax in the context of competition from the taxing authority, we could not conclude that the Due Process Clause was violated in the circumstances of this case. It was urged by the city that the private operators would not suffer because they could and would pass the tax on to their customers, who, as a class, should pay more for the services of the city that they directly or indirectly utilize in connection with the special problems incident to the twice daily movement of large numbers of cars on the streets of the city and in and out of parking garages. The response of the Pennsylvania Supreme Court was that competition from the city prevented the private operators from raising their prices and recouping their losses by collecting the tax from their customers. On the record before us, this is not a convincing basis for concluding that the parking tax effected an unconstitutional taking of respondents' property. There are undisturbed findings in the record that there were 24,300 parking places in the downtown area, that there was an overall shortage of parking facilities, and that the public authority supplied only 6,100 parking spaces. Because these latter spaces were priced substantially under the private lots it could be anticipated that they would be preferred by those seeking parking in the downtown area. Insofar as this record reveals, for the 20% tax to have a destructive effect on private operators as compared with the situation immediately preceding its enactment, the damage would have to flow chiefly, not from those who preferred the cheaper public parking lots, but from those who could no longer afford an increased price for downtown parking at all. If this is the case, we simply have another instance where the government enacts a tax at a "discouraging rate as the alternative to giving up a business," a policy to which there is no constitutional objection.

The parking tax ordinance recited that "[n]on-residential parking places for motor vehicles, by reason of the frequency rate of their use, the changing intensity of their use at various hours of the day, their location, their relationship to traffic congestion and other characteristics, present problems requiring municipal services and affect the public interest, differently from parking places accessory to the use and occupancy of residences." By enacting the tax, the city insisted that those providing and utilizing nonresidential parking facilities should pay more taxes to compensate the city for the problems incident to offstreet parking. The city was constitutionally entitled to put the automobile parker to the choice of using other transportation or paying the increased tax. * * *

OAKLAND v. OAKLAND RAIDERS

Supreme Court of California, 1982.
32 Cal.3d 60, 183 Cal.Rptr. 673, 646 P.2d 835.

RICHARDSON, JUSTICE.

The City of Oakland (City) appeals from a summary judgment dismissing with prejudice its action to acquire by eminent domain the property rights associated with respondent Oakland Raiders' (the Raiders) ownership of a professional football team as a franchise member of the National Football League (NFL). * * * When the Raiders announced its intention to move the football team to Los Angeles, City commenced this action in eminent domain. * * * The legal confrontation between the parties is sharply defined. City insists that what it seeks to condemn is "property" which is subject to established eminent domain law. City contends that whether it can establish a valid "public use" must await a determination of the court after a full trial at which all relevant facts may be adduced. In answer, respondents argue that the law of eminent domain does not permit the taking of "intangible property not connected with realty," thereby rendering impossible City's condemnation of the football franchise which respondents describe as a "network of intangible contractual rights." Further, respondents claim that the taking contemplated by City cannot as a matter of law be for any "public use" within City's authority. Thus, two issues are herein presented, the first dealing with the intangible nature of the property proposed to be taken, and the second focusing on the scope of the condemning power as limited by the doctrine of public use. * * *

Government Code section 37350.5, as amended, provides: "A city may acquire by eminent domain *any property* necessary to carry out any of its powers or functions." (Italics added.) * * * The * * * law appears to impose no greater restrictions on the exercise of the condemnation power than those which are inherent in the federal and state Constitutions. Further, the power which is statutorily extended to cities is not limited to certain types of property. * * * [W]e conclude that our eminent domain law authorizes the taking of intangible property. * * *

While broad, the eminent domain power is not entirely unlimited, section 1240.010 cautioning: "The power of eminent domain may be exercised to acquire property only for a public use." * * * Is it possible for City to prove that its attempt to take and operate the Raiders' football franchise is for a valid public use? We have defined "public use" as "a use which concerns the whole community or promotes the general interest in its relation to any legitimate object of government." (*Bauer v. County of Ventura* [1955] 45 Cal.2d 276, 284, 289 P.2d 1.) On the other hand, "It is not essential that the entire community, or even any considerable portion thereof, shall directly enjoy or participate in an improvement in order to constitute a public use." (*Fallbrook Irrigation*

District v. Bradley [1896] 164 U.S. 112, 161 162, 17 S.Ct. 56, 64, 41 L.Ed. 369.) * * *

No case anywhere of which we are aware has held that a municipality can acquire and operate a professional football team, although we are informed that the City of Visalia owns and operates a professional Class A baseball franchise in the California League; apparently, its right to do so never has been challenged in court. In our view, several decisions concerning recreation appear germane. In *City of Los Angeles v. Superior Court* (1959) 51 Cal.2d 423, 434, 333 P.2d 745, we noted that a city's acquisition of a baseball field, with recreational facilities to be constructed thereon to be used by the city, was "obviously for proper public purposes." Similarly, in *County of Alameda v. Meadowlark Dairy Corp.* (1964) 227 Cal.App.2d 80, 84, 38 Cal.Rptr. 474, the court upheld a county's acquisition by eminent domain of lands to be used for a county fair, reasoning that "Activities which promote recreation of the public constitute a public purpose." Considerably earlier, in *Egan v. San Francisco* (1913) 165 Cal. 576, 582, 133 P. 294, in sustaining a city's power to build an opera house, we declared: "Generally speaking, anything calculated to promote the education, the recreation or the pleasure of the public is to be included within the legitimate domain of public purposes."

The examples of Candlestick Park in San Francisco and Anaheim Stadium in Anaheim, both owned and operated by municipalities, further suggest the acceptance of the general principle that providing access to recreation to its residents in the form of spectator sports is an appropriate function of city government. In connection with the latter stadium, the appellate court upheld the power of the City of Anaheim to condemn land for parking facilities at the stadium on the ground that "the acquisition, construction, and operation of a stadium by a county or city represents a legitimate public purpose." * * *

Is the obvious difference between managing and owning the facility in which the game is played, and managing and owning the team which plays in the facility, legally substantial? To date, respondents have not presented a valid legal basis for concluding that it is, but we do not foreclose the trial court's reaching a different conclusion on a fuller record. * * * [W]e conclude only that the acquisition and, indeed, the operation of a sports franchise may be an appropriate municipal function. If such valid public use can be demonstrated, * * * [California] statutes * * * afford City the power to acquire by eminent domain any property necessary to accomplish that use. * * *

Respondents urge, further, that because the NFL constitution bars a city from holding a franchise and being a member, the expenditure of any public monies for acquisition of the Raiders' franchise cannot be deemed in the public interest. On the other hand, an affidavit filed by the NFL commissioner avers that "a brief interim ownership" by City "would not be inconsistent with the NFL Constitution * * *." We, of course, are not bound by such an interpretation. Assuming its validity, however, respondents answer that if City contemplates the prompt transfer to private parties of the property interests which it seeks to condemn, after such brief ownership, that transfer would vitiate any legitimate "public use" which is a prerequisite to condemnation in the first place. In turn, City points to the statute which, as previously noted, expressly authorizes that to which respondents object: "[A] person may acquire property under subdivision (a) with the intent to sell, lease, exchange or otherwise dispose of the property or an interest therein," provided such retransfer is made "subject to such reservations or restrictions as are necessary to protect or preserve the attractiveness, safety, and usefulness of the project." (§ 1240.120, subd. (b).) So long as adequate controls are imposed upon any retransfer of the condemned property, there is no reason why the "public purpose" which justifies a taking may not be so served and protected. We envision that the adequacy of any such controls can only be determined within the factual context of a specific retransfer agreement. * * *

OAKLAND v. OAKLAND RAIDERS

Court of Appeal, First District, Division Four, California, 1985.
174 Cal.App.3d 414, 220 Cal.Rptr. 153, cert. denied, 478
U.S. 1007, 106 S.Ct. 3300, 92 L.Ed.2d 714 (1986).

SABRAW, ASSOCIATE JUSTICE.

Plaintiff City of Oakland appeals from a judgment after a court trial in favor of defendants Oakland Raiders, et al. We have determined that plaintiff's proposed exercise of eminent domain power would, in this case, violate the commerce clause of the United States Constitution. Accordingly, we affirm. * * *

We turn first to the trial court's commerce clause determination. United States Constitution, article 1, section 8, clause 3, grants Congress the power "[t]o regulate commerce * * * among the several States * * *." This provision was intended to foster development and maintenance of a national common market among the states and to eradicate trade barriers. * * * It is today established that state or local regulation of interstate commerce will be upheld if it " 'regulates even-handedly to effectuate a legitimate local public interest, and its effects on interstate commerce are only incidental * * * unless the burden imposed on such commerce is clearly excessive in relation to putative local benefits.' " (*Edgar v. MITE Corp.* (1982) 457 U.S. 624, 640, 102 S.Ct. 2629, 2639, 73 L.Ed.2d 269.) * * * One additional, albeit less recently relied-on approach to review of state or local action under the commerce clause provides that burdens will be voided if the regulation governs "those phases of the national economy which, because of the need of national uniformity, demand their regulation, if any, be prescribed by a single authority." (*Southern Pacific v. Arizona* (1945) 325 U.S. 761, 767, 65 S.Ct. 1515, 1519, 89 L.Ed. 1915.) * * *

[P]laintiff contends exercise of eminent domain power can never violate the commerce clause and notes that no previous case has precluded an eminent domain taking under that constitutional provision. The lack of such case law, however, is unremarkable; it serves merely to point out that eminent domain cases have traditionally concerned real property, rarely implicating commerce clause considerations which deal primarily with products in the flow of interstate commerce. Whether the commerce clause precludes taking by eminent domain of intangible property, however, is a novel question posed, it seems, for the first time in this case.

It is well established that a state may exercise eminent domain power even though by so doing it indirectly or incidentally burdens interstate commerce. Defendants, however, contend that professional football is such a nationwide business and so completely involved in interstate commerce that acquisition of a franchise by an individual state through eminent domain would impermissibly burden interstate commerce. A recent Supreme Court decision, *Partee v. San Diego Chargers Football Co.* (1983) 34 Cal.3d 378, 194 Cal.Rptr. 367, 668 P.2d 674, supports this view.

Partee held that the NFL required nationally uniform regulation and that interstate commerce would be unreasonably burdened if state antitrust laws applied to a League franchise located in this state. Uniform nationwide regulation was called for because "Professional football teams are dependent upon the league playing schedule for competitive play. * * * The necessity of a nationwide league structure for the benefit of both teams and players for effective competition is evident as is the need for a nationally uniform set of rules governing the league structure. Fragmentation of the league structure on the basis of state lines would adversely affect the success of the competitive business enterprise, and differing state antitrust decisions if applied to the enterprise would likely compel all member teams to comply with the laws of the strictest state."

The same situation is presented here. Indeed, the trial court's findings track and amplify on *Partee*. Regarding the interdependent character of the NFL, the court noted that each member team is substantially dependent for its income on every other team: League television contract proceeds are divided equally and gate receipts nearly equally; a team's drawing power is therefore a financial benefit to the other teams as well as to itself; hence the capacity and quality of the facility in which games are played is a component of the League's financial success. The court also found evidence of the necessity of a nationwide League structure: based on the above factors, each League franchise owner has an important interest in the identity, personality, financial stability, commitment, and good faith of each other owner. Thus, under League bylaws, new members must first be approved by the current members. In short, although the clubs compete to an important degree, the League is also a joint venture of its members organized for the purpose of providing entertainment nationwide. Finally, the court found that a bar to relocation on the basis of state eminent domain law would adversely affect the League enterprise. An involuntarily acquired franchise could, at the local government's pleasure, be permanently indentured to the local entity. The League's interests would be subordinated to, or at least compromised by, the new owner's allegiance to the local public interest in matters such as lease agreements, ticket prices, concessions, stadium amenities, scheduling conflicts, etc. As the trial court found, it must also be anticipated that a single precedent of eminent domain acquisition would pervade the entire League, and even the threat of its exercise elsewhere would seriously disrupt the balance of economic bargaining on stadium leases throughout the nation.

Plaintiff's proposed action would more than indirectly or incidentally regulate interstate commerce: plaintiff claims authority—pursuant to authorization found in state eminent domain statutes—to bar indefinitely defendant's business from relocating out of Oakland. This is the precise brand of parochial meddling with the national economy that the commerce clause was designed to prohibit.

As shown above, relocation of the Raiders would implicate the welfare not only of the individual team franchise, but of the entire League. The spectre of such local action throughout the state or across the country demonstrates the need for uniform, national regulation. In these circumstances (and apart from other potential bases of commerce clause violation [3]), if relocation threatens disproportionate harm to a local entity, regulation—if necessary—should come from Congress; only then can the consequences to interstate commerce be assessed and a proper balance struck to consider and serve the various interests involved in a uniform manner.

Our supreme court in *Partee* held this state's legitimate interest in enforcing our own antitrust laws against a League franchise was outweighed by the burden such enforcement would impose on interstate commerce. Plaintiff here does not seek to promote the health or safety of its citizens, or even, as in *Partee*, promote fair economic competition. Instead it seeks to act for what may be presumed, for purposes of analysis, to be legitimate, but less compelling reasons: to promote public recreation, social welfare, and to secure related economic benefits, as well as to best utilize the stadium in which the Raiders played.

We conclude, as did *Partee* in a similar context, that the burden that would be imposed on interstate commerce outweighs the local interest in exercising statutory eminent domain authority over the Raiders franchise. * * *

---

3. * * * The trial court * * * stated, "it would seem essential to the welfare of any business in a free enterprise system that it be substantially free to relocate to a better economic environment to maintain or enhance its viability." (Cf. *Pike v. Bruce Church, Inc.,* 397 U.S. 137, 145, 90 S.Ct. 844, 849, 25 L.Ed.2d 174 ["the Court has viewed with particular suspicion state statutes requiring business operations to be performed in the home State that could more efficiently be performed elsewhere"].) Whether such a broadly stated proposition may ultimately prove correct, however, need not be decided here. We are not faced with the question of whether, consistent with the commerce clause, a local government may prevent relocation of a business that, although producing goods that eventually flow in interstate commerce, is not an interdependent component part of an interstate joint venture such as the NFL.

GERALD FRUG, PROPERTY AND POWER: HARTOG ON THE LEGAL HISTORY OF NEW YORK CITY

1984 Am. Bar Foundation Research J. 673, 687–691.

PROPERTY AND POWER

I propose below a half-dozen ways in which cities could increase their power by expanding their use of the rights of property owners. Not all of these proposals would be good ideas for every city. The point of the exercise is not to come up with an agenda for all cities in America but to help overcome the limits that our reliance on the public/private distinction imposes on our ability to imagine ways to increase city power. We need to see again that property is a mechanism for exercising city power; we need, in other words, to invent modern versions of the waterlot grants described by Professor Hartog. These versions are modern because their purpose is not to convey city land to an aristocratic elite as long as they use it according to certain conditions but to use government property rights to foster and encourage democratic decision making. My list of proposals is designed to demonstrate that city property can be a source of democratic power in America.

First, cities could operate banks, insurance companies, and other financial institutions. The importance of the role financial institutions play in modern economic life is widely recognized. In America, representatives of these institutions sit on most major corporate boards; in Mondragon, a central banking institution, the Caja Laboral Popular, has helped perpetuate and expand one of the world's major examples of worker-owned and worker-managed enterprise; in France, a socialist government recently nationalized its banks. If cities became major lenders to economic enterprise, they could influence decisions about plant closings, the democratic organization of work, the kinds of socially useful products that might be manufactured, and the job opportunities afforded racial and ethnic minorities. The power to make investment decisions is an essential ingredient in our national life, and a city's ability to loan money for some purposes rather than others can allow it to influence what these decisions are.

Second, cities could own significant amounts of residential housing, particularly apartment houses and other multiple-family dwellings. This does not mean that cities would have to manage these residential units by creating "public" housing; instead, a city's property interest could be limited to having title to the property. All decisions regarding the housing itself—who should live there, the nature of the relationship among the families, the amount of money to be spent for maintenance, and the like—could then be made by the residents themselves. The city could simply be a landlord—one that receives no rent—and a corporation consisting of (and controlled by) all current occupants could be a tenant. The housing, in other words, could be run like a condominium with the exception that legal ownership of the property would be lodged not in the residents but in the city. The reason for placing title in the city would be to ensure that the housing remains dedicated to residential purposes and to prevent profit making when a unit is transferred to new residents. Thus, as a landlord, the city could preserve housing units in the city, prevent gentrification of these units, and encourage democratic control over the operation of multiple-family housing. By retaining title, the city could also help solve property law problems that would arise if the tenants held the title themselves. The city's status as a property owner in this plan, like in others below, relies on the modern fracturing of the property right into a bundle of sticks; here the city retains title without, for example, having the right to exclude or the privilege of using the property for nonresidential purposes.

Third, cities could run a cable television system. The purpose of city ownership of such a system would be to organize it as a mechanism to help people within the city to communicate with each other. Cable could be used so that schools could provide programs for adults as well as for children; local music and drama groups could increase their audience; and individuals could work together to produce and organize shows of interest to others. Moreover, as a report on public ownership of a cable system for Cambridge, Massachusetts, suggested, it could become "a means of reintroducing our society and citizens to true 'town meeting' participation in the political process and a method of addressing the problem of limited access to government." Both the production of the programs and their content could become a focus of participatory politics. Indeed the cable system itself could be organized so as to increase democratic participation; there is no need to envision the entity as a city agency or public authority that would run the system as part of a public bureaucracy.

Fourth, cities could run profit-making businesses. If they did, they could generate income designed to promote other city functions; like the eighteenth-century city described by Professor Hartog, they could (in part) substitute a reliance on city profits for a reliance on city taxes. But the purpose of running such businesses would not simply be to generate revenue. The purpose would also be to create an alternative style of business organization. Cities could organize their businesses as workplace democracies, experimenting with the many different forms that these kinds of organizations now take. By demonstrating how life at work could be organized democratically, city businesses could become examples, within the business sector, of forms of institutional life that others could follow.

Fifth, cities could own cooperative grocery stores. Once again, cities need not be given all ingredients of the property interest in these stores; they could allow most of the prerogatives of property ownership to vest in the cooperative itself. Cities could use their resources to help establish cooperative stores, while allowing the consumers (and the employees) to manage them once they are in operation. In many cases, the stores could be required to use their revenues to pay off the city's costs over a few years, thereby preventing them from becoming a permanent drain on the city's resources. These city grocery stores could serve a number of purposes: they could ensure that stores exist in city neighborhoods where they are needed, aid in providing food to people at lower costs, and generate and promote information about nutrition. Moreover, here, as in the other examples presented above, cities could promote the democratic organization of an aspect of daily life.

Sixth, cities could purchase or condemn a property interest in those businesses within their borders that provide the bulk of employment for their citizens. The district judge in the Youngstown plant closing case [48] suggested the reason for acquiring such a property interest.

> Everything that has happened in the Mahoning Valley has been happening for many years because of steel. Schools have been built, roads have been built. Expansion that has taken place is because of steel. And to accommodate that industry, lives and destinies of the inhabitants of that community were based and planned on the basis of that institution: Steel. * * *

> * * * it seems to me that a property right has arisen from this lengthy, long-established relationship between United States Steel, the steel industry as an institution, the community in Youngstown, the people in Mahoning County and the Mahoning Valley in having given and devoted their lives to this industry.

The city interest could take the form of a servitude imposed on the businesses' property, one that required the city's consent before decisions were made about plant closing or about the future use of the property once the current owners decided to withdraw their capital.[50] Such a servitude might, for example, prevent what happened in Youngstown: United States Steel, rather than conveying the plant to the workers, demolished it.

These six proposals will no doubt generate a variety of reactions from my readers. I think most of them will agree, however, that, if these six proposals were all adopted by a city, it would gain significantly in the power it exercised in its community. Indeed, its new power would extend widely to many critical aspects of daily life: work, housing, food supply, and control over mass communications. If the cities today actually fused property with power, they could recapture a role in the creation of American society not achievable through political decentralization. They could demonstrate that the ability to exercise property rights is a major source of power in America.

---

48. United Steel Workers Local 1330 v. United States Steel Corp., 631 F.2d 1264 (6th Cir.1980).

50. Condemnation of such a servitude (or condemnation of the property itself followed by the city's leasing the property back to the owner with the servitude imposed) would, of course, require a "public" purpose. But the reasons for exercising the city's power seem to meet the rather tepid current interpretation of this public pur-

pose requirement. See Poletown Neighborhood Council v. City of Detroit, 304 N.W.2d 455 (Mich.1981). Moreover, arguments could be advanced, as they were in the *Youngstown* case itself, that no condemnation would even be necessary because a servitude existed by prescription or because an implied-in-fact contract concerning the future of the business already existed between the business and the city.

It is, of course, by no means clear that cities would use their property-power to advance the cause of democratic participation. It would be a mistake to think that cities, because they are "public," would necessarily use their power in a radically different way than "private" corporations. To ensure that cities used their power to foster democracy, efforts would have to be made to strengthen the democratic nature of cities themselves. It will take energy and imagination to transform our current city institutions into vehicles for promoting participatory democracy. It will take equal energy and imagination to overcome seeing our efforts to increase city power in terms of the public/private distinction—to overcome our preference for having a conglomerate, rather than a city, own a combination of financial, housing, food supply, and television businesses. But if cities are to become once again vital institutions, they need to be freed from the vise of the public/private distinction. They need instead to be infused with the values of participatory democracy and allowed once again to exercise genuine power. Professor Hartog's book helps us see that city property is a way for cities to exercise this power. He also helps us realize that the power of community self-government, if properly used, could significantly increase our ability to control important aspects of our daily lives. "Community self-determination," he reminds us, "is a distinctive modality of choice, serving a distinctive dimension of freedom."

3. CUTTING COSTS THROUGH PRIVATIZATION

In the preceding section, we focused on the desirability of cities taking over functions that have traditionally been performed by the private sector; in this section, we examine the opposite idea—the notion that the private sector might assume functions that have been traditionally performed by cities. Of course, the call for "privatization" of governmental functions is by no means limited to city services; on the contrary, privatization is an idea that has been widely debated not only throughout the United States but around the world. To illustrate the relevance of the topic to city services, the section begins with James Ramsey's provocative argument that the New York City subway system be sold to the private sector. Following Ramsey's argument, three excerpts—by Ronald Cass, John Donahue and myself—seek to frame the issues involved in a privatization decision. These articles introduce quite different ways of thinking about the wisdom of privatization (indeed, quite different definitions of the term). Following these readings, three cases—Colorado Assoc. of Public Employees v. Department of Highways, Professional Engineers v. Department of Transportation, and West v. Atkins—take up some of the issues about privatization that the excerpts raise: the impact of privatization on the civil service system, on the democratic control of public policymaking, and on the role of Constitutional protections in the performance of government functions. Do the excerpts help you think about how to decide the cases? Do the cases suggest limits to the kinds of analyses offered by the excerpts? What benefits of—and problems with—privatization do the excerpts and cases fail to discuss?

The final case in this section, 515 Associates v. City of Newark, deals with a very different form of privatization. In the *Newark* case, the City sought to require all large private housing complexes in the city (as well as public housing projects) to hire armed security guards. Is this an attempt to transfer the "public" function of police work to the private sector? If so, is it better analyzed in the terms advanced by the readings in this section or by those found in the readings in the previous section, dealing with city revenue-generating strategies?

JAMES RAMSEY, SELLING THE NEW YORK CITY SUBWAY: WILD–EYED RADICALISM OR THE ONLY FEASIBLE SOLUTION?

From S. Hanke, Prospects for Privatization 95–103 (1987).

ANALYSIS OF THE PROBLEM

The financial reason for the subways' difficulty is easy to state: labor costs per passenger mile have risen faster than the sum of revenues and subsidies per passenger mile. The difficult question is why. The near impossible question is what to do about it. Moreover, the problem has a puzzling aspect when one examines the situation in more detail. As labor costs rose relative to other costs, capital equipment was not substituted for labor, as would be the case in any normal profit-maximizing industry. The reason, of course, is political; the degree of pressure that a municipal union can bring to bear on a city government and the arrangements that the government can make because of its rule-making ability inevitably force bodies like the Transit Authority into trying to pay for wage increases that projected revenues do not justify by reducing maintenance and repair of capital equipment—in short, by disinvesting in capital.

A private firm's response to a higher wage rate is to substitute capital and technology for labor. Thus the full impact of the wage increment is muted through the more extensive use of capital and relatively less use of high-priced labor. In even more difficult circumstances, the private firm will reduce output, sell off nonprofitable portions of the firm, or in extremis declare bankruptcy. For purely political reasons, municipal transit authorities are not allowed these options. The ultimate response that mitigates excessive union demands—unemployment and the closing of the firm—is not available to them; worse, before the ultimate collapse of the system, labor productivity falls as the existing capital stock is depreciated so that the problem is compounded at each round of labor negotiations. Unfortunately, despite what municipal authorities seem to think, deferred maintenance is not an interest-free loan; the real interest rate of such loans is very high.

Between 1968 and 1979 total full-time [Transit Authority] employees fell from 34,649 to 34,007, a reduction of less than 2 percent. But labor costs per passenger rose from 20 cents to 63 cents over the same period. * * * Looking at increases in wages and other benefits is only one side of the coin; the other is the productivity of the labor force. Thus, if productivity grew at a faster rate than the rate of increase in wages, labor costs per unit of output could fall. An initial view of the situation is provided by the observation that in the 1960s the number of passengers per employee was between 170 and 180, but by the beginning of the 1970s that figure had fallen to 128. An optimistic estimate of the national average transit-productivity gain as a percent per year is positive, but it is as likely to be negative. Perhaps the best guess is that the national average transit-productivity gains are zero. It is reasonable to surmise that the MTA's contribution to the national average is negative. Further, while the ratio of capital to labor for the United States domestic economy has been growing at about 2.5 percent a year since 1948 and that for transit has grown at only 0.52 percent a year, and this figure does not adequately allow for the long-term deterioration of capital equipment through neglected maintenance. On balance, the change in the capital-labor ratio for the New York City Transit Authority (NYCTA) is probably negative. * * *

The initial explanation for this dismal record is the power of the unions. Federal, state, and local legislation provides transportation unions with strong powers, both economic and political. In New York City and its suburbs the Transport Worker's Union (TWU) is a monopoly whose degree of control is unmatched by any firm or even trio of firms in any industry in the country. Local 100 of the TWU bargains for eight out of ten private labor contracts and covers 93 percent of the buses and 95 percent of the bus operators. Of course, the subways are completely unionized. This gives the union enormous economic power—whether or not it has the "legal right to strike"; indeed, the legal prohibition does not seem to be much of a barrier to strikes and has been no barrier to higher wage agreements.

If the economic power of the union is combined with political leverage, the union's ability to tax the rest of society is impeded only by political reluctance to raise fares and the length of debates on tax increases. Once a municipality has taken on direct responsibility for providing a service, even through the device of an "authority," the pressure to politicize most issues is overwhelming. An ostensible strike against the TA on economic issues becomes a political battle involving the political gains and losses to the incumbent politician. In this situation, well-organized blocs of voters, like those provided by the TWU, provide a degree of political influence matched by few other groups. Better still from the union's viewpoint, settlements now have direct access to the public purse; settlements that would immediately bankrupt a private firm can be financed indefinitely by taxing the general public. While the public purse is not unlimited, a politically influential group's ability to extract large sums at the expense of anonymous taxpayers is high and is obviously in the self-interest of the politician supported by a well-organized union cadre.

One important lesson not lost on the subway riders is that the fare is only a small part of the actual cost of riding the subway. In truth, the fare is become even more irrelevant; the real total cost is already high and rising rapidly. * * * The real cost is measured in lack of safety, uncertainty as to the time of travel, filthy surroundings, overcrowding, and often some disturbing riders. One dollar is a very small part of the cost, and each time people experiment with alternative modes of getting to work, for example, during a subway strike, they discover that the real costs of the subway are greater than the use of a private car or a charter bus. In fact, ridership on the express buses is rising rapidly as commuters leave the subways—a clear indication that the riding public is willing to pay more, far more, for a quality ride. The main lesson from this discussion is that if the fare were raised and the quality of the service significantly improved, one could easily generate an increase in ridership resulting from an overall reduction in the total price to the rider. The mere substitution of clean, well-lit stations and clean, quiet trains would greatly improve the desirability of subway travel.

No mention has yet been made of management's role in the half-century decline of the subway system. Ironically, especially within the last few years, senior management has been notable for its drive, knowledge, and concern to create a useful public service. Traditionally, the first group to be blamed for poor performance is management, and in a private firm that view is quite correct. But in an organization that is highly subject to political influence, the charge is not necessarily true. By and large the senior management knows what must be done to improve the system, but for political reasons it cannot do it.

The political power of the unions has already been mentioned. But pressures for inefficiency come from the riders as well. Political pressure keeps the fare down, and when there is an allowed increase the amount is too little and too late. Subway lines and stations that economically should be closed or have their service reduced because of lack of ridership are kept open through political intervention at an enormous cost.

The reader may imagine the difficulties to be faced if he or she had to cope with a work force that cannot be effectively disciplined (MTA workers' lack of commitment to their jobs is notorious), service that cannot be changed to meet changing demands, capital projects that are a political battle, the exhausting prospect that even routine decisions face potential political intervention, and, finally, revenues that are held down until a crisis is precipitated.

Political control of a firm leads to gross economic inefficiency. The differences between alternative situations lie in how the inefficiencies are manifested. For some operations—for example, the Washington, D.C., system—the plant and equipment are modern and clean, but the subsidies are enormous. In New York, the subsidies are relatively modest by public-transportation standards, but the employee-pension burden is so egregious (it is possible to retire at nearly full pay after only twenty years of service) and work-force discipline is so negligible that the outcome is a decaying system. As the subsidies for other transportation systems decline, they will also begin to depreciate capital in order to pay for intemperate wage and pension increments.

THE ONLY FEASIBLE SOLUTION

There should be one simple but outstandingly clear lesson from the above discussion. The current system is not viable; there is no sum of money, no subsidy so great, that cannot be eaten up by union demands and political intervention. Indeed, the more the system is subsidized and the more management and the unions recognize that fact, the more inefficient the entire system will become and the higher the costs will be. Some device is needed that will limit union demands to the bounds of reason and concentrate the minds of management on trying to generate an efficient system that serves the public. The following suggestion, which is politically feasible, could produce this necessary miracle.

The proposal is to sell off the subway system line by line over a period of about five years. The fundamental elements of the scheme are that there are to be no price controls, no entry barriers to new subway firms other than those dictated by safety, and no political intervention in behalf of the unions, and the city is to share in the profits of the system. The last element is crucial to the political feasibility of the proposal.

A team of evaluators chosen in part by the city and in part by the potential bidders for the subway will evaluate the net "market value" of the current capital stock of that part of the system to be sold. This capital price must be paid in order for the bidding firm to acquire the right to provide subway service in the city. The choice of which firm is to rebuild and run the subway will be by competitive bids on net profit share to the city; that is, the highest bid share of gross profits (net of all capital costs) to be paid to the city wins the right to provide subway service on the line or lines bought. But it must be expressly agreed that no price controls and no mandated service requirements will be imposed. In a California oil lease sale where this bidding scheme was tried, the net profit share was 94.77 percent.

The city can use its profit share in any way it chooses—for example, to finance subway rides for the poor by giving them an income subsidy paid from the profit shares. Alternatively, it can pay for the provision of uneconomical service. One objective of the scheme is to separate the need for an efficient transportation system from the politically understandable wish to subsidize certain segments of the electorate.

By moving to a privately funded and operated system wherein any gains or losses are the direct responsibility of the owners, the minds of management will be concentrated on providing the service demanded by the public. Only when managers' jobs depend on their efforts and efficiency will there be a serious effort to control costs. The objective of the firm is now simply stated and easily understood—to make money. But what the general public does not understand is that this seemingly crass dictum in practice would help solve numerous complex problems and provide the rider better service at a lower cost.

The management of privately owned firms is far more efficient than that of publicly owned or controlled firms, simply because of the difference in the pressures that managers face in the two situations. In publicly owned or controlled firms, not only are there fewer and smaller personal incentives to be efficient; political control adds a further and, in the end, disastrous thrust to fiscal myopia, to the acceptance of the expedient response, and an effort to solve today's difficulty at a greater cost tomorrow. This is in part because the period for the payoff from political decisions is short, often less than a year and seldom greater than two years. It is therefore no great surprise to view the political reluctance for the long-range solutions that inevitably incur short-run difficulties. It is expedient for the politician to curry favor now and leave the problems to the next election, the next administration, or the next generation of users. It is easier to take a popular stance on low fares today than to recommend the investment needed for a viable system tomorrow. Unfortunately, the outcome of this political exchange is worse for both riders and taxpayers.

While it is well recognized that private firms face greater pressures to respond to consumer wishes and to moderate costs, it is not so well recognized that private firms can withstand union pressures more easily. This is not to say that a powerful union cannot force inefficiencies and raise wage rates above competitive levels but to say that with any degree of union power the deleterious effects will be reduced. When a public authority like the NYCTA runs the subways, the unions recognize that they have access to the public treasury and general tax revenues; any deficits created by their own demands can always be filled through public monies.

Critics will say that while the above comments are well and good, experience has shown that no private company can run a transit system unsubsidized and that no private firm can raise the funds needed to rebuild the system. The answer is that experience has shown that when transit fares are held below economic levels by government fiat, incumbent firms go broke, and no one else will be interested in the economic equivalent of self-flagellation.

What is clear to even the most skeptical of critics is that there is an enormous reservoir of demand for relatively efficient transportation. The use of a car for a typical commuter is about one hour's drive plus about $30.00 a day. A commuter bus costs $6 to $10 a day, and it is inconvenient because of the necessity of sticking to a fixed and limited schedule. This is the currently allowed competition for the subway. If there were no price constraints, the city would be flooded with proposals for providing public transportation in innovative ways. If the lack of price constraints results in a profitable situation, one need not worry about the ability to raise the necessary capital funds.

The issue of financial viability has now been reduced to one with purely emotional content. Only the "rich" will be able to afford to ride the subway; so long as the subway is a monopoly the public will be gouged unmercifully. Much colorful language can be employed in the argument, but the true situation is far more prosaic. As usual in such debates, there is a subtle propensity for those enamored of municipal control and tax-based subsidies to argue both ways simultaneously— privately run systems are not financially viable because no one will use them at the profitable price (there is strong competition) and the subway is a monopoly and people must pay any price charged (there is no competition at all).

The truth of the matter is that subways face considerable competition, although for some trips subways would clearly be the preferred mode. Insofar as the subways are sold line by line and bus lines are sold separately, subways and buses provide competition for some trips as well as opportunities for cooperative service for others; for example, crosstown bus service linked to uptown-downtown subway service. Even from the outlying boroughs, express buses, car pooling, jitney cabs (if allowed), shared limousines, nonmedallion cabs, private cars, and motorcycles provide alternative modes of transportation.

Some idea of a market-clearing price can be inferred from several items of information. The Regional Plan Association estimated in 1980 that it would take a 45–cent fare increase (plus increases on the Long Island Rail Road) to raise $1 billion a year for rebuilding the system. After eliminating all subsidies and before realizing the existing and known potential for efficiency gains, an "average fare" of about $1.20 emerged, certainly less than $1.50. But even in 1986, fares within Manhattan could be 75 to 90 cents and only fares to the ends of the outer boroughs might reach $3.00.

If express buses can operate profitably in 1986 at $3.00 to $5.00 a ride as simple commuter operations, the subway could provide far better service for much less. Consequently, from this perspective, a maximum profitable price in 1986 from the outer boroughs is less than, say, $3.00 on average; short trips should be less than the current $1.

So far this discussion has ignored technological innovations, lowering the total cost of labor by substituting relatively cheaper capital equipment, and simple efficiency gains from work-rate changes. It has been estimated that relatively minor changes of this type can lower costs by 20 percent or more. Another example would be the elimination of token clerks, about 4,000 high-paid jobs, and another 3,000 "conductors." New rail lines seem to manage with only one driver.

A counterargument that can be raised at this point is that the price increases recommended will so lower demand that costs must rise even more. This argument is invalid on two counts. First, even accurate measures of the relative price responsiveness of demand would not be of much relevance in this situation, because what is at issue is the demand for a vastly improved system, not a higher price for the existing network.

What is needed to calculate the effect on ridership is to evaluate the responsiveness of demand to increases in quality; it is the net effect of quality and price that will determine the gain in the ridership.

Second, the notion that cents per rider must rise if ridership falls can only be true for a system locked into overmanning. For most firms, if demand falls permanently, the firm shrinks to accommodate. It is usually only when demand falls to very low levels that one begins to experience serious increases in average cost to a fall in demand. The subways are by no means close to such a point.

Another argument made by those in favor of tax-supported systems is that if the subways were to charge the full economic cost, firms would relocate and New York City would lose jobs. The argument is false. First, it is true that transportation is a key issue in the decisions of firms whether to remain in the city or relocate, but it is *not* whether the fare is 60 cents or 75 cents or even $2.00 but the fact that employees are continually late, rushing off early to get a train, unwilling to work late, tired, irritable, and exhausted from inhuman conditions on the subway— in short, the abysmal level of services, or lack of them, is the problem.

Second, whatever the true costs of transportation in the city, the firm and its employees still pay the full costs no matter how low the nominal fare, because the shortfall must be made up in taxes. A viable New York City requires a viable transit system, and that requires a city government committed to open entry into the transit business, receptivity to innovative ideas, and above all the courage *not* to set price ceilings. Ironically, while this is the only strategy that can achieve a useful transportation network, it is the only one not yet tried by the city.

The most emotional issue of all concerns the poor. The nonworking poor seldom need transportation; attention here will therefore be focused on the working poor. Grant for a moment that these people would rather not work at all or would rather work locally than pay a higher subway fare. Employers would soon see their labor forces shrinking and would have to raise wages to get their workers back. In this case, then, the system is self-correcting. Further, fares based on distance traveled could lower fares for the working poor, since many work within their own neighborhoods and do not commute to Manhattan from the outer boroughs.

What can be done for the nonworking poor? The answer is not to keep fares artificially low for 95 percent of the population who can pay but to give an extra income subsidy to the nonworking poor and let them spend it how they will. Such a subsidy can be financed directly from the profits of the system paid to the city. But what if there are no profits paid in? This phenomenon can only be temporary, and there are two answers. First, since the firm is not making profits, everyone using the system is already being subsidized at the expense of the equity owners. Second, the city can finance the poor immediately in anticipation of future profit revenues.

For political reasons the city may wish to provide subway service to areas where alternative transportation is so cheap and efficient that the privately run subway system cannot compete. Under the existing scheme the city could use its profit share or any other revenue to purchase the extra service from the privately run system.

The final issue, and the most crucial one, is whether the proposed scheme is politically feasible. The opposition is powerful, but the answer can be yes. The TWU definitely does not want to see its members' pay reduced to that earned by their colleagues in private industry. All those who still believe others can be taxed to pay for their subway will be against the idea of paying their own way, no matter how inefficient and wasteful such a procedure is. There is a sizable body of people who firmly believe that only municipally provided services are desirable and that all such services should be paid for by taxing the "rich." Such people will only grudgingly compromise to accept some nonzero fare.

On the other side is the grim reality that the above proponents have reduced a once-great system to a shambles. Further, a number of people recognize that the only viable and affordable solution is to institute a private system of intracity transit like the intercity system. In any event, both New York City and the state can no longer afford to subsidize transportation at ever-increasing amounts because of the pressure of alternative and desperately needed capital expenditures on items less amenable to privatization, such as road repair, sewage plants, and street cleaning. Leadership, full discussion of the issues, and a clear recognition of the self-interest involved in many of the arguments may be the only way to escape from the transit morass.

RONALD CASS, PRIVATIZATION: POLITICS, LAW, AND THEORY

71 Marquette L. Rev. 449, 456–461, 481–488 (1988).

Privatization proposals vary along several dimensions. They suggest different *routes* to lessen government involvement in a given activity; they bring about different *degrees* of public and private control over an activity; and they leave different *types* of control in public and private hands. * * * The first group of privatization possibilities involves formal government ownership of an asset and proposes that government terminate such ownership. The classic examples are government ownership of what seems to be a "proprietary" business, that is, one that produces a product and sells the product to consumers. Conrail is such a business, as is the Tennessee Valley Authority. Government ownership makes the government the ultimate decisionmaker on the quantity of goods produced, the quality of the goods, the manner of production, the means by which (and customers to whom) the goods are distributed, and the prices at which the goods are sold. The proposal to sell the business to a nongovernment buyer usually contemplates elimination of special governmental control over all of these facets of the business. * * *

A second group of privatization proposals involves the contractual rearrangement of control over some, but not all, aspects of an activity. These arrangements fall into two categories. One is the lease of government assets to another party. One example in this category would be the lease of mineral rights in government-owned land or the lease of NASA launching vehicles to propel privately-owned satellites into Earth's orbit. In the other category, known as "contracting out," the government purchases goods or services from another party. The purchase might be of management services for a government-owned facility, such as a hospital or prison; of other services, such as trash collection, road building or even law enforcement; or of goods for use by the government, from MX missiles to paper clips. The largest group of privatization proposals suggests contracting out this middle group of services. * * * All of the contracting proposals provide for a sharing of decisionmaking responsibility between government and the other contract party. The division of control could take very different forms. At one extreme, government could lease property on long-term basis without restricting its uses. At the other extreme, government could purchase a good and provide the design and manufacturing specifications, thereby leaving only the mechanics of its production to be contracted out; but even these can be largely government controlled. * * *

Another group of privatization proposals is concerned with government restrictions on the range of choices available to private parties and suggests the reduction or removal of current constraints on private choice. * * * Deregulation addresses situations in which the government directly regulates particular private behavior. * * * The most sweeping form of deregulation abolishes an entire regulatory structure, as the recent deregulation of domestic airlines nearly did. Less wholesale approaches that eliminate specific rules—rules that, for example, preclude entry into a business or restrict enterprises' opinions and options respecting the nature of services delivered or their prices or availability—have gained currency in a variety of other fields, such as regulation of securities communications, banking, and natural gas. * * *

A related form of privatization is available when government relies less on command-and-control mechanisms than on direct provision of benefits to a class of beneficiaries. Various commentators have suggested that beneficiaries could be better off, and government would be more responsive to their needs and interests, if government allowed beneficiaries some choice among goods or services. Thus, instead of providing a publicly funded school for its residents, a locality might provide an "education voucher" redeemable at any school of the parents' (and children's) choice. The assumption is that any school, public or private, that did a good job of educating children at a reasonable price would flourish under such a system, while schools that did a poor job would go out of business, sell out to better managers or take other steps to improve their performance in order to attract voucher dollars. * * *

A final group of privatization proposals is also concerned with expanding the ambit of individual choices, focusing particularly on the choice to spend a given sum of money in exchange for given benefits. These proposals assert that private choice is restricted whenever government officials are authorized to collect a large block of funds and then, at their discretion, divide the funds over activities of their choosing. This group of privatization proposals calls for a more direct link between the payment of money and the receipt of a good or service. One example of this effort to tie costs more closely to benefits is the call for imposition of user fees, specific charges paid directly by those who elect or use particular government-provided goods or services. * * * A different route to collapsing individual decisions respecting payment for and receipt of benefits is simply to reduce general government revenues. By reducing the amount of money government has to spend, *ceteris paribus*, one increases the stock of money in private hands. * * *

The most frequently noted difference between public and private entities may be the absence in government of the sort of freely transferable property rights in residual claims that characterize ownership interests in private, profit-seeking firms. The absence of such rights reduces incentives to monitor managerial performance in line with insuring cost-minimizing, profit-maximizing performance. Beyond reducing direct monitoring, the absence of transferable rights makes replacement of poor managers difficult, limiting the effectiveness of another source of incentives to better managerial performance.

Of course, the difference between public and private enterprise is not absolute. The value of government services is capitalized into property values, and, especially within small political jurisdictions, this effect may be substantial. This creates a class of monitors for government in some measure analogous to corporate shareholders. Further, there are forces that constrain public managers in ways similar to corporate raiders. The news media invests considerable sums in monitoring government managers who, in turn, spend large amounts to resist threatened "takeover" attempts by political opponents.

But these public mechanisms are less effective than their private market counterparts. Moving out of even a relatively small jurisdiction is considerably more costly than selling shares of stock, and while news coverage of government actors may facilitate takeovers in some cases, its more general effect may be to strengthen the "brand name" advantage of incumbents. The disadvantages of public enterprise monitoring mechanisms are predicted to lead to higher agency costs (costs of behavior that depart from the enterprise's goal and costs of combating such behavior).

A second difference between public and private enterprises also suggests that the former will be characterized by higher agency costs. The private enterprise with which public agencies are compared is the profitseeking firm. Notwithstanding variation in the desires of individual firm members, these firms pursue a single, clear, *joint* goal: profit-maximization.

Public enterprises, in contrast, seldom possess a single or a clear goal. The contest for control of the government's coercive power is usually resolved by a quasi-compromise among competing interests. Rather than reach a determinate solution reduced to explicit contract terms, parties to the political process more often use ambiguous language in an effort to obscure the nature of the package offered or the deal struck. Ambiguity in this context conceals the degree to which the agreement transfers wealth from one group (usually the general public) to another group or groups, and it also allows some decisionmakers to construe the agreement honestly as promoting an abstract public interest while others regard it as serving more focused interests. Such language is not meaningless; it does serve to place general bounds on subordinate decisionmakers, but it conveys less information than would usually be required in private deals and increases friction over future action.

The absence of a single, clearly specified goal, itself in part a consequence of the absence of transferable residual claims, constitutes the second important distinction between government and private enterprise. Even without established property rights, organizations can have clearly established goals. With any well-defined goal, especially one with readily observable output measures, enterprise performance can be monitored and remedial steps taken to police departures from the goal. The public agency, lacking such a goal, should be characterized by higher agency costs than private firms. The existence of greater agency costs in public enterprises, as well as concern about them, is reflected in the greater range of constraints imposed on public managers.

The existence of greater agency costs in public enterprise also helps to explain why legal rules focus more attention on restricting the extension rather than the contraction of public power. The former imposes larger dead weight losses on society. Thus, other things equal, public interest concerns generally should be greater where public agencies play a greater role.

Moreover, private interests are unlikely to favor generic constraints on the reduction of government's role, as such constraints cannot be predicted to produce net benefits to any group. Instead, each interest will favor more focused constraints on disinvolvement from activity that serves its particular ends, which accounts for the predicted prevalence of statutory rather than constitutional requirements for government to perform certain functions.

The sole exception to this characterization of private interest groups underscores the basis for concern over government enterprise; public employees are the one group that should desire generic constraints on reduction of the government's role. The greater agency costs mean that government employees are able to appropriate rents, that is, to work less hard, to do more of what they want, or to receive more pay or greater job security than their private sector counterparts. Public employees as a group, therefore, should resist efforts to privatize. The actions of public employees appear consistent with this rent-seeking description of public employment: public employee unions, indeed, have actively opposed the concept of privatization as well as specific privatizaton proposals. * * *

If the agency-cost disadvantage of public enterprise suggests an explanation for the relative lack of concern over government disinvolvement, it neither explains why government allocates some decisions to private and others to public enterprise, nor establishes a general case for privatization. * * * As Professor Thomas Borcherding observes, the conundrum disappears when one recognizes that public and private enterprises, even when they provide nominally similar services, in fact pursue different goals and must be judged, from an agency-cost perspective, according to the efficiency with which those disparate goals are met.

Nearly all of the commentary on government's relative agency-cost disadvantage focuses on dollar efficiency. Government works less well because private enterprises generally can produce the same outputs—a given quantity of claims processing, electricity, airline services, trash collection, or whatever—at lower cost. As privatization advocates argue, private enterprise has the superior record on efficient production of goods and services in standard competitive output markets. Further, some services now offered by government on a monopoly basis can be recast in this fashion, allowing consumers to choose among different price-and-product packages from competing suppliers.

Public enterprises, however, have been asked in large measure to do a different job: superintending wealth transfers. By all accounts they have done so, although competition for those wealth transfers does not always leave the transferees as well off as they might like to be. Professor Borcherding therefore argues that—despite the claims he and others have advanced that private firms should be the preferred instruments of government policy on pure efficiency grounds—government, in fact, can be seen to operate in a waste-minimizing fashion given the wealth-redistribution goals it pursues.

This argument draws on other work suggesting that, if the enterprise mission remains the same, public reliance on private firms introduces a new source of agency costs. The private firm generally will maximize its profits from closer relation of costs and returns for each class of clients/customers than would characterize pricing policies that might provide a cross-subsidy. Private firms will resist pricing policies that allow redistribution by cross-subsidy, endeavoring either to raise price or decrease service quality on the undervalued service. Whether the private firm is subject to command-and-control regulation or direct contract, the public agent intent on maintaining a redistributive subsidy must incur substantial costs to monitor the private firms' performance. The public agent also will find it essential to exclude unregulated competitors, whose free operation would undermine the subsidy. But this strategy risks creation of monopoly rents for the preferred private supplier. The record of telephone regulation and partial deregulation over the past thirty years illustrates the difficulty of attempts to preserve subsidies while policing economic rents.

Some commentators have suggested that private enterprise need not present greater problems than public enterprise even when the public policy makers desire to create subsidy rents. Commentators have, for example, argued that appropriately designed franchise contracts let by competitive bidding can eliminate these difficulties. However, theoretical inquiries into such contracting processes and experience with such contracts in the cable television industry indicate that considerable cost and slippage attends these franchise processes. The monitoring problems associated with contracting out or regulation will be exacerbated in proportion to the public agent's unwillingness to make the terms of the subsidy or the identity of its recipients explicit.

Other commentators have suggested the introduction of limited competition with other supply sources, private or public, as an alternative to complete public or private provisions of certain services. An initial government supplier's tendency to inefficiency would be constrained by the new, competitive entrant while regulation of the additional supplier arguably would limit the undesirable by-products of regulatory friction that occurs when service is provided by a single private supplier whose profit incentives are at odds with the program's wealth-transfer goals. These proposals, too, seem problematic. In fact, the alternative suppliers, especially private entities, will have incentives to undermine the subsidy part of the public program, for instance, by serving the low-cost, high-demand segment of consumers. This appears to happen in those areas, such as education, where mixed supply has been used for some time.

In summary, the principal choice is between private or public provision of goods and services. The argument from efficiency is that public and private enterprise are employed to maximize each one's comparative advantage. In essence, private enterprise is used to produce goods and services cost effectively and public enterprise is used to produce in-kind wealth transfers cost effectively. * * *

JOHN DONAHUE, LOCAL SERVICE CONTRACTING

From J. Donahue, The Privatization Decision: Public Ends,
Private Means 135, 141–143, 146–147 (1989).

As of mid–1987, there were some twenty-eight thousand recorded instances of public services being provided by private firms under contract to local governments. Virtually every function of local government has been delegated to the private sector at some time, in some city. Shasta County in California contracts with a local law firm to provide legal counsel to the indigent while, to the south of the state, Rancho Palos Verdes contracts out for a local prosecutor. Florida and Kentucky, among other states, have private mental hospitals. The privately owned Detroit–Windsor Tunnel links Canada and the United States, while a for profit company has been authorized to build a toll road to Dulles airport. Nearly forty jurisdictions use profit-seeking fire protection companies, and a private company runs the air-traffic control tower in Farmington, New Mexico. Until tax reform cut into the implicit federal subsidies for such endeavors, dozens of communities were contemplating for-profit water or sewage treatment facilities; a few already have them. La Mirada, California, a city of some forty thousand, contracts out for more than sixty services and has a municipal work force of only fifty-five. Lakewood, California (population sixty thousand), a pioneer in contracting for services, has eight city workers, and one Dallas suburb with twenty-five hundred citizens has no city workforce at all aside from a single secretary to handle the paperwork knitting together the nexus of contracts that constitutes the town's public sector. * * *

[P]rivate contractors improve efficiency through more flexible use of labor, a richer array of incentives and penalties, and, often, a more precise allocation of accountability. Just as one would expect, they are less constrained by process; just as one would hope, they seem to be more tightly focused on results. Municipal street-sweeping crews do a better job each time they clean a street—that is, they faithfully adhere to input specifications. But they do not score so well on the *output* criterion of keeping the streets reasonably clean most of the time. Private crews sweep less thoroughly but more frequently, and, at least in the cities Stevens studied, this turns out to be the better way to keep streets looking good. Private trash collection firms suffer less downtime from equipment failures; the municipal practice of having central motor pools handle maintenance seems to dilute accountability for keeping vehicles in working order. (This problem appears in several other services as well.) Contractors also improve efficiency by paying workers on the basis of routes covered rather than hours worked. * * *

Cities take on a physical layout for complex reasons of history and politics. Only by the least likely of historical accidents will this *administrative* unit turn out to be of the ideal *economic* scale for delivering public services. A farm too small for efficient mechanization will have higher than average costs no matter how hard the farmer works; similarly, a city that must maintain its own fleet of garbage trucks, street-sweepers, and asphalt trucks is likely to be battling against the economics of scale efficiency. (The Touche Ross survey found that smaller cities were more likely than larger cities to report extremely high savings from contracting out.)

Contractors may enjoy three distinguishable advantages rooted in their freedom to let technical efficiency govern the size of their operations. The first pertains to simple scale economies: Contractors can spread the costs of capital and overhead across several cities. * * * [I]ndividual cities are too small to afford an adequate inventory of spare parts, and hence suffer from too much down-time. In the case of tree care and pruning, few cities have enough trees to keep a specialized crew busy year-round, and contractors that handle several cities get more value out of dedicated labor and equipment. * * *

The second scale-related advantage concerns incentives to innovate. Developing more efficient ways to deliver public services can be very costly, in terms of money, time, and specialized labor, and in terms of the public disgruntlement caused by failed experiments. For a municipal agency, the potential *payoff* for innovation is limited to whatever lower costs or higher quality can be achieved within the city limits. Except in the biggest cities, it seldom makes sense for public works departments to make large investments in innovation. A private contractor, however, can claim proprietary rights to innovations, diffuse new methods throughout its operations, and use technological advances as a competitive edge to expand its market. For example, the leading for-profit fire company, Rural Metro, devotes 3 percent of its gross revenues to research and development. Rural Metro innovations include fast "attack trucks" for handling small blazes, a double-hose pumper truck to deliver twice the normal volume of water to a fire, variable-pressure hoses, and a remote-controlled fire-fighting robot to spare human fire-fighters from the most dangerous tasks. Private garbage collection companies continually improve on truck design and seek competitive advantages in equipment. ServiceMaster Industries, Inc., an Illinois-based company that manages custodial services for hospitals, schools, and other institutions, spends considerable sums on improving janitorial technology, and has developed light battery-powered vacuum cleaners, ergonomically advanced mops and brooms, and other new tools and methods. This is not to say that *all* innovation comes from the private sector; there are plenty of public works departments displaying initiative and ingenuity. Civil servants in Phoenix, for example, have used technical and procedural innovation to win bid competitions with private rivals. And well-entrenched contractors may disdain research and development. But, on balance, contractors have more potent incentives for innovation.

The final scale advantage concerns management. Many things may motivate workers to exert their best efforts, including pleasure in the work, commitment to organizational goals, intimidation, self-esteem, and financial incentives. One particularly powerful inducement is the opportunity for advancement within the organization. In a municipal department, advancement usually depends in large part on seniority. Moreover, the top jobs are generally reserved for elected officials or their appointees. And room for advancement is limited by the size of the department. Private contractors, on the other hand, may be able to offer a long and flexible career ladder. Top-performing employees can be promoted upward in the hierarchy at a single site, or can be offered advancement to a larger and more challenging client city, or can rise to management jobs at divisional or corporate headquarters. Of course, if promotion decisions are seen as capricious, career mobility will do little to promote enterprise. But contractors who fail to reward good performance will be at a competitive disadvantage to those who offer attractive career ladders. * * *

The evidence and assessments in this chapter boil down to a cautious, conditional endorsement of expanding the private role in public service delivery. While there are many governmental functions that can never be delegated, a substantial portion of state and local services meet the criteria set forth in chapter 5—they can be specified in advance, subjected to competition, and monitored throughout. * * *

Some reservations remain, however. First, the losses to labor present a real problem that is too often ignored or submerged in rhetoric. On a technical economic level, the tendency of contractors to offer lower wages and benefits means that the *efficiency* advantage of privatization is usually overstated, since some of the cost difference is simply money that stays in taxpayer pockets instead of going to city workers. More generally, municipal employees have pride in their work, mortgages to pay, and a set of expectations formed before contracting out emerged as a major cost-control strategy. It is perfectly understandable that these citizens resist bearing so much of the burden of municipal austerity. Even if taxpayers' stake in efficiency takes precedence over workers' claims to their jobs, taking steps to cushion privatization's shock to municipal workers—while it will likely cut savings considerably—is both politically prudent and commendably humane.

Corruption is a second problem that is typically debated in shrill ideological terms, but that nonetheless remains a cause for concern. The trick is to determine just how big an issue it is. Public employee unions like the American Federation of State, County, and Municipal Employees suggest that bribery and kickbacks are routine in municipal contracting; privatization enthusiasts insist that they are rare. It is certainly true that illegal or unsavory dealings between municipal contractors and public officials occur. Unfortunately, there are no statistical compilations of corrupt municipal contracts by which we can calculate the respective proportions of clean and of tainted transactions. But in an environment of rampant corruption, contracting out obviously makes less sense than in a well-governed town.

The third caveat concerns competition. The good news is that there is considerable evidence that carefully structured competition with for-profit rivals can dramatically boost the efficiency of *public* organizations. The bad news is that the absence of competition can just as dramatically stifle any benefits that privatization would otherwise offer. Throughout this book, I have argued, first, that efficiency springs primarily from competition, not from privateness *per se*, and second, that competition is often difficult to arrange. * * * Municipal contracting is common enough in the Los Angeles area that the cities opting for private delivery can expect a fair degree of potential competition to discipline contractors. When services are relatively simple and observable, there is little risk that incumbent contractors will gain special advantages that protect them against challenge should their prices get out of line or their service quality erode. But if competition is lacking for any reason—and potential reasons are legion, including technical barriers to entry, corruption, mob intimidation, and such simple failings as the disinclination of public officials to keep contractors feeling appropriately insecure—there will be far less to gain from contracting out. * * *

GERALD FRUG, THE CHOICE BETWEEN PRIVATIZATION AND PUBLICAZATION

14 Current Municipal Problems 20–26 (1987).

Privatization is a fashionable idea these days in some state and local government circles. In theory at least, any governmental service could be delivered by a private business under a government contract. Garbage collection, ambulance services and health care are familiar candidates for privatization, but there is no reason to stop there. Public schools could be replaced by private schools as long as students are given government-subsidized vouchers to pay for them. Police departments could be replaced by private security guards, judges could be replaced by professional arbitrators, and fire departments could be replaced by private emergency businesses. Some states are even considering transferring their prison systems to private hands. Indeed, once you begin to take the idea of privatization seriously, you can quickly come to the view that government could be reduced to the performance of three tasks: the collection of revenue by taxation, the decision of which services this revenue should buy, and the negotiation and drafting (and, perhaps, the monitoring) of contracts with private businesses for the delivery of the chosen services. In fact, some of these jobs could be contracted out too. For example, government could hire a collection agency to enforce its laws, a private management consultant to determine what services to provide, and private lawyers to negotiate and draft its contracts. Taken to its limits, then, privatization could transform government simply into a revenue-generating mechanism run by a few people whose job would be to begin the process of contracting out, choosing the consultants and lawyers who, in turn, would continue the cycle of contracting and re-contracting. As a means of employment and delivery of services, the state really could wither away.

Why, however, would anyone *want* to go down this road to privatization? The usual answer people suggest is that private businesses are more efficient and better-run than governments are. But what do the terms "efficient" and "better"-run mean when they are invoked in this way? To some extent, private businesses are "efficient" because they do not have to comply with hundreds of laws that routinely are applied to governments, laws ranging from civil service and competitive bidding requirements to the demands of the Bill of Rights. But if any of these laws serve a valuable purpose, one would think that they should be applied to the managers of publicly funded prisons, schools, and fire departments whoever they are; conversely, if these are not good ideas, they should not be applied to anyone. Why should "private" prisons, financed solely by tax dollars, be exempt from the constitutional requirement that prisoners be treated in accordance with due process of law?

Why should the constitutional restrictions on the arbitrary expulsion of students be applied only to schools labelled "public" and not those labelled "private," when both kinds of schools would be paid for by tax revenues and charged with the task of educating the locality's population? I think the answer to these questions is that both kinds of institution should have to comply with the Bill of Rights. Moreover, I think that there is no more reason to fear corruption in a state-run police department than in a privately run police department, and that there is no more reason to tolerate abuse of employees in a "private" hospital operating pursuant to a contract with the government than in a city-run hospital. But if these contentions are true, the "efficiency" gains derived from private exemption from requirements imposed on government do not support a move to privatization. If any of these requirements are unnecessary, one should relieve governments from having to comply with them; if the requirements are desirable, one should apply them to any entity that performs a service offered in the public interest and supported by publicly generated revenue.

Indeed, any argument for privatization based on the notion that the private sector is more "efficient" than the public sector can be answered by proposing to reform the public sector instead. Some people claim, for example, that the incentive system in the private sector makes employees more productive than does the system adopted by government. But even if this is true (and its truth is much debated), the difference between their incentive systems is attributable simply to the legal rules that require government to operate differently from the way business operates. If schools would be run better if they competed against each other, such a competition could be arranged in public schools as well as in publicly financed private schools. If employees and managers in prisons and police departments could be led to act more efficiently by bonuses or profit-sharing, such a system could be installed in government as well. If private firms run better because they pay their executives more money than the government is permitted to pay, the government could revise its wage scale instead of contracting out its services. After all, it's the taxpayer who pays the bill in either case. Slogans like "competition" or "the profit motive" cannot determine the choice between having services performed by the public or private sector.

Even if the private sector is found to be more "efficient" in some sense of the word, it doesn't follow that privatization would be a good idea. Some people assert, for example, that privatization is desirable because services are cheaper when they are run by private businesses rather than by government. Before transferring services to a private concern, however, we need to find out why they are cheaper (if, indeed, they are). If the services are cheaper because private employers cut the wages or benefits of workers from below the levels offered by government, we need to determine whether such cuts promote the public interest. It's by no means obvious that the public interest is advanced by paying workers less or by providing them less adequate health or retirement benefits. Similarly, if private costs are lower because employees work harder out of fear of being fired, we need to decide whether we want to use public money to create that kind of workplace or whether, alternatively, we think that job security better contributes to a sound working environment. Fostering certain values is often worth the cost. (And—to repeat—if we find the values not worth fostering, the alternative system could be adopted in the public sector itself.)

In my opinion, privatization has become an attractive idea these days because the reform that can readily be seen as an alternative to privatization—transforming government itself—appears to be much more difficult than the process of contracting out to a private concern. Reforming government is a formidable task not only because making the tough choices about the best way to operate services is hard but also because, even after people have decided what to do, they have to get their ideas adopted. This requires dealing with state legislatures, city councils, unions, and interest groups. When confronted with such an arduous task, it's not surprising that people say, "Who needs it? Let's just contract the services out." In the current debate about state and local government services, proponents of privatization have shifted the burden of persuasion to those who favor retaining services in the public sector. The question on the public agenda has changed from "how do we make government better?" to "why not contract out?"

Posing the issue of privatization in these terms, however, does not adequately capture what is at stake in the privatization debate. That this is true can be seen just by looking in a dictionary. According to Webster's Third New International Dictionary of the English Language (the 1981 unabridged edition), the verb "privatize" means "to alter the status of (a business or industry) from public to private control or ownership." One might think, therefore, that the noun "privatization" would, in a parallel fashion, mean the alteration of a business' status from public to private control. This seems to be how people (including me, so far in this essay) are using the term these days. But look what the dictionary definition for "privatization" actually is:

> "The tendency for an individual to withdraw from participation in social and esp[ecially] political life into a world of personal concerns usu[ally] as a result of a feeling of insignificance and lack of understanding of complex social processes."

In his famous survey of America in the 1830s entitled Democracy in America, Alexis de Toqueville found that taking an active part in political life was an American's "most important business and, so to say, the only pleasure he knows * * *. If an American should be reduced to occupying himself with his own affairs, at that moment half his existence would be snatched from him; he would feel it as a vast void in his life and would become incredibly unhappy." Since Toqueville's time, the decrease in participation in public life has contributed, as Toqueville predicted, to individual feelings of insignificance and to a sense that no ordinary person can deal with the complex social problems of the modern world. These feelings have led, in turn, to further decreases in participation in public life, generating still more "feeling[s] of insignificance and lack of understanding of complex social processes." This cycle of privatization could accelerate if states and localities transferred control of their important public services to private entities. Traditionally, the political world has offered a way to engage with others that is different from private life, a form of engagement known as democracy. The sense of empowerment that we gain whenever we become participants in the creation of our social and political world will be lost if we withdraw even further into our private lives or commercial dealings. To combat this trend toward privatization—to prevent this kind of de-privation—we need to revive the sense of public involvement and connection engendered by engagement in political life. I shall call the process of reviving participatory political life "publicazation." This is not just an unfamiliar concept in the privatization debate; it's not even a word at all (according to Webster's unabridged dictionary).

These days, popular involvement in government is limited primarily to participation in the election of those who control the delivery of public services. Even those who want to transfer government services to private business seek to retain this feature of public life. The people who would provide public services would no longer work for an elected official, but they would work for someone chosen by an elected official. Such a change would attenuate, but not cut, the ties that link the electorate with the delivery of public services. But even the ties that now exist do not adequately allow for public involvement in the delivery of government services. Today our state and local government services are run bureaucratically, not in a participatory manner; if transferred to private hands, they would be run bureaucratically as well. A move toward publicazation requires more than simply the maintenance of the status quo. Government operations must be reformed in a direction opposite to that of privatization, encouraging not withdrawal from political life but more active, participatory politics.

There are various forms that publicazation could take in the operation of government services. Those who work in the public sector could be encouraged to participate more actively in the decisions about how their workplace operates. Self-government will become a meaningful contribution to people's sense of themselves only if it is part of their ordinary, day-to-day lives; workplace democracy is, therefore, an important aspect of publicazation. The increasing interest in employee self-management in the United States has not yet adequately taken hold in the delivery of government services. But there is no reason why employee self-management is more appropriate in industry than in a school system. Indeed, allowing teachers to take a greater collective role in the management of their schools could be a first step toward publicazation.

Moreover, public services could be provided in a way that involves members of the public in their planning and management. In the 1960s, public involvement in government decisionmaking took the form of citizen review panels for police departments, citizen advisory boards for public hospitals, and federally sponsored programs that required the maximum participation of those affected in the planning of specific federally funded services. Publicazation could build on the virtues, and learn from the mistakes, of these experiments in participatory decision-making. Crime watch neighborhood organizations, community-based schools, and citizen involvement in city planning and development are examples of possible forms of public participation in the delivery of government services.

Finally, some government services could be managed by groups formed on a participatory basis. Publicly funded housing projects, for example, could be organized in a way that encourages those who live in the housing to assume some of the responsibilities of its management; experiments of this kind are already taking place in a few American cities. * * * Participation could even occur in such an unlikely place as a prison system. In the political prisons of El Salvador, the political prisoners currently participate in a number of the management decisions that affect their areas of the prisons.

To be sure, the future of publicazation does not turn on whether control of public services is in the hands of the government or the private sector. The suggestions just made for government services—workplace democracy, consumer involvement in management decisions, and decentralized, participatory management of service delivery—could take place whether the services are run by government or by business. Publicazation and privatization—in the sense of transferring government services to private businesses—need not be thought of as opposites. Both could happen simultaneously. The critical choice between publicazation and privatization, therefore, is not whether government or business should run public services. The critical choice instead is whether we want public participation in the delivery of public services whoever provides them—whether we want to foster the values of publicazation. In my view, only by taking a share in governance can citizens learn how to deal with people with whom they disagree, how to wield and limit power, and how to affect the complex social processes that affect their lives. Only by taking a share in governance can a citizen overcome the feelings of insignificance and powerlessness that constitute privatization. Of course, publicazation would not be an easy undertaking, either in the government or in the private sector. But the difficult work of reformation can itself become a vehicle for citizen participation. Indeed, organizing to make government and business more participatory could become the initial project of publicazation.

COLORADO ASSOCIATION OF PUBLIC EMPLOYEES v. DEPARTMENT OF HIGHWAYS

Supreme Court of Colorado, 1991.
809 P.2d 988.

JUSTICE LOHR delivered the Opinion of the Court.

This is an appeal from a declaratory order of the Colorado State Personnel Board (Board) sustaining the authority of the Colorado Department of Highways (DOH) to contract with private sector vendors for services previously performed by state employees within the state personnel system. Certain affected state employees (employees), the Colorado Association of Public Employees and the president of its board of directors (collectively, CAPE) sought a determination that contracts with private sector vendors for such services would violate section 24–50–128, 10B C.R.S. (1988), and article XII, section 13, of the Colorado Constitution, which established the state personnel system. * * * [T]he employees * * * [are] custodial, maintenance and utility workers employed by the DOH * * *.

The state personnel system embodies a number of policies. The basic purpose of the civil service laws is to secure efficient public servants for positions in government. Two central features of the Civil Service Amendment are appointment and promotion "according to merit and fitness," Colo. Const. art. XII, § 13(1), and discharge or other discipline only for just cause, *id.* at § 13(8). The personnel system promotes competence in government by requiring the selection of public employees according to merit and fitness as ascertained by competitive tests of competence. Colo. Const. art. XII, § 13(1). Merit based selection and promotion requirements free the state personnel system from political pressures and thereby curtail political patronage. * * *

The process by which the DOH plans to obtain services from private suppliers rather than from classified state employees is commonly referred to as privatization. A primary goal of this process, as demonstrated by the record in this case, is cost savings. The DOH seeks to obtain the necessary services by contract at a lesser expense than that incurred by employing the classified state employees who previously performed this work. The DOH contracts and proposed contracts at issue here directly impact the state personnel system. Thirty-five classified positions will be eliminated, and employees of private companies will perform the work previously accomplished by state employees belonging to the state personnel system. The private sector employees will not be selected by merit and will not be subject to state personnel policies. Thus, privatization departs from traditional state employment practices.

The question before us, framed in its broadest terms, is whether the DOH is authorized to pursue its contemplated plan of privatization. To arrive at an answer, we must analyze the constitutional, statutory, and regulatory framework that creates and implements the state personnel system. * * *

The Civil Service Amendment states that the "personnel system of the state shall comprise all appointive public officers and employees of the state" with certain enumerated exceptions. Colo. Const. art. XII, § 13. It does not further specify the services that must be performed by state employees and offers no guidance concerning criteria or mechanisms for delineating, enlarging or reducing the personnel system. Embedded in the Civil Service Amendment, however, are protections against termination of employment of persons within the personnel system, including a provision that such persons shall hold their respective positions during efficient service. The DOH privatization plan would obtain services from private sector providers, thereby eliminating the need to retain the state employees currently performing those services. This would result in the termination of state employees and elimination of classified positions. This contraction of the state personnel system would implicate the tenure protection features of the Civil Service Amendment. * * *

The Colorado Constitution * * * contemplates the elaboration of the Civil Service Amendment through laws enacted by the legislature and rules adopted by the Board. * * * The general assembly has acted to "provide a sound, comprehensive, and uniform system of personnel management and administration for the employees within the state personnel system," by adopting the State Personnel System Act. * * * Notably absent from the constitutional, statutory and regulatory framework are any provisions for eliminating positions from the state personnel system and substituting private sector providers to perform under contract the services previously accomplished by persons within the state personnel system.

Privatization of government services has significant policy implications for the state personnel system. Privatization can provide important benefits by reducing costs and increasing governmental efficiency and productivity. On the other hand, privatization operates as a labor policy in that it affects the qualifications and conditions of employment of persons who will perform services for the government. Since government is a labor intensive service industry, privatization achieves savings primarily by reducing labor costs.

The competitive cost advantage of the private companies, however, may result from their freedom from the state personnel system. For example, private companies have great latitude in selecting, promoting, transferring and terminating employees; they are not required to employ competitive tests of competence. Absent specific statutory requirements, private contractors need not follow the legislatively mandated pay scales, veteran's preferences, and other employment practices that apply to the civil service. The civil service laws and regulations protect public workers from arbitrary and oppressive treatment, and require due process protections before disciplinary action or termination; private employees lack these protections. These constraints are necessary in government employment to carry out the functions of the civil service, promote competence in government, and ensure a politically independent civil service. These labor policy aspects of privatization, which are essential components of its cost efficiency, have significant consequences for the civil service.

This critical impact of privatization on the state personnel system implicates the legislature's role in structuring the system consistent with constitutional constraints, and invokes both the Board's rulemaking mandate and the Director's [of the department of personnel] duty to provide leadership in state personnel management. The scope and characteristics of any plan of privatization and means by which such a plan is to be implemented require careful consideration. Legislation, rules, or some combination thereof establishing standards will be necessary to ensure that privatization does not subvert the policies underlying the state personnel system. This requires an evaluation of the effects of the concept of privatization on the state personnel system as a whole, rather than a case specific consideration of the effect of a particular privatization plan of a single state agency on individual employees.

It is clear that before a privatization plan can be adopted, it is constitutionally necessary that the legislature, the Board and the Director exercise their respective constitutional roles in evaluating the concept and supplying the details for implementation of privatization, pursuant to their obligations to delineate the features of the state personnel system. At the time relevant to the present case, however, no one had analyzed whether or under what circumstances positions within the state personnel system can be eliminated consistent with the civil service protections in order to obtain the same services by contract with private sector providers. The legislature had not spoken concerning privatization, and no regulatory criteria or guidelines had been adopted by which an executive agency could determine whether privatization is permissible and, if so, under what circumstances. Because privatization so directly implicates both the personnel system as a whole and the specific protections accorded state personnel system employees under article XII, § 13(8), standards regulating privatization must be established by legislation, regulation, or some combination of the two. * * *

The DOH, however, contends it does have legislative authority under section 24–50–124, 10B C.R.S. (1988), to support the termination of the affected employees. That statute recognizes that certified employees can be separated from state service due to "reorganization." We do not construe that term to be so expansive. We believe the legislature had in mind a departmental reorganization that eliminates the need for the specific services previously performed by the terminated employees. Given the constitutional protections accorded civil service employees, the legislature could not have envisioned the elimination of state employees' positions by a brief reference to "reorganization" when the department continues to need the services they performed. Whatever the scope of the term, however, any reorganization must still comply with the policies and strictures of the Civil Service Amendment. * * *

The DOH also relies on section 24–50–128(2), 10B C.R.S. (1988), in support of its asserted authority to contract out for the services at issue here. Section 24–50–128 governs contracts with private sector providers for personal services and recognizes two types of personal services contracts. The first type is personal services contracts that create an employer-employee relationship. Subsection (3) governs the validity of such contracts. The second is all other personal services contracts. * * *

We consider the validity of the contracts under subsection (3) first. The subsection contains detailed standards governing the approval of personal services contracts by the Director. These detailed statutory standards constrain the Director in deciding whether to approve contracts creating an employer-employee relationship. The DOH contracts are not consistent with these detailed statutory standards. Subsection (3) states in pertinent part:

> It is declared to be the policy of the state that contracts for personal services which create an employer-employee relationship shall normally not be used to fill permanent or temporary positions in the state personnel system where the duties of such positions are classified and where such duties are commonly or historically performed by employees in regular positions under the state personnel system.

The custodial, maintenance and utility services to be supplied by the contracts at issue here were commonly and historically performed by classified state employees. The DOH has a continuing need for those services, so the duties should be considered permanent. Since the duties are permanent, proper classified positions currently exist, and the duties were historically performed by classified employees, personal services contracts cannot be used to obtain the services. The DOH contracts, therefore, violate section 24–50–128(3), and are deemed "void from the beginning," § 24–50–128(3), if they are construed to create employer-employee relationships. Moreover, under subsection (3), any personal services contract creating an employer-employee relationship outside the state personnel system cannot exceed six months in a twelve-month period, "nor shall any person be employed longer than six calendar months in any twelve-month period through any combination of a contract and any other type of temporary appointment." § 24–50–128(3). The contracts and proposed contracts at issue here exceed these durational limits and therefore, if construed to create employer-employee relationships, could not be validly approved by the Director and must be considered unauthorized and void.

The contention that the DOH contracts are authorized under section 24–50–128(2) if they do not create an employer-employee relationship does not survive close examination. Section 24–50–128(2) provides:

> Contracts for personal services for a term longer than six months in duration shall be reviewed by the state personnel director to determine whether such positions should be brought into the state personnel system.

This statute by the plain meaning of its terms is directed at a review of personal services performed by persons not in the state personnel system to determine whether the system should be expanded to encompass them. Nothing in the statutory language suggests that it was intended to permit the Director to determine whether services historically performed by state employees should be obtained instead from private providers. The need to obtain personal services for a term longer than six months raises the question whether such services could be performed to better advantage, consistent with the purposes of the Civil Service Amendment, by persons within the state personnel system. A straightforward reading of the statute itself evinces the clear and single legislative purpose to require the Director to review contracts between state agencies and private sector vendors for personal services not being performed by state employees to address that question. * * *

Finally, the DOH argues that the Civil Service Amendment applies only to personal services contracts that create an employer-employee relationship. * * * We reject this hypothesized legislative construction. * * * [T]he identification of the legal relationship created by the DOH contracts—employer-employee on the one hand and independent contractor on the other—cannot be the sole factor determining the applicability of the Civil Service Amendment. If carried to its logical extreme, the DOH's argument would permit it to replace all its classified employees with private sector providers so long as the contracts do not create an employer-employee relationship. Given the myriad applications for privatization, contracts with private sector providers could result in the elimination of a large number of state personnel positions, and thereby implicate the concerns underlying the Civil Service Amendment. Such contracts also involve the selection of persons performing personal services for the state, as well as the compensation for those personal services. Matters of this kind are firmly within the purview of the state personnel system. These fundamental personnel issues cannot be resolved without legislative or regulatory guidance. * * *

PROFESSIONAL ENGINEERS IN CALIFORNIA GOVERNMENT v. DEPARTMENT OF TRANSPORTATION

Court of Appeal, First District, 1993.
13 Cal.App.4th 585, 16 Cal.Rptr.2d 599.

ANDERSON, PRESIDING JUSTICE.

In 1989 our Legislature enacted an urgency measure empowering the California Department of Transportation (Caltrans) to contract with private developers to construct and operate tollway facilities under lease agreements with the state. (Assem. Bill No. 680 [Stats. 1989, ch. 107, pp. 1017–1019, eff. July 10, 1989].) This legislation arose from a legislative determination that "public sources of revenues to provide an efficient transportation system have not kept pace with California's growing transportation needs, and alternative funding sources should be developed to augment or supplement available public sources of revenue." The Legislature envisioned that privately financed projects could "take advantage of private sector efficiencies" and "more quickly bring reductions in congestion in existing transportation corridors." Finally, through authorized demonstration projects, Caltrans could test the feasibility and efficiency of the private financing and construction model.

Pursuant to the enabling legislation in 1990 Caltrans entered into contracts with four entities for development and construction of the four demonstration projects. Appellants[2] sought extraordinary, injunctive and declaratory relief in a multifaceted challenge to Caltrans's constitutional and statutory authority to enter into these agreements. * * *

Section 143 specifically authorizes Caltrans to "solicit proposals and enter into agreements with private entities, or consortia thereof, for the construction by, and lease to, private entities of four public transportation demonstration projects, at least one of which shall be in northern California and one in southern California." Facilities constructed pursuant to the agreements would at all times be owned by the state and the state in turn would lease them to the private developers for up to 35 years. During the lease term the developer would operate the facility and collect tolls to be applied to payment of its capital outlay, costs, and a reasonable rate of return on investment. The facility would revert to the state upon expiration of the lease. In order to implement the statutory directives, Caltrans is authorized to "exercise any power possessed by it with respect to the development and construction of state transportation projects." * * *

In response to its mandate, Caltrans solicited proposals for the demonstration projects, selected four entities, and entered into contracts with each. They are: California Toll Road Company (CTRC), for an 85–mile expressway between Sunol and Vacaville; National Toll Road Authority Corporation, for an 11–mile extension of Route 57 in Orange County utilizing the Santa Ana River Flood Control Channel; California Private Transportation Corporation for a 10–mile, 4–lane road in the median of Route 91 from the Riverside County line to Route 55 in Orange County; and California Transportation Ventures, Inc., for a 10–mile limited access highway in San Diego County. * * *

Each agreement designates a "franchise zone," "absolute protection zone" or "non-competition zone" along corridors of the proposed facilities. Within these zones, Caltrans grants certain exclusive development rights to the project sponsors. In particular, Caltrans agrees not to issue any competing franchise or open or operate any competitive transportation facility within the special zone for the term of the lease or agreement.

Appellants object that these noncompetition provisions amount to a contracting away, for some 35–plus years, of the state's police powers to determine how land should be used to serve the health and general welfare of the community within the franchise zones.

---

2. Appellants are (1) Professional Engineers in California Government, a labor organization which represents engineers employed by the State of California and (2) Richard Baker and Bruce Blanning, California taxpayers and residents of Northern and Southern California respectively.

Without question, "the government may not contract away its right to exercise the police power in the future" and an agreement attempting to do so is "invalid and unenforceable as contrary to public policy." (*Avco Community Developers, Inc. v. South Coast Regional Com.* (1976) 17 Cal.3d 785, 800 [132 Cal.Rptr. 386, 553 P.2d 546].)

A turn of the century case involving a cemetery association's continued right to make interments on certain property is instructive. There, the plaintiff association argued that since the city and county had granted land to it for purposes of a cemetery, and knew of and acquiesced in the cemetery's establishment and existence for many years, the city was estopped to enforce an ordinance preventing the interment of dead bodies within its borders. (*Laurel Hill Cemetery v. City and County* (1907) 152 Cal. 464, 475 [93 P. 70].) To this the court said: "Even if the city and county had made an express contract granting to the plaintiff the right to make interments in this ground in perpetuity, such contract would have no force as against a future exercise by the legislative branch of the government of its police power. This power cannot be bargained or contracted away, and all rights and property are held subject to it. The alleged estoppel relied on can have no greater force than would a contract such as the one supposed." (*Id.* at pp. 475–476, 93 P. 70).

The agreements here do not expressly bargain away the state's police power to legislate for the welfare and safety of its people. Instead, Caltrans has granted real parties in interest certain exclusive development rights within certain franchise zones. We will not read into the contracts an abrogation of the potential future exercise of the sovereign police power. However, we emphasize, as did the trial court below, that the reservation of this power is implicit in all government contracts and private parties take their rights subject to it. Thus, within constitutional boundaries of procedural due process, just compensation for the taking of private property and the like, all private contractual rights must give way to compelling state necessity. For instance, were a legitimate, compelling public need to arise for a transportation facility within a franchise zone that would compete with one of the demonstration projects, the Legislature, acting to attain this public welfare object, could use its power of eminent domain to condemn the franchise. (*City of Oakland v. Oakland Raiders* (1982) 32 Cal.3d 60, 64–68, 183 Cal.Rptr. 673, 646 P.2d 835.) The trial court recognized this, as do real parties in interest. The agreements do not attempt to abrogate the police power.

Finally, were we to follow appellants' argument to its logical conclusion, *all* exclusive franchises would be void because any granting of exclusive rights inherently precludes other approaches to the problem. When granted explicitly, the validity of exclusive franchises for provision of public services and benefits is well settled. * * *

Article VII of the California Constitution establishes a system of civil service employment for state government: "The civil service includes every officer and employee of the State except as otherwise provided in this Constitution." (Cal. Const., art. VII, § 1, subd. (a).) The hallmark of our civil service system is that appointments and promotions are based on merit ascertained by competitive examination. * * *

Although article VII does not expressly limit the state's ability to contract with private firms for provision of state services, courts have implied certain limits as essential to protect the civil service mandate against dissolution and destruction. Typically courts have articulated tests for determining whether employment of noncivil service personnel violates these implied limitations. For example, under the "nature of the services test" the court inquires as to whether the nature of the contracted services is such that they could have been performed by a civil servant. If so, the agency must proceed under the civil service mandate. (*California State Employees' Assn. v. Williams* (1970) 7 Cal. App.3d 390, 395, 86 Cal.Rptr. 305.) Under the "new state function" test, courts will ask whether the contracted services displace existing state civil service functions or, instead, embrace a new state activity or function. The constitutional policy of a merit employment system "does not prohibit legislative experimentation in new forms to fit new functions." (*Id.* at p. 399, upholding the statutes and resulting contract calling for private carriers to conduct administrative tasks of the Medi–Cal program.)

Appellants' most fundamental contention below was that the agreements contemplate that the developers will contract out civil service work on state highways, in contravention of article VII. Further, to the extent section 143 itself permits design of state highways by the private sector, they maintain it also is unconstitutional.

Without question Caltrans engineers could design the roads in question and other civil servants could construct them. Nor are the design and construction of roads, new state functions or activities. But appellants take too literal an approach when they say that the demonstration projects do not translate into a new state function under *Williams*. As the trial court correctly pointed out, the novelty of the contracts and legislation lies in the privatization of project financing and management. After all, the private sector, not the state, will pay for the services engaged pursuant to the exclusive franchise agreements.

Under section 143 and the agreements, the state is embarking on a new experimental program enlisting private financing, design, construction and operation of transportation facilities to solve state transportation needs that cannot be met with available public revenue. We agree with the trial court that the constitution does not discourage this experimentation. Indeed, to strike down these efforts would denigrate a key purpose of the civil service mandate—to promote efficiency and economy in state government. Of course these efficiencies and economies remain to be proven, but the very purpose of the demonstration projects is to explore the feasibility of the private financing/management approach.

While arguably the letting of any service contract or franchise might "open[] the door to the spoils system," the Legislature can adopt other measures to prevent such abuse. We will not construe article VII as prohibiting government contract for performance of services just because of a lurking potential for political favoritism. * * *

Three of the agreements grant the developer an option to lease airspace for $1 per year, with adjustment to a market rate after 35 years. The fourth agreement contemplates a right of first offer and first refusal for the development and operation of airspace improvements. The airspace leases give the developers the right to construct commercial improvements or to sublease the airspace to third parties for such purposes. Income which the developers may enjoy under airspace leases and subleases is excluded from the calculations establishing limits on profit which the developers can retain from receipt of tolls. However, the cost of improvements erected within the airspace is also excluded from the investment base against which the maximum rate of return is measured.

Appellants complain that Caltrans's grant of airspace rights to the developers exceeds the scope of authority permitted under section 143, subdivision (b). * * * Without question, * * * [state law] empowers Caltrans to grant airspace lease rights for commercial development along the toll roads. Such grants advance the private sector's involvement in developing and constructing highways and enhancing their use. * * * [Moreover,] the initial nominal value placed on the airspace is not unreasonable. First, the developers will be purchasing (or paying condemnation awards) for the underlying real property encompassed within the right-of-way of the facilities. Thus, the "grant" of airspace rights is little more than a retention or reservation of development rights by the purchaser. Second, the trial court correctly observed that Caltrans's agreement to enter airspace leases is but one of many covenants running from Caltrans to the developers in exchange for the numerous obligations and commitments which the developers have undertaken. The consideration accruing to the state is a package of commitments to which the nominal $1 is added as is the potential market rate rentals which could accrue to the state after 35 years and after *the developers* have invested substantial private capital in airspace improvements. Any value which the leases may eventually produce results from the developers' own investment. Moreover, as Caltrans represented at trial, other airspace leases which it has entered into have failed to generate significant revenue. Thus the airspace rights represent only a modest, and speculative, potential margin of profitability. Compared with the risks the project sponsors are assuming, the airspace lease provisions are reasonable. * * *

WEST v. ATKINS

Supreme Court of the United States, 1988.
487 U.S. 42, 108 S.Ct. 2250, 101 L.Ed.2d 40.

JUSTICE BLACKMUN delivered the opinion of the Court. * * *

Petitioner, Quincy West, tore his left Achilles tendon in 1983 while playing volleyball at Odom Correctional Center, the Jackson, N.C., state prison in which he was incarcerated. A physician under contract to provide medical care to Odom inmates examined petitioner and directed that he be transferred to Raleigh for orthopedic consultation at Central Prison Hospital, the acute-care medical facility operated by the State for its more than 17,500 inmates. Central Prison Hospital has one full-time staff physician, and obtains additional medical assistance under "Contracts for Professional Services" between the State and area physicians.

Respondent, Samuel Atkins, M.D., a private physician, provided orthopedic services to inmates pursuant to one such contract. Under it, Doctor Atkins was paid approximately $52,000 annually to operate two "clinics" each week at Central Prison Hospital, with additional amounts for surgery. Over a period of several months, he treated West's injury by placing his leg in a series of casts. West alleges that although the doctor acknowledged that surgery would be necessary, he refused to schedule it, and that he eventually discharged West while his ankle was still swollen and painful, and his movement still impeded. Because West was a prisoner in "close custody," he was not free to employ or elect to see a different physician of his own choosing.

Pursuant to 42 U.S.C. § 1983, West, proceeding *pro se*, commenced this action against Doctor Atkins in the United States District Court for the Eastern District of North Carolina for violation of his Eighth Amendment right to be free from cruel and unusual punishment. West alleged that Atkins was deliberately indifferent to his serious medical needs, by failing to provide adequate treatment. * * *

Respondent, as a physician employed by North Carolina to provide medical services to state prison inmates, acted under color of state law for purposes of § 1983 when undertaking his duties in treating petitioner's injury. Such conduct is fairly attributable to the State.

The Court recognized in *Estelle*: "An inmate must rely on prison authorities to treat his medical needs; if the authorities fail to do so, those needs will not be met." [*Estelle v. Gamble,*] 429 U.S. [97], at 103. In light of this, the Court held that the State has a constitutional obligation, under the Eighth Amendment, to provide adequate medical care to those whom it has incarcerated. *Id.*, at 104. * * * North Carolina employs physicians, such as respondent, and defers to their professional judgment, in order to fulfill this obligation. By virtue of this relationship, effected by state law, Doctor Atkins is authorized and obliged to treat prison inmates, such as West. He does so "clothed with the authority of state law." *United States v. Classic*, 313 U.S., at 326. He is "a person who may fairly be said to be a state actor." *Lugar v. Edmondson Oil Co.*, 457 U.S., at 937. It is only those physicians authorized by the State to whom the inmate may turn. Under state law, the only medical care West could receive for his injury was that provided by the State. If Doctor Atkins misused his power by demonstrating deliberate indifference to West's serious medical needs, the resultant deprivation was caused, in the sense relevant for state-action inquiry, by the State's exercise of its right to punish West by incarceration and to deny him a venue independent of the State to obtain needed medical care.

The fact that the State employed respondent pursuant to a contractual arrangement that did not generate the same benefits or obligations applicable to other "state employees" does not alter the analysis. It is the physician's function within the state system, not the precise terms of his employment, that determines whether his actions can fairly be attributed to the State. Whether a physician is on the state payroll or is paid by contract, the dispositive issue concerns the relationship among the State, the physician, and the prisoner. Contracting out prison medical care does not relieve the State of its constitutional duty to provide adequate medical treatment to those in its custody, and it does not deprive the State's prisoners of the means to vindicate their Eighth Amendment rights.[14] The State bore an affirmative obligation to provide adequate medical care to West; the State delegated that function to respondent Atkins; and respondent voluntarily assumed that obligation by contract.

Nor does the fact that Doctor Atkins' employment contract did not require him to work exclusively for the prison make him any less a state actor than if he performed those duties as a full-time, permanent member of the state prison medical staff. It is the physician's function while working for the State, not the amount of time he spends in performance of those duties or the fact that he may be employed by others to perform similar duties, that determines whether he is acting under color of state law. In the State's employ, respondent worked as a physician at the prison hospital fully vested with state authority to fulfill essential aspects of the duty, placed on the State by the Eighth Amendment and state law, to provide essential medical care to those the State had incarcerated. Doctor Atkins must be considered to be a state actor. * * *

515 ASSOCIATES v. CITY OF NEWARK

Supreme Court of New Jersey, 1993.
132 N.J. 180, 623 A.2d 1366.

CLIFFORD, J. * * *

In October 1991, the City Council of Newark adopted the following ordinance:

Armed Security Guard Required. Except as is otherwise herein provided all public and private housing buildings in the City of

---

14. As the dissent in the Court of Appeals explained, if this were the basis for delimiting § 1983 liability, "the state will be free to contract out all services which it is constitutionally obligated to provide and leave its citizens with no means for vindication of those rights, whose protection has been delegated to 'private' actors, when they have been denied." 815 F.2d, at 998.

Newark, New Jersey, which contain over 100 housing units shall be required to have present on the premises an armed security guard for eight of every twenty-four hours, as well as an unarmed security guard for the remaining 16 hours, during each day of a year. Housing units which are situated on the grounds of hospitals, regularly patrolled by a security force, and wherein such grounds are revisited by a security patrol at least once per hour, shall be exempt from the requirement of maintaining an armed security guard on the premises. The provisions of this section shall not apply to any dwelling unit which is a condominium development or any rental or condominium building with units each having an individual exterior entrance. * * *

Plaintiffs, owners of certain apartment buildings in Newark affected by the ordinance, filed a complaint in lieu of prerogative writ, challenging the ordinance * * *. [P]laintiffs offer several arguments based on the New Jersey Constitution and our prior case law. * * * First, plaintiffs challenge the City's action as an arbitrary and unreasonable exercise of the municipal police power. Municipalities may enact ordinances pursuant to the police power, but police-power legislation is subject to the constitutional limitation that it be not unreasonable, arbitrary, or capricious, and that the means selected by the legislative body shall have real and substantial relation to the object sought to be attained. * * *

During hearings on the ordinance, several Council members and citizens spoke about the special circumstances and dangers presented by multiple dwellings like the plaintiffs' buildings. * * * A Newark landlord who testified against the ordinance * * * said, "I have at times gotten out of my car myself to chase people when I saw someone getting robbed in the street" near a large apartment building in Newark. Another Newark resident recounted two instances in which persons had "shot up" the high-rise apartment in which she resided.

Councilman Grant noted that "a number of high-rise buildings in this City * * * are just not protected[,] and people are walking in and out at their own risks[,] and in some instances, they walk out and don't come back because of molestation." He also said, "People are calling and complaining to us, 'I live in a high rise. We have no protection. There are attendants sitting there and they are powerless to do anything.'" * * *

The Council provided the trial court with crime statistics for plaintiffs' properties and the areas immediately adjacent to those properties for the period between January 1989 and September 1990. * * * Those statistics reveal that the following crimes had been reported for those properties during that twenty-month period: fifty-two assaults, forty-two robberies, five rapes, and one murder. Plaintiffs point to the City's failure to contrast the per capita crime rate for their properties with the rates for other areas of the City. However, that observation ignores the fact that the higher population density of the regulated properties might alone justify a distinction.

Faced with the same information and experience as the Council, we might not conclude that large apartment buildings are peculiarly dangerous or that armed security is necessary, but * * * we are not free to substitute our judgment for the Council's. The anecdotal evidence offered by citizens and the Council's knowledge and experience * * * supply a rational basis for the City's action because a reasonable person faced with the same evidence could conclude that large multiple dwellings present special security problems. Therefore, we are satisfied that the Council did not act arbitrarily or capriciously.

Next, plaintiffs challenge the ordinance as an improper attempt by the municipality to delegate its governmental duty to provide police protection. Without doubt, local governments bear the burden of providing police protection, and they may not transfer that duty to private citizens. Nevertheless, we have recognized in the past that under special circumstances municipalities may require that private parties provide assistance in the police-protection area. Because we do not perceive the requirement of armed security guards in the affected properties as constituting a wholesale transfer of the duty to provide police protection, but rather as representing a valid delegation of some portion of that duty—a delegation justified by the facts supporting the City's call for assistance—we reject plaintiffs' argument.

Undoubtedly, the duties of the guards envisioned in the Newark ordinance far exceed those that have previously received the approval of our courts. In the past, the courts have upheld an ordinance that required twenty-four-hour security services at a truck stop, *Hudson Circle Servicenter*, 70 N.J. 289, 359 A.2d 862; an ordinance requiring a uniformed security guard during certain hours at apartment complexes of 250 or more units, *Sunrise Village Assocs. v. Borough of Roselle Park*, 181 N.J.Super. 567, 438 A.2d 945 (Law Div.1980), *aff'd*, 181 N.J.Super. 565, 438 A.2d 944 (App.Div.1981), *certif. denied*, 89 N.J. 413 (1982); and an ordinance requiring security guards at an arcade, *Bonito* [*v. Bloomfield Township*,] 197 N.J.Super. 390, 484 A.2d 1319. Those cases inform our resolution of the present case. * * *

In the present case, although the guards' functions involve certain duties traditionally performed by police officers, the guards do not perform several critical police functions that this State's courts had identified in the cases discussed above. One reason supporting the passage of this ordinance was the Council's belief that the presence of an armed security guard would deter crime. Councilman Rice, for instance, noted that "armed security is very effective as a deterrent." Nevertheless, that the Council also anticipated that the armed guards would perform certain functions identified as "police functions" in *Hudson Circle Servicenter* and *Sunrise Village Associates* seems clear. Those two cases listed the following as "police" functions: (1) investigating crimes, (2) apprehending and prosecuting criminals, (3) carrying weapons, and (4) intervening in criminal activities. *Sunrise Village Associates* also observed that the security guards were not "empowered with the authority of municipal police," without, however, explaining what authority that phrase contemplates. Nevertheless, Newark's ordinance does not explicitly attempt to vest the armed security guards with the powers of municipal police.

A reading of the Council's discussion of the understood functions of the required armed guards demonstrates that the Council believed that the guards would perform duties beyond the mere deterrence function envisioned in the earlier security-guard cases. Of the four functions identified in *Hudson Circle Servicenter* and *Sunrise Village Associates*, the Council clearly envisioned that the armed guards would perform two—carrying weapons and intervening in potential crimes or crimes in progress.

Nothing in the ordinance or its legislative history suggests that the guards would have the authority to investigate crimes or apprehend and prosecute offenders. That responsibility—which is an indispensable part of the police officer's function—is not part of the security guards' duties. If an armed security guard should intervene to prevent or stop a crime, the guard would have no duty to investigate or take steps to secure the criminal's arrest beyond those of an ordinary citizen. Police officers have also the right to engage in other law-enforcement activities that security guards do not, such as conducting investigative detention or warrantless searches in appropriate circumstances. Therefore, although the duties of these guards approach the line dividing security services from police services, we are fully satisfied that they do not cross that line.

Plaintiffs' and our dissenting colleagues' arguments that the City has delegated the duty of providing police protection come down to this assertion: when you give a security guard a gun, that security guard becomes a police officer. But police officers are more than security guards with guns. We do not make light of the ordinance's requirement that security guards carry a weapon, but we emphasize that police protection involves a myriad of responsibilities. Even a requirement that a person perform some task or tasks similar to those undertaken by a police officer—even one as identified with police duties as carrying a weapon—does not transform that person into a police officer.

The requirement of an armed security guard for plaintiffs' buildings in no way constitutes an abdication of the City's own duties; rather, it manifests a rational legislative determination that a certain class of buildings poses special risks of crime and that the municipal police alone cannot possibly deal with all the crime in the City in a timely manner.
* * *

Finally, plaintiffs claim that the ordinance violates the Equal Protection Clause because it irrationally singles out certain buildings for exemption from the ordinance. Once again, the strong presumption in favor of the ordinance and the legislative history lead to a finding that the distinctions are not irrational. * * *

Councilman Grant suggested a rational basis for the decision to exclude housing units on hospital grounds, noting that "units that are excluded would be those * * * such as *hospitals and what not, where they already have armed security.*" * * * Likewise, a rational basis exists for the distinction between buildings with a common entrance and condominium complexes in which each unit has its own exterior entrance. * * * The City answers plaintiffs' challenge by contending that an armed security guard "might be very effective if he could guard an entrance used by all the tenants, but his effectiveness would decrease if he could guard only one of many exterior entrances to apartment units." The City's decision that an armed guard with responsibility for one common entrance would be more effective than the same guard if the guard were responsible for more than 100 individual entrances is not clearly irrational. * * *

O'HERN, J., dissenting.

This case illustrates further the reality that the true victims of inner-city crime are the residents themselves. When the citizens in this community cried out for police protection, the answer they received was "buy your own police." Not so long ago, in the context of a case concerning private-landlord tort liability, a Michigan justice foresaw what we now experience.

Public safety is the business of government.

Today's decision concedes the failure of government to make the streets and homes of certain areas reasonably safe and in effect transfers the governmental function of public protection to the unfortunate owners of real property in such places. * * * The intrusion of private industry into the business of public safety has been one of the most unfortunate phenomena of the 1960's and the 1970's. Already, there are subdivisions which operate their own patrol cars; private police and private guards are multiplying * * *. [*Johnston v. Harris*, 387 Mich. 569, 198 N.W.2d 409, 411–12 (1972) (Brennan, J., dissenting).]

Unlike those who can take sanctuary in privileged areas, the citizens of Newark must contend with the crushing burden of crime. Everyone shares the concerns of the City's residents. Its council members are no less concerned than those anywhere else.

But the problems that they face are seemingly beyond the financial capacity of the City. Our Court errs, however, when it denies the reality of the situation. It treats the ordinance as if it were a property-maintenance code within the general-welfare jurisdiction of the governing body.

Just as we would never tolerate an abdication by a governmental agency of its function to govern, we cannot, consistent with law, sustain an abdication of the police function by a municipal governing body. The comments of the council members who voted in favor of the ordinance demonstrate its functional significance. One councilman said:

> Now the City of Newark, likewise, has a responsibility with its Police Department, but given the limited number of policemen we have in spite of adding on each year, there is still a lack of adequate protection *City-wide*. So, this particular ordinance that I've introduced is simply one to help protect the lives of the persons that we serve. [Emphasis added.]

Another councilman stated that "the residents want more police officers and they know they have to bear the cost of that because that is a service the taxpayers pay for." Another added that in his view the presence of an armed-security guard in open spaces in an apartment complex or a high-rise with a large court would deter criminal activity. Nothing could be clearer than that the ordinance represents a well-intended desire to increase the number of police officers in the community.

Like every other function of government the cost of police service should be included within the cost of general municipal services. As enacted, the provision imposes the financial burden on the victims of crime themselves, for, as Chief Justice Weintraub once explained:

> The bill will be paid, not by the owner, but by the tenants. And if, as we apprehend, the incidence of crime is greatest in the areas in which the poor must live, they, and they alone, will be singled out to pay for their own police protection. The burden should be upon the whole community and not upon the segment of the citizenry which is least able to bear it. [*Goldberg v. Hous. Auth. of Newark*, 38 N.J. 578, 591, 186 A.2d 291 (1962).] * * *

I do not take issue with the municipal power to require some assistance from private entities in providing security, as the municipalities did in *Hudson Circle Servicenter, Bonito,* and *Sunrise Village Associates.* My concern is that the Newark ordinance goes too far, thereby permitting the City to shift its responsibility onto the shoulders of private entities. Furthermore, the ordinance is unfair to plaintiffs, or their tenants, to the extent it imposes an added financial burden on them. The ordinance calls for armed police protection, an essential function of government. As such, the financial burden of providing the service should be borne by the community as a whole. * * *

SECTION E. CITIZENS' ABILITY TO SUE THE CITY FOR A VIOLATION OF THEIR RIGHTS

In this section, our inquiry into the relationship between the city and its citizens shifts to the subject of a city's liability to its citizens for violating their Constitutional rights. In the first case reproduced below, Monell v. Department of Social Services, the Supreme Court held that cities were liable to their citizens for damages under 42 U.S.C. § 1983.[1] Section 1983 provides as follows:

> Every person who, under color of any statute, ordinance, regulation, custom, or usage, of any State or Territory, subjects, or causes to be subjected, any citizen of the United States or other persons within the jurisdiction thereof to the deprivation of any rights, privileges or immunities secured by the Constitution and laws, shall be liable to the person injured in an action of law, suit in equity, or other proper proceedings for redress.

This section explores the extent of cities' liability for Constitutional violations created by *Monell*.[2] This subject, of course, could easily have been considered in Chapter Two. The exposure of cities to damages under Section 1983 constitutes a significant federal intervention into local affairs.

Before reading the cases, it might be helpful to take note of several related aspects of legal doctrine. First of all, the liability for Constitutional violations imposed on local governments is considerably more extensive than the liability imposed on any other level of government. The liability of states for offenses similar to those for which cities are liable under Section 1983, for example, is limited by the Eleventh Amendment.[3] To be sure, the notion that the Eleventh Amendment bars suits for damages in federal court brought by citizens against their own states is itself highly controversial.[4] Nevertheless, it has been clear for 100 years that cities are given no Constitutional immunity whatsoever from damage suits by the Eleventh Amendment, while states are

1. For an analysis of *Monell* and the cases following it, see, e.g., Lewis & Blumoff, Reshaping Section 1983's Asymmetry, 140 U.Pa.L.Rev. 755 (1992); Brown, Correlating Municipal Liability and Official Immunity Under 1983, 1989 U.Ill.L.Rev. 625; Kramer & Sykes, Municipal Liability Under Section 1983: A Legal and Economic Analysis, 1987 Sup.Ct. Rev. 249; Mead, 42 U.S.C. § 1983 Municipal Liability: The Monell Sketch Becomes a Distorted Picture, 65 N.C.L.Rev. 517 (1987); Snyder, The Final Authority Analysis: A Unified Approach to Municipal Liability Under Section 1983, 1986 Wis.L.Rev. 633; M.D. Gelfand, Federal Constitutional Law and American Local Government 421–71 (1984); Freilich & Carlisle (eds.), Section 1983: Sword and Shield (1983); Kramer, Section 1983 and Municipal Liability: Selected Issues Two Years After Monell v. Department of Social Services, 12 Urban Lawyer 232 (1980).

2. After *Monell,* Maine v. Thiboutot, 448 U.S. 1, 100 S.Ct. 2502, 65 L.Ed.2d 555 (1980), made clear that cities would be liable, as the words of Section 1983 suggest, for depriving their citizens of rights secured by federal statutes as well as those secured by the federal Constitution. For further developments of this aspect of city liability, see Pennhurst State School and Hospital v. Halderman, 451 U.S. 1, 101 S.Ct. 1531, 67 L.Ed.2d 694 (1981); Middlesex County Sewerage Authority v. National Sea Clammers Ass'n, 453 U.S. 1, 101 S.Ct. 2615, 69 L.Ed.2d 435 (1981); Wright v. Roanoke Redevelopment and Housing Authority, 479 U.S. 418, 107 S.Ct. 766, 93 L.Ed.2d 781 (1987); and Wilder v. Virginia Hospital Assoc., 496 U.S. 498, 110 S.Ct. 2510, 110 L.Ed.2d 455 (1990). See also Golden State Transit Corp. v. City of Los Angeles, reproduced in Chapter Two.

3. "The Judicial power of the United States shall not be construed to extend to any suit in law or equity, commenced or prosecuted against one of the United States by Citizens of another State, or by Citizens or Subjects of any Foreign State." U.S. Constitution, Amendment XI.

4. See Welch v. Texas Dept. of Highways and Public Transp., 483 U.S. 468, 107 S.Ct. 2941, 97 L.Ed.2d 389 (1987); Atascadero State Hospital v. Scanlon, 473 U.S. 234, 105 S.Ct. 3142, 87 L.Ed.2d 171 (1985).

given a considerable degree of immunity.[5] Indeed, in its 1989 term, the Supreme Court relied on the Eleventh Amendment to explain why cities, but not states, are liable for Constitutional violations under section 1983. In Will v. Michigan Department of State Police, 491 U.S. 58, 109 S.Ct. 2304, 105 L.Ed.2d 45 (1989), the Court held that states could not be sued under section 1983 because, unlike cities, states were not "persons" within the meaning of the statute. The Court reasoned:

> [I]t does not follow that if municipalities are persons then so are the States. States are protected by the Eleventh Amendment while municipalities are not, *Monell,* 436 U.S., at 690, n.54, 98 S.Ct., at 2035, n.54, and we consequently limited our holding in *Monell* "to local government units which are not considered part of the State for Eleventh Amendment purposes," ibid. Conversely, our holding here does not cast any doubt on *Monell,* and applies only to States or governmental entities that are considered "arms of the State" for Eleventh Amendment purposes.[6]

See also Ngiraingas v. Sanchez, 495 U.S. 182, 110 S.Ct. 1737, 109 L.Ed.2d 163 (1990) (holding that a Territory is not a "person" under section 1983). Finally, although the Supreme Court has recognized that no explicit Constitutional provision limits suits for damages against the federal government, it has held that, "by reason of the established doctrine of the immunity of the sovereign from suit except upon consent, the provision of Clause one of § 2 of Article III (of the United States Constitution) does not authorize the maintenance of suits against the United States".[7] Thus the federal government can be sued only with its consent.[8]

It is also important to keep in mind the standard arguments for (and against) governmental sovereign immunity. A useful statement of these arguments has been offered—for the quite different, although related, subject of tort liability [9]—by Fleming James in his article, Tort Liability of Governmental Units And Their Officers, 22 U.Chi.L.Rev. 610, 614–15 (1955):

> Governmental immunity has sometimes been defended on grounds of policy. The argument is fourfold: (1) funds devoted to public

---

5. See Mt. Healthy City School Dist. Bd. of Ed. v. Doyle, 429 U.S. 274, 280, 97 S.Ct. 568, 572, 50 L.Ed.2d 471 (1977); Lincoln County v. Luning, 133 U.S. 529, 10 S.Ct. 363, 33 L.Ed. 766 (1890).

6. By contrast, in another case decided during the 1989 term, the Court strengthened the importance of the application of § 1983 to cities. In Jett v. Dallas Independent School District, 491 U.S. 701, 109 S.Ct. 2702, 105 L.Ed.2d 598 (1989), the Court held that the rules developed for city liability under § 1983 also applied to an action brought to enforce the equal right to make and enforce contracts provided by 42 U.S.C. § 1981. The Court rejected the contention

that a municipality could be held liable for employee actions under a theory of *respondeat superior* under § 1981 on the grounds that no such liability was possible under § 1983.

7. Principality of Monaco v. Mississippi, 292 U.S. 313, 321, 54 S.Ct. 745, 747, 78 L.Ed. 1282 (1934).

8. The extent of this federal immunity might be affected, however, by First English Evangelical Lutheran Church v. County of Los Angeles, reproduced below.

9. See generally, 4 Sands & Libonati, Local Government Law, Chapter 27 (1994).

purposes should not be diverted to compensate for private injuries: (2) "the public service would be hindered, and the public safety endangered, if the superior authority could be subjected to suit at the instance of every citizen, and, consequently, controlled in the use and disposition of the means required for the proper administration of the Government"; (3) that liability would involve the government "in all its operations, in endless embarrassments, and difficulties, and losses, which would be subversive of the public interests"; and (4) that unlike private enterprise, the government derives no profit from its activities. To these arguments it may be answered in part: (1) that since the public purposes involve injury-producing activity, the injuries thus caused should be viewed as a part of the activity's normal costs, and no one suggests that it is a diversion of public funds to pay the costs of public enterprise even if payment is made to private persons; (2) that while control of government activity by private tort litigation may be involved where the alleged tort is legislative action or the making of some high-level policy decision, no such thing is involved in ordinary accident cases; (3) that the direct cost of making compensation by the government will not exceed the sum of the losses suffered by the hapless victims of government activity, and that it is better to distribute these losses widely among the beneficiaries of government than to let them rest on the individual victims; that the embarrassments and expenses incidental to defending accident suits are also a part of the just social cost of operations that cause injuries and have never stifled comparable private enterprise; and finally (4) that, though the government as an entity does not profit from its enterprises, yet (it is devoutly to be hoped) the taxpaying public does, and it is the taxpaying public which would bear the costs of government tort liability.

Few, if any, scholars and commentators could be found today to defend the full extent of governmental immunity. On the other hand, no one today urges that a judicial remedy be given for all the injuries that may result from mistaken governmental action, or that the courts should decide when governmental action of a political nature is mistaken.

In light of this background, consider whether the following cases establish a reasonable limit on city liability for Constitutional violations. Why should cities be liable in circumstances in which states, the federal government, individual city officials (and, needless to say, private corporations) are not? What kind of impact on the exercise of local power will the Section 1983 cases have? What will be the impact on local governments of First English Evangelical Lutheran Church v. County of Los Angeles—the final case in this section which establishes another remedy, analogous to Section 1983, for Constitutional violations by cities? Is there a better way of dealing with Constitutional abuses by local officials than that offered by the cases reproduced below?

MONELL v. DEPARTMENT OF SOCIAL SERVICES

Supreme Court of the United States, 1978.
436 U.S. 658, 98 S.Ct. 2018, 56 L.Ed.2d 611.

Mr. Justice Brennan delivered the opinion of the Court.

Petitioners, a class of female employees of the Department of Social Services and of the Board of Education of the city of New York, commenced this action under 42 U.S.C. § 1983 in July 1971. The gravamen of the complaint was that the Board and the Department had as a matter of official policy compelled pregnant employees to take unpaid leaves of absence before such leaves were required for medical reasons. Cf. *Cleveland Board of Education v. LaFleur,* 414 U.S. 632, 94 S.Ct. 791, 39 L.Ed.2d 52 (1974). The suit sought injunctive relief and backpay for periods of unlawful forced leave. Named as defendants in the action were the Department and its Commissioner, the Board and its Chancellor, and the city of New York and its Mayor. In each case, the individual defendants were sued solely in their official capacities. * * *

We granted certiorari in this case to consider

"Whether local governmental officials and/or local independent school boards are 'persons' within the meaning of 42 U.S.C. § 1983 when equitable relief in the nature of back pay is sought against them in their official capacities?"

* * * [W]e now overrule *Monroe v. Pape,* [365 U.S. 167, 81 S.Ct. 473, 5 L.Ed.2d 492 (1961),] insofar as it holds that local governments are wholly immune from suit under § 1983.

In *Monroe v. Pape,* we held that "Congress did not undertake to bring municipal corporations within the ambit of [§ 1983]." The sole basis for this conclusion was an inference drawn from Congress' rejection of the "Sherman amendment" to the bill which became the Civil Rights Act of 1871, 17 Stat. 13, the precursor of § 1983. The Amendment would have held a municipal corporation liable for damage done to the person or property of its inhabitants by *private* persons "riotously and tumultuously assembled." Cong. Globe, 42d Cong., 1st Sess., 749 (1871) (hereinafter Globe). Although the Sherman amendment did not seek to amend § 1 of the Act, which is now § 1983, and although the nature of the obligation created by that amendment was vastly different from that created by § 1, the Court nonetheless concluded in *Monroe* that Congress must have meant to exclude municipal corporations from the coverage of § 1 because " 'the House [in voting against the Sherman amendment] had solemnly decided that in their judgment Congress had no constitutional power to impose any *obligation* upon county and town organizations, the mere instrumentality for the administration of state law.' " 365 U.S., at 190, 81 S.Ct. at 485 (emphasis added), quoting Globe 804 (Rep. Poland). This statement, we thought, showed that Congress doubted its "constitutional power * * * to impose *civil liability* on municipalities," 365 U.S., at 190, 81 S.Ct. at 486 (emphasis added), and that such doubt would have extended to any type of civil liability.

A fresh analysis of the debate on the Civil Rights Act of 1871, and particularly of the case law which each side mustered in its support, shows, however, that *Monroe* incorrectly equated the "obligation" of which Representative Poland spoke with "civil liability."   * * * The meaning of the legislative history can most readily be developed by first considering the debate on the report of the first conference committee. This debate shows conclusively that the constitutional objections raised against the Sherman amendment—on which our holding in *Monroe* was based—would not have prohibited congressional creation of a civil remedy against state municipal corporations that infringed federal rights. Because § 1 of the Civil Rights Act does not state expressly that municipal corporations come within its ambit, it is finally necessary to interpret § 1 to confirm that such corporations were indeed intended to be included within the "persons" to whom that section applies.   * * *

Our analysis of the legislative history of the Civil Rights Act of 1871 compels the conclusion that Congress *did* intend municipalities and other local government units to be included among those persons to whom § 1983 applies.[54] Local governing bodies, therefore, can be sued directly under § 1983 for monetary, declaratory, or injunctive relief where, as here, the action that is alleged to be unconstitutional implements or executes a policy statement, ordinance, regulation, or decision officially adopted and promulgated by that body's officers.   Moreover, although the touchstone of the § 1983 action against a government body is an allegation that official policy is responsible for a deprivation of rights protected by the Constitution, local governments, like every other § 1983 "person," by the very terms of the statute, may be sued for constitutional deprivations visited pursuant to governmental "custom" even though such a custom has not received formal approval through the body's official decisionmaking channels.   As Mr. Justice Harlan, writing for the Court, said in *Adickes v. S.H. Kress & Co.*, 398 U.S. 144, 167–168, 90 S.Ct. 1598, 1613, 26 L.Ed.2d 142 (1970): "Congress included customs and usages [in § 1983] because of the persistent and widespread discriminatory practices of state officials * * *. Although not authorized by written law, such practices of state officials could well be so permanent and well settled as to constitute a 'custom or usage' with the force of law."

---

54. There is certainly no constitutional impediment to municipal liability. "The Tenth Amendment's reservation of nondelegated powers to the States is not implicated by a federal-court judgment enforcing the express prohibitions of unlawful state conduct enacted by the Fourteenth Amendment." *Milliken v. Bradley,* 433 U.S. 267, 291, 97 S.Ct. 2749, 2762, 53 L.Ed.2d 745 (1977). For this reason, *National League of Cities v. Usery,* 426 U.S. 833, 96 S.Ct. 2465, 49 L.Ed.2d 245 (1976), is irrelevant to our consideration of this case. Nor is there any basis for concluding that the Eleventh Amendment is a bar to municipal liability. See, *e.g., Fitzpatrick v. Bitzer,* 427 U.S. 445, 456, 96 S.Ct. 2666, 49 L.Ed.2d 614 (1976); *Lincoln County v. Luning,* 133 U.S. 529, 530, 10 S.Ct. 363, 33 L.Ed. 766 (1890). Our holding today is, of course, limited to local government units which are not considered part of the State for Eleventh Amendment purposes.

On the other hand, the language of § 1983, read against the background of the same legislative history, compels the conclusion that Congress did not intend municipalities to be held liable unless action pursuant to official municipal policy of some nature caused a constitutional tort. In particular, we conclude that a municipality cannot be held liable *solely* because it employs a tortfeasor—or, in other words, a municipality cannot be held liable under § 1983 on a *respondeat superior* theory.

We begin with the language of § 1983 as originally passed:

"[A]ny person who, under color of any law, statute, ordinance, regulation, custom, or usage of any State, *shall subject, or cause to be subjected,* any person * * * to the deprivation of any rights, privileges, or immunities secured by the Constitution of the United States, shall, any such law, statute, ordinance, regulation, custom, or usage of the State to the contrary notwithstanding, be liable to the party injured in any action at law, suit in equity, or other proper proceeding for redress * * *." (emphasis added).

The italicized language plainly imposes liability on a government that, under color of some official policy, "causes" an employee to violate another's constitutional rights. At the same time, that language cannot be easily read to impose liability vicariously on governing bodies solely on the basis of the existence of an employer-employee relationship with a tortfeasor. Indeed, the fact that Congress did specifically provide that A's tort became B's liability if B "caused" A to subject another to a tort suggests that Congress did not intend § 1983 liability to attach where such causation was absent.

Equally important, creation of a federal law of *respondeat superior* would have raised all the constitutional problems associated with the obligation to keep the peace, an obligation Congress chose not to impose because it thought imposition of such an obligation unconstitutional. To this day, there is disagreement about the basis for imposing liability on an employer for the torts of an employee when the sole nexus between the employer and the tort is the fact of the employer-employee relationship. Nonetheless, two justifications tend to stand out. First is the common-sense notion that no matter how blameless an employer appears to be in an individual case, accidents might nonetheless be reduced if employers had to bear the cost of accidents. Second is the argument that the cost of accidents should be spread to the community as a whole on an insurance theory.

The first justification is of the same sort that was offered for statutes like the Sherman amendment: "The obligation to make compensation for injury resulting from riot is, by arbitrary enactment of statutes, affirmatory law, and the reason of passing the statute is to secure a more perfect police regulation." Globe 777 (Sen. Frelinghuysen). This justification was obviously insufficient to sustain the amendment against perceived constitutional difficulties and there is no reason to suppose that a more general liability imposed for a similar reason would have been thought less constitutionally objectionable. The second justification was similarly put forward as a justification for the Sherman amendment: "we do not look upon [the Sherman amendment] as a punishment * * *. It is a mutual insurance." *Id.*, at 792 (Rep. Butler). Again, this justification was insufficient to sustain the amendment.

We conclude, therefore, that a local government may not be sued under § 1983 for an injury inflicted solely by its employees or agents. Instead, it is when execution of a government's policy or custom, whether made by its lawmakers or by those whose edicts or acts may fairly be said to represent official policy, inflicts the injury that the government as an entity is responsible under § 1983. Since this case unquestionably involves official policy as the moving force of the constitutional violation found by the District Court, we must reverse the judgment below. In so doing, we have no occasion to address, and do not address, what the full contours of municipal liability under § 1983 may be. We have attempted only to sketch so much of the § 1983 cause of action against a local government as is apparent from the history of the 1871 Act and our prior cases, and we expressly leave further development of this action to another day. * * *

OWEN v. CITY OF INDEPENDENCE

Supreme Court of the United States, 1980.
445 U.S. 622, 100 S.Ct. 1398, 63 L.Ed.2d 673.

MR. JUSTICE BRENNAN delivered the opinion of the Court.

Monell v. New York City Dept. of Social Services overruled *Monroe v. Pape* insofar as *Monroe* held that local governments were not among the "persons" to whom 42 U.S.C. § 1983 applies and were therefore wholly immune from suit under the statute. *Monell* reserved decision, however, on the question whether local governments, although not entitled to an absolute immunity, should be afforded some form of official immunity in § 1983 suits. In this action * * * the Court of Appeals for the Eighth Circuit held that respondent city of Independence, Mo., "is entitled to qualified immunity from liability" based on the good faith of its officials. * * * We reverse. * * *

Petitioner named the city of Independence, City Manager Alberg, and the present members of the City Council in their official capacities as defendants in this suit. Alleging that he was discharged without notice of reasons and without a hearing in violation of his constitutional rights to procedural and substantive due process, petitioner sought declaratory and injunctive relief, including a hearing on his discharge, backpay from the date of discharge, and attorney's fees. * * *

Because the question of the scope of a municipality's immunity from liability under § 1983 is essentially one of statutory construction, the starting point in our analysis must be the language of the statute itself. By its terms, § 1983 "creates a species of tort liability that on its face admits of no immunities." *Imbler v. Pachtman,* 424 U.S. 409, 417, 96 S.Ct. 984, 988, 47 L.Ed.2d 128 (1976). Its language is absolute and unqualified; no mention is made of any privileges, immunities, or defenses that may be asserted. * * * However, notwithstanding § 1983's expansive language and the absence of any express incorporation of common-law immunities, we have, on several occasions, found that a tradition of immunity was so firmly rooted in the common law and was supported by such strong policy reasons that "Congress would have specifically so provided had it wished to abolish the doctrine." *Pierson v. Ray,* 386 U.S. 547, 555, 87 S.Ct. 1213, 1218, 18 L.Ed.2d 288 (1967). Thus in *Tenney v. Brandhove,* 341 U.S. 367, 71 S.Ct. 783, 95 L.Ed. 1019 (1951), after tracing the development of an absolute legislative privilege from its source in 16th-century England to its inclusion in the Federal and State Constitutions, we concluded that Congress "would [not] impinge on a tradition so well grounded in history and reason by covert inclusion in the general language" of § 1983.

Subsequent cases have required that we consider the personal liability of various other types of government officials. Noting that "[f]ew doctrines were more solidly established at common law than the immunity of judges from liability for damages for acts committed within their judicial jurisdiction," *Pierson v. Ray, supra,* held that the absolute immunity traditionally accorded judges was preserved under § 1983. In that same case, local police officers were held to enjoy a "good faith and probable cause" defense to § 1983 suits similar to that which existed in false arrest actions at common law. Several more recent decisions have found immunities of varying scope appropriate for different state and local officials sued under § 1983. See *Procunier v. Navarette,* 434 U.S. 555, 98 S.Ct. 855, 55 L.Ed.2d 24 (1978) (qualified immunity for prison officials and officers); *Imbler v. Pachtman,* 424 U.S. 409, 96 S.Ct. 984, 47 L.Ed.2d 128 (1976) (absolute immunity for prosecutors in initiating and presenting the State's case); *O'Connor v. Donaldson,* 422 U.S. 563, 95 S.Ct. 2486, 45 L.Ed.2d 396 (1975) (qualified immunity for superintendent of state hospital); *Wood v. Strickland,* 420 U.S. 308, 95 S.Ct. 992, 43 L.Ed.2d 214 (1975) (qualified immunity for local school board members); *Scheuer v. Rhodes,* 416 U.S. 232, 94 S.Ct. 1683, 40 L.Ed.2d 90 (1974) (qualified "good-faith" immunity for state Governor and other executive officers for discretionary acts performed in the course of official conduct).

In each of these cases, our finding of § 1983 immunity "was predicated upon a considered inquiry into the immunity historically accorded the relevant official at common law and the interests behind it." *Imbler v. Pachtman, supra,* 424 U.S., at 421, 96 S.Ct., at 990. Where the immunity claimed by the defendant was well-established at common law at the time § 1983 was enacted, and where its rationale was compatible with the purposes of the Civil Rights Act, we have construed the statute to incorporate that immunity. But there is no tradition of immunity for municipal corporations, and neither history nor policy support a construction of § 1983 that would justify the qualified immunity accorded the city of Independence by the Court of Appeals. We hold, therefore, that the municipality may not assert the good faith of its officers or agents as a defense to liability under § 1983. * * *

Since colonial times, a distinct feature of our Nation's system of governance has been the conferral of political power upon public and municipal corporations for the management of matters of local concern. As *Monell* recounted, by 1871 municipalities—like private corporations— were treated as natural persons for virtually all purposes of constitutional and statutory analysis. In particular, they were routinely sued in both federal and state courts. Local governmental units were regularly held to answer in damages for a wide range of statutory and constitutional violations, as well as for common-law actions for breach of contract. And although, as we discuss below, a municipality was not subject to suit for all manner of tortious conduct, it is clear that at the time § 1983 was enacted, local governmental bodies did not enjoy the sort of "good-faith" qualified immunity extended to them by the Court of Appeals.

As a general rule, it was understood that a municipality's tort liability in damages was identical to that of private corporations and individuals. * * * Under this general theory of liability, a municipality was deemed responsible for any private losses generated through a wide variety of its operations and functions, from personal injuries due to its defective sewers, thoroughfares, and public utilities, to property damage caused by its trespasses and uncompensated takings. * * * [I]n the hundreds of cases from that era awarding damages against municipal governments for wrongs committed by them, one searches in vain for much mention of a qualified immunity based on the good-faith of municipal officers. Indeed, where the issue was discussed at all, the courts had rejected the proposition that a municipality should be privileged where it reasonably believed its actions to be lawful. * * *

To be sure, there were two doctrines that afforded municipal corporations some measure of protection from tort liability. The first sought to distinguish between a municipality's "governmental" and "proprietary" functions; as to the former, the city was held immune, whereas in its exercise of the latter, the city was held to the same standards of liability as any private corporation. * * * The governmental-proprietary distinction owed its existence to the dual nature of the municipal corporation. On the one hand, the municipality was a corporate body, capable of performing the same "proprietary" functions as any private corporation, and liable for its torts in the same manner and to the same extent, as well. On the other hand, the municipality was an arm of the State, and when acting in that "governmental" or "public" capacity, it shared the immunity traditionally accorded the sovereign. But the principle of sovereign immunity—itself a somewhat arid fountainhead for municipal immunity—is necessarily nullified when the State expressly or impliedly allows itself, or its creation, to be sued. Municipalities were therefore liable not only for their "proprietary" acts, but also for those "governmental" functions as to which the State had withdrawn their immunity. And, by the end of the 19th century, courts regularly held that in imposing a specific duty on the municipality either in its charter or by statute, the State had impliedly withdrawn the city's immunity from liability for the nonperformance or misperformance of its obligation. Thus, despite the nominal existence of an immunity for "governmental" functions, municipalities were found liable in damages in a multitude of cases involving such activities.

That the municipality's common-law immunity for "governmental" functions derives from the principle of sovereign immunity also explains why that doctrine could not have served as the basis for the qualified privilege respondent claims under § 1983. First, because sovereign immunity insulates the municipality from unconsented suits altogether, the presence or absence of good faith is simply irrelevant. The critical issue is whether injury occurred while the city was exercising governmental, as opposed to proprietary, powers or obligations not whether its agents reasonably believed they were acting lawfully in so conducting themselves. More fundamentally, however, the municipality's "governmental" immunity is obviously abrogated by the sovereign's enactment of a statute making it amenable to suit. Section 1983 was just such a statute. By including municipalities within the class of "persons" subject to liability for violations of the Federal Constitution and laws, Congress—the supreme sovereign on matters of federal law—abolished whatever vestige of the State's sovereign immunity the municipality possessed. * * *

The second common-law distinction between municipal functions— that protecting the city from suits challenging "discretionary" decisions—was grounded not on the principle of sovereign immunity, but on a concern for separation of powers. A large part of the municipality's responsibilities involved broad discretionary decisions on issues of public policy—decisions that affected large numbers of persons and called for a delicate balancing of competing considerations. For a court or jury, in the guise of a tort suit, to review the reasonableness of the city's judgment on these matters would be an infringement upon the powers properly vested in a coordinate and coequal branch of government. * * * In order to ensure against any invasion into the legitimate sphere of the municipality's policymaking processes, courts therefore refused to entertain suits against the city "either for the non-exercise of, or for the manner in which in good faith it exercises, *discretionary powers* of a public or legislative character." 2 Dillon § 753, at 862.

Although many, if not all, of a municipality's activities would seem to involve at least some measure of discretion, the influence of this doctrine on the city's liability was not as significant as might be expected. For just as the courts implied an exception to the municipality's immunity for its "governmental" functions, here, too, a distinction was made that had the effect of subjecting the city to liability for much of its tortious conduct. While the city retained its immunity for decisions as to whether the public interest required acting in one manner or another, once any particular decision was made, the city was fully liable for any injuries incurred in the execution of its judgment. * * * Thus municipalities remained liable in damages for a broad range of conduct implementing their discretionary decisions.

Once again, an understanding of the rationale underlying the common-law immunity for "discretionary" functions explains why that doctrine cannot serve as the foundation for a good-faith immunity under § 1983. That common-law doctrine merely prevented courts from substituting their own judgment on matters within the lawful discretion of the municipality. But a municipality has no "discretion" to violate the Federal Constitution; its dictates are absolute and imperative. And when a court passes judgment on the municipality's conduct in a § 1983 action, it does not seek to second-guess the "reasonableness" of the city's decision nor to interfere with the local government's resolution of competing policy considerations. Rather, it looks only to whether the municipality has conformed to the requirements of the Federal Constitution and statutes. * * *

In sum, we can discern no "tradition so well grounded in history and reason" that would warrant the conclusion that in enacting § 1 of the Civil Rights Act, the 42d Congress *sub silentio* extended to municipalities a qualified immunity based on the good faith of their officers. Absent any clearer indication that Congress intended so to limit the reach of a statute expressly designed to provide a "broad remedy for violations of federally protected civil rights," *Monell v. New York City Dept. of Social Services,* 436 U.S., at 685, 98 S.Ct., at 2033, we are unwilling to suppose that injuries occasioned by a municipality's unconstitutional conduct were not also meant to be fully redressable through its sweep.

Our rejection of a construction of § 1983 that would accord municipalities a qualified immunity for their good-faith constitutional violations is compelled both by the legislative purpose in enacting the statute and by considerations of public policy. The central aim of the Civil Rights Act was to provide protection to those persons wronged by the " '[m]isuse of power, possessed by virtue of state law and made possible only because the wrongdoer is clothed with the authority of state law.' " *Monroe v. Pape,* 365 U.S. 167, 184, 81 S.Ct. 473, 482, 5 L.Ed.2d 492 (1961) (quoting *United States v. Classic,* 313 U.S. 299, 326, 61 S.Ct. 1031, 1043, 85 L.Ed. 1368 (1941)). By creating an express federal remedy, Congress sought to "enforce provisions of the Fourteenth Amendment against those who carry a badge of authority of a State and represent it in some capacity, whether they act in accordance with their authority or misuse it." *Monroe v. Pape,* 365 U.S., at 172, 81 S.Ct., at 476.

How "uniquely amiss" it would be, therefore, if the government itself—"the social organ to which all in our society look for the promotion of liberty, justice, fair and equal treatment, and the setting of worthy norms and goals for social conduct"—were permitted to disavow liability for the injury it has begotten. A damages remedy against the offending party is a vital component of any scheme for vindicating cherished constitutional guarantees, and the importance of assuring its efficacy is only accentuated when the wrongdoer is the institution that has been established to protect the very rights it has transgressed. Yet owing to the qualified immunity enjoyed by most government officials, see *Scheuer v. Rhodes,* 416 U.S. 232, 94 S.Ct. 1683, 40 L.Ed.2d 90 (1974), many victims of municipal malfeasance would be left remediless if the city were also allowed to assert a good-faith defense. Unless countervailing considerations counsel otherwise, the injustice of such a result should not be tolerated.

Moreover, § 1983 was intended not only to provide compensation to the victims of past abuses, but to serve as a deterrent against future constitutional deprivations, as well. The knowledge that a municipality will be liable for all of its injurious conduct, whether committed in good faith or not, should create an incentive for officials who may harbor doubts about the lawfulness of their intended actions to err on the side of protecting citizens' constitutional rights. Furthermore, the threat that damages might be levied against the city may encourage those in a policymaking position to institute internal rules and programs designed to minimize the likelihood of unintentional infringements on constitutional rights. Such procedures are particularly beneficial in preventing those "systemic" injuries that result not so much from the conduct of any single individual, but from the interactive behavior of several government officials, each of whom may be acting in good faith.

Our previous decisions conferring qualified immunities on various government officials are not to be read as derogating the significance of the societal interest in compensating the innocent victims of governmental misconduct. Rather, in each case we concluded that overriding considerations of public policy nonetheless demanded that the official be given a measure of protection from personal liability. The concerns that justified those decisions, however, are less compelling, if not wholly inapplicable, when the liability of the municipal entity is at issue.

In *Scheuer v. Rhodes,* the Chief Justice identified the two "mutually dependent rationales" on which the doctrine of official immunity rested:

> "(1) the injustice, particularly in the absence of bad faith, of subjecting to liability an officer who is required, by the legal obligations of his position, to exercise discretion; (2) the danger that the threat of such liability would deter his willingness to execute his office with the decisiveness and the judgment required by the public good."

The first consideration is simply not implicated when the damage award comes not from the official's pocket, but from the public treasury. It hardly seems unjust to require a municipal defendant which has violated a citizen's constitutional rights to compensate him for the injury suffered thereby. Indeed, Congress enacted § 1983 precisely to provide a remedy for such abuses of official power. Elemental notions of fairness dictate that one who causes a loss should bear the loss.

It has been argued, however, that revenue raised by taxation for public use should not be diverted to the benefit of a single or discrete group of taxpayers, particularly where the municipality has at all times acted in good faith. On the contrary, the accepted view is that stated in *Thayer v. Boston, supra*—"that the city, in its corporate capacity, should be liable to make good the damages sustained by an [unlucky] individual, in consequence of the acts thus done." After all, it is the public at large which enjoys the benefits of the government's activities, and it is the public at large which is ultimately responsible for its administration. Thus, even where some constitutional development could not have been foreseen by municipal officials, it is fairer to allocate any resulting financial loss to the inevitable costs of government borne by all the taxpayers, than to allow its impact to be felt solely by those whose rights, albeit newly recognized, have been violated.

The second rationale mentioned in *Scheuer* also loses its force when it is the municipality, in contrast to the official, whose liability is at issue. At the heart of this justification for a qualified immunity for the individual official is the concern that the threat of *personal* monetary liability will introduce an unwarranted and unconscionable consideration into the decisionmaking process, thus paralyzing the governing official's decisiveness and distorting his judgment on matters of public policy. The inhibiting effect is significantly reduced, if not eliminated, however, when the threat of personal liability is removed. First, as an empirical matter, it is questionable whether the hazard of municipal loss will deter a public officer from the conscientious exercise of his duties; city officials routinely make decisions that either require a large expenditure of municipal funds or involve a substantial risk of depleting the public fisc. More important, though, is the realization that consideration of the *municipality's* liability for constitutional violations is quite properly the concern of its elected or appointed officials. Indeed, a decisionmaker would be derelict in his duties if, at some point, he did not consider whether his decision comports with constitutional mandates and did not weigh the risk that a violation might result in an award of damages from the public treasury. As one commentator aptly put it, "Whatever other concerns should shape a particular official's actions, certainly one of them should be the constitutional rights of individuals who will be affected by his actions. To criticize section 1983 liability because it leads decisionmakers to avoid the infringement of constitutional rights is to criticize one of the statute's *raisons d'être*."

In sum, our decision holding that municipalities have no immunity from damages liability flowing from their constitutional violations harmonizes well with developments in the common law and our own pronouncements on official immunities under § 1983. Doctrines of tort law have changed significantly over the past century, and our notions of governmental responsibility should properly reflect that evolution. No longer is individual "blameworthiness" the acid test of liability; the principle of equitable loss-spreading has joined fault as a factor in distributing the costs of official misconduct. * * *

MR. JUSTICE POWELL, with whom THE CHIEF JUSTICE, MR. JUSTICE STEWART, and MR. JUSTICE REHNQUIST join, dissenting. * * *

Until two years ago, municipal corporations enjoyed absolute immunity from § 1983 claims. *Monroe v. Pape,* 365 U.S. 167, 81 S.Ct. 473, 5 L.Ed.2d 492 (1961). But *Monell* held that local governments are "persons" within the meaning of the statute, and thus are liable in damages for constitutional violations inflicted by municipal policies. * * * After today's decision, municipalities will have gone in two short years from absolute immunity under § 1983 to strict liability. As a policy matter, I believe that strict municipal liability unreasonably subjects local governments to damages judgments for actions that were reasonable when performed. It converts municipal governance into a hazardous slalom through constitutional obstacles that often are unknown and unknowable.

The Court's decision also impinges seriously on the prerogatives of municipal entities created and regulated primarily by the States. At the very least, this Court should not initiate a federal intrusion of this magnitude in the absence of explicit congressional action. Yet today's decision is supported by nothing in the text of § 1983. Indeed, it conflicts with the apparent intent of the drafters of the statute, with the common law of municipal tort liability, and with the current state law of municipal immunities.

The Court today abandons any attempt to harmonize § 1983 with traditional tort law. It points out that municipal immunity may be abrogated by legislation. Thus, according to the Court, Congress "abolished" municipal immunity when it included municipalities "within the class of 'persons' subject to liability" under § 1983.

This reasoning flies in the face of our prior decisions under this statute. We have held repeatedly that "immunities 'well grounded in history and reason' [were not] abrogated 'by covert inclusion in the general language' of § 1983." *Imbler v. Pachtman,* 424 U.S., at 418, 96 S.Ct., at 989. The peculiar nature of the Court's position emerges when the status of executive officers under § 1983 is compared with that of local governments. State and local executives are personally liable for bad-faith or unreasonable constitutional torts. Although Congress had the power to make those individuals liable for all such torts, this Court has refused to find an abrogation of traditional immunity in a statute that does not mention immunities. Yet the Court now views the enactment of § 1983 as a direct abolition of traditional municipal immunities. Unless the Court is overruling its previous immunity decisions, the silence in § 1983 must mean that the 42d Congress mutely accepted the immunity of executive officers, but silently rejected common-law municipal immunity. I find this interpretation of the statute singularly implausible.

Important public policies support the extension of qualified immunity to local governments. First, as recognized by the doctrine of separation of powers, some governmental decisions should be at least presumptively insulated from judicial review.   * * * The allocation of public resources and the operational policies of the government itself are activities that lie peculiarly within the competence of executive and legislative bodies.   When charting those policies, a local official should not have to gauge his employer's possible liability under § 1983 if he incorrectly—though reasonably and in good faith—forecasts the course of constitutional law.   Excessive judicial intrusion into such decisions can only distort municipal decisionmaking and discredit the courts. Qualified immunity would provide presumptive protection for discretionary acts, while still leaving the municipality liable for bad faith or unreasonable constitutional deprivations.

Because today's decision will inject constant consideration of § 1983 liability into local decisionmaking, it may restrict the independence of local governments and their ability to respond to the needs of their communities.   * * * The Court now argues that local officials might modify their actions unduly if they face personal liability under § 1983, but that they are unlikely to do so when the locality itself will be held liable.   This contention denigrates the sense of responsibility of municipal officers, and misunderstands the political process.   Responsible local officials will be concerned about potential judgments against their municipalities for alleged constitutional torts.   Moreover, they will be accountable within the political system for subjecting the municipality to adverse judgments.   If officials must look over their shoulders at a strict municipal liability for unknowable constitutional deprivations, the resulting degree of governmental paralysis will be little different from that caused by fear of personal liability.

In addition, basic fairness requires a qualified immunity for municipalities.   The good-faith defense recognized under § 1983 authorizes liability only when officials acted with malicious intent or when they "knew or should have known that their conduct violated the constitutional norm." *Procunier v. Navarette,* 434 U.S., at 562, 98 S.Ct., at 860. The standard incorporates the idea that liability should not attach unless there was notice that a constitutional right was at risk.   This idea applies to governmental entities and individual officials alike.   Constitutional law is what the courts say it is, and as demonstrated by today's decision and its precursor, *Monell*—even the most prescient lawyer would hesitate to give a firm opinion on matters not plainly settled. Municipalities, often acting in the utmost good faith, may not know or anticipate when their action or inaction will be deemed a constitutional violation.

The Court nevertheless suggests that, as a matter of social justice, municipal corporations should be strictly liable even if they could not have known that a particular action would violate the Constitution. After all, the Court urges, local governments can "spread" the costs of any judgment across the local population.   The Court neglects, however, the fact that many local governments lack the resources to withstand substantial unanticipated liability under § 1983.   Even enthusiastic proponents of municipal liability have conceded that ruinous judgments under the statute could imperil local governments. By simplistically applying the theorems of welfare economics and ignoring the reality of municipal finance, the Court imposes strict liability on the level of government least able to bear it. For some municipalities, the result could be a severe limitation on their ability to serve the public. * * *

Today's decision also conflicts with the current law in 44 States and the District of Columbia. All of those jurisdictions provide municipal immunity at least analogous to a "good faith" defense against liability for constitutional torts. Thus, for municipalities in almost 90% of our jurisdictions, the Court creates broader liability for constitutional deprivations than for state-law torts. * * * The Court turns a blind eye to this overwhelming evidence the municipalities have enjoyed a qualified immunity and to the policy considerations that for the life of this Republic have justified its retention. This disregard of precedent and policy is especially unfortunate because suits under § 1983 typically implicate evolving constitutional standards. A good-faith defense is much more important for those actions than in those involving ordinary tort liability. The duty not to run over a pedestrian with a municipal bus is far less likely to change than is the rule as to what process, if any, is due the bus driver if he claims the right to a hearing after discharge.

The right of a discharged government employee to a "name clearing" hearing was not recognized until our decision in *Board of Regents v. Roth*. That ruling was handed down 10 weeks after Owen was discharged and eight weeks after the city denied his request for a hearing. By stripping the city of any immunity, the Court punishes it for failing to predict our decision in *Roth*. As a result, local governments and their officials will face the unnerving prospect of crushing damage judgments whenever a policy valid under current law is later found to be unconstitutional. I can see no justice or wisdom in that outcome.

CITY OF ST. LOUIS v. PRAPROTNIK

Supreme Court of the United States, 1988.
485 U.S. 112, 108 S.Ct. 915, 99 L.Ed.2d 107.

JUSTICE O'CONNOR announced the judgment of the Court and delivered an opinion, in which CHIEF JUSTICE REHNQUIST, JUSTICE WHITE, and JUSTICE SCALIA join.

This case calls upon us to define the proper legal standard for determining when isolated decisions by municipal officials or employees may expose the municipality itself to liability under 42 U.S.C. § 1983. * * *

Respondent James H. Praprotnik is an architect who began working for petitioner city of St. Louis in 1968. * * * By 1980, he was serving in a management-level city planning position at petitioner's Community Development Agency (CDA). * * * In April 1980, respondent was suspended for 15 days * * * for having accepted outside employment without prior approval. Respondent appealed to the city's Civil Service

Commission, a body charged with reviewing employee grievances. Finding the penalty too harsh, the Commission reversed the suspension, awarded respondent back pay, and directed that he be reprimanded * * *. The Commission's decision was not well received by respondent's supervisors * * *. Respondent's next two annual job performance evaluations were markedly less favorable than those in previous years. * * *

In the spring of 1982, * * * the city's Heritage and Urban Design Division (Heritage) was seeking approval to hire someone who was qualified in architecture and urban planning. * * * [R]espondent [was transferred] to Heritage to fill this position. * * * Respondent objected to the transfer, and appealed to the Civil Service Commission. The Commission declined to hear the appeal because respondent had not suffered a reduction in his pay or grade. Respondent then filed suit in federal district court, alleging that the transfer was unconstitutional. * * * In December 1983, respondent was laid off from Heritage. * * * Respondent then amended the complaint in his lawsuit to include a challenge to the layoff. * * * The case went to trial on two theories: (1) that respondent's First Amendment rights had been violated through retaliatory actions taken in response to his appeal of his 1980 suspension; and (2) that respondent's layoff from Heritage was carried out for pretextual reasons in violation of due process. * * *

Ten years ago, this Court held that municipalities and other bodies of local government are "persons" within the meaning of * * * [§ 1983]. Such a body may therefore be sued directly if it is alleged to have caused a constitutional tort through "a policy statement, ordinance, regulation, or decision officially adopted and promulgated by that body's officers." *Monell v. New York City Dept. of Social Services,* 436 U.S. 658, 690 (1978). * * * At the same time, the Court rejected the use of the doctrine of *respondeat superior* and concluded that municipalities could be held liable only when an injury was inflicted by a government's "lawmakers or by those whose edicts or acts may fairly be said to represent official policy." * * * In the years since *Monell* was decided, the Court has considered several cases involving isolated acts by government officials and employees. We have assumed that an unconstitutional governmental policy could be inferred from a single decision taken by the highest officials responsible for setting policy in that area of the government's business. * * * Two terms ago, in *Pembaur* [*v. Cincinnati,* 475 U.S. 469, 106 S.Ct. 1292, 89 L.Ed.2d 452 (1986)] we undertook to define more precisely when a decision on a single occasion may be enough to establish an unconstitutional municipal policy. Although the Court was unable to settle on a general formulation, Justice Brennan's plurality opinion articulated several guiding principles. First, a majority of the Court agreed that municipalities may be held liable under § 1983 only for acts for which the municipality itself is actually responsible, "that is, acts which the municipality has officially sanctioned or ordered." Second, only those municipal officials who have "final policy-making authority" may by their actions subject the government to

§ 1983 liability. Third, whether a particular official has "final policy-making authority" is a question of *state law*. Fourth, the challenged action must have been taken pursuant to a policy adopted by the official or officials responsible under state law for making policy in *that area* of the city's business.

The Courts of Appeals have already diverged in their interpretations of these principles. Today, we set out again to clarify the issue that we last addressed in *Pembaur*.

We begin by reiterating that the identification of policymaking officials is a question of state law. "Authority to make municipal policy may be granted directly by a legislative enactment or may be delegated by an official who possesses such authority, and of course, whether an official had final policymaking authority is a question of state law." *Pembaur v. Cincinnati*, 475 U.S., at 483 (plurality opinion). Thus the identification of policymaking officials is not a question of federal law and it is not a question of fact in the usual sense. The States have extremely wide latitude in determining the form that local government takes, and local preferences have led to a profusion of distinct forms. * * * Without attempting to canvass the numberless factual scenarios that may come to light in litigation, we can be confident that state law (which may include valid local ordinances and regulations) will always direct a court to some official or body that has the responsibility for making law or setting policy in any given area of a local government's business.

We are not, of course, predicting that state law will always speak with perfect clarity. We have no reason to suppose, however, that federal courts will face greater difficulties here than those that they routinely address in other contexts. We are also aware that there will be cases in which policymaking responsibility is shared among more than one official or body. In the case before us, for example, it appears that the mayor and aldermen are authorized to adopt such ordinances relating to personnel administration as are compatible with the City Charter. See St. Louis City Charter, art. XVIII, § 7(b). The Civil Service Commission, for its part, is required to "prescribe * * * rules for the administration and enforcement of the provisions of this article, and of any ordinance adopted in pursuance thereof, and not inconsistent therewith." § 7(a). Assuming that applicable law does not make the decisions of the Commission reviewable by the mayor and aldermen, or vice versa, one would have to conclude that policy decisions made either by the mayor and aldermen or by the Commission would be attributable to the city itself. In any event, however, a federal court would not be justified in assuming that municipal policymaking authority lies somewhere other than where the applicable law purports to put it. And certainly there can be no justification for giving a jury the discretion to determine which officials are high enough in the government that their actions can be said to represent a decision of the government itself.

As the plurality in *Pembaur* recognized, special difficulties can arise when it is contended that a municipal policymaker has delegated his policymaking authority to another official. If the mere exercise of discretion by an employee could give rise to a constitutional violation, the result would be indistinguishable from *respondeat superior* liability. If, however, a city's lawful policymakers could insulate the government from liability simply by delegating their policymaking authority to others, § 1983 could not serve its intended purpose. It may not be possible to draw an elegant line that will resolve this conundrum, but certain principles should provide useful guidance.

First, whatever analysis is used to identify municipal policymakers, egregious attempts by local government to insulate themselves from liability for unconstitutional policies are precluded by a separate doctrine. Relying on the language of § 1983, the Court has long recognized that a plaintiff may be able to prove the existence of a widespread practice that, although not authorized by written law or express municipal policy, is "so permanent and well settled as to constitute a 'custom or usage' with the force of law." *Adickes v. S.H. Kress & Co.*, 398 U.S. 144, 167–168 (1970). That principle, which has not been affected by *Monell* or subsequent cases, ensures that most deliberate municipal evasions of the Constitution will be sharply limited.

Second, as the *Pembaur* plurality recognized, the authority to make municipal policy is necessarily the authority to make *final* policy. When an official's discretionary decisions are constrained by policies not of that official's making, those policies, rather than the subordinate's departures from them, are the act of the municipality. Similarly, when a subordinate's decision is subject to review by the municipality's authorized policymakers, they have retained the authority to measure the official's conduct for conformance with *their* policies. If the authorized policymakers approve a subordinate's decision and the basis for it, their ratification would be chargeable to the municipality because their decision is final. * * *

Whatever refinements of these principles may be suggested in the future, we have little difficulty concluding that the Court of Appeals applied an incorrect legal standard in this case. * * * The city cannot be held liable under § 1983 unless respondent proved the existence of an unconstitutional municipal policy. Respondent does not contend that anyone in city government ever promulgated, or even articulated, such a policy. Nor did he attempt to prove that such retaliation was ever directed against anyone other than himself. Respondent contends that the record can be read to establish that his supervisors were angered by his 1980 appeal to the Civil Service Commission; that new supervisors in a new administration chose, for reasons passed on through some informal means, to retaliate against respondent two years later by transferring him to another agency; and that this transfer was part of a scheme that led, another year and a half later, to his lay off. Even if one assumes that all this was true, it says nothing about the actions of those whom the law established as the makers of municipal policy in matters of personnel administration. The mayor and aldermen enacted no ordinance designed to retaliate against respondent or against similarly situated employees. On the contrary, the city established an independent Civil Service Commission and empowered it to review and correct improper personnel actions. Respondent does not deny that his repeated appeals from adverse personnel decisions repeatedly brought him at least partial relief, and the Civil Service Commission never so much as hinted that retaliatory transfers or lay offs were permissible. Respondent points to no evidence indicating that the Commission delegated to anyone its final authority to interpret and enforce the * * * [city charter provisions concerning personnel decisions].

This case therefore resembles the hypothetical example in *Pembaur:* "[I]f [city] employment policy was set by the [mayor and aldermen and by the Civil Service Commission], only [those] bod[ies'] decisions would provide a basis for [city] liability. This would be true even if the [mayor and aldermen and the Commission] left the [appointing authorities] discretion to hire and fire employees and [they] exercised that discretion in an unconstitutional manner * * *." A majority of the Court of Appeals panel determined that the Civil Service Commission's review of individual employment actions gave too much deference to the decisions of appointing authorities * * *. Simply going along with discretionary decisions made by one's subordinates, however, is not a delegation to them of the authority to make policy. It is equally consistent with a presumption that the subordinates are faithfully attempting to comply with the policies that are supposed to guide them. It would be a different matter if a particular decision by a subordinate was cast in the form of a policy statement and expressly approved by the supervising policymaker. It would also be a different matter if a series of decisions by a subordinate official manifested a "custom or usage" of which the supervisor must have been aware. In both those cases, the supervisor could realistically be deemed to have adopted a policy that happened to have been formulated or initiated by a lower-ranking official. But the mere failure to investigate the basis of a subordinate's discretionary decisions does not amount to a delegation of policymaking authority, especially where (as here) the wrongfulness of the subordinate's decision arises from a retaliatory motive or other unstated rationale. In such circumstances, the purposes of § 1983 would not be served by treating a subordinate employee's decision as if it were a reflection of municipal policy.

Justice Brennan's opinion, concurring in the judgment, finds implications in our discussion that we do not think necessary or correct. We nowhere say or imply, for example, that "a municipal charter's precatory admonition against discrimination or any other employment practice not based on merit and fitness effectively insulates the municipality from any liability based on acts inconsistent with that policy." Rather, we would respect the decisions, embodied in state and local law, that allocate policymaking authority among particular individuals and bodies. Refusals to carry out stated policies could obviously help to show that a municipality's actual policies were different from the ones that had been announced. If such a showing were made, we would be confronted with a different case than the one we decide today. * * *

JUSTICE BRENNAN, with whom JUSTICE MARSHALL and JUSTICE BLACKMUN join, concurring.

Despite its somewhat confusing procedural background, this case at bottom presents a relatively straightforward question: whether respondent's supervisor at the Community Development Agency, Frank Hamsher, possessed the authority to establish final employment policy for the city of St. Louis such that the city can be held liable under 42 U.S.C. § 1983 for Hamsher's allegedly unlawful decision to transfer respondent to a dead-end job. Applying the test set out two Terms ago by the plurality in *Pembaur v. Cincinnati,* I conclude that Hamsher did not possess such authority and I therefore concur in the Court's judgment reversing the decision below. I write separately, however, because I believe that the commendable desire of today's plurality to "define more precisely when a decision on a single occasion may be enough" to subject a municipality to § 1983 liability has led it to embrace a theory of municipal liability that is both unduly narrow and unrealistic, and one that ultimately would permit municipalities to insulate themselves from liability for the acts of all but a small minority of actual city policymakers. * * *

In my view, *Pembaur* controls this case. As an "appointing authority," Hamsher was empowered under the City Charter to initiate lateral transfers such as the one challenged here, subject to the approval of both the Director of Personnel and the appointing authority of the transferee agency. The Charter, however, nowhere confers upon agency heads any authority to establish city *policy,* final or otherwise, with respect to such transfers. Thus, for example, Hamsher was not authorized to promulgate binding guidelines or criteria governing how or when lateral transfers were to be accomplished. Nor does the record reveal that he in fact sought to exercise any such authority in these matters. There is no indication, for example, that Hamsher ever purported to institute or announce a practice of general applicability concerning transfers. Instead, the evidence discloses but one transfer decision—the one involving respondent—which Hamsher ostensibly undertook pursuant to a city-wide program of fiscal restraint and budgetary reductions. At most, then, the record demonstrates that Hamsher had the authority to determine how best to *effectuate* a policy announced by his superiors, rather than the power to *establish* that policy. * * * Because the [lower] court identified only one unlawfully motivated municipal employee involved in respondent's transfer and layoff, and because that employee did not possess final policymaking authority with respect to the contested decision, the city may not be held accountable for any constitutional wrong respondent may have suffered.

These determinations, it seems to me, are sufficient to dispose of this case, and I therefore think it unnecessary to decide, as the plurality does, who the actual policymakers in St. Louis are. I question more than the mere necessity of these determinations, however, for I believe that in the course of passing on issues not before us, the plurality announces legal principles that are inconsistent with our earlier cases and unduly restrict the reach of § 1983 in cases involving municipalities.

The plurality begins its assessment of St. Louis' power structure by asserting that the identification of policymaking officials is a question of state law, by which it means that the question is neither one of federal law nor of fact, at least "not in the usual sense." Instead, the plurality explains, courts are to identify municipal policymakers by referring exclusively to applicable state statutory law. Not surprisingly, the plurality cites no authority for this startling proposition, nor could it, for we have never suggested that municipal liability should be determined in so formulaic and unrealistic a fashion. In any case in which the policymaking authority of a municipal tortfeasor is in doubt, state law will naturally be the appropriate starting point, but ultimately the factfinder must determine where such policymaking authority actually resides, and not simply "where the applicable law purports to put it." As the plurality itself acknowledges, local governing bodies may take myriad forms. We in no way slight the dignity of municipalities by recognizing that in not a few of them real and apparent authority may diverge, and that in still others state statutory law will simply fail to disclose where such authority ultimately rests. Indeed, in upholding the Court of Appeals' determination in *Pembaur* that the County Prosecutor was a policymaking official with respect to county law enforcement practices, a majority of this Court relied on testimony which revealed that the County Sheriff's office routinely forwarded certain matters to the Prosecutor and followed his instructions in those areas. While the majority splintered into three separate camps on the ultimate theory of municipal liability, and the case generated five opinions in all, not a single member of the Court suggested that reliance on such extra-statutory evidence of the county's actual allocation of policymaking authority was in any way improper. Thus, although I agree with the plurality that juries should not be given open-ended "*discretion* to determine which officials are high enough in the government that their actions can be said to represent a decision of the government itself," juries can and must find the predicate facts necessary to a determination of whether a given official possesses final policymaking authority. While the jury instructions in this case were regrettably vague, the plurality's solution tosses the baby out with the bath water. The identification of municipal policymakers is an essentially factual determination "in the usual sense," and is therefore rightly entrusted to a properly instructed jury.

Nor does the "custom or usage" doctrine adequately compensate for the inherent inflexibility of a rule that leaves the identification of policymakers exclusively to state statutory law. That doctrine, under which municipalities and States can be held liable for unconstitutional practices so well settled and permanent that they have the force of law, has little if any bearing on the question whether a city has delegated *de facto* final policymaking authority to a given official. A city practice of delegating final policymaking authority to a subordinate or mid-level official would not be unconstitutional in and of itself, and an isolated unconstitutional act by an official entrusted with such authority would obviously not amount to a municipal "custom or usage." Under *Pembaur,* of course, such an isolated act *should* give rise to municipal liability. Yet a case such as this would fall through the gaping hole the plurality's construction leaves in § 1983, because state statutory law would not identify the municipal actor as a policymaking official, and a single constitutional deprivation, by definition, is not a well settled and permanent municipal practice carrying the force of law.

For these same reasons, I cannot subscribe to the plurality's narrow and overly rigid view of when a municipal official's policymaking authority is "final." Attempting to place a gloss on *Pembaur*'s finality requirement, the plurality suggests that whenever the decisions of an official are subject to some form of review—however limited—that official's decisions are nonfinal. Under the plurality's theory, therefore, even where an official wields policymaking authority with respect to a challenged decision, the city would not be liable for that official's policy decision unless *reviewing* officials affirmatively approved both the "decision and the basis for it." Reviewing officials, however, may as a matter of practice never invoke their plenary oversight authority, or their review powers may be highly circumscribed. Under such circumstances, the subordinate's decision is in effect the final municipal pronouncement on the subject. Certainly a § 1983 plaintiff is entitled to place such considerations before the jury, for the law is concerned not with the niceties of legislative draftsmanship but with the realities of municipal decisionmaking, and any assessment of a municipality's actual power structure is necessarily a factual and practical one.

Accordingly, I cannot endorse the plurality's determination, based on nothing more than its own review of the City Charter, that the mayor, the aldermen, and the CSC are the only policymakers for the city of St. Louis. While these officials may well have policymaking authority, that hardly ends the matter; the question before us is whether the officials responsible for respondent's allegedly unlawful transfer were final policymakers. * * * Under the plurality's analysis, * * * even the hollowest promise of review is sufficient to divest all city officials save the mayor and governing legislative body of final policymaking authority. While clarity and ease of application may commend such a rule, we have remained steadfast in our conviction that Congress intended to hold municipalities accountable for those constitutional injuries inflicted not only by their lawmakers, but "by those whose edicts or acts may fairly be said to represent official policy." *Monell,* 436 U.S., at 694. Because the plurality's mechanical "finality" test is fundamentally at odds with the pragmatic and factual inquiry contemplated by *Monell,* I cannot join what I perceive to be its unwarranted abandonment of the traditional factfinding process in § 1983 actions involving municipalities. * * *

JUSTICE STEVENS, dissenting. * * *

[I]n *Pembaur v. Cincinnati,* we definitively held that a "decision by municipal policymakers on a single occasion" was sufficient to support an award of damages against the municipality. In *Pembaur,* a County Prosecutor had advised County sheriffs at the doorstep of a recalcitrant doctor to "go in and get [the witnesses]" to alleged charges of fraud by the doctor. Because the sheriffs possessed only arrest warrants for the witnesses and not a search warrant for the doctor's office as well, the advice was unconstitutional, and the question was whether the County Prosecutor's isolated act could subject the County to damages under § 1983 in a suit by the doctor. * * * Since the County Prosecutor was authorized to establish law enforcement policy, his decision in that area * * * [was] attributed to the County for purposes of § 1983 liability. * * *

Both *Pembaur* and the plurality and concurring opinions today acknowledge that a high official who has ultimate control over a certain area of city government can bind the City through his unconstitutional actions even though those actions are not in the form of formal rules or regulations. Although the Court has explained its holdings by reference to the nonstatutory term "policy," it plainly has not embraced the standard understanding of that word as covering a rule of general applicability. Instead it has used that term to include isolated acts not intended to be binding over a class of situations. But when one remembers that the real question in cases such as this is not "what constitutes City policy?" but rather "when should a City be liable for the acts of its agents?", the inclusion of single acts by high officials makes sense, for those acts bind a municipality in a way that the misdeeds of low officials do not.

Every act of a high official constitutes a kind of "statement" about how similar decisions will be carried out; the assumption is that the same decision would have been made, and would again be made, across a class of cases. Lower officials do not control others in the same way. Since their actions do not dictate the responses of various subordinates, those actions lack the potential of controlling governmental decisionmaking; they are not perceived as the actions of the city itself. If a County police officer had broken down Dr. Pembaur's door on the officer's own initiative, this would have been seen as the action of an overanxious officer, and would not have sent a message to other officers that similar actions would be countenanced. One reason for this is that the County Prosecutor himself could step forward and say "that was wrong"; when the County Prosecutor authorized the action himself, only a self-correction would accomplish the same task, and until such time his action would have County-wide ramifications. Here, the Mayor, those working for him, and the agency heads are high-ranking officials; accordingly, we must assume that their actions have City-wide ramifications, both through their similar response to a like class of situations, and through the response of subordinates who follow their lead. * * *

[T]he typical retaliatory personnel action claim pits one story against another; although everyone admits that the transfer and discharge of respondent occurred, there is sharp, and ultimately central, dispute over the reasons—the motivation—behind the actions. *The very nature of the tort is to avoid a formal process.* * * * [I]f the Court is willing to recognize the existence of municipal policy in a non-rule case as long as high enough officials engaged in a formal enough process, it should not deny the existence of such a policy merely because those same officials act "underground," as it were. It would be a truly remarkable doctrine for this Court to recognize municipal liability in an employee discharge case when high officials are foolish enough to act through a "formal process," but not when similarly high officials attempt to avoid liability by acting on the pretext of budgetary concerns, which is what this jury found based on the evidence presented at trial. * * *

CITY OF CANTON v. HARRIS

Supreme Court of the United States, 1989.
489 U.S. 378, 109 S.Ct. 1197, 103 L.Ed.2d 412.

JUSTICE WHITE delivered the opinion of the Court.

In this case, we are asked to determine if a municipality can ever be liable under 42 U.S.C. § 1983 for constitutional violations resulting from its failure to train municipal employees. We hold that, under certain circumstances, such liability is permitted by the statute.

In April 1978, respondent Geraldine Harris was arrested by officers of the Canton Police Department. Harris was brought to the police station in a patrol wagon. When she arrived at the station, Harris was found sitting on the floor of the wagon. She was asked if she needed medical attention, and responded with an incoherent remark. After she was brought inside the station for processing, Mrs. Harris slumped to the floor on two occasions. Eventually, the police officers left Mrs. Harris lying on the floor to prevent her from falling again. No medical attention was ever summoned for Mrs. Harris. After about an hour, Mrs. Harris was released from custody, and taken by an ambulance (provided by her family) to a nearby hospital. There, Mrs. Harris was diagnosed as suffering from several emotional ailments; she was hospitalized for one week and received subsequent outpatient treatment for an additional year.

Some time later, Mrs. Harris commenced this action alleging many state law and constitutional claims against the city of Canton and its officials. Among these claims was one seeking to hold the city liable under 42 U.S.C. § 1983 for its violation of Mrs. Harris' right, under the Due Process Clause of the Fourteenth Amendment, to receive necessary medical attention while in police custody.

A jury trial was held on Mrs. Harris' claims. Evidence was presented that indicated that, pursuant to a municipal regulation, shift commanders were authorized to determine, in their sole discretion, whether a detainee required medical care. In addition, testimony also suggested that Canton shift commanders were not provided with any special training (beyond first-aid training) to make a determination as to when to summon medical care for an injured detainee. * * *

In *Monell v. New York City Dept. of Social Services,* 436 U.S. 658, 98 S.Ct. 2018, 56 L.Ed.2d 611 (1978), we decided that a municipality can be found liable under § 1983 only where the municipality *itself* causes the constitutional violation at issue. * * * Thus, our first inquiry in any case alleging municipal liability under § 1983 is the question of whether there is a direct causal link between a municipal policy or custom, and the alleged constitutional deprivation. The inquiry is a difficult one; one that has left this Court deeply divided in a series of cases that have followed *Monell;* one that is the principal focus of our decision again today. * * * For reasons explained below, we conclude, as have all the Courts of Appeals that have addressed this issue, that there are limited circumstances in which an allegation of a "failure to train" can be the basis for liability under § 1983. * * *

Unlike the question of whether a municipality's failure to train employees can ever be a basis for § 1983 liability—on which the courts of Appeals have all agreed—there is substantial division among the lower courts as to what *degree of fault* must be evidenced by the municipality's inaction before liability will be permitted. We hold today that the inadequacy of police training may serve as the basis for § 1983 liability only where the failure to train amounts to deliberate indifference to the rights of persons with whom the police come into contact. This rule is most consistent with our admonition in *Monell* and *Polk County v. Dodson,* 454 U.S. 312, 326, 102 S.Ct. 445, 454, 70 L.Ed.2d 509 (1981), that a municipality can be liable under § 1983 only where its policies are the "moving force [behind] the constitutional violation." Only where a municipality's failure to train its employees in a relevant respect evidences a "deliberate indifference" to the rights of its inhabitants can such a shortcoming be properly thought of as a city "policy or custom" that is actionable under § 1983. As Justice Brennan's opinion in *Pembaur v. Cincinnati,* 475 U.S. 469, 483–484, 106 S.Ct. 1292, 1300, 89 L.Ed.2d 452 (1986) (plurality) put it: "[M]unicipal liability under § 1983 attaches where—and only where—a deliberate choice to follow a course of action is made from among various alternatives" by city policy makers. Only where a failure to train reflects a "deliberate" or "conscious" choice by a municipality—a "policy" as defined by our prior cases—can a city be liable for such a failure under § 1983.

Monell's rule that a city is not liable under § 1983 unless a municipal policy causes a constitutional deprivation will not be satisfied by merely alleging that the existing training program for a class of employees, such as police officers, represents a policy for which the city is responsible. That much may be true. The issue in a case like this one, however, is whether that training program is adequate; and if it is not, the question becomes whether such inadequate training can justifiably be said to represent "city policy." It may seem contrary to common sense to assert that a municipality will actually have a policy of not taking reasonable steps to train its employees. But it may happen that in light of the duties assigned to specific officers or employees the need for more or different training is so obvious, and the inadequacy so likely to result in the violation of constitutional rights, that the policymakers of the city can reasonable be said to have been deliberately indifferent to the need.[10] In that event, the failure to provide proper training may fairly be said to represent a policy for which the city is responsible, and for which the city may be held liable if it actually causes injury.

In resolving the issue of a city's liability, the focus must be on adequacy of the training program in relation to the tasks the particular officers must perform. That a particular officer may be unsatisfactorily trained will not alone suffice to fasten liability on the city, for the officer's shortcomings may have resulted from factors other than a faulty training program. It may be, for example, that an otherwise sound program has occasionally been negligently administered. Neither will it suffice to prove that an injury or accident could have been avoided if an officer had had better or more training, sufficient to equip him to avoid the particular injury-causing conduct. Such a claim could be made about almost any encounter resulting in injury, yet not condemn the adequacy of the program to enable officers to respond properly to the usual and recurring situations with which they must deal. And plainly, adequately trained officers occasionally make mistakes; the fact that they do says little about the training program or the legal basis for holding the city liable.

Moreover, for liability to attach in this circumstance the identified deficiency in a city's training program must be closely related to the ultimate injury. Thus in the case at hand, respondent must still prove that the deficiency in training actually caused the police officers' indifference to her medical needs. Would the injury have been avoided had the employee been trained under a program that was not deficient in the identified respect? Predicting how a hypothetically well-trained officer would have acted under the circumstances may not be an easy task for the factfinder, particularly since matters of judgment may be involved, and since officers who are well trained are not free from error and perhaps might react very much like the untrained officer in similar circumstances. But judge and jury, doing their respective jobs, will be adequate to the task.

10. For example, city policy makers know to a moral certainty that their police officers will be required to arrest fleeing felons. The city has armed its officers with firearms, in part to allow them to accomplish this task. Thus, the need to train officers in the constitutional limitations on the use of deadly force, see *Tennessee v. Garner,* 471 U.S. 1, 105 S.Ct. 1694, 85 L.Ed.2d 1 (1985), can be said to be "so obvious," that failure to do so could properly be characterized as "deliberate indifference" to constitutional rights. It could also be that the police, in exercising their discretion, so often violate constitutional rights that the need for further training must have been plainly obvious to the city policy makers, who, nevertheless, are "deliberately indifferent" to the need.

To adopt lesser standards of fault and causation would open municipalities to unprecedented liability under § 1983. In virtually every instance where a person has had his or her constitutional rights violated by a city employee, a § 1983 plaintiff will be able to point to something the city "could have done" to prevent the unfortunate incident. Thus, permitting cases against cities for their "failure to train" employees to go forward under § 1983 on a lesser standard of fault would result in *de facto respondeat superior* liability on municipalities—a result we rejected in *Monell*. It would also engage the federal courts in an endless exercise of second-guessing municipal employee-training programs. This is an exercise we believe the federal courts are ill-suited to undertake, as well as one that would implicate serious questions of federalism. * * *

FIRST ENGLISH EVANGELICAL LUTHERAN CHURCH OF GLENDALE v. COUNTY OF LOS ANGELES

Supreme Court of the United States, 1987.
482 U.S. 304, 107 S.Ct. 2378, 96 L.Ed.2d 250.

CHIEF JUSTICE REHNQUIST delivered the opinion of the Court.

In this case the California Court of Appeal held that a landowner who claims that his property has been "taken" by a land-use regulation may not recover damages for the time before it is finally determined that the regulation constitutes a "taking" of his property. We disagree, and conclude that in these circumstances the Fifth and Fourteenth Amendments to the United States Constitution would require compensation for that period.

In 1957, appellant First English Evangelical Lutheran Church purchased a 21–acre parcel of land in a canyon along the banks of the Middle Fork of Mill Creek in the Angeles National Forest. The Middle Fork is the natural drainage channel for a watershed area owned by the National Forest Service. Twelve of the acres owned by the church are flat land, and contained a dining hall, two bunkhouses, a caretaker's lodge, an outdoor chapel, and a footbridge across the creek. The church operated on the site a campground, known as "Lutherglen," as a retreat center and a recreational area for handicapped children.

In July 1977, a forest fire denuded the hills upstream from Lutherglen, destroying approximately 3,860 acres of the watershed area and creating a serious flood hazard. Such flooding occurred on February 9 and 10, 1978, when a storm dropped 11 inches of rain in the watershed. The runoff from the storm overflowed the banks of the Mill Creek, flooding Lutherglen and destroying its buildings.

In response to the flooding of the canyon, appellee County of Los Angeles adopted Interim Ordinance No. 11,855 in January 1979. The ordinance provided that "[a] person shall not construct, reconstruct, place or enlarge any building or structure, any portion of which is, or will be, located within the outer boundary lines of the interim flood protection area located in Mill Creek Canyon. * * * '' The ordinance was effective immediately because the county determined that it was "required for the immediate preservation of the public health and safety. * * * '' The interim flood protection area described by the ordinance included the flat areas on either side of Mill Creek on which Lutherglen had stood.

The church filed a complaint in the Superior Court of California a little more than a month after the ordinance was adopted. * * *

We * * * have no occasion to decide whether the ordinance at issue actually denied appellant all use of its property or whether the county might avoid the conclusion that a compensable taking had occurred by establishing that the denial of all use was insulated as a part of the State's authority to enact safety regulations. These questions, of course, remain open for decision on the remand we direct today. * * *

We have recognized that a landowner is entitled to bring an action in inverse condemnation as a result of " 'the self-executing character of the constitutional provision with respect to compensation. * * * ' " *United States v. Clarke,* 445 U.S. 253, 257, 100 S.Ct. 1127, 1130, 63 L.Ed.2d 373 (1980). * * * [I]t has been established at least since *Jacobs v. United States,* 290 U.S. 13, 54 S.Ct. 26, 78 L.Ed. 142 (1933), that claims for just compensation are grounded in the Constitution itself * * *. "Temporary" takings which, as here, deny a landowner all use of his property, are not different in kind from permanent takings, for which the Constitution clearly requires compensation. It is axiomatic that the Fifth Amendment's just compensation provision is "designed to bar Government from forcing some people alone to bear public burdens which, in all fairness and justice, should be borne by the public as a whole." *Armstrong v. United States,* 364 U.S., at 49, 80 S.Ct., at 1569. In the present case the interim ordinance was adopted by the county of Los Angeles in January 1979, and became effective immediately. Appellant filed suit within a month after the effective date of the ordinance and yet when the Supreme Court of California denied a hearing in the case on October 17, 1985, the merits of appellant's claim had yet to be determined. The United States has been required to pay compensation for leasehold interests of shorter duration than this. The value of a leasehold interest in property for a period of years may be substantial, and the burden on the property owner in extinguishing such an interest for a period of years may be great indeed. Where this burden results from governmental action that amounted to a taking, the Just Compensation Clause of the Fifth Amendment requires that the government pay the landowner for the value of the use of the land during this period. Cf. *United States v. Causby,* 328 U.S., at 261, 66 S.Ct., at 1065–1066 ("It is the owner's loss, not the taker's gain, which is the measure of the value of the property taken"). Invalidation of the ordinance or its successor ordinance after this period of time, though converting the taking into a "temporary" one, is not a sufficient remedy to meet the demands of the Just Compensation Clause. * * *

Nothing we say today is intended to abrogate the principle that the decision to exercise the power of eminent domain is a legislative function, " 'for Congress and Congress alone to determine.' " *Hawaii Housing Authority v. Midkiff,* 467 U.S. 229, 240, 104 S.Ct. 2321, 2329, 81 L.Ed.2d 186 (1984), quoting *Berman v. Parker,* 348 U.S. 26, 33, 75 S.Ct. 98, 103, 99 L.Ed. 27 (1954). Once a court determines that a taking has occurred, the government retains the whole range of options already available—amendment of the regulation, withdrawal of the invalidated regulation, or exercise of eminent domain. Thus we do not, as the Solicitor General suggests, "permit a court, at the behest of a private person, to require the * * * Government to exercise the power of eminent domain * * *." Brief for United States as *Amicus Curiae* 22. We merely hold that where the government's activities have already worked a taking of all use of property, no subsequent action by the government can relieve it of the duty to provide compensation for the period during which the taking was effective.

We also point out that the allegation of the complaint which we treat as true for purposes of our decision was that the ordinance in question denied appellant all use of its property. We limit our holding to the facts presented, and of course do not deal with the quite different questions that would arise in the case of normal delays in obtaining building permits, changes in zoning ordinances, variances, and the like which are not before us. We realize that even our present holding will undoubtedly lessen to some extent the freedom and flexibility of land-use planners and governing bodies of municipal corporations when enacting land-use regulations. But such consequences necessarily flow from any decision upholding a claim of constitutional right; many of the provisions of the Constitution are designed to limit the flexibility and freedom of governmental authorities and the Just Compensation Clause of the Fifth Amendment is one of them. As Justice Holmes aptly noted more than 50 years ago, "a strong public desire to improve the public condition is not enough to warrant achieving the desire by a shorter cut than the constitutional way of paying for the change." *Pennsylvania Coal Co. v. Mahon,* 260 U.S., at 416, 43 S.Ct., at 160.

Here we must assume that the Los Angeles County ordinances have denied appellant all use of its property for a considerable period of years, and we hold that invalidation of the ordinance without payment of fair value for the use of the property during this period of time would be a constitutionally insufficient remedy. * * *

JUSTICE STEVENS, with whom JUSTICE BLACKMUN and JUSTICE O'CONNOR join as to Parts I and III, dissenting.

One thing is certain. The Court's decision today will generate a great deal of litigation. Most of it, I believe, will be unproductive. But the mere duty to defend the actions that today's decision will spawn will undoubtedly have a significant adverse impact on the land-use regulatory process. * * *

In this case, the legitimacy of the County's interest in the enactment of Ordinance No. 11,855 is apparent from the face of the ordinance and has never been challenged. It was enacted as an "interim" measure "temporarily prohibiting" certain construction in a specified area because the County Board believed the prohibition was "urgently required for the immediate preservation of the public health and safety." Even if that were not true, the strong presumption of constitutionality that applies to legislative enactments certainly requires one challenging the constitutionality of an ordinance of this kind to allege some sort of improper purpose or insufficient justification in order to state a colorable federal claim for relief. A presumption of validity is particularly appropriate in this case because the complaint did not even allege that the ordinance is invalid, or pray for a declaration of invalidity or an injunction against its enforcement. Nor did it allege any facts indicating how the ordinance interfered with any future use of the property contemplated or planned by appellant. In light of the tragic flood and the loss of life that precipitated the safety regulations here, it is hard to understand how appellant ever expected to rebuild on Lutherglen.

Thus, although the Court uses the allegations of this complaint as a springboard for its discussion of a discrete legal issue, it does not, and could not under our precedents, hold that the allegations sufficiently alleged a taking or that the County's effort to preserve life and property could ever constitute a taking. As far as the United States Constitution is concerned, the claim that the ordinance was a taking of Lutherglen should be summarily rejected on its merits. * * *

The Court recognizes that the California courts have the right to adopt invalidation of an excessive regulation as the appropriate remedy for the permanent effects of overburdensome regulations, rather than allowing the regulation to stand and ordering the government to afford compensation for the permanent taking. * * * Once it is recognized that California may deal with the permanent taking problem by invalidating objectionable regulations, it becomes clear that the California Court of Appeal's decision in this case should be affirmed. Even if this Court is correct in stating that one who makes out a claim for a permanent taking is automatically entitled to some compensation for the temporary aspect of the taking as well, the States still have the right to deal with the permanent aspect of a taking by invalidating the regulation. That is all that the California courts have done in this case. They have refused to proceed upon a complaint which sought only damages, and which did not contain a request for a declaratory invalidation of the regulation, as clearly required by California precedent. * * * As a matter of regulating the procedure in its own state courts, the California Supreme Court has decided that mandamus or declaratory relief rather than inverse condemnation provides "the appropriate relief," for one who challenges a regulation as a taking. * * *

SECTION F. CITIZENS' ABILITY TO INFLUENCE CITY POLICY THROUGH VOTING

1. VOTING EQUALITY

This section investigates the extent of citizens' ability to control governmental policy by exercising their power to vote for city officials; in the next section, we examine their power to formulate city policy through an initiative or a referendum. Our inquiry into the subject of voting begins with Avery v. Midland County, the case that extended to local governments the principle of one person/one vote originally announced for state legislatures in Reynolds v. Sims, 377 U.S. 533, 84 S.Ct. 1362, 12 L.Ed.2d 506 (1964). As Justice Harlan's dissent in *Avery* and subsequent cases suggest, applying the one person/one vote principle to local governments achieves "voter equality" only if one understands citizens simply as individuals rather than in terms of their identities as members of different groups. Yet voters often experience city politics— and their own voting—in terms of a division along racial, political or neighborhood lines (and, in county elections, along city/suburban lines as well). Although every individual has an "equal vote" under the one person/one vote formula, people can nevertheless think that even under this formula they and people like them (Blacks or Republicans or small town residents) will never have the voting strength to influence governmental policy. The following cases develop a variety of ways to confront this possibility of group disenfranchisement.[1] How do the cases articulate the standard for the protection of minority groups when the minority is understood in geographical (Avery v. Midland County, Morris v. Board of Estimate), racial (Mobile v. Bolden, Holder v. Hall, Shaw v. Reno) or political (Davis v. Bandemer) terms? Can the differences between the standards for geographic, racial and political minorities be justified? What can (and should) be done about enabling minority groups to influence city policy?

As Professor Sanford Levinson has argued, a spectre haunts the discussion of the issue of group representation in political life—"the spectre of proportional representation."[2] The term "proportional representation" is often invoked (pejoratively) to mean the claim that every group should have a right to elect representatives in proportion to the group's percentage of the city's population. Defenders of proportional representation, however, do not define the concept in this way. As a

---

1. For a general analysis of voting rights issues, see, e.g., Symposium, The Future of Voting Rights After Shaw v. Reno, 92 Mich.L.Rev. 483 (1993); Symposium, Regulating the Electoral Process, 71 Tex. L.Rev. 1409 (1993); Schuck, The Thickest Thicket: Partisan Gerrymandering and Judicial Regulation of Politics, 87 Colum.L.Rev. 1325 (1987); Symposium: Gerrymandering and the Courts, 33 U.C.L.A.L.Rev. 1 (1985); C. Davidson (ed.), Minority Vote Dilution (1984); M.D. Gelfand, Federal Constitutional Law and American Local Government 1–53 (1984).

2. Levinson, Commentary: Gerrymandering and the Brooding Omnipresence of Proportional Representation: Why Won't It Go Away? 33 U.C.L.A.L.Rev. 257 (1985).

matter of democratic theory, proportional representation simply means an electoral system characterized by elections in which seats are allocated in proportion to the number of votes received by those running for office. One form of proportional representation, for example, allows each voter to cast as many votes as there are positions to be filled in the city council. Because those who receive the largest number of votes win the available positions, members of minority groups are able to give all their votes to "their" candidate and thereby help ensure his or her election. A provocative article by Lani Guinier, excerpted after the cases, offers an argument for this version of proportional representation. An alternative version, adopted for city elections in Cambridge, Massachusetts, allows each voter to vote for as many candidates as s/he chooses as long as s/he lists them in order of preference; a minority candidate can win an election if s/he receives a sufficient number of "Number 1" votes. In both of these schemes, the "minority" group one chooses to identify oneself with is selected in the process of voting. Would one of these voting plans (or some similar scheme) better protect "minority" voices than the Constitutional and statutory tests announced in the cases? Or would such a plan lead to an undesirable splintering of city politics? [3]

This section concludes with an excerpt from an article by Jamin Raskin. Raskin reminds us that, no matter which voting scheme is adopted, some city residents remain disenfranchised in almost every city in America. He presents an argument for enfranchising one such group: residents aliens. Should aliens be entitled to vote in city elections? Is alien suffrage more appropriate for city elections than for state or federal elections?

AVERY v. MIDLAND COUNTY

Supreme Court of the United States, 1968.
390 U.S. 474, 88 S.Ct. 1114, 20 L.Ed.2d 45.

MR. JUSTICE WHITE delivered the opinion of the Court.

Petitioner, a taxpayer and voter in Midland County, Texas, sought a determination by this Court that the Texas Supreme Court erred in concluding that selection of the Midland County Commissioners Court from single-member districts of substantially unequal population did not necessarily violate the Fourteenth Amendment. We granted review because application of the one man, one vote principle of *Reynolds v.*

---

3. For discussions of these and related issues, see Guinier, The Representation of Minority Interests: The Question of Single–Member Districts, 14 Cardozo L.Rev. 1135 (1993); Issacharoff, Polarized Voting and the Political Process: The Transformation of Voting Rights Jurisprudence, 90 Mich. L.Rev. 1833 (1992); Guinier, The Triumph of Tokenism: The Voting Rights Act and the Theory of Black Electoral Success, 89 Mich.L.Rev. 1077 (1991); Engstrom, Taebel & Cole, Cumulative Voting as a Remedy for Minority Vote Dilution: The Case of Alamogordo, New Mexico, 5 J. Law & Politics 469 (1989); Schuck, The Thickest Thicket: Partisan Gerrymandering and Judicial Regulation of Politics, 87 Colum.L.Rev. 1325, 1361–77 (1987); Low–Beer, The Constitutional Imperative of Proportional Representation, 94 Yale L.J. 163 (1984); Amar, Choosing Representatives by Lottery Voting, 93 Yale L.J. 1283 (1984).

Sims, 377 U.S. 533, 84 S.Ct. 1362, 12 L.Ed.2d 506 (1964), to units of local government is of broad public importance. We hold that petitioner, as a resident of Midland County, has a right to a vote for the Commissioners Court of substantially equal weight to the vote of every other resident. * * *

Although the forms and functions of local government and the relationships among the various units are matters of state concern, it is now beyond question that a State's political subdivisions must comply with the Fourteenth Amendment. The actions of local government *are* the actions of the State. A city, town, or county may no more deny the equal protection of the laws than it may abridge freedom of speech, establish an official religion, arrest without probable cause, or deny due process of law.

When the State apportions its legislature, it must have due regard for the Equal Protection Clause. Similarly, when the State delegates lawmaking power to local government and provides for the election of local officials from districts specified by statute, ordinance, or local charter, it must insure that those qualified to vote have the right to an equally effective voice in the election process. If voters residing in oversize districts are denied their constitutional right to participate in the election of state legislators, precisely the same kind of deprivation occurs when the members of a city council, school board, or county governing board are elected from districts of substantially unequal population. If the five senators representing a city in the state legislature may not be elected from districts ranging in size from 50,000 to 500,000, neither is it permissible to elect the members of the city council from those same districts. In either case, the votes of some residents have greater weight than those of others; in both cases the equal protection of the laws has been denied.

That the state legislature may itself be properly apportioned does not exempt subdivisions from the Fourteenth Amendment. While state legislatures exercise extensive power over their constituents and over the various units of local government, the States universally leave much policy and decisionmaking to their governmental subdivisions. Legislators enact many laws but do not attempt to reach those countless matters of local concern necessarily left wholly or partly to those who govern at the local level. What is more, in providing for the governments of their cities, counties, towns, and districts, the States characteristically provide for representative government—for decisionmaking at the local level by representatives elected by the people. And, not infrequently, the delegation of power to local units is contained in constitutional provisions for local home rule which are immune from legislative interference. In a word, institutions of local government have always been a major aspect of our system, and their responsible and responsive operation is today of increasing importance to the quality of life of more and more of our citizens. We therefore see little difference, in terms of the application of the Equal Protection Clause and of the principles of *Reynolds v. Sims,* between the exercise of state power through legislatures and its exercise by elected officials in the cities, towns, and counties. * * *

MR. JUSTICE HARLAN, dissenting.

I could not disagree more with this decision. * * * There are convincing functional reasons why the *Reynolds* rule should not apply to local governmental units at all. The effect of *Reynolds* was to read a long debated political theory—that the only permissible basis for the selection of state legislators is election by majority vote within areas which are themselves equal in population—into the United States Constitution, thereby foreclosing the States from experimenting with legislatures rationally formed in other ways. Even assuming that this result could be justified on the state level, because of the substantial identity in form and function of the state legislatures, and because of the asserted practical necessities for federal judicial interference referred to above, the "one man, one vote" theory is surely a hazardous generalization on the local level. As has been noted previously, no "practical necessity" has been asserted to justify application of the rule to local governments. More important, the greater and more varied range of functions performed by local governmental units implies that flexibility in the form of their structure is even more important than at the state level, and that by depriving local governments of this needed adaptability the Court's holding may indeed defeat the very goals of *Reynolds*.

The present case affords one example of why the "one man, one vote" rule is especially inappropriate for local governmental units. The Texas Supreme Court held as a matter of Texas law:

> "Theoretically, the commissioners court is the governing body of the county and the commissioners represent all the residents, both urban and rural, of the county. But developments during the years have greatly narrowed the scope of the functions of the commissioners court and limited its major responsibilities to the nonurban areas of the county. It has come to pass that the city government * * * is the major concern of the city dwellers and the administration of the affairs of the county is the major concern of the rural dwellers."

Despite the specialized role of the commissioners court, the majority has undertaken to bring it within the ambit of *Reynolds* simply by classifying it as "a unit of local government with general responsibility and power for local affairs." Although this approach is intended to afford "equal protection" to all voters in Midland County, it would seem that it in fact discriminates against the county's rural inhabitants. The commissioners court, as found by the Texas Supreme Court, performs more functions in the area of the county outside Midland City than it does within the city limits. Therefore, each rural resident has a greater interest in its activities than each city dweller. Yet under the majority's formula the urban residents are to have a dominant voice in the county government, precisely proportional to their numbers, and little or no allowance may be made for the greater stake of the rural inhabitants in the county government.

This problem is not a trivial one and is not confined to Midland County. It stems from the fact that local governments, unlike state governments, are often specialized in function. Application of the *Reynolds* rule to such local governments prevents the adoption of apportionments which take into account the effect of this specialization, and therefore may result in a denial of equal treatment to those upon whom the exercise of the special powers has unequal impact. Under today's decision, the only apparent alternative is to classify the governmental unit as other than "general" in power and responsibility, thereby, presumably, avoiding application of the *Reynolds* rule. Neither outcome satisfies *Reynolds'* avowed purpose: to assure "equality" to all voters. The result also deprives localities of the desirable option of establishing slightly specialized, elective units of government, such as Texas' county commissioners court, and varying the size of the constituencies so as rationally to favor those whom the government affects most.   * * *

Despite the majority's declaration that it is not imposing a "straitjacket" on local governmental units, its solution is likely to have other undesirable "freezing" effects on local government. One readily foreseeable example is in the crucial field of metropolitan government. A common pattern of development in the Nation's urban areas has been for the less affluent citizens to migrate to or remain within the central city, while the more wealthy move to the suburbs and come into the city only to work. The result has been to impose a relatively heavier tax burden upon city taxpayers and to fragmentize governmental services in the metropolitan area. An oft-proposed solution to these problems has been the institution of an integrated government encompassing the entire metropolitan area. In many instances, the suburbs may be included in such a metropolitan unit only by majority vote of the voters in each suburb. As a practical matter, the suburbanites often will be reluctant to join the metropolitan government unless they receive a share in the government proportional to the benefits they bring with them and not merely to their numbers. The city dwellers may be ready to concede this much, in return for the ability to tax the suburbs. Under the majority's pronouncements, however, this rational compromise would be forbidden: the metropolitan government must be apportioned solely on the basis of population if it is a "general" government.

These functional considerations reinforce my belief that the "one man, one vote" rule, which possesses the simplistic defects inherent in any judicially imposed solution of a complex social problem, is entirely inappropriate for determining the form of the country's local governments.   * * *

BOARD OF ESTIMATE v. MORRIS
Supreme Court of the United States, 1989.
489 U.S. 688, 109 S.Ct. 1433, 103 L.Ed.2d 717.

JUSTICE WHITE delivered the opinion of the Court.

The Board of Estimate of the City of New York consists of three members elected citywide, plus the elected presidents of each of the city's five boroughs. Because the boroughs have widely disparate populations—yet each has equal representation on the board—the Court of Appeals for the Second Circuit held that this structure is inconsistent with the Equal Protection Clause of the Fourteenth Amendment. We affirm. * * *

[I]n this country the people govern themselves through their elected representatives and that "each and every citizen has an inalienable right to full and effective participation in the political processes" of the legislative bodies of the Nation, state, or locality as the case may be. *Reynolds v. Sims,* 377 U.S., at 565, 84 S.Ct., at 1378. Since "[m]ost citizens can achieve this participation only as qualified voters through the election of legislators to represent then," full and effective participation requires "that each citizen have an equally effective voice in the election of members of his * * * legislature." *Ibid.* As Daniel Webster once said, "the right to choose a representative is every man's portion of sovereign power." *Luther v. Borden,* 48 U.S. (7 How.) 1, 30, 12 L.Ed. 581 (1849) (statement of counsel). * * *

That the members of New York City's Board of Estimate trigger this constitutional safeguard is certain. All eight officials become members as a matter of law upon their various elections. The Mayor, the comptroller, and the president of the City Council, who comprise the board's citywide number, are elected by votes of the entire city electorate. Each of these three cast two votes, except that the Mayor has no vote on the acceptance of modification of his budget proposal. Similarly, when residents of the city's five boroughs—the Bronx, Brooklyn, Manhattan, Queens, and Richmond (Staten Island)—elect their respective borough presidents, the elections decide each borough's representative on the board. These five members each have single votes on all board matters.

New York law assigns to the board a significant range of functions common to municipal governments. * * * The Board manages all city property; exercises plenary zoning authority; dispenses all franchises and leases on city property; fixes generally the salaries of all officers and persons compensated through city monies; and grants all city contracts. * * * In addition, and of major significance, the board shares legislative functions with the City Council with respect to modifying and approving the city's capital and expense budgets. * * * This considerable authority to formulate the city's budget, which last fiscal year surpassed twenty-five billion dollars, as well as the board's land use, franchise, and contracting powers over the city's seven million inhabitants, situate the Board comfortably within the category of governmental bodies whose "powers are general enough and have sufficient impact throughout the district" to require that elections to the body comply with Equal Protection strictures. See *Hadley v. Junior College Dist.,* 397 U.S., at 54, 90 S.Ct., at 794. * * *

The city's primary argument is that the courts below erred in the methodology by which they determined whether, and to what extent, the method of electing the board members gives the voters in some boroughs more power than the voters in other boroughs. Specifically, the city focuses on the relative power of the voters in the various boroughs to affect board decisions, an approach which involves recognizing the weighted voting of the three city-wide members.

As described by the Court of Appeals, the method urged by the city to determine an individual voter's power to affect the outcome of a board vote first calculates the power of each member of the board to affect a board vote, and then calculates voters' power to cast the determining vote in the election of that member. This method, termed the Banzhaf Index, applies as follows: 552 possible voting combinations exist in which any one member can affect the outcome of a board vote. Each borough president can cast the determining vote in 48 of these combinations (giving him a "voting power" of 8.7%) while each city-wide member can determine the outcome in 104 of 552 combinations (18.8%). A citizen's voting power through each representative is calculated by dividing the representative's voting power by the square root of the population represented; a citizen's total voting power thus aggregates his power through each of his four representatives—borough president, Mayor, comptroller, and council president. Deviation from ideal voting power is then calculated by comparing this figure with the figure arrived at when one considers an electoral district of ideal population. Calculated in this manner, the maximum deviation in the voting power to control Board outcomes is 30.8% on non-budget matters, and, because of the Mayor's absence, a higher deviation on budget issues.

The Court of Appeals gave careful attention to and rejected this submission. We agree with the reasons given by the Court of Appeals that the population-based approach of our cases * * * should not be put aside in this case. We note also that we have once before, although in a different context, declined to accept the approach now urged by the city. *Whitcomb v. Chavis,* 403 U.S. 124, 91 S.Ct. 1858, 29 L.Ed.2d 363 (1971). In that case we observed that the Banzhaf methodology "remains a theoretical one" and is unrealistic in not taking into account "any political or other factors which might affect the actual voting power of the residents, which might include party affiliation, race, previous voting characteristics or any other factors which go into the entire political voting situation." *Id.,* at 145–146, 91 S.Ct., at 1870.

The personal right to vote is a value in itself, and a citizen is, without more and without mathematically calculating his power to determine the outcome of an election, shortchanged if he may vote for only one representative when citizens in a neighboring district, of equal population, vote for two; or to put it another way, if he may vote for one representative and the voters in another district half the size also elect one representative. Even if a desired outcome is the motivating factor bringing voters to the polls, the Court of Appeals in this case considered the Banzhaf Index an unrealistic approach to determining whether citizens have an equal voice in electing their representatives because the approach tends to ignore partisanship, race, and voting habits or other characteristics having an impact on election outcomes.

The Court of Appeals also thought that the city's approach was "seriously defective in the way it measures Board members' power to determine the outcome of a Board vote." The difficulty was that this method did not reflect the way the board actually works in practice; rather, the method is a theoretical explanation of each board member's power to affect the outcome of board actions. It may be that in terms of assuring fair and effective representation, the equal protection approach reflected in the *Reynolds v. Sims* line of cases is itself imperfect, but it does assure that legislators will be elected by and represent citizens in districts of substantially equal size. It does not attempt to inquire whether, in terms of how the legislature actually works in practice, the districts have equal power to affect a legislative outcome. This would be a difficult and ever-changing task, and its challenge is hardly met by a mathematical calculation that itself stops short of examining the actual day-to-day operations of the legislative body. The Court of Appeals in any event thought there was insufficient reason to depart from our prior cases, and we agree.

Having decided to follow the established method of resolving equal protection issues in districting and apportionment cases, the Court of Appeals then inquired whether the presence of at-large members on the board should be factored into the process of determining the deviation between the more and less populous boroughs. The court decided that they need not be taken into account because the at-large members and the borough presidents respond to different constituencies. The three at-large members obviously represent citywide interests; but, in the Court of Appeals' judgment, the borough presidents represent and are responsive to their boroughs, yet each has one vote despite the dramatic inequalities in the boroughs' populations. * * * Applying the formula that we have utilized without exception since 1971, the Court of Appeals agreed with the District Court that the maximum percentage deviation from the ideal population is 132.9%.[7]

We do not agree with the Court of Appeals' approach. In calculating the deviation among districts, the relevant inquiry is whether "the vote of any citizen is approximately equal in weight to that of any other citizen," *Reynolds v. Sims,* 377 U.S., at 579, 84 S.Ct., at 1390, the aim being to provide "fair and effective representation for all citizens," *id.,*

---

7. That percentage is the sum of the percentage by which Brooklyn, the city's most populous district (population 2,230,-936), exceeds the ideal district population (1,414,206), and the percentage by which Staten Island, the least populous (352,151), falls below this ideal. Queens' population was stipulated to be 1,891,325; Manhattan's, 1,427,533; and Bronx's, 1,169,115. The parties stipulated, therefore, that the city's total population is 7,071,030.

at 565–566, 84 S.Ct., at 1383–1384. Here the voters in each borough vote for the at-large members as well as their borough president, and they are also represented by those members. Hence in determining whether there is substantially equal voting power and representation, the citywide members are a major component in the calculation and should not be ignored.

Because of the approach followed by the District Court and the Court of Appeals, there was no judicial finding concerning the total deviation from the ideal that would be if the at-large members of the board are taken into account. In pleadings filed with the District Court, however, appellees indicated, and the city agreed, that the deviation would then be 78%. This deviation was confirmed at oral argument. And as to budget matters, when only two citywide members participate, the deviation would be somewhat larger. We accept for purposes of this case the figure agreed upon by the parties.

We note that no case of ours has indicated that a deviation of some 78% could ever be justified. At the very least, the local government seeking to support such a difference between electoral districts would bear a very difficult burden, and we are not prepared to differ with the holding of the courts below that this burden has not been carried. The city presents in this court nothing that was not considered below, arguing chiefly that the board, as presently structured, is essential to the successful government of a regional entity, the City of New York. The board, it is said, accommodates natural and political boundaries as well as local interests. Furthermore, because the board has been effective it should not be disturbed. All of this, the city urges, is supported by the city's history. The courts below, of course, are in a much better position than we to assess the weight of these arguments, and they concluded that the proffered governmental interests were either invalid or were not sufficient to justify a deviation of 132%, in part because the valid interests of the city could be served by alternative ways of constituting the board that would minimize the discrimination in voting power among the five boroughs. Their analysis is equally applicable to a 78% deviation, and we conclude that the city's proffered governmental interests do not suffice to justify such a substantial departure from the one-person one-vote ideal. * * *

CITY OF MOBILE v. BOLDEN

Supreme Court of the United States, 1980.
446 U.S. 55, 100 S.Ct. 1490, 64 L.Ed.2d 47.

MR. JUSTICE STEWART announced the judgment of the Court and delivered an opinion in which THE CHIEF JUSTICE, MR. JUSTICE POWELL, and MR. JUSTICE REHNQUIST join.

The City of Mobile, Ala., has since 1911 been governed by a City Commission consisting of three members elected by the voters of the city at-large. The question in this case is whether this at-large system of municipal elections violates the rights of Mobile's Negro voters in contravention of federal statutory or constitutional law.

The appellees brought this suit in the Federal District Court for the Southern District of Alabama as a class action on behalf of all Negro citizens of Mobile.[1] Named as defendants were the city and its three incumbent Commissioners, who are the appellants before this Court. The complaint alleged that the practice of electing the City Commissioners at-large unfairly diluted the voting strength of Negroes in violation of § 2 of the Voting Rights Act of 1965, of the Fourteenth Amendment and of the Fifteenth Amendment. * * *

In Alabama, the form of municipal government a city may adopt is governed by state law. Until 1911 cities not covered by specific legislation were limited to governing themselves through a mayor and city council. In that year, the Alabama Legislature authorized every large municipality to adopt a commission form of government. Mobile established its City Commission in the same year, and has maintained that basic system of municipal government ever since.

The three Commissioners jointly exercise all legislative, executive and administrative power in the municipality. They are required after election to designate one of their number as Mayor, a largely ceremonial office, but no formal provision is made for allocating specific executive or administrative duties among the three. As required by the state law enacted in 1911, each candidate for the Mobile City Commission runs for election in the city at-large for a term of four years in one of three numbered posts, and may be elected only by a majority of the total vote. This is the same basic electoral system that is followed by literally thousands of municipalities and other local governmental units throughout the Nation. * * *

The Court's early decisions under the Fifteenth Amendment established that it imposes but one limitation on the powers of the States. It forbids them to discriminate against Negroes in matters having to do with voting. * * * Our decisions, moreover, have made clear that action by a State that is racially neutral on its face violates the Fifteenth Amendment only if motivated by a discriminatory purpose. * * * Having found that Negroes in Mobile "register and vote without hindrance," the District Court and Court of Appeals were in error in believing that the appellants invaded the protection of that Amendment in the present case. * * *

The Court of Appeals also agreed with the District Court that Mobile's at-large electoral system violates the Equal Protection Clause of the Fourteenth Amendment. There remains for consideration, therefore, the validity of its judgment on that score. * * *

"Criticism [of multi-member districts] is rooted in their winner-take-all aspects, their tendency to submerge minorities * * *, a general preference for legislatures reflecting community interests as closely as

---

1. Approximately 35.4% of the residents of Mobile are Negro.

possible and disenchantment with political parties and elections as devices to settle policy differences between contending interests." *Whitcomb v. Chavis,* 403 U.S. 124, 158–159, 91 S.Ct. 1858, 1877, 29 L.Ed.2d 363.

Despite repeated constitutional attacks upon multimember legislative districts, the Court has consistently held that they are not unconstitutional *per se, e.g., White v. Regester,* 412 U.S. 755, 93 S.Ct. 2332, 37 L.Ed.2d 314; *Whitcomb v. Chavis,* 403 U.S. 124, 91 S.Ct. 1858, 29 L.Ed.2d 363. We have recognized, however, that such legislative apportionments could violate the Fourteenth Amendment if their purpose were invidiously to minimize or cancel out the voting potential of racial or ethnic minorities. To prove such a purpose it is not enough to show that the group allegedly discriminated against has not elected representatives in proportion to its numbers. A plaintiff must prove that the disputed plan was "conceived or operated as [a] purposeful device[ ] to further racial discrimination," *id.,* at 149, 91 S.Ct. at 1872. * * *

The District Court assessed the appellees' claims in light of the standard that had been articulated by the Court of Appeals for the Fifth Circuit in *Zimmer v. McKeithen,* 485 F.2d 1297. That case, coming before *Washington v. Davis,* 426 U.S. 229, 96 S.Ct. 2040, 48 L.Ed.2d 597, was quite evidently decided upon the misunderstanding that it is not necessary to show a discriminatory purpose in order to prove a violation of the Equal Protection Clause—that proof of a discriminatory effect is sufficient.

In light of the criteria identified in *Zimmer,* the District Court based its conclusion of unconstitutionality primarily on the fact that no Negro had ever been elected to the City Commission, apparently because of the pervasiveness of racially polarized voting in Mobile. The trial court also found that city officials had not been as responsive to the interests of Negroes as to those of white persons. On the basis of these findings, the court concluded that the political processes in Mobile were not equally open to Negroes, despite its seemingly inconsistent findings that there were no inhibitions against Negroes becoming candidates, and that in fact Negroes had registered and voted without hindrance. Finally, with little additional discussion, the District Court held that Mobile's at-large electoral system was invidiously discriminating against Negroes in violation of the Equal Protection Clause.

In affirming the District Court, the Court of Appeals acknowledged that the Equal Protection Clause of the Fourteenth Amendment reaches only purposeful discrimination, but held that one way a plaintiff may establish this illicit purpose is by adducing evidence that satisfies the criteria of its decision in *Zimmer.* Thus, because the appellees had proved an "aggregate" of the *Zimmer* factors, the Court of Appeals concluded that a discriminatory purpose had been proved. That approach, however, is inconsistent with our decisions in *Washington v. Davis.* Although the presence of the indicia relied on in *Zimmer* may afford some evidence of a discriminatory purpose, satisfaction of those criteria is not of itself sufficient proof of such a purpose. The so-called *Zimmer* criteria upon which the District Court and the Court of Appeals relied were most assuredly insufficient to prove an unconstitutionally discriminatory purpose in the present case.

First, the two courts found it highly significant that no Negro had been elected to the Mobile City Commission. From this fact they concluded that the processes leading to nomination and election were not open equally to Negroes. But the District Court's findings of fact, unquestioned on appeal, make clear that Negroes register and vote in Mobile "without hindrance," and that there are no official obstacles in the way of Negroes who wish to become candidates for election to the Commission. Indeed, it was undisputed that the only active "slating" organization in the city is comprised of Negroes. It may be that Negro candidates have been defeated but that fact alone does not work a constitutional deprivation.

Second, the District Court relied in part on its finding that the persons who were elected to the Commission discriminated against Negroes in municipal employment and in dispensing public services. If that is the case, those discriminated against may be entitled to relief under the Constitution, albeit of a sort quite different from that sought in the present case. The Equal Protection Clause proscribes purposeful discrimination because of race by any unit of state government, whatever the method of its election. But evidence of discrimination by white officials in Mobile is relevant only as the most tenuous and circumstantial evidence of the constitutional invalidity of the electoral system under which they attained their offices.

Third, the District Court and the Court of Appeals supported their conclusion by drawing upon the substantial history of official racial discrimination in Alabama. But past discrimination cannot, in the manner of original sin, condemn governmental action that is not itself unlawful. The ultimate question remains whether a discriminatory intent has been proved in a given case. More distant instances of official discrimination in other cases are of limited help in resolving that question.

Finally, the District Court and the Court of Appeals pointed to the mechanics of the at-large electoral system itself as proof that the votes of Negroes were being invidiously canceled out. But those features of that electoral system, such as the majority vote requirement, tend naturally to disadvantage any voting minority, as we noted in *White v. Regester, supra.* They are far from proof that the at-large electoral scheme represents purposeful discrimination against Negro voters.

We turn finally to the arguments advanced in Part I of Mr. Justice Marshall's dissenting opinion. The theory of this dissenting opinion—a theory much more extreme than that espoused by the District Court or the Court of Appeals—appears to be that every "political group," or at least every such group that is in the minority, has a federal constitutional right to elect candidates in proportion to its numbers. Moreover, a political group's "right" to have its candidates elected is said to be a "fundamental interest," the infringement of which may be established without proof that a State has acted with the purpose of impairing anybody's access to the political process. This dissenting opinion finds the "right" infringed in the present case because no Negro has been elected to the Mobile City Commission.

Whatever appeal the dissenting opinion's view may have as a matter of political theory, it is not the law. The Equal Protection Clause of the Fourteenth Amendment does not require proportional representation as an imperative of political organization. The entitlement that the dissenting opinion assumes to exist simply is not to be found in the Constitution of the United States. * * * It is, of course, true that the right of a person to vote on an equal basis with other voters draws much of its significance from the political associations that its exercise reflects, but it is an altogether different matter to conclude that political groups themselves have an independent constitutional claim to representation. And the Court's decisions hold squarely that they do not.

The fact is that the Court has sternly set its face against the claim, however phrased, that the Constitution somehow guarantees proportional representation. In *Whitcomb v. Chavis, supra,* the trial court had found that a multimember state legislative district had invidiously deprived Negroes and poor persons of rights guaranteed them by the Constitution, notwithstanding the absence of any evidence whatever of discrimination against them. Reversing the trial court, this Court said:

> "The District Court's holding, although on the facts of this case limited to guaranteeing one racial group representation, is not easily contained. It is expressive of the more general proposition that any group with distinctive interests must be represented in legislative halls if it is numerous enough to command at least one seat and represents a majority living in an area sufficiently compact to constitute a single-member district. This approach would make it difficult to reject claims of Democrats, Republicans, or members of any political organization in Marion County who live in what would be safe districts in a single-member district system but who in one year or another, or year after year, are submerged in a one-sided multi-member district vote. There are also union oriented workers, the university community, religious or ethnic groups occupying identifiable areas of our heterogeneous cities and urban areas. Indeed, it would be difficult for a great many, if not most, multi-member districts to survive analysis under the District Court's view unless combined with some voting arrangement such as proportional representation or cumulative voting aimed at providing representation for minority parties or interests. At the very least, affirmance of the District Court would spawn endless litigation concerning the multi-member district systems now widely employed in this country."

The judgment is reversed and the case is remanded to the Court of Appeals for further proceedings. * * *

MR. JUSTICE STEVENS, concurring in the judgment. * * *

In my view, the proper standard is suggested by three characteristics of the gerrymander condemned in *Gomillion* [*v. Lightfoot,* 364 U.S. 339, 81 S.Ct. 125, 5 L.Ed.2d 110]: (1) the 28–sided configuration was, in the Court's word, "uncouth," that is to say, it was manifestly not the product of a routine or a traditional political decision; (2) it had a significant adverse impact on a minority group; and (3) it was unsupported by any neutral justification and thus was either totally irrational or entirely motivated by a desire to curtail the political strength of the minority. These characteristics suggest that a proper test should focus on the objective effects of the political decision rather than the subjective motivation of the decisionmaker. In this case, if the commission form of government in Mobile were extraordinary, or if it were nothing more than a vestige of history, with no greater justification than the grotesque figure in *Gomillion,* it would surely violate the Constitution. That conclusion would follow simply from its adverse impact on black voters plus the absence of any legitimate justification for the system, without reference to the subjective intent of the political body that has refused to alter it.

Conversely, I am also persuaded that a political decision that affects group voting rights may be valid even if it can be proved that irrational or invidious factors have played some part in its enactment or retention. * * * [A] political decision that is supported by valid and articulable justifications cannot be invalid simply because some participants in the decisionmaking process were motivated by a purpose to disadvantage a minority group. * * *

MR. JUSTICE MARSHALL, dissenting. * * *

[A] plurality of the Court concludes that, in the absence of proof of intentional discrimination by the State, the right to vote provides the politically powerless with nothing more than the right to cast meaningless ballots. * * *

[I]n *White v. Regester,* * * * [t]he District Court identified a number of social and historical factors that, when combined with the Texas electoral structure, resulted in vote dilution: (1) a history of official racial discrimination in Texas, including discrimination inhibiting the registration, casting of ballots, and political participation of Negroes; (2) proof that minorities were still suffering the effects of past discrimination; (3) a history of gross underrepresentation of minority interests; (4) proof of official insensitivity to the needs of minority citizens, whose votes were not needed by those in power; (5) the recent use of racial campaign tactics; and (6) a cultural and language barrier inhibiting the participation of Mexican–Americans. Based "on the totality of the circumstances," we affirmed the District Court's conclusion that the use of multimember districts excluded the plaintiffs "from effective participation in political life." *Id.,* at 769, 93 S.Ct., at 2341.[7]

It is apparent that a showing of discriminatory intent in the creation or maintenance of multimember districts is as unnecessary after *White* as it was under our earlier vote-dilution decisions. Under this line of cases, an electoral districting plan is invalid if it has the effect of affording an electoral minority "less opportunity than * * * other residents in the district to participate in the political processes and to elect legislators of their choice." It is also apparent that the Court in *White* considered equal access to the political process as meaning more than merely allowing the minority the opportunity to vote. *White* stands for the proposition that an electoral system may not relegate an electoral minority to political impotence by diminishing the importance of its vote. The plurality's approach requiring proof of discriminatory purpose in the present cases is, then, squarely contrary to *White* and its predecessors. * * *

The plurality's response is that my approach amounts to nothing less than a constitutional requirement of proportional representation for groups. That assertion amounts to nothing more than a red herring: I explicitly reject the notion that the Constitution contains any such requirement. See n. 7, *supra.* The constitutional protection against vote dilution found in our prior cases does not extend to those situations in which a group has merely failed to elect representatives in proportion to its share of the population. To prove unconstitutional vote dilution, the group is also required to carry the far more onerous burden of demonstrating that it has been effectively fenced out of the political process. See *ibid.* Typical of the plurality's mischaracterization of my

---

7. *White v. Regester,* 412 U.S. 755, 93 S.Ct. 2332, 37 L.Ed.2d 314 (1973), makes clear the distinction between the concepts of vote dilution and proportional representation. We have held that, in order to prove an allegation of vote dilution, the plaintiffs must show more than simply that they have been unable to elect candidates of their choice. The Constitution, therefore, does not contain any requirement of proportional representation. When all that is proved is mere lack of success at the polls, the Court will not presume that members of a political minority have suffered an impermissible dilution of political power. Rather, it is assumed that these persons have means available to them through which they can have some effect on governmental decisionmaking. For example, many of these persons might belong to a variety of other political, social, and economic groups that have some impact on officials. In the absence of evidence to the contrary, it may be assumed that officials will not be improperly influenced by such factors as the race or place of residence of persons seeking governmental action. Furthermore, political factions out of office often serve as watchdogs on the performance of the government, bind together into coalitions having enhanced influence, and have the respectability necessary to affect public policy.

Unconstitutional vote dilution occurs only when a discrete political minority whose voting strength is diminished by a districting scheme proves that historical and social factors render it largely incapable of effectively utilizing alternative avenues of influencing public policy. In these circumstances, the only means of breaking down the barriers encasing the political arena is to structure the electoral districting so that the minority has a fair opportunity to elect candidates of its choice.

The test for unconstitutional vote dilution, then, looks only to the discriminatory effects of the combination of an electoral structure and historical and social factors. At the same time, it requires electoral minorities to prove far more than mere lack of success at the polls. * * *

position is its assertion that I would provide protection against vote dilution for "every 'political group,' or at least every such group that is in the minority." The vote-dilution doctrine can logically apply only to groups whose electoral discreteness and insularity allow dominant political factions to ignore them. In short, the distinction between a requirement of proportional representation and the discriminatory effect test I espouse is by no means a difficult one, and it is hard for me to understand why the plurality insists on ignoring it.

The plaintiffs * * * proved that no Negro had ever been elected to the Mobile City Commission, despite the fact that Negroes constitute about one-third of the electorate, and that the persistence of severe racial bloc voting made it highly unlikely that any Negro could be elected at-large in the foreseeable future. Contrary to the plurality's contention, however, I do not find unconstitutional vote dilution in this case simply because of that showing. The plaintiffs convinced the District Court that Mobile Negroes were unable to use alternative avenues of political influence. They showed that Mobile Negroes still suffered pervasive present effects of massive historical, official and private discrimination, and that the city commission had been quite unresponsive to the needs of the minority community. The City of Mobile has been guilty of such pervasive racial discrimination in hiring employees that extensive intervention by the Federal District Court has been required. Negroes are grossly underrepresented on city boards and committees. The city's distribution of public services is racially discriminatory. City officials and police were largely unmoved by Negro complaints about police brutality and "mock lynchings." The District Court concluded that "[t]his sluggish and timid response is another manifestation of the low priority given to the needs of the black citizens and of the [commissioners'] political fear of a white backlash vote when black citizens' needs are at stake." * * *

The plurality * * * fails to recognize that the maintenance of multimember districts in the face of foreseeable discriminatory consequences strongly suggests that officials are blinded by "racially selective sympathy and indifference." Like outright racial hostility, selective racial indifference reflects a belief that the concerns of the minority are not worthy of the same degree of attention paid to problems perceived by whites. When an interest as fundamental as voting is diminished along racial lines, a requirement that discriminatory purpose must be proved should be satisfied by a showing that official action was produced by this type of pervasive bias. In the present cases, the plaintiffs presented strong evidence of such bias: they showed that Mobile officials historically discriminated against Negroes, that there are pervasive present effects of this past discrimination, and that officials have not been responsive to the needs of the minority community. It takes only the smallest of inferential leaps to conclude that the decisions to maintain multimember districting having obvious discriminatory effects represent, at the very least, selective racial sympathy and indifference resulting in the frustration of minority desires, the stigmatization of the minority as second-class citizens, and the perpetuation of inhumanity. * * *

Note on Holder v. Hall

Responding to the plurality opinion in *City of Mobile v. Bolden,* Congress amended § 2 of the Voting Rights Act in 1982. "Congress substantially revised § 2," the Court said in Thornburg v. Gingles, 478 U.S. 30, 106 S.Ct. 2752, 92 L.Ed.2d 25 (1986), "to make clear that a violation [of § 2] could be proven by showing discriminatory effect alone and to establish as the relevant legal standard the 'results test'". In *Thornburg,* the Court held that a minority group must prove three conditions to establish that the creation of a multimember district had a discriminatory effect and thus violated § 2: that the minority group is large enough to constitute a majority in a single-member district; that it is politically cohesive; and that the white majority votes sufficiently as a bloc to enable it usually to defeat the minority's preferred candidate. In *Thornburg* and subsequent cases, the Court examined minority vote dilution claims under the revised § 2 in the context of legislative districting. See Johnson v. DeGrandy, ___ U.S. ___, 114 S.Ct. 2647, ___ L.Ed.2d ___ (1994); Voinovich v. Quilter, ___ U.S. ___, 113 S.Ct. 1149, 122 L.Ed.2d 500 (1993); Growe v. Emison, ___ U.S. ___, 113 S.Ct. 1075, 122 L.Ed.2d 388 (1993). Not until Holder v. Hall, ___ U.S. ___, 114 S.Ct. 2581, ___ L.Ed.2d ___ (1994), did the Court return to the issue it faced in *City of Mobile v. Bolden:* the use of an at-large electoral system, rather than single-district voting, to choose the members of a governing commission of a city or other local governmental entity.

In *Holder,* black voters from Bleckley County, Georgia, challenged under § 2 the County's system of selecting all five members of its governing commission through an at-large election. Although blacks constituted 20% of the population of the county, no black person had ever run for or been elected to the office of Bleckley County Commissioner. The District Judge, who himself had run for public office, declared that he "wouldn't run if [he] were black in Bleckley County." In a 5–4 decision, the Court held that plaintiffs could not maintain a § 2 challenge to what it called the "size of a governmental body", that is, to the choice between countywide at-large elections and single-member districting. Justices Kennedy and O'Connor and Chief Justice Rehnquist, in two separate opinions, grounded this result on statutory interpretation. The three observed that a wide variety of single-member districting schemes could conceivably be adopted in Bleckley County and that § 2 provided no benchmark for determining which of them should be used as a comparison with an at-large election. Because there was no benchmark that would provide a basis for deciding the extent of minority vote dilution, they reasoned, the size of a government body, unlike legislative districting, was not subject to a vote dilution challenge under § 2. The final two votes for the majority position were provided in an opinion by Justice Thomas, in which Justice Scalia concurred. Justice Thomas interpreted § 2 much more narrowly than the plurality, reading it as limited solely to issues involving citizens' access to the ballot (voting qualifications and the like). If accepted, Justice Thomas' interpretation would thus overrule all previous cases, such as *Thornburg,* that had interpreted § 2 to permit a challenge of legislative districting on the grounds of minority vote dilution. In his opinion, Justice Thomas made the following argument against the Court's vote dilution jurisprudence:

> Perhaps the most prominent feature of the philosophy that has emerged in vote dilution decisions * * * has been the Court's preference for single-member districting schemes, both as a benchmark for measuring undiluted minority voting strength and as a remedial mechanism for guaranteeing minorities undiluted voting power. * * * It should be apparent, however, that there is no principle inherent in our constitutional system, or even in the history of the Nation's electoral practices, that makes single-member districts the "proper" mechanism for electing representatives to governmental bodies or for giving "undiluted" effect to the votes of a numerical minority. On the contrary, from the earliest days of the Republic, multimember districts were a common feature of our political systems. The Framers left unanswered in the Constitution the question whether congressional delegations from the several States should be elected on a general ticket from each State as a whole or under a districting scheme and left that matter to be resolved by the States or by Congress. It was not until 1842 that Congress determined that Representatives should be elected from single-member districts in the States. Single-member districting was no more the rule in the States themselves, for the Constitutions of most of the 13 original States provided that representatives in the state legislatures were to be elected from multimember districts. Today, although they have come under increasing attack under the Voting Rights Act, multimember district systems continue to be a feature on the American political landscape, especially in municipal governments. See The Municipal Yearbook 14 (table) (1988) (over 60% of American cities use at-large election systems for their governing bodies).

> The obvious advantage the Court has perceived in single-member districts, of course, is their tendency to enhance the ability of any numerical minority in the electorate to gain control of seats in a representative body. * * * [T]he Court has adopted the view that members of any numerically significant minority are denied a fully effective use of the franchise unless they are able to control seats in an elected body. Under this theory, votes that do not control a representative are essentially wasted; those who cast them go unrepresented and are just as surely disenfranchised as if they had been barred from registering. Such conclusions, of course, depend upon a certain theory of the "effective" vote, a theory that is not inherent in the concept of representative democracy itself.

> In fact, it should be clear that the assumptions that have guided the Court reflect only one possible understanding of effective exercise of the franchise, an understanding based on the view that voters are "represented" only when they choose a delegate who will mirror their views in the legislative halls. But it is certainly possible to construct a theory of effective political participation that would accord greater importance to voters' ability to influence, rather than control, elections. And especial-

ly in a two-party system such as ours, the influence of a potential "swing" group of voters composing 10%–20% of the electorate in a given district can be considerable. * * * Some conceptions of representative government may primarily emphasize the formal value of the vote as a mechanism for participation in the electoral process, whether it results in control of a seat or not. * * * [T]here are undoubtedly an infinite number of theories of effective suffrage, representation, and the proper apportionment of political power in a representative democracy * * *. The matters the Court has set out to resolve in vote dilution cases are questions of political philosophy, not questions of law. As such, they are not readily subjected to any judicially manageable standards that can guide courts in attempting to select between competing theories.

But the political choices the Court has had to make do not end with the determination that the primary purpose of the "effective" vote is controlling seats or with the selection of single-member districting as the mechanism for providing that control. * * * Once one accepts the proposition that the effectiveness of votes is measured in terms of the control of seats, the core of any vote dilution claim is an assertion that the group in question is unable to control the "proper" number of seats—that is, the number of seats that the minority's percentage of the population would enable it to control in the benchmark "fair" system. The claim is inherently based on ratios between the numbers of the minority in the population and the numbers of seats controlled. * * * The ratio for which this Court has opted, and thus the mathematical principle driving the results in our cases, is undoubtedly direct proportionality. * * *

[T]he Court * * * accept[s] the one underlying premise that must inform every minority vote dilution claim: the assumption that the group asserting dilution is not merely a racial or ethnic group, but a group having distinct political interests as well. Of necessity, in resolving vote dilution actions we have given credence to the view that race defines political interest. We have acted on the implicit assumption that members of racial and ethnic groups must all think alike on important matters of public policy and must have their own "minority preferred" representatives holding seats in elected bodies if they are to be considered represented at all. * * * We have involved the federal courts, and indeed the Nation, in the enterprise of systematically dividing the country into electoral districts along racial lines—an enterprise of segregating the races into political homelands that amounts, in truth, to nothing short of a system of "political apartheid." Blacks are drawn into "black districts" and given "black representatives"; Hispanics are drawn into Hispanic districts and given "Hispanic representatives"; and so on. Worse still, it is not only the courts that have taken up this project. In response to judicial decisions and the promptings of the Justice Department, the States themselves, in an attempt to avoid costly and disruptive Voting Rights Act litigation, have begun to gerrymander electoral districts according to race. * * *

The assumptions upon which our vote dilution decisions have been based should be repugnant to any nation that strives for the ideal of a color-blind Constitution. "The principle of equality is at war with the notion that District A must be represented by a Negro, as it is with the notion that District B must be represented by a Caucasian, District C by a Jew, District D by a Catholic, and so on." *Wright v. Rockefeller*, 376 U.S. 52, 66 (1964) (Douglas, J., dissenting). Despite Justice Douglas' warning sounded 30 years ago, our voting rights decisions are rapidly progressing towards a system that is indistinguishable in principle from a scheme under which members of different racial groups are divided into separate electoral registers and allocated a proportion of political power on the basis of race. Under our jurisprudence, rather than requiring registration on racial rolls and dividing power purely on a population basis, we have simply resorted to the somewhat less precise expedient of drawing geographic district lines to capture minority populations and to ensure the existence of the "appropriate" number of "safe minority seats." * * * Justice Douglas correctly predicted the results of state sponsorship of such a theory of representation: "When racial or religious lines are drawn by the State, * * * antagonisms that relate to race or to religion rather than to political issues are generated; communities seek not the best representative but the best racial or religious partisan." *Id.,* at 67. In short, few devices could be better designed to exacerbate racial tensions than the consciously segregated districting system currently being constructed in the name of the Voting Rights Act.

As a practical political matter, our drive to segregate political districts by race can only serve to deepen racial divisions by destroying any need for voters or candidates to build bridges between racial groups or to form voting coalitions. "Black-preferred" candidates are assured election in "safe black districts"; white-preferred candidates are assured election in "safe white districts." Neither group needs to draw on support from the other's constituency to win on election day. As one judge described the current trend of voting rights cases: "We are bent upon polarizing political subdivisions by race. The arrangement we construct makes it unnecessary, and probably unwise, for an elected official from a white majority district to be responsive at all to the wishes of black citizens; similarly, it is politically unwise for a black official from a black majority district to be responsive at all to white citizens." *Dallas County Comm'n,* 850 F.2d, at 1444 (Hill, J., concurring specially).

As this description suggests, the system we have instituted affirmatively encourages a racially based understanding of the representative function. The clear premise of the system is that geographic districts are merely a device to be manipulated to establish "black representatives" whose real constituencies are defined, not in terms of the voters who populate their districts, but in terms of race. The "black representative's" function, in other words, is to represent the "black interest." * * *

The decision to rely on single-member geographic districts as a mechanism for conducting elections is merely a political choice—and one that we might reconsider in the future. * * * Already, some advocates have criticized the current strategy of creating majority-minority districts and have urged the adoption of other voting mechanisms—for example, cumulative voting or a system using transferable votes—that can produce proportional results without requiring division of the electorate into racially segregated districts. * * * In principle, cumulative voting and other non-district-based methods of effecting proportional representation are simply more efficient and straightforward mechanisms for achieving what has already become our tacit objective: roughly proportional allocation of political power according to race.

At least one court, in fact, has already abandoned districting and has opted instead for cumulative voting on a county-wide basis as a remedy for a Voting Rights Act violation. The District Court for the District of Maryland recently reasoned that, compared to a system that divides voters into districts according to race, "[c]umulative voting is less likely to increase polarization between different interests," and that it "will allow the voters, by the way they exercise their votes, to 'district' themselves," thereby avoiding government involvement in a process of segregating the electorate. *Cane v. Worcester County*, 847 F.Supp. 369, 373 (Md.1994). If such a system can be ordered on a county-wide basis, we should recognize that there is no limiting principle under the Act that would prevent federal courts from requiring it for elections to state legislatures as well. * * *

In my view, our current practice should not continue. Not for another Term, not until the next case, not for another day. The disastrous implications of the policies we have adopted under the Act are too grave; the dissembling in our approach to the Act too damaging to the credibility of the federal judiciary. The "inherent tension"—indeed, I would call it an irreconcilable conflict—between the standards we have adopted for evaluating vote dilution claims and the text of the Voting Rights Act would itself be sufficient in my view to warrant overruling the interpretation of § 2 set out in *Gingles*. When that obvious conflict is combined with the destructive effects our expansive reading of the Act has had in involving the federal judiciary in the project of dividing the Nation into racially segregated electoral districts, I can see no reasonable alternative to abandoning our current unfortunate understanding of the Act. * * *

Justices Stevens, Blackmun, Souter and Ginsburg dissented. They interpreted § 2 to apply to the size of a local government body as well as to legislative districting. Since Congress had determined such a scope for § 2, Justice Stevens declared, it would be "inappropriate" to comment on the portion of Justice Thomas' argument quoted above. The argument, according to Justice Stevens, is "best described as an argument that the statute be repealed or amended in important respects."

DAVIS v. BANDEMER

Supreme Court of the United States, 1986.
478 U.S. 109, 106 S.Ct. 2797, 92 L.Ed.2d 85.

JUSTICE WHITE announced the judgment of the Court and delivered the opinion of the Court as to Part II and an opinion in which JUSTICE BRENNAN, JUSTICE MARSHALL, and JUSTICE BLACKMUN joined as to Parts I, III, and IV.

In this case, we review a judgment from a three-judge District Court, which sustained an equal protection challenge to Indiana's 1981 state apportionment on the basis that the law unconstitutionally diluted the votes of Indiana Democrats. Although we find such political gerrymandering to be justiciable, we conclude that the District Court applied an insufficiently demanding standard in finding unconstitutional vote dilution. Consequently, we reverse. * * *

III

Having determined that the political gerrymandering claim in this case is justiciable, we turn to the question whether the District Court erred in holding that appellees had alleged and proved a violation of the Equal Protection Clause. * * * We * * * agree with the District Court that in order to succeed the Bandemer plaintiffs were required to prove both intentional discrimination against an identifiable political group and an actual discriminatory effect on that group. See, *e.g., Mobile v. Bolden,* 446 U.S., at 67–68, 100 S.Ct., at 1499–1500. Further, we are confident that if the law challenged here had discriminatory effects on Democrats, this record would support a finding that the discrimination was intentional. Thus, we decline to overturn the District Court's finding of discriminatory intent as clearly erroneous.

Indeed, quite aside from the anecdotal evidence, the shape of the House and Senate Districts, and the alleged disregard for political boundaries, we think it most likely that whenever a legislature redistricts, those responsible for the legislation will know the likely political composition of the new districts and will have a prediction as to whether a particular district is a safe one for a Democratic or Republican candidate or is a competitive district that either candidate might win. As we said in *Gaffney v. Cummings* [412 U.S. 735, 93 S.Ct. 2321, 37 L.Ed.2d 298 (1973)]. * * *

> "It may be suggested that those who redistrict and reapportion should work with census, not political, data and achieve population equality without regard for political impact. But this politically mindless approach may produce, whether intended or not, the most grossly gerrymandered results; and, in any event, it is most unlikely that the political impact of such a plan would remain undiscovered by the time it was proposed or adopted, in which event the results would be both known and, if not changed, intended."

As long as redistricting is done by a legislature, it should not be very difficult to prove that the likely political consequences of the reapportionment were intended.

We do not accept, however, the District Court's legal and factual bases for concluding that the 1981 Act visited a sufficiently adverse effect on the appellees' constitutionally protected rights to make out a violation of the Equal Protection Clause. The District Court held that because any apportionment scheme that purposely prevents proportional representation is unconstitutional, Democratic voters need only show that their proportionate voting influence has been adversely affected. Our cases, however, clearly foreclose any claim that the Constitution requires proportional representation or that legislatures in reapportioning must draw district lines to come as near as possible to allocating seats to the contending parties in proportion to what their anticipated statewide vote will be. *Whitcomb v. Chavis,* 403 U.S., at 153, 156, 160, 91 S.Ct., at 1874, 1876, 1878; *White v. Regester,* 412 U.S., at 765–766, 93 S.Ct., at 2339–2340.

The typical election for legislative seats in the United States is conducted in described geographical districts, with the candidate receiving the most votes in each district winning the seat allocated to that district. If all or most of the districts are competitive—defined by the District Court in this case as districts in which the anticipated split in the party vote is within the range of 45% to 55%—even a narrow statewide preference for either party would produce an overwhelming majority for the winning party in the state legislature. This consequence, however, is inherent in winner-take-all, district-based elections, and we cannot hold that such a reapportionment law would violate the Equal Protection Clause because the voters in the losing party do not have representation in the legislature in proportion to the statewide vote received by their party candidates. As we have said: "[W]e are unprepared to hold that district-based elections decided by plurality vote are unconstitutional in either single- or multi-member districts simply because the supporters of losing candidates have no legislative seats assigned to them." *Whitcomb v. Chavis,* 403 U.S., at 160, 91 S.Ct., at 1878. This is true of a racial as well as a political group. It is also true of a statewide claim as well as an individual district claim.

To draw district lines to maximize the representation of each major party would require creating as many safe seats for each party as the demographic and predicted political characteristics of the State would permit. This in turn would leave the minority in each safe district without a representative of its choice. We upheld this "political fairness" approach in *Gaffney v. Cummings,* despite its tendency to deny safe district minorities any realistic chance to elect their own representatives. But *Gaffney* in no way suggested that the Constitution requires the approach that Connecticut had adopted in that case.

In cases involving individual multi-member districts, we have required a substantially greater showing of adverse effects than a mere lack of proportional representation to support a finding of unconstitutional vote dilution. Only where there is evidence that excluded groups have "less opportunity to participate in the political processes and to elect candidates of their choice" have we refused to approve the use of multi-member districts. *Rogers v. Lodge,* 458 U.S. [613], at 624, 102 S.Ct. [3272], at 3279. In these cases, we have also noted the lack of responsiveness by those elected to the concerns of the relevant groups.

These holdings rest on a conviction that the mere fact that a particular apportionment scheme makes it more difficult for a particular group in a particular district to elect the representatives of its choice does not render that scheme constitutionally infirm. This conviction, in turn, stems from a perception that the power to influence the political process is not limited to winning elections. An individual or a group of individuals who votes for a losing candidate is usually deemed to be adequately represented by the winning candidate and to have as much opportunity to influence that candidate as other voters in the district. We cannot presume in such a situation, without actual proof to the contrary, that the candidate elected will entirely ignore the interests of those voters. This is true even in a safe district where the losing group loses election after election. Thus, a group's electoral power is not unconstitutionally diminished by the simple fact of an apportionment scheme that makes winning elections more difficult, and a failure of proportional representation alone does not constitute impermissible discrimination under the Equal Protection Clause. See *Mobile v. Bolden,* 446 U.S., at 111, n. 7, 100 S.Ct., at 1523, n. 7 (Marshall, J., dissenting).

As with individual districts, where unconstitutional vote dilution is alleged in the form of statewide political gerrymandering, the mere lack of proportional representation will not be sufficient to prove unconstitutional discrimination. Again, without specific supporting evidence, a court cannot presume in such a case that those who are elected will disregard the disproportionately underrepresented group. Rather, unconstitutional discrimination occurs only when the electoral system is arranged in a manner that will consistently degrade a voter's or a group of voters' influence on the political process as a whole.

Although this is a somewhat different formulation than we have previously used in describing unconstitutional vote dilution in an individual district, the focus of both of these inquiries is essentially the same. In both contexts, the question is whether a particular group has been unconstitutionally denied its chance to effectively influence the political process. In a challenge to an individual district, this inquiry focuses on the opportunity of members of the group to participate in party deliberations in the slating and nomination of candidates, their opportunity to register and vote, and hence their chance to directly influence the election returns and to secure the attention of the winning candidate. Statewide, however, the inquiry centers on the voters' direct or indirect influence on the elections of the state legislature as a whole. And, as in individual district cases, an equal protection violation may be found only where the electoral system substantially disadvantages certain voters in their opportunity to influence the political process effectively. In this context, such a finding of unconstitutionality must be supported by evidence of continued frustration of the will of a majority of the voters or effective denial to a minority of voters of a fair chance to influence the political process.

Based on these views, we would reject the District Court's apparent holding that *any* interference with an opportunity to elect a representative of one's choice would be sufficient to allege or make out an equal protection violation, unless justified by some acceptable state interest that the State would be required to demonstrate. In addition to being contrary to the above-described conception of an unconstitutional political gerrymander, such a low threshold for legal action would invite attack on all or almost all reapportionment statutes. District-based elections hardly ever produce a perfect fit between votes and representation. The one-person, one-vote imperative often mandates departure from this result as does the no-retrogression rule required by § 5 of the Voting Rights Act. Inviting attack on minor departures from some supposed norm would too much embroil the judiciary in second-guessing what has consistently been referred to as a political task for the legislature, a task that should not be monitored too closely unless the express or tacit goal is to effect its removal from legislative halls. We decline to take a major step toward that end, which would be so much at odds with our history and experience.

The view that a prima facie case of illegal discrimination in reapportionment requires a showing of more than a *de minimis* effect is not unprecedented. Reapportionment cases involving the one-person, one-vote principle such as *Gaffney v. Cummings* and *White v. Regester* provide support for such a requirement. In the present, considerably more complex context, it is also appropriate to require allegations and proof that the challenged legislative plan has had or will have effects that are sufficiently serious to require intervention by the federal courts in state reapportionment decisions. * * *

In response to our approach, Justice Powell suggests an alternative method for evaluating equal protection claims of political gerrymandering. * * * [T]he crux of Justice Powell's analysis seems to be that—at least in some cases—the intentional drawing of district boundaries for partisan ends and for no other reason violates the Equal Protection Clause in and of itself. We disagree, however, with this conception of a constitutional violation. Specifically, even if a state legislature redistricts with the specific intention of disadvantaging one political party's election prospects, we do not believe that there has been an unconstitutional discrimination against members of that party unless the redistricting does in fact disadvantage it at the polls. * * * It surely cannot be an actual disadvantage in terms of fair representation on a group level just to be placed in a district with a supermajority of other Democratic voters or a district that departs from preexisting political boundaries. Only when such placement affects election results and political power statewide has an actual disadvantage occurred. * * *

JUSTICE POWELL, with whom JUSTICE STEVENS joins, concurring in Part II, and dissenting. * * *

The Equal Protection Clause guarantees citizens that their state will govern them impartially. In the context of redistricting, that guarantee is of critical importance because the franchise provides most citizens their only voice in the legislative process. *Reynolds v. Sims,* 377 U.S., at 561–562, 565–566, 84 S.Ct., at 1381–1382, 1383–1384. Since the contours of a voting district powerfully may affect citizens' ability to exercise influence through their vote, district lines should be determined in accordance with neutral and legitimate criteria. When deciding where those lines will fall, the state should treat its voters as standing in the same position, regardless of their political beliefs or party affiliation. * * * The Court's decision in *Reynolds v. Sims* illustrates two concepts that are vitally important in evaluating an equal protection challenge to redistricting. First, the Court recognized that equal protection encompasses a guarantee of equal *representation,* requiring a State to seek to achieve through redistricting "fair and effective representation for all citizens." The concept of "representation" necessarily applies to groups: groups of voters elect representatives, individual voters do not. Gross population disparities violate the mandate of equal representation by denying voters residing in heavily populated districts, *as a group,* the opportunity to elect the number of representatives to which their voting strength otherwise would entitle them. While population disparities do dilute the weight of individual votes, their discriminatory effect is felt only when those individual votes are combined. Thus, the fact that individual voters in heavily populated districts are free to cast their ballot has no bearing on a claim of malapportionment.

Second, at the same time that it announced the principle of "one person, one vote" to compel States to eliminate gross disparities among district populations, the Court plainly recognized that redistricting should be based on a number of neutral criteria, of which districts of equal population was only one. *Reynolds v. Sims* identified several of the factors that should guide a legislature engaged in redistricting. For example, the Court observed that districts should be compact and cover contiguous territory, precisely because the alternative, "[i]ndiscriminate districting," would be "an open invitation to partisan gerrymandering." Similarly, a State properly could choose to give "independent representation" to established political subdivisions. Adherence to community boundaries, the Court reasoned, would both "deter the possibilities of gerrymandering," and allow communities to have a voice in the legislature that directly controls their local interests. Thus, *Reynolds v. Sims* contemplated that "one person, one vote" would be only one among several neutral factors that serve the constitutional mandate of fair and effective representation. It was not itself to be the only goal of redistricting.

A standard that judges the constitutionality of a districting plan solely by reference to the doctrine of "one person, one vote" may cause two detrimental results. First, as a perceived way to avoid litigation, legislative bodies may place undue emphasis on mathematical exactitude, subordinating or ignoring entirely other criteria that bear directly on the fairness of redistricting. Second, as this case illustrates, and as *Reynolds v. Sims* anticipated, exclusive or primary reliance on "one person, one vote" can betray the constitutional promise of fair and effective representation by enabling a legislature to engage intentionally in clearly discriminatory gerrymandering. * * * It may be, as the plurality suggests, that representatives will not "entirely ignore the interests" of opposition voters. But it defies political reality to suppose that members of a losing party have as much political influence over state government as do members of the victorious party. Even the most conscientious state legislators do not disregard opportunities to reward persons or groups who were active supporters in their election campaigns. * * *

The plurality relies almost exclusively on the "one person, one vote" standard to reject appellees' convincing proof that the redistricting plan had a seriously discriminatory effect on their voting strength in particular districts. The plurality properly describes the claim in this case as a denial of fair and effective "representation," but it does not provide any explanation of how complying with "one person, one vote" deters or identifies a gerrymander that unconstitutionally discriminates against a cognizable group of voters. While that standard affords some protection to the voting rights of individuals, "it protects groups only indirectly at best," *Karcher v. Daggett,* 462 U.S. [725], at 752, 103 S.Ct. [2653], at 2671 (Stevens, J., concurring), even when the group's identity is determined solely by reference to the fact that its members reside in a particular voting district. "One person, one vote" alone does not protect the voting rights of a group made up of persons affiliated with a particular political party who seek to achieve representation through their combined voting strength. Thus, the facts that the legislature permitted each Democratic voter to cast his or her one vote, erected no direct barriers to Democratic voters' exercise of the franchise, and drew districts of equal population, are irrelevant to a claim that district lines were drawn for the purpose and with the effect of substantially debasing the strength of votes cast by Democrats as a group. * * *

In *Karcher v. Daggett,* Justice Stevens, echoing the decision in *Reynolds v. Sims,* described factors that I believe properly should guide both legislators who redistrict and judges who test redistricting plans against constitutional challenges. The most important of these factors are the shapes of voting districts and adherence to established political subdivision boundaries. Other relevant considerations include the nature of the legislative procedures by which the apportionment law was adopted and legislative history reflecting contemporaneous legislative goals. To make out a case of unconstitutional partisan gerrymandering, the plaintiff should be required to offer proof concerning these factors, which bear directly on the fairness of a redistricting plan, as well as evidence concerning population disparities and statistics tending to show vote dilution. No one factor should be dispositive.

In this case, appellees offered convincing proof of the ease with which mapmakers, consistent with the "one person, one vote" standard, may design a districting plan that purposefully discriminates against political opponents as well as racial minorities. * * * The legislative process consisted of nothing more than the majority party's private application of computer technology to mapmaking. * * * [T]he District Court found that the maps "conspicuously ignore[d] traditional political subdivisions, with no concern for any adherence to principles of community interest." The court carefully described how the mapmakers carved up counties, cities, and even townships in their effort to draw lines beneficial to the majority party. Many districts meander through several counties, picking up a number of townships from each. The District Court explained why this failure to honor county boundaries could be expected to have a detrimental impact on citizens' exercise of their vote. In Indiana, the county government is the seat of local affairs. The redistricting dissects counties into strange shapes lacking in common interests, on one occasion even placing the seat of one county in a voting district composed of townships from other counties. Under these conditions, the District Court expressly found that "the potential for voter disillusion and nonparticipation is great," as voters are forced to focus their political activities in artificial electoral units. Intelligent voters, regardless of party affiliation, resent this sort of political manipulation of the electorate for no public purpose.

Deposition testimony of the Chairman of the Conference Committee revealed that the mapmakers gave no consideration to the interests of communities. In the Chairman's view, the concept of honoring community interests meant only that mapmakers should refuse to divide a small, suburban community. The shapes of the voting districts and the manner in which the districts divide established communities, from the county to the township level, illustrate that community interests were ignored by appellants. As the District Court observed, for example, "it is difficult to conceive the interests shared by blacks in Washington Township and white suburbanites in Hamilton and Boone Counties, or the shared interest of Allen and Noble County farmers with residents of downtown Fort Wayne."

In addition to the foregoing findings that apply to both the House and Senate plans, the District Court also noted the substantial evidence that appellants were motivated solely by partisan considerations. * * *

In conclusion, I want to make clear the limits of the standard that I believe the Equal Protection Clause imposes on legislators engaged in redistricting. Traditionally, the determination of electoral districts within a State has been a matter left to the legislative branch of the state government. Apart from the doctrine of separation of powers and the federal system prescribed by the Constitution, federal judges are ill-equipped generally to review legislative decisions respecting redistricting. As the plurality opinion makes clear, however, our precedents hold that a colorable claim of discriminatory gerrymandering presents a justiciable controversy under the Equal Protection Clause. Federal courts in exercising their duty to adjudicate such claims should impose a heavy burden of proof on those who allege that a redistricting plan violates the Constitution. In light of *Baker v. Carr, Reynolds v. Sims,* and their progeny, including such comparatively recent decisions as *Gaffney v. Cummings,* this case presents a paradigm example of unconstitutional discrimination against the members of a political party that happened to be out of power. The well-grounded findings of the District Court to this effect have not been, and I believe cannot be, held clearly erroneous. * * *

SHAW v. RENO

Supreme Court of the United States, 1993.
—— U.S. ——, 113 S.Ct. 2816, 125 L.Ed.2d. 511.

JUSTICE O'CONNOR delivered the opinion of the Court.

This case involves two of the most complex and sensitive issues this Court has faced in recent years: the meaning of the constitutional "right" to vote, and the propriety of race-based state legislation designed to benefit members of historically disadvantaged racial minority groups. As a result of the 1990 census, North Carolina became entitled to a twelfth seat in the United States House of Representatives. The General Assembly enacted a reapportionment plan that included one majority-black congressional district. After the Attorney General of the United States objected to the plan pursuant to § 5 of the Voting Rights Act of 1965, the General Assembly passed new legislation creating a second majority-black district. Appellants allege that the revised plan, which contains district boundary lines of dramatically irregular shape, constitutes an unconstitutional racial gerrymander. The question before us is whether appellants have stated a cognizable claim. * * *

The first of the two majority-black districts contained in the revised plan, District 1, is somewhat hook shaped. Centered in the northeast portion of the State, it moves southward until it tapers to a narrow band; then, with finger-like extensions, it reaches far into the southernmost part of the State near the South Carolina border. District 1 has been compared to a "Rorschach ink-blot test," *Shaw v. Barr*, 808 F.Supp. 461, 476 (EDNC 1992) (Voorhees, C. J., concurring in part and dissenting in part), and a "bug splattered on a windshield," Wall Street Journal, Feb. 4, 1992, p. A14.

The second majority-black district, District 12, is even more unusually shaped. It is approximately 160 miles long and, for much of its length, no wider than the I–85 corridor. It winds in snake-like fashion through tobacco country, financial centers, and manufacturing areas "until it gobbles in enough enclaves of black neighborhoods." *Shaw v. Barr, supra*, at 476–477 (Voorhees, C. J., concurring in part and dissenting in part). Northbound and southbound drivers on I–85 sometimes find themselves in separate districts in one county, only to "trade" districts when they enter the next county. Of the 10 counties through which District 12 passes, five are cut into three different districts; even towns are divided. At one point the district remains contiguous only because it intersects at a single point with two other districts before crossing over them. One state legislator has remarked that " 'if you drove down the interstate with both car doors open, you'd kill most of the people in the district.' " * * *

"The right to vote freely for the candidate of one's choice is of the essence of a democratic society * * *." *Reynolds v. Sims*, 377 U.S., at 555, 84 S.Ct., at 1378. For much of our Nation's history, that right sadly has been denied to many because of race. * * * In the 1870's, for example, opponents of Reconstruction in Mississippi "concentrated the bulk of the black population in a 'shoestring' Congressional district running the length of the Mississippi River, leaving five others with white majorities." E. Foner, Reconstruction: America's Unfinished Revolution, 1863–1877, p. 590 (1988). Some 90 years later, Alabama redefined the boundaries of the city of Tuskegee "from a square to an uncouth twenty-eight-sided figure" in a manner that was alleged to exclude black voters, and only black voters, from the city limits. *Gomillion v. Lightfoot*, 364 U.S. 339, 340, 81 S.Ct. 125, 127, 5 L.Ed.2d 110 (1960).

Alabama's exercise in geometry was but one example of the racial discrimination in voting that persisted in parts of this country nearly a century after ratification of the Fifteenth Amendment. * * * Drawing on the "one person, one vote" principle, this Court recognized that "the right to vote can be affected by a dilution of voting power as well as by an absolute prohibition on casting a ballot." *Allen v. State Board of Elections*, 393 U.S. 544, 569, 89 S.Ct. 718, 833, 22 L.Ed.2d 1 (1969) (emphasis added). Where members of a racial minority group vote as a cohesive unit, practices such as multimember or at-large electoral systems can reduce or nullify minority voters' ability, as a group, "to elect the candidate of their choice." *Ibid.* Accordingly, the Court held that such schemes violate the Fourteenth Amendment when they are adopted with a discriminatory purpose and have the effect of diluting minority voting strength. See, *e.g.*, *Rogers v. Lodge*, 458 U.S. 613, 616–617, 102 S.Ct. 3272, 3274–3275, 73 L.Ed.2d 1012 (1982); *White v. Regester*, 412 U.S. 755, 765–766, 93 S.Ct. 2332, 2339–2340, 37 L.Ed.2d 314 (1973). Congress, too, responded to the problem of vote dilution. In 1982, it amended § 2 of the Voting Rights Act to prohibit legislation that *results* in the dilution of a minority group's voting strength, regardless of the legislature's intent. 42 U.S.C. § 1973; see *Thornburg v. Gingles*, 478 U.S. 30, 106 S.Ct. 2752, 92 L.Ed.2d 25 (1986) (applying amended § 2 to vote-dilution claim involving multimember districts); see also *Voinovich v. Quilter*, 507 U.S. ___, 113 S.Ct. 1149, ___, 122 L.Ed.2d 500 (1993) (single-member districts). * * * It is against this background that we confront the questions presented here. * * * It is unsettling how closely the North Carolina plan resembles the most egregious racial gerrymanders of the past.

An understanding of the nature of appellants' claim is critical to our resolution of the case. In their complaint, appellants did not claim that the General Assembly's reapportionment plan unconstitutionally "diluted" white voting strength. They did not even claim to be white. Rather, appellants' complaint alleged that the deliberate segregation of voters into separate districts on the basis of race violated their constitutional right to participate in a "color-blind" electoral process. * * * [A]ppellants appear to concede that race-conscious redistricting is not always unconstitutional. That concession is wise: This Court never has held that race-conscious state decisionmaking is impermissible in all circumstances. What appellants object to is redistricting legislation that is so extremely irregular on its face that it rationally can be viewed only as an effort to segregate the races for purposes of voting, without regard for traditional districting principles and without sufficiently compelling justification. For the reasons that follow, we conclude that appellants have stated a claim upon which relief can be granted under the Equal Protection Clause. * * *

Appellants contend that redistricting legislation that is so bizarre on its face that it is "unexplainable on grounds other than race," *Arlington Heights* [*v. Metropolitan Housing Development Corp.*, 429 U.S. 252, 266, 97 S.Ct. 555, 564, 50 L.Ed.2d 450 (1977)] demands the same close scrutiny that we give other state laws that classify citizens by race. Our voting rights precedents support that conclusion. * * * The Court applied * * * [this] reasoning to the "uncouth twenty-eight-sided" municipal boundary line at issue in *Gomillion*. Although the statute that redrew the city limits of Tuskegee was race-neutral on its face, plaintiffs alleged that its effect was impermissibly to remove from the city virtually all black voters and no white voters. The Court reasoned:

> "If these allegations upon a trial remained uncontradicted or unqualified, the conclusion would be irresistible, tantamount for all practical purposes to a mathematical demonstration, that the legislation is solely concerned with segregating white and colored voters by fencing Negro citizens out of town so as to deprive them of their preexisting municipal vote." * * *

Gomillion thus supports appellants' contention that district lines obviously drawn for the purpose of separating voters by race require careful scrutiny under the Equal Protection Clause regardless of the motivations underlying their adoption.

The Court extended the reasoning of *Gomillion* to congressional districting in *Wright v. Rockefeller*, 376 U.S. 52, 84 S.Ct. 603, 11 L.Ed.2d 512 (1964). At issue in *Wright* were four districts contained in a New York apportionment statute. The plaintiffs alleged that the statute excluded nonwhites from one district and concentrated them in the other three. Every member of the Court assumed that the plaintiffs' allegation that the statute "segregated eligible voters by race and place of origin" stated a constitutional claim. The Justices disagreed only as to whether the plaintiffs had carried their burden of proof at trial. * * * *Wright* illustrates the difficulty of determining from the face of a single-member districting plan that it purposefully distinguishes between voters on the basis of race. A reapportionment statute typically does not classify persons at all; it classifies tracts of land, or addresses. Moreover, redistricting differs from other kinds of state decisionmaking in that the legislature always is *aware* of race when it draws district lines, just as it is aware of age, economic status, religious and political persuasion, and a variety of other demographic factors. That sort of race consciousness does not lead inevitably to impermissible race discrimination. As *Wright* demonstrates, when members of a racial group live together in one community, a reapportionment plan that concentrates members of the group in one district and excludes them from others may reflect wholly legitimate purposes. The district lines may be drawn, for example, to provide for compact districts of contiguous territory, or to maintain the integrity of political subdivisions.

The difficulty of proof, of course, does not mean that a racial gerrymander, once established, should receive less scrutiny under the Equal Protection Clause than other state legislation classifying citizens by race. Moreover, it seems clear to us that proof sometimes will not be difficult at all. In some exceptional cases, a reapportionment plan may be so highly irregular that, on its face, it rationally cannot be understood as anything other than an effort to "segregate * * * voters" on the basis of race. *Gomillion, supra. Gomillion*, in which a tortured municipal boundary line was drawn to exclude black voters, was such a case. So, too, would be a case in which a State concentrated a dispersed minority population in a single district by disregarding traditional districting principles such as compactness, contiguity, and respect for political subdivisions. We emphasize that these criteria are important not because they are constitutionally required—they are not, cf. *Gaffney v. Cummings*, 412 U.S. 735, 752, n. 18, 93 S.Ct. 2321, n. 18, 37 L.Ed.2d 298—but because they are objective factors that may serve to defeat a claim that a district has been gerrymandered on racial lines. * * *

Put differently, we believe that reapportionment is one area in which appearances do matter. A reapportionment plan that includes in one district individuals who belong to the same race, but who are otherwise widely separated by geographical and political boundaries, and who may have little in common with one another but the color of their skin, bears an uncomfortable resemblance to political apartheid. It reinforces the perception that members of the same racial group—regardless of their age, education, economic status, or the community in which the live—think alike, share the same political interests, and will prefer the same candidates at the polls. We have rejected such perceptions elsewhere as impermissible racial stereotypes. * * * By perpetuating such notions, a racial gerrymander may exacerbate the very patterns of racial bloc voting that majority-minority districting is sometimes said to counteract.

The message that such districting sends to elected representatives is equally pernicious. When a district obviously is created solely to effectuate the perceived common interests of one racial group, elected officials are more likely to believe that their primary obligation is to represent only the members of that group, rather than their constituency as a whole. This is altogether antithetical to our system of representative democracy. * * *

For these reasons, we conclude that a plaintiff challenging a reapportionment statute under the Equal Protection Clause may state a claim by alleging that the legislation, though race-neutral on its face, rationally cannot be understood as anything other than an effort to separate voters into different districts on the basis of race, and that the separation lacks sufficient justification. It is unnecessary for us to decide whether or how a reapportionment plan that, on its face, can be explained in nonracial terms successfully could be challenged. Thus, we express no view as to whether "the intentional creation of majority-minority districts, without more" always gives rise to an equal protection claim. *Post* (White, J., dissenting). We hold only that, on the facts of this case, plaintiffs have stated a claim sufficient to defeat the state appellees' motion to dismiss. * * *

The dissenters * * * suggest that a racial gerrymander of the sort alleged here is functionally equivalent to gerrymanders for nonracial purposes, such as political gerrymanders. This Court has held political gerrymanders to be justiciable under the Equal Protection Clause. See *Davis v. Bandemer*. But nothing in our case law compels the conclusion that racial and political gerrymanders are subject to precisely the same constitutional scrutiny. In fact, our country's long and persistent history of racial discrimination in voting—as well as our Fourteenth Amendment jurisprudence, which always has reserved the strictest scrutiny for discrimination on the basis of race—would seem to compel the opposite conclusion. * * *

Justice Stevens argues that racial gerrymandering poses no constitutional difficulties when district lines are drawn to favor the minority, rather than the majority. See *post* (Stevens, J., dissenting). We have made clear, however, that equal protection analysis "is not dependent on the race of those burdened or benefited by a particular classification." *Croson*, 488 U.S., at 494, 109 S.Ct., at 722 (plurality opinion). * * *

Finally, nothing in the Court's highly fractured decision in [*United Jewish Organizations of Williamsburgh, Inc. v. Carey*, 430 U.S. 144, 97 S.Ct. 996, 51 L.Ed.2d 229 (1977) (*UJO*)]—on which the District Court almost exclusively relied, and which the dissenters evidently believe controls—forecloses the claim we recognize today. *UJO* concerned New York's revision of a reapportionment plan to include additional majority-minority districts in response to the Attorney General's denial of administrative preclearance under § 5. In that regard, it closely resembles the present case. But the cases are critically different in another way. The plaintiffs in *UJO*—members of a Hasidic community split between two districts under New York's revised redistricting plan—did not allege that the plan, on its face, was so highly irregular that it rationally could be understood only as an effort to segregate voters by race. Indeed, the facts of the case would not have supported such a claim. Three Justices approved the New York statute, in part, precisely because it adhered to traditional districting principles * * *. *UJO*'s framework simply does not apply where, as here, a reapportionment plan is alleged to be so irrational on its face that it immediately offends principles of racial equality. *UJO* set forth a standard under which white voters can establish unconstitutional vote dilution. But it did not purport to overrule *Gomillion* or *Wright*. Nothing in the decision precludes white voters (or voters of any other race) from bringing the analytically distinct claim that a reapportionment plan rationally cannot be understood as anything other than an effort to segregate citizens into separate voting districts on the basis of race without sufficient justification. * * *

Racial classifications of any sort pose the risk of lasting harm to our society. They reinforce the belief, held by too many for too much of our history, that individuals should be judged by the color of their skin. Racial classifications with respect to voting carry particular dangers. Racial gerrymandering, even for remedial purposes, may balkanize us into competing racial factions; it threatens to carry us further from the goal of a political system in which race no longer matters—a goal that the Fourteenth and Fifteenth Amendments embody, and to which the Nation continues to aspire. It is for these reasons that race-based districting by our state legislatures demands close judicial scrutiny. * * *

JUSTICE WHITE, with whom JUSTICE BLACKMUN and JUSTICE STEVENS join, dissenting. * * *

[T]he notion that North Carolina's plan, under which whites remain a voting majority in a disproportionate number of congressional districts, and pursuant to which the State has sent its *first* black representatives since Reconstruction to the United States Congress, might have violated appellants' constitutional rights is both a fiction and a departure from settled equal protection principles. * * * Appellants have not presented a cognizable claim, because they have not alleged a cognizable injury. To date, we have held that only two types of state voting practices could give rise to a constitutional claim. The first involves direct and outright deprivation of the right to vote, for example by means of a poll tax or literacy test. Plainly, this variety is not implicated by appellants' allegations and need not detain us further. The second type of unconstitutional practice is that which "affects the political strength of various groups," *Mobile v. Bolden*, 446 U.S. 55, 100 S.Ct. 1490, 1508, 64 L.Ed.2d 47 (1980) (Stevens, J., concurring in judgment), in violation of the Equal Protection Clause. As for this latter category, we have insisted that members of the political or racial group demonstrate that the challenged action have the intent and effect of unduly diminishing their influence on the political process. * * *

Redistricting plans * * * reflect group interests and inevitably are conceived with partisan aims in mind. To allow judicial interference whenever this occurs would be to invite constant and unmanageable intrusion. Moreover, a group's power to affect the political process does not automatically dissipate by virtue of an electoral loss. Accordingly, we have asked that an identifiable group demonstrate more than mere lack of success at the polls to make out a successful gerrymandering claim. * * * [W]e have * * * [insisted] upon a showing that "the political processes * * * were not equally open to participation by the group in question—that its members had less opportunity than did other residents in the district to participate in the political processes and to elect legislators of their choice." *White v. Regester*, 412 U.S., at 766, 93 S.Ct., at 2339. * * *

I summed up my views on this matter in the plurality opinion in *Davis v. Bandemer*, 478 U.S. 109, 106 S.Ct. 2797, 92 L.Ed.2d 85 (1986). Because districting inevitably is the expression of interest group politics, and because "the power to influence the political process is not limited to winning elections," the question in gerrymandering cases is "whether a particular group has been unconstitutionally denied its chance to effectively influence the political process." Thus, "an equal protection violation may be found only where the electoral system *substantially disadvantages certain voters in their opportunity to influence the political process effectively.*" *Id.*, at 133, 16 S.Ct., at 2810 (emphasis added). By this, I meant that the group must exhibit "strong indicia of lack of political power and the denial of fair representation," so that it could be said that it has "essentially been shut out of the political process." In short, even assuming that racial (or political) factors were considered in the drawing of district boundaries, a showing of discriminatory effects is a "threshold requirement" in the absence of which there is no equal protection violation, and no need to "reach the question of the state interests * * * served by the particular districts."

To distinguish a claim that alleges that the redistricting scheme has discriminatory intent and effect from one that does not has nothing to do with dividing racial classifications between the "benign" and the malicious—an enterprise which, as the majority notes, the Court has treated with skepticism. Rather, the issue is whether the classification based on race discriminates against *anyone* by denying equal access to the political process. * * * The most compelling evidence of the Court's position prior to this day, for it is most directly on point, is *UJO*, 430 U.S. 144, 97 S.Ct. 996, 51 L.Ed.2d 229 (1977). * * * [F]ive Justices were of the view that, absent any contention that the proposed plan was adopted with the intent, or had the effect, of unduly minimizing the white majority's voting strength, the Fourteenth Amendment was not implicated. * * * [I]t is irrefutable that appellants in this proceeding likewise have failed to state a claim. * * * [I]t strains credulity to suggest that North Carolina's purpose in creating a second majority-minority district was to discriminate against members of the majority group by "impairing or burden[ing their] opportunity * * * to participate in the political process." *Id.*, at 179, 97 S.Ct., at 1017 (Stewart, J., concurring in judgment). * * * Whites constitute roughly 76 percent of the total population and 79 percent of the voting age population in North Carolina. Yet, under the State's plan, they still constitute a voting majority in 10 (or 83 percent) of the 12 congressional districts. Though they might be dissatisfied at the prospect of casting a vote for a losing candidate—a lot shared by many, including a disproportionate number of minority voters—surely they cannot complain of discriminatory treatment.

The majority attempts to distinguish *UJO* by imagining a heretofore unknown type of constitutional claim. * * * The logic of its theory appears to be that race-conscious redistricting that "segregates" by drawing odd-shaped lines is qualitatively different from race-conscious redistricting that affects groups in some other way. The distinction is without foundation. * * * *Gomillion* does not assist the majority, for its focus was on the alleged *effect* of the city's action, which was to exclude black voters from the municipality of Tuskegee. As the Court noted, the "inevitable effect of this redefinition of Tuskegee's boundaries" was "to deprive the Negro petitioners discriminatorily of the benefits of residence in Tuskegee." * * * In *Gomillion*, in short, the group that formed the majority at the state level purportedly set out to manipulate city boundaries in order to remove members of the minority, thereby denying them valuable municipal services. No analogous purpose or effect has been alleged in this case. * * *

Racial gerrymanders come in various shades: At-large voting schemes; the fragmentation of a minority group among various districts "so that it is a majority in none," *Voinovich v. Quilter*, 507 U.S. ___, ___, 113 S.Ct. 1149, 1155, 122 L.Ed.2d 500 (1993), otherwise known as "cracking"; the "stacking" of "a large minority population concentration * * * with a larger white population"; and, finally, the "concentration of [minority voters] into districts where they constitute an excessive majority," *Thornburg v. Gingles*, 478 U.S. 30, 46, n. 11, 106 S.Ct. 2752, 2764, n. 11, 92 L.Ed.2d 25 (1986), also called "packing," *Voinovich*, *supra*, ___ U.S., at ___, 113 S.Ct., at 1155. In each instance, race is consciously utilized by the legislature for electoral purposes; in each instance, we have put the plaintiff challenging the district lines to the burden of demonstrating that the plan was meant to, and did in fact, exclude an identifiable racial group from participation in the political process.

Not so, apparently, when the districting "segregates" by drawing odd-shaped lines. In that case, we are told, such proof no longer is needed. * * * Given two districts drawn on similar, race-based grounds, the one does not become more injurious than the other simply by virtue of being snake-like, at least so far as the Constitution is concerned and absent any evidence of differential racial impact. The majority's contrary view is perplexing in light of its concession that "compactness or attractiveness has never been held to constitute an independent federal constitutional requirement for state legislative districts." *Gaffney*, 412 U.S., at 752, n. 18, 93 S.Ct., at 2331, n. 18. It is shortsighted as well, for a regularly shaped district can just as effectively effectuate racially discriminatory gerrymandering as an odd-shaped one. By focusing on looks rather than impact, the majority "immediately casts attention in the wrong direction—toward superficialities of shape and size, rather than toward the political realities of district composition." R. Dixon, Democratic Representation: Reapportionment in Law and Politics 459 (1968).

Limited by its own terms to cases involving unusually-shaped districts, the Court's approach nonetheless will unnecessarily hinder to some extent a State's voluntary effort to ensure a modicum of minority representation. This will be true in areas where the minority population is geographically dispersed. It also will be true where the minority population is not scattered but, for reasons unrelated to race—for example incumbency protection—the State would rather not create the majority-minority district in its most "obvious" location. When, as is the case here, the creation of a majority-minority district does not unfairly minimize the voting power of any other group, the Constitution does not justify, much less mandate, such obstruction. * * *

LANI GUINIER, NO TWO SEATS: THE ELUSIVE QUEST FOR POLITICAL EQUALITY

77 U.Va.L.Rev. 1413, 1458, 1461–1475, 1487–1493 (1991).

I argue that we should redefine the unit of analysis [for claims of vote dilution] from fixed territorial constituencies to voluntary interest constituencies. * * * The term "interest" refers to self-identified interests, meaning those high salience needs, wants, and demands articulated by any politically cohesive group of voters. Interest representation emphasizes the importance of voter autonomy divorced from involuntary, fixed territorial constituencies. Using voting patterns, it measures as a politically cohesive group those voters who identify themselves with each other based on their own evaluation of their shared interests. As a statutory approach to vote dilution, interest representation measures the impact of electoral or voting rules on the legislative representation of self-identified minority voters' interests.

Interest representation attempts first to identify a violation of the right to a meaningful vote by locating politically cohesive minority interests that are submerged within winner-take-all voting structures. Interest representation identifies interest submergence by demonstrating the existence of alternative electoral systems that afford greater minority interest representation and satisfaction. Any such alternatives must recognize the intensity, as well as the existence, of minority voter preferences.

For example, in a 25% black jurisdiction with four at-large representatives, the current single-member districting model would assess the fairness of the election system against the potential representativeness of the alternative, a subdistricted system. The relative fairness of the at-large system would be challenged based on the assumption that black voters would be better represented if one majority-black district could be drawn. If blacks are numerous and concentrated enough to be a majority in one single-member district, the subdistricting strategy would use that district alternative to demonstrate the unfairness of the unmodified at-large system.

In contrast, an interest representation model would assess the fairness of the at-large system against the potential representativeness of an alternative voting system that allowed voters to cumulate their votes. I adopt a cumulative voting system because it permits recognition of both the existence and intensity of minority voter preference and allows strategic voting to enforce reciprocal coalitions. Cumulative voting modifies the at-large system to eliminate its winner-take-all characteristic.

In the modified at-large election, candidates would run jurisdiction-wide, but the threshold for election would be reduced from 51% to something less. In the case of a four person at-large council, the threshold for election would be 21%. Voters would each be given the same number of votes as open seats (four in this case) that they could distribute by their choice among the competing candidates. If black voters are a politically cohesive interest constituency, they might use all four of their votes on one candidate. In a 100 voter jurisdiction, where each black voter gave all four of her votes to one candidate, a 25% black minority could elect a representative. The intensity of their interests and their political cohesion would ensure black voters the ability to elect at least one representative.

When measured against the potential representativeness of an unmodified, winner-take-all at-large voting system at the election level, the cumulative voting system promises greater and more authentic black political representation. In addition, it offers the potential for greater black political power than the single-member districting model. The modified at-large system encourages black representation without disabling or diluting the votes of potential allies. By contrast, the single-member districting approach may require submerging Latino voters within majority-black districts or white Democratic voters within majority-white Republican districts.

Depending on strategic voting behavior, a modified at-large system could encourage coalitions of these voters to develop as a result of the choice of election system. Unlike the subdistricting model, the modified at-large system rewards cooperative, rather than competitive, behavior. Thus, interest representation offers black voters both the chance to elect candidates of their choice as well as the chance for their candidates to work in the legislature with potential legislative allies, trading votes to reflect the intensity of constituent preferences.

As an example, assume that in a jurisdiction with 1000 voters and 10 representatives, blacks are 25% of the population. A subdistrict plan provides roughly "proportionate representation" with 2 majority-black districts of 100 black voters each.

Although the subdistrict plan is a majoritarian approach, a bare majority of 51% in each district can elect a representative. The votes of 49 black voters in each district are unnecessary. In addition, of the 250 blacks in the jurisdiction, 50 of them are not "captured" in either majority-black district but are distributed randomly in the majority-white districts. They are potentially unrepresented in the governing body. Those blacks that are not geographically located in the two single-member districts are represented only "virtually," if at all.

Even more damaging, because only 51 blacks are needed to elect a representative, incumbent representatives may be able to control the electorate through political patronage, political contributions, and political control of the district lines. The black voters are not encouraged to participate actively in the political process because a low turnout still benefits the incumbent. Finally, the black voters in the two majority-black districts have no mechanism to encourage representatives from the majority-white districts virtually to represent their interests.

Whereas subdistricts reinforce authenticity and mobilization concerns by clearly removing black candidates from electoral competition with whites, as a matter of legitimacy a "winner-take-only-some," or interest representation, system actually ensures fewer disaffected voters than the subdistricted majority approach. It allows black voters and their representatives the opportunity to express the intensity of their preference for candidates and for legislative programs. Particular political transactions would depend not just on the number of supporters and opponents but on the relative intensity of preferences. This reflects the insight that if each electoral or legislative vote is insulated from every other, minority interests are consistently disadvantaged. Serial up or down voting permits "a cohesive, well financed majority community to reward itself with enhanced representation, if not outright monopoly" of representation.

In addition, the alternative, nonterritorial approach by its choice of voting arrangement encourages those minority voters or representatives whose votes are not needed to support a single candidate or a particular issue to join with sympathetic white voters to support progressive white candidates or to trade with them votes on issues of indifference. The necessity of strategic voting on salient issues may help identify and shape actual preferences, and coincidentally build cross-racial constituencies. Moreover, by disaggregating the majority, 51% of the people no longer control 100% of either the electoral or the legislative power. Thus, I would argue that the modified at-large, or interest representation, approach promises a more accountable and a more reciprocal voting system. * * *

Assuming for the moment that the approach taken by interest representation, if not better than single-member districts, at least effectively ensures black voter interest representation, the meaning of the term "interest" preference itself still requires further explication. My definition of interests refers to voluntary constituencies that self-identify their interests. Unlike a subdistricting system, interest submergence does not depend on a compulsory territorial constituency or on fixed interests. Rather, interest representation acknowledges the existence of intra-group differences as well as the importance of individual choice in choosing group affiliation. Interests, as expressed in group activity and identity, would be recognized in much the same way that geographic, territorial interests are traditionally thought to define distinct communities.

In other words, voluntary constituencies would be recognized to the extent they conceptually organize and attract sufficient numbers of like-minded voters. * * * [I]nterest representation, which requires strategic voting by a politically cohesive group, does not presume that all blacks will submerge their differences to present a monolithic front. Where voting patterns suggest overwhelming majority but not unanimous issue cohesion, interest representation would allow dissenting blacks to cast their votes as they chose. Interest representation is a phenomenon of choices, where the choices protected are the default positions of the black community: from advocacy by authentic representatives for distinctive group interests to advocacy by authentic representatives for the least well-off. Participation by *all* constituents would be encouraged. * * *

Although it is perhaps possible that interest representation could inadvertently moderate authentic representatives, alienate black voters by virtue of its complexity, or threaten black community autonomy, these fears are overstated. * * * [T]o the extent these concerns are substantial, they need to be balanced against the multiple advantages of interest representation.

First, interest representation attempts to produce citizens who are more committed to achieving political solutions to public policy problems. Because interest representation, unlike the districting strategy, depends on high voter turnout, incumbents will not be able to rely on low turnout to ensure their reelection. Instead, incumbents will find it necessary to mobilize voter interest and participation in an election, a task that will require incumbents to develop substantive programs and proposals. To counteract this, challengers will find it necessary to develop counterproposals, thereby heightening the differences between the candidates.

For their part, minorities may participate in election campaigns in greater numbers than they do in single-member districts, because elections will no longer be zero-sum solutions for minority interests. Minorities will finally have good prospects of winning some victories in the political process due to cumulative voting and the absence of territorial divisions of like-minded voters. This aggregate increase in the substantive content of campaigns will facilitate the self-identification of interest constituencies by heightening voter political awareness and participation as a result of the increased discussion and debate about policy issues. Voters who are energized in this way will actively monitor their issues agenda long after election day. Therefore, under interest representation voters may be more involved in the political process, at both the pre- and post-election stages, than are voters under a single-member district scheme.

Second, under an interest representation approach, incumbents are more accountable to constituents because the incumbents are more vulnerable to shifting alliances and regular removal. Because interest representation emphasizes issues, not the personalities of the candidates, incumbents are less likely to ignore the issues in favor of personal networking and campaigning. In addition, after the election, voter interest constituencies may be sufficiently mobilized to monitor the legislative activity of their elected representatives. Thus, interest representation does not simply reproduce the false consciousness or hierarchy of individual incumbents representing safe black districts; instead, incumbents will be constrained to reflect the policy preferences of their constituents—or else.

Third, interest representation generates incentives for community-based organizations to play a more active role in mobilizing the electorate and monitoring the legislature by both protecting and ratifying authentic representatives. In this sense, interest representation requires sustained organization in a campaign to educate, not merely turn out, voters. Representatives, chosen on the basis of shared interests rather than district proximity, would more likely affiliate with organizations or political parties to realize their goals. Strong minority political parties may then better represent minority voters, both substantively and organizationally.

Fourth, the interest representation approach avoids the resentment of race-conscious districting among groups that are not protected under the Voting Rights Act. Although majority-black single-member districts may elect some black representatives, they also submerge the interests of other groups that reside in the district, such as whites or religious minorities. Under the subdistricting strategy, winner-take-all majoritarianism precludes these voters from enjoying direct representation. This form of interest submergence does not occur under interest representation because the modified at-large system ensures representation to any politically cohesive group above the threshold of exclusion. Consequently, the resentment these voters might otherwise feel for their submergence in a single-member district will be ameliorated or eliminated altogether under interest representation.

Interest representation remedies, implemented pursuant to a voting rights claim, allow whites to form interest-based constituencies, too. Representation allows politically cohesive groups of voters, such as white women, to organize around their chosen issue agenda, without being limited for at least ten years (that is, until the next census is taken) by their own decisions about where to live or by others' arbitrary districting agendas. If geography fails to define completely the minority group interests, it also pigeonholes whites as well.

Fifth, interest representation promotes the value of consensus in group decisionmaking. As I use the term, consensus does not mean a uniform ideology. Rather, it means that participants who are satisfied a fair number of times are less likely to veto or actively fight decisions with which they may weakly disagree. In other words, because interest representation eliminates the winner-take-all feature of the single-district model, dissenters can expect some victories in the legislature or council. The modified at-large scheme will thus be viewed as fair by dissenters, who will, for that reason, be more likely to accept the majority's decision. Even if the minority loses a given vote, that vote will more likely be public-regarding because it will reflect the infusion of minority viewpoints. As a result, interest representation can produce a more informed consensus. * * *

Some may challenge interest representation as accelerating the momentum toward separatism. To its critics, interest representation, which reinforces minority group interests and creates a hospitable environment for minority political parties, arguably "thickens boundaries" between citizens, transforming elections from "occasions for seeking the broadest possible base of support by convincing divergent groups of their common interests" into events that "stress the cleavages separating their supporters from other segments of society."

These critics argue that interest representation inevitably leads to fringe parties, proliferates extremist viewpoints associated with some parliamentary or other proportionate party systems, or just results in stalemate. Critics claim all group-based remedies will promote intergroup conflict, balkanizing what instead should be a uniform, national identity built with stabilizing procedural rules. Critics say majority rule, for example, is necessary as a governing norm to finesse deep and long standing divisions. In this sense, winner-take-all majority rule is claimed to be both more stabilizing and more efficient than a proportionality principle that promotes deliberation or a "dispersed pluralism." * * *

[This argument] * * * suffers * * * from the false premise that interest representation destroys a preexisting general, common, uniform perspective or cultural understanding. For members of racial minority groups who have been, and continue to be, victimized as a result of their racial identity, a deep consensus that does not acknowledge the pervasiveness of the oppression that some, and the indignity that most, have suffered on account of race is impossible. Interest representation thus does not create conflict where none previously existed.

Moreover, a credible argument can be made that interest representation is, in fact, stabilizing. Although it makes present beneficiaries of electoral or voting rules, such as incumbents, perpetually vulnerable, such "cycling" is arguably desirable for four reasons associated with contemporary pluralist analysis. First, from the perspective of minority interests, interest representation is stabilizing when compared to existing political arrangements. For statutorily protected minorities, the stability ostensibly associated with winner-take-all majority rule is illusory, and its attendant efficiency comes at the cost of ignoring or marginalizing minority perspectives. In this sense, multiple, cross-cutting cleavages are more stabilizing than permanent, deep cleavages because the former better realize the majority rule assumption that shifting alliances are a check against the tyranny of the majority.

Indeed, recognizing the intensity of preferences need not lead to chaos because doing so will create incentives for groups presently alienated by their lack of meaningful political power to work within the political process. By giving such groups proportionate power, and consequently distributing preference satisfaction more widely, it helps compensate for their relative lack of power and legitimates the results of the political process. For example, interest representation may improve the collective decisionmaking process by promoting open discussion among a diverse set of participants and by encouraging strategies of negotiation and coalition-building with the possibility of present alliances as well as future victories. By thus giving minorities a fair share of the power, interest representation's proportionality principle surfaces antecedent racial conflict, which arguably delegitimates prejudice and limits its corrosive effect. In this way, interest representation arguably *moderates* political behavior.

Second, cycling helps reduce the tendency of politically entrenched interests to reproduce themselves or to emphasize the peculiarly trans-formative effects of their individual prestige and advancement. Such cycling arguably comports with a more participatory view of political power that potentially yields greater accountability or, at a minimum, affirms the importance of constantly renewing community-based ties. Third, interest representation may potentially reduce racial polarization by encouraging whites to identify or converge their interests with blacks. It avoids the polarizing debate about affirmative action, for example, because it does not create or impose external preferences for interests based on presumptions about group solidarity or injury. Interest prefer-ences are voluntary, self-identified needs or wants that must be realized through organizational initiative and cooperation.

Even if a proportionality principle fails consistently to produce consensus, it may be stabilizing nonetheless if it is capable of generating less conflict than current empowerment strategies. Although there will probably still be some conflict, conflict is more likely to dissipate in an interest representation setting than in a subdistricting environment. For instance, because interest representation allows all groups to self-identify their interests with like-minded groups regardless of their location within the jurisdiction, whites are not directly disadvantaged through interest representation, as they may claim to be through majori-ty-black districting remedies that construct districts in which some whites are district minorities who feel politically powerless.

Finally, the winner-take-some-but-not-all approach contemplates ''strong democracy,'' meaning an invigorated electorate that participates (as opposed to spectates) throughout the political process. For example, interest representation could encourage the development of minority political organizations that would mobilize voters directly to articulate preferences and to monitor the legislative process and that would formal-ize bargains, or at least address issues of intense interest to the minori-ty. Minority voters would thus be empowered to participate interactive-ly through the organization and resources of an accountable, community-based, minority political party, which would have the effect of increasing the accountability of minority representatives.

One need not worry that the development of minority political parties or organizations will necessarily lead to stalemate because stalemate is less probable where, as in interest representation, participants experience continuous opportunities to cooperate and compromise. Indeed, studies of coalition systems do not conclude that stalemate is inevitable. For example, some scholars have concluded from the experience of foreign countries with systems resembling interest representation that long-term government stability can and in fact does exist as a function of the underlying social forces and structural features of such a political system. Furthermore, the argument that multiplication of parties leads to instability, a charge usually levelled against parliamentary systems of government, is less legitimate on a national scale where, as in the United States, the executive is independent of the legislature and certainly is not relevant at the level of local government, which I address here.

In sum, proponents of interest representation posit that changing electoral and collective voting procedures can improve the collective decisionmaking process by including and proportionately reflecting minority interests. Whatever the substantive results, the process can be legitimated and made more deliberative by choosing decisional rules that disaggregate the disproportionate power of the permanent, homogeneous majority. Similarly, conflict between interest groups may be inescapable but need not be unproductive or destabilizing. * * *

JAMIN RASKIN, LEGAL ALIENS, LOCAL CITIZENS: THE HISTORICAL, CONSTITUTIONAL AND THEORETICAL MEANINGS OF ALIEN SUFFRAGE

141 U. Pa. L. Rev. 1391, 1393–1394, 1460–1467 (1993).

As the franchise has expanded over the centuries to take in nearly all adult citizens, one group which voted and participated, at various points over a 150–year period, in at least twenty-two states and territories, lost its historic access to the ballot: inhabitants of individual states who are not citizens of the United States or, to use the reifying but inescapable idiom of immigration law, resident aliens. Today, with the extraordinary, though still largely unwritten, history of alien suffrage safely hidden from view, the U.S. citizenship voting qualification ropes off the franchise in every American state from participation by non-U.S. citizens. As a marker at the perimeter of the American body politic, the citizenship qualification carries the aura of inevitability that once attached to property, race, and gender qualifications. * * *

[T]he current blanket exclusion of noncitizens from the ballot is neither constitutionally required nor historically normal. Moreover, the disenfranchisement of aliens at the local level is vulnerable to deep theoretical objections since resident aliens—who are governed, taxed, and often drafted just like citizens—have a strong democratic claim to being considered members, indeed citizens, of their local communities. Although democratic theory cannot resolve the foundational political question of who belongs to "the people," the ideological traditions of both liberalism and republicanism make available compelling arguments for the inclusion of noncitizens as voters in local elections. The bedrock hostility of the liberal rights tradition to taxation and governance without representation makes noncitizen voting a logically unassailable, if not clearly mandatory, democratic practice. Republicanism presents a somewhat more complicated picture given its historic compatibility with exclusionary practices, but a progressive commitment to dialogic politics and the constitutive value of participation is arguably vindicated by defining universal suffrage without regard to nation-state citizenship. These arguments are deepened by evolving international norms of community-based democracy and human rights and strengthened by important instrumental considerations relating to the surge in immigration which the United States is currently experiencing. * * *

The United States is home to some ten million aliens who work in American businesses and government offices, serve in the armed forces, pay local, state, and federal taxes, and are subject to all of the obligations of citizenship, including military conscription. Since noncitizen voting is neither constitutionally obligatory nor taboo, states and municipalities may approach it as a matter of public policy. But aliens are not presently permitted to vote, or run for office, in any state election, and are therefore shut out from formal political participation at both the state and national level. There are, however, several important examples of noncitizen voting at the local level which can serve as models for interested localities. Since 1968, New York City has granted noncitizens who are the parents of school children the right to vote and run for community school board. The City of Chicago similarly gives noncitizens the right to vote in school board elections.

More expansively, a number of smaller localities in the State of Maryland—including Somerset, Barnesville, Chevy Chase Sections 3 and 5, and Martin's Additions—have for decades extended the franchise in *all* local elections to inhabitants who are not U.S. citizens. As more intimate communities whose alien populations are apparently composed, in substantial part, of World Bank and embassy personnel working in Washington, D.C., these Maryland jurisdictions rest their policies on both natural rights understandings and the early property-based conception of local voting rights. It is necessary to note that most of the inhabitants of these small communities tend to share a similar economic and social status which dilutes the threatening image many citizens have of aliens. They also share a physical proximity which permits them to have unrushed and disarming face-to-face encounters with one another.

But noncitizen voting in Maryland is not (simply, at least) a naive throwback to nineteenth-century small-town life. For on March 31, 1992, Takoma Park, Maryland, a well-integrated city bordering the District of Columbia with a population of 16,700, formally amended its municipal charter to give all residents, regardless of citizenship, the right to vote, and run for office, in local elections. The charter change followed several months of excited political debate and controversy which spilled over into the Washington, D.C. area as a whole. The issue first arose when the Takoma Park Elections Task Force completed its 1990 city council redistricting process. The Task Force found that its new wards had equal numbers of *residents*, as required by law, but that some wards had far more eligible *voters* than others because some contained a large alien population. This imbalance focused attention on two facts: the votes of citizens in wards with high citizen populations were worth much less than votes of citizens in wards with high numbers of aliens; and many city residents with all of the obligations of Takoma Park citizenship lacked the right to vote. The Task Force, by and large unaware of the rich history of alien suffrage in the United States, proposed to the City Council that it place on the November 5, 1991 ballot a referendum question on whether the citizens of Takoma Park favored extending local voting rights to noncitizens.   * * *

The referendum debate unleashed its share of xenophobia and prejudice, but the discussion was generally remarkable for its sobriety. Advocates of the charter amendment mobilized democratic principles to argue for the change and emphasized the local nature of the proposal. The Share the Vote campaign worked to humanize the question by bringing to public attention a number of people, who had come to Takoma Park from all over the world and who would be enfranchised by the change. The Washington Post, for example, interviewed Colin Norman, a Washington correspondent for a British magazine and a citizen of the United Kingdom who came to Takoma Park in 1976.

> [Norman] says he may be more a part of the city than U.S. citizens who are newcomers to the area. "I have as much interest in the community as anyone he said * * * We're not asking for a voice at the national level or in foreign policy," Norman said. "But in local matters, we're no different than somebody who has moved to Takoma Park from California."

Supporters of the change also observed "an urgent practical side to this idea for those kept out of democracy's circle have other ways of making their grievances known * * *. It is better to confront social problems nonviolently in the halls of government than violently in the streets."

Opponents of the measure emphasized that illegal aliens would technically be able to vote along with permanent resident aliens. The former commissioner of the Immigration and Naturalization Service argued that alien suffrage "undermines the value of U.S. citizenship" and that five years "is not an unreasonable time to wait to be able to participate in our democracy." He also made a slippery slope argument that "if local voting by noncitizens is allowed, state and federal voting could be next. Either there is a policy basis for noncitizens to vote, or there is not. If we open the door, it cannot be closed halfway."

The November 5, 1991 noncitizen voting referendum passed by a vote of 1,199 to 1,107. Because the referendum was only advisory, debate continued. But on February 10, 1992, the Takoma Park City Council adopted, by a vote of five to one, a Charter Amendment removing the requirement that voters and candidates for public office in Takoma Park be U.S. citizens in order to participate in the city's biennial elections.   In the meantime, Delegate John Morgan, who represents a district outside of Takoma Park, introduced a bill in the Maryland House of Delegates to prohibit noncitizen voting in local elections. On February 11, the House Committee on Constitutional and Administrative Law conducted a lengthy and impassioned hearing on the legislation.   Bill proponents claimed that noncitizen voting would bring in a tide of unwanted immigrants, while Takoma Park and other noncitizen voting communities argued that this was a local question and home rule should not be invaded.   On March 17, 1992, the bill was defeated by a vote of 11–6 and a final local effort to block implementation of the charter amendment fizzled.   On March 31, 1992, Takoma Park became the largest and most recent municipality in the United States to adopt complete noncitizen voting.   * * *

[T]he people who have joined us on our land are generally here to stay, and the question today is whether they will be democratically integrated and assimilated into our political culture or kept apart as a disenfranchised and increasingly disaffected population.   A number of immigrant groups continue to live on the margins of American society. Recent cases of unrest, delinquency, and riot in immigrant communities, on both the east coast and the west coast, illustrate the dangers of excluding large numbers of people from political membership in their communities.   But it is no answer to say that members of these excluded groups should simply apply for United States' citizenship;   their very alienation renders improbable their participation in the citizenship naturalization process, which is more of an affirmation of a sense of social belonging than a first step towards achieving this goal.   The virtue of extending the vote in local elections to noncitizens is that it invites noncitizens to participate in, and learn about, American political culture and practices without immediately requiring the greater psychic break of surrendering one's given nationality.   Presumably the taste of democratic citizenship that some aliens get from local voting will make them hunger for a greater role in our politics.   If so, the practice of alien suffrage, sometimes derided as a threat to the naturalization process, can become once again, as it was in the last two centuries, a pathway to naturalized citizenship.   * * *

2. THE INITIATIVE AND THE REFERENDUM

The initiative and referendum are means by which voters can decide issues of city policy directly rather than by electing representatives to decide the issues for them.   An initiative is a piece of legislation placed on the ballot by means of a petition signed by a (legally-defined) number of voters.   Passing an initiative can thus be a means of enacting legislation that completely bypasses the representative process, although sometimes an initiative allows the legislature an opportunity to accept or reject the proposal.   A referendum, by contrast, is an election called after a legislative body has already acted on a piece of legislation. Sometimes a referendum election is called by the legislature and sometimes by a petition signed by (the required number of) voters.   A referendum thus enables voters to decide for themselves whether legislation passed by their representatives should be enacted.

The initiative and referendum have long been hailed as models of direct democracy, but they are not without their critics.[1] The following materials—three cases and an article by Derrick Bell—consider some of the problems critics raise about these forms of direct democracy. What aspects of the legislative—and administrative—processes are absent when decisionmaking is made by popular vote? Is there a way to organize popular decisionmaking that might (at the minimum) approximate the amount of informed attention to the public interest that now takes place in administrative or legislative decisionmaking?

CITY OF EASTLAKE v. FOREST CITY ENTERPRISES, INC.

Supreme Court of the United States, 1976.
426 U.S. 668, 96 S.Ct. 2358, 49 L.Ed.2d 132.

MR. CHIEF JUSTICE BURGER delivered the opinion of the Court.

The question in this case is whether a city charter provision requiring proposed land use changes to be ratified by 55% of the votes cast violates the due process rights of a landowner who applies for a zoning change.

The city of Eastlake, Ohio, a suburb of Cleveland, has a comprehensive zoning plan codified in a municipal ordinance. Respondent, a real estate developer, acquired an eight-acre parcel of real estate in Eastlake zoned for "light industrial" uses at the time of purchase.

In May 1971, respondent applied to the City Planning Commission for a zoning change to permit construction of a multi-family, high-rise apartment building. The Planning Commission recommended the proposed change to the City Council, which under Eastlake's procedures could either accept or reject the Planning Commission's recommendation. Meanwhile, by popular vote, the voters of Eastlake amended the city charter to require that any changes in land use agreed to by the Council be approved by a 55% vote in a referendum. The City Council approved the Planning Commission's recommendation for reclassifica-

---

1. See generally, Hsiao, Invisible Cities: The Constitutional Status of Direct Democracy in a Democratic Republic, 41 Duke L.J. 1267 (1992); Baker, Direct Democracy and Discrimination: A Public Choice Perspective, 67 Chi.-Kent L.Rev. 707 (1991); Eule, Judicial Review of Direct Democracy, 99 Yale L.J. 1503 (1990); Cronin, Direct Democracy: The Politics of Initiative, Referendum and Recall (1989); Gordon & Magleby, Pre–Election Judicial Review of Initiatives and Referendums, 64 Notre Dame L.Rev. 298 (1989); Gillette, Plebiscites, Participation and Collective Action in Local Government Law, 86 Mich.L.Rev. 930 (1988); Magleby, Direct Legislation (1984); Ranney (ed.), The Referendum Device (1981); Castello, The Limits of Popular Sovereignty: Using the Initiative Power to Control Legislative Procedure, 74 Calif.L.Rev. 491 (1986); Rosenberg, Referendum Zoning: Legal Doctrine and Practice, 53 U.Cinn.L.Rev. 381 (1984); Sirico, The Constitutionality of the Initiative and Referendum, 65 Iowa L.Rev. 637 (1980); Hogue, Eastlake and Arlington Heights: New Hurdles in Regulating Land Use?, 28 Case W.L.Rev. 41, 43–73 (1977); Trautman, Initiative and Referendum in Washington: A Survey, 49 Wash.L.Rev. 55 (1973).

tion of respondent's property to permit the proposed project. Respondent then applied to the Planning Commission for "parking and yard" approval for the proposed building. The Commission rejected the application, on the ground that the City Council's rezoning action had not yet been submitted to the voters for ratification.

Respondent then filed an action in state court, seeking a judgment declaring the charter provision invalid as an unconstitutional delegation of legislative power to the people. While the case was pending, the City Council's action was submitted to a referendum, but the proposed zoning change was not approved by the requisite 55% margin. Following the election, the Court of Common Pleas and the Ohio Court of Appeals sustained the charter provision.

The Ohio Supreme Court reversed. Concluding that enactment of zoning and rezoning provisions is a legislative function, the court held that a popular referendum requirement, lacking standards to guide the decision of the voters, permitted the police power to be exercised in a standardless, hence arbitrary and capricious manner. Relying on this Court's decisions in *Washington ex rel. Seattle Title Trust Co. v. Roberge*, 278 U.S. 116, 49 S.Ct. 50, 73 L.Ed. 210 (1928), *Thomas Cusack Co. v. Chicago*, 242 U.S. 526, 37 S.Ct. 190, 61 L.Ed. 472 (1917), and *Eubank v. Richmond*, 226 U.S. 137, 33 S.Ct. 76, 57 L.Ed. 156 (1912), but distinguishing *James v. Valtierra*, 402 U.S. 137, 91 S.Ct. 1331, 28 L.Ed.2d 678 (1971), the court concluded that the referendum provision constituted an unlawful delegation of legislative power.   * * *

The conclusion that Eastlake's procedure violates federal constitutional guarantees rests upon the proposition that a zoning referendum involves a delegation of legislative power. A referendum cannot, however, be characterized as a delegation of power. Under our constitutional assumptions, all power derives from the people, who can delegate it to representative instruments which they create. See, *e.g.,* The Federalist No. 39 (Madison). In establishing legislative bodies, the people can reserve to themselves power to deal directly with matters which might otherwise be assigned to the legislature. *Hunter v. Erickson,* 393 U.S. 385, 392, 89 S.Ct. 557, 561, 21 L.Ed.2d 616 (1969).

The reservation of such power is the basis for the town meeting, a tradition which continues to this day in some States as both a practical and symbolic part of our democratic processes. The referendum, similarly, is a means for direct political participation, allowing the people the final decision, amounting to a veto power, over enactments of representative bodies. The practice is designed to "give citizens a voice on questions of public policy." *James v. Valtierra, supra,* 402 U.S., at 141, 91 S.Ct., at 1333.

In framing a state constitution, the people of Ohio specifically reserved the power of referendum to the people of each municipality within the State.

"The initiative and referendum powers are hereby reserved to the people of each municipality on all questions which such municipalities may now or hereafter be authorized by law to control by legislative action * * *."

To be subject to Ohio's referendum procedure, the question must be one within the scope of legislative power. The Ohio Supreme Court expressly found that the City Council's action in rezoning respondent's eight acres from light industrial to high-density residential use was legislative in nature. Distinguishing between administrative and legislative acts, the court separated the power to zone or rezone, by passage or amendment of a zoning ordinance, from the power to grant relief from unnecessary hardship. The former function was found to be legislative in nature. * * *

The Ohio Supreme Court further concluded that the amendment to the city charter constituted a "delegation" of power violative of federal constitutional guarantees because the voters were given no standards to guide their decision. Under Eastlake's procedure, the Ohio Supreme Court reasoned, no mechanism existed, nor indeed could exist, to assure that the voters would act rationally in passing upon a proposed zoning change. This meant that "appropriate legislative action [would] be made dependent upon the potentially arbitrary and unreasonable whims of the voting public." The potential for arbitrariness in the process, the court concluded, violated due process.

Courts have frequently held in other contexts that a congressional delegation of power to a regulatory entity must be accompanied by discernible standards, so that the delegatee's action can be measured for its fidelity to the legislative will. Assuming, *arguendo,* their relevance to state governmental functions, these cases involved a delegation of power by the legislature to regulatory bodies, which are not directly responsible to the people; this doctrine is inapplicable where, as here, rather than dealing with a delegation of power, we deal with a power reserved by the people to themselves.[10]

In basing its claim on federal due process requirements, respondent also invokes *Euclid v. Ambler Realty Co.,* 272 U.S. 365, 47 S.Ct. 114, 71 L.Ed. 303 (1926), but it does not rely on the direct teaching of that case. Under *Euclid,* a property owner can challenge a zoning restriction if the measure is "clearly arbitrary and unreasonable, having no substantial relation to the public health, safety, morals, or general welfare." If the substantive result of the referendum is arbitrary and capricious, bearing no relation to the police power, then the fact that the voters of Eastlake

---

10. The Ohio Supreme Court's analysis of the requirements for standards flowing from the Fourteenth Amendment also sweeps too broadly. Except as a legislative history informs an analysis of legislative action, there is no more advance assurance that a legislative body will act by conscientiously applying consistent standards than there is with respect to voters. For example, there is no certainty that the City Council in this case would act on the basis of "standards" explicit or otherwise in Eastlake's comprehensive zoning ordinance. Nor is there any assurance that townspeople assembling in a town meeting, as the people of Eastlake could do, *Hunter v. Erickson,* 393 U.S. 385, 392, 89 S.Ct. 557, 561, 21 L.Ed.2d 616 (1969), will act according to consistent standards. The critical constitutional inquiry, rather, is whether the zoning restriction produces arbitrary or capricious results.

wish it so would not save the restriction. As this Court held in invalidating a charter amendment enacted by referendum:

> "The sovereignty of the people is itself subject to those constitutional limitations which have been duly adopted and remain unrepealed." *Hunter v. Erickson,* 393 U.S., at 392, 89 S.Ct., at 561.

But no challenge of the sort contemplated in *Euclid v. Ambler Realty* is before us. The Ohio Supreme Court did not hold, and respondent does not argue, that the present zoning classification under Eastlake's comprehensive ordinance violates the principles established in *Euclid v. Ambler Realty.* If respondent considers the referendum result itself to be unreasonable, the zoning restriction is open to challenge in state court, where the scope of the state remedy available to respondent would be determined as a matter of state law, as well as under Fourteenth Amendment standards. That being so, nothing more is required by the Constitution.

Nothing in our cases is inconsistent with this conclusion. Two decisions of this Court were relied on by the Ohio Supreme Court in invalidating Eastlake's procedure. The thread common to both decisions is the delegation of legislative power, originally given by the people to a legislative body, and in turn delegated by the legislature to a *narrow segment* of the community, not to the people at large. In *Eubank v. Richmond,* 226 U.S. 137, 33 S.Ct. 76, 57 L.Ed. 156 (1912), the Court invalidated a city ordinance which conferred the power to establish building setback lines upon the owners of two-thirds of the property abutting any street. Similarly, in *Washington ex rel. Seattle Title Trust Co. v. Roberge,* 278 U.S. 116, 49 S.Ct. 50, 73 L.Ed. 210 (1928), the Court struck down an ordinance which permitted the establishment of philanthropic homes for the aged in residential areas, but only upon the written consent of the owners of two-third of the property within 400 feet of the proposed facility.

Neither *Eubank* nor *Roberge* involved a referendum procedure such as we have in this case; the standardless delegation of power to a limited group of property owners condemned by the Court in *Eubank* and *Roberge* is not to be equated with decisionmaking by the people through the referendum process. The Court of Appeals for the Ninth Circuit put it this way:

> "A referendum, however, is far more than an expression of ambiguously founded neighborhood preference. It is the city itself legislating through its voters—an exercise by the voters of their traditional right through direct legislation to override the views of their elected representatives as to what serves the public interest."

Our decision in *James v. Valtierra,* upholding California's mandatory referendum requirement, confirms this view. Mr. Justice Black, speaking for the Court in that case, said:

> "This procedure ensures that *all the people* of a community will have a voice in a decision which may lead to large expenditures of

local governmental funds for increased public services * * *." (emphasis added).

Mr. Justice Black went on to say that a referendum procedure, such as the one at issue here, is a classic demonstration of "devotion to democracy * * *." As a basic instrument of democratic government, the referendum process does not, in itself, violate the Due Process Clause of the Fourteenth Amendment when applied to a rezoning ordinance. Since the rezoning decision in this case was properly reserved to the People of Eastlake under the Ohio Constitution, the Ohio Supreme Court erred in holding invalid, on federal constitutional grounds, the charter amendment permitting the voters to decide whether the zoned use of respondent's property could be altered. * * *

JUSTICE STEVENS, with whom MR. JUSTICE BRENNAN joins, dissenting * * *.

As the Justices of the Ohio Supreme Court recognized, we are concerned with the fairness of a provision for determining the right to make a particular use of a particular parcel of land. In such cases, the state courts have frequently described the capricious character of a decision supported by majority sentiment rather than reference to articulable standards. Moreover, they have limited statutory referendum procedures to apply only to approvals of comprehensive zoning ordinances as opposed to amendments affecting specific parcels. This conclusion has been supported by characterizing particular amendments as "administrative" and revision of an entire plan as "legislative."

In this case the Ohio Supreme Court characterized the Council's approval of respondent's proposal as "legislative." I think many state courts would have characterized it as "administrative." The courts thus may well differ in their selection of the label to apply to this action, but I find substantial agreement among state tribunals on the proposition that requiring a citywide referendum for approval of a particular proposal like this is manifestly unreasonable. Surely that is my view.

The essence of fair procedure is that the interested parties be given a reasonable opportunity to have their dispute resolved on the merits by reference to articulable rules. If a dispute involves only the conflicting rights of private litigants, it is elementary that the decision-maker must be impartial and qualified to understand and to apply the controlling rules.

I have no doubt about the validity of the initiative or the referendum as an appropriate method of deciding questions of community policy. I think it is equally clear that the popular vote is not an acceptable method of adjudicating the rights of individual litigants. The problem presented by this case is unique, because it may involve a three-sided controversy, in which there is at least potential conflict between the rights of the property owner and the rights of his neighbors, and also potential conflict with the public interest in preserving the city's basic zoning plan. If the latter aspect of the controversy were predominant, the referendum would be an acceptable procedure. On the other hand, when the record indicates without contradiction that there is no threat to the general public interest in preserving the city's plan as it does in this case, since respondent's proposal was approved by both the Planning Commission and the City Council and there has been no allegation that the use of this eight-acre parcel for apartments rather than light industry would adversely affect the community or raise any policy issue of citywide concern—I think the case should be treated as one in which it is essential that the private property owner be given a fair opportunity to have his claim determined on its merits.

As Justice Stern points out in his concurring opinion, it would be absurd to use a referendum to decide whether a gasoline station could be operated on a particular corner in the city of Cleveland. The case before us is not that clear because we are told that there are only 20,000 people in the city of Eastlake. Conceivably, an eight-acre development could be sufficiently dramatic to arouse the legitimate interest of the entire community; it is also conceivable that most of the voters would be indifferent and uninformed about the wisdom of building apartments rather than a warehouse or factory on these eight acres. The record is silent on which of these alternatives is the more probable. Since the ordinance places a manifestly unreasonable obstacle in the path of every property owner seeking any zoning change, since it provides no standards or procedures for exempting particular parcels or claims from the referendum requirement, and since the record contains no justification for the use of the procedure in this case, I am persuaded that we should respect the state judiciary's appraisal of the fundamental fairness of this decisionmaking process in this case.

MEYER v. GRANT

Supreme Court of the United States, 1988.
486 U.S. 414, 108 S.Ct. 1886, 100 L.Ed.2d 425.

Justice Stevens delivered the opinion of the Court.   * * *

Colorado is one of several States that permits its citizens to place propositions on the ballot through an initiative process. Under Colorado law, proponents of an initiative measure must submit the measure to the State Legislative Council and the Legislative Drafting Office for review and comment. The draft is then submitted to a three-member title board, which prepares a title, submission clause, and summary. After approval of the title, submission clause, and summary, the proponents of the measure then have six months to obtain the necessary signatures, which must be in an amount equal to at least five percent of the total number of voters who cast votes for all candidates for the Office of Secretary of State at the last preceding general election. If the signature requirements are met, the petitions may be filed with the Secretary of State, and the measure will appear on the ballot at the next general election.

State law requires that the persons who circulate the approved drafts of the petitions for signature be registered voters. Before the signed petitions are filed with the Secretary of State, the circulators must sign affidavits attesting that each signature is the signature of the person whose name it purports to be and that, to the best of their knowledge and belief, each person signing the petition is a registered voter. The payment of petition circulators is punished as a felony.

Appellees are proponents of an amendment to the Colorado Constitution that would remove motor carriers from the jurisdiction of the Colorado Public Utilities Commission. In early 1984 they obtained approval of a title, submission clause, and summary for a measure proposing the amendment and began the process of obtaining the 46,737 signatures necessary to have the proposal appear on the November 1984 ballot. Based on their own experience as petition circulators, as well as that of other unpaid circulators, appellees concluded that they would need the assistance of paid personnel to obtain the required number of signatures within the allotted time. They then brought this action under 42 U.S.C. section 1983 against the Secretary of State and the Attorney General of Colorado seeking a declaration that the statutory prohibition against the use of paid circulators violates their rights under the First Amendment. * * *

We fully agree with the Court of Appeals' conclusion that this case involves a limitation on political expression subject to exacting scrutiny. * * * The circulation of an initiative petition of necessity involves both the expression of a desire for political change and a discussion of the merits of the proposed change. Although a petition circulator may not have to persuade potential signatories that a particular proposal should prevail to capture their signatures, he or she will at least have to persuade them that the matter is one deserving of the public scrutiny and debate that would attend its consideration by the whole electorate. This will in almost every case involve an explanation of the nature of the proposal and why its advocates support it. Thus, the circulation of a petition involves the type of interactive communication concerning political change that is appropriately described as "core political speech."

The refusal to permit appellees to pay petition circulators restricts political expression in two ways: First, it limits the number of voices who will convey appellees' message and the hours they can speak and, therefore, limits the size of the audience they can reach. Second, it makes it less likely that appellees will garner the number of signatures necessary to place the matter on the ballot, thus limiting their ability to make the matter the focus of statewide discussion. The Colorado Supreme Court has itself recognized that the prohibition against the use of paid circulators has the inevitable effect of reducing the total quantum of speech on a public issue. When called upon to consider the constitutionality of the statute at issue here in another context in *Urevich v. Woodard*, 667 P.2d 760, 763 (Colo.1983), that court described the burden the statute imposes on First Amendment expression: * * *

" 'The securing of sufficient signatures to place an initiative measure on the ballot is no small undertaking. Unless the proponents of a measure can find a large number of volunteers, they must hire persons to solicit signatures or abandon the project. I think we can take judicial notice of the fact that the solicitation of signatures on petitions is work. It is time-consuming and it is tiresome—so much so that it seems that few but the young have the strength, the ardor and the stamina to engage in it, unless, of course, there is some remuneration.' ''

We agree with the Court of Appeals' conclusion that the statute trenches upon an area in which the importance of First Amendment protections is "at its zenith." For that reason the burden that Colorado must overcome to justify this criminal law is well-nigh insurmountable. * * *

We are not persuaded by the State's arguments that the prohibition is justified by its interest in making sure that an initiative has sufficient grass roots support to be placed on the ballot, or by its interest in protecting the integrity of the initiative process. As the Court of Appeals correctly held, the former interest is adequately protected by the requirement that no initiative proposal may be placed on the ballot unless the required number of signatures has been obtained.[7]

The State's interest in protecting the integrity of the initiative process does not justify the prohibition because the State has failed to demonstrate that it is necessary to burden appellees' ability to communicate their message in order to meet its concerns. The Attorney General has argued that the petition circulator has the duty to verify the authenticity of signatures on the petition and that compensation might provide the circulator with a temptation to disregard that duty. No evidence has been offered to support that speculation, however, and we are not prepared to assume that a professional circulator—whose qualifications for similar future assignments may well depend on a reputation for competence and integrity—is any more likely to accept false signatures than a volunteer who is motivated entirely by an interest in having the proposition placed on the ballot.

Other provisions of the Colorado statute deal expressly with the potential danger that circulators might be tempted to pad their petitions with false signatures. It is a crime to forge a signature on a petition, to

<hr/>

7. Colorado also seems to suggest that it is permissible to mute the voices of those who can afford to pay petition circulators. See Brief for Appellants 17. "But the concept that government may restrict the speech of some elements of our society in order to enhance the relative voice of others is wholly foreign to the First Amendment." *Buckley [v. Valeo],* 424 U.S. 1, 48–49 (1976). The concern that persons who can pay petition circulators may succeed in getting measures on the ballot when they might otherwise have failed cannot defeat First Amendment rights. As we said in *First National Bank of Boston v. Belotti,* 435 U.S. 765, 790–791 (1978), paid advocacy "may influence the outcome of the vote; this would be

its purpose. But the fact that advocacy may persuade the electorate is hardly a reason to suppress it * * *. '[T]he concept that government may restrict the speech of some elements of our society in order to enhance the relative voice of others is wholly foreign to the First Amendment * * *.' *Buckley,* 424, U.S., at 48–49 * * *. [T]he people in our democracy are entrusted with the responsibility for judging and evaluating the relative merits of conflicting arguments." Cf. *Brown v. Hartlage,* 456 U.S. 45, 60 (1982) ("[t]he State's fear that voters might make an ill-advised choice does not provide the State with a compelling justification for limiting speech").

make false or misleading statements relating to a petition, or to pay someone to sign a petition. Further, the top of each page of the petition must bear a statement printed in red ink warning potential signatories that it is a felony to forge a signature on a petition or to sign the petition when not qualified to vote and admonishing signatories not to sign the petition unless they have read and understand the proposed initiative. These provisions seem adequate to the task of minimizing the risk of improper conduct in the circulation of a petition, especially since the risk of fraud or corruption, or the appearance thereof, is more remote at the petition stage of an initiative than at the time of balloting. *Cf. First National Bank of Boston v. Bellotti*, 435 U.S., at 790 ("[t]he risk of corruption perceived in cases involving candidate elections * * * simply is not present in a popular vote on a public issue").

"[L]egislative restrictions on advocacy of the election or defeat of political candidates are wholly at odds with the guarantees of the First Amendment." *Buckley v. Valeo*, 424 U.S., at 50. That principle applies equally to "the discussion of political policy generally or advocacy of the passage or defeat of legislation." *Id.*, at 48. The Colorado statute prohibiting the payment of petition circulators imposes a burden on political expression that the State has failed to justify. The Court of Appeals correctly held that the statute violates the First and Fourteenth Amendments. * * *

BUILDING INDUSTRY ASSOCIATION OF SOUTHERN CALIFORNIA v. CITY OF CAMARILLO

Supreme Court of California, 1986.
41 Cal.3d 810, 226 Cal.Rptr. 81, 718 P.2d 68.

LUCAS, JUSTICE.

This case presents two issues for review: (1) Is Evidence Code section 669.5, which shifts the burden of proof in actions challenging the validity of growth control ordinances, applicable to such an ordinance enacted by the initiative process? (2) Is Government Code section 65863.6, which requires cities and counties to balance housing needs against public service needs before passing growth control ordinances, and to list in those ordinances findings as to the public health, safety, and welfare to be promoted which justify reducing the housing opportunities of the region, applicable to a growth control ordinance enacted by means of the initiative process?

We conclude that Evidence Code section 669.5 applies to ordinances enacted by initiative after the effective date of that section, but that Government Code section 65863.6 does not apply to such ordinances. * * *

On June 2, 1981, the voters of the City of Camarillo (City) adopted an initiative for a growth control ordinance, which was referred to as Measure A. The stated purpose of the ordinance was to achieve a steady

rate of residential growth and insure the adequacy of city, school, and recreation facilities. Measure A limited the number of "dwelling units" constructed in City to 400 per year for the years 1982 to 1995. Single family homes, subsidized low income and senior citizen housing, remodelling of existing dwellings, and fourplexes or lesser numbered multiple dwellings on a single lot were exempted from the ordinance. Developers must compete each year for the right to construct these 400 units.
* * *

In 1980, the Legislature adopted Evidence Code section 669.5, which establishes a presumption that growth limitation ordinances adversely affect regional housing needs and places the burden of proof on the city or county to show that the ordinance is necessary to promote public health, safety, and welfare. It is clear from section 1 of Assembly Bill No. 3252 (which added § 669.5 to the Evidence Code) that the Legislature intended to shift the burden of proof to the proponents of growth control legislation as a matter of public policy in order to counteract unjustified limitations on the supply of local housing sufficient to meet the municipality's share of regional housing needs. * * *

Amicus San Clementeans for Managed Growth argues that section 669.5 substantially impairs the ability of the people to exercise initiative power because the proponents of the initiative would not have an effective way to defend it. Despite the fact that the city or county would have a duty to defend the ordinance, a city or county might not do so with vigor if it has underlying opposition to the ordinance. Furthermore, the proponents of the initiative have no guarantee of being permitted to intervene in the action, a matter which is discretionary with the trial court. This argument would have merit if intervention was unavailable. But when a city or county is required to defend an initiative ordinance and, because of Evidence Code section 669.5, must shoulder the burden of proving reasonable relationship to public health, safety or welfare, we believe the trial court in most instances should allow intervention by proponents of the initiative. To fail to do so may well be an abuse of discretion. Permitting intervention by the initiative proponents under these circumstances would serve to guard the people's right to exercise initiative power, a right that must be jealously defended by the courts.

City suggests that local governments might not be able to bear the burden of proof needed to sustain an initiative measure because they would not possess the necessary planning data. This suggestion largely ignores the reality of land use planning in this state. For example, prior to its adoption, Measure A was debated at public forums and in the newspapers. Over $107,000 was spent by proponents and opponents of Measure A in the campaign. The information generated by such campaigns can serve as data for the local government to use in defending the ordinance. In addition, cities are required by state law to develop a housing element as part of a general plan. This process develops additional and substantial data concerning housing within the city and the general area, all of which is readily available to the local government.

Evidence Code section 669.5 will not impede the adoption of growth control ordinances. It simply shifts to the local government the burden of proving that the growth control ordinance is necessary for the protection of the public health, safety, or welfare if the ordinance is challenged. Because local government is capable of carrying out the requirement of section 669.5, whether or not the growth control ordinance originated as an initiative measure, we conclude that no unconstitutional impediment of the initiative process occurs. * * *

Government Code section 65863.6 is contained in a chapter of the code relating to zoning regulations. The section requires a city or county to "consider the effect of ordinances" on local housing needs and to balance those housing needs against the public service needs and the available fiscal and environmental services. Any ordinance adopted must contain findings as to the public health, safety, and welfare factors which justify restricting the housing opportunities. * * *

When the Legislature wrote that "each county and city shall consider the effect of ordinances adopted pursuant to this chapter on the housing needs of the region * * * and balance these needs against the public service needs of its residents and available fiscal and environmental resources," it could not have intended the *electorate* to undertake this process when enacting legislation by initiative. How can one prove that the voters weighed and balanced the regional housing needs against the public service, fiscal, and environmental needs? We agree with *Arnel Development Co. v. City of Costa Mesa* (1981) 126 Cal.App.3d 330, 335, 178 Cal.Rptr. 723, that "what was in the minds of the electorate in adopting the initiative is * * * immaterial." It is simply not logical or feasible to place this balancing requirement on the voters.

The second requirement of section 65863.6, that findings be contained in the ordinance which detail the public health, safety, and welfare factors which justify reducing housing opportunities, is merely a requirement to specify the results of the consideration and balancing process required by the first part of the section. The fact that supposed "findings" are set forth in an initiative measure which is passed by the electorate does not really show that the statutory consideration and balancing process actually took place. To so assume would place form over substance. "Findings" drawn up by the drafters of an initiative cannot truly satisfy the requirements of this statute. The section lays out procedures for a governing body to follow before enacting a growth control ordinance, but the words cannot be stretched to apply to a measure passed by initiative.

Section 65863.6 establishes guidelines that can be carried out by a city or county government, but which reasonably cannot be satisfied by the initiative process. For this reason, we conclude that the section does not apply to initiative measures. To hold otherwise would place an insurmountable obstacle in the path of the initiative process and effectively give legislative bodies the only authority to enact this sort of zoning ordinance. Nevertheless, growth control ordinances must meet certain other requirements. An initiative ordinance such as Measure A still must comply with the requirement that it be substantially and reasonably related to the welfare of the region affected. It cannot unfairly discriminate against a particular parcel of property and it cannot be arbitrary or capricious. * * *

DERRICK BELL, THE REFERENDUM: DEMOCRACY'S BARRIER TO RACIAL EQUALITY

54 Wash.L.Rev. 1, 1, 2–3, 6, 8, 9, 13–21, 24–26 (1978).

"Provisions for referendums demonstrate devotion to democracy, not to bias, discrimination, or prejudice."

—Justice Hugo Black

For most Americans, whether or not legally trained, Justice Black's statement is unexceptional, accepted as a truism in harmony with the principles of life in a free society. As proponents of referenda and initiatives never tire of asking, if voters are smart enough to elect representatives to make their laws, are they not just as able to make the laws themselves? At first glance, this seems logical. But blacks and other nonwhite groups in this society cannot afford the luxury of reliance on either truisms or the appearance of logic. Their status, success, and sometimes even survival may depend on an instant recognition of the real danger lurking behind what whites might consider "generally accepted principles." Experience is a far safer guide than rhetoric; and the experience of blacks with the referendum has proved ironically that the more direct democracy becomes, the more threatening it is. * * *

When Justice Black hailed referendum provisions as reflecting a devotion to democracy, and not proof of "bias, discrimination, or prejudice," his was not simply a rhetorical flourish. The statement embodied a central principle of his 1971 majority opinion in *James v. Valtierra*. In that case, black and Mexican–American indigents had challenged Article 34 of the California constitution, which required prior approval in a local referendum before a state public body could develop a federally financed low-rent housing project. They argued that Article 34 unreasonably discriminated, explicitly against the poor and implicitly against minority groups, because it mandated special voter approval for low-income housing. A three-judge federal court held that the provision imposed a special procedural burden on the legislative capacity to assist minorities, an action previously barred by the Supreme Court in *Hunter v. Erickson*. Consequently, the lower court ruled that Article 34 denied the plaintiffs equal protection. * * *

The Supreme Court, however, reversed. Justice Black, writing for a 5–3 majority, distinguished *Hunter* as involving a referendum that specifically burdened racial minorities. He perceived little evidence that the housing referendum required by Article 34 relied on "distinctions based on race." Noting that mandatory referenda were required by California law for other actions, albeit not connected with housing, Justice Black viewed the referendum as a legitimate vehicle for ensuring "that all the people of a community will have a voice in a decision which may lead to large expenditures of local governmental funds for increased public services and to lower tax revenues." * * *

Chief Justice Burger relied heavily on Justice Black's *Valtierra* opinion in *City of Eastlake v. Forest City Enterprises, Inc.* That decision upheld a charter provision of the suburban town of Eastlake, Ohio, which required approval of all zoning changes by a fifty-five percent referendum vote. The Ohio Supreme Court had found that the requirement frustrated a multifamily, high rise apartment project, in violation of the owner-developer's due process rights. Calling the referendum process "a basic instrument of democratic government," Chief Justice Burger adopted Justice Black's view that "[t]his procedure ensures that *all the people* of a community will have a voice in a decision which may lead to large expenditures of local governmental funds for increased public services." * * *

Referendum provisions simply repealing fair housing ordinances or laws and upsetting city council or zoning commission approval to build low-income housing have become a standard means of barring minorities from suburban, residential communities. * * * The question then is whether, in the practice of popular sovereignty, there are unacknowledged aspects of racial discrimination or some other basis, such as a serious danger to our legislative form of government, which entitle minority groups to special protection when their interests are disadvantaged by repeal of protective legislation through the use of initiative or referendum. * * *

Public officials, even those elected on more or less overtly racist campaigns, may prove responsive to minority pressures for civil rights measures once in office or, at least, be open to the negotiation and give-and-take that constitutes much of the political process. Thus, legislators may vote for, or executive officials may sign, a civil rights or social reform bill with full knowledge that a majority of their constituents oppose the measure. They are in the spotlight and do not wish publicly to advocate racism; they cannot openly attribute their opposition to "racist constituents." The more neutral reasons for opposition are often inadequate in the face of serious racial injustices, particularly those posing threats not confined to the minority community.

When the legislative process is turned back to the citizenry either to enact laws by initiative or to review existing laws through the referendum, few of the concerns that can transform the "conservative" politician into a "moderate" public official are likely to affect the individual voter's decision. No political factors counsel restraint on racial passions emanating from longheld and little considered beliefs and fears. Far from being the pure path to democracy that Justice Black proclaimed, direct democracy, carried out in the privacy of the voting booth, has diminished the ability of minority groups to participate in the democratic process. Ironically, because it enables the voters' racial beliefs and fears to be recorded and tabulated in their pure form, the referendum has been a most effective facilitator of that bias, discrimination, and prejudice which has marred American democracy from its earliest day.

Courts have been reluctant to grapple with or even acknowledge the plethora of racist influences and status and class concerns which come into play when the future of a fair housing law is to be decided at the voting booth, or when the electorate must approve, perhaps as in *City of Eastlake* by some super-majority, a legislative or administrative decision to construct a low-income housing project. Any serious consideration of the degree to which prejudice affects the outcome of race-related referenda must at the very least bring an end to the uncritical acceptance and repetition of the unproved assumptions that direct voting techniques are fair and faithful reflections of the country's highest democratic values.

Chief Justice Burger's majority opinion in *City of Eastlake,* for example, relied too heavily on the fiction that the referendum process is the exercise of a nondelegated legislative power which, for some unexplained reason, gains legitimacy and need not even be scrutinized to insure regularity, merely because it is exercised directly by the people. For support, the Chief Justice turned to history, comparing the referendum with the New England town meeting, which he deemed "both a practical and symbolic part of our democratic processes." But, as several historians have pointed out, the colonial town meeting's effectiveness was due largely to the cultural and political homogeneity of its participants. The town meeting was less a forum for conflicting opinions than a place for ratifying, usually by unanimous vote, prior understandings of the community. The meeting expressed the will of a homogenous electorate shaped by exclusionary controls on the admission of new residents. Such exclusionary controls were as tight as those now achieved by zoning referenda in modern suburbs.

Subtle social pressures in those small communities tended to minimize dissent, and even though the communities were small, they often lacked adequate information. James Madison, who preferred representative government because it fostered consideration and compromise of competing interests, believed that popular democracy was prone to majority dictatorship because there were few checks on the temptation to sacrifice minority interests or disadvantage unpopular individuals.

Madison's eighteenth-century fears became nineteenth-century reality when, for example, voters in the Oregon territory overwhelmingly approved an 1857 referendum law intended to exclude all free blacks. Despite its very small black population, residents of the territory had discussed barring blacks for several years, but neither the legislature nor constitutional conventions would approve such a measure because each political party feared that another would be able to exploit the issue. When the proposal was finally submitted to a popular vote, however, it received more support than an accompanying antislavery proposition.

Voting on both issues reflected the whites' belief that they should not have to compete with slaves or free blacks for jobs, that blacks would bring crime and disease, and that Oregon should be preserved for the white race. The same motivation prompted the citizens of Kansas to adopt a similar restriction against blacks in 1855. Even earlier, Indiana and Illinois had voted by large majorities to include anti-black immigration provisions in their constitutions. Although anti-black immigration laws were seldom enforced, historian Leon Litwack regards them both as a constant reminder to Negroes of their inferior position in society and as a convenient excuse for whites to engage in mob violence and frequent harassment of the black population.

No court seems to have considered the potential of present-day barriers against low-income housing to convey the same message or similarly to encourage harassment of those minority families who manage to move into such areas. Certainly, the Court majorities in *Valtierra* and *City of Eastlake* failed to grasp the point, although Justice Stevens, dissenting in the *Eastlake* case, recognized the exclusionary impact of the referendum requirement.

A realistic assessment of referenda and initiatives must include an examination of how they have developed in practice as well as a description of their theoretical democratic virtues. Direct legislation, the creation of progressives of another era, today poses more danger to social progress than the problems of governmental unresponsiveness it was intended to cure. This is not to suggest that we ought to ignore the defects and disappointments of the representative system which today, as in the past, have spurred public recourse to direct legislation. All too often, both Congress and the President become targets and, one fears, the captives of powerful business interests. It is also undeniable that representatives may vote on bills which they do not understand or concerning which they have been improperly influenced.

Nevertheless, our distrust and dissatisfaction with the Congress, with state and local representatives, and with executive officials should not so quickly lead us to conclude that increased reliance on direct democracy will avoid those evils to which legislatures and Congress seem so vulnerable. Supporters of minority rights must be concerned that both the initiative and the referendum often serve those opposed to reform. It is clear, for example, that direct legislation is used effectively by residents of homogenous middle-class communities to prevent unwanted development—especially development that portends increased size or heterogeneity of population.

Today, direct democracy is used comparatively infrequently to curb abuses in government or otherwise to control elected officials. Rather, intense interest is generated when the issues are seemingly clear-cut and often emotional matters such as liquor, gun control, pollution, pornography, or race. Complicated taxation problems and matters of governmental structure, on the other hand, typically evoke little voter response.

The emotionally charged atmosphere often surrounding referenda and initiatives can easily reduce the care with which the voters consider the matters submitted to them. Tumultuous, media-oriented campaigns, such as the ones successfully used to repeal ordinances recognizing the rights of homosexuals in Dade County, Florida, St. Paul, Minnesota, and Eugene, Oregon, are not conducive to careful thinking and voting. A similar furor surrounded the innovative "anti-pornography" law enacted by initiative in the State of Washington but promptly declared unconstitutional in *Spokane Arcades, Inc. v. Ray.*

Appeals to prejudice, oversimplification of the issues, and exploitation of legitimate concerns by promising simplistic solutions to complex problems often characterize referendum and initiative campaigns. Of course, politicians, too, may offer quick cure-alls to gain electoral support and may spend millions on election campaigns that are as likely to obfuscate as to elucidate the issues. But we vote politicians into office, not into law. Once in office, they may become well-informed, responsible representatives; at the least, their excesses may be curtailed by the checks and balances of the political process.

The success or failure of ballot-box legislation, therefore, may depend less on the merits of the issue than on who is financing the campaign. One California public relations official boasted that he could put any issue on the California state ballot for $325,000. Even before the Supreme Court's rejection of spending regulations in *First National Bank of Boston v. Bellotti,* large corporations were investing huge sums in referenda campaigns. With so much at stake it is not surprising to find direct voting procedures criticized for phrasing proposals deceptively, for abusing the signature gathering process, especially by professional signature gathering organizations, and for political sloganeering intended to obscure and confuse public discussion.

The Court's failure to review more closely the many opportunities for misrepresentation, financial abuse, and outright fraud can only encourage campaigners to appeal to prejudice. The record of recent ballot legislation reflects all too accurately the conservative, even intolerant, attitudes citizens display when given the chance to vote their fears and prejudices, especially when exposed to expensive media campaigns. The security of minority rights and the value of racial equality which those rights affirm are endangered by the possibility of popular repeal.
* * *

Unfortunately, the racial motivations and discriminatory impact of many modern referenda and initiatives cannot similarly be attacked directly because the measures are couched in racially neutral terms and may be viewed as serving some legitimate, nonracial public purpose. The current Court has refused to invalidate laws as invidiously discriminatory merely because they have discriminatory impact; the Court insists that a discriminatory purpose must be shown. Blacks and other minorities will encounter substantial difficulty when they challenge a referendum on race discrimination grounds because, as in *Valtierra,* they must show "that a law seemingly neutral on its face is in fact aimed at a racial minority."

However, the racially discriminatory impact of ballot legislation is not the only constitutional problem presented. The initiative and referendum are participatory political processes; they involve *voting*. Therefore, the cases protecting the right to vote and the equal power of every person's vote can be brought to bear, and the reasoning of those cases applied. Although the Court's dominant concern in the "one person, one vote" cases was to prevent the dilution of the individual citizen's vote, the Court was also concerned with the proper functioning of the republican form of government by insuring equally weighted votes. This concern for republicanism was articulated by Chief Justice Warren in *Reynolds v. Sims:* "The right to vote freely for the candidate of one's choice is of the essence of a democratic society, and any restrictions on that right strike at the heart of representative government."

This theme of protection of the republican system of government—and impliedly the protection of the society vouchsafed by that republican system—was announced more clearly in the cases involving at-large elections in multi-member districts. The Warren Court often expressed concern that at-large election schemes had long been used as a means of diluting the votes of minority groups or political parties. On more than one occasion, the Court warned that such legislative or local districts would be found unconstitutional where they were shown to operate "designedly or otherwise * * * under the circumstances of a particular case [to] minimize or cancel out the voting strength of racial or political elements of the voting population."

Referenda and initiatives are "at-large elections" on issues instead of candidates. Just as multi-member districts have the potential of minimizing or cancelling out the voting strength of racial or political groups in the election of officials, referenda and initiatives have a similar effect on direct legislation. In both cases the strength of the minority will be diluted.

The same danger to the republican process which was present in the multi-district cases is present here. The danger is twofold. First, in a particular referendum on a particular issue, a matter extremely harmful to minority interests but only moderately beneficial to non-minority interests may be passed; the ballot does not easily register intensity of interest as the legislative process does. Second, the initiative and referendum processes in general prevent meaningful participation by minority groups. As more legislation is passed through direct ballot, minorities are increasingly excluded from participating in decisions affecting the entire society. Of what value is it to protect an individual's right to vote for elected officials if the important decisions are made in referenda rather than in the legislature?

Thus, there is reason to scrutinize measures passed by initiative or referendum. In doing so the Court would be protecting participation in the political process and the integrity of the representational system, rather than directly remedying racial discrimination, with the belief that as long as the representational system is sound and minorities are effectively participating in the decisionmaking process, minorities can safeguard their own interests. Although in one sense any referendum or initiative operates counter to the representative system, the need for court protection of that system is strongest when the majority attempts through the direct ballot to take away something the minority obtained through the representative system. As a first step, Court scrutiny of ballot legislation might arguably be limited to such cases. * * *

SECTION G. CITIZENS' ABILITY TO INFLUENCE CITY POLICY THROUGH ACCESS TO INFORMATION OR PARTICIPATION

1. GOVERNMENT IN THE SUNSHINE

One way for citizens to influence governmental policy—or, at a minimum, to facilitate their ability to influence it through participation, voting, or litigation—is by obtaining information about what their government is doing. Acquiring information might take the form either of giving citizens access to governmental records (through local equivalents to the federal Freedom of Information Act) or of enabling them to attend the meetings at which governmental policy is formulated. This section investigates the second of these mechanisms for creating a more open government—statutes that require governmental meetings to be open to the public. These statutes—often called "sunshine laws"—have been adopted in every state.[1] Of course, none of these statutes opens every governmental meeting to the public. No one is entitled to be present when the Mayor meets with his or her staff. The case that follows—requiring an open search process for selecting a university president—thus represents only one possible position about the desirability of sunshine laws. Does either opinion in the case adequately deal with the problems engendered by opening a search process to the media? In what ways are open meeting statutes likely to influence governmental policy? Is something valuable lost if at least *some* discussions among government decisionmakers are not off-the-record? Should members of the public sometimes be feared (and government trusted) while, at other times, the government be feared (and the public trusted)?

---

1. For an analysis of sunshine laws, see, e.g., Bensch, Government in the Sunshine Act Seventeen Years Later: Has Government Let the Sunshine In?, 61 Geo.Wash. L.Rev. 1475 (1993); Note, Facilitating Government Decision Making: Distinguishing Between Meetings and Nonmeetings Under the Federal Sunshine Act, 66 Tex.L.Rev. 1195 (1988); White, The Ohio "Sunshine" Act: An Appraisal, 16 Akron L.Rev. 243 (1982); Sentell, Omen of "Openness" in Local Government Law, 13 Ga.L.Rev. 97, 98 107 (1978); Little & Tompkins, Open Government Laws: An Insider's View, 53 N.C.L.Rev. 451 (1975); Wickham, Tennessee's Sunshine Law: A Need for Limited Shade and Clearer Focus, 42 Tenn.L.Rev. 557 (1975); Wickham, Let the Sun Shine In! Open–Meeting Legislation Can Be Our Key to Closed Doors in State and Local Government, 68 Nw.U.L.Rev. 480 (1973); Note, Open Meeting Statutes: The Press Fights for the "Right to Know," 75 Harv. L.Rev. 1199 (1962).

BOOTH NEWSPAPERS, INC. v. UNIVERSITY OF MICHIGAN BOARD OF REGENTS

Supreme Court of Michigan, 1993.
444 Mich. 211, 507 N.W.2d 422.

MALLETT, JUSTICE.

The dispositive issues in this case are whether the presidential selection procedure adopted by the University of Michigan Board of Regents violated the Open Meetings Act * * *.

On April 28, 1987, Harold Shapiro announced his resignation as President of the University of Michigan, effective January 3, 1988. In May of 1987, the Board of Regents, consisting of eight members, appointed itself as the presidential Selection Committee and began the process of choosing a new university president. The committee appointed Regent Paul W. Brown as chairman and formed three advisory committees to assist it: a student committee, a faculty committee, and an alumni committee.

By the fall of 1987, the presidential Selection Committee had compiled an informal list of 250 potential candidates to replace President Shapiro. * * * The first cut reduced the number of candidates from 250 to 70. The Presidential Selection Committee entrusted Regent Brown with sole authority to make the first cut, and he did so after numerous telephone calls and meetings with the advisory committees and informal subquorum groups of regents. * * * The second phase of cuts employed essentially the same procedure as the first. During this phase, the presidential Selection Committee narrowed the candidate list from seventy to thirty. Again, Regent Brown telephoned individual regents, and all regents participated in the reduction process. Subquorum-sized groups of regents met to discuss the candidates and to reach a consensus regarding the desired individuals. One regent testified that candidates were rated, the ratings were tallied and circulated, and Brown discussed the results privately with each regent to insure that the list of thirty would be acceptable to the entire committee.

The candidates themselves made the third cut. Brown called the thirty remaining candidates and asked if they would be interested in the position. At this point, more than half the candidates removed themselves from consideration, but twelve candidates expressed their desire to remain on the list.

In March and April of 1988, groups of two, three, or four regents conducted private interviews in the candidates' home cities. Although the Presidential Selection Committee referred to these meetings as "visits," at least one regent conceded that, like any interview, these meetings were to assess and possibly recruit candidates.

Before these interviews, candidates informed the regents that they desired their candidacy to remain confidential by signing a form letter that the board had prepared in advance. Subsequently, the candidates and the groups of visiting regents met to discuss the position and the candidates' interests and qualifications. After these meetings, some regents submitted written reports of their impressions of the candidates to the other regents, while others telephoned Brown with their impressions.

The fourth cut followed a number of closed meetings held by the board to discuss the remaining twelve candidates, those "most seriously considered" by the presidential Selection Committee. The board believed that it could now justifiably convene in closed sessions because of the candidates' request for confidentiality. Following these closed sessions, Brown reduced the list of candidates from twelve to five. Although the regents contended that no voting occurred at these closed meetings, they agreed that they reached a general consensus and that Brown's list of five candidates reflected the views of the entire Presidential Selection Committee.

On May 20, 1988, the board resolved to form a "nominating committee" to decide which candidates would be placed in nomination for action by the board. On May 24, 1988, before the nominating committee met, seven of the regents held a closed meeting to discuss the results of the interviews and to reveal their opinions regarding each of the remaining candidates. The board insisted that no voting took place at this time. It conceded, however, that, on the basis of a consensus, two of the candidates were preferred over the other three.

Immediately following this closed meeting, the nominating committee met, considered the entire candidate list, and decided that only two preferred candidates would remain. This was the fifth cut. After this decision and various informal discussions between committee members and the two remaining candidates, the nominating committee unanimously decided to recommend one candidate, Dr. James Duderstadt, to the board. Dr. Duderstadt was interviewed in an open session by the regents and by selected student, faculty, and alumni representatives. Following this open interview, the nominating committee met in a closed session, and recommended the nomination of Dr. Duderstadt. The board subsequently reconvened in a public session and voted to elect Dr. Duderstadt president of the University of Michigan.

Booth Newspapers, Inc., doing business as the Ann Arbor News, and the Detroit Free Press, Inc., brought an action in Washtenaw Circuit Court, alleging that the Board of Regents had violated the Open Meetings Act * * *.

In 1968, the Legislature * * * [enacted] an open meetings statute applicable to most public bodies. The statute required only that public entities conduct final votes on certain subjects at meetings open to the public. Consequently, all other decisions and deliberations by public bodies could lawfully be held in closed sessions. * * * In 1973, the Michigan Senate established the Special Senate Study Committee on Political Ethics * * * [which] concluded that revisions to the open meetings law were necessary. It stated:

* * * "Since final decisions of a public body are the only items that must be made public, nothing in Michigan law prevents members of any public body, even including school boards, from discussing a proposal, adjourning to an executive session where members can agree privately on the action to be taken and then reconvene the 'public' meeting for the one or two minutes required to formally vote on their privately-arranged agreement. Actually, under existing law it is really not necessary for a public body in Michigan to go through even this semblance of openness if it doesn't want to."

To rectify the ineffectiveness of the 1968 statute, legislators introduced bills to comprehensively revise and substantially improve the law. The current Open Meetings Act resulted from these legislative efforts. * * *

Legislators hailed the act as "a major step forward in opening the political process to public scrutiny." During this period, lawmakers perceived openness in government as a means of promoting responsible decision making. Moreover, it also provided a way to educate the general public about policy decisions and issues. It fostered belief in the efficacy of the system. Legal commentators noted that "open government is believed to serve as both a light and disinfectant in exposing potential abuse and misuse of power. The deliberation of public policy in the public forum is an important check and balance on self-government." * * *

[T]he legislative reforms during the 1970s resulted in an OMA with broad inclusive language that required a public meeting for "all decisions of a public body" and "[a]ll deliberations of a public body constituting a quorum of its members * * *."

The gist of our analysis is whether, on the basis of the OMA's plain meaning, the Presidential Selection Committee (a) constituted a public body that (b) made closed session decisions and deliberations, and (c) conducted closed-session interviews in violation of the act. * * *

The OMA defines a "public body" to include a "committee, subcommittee, authority, or council, which is empowered by state constitution, statute, charter, ordinance, resolution, or rule to exercise governmental or proprietary authority * * *." * * * In this case, it is beyond question that the University of Michigan Board of Regents is a public body charged by law and financed by Michigan taxpayers to govern an institute of higher education. * * *

Section 2(d) of the OMA provides:

" 'Decision' means a determination, action, vote, or disposition upon a motion, proposal, recommendation, resolution, order, ordinance, bill, or measure on which a vote by members of a public body is required and by which a public body effectuates or formulates public policy."

The board insists that the process of reducing the candidate list resulted from recommendations by subquorum groups of regents, the nominating committee of board members, or by Regent Brown acting alone after consultation with individual regents. It maintains that none of these actions constituted formal "decisions" that bound the board because the possibility existed that the board might reconsider their candidate evaluations and reexamine a previously rejected candidate. On each occasion, the board claims that they merely reached a consensus regarding the action that they would take or the candidates that they preferred. In short, the board insists that their actions, in reducing the list of viable candidates, were not subject to the OMA because it did not take action by a "vote" as required under the act's definition of "decision." It maintains that the only decision that required a public meeting was held on June 10, 1988, when the board actually voted to elect Dr. Duderstadt. * * *

As currently worded, the OMA's plain meaning clearly applies to "all decisions" by public bodies. The act does not modify the word "vote" by the term "formal." If this provision were now read into the current OMA, it would resurrect the amended 1968 statute, which has been discredited by the Legislature. The board cannot read into the statute what the Legislature has seen fit to exclude.

Regardless of how the Presidential Selection Committee wishes to categorize its actions, the fact remains that the board adopted a procedure that violated the OMA. The OMA does not contain a "voting requirement" or any form of "formal voting requirement." Consequently, arguments that the Presidential Selection Committee's actions were a consensus building process, rather than a mere vote or "formal" vote, are irrelevant. Furthermore, any alleged distinction between the committee's consensus building and a determination or action, as advanced in the OMA's definition of "decision," is a distinction without a difference. Even members of the committee acknowledged that its "round-the-horn" decisions and conferences achieved the same effect as if the entire board had met publicly, received candidate ballots, and "formally" cast their votes. Moreover, testimony of various regents even raises the question whether the board did in fact vote through the use of tallies and a rating system. * * * In sum, the board's actions must be considered closed session decisions under the OMA. Any other interpretation of its actions would contradict the act's letter and spirit. This Court's failure to recognize this fact would undermine the legislative intent to promote responsible and open government. * * *

Although § 3(3) of the OMA requires a public body to hold all deliberations at an open meeting, § 8(f) does permit closed session deliberations "to review the specific contents of an application for employment or appointment to a public office if the candidate requests that the application remain confidential." The OMA further provides, however, that "all interviews by a public body for employment or appointment to a public office shall be held in an open meeting pursuant to this act."

The board maintains that this "application exception" permitted it to withhold the candidates' identities and to justify closure of discussions comparing the candidates' qualifications for the purpose of reducing the list of viable individuals. The board's deliberation, however, far exceeded the exemption's scope. The OMA exception permitting closed sessions to review the "specific contents" of an application would entail discussions about the applicant's qualifications on the basis of information contained in the application.

In the instant case, the Court of Appeals construed the "specific contents" exemption narrowly and held that the OMA permitted closed sessions only to review personal matters contained in a candidate's application. We agree. Considering the OMA's prodisclosure nature, the requirement to strictly construe exemptions and the mandate for open candidate interviews, it is reasonable to assume that the Legislature intended this exemption to be a limited compromise, allowing privacy rights to dictate in instances where boards were not engaged in decision-making activities. Here we agree with the panel that the board went beyond this limitation and made reduction decisions under the guise of this exemption. Clearly, however, the OMA requires that "all decisions of a public body" be made in public. Consequently, the act mandates that the Presidential Selection Committee make any reduction decisions in public.

With regard to the interviews, or "visits" as termed by the board, there is no statutory exception permitting a subcommittee to conduct closed interviews. On the contrary, the Legislature expressly mandated open interviews. In doing so, the Legislature must have recognized that candidates' identities would become public, and that it was in the greater public interest to know the qualifications of candidates for public positions and the hiring procedures of public officials.

Therefore, we hold that the Board of Regents is a public body that made closed session deliberations and decisions and held private interviews in violation of the OMA. * * * [W]e remand this case to the circuit court for entry of a judgment providing injunctive relief and compelling disclosure in conformity with this opinion.

BOYLE, JUSTICE (concurring in part and dissenting in part). * * *

I cannot agree with the majority's determination that the Open Meetings Act requires that the entire presidential selection process be conducted in public view. I would hold that the OMA does not compel that information gathered in the initial candidate screening process be disclosed to the public, nor does it dictate the revelation of a candidate's identity without consent or before the scheduling of a public interview. * * *

The compiling of a list of names, reviewing qualifications, and identifying a limited number of persons for interviews to further assess their capability and interest in the position, are tasks that are ministerial in nature and not "public business" within the purview of the OMA. Screening from the original inventory of 250 names, a list of thirty potential candidates who were more qualified than the others was not a public body meeting, deliberation, or decision effectuating public policy.

Whether performed by administrative staff, a third party, or the Board of Regents itself, does not change the technical and qualitative nature of the task. At no time during this initial screening process was there any "decision" by any person or public body to eliminate or remove any person from the list of 250 potential candidates. Rather, the assignment involved the gathering and sorting of submitted names to locate those persons who might be best qualified for the position of president of the university.

Tapering the list from the thirty most qualified "potential" candidates to twelve "actual" candidates was executed by the candidates themselves and not through any action of a public body or official. These twelve candidates expressed an interest in the position and, when asked, requested that their preliminary candidacy remain confidential. Although no "applications" per se were submitted, a logical inference follows that when the potential candidates affirmed an interest in pursuing the position, they became "applicants" within the meaning of the OMA. Pursuant to MCL 15.268(f), authorizing closed meetings by the full public body to deliberate and review applications for appointment when the applicant requests confidentiality, the board met in a private session to evaluate the twelve candidates' curricula vitae. Hence, no violation of the OMA by the President Selection Committee or the board occurred at this stage of the selection process.

Although § 8(f) enables a public body to meet in closed session to review the specific contents of an employment application, the second sentence of the same provision provides that all interviews by a public body for employment shall be held in an open meeting. The tension between the sentences is apparent when a public body, authorized to review and discuss a candidate's application at a closed meeting, is unable to render any "decision" concerning the candidate without violating the open meeting requirement that all "decisions" of the public body be made in an open forum. In an attempt to reconcile this conflict, it has been suggested that the public body create a committee composed of outside members or a subquorum of public officials, and charge the group with recommending a final list of candidates who are most qualified and suited for the position. As a nonpublic body without authority to exercise a government function, it has been contended that the committee would be free to meet in private and to conduct confidential interviews with some or all of the candidates to facilitate the development of its recommendation of final candidates to the full public body.

The President Selection Committee was not a committee empowered solely with authority to advise or make a recommendation to the full board because, as indicated above, the committee was "itself" the board. The committee therefore could not accomplish in subquorum groups what it was prohibited by the OMA from performing as a quorum public body. At the juncture in the process when the board conducted subquorum private interviews, deliberations, and decisions concerning the twelve applicants for employment, it violated the mandates of the OMA.

The board does not deny, and it is unclear from the record, whether a quorum of the regents as President Selection Committee members may have interviewed any single applicant, albeit at different times. Nevertheless, even absent a quorum of regents interviewing any one candidate, the board violated the OMA's public interview requirement. * * *

The overall purpose of the interviews and follow-up discussions were to narrow the list of candidates for final consideration. Unable to make an advisory recommendation to itself because its membership included the entire public body, the President Selection Committee, as a public body, was required by the OMA to conduct open interviews and decisions. The recommendation by Regent Brown, as chair of the committee, to further interview five candidates in private with participation from the three advisory groups and, finally, to interview two candidates in public was, in reality, the general consensus and view of the entire board after discussing the candidates in several closed meetings and phone conversations with all the regents. Such decision making violated the act by not taking place in a public forum. * * *

The majority opinion rests on the explicit premise that the prodisclosure purpose of the act requires broad application of the OMA to all phases of the public hiring process. This approach overlooks the fact that, as enacted, the OMA is actually less comprehensive than the act originally proposed. The initial draft of the act would have included within the definition of a public body "any * * * state or local government entity to make recommendations concerning the exercise of governmental authority." The applicability of the act to such recommending entities was stricken by the first amendment of the bill. * * * Having specifically considered and rejected the idea that "recommendations" by a committee or subcommittee of a public body concerning the exercise of government authority be included in the act's definition of a "public body," it can safely be concluded that the Legislature intended to exempt such entities from the OMA's public forum requirements. The public body could create such an advisory committee to maintain the confidentiality of preliminary candidates and to recommend a pool of finalists for its consideration. Although the OMA imposes no literal restrictions or reporting requirements on advisory committees, to effectuate the purpose of the OMA, the committee should provide with its recommendation reasons for its recommendation and the procedures and methods used in reaching it. As always, the public body would be free to reject, accept, or modify the committee's nonbinding recommendation.

I also disagree with the majority's conclusion that the OMA requires that a public body disclose the identity of a candidate yet allows it to meet in a closed session to review "personal matters contained in a candidate's application." To read the OMA in this manner is nonsensical. * * * [T]he position of president of a major public university customarily attracts well-qualified, prominent, and distinguished persons. The information submitted and reviewed generally includes the candidate's curriculum vitae, rather than an employment "application" per se filled out by a hopeful applicant. It is only logical to assume that the Legislature understood that in hiring situations for high level positions, the most sensitive information, and that most in need of being defined as confidential, is the candidate's identity. The Legislature's highly sophisticated experience in such matters must be deemed to have contemplated that once the identity of a candidate who is generally well-known and respected within a given community is made public, the candidate's biographical resume is often an open book and easily obtainable. Given that the result of such disclosure is to serve notice upon the candidate's current employer that the person is contemplating other employment and to discourage the best candidates from pursuing an interest in the position, it strains credulity to believe that the Legislature intended a result so inconsistent with public interest and the hiring needs of public bodies.

For the above reasons, the OMA should be construed to grant a public body the power to refuse to disclose the identity of a preliminary candidate when confidentiality is requested and to permit the review and deliberation of the candidate's qualifications to occur in a closed meeting. If recommended as a finalist for the position, the candidate should be afforded the opportunity to withdraw before a formal public recommendation to the hiring body. Any candidate who consents to further consideration by the full public body must be deemed to have waived the right to privacy, yielding to the public's right to know the qualifications of the candidate and satisfying the act's requirement that where the public body reserves to itself the final decision for appointment to certain levels of employment, without exception, those interviews must be conducted in public. * * *

2. CITIZEN PARTICIPATION IN GOVERNMENT DECISION-MAKING

As an alternative or a supplement to voting or attending government meetings, citizens might actually participate in the formulation of governmental policy.[1] In the 1960's and 1970's, a series of federal statutes sought to encourage direct citizen participation in a number of different local programs. For example, in setting up community action agencies under the Office of Economic Opportunity in 1964, Congress specified, in 42 U.S.C. § 2781, that one of its purposes was:

> the development and implementation of all programs and projects to serve the poor or low-income areas with the maximum feasible participation of residents of the areas and members of the groups served, so as to best stimulate and take full advantage of capabilities for self-advancement and assure that those programs and projects are otherwise meaningful to and widely utilized by their intended

---

1. See generally, Liebmann, Devolution of Power to Community and Block Associations, 25 The Urban Lawyer 335 (1993); Steinberger, Ideology and the Urban Crisis 63–98 (1985); Advisory Commission on Intergovernmental Relations, Citizen Participation in the American Federal System (1979).

beneficiaries.[2]

The first two cases reproduced below deal with the interpretation of another federal statute that similarly encouraged popular participation in the formulation of public policy, the Demonstration Cities and Metropolitan Development Act of 1966, popularly known as the Model Cities Act.[3] The two cases confront problems raised by the Model Cities Act's attempt to create community boards: North City Area–Wide Council v. Romney deals with the kind of power the community boards could exercise; Hairston v. Model Cities Agency of the City of New York concerns how the board members were to be selected. The final case in this section, Fumarolo v. Chicago Board of Education, raises an issue similar to that confronted in the *Hairston* case in a much more recent context—the attempt to decentralize control of Chicago's public schools. In reading these cases, consider the functions community boards might perform and how they might be organized. Is it wrong both to participate in the formulation of governmental policy and to implement the program decided upon? Was the *Fumarolo* court right to apply the one person/one vote formula to these participatory efforts? Are the problems that the cases confront generated by defects in the community board structure that the relevant statutes adopted or by defects in the very notion that the public can participate in formulating governmental policy?

NORTH CITY AREA–WIDE COUNCIL, INC. v. ROMNEY

United States Court of Appeals, Third Circuit, 1972.
456 F.2d 811, cert. denied, 406 U.S. 963, 92 S.Ct. 2063, 32 L.Ed.2d 351.

BIGGS, CIRCUIT JUDGE.

The determination of this case depends, as we stated previously in 428 F.2d 754, 755 (1970), on the meaning of the requirements in the Demonstration Cities and Metropolitan Development Act of 1966 (the "Act"). The complaint in this case, filed August 15, 1969, has as plaintiffs North City Area–Wide Council, Inc., and various persons living within the so-called "target area" of the Philadelphia Model Cities Program, referred to collectively as "AWC," and is brought on their own behalf and on behalf of all other persons similarly situated. The defendants are George W. Romney, Secretary of Housing and Urban Development, the Department of Housing and Urban Development (HUD), Mayor James H.J. Tate, of Philadelphia, Goldie E. Watson, Model Cities Administrator for Philadelphia, and the City of Philadelphia (City or Philadelphia). * * * The complaint describes the Model Cities Program to be made operational pursuant to the Act which authorized the Secretary of Housing and Urban Development to make

---

2. 42 U.S.C. § 2781 was repealed on August 13, 1981. Pub.L. 97–35, Title VI, § 683(a), August 13, 1981, 95 Stat. 519.

3. For an analysis of the Act, see Hetzel & Pinsky, The Model Cities Program, 22 Vand.L.Rev. 727 (1969).

grants to local governments to plan and implement comprehensive Model Cities Demonstration Programs.

The gravamen of the complaint is that the defendants proceeded to implement the Model Cities Program in Philadelphia without regard for AWC and the provisions of the Act. The plaintiffs sought, *inter alia,* temporary and permanent injunctions to prevent the defendants from proceeding with the implementation of the Philadelphia Model Cities Program. The case came on for hearing before the District Court on a stipulation of facts, the defendants moving for summary judgment. The motion was granted and an appeal was taken to this court. We reversed, *sub nom. North City Area–Wide Council, Inc. v. Romney,* 428 F.2d 754 (1970), and remanded the case for further proceedings in accordance with our opinion. The District Court proceeded to final hearing on an extensive record and ordered the complaint dismissed. The appeal at bar followed.

In our previous opinion we defined the requirements of the Act. We said that "to be eligible for Federal aid, a 'comprehensive city demonstration program,' must 'provide * * * widespread citizen participation in the program' and the Secretary of Housing and Urban Development must 'emphasize local initiative in the planning * * * [of it].' "

We also stated: "These requirements form a central and novel feature of the Demonstration Cities Act, in whose prologue the Congress declared: ' * * * that improving the quality of urban life is the most critical domestic problem facing the United States. The persistence of widespread urban slums and blight, the concentration of persons of low income in older urban areas, and the unmet needs for additional housing and community facilities and services arising from rapid expansion of our urban population have resulted in a marked deterioration in the quality of the environment and lives of large numbers of our people while the nation as a whole prospers. * * *'

"The purpose of the Act stated by Congress was 'to provide additional financial and technical assistance to enable cities of all sizes * * * to plan, develop and carry out locally prepared and scheduled comprehensive city demonstration programs. * * *' The basic philosophy of the Act was well-expressed by the Department of Housing and Urban Development ('HUD') in a statement of its policy concerning citizen participation: ' * * * improving the quality of life of the residents of a model neighborhood can be accomplished only by the affirmative action of the people themselves. This requires a means of building self-esteem, competence and a desire to participate effectively in solving the social and physical problems of their community.' " * * * Perhaps the best expression of Congress' intent in passing the Act was employed by plaintiffs' counsel in oral argument in this court: *viz.,* "Power to the powerless," that is to say, it was the intention of Congress to cause the poverty-stricken citizens of our larger cities to improve their lot by their own efforts. * * *

Pursuant to the Act, on March 3, 1967 Philadelphia applied to the Secretary for a grant to enable the planning of a Model Cities Program. Soon thereafter AWC was organized in the so-called "Target area." The AWC consisted of approximately 458 associated persons from approximately 145 organizations within the target area. This was intended to provide the local "citizen participation" in the Philadelphia program. Shortly thereafter a contract was entered into to provide the required citizen participation.

On November 16, 1967 the City received a grant of $203,000 from the Secretary for the planning and development of its Model Cities Program and after extensive planning for a period in excess of a year, by consultation between the City and AWC, the City on December 31, 1968 submitted to the Secretary an application for a grant to implement a Model Cities Program for Philadelphia.

On February 5, 1969, a Regional Inter–Agency Coordinating Committee meeting was held in Philadelphia to review with the City and AWC Philadelphia's proposed 1968 submission for Model Cities funds. This meeting was attended by HUD representatives, by members of the Philadelphia City Demonstration Agency (CDA), and AWC. At this meeting, apparently for the first time, an issue of conflict of interest was raised by HUD. In this connection the District Judge stated in his opinion: "By conflict of interest, HUD meant the problems which might arise if the same citizen participation unit which was planning and evaluating the Model Cities Program, namely AWC, was also to operate the program. Mr. William Meek, Executive Director of the AWC, attended the February 5th meeting and was aware of the HUD policy." The accuracy of these statements cannot be doubted. The issue of conflict of interests has become the guiding star of the arguments of AWC's opponents. A conflict was undoubtedly present and was a contributing factor to the actions of the defendants complained of by AWC and set out hereinafter. It must be borne in mind that the City was required to approve all plans.

On March 19, 1969 Mayor Tate received a letter from Assistant Secretary Floyd H. Hyde of HUD. A similar letter was sent to the Mayors of other cities engaged in the Model Cities Program and was an expression of participation policy as of that date. The letter as quoted in our previous opinion stated: " ' * * * HUD's policy is that local City Demonstration Agencies (and their Model Cities staff and citizen participation arms) are not intended to serve as program operators. CDA Letter Number 6 specifically states that "the CDA is not meant to be a multi-functional operating agency." CDA's are expected to coordinate the activities of the various existing agencies whose new or existing functions impact on the model neighborhood. CDA's are expected to use their supplemental funds to influence and persuade these existing agencies to modify present practices, priorities and programs identified and goals established as a result of Model Cities planning.

" 'Where there is no appropriate existing agency to carry out a new program which has been planned as part of the Model Cities effort, the City can certainly organize a new operating agency—such as a nonprofit corporation. The CDA or its citizen board should be a program operator only as the last resort and then only as a transition matter. If the CDA becomes a program operator, your Model Cities program could easily become just another local program competing for scarce resources and incapable of effectively performing the coordination, recourse [*sic, re-source*] allocation, and institutional change role for which it is intended.' " This letter was discussed by Mr. William Meek, Executive Director of AWC, with AWC's Executive Board but no position was taken by the Board insofar as the record indicates.

On April 15, 1969, Mr. John Buggs, then Deputy Director of the Model Cities Administration, and Mr. Chester Jones, a staff member of HUD, had a meeting with Mrs. Watson, officials from the HUD Regional Office, Mr. Meek and the AWC staff. There was a discussion of fiscal and administrative policies and of the Hyde letter of March 19. On April 18, 1969, Mr. Buggs sent a "Memorandum of Understanding" to the persons he had met on April 15, 1969, stating that "Mr. Meek agreed that AWC would not present a plan which involved that organization in extensive program operation."

On April 30, 1969 the City's application to HUD was supplemented after further consultation between HUD, the City, and AWC. The April 30, 1969 supplement clearly demonstrated the powerlessness of the citizens to influence decisions affecting their community as the factor most responsible for perpetuating the undesirable conditions existing in the target area. A large part of this Program was to be administered by seven non-profit corporations. A majority of the directors of four of the corporations and large minorities of the directors of the other three corporations were to be chosen by AWC.

On May 27, 1969, by a letter addressed to Mayor Tate, Assistant Secretary Hyde objected to the Philadelphia Model Cities Program because of the heavy involvement of the AWC in the non-profit corporations and because of the insufficient involvement in the Program on the part of the City of Philadelphia. On June 2, 1969, Deputy Assistant Secretary of HUD, Robert H. Baida, came to Philadelphia to meet Mrs. Goldie Watson, Philadelphia Model Cities Administrator, to discuss the problems outlined in Assistant Secretary Hyde's letter of May 27. AWC attaches much significance to the fact that no AWC representative attended this meeting, asserting that this was because Deputy Assistant Secretary Baida did not want any representative of AWC to be present and for this reason requested a meeting only with Mrs. Watson and her staff. It is clear that this assertion is not completely borne out by the record. It does appear that HUD asked for a meeting with Mrs. Watson and that she did not invite any member or representative of AWC to be present at her meeting with Mr. Baida. At that meeting, a "new policy" was discussed. The "new policy" is that set out in the March 19 letter of Secretary Hyde to Mayor Tate quoted above but we think it cannot be successfully maintained that that policy was made crystal clear. It seems, however, to have been directed toward excluding AWC from exercising a direct operational function as we think was required by CDA Letter No. 3. AWC's role was to be reduced to an advisory capacity. At her meeting with Mr. Baida, Mrs. Watson protested the new policy but apparently finally acceded to it. Mr. Baida insisted that a proper plan would have to be submitted to HUD within ten days. No adequate reason for this very short time limit appears from the record.

On the following day, June 3, Mrs. Watson had a meeting with President Patton of AWC and Mr. Meek, and explained to them that a reply was expected to the Hyde letter of May 27th within ten days. Mrs. Watson testified that at that meeting she gave to all persons present a copy of the May 27th letter and stated that she would be willing to cooperate with AWC in responding to the letter. President Patton expressed a willingness to cooperate in preparing a reply but Mr. Meek at that time refused cooperation. Thereafter, with the express authorization of AWC's Executive Committee, on June 6, Mr. Meek sent identical telegrams to Mayor Tate and Mrs. Watson, as follows: "URGENTLY REQUEST REPLY TO SECT. HYDE'S LETTER BE POSTPONED UNTIL AUDIENCE WITH YOU BE HELD BY AREA–WIDE COUNCIL BOARD REPRESENTATIVES. REQUEST THIS MEETING ON MONDAY JUNE 9TH IF POSSIBLE. SINCERELY, WILLIAM R. MEEK, AREA EXECUTIVE DIRECTOR, AREA–WIDE COUNCIL." It was earnestly contended by counsel for the Federal defendants at the argument before us that the wire had been sent to Mayor Tate only and not to Mrs. Watson. Counsel's contention was erroneous. This substantially is the end of the story insofar as AWC is concerned for Mrs. Watson seems to have assumed the position that no cooperation was possible with AWC and dispatched her reply to the May 27th letter on June 9. The District Judge states by way of explanation for Mrs. Watson's action that: "[She] explained to Messrs. Meek and Patton that a reply to the May 27 letter was expected within 10 days. Mrs. Watson told them she had Mr. Baida standing by for a meeting with AWC on June 9 and requested a list of AWC board members so she could send out invitations. Messrs. Meek and Patton refused to hand over the list on the grounds that it was AWC policy not to give the Model Cities Administrator a list of AWC board members. Mrs. Watson pressed her demand for the list saying that she did not want to meet with people she did not know. * * * AWC finally reversed its 'policy' against giving out a list of members, but the list was not transmitted to Mrs. Watson until June 23, 1969." She further stated in her communication of June 9 to HUD with respect to the revised proposal: *"It must be emphasized that this statement has been prepared by the [Model Cities] Administrator [of defendant Philadelphia] without the participation, review or endorsement of the Area–Wide Council."* (Emphasis in original).

The opinion of the District Court states at the meeting of June 3, 1969, "[T]he City told AWC it was willing to convene a meeting with Mr. Hyde's Deputy, Mr. Baida, on June 9, 1969, but AWC refused to participate in such a meeting. AWC, instead, adopted a strategy of by-passing the Model Cities Administrator and appealing to the City and HUD in an attempt to procure a reversal of the policies stated in the Hyde letter. AWC sent its own telegrams to the Mayor seeking to arrange a meeting, and to Mrs. Perry, HUD coordinator, asking her to arrange a meeting with Mr. Baida. [Mayor Tate] declined to meet with AWC at that time, and there is no indication of the reaction from Mrs. Perry." We conclude that this finding is not supported by the evidence. There is no showing that the telegram sent by AWC to Mrs. Watson was not sent in good faith.

AWC's contract with the City was allowed to expire on June 30, 1969 and after further contract negotiations ceased, on July 10, 1969, Mrs. Watson took steps to organize a new citizen participation commit-tee, three of the seven AWC Hubs expressing a desire to remain affiliated with the Model Cities Program. The new committee consisted of 47 persons, at least 15 of whom were formerly associated with AWC. In connection with this the District Court made the following conclusion, stating: " * * * [A]t the present moment, Philadelphia's Model Cities program is functioning with the 'wide-spread citizen participation re-quired by 42 U.S.C.A. § 3303.' " The court went on to say: "In light of all the facts presented in this case, this Court finds that the Philadelphia Model Cities Program is now, and has been, operating in accordance with the statutory mandate."

The Federal defendants insist that the supplemental submission by the City of June 9, 1969 did not constitute a major change in the program and "In fact, it did not create any change at all." We cannot agree.

The issue which we have before us is clearly stated by the plaintiffs as follows: "The central issue in this case is whether the changes made in the Philadelphia Model Cities Program by means of the letter of Assistant Secretary Hyde of May 27, 1969, Mrs. Watson's supplementary statement of June 9, 1969, and the July 3, 1969 letter of Deputy Assistant Secretary Baida were made with the citizen participation required by the Model Cities Act and the regulations thereunder. In its decision in this matter, on the basis of the April 30, 1969 supplement to the Philadelphia application and the three documents by which the changes were made this Court concluded [*North City Area–Wide Council v. Romney*, 428 F.2d 758]: ' * * * [T]he issue is not citizen veto or even approval, but citizen participation, negotiation, and consultation in the major decisions which are made for a particular Model Cities Program. While not every decision regarding a Program may require full citizen participation, certainly decisions which change the basic strategy of the Program do require such participation. The June 9th decision of the City and the July 3rd statement of HUD made such fundamental changes in the Philadelphia Program. Previously, that Program had contemplated a much heavier involvement by the designated citizen participation component, AWC. This involvement was drastically re-duced by the unilateral actions of the City and HUD. The Secretary therefore violated the Act when he accepted a proposal for major modification of the Model Cities Program from the City which made clear on its face there had been no citizen participation in its formulation. * * * '"

The very essence of the Act is participation by the inhabitants of the affected community, and AWC's position was correctly stated by Mrs. Watson when she said and we repeat, "It must be emphasized that this statement [*i.e.*, the supplementary proposal of June 9, 1969] has been prepared by the [Model Cities] Administrator [of Philadelphia] without the participation, review or endorsement of the Area–Wide Council." Manifestly the various programs have continued for a considerable length of time under the auspices of the Interim Committee which eventually ceased to be "interim" and became a committee created from the target area. A misunderstanding of the law by the District Court has not inhibited the HUD programs. Nonetheless, we find ourselves unwilling to accept what we deem to be error to prevent or to avoid the operation of the Act as intended by Congress. Perhaps a workable solution to the difficulties presented by the attitudes of the respective parties can be arrived at. It is possible and we hope probable that the passage of time may have sweetened the minds of the parties to this suit and their representatives.

We must reverse the judgment and we will direct the District Court upon remand to enter an order providing:

1. That plaintiff, Area–Wide Council, be reinstated forthwith insofar as it may be the citizen participation organization for the Philadelphia Model Cities Program.

2. That Area–Wide Council as such citizen representation organization negotiate in good faith with the existing citizen structure for the purpose of integrating that structure into the organization of the Area–Wide Council.

3. That the City of Philadelphia negotiate with the Area–Wide Council in good faith for the purpose of entering into an agreement with it for the Council to act as the citizen representation organization for the Philadelphia Model Cities Program, the form of contract dated June 30, 1969 to serve as a basis for these negotiations, it being understood, however, that in accepting any contract, Area–Wide Council will not be bound by the illegal changes made in the Philadelphia Model Cities Program by the Hyde letter of May 27, 1969, the Watson memorandum of June 9, 1969, or the Baida letter of July 3, 1969.

4. That HUD and the City negotiate in good faith with the Area–Wide Council concerning all changes made in the Philadelphia Model Cities Program since May 27, 1969.

HAIRSTON v. MODEL CITIES AGENCY OF THE CITY OF NEW YORK

Supreme Court, Kings County, 1971.
66 Misc.2d 443, 321 N.Y.S.2d 498.

MILES F. MCDONALD, JUDGE.

Petitioners, members of the board of directors of the Brownsville Community Council, an antipoverty agency, initiated this proceeding to restrain respondents, from conducting the proposed elections for the Local Policy Committee of the Model Cities Agency, and restraining respondents from circulating petitions for candidates in such elections. Petitioners also seek public hearings with reference to the proposed plan of elections. * * *

The Model Cities Program is a comprehensive approach to rebuild and revitalize blighted and slum areas in our cities under the Demonstration Cities and Metropolitan Development Act of 1966, which makes available grants and technical assistance to enable city demonstration agencies to plan and carry out programs to effectuate the legislative intent. * * * Central Brooklyn Model Cities Area involved in this proceeding comprises the area designated Brownsville, East New York and Bedford–Stuyvesant.

The enabling legislation enacted by Congress * * * specifically direct "widespread citizen participation". How such participation is to be obtained is not mandated. Thus, there is no obligation upon the Model Cities Administration to conduct elections for membership on the local planning committee. However, it was decided by the Model Cities Administration that an election was the best procedure to secure broad based citizens' support. Accordingly the election method was utilized at the inception of the Model Cities Program in the early spring of 1968. Each of the designated areas conducted its own elections in a series of convention meetings. Members and delegates were elected for a term of five years *or until the next election, whichever occurred first,* thus tenure of the present board would terminate upon the happening of alternate contingencies. A call for new elections and designations having been made, the terms of office of the entire present sitting body are considered expired, leaving the way open for new elections and appointments for all members including those 12 of the present board who are to be nominated and appointed to provide continuity and experience to the new body. Information concerning the elections was distributed to eight hundred organizations throughout the central Brooklyn area.

The plan as amended would establish a local planning committee of 38 members, an increase of 3 over the present 35–member committee. There are three districts in the Central Brooklyn Model Cities area, each of which contains three subdistricts. The proposed plan would retain 12 of the existing board members to be selected by the present board. The chairman of each Community Corporation (antipoverty agency) operating in the area would be entitled to full voting membership; members of the board of directors and the executive staff of the Community Corporations are specifically disqualified from holding any office. Five members would represent special community interests (business, religious, educational, community health and social welfare). To reconstitute the three area policy committees, the Citywide Model Cities Board (which is composed of both the city government officials appointed by the Mayor and of representatives selected by and from the three existing local policy committees) met on several occasions to formulate and ultimately approve and adopt a set of election policies and procedures which is the subject of this proceeding. In the business and religious category, any group of at least three of their respective number may nominate one candidate for appointment to the local planning committee. Any nominee seeking to represent the educational interest must submit ten nominating signatures of professional educators who are residents of the Model Cities area. A community health nominee must be a doctor, dentist or registered nurse and must obtain five signatures of members of their profession. The board of directors of any local social welfare agency may nominate one of its officers or one of its full time employees. The administrator, in consultation with the neighborhood directors of the respective Model Cities areas, shall then appoint one from each of the classes mentioned from the list of nominees compiled. One adult representative (over the age of 18) would be elected from each subdistrict. To be nominated, a candidate of such district must present a petition bearing the valid signatures of 100 residents of the subdistrict which he seeks to represent. Also to be elected [are] six youth representatives (aged 16 to 18), two of whom would come from each district. Voters would be permitted to vote for only one youth representative from each district and the one receiving the highest number of votes to serve a term of one year.

Finally, three senior citizens (over the age of 65) would be elected, one from each of these districts. A senior citizen candidate, like the other two classes of representatives, in order to have his name placed on the ballot, must present a nominating petition signed by 100 residents of the district he seeks to represent, with the provision that no person may sign more than one nominating petition for each class of representatives. One shall be elected from each district to serve a term of two years.

While the complexity of the plan is not one that would recommend it to the court, it is lawful and it is not within the court's province to substitute its judgment for that of the Model Cities Administration.
* * *

Petitioners challenge the election guidelines on the broad general principle that they do not encourage maximum feasible participation of the poor. Specifically, petitioners allege that retaining 12 members of the present board without requiring an election of those members deprives the residents of the opportunity to elect the required members of the Local Policy Committee and further reducing the number of eligible candidates that may be elected from the area. Petitioners also challenge that portion of the guidelines which disqualifies the antipoverty board members and their executive staff from holding office. They argue that this exclusionary provision would deprive the residents of the Central Brooklyn area from electing representatives of their choice and prevents the representation of a number of residents who are actively participating in the improvement of the community. Petitioners further question the validity of having the youth representatives and senior citizens elected at large. They question the manner in which the various classes of persons shall be nominated. Specifically, they object to those provisions which limit the voter to nominating only one of each class.

The court is of the opinion that there is no merit to petitioners' objections. The enabling legislation and subsequent executive pronouncements require only that there be "active citizen participation". * * * [I]n the case of *North City Area–Wide Council v. Romney*, 3 Cir., 428 F.2d 754, the Federal court had occasion to interpret the meaning of the term "active citizen participation" under the statute in question and declared, "the issue is not citizen veto or even approval, but citizen participation, negotiation and consultation in the major decisions which are made for the particular Model Cities Program". The statute is discretionary in nature, limited only to the extent that there be active citizen participation. The election proposals submitted clearly show that a determined effort was made here to provide widespread citizen participation in the election procedures. The plan provided for appointive and elective devices to insure the election of a wide segment of the population in the area. Provisions are made for the election of the very young and the old, special interests, as well as the public at large.

Constitutionally, it is only when the initial legislation directs the use of popular elections that there must then be compliance with constitutional safeguards (*Hadley v. Junior Coll. Dist.*, 397 U.S. 50, 90 S.Ct. 791, 25 L.Ed.2d 45). In the case at bar, the enabling legislation does not require elections, on the contrary, the statute uses the word "participation" not "representation", a subtle but pertinent distinction. The plan adopted herein is merely an extension of the discretionary power granted to the local administrator under the statute.

Moreover, the Supreme Court has upheld against constitutional challenge an election plan that required that candidates be residents of certain districts that did not contain equal numbers of people (*Dusch v. Davis*, 387 U.S. 112, 87 S.Ct. 1554, 18 L.Ed.2d 656). It has also been held that where a State chooses to select members of an official body by appointment rather than election, and that choice does not itself offend the Constitution, the fact that each official does not "represent" the same number of people does not deny those people equal protection of the laws (*Sailors v. Board of Educ.*, 387 U.S. 105, 87 S.Ct. 1549, 18 L.Ed.2d 650).

Finally, the words of Mr. Justice Black in the *Hadley* case, supra, seem most appropriate, " * * * viable local governments may need many innovations, numerous combinations of old and new devices, great flexibility in municipal arrangements to meet changing urban conditions. We see nothing in the Constitution to prevent experimentation". The proposal under attack is such an innovative experiment; the proposal amply provides for widespread citizen participation called for by the statute. * * *

FUMAROLO v. CHICAGO BOARD OF EDUCATION

Supreme Court of Illinois, 1990.
142 Ill.2d 54, 153 Ill.Dec. 177, 566 N.E.2d 1283.

JUSTICE WARD delivered the opinion of the court:

The plaintiffs, individuals serving as principals, an individual serving as a subdistrict superintendent in the Chicago public school system and individuals who are registered voters and property owners-taxpayers in the City of Chicago, filed a complaint in the circuit court of Cook County, challenging the constitutionality of the Chicago School Reform Act (the Act). * * * The * * * Act was enacted in 1988 in an attempt to resolve * * * problems [in the public school system]. The Act makes significant changes in school governance and administration by decentralizing the school system and by imposing primary responsibility for local school governance on parents, community residents, teachers and school principals. The plaintiffs do not dispute the need for change in the Chicago public school system, but they * * * allege that the Act's voting scheme for electing members of the local school councils violates the equal protection clauses of the State and Federal Constitutions because it denies an equal vote in local school council elections to large portions of the electorate. * * *

A brief overview of the contested portions of the Act will be necessary. * * * Although the board of education retains many general administrative powers and responsibilities, its powers and responsibilities under the Act have been substantially altered. To place increased authority for individual school decisions at the individual school level, the Act provides for the creation of a local school council for each grammar school and each high school in the Chicago public school system (there are 539 schools in the Chicago public school system). The local school council is composed of the school principal and 10 elected members. The elected members are: six parents of currently enrolled students who are elected by parents of currently enrolled students, two residents of the attendance area served by the school who are elected by the residents of that area (except in multiarea districts—districts which draw and admit students from more than a single attendance area— where the community residents to be elected are elected by the parents of currently enrolled students, the principal of the multiarea school and the school staff) and two teachers of the school who are elected by the school staff. Each local school council elects the principal who will serve at the school for a contract period of four years and may retain the principal for another four-year period when the contract expires. Should a principal not be retained, the local school council will select a new principal. The local school council also develops specific performance criteria for its principal and has responsibility for approving the budget plan drawn up and administered by the principal. In addition, the local school council has substantial advisory responsibilities. * * *

The plaintiffs (registered voters and taxpayers) first state that the Act's voting scheme for electing local school council members * * * violates the equal protection guarantees of the United States Constitution * * * because voters who are otherwise qualified to vote, but do not currently have children attending Chicago schools, are denied a vote in local school council elections that is equal to that of voters who do have children in attendance at the public schools. * * * The plaintiffs argue that the Act's differentiated allocation of votes among parents, community residents and teachers in local school council elections impermissibly interferes with their fundamental right to have an equal voice in an election involving a governmental matter of general interest, namely, the operation of local schools. Under the Act, community residents who reside in multiarea districts and do not have children in attendance at the public schools are unable to vote for any local school council members. Community residents in single district attendance centers who do not have children in attendance in a public school are entitled to vote for only two members of the council. Parents, however, who have children in the school, are entitled to vote for six members of the council. The defendants, in response, contend that a voting scheme which results in differentiated treatment of voters will not be found to violate constitutional assurances of equal protection if the voters given the weighted vote have a greater interest in and are more greatly benefited by the particular activities of the governmental unit which is the subject of the election.

From an analysis of the Act and from the argument of the plaintiffs, it is clear that the local school councils are elected by citizens who have different voting powers, i.e., with votes of unequal weight. The one person, one vote rule announced by the United States Supreme Court * * * means that a person is entitled to have his or her vote regarded as equal to every other voter's vote. The one person, one vote rule has been held to be applicable in elections of governmental bodies or units which exercise general governmental powers. See, *e.g., Avery v. Midland County* (1968), 390 U.S. 474, 88 S.Ct. 1114, 20 L.Ed.2d 45; *Hadley v. Junior College District* (1970), 397 U.S. 50, 90 S.Ct. 791, 25 L.Ed.2d 45; *Kramer v. Union Free School District No. 15* (1969), 395 U.S. 621, 89 S.Ct. 1886, 23 L.Ed.2d 583; *Board of Estimate v. Morris* (1989), 489 U.S. 688, 109 S.Ct. 1433, 103 L.Ed.2d 717. * * *

The trial court here did not analyze the legislation under the strict scrutiny test; rather, it applied the rational basis test. Under the rational basis test, the court simply inquires whether the method or means employed in the statute to achieve the stated goal or purpose of the legislation is rationally related to that goal. (*Ball v. James* (1981), 451 U.S. 355, 371, 101 S.Ct. 1811, 1821, 68 L.Ed.2d 150, 163.) The trial court held that local school councils were special limited-purpose bodies that did not exercise general governmental powers and that their elections, therefore, did not have to comply with the one person, one vote rule. The trial court stated that giving parents of children currently attending the public schools a weighted vote was rationally related to the legislative goal of improving the school system because parents were more greatly affected by and interested in the local school council's decisions.

The trial court erred in finding that the local school councils did not exercise general governmental powers and in its resulting decision to apply the rational basis test, instead of strict scrutiny. * * * That the powers exercised by the local school councils differ from those in the cases in which the Supreme Court has applied the one person, one vote principle or the exception to it is understandable. * * * [T]here does not appear to be a comparable statute in the United States or a comparable public education structure. Because they do not have powers similar to the boards in *Hadley* and *Kramer*, such as the authority to tax, to contract or to issue bonds, the local school councils' powers, upon a superficial viewing, may appear to be of a limited nature. Upon a reading of the whole Act, however, it is clear that the local school councils perform functions which are at the heart of a traditional and vital governmental function: the operation of public education. The legislature has made the local school councils the indispensable foundation of the school system. In a school system as large as Chicago's, it is obvious that powers such as issuing bonds, contracting with unions and imposing taxes must be centralized and given to one administrative body. Because these powers are lodged with the board of education, however, does not suggest that the legislature intended that sole responsibility for operation of the schools be lodged in the board. The system is structured so that responsibility for operation of the schools is divided between the board and the local school councils, with the local school to be the essential unit for educational governance and improvement. To say that the local school councils do not exercise general governmental functions simply because they do not, like the governmental bodies in *Avery*, *Hadley* or *Kramer*, have the power to tax, issue bonds or contract is to ignore the structure and legislative intention of this seemingly unique Act. The power to tax, issue bonds, contract and the like, as stated, was purposely vested by the legislature in a centralized administrative body, the board of education, because the board could more efficiently perform these functions. Control and supervision over the operation of the local schools was vested in the local school councils. The Act specifically created a system in which both the board and the local school councils play different roles. The record shows that the Act was specifically structured in this way because it was felt that the board of education had not been sufficiently responsive to problems experienced by the local schools. * * *

The local school councils are readily distinguishable from the water district[ ] at issue in *Ball* * * *. The local school councils are the cornerstone, in a real sense, of the operation of the city's schools and they play a significant role in the Act's scheme to improve education in the City of Chicago. They have important and multiple powers that affect the whole community. * * * The administration of education through the operation of our schools is a fundamental governmental activity in which all members of society have an interest. Furthermore, educational activities are financed by and affect virtually every resident. The local school councils perform an indispensable role in administering the board's educational policy at the local level and in carrying out the legislature's intent to create a dominant force at that level. We hold, therefore, that the local school councils exercise general governmental functions, as that term has been defined in *Hadley* and *Kramer*.

The question now to be addressed is whether the restriction causing unequal powers of voting in the legislative scheme for the election of local school councils can satisfy a strict scrutiny analysis. * * * The situation here is not unlike that in *Kramer*. Here certain classes of voters (those in multiarea districts) are completely denied the opportunity to participate in local school council elections. In single-area districts, although the Act does not disqualify any voter, certain classes of voters are given a clearly reduced vote. The Act plainly gives certain voters who may have little or no interest in the local school a weighted vote, *e.g.*, a parent who has left the family and has no significant contact with or interest in the child, the community or its local school, while significantly limiting the weight of the vote of a section of the community that may have a strong interest in the school, *e.g.*, property owners concerned with the value of their property and families with children of preschool age. The fact that a voter does not currently have a child attending a public school does not demonstrate a lack of attachment to or interest in the community and its educational values and certainly not to the degree that the Act assumes in giving a substantially weighted vote to parents with children in the public schools.

It is certainly not unreasonable to assume that parents with children attending the public schools possess an interest in the schools and in the educational process, but it is unreasonable and not necessary for purposes of the Act that those citizens who do not, at the time, have children in the public schools are denied an equal voice in the selection of local school council members. Here the General Assembly, without its being necessary to attain the goal of the legislation, built into the Act a substantial bias in favor of certain voters and denied or substantially restricted the weight of the vote of others. We consider that the restrictions on voting in the Act are not necessary to effect its purpose and, in any event, the restrictions as drawn in the Act are not the least restrictive means of attaining the General Assembly's goal. We hold that the Act does not meet the strict scrutiny standard and is violative of the equal protection clauses of the Federal and State Constitutions. * * *

JUSTICE CLARK, dissenting: * * *

To determine whether the local school councils exercise general governmental powers, it is necessary to analyze the powers granted to the local school councils. A local school council has the authority to: select the principal, who will serve under a four-year performance contract; evaluate the performance of the principal to determine whether the contract should be renewed; establish criteria to be included in the principal's performance contract; approve the expenditure plan prepared by the principal with respect to all funds allocated and distributed to the attendance center by the board; make *recommendations* to the principal concerning textbook selection; *advise* the principal concerning the attendance and disciplinary policies; approve a school improvement plan developed by the principal in conjunction with the local school council, school staff, parents and community residents; *evaluate* and make *recommendations* regarding the allocation of teaching resources; make *recommendations* to the principal and subdistrict superintendent concerning the appointment of persons to fill any vacant, additional or newly created teaching positions; and request training and assistance for the local school council.

As is evident in the list of powers granted to the local school councils, it is the overall function and duty of the local school councils to "advise," "recommend," or "evaluate." The local school councils have some actual decisionmaking authority, but this authority is limited to three areas and is relatively narrow. First, although a local school council has the authority to select a principal, the choice is limited to those persons certified by the State of Illinois. * * * Second, while the local school council must approve a local school expenditure plan, it is the principal who prepares this expenditure plan after consultation with "the local school council, the professional personnel advisory committee and with all other school personnel." Further, the amount allocated to each local school is determined by the board of education, and the local school council has no authority to increase the amount appropriated to the local school. Third, although the local school council must approve a school improvement plan, it is the principal who develops the plan after consultation with the "local school council, all categories of school staff, parents and community residents."

The holdings in *Avery*, *Hadley*, and *Board of Estimate* do not support the majority's conclusion that the local school councils exercise general governmental powers. In each of those cases, the local unit of government was granted extensive governmental powers. Thus, the Court refused to apply the exception to the one person, one vote rule. In this case, however, the local school councils have none of the powers the Court deemed general governmental powers in *Avery*, *Hadley*, and *Board of Estimate*. The local school councils cannot levy taxes, issue bonds, enter into employment contracts, purchase, lease or acquire by condemnation buildings or real estate, divide the city into districts and apportion the pupils, etc. In fact, the local school councils not only cannot perform these general governmental functions, but these are precisely the powers granted to the Chicago board of education. * * *

The School Reform Act recognizes that while all residents in the attendance area have an interest in the local schools, these interests are not identical in their nature or weight. * * * In this case, the parents of children in the public schools have a greater interest in the decisions of the local school council than that of nonparent residents in the school attendance area. Nonparent residents do have legitimate interests in the decisions of the local school council, but their interests are not equal to that of parents of children in the public schools. The Supreme Court has specifically recognized the special interest of parents in their children's education. (See *Pierce v. Society of the Sisters of the Holy Names of Jesus and Mary* (1925), 268 U.S. 510, 534–35, 45 S.Ct. 571, 69 L.Ed. 1070, 1078 (parents have a special interest in and a right to "direct the upbringing and education of children under their control").) The interests of the parents with children in the public schools, as opposed to those of the nonparent residents, are distinct from and greater than those of nonparent residents.

Because the local school council is a special purpose unit of government which affects definable groups of citizens more than other citizens, the election scheme in the School Reform Act fits the exception to the one person, one vote rule. Consequently, the School Reform Act should be analyzed under the rational basis test rather than the strict scrutiny test. (See *Ball*, 451 U.S. at 371, 101 S.Ct. at 1821, 68 L.Ed.2d at 163.) Under the rational basis test, the School Reform Act—which grants parents of children in the public schools a greater say in the election of local school council members—is rationally related to the statutory objective of improving the Chicago public school system, and is therefore constitutional.

In November 1987, United States Secretary of Education William Bennett labeled the Chicago public schools the "worst in the nation." Statistics, cited by the appellees in their briefs, substantiate the conclusion that the Chicago public school system is failing miserably in its responsibility to educate the City's youths. Currently, only 15% of Chicago high school students both graduate and read at or above the national average for twelfth graders. According to a study comparing the reading test results of Chicago public high schools with suburban high schools, only 2.9% of the Chicago public high schools scored at or above the national average in reading achievement whereas all reporting suburban high schools scored at or above the national average. One-half of the City's public high schools have average ACT scores that fall in the lowest 1% of all United States high schools.

These statistics, which depict the dire condition of the Chicago public schools, provoked the legislature in Springfield to completely restructure public education in Chicago. * * * In developing the School Reform Act, the legislature listened closely to the advice of leading researchers and education policy analysts. * * * [T]he innovative School Reform Act is responding to the needs of the thousands of children attending public schools in Chicago. The local school councils are being elected in the communities, and the newly appointed board of education is beginning to implement reform policies in the public schools. I agree with the circuit court's ruling that the School Reform Act is a proper and constitutional response to the educational crisis facing the City of Chicago. * * *

SECTION H. THE CITY AND DEMOCRATIC THEORY: PART FOUR

The five readings that conclude this chapter present a conception of local democracy that differs from the one that has been emphasized in most of the chapter's cases and materials. The cases and materials have concentrated on protecting citizens from city governmental power (particularly in the sections dealing with Constitutional violations of citizens' rights) or on mechanisms for citizen control of government, such as voting or access to governmental information, that perpetuate a sharp distinction between those who govern and those who are governed. In the following readings, by contrast, the emphasis is on citizen participation as the basis for the relationship between a city and its citizens— or, more accurately, as the basis for the relationships among the citizens themselves. To be sure, the notion of participation has often been referred to in this chapter, especially in the section just completed. Here, however, a fuller discussion of the idea is offered. Benjamin Barber expands on the values of participation as a way of defining oneself and one's community; Jeffrey Berry, Kent Portney and Ken Thompson describe current efforts in five American cities to institutionalize what the Barber excerpt calls "strong democracy"; John Gaventa presents an argument against the conventional reason advanced for lack of participation ("if they wanted to participate, they would"); and Hanna Pitkin and Sara Shumer sketch how the notion of participatory democracy might connect with current ideas about the necessity of bureaucratic organization, representative democracy, and technological expertise. What changes in the legal doctrine covered in the chapter would be necessary to promote the ideal these readings advance? Is the argument for participatory democracy simply a romantic fantasy or could it be put into practice in one's own community (or workplace or law school)? Even if it were put into practice, would it create a city of justice without its own defects? On this final question, Italo Calvino, appropriately enough, has the last word.

BENJAMIN BARBER, STRONG DEMOCRACY

Pp. 150–155, 173–193, 197–198 (1984).

STRONG DEMOCRACY: POLITICS IN THE PARTICIPATORY MODE

The future of democracy lies with strong democracy—with the revitalization of a form of community that is not collectivistic, a form of public reasoning that is not conformist, and a set of civic institutions that is compatible with modern society. Strong democracy is defined by politics in the participatory mode: literally, it is self-government by citizens rather than representative government in the name of citizens. Active citizens govern themselves directly here, not necessarily at every level and in every instance, but frequently enough and in particular when basic policies are being decided and when significant power is being deployed. Self-government is carried on through institutions designed to facilitate ongoing civic participation in agenda-setting, deliberation, legislation, and policy implementation (in the form of "common work"). Strong democracy does not place endless faith in the capacity of individuals to govern themselves, but it affirms with Machiavelli that the multitude will on the whole be as wise as or even wiser than princes and with Theodore Roosevelt that "the majority of the plain people will day in and day out make fewer mistakes in governing themselves than any smaller body of men will make in trying to govern them."

Considered as a response to the dilemmas of the political condition, strong democracy can be given the following formal definition: *strong democracy in the participatory mode resolves conflict in the absence of an independent ground through a participatory process of ongoing, proximate self-legislation and the creation of a political community capable of transforming dependent private individuals into free citizens and partial and private interests into public goods.*

The crucial terms in this strong formulation of democracy are *activity, process, self-legislation, creation,* and *transformation.* Where weak democracy eliminates conflict (the anarchist disposition), represses it (the realist disposition), or tolerates it (the minimalist disposition), strong democracy *transforms conflict.* It turns dissensus into an occasion for mutualism and private interest into an epistemological tool of public thinking.

Participatory politics deals with public disputes and conflicts of interest by subjecting them to a never-ending process of deliberation, decision, and action. Each step in the process is a flexible part of ongoing procedures that are embedded in concrete historical conditions and in social and economic actualities. In place of the search for a prepolitical independent ground or for an immutable rational plan, strong democracy relies on participation in an evolving problem-solving community that creates public ends where there were none before by means of its own activity and of its own existence as a focal point of the quest for mutual solutions. In such communities, public ends are neither extrapolated from absolutes nor "discovered" in a preexisting "hidden consensus." They are literally forged through the act of public participation, created through common deliberation and common action and the effect that deliberation and action have on interests, which change shape and direction when subjected to these participatory processes.

Strong democracy, then, seems potentially capable of transcending the limitations of representation and the reliance on surreptitious independent grounds without giving up such defining democratic values as liberty, equality, and social justice. Indeed, these values take on richer and fuller meanings than they can ever have in the instrumentalist setting of liberal democracy. For the strong democratic solution to the political condition issues out of a self-sustaining dialectic of participatory civic activity and continuous community-building in which freedom and equality are nourished and given political being. Community grows out of participation and at the same time makes participation possible; civic activity educates individuals how to think publicly as citizens even as citizenship informs civic activity with the required sense of publicness and justice. Politics becomes its own university, citizenship its own training ground, and participation its own tutor. Freedom is what comes out of this process, not what goes into it. Liberal and representative modes of democracy make politics an activity of specialists and experts whose only distinctive qualification, however, turns out to be simply that they engage in politics—that they encounter others in a setting that requires action and where they have to find a way to act in concert. Strong democracy is the politics of amateurs, where every man is compelled to encounter every other man without the intermediary of expertise.

This universality of participation—every citizen his own politician—is essential, because the "Other" is a construct that becomes real to an individual only when he encounters it directly in the political arena. He may confront it as an obstacle or approach it as an ally, but it is an inescapable reality in the way of and on the way to common decision and common action. *We* also remains an abstraction when individuals are represented either by politicians or as symbolic wholes. The term acquires a sense of concreteness and simple reality only when individuals redefine themselves as citizens and come together directly to resolve a conflict or achieve a purpose or implement a decision. Strong democracy creates the very citizens it depends upon *because* it depends upon them, because it permits the representation neither of *me* nor of *we,* because it mandates a permanent confrontation between the *me* as citizen and the "Other" as citizen, forcing *us* to think in common and act in common. The citizen is by definition a *we*-thinker, and to think of the *we* is always to transform how interests are perceived and goods defined.

This progression suggests how intimate the ties are that bind participation to community. Citizenship is not a mask to be assumed or shed at will. It lacks the self-conscious mutability of a modern social "role" as Goffman might construe it. In strong democratic politics, participation is a way of defining the self, just as citizenship is a way of living. The old liberal notion, shared even by radical democrats such as Tom Paine, was that a society is "composed of distinct, unconnected individuals [who are] continually meeting, crossing, uniting, opposing, and separating from each other, as accident, interest, and circumstances shall direct." Such a conception repeats the Hobbesian error of setting participation and civic activity apart from community. Yet participation without community, participation in the face of deracination, participation by victims or bondsmen or clients or subjects, participation that is uninformed by an evolving idea of a "public" and unconcerned with the nurturing of self-responsibility, participation that is fragmentary, part-time, half-hearted, or impetuous—these are all finally sham, and their failure proves nothing.

It has in fact become a habit of the shrewder defenders of representative democracy to chide participationists and communitarians with the argument that enlarged public participation in politics produces no great results. Once empowered, the masses do little more than push private interests, pursue selfish ambitions, and bargain for personal gain, the liberal critics assert. Such participation is the work of prudent beasts and is often less efficient than the ministrations of representatives who have a better sense of the public's appetites than does the public itself. But such a course in truth merely gives the people all the insignia and none of the tools of citizenship and then convicts them of incompetence. Social scientists and political elites have all too often indulged themselves in this form of hypocrisy. They throw referenda at the people without providing adequate information, full debate, or prudent insulation from money and media pressures and then pillory them for their lack of judgment. They overwhelm the people with the least tractable problems of mass society—busing, inflation, tax structures, nuclear safety, right-to-work legislation, industrial waste disposal, environmental protection (all of which the representative elites themselves have utterly failed to deal with)—and then carp at their uncertainty or indecisiveness or the simple-mindedness with which they muddle through to a decision. But what general would shove rifles into the hands of civilians, hurry them off to battle, and then call them cowards when they are overrun by the enemy?

Strong democracy is not government by "the people" or government by "the masses," because a people are not yet a citizenry and masses are only nominal freemen who do not in fact govern themselves. Nor is participation to be understood as random activity by maverick cattle caught up in the same stampede or as minnow-school movement by clones who wiggle in unison. As with so many central political terms, the idea of participation has an intrinsically normative dimension a dimension that is circumscribed by citizenship. Masses make noise, citizens deliberate; masses behave, citizens act; masses collide and intersect, citizens engage, share, and contribute. At the moment when "masses" start deliberating, acting, sharing, and contributing, they cease to be masses and become citizens. Only then do they "participate."

Or, to come at it from the other direction, to be a citizen *is* to participate in a certain conscious fashion that presumes awareness of and engagement in activity with others. This consciousness alters attitudes and lends to participation that sense of the *we* I have associated with community. To participate *is* to create a community that governs itself, and to create a self-governing community *is* to participate. Indeed, from the perspective of strong democracy, the two terms *participation* and *community* are aspects of one single mode of social being: citizenship. Community without participation first breeds unreflected consensus and uniformity, then nourishes coercive conformity, and finally engenders unitary collectivism of a kind that stifles citizenship and the autonomy on which political activity depends. Participation without community breeds mindless enterprise and undirected, competitive interest-mongering. Community without participation merely rationalizes collectivism, giving it an aura of legitimacy. Participation without community merely rationalizes individualism, giving it the aura of democracy.

This is not to say that the dialectic between participation and community is easily institutionalized. Individual civic activity (participation) and the public association formed through civic activity (the community) call up two strikingly different worlds. The former is the world of autonomy, individualism, and agency; the latter is the world of sociability, community, and interaction. The world views of individualism and communalism remain at odds; and institutions that can facilitate the search for common ends without sabotaging the individuality of the searchers, and that can acknowledge pluralism and conflict as starting points of the political process without abdicating the quest for a world of common ends, may be much more difficult to come by than a pretty paragraph about the dialectical interplay between individual participation and community. Yet it is just this dialectical balance that strong democracy claims to strike. To justify this claim in detail is the task of the remaining part of this study. * * *

At the heart of strong democracy is talk. As we shall see, talk is not mere speech. It refers here to every human interaction that involves language or linguistic symbols. Talk has been at the root of the Western idea of politics since Aristotle identified *logos* as the peculiarly human and peculiarly social faculty that divided the human species from animals otherwise defined by similar needs and faculties. But as talk became a synonym for politics, its meanings became as multifarious as those of politics.

Modern democratic liberals certainly maintain the close identity of politics and talk, but they do so by reducing talk to the dimensions of their smallish politics and turning it into an instrument of symbolic exchange between avaricious but prudent beasts. "Descartes, Locke, and Newton took away the world," laments Yeats in his *Explorations,* "and gave us its excrement instead." Hobbes, Bentham, and Laswell take away talk and give us instead noise: animal expletives meant to signify bargaining positions in a world of base competition. The first ten books of *Leviathan* offer a scrupulously reductionist lexicography that gives to every term in the language of rhetoric an austere referent in the physics of psychology. Within three centuries, abetted by stimulus-response models of social behavior, by nominalist and behaviorist models of linguistics, and by logical-positivist models of social science, this lexicography has impoverished political talk, both as a medium of politics itself and as a tool for rendering political processes intelligible. Yet talk remains central to politics, which would ossify completely without its creativity, its variety, its openness and flexibility, its inventiveness, its capacity for discovery, its subtlety and complexity, its eloquence, its potential for empathy and affective expression, and its deeply paradoxical (some would say dialectical) character that displays man's full nature as a purposive, interdependent, and active being.

Before embarking on a detailed discussion of the functions of talk in democracy, I want to make three general observations. First, strong democratic talk entails listening no less than speaking; second, it is affective as well as cognitive; and third, its intentionalism draws it out of the domain of pure reflection into the world of action.

In considering recent liberal theory and the idea of democracy as the politics of interest, one finds it easy enough to see how talk might be confused with speech and speech reduced to the articulation of interest by appropriate signs. Yet talk as communication obviously involves receiving as well as expressing, hearing as well as speaking, and empathizing as well as uttering. The liberal reduction of talk to speech has unfortunately inspired political institutions that foster the articulation of interests but that slight the difficult art of listening. It is far easier for representatives to speak for us than to listen for us (we do not send representatives to concerts or lectures), so that in a predominantly representative system the speaking function is enhanced while the listening function is diminished. The secret ballot allows the voter to express himself but not to be influenced by others or to have to account for his private choices in a public language. The Anglo American adversary system, expressed in legislative politics, in the judicial system, and even in the separation of powers into contending branches, also puts a premium on speaking and a penalty on listening. The aim in adversarial proceedings is to prevail—to score verbal points and to overcome one's interlocutors. In fact, speech in adversary systems is a form of aggression, simply one more variety of power. It is the war of all against all carried on by other means.

The participatory process of self-legislation that characterizes strong democracy attempts to balance adversary politics by nourishing the mutualistic art of listening. "I will listen" means to the strong democrat not that I will scan my adversary's position for weaknesses and potential trade-offs, nor even (as a minimalist might think) that I will tolerantly permit him to say whatever he chooses. It means, rather, "I will put myself in his place, I will try to understand, I will strain to hear what makes us alike, I will listen for a common rhetoric evocative of a common purpose or a common good."

Good listeners may turn out to be bad lawyers, but they make adept citizens and excellent neighbors. Liberal democrats tend to value speech, and are thus concerned with formal equality. Listeners, on the other hand, feel that an emphasis on speech enhances natural inequalities in individuals' abilities to speak with clarity, eloquence, logic, and rhetoric. Listening is a mutualistic art that by its very practice enhances equality. The empathetic listener becomes more like his interlocutor as the two bridge the differences between them by conversation and mutual understanding. Indeed, one measure of healthy political talk is the amount of *silence* it permits and encourages, for silence is the precious medium in which reflection is nurtured and empathy can grow. Without it, there is only the babble of raucous interests and insistent rights vying for the deaf ears of impatient adversaries. The very idea of rights—the right to speak, the right to get on the record, the right to be heard—precludes silence. The Quaker meeting carries a message for democrats, but they are often too busy articulating their interests to hear it.

A second major requirement of talk in strong democracy is that it encompass the affective as well as the cognitive mode. Philosophers and legal theorists have been particularly guilty of overrationalizing talk in their futile quest for a perfectly rational world mediated by perfectly rational forms of speech. Having abandoned Wittgenstein's later wariness about language and its limits, they are forever trying to domesticate unruly words with the discipline of logic, trying to imprison speech in reason, trying to get talk not merely to reveal but to define rationality. Bruce Ackerman's is only the most candid and explicit of the recent attempts to impose on language a set of "neutral constraints" that make speech the parent of justice. This verbal eugenics, in which justice is produced by the controlled breeding of words, threatens to displace entirely the idea of justice as the product of political judgment. Most philosophers would agree with Bertrand Russell that "real life" is "a long second-best, a perpetual compromise between the ideal and the possible," whereas the "world of pure reason knows no compromise, no practical limitations, no barrier to the creative activity embodying in splendid edifices the passionate aspirations after the perfect form." Thus the quest for philosophical justice becomes "an escape from the dreary exile of the actual world." Talk disciplined by philosophy is not only fit to enter the world of pure reason, it is capable, as the common denominator between politics and philosophy, of taking politics with it. However, for the most part this brave experiment in other-worldliness has only impoverished politics without ever achieving the elevation of talk.

The philosophers are not really the primary culprits, however. They follow even as they lead, and if they have not always recognized, in Kolakowski's words, that "man as a cognitive being is only part of man as a whole," it is in part because the political liberals whom they wish to succor have persuaded them that man as a creature of interest is the whole man and that the rationalization of interest is the philosophical task that needs doing. The philosophers can hardly be blamed then for developing notions of rationality rooted in instrumental prudence and notions of justice legitimized by enlightened self-interest. How can speech be anything but cognitive under these circumstances?

Stripped of such artificial disciplines, however, talk appears as a mediator of affection and affiliation as well as of interest and identity, of patriotism as well as of individuality. It can build community as well as maintain rights and seek consensus as well as resolve conflict. It offers, along with meanings and significations, silences, rituals, symbols, myths, expressions and solicitations, and a hundred other quiet and noisy manifestations of our common humanity. Strong democracy seeks institutions that can give these things a voice—and an ear.

The third issue that liberal theorists have underappreciated is the complicity of talk in action. With talk we can invent alternative futures, create mutual purposes, and construct competing visions of community. Its potentialities thrust talk into the realm of intentions and consequences and render it simultaneously more provisional and more concrete than philosophers are wont to recognize. Their failure of imagination stems in part from the passivity of thin democratic politics and in part from the impatience of speculative philosophy with contingency, which entails possibility as well as indeterminateness. But significant political effects and actions are possible only to the extent that politics is embedded in a world of fortune, uncertainty, and contingency.

Political talk is not talk *about* the world; it is talk that makes and remakes the world. The posture of the strong democrat is thus "pragmatic" in the sense of William James's definition of pragmatism as "the attitude of looking away from first things, principles, 'categories,' supposed necessities; and of looking toward last things, fruits, consequences, facts." James's pragmatist "turns toward concreteness and adequacy, toward facts, toward action, and toward power. * * * [Pragmatism thus] means the open air and possibilities of nature, as against dogma, artificiality and the pretense of finality in truth." Strong democracy is pragmatism translated into politics in the participatory mode. Although James did not pursue the powerful political implications of his position, he was moved to write: "See already how democratic [pragmatism] is. Her manners are as various and flexible, her resources as rich and endless, and her conclusions as friendly as those of mother nature." The active, future-oriented disposition of strong democratic talk embodies James's instinctive sense of pragmatism's political implications. Future action, not a priori principle, constitutes such talk's principal (but not principled) concern.

Strong democratic talk, then, always involves listening as well as speaking, feeling as well as thinking, and acting as well as reflecting. These characteristics are evident in and help to explain the particular political functions of talk in a strong democratic system. What follows is an inventory of these functions. * * *

The functions of talk in the democratic process fall into at least nine major categories. The first two are familiar to liberals and encompass most of what they understand as the functions of talk. The next six are muted and undervalued in liberal theory, in part because they are not well served by representative institutions and by the adversary system. The last summarizes the overall function of talk. The nine functions are:

1. The articulation of interests; bargaining and exchange
2. Persuasion
3. Agenda-setting
4. Exploring mutuality
5. Affiliation and affection

6. Maintaining autonomy

7. Witness and self-expression

8. Reformulation and reconceptualization

9. Community-building as the creation of public interests, common goods, and active citizens

1. The Articulation of Interests; Bargaining and Exchange. In most liberal polities, talk is understood as a primary medium of exchange among competing individuals who seek to maximize their self-interests through market interaction. Contracts are one good example. The model here is economic, and speech is little more than a system of mathematical signs—quantifications of competing expressions such as "I want" and "How much will you pay?"—that make possible the adjudication, aggregation, and exchange that is presumed to lie at the heart of politics. The term *interest* is crucial here, because it embodies the idea of the individual and his adversary social role * * *. This narrow construction of talk certainly depicts one of the aspects it has in all democratic regimes. But this interpretation also raises problems. By reducing talk to the hedonistic speech of bargaining, it creates a climate hostile to the affective uses of talk and invulnerable to the subtle claims of mutualism. These limitations are most clearly evident in the "free-rider" problem, which continues to bedevil the shapers of public policy and of economic choice. Free-riders are self-interested individuals who do not care to comply with public policies and common decisions in the absence of careful policing and external coercion. Since they act exclusively out of self-interest and obey regulations only as the necessary price for winning the compliance of others, they are content to ride for nothing on the back of the "public" as long as they can get away with it. As we will see when we discuss the nature of public interests below, free-riders can exist only in a thin democracy where obligation is the provisional consequence of a bargain. Citizens do not and cannot ride for free, because they understand that their freedom is a consequence of their participation in the making and acting out of common decisions. To ride for free is to betray not others or an abstract promise but themselves.

2. Persuasion. Liberal democrats favor economic models of political interaction, but they are far too sophisticated to think that the shouting on the floor of the stock exchange and the bargains that such shouting seals exhaust the possibilities of political talk. They recognize persuasion and rhetoric as well, although they tend to regard these as tools to be used in convincing others of the legitimacy of one's own interests. Persuasion thus constitutes a second major function of talk in all democratic regimes. Among liberals, this function is conventionally associated with the idea of the "rationality of interests," a notion of talk that falls short of a truly public interest but that does envision a web of interest linking private to more general goods. Bentham's principle of greatest happiness, Smith's invisible hand, and Rawls's original position involve the idea of a web of interest. Such reasoning gives to mere interest the persuasive ring of generality and a rhetorical suggestion of justice, without actually relinquishing radical individualism or psychological hedonism.

The rhetorical functions of talk lend themselves to representation. Individuals and groups who wish to exhibit the public utility of their private interests employ suitably talented "mouthpieces"—rhetoricians, barristers, and senators—who deploy the arts of logic, litigation, and legislation to cloak the private in pseudopublic talk. Nonetheless, the rhetorician's resort to public arguments suggests something of the ability that the idea of a public has to legitimize politics, even in liberal democratic theory. The senator weaving a mantle of public talk around a purely private interest still does a small service to the very idea of the public, though he may be putting it to a scoundrel's use. In this way, even the narrowest construction of persuasion moves the policy beyond talk as the expression of wholly private interests and becomes a link to stronger forms of democracy.

3. Agenda–Setting. In liberal democracies, agendas are typically regarded as the province of elites—of committees, or executive officers, or (even) pollsters. This is so not simply because representative systems delegate the agenda-setting function or because they slight citizen participation, but because they conceive of agendas as fixed and self-evident, almost natural, and in this sense incidental to such vital democratic processes as deliberation and decision-making.

Yet a people that does not set its own agenda, by means of talk and direct political exchange, not only relinquishes a vital power of government but also exposes its remaining powers of deliberation and decision to ongoing subversion. What counts as an "issue" or a "problem" and how such issues or problems are formulated may to a large extent predetermine what decisions are reached. For example, the choice between building a small freeway and a twelve-lane interstate highway in lower Manhattan may seem of little moment to those who prefer to solve the problems of urban transportation with mass rail transit. Or the right to choose among six mildly right-of-center candidates may fail to exercise the civic imagination of socialists. Nor is it sufficient to offer a wide variety of options, for what constitutes an option—how a question is formulated—is as controversial as the range of choices offered. Abortion is clearly an issue that arouses intense public concern at present, but to say that it belongs on the public agenda says too little. The vital question remains: How is it presented? In this form: "Do you believe there should be an amendment to the Constitution protecting the life of the unborn child?" Or in this form: "Do you believe there should be an amendment to the Constitution prohibiting abortions?" When asked the first question by a *New York Times*-CBS poll, over one-half responded "yes," whereas when asked the second question only 29 percent said "yes." He who controls the agenda—if only its wording—controls the outcome. The battle for the Equal Rights Amendment was probably lost because its enemies managed to place it on the public agenda as calling for "the destruction of the family, the legitimization of homosexuality, and the compulsory use of coed toilets." The ERA's supporters never succeeded in getting Americans to see it as "the simple extension of the Constitution's guarantees of rights to women"—a goal that most citizens would probably endorse. * * *

For these reasons, strong democratic talk places its agenda at the center rather than at the beginning of its politics. It subjects every pressing issue to continuous examination and possible reformulation. Its agenda *is,* before anything else, its agenda. It thus scrutinizes what remains unspoken, looking into the crevices of silence for signs of an unarticulated problem, a speechless victim, or a mute protester. The agenda of a community tells a community where and what it is. It defines that community's mutualism and the limits of mutualism, and draws up plans for pasts to be institutionalized or overcome and for futures to be avoided or achieved. Far from being a mere preliminary of democracy, agenda-setting becomes one of its pervasive, defining functions.

4. Exploring Mutuality. When talk is reduced to mere signing in a bargaining process, it can permit us at best only to explore our differences in the search for mutually beneficial exchanges. Rational-choice models such as the "prisoner's dilemma" translate even altruism into the language of interest. But because it permits us to treat our interlocutors as kin by virtue of our common language, rather than as adversaries by virtue of our divergent interests, strong democratic talk becomes a medium of mutual exploration. The functions of talk in deliberation (airing choices), bargaining (exchanging benefits), and decision-making (choosing goals) are complemented by the more complex, open-ended art of conversation.

Because liberals have been set on securing rights, realizing purposes, protecting interests, and in general getting things done, they have had a difficult time making sense of conversation as a political art. They have let the graceful proponents of the conservative tradition pay tribute to conversation as a basic art of civility and have thereby abandoned what might have been an important tool of democracy. Michael Oakeshott's portrait of conversation goes to the heart of the dialectical function of talk:

> In conversation, "facts" appear only to be resolved once more into the possibilities from which they were made: "certainties" are shown to be combustible, not by being brought into contact with other "certainties" or with doubts, but by being kindled by the presence of ideas of another order; approximations are revealed between notions normally remote from one another. Thoughts of different species take wing and play around one another, responding to each other's movements and provoking one another to fresh exertion.

Conversation as part of a politics that acknowledges the absence of independent grounds and, refusing the arbitration of extrinsic authority, acts as its own epistemology exactly meets Oakeshott's standard for conversation. "There is no symposiarch or arbiter," he concludes, "not even a doorkeeper to examine credentials * * * *voices which speak in conversation do not compose a hierarchy*." So it is with democratic talk, where no voice is privileged, no position advantaged, no authority other than the process itself acknowledged. Every expression is both legitimate and provisional, a proximate and temporary position of a consciousness in evolution.

Fixing its own rules as it conducts itself, a conversation follows an informal dialectic in which talk is used not to chart distinctions in the typical analytic fashion but to explore and create commonalities. Analytic reason yields contradictions such as individual versus society, or freedom versus authority. Conversation gives life to a notion of "citizen" in which such antinomies are superseded. "The vagaries of me and you" (Peirce) dissolve in a form of talk possible only for "us." *Right* and *wrong* cease to be viable terms of judgment in an interchange that makes no claim to certainty or truth. Think of two neighbors talking for the first time over a fence, or two college freshmen talking over a first cup of coffee: there are no debates, no arguments, no challenges, no setting of priorities, no staking out of positions, no inventorying of interests, no distribution of goods, no awarding of prizes. There is only a "getting to know you" and thereby "getting to know *us* "—exploring the common context, traits, circumstances, or passions that make of two separate identities one single *we*. World leaders meeting at a summit will frequently devote an initial session to getting to know one another in very much this fashion, before they get down to the business of bargaining and exchange. And it is much more than protocol that motivates them; indeed, even protocol is a form of ritual in which civility is given its due, where there may be little more than civility to hold adversaries together. * * *

In juries and multimember courts, in committees, and in diplomacy, ambiguity and novel formulations often produce agreements that legalistic speech or economic bargaining could not hope to yield. A vague but encompassing phrase that is susceptible to several interpretations may serve mutuality far better than an exact phrase weighed down with all the baggage of historical stipulation and fixed usage. Yet where diplomats, politicians, and judges are encouraged to fudge in search of agreement or at least of understanding, voters, constituents, and citizens are urged to follow the polarizing example of rational-choice models. Harold Nicolson thus chides democrats in his classic study *Diplomacy* by assailing "the vagueness and fluidity of democratic policy" as one of "its salient vices. * * * [T]here is the tendency of all democracies to prefer a vague and comforting formula to a precise and binding definition." But "precise and binding" language implies clear winners and losers and sets a schedule of gains and losses that must be publicly acknowledged by all parties. The clarity of the Versailles Treaty that ended World War I was surpassed only by its potential for disaster. In keeping with the Wilsonian model of unambiguous diplomacy, it assigned the roles of winner and loser with perfect precision and thereby helped create not a world safe for democracy but a world doomed to enmity and to the eventual resumption of armed conflict. The Middle East accord worked out by Carter, Begin, and Sadat, in contrast, developed language that each of the parties could interpret in its own way, so that each could view the agreement as a victory for its side.

The art of conversation is the art of finding language that is broad and novel enough to bridge conflicting perceptions of the world yet sufficiently genuine to withstand the later pounding of the subscribing parties. Although language alone can hardly hold the dike against a tide of adversary interests, it can often transform interests over time—as appears to have happened in the case of Israel and Egypt. Words can have a limited but potent magic, either to divide or to unite; and silence too has a magic, if only to soothe too-often iterated passions. Diplomats and labor negotiators use both talk and silence with a studious regard for ambiguity; conference committees and the professional legislators who people them can move party ideologues to consensus by moving commas in a legislative preamble. These are the conversational skills needed by citizens who wish to be self-governing, if they are to achieve mutuality without surrendering their autonomy.

5. *Affiliation and Affection.* Conversation enables us to know and even to understand one another, but we do not necessarily like what we know and understand. Thus it is useful to separate the exploratory from the affective uses of talk in democracy, even though these obviously overlap a good deal. For whereas in exploring mutuality, talk retains its cognitive structure (though it may stretch it for the sake of ambiguity), in serving affection and affiliation talk takes advantage of its potential for emotive expression, musical utterance, inflection, feeling, ritual, and symbolism (or myth). We talk to infants, to animals, to lovers, to ourselves, and to God in sounds for which neither economists nor analytic philosophers would find much use. Yet the sound of music and the sound of poetry move and bind with a power that belongs to talk. Through words we convey information, articulate interests, and pursue arguments, but it is through tone, color, volume, and inflection that we feel, affect, and touch each other. We reassure, we frighten, we unsettle, we comfort, we intimidate, we soothe, we hate, and we love by manipulating the medium rather than the content of speech. Indeed, we can use the medium to contradict its message—as in Ring Lardner's whimsical line, " 'Shut up!' he explained"—or to create irony, that irksome tribute to the deeply layered texture (the deep structure) of all speech. And our talk is peppered with ritual speech: greetings and goodbyes, prayers and incantations, exclamations and expletives, all of which in their banality and conventionality express and reinforce the daily structures of common life.

In politics, noncognitive speech is less appreciated, perhaps once again because formal rationality and liberal democracy have forged so close a partnership. But in practice, ritual is not to be denied, particularly in the bodies of government where talk is most valued. The United States Senate is full of invaluable sound and fury signifying nothing.

Meaningless hortatory phrases insinuate themselves into debate and bring with them a civility that helps to attenuate the force of divisive passions. The senator from New York who yields "to the honorable and loquacious gentleman from the great farm state of Iowa," so that the gentleman can launch into a diatribe against New York's financial mismanagement, is testifying to his respect for regionalism, his belief in federalism and variety, and his willingness to listen to and work with adversaries in a common body that is responsible for the nation's welfare—all this with a puffed-up phrase or two drawn from the hyperbole of parliamentary grandiloquence.

Grass-roots politics and participatory democracy need this quaint language of affiliation and affection no less than do the great legislative houses and courts of the world. Voting—which is already the least significant act of citizenship in a democracy—has in America been stripped of almost all pomp and ritual, largely in the name of the kind of efficiency symbolized by voting machines and the kind of privatism represented by the secret ballot. Voting should be an occasion for celebration as well as for choice, just as the exercise of freedom should be a rite as well as a right. In some localities, the Swiss still choose their representatives and vote on policies in day-long assemblies in which festive games, theater, drinking, and camaraderie accompany the formal voting process. Rousseau notes the invigorating effect that such celebrations have on the community's sense of identity as well as on individual citizens' autonomy and capacity for action. In contrast, our primary electoral act, voting, is rather like using a public toilet: we wait in line with a crowd in order to close ourselves up in a small compartment where we can relieve ourselves in solitude and in privacy of our burden, pull a lever, and then, yielding to the next in line, go silently home. Because our vote is secret—"private"—we do not need to explain or justify it to others (or, indeed, to ourselves) in a fashion that would require us to think publicly or politically. The public rites of voting can have an affiliating effect that is as valuable to democracy as the decision itself. In strong democracy, affect and effect are Siamese twins; neither can thrive without the other. After all, the right to choose belongs to citizens not to individuals, and citizens are defined by their membership in a community not by their capacity to vote, which follows only from membership.

The affective and affiliative functions of talk are not limited to ceremonial community-building or to entirely noncognitive aspects of emotive speech. Talk of every kind—cognitive, prudential, exploratory, conversational, and affective—can enhance empathy, and there is perhaps no stronger social bond and no more significant ally of public thinking than the one fashioned by empathy. * * *

Empathy has a politically miraculous power to enlarge perspectives and expand consciousness in a fashion that not so much accommodates as transcends private interests and the antagonisms they breed. A neighbor is a stranger transformed by empathy and shared interests into a friend—an *artificial* friend, however, whose kinship is a contrivance of politics rather than natural or personal and private. This distinction is crucial in the civil process, for the attachments we feel toward natural kith and kin can be constricting and parochializing; they can exclude and subvert rather than nourish citizenship. Empathy, however, as an artificial product of political talk, arouses feelings that attach precisely to "strangers," to those who do not belong to our private families or clubs or churches. The leap out of privatism and self-interest that democratic participation promotes is a leap to embrace strangers whose commonality with us arises less out of blood or geography or culture than out of talk itself.

Talk thus breaks through the walls of the private world of family, friends, and neighbors and ordains concourse with strangers in a larger artificial world of political citizenship. Politics is the art of engaging strangers in talk and of stimulating in them an artificial kinship made in equal parts of empathy, common cause, and enlightened self-interest. The affective power of talk is, then, the power to stretch the human imagination so that the *I* of private self-interest can be reconceptualized and reconstituted as a *we* that makes possible civility and common political action.

6. *Maintaining Autonomy.* Talk helps us overcome narrow self-interest, but it plays an equally significant role in buttressing the autonomy of individual wills that is essential to democracy. It is through talk that we constantly reencounter, reevaluate, and repossess the beliefs, principles, and maxims on the basis of which we exert our will in the political realm. To be free, it is not enough for us simply to will what we choose to will. We must will what we possess, what truly belongs to us. John Stuart Mill commented on the "fatal tendency of mankind to leave all thinking about a thing when it is no longer doubtful." He ascribed to this tendency "the cause of about half [men's] errors." Mindless convictions not only spawn errors, they turn those who hold them into charlatans of liberty. Today's autonomously held belief is tomorrow's heteronomous orthodoxy unless, tomorrow, it is reexamined and repossessed.

Talk is the principal mechanism by which we can retest and thus repossess our convictions, which means that a democracy that does not institutionalize talk will soon be without autonomous citizens, though men and women who call themselves citizens may from time to time deliberate, choose, and vote. Talk immunizes values from ossification and protects the political process from rigidity, orthodoxy, and the yoke of the dead past.

This, among all the functions of talk, is the least liable to representation, since only the presence of our own wills working on a value can endow that value with legitimacy and us with our autonomy. Subjecting a value to the test of repossession is a measure of legitimacy as well as of autonomy: forced knowingly to embrace their prejudices, many men falter. Prejudice is best practiced in the dark by dint of habit or passion. Mobs are expert executors of bigotry because they assimilate individual wills into a group will and relieve individuals of any responsibility for their actions. It is above all the imagination that dies when will is subordinated to instinct, and as we have seen, it is the imagination that fires empathy.

Values will, naturally, conflict even where they are thoughtfully embraced and willed; and men's souls are sufficiently complex for error or even evil to dwell comfortably in the autonomous man's breast. Autonomy is no guarantee against moral turpitude; indeed, it is its necessary condition. But in the social setting, it seems evident that maxims that are continuously reevaluated and repossessed are preferable to maxims that are embraced once and obeyed blindly thereafter. At a minimum, convictions that are reexamined are more likely to change, to adapt themselves to altered circumstances and to evolve to meet the challenges offered by competing views. Political willing is thus never a one-time or sometime thing (which is the great misconception of the social-contract tradition), but an ongoing shaping and reshaping of our common world that is as endless and exhausting as our making and remaking of our personal lives. A moment's complacency may mean the death of liberty; a break in political concentration may spell the atrophy of an important value; a pleasant spell of privatism may yield irreversible value ossification. Democratic politics is a demanding business.

Perhaps this is why common memory is even more important for democracy than for other forms of political culture. Not every principle of conduct can be tested at every moment; not every conviction can be exercised on every occasion; not every value can be regarded as truly ours at a given instant. Thus remembrance and imagination must act sometimes as surrogates for the actual testing of maxims. Founding myths and the rituals associated with them (July 14 in France or August 1 in Switzerland), representative political heroes who embody admired convictions (Martin Luther King or Charles de Gaulle), and popular oral traditions can all revivify citizens' common beliefs and their sense of place in the political culture. These symbols are no substitute for the citizenry's active reexamination of values through participation in political talk, but they can and do supplement such talk through the imaginative reconstruction of the past in live images and through the cultivation of beliefs that are not necessarily involved in a given year's political business.

7. *Witness and Self–Expression.* There is a second feature of talk that undergirds the autonomous individual and secures his place in a community of talk. The fact that an individual belongs to a political community and assents to common decisions means ideally that he reformulates his personal interests and beliefs in terms commensurable with public interests and beliefs. But realistically, that fact may also mean that the individual is outtalked or outvoted or even overruled by a collective will that seems less likely to serve the public good than would the individual's own will. A healthy democratic community will therefore leave room for the expression of distrust, dissent, or just plain opposition, even in lost causes where dissenters are obviously very much

in the minority. Here the function of talk is to allow people to vent their grievances or frustration or opposition, not in hopes of moving others but in order to give public status to their strongly held personal convictions. The cry "In spite of all, *I believe* * * * "is the hallmark of such usage, and conscientious objection to military service is an illuminating example.

This form of self-expression involves much more than merely letting off steam, though we would be foolish to undervalue the safety-valve function. It is a symbol of the community's heterogeneity and an acknowledgment that, though political decisions must be taken and common grounds for these decisions contrived in the absence of independent measures, the common will may comprise individuals whose compliance is reluctant. "I am part of the community, I participated in the talk and deliberation leading to the decision, and so I regard myself as bound; but let it be known that I do not think we have made the right decision," says the dissenter in a strong democracy. He means thus not to change the decision this time, for it has been taken, but to bear witness to another point of view (and thereby to keep the issue on the public agenda).

Our present liberal democratic institutions obstruct this sort of talk in two ways. First, through representation, they make it impossible for losers and dissenters to voice their postelectoral regrets in a public place where it will be heard. As a consequence, disappointed participants are often transformed into voiceless aliens. Legislators who lose can take to the floor of their parliamentary houses or call a press conference and shout their sorrow to the listening world. Citizens who lose actually lose twice, first by being outvoted and then by being relegated to silence.

Liberal institutions also slight the witnessing function of talk by presuming (in keeping with the rational-choice model) that views should be aired only before the decision is made and that such self-expression has no rational function afterwards. But it is in the aftermath of a vote that dissenters may feel the greatest need to speak their pain. The character and intensity of talk after a vote may well be a measure of how effectively a decision has coped with an issue. The citizen bearing witness to his disappointment also serves notice on the community that it is in danger of fragmentation. There is simply no day in the life of a democracy when citizens can afford either to stop talking themselves or to stop others from talking to them.

8. *Reformulation and Reconceptualization.* As we have seen, the reformulation of terms and values insinuates itself into each of the other functions of talk. Agenda-setting as an ongoing function involves the persistent reconceptualization of public business, of the very idea of the public; the exploration of mutuality entails an enlargement of consciousness that brings with it new and broader understandings of common language; affiliation and affection depend on an empathy that changes how we view our interests and our separate identities; autonomy means rethinking our values and beliefs in a changing world; and witness

suggests a challenge to common decisions commonly taken that may facilitate reevaluation. Only bargaining and persuasion (narrowly understood) are free of reformulation—which is, of course, exactly what is the matter with them.

"My language is the sum total of myself," writes Peirce, "for the man is the thought." But language is ineluctably communal and its evolution determines the evolution of self and other, of the communal we. Those who control language thus control the communal we. If the definition of democracy as popular sovereignty has any meaning, then it is sovereignty over language—over talk fashioned by and for the talkers themselves. Democratize language, give each citizen some control over what the community will mean by the crucial terms it uses to define all the citizens' selves and lives in public and private, and other forms of equality will follow. We may redistribute goods and make power accountable, but if we reserve talk and its evolution to specialists—to journalists or managers or clerics or packagers or bureaucrats or statesmen or advertisers or philosophers or social scientists—then no amount of equality will yield democracy. * * *

9. Community–Building as the Creation of Public Interests, Common Goods, and Active Citizens. All of the functions of talk discussed above converge toward a single, crucial end—the development of a citizenry capable of genuinely public thinking and political judgment and thus able to envision a common future in terms of genuinely common goods * * *. [T]alk is ultimately a force with which we can create a community capable of creating its own future and that talk is nourished by community even as it helps establish the conditions for community. * * *

JEFFREY BERRY, KENT PORTNEY, & KEN THOMSON, THE REBIRTH OF URBAN DEMOCRACY

Pp. 10–14, 294–296 (1993).

The literature on face-to-face interaction is of crucial importance to constructing a plausible case for participatory democracy because it attacks the notion that individual behavior is based on self-interest. It offers a rationale for why people might be more likely to gravitate toward solutions that are best for the broader community rather than single-mindedly pursuing what is best for themselves. Experimental research shows that group identity is a critical variable in leading people away from self-interested behavior. People place a high value on benefits accruing to groups they identify with, and thus having the group reach a good decision can take on greater importance than having one's own preference chosen. Behavioral research has also shown that "ingroup biasing is a remarkably robust and easily elicited psychological phenomenon."

Another important finding from this research is that the frequency of interaction is strongly related to the propensity for cooperative behavior. In his study of the prisoner's dilemma, Robert Axelrod concludes: "Here is the argument in a nutshell. The evolution of cooperation requires that individuals have a sufficiently large chance to meet again so that they have a stake in their future interaction." It is simple human nature for individuals to behave differently with other people when they know they will be in extensive contact in the months or years to come.

Cooperation is also facilitated by the opportunity for discussion. Experimental research that places strangers in group situations and forces them to choose between courses of action that benefit themselves and those that benefit the group finds dramatic differences in outcomes when discussion is allowed. In one set of experiments, people could defect from the group anonymously by choosing an option on a secret ballot that could give them an individual financial payoff larger than the one they would get by choosing the option that would benefit the whole group. Discussion was the critical variable that bonded the group and led to cooperative rather than egoistic choices. Personal interaction and discussion lead to trust, and trust underlies cooperation. Trust is an emotional commitment as well as a rational calculation of likely outcomes.

It is important not to overstate the case: face-to-face interaction does not inevitably lead to cooperative, public-spirited behavior. A majority faction may use its numerical strength to override the concerns of others. In addition, face-to-face forums allow for peer pressure and decisions mask real disagreements. And cooperative behavior does not necessarily signify completely altruistic behavior. In much of the theoretical work, self-interest and altruistic behavior are placed at opposite poles, but political behavior can incorporate both motives. Moreover, for people to bring their own self-interested concerns to the political process is not inherently wrong. But if self-interest is assumed to be the dominant incentive that drives political behavior, then institutions and policymaking processes will be designed to facilitate the politics of self-interest. If it is assumed instead that self-interest is an important but not a dominant motivating factor in politics, then government may be structured quite differently.

A decentralized city government, with considerable authority placed in the hands of the neighborhoods, represents a sensible compromise between the realistic needs of efficiency and scale for some services and the requirements of participatory democracy. Neighborhood-based government draws easily on people's sense of identity with the area they live in. People know they are going to have frequent interactions with their neighbors, so even if they attend meetings infrequently they have a powerful incentive to think about long-term relationships in addition to the policy questions at hand. The primary decisionmaking tool in neighborhood associations is, quite simply, discussion among the community residents who attend the regular open meetings. Thus neighborhood associations are institutions that are well suited to the face-to-face interaction that can nurture cooperative behavior. * * *

This book is a study of five cities that take face-to-face democracy seriously. In these cities neighborhood organizations are the primary agent of political dialogue and citizen influence. This type of neighborhood system is a significant step toward strong democracy. And the systems work.

Each city has built a system of support and policy connections around the following neighborhood groups.

—Birmingham has a three-tiered system in which neighborhood officers in over ninety-five neighborhoods are elected every two years at the polls. The neighborhood associations form the base of the system. Broader "communities" encompass several neighborhoods apiece, and a citywide Citizens Advisory Board (CAB) is composed of representatives from each of these communities. Each association communicates with all households in its neighborhood through a monthly newsletter, decides how its community development block grant (CDBG) allocations will be used, and works with community resource staff to find solutions to neighborhood concerns. This structure was the first to bring blacks and whites in Birmingham together in a common vision for the city.

—Dayton has a system of seven Priority Boards whose members are elected by precinct through the use of mail ballots. Each Priority Board area is divided into neighborhoods, which overlap the precinct boundaries. The system is seen explicitly as a two-way communication channel between government and citizens. Through leadership training; a monthly council meeting of each board and representatives of major city agencies; annual neighborhood needs statements; and a wide range of neighborhood-oriented planning, initiatives, and self-help programs, citizens learn how to make their voices heard. In return, the city communicates its plans and progress to all the neighborhoods through a Priority Board staff based in a neighborhood office and makes its case for needed change on a wide range of matters from bond issues to city employee residency requirements.

—Portland has grown into a citywide system of autonomous neighborhood associations, with seven District Coalition Boards pulling together more than ninety neighborhood representatives. Each board, hiring its own staff and working out of its own office, is under contract with the city to provide "citizen participation services" to its own community. The administrative budget alone was more than $1.2 million in 1986–87. The system consciously balances the coalition advocacy, annual neighborhood needs reports, crime prevention teams, and individual neighborhood issues with a wide range of citywide participation initiatives. These initiatives include Budget Advisory Committees for every major agency plus the "big BAC" for the city as a whole, comprehensive neighborhood-based planning, self-help development grants, technical assistance, and a citizen mediation program. City officials take pride in the multiplicity of participation routes.

—St. Paul is divided into seventeen District Councils, each elected by residents of the council area. Every council has a city-paid community organizer and neighborhood office, but virtually all other efforts come from volunteers or additional funds raised by the council itself. The District Councils have substantial powers, including jurisdiction over zoning, authority over the distribution of various goods and services, and substantial influence over capital expenditures. A citywide Capital Improvement Budget Committee (CIB), composed solely of neighborhood representatives, is responsible for the initiation and priority ranking of most capital development projects in the city. Community centers, crime prevention efforts, an early notification system for all major city agencies, and a district newspaper in virtually every council area help to make the system one of the most coherent and comprehensive of any city we have seen.

—In San Antonio, Communities Organized for Public Service (COPS) is structured along parish boundaries of the Catholic church in the Hispanic sections of the city. Parallel but much weaker organizations exist in the remainder of the city, competing with independent neighborhood organizations. Citywide conventions and "actions" (demonstrations, meetings, and confrontations with public officials) of several hundred to several thousand people characterize COPS activity. The city initiates fewer programs in support of the neighborhood groups than do the other four cities, but over the course of twenty years, COPS has provided the Hispanic community, which had virtually no clout at city hall, with an organization that arguably has more political power than any other single community group in the nation.

In contrast to the critics' predictions, these strong participation systems have not functioned at the expense of governability. They do not produce policy gridlock or increased political conflict. The systems do not seem to introduce racial or economic biases into the policymaking process. There is no evidence that the city-supported neighborhood associations at the core of the systems in four of the five cities are less effective in translating citizen demands into governmental action than are independent citizen groups.

Instead of chaos, there is a degree of empowerment. Participation in these systems tends to increase confidence in government and sense of community. Within a certain range of issues—particularly land use and planning issues—neighborhoods generate city policy. High levels of face-to-face participation are linked to increased responsiveness by city hall.

After many years of operation, however, many participants and nonparticipants alike have criticisms of these systems. Some feel that they do not go far enough: the city does not listen to them on the important issues, the participation structures have become rigid, and too few people are involved. Indeed, our comparison surveys show that the overall numbers of people active in their community are little different in these cities from those in comparable cities with less extensive participation efforts, although more of this activity in the five cities is directed toward community and political issues than purely social interaction. Low-income people and those with lower education levels are still much less involved than higher income, more highly educated people. Many remain unaware of an opportunity to participate and skeptical of their ability to influence any political decision. Even the five cities are still far from achieving the ideals of strong democracy. * * *

The success of the citizen participation systems in the five core study cities is unusual. Our preliminary screening turned up few other cities that even came close to the five cities in the scope of neighborhood-based citizen participation. It is not that other cities have not tried: many have created a citizen participation system on paper only to see it fail miserably in operation.

Given the frequency of failure, does it make sense for cities to invest scarce resources to emulate the four citywide systems depicted here? The potential payoff is high, but the risk is substantial too. Involving people in systems that are ineffectual is sure to alienate them and damage the reputation of the incumbent administration. Given the negative legacy of failure for citizen participation in urban politics, the paucity of inspired efforts in recent years to create new systems is not surprising. Parental control of neighborhood schools in Chicago is one visible exception to this. More often than not, citizen participation has earned little more than empty rhetoric or lame efforts, such as the open office hours New York Mayor David Dinkins held for one day. Twenty-two hundred people showed up to tell him how to improve city government, and fifty-four were permitted brief audiences with the mayor. * * *

Cities should not attempt to create citizen participation programs unless they are willing to meet three important conditions. First, exclusive powers must be turned over to the citizen participation structures. The primary participation structures must not be merely planning boards or advisory committees; they must have authority to allocate some significant goods and services in their communities. This means that powers must be taken away from the agencies at city hall that currently exercise such authority and transferred unequivocally to neighborhood organizations. As the four citywide systems have shown, control over zoning, a key to establishing authority over the neighborhood, should be among the powers transferred to the community. More broadly, what neighborhood associations do must be integrated into the existing administrative structure of the city. Interaction between the neighborhood associations and city administrators must be routinized, so that in areas where powers are shared between neighborhood and city hall, the neighborhoods are not dependent on administrators' willingness to meet with them.

Second, accompanying such structural changes must be an administrative plan that creates sanctions and rewards for city hall administrators who must interact with the neighborhood groups. If people running agencies are able to fight a rearguard action to try to prevent the neighborhood associations from encroaching on their authority, they may very well sink the citizen participation program. In the absence of proper incentives and sanctions, agency managers are the "losers" when citizen participation systems succeed; they are the ones who must give up power. Consequently, their incentives for cooperation must be realistically assessed. It has to be worth their while to buy into the system so that they have a stake in its success. Thus their personal future in city government must be tied to the success of the citizen participation system.

Third, citizen participation systems must be citywide in nature. Each community should have a single, officially recognized neighborhood association that represents an area with well-defined boundaries. They should not be explicitly designed as programs to help low-income or minority neighborhoods. As William Julius Wilson has pointed out, the best way to help poor minority groups in cities is to create "programs to which the more advantaged groups of all races and class backgrounds can positively relate." Programs that are aimed at disadvantaged neighborhoods will not have the same credibility or legitimacy as citywide programs. * * *

JOHN GAVENTA, POWER AND POWERLESSNESS
Pp. 3–25 (1980).

POWER AND PARTICIPATION

This is a study about quiescence and rebellion in a situation of glaring inequality. Why, in a social relationship involving the domination of a non-elite by an elite, does challenge to that domination not occur? What is there in certain situations of social deprivation that prevents issues from arising, grievances from being voiced, or interests from being recognized? Why, in an oppressed community where one might intuitively expect upheaval, does one instead find, or appear to find, quiescence? Under what conditions and against what obstacles does rebellion begin to emerge?

The problem is significant to classical democratic and Marxist theories alike, for, in a broad sense, both share the notion that the action of the dispossessed will serve to counter social inequities. Yet, as these views move from political theory to political sociology, so, too, do they appear to move—particularly with reference to the United States—from discussing the necessities of widespread participation and challenge to considering the reasons for their non-occurrence. In their wake, other more conservative theories of democracy present the appearance of quiescence in the midst of inequality as evidence of the legitimacy of an existing order, or as an argument for decision-making by the few, or at least as a phenomenon functional to social stability. More recently, these 'neo-elitists' have in turn been challenged by others who, with C. Wright Mills, argue that the appearance of quiescence need neither suggest consent nor refute the classical ideals. Rather, it may reflect the use or misuse of modern-day power.

While the theories of democracy turn, at least to a degree, upon disputes as to the significance of quiescence, the sociological literature of industrial societies offers an array of explanations for its roots: embourgeoisement, hegemony, no real inequality, low rank on a socio-economic status scale, cultural deficiencies of the deprived, or simply the innate apathy of the human race—to name but a few. Rather than deal with these directly, this study will explore another explanation: in situations of inequality, the political response of the deprived group or class may be seen as a function of power relationships, such that power serves for the development and maintenance of the quiescence of the non-elite. The emergence of rebellion, as a corollary, may be understood as the process by which the relationships of power are altered.

The argument itself immediately introduces a further set of questions to be explored: what is the nature of power? How do power and powerlessness affect the political actions and conceptions of a non-elite?

In his recent book, *Power: A Radical View,* Lukes has summarized what has been an extended debate since C. Wright Mills, especially in American political science, about the concept and appropriate methods for its study.[4] Power, he suggests, may be understood as having three dimensions, the first of which is based upon the traditional pluralists' approach, the second of which is essentially that put forward by Bachrach and Baratz in their consideration of power's second face,[5] and the third of which Lukes develops. In this chapter, I shall examine the dimensions briefly, arguing that each carries with it, implicitly or explicitly, differing assumptions about the nature and roots of participation and non-participation. I shall argue further that together the dimensions of power (and powerlessness) may be developed into a tentative model for more usefully understanding the generation of quiescence, as well as the process by which challenge may emerge. * * *

THE NATURE OF POWER AND ROOTS OF QUIESCENCE

The One–Dimensional Approach. The one-dimensional approach to power is essentially that of the pluralists, developed in American political science most particularly by Robert Dahl and Nelson Polsby. 'My intuitive idea of power', Dahl wrote in an early essay, 'is something like this: A has power over B to the extent that he can get B to do something that B would not otherwise do.' In the politics of a community, Polsby later added, power may be studied by examining 'who participates, who gains and loses, and who prevails in decision-making'.

The key to the definition is a focus on behaviour—doing, participating—about which several assumptions are made * * *. First, grievances are assumed to be recognized and acted upon. Polsby writes, for instance, that 'presumably people participate in those areas they care about the most. Their values, eloquently expressed by their partic-

4. Steven Lukes, *Power: A Radical View* (Macmillan, London, 1974).
5. Peter Bachrach and Morton S. Baratz, "The Two Faces of Power", *American Political Science Review,* 56 (1962), 947–52; and Bachrach and Baratz, *Power and Poverty: Theory and Practice* (Oxford University Press, New York, 1970).

ipation, cannot, it seems to me, be more effectively objectified.' Secondly, participation is assumed to occur within decision-making arenas, which are in turn assumed to be open to virtually any organized group. Again, Polsby writes, 'in the decision-making of fragmented government—and American national, state and local government are nothing if not fragmented—the claims of small intense minorities are usually attended to'. In his study of New Haven Dahl takes a similar view:

> In the United States the political system does not constitute a homogenous class with well-defined class interests. In New Haven, in fact, the political system is easily penetrated by anyone whose interests and concerns attract him to the distinctive political culture of the stratum * * * The independence, penetrability and heterogeneity of the various segments of the political stratum all but guarantee that any dissatisfied group will find a spokesman * * *

Thirdly, because of the openness of the decision-making process, leaders may be studied, not as elites, but as representative spokesmen for a mass. Polsby writes, 'the pluralists want to find about leadership's role, presumed to be diverse and fluid'. Indeed, it is the conflict amongst various leaders that ensures the essential responsiveness of the political game to all groups or classes. As Dahl puts it, 'to a remarkable degree, the existence of democratic ceremonials that give rise to the rules of combat has insured that few social elements have been neglected for long by one party or the other'.

Within the one-dimensional approach, because a) people act upon recognized grievances, b) in an open system, c) for themselves or through leaders, then *non-participation* or *inaction* is not a political problem. For Polsby it may be explained away with 'the fundamental presumption that human behaviour is governed in large part by inertia'. Dahl distinguishes between the activist, *homo politicus,* and the non-activist, *homo civicus,* for whom 'political action will seem considerably less efficient than working at his job, earning more money, taking out insurance, joining a club, planning a vacation, moving to another neighbourhood or city, or coping with an uncertain future in manifold other ways * * *'. The pluralists argue that by assuming political action rather than inaction to be the problem to be explained, their methodology avoids the 'inappropriate and arbitrary assignment of upper and middle class values to all actors in the community'—i.e. the value of participation. Yet, the assumption itself allows class-bound conclusions. Dahl's characterization of *homo civicus* is certainly one of a citizen for whom there are comfortable alternatives to participation and relatively low costs to inaction. And for Polsby, the assumption of inertia combines with the assumption of an open system to allow the conclusion, without further proof, that class consciousness has not developed in America because it would be 'inefficient' or 'unnecessary'.

The biases of these assumptions might appear all the more readily were this approach strictly applied to the quiescence of obviously deprived groups. Political silence, or inaction, would have to be taken to reflect 'consensus', despite the extent of the deprivation. Yet, rarely is the methodology thus applied, even by the pluralists themselves. To make plausible inaction among those for whom the status quo is not comfortable, other explanations are provided for what appears 'irrational' or 'inefficient' behaviour. And, because the study of non-participation in this approach is sequestered by definition from the study of power, the explanations must generally be placed within the circumstance or culture of the non-participants themselves. The empirical relationship of low socio-economic status to low participation gets explained away as the apathy, political inefficacy, cynicism or alienation of the impoverished. Or other factors—often thought of as deficiencies—are put forward in the non-political culture of the deprived group, such as in the 'amoral familism' argument of Banfield in reference to Southern Italy. Rather than examining the possibility that power may be involved, this approach 'blames the victim' for his non-participation. And it also follows that by changing the victim—e.g. through remedial education or cultural integration—patterns of non-participation will also be changed. Increased participation, it is assumed, will not meet power constraints.

Even within its own assumptions, of course, this understanding of the political behaviour of deprived groups is inadequate. What is there inherent in low income, education or status, or in rural or traditional cultures that itself explains quiescence? If these are sufficient components of explanation, how are variations in behaviour amongst such groups to be explained? Why, for instance, do welfare action groups spring up in some cities but not in others? * * * If most blacks are of a relatively low socio-economic status, why did a highly organized civil rights movement develop, and itself alter patterns of political participation?

In short, as operationalized within this view, the power of A is thought to affect the action of B, but it is not considered a factor relevant to why B does not act in a manner that B otherwise might, were he not powerless relative to A. That point, among others, is well made by those who put forward the two-dimensional view of power.

The Two–Dimensional Approach. 'It is profoundly characteristic', wrote Schattschneider, that 'responsibility for widespread nonparticipation is attributed wholly to the ignorance, indifference and shiftlessness of the people.' But, he continued:

> There is a better explanation: absenteeism reflects the suppression of the options and alternatives that reflect the needs of the nonparticipants. It is not necessarily true that people with the greatest needs participate in politics most actively—whoever decides what the game is about also decides who gets in the game.

In so writing, Schattschneider introduced a concept later to be developed by Bachrach and Baratz as power's 'second face', by which power is exercised not just upon participants within the decision-making process but also towards the exclusion of certain participants and issues altogether. Political organizations, like all organizations, develop a 'mobilization of bias * * * in favour of the exploitation of certain kinds of conflict and the suppression of others * * * Some issues are organized into politics while others are organized out.' And, if issues are prevented from arising, so too may actors be prevented from acting. The study of politics must focus 'both on who gets what, when and how and who gets left out and how'—and how the two are interrelated.

When this view has been applied (explicitly or implicitly) to the political behaviour of deprived groups, explanations for quiescence in the face of inequalities have emerged, which are quite different from those of the one-dimensional view. For instance, Matthew Crenson, in his extended empirical application of the 'non-issues' approach, *The Un–Politics of Air Pollution,* states that 'while very few investigators have found it worthwhile to inquire about the political origins of inaction * * *', in Gary, Indiana, 'the reputation for power may have been more important than its exercise. It could have enabled U.S. Steel to prevent political action without taking action itself, and may have been responsible for the political retardation of Gary's air pollution issue.' Or, Parenti, in his study of urban blacks in Newark, found that in city hall the 'plurality of actors and interests * * * displayed remarkable capacity to move against some rather modest lower-class claims'. 'One of the most important aspects of power', he adds, is 'not to prevail in a struggle but to predetermine the agenda of struggle—to determine whether certain questions ever reach the competition stage.' Salamon and Van Evera, in their work on voting in Mississippi, found patterns of participation and non-participation not to be related to apathy amongst low status blacks as much as to 'fear' and 'vulnerability' of these blacks to local power elites. Similarly, in his extensive study, *Peasant Wars,* Wolf found acquiescence or rebellion not to be inherent in the traditional values or isolation of the peasantry, but to vary 'in the relation of the peasantry to the field of power which surrounds it'.

In this view, then, apparent inaction within the political process by deprived groups may be related to power, which in turn is revealed in participation and non-participation, upon issues and non-issues, which arise or are prevented from arising in decision-making arenas. But though the second view goes beyond the first, it still leaves much undone.

Empirically, while the major application of the approach, that by Crenson, recognizes that 'perceived industrial influence, industrial inaction, and the neglect of the dirty air issue go together', it still adds 'though it is difficult to say how'.

Even conceptually, though, this second approach stops short of considering the full range of the possibilities by which power may intervene in the issue-raising process. While Bachrach and Baratz insist that the study of power must include consideration of the barriers to action upon grievances, they equally maintain that it does not go so far as to include how power may affect conceptions of grievances themselves.

If 'the observer can uncover no grievances', if 'in other words, there appears to be universal acquiescence in the status quo', then, they argue, it is not 'possible, in such circumstances, to determine empirically whether the consensus is genuine or instead has been enforced'.

However difficult the empirical task, though, their assumption must be faulted on two counts. First, as Lukes points out, 'to assume the absence of grievance equals genuine consensus is simply to rule out the possibility of false or manipulated consensus by definitional fiat'. Secondly, though, the position presents an inconsistency even within their own work. They write further:

> For the purposes of analysis, a power struggle exists, overtly or covertly, either when both sets of contestants are aware of its existence *or when only the less powerful party is aware* of it. The latter case is relevant where the domination of status quo defenders is so secure and pervasive that they are oblivious of any persons or groups desirous of challenging their preeminence.

But, if the power of the 'defenders of the *status quo*' serves to affect their awareness that they are being challenged, why cannot the powerlessness of potential challengers similarly serve to affect their awareness of interests and conflict within a power situation? That is, just as the dominant may become so 'secure' with their position as to become 'oblivious', so, too, may such things as routines, internalization of roles or false consensus lead to acceptance of the *status quo* by the dominated. In short, I shall agree with Lukes that the emphasis of this approach upon observable conflict may lead it to neglect what may be the 'crucial point': 'the most effective and insidious use of power is to prevent such conflict from arising in the first place'.

The Three–Dimensional Approach. In putting forward a further conception of power, Lukes argues that 'A exercises power over B when A affects B in a manner contrary to B's interests.' The means by which A may do so go significantly beyond those allowed within the first two approaches.

First, 'A may exercise power over B by getting him to do what he does not want to do, but *he also exercises power over him by influencing, shaping or determining his very wants.*' Not only might A exercise power over B by prevailing in the resolution of key issues or by preventing B from effectively raising those issues, but also through affecting B's conceptions of the issues altogether. Secondly, 'this may happen in the absence of observable conflict, which may have been successfully averted', though there must be latent conflict, which consists, Lukes argues, 'in a contradiction between the interests of those exercising power and the *real interests* of those they exclude'. Thirdly, the analysis of power must avoid the individualistic, behavioral confines of the one- and to some extent the two-dimensional approaches. It must allow 'for consideration of the many ways in which *potential issues* are kept out of politics, whether through the operation of social forces and institutional practices or through individuals' decisions'. In so extending the concept of power, Lukes suggests, 'the three-dimensional view * * * offers the prospect of a serious sociological and not merely personalized explanation of how political systems prevent demands from becoming political issues or even from being made'.

Though the prospect has been offered, the task has yet to have been carried out. To do so, though, might bring together usefully approaches often considered separately of the relationship of political conceptions to the social order. For instance, following in a line of American political scientists (beginning perhaps with Lasswell), the emphasis upon consciousness allows consideration of the subjective effects of power, including Edelman's notion that 'political actions chiefly arouse or satisfy people not by granting or withholding their stable, substantive demands but rather by changing their demands and expectations'. At the same time, by not restricting power to individuals' actions, the three-dimensional definition allows consideration of the social forces and historical patterns involved in Gramsci's concept of hegemony, or what Milliband develops as the use of ideological predominance for the 'engineering of consent' amongst the subordinate classes.

Perhaps more significant, however, are the implications of this three-dimensional approach for an understanding of how power shapes participation patterns of the relatively powerless. In a sense, the separation by the pluralists of the notion of power from the phenomenon of quiescence has indicated the need for such a theory, while in the second and third approaches are its beginnings. In the two-dimensional approach is the suggestion of barriers that prevent issues from emerging into political arenas—i.e. that constrain conflict. In the three-dimensional approach is the suggestion of the use of power to pre-empt manifest conflict at all, through the shaping of patterns or conceptions of non-conflict. Yet, the two-dimensional approach may still need development and the three-dimensional prospect has yet to be put to empirical test.

This book therefore will pick up the challenge of attempting to relate the three dimensions of power to an understanding of quiescence and rebellion of a relatively powerless group in a social situation of high inequality. Through the empirical application further refinements of the notion of power may develop, but, of equal importance, more insights may be gleaned as to why non-elites in such situations act and believe as they do.

THE MECHANISMS OF POWER

What are the mechanisms of power? How might its components be wielded in the shaping or containment of conflict?

First Dimension. In the first-dimensional approach to power, with its emphasis on observable conflict in decision-making arenas, power may be understood primarily by looking at who prevails in bargaining over the resolution of key issues. The mechanisms of power are important, but relatively straightforward and widely understood: they involve the political resources—votes, jobs, influence—that can be brought by political actors to the bargaining game and how well those resources can be wielded in each particular play through personal efficacy, political experience, organizational strength, and so on.

Second Dimension. The second-dimensional approach adds to these resources those of a 'mobilization of bias',

> A set of predominant values, beliefs, rituals, and institutional proce-dures ('rules of the game') that operate systematically and consis-tently to the benefit of certain persons and groups at the expense of others. Those who benefit are placed in a preferred position to defend and promote their vested interests.

Bachrach and Baratz argue in *Power and Poverty* that the mobilization of bias not only may be wielded upon decision-making in political arenas, but it in turn is sustained primarily through 'non-decisions', defined as:

> A decision that results in suppression or thwarting of a latent or manifest challenge to the values or interests of the decision maker. To be more nearly explicit, nondecision-making is a means by which demands for change in the existing allocation of benefits and privi-leges in the community can be suffocated before they are voiced, or kept covert; or killed before they gain access to the relevant decision-making arena; or, failing all of these things, maimed or destroyed in the decision-implementing stage of the policy process.

One form of non-decision-making, they suggest, may be force. A second may be the threat of sanctions, 'negative or positive', 'ranging from intimidation * * * to co-optation'. A third may be the 'invocation of an existing bias of the political system—a norm, precedent, rule or proce-dure—to squelch a threatening demand or incipient issue'. This may include the manipulation of symbols, such as, in certain political cul-tures, 'communist' or 'troublemaker'. A fourth process which they cite 'involves reshaping or strengthening the mobilization of bias' through the establishment of new barriers or new symbols 'against the challeng-ers' efforts to widen the scope of conflict'.

While the above mechanisms of power involve identifiable actions which prevent issues from entering the decision-making arenas, there may be other processes of non-decision-making power which are not so explicitly observable. The first of these, 'decisionless decisions', grows from institutional inaction, or the unforeseen sum effect of incremental decisions. A second process has to do with the 'rule of anticipated reactions', 'situations where B, confronted by A who has greater power resources decides not to make a demand upon A, for fear that the latter will invoke sanctions against him'. In both cases, the power process involves a non-event rather than an observable non-decision.

Third Dimension. By far the least developed and least understood mechanisms of power—at least within the field of political science—are those of the third dimension. Their identification, one suspects, involves specifying the means through which power influences, shapes or determines conceptions of the necessities, possibilities, and strategies of challenge in situations of latent conflict. This may include the study of social myths, language, and symbols, and how they are shaped or manipulated in power processes. It may involve the study of communication of information—both of what is communicated and how it is done. It may involve a focus upon the means by which social legitimations are developed around the dominant, and instilled as beliefs or roles in the dominated. It may involve, in short, locating the power processes behind the social construction of meanings and patterns that serve to get B to act and believe in a manner in which B otherwise might not, to A's benefit and B's detriment.

Such processes may take direct observable forms, as Lukes suggests. 'One does not have to go to the lengths of talking about Brave New World, or the world of B.F. Skinner to see this: thought control takes many less total and more mundane forms, through the control of information, through the mass media, and through the process of socialization.' * * *

In addition to these processes of information control or socialization, there may be other more indirect means by which power alters political conceptions. They involve psychological adaptations to the state of being without power. They may be viewed as third-dimensional effects of power, growing from the powerlessness experienced in the first two dimensions. Especially for highly deprived or vulnerable groups, three examples might be given of what shall be called the *indirect* mechanisms of power's third dimension.

In the first instance, the conceptions of the powerless may alter as an adaptive response to continual defeat. If the victories of A over B in the first dimension of power lead to non-challenge of B due to the anticipation of the reactions of A, as in the second-dimensional case, then, over time, the calculated withdrawal by B may lead to an unconscious pattern of withdrawal, maintained not by fear of power of A but by a sense of powerlessness within B, regardless of A's condition. A sense of powerlessness may manifest itself as extensive fatalism, self-deprecation, or undue apathy about one's situation. Katznelson has argued, for instance, in *Black Men, White Cities* that 'given the onus of choice, the powerless internalize their impossible situation and internalize their guilt * * * The slave often identified with his master and accepted society's estimate of himself as being without worth * * * The less complete but nonetheless pervasive powerlessness of blacks in America's northern ghettos * * * has had similar effects.' Or, the powerless may act, but owing to the sense of their powerlessness, they may alter the level of their demands. The sense of powerlessness may also lead to a greater susceptibility to the internalization of the values, beliefs, or rules of the game of the powerful as a further adaptive response—i.e. as a means of escaping the subjective sense of powerlessness, if not its objective condition.

The sense of powerlessness may often be found with, though it is conceptually distinct from, a second example of the indirect mechanisms of power's third dimension. It has to do with the interrelationship of participation and consciousness. As has been seen in the pluralists' literature, it is sometimes argued that participation is a consequence of a high level of political awareness or knowledge, most often associated with those of a favourable socio-economic status. However, it might also be the case, as is argued by the classical democratic theorists, that it is participation itself which increases political consciousness—a reverse argument from the one given above. Social psychology studies, for instance, have found that political learning is dependent at least to some degree of political participation within and mastery upon one's environment. And, as Pizzorno points out, there is a 'singular relationship, well known by all organizers of parties and political movements: class consciousness promotes political participation, and in its turn, political participation increases class consciousness'. If this second understanding of the relationship to participation and consciousness is the case, then it should also be the case that those denied participation—unable to engage actively with others in the determination of their own affairs— also might not develop political consciousness of their own situation or of broader political inequalities.

This relationship of non-participation to non-consciousness of deprived groups is developed by Paulo Freire, one of the few writers to have considered the topic in depth. 'Consciousness', he writes, 'is constituted in the dialectic of man's *objectification* and *action* upon the world.' In situations of highly unequal power relationships, which he terms 'closed societies', the powerless are highly dependent. They are prevented from either self-determined action or reflection upon their actions. Denied this dialectic process, and denied the democratic experience out of which the 'critical consciousness' grows, they develop a 'culture of silence'. 'The dependent society is by definition a silent society.' The culture of silence may preclude the development of consciousness amongst the powerless thus lending to the dominant order an air of legitimacy. As in the sense of powerlessness, it may also encourage a susceptibility among the dependent society to internalization of the values of the dominant themselves. 'Its voice is not an authentic voice, but merely an echo of the metropolis. In every way the metropolis speaks, the dependent society listens.' Mueller similarly writes about groups which 'cannot articulate their interests or perceive social conflict. Since they have been socialized into compliance, so to speak, they accept the definitions of political reality as offered by dominant groups, classes or government institutions.'

Even as the 'silence' is broken, the initial demands of the dominated may be vague, ambiguous, partially developed. This might help to explain the phenomenon of the 'multiple' or 'split' consciousness often cited in the literature for poor or working-class groups. As long as elements of the sense of powerlessness or the assuming consciousness that grow from non-participation can be maintained, then although there may be a multitude of grievances, the 'unified' or 'critical' consciousness will likely remain precluded. And, in turn, the inconsistencies themselves may re-enforce the pattern of non-challenge. In Gramsci's terms, 'it can reach the point where the contradiction of conscience will not permit any decision, any choice, and produce a state of moral and political passivity'.

This understanding gives rise to a final indirect means through which power's third dimension may work. Garson has described the 'multiple consciousness' as being characterized by 'ambiguity and overlays of consciousness; different and seemingly contradictory orientations will be evoked *depending upon the context*'. If such is the case, then the consciousness of the relatively powerless, even as it emerges, may be malleable, i.e. especially vulnerable to the manipulation of the power field around it. Through the invocation of myths or symbols, the use of threat or rumours, or other mechanisms of power, the powerful may be able to ensure that certain beliefs and actions emerge in one context while apparently contradictory grievances may be expressed in others. From this perspective, a consistently expressed consensus is not required for the maintenance of dominant interests, only a consistency that certain potentially key issues remain latent issues and that certain interests remain unrecognized—at certain times more than at others.

These direct and indirect mechanisms of power's third dimension combine to suggest numerous possibilities of the means through which power may serve to shape conceptions of the necessities, possibilities, or strategies of conflict. Not only, as in the two-dimensional approach, might grievances be excluded from entering the political process, but they might be precluded from consideration altogether. Or, B, the relatively powerless, may recognize grievances against A, the relatively powerful, but desist from challenge because B's conceptions of self, group, or class may be such as to make actions against A seem inappropriate. Or, B may recognize grievances, be willing to act upon them, but not recognize A as the responsible agent towards which action should be directed—e.g. because of the mystifications or legitimations which surround A. Or, B may recognize grievances against A and be willing to act, but may not through viewing the order as immutable or through lacking conceptions of possible alternatives. Or, B may act, but do so on the basis of misconceived grievances, against the wrong target, or through an ineffective strategy. Any or all of these possibilities may serve the same purpose of protecting A's interests owing to B's shaped conceptions of potential conflict, to B's detriment.

But the indirect mechanisms of power's third dimension, seen as a consequence of the powerlessness experienced in the first two, have suggested yet a further consideration: the dimensions of power, each with its sundry mechanisms, must be seen as interrelated in the totality of their impact. In that simple idea lies the basis for developing a more coherent theory about the effects of power and powerlessness upon quiescence and rebellion in situations of great inequality.

POWER AND POWERLESSNESS: QUIESCENCE AND
REBELLION—A TENTATIVE RELATIONSHIP

Power, it has been suggested, involves the capacity of A to prevail over B both in resolution of manifest conflict and through affecting B's actions and conceptions about conflict or potential conflict. Intuitively, if the interests of A and B are contrary, and if A (individual, group, class) exercises power for the protection of its interests, then it will also be to A's advantage if the power can be used to generate and maintain quiescence of B (individual, group, class) upon B's interests. In that process, the dimensions of power and powerlessness may be viewed as interrelated and accumulative in nature, such that each dimension serves to re-enforce the strength of the other. The relationships may be schematized * * * as follows:

As A develops power, A prevails over B in decision-making arenas in the allocation of resources and values within the political system. If A prevails consistently, then A may accumulate surplus resources and values which may be allocated towards the construction of barriers around the decision-making arenas—i.e. towards the development of a mobilization of bias, as in the second dimension of power. The consistent prevalence of A in the decision-making arenas plus the thwarting of challenges to that prevalence may allow A further power to invest in the development of dominant images, legitimations, or beliefs about A's power through control, for instance, of the media or other socialization institutions. The power of A to prevail in the first dimension increases the power to affect B's actions in the second dimension, and increases the power to affect B's conceptions in the third.

The power of A is also strengthened by the fact that the powerlessness of B is similarly accumulative, and that power and powerlessness may each re-enforce the other towards the generation of B's quiescence. In the decision-making arena, B suffers continual defeat at the hands of A. Over time, B may cease to challenge A owing to the anticipation that A will prevail. But B's non-challenge allows A more opportunity to devote power to creating barriers to exclude participation in the future. The inaction of B in the second-dimensional sense becomes a sum of the anticipation by B of defeat and the barriers maintained by A over B's entering the decision-making arena anyway, and the re-enforcing effect of one upon the other.

In turn, the second-dimensional relationship may re-enforce the sense of powerlessness, the maintained non-participation, the ambiguous consciousness, or other factors which comprise the indirect mechanisms of power's third dimension. Further withdrawal of B though, in turn, allows more security for A to develop further legitimations or ideologies which may be used indirectly to affect the conceptions of B. And, as has been seen, the powerlessness of B may also increase the susceptibility of B to introjection of A's values. In the third-dimensional sense, then, B's response becomes understood as the sum of B's powerlessness and A's power, and the re-enforcing effects of the one upon the other.

Once such power relationships are developed, their maintenance is self-propelled and attempts at their alteration are inevitably difficult. In order to remedy the inequalities, B must act, but to do so B must overcome A's power, and the accumulating effects of B's powerlessness. In order to benefit from the inequalities, A need not act, or if acting, may devote energies to strengthening the power relationships. Indeed, to the extent that A can maintain conflict within the second- or third-dimensional arenas, then A will continue to prevail simply through the inertia of the situation. Pocock describes what may have been such a relationship with reference to the maintenance of power by Ancient Chinese rulers:

> Where A has the power and B has not, it is a sign of weakness for either to take initiative, but B must take it and A need not * * * Once acquired, it (power) is maintained not by exertion but by inaction; not by imposing norms, but by being prerequisite to their imposition; not by the display of virtue, but by the characterless force of its own necessity. The ruler rules not by solving other's problems, but by having none of his own; others have problems—i.e. they desire the power he has—and by keeping these unsolved he retains the power over them.

In such a situation, power relationships can be understood only with reference to their prior development and their impact comprehended only in the light of their own momentum.

Challenge, or rebellion, may develop if there is a shift in the power relationships—either owing to loss in the power of A or gain in the power of B. (The two need not be the same owing to the possibility of intervention by other actors, technological changes, external structural factors, etc.) But even as challenge emerges, several steps in overcoming powerlessness by B must occur before the conflict is on competitive ground. B must go through a process of *issue and action formulation* by which B develops consciousness of the needs, possibilities, and strategies of challenge. That is, B must counter both the direct and indirect effects of power's third dimension. And, B must carry out the process of *mobilization of action upon issues* to overcome the mobilization of bias of A against B's actions. B must develop its own resources—real and symbolic—to wage the conflict. Only as the obstacles to challenge by B in the second and third dimensions are overcome can the conflict which emerges in the first dimension be said to reflect B's genuine participation—i.e. self-determined action with others similarly affected upon clearly conceived and articulated grievances.

This formulation of the steps in the emergence of effective challenge provides further understanding of the means by which A may prevail over the outcome of any latent or manifest conflict. In the first instance, A may simply remain aloof from B, for to intervene in a situation of potential conflict may be to introduce the notion of conflict itself. But, if conceptions or actions of challenge do arise on the part of B, A may respond at any point along the process of issue-emergence.

That is, the powerless may face barriers to effective challenge in the processes of the formulation of issues, of the mobilization of action upon issues, or in the decision-making about issues—any or all of which may affect the outcome of the conflict. What are for B barriers to change are for A options for the maintenance of the status quo.

But, by the same token, as the barriers are overcome, so, too, do A's options for control lessen. And, just as the dimensions of power are accumulative and re-enforcing for the maintenance of quiescence, so, too, does the emergence of challenge in one area of a power relationship weaken the power of the total to withstand further challenges by more than the loss of a single component. For example, the development of consciousness of an issue re-enforces the likelihood of attempted action upon it, in turn re-enforcing consciousness.

A single victory helps to alter inaction owing to the anticipation of defeat, leading to more action, and so on. Once patterns of quiescence are broken upon one set of grievances, the accumulating resources of challenge—e.g. organization, momentum, consciousness—may become transferable to other issues and other targets.

For this reason, the development and maintenance of a generalized pattern of quiescence of B by A in situations of latent conflict will always be in A's interests. A will act to thwart challenges by B regardless of whether they appear, in the immediate sense, to be directed against A; for once the patterns are broken, the likelihood of further action by B increases and the options for control wielded by A decrease. For this reason, too, A will support A' on matters of common interest *vis-à-vis* the behaviour and conceptions of B; and B must ally with B' for the emergence of effective challenge against A—giving rise over time to social grouping and social classes of the relatively powerful and the relatively powerless. * * *

HANNA PITKIN & SARA SHUMER, ON PARTICIPATION

2 democracy 43, 50–54 (1982).

When people say that democracy is "obviously" not suitable for a large population, they fall captive to an abstract notion of assembling more and more people in one place: "no room can hold them all." But that is not how democratic movements grow, nor how real democratic polities function. Consider the American Tocqueville discovered in the 1830s, a people deeply engaged in democratic self-government: their "most important business" and their greatest pleasure. Take away politics from the American, Tocqueville said, and you rob him of half his existence, leaving a "vast void in his life" and making him "incredibly unhappy." Yet Tocqueville's America was no city-state, nor could its citizens assemble in one place. If size was no bar then to so lively a democratic engagement, it need not be now.

Face-to-face citizen assemblies are indeed essential to democracy, but one single assembly of all is not. Representation, delegation, cooperation, coordination, federation, and other kinds of devolution are entirely compatible with democracy, though they do not constitute and cannot guarantee it. Disillusioned democrats from Robert Michels to Frances Fox Piven and Richard A. Cloward have argued that any large organization and any differentiated leadership necessarily must take the life out of democracy, rigidifying into bureaucratic hierarchy. But formless, spontaneous mobs in the streets disrupting an established order cannot by themselves be a source of enduring change or even enduring challenge. Even if ossification were ultimately inevitable for any democratic engagement, surely the democrat's task would still be to prolong and revitalize the early, militant stage of popular involvement. The point is not to eschew all organization and all differentiated leadership, confining democracy to the local and spontaneous, but to develop those organizational forms and those styles of authority that sustain rather than suppress member initiative and autonomy. From historical examples we know that such forms and styles exist; it has sometimes been done.

Democrats need to think hard—both historically and theoretically—about the circumstances and the institutions by which large-scale collective power can be kept responsible to its participatory foundations. In the new American states, for example, after the disruption of British rule, radicals insisted on unicameral legislatures, weak or collective executives, frequent elections, rotation in office to prevent formation of a class of professional politicians. Most important, representatives were elected by participatory town or country meetings, thus by political bodies with an identity and some experience in collective action, rather than by isolated voters. Consequently, dialogue between representatives and their constituencies was frequent and vigorous; representatives were often instructed and sometimes recalled. But there are many possibilities for vital and fruitful interaction between the local and the national community. Recent resolutions on nuclear disarmament passed by New England town meetings are a promising experiment. All such devices, however, depend ultimately on the character of the citizenry, their love of and skill in exercising freedom; and these, in turn, rest mainly on the direct experience of meaningful local self-government.

Tocqueville argued that what made the American nation democratic was the vitality of direct participation in small and local associations. Face-to-face democracy was the foundation—not a substitute—for representative institutions, federalism, and national democracy. In direct personal participation, Tocqueville observed, people both learn the skills of citizenship and develop a taste for freedom; thereafter they form an active rather than deferential, apathetic, or privatized constituency for state and national representation, an engaged public for national issues. Size is not an insurmountable problem. On the basis of local, face-to-face politics, all sorts of higher and more distant structures of representation and collective power can be erected without destroying democracy—indeed, they can enhance it. Lacking such a basis, no institutional structures or programs of indoctrination can produce democracy.

From the question of size, turn next to that of technology. Has the technological complexity of modern society, requiring specialized expertise, rendered democracy obsolete? Here it is useful to remember that while the technological society may be new, the claims for expertise against democracy are very old, at least as old as Plato's *Republic*. The idea that ordinary people are incompetent to deal intelligently with the issues affecting their lives rests now, as it always has, on an overly narrow idea of what constitutes politically relevant knowledge, and a confusion between knowledge and decision.

First off, stupidity knows no class. Maybe most people are foolish, but foolishness is found in all social strata. Education removes some kinds of ignorance, but may entrench or instill others. The cure is not to exclude some but to include as diverse a range of perspectives and experience as possible in political deliberation. Second, expertise cannot solve political problems. Contemporary politics is indeed full of technically complex topics, about which even the educated feel horribly ignorant. But on every politically significant issue of this kind, the "experts" are divided; that is part of what makes the issues political. Though we may also feel at a loss to choose between them, leaving it to the experts is no solution at all.

Finally, while various kinds of knowledge can be profoundly useful in political decisions, knowledge alone is never enough. The political question is what we are to *do;* knowledge can only tell us how things are, how they work, while a political resolution always depends on what we, as a community, want and think right. And those questions have no technical answer; they require collective deliberation and decision. The experts must become a part of, not an alternative to, the democratic political process.

Technology as such is not the problem for democracy; the problems here are popular deference to experts, and the belief in technology as an irresistible force, an "imperative" beyond human control. Since such deference and fatalism originate in people's experience, which is rooted in social conditions, they may be fought wherever they arise; and that is reason for hope and perseverence. The apathetic oppressed constitute an enormous pool of potential democratic energy. And as the historical examples remind us, even the most oppressed people sometimes rediscover within themselves the capacity to act. Democrats today must seek out and foster every opportunity for people to experience their own effective agency: at work, at school, in family and personal relations, in the community. Democratic citizenship is facilitated by democratic social relations and an autonomous character structure; dependency and apathy must be attacked wherever people's experience centers. Yet such attacks remain incomplete unless they relate personal concerns to public issues, extend individual initiative into shared political action. A sense of personal autonomy, dignity, and efficacy may be requisite for, but must not be confused with, citizenship.

And so we return to the need for direct, personal political participation. As Tocqueville already made clear, not just any kind of small or local group can provide the democratic experience: the point is not gregariousness but politicization. To support democracy, face-to-face groups must themselves be internally democratic in ways already discussed, must deal with issues that really matter in their members' lives, and must have genuine power to affect the outcomes of those issues. One can experience freedom or learn citizenship no better in a "Mickey Mouse" group where nothing of importance is at stake than in a hierarchical organization.

Tocqueville's America was already big, but many important matters could still be addressed and resolved on the small scale. Confronting the realities of large-scale private power and social problems today requires national and even international organization. Such organization can be democratic, we have argued, if it rests on an active, engaged citizenry. Technology, too, can be democratically handled by such a citizenry. But such a citizenry emerges only from *meaningful* small-scale participation. Is that still a realistic possibility in a society such as ours?

To answer that crucial question, one must distinguish between short- and long-run requirements. In the long run, if we truly want full democracy, there is no doubt that we shall have to change our society and economy in fundamental ways. But in the short run, the right means toward that goal are participatory democratic movements. That such movements can still occur was shown in the 1960s; nothing fundamental has changed since then. Today's democrat must hope that in the brief experience of active participation that follows a flaring up of the democratic impulse, ordinary people, discovering the connections between local problems and national structures, coming up against the repressive power of established privilege, will themselves discover the need for more fundamental changes. We must be prepared to use the impulses toward and the experience of democracy, where they occur and while they last, to produce the social and economic changes that will further facilitate democracy. Each time it is, one might say, a race between the radicalizing and liberating potential of political action, and the dispiriting and paralyzing effects of the repression and political defeat likely to follow.

Confronting this most central and difficult problem, we need to recall not only Tocqueville and Revolutionary America, but also the movements of the 1960s, to build on their achievements and learn from their mistakes. On the whole, these movements did not see themselves as building participatory alternatives, nor as engaged in a long-term transformation of consciousness and social conditions to make possible a more democratic America. They looked for immediate changes on specific issues, mobilized people for short-term successes, and saw their own internal organization largely in instrumental terms. Even the Students for a Democratic Society, which did begin with a larger vision and did value internal democracy, eventually became absorbed in ending the Vietnam War. Neglecting democratic organization for immediate policy changes, the 1960s movements failed in what Goodwyn has called "democratic patience," the capacity to sustain democratic momentum for the long haul. Yet they left behind a changed America, and many less conspicuous yet active neighborhood groups, and radical opposition groups in unions, the professions, and among consumers.

A democratic movement for the 1980s must come out of such groups, out of local organizing around the grievances and aspirations people now feel. It must encourage local autonomy, ways of doing for ourselves and doing without, so as to cut loose from the system. Yet it must also encourage a widening perspective on the issues, their connections with the larger social structures of private power; it must foster alliances and debate among such groups. People must organize in ways that constantly enlarge rather than suppress movement members' active engagement, independent judgment, and preparedness for continued struggle.

Such local and ad hoc beginnings by no means preclude a commitment to radical systemic social and economic change. In the long run, democracy's full realization might well entail abolishing the joint-stock limited-liability corporation; or abolishing private ownership of the means of production; or even abandoning the Faustian dream of mastering and exploiting nature to gain infinitely expanding wealth.

But that is to get ahead of ourselves. For surely the privileged elites of corporate power will not permit such radical changes today or tomorrow, nor are our fellow citizens ready to fight on such grounds. We must not postpone the practice of participatory democracy until after such changes are achieved, nor expect it to emerge automatically from them. Democracy is our best means for achieving social change and must remain our conscious goal. Then the vicious circle of social process, in which democracy seems to presuppose the conditions that only democracy can bring about, can become grounds for hope: wherever we do cut into the circle, we thereby transform all the rest of its course. We can begin where we are.

ITALO CALVINO, INVISIBLE CITIES

Pp. 161–163 (1974).

I should not tell you of Berenice, the unjust city, which crowns with triglyphs, abaci, metopes the gears of its meat-grinding machines (the men assigned to polishing, when they raise their chins over the balustrades and contemplate the atria, stairways, porticos, feel even more imprisoned and short of stature). Instead, I should tell you of the hidden Berenice, the city of the just, handling makeshift materials in the shadowy rooms behind the shops and beneath the stairs, linking a network of wires and pipes and pulleys and pistons and counterweights that infiltrates like a climbing plant among the great cogged wheels (when they jam, a subdued ticking gives warning that a new precision mechanism is governing the city). Instead of describing to you the perfumed pools of the baths where the unjust of Berenice recline and weave their intrigues with rotund eloquence and observe with a proprietary eye the rotund flesh of the bathing odalisques, I should say to you how the just, always cautious to evade the spying sycophants and the Janizaries' mass arrests, recognize one another by their way of speaking, especially their pronunciation of commas and parentheses; from their habits which remain austere and innocent, avoiding complicated and nervous moods; from their sober but tasty cuisine, which evokes an ancient golden age: rice and celery soup, boiled beans, fried squash flowers.

From these data it is possible to deduce an image of the future Berenice, which will bring you closer to knowing the truth than any other information about the city as it is seen today. You must nevertheless bear in mind what I am about to say to you: in the seed of the city of the just, a malignant seed is hidden, in its turn: the certainty and pride of being in the right—and of being more just than many others who call themselves more just than the just. This seed ferments in bitterness, rivalry, resentment; and the natural desire of revenge on the unjust is colored by a yearning to be in their place and to act as they do. Another unjust city, though different from the first, is digging out its space within the double sheath of the unjust and just Berenices.

Having said this, I do not wish your eyes to catch a distorted image, so I must draw your attention to an intrinsic quality of this unjust city germinating secretly inside the secret just city: and this is the possible awakening—as if in an excited opening of windows—of a later love for justice, not yet subjected to rules, capable of reassembling a city still more just than it was before it became the vessel of injustice. But if you peer deeper into this new germ of justice you can discern a tiny spot that is spreading like the mounting tendency to impose what is just through what is unjust, and perhaps this is the germ of an immense metropolis.
* * *

From my words you will have reached the conclusion that the real Berenice is a temporal succession of different cities, alternately just and unjust. But what I wanted to warn you about is something else: all the future Berenices are already present in this instant, wrapped one within the other, confined, crammed, inextricable.

*

Index

References are to Pages

References are to Pages

†